About the cover

Edgar Degas, *The Cotton Exchange, New Orleans,* 1873

The cover image presents a portion of the larger painting that appears below. When they explore American histories, scholars consider many different aspects of America's past and connect them for a rich, fresh synthesis. This painting by the French artist Edgar Degas, whose aunt and uncle lived in Louisiana, appears to depict a thriving cotton business. However, the full picture includes a young man (Degas's brother René) reading *The Daily Picayune,* which reported the business's bankruptcy in 1873. Moreover, the painting does not show either the establishment in 1871 of the centralized New Orleans Cotton Exchange, which pushed out smaller competitors, or the laborers, including millions of newly freed African Americans, who produced the cotton sold by white entrepreneurs.

Seattle

Olympia
WASHINGTON

Mt. Rainier
(14,411 ft.; 4,392 m)

Mt. St. Helens
(8,366 ft.; 2,550 m)

MTS.

Portland

CASCADE

Salem

Eugene

OREGON

COAST RANGES

Columbia River

Columbia River

Helena

MONTANA

Missouri River

Yellowstone River

Billings

NORTH DAKOTA

Bismarck

BADLANDS

SOUTH DAKOTA

Pierre

Boise

IDAHO

Snake River

ROCKY

WYOMING

GREAT DIVIDE BASIN

BLACK HILLS

GREAT

Siou Fa

40°N

50°N   120°W   110°W   100°W

SIERRA

Carson City

Great Salt Lake

Salt Lake City

Cheyenne

Sacramento River

San Francisco

Oakland

Sacramento

NEVADA

GREAT BASIN

UTAH

Mt. Elbert
(14,433 ft.; 4,399 m)

COLORADO

Denver

Colorado Springs

Pikes Peak
(14,110 ft.; 4,301 m)

PLAINS

NEBRASKA

Platte River

KANSAS

San Jose

San Joaquin River

Fresno

NEVADA

Mt. Whitney
(14,494 ft.; 4,418 m)

Las Vegas

Colorado River

MOUNTAINS

Arkansas River

Wichi

CALIFORNIA

MOJAVE DESERT

ARIZONA

Santa Fe

Albuquerque

NEW MEXICO

OKLAHOMA

Oklahoma City

Los Angeles

San Diego

PACIFIC OCEAN

Phoenix

Tucson

Pecos River

Lubbock

LLANO ESTACADO

Red River

Fort Wor

TEXAS

El Paso

Colorado River

EDWARDS PLATEAU

Austin

Rio Grande

San Antonio

170°W   130°W   70°W

ARCTIC OCEAN

RUSSIA

BROOKS RANGE

ALASKA

Mt. McKinley
(20,320 ft.; 6,194 m)

Arctic Circle

ALASKA RANGE

CANADA

60°N

Anchorage

Yukon River

Bering Sea

Gulf of Alaska

Juneau

ALEUTIAN ISLANDS

160°W   150°W   140°W

0   250   500 miles

0   250   500 kilometers

Kauai

Niihau

Oahu

Honolulu

Molokai

HAWAII

22°N

PACIFIC OCEAN

Lanai

Kahoolawe

Maui

20°N

Hawaii

160°W   158°W   156°W

0   50   100 miles

0   50   100 kilometers

30°N

MEXICO

CANADA

MINNESOTA

Lake Superior

St. Paul
Minneapolis

WISCONSIN

Milwaukee
Madison

Lake Michigan

MICHIGAN
Lansing

Detroit

Lake Huron

Lake Ontario

Buffalo

NEW
YORK

Albany

VERMONT
Burlington   Montpelier
Mt. Washington
(6,288 ft.; 1,917 m)   Concord
Manchester

Hartford

MAINE
Augusta

Portland

NEW
HAMPSHIRE
Boston
MASS.
Providence
R.I.
CONNECTICUT

IOWA
Des Moines

Chicago

Lake Erie

Cleveland

OHIO

PENNSYLVANIA

Pittsburgh
Wheeling

Harrisburg

New York
Trenton

Philadelphia

NEW JERSEY

Omaha
Lincoln

CENTRAL
LOWLAND

INDIANA
Indianapolis

Columbus

APPALACHIAN MTS.

Baltimore

Dover

DELAWARE

Annapolis

WASHINGTON, D.C.

MISSOURI

Springfield

Cincinnati

W.
VA.

Charleston

MARYLAND

Missouri River

Kansas City
St. Louis

ILLINOIS

Louisville
Frankfort

Ohio River

KENTUCKY

Richmond

VIRGINIA

Potomac
River

Chesapeake
Bay

Norfolk

Topeka
Jefferson
City

Cumberland
River

Knoxville

Raleigh

NORTH CAROLINA

ATLANTIC
OCEAN

Tulsa

ARKANSAS

Little
Rock

Nashville
Mt. Mitchell
(6,684 ft.; 2,037 m)

TENNESSEE

Memphis

Tennessee River

Charlotte

SOUTH CAROLINA

Columbia

TIDEWATER

Mississippi River

Birmingham

Atlanta

Charleston

THE
UNITED STATES

Elevation
Feet   Meters

Over 13,001   Over 3,001

6,561–13,000   2,001–3,000

3,281–6,560   1,001–2,000

1,641–3,280   501–1,000

661–1,640   201–500

0–660   0–200

Below   Below
sea level   sea level

Dallas

LOUISIANA

MISSISSIPPI

Jackson

ALABAMA

Montgomery

GEORGIA

Alabama River

Jacksonville

Houston

Baton Rouge

New Orleans

Tallahassee

Orlando

FLORIDA

Gulf
of
Mexico

Lake
Okeechobee

Miami

B
A
H
A
M
A
S

ATLANTIC OCEAN

67°W   65°W

San Juan

PUERTO
RICO

18°N

VIRGIN
ISLANDS

Caribbean Sea

0   50   100 miles

0   50   100 kilometers

0   150   300 miles

0   150   300 kilometers

90°W   80°W   70°W

St. Lawrence River

Hudson River

N
W   E
S

CUBA

EXPLORING AMERICAN HISTORIES

EXPLORING AMERICAN HISTORIES

A BRIEF SURVEY WITH SOURCES

Nancy A. Hewitt

Rutgers University

Steven F. Lawson

Rutgers University

Bedford/St. Martin's

Boston • New York

**To Mary and Charles Takacs, Florence and Hiram Hewitt,
Sarah and Abraham Parker, Lena and Ben Lawson,
who made our American histories possible.**

For Bedford/St. Martin's

Publisher for History: Mary V. Dougherty
Senior Executive Editor for History: William J. Lombardo
Director of Development for History: Jane Knetzger
Senior Developmental Editor: Sara Wise
Senior Production Editor: Christina M. Horn
Senior Production Supervisor: Jennifer Peterson
Senior Marketing Manager for U.S. History: Amy Whitaker
Associate Editor: Jennifer Jovin
Editorial Assistant: Arrin Kaplan
Production Assistant: Elise Keller
Copy Editor: Linda McLatchie
Map Editor: Charlotte Miller
Indexer: Leoni McVey
Cartography: Mapping Specialists, Ltd.
Photo Researcher: Naomi Kornhauser
Permissions Manager: Kalina K. Ingham

Senior Art Director: Anna Palchik
Text Designer: Jerilyn Bockorick
Cover Designer: Billy Boardman
Cover Art: Edgar Degas (1834–1917), *The Cotton Exchange, New Orleans, 1873* (oil on canvas). Musée des Beaux-Arts, Pau, France/Giraudon/The Bridgeman Art Library.
Composition: Cenveo Publisher Services
Printing and Binding: RR Donnelley and Sons

President, Bedford/St. Martin's: Denise B. Wydra
Presidents, Macmillan Higher Education: Joan E. Feinberg and Tom Scotty
Director of Marketing: Karen R. Soeltz
Production Director: Susan W. Brown
Associate Production Director: Elise S. Kaiser
Managing Editor: Elizabeth M. Schaaf

For information, write: Bedford/St. Martin's, 75 Arlington Street, Boston, MA 02116   (617-399-4000)

ISBN 978-0-312-40998-2 (Combined Edition)
ISBN 978-1-4576-4194-7 (Loose-leaf Edition)
ISBN 978-0-312-41000-1 (Volume 1)
ISBN 978-1-4576-4195-4 (Loose-leaf Edition, Volume 1)
ISBN 978-0-312-41001-8 (Volume 2)
ISBN 978-1-4576-4196-1 (Loose-leaf Edition, Volume 2)

Exploring American Histories is a new kind of U.S. history survey text. Unique among textbooks, its innovative format makes a broad and diverse American history accessible to a new generation of students and instructors interested in a more active learning and teaching style. To accomplish this, our book joins an inclusive yet brief narrative text with an integrated documents reader; together, these two elements create unsurpassed opportunities for exploring American history in ways best suited for the twenty-first-century classroom.

Format

Our extensive experience teaching American history in a wide variety of classrooms has led us to conclude that students learn history most effectively when they read historical narrative in conjunction with primary sources. Sources bring the past to life in ways that narrative alone cannot, while narrative offers the necessary framework, context, and chronology that documents by themselves do not typically provide. We believe that the most engaging entry to the past starts with individuals and how people in their daily lives connect to larger political, economic, cultural, and international developments. This approach makes the history relevant and memorable. The available textbooks left us unsatisfied, compelling us to assign additional books, readers, and documents we found on the Web. However, these supplementary texts raised costs for our students, and too often students had difficulty seeing how the different readings related to one another. Simply remembering what materials to bring to class became too unwieldy. So we decided to write our own book.

For *Exploring American Histories*, we sought to reconceive the relationship of the textbook and reader to create a mutually supportive set of course materials designed to help our students appreciate the diversity of America's history, to help instructors teach that primary sources are the building blocks of historical interpretation, and to encourage students to see that every past event can and should be considered from multiple perspectives. The people of the past experienced the events of their lifetimes in a variety of ways and from multiple vantage points, and historians debate continually among themselves and the general public about what actually happened and why it matters for us today. Consequently, there is no one story about the past; there are many stories, and so we wanted to emphasize these plural *Histories* in the book's title. Indeed, on the last day of our own survey classes, we measure our

success by how well our students can demonstrate that they understand this rich complexity that is central to the discipline, and whether they can put the multiple stories they have come to understand into the context of the larger whole. Instructors at all types of schools share our goal, and we hope that *Exploring American Histories* will help them enrich their students' understanding of events of the past.

For *Exploring American Histories*, we have selected an extensive and diverse array of primary-source materials that highlight multiple perspectives, and we have integrated them at key points as teaching moments within the narrative text. Each chapter contains numerous featured primary sources with a distinctive pedagogy designed to help students make connections between the documents and the text's big themes. Every document is clearly cross-referenced within the narrative so that students can easily incorporate them into their reading as well as reflect on our interpretation. A specially selected set of interrelated documents placed at the end of each chapter addresses an important historical question related to the chapter.

Exploring American Histories also opens up a new dimension to the familiar textbook format by expanding beyond its printed pages to grant students and teachers access to a wealth of online tools and resources built specifically for our text to enhance reading comprehension and promote in-depth study. Of special note, every chapter includes an additional document set that instructors can order packaged with the book; each set of documents focuses on a particular theme and is available only online. Many of these projects incorporate multimedia sources such as audio and video files that until recently were unavailable to work with in class. In addition, *Exploring American Histories* features LearningCurve, an easy-to-assign adaptive learning tool that helps students rehearse the material in the narrative so that they come to class better prepared. Students receive access to LearningCurve, described more fully below, when they purchase a new copy of the book. And because textbook prices are a big concern, our "two-in-one" survey text—a combination of brief narrative plus reader—offers attractive cost savings for students.

Approach

During the last thirty years, scholarship in history has transformed our vision of the past, most notably by dramatically increasing the range of people historians study, and thus deepening and complicating traditional under-standings of change over time. Creating a story of the past was easier to do when it was limited to the study of great white men engaged in national politics and high-level diplomacy, but it was also stunted in its explanatory power and disconnected from the life experiences of nearly all our students. Over the last several decades, the historical profession itself has made huge strides in becoming more inclusive in membership, with teachers and scholars increasingly reflecting the diverse face of America. The range of new research has been vast, with a special focus on gender, race, ethnicity, and class, and histori-ans have produced landmark work in women's history, African American history, American Indian history, and labor history.

All of these changes in the historical profession have greatly influenced how the American history survey course is taught in two fundamental ways. First, many instructors now try to help their students see that ordinary people, from all walks of life, can and do affect the course of historical change. Second, many historians have become increasingly transparent about their methodology and have a strong desire to teach their students that history is an interpretive discipline and open to multiple perspectives. Since the 1970s, survey textbooks have changed in coverage, organization, and pedagogy, but they have struggled to get it right—becoming overwhelming in their scope, difficult to read, and losing the sense of story that makes the past accessible, engaging, and comprehensible. As more instructors have embraced teaching with documents, they have come to see these shortcomings in the available survey textbooks. Along with many of our colleagues, we came to the same conclusion ourselves. Many current texts are too long, so we've made ours brief. *Exploring American Histories* is comprehensive, but with a carefully selected amount of detail that is more in tune with what instructors can realistically expect their students to remember. Many texts include some documents, but the balance between narrative (too much) and primary sources (too few) was off-kilter, so we have included more documents and integrated them in creative ways that help students make the necessary connections and that spur them to think critically. But the most innovative aspect of *Exploring American Histories*, and what makes it a true alternative, is that its format introduces a unique textbook structure organized around the broad theme of *diversity*.

Diversity as a theme works in *Exploring American Histories* in several ways. First, diversity supports our presentation of an inclusive historical narrative, one that recognizes the American past as a series of interwoven stories made by a multiplicity of historical actors. We do this within a strong national framework that allows our readers to see how the various stories fit together and to understand why they matter. Our narrative is comple-mented by a wide variety of documents that challenge students to consider multiple points of view. In chapter 4, students hear from both a woman accused of witchcraft and a minister who defended the Salem witch trials. In chapter 25, we ask our readers to contrast an idyllic, inviting depiction of 1950s suburbia with a racially restrictive covenant of the same period.

Second, our theme of diversity allows us to foreground the role of individual agency as we push readers to consider the reasons behind historical change. Each chapter opens with a pair of American Histories, biographies that showcase indi-viduals who experienced and influenced events in a particular period, and then returns to them throughout the chapter to strengthen the connections and highlight their place in the bigger picture. These biographies cover both well-known Americans—such as Daniel Shays, Frederick Douglass, Andrew Carnegie, and Eleanor Roosevelt—and those who never gained fame or fortune—such as the activist Amy Kirby Post, organizer Luisa Moreno, and World War II internee Fred Korematsu. Introducing such a broad range of biographical subjects illuminates the many ways that individuals shaped and were shaped by historical events. This strategy also works to make visible throughout the chapter the intersections where history from the top down meets history from the bottom up and to connect social and political histories to their relation-ships with economic, cultural, and diplomatic developments. We work to show that events at the national level, shaped by elite political and economic leaders, have a direct impact on the lives of ordinary people; at the same time, we demonstrate that actions at the local level often have a significant influence on decisions made at the centers of national government and commerce. The discussions of the interrelationship among international, national, and local theaters and actors incorpo-rate the pathbreaking scholarship of the last three decades, which has focused on gender, race, class, and ethnicity in North America and the United States, and on colonization, empire, and globalization in the larger world.

Primary Sources

The heart of *Exploring American Histories* is its primary sources, and in every chapter we supply students with numer-ous and carefully selected documents from which they can evaluate the text's interpretations and construct their own versions of history. These firsthand accounts include maps, drawings, material artifacts, paintings, speeches, sermons, letters, diaries, memoirs, newspaper articles, political cartoons, laws, wills, court cases, petitions, advertisements, photographs, and blogs. In selecting documents, we have provided multiple perspectives on critical issues, including both well-known sources and those that are less familiar. But our choices were also influenced by the kinds of primary sources that exist. For some periods of American history and some topics, the available primary sources are limited and fragmentary.

For other eras and issues, the sources are varied and abundant, indeed sometimes overwhelming, especially as we move into the twentieth century. In all time periods, some groups of Americans are far better represented in primary sources than others. Those who were wealthy, well educated, and politically powerful produced and preserved many sources about their lives. And their voices are well represented in this textbook. But we have also provided documents by American Indians, enslaved Africans, colonial women, rural residents, immigrants, working people, and young people. Moreover, the lives of those who left few sources of their own can often be illuminated by reading documents written by elites to see what information they yield, intentionally or unintentionally, about less well-documented groups.

Individual documents are embedded throughout every chapter and connected to the narrative text with Explore prompts, and within each chapter these documents are treated in the following three ways:

- Each chapter has one annotated textual or visual source, with questions in the margins to help students consider a specific phrase or feature and analyze the source as a whole. These questions and annotations are intended to train students in historical habits of mind. A Put It in Context question prompts students to consider the source in terms of the broad themes of the chapter.
- Each chapter contains Two Views, a paired set of documents that show contrasting perspectives. Two Views documents are introduced by a single headnote and are followed by Interpret the Evidence and Put It in Context questions that prompt students to analyze and compare both items and place them in a larger historical framework.
- Each chapter also presents one or more additional documents consisting of excerpts or images of classic or lesser-known sources. These are provided to encourage more practice working with sources and to offer additional perspectives to compare with the narrative. These documents are accompanied by informative headnotes and conclude with Interpret the Evidence and Put It in Context questions.

A Document Project at the end of every chapter is the capstone of our integrated primary-sources approach. Each Document Project is a collection of five or six documents focused on a critical issue central to that chapter. It is introduced by a brief overview and ends with interpretive questions that ask students to draw conclusions based on what they have learned in the chapter and read in the sources.

We understand that the instructor's role is crucial in teaching students how to analyze primary-source materials and develop interpretations. Teachers can use the documents to encourage critical thinking and also to measure students' understanding and assess their progress. The integration of the documents in the narrative should prompt students to read more closely than they usually do, as they will see more clearly the direct connection between the two. We have organized the documents to give instructors the flexibility to use them in many different ways—as in-class discussion prompts, for take-home writing assignments, and even as the basis for exam questions—and also in different combinations, as the documents throughout the chapter can be compared and contrasted with one another. An instructor's manual for *Exploring American Histories* provides a wealth of creative suggestions for using the documents program effectively (see the Versions and Supplements description on pages xv–xviii for more information on all the available instructor resources).

More Help for Students

We know that students often need help making sense of their reading. As instructors, all of us have had students complain that they cannot figure out what's important in the textbooks we assign. For many of our students, especially those just out of high school, their college history survey textbook is likely the most difficult book they have ever encountered. We understand the challenges that our students face, so in addition to the extensive document program, we have included the following pedagogical features designed to aid student learning:

- Review and Relate questions help students focus on main themes and concepts presented in each major section of the chapter.
- Key terms in boldface highlight important content. All terms are defined in a glossary at the end of the book.
- Clear conclusions help students summarize what they've read.
- A full-page Chapter Review lets students review key terms, important concepts, and notable events.

In addition, the book includes access to LearningCurve, an online adaptive learning tool that promotes engaged reading and focused review. Cross-references at the end of every major section and chapter in the text prompt students to log in and rehearse their understanding of the material they have just read. Students move at their own pace and accumulate points as they go, giving the interaction a game-like feel. Feedback for incorrect responses explains why the answer is incorrect and directs students back to the text to review before they attempt to answer the question again. The end result is a better understanding of the key elements of the text. See the inside front cover for more details.

We imagine *Exploring American Histories* as a new kind of American history textbook, one that not only offers a strong, concise narrative but also challenges students to construct their own interpretations through primary-source analysis. We are thrilled that our hopes have come to fruition, and we believe that our textbook will provide a thought-provoking and highly useful foundation for every U.S. history survey course and will benefit students and faculty alike. The numerous opportunities provided for active learning will allow teachers to engage students in stimulating ways and help them experience the past in closer connection to the present. After all, active learning is the basis for active citizenship, and teaching the survey course is our chance as historians, whose work is highly specialized, to reach the greatest number of undergraduates. We hope not only to inspire the historical imaginations of those who will create the next generation of American histories but also to spur them to consider the issues of today in light of the stories of yesterday.

Acknowledgments

We wish to thank the talented scholars and teachers who were kind enough to give their time and knowledge to review the manuscript:

Benjamin Allen, *South Texas College*
Christine Anderson, *Xavier University*
Uzoamaka Melissa C. Anyiwo, *Curry College*
Anthony A. Ball, *Housatonic Community College*
Terry A. Barnhart, *Eastern Illinois University*
Edwin Benson, *North Harford High School*
Paul Berk, *Christian Brothers University*
Deborah L. Blackwell, *Texas A&M International University*
Thomas Born, *Blinn College*
Margaret Bramlett, *St. Andrews Episcopal High School*
Lauren K. Bristow, *Collin College*
Tsekani Browne, *Duquesne University*
Jon L. Brudvig, *Dickinson State University*
Dave Bush, *Shasta College*
Barbara Calluori, *Montclair State University*
Julia Schiavone Camacho, *The University of Texas at El Paso*
Jacqueline Glass Campbell, *Francis Marion University*
Amy E. Canfield, *Lewis-Clark State College*
Dominic Carrillo, *Grossmont College*
Mark R. Cheathem, *Cumberland University*
Laurel A. Clark, *University of Hartford*
Myles L. Clowers, *San Diego City College*
Hamilton Cravens, *Iowa State University*
Audrey Crawford, *Houston Community College*
John Crum, *University of Delaware*
Alex G. Cummins, *St. Johns River State College*
Susanne Deberry-Cole, *Morgan State University*
Julian J. DelGaudio, *Long Beach City College*

Patricia Norred Derr, *Kutztown University*
John Donoghue, *Loyola University Chicago*
Timothy Draper, *Waubonsee Community College*
David Dzurec, *University of Scranton*
Keith Edgerton, *Montana State University Billings*
Blake Ellis, *Lone Star College*
Christine Erickson, *Indiana University–Purdue University Fort Wayne*
Todd Estes, *Oakland University*
Gabrielle Everett, *Jefferson College*
Julie Fairchild, *Sinclair Community College*
Randy Finley, *Georgia Perimeter College*
Kirsten Fischer, *University of Minnesota*
Michelle Fishman-Cross, *College of Staten Island*
Jeffrey Forret, *Lamar University*
Kristen Foster, *Marquette University*
Susan Freeman, *Western Michigan University*
Nancy Gabin, *Purdue University*
Kevin Gannon, *Grand View University*
Benton Gates, *Indiana University–Purdue University Fort Wayne*
Bruce Geelhoed, *Ball State University*
Mark Gelfand, *Boston College*
Jason George, *The Bryn Mawr School*
Judith A. Giesberg, *Villanova University*
Sherry Ann Gray, *Mid-South Community College*
Patrick Griffin, *University of Notre Dame*
Aaron Gulyas, *Mott Community College*
Scott Gurman, *Northern Illinois University*
Melanie Gustafson, *University of Vermont*
Brian Hart, *Del Mar College*
Paul Hart, *Texas State University*
Paul Harvey, *University of Colorado Colorado Springs*
Woody Holton, *University of Richmond*
Vilja Hulden, *University of Arizona*
Colette A. Hyman, *Winona State University*
Brenda Jackson-Abernathy, *Belmont University*
Troy R. Johnson, *California State University–Long Beach*
Shelli Jordan-Zirkle, *Shoreline Community College*
Jennifer Kelly, *The University of Texas at Austin*
Kelly Kennington, *Auburn University*
Andrew E. Kersten, *University of Wisconsin–Green Bay*
Janilyn M. Kocher, *Richland Community College*
Max Krochmal, *Duke University*
Peggy Lambert, *Lone Star College*
Jennifer R. Lang, *Delgado Community College*
John S. Leiby, *Paradise Valley Community College*
Mitchell Lerner, *The Ohio State University*
Matthew Loayza, *Minnesota State University, Mankato*
Gabriel J. Loiacono, *University of Wisconsin Oshkosh*
John F. Lyons, *Joliet Junior College*
Lorie Maltby, *Henderson Community College*

Christopher Manning, *Loyola University Chicago*
Marty D. Matthews, *North Carolina State University*
Eric Mayer, *Victor Valley College*
Suzanne K. McCormack, *Community College of Rhode Island*
David McDaniel, *Marquette University*
J. Kent McGaughy, *Houston Community College, Northwest*
Alan McPherson, *Howard University*
Sarah Hand Meacham, *Virginia Commonwealth University*
Brian Craig Miller, *Emporia State University*
Brett Mizelle, *California State University Long Beach*
Mark Moser, *The University of North Carolina at Greensboro*
Jennifer Murray, *Coastal Carolina University*
Peter C. Murray, *Methodist University*
Steven E. Nash, *East Tennessee State University*
Chris Newman, *Elgin Community College*
David Noon, *University of Alaska Southeast*
Richard H. Owens, *West Liberty University*
David J. Peavler, *Towson University*
Laura A. Perry, *University of Memphis*
Wesley Phelps, *University of St. Thomas*
Merline Pitre, *Texas Southern University*
Eunice G. Pollack, *University of North Texas*
Kimberly Porter, *University of North Dakota*
Cynthia Prescott, *University of North Dakota*
Gene Preuss, *University of Houston*
Sandra Pryor, *Old Dominion University*
Rhonda Ragsdale, *Lone Star College*
Michaela Reaves, *California Lutheran University*
Peggy Renner, *Glendale Community College*
Steven D. Reschly, *Truman State University*
Barney J. Rickman, *Valdosta State University*
Pamela Riney-Kehrberg, *Iowa State University*
Paul Ringel, *High Point University*
Timothy Roberts, *Western Illinois University*
Glenn Robins, *Georgia Southwestern State University*
Alicia E. Rodriquez, *California State University Bakersfield*
Mark Roehrs, *Lincoln Land Community College*
Patricia Roessner, *Marple Newtown High School*
John G. Roush, *St. Petersburg College*
James Russell, *St. Thomas Aquinas College*
Eric Schlereth, *The University of Texas at Dallas*
Ronald Schultz, *University of Wyoming*
Stanley K. Schultz, *University of Wisconsin–Madison*
Sharon Shackelford, *Erie Community College*
Donald R. Shaffer, *American Public University System*
David J. Silverman, *The George Washington University*
Andrea Smalley, *Northern Illinois University*
Molly Smith, *Friends School of Baltimore*
David L. Snead, *Liberty University*
David Snyder, *Delaware Valley College*
Jodie Steeley, *Merced College*
Bryan E. Stone, *Del Mar College*

Emily Straus, *SUNY Fredonia*
Jean Stuntz, *West Texas A&M University*
Nikki M. Taylor, *University of Cincinnati*
Heather Ann Thompson, *Temple University*
Timothy Thurber, *Virginia Commonwealth University*
T. J. Tomlin, *University of Northern Colorado*
Laura Trauth, *Community College of Baltimore County–Essex*
Russell M. Tremayne, *College of Southern Idaho*
Laura Tuennerman-Kaplan, *California University of Pennsylvania*
Vincent Vinikas, *The University of Arkansas at Little Rock*
David Voelker, *University of Wisconsin–Green Bay*
Ed Wehrle, *Eastern Illinois University*
Gregory Wilson, *University of Akron*
Maria Cristina Zaccarini, *Adelphi University*
Nancy Zens, *Central Oregon Community College*
Jean Hansen Zuckweiler, *University of Northern Colorado*

We also appreciate the help the following scholars and students gave us in providing the information we needed at critical points in the writing of this text: Leslie Brown, Andrew Buchanan, Gillian Carroll, Susan J. Carroll, Paul Clemens, Dorothy Sue Cobble, Jane Coleman-Harbison, Alison Cronk, Elisabeth Eittreim, Phyllis Hunter, Tera Hunter, William Link, James Livingston, Julia Livingston, Gilda Morales, Vicki L. Ruiz, Susan Schrepfer, Bonnie Smith, Melissa Stein, Margaret Sumner, Jessica Unger, and Anne Valk. Jacqueline Castledine and Julia Sandy-Bailey worked closely with us in finding documents and creating the Document Projects. Without them, this would not be a docutext.

We would particularly like to applaud the many hardworking and creative people at Bedford/St. Martin's who guided us through the labyrinthine process of writing a textbook from scratch. No one was more important to us than the indefatigable and unflappable Sara Wise, our developmental editor. We are also deeply grateful to Patricia Rossi, who first persuaded us to undertake this project. Joan Feinberg had the vision that guided us through every page of this book. We could not have had a better team than Denise Wydra, Mary Dougherty, William Lombardo, Jane Knetzger, Christina Horn, Jennifer Jovin, Katherine Bates, Amy Whitaker, Jenna Bookin Barry, Daniel McDonough, and Arrin Kaplan. They also enlisted Naomi Kornhauser, Charlotte Miller, Linda McLatchie, Heidi Hood, Rob Heinrich, Shannon Hunt, John Reisbord, and Michelle McSweeney to provide invaluable service. Finally, we would like to thank our friends and family who have been asking us these past years, "When will you be finished?" We are very pleased to be able to respond, "The time is now."

Nancy A. Hewitt and Steven F. Lawson

Adopters of **Exploring American Histories** and their students have access to abundant resources, including documents, presentation and testing materials, volumes in the acclaimed Bedford Series in History and Culture, and much more. For more information on the offerings described below, visit the book's catalog site at bedfordstmartins.com/hewittlawson/catalog, or contact your local Bedford/St. Martin's sales representative.

Get the Right Version for Your Class

To accommodate different course lengths and course budgets, *Exploring American Histories* is available in several different formats, including three-hole punched loose-leaf Budget books versions and e-books, which are available at a substantial discount.

- Combined edition (chapters 1–29)—available in paperback, loose-leaf, and e-book formats
- Volume 1: To 1877 (chapters 1–14)—available in paperback, loose-leaf, and e-book formats
- Volume 2: Since 1865 (chapters 14–29)—available in paperback, loose-leaf, and e-book formats

Assign the online, interactive Bedford x-Book. With all the content of the print book—plus integrated LearningCurve and the 29 extra Document Projects, some with audio or video—the *x-Book for Exploring American Histories* features a robust search engine, navigation tools, easy ways to take and share notes, and interactive exercises. And with fast ways to rearrange chapters and add new pages, sections, or links, it lets teachers build just the right book for their course.

Let students choose their e-book format. Students can purchase the downloadable *Bedford e-Book to Go for Exploring American Histories* from our Web site or find other PDF versions of the e-book at our publishing partners' sites: CourseSmart, Barnes & Noble NookStudy; Kno; CafeScribe; or Chegg.

Assign LearningCurve So That Your Students Come to Class Prepared

As described in the preface and on the inside front cover, students purchasing new books receive access to Learning Curve for *Exploring American Histories*, an online learning tool designed to help students rehearse content at their own pace in a nonthreatening, game-like environment. The feedback for wrong answers provides instructional coaching and sends students back to the book for review. Students answer as many questions as necessary to reach a target score, with repeated chances to revisit material they haven't mastered. Assigning LearningCurve is easy for instructors, and the reporting features help instructors track overall class trends and spot topics that are giving students trouble.

Send Students to Free Online Resources

The book's companion site at bedfordstmartins.com/hewittlawson gives students a way to read, write, and study by providing plentiful quizzes and activities, study aids, and history research and writing help.

FREE Online Study Guide. Available at the companion site, this popular resource provides students with quizzes and activities for each chapter, including multiple-choice self-tests that focus on important concepts; flash cards that test students' knowledge of key terms; timeline activities that emphasize causal relationships; and map quizzes intended to strengthen students' geography skills. Instructors can monitor students' progress through an online Quiz Gradebook or receive email updates.

FREE Research, Writing, and Anti-plagiarism Advice. Available at the companion site, Bedford's **History Research and Writing Help** includes **History Research and Reference Sources**, with links to history-related databases, indexes, and journals; **More Sources and How to Format a History Paper**, with clear advice on how to integrate primary and secondary sources into research papers and how to cite and format sources correctly; **Build a Bibliography**, a simple Web-based tool known as The Bedford Bibliographer that generates bibliographies in four commonly used documentation styles; and **Tips on Avoiding Plagiarism**, an online tutorial that reviews the consequences of plagiarism and features exercises to help students practice integrating sources and recognize acceptable summaries.

Take Advantage of Instructor Resources

Bedford/St. Martin's has developed a rich array of teaching resources for this book and for this course. They range from lecture and presentation materials and assessment tools to course management options. Most can be downloaded or ordered at **bedfordstmartins.com/hewittlawson/catalog**.

HistoryClass for *Exploring American Histories*. *History-Class*, a Bedford/St. Martin's Online Course Space, puts the online resources available with this textbook in one convenient and completely customizable course space. There you and your students can access the interactive x-book; video clips, maps, images, documents, and links; chapter review quizzes; and research and writing help. In *HistoryClass* you can get all our premium content and tools, which you can assign, rearrange, and mix with your own resources. *HistoryClass* also includes LearningCurve, Bedford/St. Martin's adaptive tool for quizzing to learn, and the additional Document Project for each chapter. For more information, visit **yourhistoryclass.com**.

Instructor's Resource Manual. The instructor's manual offers both experienced and first-time instructors tools for preparing lectures and running discussions. It includes chapter-review material, teaching strategies, and a guide to chapter-specific supplements available for the text, plus suggestions on how to get the most out of LearningCurve.

Computerized Test Bank. The test bank includes a mix of carefully crafted multiple-choice, short-answer, and essay questions for each chapter. It also contains the Interpret the Evidence and Put It in Context questions from the textbook and model answers for each. All questions appear in Microsoft Word format and in easy-to-use test bank software that allows instructors to add, edit, re-sequence, and print questions and answers. Instructors can also export questions into a variety of formats, including WebCT and Blackboard.

The Bedford Lecture Kit: PowerPoint Maps, Images, Lecture Outlines, and i>clicker Content. Look good and save time with *The Bedford Lecture Kit*. These presentation materials are downloadable individually from the Instructor Resources tab at **bedfordstmartins.com/hewittlawson/catalog** and are available on *The Bedford Lecture Kit* Instructor's Resource CD-ROM. They provide ready-made and fully customizable PowerPoint multimedia presentations that include lecture outlines with embedded maps, figures, and selected images from the textbook and extra background for instructors. Also available are maps and selected images in JPEG and PowerPoint formats; content for i>clicker, a classroom response system, in Microsoft Word and PowerPoint formats; the Instructor's Resource Manual in Microsoft Word format; and outline maps in

PDF format for quizzing or handing out. All files are suitable for copying onto transparency acetates.

Make History—Free Documents, Maps, Images, and Web Sites. *Make History* combines the best Web resources with hundreds of maps and images, to make it simple to find the source material you need. Browse the collection of thousands of resources by course or by topic, date, and type. Each item has been carefully chosen and helpfully annotated to make it easy to find exactly what you need. Available at **bedfordstmartins.com/makehistory**.

America in Motion: Video Clips for U.S. History. Set history in motion with *America in Motion,* an instructor DVD containing dozens of short digital movie files of events in twentieth-century American history. From the wreckage of the battleship *Maine*, to FDR's fireside chats, to Oliver North testifying before Congress, *America in Motion* engages students with dynamic scenes from key events and challenges them to think critically. All files are classroom-ready, edited for brevity, and easily integrated with PowerPoint or other presentation software for electronic lectures or assignments. An accompanying guide provides each clip's historical context, ideas for use, and suggested questions.

Videos and Multimedia. A wide assortment of videos and multimedia CD-ROMs on various topics in U.S. history is available to qualified adopters through your Bedford/St. Martin's sales representative.

Package and Save Your Students Money

For information on free packages and discounts up to 50%, visit **bedfordstmartins.com/hewittlawson/catalog** or contact your local Bedford/St. Martin's sales representative.

Online Document Projects for *Exploring American Histories*. A complete set of additional 29 Document Projects—one per chapter—is available to provide students with more opportunities to work with primary sources. Each set mirrors the pedagogy in the text with overviews, headnotes, and Interpret the Evidence and Put It in Context questions, and many sets include audio and video sources. Topics include loyalists in the American Revolution, abolitionist debates, women's liberation, and the Reagan Revolution. Automatically available online to all students who purchase the x-Book or *HistoryClass* and free when packaged with the text.

The Bedford Series in History and Culture. More than 150 titles in this highly praised series combine first-rate scholarship, historical narrative, and important primary documents for undergraduate courses. Each book is brief, inexpensive, and focused on a specific topic or period. For a complete list of titles, visit bedfordstmartins.com/history/series. Package discounts are available.

Rand McNally Historical Atlas of American History. This collection of more than 84 full-color maps illustrates key events and eras, from early exploration, settlement, expansion, and immigration to U.S. involvement in wars abroad and on U.S. soil. Introductory pages for each section include a brief overview, timelines, graphs, and photographs to quickly establish a historical context. Available for $3.00 when packaged with the print text.

Maps in Context: A Workbook for American History. Written by historical cartography expert Gerald A. Danzer (University of Illinois at Chicago), this skill-building workbook helps students comprehend essential connections between geographic literacy and historical understanding. Organized to correspond to the typical U.S. survey course, *Maps in Context* presents a wealth of map-centered projects and convenient pop quizzes that give students hands-on experience working with maps. Available free when packaged with the print text.

The Bedford Glossary for U.S. History. This handy supplement for the survey course gives students historically contextualized definitions for hundreds of terms—from *abolitionism* to *zoot suit*—that they will encounter in lectures, reading, and exams. Available free when packaged with the print text.

U.S. History Matters: A Student Guide to U.S. History Online. This resource, written by Kelly Schrum, Alan Gevinson, and the late Roy Rosenzweig (all of George Mason University), provides an illustrated and annotated guide to 250 of the most useful Web sites for student research in U.S. history as well as advice on evaluating and using Internet sources. This essential guide is based on the acclaimed "History Matters" Web site developed by the American Social History Project and the Center for History and New Media. Available free when packaged with the print text.

Trade Books. Titles published by sister companies Hill and Wang; Farrar, Straus and Giroux; Henry Holt and Company; St. Martin's Press; Picador; and Palgrave Macmillan are available at a 50% discount when packaged with Bedford/St. Martin's textbooks. For more information, visit bedfordstmartins.com/tradeup.

A Pocket Guide to Writing in History. This portable and affordable reference tool by Mary Lynn Rampolla, now also available as a searchable e-book, provides reading, writing, and research advice useful to students in all history courses. Concise yet comprehensive advice on approaching typical history assignments, developing critical-reading skills, writing effective history papers, conducting research, using and documenting sources, and avoiding plagiarism—enhanced with practical tips and examples throughout—have made this slim reference a best seller. Package discounts are available.

A Student's Guide to History. This complete guide to success in any history course provides the practical help students need to be effective. In addition to introducing students to the nature of the discipline, author Jules Benjamin teaches a wide range of skills from preparing for exams to approaching common writing assignments, and he explains the research and documentation process with plentiful examples. Package discounts are available.

Going to the Source: The Bedford Reader in American History. Developed by Victoria Bissell Brown and Timothy J. Shannon, this reader's strong pedagogical framework helps students learn how to ask fruitful questions in order to evaluate documents effectively and develop critical-reading skills. The reader's wide variety of chapter topics that complement the survey course and its rich diversity of sources—from personal letters to political cartoons—provoke students' interest as it teaches them the skills they need to successfully interrogate historical sources. Package discounts are available.

America Firsthand. With its distinctive focus on ordinary people, this primary documents reader, by Anthony Marcus, John M. Giggie, and David Burner, offers a remarkable range of perspectives on American history from those who lived it. Popular Points of View sections expose students to different perspectives on a specific event or topic, and Visual Portfolios invite analysis of the visual record. Package discounts are available.

Explore Other Docutexts from Bedford/St. Martin's

Bedford/St. Martin's has been a leader in pioneering new ways to bring primary sources into the undergraduate classroom, beginning with the Bedford Series in History and

Culture, described above. The "docutext" format of *Exploring American Histories,* which combines a brief narrative with themed collections of written and visual sources, represents another innovation in making documents accessible for students. Docutexts authored by leading historians are now available from Bedford for a variety of history courses.

World History Survey. Find out about *Ways of the World: A Brief Global History with Sources,* by Robert W. Strayer, at bedfordstmartins.com/strayersources/catalog.

African American History. Find out about *Freedom on My Mind: A History of African Americans, with Documents,* by Deborah Gray White, Mia Bay, and Waldo E. Martin Jr., at bedfordstmartins.com/graywhite/catalog.

U.S. Women's History. Find out about *Through Women's Eyes: An American History with Documents,* by Ellen Carol DuBois and Lynn Dumenil, at bedfordstmartins.com/duboisdumenil/catalog.

Native American History. Find out about *First Peoples: A Documentary Survey of American Indian History,* by Colin G. Calloway, at bedfordstmartins.com/calloway/catalog.

Twentieth-Century European History. Find out about *Europe in the Contemporary World, 1900 to the Present: A Narrative History with Documents,* by Bonnie G. Smith, at bedfordstmartins.com/smitheurope/catalog.

Brief Contents

3
Global Changes Reshape Colonial America
1680–1750   64

4
Religious Strife and Social Upheavals
1680–1750   96

5
Wars and Empires
1750–1774   128

6
Revolutions
1775–1783   160

7

Political Cultures
1783–1800   192

AMERICAN HISTORIES
Daniel Shays and Alexander Hamilton   193

DOCUMENT PROJECT 7

The Whiskey Rebellion   218

Document 7.5 Resolution to the Pennsylvania Legislature,
1791 | Document 7.6 The Pittsburgh Resolution, 1794 |
Document 7.7 George Washington, Proclamation against the
Rebels, 1794 | Document 7.8 Alexander Hamilton, Letter to
George Washington, August 5, 1794 | Document 7.9 Alexander
Hamilton, Tully's Pamphlet, 1794 | Document 7.10 James
Madison, Letter to James Monroe, December 4, 1794

8

New Frontiers
1790–1820   226

AMERICAN HISTORIES
Parker Cleaveland and Sacagawea   227

9
Defending and Redefining the Nation
1809–1832   258

10
Slavery Expands South and West
1830–1850   292

11
Social and Cultural Ferment in the North
1820–1850   326

AMERICAN HISTORIES
Charles Grandison Finney and Amy Kirby Post   327

14
Emancipations and Reconstructions
1863–1877 424

15
Frontier Encounters
1865–1896 458

26
The Liberal Consensus and Its Challengers
1960–1973   822

27
The Conservative Ascendancy
1968–1992   858

Maps, Figures, and Tables

Maps

Figures and Tables

How to Use This Book

Start by reading the narrative and using the chapter tools to help you focus on what's important.

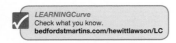
LEARNINGCurve
Check what you know.
bedfordstmartins.com/hewittlawson/LC

Scan the **chapter outline** for a preview of the chapter's big topics and themes.

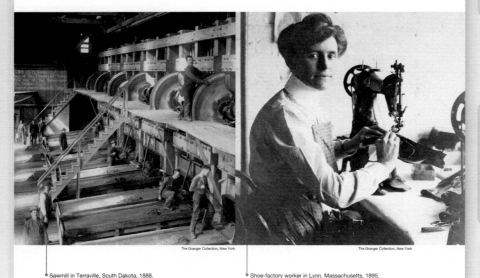
The Granger Collection, New York
The Granger Collection, New York
• Sawmill in Terraville, South Dakota, 1888.
• Shoe-factory worker in Lynn, Massachusetts, 1895.

As you read, pay attention to the **boldfaced key terms**, which highlight important concepts you'll likely see on an exam. All terms are defined in the glossary of Key Terms at the end of the book.

oslavery document. Some Garrisonians a
work of the **underground railroad**, a se
ivists who assisted fugitives fleeing ensla
In 1835 Sarah and Angelina Grimké j
d soon began lecturing for the organiza
rominent South Carolina planter, they

new leisure pursuits. Many joined colleagues at restaurants, the theater, or sporting events. They also attended plays and lectures with their wives, visited museums, and took their children to the circus.

REVIEW & RELATE

At the end of each major section, answer the **Review & Relate** questions to check your understanding of key concepts.

• Why did American cities become larger and more diverse in the first half of the nineteenth century?

• What values and beliefs did the emerging American middle class embrace?

✓ *LEARNINGCurve* bedfordstmartins.com/hewittlawson/LC

Then log on to **LearningCurve** to review the section you've just read. LearningCurve lets you move at your own pace and earn points as you go.

Use the Chapter Review to draw connections across all the sections of the narrative and identify significant historical developments.

Return to **LearningCurve** to review chapter material.

Test your knowledge of important concepts from the **Key Terms** list. See if you can not only define each term but also describe its significance.

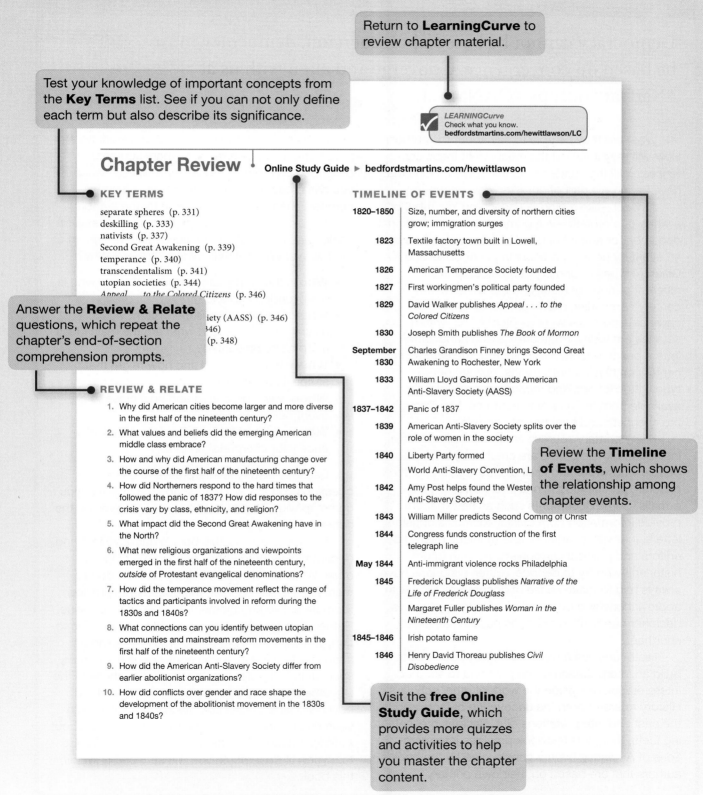

✓ **LEARNINGCurve**
Check what you know.
bedfordstmartins.com/hewittlawson/LC

Chapter Review

Online Study Guide ▶ bedfordstmartins.com/hewittlawson

KEY TERMS

separate spheres (p. 331)
deskilling (p. 333)
nativists (p. 337)
Second Great Awakening (p. 339)
temperance (p. 340)
transcendentalism (p. 341)
utopian societies (p. 344)
Appeal . . . to the Colored Citizens (p. 346)

Answer the **Review & Relate** questions, which repeat the chapter's end-of-section comprehension prompts.

...iety (AASS) (p. 346)
...46)
... (p. 348)

REVIEW & RELATE

1. Why did American cities become larger and more diverse in the first half of the nineteenth century?

2. What values and beliefs did the emerging American middle class embrace?

3. How and why did American manufacturing change over the course of the first half of the nineteenth century?

4. How did Northerners respond to the hard times that followed the panic of 1837? How did responses to the crisis vary by class, ethnicity, and religion?

5. What impact did the Second Great Awakening have in the North?

6. What new religious organizations and viewpoints emerged in the first half of the nineteenth century, *outside* of Protestant evangelical denominations?

7. How did the temperance movement reflect the range of tactics and participants involved in reform during the 1830s and 1840s?

8. What connections can you identify between utopian communities and mainstream reform movements in the first half of the nineteenth century?

9. How did the American Anti-Slavery Society differ from earlier abolitionist organizations?

10. How did conflicts over gender and race shape the development of the abolitionist movement in the 1830s and 1840s?

TIMELINE OF EVENTS

1820–1850	Size, number, and diversity of northern cities grow; immigration surges
1823	Textile factory town built in Lowell, Massachusetts
1826	American Temperance Society founded
1827	First workingmen's political party founded
1829	David Walker publishes *Appeal . . . to the Colored Citizens*
1830	Joseph Smith publishes *The Book of Mormon*
September 1830	Charles Grandison Finney brings Second Great Awakening to Rochester, New York
1833	William Lloyd Garrison founds American Anti-Slavery Society (AASS)
1837–1842	Panic of 1837
1839	American Anti-Slavery Society splits over the role of women in the society
1840	Liberty Party formed
	World Anti-Slavery Convention, L...
1842	Amy Post helps found the Wester... Anti-Slavery Society
1843	William Miller predicts Second Coming of Christ
1844	Congress funds construction of the first telegraph line
May 1844	Anti-immigrant violence rocks Philadelphia
1845	Frederick Douglass publishes *Narrative of the Life of Frederick Douglass*
	Margaret Fuller publishes *Woman in the Nineteenth Century*
1845–1846	Irish potato famine
1846	Henry David Thoreau publishes *Civil Disobedience*

Review the **Timeline of Events**, which shows the relationship among chapter events.

Visit the **free Online Study Guide**, which provides more quizzes and activities to help you master the chapter content.

Apply these principles to your analysis of the chapter's primary sources.

What will historians fifty years from now make of this tweet from @er0tikka?

> Democracy cannot be based upon coercion, democracy must be based on convergence. Converge and align with us at #NatGat #occupy #OANatGat.

What will they be able to say about the author? How will they interpret the meaning of these sentences? Will they understand the abbreviations that have become a part of our everyday language?

A tweet—like a blog, a speech on YouTube, or a video of a protest—is a primary source, an original document or artifact created at or near the time of an event by people participating in or observing it. Different types of primary sources exist from different periods of history. In the seventeenth century and earlier, drawings, paintings, stone carvings, and relics were as plentiful as written sources are today. Printed texts and handwritten letters became more available from the eighteenth century on, while photographs, newspapers, typewritten letters, and recordings are widely available from the mid-nineteenth century through the twentieth and twenty-first centuries.

Many primary sources are produced by official institutions, while others are created by ordinary people who wrote and kept diaries and letters, took pictures, participated in oral interviews, or sent e-mails. Some documents such as newspapers provide information from official sources alongside letters, interviews, articles, and opinions offered by editors and political cartoonists. As with future historians who try to decode Twitter, historians have always had to make sense of documents filled with abbreviations and peculiarities of language and to decipher handwriting styles as puzzling as digital shorthand.

Historians use a wealth of primary sources to build an interpretation of the past and to set that interpretation alongside the work of other scholars. History refers to both the uncovering of facts about the past and interpretations of it. Besides presenting facts, then, this textbook provides interpretations of American history constructed by the book's authors that are based on their own primary research as well as the work of other historians. But it also offers a large array of primary sources, described on the next several pages, from which you can create your own interpretations and compare them with those offered by the authors.

To guide your analysis, begin by asking several basic questions that can be succinctly thought of as the five Ws: Who? What? Where? When? Why?

- **Who** is the author of the document and who is the intended audience?
- **What** kind of source is it—written, visual, official, unofficial—and what are the main ideas or opinions presented?
- **Where** was it created and how might that shape its meaning?
- **When** was it produced and how close to the event being recorded?
- **Why** was it created and how does that influence your interpretation of it?

Because history is interpretive, the kind of questions you ask will help shape the answers you come up with. The more questions you explore, the richer the history you produce will be.

Keep in mind that this book's narrative text and documents work together, each reinforcing the other. While the narrative helps place the documents in a larger context, the documents provide for more active engagement with an event or issue. Rather than merely receiving a collection of information, you will be able to participate in shaping an account of the past. If you consider all the primary sources in a chapter together, including those in the Document Project, you can begin to understand how historians assess and piece together diverse sources of evidence to forge a larger narrative about American history. The next pages introduce you to the types of documents you will be working with in this book.

Get to work exploring the documents.

Individual documents are easy to find and well integrated into every chapter.

Red **Explore** boxes tell you where to find the source and where to return to the text to continue the story.

the issue opposing the measure. John C. Calhoun, a proslavery senator from South Carolina, refused to support any compromise that allowed Congress to decide the fate of slavery in the western territories. Meanwhile William H. Seward, an antislavery Whig senator from New York, proclaimed that in all good conscience he could not support a compromise that forced Northerners to help hunt down fugitives from slavery. Daniel Webster, a Massachusetts Whig and an elder statesman, appealed to his fellow senators to support the compromise in order to preserve the Union, but Congress adjourned with the fate of California undecided.

Explore

See Document 12.2 for Calhoun's final attempt to reject a compromise.

Before the Senate reconvened in the fall of 1850, however, the political landscape changed in unexpected ways. Henry Clay retired in the spring of 1850, leaving the Capitol with his last great legislative effort unfinished. On March 31, Calhoun died; his absence from the Senate made compromise more likely. In July, President Taylor died unexpectedly, and his vice president, Millard Fillmore of Buffalo, New York, was elevated to the presidency. Fillmore then appointed Webster as secretary of state, removing him from the Senate as well.

In September 1850, with President Fillmore's support, a younger cohort of senators and representatives steered the **Compromise of 1850** through Congress, one clause at a time, thereby allowing legislators to support only those parts of the compromise they found palatable. In the end, all the provisions passed, and Fillmore quickly signed the bills into law. California entered the Union as a free state, and John C. Frémont entered Congress as one of that state's first two senators. The Compromise of 1850, like the Missouri Compromise thirty years earlier, fended off a sectional crisis, but it also signaled future problems. Would popular sovereignty prevail when later territories sought admission to the Union, and would Northerners abide by a fugitive slave law that called on them to aid directly in the capture of runaway slaves?

The Fugitive Slave Act Inspires Northern Protest

The fugitive slave laws of 1793 and 1824 mandated that all states aid in apprehending and returning runaway slaves to their owners. The **Fugitive Slave Act of 1850** was different in two important respects. First, it eliminated jury trials for alleged fugitives. Second, the law required individual citizens, not just state officials, to help return runaways or

---

DOCUMENT 12.2

John C. Calhoun | On the Compromise of 1850, 1850

California's application for statehood in 1849 prompted another crisis over slavery. Southerners feared that admitting California as a free state would tip the balance in Congress against them. Senator Henry Clay tried to broker a compromise that would admit California as a free state but toughen the fugitive slave law. Amid vigorous congressional debate, South Carolina senator John C. Calhoun insisted that slavery be preserved. A colleague read Calhoun's address for the aging and ill senator. Calhoun's death a few weeks later helped pave the way for final passage of the Compromise of 1850.

Explore

How can the Union be saved? To this I answer, there is but one way by which it can be, and that is, by adopting such measures as will satisfy the States belonging to the Southern section that they can remain in the Union consistently with their honor and their safety. . . .

. . . The South asks for justice, simple justice, and less she ought not to take. She has no compromise to offer but the Constitution, and no concession or surrender to make. She has already surrendered so much that she has little left to surrender. Such a settlement would go to the root of the evil, and remove all cause of discontent, by satisfying the South that she could remain honorably and safely in the Union, and thereby restore the harmony and fraternal feelings between the sections which existed anterior to the Missouri agitation. . . .

But can this be done? Yes, easily; not by the weaker party, for it can of itself do nothing—not even protect itself—but by the stronger. The North has only to will it to accomplish it—to do justice by conceding to the South an equal right in the acquired territory, and to do her duty by causing the stipulations relative to fugitive slaves to be faithfully fulfilled—to cease the agitation of the slave question, and to provide for the insertion of a provision in the Constitution, by an amendment, which will restore to the South in substance the power she possessed of protecting herself, before the equilibrium between the sections was destroyed by the action of this Government. There will be no difficulty in devising such a provision—one that will protect the South, and which at the same time will improve and strengthen the Government, instead of impairing and weakening it.

Source: *The Congressional Globe*, 31st Cong., 2nd Sess. (1850), 453, 455.

Interpret the Evidence

- Calhoun objects to the Compromise of 1850 because it does not sufficiently protect southern rights. Which rights does he think need protection, and why does he think those rights are in jeopardy?
- Calhoun wants to regain the "harmony and fraternal feelings" between the sections that existed before "the Missouri agitation." Why does he pinpoint the Missouri Compromise as the moment when sectional divisions took hold?

Put It in Context

What developments in the 1840s led Calhoun and other southern leaders to fear that the South was becoming weaker, at least politically, compared to the North? Would northern senators have agreed?

---

else risk being fined or imprisoned. The act angered many Northerners who believed that the federal government had gone too far in protecting the rights of slaveholders and thereby aroused sympathy for the abolitionist cause.

Before 1850, the most well-known individuals aiding fugitives were free blacks such as David Ruggles in New York City; Jermaine Loguen in Syracuse, New York; and, after his own successful escape, Frederick Douglass in Rochester, New York. Their main allies in this work were white Quakers such as Amy and Isaac Post in Rochester; Thomas Garrett in Chester County, Pennsylvania; and Levi and Catherine Coffin in Newport, Indiana. The work was

---

Two **Interpret the Evidence** questions help you analyze the source.

A **Put It in Context** question helps you connect the primary source to the larger historical narrative.

Annotated documents help you examine sources closely by breaking them down into smaller components.

Annotations direct you to points of interest—either specific text passages or visual details—to help you analyze the document and to model what to look for when you approach similar types of documents on your own.

DOCUMENT 14.4

Sharecropping Agreement, 1870

Because Congress did not generally provide freedpeople with land, African Americans lacked the capital to start their own farms. At the same time, plantation owners needed labor to plant and harvest their crops for market. Out of mutual necessity, white plantation owners entered into sharecropping contracts with blacks to work their farms in exchange for a portion of the crop, such as the following contract between Willis P. Bocock and several of his former slaves. Bocock owned Waldwick Plantation in Marengo County, Alabama.

Explore

What are the farmers' responsibilities?

Why would Bocock want to clarify that his laborers would work equally hard throughout the year?

How might putting a lien on crops for debts owed create difficulties for the black farmer?

Contract made the 3rd day of January in the year 1870 between us the free people who have signed this paper of one part, and our employer, Willis P. Bocock, of the other part. We agree to take charge of and cultivate for the year 1870, a portion of land, say [left blank] acres or thereabouts, to be laid off to us by our employer on his plantation, and to tend the same well in the usual crops, in such proportions as we and he may agree upon. We are to furnish the necessary labor, say an average hand to every 15 acres in the crops, making in all average hands; and are to have all proper work done, ditching, fencing, repairing, etc., as well as cultivating and saving the crops of all kinds, so as to put and keep the land we occupy and tend in good order for cropping, and to make a good crop ourselves; and to do our fair share of job work about the place. . . . We are to be responsible for the good conduct of ourselves, our hands, and families, and agree that all shall be respectful to employer, owners, and manager, honest, industrious, and careful about every thing, and shall not interrupt any thing about the place, working as industriously the last part of the year as the first; and then our employer agrees that he and his manager shall treat us kindly, and help us to study our interest and do our duty. If any hand or family proves to be of bad character, or dishonest, or lazy, or disobedient, or any way unsuitable our employer or manager has the right, and we have the right, to have such turned off. . . .

For the labor and services of ourselves and hands rendered as above stated, we are to have one third part of all the crops, or their net-proceeds, made and secured, or prepared for market by our force. . . .

We are to be furnished by our employer through his manager with provisions if we call for them: not over one peck of meal or corn, and $3\frac{1}{2}$ pounds of meat or its equivalent per week, for every 15 acres of land or average hand, to be charged to us at fair market prices.

And whatever may be due by us, or our hands to our employer for provisions or any thing else, during the year, is to be a lien on our share of the crops, and is to be retained by him out of the same before we receive our part.

Source: Waldwick Plantation Records, 1834–1971, LPR174, box 1, folder 9, Alabama Department of Archives and History.

Put It in Context

Why would free blacks and poor whites be willing to enter into such a contract?

DOCUMENT 11.4

Drunkard's Home, 1850

Temperance societies undertook a variety of activities to publici[z]... and parades were popular venues, as were newspapers and boo... *Temperance Offering*, an 1850 publication of the Sons of Temper... 1842, the Sons of Temperance was one of the oldest temperance... mutual aid society that offered members life insurance, funeral b...

Explore

How does the father's drinking seem to affect the family's economic situation?

In this illustration, what is the source of the father's violence?

How... me...

The National Temperance Offering, and Sons and Daughters of Temperance Gift (PS1265.N3 1850), University of Virginia Library

All annotated documents conclude with **Put It in Context** questions that ask you to figure out how the document fits in—or doesn't fit in—with the narrative you're reading.

Put It in Context

What moral arguments did members of the temperance movement use to support their cause?

"Two Views" comparison documents present contrasting or complementary perspectives on a single topic so that you can form your own interpretation.

DOCUMENTS 11.1 AND 11.2

Life in the Mills: Two Views

In the 1820s, the textile mills of Lowell, Massachusetts, provided the daughters of local farmers a way to contribute to their family incomes and experience some adventure. Soon, however, a slowing economy led to reduced wages, longer hours, and demands for increased productivity. The Lowell workers organized to protest these changes and went on strike several times during the late 1820s and the 1830s. The first selection below is from an 1844 edition of *The Lowell Offering*, a magazine to which mill workers contributed stories and poems. Factory owners controlled the content of the magazine to ensure an idealized vision of life in the mills. Still, the letter from "Susan" below does highlight the physical toll of industrial labor. Susan was a pseudonym for Harriet Farley, a weaver and the editor of *The Lowell Offering*. The selection at right is by Harriet Robinson, who entered the mills at age ten in 1834. She published a memoir in 1898 in which she recalls the growing dissatisfaction of the women workers and her critical role in a strike in 1836.

Explore

11.1 Letter from a Lowell Factory Worker, 1844

It makes my feet ache and swell to stand so much, but I suppose I shall get accustomed to that too. The girls generally wear old shoes about their work, and you know nothing is easier; but they almost all say that when they have worked here a year or two they have to procure shoes a size or two larger than before they came. The right hand, which is the one used in stopping and starting the loom, becomes larger than the left; but in other respects the factory is not detrimental to a young girl's appearance. Here they look delicate, but not sickly; they laugh at those who are much exposed, and get pretty brown; but I, for one, had rather be brown than pure white. I never saw so many pretty looking girls as there are here. Though the number of men is small in proportion there are many marriages here, and a great deal of courting. I will tell you of this last sometime. . . .

You ask if the work is not disagreeable. Not when one is accustomed to it. It tried my patience sadly at first, and does now when it does not run well; but, in general, I like it very much. It is easy to do, and does not require very violent exertion, as much of our farm work does.

You also ask how I get along with the girls here. Very well indeed.

and workingmen started joining forces throughout the North to advocate for principles of liberty and equality. Self-educated artisans like Thomas Skidmore of New York City argued for the redistribution of property and the abolition of inheritance to equalize wealth in the nation. However, most workingmen's parties focused on more practical proposals: government distribution of free land in the West, the abolition of compulsory militia service and imprisonment for debt, public funding for education, and the regulation of banks and corporations. Although the

Explore

11.2 Harriet Robinson | Reflections on the 1836 Lowell Mills Strike, 1898

My own recollection of this first strike (or "turn out" as it was called) is very vivid. I worked in a lower room, where I had heard the proposed strike fully, if not vehemently, discussed; I had been an ardent listener to what was said against this attempt at "oppression" on the part of the corporation, and naturally I took sides with the strikers. When the day came on which the girls were to turn out, those in the upper rooms started first, and so many of them left that our mill was at once shut down. Then, when the girls in my room stood irresolute, uncertain what to do, asking each other, "Would you?" or "Shall we turn out?" and not one of them having the courage to lead off, *I*, who began to think they would not go out, after all their talk, became impatient, and started on ahead, saying, with childish bravado, "I don't care what you do, I am going to turn out, whether any one else does or not"; and I marched out, and was followed by the others.

As I looked back at the long line that followed me, I was more proud than I have ever been since at any success I may have achieved, and more proud than I shall ever be again until my own beloved State gives to its women citizens the right of suffrage.

The agent of the corporation where I then worked took some small revenges on the supposed ringleaders; on the principle of sending the weaker to the wall, my mother [a landlady] was turned away from her boarding-house, that functionary saying, "Mrs. Hanson, you could not prevent the older girls from turning out, but your daughter is a child, and *her* you could control."

It is hardly necessary to say that so far as results were concerned this strike did no good. The dissatisfaction of the operatives subsided, or burned itself out, and though the authorities did not accede to their demands, the majority returned to their work, and the corporation went on cutting down the wages.

Source: Harriet H. Robinson, *Loom and Spindle; or, Life among the Early Mill Girls* (New York: Thomas Y. Crowell, 1898), 84–86.

Interpret the Evidence questions help you analyze the sources.

Interpret the Evidence

- How did life on the farm differ from life in the factory? How does "Susan" describe her own adjustment to industrial work?
- What connections does Robinson make between the strike and the larger social and political context of 1830s Massachusetts? How does she see herself and her actions?

Put It in Context

Were "Susan" and Robinson typical factory workers in this period? Why or why not?

Trades Union was established later that year, with delegates representing more than twenty-five thousand workers across the North. These organizations aided skilled workers but refused admission to women and unskilled men.

panic of 1837, the common plight of workers became clearer. But the economic crisis made unified action nearly impossible as individuals sought to hold on to what little they had by any means available.

A **Document Project** concludes each chapter.

Each project provides multiple perspectives on a particular issue or development along with an **introduction** and **questions** to guide you through the process of interpretation. The chapter itself offers the background material for your interpretation.

and grasses that would have kept the earth from eroding and turning into dust. Instead, dust storms brought life to a grinding halt, blocking out the midday sun. **See Document Project 22: The Depression in Rural America, page 712.**

As the storms continued through the 1930s, most residents—approximately 75 percent—remained on

Red **cross-references** at the relevant point in the chapter direct you to the chapter's Document Project.

DOCUMENT 22.6
The Life of a White Sharecropper, 1938

In 1936 workers in the WPA's Federal Writers Project began the Folklore Project. Interviewers spoke with thousands of ordinary individuals to document their home lives, education, occupations, political and religious views, and the impact of the Great Depression on their families. Folklore Project worker Claude Dunnagan collected the following story from a white sharecropping family in Longtown, North Carolina.

I guess we been hard luck renters all our lives—me and Morrison both. They was ten young'uns in my family, and I was next to the youngest. We had it awful hard. . . . We went to Yadkin County and rented an old rundown farm for a share of what we could raise. The crops wasn't any good that year, the landlord came and got what we had raised and had the auctioneers come and sell our tools and furniture. They was a bunch of people at the sale that day from all around. I was standin' there watchin' the man sell the things when I saw a good lookin' man in overalls lookin' toward me. He watched me all durin' the sale and I knew what he was thinkin'. That was the first time I ever saw Allison. I reckon he fell in love with me right off, for we was married a few days later. Allison didn't have no true father. His mother wasn't married, and he was raised up by his kin folks. Then we moved to a little farm near Longtown, about ten miles away. The owner said we could have three-fourths of what we raised. The first two years the crops turned out pretty good so we could pay off the landlord and buy a little furniture . . . a bed and table and some chairs. Then the first baby came on. That was Hildreth. He's out in the field workin' now, suckerin' [removing sprouts] tobacco. . . . By that time, we was able to get a cow, and that came in good, for the baby was awful thin and weak. . . .

Hildreth was only six, but he could help a lot, pullin' and tyin' the tobacco, and helpin' hang it in the barn. We got out more tobacco that year than any other, but when we took it to market in Winston, they wasn't payin' but about twelve cents a pound for the best grade, so when we give the landlord his share and paid the fertilizer bill, we didn't have enough left to pay the doctor and store bill. We didn't know what we was goin' to do durin' the winter. Allison had raised a few vegetables and apples, so we canned what we could and traded the rest for some cotton cloth up at the store so the children would have something to wear that winter. Allison got a job helpin' build a barn for a neighbor, but it didn't last but two days. The neighbor gave him two second hand pairs of overalls for the work. . . .

Things are a lot better for the renter today than in the past. It used to be we couldn't get enough to eat and wear. Now we got a cow, a hog, and some chickens. Allison bought a second-hand car and every Sunday afternoon we ride somewhere. It's the only time we ever get away from home.

The landlord gives us five-sixths of what we raise, so we get along pretty good when the crops are fair. Of course we have to furnish the fertilizer and livestock. This year we had seven barns of tobacco and four acres of corn. Wheat turned out pretty good, too. We raised forty-three bushels, and I hear the price is going to be fair at the roller mill. I canned about all our extra fruits and vegetables. I reckon we still got about a hundred cans in the pantry.

Source: Library of Congress, Manuscript Division, WPA Federal Writers Project Collection.

DOCUMENT PROJECT **22**

The Depression in Rural America

During the 1930s, rural Americans' lives were devastated by the twin disasters of the Great Depression and, in the Great Plains, the most sustained drought in American history. But both problems only deepened the already difficult lives of many farmers. Agriculture in the South had long been dominated by sharecropping, a system that hampered crop diversification and left many African American tenant farmers vulnerable to exploitation by white landowners. In the Midwest, farmers had spent decades overgrazing pastures and exhausting the soil through overproduction. Prices dropped dramatically throughout the 1920s, and farmers were the only group whose incomes fell during that decade.

When the depression hit, many farmers did not have the resources to stay on their land, and farm foreclosures tripled in the early 1930s. Sharecroppers, tenant farmers, and former farm owners left their homes to find better opportunities, and a million people left the Great Plains alone. Most ended up as migrant agricultural laborers in farms and orchards on the West Coast. Feeling overrun by refugees, California passed a law in 1937 making it a misdemeanor to bring into California any indigent person who was not a state resident. This law remained in effect until 1941.

Under the New Deal, the federal government acted in a number of ways to relieve the plight of farmers around the country. The Agricultural Adjustment Act attempted to raise crop prices and stabilize agricultural incomes by encouraging farmers to cut production. The Farm Credit Act helped some farmers refinance mortgages at a lower rate, the Rural Electrification Administration brought electricity to farm areas previously without it, and the Soil Conservation Service advised farmers on how to properly cultivate their hillsides. The report of the Great Plains Committee (Document 22.10), another Roosevelt creation, details additional recommendations for helping the agricultural economy in the Midwest.

The following documents on the lives of farmers, sharecroppers, migrants, and labor organizers during the 1930s shed light on many aspects of the Great Depression. Consider what they reveal about the challenges faced by rural Americans and how different individuals and groups responded to those problems.

Document Project 22: The Depression in Rural America   **713**

DOCUMENT 22.5
Ann Marie Low | Dust Bowl Diary, 1934

When massive dust storms swept through the Midwest beginning in the early 1930s, they blew away the topsoil of a once productive farm region and created hazardous living conditions. Residents needed to clean and wash repetitively to perform even simple daily tasks. Ann Marie Low, a young woman living with her family in southeastern North Dakota, describes in her diary the monotony and difficulty of life in the Dust Bowl.

May 21, 1934, Monday . . .
Saturday Dad, Bud, and I planted an acre of potatoes. There was so much dirt in the air I couldn't see Bud only a few feet in front of me. Even the air in the house was just a haze. In the evening the wind died down, and Cap came to take me to the movie. We joked about how hard it is to get cleaned up enough to go anywhere.

The newspapers report that on May 10 there was such a strong wind the experts in Chicago estimated 12,000,000 tons of Plains soil was dumped on that city. By the next day the sun was obscured in Washington, D.C., and ships 300 miles out at sea reported dust settling on their decks.

Sunday the dust wasn't so bad. Dad and I drove cattle to the Big Pasture. Then I churned butter and baked a ham, bread, and cookies for the men, as no telling when Mama will be back.

May 30, 1934, Wednesday
Ethel got along fine, so Mama left her at the hospital and came to Jamestown by train Friday. Dad took us both home.

The mess was incredible! Dirt had blown into the house all week and lay inches deep on everything. Every towel and curtain was just black. There wasn't a clean dish or cooking utensil. There was no food. Oh, there were eggs and milk and one loaf left of the bread I baked the weekend before. I looked in the cooler box down the well (our refrigerator) and found a little ham and butter. It was late, so Mama and I cooked some ham and eggs for the men's supper because that was all we could fix in a hurry. It turned out they had been living on ham and eggs for two days.

Mama was very tired. After she had fixed starter for bread, I insisted she go to bed and I'd do all the dishes. It took until 10 o'clock to wash all the dirty dishes. That's not wiping them—just washing them. The cupboards had to be washed out to have a clean place to put them.

Saturday was a busy day. Before starting breakfast I had to sweep and wash all the dirt off the kitchen and dining room floors, wash the stove, pancake griddle, and dining room table and chairs. There was cooking, baking, and churning to be done for those hungry men. Dad is 6 feet 4 inches tall, with a big frame. Bud is 6 feet 3 inches and almost as big-boned as Dad. We say feeding them is like filling a silo.

Mama couldn't make bread until I carried water to wash the bread mixer. I couldn't churn until the churn was washed and scalded. We just couldn't do anything until something was washed first. Every room had to have dirt almost shoveled out of it before we could wash floors and furniture.

We had no time to wash clothes, but it was necessary. I had to wash out the boiler, wash tubs, and the washing machine before we could use them. Then every towel, curtain, piece of bedding, and garment had to be taken outdoors to have as much dust as possible shaken out before washing. The cistern is dry, so I had to carry all the water we needed from the well.

Source: Ann Marie Low, *Dust Bowl Diary* (Lincoln: University of Nebraska Press, 1984), 96–97.

DOCUMENT 22.7
Sharecropping Family in Washington County, Arkansas, 1935

The Resettlement Administration (later the Farm Security Administration) documented the plight of migrant farmworkers and sharecroppers in numerous photographs. The following photo, taken by the noted photojournalist Arthur Rothstein, depicts a sharecropper's wife and daughters in Washington County, Arkansas, in 1935.

DOCUMENT 22.9
Frank Stokes | Let the Mexicans Organize, 1936

While union organizers made some gains in the industrial sector, they made little headway in the agricultural fields of California. Frank Stokes was a citrus grower who broke with his fellow farmers to support migrant labor organizing. In the following selection, Stokes argues in favor of unionization among migrant Mexican farmworkers.

The Mexican is to agricultural California what the Negro is to the medieval South. His treatment by the vegetable growers of the Imperial Valley is well known. What has happened to him in the San Joaquin has likewise been told. But for a time at least it appeared that the "citrus belt" was different. Then came the strike of the Mexican fruit pickers in Orange County. In its wake came the vigilantes, the night riders, the strike-breakers, the reporters whose job it was to "slant" all the stories in favor of the packers and grove owners. There followed the State Motor Patrol, which for the first time in the history of strike disorders in California set up a portable radio broadcasting station "in a secret place" in the strike area "to direct law-and-order activities." And special deputy badges blossomed as thick as Roosevelt buttons in the recent campaign.

Sheriff Jackson declared bravely: "It was the strikers themselves who drew first blood so from now on we will meet them on that basis." "This is no fight," said he, "between orchardists and pickers. It is a fight between the entire population of Orange County and a bunch of Communists." However, dozens and dozens of non-Communist Mexican fruit pickers were jailed; 116 were arrested en masse while traveling in automobiles along the highway. They were charged with riot and placed under bail of $500 each. . . . After fifteen days in jail the hearing was finally held—and the state's witnesses were able to identify only one person as having taken part in the trouble. . . . Judge Ames of the Superior Court ordered the release of all but one identified prisoner and severely criticized the authorities for holding the Mexicans in jail for so long a time when they must have known it would not be possible to identify even a small portion of the prisoners.

For weeks during the strike newspaper stories described the brave stand taken by "law-abiding citizens." These stories were adorned with such headlines as "Vigilantes Battle Citrus Strikers in War on Reds." During all this time, so far as I know, only one paper—the Los Angeles *Evening News*—defended the fruit pickers. . . .

These Mexicans were asking for a well-deserved wage increase and free transportation to and from the widely scattered groves; they also asked that tools be furnished by the employers. Finally they asked recognition of their newly formed union. Recognition of the Mexican laboring man's union, his cooperative organization formed in order that he might obtain a little more for his commodity, which is labor—here was the crucial point. The growers and packers agreed to furnish tools; they agreed to furnish transportation to and from the groves. They even agreed to a slight wage increase, which still left the workers underpaid. But recognition of the Mexican workers' union? Never! . . .

Not only in the fields are the Mexican people exploited. Not only as earners but as buyers they are looked upon as legitimate prey—for old washing machines that will not clean clothes, for old automobiles that wheeze and let down, for woolen blankets made of cotton, for last season's shop-worn wearing apparel. Gathered in villages composed of rough board shanties or drifting with the seasons from vegetable fields of the Imperial Valley to the grape vineyards of the San Joaquin, wherever they go it is the same old, pathetic story. Cheap labor!

Source: Frank Stokes, "Let the Mexicans Organize," *The Nation*, December 19, 1936, 731–32.

DOCUMENT 22.10
Report of the Great Plains Committee, 1937

In 1936 President Roosevelt established the Great Plains Committee to investigate the causes of the Dust Bowl and possible solutions for the region. The committee's report, submitted the following year, outlined how federal, state, and local government agencies could work together to restore the Great Plains to economic health. One of the witnesses the committee called to testify was Otis Nation, an organizer for the Oklahoma Tenant Farmers' Union, whose testimony follows.

Much has been written of our droughts here in Oklahoma, and how they have driven the farmers from the land. But little has been said of the other tentacles that choke off the livelihood of the small owner and the tenant. We do not wish to minimize the seriousness of these droughts and their effects on the farming population. But droughts alone would not have permanently displaced these farmers. The great majority of migrants had already become share-tenants and sharecroppers. The droughts hastened a process that had already begun. We submit the following as the cases for migratory agricultural workers:

1. *High interest rates.* Often a farmer borrows money for periods of 10 months and is charged an interest rate of 10 percent. These rates are charged when crops are good and when they fail. Through such practices the farmer loses his ownership; he becomes a tenant, then a sharecropper, then a migrant.
2. *The tenant and sharecropping system.* When share tenants are charged 33⅓ percent of all corn or feed crops and 25 percent or more on cotton, plus 10 percent on all money borrowed at the bank, when sharecroppers are charged 50 to 75 percent of all he produces to the landlords, plus 10 percent for the bank's share on money invested; when these robbing practices are carried on in a community or a State, is it surprising that 33,241 farm families have left Oklahoma in the past 5 years?
3. *Land exhaustion, droughts, soil erosion, and the one-crop system of farming.* Lacking capital and equipment, small farmers have been unable to terrace their land or conduct other soil-conservation practices. The tenant and sharecropping system is chiefly responsible for the one-crop system. The landlord dictates what crops are to be planted—invariably cotton—and the tenant either plants it or gets off.
4. *Unstable markets.* Approximately a month and a half before the wheat harvest this year the price for this product was 93 cents here in Oklahoma City. But at harvest time the farmer sold his wheat for 46 cents to 60 cents per bushel, depending on the grade. . . . Kaffir [a grain sorghum] was selling

for $1.30 one month ago, and yesterday we sold some for 85 cents per hundred. . . .

It is obvious to all of us that farm prices are set by speculators. The farmer's losses at the market have contributed in no small part to the farmer losing his place on the land. Higher prices for farm products are quoted when the farmer has nothing to sell.

5. *Tractor farming.* In Creek County, Okla., we have the record of one land-owner purchasing 3 tractors and forcing 31 of his 34 tenants and croppers from the land. Most of these families left the State when neither jobs nor relief could be secured. This is over 10 families per machine, 10 families who must quit their profession and seek employment in an unfriendly, industrialized farming section of Arizona or California. Many of these families were even unable to become "Joads" [the fictional family in *The Grapes of Wrath*] in these other States, and had to seek relief from an unfriendly national administration and a more unfriendly State administration. . . .

At this hearing we will have all kinds of statistical material presented and arguments based on this material. But I am one of those who is more interested in the people, my people, than in mere figures. I do not agree with those who say "the no-good must always be weeded out." I say that all of these people, casually referred to in statistical sums, are 100-percent Americans. There are no more important problems facing us than the problem of stopping this human erosion and rehabilitating those unfortunates who have already been thrown off the land. Certainly it is un-American for Americans to be starved and dispossessed of their homes in our land of plenty. Those who seek to exploit and harass these American refugees, the migratory workers, are against our principles of democracy.

Source: U.S. Congress, House Select Committee to Investigate the Interstate Migration of Destitute Citizens (Washington: Government Printing Office, 1940–1941), 2102.

Interpret the Evidence

1. What does Ann Marie Low's description of a typical day suggest about the particular challenges women faced during the Dust Bowl era (Document 22.5)?
2. Compare the living conditions described by a white southern sharecropper (Document 22.6) to those of the migrant family described by John Steinbeck (Document 22.8). How does the poverty of the two families differ? How would you explain the differences you note?
3. Compare the sharecropper's story (Document 22.6) with the photograph of the Arkansas family (Document 22.7). Do the subjects seem to react to the Great Depression in the same way? Do they seem hopeful or hopeless?
4. According to Frank Stokes, how did the fruit packers and grove owners characterize their conflict with the Mexican farmworkers (Document 22.9)? In what ways did their characterization draw on more general conservative criticisms of the New Deal?
5. According to the Great Plains Committee testimony (Document 22.10), what role did human-caused factors play in producing the misery that accompanied the dust storms of the early 1930s?

Put It in Context

- What do these documents tell us about expectations regarding government help during the Great Depression?

EXPLORING AMERICAN HISTORIES

A map showing the arrival of the English in Virginia, 1585–1588.

Aztec feather artisans at work, from the Florentine Codex, c. 1540–1585.

1
Mapping Global Frontiers
to 1585

Biblioteca Nacional, Madrid, Spain/Giraudon/The Bridgeman Art Library

Meeting of Hernán Cortés and Montezuma, from the Duran Codex, 1579.

AMERICAN HISTORIES

In 1519 a young Indian woman named Malintzin was thrust into the center of dramatic events that transformed not only her world but also the world at large. As a young girl, Malintzin, whose birth name is lost to history, lived in the rural area of Coatzacoalcos on the frontier between the expanding kingdom of the Mexica and the declining Mayan states of the Yucatán peninsula. Raised in a noble household, Malintzin was fluent in Nahuatl, the language of the Mexica.

In 1515 or 1516, when she was between the ages of eight and twelve, Malintzin was taken by or given to Mexica merchants, perhaps as a peace offering to stave off military attacks. She then entered a well-established trade in slaves, consisting mostly of women and girls, who were sent eastward to work in the expanding cotton fields. Malintzin was apparently sold to a Chontal Mayan village along the Tabasco River near the Gulf of Mexico. As a slave, Malintzin was among thousands of workers who planted, watered, weeded, and harvested the cotton or beat and carded the raw fibers into thread and spun and dyed the yarn. She may also have been forced into a sexual relationship as the concubine of a landowner. Whatever her situation, Malintzin learned the Mayan language during her captivity.

In 1517 Mayan villagers sighted Spanish adventurers along local rivers and drove them off. But in 1519 the Spaniards returned. Well armed and sailing huge boats, they traveled up the Tabasco River and attacked local villages. The Maya's cotton armor and wooden arrows were no match for the invaders' steel swords, guns, and horses. Forced to surrender, the Maya offered the Spaniards food, gold, and twenty enslaved women, including Malintzin. The Spanish leader, Hernán Cortés, baptized the enslaved women as Christians, though they neither understood nor consented to the ritual. He assigned each of them Christian names, including Marina, which was later changed to Malintzin. Cortés then divided the women among his senior officers, giving Malintzin to the highest-ranking noble.

Already fluent in Nahuatl and Mayan, Malintzin soon learned Spanish. Within a matter of months, she became the chief translator between the Spaniards and native peoples. As Cortés moved into territories ruled by the Mexica (whom the Spaniards called Aztecs), his success depended on his ability to understand Aztec ways of thinking and to convince subjugated groups to fight against their despotic rulers. Malintzin thus accompanied Cortés at every step, including his triumphant conquest of the Aztec capital in the fall of 1521.

At the same time that Malintzin played a key role in the conquest of the Aztecs, Martin Waldseemüller sought to map the frontiers along which these conflicts erupted. Born in present-day Germany in the early 1470s, Waldseemüller enrolled at the University of Fribourg in 1490, where he probably studied theology. He would gain fame, however, not as a cleric but as a cartographer, or mapmaker.

In 1507 Waldseemüller and Mathias Ringmann produced a map of the world, a small globe, and a Latin translation of the four voyages of the Italian explorer Amerigo Vespucci. The map and the globe, entitled *Universalis Cosmographia*, depict the "known" world as well as the "new" worlds recently discovered by European explorers. The latter include an elongated territory labeled America, set between the continents of Africa and Asia. A thousand copies of the map were produced, each consisting of twelve sections engraved on wood and covering some 36 square feet. The map offered a view of the world never before attempted.

In 1513 Waldseemüller and Ringmann published the world's first atlas, which included a Latin edition of the works of Ptolemy, the Greco-Egyptian mathematician and astronomer. Three years later, Waldseemüller produced an updated map of the world, the *Carta Marina*. Apparently in response to challenges regarding Vespucci's role in discovering new territories, he substituted the term *Terra Incognita* ("unknown land") for the region he had earlier labeled America. But the 1507 map had already circulated widely, and *America* became part of the European lexicon. •

THE PERSONAL HISTORIES of Malintzin and Martin Waldseemüller were both shaped by the profound consequences of contact between the peoples of Europe and those of the Americas. Both Malintzin and Waldseemüller helped to map the frontiers of an increasingly global society. **See Document Project 1: Mapping America, page 27**. It took much longer in the sixteenth century than today to travel from continent to continent and to communicate across such vast distances. Nonetheless, animals, plants, goods, ideas, and people began circulating regularly among Asia, Africa, Europe, and the Americas during the sixteenth century. Malintzin and Waldseemüller, in their very different ways, were part of these dramatic transformations.

Native Peoples in the Americas

It is likely that the first migrants to the Americas were northeast Asians who arrived some 13,000 to 15,000 years ago. By the time Malintzin participated in the Spanish conquest of the Aztecs in the early sixteenth century, the Americas probably had a population of 60 million to 70 million people. The Nahuatl- and Mayan-speaking groups whose lands bordered the Gulf of Mexico were among hundreds of native societies that covered this vast landmass. Most lived within a few hundred miles of the equator, while only about 6 million to 7 million people likely lived in present-day North America. Despite its isolation, the Americas, like other regions of the world, were home to diverse and dynamic societies, ranging from nomadic hunter-gatherers to large and sophisticated city-centered empires.

Native Peoples Develop Diverse Cultures

Much of what we know as the Americas was probably first settled by peoples from northeast Asia. Between about 16,000 and 14,000 B.C.E., the growth of glaciers during the Wisconsin period led to a dramatic drop in sea levels and created a land bridge in the Bering Straits, between present-day Siberia and Alaska. Early settlers probably traveled over this bridge, known as **Beringia**, following herds of mammoths, musk oxen, and woolly rhinoceroses.

While most of these groups settled along the coast or gradually pushed inland, others probably used boats, hugging the shore and landing at various points along the Pacific coastline. Whether on foot or by boat, most groups traveled southward, skirting melting glaciers and seeking better hunting grounds and more abundant plant life. The mammoths and other large game disappeared about 10,000 years ago, and many groups then depended on smaller game, fish, roots, berries, and other plant foods to survive. At the same time, migrations continued across the Bering Straits, with Inuit and Aleut peoples arriving in present-day Alaska about 5,000 years ago (Map 1.1).

About 3,000 years ago, some communities in the Americas began establishing agricultural systems that encouraged more stable settlements, population growth, and the accumulation of possessions. In the Americas, **horticulture**—a form of agriculture in which people work small plots of land with simple tools—first developed in present-day Mexico. There men and women developed strains of maize (or Indian corn) with larger kernels and higher yields than those that grew in the wild. They also cultivated beans, squash, tomatoes, potatoes, and manioc (a root vegetable), providing rich sources of protein. The combination of beans, squash, and corn offered an especially nutritious diet while maintaining the fertility of the soil. Moreover, high yields produced surplus food that could be stored or traded to neighboring communities.

By 500 C.E., complex societies, rooted in intensive agriculture, began to thrive in the equatorial region. Between 500 and 1500 C.E., thousands of separate societies and cultures speaking hundreds of distinct languages developed in the Americas. Small bands of hunters and gatherers continued to thrive in deserts and forests while impressive civilizations marked by gigantic stone statuary, complex irrigation systems, and ornate gold and silver ornaments arose on swamplands and in the mountains.

The Aztecs, the Maya, and the Incas

Three significant civilizations had developed by the early sixteenth century: Aztec and Mayan societies in the equatorial region and the Inca society along the Pacific coast in present-day Peru. Technologically advanced and with knowledge of mathematics and astronomy, these societies were characterized by vast mineral wealth, large urban centers, highly ritualized religions, and complex political systems. Unlike their counterparts in Europe, Asia, and Africa, they did not develop the wheel to aid in transportation, nor did they have steel tools and weapons. Since most of their commerce was carried out over land or along rivers and coastlines, they did not build large boats. They also lacked horses, which had disappeared from the region thousands of years earlier. Still, the Aztecs, Maya, and Incas established grand cities and civilizations that rivaled those of the most sophisticated societies in the world.

Around 1325 C.E., the **Aztecs**, who called themselves Mexica, built their capital, Tenochtitlán, on the site of present-day Mexico City. As seminomadic warriors who had invaded and then settled in the region, the Aztecs drew on local residents' knowledge of irrigation and cultivation and adopted their written language. Aztec commoners,

Figure Whistle, Peru, 3rd–7th Century

This figure whistle made of hammered gold was produced by the Moche (pre-Inca) civilization in northern Peru. The man pictured here is a warrior and once held an object in his right hand. Moche people used figure whistles to communicate with their ancestors when a human offering was made.   Image © Metropolitan Museum of Art/Art Resource, NY

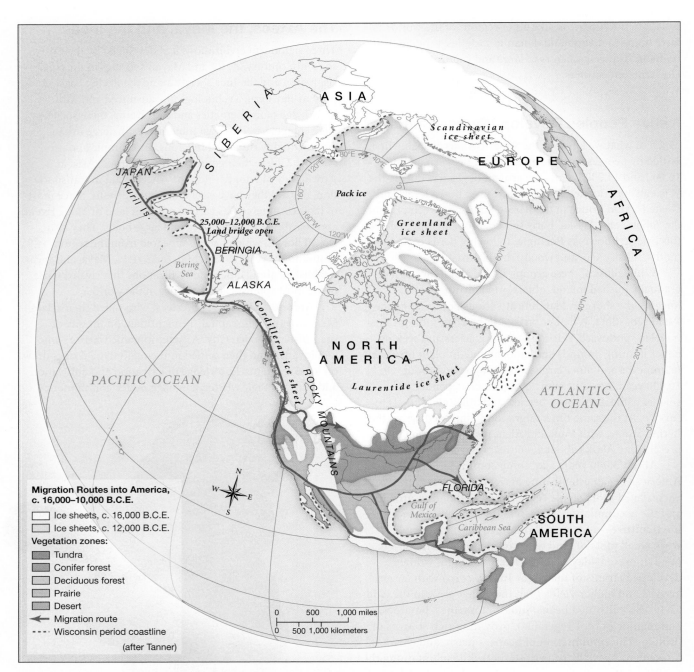

MAP 1.1   The Wisconsin Glaciation and the Settling of the Americas

In roughly 16,000 B.C.E., ice covered most of North America. Its presence lowered the depth of the world's oceans, creating a land bridge called Beringia between Siberia and Alaska. Asian peoples likely migrated to North America across this bridge, hunting woolly mammoths and other game, and then slowly moved south and east as the ice retreated over the next four thousand years.

who tilled communally owned lands, were ruled over by priests and nobles. The nobles formed a warrior class and owned vast estates on which they employed both serfs and slaves captured from non-Aztec communities in the region. Priests promised fertility—for the land and its people—but demanded human sacrifices, including thousands of men

and women from captured tribes. To sustain their society, Aztecs extended their trade networks into surrounding areas. Aztec artisans produced valuable trade goods like pottery, cloth, and leather goods that were exchanged for textiles, food items, and obsidian (the volcanic rock used to make sharp-edged tools) as well as bird feathers, tortoiseshells, and other luxury goods. As Malintzin's story illustrates, Aztecs also traded in slaves.

When Malintzin was sold to a Chontal Mayan village by Aztec merchants, she was being traded from one grand civilization to another. The **Maya** had slowly settled the Yucatán peninsula and the rain forests of present-day Guatemala between roughly 900 B.C.E. and 300 C.E. They established large cities that were home to skilled artisans and developed elaborate systems for irrigation and water storage. Farmers worked the fields and labored to build huge stone temples and palaces for rulers who claimed to be descended from the gods. Learned men developed mathematical calculations, hieroglyphic writing, and a calendar. Mayan astronomers also developed an amazingly accurate system for predicting eclipses of the sun and the moon.

Yet the Mayan civilization began to decline around 800 C.E. An economic crisis, likely the result of a drought and exacerbated by heavy taxation, probably drove peasant families into the interior. Many towns and religious sites were abandoned. Yet some communities survived the crisis and reemerged as thriving city-states. By the early sixteenth century, they traded with the Aztecs.

The **Incas** developed an equally impressive civilization in the Andes Mountains along the Pacific coast. The Inca empire, like the Aztec empire, was built on the accomplishments of earlier societies. At the height of their power, in the fifteenth century, the Incas controlled some sixteen million people spread over 350,000 square miles. They constructed an expansive system of roads and garrisons to ensure the flow of food, trade goods, and soldiers from their capital at Cuzco through the surrounding mountains and valleys. Pack trains of llamas hauled tribute from conquered tribes to provincial centers and then on to Cuzco.

The key to Inca success was the cultivation of fertile mountain valleys. Cuzco, some eleven thousand feet above sea level, lay in the center of the Inca empire, with the Huaylas and Titicaca valleys on either side. Here residents cut timber from dense forests and cultivated potatoes and other crops on terraces watered by an elaborate irrigation system. Some artisans crafted gold and silver from the rich mountains into jewelry and decorative items, while others excelled at stone carving, pottery, and weaving. Thousands of laborers constructed elaborate palaces and temples. And like the Aztecs, Inca priests sacrificed humans to the gods to stave off natural disasters and military defeat.

Native Cultures to the North

To the north of these grand civilizations, smaller societies with less elaborate cultures thrived. In present-day Arizona and New Mexico, the Mogollon and Hohokam established communities around 500 C.E. The Mogollon were expert potters while the Hohokam developed extensive irrigation systems. Farther north, in present-day Utah and Colorado, the ancient Pueblo people built adobe and masonry homes cut into cliffs around 750 C.E. The homes clustered around a sunken ceremonial room, the kiva. A century later, the center of this culture moved south to the San Juan River Basin, where the Pueblo constructed large buildings that housed the people and their rulers along with administrative offices, religious centers, and craft shops. When a prolonged drought settled on the region in the early twelfth century, many Pueblo moved back north into cliff dwellings that offered greater protection from invaders as well as from the heat and sun. By 1300 these areas, too, were gripped by drought, and the residents appear to have dispersed into smaller groups.

Farther north on the plains that stretched from present-day Colorado into Canada, hunting societies developed around herds of bison. A weighted spear-throwing device, called an *atlatl*, allowed hunters to capture smaller game, while nets, hooks, and snares allowed them to catch birds, fish, and small animals. For many such groups, hunting was supplemented by the gathering of berries, roots, and other edible plants. These Plains societies generally remained small and widely scattered since they needed a large expanse of territory to ensure their survival as they traveled to follow migrating animals or seasonal plant sources.

Hunting-gathering societies also emerged along the Pacific coast, but the abundance of fish, small game, and plant life there provided the resources to develop permanent settlements. The Chumash Indians, near present-day Santa Barbara, California, harvested resources from the land and the ocean. Women gathered acorns and pine nuts, while men fished along the coastal waters and in rivers and hunted deer and smaller animals. The Chumash, whose villages sometimes held a thousand inhabitants, participated in regional exchange networks up and down the coast. As many as 300,000 people may have lived along the Pacific in a diverse array of societies before the arrival of Europeans.

Even larger societies with more elaborate social, religious, and political systems developed near the Mississippi River. A group that came to be called the **Hopewell people** established a thriving culture there in the early centuries C.E. The river and its surrounding lands provided fertile fields and easy access to distant communities. Centered in present-day southern Ohio and western Illinois, the Hopewell constructed towns of four thousand to six thousand people. Artifacts from their burial sites reflect extensive trading networks that stretched from the Missouri River to Lake Superior, and from the Rocky Mountains to the Appalachian region and Florida.

Serpent Mound

This mound was most likely constructed sometime between 950 and 1200 C.E. by the Mississippian society found in present-day southern Ohio. A sun-worshipping culture, the Mississippians aligned the head of the serpent with the sunset of the summer solstice (June 20 or 21). Goods found at such sites indicate that Hopewell networks were further extended by the Mississippians.   Mark C. Burnett/Photo Researchers

Beginning around 500 C.E., the Hopewell culture gave birth to larger and more complex societies that flourished in the Mississippi River valley and to the south and east. As bows and arrows spread into the region, people hunted more game in the thick forests. But Mississippian groups also learned to cultivate corn. The development of corn as a staple crop allowed the population to expand dramatically, and more complex political and religious systems developed in which elite rulers gained greater control over the labor of farmers and hunters.

Mississippian peoples created massive earthworks sculpted in the shape of serpents, birds, and other creatures. Still visible in present-day north Georgia, eastern Oklahoma, and southern Ohio and at Cahokia Creek near modern East St. Louis, Illinois, some earthen sculptures stood over 70 feet high and stretched more than 1,300 feet in length. Mississippians also constructed huge temple mounds that could cover nearly 16 acres.

By about 1100 C.E., the community around Cahokia Creek had grown to some fifteen thousand inhabitants. Powerful chieftains extended their trade networks, conquered smaller villages, and created a centralized government. But the rulers proved too weak to maintain their control over numerous scattered towns. To the south, near present-day Tuscaloosa, Alabama, more than twenty flat-topped mounds formed an important ceremonial center in the thirteenth century. By 1400, however, the Mississippians began to lose power there as well. Over the next century, this once-flourishing culture declined, leaving behind vast temple mounds and stunning earthen sculptures.

REVIEW & RELATE

Compare and contrast the Aztecs, Incas, and Maya. What similarities and differences do you note?

How did the societies of North America differ from those of the equatorial zone and the Andes?

LEARNINGCurve **bedfordstmartins.com/hewittlawson/LC**

Europe Expands Its Reach

The complex societies that emerged in the Americas were made possible by an agricultural revolution that included the establishment of crop systems, the domestication of animals, and the development of tools. These developments had occurred 4000–3000 B.C.E. in the Fertile Crescent (see Map 1.2) in southwest Asia and in China. The increased productivity in these areas ensured population growth and allowed attention to science, trade, politics, religion, and the arts. Over millennia, knowledge from these civilizations made its way northward and westward into Europe, and at the height of the Roman empire in the early centuries C.E., Europe was part of dense global trade networks that connected the peoples of Europe, Africa, and Asia. With the decline of Roman power in western Europe, however, those connections broke down, and Europeans turned inward. It would take many centuries for European societies to recover. When they did, motivated by a desire to gain access to the riches of the East, they began to search for ways to regain their connections to the larger world.

The Mediterranean World

For several centuries before 1500, Islam proved one of the most dynamic cultural, political, and military forces in the world. By the ninth century, Islamic (also known as Muslim) regimes controlled most of southwest Asia and North Africa and conquered parts of the Iberian peninsula. The Muslims' greatest competitors were the Ottoman Turks, not European Catholics (Map 1.2). Still, in the eleventh and twelfth centuries, Catholic leaders launched several military and religious campaigns to reclaim the Holy Land for the church. Later known as the **Crusades**, these campaigns largely failed in establishing Christian settlements in the East and exacerbated conflicts with Greek Orthodox and Jewish communities. But they enhanced the roles of Italian merchants, who profited from both outfitting Crusaders and opening new trade routes to the East.

Moreover, these campaigns inspired explorers and adventurers throughout Europe.

Medieval European elites were first introduced to goods and ideas from the East by merchant adventurers such as Marco Polo. He traveled to Cathay (his name for China) during the 1270s and published his *Travels* in 1292. Describing his adventures along the Silk Road, Polo introduced Europeans to "burning rocks" (coal), spices that preserved meat, and other wonders of the Far East.

Europeans also learned of successful civilizations in the Middle East, where inhabitants had managed to survive droughts and other ecological crises, largely because of their productive economic systems. In the Mediterranean world, this productivity depended on technological advances in irrigation and navigation and on adequate labor in the form of slavery. Earlier European societies as well as the Aztecs, Incas, and Maya had put

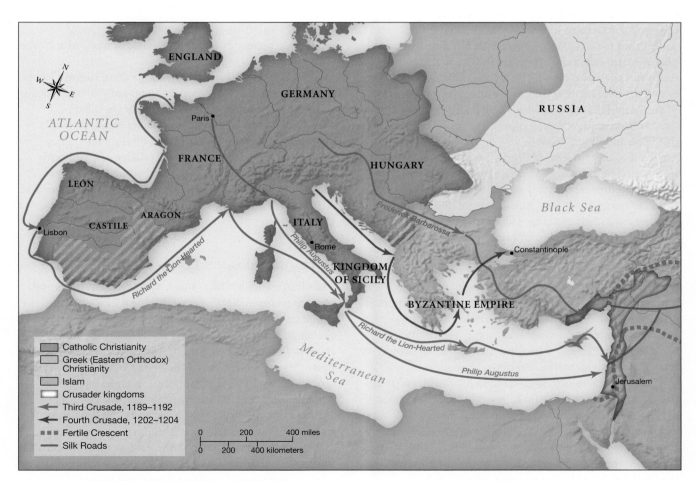

MAP 1.2 The Mediterranean World, c. 1150–1300

The Mediterranean Sea sat at the center of dynamic religious, political, and commercial networks. Crusaders traveled from Europe to Turkey, Arabia, and Persia, hoping to spread Christianity among Islamic peoples. In the thirteenth century, Marco Polo and other adventurers followed the Silk Road deeper into Asia, returning with goods, technologies, and diseases from the eastern Mediterranean, India, and China.

conquered peoples to work as slaves, but none compared to the vast network of slave-trading centers that fueled agricultural development in the Middle East. And it was the productivity of agriculture—developed centuries earlier than in Europe or America—that allowed societies along the southern Mediterranean, in northern Africa, and in southwest Asia to excel in astronomy, mathematics, architecture, and the arts.

Medieval European states proved far less adept at staving off human and environmental disasters than their counterparts to the south. Besieged by drought and disease as well as wars and peasant rebellions, rulers across the continent expended most of their resources on trying to sustain their population and protect their borders. Even launching trade with Asia led to disaster: In the 1340s, the bubonic plague was carried from Central Asia to Middle Eastern and European seaports by rats stowed away on ships. Sailors who contracted the disease at sea also spread the infection far and wide. From the 1340s to the early fifteenth century, the plague—later called the **Black Death**—periodically ravaged European cities and towns. During the initial outbreak between 1346 and 1350, about 36 million people—half of Europe's population—perished. At the same time, France and England engaged in a century-long war that added to the death and destruction.

By the early fifteenth century, the plague had retreated from much of Europe, and the climate had improved. Only then were European peoples able to benefit significantly from the riches of the East. Smaller populations led to an improved standard of living. Then rising birthrates and increased productivity, beginning in Italian city-states, fueled a resurgence of trade with other parts of the world. The profits from agriculture and commerce allowed the wealthy and powerful to begin investing in painting, sculpture, music, and literature and to pay jewelers, potters, and other craftsmen for their wares. Indeed, a cultural **Renaissance** (from the French word for "rebirth") flourished in the Italian city-states and then spread to France, Spain, the Low Countries, and central Europe.

The cultural rebirth went hand in hand with political unification as more powerful rulers extended their control over smaller city-states and principalities. In 1469, for example, the marriage of Isabella of Castile and Ferdinand II of Aragon led to the unification of Spain. By 1492 their combined forces expelled the last Muslim conquerors from the Iberian peninsula. Promoting Catholicism to create a more unified national identity, Isabella and Ferdinand also launched a brutal Inquisition against supposed heretics and executed or expelled Jews and Muslims. This reconquest of

Comparing Chinese and European Sailing Ships
The lateen sail used by the Chinese in the early fifteenth century marked a considerable improvement over the square sails used by Europeans such as Columbus, illustrated in the lower right corner by a contemporary artist. The lateen sail was developed as early as the sixth century C.E. by Byzantine ship-builders in the Mediterranean region.   © Dugald Stermer

the Iberian peninsula fueled the revival of trade with North Africa, India, and other Asian lands.

Yet Italy controlled the most important routes through the Mediterranean, so leaders in Spain and Portugal sought alternate paths to riches. Their efforts were aided by explorers, missionaries, and merchants who traveled to Morocco, Turkey, India, and other distant lands. They brought back trade goods and knowledge of astronomy, shipbuilding, mapmaking, and navigation that allowed Iberians to venture farther south along the Atlantic coast of Africa and, eventually, west into the uncharted Atlantic Ocean.

Portugal Pursues Long-Distance Trade

Cut off from the Mediterranean by Italian city-states and Muslim forces in North Africa, Portugal looked toward the Atlantic. Motivated by dreams of wealth and a desire to challenge Muslim power, Portuguese rulers sought another route to India and the Far East. Although a tiny nation, Portugal benefited from the leadership of its young prince, Henry (1394–1460), who launched an effort to explore the African coast and find a passage to India via the Atlantic Ocean. Prince Henry—known as Henry the Navigator—gathered information from astronomers, geographers, mapmakers, and craftsmen in the Arab world and recruited Italian cartographers and navigators along with Portuguese scholars, sailors, and captains. He then launched a systematic campaign of exploration, observation, shipbuilding, and long-distance trade that revolutionized Europe and shaped developments in Africa and the Americas.

Prince Henry and his colleagues developed ships known as caravels—vessels with narrow hulls and triangular sails that were especially effective for navigating the coast of West Africa. His staff also created state-of-the-art maritime charts, maps, and astronomical tables; perfected navigational instruments; and mastered the complex wind and sea currents along the African coast. Soon Portugal was trading in gold, ivory, and slaves from West Africa. By the time Prince Henry died in 1460, his ships had ventured as far east as the Canary Islands and Cape Verde and as far south as Sierra Leone.

In 1482 Portugal built Elmina Castle, a trading post and fort on the Gold Coast (present-day Ghana). The castle served as a launching point for further expeditions and as protection against Spanish competitors. Five years later, a fleet led by Bartolomeu Dias rounded the Cape of Good Hope, on the southernmost tip of Africa, demonstrating the possibility of sailing directly from the Atlantic to the Indian Ocean. Vasco da Gama followed this route to India in 1497, returning to Portugal in 1499, his ships laden with cinnamon and pepper.

By the early sixteenth century, Portuguese traders wrested control of the India trade from Arab fleets. They established fortified trading posts at key locations on the Indian Ocean and extended their expeditions to Indonesia, China, and Japan. Within a decade, the Portuguese had become the leaders in international trade. Spain, England, France, and the Netherlands competed for a share of this newfound wealth by developing long-distance markets that brought spices, ivory, silks, cotton cloth, and other luxury goods to Europe.

With expanding populations and greater agricultural productivity, European nations developed more efficient systems of taxation, built larger military forces, and adapted gunpowder to new kinds of weapons. The surge in population provided the men to labor on merchant vessels, staff forts, and protect trade routes. More people began to settle in cities like London, Bristol, Amsterdam, and Venice, which became important commercial centers. Slowly, a form of capitalism based on market exchange, private ownership, and capital accumulation and reinvestment developed across much of Europe.

African slaves were among the most lucrative goods traded by European merchants. Slavery had been practiced in Europe and other parts of the world, including Africa, for centuries. But in most times and places, slaves were

Elmina Castle, 1603

This engraving by Johann Theodor de Bry depicts the fortress of São Jorge da Mina, known as Elmina Castle, on the African Gold Coast. Built in 1482 at the order of King John II of Portugal, the fort served as a supply base for Portuguese navigators and housed thousands of Africans bound for slavery in the Americas.   The Granger Collection, New York captives of war or individuals sold in payment for deaths or injuries to conquering enemies. Under such circumstances, slaves generally retained some legal rights, and bondage was rarely permanent and almost never inheritable. With the advent of large-scale European participation in the African slave trade, however, the system of bondage began to change, transforming Europe and Africa and eventually the Americas.

European Encounters with West Africa

In the 1440s, Portuguese ships began to trade along the West African (or Guinea) coast. The Portuguese established bases in port cities like Benin to collect trade goods, including slaves, for sale in Europe. The slave trade expanded with the building of Elmina Castle and by the early sixteenth century had increased significantly. Initially, Africans were viewed as "exotic" objects and were often put on display at courts or for popular entertainment. Increasingly, however, African slaves were put to work in households and shops or on large estates.

Still, Europeans were most familiar with North Africa, a region deeply influenced by Islam and characterized by large kingdoms, well-developed cities, and an extensive network of trading centers. In northeast Africa, including Egypt, city-states flourished, with ties to India, the Middle East, and China. In northwest Africa, Timbuktu linked North Africa to empires south of the Great Desert as well as to Europe. Here African slaves labored for wealthier Africans in a system of bound labor long familiar to Europeans.

As trade with western Africa increased, however, Europeans learned more about communities that lived by hunting and subsistence agriculture. By the mid-sixteenth century, European nations established competing forts along the African coast from the Gold Coast and Senegambia in the north to the Bight of Biafra and West Central Africa farther south. The men and women shipped from these forts to Europe generally came from communities that had been raided or conquered by more powerful groups. They arrived at the coast exhausted, hungry, dirty, and with few clothes. They worshipped gods unfamiliar to Europeans, and their cultural customs and social practices seemed strange and often frightening. Over time, it was the image of the captured West African slave that came to dominate European visions of the entire continent.

As traders from Portugal, Spain, Holland, and England brought back more stories and more African slaves, these negative portraits took deeper hold. Woodcuts and prints circulated in Europe that showed half-naked Africans who looked more like apes than humans. These images resonated with biblical stories like that of Ham, who sinned against his father, Noah. Noah then cursed Ham's son Canaan to a life of slavery. Increasingly, European Christians considered Africans the "sons of Ham," infidels rightly assigned by God to a life of bondage. This self-serving idea then justified the enslavement of black men, women, and children.

> **Explore**
>
> For one English captain's impression of Africans during this period, see Document 1.1.

Of course, these images of West Africa failed to capture the diverse peoples who lived in the area's tropical rain forests, plains, and savannas. By the fourteenth century, agricultural productivity in the region fueled population growth and the rise of both city-states and trade networks. The Yoruba people developed walled towns ruled by *obas*, many of whom were women, who served as religious and political leaders. To the south lay the highly centralized kingdom of Benin. Its warrior king, Euware, had conquered some two hundred villages to create his kingdom and then used his power and wealth to promote trade and patronize the arts. Nearby the Igbo people rejected kingships in favor of title societies composed of wealthy men, women's associations tied to kinship, and hereditary organizations that created cohesion among competing groups. Despite their political and social differences, the Yoruba, Beni, and Igbo traded with one another and with more distant African kingdoms.

In addition to these powerful kingdoms, smaller societies based on farming or herding existed across western and central Africa. These communities were sometimes conquered by expanding kingdoms and their members sold as slaves within Africa. But once trade developed with Portugal, Spain, and other nations, these communities were increasingly raided to provide slaves for European markets. As the slave trade expanded in the sixteenth and seventeenth centuries, it destabilized large areas of western and central Africa, with smaller societies decimated by raids and even larger kingdoms damaged by the extensive commerce in human beings. As early as 1526, Afonso, the king of the Kongo people and a convert to Christianity, begged the Portuguese to end the slave trade: "Merchants are taking everyday our natives, sons of the land and the sons of our noblemen and vassals and our relatives."

Still, rulers of the most powerful African societies helped shape the slave trade. For instance, because women were more highly valued by Muslim traders in North Africa and Asia, African traders steered women to these profitable markets. At the same time, African societies organized along matrilineal lines—where goods and political power passed through the mother's line—often tried to protect

DOCUMENT 1.1

John Lok | The Second Voyage to Guinea, 1554

By the mid-fifteenth century, Europeans had developed a lucrative trading relationship with Africa, which included gold, ivory, and slaves. African slaves were first seen as exotic oddities, but increasingly they were bought as laborers to work in shops or on agricultural estates. As the slave trade increased, Europeans developed a vision of Africans as heathen, savage, and vastly inferior to themselves. The following passage, taken from the descriptions of John Lok, the captain of an English expedition to Africa in 1554, represents common European depictions of Africans in the sixteenth century.

Explore

> It is to be understood, that the people which now inhabite the regions of the coast of Guinea, and the midle parts of Africa, as Libya the inner, and Nubia, with divers other great and large regions about the same, were in old time called Æthiopes and Nigritæ, which we now call Moores, Moorens, or Negroes, a people of beastly living, without a God, lawe, religion, or common wealth, and so scorched and vexed with the heat of the sunne, that in many places they curse it when it riseth. . . .
>
> There are also other people of Libya called Garamantes, whose women are common: for they contract no matrimonie, neither have respect to chastitie.
>
> Source: "The Second Voyage of M. John Lok to Guinea, Anno 1554," in Richard Hakluyt, *The Principal Navigations, Voyages, Traffiques & Discoveries of the English Nation* (Glasgow: James MacLehose and Sons, 1904), 6:167–68.

Interpret the Evidence

- What characteristics does the author associate with Africans? To what extent, if any, does the author differentiate among African peoples?
- Do Lok's characterizations seem to be based on firsthand observation? Why or why not?

Put It in Context

How did descriptions such as these justify African enslavement?

---

women against enslavement. Other groups sought to limit the sale of men.

Ultimately, men, women, and children were captured by African as well as Portuguese, Spanish, Dutch, and English traders. Still, Europeans did not institute a system of perpetual slavery, in which enslavement was inherited from one generation to the next. Instead, Africans formed another class of bound labor, alongside peasants, indentured servants, criminals, and apprentices. Slavic-speaking workers imported from areas around the Black Sea were especially prominent on sugar plantations in the Mediterranean region. Indeed, the term *Slav* became the basis for the word *slave*. When the Ottoman Turks cut off access to Slavic laborers, Europeans increased their slave trade with Africa.

Distinctions among bound laborers on the basis of race had not yet fully developed. Thus affluent Europeans condemned pagan rituals, sexual licentiousness, and ignorance among both Slavic and African laborers. They also considered such traits common among their own peasants. When the English entered the African slave trade in the 1560s, via the privateer John Hawkins, they quickly put their own spin on such comparisons. In the sixteenth century, they viewed both Africans and the conquered Irish as "rude, beastly, ignorant, cruel, and unruly infidels."

REVIEW & RELATE

How and why did Europeans expand their connections with Africa and the Middle East in the fifteenth century?

How did early European encounters with West Africans lay the foundation for later race-based slavery?

 LEARNINGCurve bedfordstmartins.com/hewittlawson/LC

Worlds Collide

In the 1520s and 1530s, Spain and Portugal chartered traders to ship enslaved Africans to the Caribbean, Brazil, Mexico, and Peru. The success of this trade relied heavily on the efforts of European cartographers, who began to chart the coastlines, rivers, and inland territories of the Western Hemisphere described by explorers and adventurers. Their maps illustrated the growing connections among Europe, Africa, and the Americas even as they also reflected the continued dominance of the Mediterranean region, the Middle East, India, and China in European visions of the world. Yet that world was changing rapidly as Europeans introduced guns, horses, and new diseases to the Americas and came in contact with previously unknown flora and fauna. The resulting exchange of plants, animals, and germs transformed the two continents as well as the wider world.

Europeans Cross the Atlantic

The first Europeans to discover lands in the western Atlantic were Norsemen. In the early ninth century, Scandinavians colonized Ireland, and in the 870s they settled Iceland. A little more than a century later, seafarers led by Erik the Red reached Greenland. Sailing still farther west, Erik's son Leif led a party that discovered an area that they called Vinland, near the Gulf of St. Lawrence. The Norse established a small settlement there around 1000 C.E., and people from Greenland continued to visit Vinland for centuries. By 1450, however, the Greenland settlements had disappeared.

Nearly a half century after Norse settlers abandoned Greenland, a Genoese navigator named Christopher Columbus visited the Spanish court of Ferdinand and Isabella and proposed an **Enterprise of the Indies**. He planned to sail west across the Atlantic to Cipangu (Japan) and Cathay (China). Because Italian city-states controlled the Mediterranean and Portugal dominated the routes around Africa, Spain sought a third path to the rich Eastern trade. Columbus claimed he could find it.

Columbus's 1492 proposal was timely. Having just expelled the last Muslims from Granada and imposed Christian orthodoxy on a now-unified nation, the Spanish monarchs sought to expand their empire. Queen Isabella, ignoring the advice of two royal committees that had rejected Columbus's plan, decided to fund his initial venture. With her support, the Genoese captain headed off in three small ships with ninety men. They stopped briefly at the Canary Islands and then headed due west on September 6, 1492.

Columbus had calculated the distance to Cipangu based on Ptolemy's division of the world into 360 degrees of north-south lines of longitude. But in making his calculations, Columbus made a number of errors that led him to believe that it was possible to sail from Spain to Asia in about a month. The miscalculations nearly led to mutiny when Columbus's crew had not sighted land after more than four weeks at sea. Disaster was averted, however, when on October 12 a lookout spotted a small island. Columbus named the island San Salvador and made contact with local residents, whom he named Indians in the belief that he had found the East Indies. These "Indians" offered the newcomers food, drinks, and gifts. Columbus was impressed with their warm welcome and viewed their gold jewelry as a sign of greater riches in the region.

Although the native inhabitants and Columbus's men did not speak a common language, they communicated sufficiently to explore San Salvador as well as a larger island nearby, present-day Cuba. The crew then sailed on to an island they named Hispaniola. Nothing they saw resembled contemporary descriptions of China or the East Indies, but Columbus was convinced he had reached his destination. Leaving a small number of men behind, he sailed for Spain with samples of gold jewelry and tales of more wonders to come.

> **Explore**
>
> Read part of Columbus's account of his first encounter with native people in Hispaniola in Document 1.2.

Columbus and his crew were welcomed as heroes when they returned to Spain in March 1493. Their discovery of islands seemingly unclaimed by any known power led the pope to confer Spanish sovereignty over all lands already claimed or to be claimed 100 leagues west of the Cape Verde Islands. A protest by Portugal soon led to a treaty that moved the line 270 leagues farther west, resulting ultimately in Portugal's control of Brazil and Spain's control of the rest of what would become known as South America.

Europeans Explore the Americas

Columbus made two more voyages to the Caribbean to claim land for Spain and sought to convince those who accompanied him to build houses, plant crops, and cut logs for forts. But the men had come for gold, and when the Indians stopped trading willingly, the Spaniards used force to claim their riches. Columbus sought to impose a more rigid discipline but failed. On his final voyage, he was forced to introduce a system of *encomiendas*, by which leading men received land and the labor of all Indians

DOCUMENT 1.2

Christopher Columbus | Reaching the West Indies, 1492

On October 12, 1492, five weeks after heading into the Atlantic Ocean, Christopher Columbus landed on an island in the West Indies that he named San Salvador. The exact location and name of the island where Columbus first made landfall is in dispute, but we do know that it is in the Bahamas, although Columbus believed it to be India. Columbus spent five days exploring the area where he and his men first encountered native people and kept a detailed journal of his experiences. Although the original journal was lost, large parts of it had been copied by the Catholic friar Bartolomé de Las Casas, including the following journal entry.

Explore

What motivates Columbus to give gifts to the people he meets?

Why does Columbus think the people he encounters are very poor?

Why does Columbus think the people that he meets will be good servants?

October 12, 1492

I, . . . that we might form great friendship, for I knew that they were a people who could be more easily freed and converted to our holy faith by love than by force, gave to some of them red caps, and glass beads to put round their necks, and many other things of little value, which gave them great pleasure, and made them so much our friends that it was a marvel to see. They afterwards came to the ship's boats where we were, swimming and bringing us parrots, cotton threads in skeins, darts, and many other things; and we exchanged them for other things that we gave them, such as glass beads and small bells. In fine [In short], they took all, and gave what they had with good will. It appeared to me to be a race of people very poor in everything. They go as naked as when their mothers bore them, and so do the women, although I did not see more than one young girl. . . . They have no iron, their darts being wands without iron, some of them having a fish's tooth at the end. . . . They should be good servants and intelligent, for I observed that they quickly took in what was said to them, and I believe that they would easily be made Christians, as it appeared to me that they had no religion. I, our Lord being pleased, will take hence, at the time of my departure, six natives for your Highnesses, that they may learn to speak.

Source: *The Journal of Christopher Columbus (during His First Voyage, 1492–93) and Documents Relating to the Voyages of John Cabot and Gaspar Corte Real* (London: Hakluyt Society, 1893), 37–38.

Put It in Context

How might Columbus's journal entry, which was circulated among clerics and officials, have shaped Spanish views about native peoples?

residing on it. Although he boasted to the Spanish crown that he had "placed under their Highnesses' sovereignty more land than there is in Africa and Europe," Columbus had lost the support of the Spanish authorities by the time he died in 1506. The islands he discovered were quickly dissolving into chaos as traders and adventurers fought with Indians and one another over the spoils of conquest.

By then, no one believed that he had discovered a route to China, and few people understood the revolutionary importance of the lands he had found.

Nonetheless, Columbus's voyages inspired others to head across the Atlantic (Map 1.3). In 1497 another Genoese navigator, John Cabot (or Caboto), sailing under the English flag, headed into the northern Atlantic in a tiny

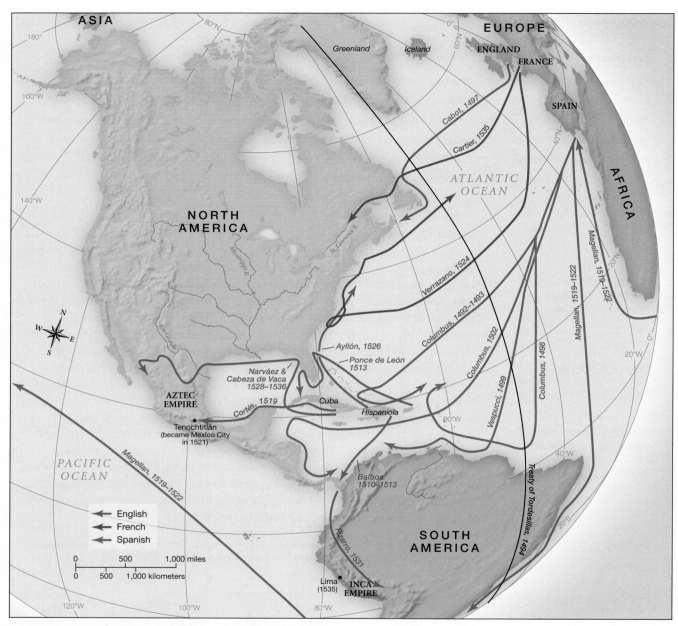

MAP 1.3   European Explorations in the Americas, 1492–1536

Early explorers, funded by Spain, sought trade routes to Asia or gold, silver, and other riches in the Americas. The success of these voyages encouraged adventurous Spaniards to travel throughout the West Indies and across South America and southern North America. It also inspired the first expeditions by the French and the English, who sought treasures farther north.

ship with only eighteen men. He reached an island off Cape Breton, where he discovered good cod fishing but met no local inhabitants. Over the next several years, Cabot and his son Sebastian made more trips to North American shores, but England failed to follow up on their discoveries.

More important at the time, Portuguese and Spanish mariners continued to explore the western edges of the Caribbean. Amerigo Vespucci, a Florentine merchant, joined one such voyage in 1499. It was Vespucci's account of his journey that led Martin Waldseemüller to identify the new continent he charted on his 1507 *Universalis Cosmographia* as "America." Meanwhile, Spanish explorers subdued tribes like the Arawak and Taino in the Caribbean and headed toward the mainland. In 1513 Vasco Nuñez de

Balboa traveled across the Isthmus of Darien (now Panama) and became the first European to see the Pacific Ocean. That same year, Juan Ponce de León launched a search for gold and slaves along a peninsula to the north. Although he did not find riches there, he named the region Florida, meaning "flowery land," and claimed it for Spain.

Ferdinand Magellan launched an even more impressive expedition in August 1519 when he, with the support of Charles V of Spain, sought a passageway through South America to Asia. In the first fifteen months, Magellan faced bad weather, disappointments, hostile Indians, and open mutiny. But he managed to maintain his authority, and in October 1520 his crew discovered a strait at the southernmost tip of South America that connected the Atlantic and Pacific Oceans. Ill with scurvy and near starvation, the crew reached Guam and then the Philippines in March 1521. Magellan died there a month later, but one of his five ships and eighteen of the original crew finally made it back to Seville in September 1522, having successfully circumnavigated the globe. Despite the enormous loss of life and equipment, Magellan's lone ship was loaded with valuable spices, his venture allowed Spain to claim the Philippine Islands, and his journals provided cartographers with vast amounts of knowledge about the world's oceans and landmasses.

Mapmaking and Printing

Waldseemüller's 1507 map reflected the expanding contacts among Europe, Africa, and the Americas. Over the following decades, as ships from Europe sailed back and forth across the Atlantic, cartographers charted newly discovered islands, traced coastlines and bays, and situated each new piece of data in relation to lands already known.

The dissemination of geographical knowledge was greatly facilitated by advances in information technology. The Chinese had developed a form of printing with wood blocks in the tenth century, and woodcut pictures appeared in Europe in the fifteenth century. In the 1440s, German craftsmen invented a form of movable metal type in which each letter was created in a separate mold. This allowed printers to rearrange the type for each page and create multiple copies of a single manuscript more quickly and more cheaply than ever before. Between 1452 and 1455, Johannes Gutenberg, a German goldsmith, printed some 180 copies of the Bible with movable type. Although this was not the first book printed using the new system, Gutenberg's Bible marked a revolutionary change in the production and circulation of written texts.

Innovations in printing helped publicize Portuguese and Spanish explorations, the travels of European adventurers, and the atlases created by Waldseemüller and other cartographers. Italian craftsmen contributed by manufacturing paper

Printing Press

This woodcut of a printing press from Leipzig, Germany, in 1520 illustrates typical printing equipment of the sixteenth century. A craftsman applies inked type to the paper using a screw press, and a second worker gathers and stacks the printed pages. This process accelerated the publication and distribution of books and pamphlets throughout early modern Europe.   © Mary Evans Picture Library/The Image Works

that was thinner and cheaper than traditional vellum and parchment. Books were still expensive, and they could be read only by the small minority of Europeans who were literate. Still, mechanical printing rapidly increased the speed with which knowledge was circulated, allowing a German mapmaker like Waldseemüller to read the journals of the Italian mariner Vespucci. Of course, not everything that was printed was accurate, but the ability to exchange ideas encouraged their expression and ensured the flow of information among scholars and rulers across Europe.

The peoples of the Americas had their own ways of charting land, waterways, and boundary lines and for circulating information. The Maya, for instance, developed a system of glyphs—images that represented prefixes, suffixes, numbers, people, or words. Scribes carved glyphs

The Aztec City of Tenochtitlán

German geographers drew this map of Tenochtitlán in 1524 based on Aztec sources. At its peak, the city contained some 100,000 people, and at its center stood temples, a marketplace, schools, the palace of the Aztec chief Montezuma, and a ball-game court. The Aztecs viewed Tenochtitlán as the intersection of the secular and divine worlds.

Bildarchiv Preussischer Kulturbesitz/Dietmar Katz/Art Resource, NY

into large flat stones, or *stela*, providing local residents with histories of important events. In settled farming villages, this system communicated information to a large portion of the population. But it could not serve, as printed pages did, to disseminate ideas more widely. Similarly, the extant maps created by the Maya, Aztecs, and other native groups tended to focus on specific locales. Still, we know that these groups traded across long distances, so they must have had some means of tracing rivers, mountains, and villages beyond their own communities.

The Columbian Exchange

Even as maps documented Europeans' expanded knowledge of the Americas, they could not capture the experience of contact between peoples separated for centuries by the Atlantic Ocean. Most important, the Spaniards were aided in their conquest of the Americas as much by germs as by maps, guns, or horses. Because native peoples in the Western Hemisphere had had almost no contact with the rest of the world for millennia, they lacked immunity to most germs

carried by Europeans. Disease along with warfare first eradicated the Arawak and Taino on Hispaniola, wiping out some 300,000 people. In the Inca empire, the population plummeted from about 9 million in 1530 to less than half a million by 1630. Among the Aztecs, the Maya, and their neighbors, the population collapsed from some 40 million people around 1500 to about 3 million a century and a half later. The germs spread northward as well, leading to catastrophic epidemics among the Pueblo peoples of the Southwest and the Mississippian cultures of the Southeast.

These demographic disasters—far more devastating even than the bubonic plague in Europe—were part of what historians call the **Columbian exchange**. But this exchange also involved animals, plants, and seeds and affected Africa and Asia as well as Europe and the Americas. The transfer of flora and fauna and the spread of diseases transformed the economies and environments of all four continents. Initially, however, it was the catastrophic decline in Indian populations that ensured the victory of Spain and other European powers over American populations, facilitating their subsequent exploitation of American land, labor, and resources.

The diseases that swept across the Americas came from Africa as well as Europe. Indeed, it was Africans' partial immunity to malaria and yellow fever that made them so attractive to European traders seeking laborers for Caribbean islands after the native population was decimated. African coconuts and bananas had already been introduced to Europe, while European traders had provided their African counterparts with iron and pigs. Asia also participated in the exchange, introducing Europe and Africa not only to the bubonic plague but also to sugar, rice, tea, and highly coveted spices.

America provided Europeans with high-yielding, nutrient-rich foods like maize and potatoes, as well as new indulgences like tobacco and cacao. The conquered Inca and Aztec empires also provided vast quantities of gold and silver, making Spain the treasure-house of Europe and ensuring its dominance on the continent for several decades. Sugar was first developed in the East Indies, but once it took root in the West Indies, it, too, became a source of enormous profits and, when mixed with cacao, created an addictive drink known as chocolate.

In exchange for products that America offered to Europe and Africa, these continents sent rice, wheat, rye, lemons, and oranges as well as horses, cattle, pigs, chickens, and honeybees to the Western Hemisphere (Map 1.4). The grain crops transformed the American landscape, particularly in North America, where wheat became a major food source. Cattle and pigs, meanwhile, changed native diets, while horses inspired new methods of farming, transportation, and warfare throughout the Americas.

The Columbian exchange benefited Europe far more than the Americas. Initially, it also benefited Africa, providing new crops with high yields and rich nutrients. Ultimately, however, the spread of sugar and rice to the West Indies and European cravings for tobacco and cacao increased the demand for labor, which could not be met by the declining population of Indians. This situation ensured the expansion of the African slave trade. The consequences of the Columbian exchange were thus monumental for the peoples of all three continents.

REVIEW & RELATE

What were the short-term consequences in both Europe and the Americas of Columbus's voyages?

How did the Columbian exchange transform both the Americas and Europe?

✓ LEARNINGCurve bedfordstmartins.com/hewittlawson/LC

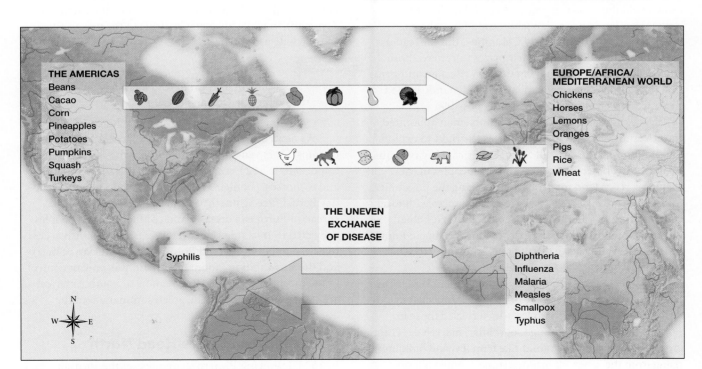

MAP 1.4   The Columbian Exchange, 16th Century

When Europeans made contact with Africa and the Americas, they initiated an exchange of plants, animals, and germs that transformed all three continents. The contact among these previously isolated ecosystems caused dramatic transformations in food, labor, and mortality. American crops changed eating habits across Europe, while foreign grains and domesticated animals thrived in the Americas even as diseases devastated native populations.

Europeans Make Claims to North America

With the help of native translators, warriors, and laborers, Spanish soldiers called **conquistadors** conquered some of the richest and most populous lands in South America in the early sixteenth century. Others then headed north, hoping to find gold in the southern regions of North America or develop new routes to Asia. At the same time, rulers of other European nations, jealous of Spanish wealth, began to fund expeditions to North America. However, both France and England were ruled by weak monarchs and divided both religiously and politically. Consequently, their early efforts met with little success. By the late sixteenth century, Spanish supremacy in the Americas and the wealth acquired there transformed the European economy. But conquest also raised critical questions about Spanish responsibilities to God and humanity.

Spaniards Conquer Indian Empires

Although rulers in Spain supposedly set the agenda for American ventures, it was difficult to control the campaigns of their emissaries at such a distance. The Spanish crown held the power to grant successful leaders vast amounts of land and Indian labor, expanding the encomienda system introduced by Columbus. But the leaders themselves then divided up their prizes to reward those who served under them, giving them in effect an authority that they sometimes lacked in law. This dynamic helped make Cortés's conquest of the Aztecs possible.

Diego de Velásquez, a Spanish nobleman appointed the governor of Cuba, granted Cortés the right to explore and trade along the coast of South America. He gave him no authority, however, to attack native peoples in the region or claim land for himself. But seeing the possibility for gaining great riches, Cortés forged alliances with local rulers willing to join the attack against the Aztec chief, Montezuma. From the perspective of local Indian communities, Cortés's presence offered an opportunity to strike back against the brutal Aztec regime.

Despite their assumption of cultural superiority, many Spaniards who accompanied Cortés were astonished by Aztec cities, canals, and temples, which rivaled those in Europe. Bernal Díaz, a young foot soldier, marveled, "These great towns and cues [pyramid-like temples] and buildings rising from the water, all made of stone, seemed like an enchanted vision. . . . Indeed, some of our soldiers asked if it were not all a dream." Seeing these architectural wonders may have given some soldiers pause about trying to conquer the Indian kingdom. But when Montezuma presented Cortés with large quantities of precious objects, including gold-encrusted jewelry, as a peace offering, he alerted Spaniards to the vast wealth awaiting them in the Aztec capital.

When Cortés and his men marched to Tenochtitlán in 1519, Montezuma was indecisive in his response. After an early effort to ambush the Spaniards failed, the Aztec leader allowed Cortés to march his men into the capital city, where the Spanish conquistador took Montezuma hostage. In response, Aztec warriors attacked the Spaniards, but Cortés and his men managed to fight their way out of Tenochtitlán. They suffered heavy losses and might have been crushed by their Aztec foes but for the alliances they had made among native groups in the surrounding area. Given time to regroup, the remaining Spanish soldiers and their allies attacked the Aztecs with superior steel weapons, horses, and attack dogs and gained a final victory.

The Spanish victory was also aided by the germs that soldiers carried with them. The invaders unintentionally introduced smallpox to the local population, which led to a staggering epidemic. It swept through Tenochtitlán in 1521, killing thousands and leaving Montezuma's army dramatically weakened. This human catastrophe as much as military resources and strategies allowed Cortés to conquer the capital. He then claimed the entire region as New Spain, asserting Spanish authority over the native groups that had allied with him. The Spanish conquistador then settled in Tenochtitlán while his men constructed the new capital of Mexico City around him.

> **Explore**
>
> For an illustration of the devastating effects of smallpox on an Aztec victim, see Document 1.3.

As news of Cortés's victory spread, other Spanish conquistadors sought gold and glory in the Americas. Most important, in 1524 Francisco Pizarro, with only 168 men and 67 horses, conquered the vast Inca empire in present-day Peru. Once again, the Spaniards were aided by the spread of European diseases and conflicts among peoples subjected to Inca rule. This victory ensured Spanish access to vast supplies of silver in Potosí (in present-day Bolivia) and the surrounding mountains. Spain was now in control of the most densely populated regions of South America, areas that also contained the greatest mineral wealth.

Spanish Adventurers Head North

In 1526, following Pizarro's conquest of the Incas, a company of Spanish women and men traveled from the West Indies as far north as the Santee River in present-day South Carolina. They planned to settle in the region and then search for gold and other valuables. The effort failed, but two years later Pánfilo de Narváez—one of the survivors—led four hundred soldiers from Cuba to Florida's Tampa Bay. Seeking precious metals, the party instead confronted hunger, disease, and hostile Indians. The ragtag group continued to journey along the Gulf coast,

until only four men, led by Álvar Núñez Cabeza de Vaca, made their way from Galveston Bay back to Mexico City.

A decade later, in 1539, a survivor of Narváez's ill-fated venture—a North African named Esteban—led a party of

---

DOCUMENT 1.3

Aztec Smallpox Victim, 1540

Between 1519 and 1521, the Spanish explorer Hernán Cortés led a war of conquest against the Aztecs. His eventual victory was greatly aided by advanced military technology, native allies, and the unintended introduction of European diseases into the Aztec population. Spanish contact spread smallpox to the region, killing thousands and weakening a once-powerful Aztec military. The image below, from a treatise written by a Franciscan missionary, shows the different stages suffered by a smallpox victim.

Explore

The Granger Collection, New York

Interpret the Evidence

- What does this image tell us about the role of the Aztec healer, standing before one of the victims, in the face of a smallpox epidemic?
- What does this group of five panels imply about the way that smallpox victims experienced the disease?

Put It in Context

What message do you think Bernardino de Sahagun, the Franciscan missionary, meant to convey in using this image in his history of New Spain?

Spaniards from Mexico back north. Lured by tales of Seven Golden Cities, the party instead encountered Zuñi Indians, who attacked the Spaniards and killed Esteban. Still, the men who returned to Mexico passed on stories about an extensive system of pueblos, where many Spaniards believed mountains of gold were hidden. Hoping to find fame and fortune, Francisco Vásquez de Coronado launched a grand expedition northward in 1540. Angered when they discovered that the fabled "Seven Cities are seven little villages," Coronado and his men terrorized the region, burning towns and stealing food and other goods before returning to Mexico.

Hernando de Soto headed a fourth effort to find wealth in North America. He had first sailed to America in 1514 and participated in conquests around present-day Panama. There he achieved a reputation for brutality and gained wealth through the Indian slave trade and by looting native treasures. Then in 1539 de Soto received royal authority to explore Florida, and that spring he established a village near Tampa Bay with more than six hundred Spanish, Indian, and African men, a few women, and more than two

hundred horses. A few months later, de Soto and the bulk of his company traveled up the west Florida coast with Juan Ortiz. Ortiz, a member of the Narváez expedition, was an especially useful guide and interpreter. That winter, the expedition traveled into present-day Georgia and the Carolinas in an unsuccessful search for riches (Map 1.5).

On their return trip, de Soto's men engaged in a brutal battle with local Indians led by Chief Tuskaloosa. Although the Spaniards claimed victory, they lost a significant number of men and horses and most of their equipment. Fearing that word of the disaster would reach Spain, de Soto steered his men away from supply ships in the Gulf of Mexico and headed back north. The group continued through parts of present-day Tennessee, Arkansas, Oklahoma, and Texas, and in May 1541 they became the first Europeans to report seeing the vast Mississippi River. By the winter of 1542, the expedition had lost more men and supplies to Indians, and de Soto had died. The remaining members finally returned to Spanish territory in the summer of 1543.

The lengthy journey of de Soto and his men brought European diseases into new areas, leading to epidemics

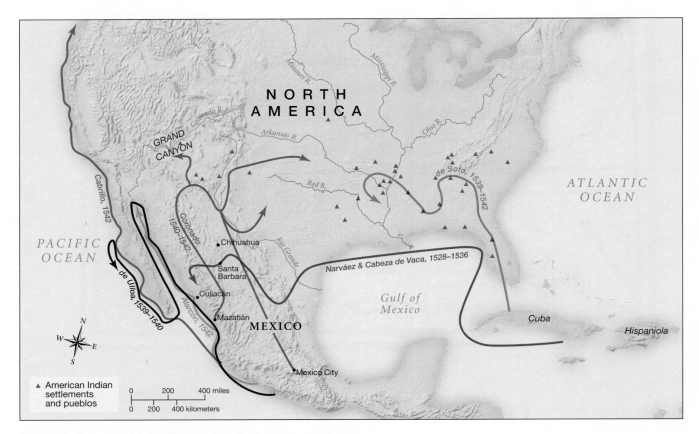

MAP 1.5   Spanish Explorations in North America, 1528–1542

Spanish explorers in North America hoped to find gold and other treasures. Instead, they encountered difficult terrain and native peoples hostile to Spanish intrusions. Many Spaniards died on these expeditions, and they failed to discover new sources of wealth. But they laid the foundations for Spanish settlements in Florida, northern Mexico, and California, in part by devastating local Indian populations.

and the depopulation of once-substantial native communities. At the same time, the Spaniards left horses and pigs behind, creating new sources of food and transportation for native peoples. Although most Spaniards considered de Soto's journey a failure, the Spanish crown claimed vast new territories. Two decades later, in 1565, Pedro Menéndez de Avilés established a mission settlement on the northeast coast of Florida, named St. Augustine. It became the first permanent European settlement in North America and served as a model for missions later founded by Spaniards in Santa Fe, New Mexico, and in California.

Europeans Compete in North America

Spain's early ventures in North America helped inspire French and English explorers to establish their own footholds on the continent. The French entered the race for empire in 1524, when an Italian navigator named Giovanni da Verrazano led a French company along the coast of North America. Landing initially near Cape Fear on the Carolina coast, the expedition headed north, sailing into what would become New York harbor. Verrazano then continued north, claiming lands all along the coast for France.

A decade later, in 1534, the Frenchman Jacques Cartier sailed to the Gulf of St. Lawrence and traded for furs with the Micmac Indians. In two subsequent expeditions, Cartier pushed deeper into the territory known as Canada. Although he failed to discover precious metals or the elusive passage to the Pacific Ocean, Cartier's adventures inspired a French nobleman, the Sieur de Roberval, and several hundred followers to attempt a permanent settlement at Quebec in 1542. But the project was abandoned within a year because of harsh weather, disease, and high mortality.

English interest in North America was ignited by Spanish and French challenges to claims Cabot had made along the North Atlantic coast in the 1490s. To secure these rights, the English needed to colonize the disputed lands. Since the English crown did not have funds to support settlement, the earliest ventures were financed by minor noblemen who hoped to gain both wealth and the crown's favor. But early efforts failed. In 1583 inadequate financing doomed Sir Humphrey Gilbert's effort to plant a colony in Newfoundland, and inadequate supplies along with the harsh climate undercut Sir Ferdinando Gorge's settlement on the Maine coast the next year.

The most promising effort to secure an English foothold in North America was organized by Sir Walter Raleigh, a half-brother of Humphrey Gilbert. Claiming all the land north of Florida for England, Raleigh called the vast territory Virginia (after Elizabeth I, "the Virgin Queen"). Although he did not set foot in North America himself, in 1585 Raleigh sent a group of soldiers to found a colony on Roanoke Island, off the coast of present-day North Carolina. The colony would establish England's claims and serve as a launching point for raids against Spanish ships laden with valuables. This venture lasted less than a year before the company returned to England. But in 1587 Raleigh tried again to colonize the area, sending a group of 117 men, women, and children to Roanoke. When supply ships came to fortify the settlement in 1590, no trace of the English settlers remained.

By 1590, then, nearly a century after Columbus's initial voyage, only Spain had established permanent colonies in the Americas, mostly in the West Indies, Mexico, and South America. St. Augustine remained the only European outpost in North America. The French and the English, despite numerous efforts, had not sustained a single ongoing settlement by the end of the sixteenth century. Yet neither nation gave up hope of benefiting from the wealth of the Americas.

Spain Seeks Dominion in Europe and the Americas

The continued desire of European nations to gain colonies in the Americas resulted from the enormous wealth garnered by Spanish conquests. That wealth transformed economies throughout Europe. Between 1500 and 1650, Spanish ships carried home more than 180 tons of gold and 16,000 tons of silver from Mexico and Potosí. About one-fifth of this amount was taken by the Spanish crown for taxes; the rest was spent on goods imported from the Americas, Asia, or other European nations. Very little of this wealth was invested in improving conditions at home. Instead, the elite displayed their wealth in ostentatious ways: elaborate silver candelabras, dresses drenched in jewels, and lavish tapestries imported from Asia. Meanwhile the rapid infusion of gold and silver fueled inflation, making it harder for ordinary people to afford the necessities of life.

In one area, however, employment for the poor expanded rapidly. King Philip II, who ruled Spain from 1556 to 1598, used American gold and silver to fund a variety of military campaigns, ensuring an endless demand for soldiers and sailors. The king, a devout Catholic, claimed to be doing God's work as Spain conquered Italy and Portugal, including the latter's colonies in Africa, and tightened its grip on the Netherlands, which had been acquired by Spain through marriage in the early sixteenth century. In response, the English aristocrat Sir Walter Raleigh warned, "It is his [Philip's] Indian Gold that . . . endangereth and disturbeth all the nations of Europe."

Despite the obvious material benefits, the Spaniards were not blind to the enormous human costs of colonization, and the conquest of the Americas inspired heated debates within Spain. Roman Catholic bishops and priests, royal officials, and colonial leaders disagreed vehemently about whether Spanish conquerors could simply acquire riches from foreign lands or were required to Christianize those they conquered for the glory of God. While Catholic leaders believed that the conversion of native peoples was critical to Spanish success in the Americas, most royal officials and colonial agents viewed the extraction of precious metals as far more important. They argued that cheap labor was essential to creating wealth. Yet brutal conditions led to the death of huge numbers of Indians, and many church officials insisted that such conditions made it nearly impossible to gain new converts to Catholicism.

By 1550, tales of the widespread torture and enslavement of Indians convinced the Spanish king Carlos V to gather a group of theologians, jurists, and philosophers at Valladolid to discuss the moral and legal implications of conquest. From Mexico, Hernán Cortés sent the king a message, insisting that there was no need to consider the natives' views since they "must obey the royal orders of Your Majesty, whatever their nature." But not all the participants at Valladolid agreed. Bartolomé de Las Casas, a former conquistador and Dominican friar, spent many years preaching to Indians in America. He asked, "And so what man of sound mind will approve a war against men who are harmless, ignorant, gentle, temperate, unarmed, and destitute of every human defense?" Las Casas reasoned that even if Spain defeated the Indians, the souls of those killed would be lost to God, while among the survivors "hatred and loathing of the Christian religion" would prevail. He even suggested replacing Indian labor with African labor, apparently less concerned with the souls of black people.

Juan Ginés de Sepúlveda, the royal historian, attacked Las Casas's arguments. Although he had never set foot in America, he read reports of cannibalism and other violations of "natural law" among native peoples. Since the Indians were savages, the civilized Spaniards were obligated to "destroy barbarism and educate these people to a more humane and virtuous life." If they refused such help, Spanish rule "can be imposed upon them by force of arms." Like Ginés de Sepúlveda, Theodor de Bry, the well-known illustrator of Documents 1.4 and 1.5, never visited the Americas, yet his depictions of the region shaped European impressions. Although Ginés de Sepúlveda spoke for the majority at Valladolid, Las Casas and his supporters continued to press their case as Spain expanded its reach into North America.

Explore

To examine two European depictions of interactions between Spanish and native peoples, see Documents 1.4 and 1.5.

At the same time, American riches increasingly flowed beyond Spain's borders. The Netherlands was a key beneficiary of this wealth, becoming a center for Spanish shipbuilding and trade. Still, the Dutch were never completely under Spanish control, and they traded independently with their European neighbors. Thus gold, silver, and other items made their way to France, England, and elsewhere. Goods also followed older routes across the Mediterranean to the Ottoman empire, where traders could make huge profits on exotic items from the Americas. Thus, while some Europeans suffered under Spanish power, others benefited from the riches brought to the continent. By the late sixteenth century, the desire for a greater share of those riches revitalized imperial dreams among the French and English as well as the Dutch.

REVIEW & RELATE

What motives were behind the Spanish conquest and colonization of the Americas?

What were the consequences in Europe of Spain's acquisition of an American empire?

LEARNINGCurve bedfordstmartins.com/hewittlawson/LC

Conclusion: A New America

When Spanish explorers happened upon the Americas, they brought Europeans into contact with native peoples who had inhabited the two continents for thousands of years. But these explorations and the conquests that followed did transform North and South America in dramatic ways. Martin Waldseemüller died in 1521 or 1522, so he was not able to incorporate into his maps the coastlines, waterways, and mountains reported by Magellan, Balboa, Cortés, Coronado, de Soto, Cartier, and other European adventurers. He would no doubt have been amazed to see the increasingly detailed maps that cartographers created of the elongated continent he first named America.

While mapmakers benefited from Europeans pushing deeper and deeper into the Americas, native residents were rarely asked if they wanted the plants, animals, goods, and germs offered by these invaders. Even Europeans seeking permanent settlements and peaceful trade relations with the Indians brought diseases that devastated local populations along with plants and animals that transformed their landscape, diet, and traditional ways of life.

Malintzin saw these changes firsthand. She watched as disease ravaged not only rural villages but even the capital city of Tenochtitlán. She encountered horses, pigs, attack dogs, and other European animals. She ate the foods and

DOCUMENTS 1.4 AND 1.5

European Depictions of the Americas: Two Views

In the late 1500s, the engraver Theodor de Bry and his sons began creating a series of copperplate illustrations depicting the exploration of the Americas. Because de Bry had never visited the New World, his illustrations came from descriptions and pictures by explorers. He got a number of cultural facts wrong, but his scenes were detailed and graphic and enormously popular. The de Bry family created hundreds of illustrations, which were used in their own books and those of others, including Bartolomé de Las Casas. These scenes figured into discussions about the legitimacy of Spanish actions in the Americas, as well as popular views of native populations. The first illustration below depicts Spanish cruelty against Indians; the second one shows Indian torture of Spanish explorers.

Explore

1.4 Theodor de Bry | Engraving of the Black Legend, 1598

Beinecke Rare Book and Manuscript Library, Yale University

1.5 Theodor de Bry | Indians Torturing Spaniards, 1594

Beinecke Rare Book and Manuscript Library, Yale University

Interpret the Evidence

• What do these images tell us about public perceptions of Indians and Spanish explorers?

• What details reveal that de Bry never went to the Americas?

Put It in Context

Who would have used these images in debates over Spanish exploration in the Americas and for what purpose?

---

wore the clothes that her Spanish captors provided. Malintzin accompanied Cortés and his men as they conquered the Aztecs, and she watched as more Spaniards, including the first women, settled in New Spain. In 1522 she gave birth to Cortés's son; two years later, she served as interpreter when he ventured north from Mexico City to conquer more territory. In 1526 or 1527, however, she married a Spanish soldier, Juan Jaramillo, and settled in Mexico City. She soon had a daughter, Maria, and in 1528

Jaramillo and "his wife, doña Marina" were granted lands for an orchard and a farm. We do not know how long Malintzin lived or what she thought of her life as the wife of a Spanish gentleman. But her children would grow up in a world that was very different from the one in which their mother was raised. In the century to come, the contacts and conflicts between native peoples and Europeans escalated, especially in North America. So, too, did conflicts among European nations seeking to gain control of North American lands.

LEARNINGCurve
Check what you know.
bedfordstmartins.com/hewittlawson/LC

Chapter Review

Online Study Guide ▶ bedfordstmartins.com/hewittlawson

KEY TERMS

Beringia (p. 5)
horticulture (p. 5)
Aztecs (p. 5)
Maya (p. 7)
Incas (p. 7)
Hopewell people (p. 7)
Crusades (p. 9)
Black Death (p. 10)
Renaissance (p. 10)
Enterprise of the Indies (p. 14)
encomiendas (p. 14)
Columbian exchange (p. 18)
conquistadors (p. 20)

REVIEW & RELATE

1. Compare and contrast the Aztecs, Incas, and Maya. What similarities and differences do you note?

2. How did the societies of North America differ from those of the equatorial zone and the Andes?

3. How and why did Europeans expand their connections with Africa and the Middle East in the fifteenth century?

4. How did early European encounters with West Africans lay the foundation for later race-based slavery?

5. What were the short-term consequences in both Europe and the Americas of Columbus's voyages?

6. How did the Columbian exchange transform both the Americas and Europe?

7. What motives were behind the Spanish conquest and colonization of the Americas?

8. What were the consequences in Europe of Spain's acquisition of an American empire?

TIMELINE OF EVENTS

13,000–11,000 B.C.E.	First northeast Asians migrate to the Americas
1000 B.C.E.	Agriculture develops in some parts of the Americas
900 B.C.E.–300 C.E.	Maya settle Yucatán peninsula
500 C.E.	Mogollon and Hohokam communities established in present-day Arizona and New Mexico
500–1400	Mississippian people establish complex societies centered on towns and massive earthworks
800	Mayan civilization begins to decline
1000	Norse establish small settlement in North America
1292	Marco Polo publishes his *Travels*
1325	Aztecs build Tenochtitlán
1340s	Bubonic plague arrives in Europe from Asia
1400–1500	Inca empire reaches the height of its power
1440s	Portuguese begin to trade along the coast of West Africa
1452–1455	Johannes Gutenberg uses movable type to produce 180 copies of the Bible
1469	Marriage of Isabella of Castile and Ferdinand II of Aragon leads to unification of Spain
1482	Portugal builds Elmina Castle on the Gold Coast of West Africa
1487	Bartolomeu Dias rounds the Cape of Good Hope
1492	Isabella and Ferdinand expel last Muslim conquerors from the Iberian peninsula
	Columbus launches Enterprise of the Indies
1497	Vasco da Gama reaches India by sailing around Africa
1507	Martin Waldseemüller and Mathias Ringmann publish *Universalis Cosmographia*
1519	Malintzin captured by Spaniards
1519–1521	Spanish and Indian army led by Cortés conquers the Aztecs
1519–1522	Fleet led by Ferdinand Magellan circumnavigates the globe sailing west
1524	Francisco Pizarro conquers the Incas
1587	English colony of Roanoke established in North America

Mapping America

As Europeans expanded their trade and exploration in the fifteenth century, they gathered information about navigational routes and the regions they encountered. Cartographers used this information to create increasingly accurate maps of the known world. One of the leading efforts in mapmaking was conducted under the leadership of Prince Henry of Portugal. His assemblage of cartographers, geographers, astronomers, and explorers helped revolutionize European understandings of the western coast of Africa and nearby islands in the Atlantic. The 1513 Piri Reis map (Document 1.8), in particular, used Portuguese maps to chart Africa and the Atlantic.

Columbus's discovery of the Western Hemisphere in 1492 redrew the map of the world. Although he believed he had found a route to Asia, by 1507 when the *Universalis Cosmographia* (Document 1.7) appeared, cartographers understood this as an entirely new region. Throughout the early sixteenth century, maps of the Americas continued to expand and modify knowledge of what was termed the "New World," whose territory would be claimed by Spain, Portugal, England, France, and other European powers. Of course, the Western Hemisphere was not a "new" world but instead one inhabited by millions of indigenous peoples with complex societies of their own. Document 1.10 is an example of a map created by indigenous people in what is now Mexico; they often used maps not only to depict an area but also to record developments in that region that had occurred over decades or even centuries.

The following maps depict changing understandings of Europe, Africa, and the Americas from 1490 to the mid-sixteenth century, as well as the increasing interconnectedness of these regions. They represent not only attempts to chart territory and navigational routes but also cultural beliefs about the world and the people encountered by Europeans. As you examine them, think about what their creators chose to include, what they left out, and how these maps helped shape European attitudes toward Africa and the Western Hemisphere.

Library of Congress

DOCUMENT 1.6

Christopher and Bartolomeo Columbus |
Map of Europe and North Africa, c. 1490

While Christopher Columbus's discovery of the Americas is well known, his younger brother, Bartolomeo, also played a part in the early discovery and exploration of the Western Hemisphere. Bartolomeo was a cartographer and navigator who accompanied Christopher on several explorations. This map is believed to have been produced in the Lisbon workshop of Christopher and Bartolomeo Columbus in 1490, two years before Columbus set sail on his first voyage. It depicts Europe and North Africa and also includes a circular world map on the left.

DOCUMENT 1.7

Martin Waldseemüller and Mathias Ringmann | *Universalis Cosmographia*, 1507

In 1507 German cartographers Martin Waldseemüller and Mathias Ringmann produced a map of the "known" world, which included those areas in the Western Hemisphere recently discovered by European explorers. They were the first to use the term *America*, and their *Universalis Cosmographia* was also the first map to show the Americas as separate from Asia. The map was printed from wood engravings and produced in twelve sections.

Library of Congress

DOCUMENT 1.8

Piri Reis Map, 1513

The Turkish admiral and cartographer Piri Reis produced another early-sixteenth-century map. While much of the map does not survive, the remaining part includes the western coasts of Europe and North Africa, the eastern coast of South America, and the northern coast of Antarctica. Reis used Portuguese, Ptolemaic, and Arabic maps to produce his version of the world, and the illustrations are detailed and reasonably accurate.

DOCUMENT 1.9

Dauphin Map of Canada, c. 1543

Although Jacques Cartier was not the first European to explore present-day Canada, he was the first to penetrate into the eastern interior, aided by two Iroquois guides whom he had kidnapped. The French explorer claimed the region for France in the 1530s, and over the next decade he completed three voyages to explore and map the Gulf of St. Lawrence region. He also sought what he believed were great riches at a legendary Indian kingdom named Saguenay. The map shown here, known as the Dauphin Map of Canada and based on Cartier's explorations, includes French Canada and the entire east coast of North America. Created in 1543, this map includes the largest Indian settlements (Hochelaga and Stadaconna) but also names and claims numerous rivers, inlets, harbors, and the lands surrounding them for the French. Finally, it also illustrates some of the land claims of England and Spain in the region.

DOCUMENT 1.10

Map of Cuauhtinchan, 1550

The *Historia Tolteca-Chichimeca* is a series of Nahuatl-language annals written in the mid-sixteenth century. Covering the history of the Cuauhtinchan region (in present-day Mexico) during the previous four hundred years, the text focuses mainly on the area's social and political history. Most of the narrative deals with events that occurred before, or were unrelated to, Spanish activity in the region. Illustrations accompanied the text, including the map shown here. This map, covered with some seven hundred glyphs, depicts how the Toltec-Chichimeca peoples of the Puebla valley left their seven-chambered cave of Chicomoztoc, conquered their enemies, and established their new home at Cuauhtinchan in 1183 C.E. Like many native maps, it combines myth and history with geography and tells a story across time and space. Yet this territorial map was considered so reliable that it was used as evidence in Spanish colonial courts in the sixteenth century.

Nettie Lee Benson Latin American Collection, University of Texas Libraries, The University of Texas at Austin

Interpret the Evidence

1. How did the mapmakers in Documents 1.7, 1.8, and 1.9 represent the lands being discovered and claimed by various European nations?

2. What were the different purposes of the various maps included here?

3. What elements other than geographical features appear on these maps, and what were they intended to symbolize?

4. Compare the Cuauhtinchan map (Document 1.10) with those created by Europeans. What are the major differences? What do you think these differences reveal about the cultures of the mapmakers?

Put It in Context

- What are the strengths and weaknesses of modern mapmaking compared with older mapmaking?

- What is gained and what is lost in the transition from one to the other?

HIP/Art Resource, NY

© Burstein Collection/CORBIS

English Captain Bartholomew Gosnold trading with Indians, Virginia, 1634.

Portrait of Elizabeth Paddy Wensley by unknown artist, c. 1670–1680.

2
Colonization and Conflicts
1550–1680

HIP/Art Resource, NY

Village of Pomeiooc, Virginia, 1618.

Born in 1580 to a yeoman farm family in Lincolnshire, the adventurer John Smith left England as a young man "to learne the life of a Souldier." After fighting and traveling in Europe, the Mediterranean, and North Africa for several years, Captain Smith returned to England around 1605. There he joined the Virginia Company, whose investors planned to establish a private settlement on mainland North America. In December 1606, Captain Smith sailed with a contingent of 104 men, arriving in Chesapeake Bay the following April. The group founded Jamestown, named in honor of King James I. In doing so, they claimed the land for themselves and their country. However, whatever abstract claims Captain Smith and his comrades believed they were making to the region, their settlement was located in an area already controlled by a powerful leader, Chief Powhatan, who headed a confederation of local tribes.

In December 1607, when Powhatan's younger brother discovered Smith and two of his Jamestown comrades in the chief's territory, the Indians executed the two comrades but eventually released Smith. It is likely that before sending him back to Jamestown, Powhatan performed an adoption ceremony in an effort to bring Smith and the English under his authority. A typical ceremony would have involved Powhatan sending out one of his daughters—in this case, Pocahontas, who was about twelve years old—to indicate that the captive was spared. But Smith either did not understand or refused to accept his new status. He later claimed that

35

John Smith and Anne Hutchinson

Pocahontas saved him out of love. At the time, however, he simply returned to Jamestown and urged the residents to build fortifications to enhance their strength and security.

The following fall, the colonists elected Smith president of the Jamestown council. Holding the power of a colonial governor, he argued that intimidating the Indians was the way to win Powhatan's respect. He also demanded that the English labor on farms and fortifications six hours a day. Many colonists resisted. Like Smith himself, most of the men were adventurers; they had little skill—and even less interest—in farming. They came to America not to settle down but to gain wealth and glory. Despite improvements in conditions in the colony under Smith's regime, the Virginia Company soon replaced him with a new set of leaders. In October 1609, angry and bitter, Smith returned to England.

Captain Smith criticized Virginia Company policies on a number of fronts, publishing his views in 1612, which brought him widespread attention. Smith then set out to map the northern Atlantic coast, and in 1616 he published a tract that emphasized the similarity of the area's climate and terrain to the British Isles, calling it New England. He argued that colonies there could be made commercially viable but that success depended on recruiting settlers with the necessary skills and offering them land and a say in the colony's management.

English men and women settled New England in the 1620s, but they did not invite Smith to join them. The first colonists to the region sought religious sanctuary, not commercial success or military dominance. Yet they, too, suffered schisms in their ranks. Anne Hutchinson, a forty-five-year-old wife and mother, was at the center of one such division. Also born in Lincolnshire, England, in 1591, about a decade after Smith, Anne was well educated by her father, a minister in the Church of England.

In 1612 she married William Hutchinson, a merchant, and over the next twenty years she gave birth to thirteen children. The Hutchinsons began attending Puritan sermons and by 1630 had embraced the new faith. Four years later, they followed the Reverend John Cotton to Massachusetts Bay.

The Reverend Cotton was soon urging Anne Hutchinson to use her exceptional knowledge of the Bible to hold prayer meetings in her home on Sundays for pregnant and nursing women who could not attend regular services. Hutchinson, like Cotton, preached a covenant of grace, by which individuals must rely solely on God's grace and could play no part in their own salvation. By contrast, mainstream Puritan leaders claimed that a man or woman could cooperate with God's grace by leading a saintly life and performing good works.

Hutchinson began challenging Puritan ministers who opposed a pure covenant of grace, charging that they posed a threat to their congregations. She soon attracted a loyal following that included men as well as women. The growing size of her Sunday meetings helped convince Puritan leaders to call the first synod of their Congregational Church in August 1637. The synod denounced Hutchinson's views and condemned her Sunday meetings. When she refused to recant, she was put on trial. Standing alone to face a panel of forty-nine powerful men in November 1637, Hutchinson defended herself against charges that she presumed to teach men and failed to honor the ministers of the colony. Unmoved by her defense, the Puritan judges convicted her of heresy and banished her from Massachusetts Bay. Hutchinson, her husband, and their six youngest children, along with dozens of followers, then settled in the recently established colony of Rhode Island. ●

bottom photo: Schlesinger Library, Radcliffe Institute, Harvard University/The Bridgeman Art Library

THE AMERICAN HISTORIES of John Smith and Anne Hutchinson illustrate the diversity of motives that drew English men and women to North America in the seventeenth century. Smith led a group of soldiers and adventurers seeking wealth and glory, both for themselves and for their king. In many ways, their efforts to colonize Virginia were an extension of a larger competition between European states. The roots of Hutchinson's journey to North America can be traced to the Protestant Reformation of the sixteenth century, a massive religious upheaval that divided Europe into rival religious factions. The Puritan faith that was so central to her life was an outgrowth of the Reformation. Yet as different as these two people and their motives were, both worked to further English settlement in North America even as they generated conflict within their own communities. At the same time, those communities confronted the needs and desires of diverse native peoples as well as the colonial aspirations of other Europeans. These contending forces reshaped the landscape of North America between 1550 and 1680.

Religious and Imperial Transformations

The Puritans were part of a relatively new religious movement known as **Protestantism** that had emerged around 1520. Protestants challenged Catholic policies and practices but did not form a single church of their own. Instead, a number of theologians, including Martin Luther and John Calvin, formed distinct denominations in various regions of Europe, especially the German states, Switzerland, France, England, and the Netherlands. Catholics sought to counter their claims by revitalizing their faith and reasserting control. These religious conflicts shaped developments in North America as groups with competing visions worked to claim lands and sometimes souls.

The Protestant Reformation

Critiques of the Catholic Church multiplied in the early sixteenth century, driven by papal involvement in conflicts among monarchs and corruption among church officials. But the most vocal critics focused on immorality, ignorance, and absenteeism among clergy. These anticlerical views appeared in popular songs and printed images as well as in learned texts by theologians such as Martin Luther.

Luther, a professor of theology in Germany, believed that faith alone led to salvation, which could be granted only by God. He challenged the claims of Pope Leo X and his bishop in Germany that individuals could achieve salvation by buying indulgences, which were documents that absolved the buyer of sin. The church profited enormously from these sales, but they suggested that God's grace could be purchased. In 1517 Luther wrote an extended argument against indulgences and sent it to the local bishop. Although intended for learned clerics and academics, his writings soon gained a wider audience.

Luther's followers, who protested Catholic practices, became known as Protestants. His teachings circulated widely through sermons and printed texts, and his claim that ordinary people should read and reflect on the Scriptures appealed to the literate middle classes. Meanwhile his attacks on indulgences and corruption attracted those who resented the church's wealth and priests' lack of attention to their flock. In Switzerland, John Calvin developed a version of Protestantism in which civil magistrates and reformed ministers ruled over a Christian society. According to Calvinist beliefs, God was all-knowing and absolutely sovereign, while man was weak and sinful. Calvin argued that God had decided at the beginning of time who was saved and who was damned. Calvin's idea, known as predestination, energized Protestants who understood salvation as a gift from an all-knowing God in which human "works" played no part.

The Protestant Reformation quickly spread through central and northern Europe. England, too, came under the influence of Protestantism in the 1530s, although for different reasons. When the pope refused to annul the marriage of King Henry VIII and Catherine of Aragon, Henry denounced papal authority and established the **Church of England**, or Anglicanism, with himself as "defender of the faith." Despite the king's conversion to Protestantism, the Church of England retained many Catholic practices.

In countries like Spain and France with strong central governments and powerful ties to the Catholic Church, a strong Catholic Counter-Reformation largely quashed Protestantism. At the same time, Catholic leaders initiated reforms to counter their critics. In 1545 Pope Paul II called together a commission of cardinals, known as the Council of Trent (1545–1563), to address contentious issues such as corrupt bishops and priests, indulgences, and other financial abuses. The council initiated reforms, such as the founding of seminaries to train priests and the return of monastic orders to their spiritual foundations.

Religious upheavals in Europe contributed significantly to empire building in North America. Protestant and Catholic leaders urged followers to spread their faith across the Atlantic, while religious minorities sought a safe haven in North America. Just as important, political struggles erupted between Catholic and Protestant rulers in Europe following the Reformation. The politicization of religious divisions resulted in peasant unrest, economic crises, and military conflicts that pushed (or forced) people to seek new opportunities in the Americas. Thus in a variety of ways, religious transformations in Europe fueled the construction of empires in America.

Spain's Global Empire Declines

As religious conflicts escalated in Europe, the Spaniards in America continued to push north from Florida and Mexico in hopes of expanding their empire. At times, they confronted Protestants seeking to gain a foothold in the New World. For example, French Protestants, known as Huguenots, settled in Florida in the 1550s. By 1565, Spanish soldiers had constructed a fort at St. Augustine and massacred some three hundred Huguenots. The fort's main purpose, however, was to limit raids on Spanish ships by French and English privateers seeking to enrich themselves and their monarchs.

Yet as a result of the Council of Trent and the Catholic Counter-Reformation, Spain increasingly emphasized its religious mission. Thus Spanish authorities decided in 1573 that missionaries rather than soldiers should direct all new settlements. Franciscan priests began founding missions on the margins of Pueblo villages north of Mexico. They named the area Nuevo México (New Mexico), and many learned Indian languages. Over the following decades, as many as twenty thousand Pueblos officially converted to Catholicism, although many still retained traditional beliefs and practices. Thus they continued to practice religious ceremonies at sacred shrines known as kivas. Missionaries periodically destroyed the shrines and flogged Pueblo ceremonial leaders, but to no avail.

At the same time, the Franciscans tried to force the Pueblo people to adopt European ways. They insisted that men rather than women farm the land and that the Pueblos speak, cook, and dress like the Spaniards. Yet the missionaries largely ignored Spanish laws intended to protect Indians from coerced labor. Indeed, the Franciscans forced the Pueblos to build churches, provide the missions with food, and carry their goods to market. Wealthy landowners who followed the missionaries into New Mexico also demanded tribute in the form of goods and labor.

Then in 1598 Juan de Oñate, a member of a wealthy mining family, established a trading post and fort in the upper Rio Grande valley. The 500 soldiers who accompanied him seized corn and clothing from Pueblo villages and murdered or raped those who resisted. When the Spanish force was confronted by Indians at the Acoma pueblo, 11 soldiers were killed. The Spanish retaliated, slaughtering 500 men and 300 women and children. But fearing reprisals

San Esteban del Rey Mission

Opened in 1644 after fourteen years of construction, this Spanish mission in present-day New Mexico provided instruction in Christianity and Hispanic customs for the Acoma (Pueblo) people. To this end, Spanish missionaries prohibited traditional Pueblo practices such as dances and wearing masks. The mission was one of the few to survive Pueblo revolts in the late seventeenth century.
© age fotostock/SuperStock

from outraged Indians, most Spanish settlers withdrew from the region.

In 1610 the Spanish returned, founded Santa Fe, and established a network of missions and estates owned by *encomenderos*, Spanish elites granted land and the right to exploit local Indian labor. The Pueblo people largely accepted the new situation. In part, they feared military reprisals if they challenged Spanish authorities. But they were also faced with droughts and disease, as well as raids by hostile Apache and Navajo tribes. The Pueblos hoped to gain protection from Spanish soldiers and priests. Yet their faith in the Franciscans' spiritual power soon began to fade when conditions did not improve. Although Spain maintained a firm hold on Florida and its colonies in the West Indies, it began focusing most of its efforts on staving off growing resistance among the Pueblo people. Thus as other European powers expanded their reach into North America, the Spaniards were left with few resources to protect their eastern frontier.

France Enters the Race for Empire

In the late sixteenth century, French, Dutch, and English investors became increasingly interested in gaining a foothold in North America. But until Catholic Spain's grip on the Atlantic world was broken, other nations could not hope to compete for an American empire. It was the Protestant Reformation that helped shape the alliances that shattered Spain's American monopoly. As head of the Church of England, King Henry VIII and then his daughter Queen Elizabeth I sought closer political and commercial ties with Protestant nations like the Netherlands. At the same time, the queen assented to, and benefited from, Francis Drake's raids on Spanish ships. She rewarded him with a knighthood for services to the crown. In 1588 King Philip II of Spain decided to punish England for its attacks against Spanish shipping and intervention in the Netherlands and sent a massive armada to spearhead the invasion of England. Instead, the English, aided by Dutch ships that were smaller and more mobile, defeated the armada and ensured that other nations could compete for riches and colonies in North America.

Although French rulers shared Spain's Catholic faith, the two nations were rivals, and the defeat of the armada provided them as well as the Dutch and English with greater access to North American colonies. Moreover, once in North America, the French adopted attitudes and policies that were significantly different from those of Spain. This was due in part to their greater interest in trade than in conquest. They needed to develop alliances with local inhabitants who could supply them with fish and furs to be sold in Europe. The French had fished the North Atlantic since the mid-sixteenth century, but in the 1580s

they built stations along the Newfoundland coast for drying codfish. French traders then established relations with local Indians and eagerly exchanged iron kettles, which the native peoples desired, for beaver skins, which were highly prized in Europe.

By the early seventeenth century, France's King Henry IV sought to profit more directly from the resources in North America. With the Edict of Nantes (1598), the king ended decades of religious wars by granting political rights and limited toleration to French Protestants, the Huguenots. Now he could focus on developing the increasingly lucrative trade in American fish and furs. Samuel de Champlain, an experienced soldier and sailor, founded the first permanent French settlement in North America in 1608 at Quebec. Accompanied by several dozen of his men, Champlain joined a Huron raid on the Iroquois, who resided south of the Great Lakes. Using guns, which had rarely been seen in the region, the French helped ensure a Huron victory and a powerful ally for the French. But the battle also fueled lasting bitterness among the Iroquois.

Trade relations flourished between the French and their Indian allies, but relatively few French men and even fewer French women settled in North America in the seventeenth century. Government policies discouraged mass migration, and peasants were also concerned by reports of short growing seasons and severe winters in Canada. Cardinal Richelieu, the king's powerful chief minister, urged priests and nuns to migrate to New France and establish missions among the Indians, but he barred Huguenots from emigrating, which further limited colonization. Thus into the 1630s, French settlements in North America consisted largely of fishermen, fur traders, and Catholic missionaries.

Fur traders were critical to sustaining the French presence and warding off encroachment by the English. They journeyed along lakes and rivers throughout eastern Canada, aided by the Huron tribe. Some Frenchmen took Indian wives, who provided them with both domestic labor and kinship ties to powerful trading partners. These marriages also helped forge a middle ground in the Great Lakes region as French traders pushed westward and gained new Indian allies among the Ojibwe and Dakota tribes. The middle ground was a space in which shared economic interest motivated a remarkable degree of cultural exchange and mutual adaptation. Some French learned native languages and recognized the incredible value of canoes to their trade. They also came to appreciate Indian women's importance in gathering and preparing food, scraping beaver pelts, and weaving. At the same time, Indian communities adopted iron cooking pots and needles and European cloth. Jesuit missionaries, who entered New France in 1625, frowned on these marriages and the cultural exchanges they fostered. Nonetheless, they followed the path set out by fur traders and established missions among the Hurons and later the Ojibwes.

Explore

In Documents 2.1 and 2.2, compare a Huron woman's concerns about the Jesuits' presence in New France with a French priest's speech on the Jesuits' motivations.

In their ongoing search for new sources of furs, the French established a fortified trading post at Montreal in 1643, and over the next three decades they continued to push farther west. However, in extending the fur trade beyond the St. Lawrence River valley, the French left their Huron allies open to attacks from the Iroquois. The Iroquois suffered from the same diseases that decimated other tribes, and they also wanted to keep the Huron tribe from trading their high-quality furs to the Dutch. With guns supplied by Dutch merchants, the Iroquois could fend off economic competition and secure captives to restore their population. The result was a series of devastating assaults on Huron villages in which dozens of Jesuits died alongside the Indians they had converted.

The ongoing wars among native rivals limited the ability of France to capitalize on its North American colonies. Indeed, the only hope of maintaining profits from the fur trade was to continue to move westward. But in doing so, the French carried European diseases into new areas, ignited warfare among more native groups, and stretched their always small population of settlers ever thinner. Still, French explorers, traders, and priests extended their reach across Canada and by 1681 moved southward along the Mississippi to a territory they named Louisiana in honor of King Louis XIV. There they would find themselves face-to-face with Spanish adventurers heading east from New Mexico.

The conflicts between commerce and conversion so evident in Spanish America were far less severe in New France. Not only did French traders rely on Indian allies, but French missionaries also sought to build on native beliefs and to learn their language and customs. Although the Jesuits assumed that their own religious beliefs and cultural values were superior to those of the Indians, they did seek to engage Indians on their own terms. Thus one French Jesuit employed the Huron belief that "our souls have desires which are inborn and concealed" to explain Christian doctrines of sin and salvation to potential converts. Still, French traders and missionaries carried deadly germs, and Catholics sought conversion, not mutual adaptation. Thus while Indians clearly benefited from their alliances with the French in the short term, the long-term costs were devastating.

The Dutch Expand into North America

The Dutch, who eagerly embraced the Protestant Reformation at home, made no pretense of bringing religion to Indians in America. From the beginning, their goals were primarily economic. As Spain's shipbuilding center, the Netherlands benefited from the wealth pouring in from South America. The affluent merchant class that emerged among the Dutch promoted the arts, and artists like Salomon van Ruysdael and Johannes Vermeer in turn captured the importance of trade in their work. But the Dutch also embraced Calvinism and sought to separate themselves from Catholic Spain. In 1581 the Netherlands declared its independence from King Philip II, although Spain refused to recognize the new status for several decades. Still, by 1600 the Netherlands was both a Protestant haven and the trading hub of Europe. Indeed, the Dutch East India Company controlled trade routes to much of Asia and parts of Africa.

With the technology and skills developed under Spanish control, the Dutch decided to acquire their own American colonies. In 1609 the Dutch established a trading center on the Hudson River in present-day New York, where they could trade with Iroquois to the west as well as with Indians who gathered beaver skins along Lake Champlain and farther north. The small number of Dutch traders developed especially friendly relations with the powerful Mohawk nation, and in 1614 the trading post was relocated to Fort Orange, near present-day Albany.

In 1624, to fend off French and English raids on ships sent downriver from Fort Orange, the Dutch established New Amsterdam on Manhattan Island, which they purchased from the Lenape Indians. The new settlement was organized by the Dutch West Indies Company, which had been chartered three years earlier. New Amsterdam was the centerpiece of the larger New Netherland colony and attracted a diverse community of traders, fishermen, and farmers. It was noted for its representative government and religious toleration, which ensured that religious differences did not get in the way of making money.

The European settlers of New Netherland may have gotten along with one another, but the same could not be said for the settlers and the local Indian populations. Tensions increased as Dutch colonists carved out farms north of New Amsterdam where larger communities of Algonquian Indians lived and where European pigs and cattle foraged in Indian cornfields. Algonquians in turn killed and ate Dutch livestock. In 1639 conflict escalated when Governor William Kieft demanded an annual tribute in wampum or grain. Local Algonquians resisted, raiding Dutch farms on the frontier and killing at least two colonists. Then in 1643 Kieft launched a surprise attack on an

DOCUMENTS 2.1 AND 2.2

Indians and Jesuit Missionaries in New France: Two Views

The arrival of Jesuit missionaries further exposed the cultural differences between Indians and Europeans in New France. In Document 2.1, an elder Huron woman advises her village to reject the Jesuits' preaching and suggests that the Black Robes, as the missionaries were called, be put to death. Although her sentiments were relayed by a third party to a French nun, Marie de L'Incarnation, who then quoted them in a letter sent to France, they seem to accurately reflect the views of many Indians in New France. Document 2.2 indicates that, despite Indian resistance, French Jesuits continued to proselytize in New France. In 1656 Father Pierre Chaumont spoke to a group of Iroquois assembled on the shores of Lake Onondaga. Like many Jesuits, he had learned several Indian languages and spoke to the assembled Iroquois in their own language.

Explore

2.1 Statement from a Huron Woman, 1640

It is the Black Robes that make us die by their spells. Harken to me. I am proving it by arguments you will know to be true. They lodged in a certain village where everyone was well. As soon as they were established there, everyone was dead except for three or four persons. They went elsewhere and the same thing happened. They visited the cabins in other villages and only those they did not enter were free of mortality and sickness. Do you not see that when they move their lips—what they call prayers—those are spells that come from their mouths? It is the same way when they read in their books. Besides, in their cabins they have big pieces of wood [those are guns] with which they make a great noise and spread their magic everywhere. If they are not promptly put to death, they will finally ruin the country so that neither small nor great will remain.

Source: Joyce Marshall, ed. and trans., *Word from New France: The Selected Letters of Marie de L'Incarnation* (Toronto: Oxford University Press, 1967), 82.

Explore

2.2 Father Pierre Chaumont | Speech to the Iroquois, 1656

For the Faith, we have departed from our country; for the Faith, we have abandoned our relatives and our friends; for the Faith, we have crossed the Ocean; for the Faith, we have left behind the great ships of the French to set off on your small canoes; for the Faith, we have relinquished our fine houses to live in your bark cabins; for the Faith, we have deprived ourselves of our natural nourishment and the delicious foods that we could have enjoyed in France to eat your boiled meal and your other victuals, which the animals of our country would hardly touch.

Source: Natalie Zemon Davis, *Women on the Margins: Three Seventeenth Century Lives* (Cambridge, MA: Harvard University Press, 1995), 94.

Interpret the Evidence

- According to the Huron woman, why should Native Americans reject the efforts of Jesuit missionaries?
- How does Father Pierre Chaumont characterize the lives of Jesuit missionaries?

Put It in Context

What do these documents reveal about how Native Americans and Jesuit missionaries perceived each other? How do these perceptions compare with Indian-European relations in English and Spanish colonies?

Nieuw Nederlandt.

New Amsterdam

This engraving from the 1620s provides the oldest view of the Dutch colony of New Amsterdam. Located at the tip of present-day Manhattan, the Dutch settlement consisted mainly of a fort and trading post. The ships suggest the importance of commerce, and the Indians, from whom the island was purchased, demonstrate their significant presence in the region.   Culver Pictures/The Art Archive at Art Resource, NY

Indian encampment on Manhattan Island, murdering eighty people, mostly women and children. Outraged Algonquians burned and looted homes north of the city, killed livestock, and murdered settlers. For two decades, sporadic warfare continued, but eventually the Algonquians were defeated.

At the same time, the Dutch eagerly traded for furs with Mohawk Indians along the upper Hudson River. The Mohawks were a powerful tribe that had the backing of the even more powerful Iroquois Confederacy. Their ties to Indian nations farther west allowed them to provide beaver skins to Dutch traders long after beavers had died out in the Hudson valley. Still, the Mohawk people did not deceive themselves. As one chief proclaimed in 1659, "The Dutch say we are brothers and that we are joined together with chains, but that lasts only so long as we have beavers."

Meanwhile reports of atrocities by both Indians and the Dutch circulated in the Netherlands. These damaged New Amsterdam's reputation and slowed migration dramatically. Exhausted by the unrelenting conflicts, the Dutch surrendered New Amsterdam to the English without a fight when the latter sent a convoy to oust their former allies in 1664.

REVIEW & RELATE

How did the Protestant Reformation shape the course of European expansion in the Americas?

How did the French and Dutch colonies in North America differ from the Spanish empire to the south?

LEARNINGCurve bedfordstmartins.com/hewittlawson/LC

The English Seek an Empire

The English, like the French and the Dutch, entered the race for an American empire late. England's failed efforts to colonize North America in the sixteenth century had left them without a permanent settlement until the founding of **Jamestown** on the Chesapeake River in 1607. In the 1620s, the English also established settlements in the West Indies, which quickly became the economic engine of English colonization. Expansion into these areas demanded new modes of labor to ensure a return on investment. Beginning in the mid-sixteenth century, large numbers of European indentured servants and growing numbers of African men and women crossed the Atlantic, some voluntarily, many involuntarily.

The English Establish Jamestown

England's success in colonizing North America depended in part on a new economic model in which investors sold shares in joint-stock companies and sought royal support for their venture. In 1606 a group of London merchants formed the Virginia Company, and King James I granted them the right to settle a vast area of North America, from present-day New York to North Carolina. The proprietors promised to "propagate the *Christian* religion" among native inhabitants in the region, but they were far more interested in turning a profit.

Most of the men that the Virginia Company recruited as colonists were, like John Smith, adventurers who hoped to get rich through the discovery of precious metals. Arriving on the coast of North America in April 1607 after a four-month voyage, the weary colonists established Jamestown on a site they chose for its easy defense. Although bothered by the settlement's mosquito-infested environment, the colonists focused their energies on the search for gold and silver.

The Englishmen also made contact with the Indian chief Powhatan, who presided over a confederation of some 14,000 Algonquian-speaking Indians from 25 to 30 tribes. The **Powhatan Confederacy** was far more powerful than its English neighbors, and, indeed, for the first two years the settlers depended on the Indians to survive. Although the Jamestown settlers were often hungry, few of them engaged in farming. Moreover, the nearby water was tainted by salt from the ocean, and diseases that festered in the low-lying area ensured a high death toll. Nine months after arriving in Virginia, only 38 of the original 105 settlers remained alive.

Despite the Englishmen's aggressive posture and inability to feed themselves, Powhatan initially assisted the settlers in hopes they could provide him with English cloth, iron hatchets, and even guns. His capture and subsequent release of John Smith in 1607 suggests his interest in developing trade relations with the newcomers even as he sought to subordinate them. But leaders like Captain Smith considered Powhatan and his warriors a threat rather than an asset. Although Jamestown residents could not afford to engage in open hostilities with local natives, they did raid villages for corn and other food, making Powhatan increasingly wary. The settlers' decision to construct a fort under Smith's direction only increased the Indians' concern.

Meanwhile the Virginia Company devised a new plan to stave off the collapse of its colony. It started selling seven-year joint-stock options to raise funds and recruited new settlers to produce staple crops—grapes, sugar, cotton, or tobacco—for export since the search for precious metals had failed. Interested individuals who could not afford to invest cash could sign on for service in Virginia. After seven years, these colonists would receive a hundred acres of land. In June 1609, a new contingent of colonists attracted by this plan—five hundred men and a hundred women—sailed for Jamestown (Map 2.1).

The new arrivals, however, had not brought enough supplies to sustain the colony through the winter. Powhatan did offer some aid, but a severe dry spell meant that the Indians, too, suffered from shortages in the winter of 1609–1610. A "starving time" settled on Jamestown. By the spring of 1610, seven of every eight settlers who had arrived in Jamestown since 1607 were dead. One colonist noted that settlers "were destroyed by cruell diseases, as Swellings, Fluxes, [and] Burning Fevers," though most "died of mere famine."

That June, the sixty survivors decided to abandon Jamestown and sail for home. But in the harbor, they met three English ships loaded with supplies and three hundred more settlers. Fresh supplies and a larger population inspired the English to take a much more confrontational

MAP 2.1 Jamestown, c. 1615

After eight years, the English settlement at Jamestown was finally expanding. Most important for the future, John Rolfe's experiments with tobacco promised a profitable cash crop. Still, English colonists remained a small minority huddled along the James River. Numerous Indian tribes, many of them members of the Powhatan Confederacy, surrounded them on all sides.

approach. Jamestown's new leaders adopted an aggressive military posture, attacking native villages, burning crops, killing many Indians, and taking others captive. They believed that such brutality would horrify neighboring tribes and convince them to obey English demands for food and labor.

Tobacco Fuels Growth in Virginia

It was not, however, military aggression but the discovery of a viable cash crop that saved the colony. Orinoco tobacco, a sweet-flavored leaf grown in the West Indies and South America, sold well in England and Europe. One Virginia colonist, John Rolfe, began to experiment with its growth in 1612. Within two years, it was clear that Orinoco tobacco prospered in Virginia soil. Production of the leaf soared as eager investors poured seeds, supplies, and labor into Jamestown. Exports multiplied rapidly, from 2,000 pounds in 1615 to 40,000 five years later and an incredible 1.5 million pounds by 1629. Although high taxes and overproduction led to declining prices in the 1630s, tobacco remained the most profitable cash crop on mainland North America throughout the seventeenth century.

Tobacco cultivation transformed relations between the English and the Indians. Farmers could increase their profits only by obtaining more land and more laborers. The Virginia Company sought to supply the laborers by offering those who could pay their own way land for themselves and their families. Those who could not afford passage could labor for landowners for seven years and then gain their independence and perhaps land of their own. Yet the land the Virginia Company so generously offered would-be colonists was, in most cases, already settled by members of the Powhatan Confederacy. Thus the rapid increase in tobacco cultivation intensified competition for land between colonists and Indians.

As circumstances began to change, Powhatan tried one last time to create an alliance between his confederacy and the English settlers. In 1614 he agreed to allow his daughter Pocahontas to marry John Rolfe. Pocahontas converted to Christianity, took the name Rebecca, and two years later traveled to England with Rolfe and their infant son. Rebecca was treated royally, but she fell ill and died in 1617. After her death, Rolfe returned to Virginia and continued to develop successful strains of tobacco. Soon after his return, Powhatan died, and his younger brother Opechancanough took over as chief.

Explore

To examine the only image of Pocahontas drawn from life, see Document 2.3.

In 1619 the English crown granted Virginia the right to establish a local governing body, the **House of Burgesses**. Its members could make laws and levy taxes, although the English governor or the company council in London held veto power. At the same time, the Virginia Company resolved to recruit more female settlers as a way to increase the colony's population so that it "may spread into generations." Other young women and men arrived as **indentured servants**, working in the fields and homes of more affluent Englishmen for a set period of time, often seven years, in exchange for the price of passage to America. The first boatload of twenty Africans also arrived in Jamestown aboard a Dutch ship in 1619, bound as indentured servants to farmers desperate for labor.

Although the English colony still hugged the Atlantic coast, its expansion increased conflict with native inhabitants. In March 1622, after repeated English incursions on land cleared and farmed by Indians, Chief Opechancanough mobilized area tribes for a surprise attack on English settlements. The Indians killed nearly a third of the colonists. In retaliation, Englishmen assaulted native villages, killed inhabitants, burned cornfields, and sold captives into slavery.

Announcing victory in 1623, the English claimed they owned the land "by right of Warre." But hostilities continued for nearly a decade. In 1624, in the midst of the crisis, King James annulled the Virginia Company charter and took control of the colony. He appointed the governor and a small advisory council, required that legislation passed by the House of Burgesses be ratified by the Privy Council, and demanded that property owners pay taxes to support the Church of England. These regulations became the model for royal colonies throughout North America. Still, royal proclamations could not halt Indian opposition. In 1644 Opechancanough launched a second uprising against the English, in which some five hundred colonists were killed. However, after two years of bitter warfare, the Powhatan chief was finally captured and then killed. With the English population now too large to eradicate, the Chesapeake Indians finally submitted to English authority in 1646, paying tribute to remain on lands they had lived on for generations.

Expansion, Rebellion, and the Emergence of Slavery

By the 1630s, despite continued conflicts with Indians, Virginia was well on its way to commercial success. The most successful tobacco planters utilized indentured servants, including some Africans as well as thousands of English and Irish immigrants. Between 1640 and 1670, some 40,000 to 50,000 of these migrants settled in Virginia and neighboring Maryland (Map 2.2). Maryland was

DOCUMENT 2.3

Simon van de Passe | Engraving of Pocahontas, 1616

Simon van de Passe created this portrait of Pocahontas during her visit to England in 1616. The engraving was commissioned by the Virginia Company as a way to market settlement in Jamestown. It was the only depiction of Pocahontas drawn from life because she died in London the following year. This engraving was copied, though not always accurately, many times during the eighteenth and nineteenth centuries.

Explore

While most portraits of English women from this period show the women looking down or to the side, Pocahontas looks directly at the viewer. Why might Simon van de Passe have portrayed Pocahontas in this way?

What does the elaborate clothing suggest about the parallels Simon van de Passe intends to draw between Indian royalty and English royalty?

What possible messages did the Virginia Company hope to promote with this image and its caption?

Library of Congress

Put It in Context

This image suggests both the possibility for establishing a long-term alliance between the Powhatan Indians and the English and the Virginia Company's desire to promote further English settlement in the Chesapeake. What is the relationship between the two messages offered by Pocahontas's portrait?

founded in 1632 when King Charles I, the successor to James I, granted most of the territory north of Chesapeake Bay and the title of Lord Baltimore to Cecilius Calvert. Calvert was among the minority of English who remained a Catholic, and he planned to create Maryland as a refuge for his persecuted coworshippers. Appointing his brother Leonard Calvert as governor, he carefully prepared for the first settlement. The Calverts recruited skilled artisans and farmers (mainly Protestant) as well as wealthy merchants and aristocrats (mostly Catholic) to establish St. Mary's City on the mouth of the Potomac River. Although conflict continued to fester between the Catholic elite and the Protestant majority, Governor Calvert convinced the Maryland assembly to pass the Act of Religious Toleration in 1649, granting religious freedom to all Christians.

Taken together, Maryland and Virginia formed the Chesapeake region of the English empire. Both colonies relied on tobacco to produce the wealth that fueled their growth, and both introduced African labor to complement the supply of white indentured servants. This proved especially important from 1650 on, as improved economic conditions in England meant fewer English men and women were willing to gamble on a better life in North America. Although the number of African laborers remained small until late in the century, there was a growing effort on the part of colonial leaders to increase their control over this segment of the workforce. Thus in 1660 the House of Burgesses passed an act that allowed African laborers to be enslaved. In 1664 Maryland followed suit. A slow if unsteady march toward full-blown racial slavery had begun.

Explore

See Document 2.4 for the Virginia law that made slavery an inherited condition passed from mother to child.

In legalizing human bondage, Virginia legislators followed a model established in Barbados, where the booming sugar industry spurred the development of plantation slavery. By 1660 Barbados had become the first English colony with a black majority population. Twenty years later, there were seventeen slaves for every white indentured servant on Barbados. The growth of slavery on the island depended almost wholly on imports from Africa since slaves there died faster than they could reproduce themselves. In the context of high death rates, brutal working conditions, and massive imports, Barbados systematized its slave code, defining enslaved Africans as chattel—that is, as mere property more akin to livestock than to human beings. Slaves existed to enrich their masters, and masters could do with them as they liked.

While African slaves would, in time, become a crucial component of the Chesapeake labor force, indentured servants made up the majority of bound workers in Virginia and Maryland for most of the seventeenth century. They labored under harsh conditions, and punishment for even minor infractions could be severe. Servants had holes bored in their tongues for complaining against their masters; they were beaten, whipped, and branded for a variety of "crimes"; and female servants who became pregnant had two years added to their contracts. Some white servants made common cause with black laborers who worked side by side with them on tobacco plantations. They ran away together, stole goods from their masters, and planned uprisings and rebellions.

By the 1660s and 1670s, the population of former servants who had become free formed a growing and increasingly unhappy class. Most were struggling economically, working as common laborers or tenants on large estates. Those who managed to move west and claim land on the frontier were confronted by hostile Indians like the Susquehannock. Virginia governor Sir William Berkeley had little patience with the complaints of these colonists. The labor demands of wealthy tobacco planters needed to be met, and

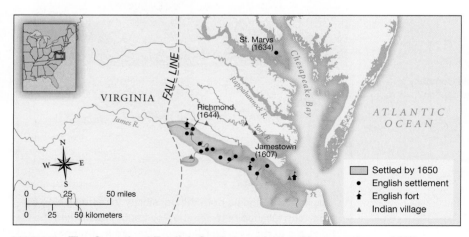

MAP 2.2 The Growth of English Settlement in the Chesapeake, c. 1650
With the success of tobacco, English plantations and forts spread along the James River and north to St. Mary's. By 1650 most Chesapeake Indian tribes had been vanquished or forced to move north and west. While the fall line, which marked the limit of navigable waterways, kept English settlements close to the Atlantic coast, it also ensured easy shipment of goods.

DOCUMENT 2.4

Virginia Slave Law, 1662

When the flow of white indentured servants to the Virginia colony slowed at midcentury, tobacco planters imported Africans to fill their labor needs. Anxious to define the status of these new workers, in the 1660s Virginia legislators passed a series of slave-related laws, such as the 1662 legislation that defined slavery as an inherited position, thus ensuring the perpetual enslavement of Africans and therefore a steady supply of workers. The act differed significantly from English common law, in which legal status and inheritance passed through the father.

Explore

Whereas some doubts have arisen whether children got by any Englishman upon a Negro woman should be slave or free, *Be it therefore enacted and declared by this present grand assembly,* that all children born in this country shall be held bond or free only according to the condition of the mother; and that if any Christian shall commit fornication with a Negro man or woman, he or she so offending shall pay double the fines imposed by the former act.

Source: William W. Hening, ed., *The Statutes at Large; Being a Collection of All Laws of Virginia, from the First Session of the Legislature in the Year 1619* (New York and Philadelphia, 1819–1823), 2:170.

Interpret the Evidence

- Why would the Virginia General Assembly make slavery an inheritable condition passed down through the mother instead of the father?
- What might explain the Assembly's decision to double the fine for fornication between a "Christian" and an African American?

Put It in Context

How did such laws create clearer distinctions between white indentured servants and enslaved Africans and African Americans?

frontier settlers' call for an aggressive Indian policy would hurt the profitable deerskin trade with the Algonquian Indians. Adopting a defensive strategy, Berkeley maintained a system of nine forts along the frontier that was supported by taxes, providing another aggravation for poorer colonists.

In late 1675, conflict erupted when frontier settlers attacked not the Susquehannock nation but rather Indian communities allied with the English since 1646. An even larger force of Virginia militiamen then surrounded a Susquehannock village and murdered five chiefs who tried to negotiate for peace. Susquehannock warriors retaliated with deadly raids on frontier farms. Despite the outbreak of open warfare, Governor Berkeley still refused to send troops, so disgruntled farmers turned to Nathaniel Bacon. Bacon, only twenty-nine years old and a newcomer to Virginia, came from a wealthy family and was related to Berkeley by marriage. But he defied the governor's authority and called up an army to attack all of the region's Indians, whether Susquehannocks or English allies. **Bacon's Rebellion** had begun. Frontier farmers formed an important part of Bacon's coalition. But affluent planters who had been left out of Berkeley's inner circle also joined Bacon in hopes of gaining access to power and profits. And bound laborers, black and white, assumed that anyone who opposed the governor was on their side.

In the summer of 1676, Governor Berkeley declared Bacon guilty of treason. Rather than waiting to be captured, Bacon led his army toward Jamestown. Berkeley then arranged a hastily called election to undercut the rebellion. Even though Berkeley had rescinded the right of men without property to vote, Bacon's supporters won control of the House of Burgesses, and Bacon won new adherents. These included "news wives," lower-class women who spread information (and rumors) about oppressive conditions, thereby aiding the rebels. As Bacon and his followers marched across Virginia, his men plundered the plantations of Berkeley supporters and captured Berkeley's estate at Green Spring. In September they reached Jamestown after the governor and his administration fled across Chesapeake Bay. The rebels burned the capital to the ground, victory seemingly theirs.

Only a month later, however, Bacon died of dysentery, and the movement he formed unraveled. Governor Berkeley, with the aid of armed ships from England, quickly reclaimed power. Outraged by the rebellion, he hanged twenty-three rebel leaders and incited his followers to plunder the estates of planters who had supported Bacon. But he could not undo the damage to Indian relations on the Virginia frontier. Bacon's army had killed or enslaved hundreds of once-friendly Indians and left behind a tragic and bitter legacy.

An even more important consequence of the rebellion was that wealthy planters and investors realized the depth of frustration among poor white men and women who were willing to make common cause with their black counterparts. Having regained power, the planter elite worked to crush any such interracial alliance. They promised most white rebels who put down arms the right to return home peacefully, and most complied. Virginia legislators then began to improve the conditions and rights of poorer white settlers while imposing new restrictions on blacks. At nearly the same time, in an effort to meet the growing demand for labor in the West Indies and the Chesapeake, King Charles II chartered the Royal African Company in 1672 to carry enslaved women and men from Africa to North America.

The English Compete for West Indies Possessions

While tobacco held great promise in Virginia, investors were eager to find other lucrative exports. Some turned their sights on the West Indies, where the English, the French, and the Dutch had all established bases on small islands during the sixteenth century. In the 1620s, the English developed more permanent settlements on St. Christopher, Barbados, and Nevis. Barbados quickly became the most attractive of these West Indies colonies. English migrants settled Barbados in growing numbers, clearing land and bringing in indentured servants from England, Ireland, and Scotland to cultivate tobacco and cotton and raise livestock.

The Dutch and the French also began establishing more permanent settlements in the West Indies. The Dutch colonized St. Martin and Curaçao, while the French settled Guadalupe, Martinique, and later Saint Domingue. The Dutch, however, profited mainly from carrying trade goods for other nations, while the French faced significant resistance from Carib Indians who resided on their island colonies. Thus neither developed their West Indies outposts to the same extent as the English. But even the English faced economic stagnation on Barbados as tobacco prices fell in the 1630s.

A few forward-looking planters were already considering another avenue to wealth: sugarcane. English and European consumers absorbed as much of the sweet gold as the market could provide, but producing sugar required

Sugar Manufacturing in the West Indies

This 1665 engraving depicts the use of slave labor in the production of sugar in the Antilles (West Indies). As shown in the illustration, the Dutch and English used slaves to plant sugarcane and then cut, press, and boil it to produce molasses. The molasses was turned into rum and refined sugar, which were among America's most profitable exports.   Private Collection/The Bridgeman Art Library expensive equipment and technical know-how as well as a large number of laborers. In addition, the sugar that was sent from America needed further refinement in Europe before being sold to consumers. The Dutch had learned the secrets of sugar cultivation from the Portuguese in Brazil, and they built the best refineries in Europe. But their small West Indies colonies could not supply sufficient raw material. By 1640 they decided to form a partnership with English planters, offering them the knowledge and financing to establish sugar plantations and mills on Barbados. That decision would reshape the economic and political landscape of North America and intensify competition for both land and labor.

REVIEW & RELATE

How did the Virginia colony change and evolve between 1607 and the 1670s?	How did the growth of the English colonies on the mainland and in the West Indies shape conflicts in Virginia and demands for labor throughout North America?

 LEARNINGCurve bedfordstmartins.com/hewittlawson/LC

Pilgrims and Puritans Settle New England

Along with merchants, planters, and indentured servants, religious dissenters also traveled to North America. Critics of the Church of England formed a number of congregations in the early seventeenth century, and some sought refuge in New England. One such group, the Pilgrims (also known as Separatists), landed on the Massachusetts coast in 1620 and established a permanent settlement at Plymouth. Their goal was to establish a religious community wholly separate from the Anglican Church. The Puritans, who hoped to purify rather than separate from the Church of England, arrived a decade later with plans to develop their own colony. Over the next two decades, New England colonists prospered, but they also confronted internal dissent and conflicts with local Indians.

Pilgrims Arrive in Massachusetts

In the 1610s, to raise capital, the Virginia Company began offering legal charters to groups of private investors, who were promised their own tract of land in the Virginia colony with minimal oversight by the governor or the company council. One such charter was purchased by a group of English **Pilgrims** who wanted to form a separate church and community in a land untainted by Catholicism, Anglicanism, or European cosmopolitanism. Thirty-five Pilgrims from Leiden in the Dutch Republic and several dozen from England signed on to the venture and set sail on the *Mayflower* from Plymouth, England, in September 1620.

Battered by storms, the ship veered off course, landing at Cape Cod in present-day Massachusetts in early December. With winter closing in, the exhausted passengers decided to disembark. Before leaving the ship, the settlers, led by William Bradford, signed a solemn pact, which they considered necessary because they were settling in a region where they had no legal authority. The Pilgrims agreed to "combine ourselves together into a civill body politick." The **Mayflower Compact** was the first written constitution adopted in North America. It followed the Separatist model of a self-governing religious congregation.

After several forays along the coast, the Pilgrims located an uninhabited village surrounded by cornfields where they established their new home, Plymouth. Uncertain of native intentions, the Pilgrims were unsettled by sightings of Indians near their hastily built fort. They did not realize that a smallpox epidemic in the area only two years earlier had killed nearly 90 percent of the local Wampanoag population, leaving them too weak to launch an assault on the Pilgrims. Indeed, fevers and other diseases proved far more deadly to the settlers than did Indians. By the spring of 1621, only half of the 102 Pilgrims remained alive.

Desperate to find food, the survivors were stunned when two English-speaking Indians—Samoset and Squanto—appeared at Plymouth that March. Both had been captured as young boys by English explorers, and they now negotiated a fragile peace between the Pilgrims and Massasoit, chief of the Wampanoag tribe. Although concerned by the power of English guns, Massasoit hoped to create an alliance that would assist him against his traditional native enemies. The Wampanoags supplied the English with seeds, fishing gear, and other goods that allowed them to take advantage of the short growing season and the abundant fish and wildlife in the region. The surviving Pilgrims soon regained their health.

In the summer of 1621, reinforcements arrived from England, and the next year the Pilgrims received a charter granting them rights to Plymouth Plantation and a degree of self-government. The region's cold climate turned out to be a boon as well, minimizing the spread of disease. These developments encouraged the Pilgrims to take a more aggressive stance toward Indians, like the Massachusetts tribe, who posed a threat to them. In 1623 Captain Miles Standish led an attack on a Massachusetts village after kidnapping and killing the chief and his younger brother. The survivors fled north and west, alerting other Indians to the Pilgrims' presence. Although Separatist leaders in

Leiden were appalled that their brethren were assaulting rather than converting Indians, Standish's strategy ensured that Massasoit, the colonists' Wampanoag ally, was now the most powerful chief in the region.

The Puritan Migration

As the Pilgrims gradually expanded their colony during the 1620s, a new group of English dissenters, the **Puritans**, made plans to develop their own settlement. As religious dissenters, Puritans faced persecution in England. However, persecution was only one reason the Puritans chose to leave England. They believed that their country's church and government had grown corrupt and was being chastened by an all-powerful God. During the early seventeenth century, the English population boomed but harvests failed, the poor suffered from famine and rising prices, the number of beggars multiplied, and crime and taxes rose.

The enclosure movement, in which landlords fenced in fields and hired a few laborers and tenants to replace a large number of peasant farmers, increased the number of landless vagrants. At the same time, the English cloth industry nearly collapsed under the weight of competition from abroad. In the Puritans' view, all of these problems were divine punishments for the nation's sins.

Thus, from the Puritans' perspective, New England was a safe haven from God's wrath. Puritan lawyer John Winthrop claimed that God offered New England as "a refuge for manye, whom he meant to save out of the general destruction." Consequently, under his leadership a group of affluent Puritans sought and received a royal charter for the Massachusetts Bay Company. To the Puritans, however, New England was more than just a place of safety. Unlike the Pilgrims, they believed that England and the Anglican Church could be redeemed. By prospering spiritually and materially in America, they could establish a model "City

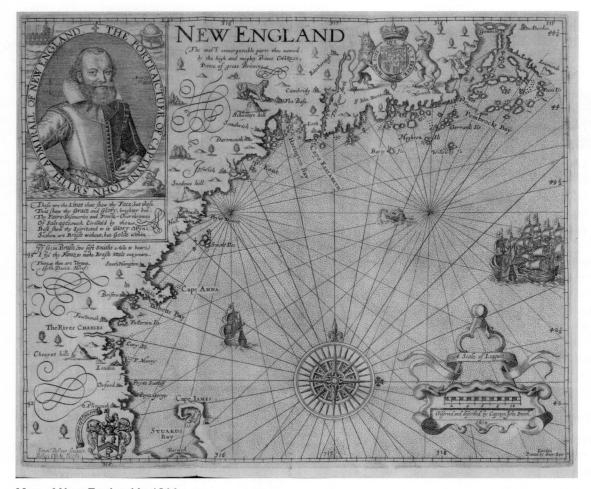

Map of New England in 1614

This engraving by the Dutchman Simon van de Passe in 1616 is based on a map drawn by the English explorer John Smith two years earlier. After leaving Jamestown, Smith, who is pictured in the upper left corner, sailed along the Atlantic coast of North America, a region he named New England.   Beinecke Rare Book and Manuscript Library, Yale University upon a Hill" that would then inspire reform among residents of the mother country.

About one-third of English Puritans chose to leave their homeland for North America. They were better supplied, more prosperous, and more numerous than either their Pilgrim or Jamestown predecessors. Arriving in an armada of seventeen ships, the settlers included ministers, merchants, craftsmen, and farmers. Many Puritans sailed with entire families in tow, ensuring the rapid growth of the colony. Having seen the risks of settling in unhealthy or unknown locales, they studied John Smith's map of the New England coast to select the best site for their community.

The first Puritan settlers arrived on the coast north of Plymouth in 1630 and named their community Boston, after the port city in England from which they had departed. Once established, they relocated the Massachusetts Bay Company's capital and records to New England, thereby converting their commercial charter into the founding document of a self-governing colony. They instituted a new kind of polity in which all adult males participated in the election of a governor (John Winthrop), deputy governor, and legislature. Although the Puritans suffered a difficult first winter, they quickly recovered and soon cultivated sufficient crops to feed themselves and a steady stream of new migrants. During the 1630s, some eighteen thousand Puritans migrated to New England, fourteen thousand of those to Massachusetts. Even without a cash crop like tobacco or sugar, the Puritan colony flourished.

Eager to take advantage of the abundant land, the close-knit community spread quickly beyond its original boundaries. The legislature, known as the General Court, was thus forced early on to develop policies for establishing townships with governing bodies that supported a local church and school. By the time the migration of Puritans slowed around 1640, the settlers had turned their colony into a thriving commercial center. They shipped codfish, lumber, wheat, rye, oats, pork, cheese, and other agricultural products to England in exchange for cloth, iron pots, and other manufactured goods and to the West Indies for rum and molasses. This trade, along with the healthy climate, relatively egalitarian distribution of property, and more equal ratio of women to men, ensured a stable and prosperous colony.

Puritans also sought friendly relations with some local natives; in their case it was with the neighboring Massachusetts tribe, who were longtime enemies of the

Thomas Smith, Self-Portrait

This self-portrait of the Massachusetts painter Thomas Smith, dating from around 1680, remains both the earliest seventeenth-century New England painting attributed to a specific person and the only surviving self-portrait from that period. Little is known about Smith, but the battle scene in the background hints that he may once have been a naval officer. Worcester Art Museum, Worcester, Massachusetts

Pilgrims' allies, the Wampanoags. Many Puritans hoped that their Indian neighbors could be converted to Christianity. Such efforts were made easier by the death of many of the Massachusetts tribe's religious leaders in the Pilgrim attack of 1623. Puritan missionaries taught their pupils how to read the Bible, and a few students attended Harvard College, founded in 1636. In an effort to wean converts from their traditional customs and beliefs, missionary John Eliot created "praying towns." There Christian Indians could live among others who shared their faith while being protected from English settlers seeking to exploit them. Yet most "praying Indians" continued to embrace traditional rituals and beliefs alongside Christian practices.

The Puritan Worldview

Opposed to the lavish rituals and hierarchy of the Church of England and believing that few Anglicans truly felt the grace of God, Puritans set out to establish a simpler form of worship. They focused on their inner lives and on the purity of their church and community. Puritans followed Calvin, believing in an all-knowing God who had seen his flock wander away from his most basic teachings. The true Word of God was presented in the Bible, not in the Anglican Book of Common Prayer or hymns written by modern composers. The biblically sanctioned church was a congregation formed by a group of believers who made a covenant with God. Only a small minority of people, known as Saints, were granted God's grace, and Puritans believed (or at least hoped) that their churches were filled with Saints.

Saints were granted God's grace even though all humans since the fall of Adam were deserving of perpetual damnation. Whether one was a Saint and thereby saved was predetermined by and known only to God. Yet Puritans believed that those who were chosen led a godly life. Visible signs included individuals' passionate response to the preaching of God's Word, their sense of doubt and despair over their own soul, and that wonderful sense of reassurance that came with God's "saving grace." Saints were also expected to be virtuous, neighborly, benevolent, and successful.

Puritans, like most Christians at the time, believed that signs of God's hand in the world were everywhere. They appeared in natural phenomena like comets, eclipses, and deformed births as well as in "remarkable providences" that eased believers' way. Thus when a smallpox epidemic killed several thousand Massachusetts Indians in 1633–1634, a Puritan town council observed: "Without this remarkable and terrible stroke of God upon the native, we would with much more difficulty have found room, and at a far greater charge have obtained and purchased land." Clearly God was shining his light on the Puritans, rather than on the Massachusetts.

Shared religious beliefs helped forge a unified community where faith guided civil as well as spiritual decisions. Most political leaders were devout Puritans. Indeed, ministers often served as members of the General Court or presided over town meetings. Puritan leaders determined who got land, how much, and where; they also served as judge and jury for those accused of crimes or sins. Their leadership was largely successful. Even if colonists differed over who should get the most fertile strip of land, they agreed on basic principles. Still, almost from the beginning, certain Puritans challenged some of the community's fundamental beliefs, and in the process, the community itself.

Dissenters Challenge Puritan Authority

In the early 1630s, Roger Williams, a Salem minister, criticized Puritan leaders for not being sufficiently pure in their rejection of the Church of England and the English

monarchy. He preached that not all the Puritan leaders were Saints and that some were bound for damnation. Despite admonitions from the Massachusetts Bay authorities, Williams continued to rail against what he saw as deviations from the one true faith. By 1635 he was forced out of Salem and moved south with his followers to found Providence in the area that became Rhode Island. Believing that there were very few Saints in the world, Williams and his followers accepted that one must live among those who were not saved. Thus unlike Massachusetts Bay, Williams welcomed Quakers, Baptists, and Jews to the community, and his followers insisted on a strict separation of church and state. Williams also forged alliances with the Narragansetts, the most powerful Indian nation in the region, trading with them and securing land for a growing number of English settlers.

A year later, Anne Hutchinson and her followers joined Williams's Rhode Island colony. When put on trial in November 1637, Hutchinson was initially accused of sedition, or trying to overthrow the government by challenging colonial leaders, such as Governor John Winthrop, who were devout Puritans. An eloquent orator,

Anne Hutchinson

This drawing of Anne Hutchinson is based on a 1620 portrait made while she still lived in England. Here she appears as a proper matron, but sixteen years later she would be tried for heresy by Puritan leaders in Massachusetts Bay and banished from the colony.   Schlesinger Library, Radcliffe Institute, Harvard University/The Bridgeman Art Library

Hutchinson ultimately claimed that her authority to challenge the Puritan leadership came from "an immediate revelation" from God, "the voice of his own spirit to my soul." Since Puritans believed that God spoke only through the intermediary of properly appointed male ministers, her claim was condemned as heretical.

Hutchinson was seen as a threat not only because of her religious beliefs but also because she was a woman. The Reverend Hugh Peter, for example, reprimanded her at trial: "You have stept out of your place, you have rather bine a Husband than a Wife and a preacher than a Hearer; and a Magistrate than a Subject." Thus the accusations against her were rooted as much in her challenge to gender hierarchies as to Puritan authority, although her accusers no doubt viewed these as synonymous.

Wars in Old and New England

As Anne Hutchinson and Roger Williams confronted the religious hierarchy, Puritans and Pilgrims faced another serious threat from the Pequot nation. Among the most powerful tribes in New England, the Pequots had been allies of the English for several years. Yet some Puritans feared that the Pequots, who opposed the colonists' continued expansion, "would cause all the Indians in the country to join to root out all the English." Using the death of two Englishmen in 1636 to justify a military expedition against the Pequots, the colonists went on the attack. The Narragansetts, whom Roger Williams had befriended, fought with the English in the **Pequot War**. After months of bloody conflict, the English and their Indian allies launched a brutal attack on a Pequot fort in May 1637 that left some four hundred men, women, and children dead. The English saw the victory as a sign of God's grace, and the Narragansetts saw it as the defeat of a powerful rival.

Explore

To examine an illustration of an attack on the Pequots as depicted by the English captain who led the assault, see Document 2.5.

Puritans in England were soon engaged in armed conflict as well, but this time against other Englishmen. Differences over issues of religion, taxation, and royal authority had strained relations between Parliament and the crown for decades, as James I (r. 1603–1625) and his son Charles I (r. 1625–1649) sought to consolidate their own power at Parliament's expense. In 1642 the relationship between Parliament and King Charles I broke down completely, and the country descended into civil war. Oliver Cromwell, a Puritan, emerged as the leader of the Protestant parliamentary forces, and after several years of fighting, he claimed victory. Charles I was executed,

Parliament established a republican commonwealth, and bishops and elaborate rituals were banished from the Church of England. Cromwell ruled England as a military dictator until his death in 1658. By then, much of England had tired of religious conflict and Puritan rule, so Charles I's son, Charles II (r. 1660–1685), was invited to return from exile on the continent and restore the monarchy and the Church of England. In 1660, when Charles II acceded to the throne, the Puritans recognized that their only hope for building a godly republic lay in North America.

During the civil war of the 1640s, English settlements had quickly spread throughout Connecticut, Massachusetts, and Rhode Island, as well as into Maine and what became New Hampshire. The English king and Parliament, embroiled in war, paid little attention to events in North America, allowing these New England colonies to develop with little oversight. In 1664, after the restoration of the monarchy, the English wrested control of New Amsterdam from the Dutch and renamed it New York. Although it would be another decade before they fully subordinated the Dutch to their rule, by 1674 the English could claim dominance—in population, trade, and politics—over the other European powers vying for empires along the northern Atlantic coast.

The spread of English control was, however, still contested by various Indian groups. In New England, only 15,000 to 16,000 native people remained by 1670, a loss of about 80 percent over fifty years. Meanwhile the English population soared from a few hundred to more than 50,000, with settlers expanding into new territories and encroaching on native hunting grounds. In 1671 the English demanded that the Wampanoags, who had been their allies since the 1620s, surrender their guns and be ruled by English law. Instead, many Indians hid their weapons and, over the next several years, raided frontier farms and killed several settlers. English authorities responded by hanging three Wampanoag men.

By 1675 the Wampanoag chief Metacom, called King Philip by the English, came to believe that Europeans had to be forced out of New England if Indians were going to survive. As conflict escalated between the English and the Wampanoags, Metacom gained the support of the Narragansett and Nipmuck Indians. Together warriors from the three tribes attacked white settlements throughout the region. Armed with hundreds of guns as well as more traditional knives, hatchets, and arrows, Indians terrorized frontier communities. They burned fields, killed male settlers, and took women and children captive.

Initially, the English were convinced they could win an easy victory over their Indian foes, but the war dragged on and became increasingly brutal on both sides. Some 1,000 English settlers were killed and dozens were taken captive

DOCUMENT 2.5

Captain John Underhill | Attack at Mystic, Connecticut, 1638

Determined to expand westward, the English went to war with the Pequot Indians. The Pequot War culminated when the English and their Narragansett allies brutally attacked a Pequot fort at Mystic, Connecticut, in 1637. John Underhill, an English captain who helped lead the raid, claimed that four hundred Pequots were killed during the short but bloody battle. By the end of the war, most Pequots had either died, been sold into slavery, or fled the region. The following image, an engraving created by Underhill himself, gives the English perspective on the attack.

Explore

Library of Congress

Interpret the Evidence

- According to this image, how did the English defeat the Pequots, and what role did their Narragansett allies play?
- How had the Pequots attempted to defend themselves and their community?

Put It in Context

How might this image support the English view of the Pequots as a threat to English expansion that needed to be contained?

during the war. Eighteen New England towns were destroyed, almost 1,200 homes were burned, and 8,000 cattle were slaughtered. Metacom's forces attacked Plymouth and Providence and marched within twenty miles of Boston. The English meanwhile made an alliance with Mohawks, Pequots, Mohegans, and praying Indians (mostly Christian Wampanoags) in the region, who ambushed Narragansett forces. The English also attacked enemy villages, killing hundreds of Indians and selling hundreds more into slavery in the West Indies, including Metacom's wife and son. Indian losses were catastrophic on both sides of the conflict, as food shortages and disease combined with military deaths to kill as many as 4,500 men, women, and children. About a quarter of the remaining Indian population of New England died in 1675–1676.

The war, called **King Philip's War** by the English, finally ended when Wampanoag, Narragansett, and Nipmuck forces ran short of guns and powder and the Mohawks ambushed and killed Metacom. **See Document Project 2: King Philip's War, page 57**. The remaining Algonquian-speaking Indians moved north and gradually intermarried with tribes allied with the French. As the carnage of the war spilled into New York, Iroquois leaders and colonists met at Albany in 1677. There they formed an alliance, the Covenant Chain, in hopes of forestalling future conflict so that they could continue their profitable fur trade. In the following decades, furs and land would continue to define the complex relations between Indians and Europeans across the northern regions of North America.

REVIEW & RELATE

How did the Puritans' religious views shape New England's development?

Why did conflict between New England settlers and the region's Indians escalate over the course of the seventeenth century?

 LEARNINGCurve bedfordstmartins.com/hewittlawson/LC

Conclusion: European Empires in North America

When John Smith died in 1631, the English were just beginning to establish colonies in North America. Despite Smith's love of adventure, he realized early on that a successful empire in Virginia required a different approach than the Spanish had taken in Mexico and Peru. North American colonies demanded permanent settlement, long-term investment, and hard work. Liberal land policies, self-government, and trade formed the touchstones of colonies along the north Atlantic coast.

Yet as European colonists found different ways to prosper in Virginia, Massachusetts Bay, Quebec, and New Amsterdam, they faced daunting choices. Most important, should they create alliances with local Indians for sustenance and trade, or should they seek to dominate them and take what they needed? Smith, Miles Standish, and many other early settlers supported an aggressive policy, much like that of Spain. In Virginia this policy ended persistent threats from the Powhatan Confederacy by the 1640s. But many Europeans, especially in New England, New Amsterdam, and Canada, advocated a different approach. Some, like French Jesuit priests and Puritan missionaries, focused on the spiritual and material benefits of conversion. Far more argued that building alliances was the most effective means of advancing trade and gaining land, furs, and other goods valued by Europeans.

Throughout the early and mid-seventeenth century, English, Dutch, and French colonists profited from trade relations and military alliances with Indian nations. Nonetheless, European demands for land fueled repeated conflicts with tribes like the Pequots in the 1630s and the Wampanoags and Narragansetts in the 1670s. The exhaustion of furs along the Atlantic coast only increased the vulnerability of those Indians who could no longer provide this valuable trade item. Already devastated by European-borne diseases, their very survival was at stake. Indians in New Amsterdam as well as New England resisted the loss of their land and livelihood, often with violence. It was such violence that led to the death of Anne Hutchinson. In 1642 she and her six youngest children moved to the outskirts of New Netherland after the death of her husband. They lived on an isolated farm on what is now Pelham Bay in the Bronx. A year later, Anne and all but one of her children were massacred by Indians outraged by Dutch governor William Kieft's 1643 slaughter of peaceful Indians on Manhattan Island.

Still, as European settlements reached deeper into North America in the late seventeenth century and early eighteenth century, their prosperity continued to depend on trade goods and land that were often in Indian hands. At the same time, a growing demand for labor led wealthier settlers to seek an increased supply of indentured servants from Europe and enslaved workers from Africa. Over the next half century, relations between wealthy and poor settlers, between whites and blacks, between settlers and Indians, and among the European nations that vied for empire would only grow more complicated.

LEARNINGCurve
Check what you know.
bedfordstmartins.com/hewittlawson/LC

Chapter Review

Online Study Guide ▶ bedfordstmartins.com/hewittlawson

KEY TERMS

Protestantism (p. 37)
Church of England (p. 37)
Jamestown (p. 42)
Powhatan Confederacy (p. 43)
House of Burgesses (p. 44)
indentured servants (p. 44)
Bacon's Rebellion (p. 47)
Pilgrims (p. 49)
Mayflower Compact (p. 49)
Puritans (p. 50)
Pequot War (p. 53)
King Philip's War (p. 55)

REVIEW & RELATE

1. How did the Protestant Reformation shape the course of European expansion in the Americas?

2. How did the French and Dutch colonies in North America differ from the Spanish empire to the south?

3. How did the Virginia colony change and evolve between 1607 and the 1670s?

4. How did the growth of the English colonies on the mainland and in the West Indies shape conflicts in Virginia and demands for labor throughout North America?

5. How did the Puritans' religious views shape New England's development?

6. Why did conflict between New England settlers and the region's Indians escalate over the course of the seventeenth century?

TIMELINE OF EVENTS

1517	Martin Luther denounces indulgences, sparking the Protestant Reformation
1530s	England breaks with the Roman Catholic Church
1545–1563	Council of Trent (Catholic Church)
1598	Acoma pueblo uprising in New Mexico
	Edict of Nantes (France)
1607	Jamestown founded under leadership of Captain John Smith
1608	First permanent French settlement in North America founded at Quebec
1609	Dutch traders establish a settlement on the Hudson River
1612	John Rolfe experiments with tobacco cultivation in Virginia
1619	House of Burgesses established in Virginia First Africans arrive in Virginia
1620	Pilgrims found Plymouth settlement in Massachusetts
1624	Dutch establish New Amsterdam on Manhattan Island
1630	Puritans found Massachusetts Bay colony
1632	Maryland founded
1635	Roger Williams moves with followers to Rhode Island
1636–1637	Pequot War
1637	Anne Hutchinson banished from Massachusetts Bay colony
1642–1649	English civil war
1660	Monarchy restored in England
1660–1664	House of Burgesses passes acts that allow enslavement of African laborers
1664	Dutch surrender New Amsterdam to the English
1675–1676	King Philip's War
1676	Bacon's Rebellion

DOCUMENT PROJECT 2

King Philip's War

King Philip's War was proportionally one of the bloodiest conflicts in American history. Although Indians and whites had lived in relative peace for nearly forty years, tensions escalated during the mid-seventeenth century due to a steady decline in Indian population, territory, and cultural integrity. Metacom, whom the colonists called King Philip, became grand sachem of the Wampanoag Confederacy in 1662 after the death of his brother. Troubled by English encroachments on native lands and hunting grounds, King Philip negotiated an alliance with two-thirds of the region's Indian population, including the Narragansett and Nipmuck tribes. They began coordinating attacks on white settlements in New England, burning fields, taking captives, and killing male colonists.

In 1675 Indian attacks on New England towns escalated. In Document 2.10, Mary Rowlandson describes her experiences when she was taken captive during an Indian raid on Lancaster, Massachusetts, in February of that year. As relations between settlers and Indians deteriorated, the Rhode Island colony sent representatives to meet with King Philip in June (Document 2.6). The colonists were hoping for a diplomatic solution, but the meeting was unsuccessful, and Indian attacks increased throughout the summer. The New England Confederation declared war in September, and fighting continued for a year, with one thousand whites and more than four thousand Indians killed in the conflict. The English, who had forged alliances with the surviving Pequots and powerful Mohawks, finally gained the upper hand in August 1676 when King Philip was ambushed in a swamp near Bristol, Rhode Island, by soldiers led by Captain Benjamin Church. Philip was shot and killed by John Alderman, an Indian ally of the colonists, which signaled the end of the war in southern New England.

Because there are fewer Indian written sources, historians have struggled to develop a balanced picture of the war. William Nahaton (Document 2.9) learned firsthand that the English would go to great lengths to infiltrate Indian communities, Christian or otherwise. Which other documents provide information about Indian perceptions of the war? What do disagreements among Englishmen reveal about English-Indian relations?

DOCUMENT 2.6

John Easton | A Relation of the Indian War, 1675

As relations between English settlers and Indians grew more tense, a meeting was arranged for June 1675 between King Philip and John Easton, attorney general of the Rhode Island colony. At this meeting, Philip related the Indians' many complaints, which included the sale of liquor to Indians, the destruction of their crops, and their mistreatment under the colonial justice system. This meeting was unsuccessful in preventing further violence, however, and by the end of the month King Philip's War began.

Another Grievance was, when their King sold Land, the English would say, it was more than they agreed to, and a Writing must be prove against all them, and some of their Kings had dun Rong [done wrong] to sell so much. He left his Peopell [people] none, and some being given to Drunknes the English made them drunk and then cheated them in Bargains, but now their Kings were forewarned not for to part with Land, for nothing in Comparison to the Value thereof. Now home [some] the English had owned for King or Queen, they would disinherit, and make another King that would give or sell them these Lands; that now they had no Hopes left to keep any Land. Another Grievance, the English Catell [cattle] and Horses still increased; that when they removed 30 Miles from where English had any thing to do, they could not keep their Corn from being spoiled, they never being used to fence, and thought when the English bought Land of them they would have kept their Catell upon their owne Land. Another Grievance, the English were so eager to sell the Indians Lickers [liquor], that most of the Indians spent all in Drunknes, and then ravened upon the sober Indians, and they did believe often did hurt the English Cattel, and their King could not prevent it.

Source: John Easton, "A Relation of the Indian War," in *A Narrative of the Causes Which Led to Philip's Indian War, of 1675 and 1676* (Albany: J. Munsell, 1858), 13–15.

DOCUMENT 2.7

Benjamin Church | Passages Relating to Philip's War, 1716

Benjamin Church was an aide to Plymouth governor Josiah Winslow. But Church was also viewed as a fair man by local Indian leaders. Thus in June 1675, before the outbreak of war, Awashonks, the sachem of the Sakonnet Indians, invited Church to meet with her. He offered his advice on how best to secure the protection of her people. Despite his advice, the Sakonnets initially allied with King Philip but later switched to the English side. Meanwhile, as captain in the Plymouth colony militia, Church adopted Indian fighting tactics, and his unit conducted successful raids against King Philip and his allies. In 1716 Church's son, Thomas, published an account of the war from his father's notes. The following passage recalls his visit with Awashonks.

The next Spring advancing, while Mr. Church was diligently settling his new Farm, stocking, leasing, and disposing of his Affairs, and had a fine prospect of doing no small things; and hoping that his good success would be inviting unto other good Men to become his Neighbours; Behold! the rumor of a War between the English and the Natives gave check to his projects. People began to be very jealous of the Indians, and indeed they had no small reason to suspect that they had form'd a design of War upon the English. Mr. Church had it daily suggested to him that the Indians were plotting a bloody design. That Philip the great Mount-hope Sachem was leader therein: and so it prov'd, he was sending his Messengers to all the Neighbouring Sachems, to ingage them in a Confederacy with him in the War.

Among the rest he sent Six Men to Awashonks Squaw-Sachem of the Sogkonate [Sakonnet] Indians, to engage her in his Interests: Awashonks so far listened unto them as to call her Subjects together, to make a great Dance, which is the custom of that Nation when they advise about Momentous Affairs. But what does Awashonks do, but sends away two of her Men that well understood the English Language . . . to invite Mr. Church to the Dance. Mr. Church upon the Invitation, immediately takes with him Charles Hazelton his Tennants Son, who well understood the Indian Language, and rid [rode] down to the Place appointed: Where they found hundreds of Indians gathered together from all Parts of her Dominion. Awashonks her self in a foaming Sweat was leading the Dance. But she was no sooner sensible of Mr. Churches arrival, but she broke off, sat down, calls her Nobles round her, orders Mr. Church to be invited into her presence. Complements being past, and each one taking Seats. She told him, King Philip had sent Six Men of his with two of her People that had been over at Mount-hope, to draw her into a confederacy with him in a War with the English. . . .

Then Mr. Church turn'd to Awashonks, and told her, if Philip were resolv'd to make War, her best way would be to knock those Six Mount-hopes on the head, and shelter her self under the Protection of the English: upon which the Mount-hopes were for the present Dumb. . . .

Then he told Awashonks he thought it might be most advisable for her to send to the Governour of Plymouth, and shelter her self, and People under his Protection. She lik'd his advice, and desired him to go on her behalf to the Plymouth Government, which he consented to: And at parting advised her what ever she did, not to desert the English Interest, to joyn with her Neighbours in a Rebellion which would certainly prove fatal to her. He mov'd none of his Goods from his House that there might not be the least umbrage from such an Action. She thank'd him for his advice, and sent two of her Men to guard him to his House; which when they came there, urged him to take care to secure his Goods, which he refused for the reasons before mentioned. But desired the Indians that if what they feared should happen, they would take care of what he left, and directed them to a Place in the woods where they should dispose them; which they faithfully observed.

Source: Benjamin Church, *The History of King Philip's War* (Boston: John Kimball Wiggin, 1865), 5–11.

DOCUMENT 2.8

Edward Randolph | Report on the War, 1676

Edward Randolph was an English customs official sent to the colonies to investigate colonial compliance with English laws. He criticized the Puritan colonies for pursuing political autonomy, like coining money and administering their own oath of allegiance, and called for greater control by Parliament. Randolph's reports to his superiors in London also described the outbreak of violence. He reported on what he saw as the causes of the war, criticizing the actions of both colonists and Indians.

Various are the reports and conjectures of the causes of the late Indian wars. Some impute it to an imprudent zeal in the magistrates of Boston to Christianize those heathens, before they were civilized, and enjoining them to the strict observation of their laws, which, to people so rude and licentious hath proved even intolerable; and that the more, for while the magistrates, for their profit, severely put the laws in execution against the Indians, the people on the other side, for lucre [money] and gain, intice and provoke the Indians to the breach thereof, especially to drunkenness, to which these people are so generally addicted, that they will strip themselves to the skin to have their fill of rum and brandy.

The Massachusetts government having made a law that every Indian being drunk should pay ten shillings or be whipped, according to the discretion of the magistrate, many of these poor people willingly offered their backs to the lash, to save their money. Upon the magistrate finding much trouble and no profit to arise to the government by whipping, did change that punishment of the whip into ten days' work, for such as would not or could not pay the fine of ten shillings; which did highly incense the Indians. . . .

Others impute the cause to arise from some injuries offered to the Sachem Philip; for he being possessed of a tract of land called Mount Hope, a very fertile, pleasant and rich soil, some English had a mind to dispossess him thereof, who, never wanting some pretence or other to attain their ends, complained of injuries done by Philip and his Indians to their stock and cattle. Whereupon the Sachem [King] Philip was often summoned to appear before the magistrates, sometimes imprisoned, and never released but upon parting with a considerable part of his lands.

But the government of the Massachusetts . . . do declare [the following acts] are the great and provoking evils which God hath given the barbarous heathen commission to rise against them: . . .

For men wearing long hair and perriwigs made of women's hair.

For women wearing borders of hair and cutting, curling and laying out their hair and disguising themselves by following strange fashions in their apparel.

For profaneness of the people in not frequenting their [church] meetings, and others going away before the blessing is pronounced.

For suffering the Quakers to dwell among them, and to set up their thresholds by God's thresholds, contrary to their old laws and resolutions, with many such reasons.

But whatever was the cause, the English have contributed very much to their misfortunes, for they first taught the Indians the use of arms and admitted them to be present at all their musters and trainings, and showed them how to handle, mend and fix their muskets, and have been constantly furnished with all sorts of arms by permission of the government, so that the Indians are become excellent fire-men.

Source: John Norris McClintock, *History of New Hampshire* (Boston: B. B. Russell, 1888), 79–80.

DOCUMENT 2.9

William Nahaton | Petition to Free an Indian Slave, 1675

The English sold a number of Indians into slavery during King Philip's War. Many English colonists petitioned the government of Massachusetts Bay to stop this practice. As the following document indicates, Indians also tried to find recourse through petitions. William Nahaton, an Indian who had embraced Christianity, sent this petition to convince colonial leaders to release a relative who was about to be sold into slavery in the West Indies.

To the honored counsel now siting at boston to the humble petition of william [n]ahaton hee humbly sheweth.

I have seing a woman taken by the mohegins and now brought to boston which woman although she did belong to [King] phillip his Company yet shee is a kinn to me and all so to john huntar as severall of the indians of punkapoag do know[.] my humble and right request there fore to the Renowned Counsel is that if it may stand with there plesure and with out futur inconvenience her Life may be spared and her Liberty granted under such conditions as the honored Counsel see most fit: shee being a woman whatever her mind hath been it is very probable she hath not dun much mischefe and if the honored counsel shall plese so grant me that favor I shall understand to leve her at punkapoag[.] . . . I shall obtaine so much favor from the honored counsel which will further oblige him who is your honored to command william [n]ahaton.

Source: Jill Lepore, *Encounters in the New World: A History in Documents* (New York: Oxford University Press, 2000), 154–55.

Upon a *Friday*, a little after noon we came to this River. When all the company was come up, and were gathered together, I thought to count the number of them, but they were so many, and being somewhat in motion, it was beyond my skil. In this travel, because of my wound, I was somewhat favored in my load; I carried only my knitting work and two quarts of parched meal: Being very faint I asked my mistriss to give me one spoonfull of the meal, but she would not give me a taste. They quickly fell to cutting dry trees, to make Rafts to carry them over the river: and soon my turn came to go over: By the advantage of some brush which they had laid upon the Raft to sit upon, I did not wet my foot (which many of themselves at the other end were mid-leg deep) which cannot but be acknowledged as a favour of God to my weakened body, it being a very cold time. I was not before acquainted with such kind of doings or dangers. *When thou passeth through the waters I will be with thee, and through the rivers they shall not overflow thee,* Isai. 43.2. A certain number of us got over the River that night, but it was the night after the Sabbath before all the company was got over. On the *Saturday* they boyled [boiled] an old Horses leg which they had got, and so we drank of the broth, as soon as they thought it was ready, and when it was almost all gone, they filled it up again.

The first week of my being among them, I hardly ate any thing; the second week, I found my stomach grow very faint for want of something; and yet it was very hard to get down their filthy trash: but the third week, though I could think how formerly my stomach would turn against this or that, and I could starve or die before I could eat such things, yet they were sweet and savory to my taste. I was at this time knitting a pair of white cotton stockins for my mistriss: and had not yet wrought upon a Sabbath day; when the Sabbath came they bade me go to work; I told them it was the Sabbath-day, and desired them to let me rest, and told them I would do as much more tomorrow; to which they answered me, they would break my face. And here I cannot but take notice of the strange providence of God in preserving the heathen: They were many

DOCUMENT 2.10

Mary Rowlandson | Narrative of Captivity, 1682

In February 1675, the Wampanoags and their allies attacked Lancaster, Massachusetts, setting fire to the town and killing many residents. Mary Rowlandson and her three children were captured and forced to flee with the Indians as they tried to outrun colonial forces. Mary's six-year-old daughter Sarah died, but she and her other children survived and were sold for ransom after eleven weeks and reunited with her husband, Joseph. After the war, she published an account of her captivity that highlighted the ways in which her Puritan faith helped her survive the ordeal. The book became one of the most popular publications of its era.

hundreds, old and young, some sick, and some lame, many had *Papooses* [infants] at their backs, the greatest number at this time with us, were *Squaws*, and they travelled with all they had, bag and baggage, and yet they got over this River aforesaid; and on *Munday* they set their *Wigwams* on fire, and away they went: On that very day came the *English* Army after them to this River, and saw the smoak of their *Wigwams*, and yet this River put a stop to them. God did not give them courage or activity to go over after us; we were not ready for so great a mercy as victory and deliverance; if we had been, God would have found out a way for the *English* to have passed this River, as well as for the *Indians* with their *Squaws* and *Children*, and all their Luggage. . . .

On Munday *(as I said) they set their* Wigwams *on fire, and went away*. It was a cold morning, and before us there was a great Brook with ice on it; some waded through it, up to the knees & higher, but others went till they came to a Beaver dam, and I amongst them, where through the good providence of God, I did not wet my foot. I went along that day mourning and lamenting, leaving farther my own Country, and travelling into the vast and howling *Wilderness,* and I understood something of *Lot's* Wife's Temptation, *when she looked back.* We came that day to a great Swamp, by the side of which we took up our lodging that night. When I came to the brow of the hill, that looked toward the Swamp, I thought we had been come to a great *Indian* Town (though there were none but our own Company). The *Indians* were as thick as the trees: it seemed as if there had been a thousand Hatchets going at once: if one looked before one, there was nothing but *Indians,* and behind one, nothing but *Indians,* and so on either hand, I my self in the midst, and no Christian soul near me, *and yet how hath the Lord preserved me in safety! Oh the experience that I have had of the goodness of God, to me and mine!*

Source: Henry S. Nourse, ed., *The Narrative of the Captivity and the Restoration of Mrs. Mary Rowlandson* (Lancaster, MA, 1903), 17–20.

Interpret the Evidence

1. What types of complaints did the Wampanoags have against the English (Documents 2.6 and 2.8)? Which seem the most grievous to the Indians? What do these complaints reveal about how the colonists viewed the Wampanoags?

2. What does Edward Randolph's description of the causes of the war (Document 2.8) reveal about how this war might be viewed by Englishmen who were not colonists?

3. What does Benjamin Church's meeting with Awashonks (Document 2.7) suggest about the difficult choices faced by some Indians and some colonists as war approached?

4. In what ways did the English disagree among themselves over the causes of war? What do these differences tell us about the era and the war?

5. What does William Nahaton's petition (Document 2.9) reveal about English leaders' main goal when dealing with the Indians? Do you think the English differentiated between Christian and non-Christian Indians?

6. How does Mary Rowlandson employ religion to explain the events that happen to her during her captivity? What does the enormous popularity of her book indicate about the place of religion in New England in the 1680s?

Put It in Context

- King Philip's War was one of the bloodiest in American history. From these documents, what do you think accounts for its ferociousness?

background photos: pages 58 and 61, HIP/Art Resouce, NY

Bibliothèque Nationale, Paris, France/Giraudon/The Bridgeman Art Library

Virginia Historical Society, Richmond, Virginia, USA/The Bridgeman Art Library

● View of Boston Town Hall, 18th century.

● Tobacco label showing two Native Americans with pipes, 18th century.

3

Global Changes Reshape Colonial America

1680–1750

© Pictorial Press Ltd./Alamy

English cartoon of industrious American colonists, mid-18th century.

AMERICAN HISTORIES

In 1729, at age thirty, William Moraley Jr. signed an indenture to serve a five-year term as a "bound servant" in the "American Plantations." This was not what his parents had imagined for him. The only child of a journeyman watchmaker and his wife, Moraley received a good education and was offered a clerkship with a London lawyer. But Moraley preferred London's pleasures to legal training. At age nineteen, out of money, he was forced to return home and become an apprentice watchmaker for his father. Moraley's apprenticeship went no better than his clerkship, and in 1725, fed up with his son's lack of enterprise, Moraley's father rewrote his will, leaving him just 20 shillings. When Moraley's father died unexpectedly, his wife gave her son 20 pounds, and in 1728 Moraley headed back to London.

But London was in the midst of a prolonged economic crisis, and Moraley failed to find work. By May 1729, he was imprisoned for debt. Three months later, he sold his labor for five years in return for passage to America. Moraley sailed for Philadelphia in September and was indentured in January to a Quaker clockmaker in Burlington, New Jersey. Eventually, he tired of this situation as well, and he ran away. But when he was caught, he was not punished by having his contract extended, as happened to most fugitive servants. Instead, he was released before his indenture was up, after serving only three years.

Moraley spent the next twenty months traveling the northern colonies, but found no steady employment. Hounded by creditors, he boarded a ship in Philadelphia bound for Ireland. He returned to his mother's home, penniless and unemployed. In 1743, hoping to cash in on popular interest in adventure tales, he published an account of his travels. In the book, entitled *The Infortunate, the Voyage and Adventures of William Moraley, an Indentured Servant,* he offered a poor man's view of eighteenth-century North America. Like so much else in Moraley's life, the book was not a success.

In 1738, while Moraley was back in England trying to carve out a career as a writer, sixteen-year-old Eliza Lucas, the eldest daughter of a career British military officer, arrived in South Carolina. Her father, Colonel George Lucas, had inherited a 600-acre plantation, called Wappoo, six miles south of Charles Town (later Charleston), and moved his family there in hopes that the climate would improve his wife's health. Eliza had been born on Antigua, where her father served with the British army and owned a sugar plantation. Although the move north did not benefit his wife, it created an unusual opportunity for his daughter, who was left in charge of the estate when Colonel Lucas was called back to Antigua in May 1739.

For the next five years, Eliza Lucas managed Wappoo and two other Carolina plantations owned by her father. Rising each day at 5 a.m., she checked on the fields and the enslaved laborers who worked them, balanced the books, nursed her mother, taught her younger sister to read, and wrote to her younger brothers at school in England. In a large bound book, she kept the accounts; copies of her letters to family, friends, commercial agents, and fellow planters; and information on legal affairs.

She also embarked on plans to improve her family estates. With her father's enthusiastic support, Lucas began experimenting with new crops, particularly indigo. The indigo plant, which was first imported to Europe from India in the seventeenth century, produced a blue dye popular for coloring textiles. When her experiments proved successful, Lucas encouraged other planters to follow her lead, and with financial aid from the colonial legislature and Parliament, indigo became a profitable export from South Carolina, second only to rice. •

THE AMERICAN HISTORIES of William Moraley and Eliza Lucas were shaped by a profound shift in global trading patterns that resulted in the circulation of labor and goods among Asia, Africa, Europe, and the Americas. Between 1680 and 1750, indentured servants, enslaved Africans, planters, soldiers, merchants, and artisans traveled along these new trade networks. So, too, did sugar, rum, tobacco, indigo, cloth, and a host of other items. As England, France, and Spain expanded their empires, colonists developed new crops for export and increased the demand for manufactured goods from home. Yet the vibrant, increasingly global economy was fraught with peril. Economic crises, the uncertainties of maritime navigation, and outbreaks of war caused constant disruptions. For some, the opportunities offered by colonization outweighed the dangers; for others, fortune was less kind, and the results were disappointing, even disastrous.

Europeans Expand Their Claims

Beginning with the restoration of Charles II to the throne in 1660, English monarchs began granting North American land and commercial rights to men who were loyal to the crown. Shaped in part by rebellions at home and abroad, the policies of English monarchs aimed to expand England's imperial reach at the lowest possible cost. France and Spain also expanded their empires in North America, frequently coming into conflict with each other in the late seventeenth and early eighteenth centuries. At the same time, American Indians challenged various European efforts to displace them from their homelands. A Pueblo rebellion against Spanish authorities in New Mexico provided other Indian nations with access to guns and horses. In Florida, Indian-Spanish conflicts allowed England to gain native allies.

English Colonies Grow and Multiply

To repay the men who helped him return to power, Charles II granted them land and commercial rights in North America (see chapter 2). The king rewarded his most important allies with positions on the newly formed Councils for Trade and Plantations. Many of the appointees also gained other benefits: partnerships in the Royal African Company, vast lands along the South Atlantic coast, or charters for territory in Canada. In addition, he gave his brother James, the Duke of York, control over all the lands between the Delaware and Connecticut Rivers, once known as New Netherland, but now known as New York. He then conveyed the adjacent lands to investors who established the colonies of East and West Jersey. Finally, Charles II repaid debts to Admiral Sir William Penn by granting his son huge tracts of land in the Middle Atlantic region. Six years later, William Penn Jr. left the Church of England and joined the Society of Friends, or Quakers. This radical Protestant sect was severely persecuted in England, so the twenty-two-year-old Penn turned his holdings into a Quaker refuge named Pennsylvania.

Between 1660 and 1685, Penn and other English gentlemen were established as the proprietors of a string of **proprietary colonies** from Carolina to New York. These powerful aristocrats could govern largely as they wished as long as they conformed broadly to English traditions. Most envisioned a manorial system in which they and other gentry presided over workers producing goods for export. In practice, however, local conditions dictated what was possible, and by the 1680s a range of labor relationships had emerged. Following Bacon's Rebellion in Virginia (see chapter 2), small farmers and laborers in northern Carolina rose up and forced proprietors there to offer land at reasonable prices and a semblance of self-government. In the southern part of Carolina, however, English West Indian planters dominated. They created a mainland version of Barbados by introducing enslaved Africans as laborers, carving plantations out of coastal swamps, and trading with the West Indies.

William Penn provided a more progressive model of colonial rule. He established friendly relations with the local Lenni-Lenape Indians and drew up a Frame of Government in 1681 that recognized religious freedom for all Christians. It also allowed all property-owning men to vote and hold office. Under Penn's leadership, Pennsylvania attracted thousands of middling farm families, most of them Quakers, as well as artisans and merchants. By the time Charles II died in 1685, Pennsylvania was the most successful of his proprietary colonies.

Charles's death marked an abrupt shift in crown-colony relations. Charles's successor, James II, instituted a more authoritarian regime both at home and abroad. He consolidated the colonies in the Northeast and established tighter controls. His royal officials banned town meetings, challenged land titles granted under the original colonial charters, and imposed new taxes. Fortunately for the colonists, the Catholic James II alienated his subjects in England as well as in the colonies, inspiring a bloodless coup in 1688. His Protestant daughter Mary and her husband William of Orange (r. 1689–1702) then ascended the throne, introducing more democratic systems of governance in England and the colonies. This so-called **Glorious Revolution** inspired John Locke to write his famous treatise justifying the changes made by William and Mary. Locke challenged the divine right of monarchs and insisted that government depended on the consent of the governed.

> **Explore**
>
> For Locke's thoughts on property and the rule of law, see Document 3.1.

Eager to restore political order and create a commercially profitable empire, William and Mary established the new colony of Massachusetts (which included Plymouth, Massachusetts Bay, and Maine) and restored town meetings and an elected assembly. But the 1692 charter also granted the English crown the right to appoint a royal governor and officials to enforce customs regulations. It ensured religious freedom to members of the Church of England and allowed all male property owners (not just Puritans) to be elected to the assembly. In Maryland, too, the crown imposed a royal governor and replaced the Catholic Church with the Church of England as the established religion. And in New York, wealthy English merchants won the backing of the newly appointed royal governor, who instituted a representative assembly and supported a merchant-dominated Board of Aldermen. Thus, taken as a whole, William and Mary's policies asserted royal authority at the same time that they sought to create a partnership between England and colonial elites by allowing colonists to retain long-standing local governmental institutions (Table 3.1).

In the early eighteenth century, England's North American colonies took the form that they would retain until the revolution in 1776. In 1702 East and West Jersey united into the colony of New Jersey. Delaware separated from Pennsylvania in 1704. By 1710 North Carolina became fully independent of South Carolina, forming its own assembly and receiving its own charter. Finally, in 1732, the colony of Georgia was established as a buffer between Spanish Florida and the increasingly lucrative plantations of South Carolina. At the same time, settlers pushed back the frontier in all directions. Wealthy Englishmen like Robert Livingston bought up land on the upper Hudson River and

DOCUMENT 3.1

John Locke | On the State of Nature, 1690

John Locke was an English physician and philosopher whose ideas influenced England's Glorious Revolution, as well as the development of Enlightenment thought. In the late eighteenth century, revolutionaries such as Thomas Jefferson and Benjamin Franklin incorporated his ideas into their justifications for revolution and, especially, the Declaration of Independence. The following selection is from "Of the Ends of Political Society and Government."

Explore

Section 123. If man in the state of nature be so free, as has been said; if he be absolute lord of his own person and possessions, equal to the greatest, and subject to nobody, why will he part with his freedom? why will he give up his empire, and subject himself to the dominion and control of any other power? To which it is obvious to answer, that though in the state of nature he hath such a right, yet the enjoyment of it is very uncertain, and constantly exposed to the invasion of others; for all being kings as much as he, every man his equal, and the greater part no strict observers of equity and justice, the enjoyment of the property he has in this state is very unsafe, very unsecure. This makes him willing to quit a condition, which, however free, is full of fears and continual dangers; and it is not without reason, that he seeks out, and is willing to join in society with others, who are already united, or have a mind to unite, for the mutual preservation of their lives,

liberties, and estates, which I call by the general name, property.

Section 124. The great and chief end, therefore, of men's uniting into commonwealths, and putting themselves under government, is the preservation of their property. To which in the state of nature there are many things wanting.

First, There wants an established, settled, known law, received and allowed by common consent to be the standard of right and wrong, and the common measure to decide all controversies between them: for though the law of nature be plain and intelligible to all rational creatures; yet men being biassed by their interest, as well as ignorant for want of studying it, are not apt to allow of it as a law binding to them in the application of it to their particular cases.

Source: John Locke, *Two Treatises on Government* (London: C. and J. Rivington, 1824), 203–4.

Interpret the Evidence

- According to Locke, why would man leave the state of nature?
- By leaving the state of nature, what does man gain? What does he give up?

Put It in Context

How did Locke's theories strengthen calls for greater autonomy among British colonists in America?

---

joined Dutch *patroons* who had earlier established vast estates in the region. Meanwhile families in Massachusetts carved out farms and villages on the New Hampshire and Maine frontier, while migrants and immigrants pushed the boundaries of Pennsylvania, Virginia, and the Carolinas westward.

France Seeks Lands and Control

When James II became king of England, he modeled himself after Louis XIV of France. Like Louis, James saw

himself as ruling by divine right and with absolute power, but the French king was far more successful in establishing and sustaining his authority. During his long reign from 1661 to 1715, Louis XIV dominated European affairs and oversaw an expansion of North American possessions. Still, in 1680 New France comprised only ten thousand inhabitants, and one potential source of settlers—Protestant Huguenots—was denied the right to emigrate.

The French government thus extended the boundaries of its North American colonies more through exploration and trade than through settlement. In 1682 French

TABLE 3.1   English Colonies Established in North America, 1607–1750

Colony	Date	Original Colony Type	Religion	Status in 1750	Economic Activity
Virginia	1624	Proprietary	Church of England	Royal	Tobacco, wheat
Massachusetts	1630	Proprietary	Congregationalist	Royal	Fishing, mixed farming, shipbuilding materials, shipping
Maryland	1632	Royal	Catholic	Royal	Tobacco, wheat
Carolina	1663	Proprietary	Church of England	Royal	
North	1691				Shipbuilding materials, farming
South	1691				Rice, indigo
New Jersey	1664	Proprietary	Church of England	Royal	Wheat
New York	1664	Proprietary	Church of England	Royal	Furs, naval stores, mixed farming, shipping
Pennsylvania	1681	Proprietary	Quaker	Proprietary	Wheat
Delaware	1704	Proprietary	Lutheran/Quaker	Proprietary	Furs, farming, shipping
Georgia	1732	Trustees	Church of England	Royal	Rice
New Hampshire (separated from Massachusetts)	1741	Royal	Congregationalist	Royal	Mixed farming, lumber, shipbuilding materials

adventurers and their Indian allies journeyed down the lower Mississippi River. Led by René-Robert Cavelier, Sieur de La Salle, the party traveled to the Gulf of Mexico and claimed all the land drained by its tributaries for Louis XIV. The new territory of Louisiana (named for the king) promised great wealth, but its development stalled when La Salle failed in his attempt to establish a colony.

Still eager for a southern outlet for furs, the French did not give up. After several more attempts at colonization in the early eighteenth century, French settlers maintained a toehold along Louisiana's Gulf coast. Most important, Pierre LeMoyne d'Iberville, a Canadian military officer, and his brother established forts at Biloxi and Mobile bays, where they traded with local Choctaw Indians. They recruited settlers from Canada and France, and the small outpost survived despite conflicts among settlers, pressure from the English, a wave of epidemics, and a lack of supplies from France. Still, Louisiana counted only three hundred French settlers by 1715.

Continuing to promote commercial relations with diverse Indian nations, the French built a string of missions and forts along the upper Mississippi and Illinois Rivers. These outposts in the continent's interior allowed France to challenge both English and Spanish claims to North America. And extensive trade with a range of Indian nations ensured that French power was far greater than the small number of French settlers would suggest.

The Pueblo Revolt and Spain's Fragile Empire

As New France pushed westward and southward, Spain continued to oversee an empire that was spread dangerously thin on its northern reaches. In New Mexico, tensions between Spanish missionaries and *encomenderos* and the Pueblo nation had simmered for decades (see chapter 2). Relations worsened in the 1670s when a drought led to famine among many area Indians and brought a revival of Indian rituals that the Spaniards viewed as a threat to Christianity. In addition, Spanish forces failed to protect the Pueblos against devastating raids by Apache and Navajo warriors. Finally, Catholic prayers proved unable to stop Pueblo deaths in a 1671 epidemic. When some of the Pueblos returned to their traditional priests, Spanish officials hanged three Indian leaders for idolatry and whipped and incarcerated forty-three others. Among those punished was Popé, a militant Pueblo who upon his release began planning a broad-based revolt.

On August 10, 1680, seventeen thousand Pueblo Indians initiated a coordinated assault on numerous Spanish missions and forts. They destroyed buildings and farms, burned crops and houses, and smeared excrement on Christian altars. The Spaniards retreated to Mexico without launching any significant counterattack.

Yet the Spaniards returned in the 1690s and reconquered parts of New Mexico, aided by growing internal

Battling the Spaniards
After the Pueblo revolt in 1680 drove out the Spaniards, the Pueblos established close contact with the Navajo people. In 1692 Spain reconquered the region, and skirmishes continued. This Navajo petroglyph (rock engraving) in One Crow Canyon near Farmington, New Mexico, records one such battle, with Spanish soldiers on horseback wielding swords.   Photograph © George Oxford Miller

conflict among the Pueblos and fierce Apache raids. The governor general of New Spain worked hard to subdue the province and in 1696 crushed the rebels and opened new lands for settlement. Meanwhile Franciscan missionaries established better relations with the Pueblos by allowing them to retain more indigenous practices and built new missions in the region.

Yet despite the Spanish reconquest, in the long run the **Pueblo revolt** limited Spanish expansion by strengthening other indigenous peoples in the region. In the aftermath of the revolt, some Pueblo refugees moved north and taught the Navajos how to grow corn, raise sheep, and ride horses. Through the Navajos, the Ute and Comanche peoples also gained access to horses. By the 1730s, the Comanches, who had become a fully equestrian society, launched mounted bison hunts and traded over vast areas. One key trading center formed at Taos in northern New Mexico, where Spanish control was weak. There Comanches sold captives as slaves and gained more horses, metal tools, and guns. Thus the Pueblos provided other Indian nations with the means to support larger populations, wider commercial networks, and more warriors. These nations would continue to contest Spanish rule.

At the same time, Spain sought to reinforce its claims to Texas (named after the Tejas Indians) in response to French settlements in the lower Mississippi valley. Thus, in the early eighteenth century, Spanish missions and forts appeared along the route from San Juan Batista to the border of present-day Louisiana. Although small and scattered, these outposts were meant to ensure Spain's claim to Texas. But the presence of large and powerful Indian nations, including the Caddo and the Apache, forced Spanish residents to accept many native customs in order to maintain their presence in the region.

Spain also faced challenges to its authority in Florida, where Indians resisted the spread of cattle ranching in the 1670s. Authorities imposed harsh punishments on those killing cows or raiding herds and forced hundreds of Indians to construct a stone fortress, San Marcos, at St. Augustine. Meanwhile the English wooed Florida natives by exchanging European goods for deerskins. Some Indians then moved their settlements north to the Carolina border. The growing tensions along this Anglo-Spanish border would turn violent when Europe itself erupted into war.

REVIEW & RELATE

- What role did the crown play in the expansion of the English North American colonies in the second half of the seventeenth century?

- How did the development of the Spanish and French colonies in the late seventeenth century differ from that of the English colonies?

 LEARNINGCurve **bedfordstmartins.com/hewittlawson/LC**

European Wars and American Consequences

Developments in North America in the late seventeenth and early eighteenth centuries were driven as much by events in Europe as by those in the colonies. From 1689 until 1713, Europe was in an almost constant state of war, with continental conflicts spilling over into colonial possessions in North America. The result was increased tensions between colonists of different nationalities, Indians and colonists, and colonists and their home countries.

Colonial Conflicts and Indian Alliances

France was at the center of much of the European warfare of the period. Louis XIV hoped to expand France's borders and gain supremacy in Europe. To this end, he built a powerful professional army under state authority. By 1689 more than 300,000 well-trained troops had been outfitted with standardized uniforms and weapons. Having gained victories in the Spanish Netherlands, Flanders, Strasbourg, and Lorraine, the French army seemed invincible.

In the 1690s, France and England fought their first sustained war in North America, **King William's War** (1689–1697). The war began over conflicting French and English interests on the European continent, but it soon spread to the American frontier when English and Iroquois forces attacked French and Huron settlements around Montreal and northern New York. English and Iroquois forces captured Fort Royal in Acadia (present-day Nova Scotia), while the French destroyed Schenectady, New York, and attacked settlers in Maine and New Hampshire.

Although neither side had gained significant territory when peace was declared in 1697, the war had important consequences. Many colonists serving in the English army died of battle wounds, smallpox, and inadequate rations. Those who survived resented their treatment and the unnecessary deaths of so many comrades. The Iroquois fared even worse. Their fur trade was devastated, and hundreds of Mohawks and Oneidas were forced to flee from France's Indian allies along the eastern Great Lakes. "French Indians" and Iroquois continued to attack each other after the peace settlement, but in 1701 the Iroquois agreed to end the raids and remain neutral in all future European conflicts. Wary of further European entanglements, Iroquois leaders focused on rebuilding their tattered confederacy.

A second protracted conflict, known as the **War of the Spanish Succession** (1702–1713) or Queen Anne's War, had even more devastating effects on North America. The conflict erupted in Europe when Charles II of Spain died without an heir, launching a contest for the Spanish

kingdom and its colonies. France and Spain squared off against England, the Netherlands, Austria, and Prussia. In North America, however, it was England alone that faced France and Spain, with each nation hoping to gain additional territory. Both sides recruited Indian allies.

After more than a decade of savage fighting, Queen Anne's War ended in 1713 with the Treaty of Utrecht, which sought to secure a prolonged peace by balancing the interests of the great powers in Europe and their colonial possessions. Yet England benefited the most in North America even as it consolidated power at home by incorporating Scotland into Great Britain through the 1707 Act of Union. Just six years later, France surrendered Newfoundland, Nova Scotia, and the Hudson Bay Territory to England, while Spain granted England control of St. Kitts in the West Indies, Gibraltar, and Minorca as well as the right to sell African slaves in its American colonies. Yet neither the treaty nor Britain's consolidation forestalled further conflict. Indeed, Spain, France, and Britain all strengthened fortifications along their North American borders (Map 3.1).

Indians Resist European Encroachment

The European conflicts in North America put incredible pressure on Indian peoples to choose sides. It was increasingly difficult for native peoples in colonized areas to remain autonomous, yet Indian nations were not simply pawns of European powers. Some sought European allies against their native enemies, and most improved their situation by gaining cloth, metal tools, guns, or horses from their European trading partners. However, many Indian nations suffered growing internal conflicts as war, trade, and colonial expansion increased the power of male warriors. In societies like the Cherokee and Iroquois, in which older women had long held significant economic and political authority, the rising power of young men threatened traditional gender and generational relations. In addition, struggles between the English and the French often fostered conflict among Indian peoples, reinforcing grievances that existed before European settlement.

The tensions among Indians escalated during the late seventeenth century as southern tribes like the Tuscarora, Yamasee, Creek, Cherokee, Caddo, and Choctaw gained European goods, including guns. As deer disappeared from the Carolinas and the lower Mississippi valley, the most precious commodity for trade became Indian captives sold as slaves. Indians had always taken captives in war, but some of those captives had been adopted into the victorious nation. Now, however, war was almost constant in some areas, and captives were more valuable for sale as slaves than as adopted tribesmen. Moreover, slave raiding occurred outside formal conflicts, intensifying hostilities across the southern region.

MAP 3.1   European Empires in North America, 1715–1750
France, Great Britain, and Spain competed with one another and with numerous Indian nations for control of vast areas of North America. Although European wars repeatedly spilled over into North America in the early to mid-eighteenth century, this map shows the general outlines of the empires claimed by each European nation in this period and the key forts established to maintain those claims.

Still, during the 1710s, some southern Indians tried to develop a pan-Indian alliance similar to that forged by New England Indians in the 1670s (see chapter 2). First, a group of Tuscarora warriors, hoping to gain support from other tribes, launched an attack on North Carolina settlements in September 1711. Over the next several months, hundreds of settlers were killed and hundreds more fled. However, South Carolina colonists came to the aid of their North Carolina countrymen and persuaded Indian allies among the Yamasee, Catawba, and Cherokee nations to join forces against the Tuscaroras. Although some of these allies had traditionally been enemies, they now cooperated. Meanwhile political leaders in North Carolina convinced a competing group of Tuscaroras to ally with the colonists. By 1713 the war was largely over, and in 1715 the Tuscaroras signed a peace treaty and forfeited their lands. Many then migrated north and were accepted as the sixth nation of the Iroquois Confederacy.

Explore

See Document 3.2 to read a Tuscarora appeal to British colonial officials.

DOCUMENT 3.2

The Tuscarora Appeal to the Pennsylvania Government, 1710

Shortly before the outbreak of the Tuscarora War, a delegation of Tuscaroras traveled to Pennsylvania to negotiate with British colonial officials and representatives of the Iroquois Confederacy. These representatives included Iwaagenst Terrutawanaren and Teonnottein. Although summarized by two white officials, John French and Henry Worley, the following document clearly presents the views of the Tuscarora Indians. The Pennsylvania government subsequently denied their requests, but the meeting did produce one important benefit for the Tuscaroras. When the war ended in 1715, members of the tribe moved to New York and became the sixth nation of the Iroquois Confederacy.

Explore

At Conestogo, June 8th, 1710.

The Indians were told that according to their request we were come from the Govr. and Govmt. to hear what proposals they had to make anent [about] a peace, according to the purport of their Embassy from their own People.

They signified to us by a Belt of Wampum, which was sent from their old Women, that those Implored their friendship of the Christians & Indians of this Govmt., that without danger or trouble they might fetch wood & Water.

The second Belt was sent from their Children born, & those yet in the womb, Requesting that Room to sport & Play without danger of Slavery, might be allowed them.

The third Belt was sent from their young men fitt to Hunt, that privilege to leave their Towns, & seek provision for their aged, might be granted to them without fear of Death or Slavery.

The fourth was sent from the men of age, Requesting that the Wood, by a happy peace, might be as safe for them as their forts.

The fifth was sent from the whole nation, requesting peace, that thereby they might have Liberty to visit their Neighbours.

The sixth was sent from their Kings and Chiefs, Desiring a lasting peace with the Christians & Indians of this Govmt., that thereby they might be secured against those fearful apprehensions they have for these several years felt. . . .

These Belts (they say) are only sent as an Introduction, & in order to break off hostilities till next Spring, for then their Kings will come and sue for the peace they so much Desire.

We acquainted them that . . . if they intend to settle & live amiably here, . . . to Confirm the sincerity of their past Carriage towards the English, & to raise in us a good opinion of them, it would be very necessary to procure a Certificate from the Govmt. they leave, to this, of their Good behaviour, & then they might be assured of a favourable reception.

Source: Sherman Day, *Historical Collections of the State of Pennsylvania* (Philadelphia: George W. Gorton, 1853), 391–92.

Interpret the Evidence

- What gifts did the Tuscarora delegation present to the Pennsylvania officials? What did the gifts symbolize?
- What did French and Worley require of the Tuscaroras before allowing them to move to Pennsylvania?

Put It in Context

Why was it important for many American Indian nations to negotiate with both Europeans and other Indian tribes simultaneously?

The end of the war did not mean peace in the Carolinas, however. For the next two years, fierce battles erupted between a Yamasee-led coalition and the South Carolina militia. The Yamasee people remained deeply in debt to British merchants even as the trade in deerskins and slaves moved farther west. They thus secured allies among the Creeks and launched an all-out effort to force the British out. The Yamasee War marked the Indians' most serious challenge to European dominance. Indeed, it was even bloodier than King Philip's War. The British gained victory only after the Cherokees switched their allegiance to the colonists in early 1716 and thus ended the possibility of a major Creek offensive. The final Indian nations withdrew from the conflict in 1717, and a fragile peace followed.

The Yamasee War did not oust the British, but it did transform the political landscape of native North America. In its aftermath, the Creek and Catawba tribes emerged as powerful new confederations, the Cherokees became the major trading partner of the British, and the Yamasee nation was seriously weakened. And as the Cherokees allied with the British, the Creek and the Caddo tribes strengthened their alliance with the French. Meanwhile many Yamasees migrated to Spanish Florida, joining the Seminole nation.

Despite the British victory, colonists on the Carolina frontier faced raids on their settlements for decades to come. In the 1720s and 1730s, settlers in the Middle Atlantic colonies also experienced fierce resistance to their westward expansion. And attacks on New Englanders along the Canadian frontier periodically disrupted settlement there. Still, many Indian tribes were pushed out of their homelands. As they resettled in new regions, they alternately allied and fought with native peoples already living there. At the same time, the trade in Indian slaves expanded in the west as the French and the Spanish competed for economic partners and military allies.

Global Conflicts on the Southern Frontier

Indians were not the only people to have their world shaken by war. By 1720 years of warfare and upheaval had transformed the mind-set of many colonists, from New England to the Carolinas. Although most considered themselves loyal British subjects, many believed that British proprietors remained largely unconcerned with the colonies' welfare. Others resented the British army's treatment of colonial militia and Parliament's unwillingness to aid settlers against Indian attacks. Moreover, the growing numbers of settlers who arrived from other parts of Europe had little investment in British authority.

The impact of Britain's ongoing conflicts with Spain during the 1730s and 1740s on southern colonists illustrates this development. Following the Yamasee War, South

Carolina became a royal colony, and its profitable rice and indigo plantations spread southward. Then, in 1732, Parliament established Georgia (named after King George II) on lands north of Florida as a buffer between Carolina colonists and their longtime Spanish foes. The colony was initiated by social reformers like James Oglethorpe who hoped to provide small farms for Britain's poor. Initially slavery was outlawed, and land grants usually consisted of 50 to 100 acres.

Despite the noble intentions of Georgia's founders, Spanish authorities were furious at this expansion of British territorial claims. Thus in August 1739, a Spanish naval ship captured an English ship captain who was trading illegally in the Spanish West Indies and severed his ear. In response, Great Britain attacked St. Augustine and Cartagena (in present-day Colombia), but its troops were repulsed. In 1742 Spain sent troops into Georgia, but Oglethorpe's militia pushed back the attack. By then, the American war had become part of a more general European conflict. Once again France and Spain joined forces while Great Britain supported Germany in Europe. When the war ended in 1748, Britain had ensured the future of Georgia and reaffirmed its military superiority. Once again, however, victory had come at the cost of the lives of many colonial settlers and soldiers, a fact that was not lost on the colonists, some of whom began to wonder if their interests and those of the British government were truly the same.

Southern Indians were also caught up in ongoing disputes among Europeans. While both French and Spanish forces attacked the British along the Atlantic coast, they sought to outflank each other in the lower Mississippi River valley and Texas. With the French relying on Caddo, Choctaw, and other Indian allies for trade goods and defense, the Spaniards needed to expand their alliances beyond the Tejas. Initially, however, Apache raids on Spanish missions led Spanish settlers to sell captured Apache women and children into slavery in Mexico. In 1749, however, Father Santa Ana convinced a Spanish general to send two Apache women and a man back to their village with a peace proposal. Shortly afterward, in an elaborate ceremony at the mission, the two sides literally buried their differences in a large pit and negotiated peace.

The British meanwhile became increasingly dependent on European immigrants to defend colonial frontiers against the French, Spaniards, and Indians. Certainly many Anglo-Americans moved westward as coastal areas became overcrowded, but frontier regions also attracted immigrants from Scotland and Germany who sought refuge and economic opportunity in the colonies. Many headed to the Virginia and Carolina frontier and to Georgia in the 1730s and 1740s. Meanwhile South

Carolina officials recruited Swiss, German, and French Huguenot as well as Scots-Irish immigrants in the 1740s to settle along the Pee Dee River and other inland waterways. Small communities of Jews settled in Charleston as well. Gradually many of these immigrants moved south into Georgia, seeking more and cheaper land. Thus when Spanish, French, or Indian forces attacked the British colonial frontier, they were as likely to face Scots-Irish and German immigrants as Englishmen.

REVIEW & RELATE

How did the European wars of the late seventeenth and early eighteenth centuries impact relations between colonists and England?

How and why were Indians pulled into the wars between European powers fought in North America?

✓ *LEARNINGCurve* bedfordstmartins.com/hewittlawson/LC

The Benefits and Costs of Empire

The combined forces of global trade and international warfare altered the political and economic calculations of imperial powers. This was especially true for British North America, where colonists settled as families and created towns that provided key markets for Britain's commercial expansion. Over the course of the eighteenth century, British colonists became increasingly avid consumers of products from around the world. Meanwhile the king and Parliament, determined to reap the benefits of their costly empire, sought greater control over these far-flung commercial networks.

Colonial Traders Join Global Networks

In the late seventeenth and early eighteenth centuries, trade became truly global. Not only did goods from China, India, the Middle East, Africa, and North America gain currency in England and the rest of Europe, but the tastes of European consumers also helped shape goods produced in other parts of the world. For instance, wealthy Englishmen had long desired fine porcelain from China, and by the early eighteenth century the Chinese were making teapots and bowls specifically

for that market. The trade in cloth, tea, and sugar was similarly influenced by European tastes. The exploitation of African laborers contributed significantly to this global commerce. They were a crucial item of trade in their own right, and their labor in the Americas ensured steady supplies of sugar, rice, tobacco, indigo, and other goods for the world market.

By the early eighteenth century, both the volume and the diversity of goods multiplied. Silk, calico, porcelain, olive oil, wine, and other goods were carried from the East to Europe and the American colonies, while cod, mackerel, shingles, pine boards, barrel staves, rum, sugar, rice, and indigo filled ships returning west. A healthy trade also grew up within North America as New England fishermen, New York and Charleston merchants, and Caribbean planters met one another's needs. Salted cod and mackerel flowed to the Caribbean, and rum, molasses, and slaves flowed back to the mainland. This commerce required ships, barrels, docks, warehouses, and wharves, all of which ensured a lively trade in lumber, tar, pitch, and rosin. The volume of trade originating in British North America was impressive. Between April and December 1720, for example, some 425 ships sailed in and out of Boston harbor alone (Map 3.2).

The flow of information was critical to the flow of goods and credit. By the early eighteenth century, coffeehouses flourished in port cities around the Atlantic, providing access to the latest news. Merchants, ship captains, and traders met in

London Coffeehouse, 1725

This London coffeehouse, situated in the courtyard of the Royal Exchange (bank), was one among many such establishments in port cities on both sides of the Atlantic. In this setting, patrons conducted business related to overseas trade. They read the *Spectator* and *London Times* among other newspapers and swapped stories about politics, business, and other events of the day.
© The Trustees of the British Museum/Art Resource, NY

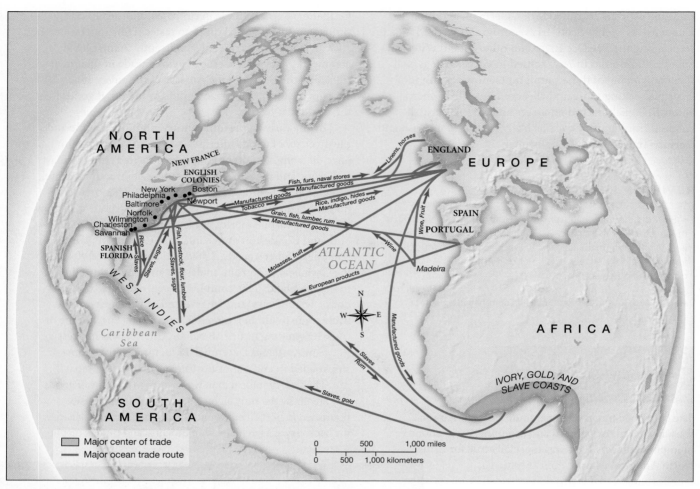

MAP 3.2   North Atlantic Trade in the 18th Century

North Atlantic trade provided various parts of the British empire with raw materials, manufactured goods, and labor. Many ships traveled between only two regions because they were equipped to carry particular kinds of goods—slaves, grains, or manufactured goods. Ultimately, however, people and goods were exchanged among four key points: the West Indies, mainland North America, West Africa, and Great Britain.

person to discuss new ventures and to keep apprised of recent developments. British and American periodicals reported on parliamentary legislation, commodity prices in India and Great Britain, the state of trading houses in China, the outbreak of disease in foreign ports, and stock ventures in London. Thus colonists from Boston to Charleston could follow the South Seas Bubble in 1720, when shares in the British South Seas Company rose to astronomical heights and then collapsed. William Moraley's father was among the thousands of British investors who lost a great deal of money in this venture. But colonists could also track the rising price of wheat.

Imperial Policies Focus on Profits

In the midst of this growing international trade, European sovereigns worked to ensure that colonial possessions

benefited their own treasuries. In the late seventeenth century, both Louis XIV and his English rivals embraced a system known as **mercantilism**, which centered on the maintenance of a favorable balance of trade, with more gold and silver flowing into the home country than flowed out. In France, finance minister Jean-Baptiste Colbert honed the system. Beginning in the 1660s, he taxed foreign imports while removing all barriers to trade within French territories. Colonies like New France provided valuable raw materials— furs, fish, lumber—that could be used to produce manufactured items for sale to foreign nations and to colonists.

While France's mercantile system was limited by the size of its empire, England benefited more fully from such policies. The English crown had access to a far wider array of natural resources and a larger market for its manufactured goods. As early as 1660, Parliament passed a

Navigation Act that required merchants to conduct trade with the colonies only in English-owned ships. In addition, certain items imported from foreign ports—salt, wine, and oil, for instance—had to be carried in English ships or in ships with predominantly English crews. Finally, a list of "enumerated articles"—from tobacco and cotton to sugar and indigo—had to be shipped from the colonies to England before being re-exported to foreign ports. Thus the crown benefited directly or indirectly from nearly all commerce conducted by its colonies. But colonies, too, often benefited, as when Parliament helped subsidize the development of indigo in South Carolina. **See Document Project 3: The Production of Indigo, page 90.**

In 1663 Parliament expanded its imperial reach by requiring that goods sent from Europe to English colonies also pass through its ports. And a decade later, ship captains had to pay a duty or post bond before carrying enumerated articles between colonial ports. Despite the Great Plague of 1665 and the London fire of 1666, England's overseas colonies fueled an economic upsurge. Indeed, when London was rebuilt after the fire, its wide boulevards, massive mercantile houses, crowded wharves, and bustling coffee shops marked it as the hub of an expanding commercial empire. Beginning in 1673, England sent customs officials to the colonies to enforce the various parliamentary acts. And by 1680, London, Bristol, and Liverpool all thrived as barrels of sugar, cases of indigo, and stacks of deerskin were unloaded and bolts of dyed cloth and cartons of felt hats were put on board for the return voyage. At the same time, the transformation of New Amsterdam into New York allowed England to incorporate the diverse commercial ventures that thrived in the Dutch colony into its imperial network.

Parliament then sought to quash nascent manufacturing in the colonies by prohibiting the sale of products such as American-made textiles (1699), hats (1732), and iron goods (1750). In addition, Parliament worked to restrict trade among the North American colonies. Settlers in the British West Indies had begun selling surplus fish, flour, and meat arriving from the mainland to their French neighbors. Meanwhile mainland colonists bought growing quantities of molasses, which they made into rum, from those same French islands at a much lower price than British West Indians could offer. Fearing French planters would dominate the sugar and molasses trade, Parliament passed the 1733 Molasses Act, which allowed mainland merchants to export fish and agricultural goods directly to the French West Indies but required them to pay a high import tariff on French molasses. The law might have crippled the American distilling industry, but mainland colonists instead began smuggling cheap French molasses into their ports and bribing customs officials to look the other way.

Despite the increasing regulation, American colonists could own British ships and transport goods produced in the colonies. Indeed, by the mid-eighteenth century, North American merchants oversaw 75 percent of the trade in manufactures sent from Bristol and London to the colonies and 95 percent of the trade with the West Indies. Ironically, then, a system established to benefit Great Britain ended up creating a mercantile elite in British North America. Most of those merchants traded in goods, but some traded in human cargo.

The Atlantic Slave Trade

Parliament chartered the Royal African Company in 1672, and England slowly expanded its role in the slave trade as the Dutch commercial empire waned. In 1713, when the British gained the right to sell slaves to Spanish colonies, that nation became a major player in the horrific trade in human cargo. Between 1700 and 1808, some 3 million captive Africans were carried on British and Anglo-American ships, about 40 percent of the total of those sold in the Americas in this period (Figure 3.1). Half a million Africans died on the voyage across the Atlantic. Huge numbers also died in Africa, while being marched to the coast or held in forts waiting to be forced aboard ships. Yet despite this astounding death rate, the slave trade yielded enormous profits and had far-reaching consequences: The Africans that British traders bought and sold transformed labor systems in the colonies, fueled international trade, and enriched merchants, planters, and their families and partners.

European traders worked closely with African merchants to gain their human cargo. Where once they had traded textiles and alcohol for gold and ivory, Europeans now traded muskets, metalware, and linen for men, women, and children. Originally many of those sold into slavery were war captives. But by the time British and Anglo-American merchants became central to this notorious trade, their contacts in Africa were procuring labor in any way they could. The cargo included war captives, servants, and people snatched in raids specifically to secure slaves. Over time, African traders moved farther inland to fill the demand, devastating large areas of West Africa, particularly the Congo-Angola region, which supplied some 40 percent of all Atlantic slaves.

The trip across the Atlantic, known as the **Middle Passage**, was a brutal and often deadly experience for Africans. Exhausted and undernourished by the time they boarded the large oceangoing vessels, the captives were placed in dark and crowded holds. Most had been poked and prodded by slave traders, and some had been branded to ensure that a trader received the exact individuals he

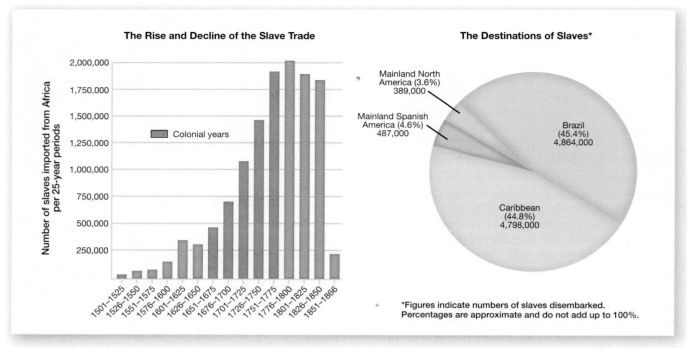

FIGURE 3.1   The Slave Trade in Numbers, 1501–1866

Extraordinary numbers of Africans were shipped as slaves to other parts of the world from the sixteenth to the nineteenth century. These shipments increased dramatically during North America's colonial era (1601–1775). Although the slave trade transformed mainland North America, the vast majority of enslaved Africans were sent to Brazil and the West Indies.

Source: Trans-Atlantic Slave Trade Database, http://www.slavevoyages.org/tast/assessment/estimates.faces.

had purchased. Once in the hold, they might wait for weeks before the ship finally set sail. By that time, the foul-smelling and crowded hold became a nightmare of disease and despair. There was never sufficient food or fresh water for the captives, and women especially were subject to sexual abuse and rape by crew members. Many captives could not communicate with each other since they spoke different languages, and none of them knew exactly where they were going or what would happen when they arrived.

Explore

See Document 3.3 for a look inside a slave ship.

Those who survived the voyage were likely to find themselves in the slave markets of Barbados or Jamaica, where they were put on display for potential buyers. Once purchased, the slaves went through a period of **seasoning** as they regained their strength, became accustomed to their new environment, and learned commands in a new language. In this period of acculturation, enslaved laborers

also confronted strange foods, new diseases, and unfamiliar tasks. Most were also given new names. Some did not survive seasoning, falling prey to malnutrition and disease or committing suicide. Others adapted to the new circumstances and adopted enough European or British ways to carry on even as they sought means to resist the shocking and oppressive conditions.

More than half of the slaves imported to the Lower South entered the mainland at Charleston, South Carolina. Beginning around 1700, enslaved Africans were shipped directly to Charleston rather than transshipped from the West Indies. Successful planters like Eliza Lucas likely had first choice of the new arrivals, sending agents to the wharves to buy Africans.

Seaport Cities and Consumer Cultures

The same trade in human cargo that brought misery to millions of Africans provided traders, investors, and plantation owners with huge profits that helped turn America's seaport cities into centers of culture and consumption. When Eliza Lucas arrived in Charleston in 1738, she

DOCUMENT 3.3

Plan of a Slave Ship, 1789

To increase the profitability of the slave trade, cargo ships by the mid-eighteenth century had been replaced by ships built specifically to transport African slaves. Designed to hold as many people as possible in the lower decks, these ships were scenes of horror, disease, and death for Africans during the Middle Passage. This image of the slave ship *Brookes* vividly portrays the business of transporting human cargo. It was widely used by British abolitionists in their campaign against slavery and the slave trade.

Explore

Would this visual representation of enslaved Africans have been more or less effective than written descriptions of the Middle Passage? Why or why not?

Why did the artist include the insurrection? What purpose does it serve?

How might this image make viewers identify and sympathize with captured Africans?

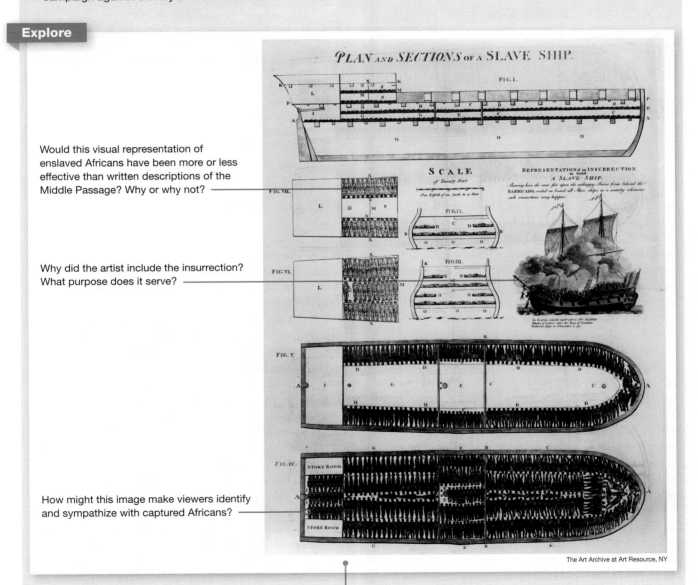

The Art Archive at Art Resource, NY

Put It in Context

What does this image tell the viewer about slavery and the Middle Passage?

Charleston, 1739

This 1739 engraving offers a view of Charleston harbor from the Battery, where heavy rocks fortified the banks of the Cooper River and artillery later was placed in the American Civil War. Some of the ships in this scene carried slaves and consumer goods that made Charleston one of the great commercial centers in the South.   The Granger Collection, New York

noted that "the Metropolis is a neat pretty place. The inhabitants [are] polite and live in a very gentile [genteel] manner." Throughout British North America, seaports, with their elegant homes, fine shops, and lively social seasons, captured the most dynamic aspects of colonial life. Although cities like New York, Boston, Philadelphia, Baltimore, and Charleston contained less than 10 percent of the colonial population, they served as focal points of economic, political, social, and cultural activity.

Many affluent urban families shed the religious strictures or financial constraints that shaped the lives of their colonial forebearers and created a consumer revolution in North America. Changing patterns of consumption challenged traditional definitions of status. Less tied to birth and family pedigree, status in the colonies became more closely linked to financial success and a genteel lifestyle. Successful men of humble origins and even those of Dutch, Scottish, French, and Jewish heritage might join the British-dominated colonial gentry.

Of those who made the leap in the early eighteenth century, Benjamin Franklin was the most notable. He might have taken the path of the "infortunate" William Moraley Jr., but Franklin was apprenticed to his brother, a printer, an occupation that matched his interest in books, reading, and politics. At age sixteen, Franklin published (anonymously) his first essays in his brother's paper, the *New England Courant*. Two years later, a family dispute led Franklin to try his luck in New York and then Philadelphia. His fortunes were fragile, but hard work, a quick wit, good luck, and political connections led to success. In 1729 Franklin

purchased the *Pennsylvania Gazette* and became the colony's official printer.

While Franklin worried about the concentration of wealth in too few hands, most colonial elites happily displayed their profits. Thus in the early eighteenth century, leading merchants in Boston, Salem, New York, and Philadelphia emulated British styles and built fine two- and three-story brick homes that had separate rooms for sleeping, eating, and entertaining guests. Mercantile elites also redesigned the urban landscape in the early eighteenth century. They donated money for brick churches and stately town halls. They constructed new roads, wharves, and warehouses to facilitate trade, and they invested in bowling greens and public gardens that beckoned affluent families on a Sunday afternoon.

Many Anglo-American elites used their knowledge of London fashions to reassert their British identity. Tea drinking was especially important in this regard, and families who could afford the finest furnishings and the time for extended social rituals made teatime a daily event. Yet the tea served at the home of Boston merchant Anthony Stoddard was imported from East Asia; the cups, saucers, and teapot were from China; and a handsome bowl held sugar from the West Indies. Stoddard decorated his home with heavily lacquered "japanned" boxes, French-patterned wallpaper, Indian calico bedding, and Italian silk curtains—all of which demonstrated that he was a successful merchant as well as a fashionable British citizen.

The spread of international commerce created a lively cultural life and great affluence in colonial cities. But it also created deep divisions between rich and poor. Wealthy merchants and professionals congregated in urban areas along with a middling group of artisans and shopkeepers and a growing class of unskilled laborers, widows, orphans, the elderly, the disabled, and the unemployed. The frequent wars of the late seventeenth and early eighteenth centuries contributed to these divisions by boosting the profits of merchants, shipbuilders, and artisans. They also improved the wages of seamen temporarily. But in their aftermath, rising prices, falling wages, and a lack of jobs led to the concentration of wealth in fewer hands.

REVIEW & RELATE

What place did North American colonists occupy in the eighteenth-century global trade network?

How did the British government seek to maintain control over the colonial economy and ensure that its colonies served Britain's economic and political interests?

 LEARNINGCurve **bedfordstmartins.com/hewittlawson/LC**

Labor in North America

What brought the poor and the wealthy together was the demand for labor. Labor was sorely needed in the colonies, but this did not mean that it was easy to find steady, high-paying employment. Many would-be laborers had few skills and faced fierce competition from other workers for limited, seasonal manual labor. Moreover, a majority of immigrants, both European and African, arrived in America with significant limits on their freedom.

Finding Work in the Colonies

The demand for labor did not necessarily help free laborers find work. Many employers preferred indentured servants, apprentices, or others who came cheap and were bound by contract. Others employed criminals or purchased slaves, who would provide years of service for a set price. Free laborers who sought a decent wage and steady employment needed to match their desire to work with skills that were in demand.

When William Moraley ended his indenture and sought work, he discovered that far fewer colonists than Englishmen owned timepieces, leaving him without a useful trade. So he tramped the countryside, selling his labor when he could, but found no consistent employment. Returning to New York and Philadelphia, William begged lodging from friends, considered marrying an elderly widow, was imprisoned for

minor offenses, and accepted Quaker charity. But he fell ever deeper in debt. Thousands of other men and women, most without Moraley's education or skills, also found themselves at the mercy of unrelenting economic forces.

Many poor men and women found jobs building homes, loading ships, or spinning yarn. But they were usually employed for only a few months a year. The rest of the time they scrounged for bread and beer, begged in the streets, or stole what they needed. Most lived in ramshackle buildings filled with cramped and unsanitary rooms. Freezing in winter and sweltering in summer, these quarters served as breeding grounds for smallpox, scarlet fever, and other diseases. Children born into such squalid circumstances were lucky to survive their first year. Those who survived could watch ships sail into port and earn a few pence running errands for captains or sailors, but they would never have access to the bounteous goods intended for those who lived in stately mansions.

By the early eighteenth century, older systems of labor, like indentured servitude, began to decline in many areas. In some parts of the North and across the South, white servants were gradually replaced by African slaves. At the same time, farm families who could not usefully employ all their children began to bind out sons and daughters to more prosperous neighbors. Apprentices, too, competed for positions. Unlike most servants, apprentices contracted to learn a trade. They trained under the supervision of a craftsman, who gained cheap labor by promising to teach a young man (and most apprentices were men) his trade. But master craftsmen limited the number of apprentices they accepted to maintain the value of their skills.

Another category of laborers emerged in the 1720s. A population explosion in Europe and the rising price of wheat and other items convinced many people to seek passage to America. Shipping agents offered them loans that were repaid when the immigrants found a colonial employer who would redeem (that is, repay) the original loan. In turn, these **redemptioners** labored for the employer for a set number of years, though they could live independently with their own family. The redemption system was popular in the Middle Atlantic colonies, especially among German immigrants who hoped to establish farms on the Pennsylvania frontier. While many succeeded, their circumstances could be extremely difficult.

> **Explore**
>
> Read two immigrants' descriptions of their varying experiences in Documents 3.4 and 3.5.

Large numbers of convicts, too, entered the British colonies in the eighteenth century. Jailers in charge of Britain's overcrowded prisons offered inmates the option of transportation to the colonies. Hundreds were thus bound out each year to American employers. The combination of indentured servants, redemptioners, apprentices, and convicts ensured that as late as 1750 the majority of white workers—men and women—were bound to some sort of contract.

Sometimes white urban workers also competed with slaves, especially in the northern colonies. Africans and African Americans formed only a small percentage of the northern population, just 5 percent from Pennsylvania to New Hampshire in 1750. In the colony of New York, however, blacks formed about 14 percent of inhabitants.

While some enslaved blacks worked on agricultural estates in the Hudson River valley and New Jersey, even more labored as household servants, dockworkers, seamen, and blacksmiths in New York City alongside British colonists and European immigrants (Figure 3.2). Considered a status symbol by many wealthy merchants, urban slaves were usually discouraged from marrying or bearing large numbers of children. However, some masters allowed their slaves to marry and set up independent households or to hire themselves out to other employers, as long as their wages were paid to their owners.

DOCUMENTS 3.4 AND 3.5

Pennsylvania as Promised Land? Two Views

German colonists began moving to Pennsylvania in the late seventeenth century, encouraged by reports of rich land and religious freedom. Francis Pastorius was an agent for the Frankfort Land Company who successfully promoted German settlement in the colony. In Document 3.4, he describes life in Pennsylvania as lush and prosperous. Document 3.5, published more than fifty years later, offers a very different depiction of life for German settlers. Gottlieb Mittelberger left his home in Germany to move to Pennsylvania in 1750. When he returned to Germany in 1754, he wrote a book (published two years later) warning others against settling in the American colonies. Although Mittelberger was not an indentured servant, his book focused on the hardships brought about by this practice.

Explore

3.4 Francis Pastorius | Description of Pennsylvania, 1700

Inasmuch as this region lies in the same degree of latitude as Montpelier and Naples, but has a much richer soil, and that better watered by its many springs and rivulets, it is but reasonable to suppose that such a country must be well calculated to produce all kinds of fruit. The air is pure and serene, the summer is longer and warmer than it is in Germany, and we are cultivating many kinds of fruits and vegetables, and our labors meet with rich reward.

Of cattle we have a great abundance, but for want of proper accommodation they roam at large for the present. . . .

Although this far-distant land was a dense wilderness—and it is only quite recently that it has come under the cultivation of the Christians—there is much cause of wonder and admiration how rapidly it has already, under the blessing of God, advanced, and is still advancing, day by day. The first part of the time we were obliged to obtain our provisions from the Jerseys for money, and at a high price; but now we not only have enough for ourselves, but a considerable surplus to dispose of among our neighboring colonies. Of the most needful mechanics we have enough now; but day-laborers are very scarce, and of them we stand in great need. . . .

Our surplus of grain and cattle we trade to Barbados for rum, syrup, sugar, and salt. The furs, however, we export to England for other manufactured goods.

Source: Francis Daniel Pastorius, *A Particular Geographical Description of the Lately Discovered Province of Pennsylvania*, trans. Lewis H. Weiss (1700), reprinted in *Old South Leaflets*, No. 95 (Boston, 1898), 8–9.

Coping with Economic Distress

White workers who were bound by contracts might have felt common cause with slaves, but most recognized that eventually they would be free. Despite the challenges faced by white workers who migrated to British North America in the early eighteenth century, many still improved their lives. Most servants, apprentices, redemptioners, and convicts hoped one day to purchase land, open a shop, or earn a decent wage. Yet gaining freedom did not promise economic success.

Several challenges confronted those looking to succeed. First, white women and men who gained their freedom from indentures or other contracts had to compete for jobs with a steady supply of redemptioners, convicts, and apprentices as well as other free laborers. Second, by the early eighteenth century, many areas along the Atlantic coast faced a land shortage that threatened the fortunes even of long-settled families. Finally, a population boom in Britain's North American colonies produced growing numbers of young people seeking land and employment. Thus many free laborers migrated from town to town and from country to

Explore

3.5 Gottlieb Mittelberger | Journey to Pennsylvania, 1756

Our Europeans, who are purchased [indentured servants and redemptioners], must always work hard, for new fields are constantly laid out; and so they learn that stumps of oak-trees are in America certainly as hard as in Germany. In this hot land they fully experience in their own persons what God has imposed on man for his sin and disobedience; for in Genesis we read the words: In the sweat of thy brow shalt thou eat bread. Who therefore wishes to earn his bread in a Christian and honest way, and cannot earn it in his fatherland otherwise than by the work of his hands, let him do so in his own country, and not in America; for he will not fare better in America. However hard he may be compelled to work in his fatherland, he will surely find it quite as

hard, if not harder, in the new country. Besides, there is not only the long and arduous journey lasting half a year, during which he has to suffer, more than with the hardest work; he has also spent about 200 florins which no one will refund to him. If he has so much money, it will slip out of his hands; if he has it not, he must work his debt off as a slave and poor serf. Therefore let every one stay in his own country and support himself and his family honestly. Besides I say that those who suffer themselves to be persuaded and enticed away by the man-thieves, are very foolish if they believe that roasted pigeons will fly into their mouths in America or Pennsylvania without their working for them.

Source: Gottlieb Mittelberger, *Gottlieb Mittelberger's Journey to Pennsylvania in the Year 1750 and Return to Germany in the Year 1754*, trans. Carl Theo. Eben (Philadelphia: John Jos. McVey, 1898), 30–31.

Interpret the Evidence

- What might Pastorius's readers have found most appealing about the land he describes? How did his description differ from the experience of the average agricultural worker in Germany?
- What myths about America did Mittelberger try to dispel?
- How would you account for the differences between Pastorius's and Mittelberger's accounts of Pennsylvania?

Put It in Context

What do these accounts tell us about the experiences of colonial settlers in the early and mid-eighteenth century?

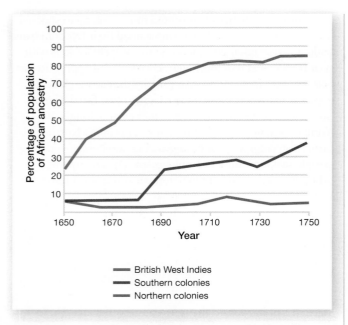

FIGURE 3.2   African Populations in the British West Indies, Northern Colonies, and Southern Colonies, 1650–1750

In 1650 the African population in the British West Indies already far exceeded that in mainland North America. Over the next century, the number of Africans and African Americans increased significantly on the mainland. But the growth was far greater in the southern than in the northern colonies, reaching 40 percent in the Chesapeake and Lower South colonies by the mid-eighteenth century. Source: Data from Robert William Fogel and Stanley L. Engerman, *Time on the Cross: The Economics of American Negro Slavery.*

city seeking work. They hoped to find farmers who needed extra hands for planting and harvesting or ship captains and contractors who would hire them to load or unload cargo or assist in the construction of homes and churches. The Royal Army and Navy also periodically sought colonial recruits, though mostly in times of war. Women meanwhile hoped for employment spinning yarn or working as cooks, laundresses, or nursemaids.

Seasonal and temporary demands for labor created a corps of transient workers. Many New England towns developed systems to "warn out" those who were not official residents. Modeled after the British system, warning-out was meant to ensure that strangers did not become public dependents. Still, being warned did not mean immediate removal. Sometimes transients were simply warned that they were not eligible for poor relief. At other times, constables returned them to an earlier place of residence. In many ways, warning-out served as an early registration system, allowing authorities to encourage the flow of labor, keep residents under surveillance, and protect the town's coffers. But it rarely aided those in need of work.

Residents who were eligible for public assistance might be given food and clothing or boarded with a local family.

Many towns began appointing Overseers of the Poor to deal with the growing problem of poverty. By 1750 every seaport city had constructed an almshouse that sheltered residents without other means of support. In 1723 the Bridewell prison was added to Boston Almshouse, built in 1696. Then in 1739 a workhouse was opened on the same site to employ the "able-bodied" poor in hopes that profits from it would help fund the almshouse and prison. Overseers in each city believed that a workhouse would "simultaneously correct the idle poor and instill in them a habit of industry by obliging them to work to earn their keep." Still, these efforts at relief fell far short of the need, especially in hard economic times.

Rural Americans Face Changing Conditions

While seaport cities and larger towns fostered a growing cohort of individuals who lived outside traditional households, families remained the central unit of economic organization in rural areas, where the vast majority of Americans lived. Yet even farms were affected by the transatlantic circulation of goods and people.

In areas along the Atlantic coast, rural families were drawn into commercial networks in a variety of ways. Towns and cities needed large supplies of vegetables, meat, butter, barley, wheat, and yarn. Farm families sold produce or homemade goods to residents and bought sugar, tea, and other imported items that diversified their diet. Few rural families purchased ornamental or luxury items, but cloth or cheese bought in town saved hours of labor at home. Just as important, coastal communities like Salem, Massachusetts, and Wilmington, Delaware, that were once largely rural became thriving commercial centers in the late seventeenth century.

In New England, the land available for farming shrank as the population soared. In the original Puritan colonies, the population rose from 100,000 in 1700 to 400,000 in 1750, and many parents were unable to provide their children with sufficient land for profitable farms. The result was increased migration to the frontier, where families were more dependent on their own labor and a small circle of neighbors. And even this option was not accessible to all. Before 1700, servants who survived their indenture had a good chance of securing land, but by the mid-eighteenth century only two of every ten were likely to become landowners.

In the Middle Atlantic region, the population surged from 50,000 in 1700 to 250,000 in 1750. The increase was due in part to the rapid rise in wheat prices, which leaped by more than 50 percent in Europe. Hoping to take advantage of this boon, Anglo-Americans, Germans, Scots-Irish, and other non-English groups flooded into western Pennsylvania, New

York's Mohawk River valley, and the Shenandoah valley of Virginia in the early eighteenth century. By the 1740s, German families had created self-contained communities in these areas. They worshipped in German churches, read German newspapers, and preserved German traditions. Meanwhile Scots-Irish immigrants, most of them Presbyterians, established churches and communities in New Jersey, central Pennsylvania, and western Maryland and Virginia (Map 3.3).

In the South, immigrants could acquire land more easily, but their chances for economic autonomy were increasingly influenced by the spread of slavery. As hundreds and then thousands of Africans were imported into the Carolinas in the 1720s and 1730s, economic and political power became more entrenched in the hands of planters and merchants. Increasingly, they controlled the markets, wrote the laws, and set the terms by which white as well as black families lived. Farms along inland waterways and on the frontier were crucial in providing food and other items for urban residents and for planters with large labor forces. But farm families depended on commercial and planter elites to market their goods and help defend their communities against hostile Indians or Spaniards.

Slavery Takes Hold in the South

The rise of slavery reshaped the South in numerous ways. The shift from white indentured servants to black slaves began in Virginia after 1676 (see chapter 2) and soon spread across the Chesapeake. The Carolinas, meanwhile, developed as a slave society from the start. Slavery in turn allowed for the expanded cultivation of cash crops like tobacco, rice, and indigo, which promised high profits for planters as well as merchants. But these developments also made southern elites more dependent on the global market and limited opportunities for poorer whites and all blacks. They also ensured that Indians and many whites were pushed farther west as planters sought more land for their ventures.

In the 1660s, the Virginia Assembly passed a series of laws that made slavery a status inherited through the mother, denied that the status could be changed by converting to Christianity, and granted masters the right to kill slaves who resisted their authority (see chapter 2). In 1680 the Assembly made it illegal for "any negro or other slave to carry or arme himself with any club, staffe, gunn, sword, or

any other weapon of defence or offence." Nor could slaves leave their master's premises without a certificate of permission. Those who disobeyed were whipped or branded. Increasingly harsh laws in Virginia and Maryland, modeled on those in Barbados, coincided with a rise in the number of slaves imported to the colony. The statutes also ensured the decline of the free black population in the Chesapeake. In 1668 one-third of all Africans and African Americans in Virginia and Maryland were still free, but the numbers dwindled year by year. Once the Royal African Company started supplying the Chesapeake with slaves directly from Africa in the 1680s, the pace of change quickened. By 1750, 150,000 blacks resided in the Chesapeake, and only about 5 percent remained free.

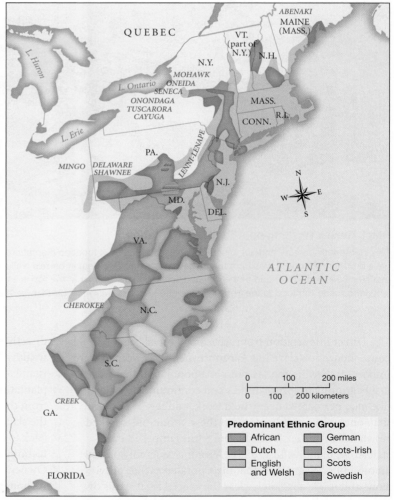

MAP 3.3 Ethnic and Racial Diversity in British North America, 1750

By 1750 British North America was a far more diverse region than it had been fifty years earlier. In 1700 the English dominated most regions, while the Dutch controlled towns and estates in the Hudson River valley. By 1750, however, growing numbers of African Americans, German and Scots-Irish immigrants, and smaller communities of other ethnic groups predominated in various regions.

Black Slaves Working on a Tobacco Plantation
This eighteenth-century engraving shows slaves laboring on a tobacco plantation. The bare-chested slaves
have brought tobacco leaves from the fields and are packing them in barrels while well-dressed whites
oversee their work. The head of the Indian displayed in the banner at the top is a reminder of the people
who introduced tobacco to the English colonists. Peter Newark American Pictures/The Bridgeman Art Library

Direct importation from Africa had other negative consequences on slave life. Far more men than women were imported, skewing the sex ratio in a population that was just beginning to form families and communities. Women like men performed heavy field work, and few bore more than one or two children. When these conditions sparked resistance by the enslaved, fearful whites imposed even stricter regulations. In 1705 the Virginia Assembly passed an omnibus "Negro Act" that incorporated earlier provisions and made absolutely clear the special legal status of the enslaved. For instance, while mistreated white servants could sue in court, black slaves could not. And a slave who ran away and was captured could be tortured and dismembered in hopes of "terrifying others from the like practices."

While slavery in the Carolinas was influenced by developments in the Chesapeake, it was shaped even more

directly by practices in the British West Indies. Many wealthy families from Barbados, Antigua, and other sugar islands—including that of Colonel Lucas—established plantations in the Carolinas. At first, they brought slaves from the West Indies to oversee cattle and pigs and assist in the slaughter of livestock and curing of meat for shipment back to the West Indies. Some of the slaves grew rice, using techniques learned in West Africa, to supplement their diet. Owners soon realized that rice might prove very profitable. Although not widely eaten in Europe, rice could provide cheap and nutritious food for sailors, orphans, convicts, and peasants. Relying initially on Africans' knowledge, planters began cultivating rice for export.

The need for African rice-growing skills and the fear of attacks by Spaniards and Indians led Carolina owners to grant slaves rights unheard of in the Chesapeake or the West

Indies. Initially slaves were allowed to carry guns and serve in the militia. For those who nonetheless ran for freedom, Spanish and Indian territories offered refuge. Still, most stayed, depending for support on bonds they had developed in the West Indies. The frequent absence of owners also offered Carolina slaves greater autonomy.

As rice cultivation expanded, however, slavery in the Carolinas turned more brutal. The Assembly enacted harsher and harsher slave codes to ensure control of the growing labor force. No longer could slaves carry guns, join militias, meet in groups, or travel without a pass. As planters began to import more slaves directly from Africa, sex ratios, already male dominated, became even more heavily skewed. In addition, older community networks from the West Indies were disrupted. Military patrols by whites were initiated to enforce laws and labor practices. Some plantations along the Carolina coast turned into virtual labor camps, where thousands of slaves worked under harsh conditions with no hope of improvement.

By 1720 blacks outnumbered whites in the Carolinas, and fears of slave rebellions inspired South Carolina officials to impose even harsher laws and more brutal enforcement measures. When indigo joined rice as a cash crop in the 1740s, the demand for slave labor increased further. Although far fewer slaves—about 40,000 by 1750—resided in South Carolina than in the Chesapeake, they constituted more than 60 percent of the colony's total population.

Africans Resist Their Enslavement

Enslaved laborers in British North America resisted their subjugation in a variety of ways. They sought to retain customs, foods, belief systems, and languages from their homelands. They tried to incorporate work patterns passed down from one generation to the next into new environments. They challenged masters and overseers by refusing to work, breaking tools, feigning illness, and other means of disputing whites' authority. Some ran for freedom, others fought back in the face of punishment, and still others used arson, poison, or other means to defy owners. A few planned revolts.

The consequences for resisting were severe, from whipping, mutilation, and branding to summary execution. Because whites were so fearful of rebellion, they often punished people falsely accused of planning revolts. Yet some slaves did plot ways to rise up against their owners or whites in general. Southern whites, living amid large numbers of blacks, were most deeply concerned about resistance and rebellion. But even in the North, whites did not doubt slaves' desire for freedom. As more slaves were imported directly from Africa, both the fear and the reality of rebellion increased.

In New York City in 1712, several dozen enslaved Africans and Indians set fire to a building. When whites rushed to the scene, the insurgents attacked them with clubs, pistols, axes, and staves, killing 8 and injuring many more. The rebels were soon defeated by the militia, however. Authorities executed 18 insurgents, burning several at the stake as a warning to others, while 6 of those imprisoned committed suicide. In 1741 a series of suspicious fires in the city led to accusations against a white couple who owned an alehouse where blacks gathered to drink. To protect herself from prosecution, an Irish indentured servant testified that she had overheard discussions of an elaborate plot involving black and white conspirators. Frightened of any hint that poor whites and blacks might make common cause, authorities immediately arrested suspects and eventually executed 34 people, including 4 whites. They also banished 72 blacks from the city. Among those executed was Cuffee, a slave who claimed that "a great many people have too much, and others too little."

The most serious slave revolt, however, erupted in South Carolina, just a few miles from Wappoo, the Lucas plantation. A group of recently imported Africans led the **Stono rebellion** in 1739. On Sunday, September 9, a group of enslaved men stole weapons from a country store and killed the owners. They then marched south, along the Stono River, beating drums and recruiting others to join them. Torching plantations and killing whites along the route, they had gathered more than fifty insurgents when armed whites overtook them. In the ensuing battle, dozens of rebels died. The militia, along with Indians hired to assist them, killed another twenty over the next two days and then captured a group of forty, who were executed without trial.

This revolt reverberated widely in a colony where blacks outnumbered whites nearly two to one, direct importation from Africa was at an all-time high, and Spanish authorities in Florida promised freedom to runaway slaves. In 1738 the Spanish governor formed a black militia company, and he allowed thirty-eight fugitive families to settle north of St. Augustine and build Fort Mose for their protection. When warfare erupted between Spain and Britain over commercial rivalries in 1739, Carolina slaves may have seen their chance to gain freedom en masse. But as with other rebellions, this one failed, and the price of failure was death.

REVIEW & RELATE

What were the sources of economic inequality in North America in the early eighteenth century?

Under what kinds of contracts and conditions did poor people, both white and black, work?

Conclusion: Changing Fortunes in British North America

Global commerce, international wars, and immigration reshaped the economy and geography of North America between 1680 and 1750. Many colonists thrived, initiating a consumer revolution that transformed daily life and ensured the growth of seaport cities. Others found greater opportunities by pushing inland and establishing farms and communities along new frontiers. But many failed to benefit from either land or trade. White workers caught in a downward economic spiral, enslaved Africans, and Indians on the wrong side of a war—all became victims of international trade and imperial conflicts.

The development of manufacturing in England shaped the lives of working people on both sides of the Atlantic Ocean. William Moraley Jr., for example, lived out his life in Newcastle-upon-Tyne, making and repairing watches at a time when cheap watches were being turned out in large numbers. While master craftsmen and shop owners could make a good living, those with less skill and fewer funds commanded far lower wages. When Moraley died in January 1762, his only claim to fame was his "adventures" in the American colonies. Yet the nascent industrial revolution had far more positive effects for some colonists. The mechanization of cloth production in England demanded vast amounts of raw material from the English countryside and the colonies. It ensured, for example, the profitability of indigo. This crop benefited many South Carolina planters, including Eliza Lucas and—after her marriage in 1744—her husband, Charles Pinckney, a successful planter himself. Still, profits from indigo could be gained only through the labor of hundreds of slaves.

Eliza Pinckney's sons became important leaders in the colony, and despite their English education and the benefits they gained through British trade, both developed a strong belief in the rights of the colonies to control their own destinies. Like many American colonists, they were spurred by the consumer revolution, geographical expansion, growing religious and ethnic diversity, and conflicts with Indian and European enemies to develop a mind-set that differed significantly from their counterparts back home. As the fortunes of colonists rose or fell with the changing dynamics of global trade and as they grappled with the claims of Indians and the growth of slavery, some reimagined their relationships not only to production and consumption, agriculture and commerce, but also to the religious and political beliefs that had sustained them for generations.

LEARNINGCurve
Check what you know.
bedfordstmartins.com/hewittlawson/LC

Chapter Review

Online Study Guide ▶ bedfordstmartins.com/hewittlawson

KEY TERMS

proprietary colonies (p. 67)
Glorious Revolution (p. 67)
Pueblo revolt (p. 70)
King William's War (p. 71)
War of the Spanish Succession (p. 71)
mercantilism (p. 76)
Middle Passage (p. 77)
seasoning (p. 78)
redemptioners (p. 81)
Stono rebellion (p. 87)

REVIEW & RELATE

1. What role did the crown play in the expansion of the English North American colonies in the second half of the seventeenth century?

2. How did the development of the Spanish and French colonies in the late seventeenth century differ from that of the English colonies?

3. How did the European wars of the late seventeenth and early eighteenth centuries impact relations between colonists and England?

4. How and why were Indians pulled into the wars between European powers fought in North America?

5. What place did North American colonists occupy in the eighteenth-century global trade network?

6. How did the British government seek to maintain control over the colonial economy and ensure that its colonies served Britain's economic and political interests?

7. What were the sources of economic inequality in North America in the early eighteenth century?

8. Under what kinds of contracts and conditions did poor people, both white and black, work?

TIMELINE OF EVENTS

1660	Monarchy restored in England
	Parliament passes first of a series of Navigation Acts to regulate colonial commerce
1660–1685	Charles II rewards his most important allies with proprietorships in North America
1672	Royal African Company chartered
1680	Pueblo revolt against Spanish rule in New Mexico
1688	Glorious Revolution
1689–1697	King William's War
1692	New colony of Massachusetts established
1700–1750	New England colonial population increases from 100,000 to 400,000
	Middle Atlantic colonial population increases from 50,000 to 250,000
1700–1808	British and Anglo-American ships transport 3 million African slaves to the Americas
1702	East and West Jersey unite into colony of New Jersey
1702–1713	War of the Spanish Succession
1704	Delaware separates from Pennsylvania
1705	Virginia passes "Negro Act" consolidating and tightening earlier slave laws
1710	North Carolina becomes fully independent of South Carolina
1711–1715	Tuscaroras lead pan-Indian war against settlers in the Carolinas
1715–1717	Yamasee War
1729	Benjamin Franklin becomes Pennsylvania's official printer
1732	Colony of Georgia established
1739	Eliza Lucas takes charge of her father's South Carolina estates
	Stono rebellion
1743	William Moraley publishes an account of his time in America
1749	Spanish settlers in Texas make peace with the Apaches

DOCUMENT PROJECT 3

The Production of Indigo

Indigo dye was a very popular commodity in seventeenth-century Europe, but it was notoriously difficult to produce and indigo plants grew only in tropical climates. Most European nations, therefore, relied on their colonies to produce indigo, with the British government even paying subsidies to indigo planters. While British colonies in the West Indies took advantage of this financial incentive, those in North America were slow to develop the product. Attempts in the early eighteenth century produced poor yields, and most planters switched to the ease and profitability of rice as an export crop.

Those who attempted to grow indigo faced many obstacles. First, indigo plants were fragile, and their cultivation required a significant capital investment, including money to purchase and clear land, create irrigation systems, and build processing vats and drying sheds. Second, the work was extremely labor intensive. It was rendered even more unpleasant, even dangerous, by the sickening fumes that emanated from fermenting indigo and attracted hordes of flies and other insects (see Document 3.7). As a result, planters would invest in indigo only if they could be assured the use of slave labor. In fact, some slaves from Africa or the West Indies brought with them prior knowledge about how to grow and process indigo.

In the early 1740s, Eliza Lucas Pinckney produced the first successful crop in South Carolina (see Document 3.6). She donated seeds to other planters in the area, and South Carolina indigo became extremely popular in Great Britain. By 1755 the colony's annual indigo exports exceeded 200,000 pounds, making it the second most exported crop behind rice. In addition, the cycle of indigo planting, harvesting, and production could be integrated with the cycles of rice cultivation, ensuring the optimum use of enslaved labor year-round (see Document 3.9). Georgia planters also grew and exported indigo, although far less than those in South Carolina (see Document 3.10).

The following documents explore the history of indigo production in the American colonies. They highlight the challenges that planters and laborers encountered and the benefits of indigo for local economies (see Documents 3.7 and 3.8). Although no slave left us a direct description of cultivating the crop, consider what these documents tell us about the role of slave labor in producing indigo.

DOCUMENT 3.6

Eliza Lucas Pinckney | Letter to Charles Cotesworth Pinckney, 1785

In the early 1740s, Eliza Lucas was looking for a cash crop to grow on her family's South Carolina plantation. Her father, then the lieutenant governor of Antigua, sent her various seeds to try, including indigo. Her first few attempts were unsuccessful, but she continued her efforts and hired an expert in indigo production from Montserrat. After marrying Charles Pinckney, Eliza expanded her cultivation of indigo to his plantations as well. In the following letter, Eliza Lucas Pinckney recalls for her son some of the difficulties she encountered in her first few attempts to produce a successful indigo crop. Among her problems was the sabotage of her crop by her hired expert, Mr. Cromwell.

September 10, 1785

My Dear Child,

You wish me to inform you what I recollect of the introducing and culture of indigo in this country. You have heard me say I was very early fond of the vegetable world, my father was pleased with it and encouraged it, he told me the turn I had for those amusements might produce something of real and public utility, if I could bring to perfection the plants of other countries which he would procure me. Accordingly when he went to the West Indies he sent me a variety of seeds, among them the indigo. I was ignorant both of the proper season for sowing it, and the soil best adapted to it. To the best of my recollection I first try'd it in March 1741, or 1742; it was destroyed (I think by a frost). The next time in April, and it was cut down by a worm; I persevered to a third planting and succeeded, and when I informed my father it bore seed and the seed ripened, he sent a man from the Island of Monserat by the name of Cromweel [Cromwell] who had been accustomed to making indigo there, and gave him high wages; he made some brick vats on my fathers plantation on Wappo Creek and then made the first indigo; it was very indifferent, and he made a great mistery of it, said he repented coming as he should ruin his own country by it, for my father had engaged him to let me see the whole process. I observed him as carefully as I could and informed Mr. Deveaux an old gentleman a neighbour of ours of the little knowledge I had gain'd and gave him notice when the indigo was to be beat; he saw and afterwards improved upon it, not withstanding the churlishness of Cromwell, who wished to deceive him, and threw in so large a quantity of lime water as to spoil the colour. In the year 1744 I married, and my father made Mr. Pinckney a present of all the indigo then upon the ground as the fruit of my industry. The whole was saved for seed, and your father gave part of it away in small quantities to a great number of people that year, the rest he planted the next year at Ashipo for seed, which he sold, as did some of the gentlemen to whom he had given it the year before; by this means there soon became plenty in the country. Your father gained all the information he could from the French prisoners brought in here, and used every other means of information, which he published in the Gazette for the information of the people at large.

The next year Mr. Cattle sent me a present of a couple of large plants of the wild indigo which he had just discovered. Experiments were afterwards made upon his sort, which proved to be good indigo, but it did not produce so large a quantity as the cultivated sort.

I am your truly affectionate mother,

Eliza Pinckney

Source: "A Letter from Eliza Lucas Pinckney, 1785," in *The Colonial South Carolina Scene: Contemporary Views, 1697–1774*, ed. H. Roy Merrens (Columbia: University of South Carolina Press, 1977), 145–46.

DOCUMENT 3.7

George Milligen-Johnston | A Description of South Carolina, 1770

Colonial officials encouraged planters to invest in indigo production by providing subsidies and assurances that it would be a lucrative venture. Harvesting and processing a successful crop, however, required skill and tremendous physical labor. In the following passage, George Milligen-Johnston, a Scottish-born physician who immigrated to South Carolina as a young man, explains the processes required to ferment and dry indigo. His description indicates some of the challenges that indigo planters faced and the work required of their slaves, though he does not state who is performing the tasks he describes.

In Carolina we generally begin to plant about the beginning of April, in the following manner: The ground being well prepared, furrows are made with a drill-plough, or hoe, two inches deep, and eighteen inches distant from each other, to receive the seed, which is sown regularly, and not very thick, after which it is covered lightly with earth. A bushel of seeds will sow four English acres. If the weather proves warm and serene, the plant will appear above ground in ten or fourteen days. After the plant appears, the ground, though not grassy, should be hoed to loosen the earth about it, which otherwise would much hinder its growth. In good seasons it grows very fast, and must all the while be kept perfectly clean of weeds. Whenever the plant is in full bloom it must be cut down, without paying any regard to its height, as its leaves are then thick and full of juice, and this commonly happens in about four months after planting. . . . When everything is ready, the weed must be cut and laid regularly in the steeper [vat] with the stalk upward, which will hasten the fermentation; then long rails must be laid the length of the vat, at eighteen inches distance from one another, and wedged down to the weed, to prevent its buoying up when the water is pumped into the steeper. For this purpose the softest water answers best, and the quantity of it necessary must be just sufficient to cover all the weed. In this situation it is left to ferment, which will begin sooner or later in proportion to the heat of the weather and the ripeness of the plant, but for the most part takes twelve or fifteen hours. After the water is loaded with the salts and substance of the weed, it must be let out of the steeper into the battery, there to be beat; in order to perform which operation, many different machines have been invented; but for this purpose any instrument that will agitate the water with great violence may be used. When the water has been violently agitated for fifteen or twenty minutes in the battery, by taking a little of the liquor up in a plate it will appear full of small grain or curdled; then you are to let in a quantity of lime-water kept in a vat for the purpose, to augment and precipitate the fæculæ [starch], still continuing to stir and beat vehemently the indigo water, till it becomes of a strong purple colour, and the grain hardly perceptible. Then it must be left to settle, which it will do in eight or ten hours. After which the water must be gently drawn out of the battery through plug-holes contrived for that purpose, so that the fæculæ may remain at the bottom of the vat. It must then be taken up, and carefully strained through a horsehair sieve, to render the indigo perfectly clean, and put into bags . . . and suspended for six hours, to drain the water out of it. After which the mouths of these bags being well fastened, it must be put into a press to be entirely freed from any remains of water, which would otherwise greatly hurt the quality of the indigo. The press commonly used for this purpose is a box of five feet in length, two and a half wide, and two deep, with holes at one end to let out the water. In this box the bags must be laid, one upon another, until it is full, upon which a plank must be laid, fitted to go within the box, and upon all a sufficient number of weights to squeeze out the water entirely by a constant and gradual pressure so that the indigo may become a fine stiff paste; which is then taken out and cut into small pieces, each about two inches square, and laid out to dry. A house made of logs must be prepared on purpose for drying it, and so constructed that it may receive all the advantages of an open and free air, without being exposed to the sun, which is very pernicious to the dye. For here indigo placed in the sun in a few hours will be burnt up to a perfect cinder. While the indigo remains in the drying house, it must be carefully turned three or four times in a day, to prevent its rotting. Flies should likewise be carefully kept from it, which at this season of the year are hatched in millions, and infest an indigo plantation like the plague. After all, great care must also be taken, that the indigo be sufficiently dry before it is packed, lest after it is headed up in barrels it should sweat, which will certainly spoil and rot it.

Source: B. R. Carroll, *Historical Collections of South Carolina* (New York: Harper and Brothers, 1836), 1:387–89.

DOCUMENT 3.8

Pamphlet on Cultivating Indigo, 1746

Promoters of indigo highlighted the profits to be gained by producing the crop, and some detailed the steps in its cultivation and the problems posed for planters. But almost none of them described the intensive labor demanded of the slaves who produced the crop or the putrid smell of the fermented plant and the swarms of flies it attracted. However, in this pamphlet, dedicated to "A Friend to Carolina," the author briefly describes the backbreaking labor required for planting and the dangers of imbibing indigo dust in the drying process.

They [the slaves] weed and cleanse the Ground where they intend to plant the Indigo-seed, five times over. They sometimes carry their Neatness to such a Pitch, that they sweep the Piece of Ground, as they do a Room. After that, they make the Holes or Pits, wherein the Seeds are to be put; for this Purpose, the Slaves . . . range themselves in the same Line . . . and going backwards, they make little Pits of the Breadth of their Hough, of the Depth of three or four Inches, at about a Foot Distance every Way, and as much as possible in a strait Line. When they are come to the End of the Ground, each furnishes himself with a little Bag of Seeds, and returning that Way they came, they put eleven or thirteen Seeds into each of the Holes. . . .

This Work is the most toilsom of any in the Manufacture of Indigo; for those who plant it, must be always stooping, without riseing up, till the planting of the whole Length of the Piece is ended; so that, when that is large, (which almost always happens) they are obliged to remain two Hours, and often more, in this Posture. . . .

[*The indigo is then soaked, fermented, and dried.*]

. . . M. Tavernier observes, in his Book, Page 242, that the Indigo Dust is so subtile [subtle], and so penetrating, that those who sift it are obliged to have their Faces covered, and drink Whey very often: And to confirm this, and make good the Penetration of the Indigo-Powder, he says, having put several Times an Egg, in the Morning, near the Sifters of Indigo, and at Night breaking it, the Inside should be all stained thro' with a blue Colour.

Source: "Observations Concerning Indigo and Cochineal" (London, 1746), 7–8, 21–22.

DOCUMENT 3.9
Laboring for Indigo, 1773

Henry Mouzon Jr. was born in 1741 on his family's South Carolina plantation. Sent to France for his education, Mouzon returned to the colonies and became an important civil engineer and surveyor. In 1771 he was commissioned to survey the boundaries of North and South Carolina. As was the custom at the time, Mouzon's map contained visual depictions of local society. This image from his map shows slaves working on a South Carolina indigo plantation.

DOCUMENT 3.10

James Habersham | Letter to Benjamin Martyn, June 13, 1751

In 1738 James Habersham accompanied the Reverend George Whitefield to Georgia, agreeing to help establish an orphanage at Bethesda. He soon became a leading merchant and by the 1750s was active in Georgia's colonial government. He was also instrumental in establishing slavery in the colony. The following selection is from a letter Habersham wrote to Benjamin Martyn, secretary to the Trustees of Georgia, in which he discusses his hopes for the production of indigo by Georgia planters.

Before the Conclusion of the late War, when Rice [was] a very low Price, the Planters in the neighbouring Province were very Sanquine in raising of Indicoe [indigo], and several made very good, which answered their Expectations in England, but most rather endeavouring to make a large Quantity, than a good Quality brought it into Disrepute, some being sold so low in England as Eight Pence per Pound, and a great deal from one to two Shillings per Pound, which struck almost a universal Damp on it; and [after] riseing in Price after the Conclusion of the Peace, most People dropt planting Indicoe, and employed their Strength in raising Rice, which is indeed a most usefull Commodity to the Planter, as their greatest Staple, as well as Fodder are produced by one Expence; and its said Indicoe very much impoverishes Land, and its certain affords nothing for the Subsistance of any living Creature about a Plantation; however I now hear several are renewing their former Industry in producing this Article, having had extraordinary Accounts of the Sale of the last in England—I don't hear of but only one of our Planters . . . who have attempted to make any this Year, and He purposes employing his few Hands (except planting Provisions for his Family) in this Produce and Silk, for which he has got a fine Quantity of young Mulberry Trees. It seems highly necessary that People should turn their Thoughts on different Cultures, and what their Genius's leads them to, and I could wish more would go upon Indicoe (as it will prevent our depending so much on the French for it) but there is no forcing them to do, what they don't see to be their Interest, however I hope the Production of this Article will in Time appear so, as well as that of Silk which now seems to engage the Attention of our Planters.

Source: *The Colonial Records of the State of Georgia, 1750–1752* (Atlanta, 1916), 26:235–36.

Interpret the Evidence

1. What seem to be the biggest challenges that indigo planters faced, and how did they overcome those challenges?

2. What advantages did indigo production have for planters and for the American colonies?

3. How would you compare the descriptions of growing indigo by Eliza Lucas Pinckney (Document 3.6), George Milligen-Johnston (Document 3.7), and the London pamphleteer (Document 3.8)? What different insights do you gain about the importance of slave labor in these three documents, and why does only the London pamphleteer mention slave labor directly?

4. On what grounds does James Habersham (Document 3.10) promote the introduction of indigo into Georgia?

5. What does the image of slaves working on an indigo plantation (Document 3.9) convey about indigo's production and about the experience of slaves? How would you compare it with the written descriptions in Documents 3.7 and 3.8?

Put It in Context

- How did the initiative of North American planters in developing new crops for export shape the development of the southern colonies and the economic relations between the colonies and Great Britain?

- How did planters respond to their vital need for more labor, and how did enslaved laborers respond to the harsh demands of cultivating cash crops like rice and indigo?

LEARNINGCurve
Check what you know.
bedfordstmartins.com/hewittlawson/LC

Gianni Dagli Orti/The Art Archive at Art Resource, NY

Private Collection/Peter Newark American Pictures/The Bridgeman Art Library

Niagara Falls, 18th century.

The New Dutch Reformed Church, New York City, 1731.

4

Religious Strife and Social Upheavals

1680–1750

Image copyright © The Metropolitan Museum of Art. Image source: Art Resource, NY

Linen embroidered with wool and silk thread, 1750s.

AMERICAN HISTORIES

In the 1730s Gilbert Tennent, a leading preacher in the American colonies, outraged more traditional ministers with his evangelical zeal. The son of a Scots-Irish clergyman, Gilbert Tennent was born in Vinecash, Ireland, in 1703 and at age fifteen moved with his family to Philadelphia. After receiving an M.A. from Yale College in 1725, Gilbert was ordained a Presbyterian minister in New Brunswick, New Jersey, with little indication of the role he would play in a major denominational schism.

Tennent entered the ministry at a critical moment, when leaders of a number of denominations had become convinced that the colonies were descending into spiritual apathy. Tennent dedicated himself to sparking a rebirth of Christian commitment, and by the mid-1730s the pastor had gained fame as a revival preacher. At the end of the decade, he journeyed through the middle colonies with Englishman George Whitefield, an Anglican preacher known for igniting powerful revivals. Then in the fall of 1740, following the death of his wife, Tennent launched his own evangelical "awakenings."

Revivals inspired thousands of religious conversions across denominations, but they also fueled conflicts within established churches. Presbyterians in Britain and America disagreed about whether only those who had had a powerful, personal conversion experience were qualified to be ministers. Tennent made his opinion clear by denouncing unconverted ministers in his sermons, a position that led to his expulsion from the Presbyterian Church in 1741. But many local churches sought converted preachers, and four years later a group of ejected pastors formed a rival synod that trained its own evangelical ministers. During these upheavals, Tennent married a widow with children and became pastor of the New Building of Philadelphia, a church founded by Whitefield supporters. But he proved too moderate for many of the more enthusiastic congregants, who left to join the Baptist Church.

While ministers debated the proper means of saving sinners, ordinary women and men searched their souls. In Pomfret, Connecticut, Sarah Grosvenor certainly feared for hers in the summer of 1742 when the unmarried nineteen-year-old realized she was pregnant. Her situation was complicated by her status in the community. She was the daughter of Leicester Grosvenor, an important local landowner and town official, and Sarah's family regularly attended Pomfret's Congregational church.

The pew next to Sarah and her family was occupied by Nathaniel Sessions and his sons, including the twenty-six-year-old Amasa, who had impregnated Sarah. Many other young women became pregnant out of wedlock in the 1740s, but families accepted the fact as long as the couple married before the child was born. In Sarah's case, however, Amasa refused to marry her and suggested instead that she have an abortion.

For centuries, women had sought to end unwanted pregnancies by using herbal potions. Although Sarah was reluctant to follow this path, Amasa insisted. When the herbs failed to induce a miscarriage, he introduced Sarah to John Hallowell, a doctor who claimed he could remove the fetus with forceps, a recently developed instrument to aid in delivery. After admitting her agonizing situation to her older sister Zerviah and her cousin Hannah, Sarah allowed Hallowell to proceed. He finally induced a miscarriage, but Sarah soon grew feverish, suffered convulsions, and died ten days later.

Apparently Sarah's and Amasa's parents were unaware of the events leading to her demise. Then in 1745, a powerful religious revival swept through the region, and Zerviah and Hannah suffered great spiritual anguish. We are not sure whether they finally confessed their part in the affair, but that year officials finally brought charges against Sessions and Hallowell for Sarah's death. At the resulting trial, Zerviah and Hannah testified about their roles and those of Sessions and Hallowell. Still, their spiritual anguish did not lead to earthly justice. Hallowell was found guilty but escaped punishment by fleeing to Rhode Island. Sessions was acquitted and remained in Pomfret, where he married and became a prosperous farmer. ●

T HE AMERICAN HISTORIES of Gilbert Tennent and Sarah Grosvenor were shaped by powerful religious forces—later called the Great Awakening—that swept through the colonies in the early eighteenth century. Those forces are best understood in the context of larger economic and political changes. Many young people became more independent of their parents and developed tighter bonds with siblings, cousins, and neighbors their own age. Towns and cities developed clearer hierarchies by class and status, which could protect wealthier individuals from being punished for their misdeeds. A double standard of sexual behavior became more entrenched as well, with women subject to greater scrutiny than men for their sexual behavior. Of course, most young women did not meet the fate of

Sarah Grosvenor. Still, pastors like Gilbert Tennent feared precisely such consequences if the colonies—growing ever larger and more diverse—did not reclaim their religious foundations.

An Ungodly Society?

The upheavals that marked the lives of Gilbert Tennent and Sarah Grosvenor were shaped in part by economic and political changes that began several decades earlier. As American colonists became more engaged in international and domestic commerce, spiritual commitments appeared to wane. In New England, Congregational ministers condemned the apparent triumph of worldly ambition over religiosity. Nonetheless, some ministers saw economic success as a reward for godly behavior even as they worried that wealth and power opened the door to sin. In the late seventeenth century, these anxieties deepened when accusations of witchcraft erupted across southern New England.

The Rise of Religious Anxieties

In 1686 the Puritan minister Samuel Sewell railed against the behavior of Boston mercantile elites, many of whom spent more time at the counting house than the house of worship. Citing examples of their depravity in his diary, including drunkenness and cursing, he claimed that such "high-handed wickedness has hardly been heard of before." Sewell was outraged as well by popular practices such as donning powdered wigs in place of God-given hair, wearing scarlet and gold jackets rather than simple black cloth, and offering toasts rather than prayers.

While Sewell spoke for many Puritans concerned with the consequences of commercial success, other religious leaders tried to meld old and new. The Reverend Cotton Mather bemoaned the declining number of colonists who participated in public fast days and their greater interest in the latest fashions than in the state of their souls. Yet he was attracted by the luxuries available to colonists and hoped to make his son "a more finished Gentleman." Mather was also fascinated by new scientific endeavors and supported inoculations for smallpox, which others viewed as challenging God's power.

Certainly news of the Glorious Revolution in England (1688) offered Puritans hope of regaining their customary authority (see chapter 3). But the outbreak of King William's War in 1689 quickly ended any notion of an easy return to peace and prosperity. Instead, continued conflicts and renewed fears of Indian attacks on rural settlements heightened the sense that Satan was at work in the region. Soon, accusations of witchcraft joined outcries against other forms of ungodly behavior.

Cries of Witchcraft

Belief in witchcraft had been widespread in Europe and England for centuries. It was part of a general belief in supernatural causes for events that could not otherwise be explained—severe storms, a suspicious fire, a rash of deaths among livestock. God sent signs through nature, but so, too, did Satan. Thus people searched babies for deformities, scheduled important events using astrological charts, and feared eclipses of the sun. When a community began to suspect witchcraft, they often pointed to individuals who challenged cultural norms. Women who were quarrelsome, eccentric, or poor were especially easy to imagine as cavorting with evil spirits and invisible demons.

Witchcraft accusations tended to be most common in times of change and uncertainty. Over the course of the seventeenth century, colonists had begun to spread into new areas seeking more land and greater economic opportunities. But expansion brought with it confrontations with Indians, exposure to new dangers, and greater vulnerability to a harsh and unforgiving environment. As the stress of expansion mounted, witchcraft accusations emerged. Some 160 individuals, mostly women, were accused of witchcraft in Massachusetts and Connecticut between 1647 and 1692, although only 15 were put to death. They were linked to ruined crops, sickened neighbors, and the death of cattle. Many of the accused were poor, childless, or disgruntled women, but widows who inherited property also came under suspicion, especially if they fought for control against male relatives and neighbors.

The social and economic complexities of witchcraft accusations are well illustrated by the most famous of American witch-hunts, the Salem witch trials of the early 1690s. In 1692 Salem confronted conflicts between long-settled farmers and newer mercantile families, political uncertainties following the Glorious Revolution, ongoing fear of threats from Indians, and local quarrels over the choice of a new minister. These tensions were brought to a head when the Reverend Samuel Parris's daughter and niece learned voodoo lore and exotic dances from the household's West Indian slave, Tituba. The daughters and servants of neighboring families also became entranced by Tituba's tales and began to tell fortunes, speak in gibberish, and contort their bodies into painful positions. When the girls were questioned about their strange behavior, they pointed not only to Tituba but also to other people in the community. They first accused an elderly female pauper and a homeless widow of bewitching them, but soon they singled out respectable churchwomen as well as a minister, a wealthy merchant, and a four-year-old child.

Within weeks, more than one hundred individuals, 80 percent of them women, stood accused of witchcraft. When the new governor, William Phips, took office in May 1692, he set up a special court to handle the cases and appointed eight Puritan leaders, including Samuel Sewell, to preside. Twenty-seven of the accused came to trial, and twenty were found guilty based on testimony from the girls and on **spectral evidence**—whereby the girls were seen writhing, shaking, and crying out in pain when they came in contact with invisible spirits sent by the accused. Nineteen people were hanged, and one was pressed to death with stones.

But when accusations reached into prominent Salem and Boston families, Governor Phips stepped in. He ended the proceedings and released the remaining suspects. In the following months, leading ministers and colonial officials condemned the use of spectral evidence, and some of the young accusers recanted their testimony. Witch-hunts in North America were small affairs compared to those in Europe, rarely occurred outside New England, and died out by 1700. Yet for those caught up in the trials, the consequences were severe.

Explore

Compare the statement of an accused woman and one minister's defense of the trials in Documents 4.1 and 4.2.

The Salem trials illuminate far more than beliefs in witchcraft, however. The trials pitted the daughters and servants of prosperous farmers against the wives and widows of recently arrived merchants. The accusers

---

DOCUMENTS 4.1 AND 4.2

The Devil's Work: Two Views

Abigail Faulkner, the daughter of a minister and the wife of a large landowner, was among those accused of witchcraft during the frenzied hysteria that occurred in Salem, Massachusetts, in 1692. Although she maintained her innocence, Faulkner was declared guilty, entirely on the basis of coerced confessions and spectral evidence. Because she was pregnant, however, her execution was postponed, and she petitioned Governor Phips to be released (Document 4.1). Faulkner was released, but only after Massachusetts officials stepped in and ended the trials. Still, the belief in witches

Explore

4.1 Petition of Abigail Faulkner, 1692

The humblee Petition of Abigall: Falkner unto his Excellencye S'r W'm Phipps knight and Govern'r of their Majestyes Dominions in America: humbly sheweth

That your poor and humble Petitioner having been this four monthes in Salem Prison and condemned to die having had no other evidences against me but the Spectre Evidences and the Confessors w'ch Confessors have lately since I was condemned owned to my selfe and others and doe still own that they wronged me and what they had said against me was false: and that they would not that I should have been put to death for a thousand worldes for they never should have enjoyed themselves againe in this world; w'ch undoubtedly I shouled have been put to death had it not pleased the Lord I had been with child. Thankes be to the Lord I know my selfe altogether Innocent & Ignorant of the crime of witchcraft w'ch is layd to my charge: as will appeare at the great day of Judgment (May it please yo'r Excellencye) my husband about five yeares a goe was taken w'th fitts w'ch did very much impaire his memory and understanding but w'th the blessing of the Lord upon my Endeavors did recover of them againe but now through greife and sorrow they are returned to him againe as bad as Ever they were: I having six children and having little or nothing to subsist on being in a manner without a head [husband] to doe any thinge for my selfe or them and being closely confined can see no otherwayes but we shall all perish Therfore may it please your Excellencye your poor and humble petition'r doe humbly begge and Implore of yo'r Excellencye to take it into yo'r pious and Judicious consideration that some speedy Course may be taken w'th me for my releasement that I and my children perish not through meanes of my close confinement here w'ch undoubtedly we shall if the Lord does not mightily prevent and yo'r poor petitioner shall for ever pray for your health and happinesse in this life and eternall felicity in the world to come.

Source: Paul Boyer and Stephen Nissenbaum, eds., *The Salem Witchcraft Papers, Verbatim Transcripts of the Legal Documents of the Salem Witchcraft Outbreak of 1692* (New York: Da Capo Press, 1977), 1:333–34.

included young women like nineteen-year-old Mercy Lewis, who was bound out as a servant when her parents were killed by Indians. Fear of attack from hostile Indians, hostile officials in England, or hostile neighbors fostered anxieties in Salem, as it did in many colonial communities. Other anxieties also haunted the accusers. A shortage of land led many New England men to seek their fortune farther west, leaving young women with few eligible

bachelors to choose from. Marriage prospects were affected as well by battles over inheritance. Thomas Putnam Jr., who housed three of the accusers, was in the midst of one such battle, which left his three sisters—the accusers' aunts—in limbo as they awaited legacies that could enhance their marriage prospects. As young women in Salem forged tight bonds in the face of such uncertainties, they turned their anger not against men, but instead

persisted. Cotton Mather, a prominent Puritan minister, defended the trials and his role in them in *Wonders of the Invisible World*, published the following year (Document 4.2). His justifications for the trials and their outcome reveal some awareness of the problems associated with the evidence used against the accused. Nonetheless, his writings indicate his belief that Satan was actively working to undermine colonial communities and that godly Christians needed to take extreme measures to save their communities.

Explore

4.2 Cotton Mather | *The Wonders of the Invisible World,* 1693

These our poor afflicted neighbours, quickly after they become infected and infested with these dæmons, arrive to a capacity of discerning those which they conceive the shapes of their troublers; and notwithstanding the great and just suspicion, that the dæmons might impose the shapes of innocent persons in their spectral exhibitions upon the sufferers (which may perhaps prove no small part of the witch-plot in the issue), yet many of the persons thus represented, being examined, several of them have been convicted of a very damnable witchcraft: yea, more than one twenty have confessed, that they have signed unto a book, which the devil show'd them, and engaged in his hellish design of bewitching, and ruining our land. We know not, at least I know not, how far the delusions of Satan may be interwoven into some

circumstances of the confessions; but one would think, all the rules of understanding humane affairs are at an end, if after so many most voluntary harmonious confessions, made by intelligent persons of all ages, in sundry towns, at several times, we must not believe the main strokes wherein those confessions all agree: especially when we have a thousand preternatural things every day before our eyes, wherein the confessors do acknowledge their concernment, and give demonstration of their being so concerned. If the devils now can strike the minds of men with any poisons of so fine a composition and operation, that scores of innocent people shall unite, in confessions of a crime, which we see actually committed, it is a thing prodigious, beyond the wonders of the former ages, and it threatens no less than a sort of a dissolution upon the world.

Source: Cotton Mather, *The Wonders of the Invisible World: Being an Account of the Tryals of Several Witches Lately Executed in New-England* (London: John Russell Smith, 1862), 15–16.

Interpret the Evidence

- On what grounds did Abigail Faulkner defend herself?
- How does Mather both defend and question the events in Salem, including the use of spectral evidence?

Put It in Context

What circumstances might have convinced innocent people to confess to witchcraft?

against older women, including respectable "goodwives" like Abigail Faulkner.

REVIEW & RELATE

What factors led to a rise in tensions within colonial communities in the early 1700s?

How did social, economic, and political tensions contribute to an increase in accusations of witchcraft?

✔ *LEARNINGCurve* bedfordstmartins.com/hewittlawson/LC

Family and Household Dynamics

Concerns about marriage, property, and inheritance were not limited to Salem or to New England. As the American colonies became more populous and the numbers of women and men more balanced, husbands gained greater control over the behavior of household members, and the legal and economic rewards available to most women declined. Colonial women with wealth, education, or special skills like midwifery or beer brewing might hold some power in their household and community. But those saddled with abusive husbands or masters quickly discovered that their rights and resources were severely limited.

Women's Changing Status

In most early American colonies, the scarcity of women and workers ensured that many white women gained economic and legal leverage. In the first decades of settlement in the Chesapeake, where women were in especially short supply and mortality was high, young women who arrived as indentured servants and completed their term might marry older men of property. If the husbands died first, widows often took control of the estate and passed on the property to their children. Even in New England, where the numbers of men and women were more balanced from the beginning, the crucial labor of wives in the early years of settlement was sometimes recognized by their control of family property after a husband's death.

By the late seventeenth century, however, as the sex ratio in the Chesapeake evened out, women lost the opportunity to marry "above their class" (Table 4.1). And across the colonies, widows lost control of family estates. Even though women still performed vital labor, the spread of indentured servitude and slavery lessened the recognition of their contributions, while in urban areas the rise of commerce highlighted their role as consumers rather than as producers. As a result, most wives and daughters of white settlers were assigned primarily domestic roles. While domestic chores involved hard physical labor, many women welcomed the change from the more arduous tasks performed by their mothers and grandmothers. Yet they also found their legal and economic rights restricted to those accorded their female counterparts in Great Britain.

According to English common law, a wife's status was defined as *feme covert*, which meant that she was legally covered over by (or hidden behind) her husband. The husband controlled his wife's labor, the house in which she lived, the property she brought into the marriage, and any wages she earned. He was also the legal guardian of their children, and through the instrument of a will he could continue to control the household after his death. In many ways, a wife's legal status was that of a child, with her husband acting in this context as her father.

With the growth and diversity of colonial towns and cities, the **patriarchal family**—a model in which fathers have absolute authority over wives, children, and servants—came to be seen as a crucial bulwark against disorder. Families with wealth were especially eager to control the behavior of their sons and daughters as they sought to build commercial and political alliances. The refusal of Amasa Sessions to marry Sarah Grosvenor, for instance, may have resulted from his belief that his father expected a better match. Although a few women escaped the worst strictures of patriarchal households, most were expected to comply with the wishes of their fathers and then their husbands. Even as widows, many found their finances and daily life shaped by a husband's will and its implementation by male executors.

TABLE 4.1   Sex Ratios in the White Population for Selected Colonies, 1624–1755

Date	Colony	White Male Population	White Female Population	Females per 100 Males
1624–1625	Virginia	873	222	25
1660	Maryland	c. 600	c. 190	32
1704	Maryland	11,026	7,136	65
1698	New York	5,066	4,677	92
1726	New Jersey	15,737	14,124	90
1755	Rhode Island	17,860	17,979	101

Explore

Read the will of a New York farmer in Document 4.3.

Working Families

For most colonial women and men, daily rounds of labor shaped their lives more powerfully than legal statutes or inheritance rights. Whatever their official status, husbands and wives depended on each other to support the family. By the early eighteenth century, many colonial writers promoted the idea of marriage as a partnership, even if the wife remained the junior partner. In 1712 Benjamin Wadsworth published his advice for *The Well-Ordered Family,* in which he urged couples to "delight in each other's company," "be helpful to each other," and "bear one another's burdens."

This concept of marriage as a partnership took practical form in communities across the colonies. In

---

DOCUMENT 4.3

Will of Edmund Titus, Oyster Bay, New York, 1754

The treatment of widows indicates the limited rights that colonial women held by the mid-eighteenth century. Wills provide detailed examples of wives' lack of control over property, even after the death of their husbands. Instead of directly inheriting land, houses, and goods, widows were often placed under the legal protection (and control) of male relatives, whose decisions would regulate their finances and daily lives. The will of New York farmer Edmund Titus shows the customary arrangements of the era.

Explore

How does Titus view the ownership of his family's property and possessions?

In what ways will Titus's wife and daughters have power over their own lives after his death?

Who is left in charge of Titus's estate, and what does this choice tell you about gender relations in mid-eighteenth-century New York?

"I, Edmund Titus, of Wheatly, in the bounds of Oyster Bay, in Queens County, yeoman, being this 5 day of the 3d month, called March, in the year 1754, in a feeble condition of body, and willing to set my house in order before my final change." I leave to my wife Sarah one of the choicest of my beds, with full furniture, and one of the choicest of my horses, and her riding saddle, and my cupboard and oval table, and my Great Bible, and all bed linnen. I will that all my lands and meadows, both divided and undivided, lying in the Town of Hempstead, be sold by my executors, and the money to go towards payment of debts. My executors are to set apart so much of my household goods and utensils of husbandry [farming] as they shall find expedient for my wife and family to keep house with, and the rest to be sold. My will and desire is that my wife is to have liberty to carry on farming for the support of herself and family so long as my wife shall think it profitable, and my executors may sell lands at discretion. My 4 daughters, Sarah, Martha, Mary, and Hannah, shall each have so much money as to be equal to what I have given to my eldest daughter, Phebe Pryer, and when my youngest daughter is of age or married, then the estate to be divided between my wife and my 5 daughters. I make my brother in law, Jacob Titus, and my cousin, Samuel Willis, of Jericho, and Thomas Seaman, of Westbury, executors.

Source: "Abstracts of Wills on File in the Surrogate's Office, City of New York. Vol. V 1754–1760," in *Collections of the New-York Historical Society for the Year 1896* (New York: New-York Historical Society, 1897), 30–31.

Put It in Context

What does Edmund Titus's will indicate about the lifestyle and the gender and generational relations within middling farm families?

towns, the wives of artisans often learned aspects of their husband's craft and assisted their husbands in a variety of ways. Given the overlap between homes and workplaces in the eighteenth century, women often cared for apprentices, journeymen, and laborers as well as their own children. Husbands meanwhile labored alongside their subordinates and represented their family's interests to the larger community. Both spouses were expected to provide models of godliness and to encourage prayer and regular church attendance among household members.

On farms, where the vast majority of colonists lived, women and men played crucial if distinct roles. In general, wives and daughters labored inside the home as well as in the surrounding yard with its kitchen garden, milk house, chicken coop, dairy, or washhouse. Husbands and sons worked the fields, kept the livestock, and managed the orchards. However, we should not imagine such farm families as self-sufficient units. Many families supplemented their own labor with that of servants, slaves, or hired field hands. And surplus crops—from corn to apples to eggs—and manufactured goods, such as cloth, sausage, or nails, were exchanged with neighbors or sold at market, creating a linked economic community of small producers.

Indeed, in the late seventeenth and early eighteenth centuries, many farm families in long-settled areas participated in a household mode of production. Men lent each other tools and draft animals and shared grazing land, while women gathered together to spin, sew, and quilt.

Farm Life

This colorful piece of needlework embroidered by Mehitable Starkey of Boston around 1760 portrays three farmers harvesting grain. A woman at the center holds up a sickle, while a man at her right cuts the wheat and a man at her left bundles it. The frontier environment is suggested by the wild game running about the field at the bottom. Image copyright © The Metropolitan Museum of Art. Image source: Art Resource, NY

Individuals with special skills like midwifery or blacksmithing assisted neighbors, adding farm produce or credit to the family ledger. Surplus corn, wheat, beef, or wool might be exchanged for sugar and tea from traveling salesmen or for an extra hand from neighbors during the harvest. One woman's cheese might be bartered for another woman's jam. A family that owned the necessary equipment might brew barley and malt into beer, while a neighbor with a loom would turn yarn into cloth. The system of exchange, managed largely through barter, allowed individual households to function even as they became more specialized in what they produced.

Reproduction and Women's Roles

Maintaining a farm required the work of both women and men, which made marriage an economic as well as a social and religious institution. In the early eighteenth century, more than 90 percent of white women married. And as mortality declined in the South and remained low in the North, most wives spent the first twenty years of marriage bearing and rearing children. By 1700 a New England wife who married at age twenty and survived to forty-five bore an average of eight children, most of whom lived to adulthood. In the Chesapeake, where mortality rates remained higher and the sex ratio still favored men, marriage and birth rates were slightly lower and infant mortality higher. Still, by the 1720s, southern white women nearly matched the reproductive rates of their northern counterparts.

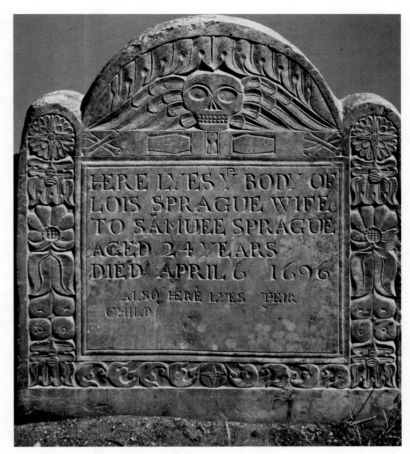

The Perils of Maternal Health

Women often died in childbirth in the late seventeenth century. In this instance, neither mother nor newborn survived. Lois Sprague, twenty-four years old, and her unnamed infant died on April 6, 1696. The skull with wings at the top of the gravestone was a typical symbol of death and heavenly ascension.   Courtesy American Antiquarian Society

Fertility rates among enslaved Africans and African Americans were much lower than those among whites in the early eighteenth century, and fewer infants survived to adulthood. It was not until the 1740s that the majority of slaves were born in the colonies rather than imported. But slowly some slave owners began to realize that encouraging reproduction made good economic sense. Still, enslaved women, most of whom worked in the fields, gained only minimal relief from their labors during pregnancy. Female slaves who lived in seaport cities were more likely to work in homes or shops, a healthier environment than the fields. But owners in already-crowded urban households often discouraged marriage and childbearing.

Immigrants from Scotland, Ireland, and Europe, many of whom lived in the Middle Atlantic colonies, often bore large numbers of children. Quakers, German Mennonites, Scots-Irish Presbyterians, and other groups flowed into New Jersey, Pennsylvania, and Delaware. Some settled in New York City and Philadelphia, but even more spread into rural areas, filling the interior of New Jersey and populating the Pennsylvania frontier. As they pushed westward, growing families replicated the experiences of early colonists, depending on their own resources and those of their immediate neighbors to carve farms and communities out of the wilderness.

Wherever they settled, mothers combined childbearing and child rearing with a great deal of other work. While some affluent families could afford wet nurses and nannies, most colonial women fended for themselves or hired temporary help for particular tasks. Mothers with babies on hip and children under foot hauled water, fed chickens, collected eggs, picked vegetables, prepared meals, spun thread, and manufactured soap and candles. Children were at constant risk of disease and injury, but physicians were rare in many rural areas. Still, farm families were spared from the overcrowding, raw sewage, and foul water that marked most urban neighborhoods.

Colonists feared the deaths of mothers as well as of infants. In 1700 roughly one out of thirty births ended in the mother's death. Women who bore six to eight children thus faced death on a regular basis. Many prayed intensely before and during labor, hoping to survive the ordeal. One minister urged pregnant women to prepare their souls, claiming, "For ought you to know your Death has entered into you."

When a mother died when her children were still young, her husband was likely to remarry soon afterward in order to maintain the family and his farm or business. Even though fathers held legal guardianship over their children, there was little doubt that child rearing, especially for young children and for daughters, was women's work. Many husbands acknowledged this role, prayed for their wife while in labor, and sought to ease her domestic burdens near the end of a pregnancy. But some women received only hostility and abuse from their husbands. In these cases, wives and mothers had few means to protect their children or themselves.

The Limits of Patriarchal Order

Sermons against fornication; ads for runaway spouses, servants, and slaves; reports of domestic violence; poems about domineering wives; petitions for divorce; and legal suits charging rape, seduction, or breach of contract—all of these make clear that ideals of patriarchal authority did not always match the reality. It is impossible to quantify precisely the frequency with which women experienced or resisted abuse at the hands of men. Still, a variety of evidence points to increasing tensions in the early eighteenth century around issues of control—by husbands over wives, fathers over children, and men over women.

Women's claims about men's misbehavior were often demeaned as gossip, but gossip could be an important weapon for those who had little chance of legal redress. In colonial communities, credit and thus trust were central to networks of exchange, so damaging a man's reputation could be a serious matter. Still, gossip was not as powerful as legal sanctions. Thus in cases in which a woman bore an illegitimate child, suffered physical and sexual abuse, or was left penniless by a husband who drank and gambled, she or her family might seek assistance from the courts.

Divorce was as rare in the colonies as it was in England. In New England, colonial law allowed for divorce, but few were granted and almost none to women before 1750. In other colonies, divorce could be obtained only by an act of the colonial assembly and was therefore confined to the wealthy and powerful. If a divorce was granted, the wife usually received "maintenance," an allowance that provided her with funds to feed and clothe herself. Yet without independent financial resources, she nearly always had to live with relatives. Custody of any children was awarded to the father because he had the economic means to support them, although infants or young girls might be assigned to

Advertising a Married Couple's Separation

Although it was difficult to obtain a legal divorce, husbands and wives sometimes abandoned each other or agreed to separate. In this November 1768 notice in the *Boston-Gazette and County Journal,* John Crede notified merchants and other creditors that he would not pay debts contracted by his wife Elizabeth, from whom he claimed to have been separated for twenty years. Library of Congress live with the mother. Some couples were granted a separation of bed and board, which meant they lived apart but could not remarry. Here, too, the wife remained dependent on her estranged husband or on family members for economic support. A quicker and cheaper means of ending an unsatisfactory marriage was to abandon one's spouse. Again wives were at a disadvantage since they had few means to support themselves or their children. Colonial divorce petitions citing desertion and newspaper ads for runaway spouses suggest that husbands fled in at least two-thirds of such cases.

In the rare instances when women did obtain a divorce, they had to bring multiple charges against their husband. Domestic violence, adultery, or abandonment alone was insufficient to gain redress. Indeed, ministers and relatives were likely to counsel abused wives to change their behavior or suffer in silence since by Scripture and law a wife was subject to her husband's will. Even evidence of brutal assaults on a wife rarely led to legal redress. Because husbands had the legal right to "correct" their wives and children and because physical punishment was widely accepted, it was difficult to distinguish between "correction" and abuse.

Single women also faced barriers in seeking legal redress. By the late seventeenth century, church and civil courts in New England gave up on coercing sexually active couples to marry. Judges, however, continued to hear complaints of seduction or breach of contract brought by the fathers of single women who were pregnant but unmarried. Had Sarah Grosvenor survived the abortion, her family could have sued Amasa Sessions on the grounds that he gained "carnal knowledge" of her through "promises of marriage." If the plaintiffs won, the result was no longer marriage, however, but financial support for the child. In 1730 the Court of Common Pleas in Concord, Massachusetts, heard testimony from Susanna Holding that a local farmer, Joseph Bright, who was accused of fathering her illegitimate child, had "ruined her Reputation and Fortunes." When Bright protested his innocence, Holding found townsmen to testify that the farmer, "in his courting of her . . . had designed to make her his Wife." In this case, the abandoned mother mobilized members of the community, including men, to uphold popular understandings of patriarchal responsibilities. Without such support, women were less likely to win their case. Still, towns were eager to make errant men support their offspring so that the children did not become a public burden. And at least in Connecticut, a growing number of women initiated civil suits from 1740 on, demanding that men face their financial and moral obligations.

Women who were raped faced even greater legal obstacles than those who were seduced and abandoned. In most colonies, rape was a capital crime, punishable by death, and all-male juries were reluctant to find men guilty. In addition, men were assumed to be the aggressor in sexual encounters. Although bawdy women were certainly a part of colonial lore, it was assumed that most women needed persuading to engage in sex. Precisely when persuasion turned to coercion was less clear. Unlikely to win and fearing humiliation in court, few women charged men with rape. Yet more did so than the records might show since judges and justices of the peace sometimes downgraded rape charges to simple assault or fornication, that is, sex outside of marriage (Table 4.2).

TABLE 4.2   Sexual Coercion Cases Downgraded in Chester County, Pennsylvania, 1731–1739

Date	Defendant/Victim	Charge on Indictment in Testimony	Charge in Docket
1731	Lawrence MacGinnis/Alice Yarnal	Assault with attempt to rape	None
1731	Thomas Culling/Martha Claypool	Assault with attempt to rape	Assault
1734	Abraham Richardson/Mary Smith	Attempted rape	Assault
1734	Thomas Beckett/Mindwell Fulfourd	Theft (testimony of attempted rape)	Theft
1734	Unknown/Christeen Pauper	(Fornication charge against Christeen)	None
1735	Daniel Patterson/Hannah Tanner	Violent assault to ravish	Assault
1736	James White/Hannah McCradle	Attempted rape/adultery	Assault
1737	Robert Mills/Catherine Parry	Rape	None
1738	John West/Isabella Gibson	Attempt to ravish/assault	Fornication
1739	Thomas Halladay/Mary Mouks	Assault with intent to ravish	None

Source: Sharon Block, *Rape and Sexual Power in Early America* (Chapel Hill: University of North Carolina Press). Data from Chester County Quarter Sessions Docket Books and File Papers, 1730–1739.

White women from respectable families had the best chance of gaining support from local authorities, courts, and neighbors when faced with seduction, breach of contract, or rape. Yet such support depended on young people confiding in their elders. By the mid-eighteenth century, however, children were seeking more control over their sexual behavior and marriage prospects, and certain behaviors—for example, sons settling in towns distant from the parental home, younger daughters marrying before their older sisters, and single women finding themselves pregnant—increased noticeably. In part, these trends were natural consequences of colonial growth and mobility. The bonds that once held families and communities together began to loosen. But in the process, young women's chances of protecting themselves against errant men diminished. Just as important, even when they faced desperate situations, young women like Sarah Grosvenor increasingly turned to sisters and friends rather than fathers or ministers.

If women in respectable families found it difficult to redress abuse from suitors or husbands, the poor and those who labored as servants or slaves had even fewer options. Slaves in particular had little hope of prevailing against brutal owners. Even servants faced tremendous obstacles in obtaining legal independence from masters or mistresses who beat or sexually assaulted them. Colonial judges and juries generally refused to declare a man who was wealthy enough to support servants guilty of criminal acts against them. Moreover, female servants and slaves were regularly depicted in popular culture as lusty and immoral, making it even less likely that they would gain the sympathy of white male judges or juries. Thus for most servants and slaves, running away was their sole hope for escape from abuse; however, if they were caught, their situation would likely worsen. Even poor whites who lived independently had little chance of addressing issues of domestic violence, seduction, or rape through the courts. For unhappy couples beyond the help or reach of the law, abandonment was no doubt the most likely option. And as the colonies grew and diversified, leaving a wife and children or an abusive husband or master behind may have become a bit easier than it was in the small and isolated communities of earlier periods.

REVIEW & RELATE

Why and how did the legal and economic status of colonial women decline between 1650 and 1750?

How did patriarchal ideals of family and community shape life and work in colonial America? What happened when men failed to live up to those ideals?

LEARNINGCurve bedfordstmartins.com/hewittlawson/LC

Diversity and Competition in Colonial Society

As the English colonies in North America expanded, divisions increased between established families living in long-settled regions—whether on rural farmsteads or in urban homesteads—and the growing population of women and men with few resources. Although most colonists still hoped to own their own land and establish themselves as farmers, artisans, or shopkeepers, fewer were likely to succeed than in the past. By 1760 half of all white men in North America were propertyless. This growing class cleavage was accompanied by increasing racial, national, and religious diversity.

Population Growth and Economic Competition

After 1700, the population grew rapidly across the colonies. In 1700 about 250,000 people lived in England's North American colonies. By 1725 that number had doubled, and fifty years later it had reached 2.5 million. Much of the increase was due to natural reproduction, but in addition nearly 250,000 immigrants and Africans arrived in the colonies between 1700 and 1750.

Because more women and children arrived than in earlier decades, higher birthrates and a more youthful population resulted. At the same time, most North American colonists enjoyed a better diet than their counterparts in Europe and had access to more abundant timber, furs, fish, and other resources. Thus colonists in the eighteenth century began living longer, with more adults surviving to watch their children and grandchildren grow up.

As the population soared, the chance for individuals to obtain land or start a business of their own diminished. Even those with land did not always thrive: Farmers living in New England where the soil was exhausted or in swampy frontier regions or in areas already claimed by Indian, French, or Spanish settlers found that owning land did not automatically lead to prosperity. In the South Carolina backcountry, a visitor in the mid-eighteenth century noted that many residents "have nought but a Gourd to drink out of, nor a Plate, Knive or Spoon, a Glass, Cup, or anything." In the Carolinas and along the Hudson River, many farmers rented land from large landowners, thus ensuring limited profits even in years of relative abundance.

In prosperous parts of Middle Atlantic colonies like Pennsylvania, many landless laborers abandoned rural life and searched for urban opportunities. They moved to Philadelphia or other towns and cities in the region, seeking jobs as dockworkers, street vendors, or servants, or as apprentices in one of the skilled trades. But newcomers found the job market flooded and the chances for advancement growing slim (Figure 4.1).

In the South, too, divisions between rich and poor became more pronounced in the early decades of the eighteenth century. Tobacco was the most valuable product in the Chesapeake, and the largest tobacco planters lived in relative luxury. Families with extensive landholdings and large numbers of slaves grew rich. They developed mercantile contacts in seaport cities on the Atlantic coast and in the Caribbean and imported luxury goods from Europe. They also began training some of their slaves as domestic workers to relieve wives and daughters of the strain of household labor.

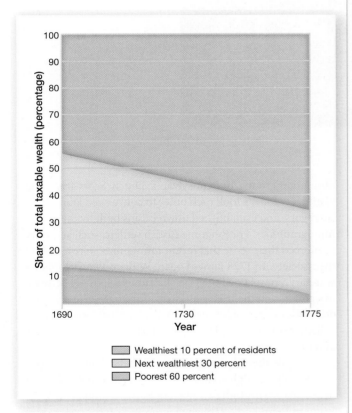

FIGURE 4.1 Wealth Inequality in Northern Cities, 1690–1775

During the eighteenth century, the wealth of merchants rose much faster than that of artisans and laborers. By 1750 the wealthiest 10 percent of the taxable residents of major northern cities owned 60 percent of the taxable wealth, while the poorest 60 percent owned less than 10 percent. This gap between rich and poor only increased over the next quarter century.

Source: Gary B. Nash, *The Urban Crucible: Social Change, Political Consciousness, and the Origins of the American Revolution* (Cambridge, MA: Harvard University Press, 1979).

The profits from tobacco allowed a larger percentage of southern than northern whites to own land. In 1750 two-thirds of white families farmed their own land in Virginia, and an even higher percentage did so in the Carolinas. Yet small farmers became increasingly dependent on large landowners, who controlled markets, political authority, and the courts. Many artisans, too, depended on wealthy planters for their livelihood, working either for them directly or for the shipping companies and merchants that relied on plantation orders. And the growing number of tenant farmers relied completely on large landowners for their sustenance.

Some southerners fared far worse. One-fifth of all white southerners owned little more than the clothes on their backs in the mid-eighteenth century. Thus those with small plots of land could easily imagine what their future would be if they suffered a bad season, a fall in tobacco prices, or the death of a father or husband. At the same time, free blacks in the South found their opportunities for landownership and economic independence increasingly curtailed, while enslaved blacks had little hope of gaining their freedom and held no property of their own.

Increasing Diversity

Population growth and economic divisions were accompanied by increased diversity in the North American colonies. Indentured servants arrived from Ireland and Scotland as well as England. Africans were imported in growing numbers and entered a more highly structured system of slavery, whether laboring on southern farms, on northern estates, or in seaport cities. In addition, free families and redemptioners from Ireland, Scotland, the German states, and Sweden came in ever-larger numbers and developed their own communities and cultural institutions. There were also more colonists who had spent time in the Caribbean before settling on the mainland, and the frontiers of British North America were filled with American Indians and French and Spanish settlers as well as European immigrants.

As the booming population increased the demand for land in the colonies, diverse groups of colonists pushed westward to find territory that either was not claimed by others or could be purchased. In Pennsylvania in the early eighteenth century, Moravian and Scots-Irish immigrants settled in areas like Shamokin that were dotted with Iroquois, Algonquian, and Siouan towns, negotiating with Indians to obtain farmland. At the same time, Delaware and Shawnee groups moved into Pennsylvania from New Jersey and the Ohio River valley and negotiated with colonists and the colonial government to establish communities for themselves. All along the Pennsylvania

Fraktur Birth and Baptismal Certificate

Frakturs were an elaborate form of German folk art and style of lettering adapted by the Pennsylvania Dutch (from *Deutsch*, meaning "German"). They were first used in North America in the 1740s to commemorate births, baptisms, weddings, and other life events. This birth and baptismal certificate for Eva Eissenhaer from around 1773 likely shows the infant's parents in their finest dress.   Used by permission of the Rare Book Department, Free Library of Philadelphia

frontier, the lines between Indian and immigrant settlements blurred, and neither Indian chiefs nor colonial authorities seemed able to demarcate clear boundaries. Still, many communities prospered in the region, with white settlers exchanging European and colonial trade goods for access to Indian-controlled orchards, waterways, and lands (Map 4.1).

In the 1720s and 1730s, however, a flood of Scots-Irish settlers arrived in Pennsylvania when bad harvests and high rents caused them to flee oppressive conditions back home. The new immigrants overwhelmed native communities that had welcomed earlier settlers. The death of William Penn in 1718 exacerbated the situation as his sons and closest advisers struggled to gain political and economic control over the colony, but this did not halt the flow of white settlers into the region. Indeed, as Indians were pushed to the margins, more diverse groups of European settlers moved into frontier territories.

Expansion and Conflict

As more and more colonists sought economic opportunities on the frontier, conflicts erupted regularly between earlier British and newer immigrant settlers as well as among immigrant groups. In Pennsylvania, Dutch, Scots-Irish, and German colonists took each other to court, sued land surveyors, and even burned down cabins built by their immigrant foes. For longtime British settlers, such acts only reinforced their sense that recent immigrants were a threat to their society. In 1728 James Logan, William Penn's longtime secretary, complained that the "Palatines [Germans] crowd in upon us and the Irish yet faster." For Logan, these difficulties were exacerbated by what he considered the "idle," "worthless," and "indigent" habits of Scots-Irish and other recent arrivals.

Despite their disparagement of others, Anglo-Americans hardly set high standards themselves, especially when negotiating with Indians. Even in Pennsylvania, where William Penn had established a reputation for (relatively) fair dealing, the desire for Indian land led to dishonesty and trickery. Colonial leaders' success in prying more territory from Indians, however, also resulted from conflicts within the Iroquois Confederacy. Hoping to assert their authority over the independent-minded Delaware Indians, Iroquois chiefs negotiated with Pennsylvania officials in the 1720s, claiming they held rights to much of the Pennsylvania territory. Colonial authorities then produced a questionable treaty supposedly drafted by

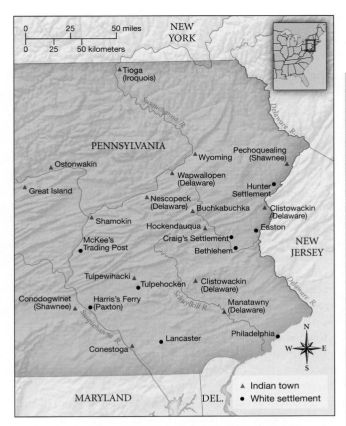

MAP 4.1 Frontier Settlements and Indian Towns in Pennsylvania, 1700–1740

German and Scots-Irish immigrants to Pennsylvania mingled with Indian settlements in the early eighteenth century as Delaware and Shawnee groups pushed east from New Jersey. In the 1720s and 1730s, however, European migration escalated dramatically in the fertile river valleys. In response, once-independent Indian tribes joined the Delaware and Shawnee nations to strengthen their position against the influx of colonists.

Source: Jane T. Merritt, *At the Crossroads: Indians & Empires on a Mid-Atlantic Frontier, 1700–1763* (Chapel Hill: University of North Carolina Press, 2003), 35.

Penn in 1686 to claim that large portions of that territory had already been ceded to settlers. James Logan "discovered" a copy of the treaty deed that allowed the English to control an area that could be walked off in a day and a half. The Iroquois finally agreed to this **Walking Purchase**, giving Pennsylvania officials the leverage they needed to persuade the Delawares to allow them to walk off the boundaries. By the time the Delawares acquiesced in the fall of 1737, Pennsylvania surveyors had already marked off the "shortest and best course," which allowed them to extend the boundaries by at least thirty miles beyond those set in the original, and questionable, treaty.

While extending colonial boundaries provided more land for hungry settlers, the rapid expansion of the colonial population ensured that conflicts would continue to erupt. Indian and British authorities repeatedly argued over treaty rights, boundary lines, and the power to cede or purchase land. Meanwhile migrants and immigrants on the Anglo-American frontier claimed land simply by taking control of it, building houses, and planting crops. This led to conflicts with local Indian communities that still considered the territory their own, with English officials who demanded legal contracts and deeds, and among immigrants who settled in the same area.

Immigrants also introduced greater religious diversity into the British colonies. But in Pennsylvania, several religious groups sought friendly relations with local Indians in order to secure land and trade goods. Some early immigrants, such as William Penn's Quakers, accepted Indian land claims and tried to pursue honest and fair negotiations. German Moravians who settled in eastern Pennsylvania in the 1740s also developed good trade relations with area tribes, shared in burial rituals, and acquiesced when the local Iroquois chief demanded the services of a blacksmith to make and repair guns. Meanwhile Scots-Irish Presbyterians settled along the western frontier and established alliances with Delaware and Shawnee groups there. These alliances were rooted less in religious principles, however, than in the hope of profiting from the fur trade when area Indians pursued new commercial partners after their former French allies became too demanding.

As tensions escalated between English and French authorities in the region, conflicts intensified among the various immigrant and religious communities and with Indians. Although colonists had disagreed many times before over policies toward native people, the dramatically different visions of Indian-settler relations rooted in distinct religious traditions magnified these differences and made it more difficult to find common ground. Growing religious diversity also created sharper boundaries within and between colonial communities. German Moravians and Scots-Irish Presbyterians in Pennsylvania established churches and schools separate from their Quaker neighbors, while Puritan New Englanders remained suspicious of Quakers as well as other Protestant sects. Moravians and other German sects also flourished in Georgia and the Carolinas, and nearly all sought to isolate themselves from the influences of other religious and ethnic groups.

Some religious groups were isolated as much by force as by choice. While most early Irish immigrants were Protestant, by the early eighteenth century more Irish Catholics began to arrive. Then in 1745 some forty thousand Scots who had supported the Catholic monarchs in England prior to the Glorious Revolution (see chapter 3) were shipped to the Carolinas after a failed rebellion. As traitors to the crown, they were doubly marginalized. But even long-settled Catholics, like those in Maryland, were looked on with suspicion by many Protestants. Jewish families also multiplied, founding the first American synagogues in Newport, Rhode Island; Savannah; Charleston; and Philadelphia. Although only a few hundred Jewish families resided in the colonies by 1750, they formed small but enduring communities in a number of seaport cities, where they developed a variety of mercantile ventures and practiced their faith.

Africans, too, brought new ideas and practices to North America. Transported by force to an unknown land, they may have found religious faith particularly important. Enslaved blacks included some Catholics from regions long held by the Portuguese and a few thousand Muslims, but many Africans embraced religions that were largely unknown to their Anglo-American masters. Even those planters who allowed Protestants to minister to their slaves discovered that many Africans and African Americans retained beliefs and rituals handed down across generations.

As religious affiliations in the colonies multiplied, they reinforced existing concerns about spiritual decline. Moreover, spiritual differences often exacerbated cleavages rooted in nationality and class. And they heightened concerns among many well-established families over the future of British culture and institutions in North America.

REVIEW & RELATE

How and why did economic inequality in the colonies increase in the first half of the eighteenth century?

How did population growth and increasing diversity contribute to conflict among and anxieties about the various groups inhabiting British North America?

 LEARNINGCurve bedfordstmartins.com/hewittlawson/LC

Religious Awakenings

Whether rooted in fears that worldly concerns were overshadowing spiritual devotion or that growing religious diversity was undermining the power of the church, Protestant ministers lamented the state of faith in eighteenth-century America. Many church leaders in Britain and the rest of Europe shared their fears. Ministers eager to address this crisis of faith—identified in the colonies as **New Light clergy**—worked together to re-energize the faithful and were initially welcomed, or at least tolerated, by more traditional **Old Light clergy**. But by the 1740s, fears that revivalists had gone too far led to a backlash. Still, for a time, the religious awakenings of the early eighteenth century created a powerful sense of common cause among Protestant colonists of different faiths, nationalities, and classes and promised a rebirth of commitment to both spiritual values and the larger society.

The Roots of the Great Awakening

The European religious landscape had grown remarkably more diverse in the two hundred years following the Reformation as Presbyterians, Lutherans, Methodists, Baptists, Quakers, and a variety of smaller sects competed for followers. Another current also had an impact: By the eighteenth century, the **Enlightenment**, a cultural movement that emphasized rational and scientific thinking over traditional religion and superstition, had taken root, particularly among elites. As North American colonies attracted settlers from new denominations and as more and more colonists were influenced by Enlightenment thought, the colonists as a whole became more accepting of religious diversity.

There were, however, countervailing forces. The German **Pietists** in particular challenged Enlightenment ideas that had influenced many Congregational and Anglican leaders in Europe and the colonies. Pietists not only decried the power of established churches but also urged individuals to follow their heart rather than their head in spiritual matters. Only by restoring intensity and emotion to worship, they believed, could spiritual life be revived. Persecuted in Germany, Pietists migrated to Great Britain and North America, where their ideas influenced Scots-Irish Presbyterians, French Huguenots, and members of the Church of England. John Wesley, the founder of Methodism and a professor of theology at Oxford University, taught Pietist ideas to his students. George Whitefield was inspired by Wesley. Like the German Pietists whose ideas he embraced, Whitefield believed that the North American colonies offered an important opportunity to implement these ideas.

But not all colonists waited for Whitefield or the German Pietists to rethink their religious commitments. By 1700 both laymen and ministers voiced growing concern with the state of colonial religion. Preachers educated in England or at the few colleges established in the colonies, like Harvard College (1636) and the College of William and Mary (1693), often emphasized learned discourse over passion. At the same time, there were too few clergy to meet the demands of the rapidly growing population in North America. Many rural parishes covered vast areas, and residents grew discouraged at the lack of ministerial attention. Meanwhile urban churches increasingly reflected the class divisions of the larger society. In many meetinghouses, wealthier members paid substantial rents to seat their families in the front pews. Small farmers and shopkeepers rented the cheaper pews in the middle of the church, while the poorest congregants—including landless laborers, servants, and slaves—sat on free benches at the very back or in the gallery. Educated clergy might impress the richest parishioners with their learned sermons, but they did little to move the spirits of the congregation at large.

In 1719 the Reverend Theodorus Freylinghuysen, a Dutch Reformed minister in New Brunswick, New Jersey, began emphasizing parishioners' emotional investment in Christ. The Reverend William Tennent arrived in neighboring Pennsylvania with his family about the same time. He despaired that Presbyterian ministers were too few in number to reach the growing population and, like Freylinghuysen, feared that their approach was too didactic and cold. Tennent soon established his own academy—one room in a log cabin—to train his four sons and other young men for the ministry. Though disparaged by Presbyterian authorities, the school attracted devout

students. A decade later, in 1734–1735, Jonathan Edwards, a Congregational minister in Northampton, Massachusetts, made clear the value of religious appeals that emphasized emotion over logic. Proclaiming that "our people do not so much need to have their heads stored [with knowledge] as to have their hearts touched," he initiated a local revival that reached hundreds of colonists.

Like Edwards, William Tennent's son Gilbert urged colonists to embrace "a true living faith in Jesus Christ." Assigned a church in New Brunswick in 1726, Tennent met Freylinghuysen, who viewed conversion as a three-step process: Individuals must be convinced of their sinful nature, experience a spiritual rebirth, and then behave piously as evidence of their conversion. Tennent embraced these measures, believing they could lance the "boil" of an unsaved heart and apply the "balsam" of grace and righteousness. Then in 1739 Tennent met Whitefield, who launched a wave of revivals that revitalized and transformed religion across the colonies.

A North-West Prospect of Nassau-Hall, with a Front View of the Presidents House, in New Jersey.

The College of New Jersey

The College of New Jersey, which later became Princeton University, developed out of the Reverend William Tennent's Log Cabin College and was established to train New Light ministers. This engraving by Henry Dawkins shows the campus in 1764 and is based on drawings by William Tennent Jr., the minister's son. © Corbis

An Outburst of Revivals

Whitefield was perfectly situated to initiate the series of revivals that scholars later called the **Great Awakening**. Gifted with a powerful voice, he understood that the expanding networks of communication and travel—developed to promote commerce—could also be used to promote religion. Advertising in newspapers and broadsides and traveling by ship, coach, and horseback, Whitefield made seven trips to the North American colonies during his career, beginning in 1738. He reached audiences from Georgia to New England to the Pennsylvania backcountry and inspired ministers in the colonies to extend his efforts.

In 1739 Whitefield launched a fifteen-month preaching tour that reached tens of thousands of colonists. Like Edwards, Freylinghuysen, and Tennent, he asked individuals to invest less in material goods and more in spiritual devotion. **See Document Project 4: Awakening Religious Tensions, page 122**. If they admitted their depraved and sinful state and truly repented, God would hear their prayers. The droughts and locusts that plagued farmers and the epidemics and fires that threatened city folk were signs of God's anger at the moral decay that marked colonial life. Whitefield danced across the platform, shouted and raged, and gestured dramatically, drawing huge crowds everywhere he went. And he went everywhere, preaching on 350 separate occasions in 1739–1740. He attracted 20,000 people to individual events, at a time when the entire city of Boston counted just 17,000 residents.

Explore

Read one follower's impression of Whitefield in Document 4.4.

Whitefield encouraged local ministers like Tennent to join him in his efforts to revitalize Protestantism. Less concerned with denominational affiliation than with core beliefs and passionate preaching, Whitefield hailed his fellow revivalists as "burning and shining lights" and embraced the vitality (and disruption) that followed in their wake. New Light ministers carried on Whitefield's work throughout the 1740s, honing their methods and appeal. They denounced urbane and educated clergy, used extemporaneous oratorical styles and outdoor venues to attract crowds, and invited colonists from all walks of life to build a common Christian community. Some became itinerant preachers, preferring the freedom to carry their message throughout the colonies to the security of a traditional pulpit.

New Light clergy brought young people to religion by the thousands. In addition, thousands of colonists who were already church members were "born again,"

recommitting themselves to their faith. Poor parishioners who felt little connection to preaching when they sat on the back benches eagerly joined the crowds at outdoor revivals, where they could stand as close to the pulpit as a rich merchant. Indeed, Tennent appealed especially to poor and single women and girls when he preached with Whitefield in Boston. Enthusiastic parishioners from a wide range of denominations formed new churches. Some, like the New Building of Philadelphia, sought interdenominational communion, but most expanded the reach of particular denominations, whether Presbyterian, Congregational, Methodist, Baptist, or Anglican.

Religious Dissension

Initially, the Great Awakening drew support from large numbers of ministers because it increased religious enthusiasm and church attendance throughout the colonies. After decades of decline, religion once again took center stage. But the early embrace by Old Light clergy diminished as revivals spread farther afield, as critiques of educated clergy became more pointed, and as New Light clergy began carrying parts of older congregations into new churches. A growing number of ministers and other colonial leaders began to fear that revivalists were providing lower-class whites, free blacks, and even women and slaves with compelling critiques of those in power. As the Great Awakening peaked in 1742, a backlash developed among more settled ministers and their congregations.

Itinerant preachers traveling across the South seemed especially threatening as they invited blacks and whites to attend revivals together and proclaimed their equality before God. Although it was rare that New Light clergy directly attacked slavery—indeed, many preached that worldly status was irrelevant to salvation—they implicitly challenged racial hierarchies. New Light preachers also gained more adherents among African Americans and American Indians than had earlier clergy by emphasizing communal singing and emotional expressions of the spirit, both of which echoed traditional African and Indian practices. Combined with their recruitment of young, poor, and female converts, such a broad appeal came to seem more dangerous than beneficial.

In the North, too, Old Light ministers and local officials began to question New Light techniques and influences. One of the most radical New Light preachers, James Davenport, attracted huge crowds when he preached in Boston in the early 1740s. Drawing thousands of colonists to Boston Common day after day, Davenport declared that the people "should drink rat poison rather than listen to corrupt, unconverted clergy." Claiming that Davenport's followers were "idle or ignorant Persons, [and] those of the Lowest

DOCUMENT 4.4

Nathan Cole | On George Whitefield Coming to Connecticut, 1740

The evangelical religious movement known as the Great Awakening swept through British North America in the 1730s and 1740s. Thousands flocked to revivals led by traveling ministers, especially George Whitefield, an evangelical Anglican whose religious ideas were shaped by the teachings of John Wesley. Whitefield launched an extensive speaking tour of the colonies in 1739. In the following passage, Nathan Cole, a Connecticut farmer, describes the crowd assembled at Wethersfield to hear Whitefield preach.

Explore

We went down in the Stream; I heard no man speak a word all the way three mile but every one pressing forward in great haste and when we got down to the old meeting house there was a great multitude; it was said to be 3 or 4000 of people assembled together. We got off from our horses and shook off the dust and the ministers were then coming to the meeting house. I turned and looked toward the great river and saw the ferry boats running swift forward and backward bringing over loads of people; the oars rowed nimble and quick. Every thing men horses and boats all seemed to be struggling for life; the land and the banks over the river looked black with people and horses all along the 12 miles. I see no man at work in his field but all seemed to be gone—when I saw Mr. Whitefield come upon the Scaffold [platform] he looked almost angelical, a young slim slender youth before some thousands of people and with a bold undaunted countenance, and my hearing how God was with him every where as he came along it solemnized my mind and put me in a trembling fear before he began to preach; for he looked as if he was clothed with authority from the great God, and a sweet solemn solemnity sat upon his brow. And my hearing him preach gave me a heart wound; by God's blessing my old foundation was broken up and I saw that my righteousness would not save me; then I was convinced of the doctrine of Election and went right to quarreling with God about it because all that I could do would not save me; and he had decreed from Eternity who should be saved and who not.

Source: George Leon Walker, *Some Aspects of the Religious Life of New England* (New York: Silver, Burnett, 1897), 91–92.

Interpret the Evidence

- How does Cole describe Whitefield, and what does this description tell us about Whitefield's popularity among the colonists?
- What messages does Cole take away from Whitefield's sermon?

Put It in Context

How might colonists' religious experience have been affected by hearing Whitefield and others preach to such a large audience?

Rank," Boston officials finally called a grand jury into session to silence him "on the charge of having said that Boston's ministers were leading the people blindfold to hell."

Although Davenport was unusual in directly linking corrupt clergy to a corrupt social order, he suggested to authorities the dangers of allowing revivalists to go unanswered. The extremes to which a few revivalists went also disturbed some New Light ministers, including Tennent, who eventually sought to reunite the Presbyterian Church

he had helped to divide. From the beginning, he had celebrated Christian love and fellowship. In 1757 Tennent wrote a sacramental sermon entitled "Love to Christ" that emphasized pietistic communion. He then worked earnestly to reunite the New York and Philadelphia synods, and his efforts succeeded a year later.

Not all churches reconciled their differences so easily, however. Revivals continued throughout the 1740s, as the awakening in Pomfret, Connecticut, indicates. Yet over time, they lessened in intensity as churches and parishioners settled back into a more ordered religious life. Moreover, the central tenets of revivalist preaching—criticisms of educated clergy, itinerancy, and extemporaneous preaching—worked against the movement's institutionalization. The Great Awakening echoed across the colonies for at least another generation, but its influence was felt more often in attitudes and practices than in institutions.

For example, when, in 1750, King George II threatened to appoint an Anglican bishop for the North American colonies, many North American ministers, both Old Light and New, resisted the appointment. Most colonists had become used to religious diversity and toleration, at least for Protestants, and had little desire to add church officials to the existing hierarchies of colonial authorities. In various ways, revivalists also highlighted the democratic tendencies in the Bible, particularly in the New Testament. Thus even as they proclaimed God's wrath against sinners, they also preached that a lack of wealth and power did not diminish a person in God's eyes. Indeed, it was often the well educated, the wealthy, and the powerful who had the most to fear from the righteous. And revivalists honed a style of passionate and popular preaching that would shape American religion and politics for centuries to come. This mode of communication had immediate application as colonists mobilized to resist what they saw as tyrannical actions by colonial officials and others in authority.

REVIEW & RELATE

What groups were most attracted to the religious revivals of the early eighteenth century? Why?

What were the legacies of the Great Awakening for American religious and social life?

✓ *LEARNINGCurve* bedfordstmartins.com/hewittlawson/LC

Political Awakenings

The effects of eighteenth-century religious awakenings rippled out from churches and revivals to influence social and political relations. In various areas of life, colonists began to question the right of those in power to impose their will on the community as a whole. Similar issues had surfaced before the revivals, but New Light clergy gave greater weight to political and social challenges, allowing colonists to view their resistance to traditional authorities as part of their larger effort to create a better and more just world.

Changing Political Relations

The settlements of the seventeenth century could be regulated with a small number of officials, and in most colonies male settlers agreed on who should rule. However, with geographical expansion, population growth, and commercial development, colonial officials—whether appointed by the crown or selected by local residents—found themselves confronted with a more complex, and more contentious, situation. Most officials were educated men who held property and had family ties to other colonial elites. Although they made decisions locally, ultimate political authority—or sovereignty—rested with the king and Parliament. The crown appointed governors, judges, and other royal officials and approved those elected locally. The king and Parliament held veto power over colonial legislation and made all decisions about war and peace. Finally, they set policy for the colonies in such critical areas as taxes and duties and military service.

While ultimate political sovereignty rested with authorities in England, the king and Parliament were too distant to have a hand in the daily workings of colonial life. Even royal officials appointed to carry out official policies often discovered that what sounded good in London was not practicable in North America. Another factor that weakened the power of royal officials was the tradition of town meetings and representative bodies, like the Virginia House of Burgesses, that had emerged within the colonies, giving colonists a stake in their own governance. Officials in England and the colonies assumed that most people would defer to those in authority, and they minimized resistance by holding public elections in which freemen cast ballots by voice vote. Not surprisingly, those with wealth and power, who often treated voters with food and drink on election days, continued to win office.

Still, evidence throughout the colonial period indicates that deference to authority was not always sufficient to maintain order. Roger Williams and Anne Hutchinson, Bacon's Rebellion, the Stono rebellion, the Salem witchcraft trials, and the radical preaching of James Davenport make clear that not everyone willingly supported their supposed superiors. These episodes of dissent and protest were widely scattered across time and place. But as the ideas disseminated by New Light clergy converged with changing political relations, resistance to established authority became more frequent and more collective.

Dissent and Protest

Protests against colonial elites multiplied from the 1730s on. The issues and methods varied, but they indicate a growing sense of political and economic autonomy among

Virginia House of Burgesses

This engraving depicts the Virginia House of Burgesses as it looked around 1740. Established in 1619, this legislature was the oldest institution of self-government in British North America. White men over the age of seventeen who owned land could vote for its members. After 1699, the House of Burgesses met in Williamsburg, where it remained throughout the colonial period.   The Granger Collection, New York

North American colonists. Some protests focused on royal officials like governors and Royal Navy captains; others focused on local authorities, merchants, or large landowners. Whatever the target of resistance, protests demonstrated colonists' belief that they had rights that were worth protecting, even against those who held legitimate authority. Just as importantly, dissenters included the poor, women, and African Americans as well as property-owning white men.

Access to reasonably priced food, especially bread, inspired regular protests in the eighteenth century. During the 1730s, the price of bread—a critical staple in colonial diets—rose despite falling wheat prices and a recession in seaport cities. Bread rioters attacked grain warehouses, bakeries, and shops, demanding more bread at lower prices. Like similar protests in Europe, these riots were often successful in the short run, though eventually prices began to rise again. They were often led by women, who were responsible for putting bread on the table; thus when grievances involved domestic or consumer issues, women felt they had the right to make their voices heard.

Public markets were another site where struggles over food led to collective protests. In 1737, for instance, Boston officials decided to construct a public market and charge fees to farmers who sold their goods there. Small farmers, who were used to selling produce from the roadside for free, clashed with officials and with larger merchants over the venture. Many Boston residents supported the protesters because the market fees would lessen competition and raise prices for consumers. When petitions to city officials had no effect, opponents demolished the market building and stalls in the middle of the night. Local authorities could find no witnesses to the crime. Like bread riots, the success of this protest was short-lived. Officials built another market; nonetheless, the protest had demonstrated the collective power of those with limited resources.

Access to land was also a critical issue in the colonies. Beginning in the 1740s, protests erupted on estates in New Jersey and along the Hudson River in New York over the leasing policies of landlords as well as the amount of land controlled by speculators. When tenants and squatters petitioned colonial officials and received no response, they took collective action. They formed groups, targeted specific landlords, and then burned barns, attacked livestock, and emptied houses and farm buildings of furniture and tools. Eventually, they established regional committees to hear grievances and formed "popular" militia companies and courts to mete out justice to those who refused to renegotiate rental agreements and prices. When landlords and colonial officials called out local militia to arrest the perpetrators, they failed to consider that militia members were often the same poor men whose protests they ignored.

In seaport cities, a frequent source of conflict was the **impressment** of colonial men who were forcibly drafted into service in the Royal Navy. British officials, caught up in nearly continuous warfare in Europe, periodically raided portside communities in order to fill their complement of sailors. Not only sailors but also dockworkers and men drinking at taverns along the shore might find themselves suddenly inducted into military service. Facing high mortality rates, bad food, rampant disease, and harsh discipline on navy ships, these impressed men were unwilling to wait while colonial officials complained to the British government about the labor shortages that impressment caused. Instead, they fought back. In 1747 in Boston, a general impressment led to three days of rioting. An observer noted that "Negros, servants, and hundreds of seamen seized a naval lieutenant, assaulted a sheriff, and put his deputy in stocks, surrounded the governor's house, and stormed the Town House (city hall)." Such riots did not end the system of impressment, but they showed that colonists would battle those who sought to deprive them of their liberty.

The religious upheavals and economic uncertainties of the 1730s and 1740s led colonists to challenge colonial and British officials with greater frequency than in earlier decades. But most protests also accentuated class lines as the poor, small farmers, and craftsmen fought against merchants, landowners, and local officials. Still, the resistance to impressment proved that colonists could mobilize across economic differences when British policies affected diverse groups of colonial subjects.

Transforming Urban Politics

The development of cross-class alliances in the 1730s and 1740s was also visible in the more formal arena of colonial politics. Beginning in the 1730s, some affluent political leaders in cities like New York and Philadelphia began to seek support from a wider constituency. In most cases, it

was conflicts among the elite that led to these appeals to the "popular" will. In 1731, for instance, a new royal charter confirmed New York City's existence as a "corporation" and stipulated the rights of freemen (residents who could vote in local elections after paying a small fee) and freeholders (individuals, whether residents or not, who held property worth £40 and could vote on that basis). A large number of artisans, shopkeepers, and laborers acquired the necessary means to vote, and shopkeepers and master craftsmen now sat alongside wealthier men on the Common Council. Yet most laboring men did not participate actively in elections until 1733, when local elites led by Lewis Morris sought to mobilize the mass of voters against royal officials, like Governor William Cosby, appointed in London.

Morris, a wealthy man and a judge, joined other colonial elites in believing that the royal officials recently appointed to govern New York were tied to ministerial corruption in England. Morris thus presented himself as the voice of the common man when he ran against a candidate approved by Cosby. On election day, hundreds of his supporters marched across the town green of Eastchester behind "two Trumpeters and 3 Violines." His opponent also mustered followers on horseback, escorted by royal officials, including the "high sheriff." But the voters chose Morris. The Morrisites then helped launch a newspaper, published by John Peter Zenger, a printer, to mobilize laborers, shopkeepers, and artisans on their behalf.

In his *New-York Weekly Journal*, Zenger leaped into the political fray, accusing Governor Cosby and his cronies of corruption, incompetence, election fraud, and tyranny. The vitriolic attacks led to Zenger's indictment for seditious libel and his imprisonment in November 1734. At the time, libel related only to whether published material undermined government authority, not whether it was true or false. But Zenger's lead attorney, Andrew Hamilton of Philadelphia, argued that truth must be recognized as a defense against charges of libel. Appealing to a jury of Zenger's peers, Hamilton proclaimed, "It is not the cause of a poor printer, nor of New York alone, which you are now trying. . . . It is the best cause. It is the cause of liberty." In response, jurors ignored the law as written and acquitted Zenger. A pamphlet about the case, authored by one of his lawyers and printed by Zenger in 1736, gained a wide readership in Britain and America.

> **Explore**
>
> See part of Hamilton's defense of Zenger in Document 4.5.

Although the decision in the Zenger case did not lead to a change in British libel laws, it did signal the willingness of colonial juries to side with fellow colonists against king and

DOCUMENT 4.5

The Trial of John Peter Zenger, 1736

In 1734 John Peter Zenger, the publisher of the *New-York Weekly Journal*, was arrested for printing articles accusing New York's colonial governor of corruption and fraud. Colonists widely protested Zenger's arrest and followed his trial closely. Zenger's attorney, Andrew Hamilton, argued that his client's accusations against the governor were true and therefore not libel. Since English common law defined libel as a statement undermining government authority, regardless of whether or not it was truthful, Hamilton's successful defense of Zenger signaled an important moment in the history of free speech and the press.

Explore

Mr. Hamilton. May it please Your Honour; I agree with Mr. Attorney, that Government is a sacred Thing, but I differ very widely from him when he would insinuate, that the just Complaints of a Number of Men, who suffer under a bad Administration, is libelling that Administration. Had I believed that to be Law, I should not have given the Court the Trouble of hearing any Thing that I could say in this cause. . . . What strange Doctrine is it, to press every Thing for Law here which is so in England? I believe we should not think it a Favour, at present at least, to establish this Practice. In England so great a Regard and Reverence is had to the Judges, that if any man strike another in Westminster Hall, while the Judges are sitting, he shall lose his Right Hand, and forfeit his Land and Goods, for so doing. And tho' the Judges here claim all the Powers and Authorities within this Government, that a Court of King's Bench has in England, yet I believe Mr. Attorney will scarcely say, that such a Punishment could be legally inflicted on a Man for committing such an Offence, in the Presence of the Judges sitting in any Court within the Province of New-York. The Reason is obvious; a Quarrel or Riot in New-York cannot possibly be attended with those dangerous Consequences that it might in Westminster Hall; nor (I hope) will it be alledged, that any Misbehaviour to a Governor in the Plantations will, or ought to be, judged of or punished, as a like Undutifulness would be to Our Sovereign.

Source: Livingston Rutherfurd, ed., *John Peter Zenger, His Press, His Trial, and a Bibliography of Zenger Imprints* (New York: Dodd, Mead, 1904), 74, 77.

Interpret the Evidence

- What do Hamilton's arguments tell us about colonial perceptions of government?
- What argument is Hamilton making about the relationship between the colonies and Britain?

Put It in Context

Why were jurors willing to ignore English common law in finding Zenger innocent and to thereby set a novel legal precedent?

Parliament, at least when it came to their right to censure public officials. Building on their success, Morris and his followers continued to gain popular support. In 1737 his son, Lewis Morris Jr., was appointed speaker of the new Assembly, and the Assembly appointed Zenger as its official printer. But soon after this victory, the group fell into disarray when royal officials offered political prizes to a few of their leaders. Indeed, the elder Morris accepted appointment as royal governor of New Jersey, after which he switched allegiances and became an advocate of executive authority. Nonetheless, the political movement he led had aroused ordinary freemen to participate in elections, and newspapers and pamphlets now readily attacked corrupt officials and threats to the rightful liberties of British colonists.

Even as freemen gained a greater voice in urban politics, they could challenge the power of economic and political leaders only when the elite were divided. Moreover, the rewards they gained sometimes served to reinforce class divisions. Thus many city workers had benefited when the elder Morris used his influence to ensure the building of the city's first permanent almshouse in 1736. The two-year project employed large numbers of artisans and laborers in a period of economic contraction. Once built, however, the almshouse became a symbol of the growing gap between rich and poor in the city and in the colonies more generally. Its existence was also used by future city councils as a justification to eliminate other forms of relief, leaving the poor in worse shape than before.

Conclusion: A Divided Society

By 1750 religious and political awakenings had transformed colonists' sense of their relation to spiritual and secular authorities. Both Gilbert Tennent and Sarah Grosvenor were caught up in these transitions. Like most colonists, they did not conceive of themselves as part of a united body politic but rather identified most deeply with their family, town, or church. Indeed, most colonists thought of themselves as English, or Scots-Irish, or German, rather than American. At best, they claimed identity as residents of Massachusetts, New Jersey, or South Carolina rather than British North America. By 1750 the diversity and divisions among colonists were greater than ever as class, racial, religious, and regional differences multiplied across the colonies. Still, by midcentury, religious leaders had gained renewed respect, colonial assemblies had wrested more autonomy from royal hands, freemen participated more avidly in political contests and debates, printers and lawyers insisted on the rights and liberties of colonists, and local communities defended those rights in a variety of ways. When military conflicts brought British officials into more direct contact with their colonial subjects in the following decade, they sought to check these trends, with dramatic consequences.

REVIEW & RELATE

How did ordinary colonists, both men and women, black and white, express their political opinions and preferences in the first half of the eighteenth century?	How did politics bring colonists together across economic lines in the first half of the eighteenth century? How did politics highlight and reinforce class divisions?

 LEARNINGCurve **bedfordstmartins.com/hewittlawson/LC**

LEARNINGCurve
Check what you know.
bedfordstmartins.com/hewittlawson/LC

Chapter Review   Online Study Guide ▶ bedfordstmartins.com/hewittlawson

KEY TERMS

spectral evidence (p. 99)
patriarchal family (p. 102)
Walking Purchase (p. 111)
New Light clergy (p. 112)
Old Light clergy (p. 112)
Enlightenment (p. 112)
Pietists (p. 112)
Great Awakening (p. 114)
impressment (p. 118)

REVIEW & RELATE

1. What factors led to a rise in tensions within colonial communities in the early 1700s?

2. How did social, economic, and political tensions contribute to an increase in accusations of witchcraft?

3. Why and how did the legal and economic status of colonial women decline between 1650 and 1750?

4. How did patriarchal ideals of family and community shape life and work in colonial America? What happened when men failed to live up to those ideals?

5. How and why did economic inequality in the colonies increase in the first half of the eighteenth century?

6. How did population growth and increasing diversity contribute to conflict among and anxieties about the various groups inhabiting British North America?

7. What groups were most attracted to the religious revivals of the early eighteenth century? Why?

8. What were the legacies of the Great Awakening for American religious and social life?

9. How did ordinary colonists, both men and women, black and white, express their political opinions and preferences in the first half of the eighteenth century?

10. How did politics bring colonists together across economic lines in the first half of the eighteenth century? How did politics highlight and reinforce class divisions?

TIMELINE OF EVENTS

1636	Harvard College established
1647–1692	Some 160 individuals tried for witchcraft in Massachusetts and Connecticut
1688	Glorious Revolution
1692	Salem witch trials
1693	College of William and Mary established
1700–1750	250,000 immigrants and Africans arrive in the colonies
1700–1775	Population of British North America grows from 250,000 to 2.5 million
1712	Benjamin Wadsworth publishes *The Well-Ordered Family*
1720–1740	Large numbers of Scots-Irish arrive in Pennsylvania
1734	John Peter Zenger acquitted of libel in New York City
1736	First permanent almshouse built in New York City
1737	Delaware Indians acquiesce to Walking Purchase
	Protest against public market in Boston
1739	George Whitefield launches fifteen-month preaching tour of the colonies
1741	Gilbert Tennent expelled from the Presbyterian Church
1742	Sarah Grosvenor dies as a result of a botched abortion
1745	40,000 Scottish Catholics shipped to the Carolinas after a failed rebellion
1747	Impressment leads to three days of rioting in Boston
1750	American colonists resist appointment of an Anglican bishop for the North American colonies
1757	George Tennent initiates effort to reunite the Presbyterian Church

Awakening Religious Tensions

The Great Awakening reveals many of the tensions present in British North America in the mid-eighteenth century. Many upper-class and educated Americans embraced the Enlightenment and deism, which viewed God as a kind of rational "watchmaker" who had set the world in motion but did not directly intervene in its daily workings. Other colonists rejected this intellectual approach in favor of the emotional connections they found in evangelical revivals. The Great Awakening challenged the authority of legally established churches and their ministers, whose congregations began flocking to New Light preachers. These "separatist" groups criticized state-sponsored churches and proposed, instead, that churches be supported through voluntary contributions by church members. Some denominations, such as the Presbyterian Church, split over the controversies engendered by the religious revivals in their midst. The Great Awakening also threw established relations of class and social status into question. Women and men, old and young, upper and lower classes, and even blacks and whites mingled together at revivals, where religious instruction blended with sometimes pointed critiques of colonial power structures. (See Document 4.4 on page 115 for one participant's description of a revival.)

At first, established clergy, known as the Old Lights, embraced the Awakening as a way to promote church attendance and religious practices. However, as revivalist preachers grew more popular, Old Lights became increasingly uneasy about their messages (Documents 4.9 and 4.10). The powerful preaching of George Whitefield of England initiated a wave of revivals across the colonies (Document 4.6). New Light minister Gilbert Tennent, for example, argued that a minister's authority rested on his conversion experience, not his education and training (Document 4.7). By 1742 the controversial actions of itinerant preachers such as James Davenport (Document 4.8) led to a backlash from Old Light ministers and their congregations. The following selections reflect the competing religious views of the Old Lights and the New Lights. As you read, consider the issues at stake in the Great Awakening. Why was the conversion experience espoused by New Lights embraced by some but rejected by others? How do these documents reveal the religious, social, and economic tensions that were a part of eighteenth-century colonial society?

DOCUMENT 4.6

George Whitefield | Marks of a True Conversion, 1739

When George Whitefield was first ordained as a minister in the Anglican Church, he began open-air preaching in parks and fields to reach those who did not regularly attend church. Whitefield used dramatic gestures, a commanding speaking voice, and personal charisma to inspire an emotional response from his audiences. In 1738 he brought his revivals to the American colonies, attracting audiences by the tens of thousands. "Marks of a True Conversion," excerpted here, was one of his most famous sermons.

If a person is what the world calls an honest moral man, if he does justly, and, what the world calls, loves a little mercy, is now and then good-natured, reacheth out his hand to the poor, receives the sacrament once or twice a year, and is outwardly sober and honest; the world looks upon such a one as a Christian indeed, and doubtless we are to judge charitably of every such person. There are many likewise who go on in a round of duties, a model of performances, that think they shall go to heaven; but if you examine them, though they have a Christ in their heads, they have no Christ in their hearts.

The Lord Jesus Christ knew this full well; he knew how desperately wicked and deceitful men's hearts were; he knew very well how many would go to hell even by the very gates of heaven, how many would climb up even to the door, and go so near as to knock at it, and yet after all be dismissed with a "Verily, I know thee not." The Lord, therefore, plainly tells us, what great change must be wrought in us, and what must be done for us, before we can have any well-grounded hopes of entering into the kingdom of heaven. Hence, he tells Nicodemus, "that unless a man be born again, and from above, and unless a man be born of water and of the Spirit, he cannot enter into the kingdom of God." And of all the solemn declarations of our Lord, I mean with respect to this, perhaps, the words of the text are one of the most solemn, "Except, (says Christ) ye be converted, and become as little children, ye shall not enter into the kingdom of heaven." The words, if you look back to the context, are plainly directed to the disciples; for we are told, "that at the same time came the disciples unto Jesus." And I think it is plain from many parts of scripture, that these disciples, to whom our Lord addressed himself at this time, were in some degree converted before. If we take the words strictly, they are applicable only to those, that have already gotten some, though but weak, faith in Christ. Our Lord means, that though they had already tasted the grace of God, yet there was so much of the old man, so much indwelling sin, and corruption, yet remaining in their hearts, that unless they were more converted than they were, unless a greater change past upon their souls, and sanctification was still carried on, they could give but very little evidence of their belonging to his kingdom, which was not to be set up in outward grandeur, as they supposed, but was to be a spiritual kingdom, begun here, but completed in the kingdom of God hereafter.

Source: George Whitefield, *Sermons on Important Subjects* (London: Henry Fisher, Son, and P. Jackson, 1832), 269.

DOCUMENT 4.7

Gilbert Tennent | The Danger of an Unconverted Ministry, 1739

Gilbert Tennent, one of the most important New Light ministers of the Great Awakening, underwent a religious conversion at the age of twenty. Tennent became convinced that all true believers—especially ministers—needed to undergo the same type of conversion experience. His attacks on the intellectualism of Old Light ministers, highlighted in his famous sermon "The Danger of an Unconverted Ministry," contributed to the division of the Presbyterian Church into the Old Lights and the New Lights. Tennent eventually tried to heal this divide and helped to reunite the New York and Philadelphia synods in 1758.

And let gracious Souls be exhorted, to express the most tender Pity over such as have none but Pharisee-Teachers; and that in the Manner before described: To which let the Example of our LORD in the Text before us, be an inducing and effectual Incitement; as well as the gracious and immense Rewards, which follow upon so generous and noble a Charity, in this and the next State.

And let those who live under the Ministry of dead Men, whether they have got the Form of Religion or not, repair to the Living, where they may be edified. Let who will, oppose it. What famous Mr. Jenner observes upon this Head, is most just, "That if there be any godly Souls, or any that desires the Salvation of his Soul, and lives under a blind Guide, he cannot go out (of his Parish) without giving very great Offence; it will be tho't a Giddiness, and a Slighting of his own Minister at home. When People came out of every Parish round about, to John [The Baptist], no Question but this bred Heart-burning against John, ay, and Ill-will against those People, that would not be satisfied with that Teaching they had in their own Synagogues." . . . But tho' your Neighbors growl against you, and reproach you for doing your Duty, in seeking your Souls Good; bear their unjust Censures with Christian Meekness, and persevere; as knowing that Suffering is the Lot of Christ's Followers, and that spiritual Benefits do infinitely overbalance all temporal Difficulties.

And O! that vacant Congregations would take due Care in the Choice of their Ministers! Here indeed they should hasten slowly. The Church of Ephesus . . . is commended, for Trying them which said they were Apostles, and were not; and for finding them Liars. Hypocrits are against all Knowing of others, and Judging, in order to hide their own Filthiness; like Thieves they flee a Search, because of their stolen Goods. But the more they endeavour to hide, the more they expose their Shame.

Source: Gilbert Tennent, *The Danger of an Unconverted Ministry Considered in a Sermon on Mark VI. 34* (Philadelphia: Benjamin Franklin, 1740).

DOCUMENT 4.8

Newspaper Report on James Davenport, 1743

James Davenport, whose popular sermons denounced Old Light clergy as corrupt and worldly, was one of the more controversial New Light ministers. Throughout the early 1740s, his behavior became increasingly erratic, culminating in a public book burning in New London, Connecticut, in 1743. After leading his audience in the burning of what he termed "immoral books," Davenport then urged them to throw luxury items and clothing into the fire. In the excitement of the event, Davenport even took off his own pants and threw them into the fire. His actions, and the ensuing controversy, caused even New Light ministers to turn against Davenport, and by 1744 he issued a public apology for his extreme behavior. The following selection from a Boston newspaper describes the incident in New London.

Multitudes hasten'd toward the Place of Rendezvous, directing themselves by the Clamor and Shouting, which together, with the ascending Smoak [smoke] bro't them to one of the most public Places in the Town, and there found these good People encompassing a Fire which they had built up in the Street, into which they were casting Numbers of Books, principally on Divinity, and those that were well-approved by Protestant Divines, viz. . . . Mr. Russel's Seven Sermons, one of Dr. Colman's, and one of Dr. Chauncy's Books, and many others. Nothing can be more astonishing than their insolent Behaviour was during the Time of their Sacrifice, as 'tis said they call'd it; whilst the Books were in the Flames they cry'd out, *Thus the Souls of the Authors of those Books, those of them that are dad [dead], are roasting in the Flames of Hell;* and that *the Fate of those surviving, would be the same, unless speedy Repentance prevented*: On the next Day they had at the same Place a second Bonfire of the like Materials, and manag'd in the same manner. Having given this fatal Stroke to Heresy, they made ready to attack Idolatry, and sought for Direction, as in the Case before; and then Mr. [Davenport] told them to look at Home first, and that they themselves were guilty of idolizing their Apparel, and should therefore divest themselves of those Things especially which were for Ornament, and let them be burnt: Some of them in the heighth of their Zeal, conferred not with Flesh and Blood, but fell to stripping and cast their Cloaths [clothes] down at their Apostle's Feet; one or two hesitated about the Matter, and were so bold as to tell him they had nothing on which they idoliz'd: He reply'd, that such and such a Thing was an Offence to him; and they must down with them. One of these being a Gentleman of Learning and Parts ventur'd to tell Mr. [Davenport], that he could scarce see how his disliking the Night-Gown that he had on his Back, should render him guilty of Idolatry. However, This carnal Reasoning avail'd nothing; strip he must, and strip he did. . . . Next Mr. [Davenport] pray'd himself; and now the Oracle spake clear to the Point, without Ambiguity, and utter'd that *the Things must be burnt*; and to confirm the Truth of the Revelation, took his wearing Breeches, and hove them with Violence into the Pile, saying, *Go you with the Rest.*

Source: "Religious Excess at New London," *The Boston Weekly Post-Boy*, March 28, 1743, in *The Great Awakening: Documents on the Revival of Religion, 1740–1745*, ed. Richard L. Bushman (New York: Institute of Early American History and Culture, 1970), 51–52.

DOCUMENT 4.9

Charles Chauncy | Letter to Scottish Minister George Wishart, 1742

As the Great Awakening gained strength, it was increasingly attacked by Old Light ministers. The leader of the Old Lights was Charles Chauncy, a Harvard-educated minister who led the First Church of Boston for more than sixty years. Chauncy detested the emotionalism of the Great Awakening, preferring instead a rationalist and intellectual approach to faith. The following selection is from a letter he wrote to a Scottish minister describing George Whitefield's reception in the colonies.

The minds of people in this part of the world had been greatly prepossessed in favor of Mr. Whitefield, from the accounts transmitted of him, from time to time, as a wonder of piety, a man of God, so as no one was like him. Accordingly, when he came to town, about two years since, he was received as though he had been an angel of God; yea, a god come down in the likeness of man. He was strangely flocked after by all sorts of persons, and much admired by the vulgar, both great and small. The ministers had him in veneration, at least in appearance, as much as the people; encouraged his preaching, attended it themselves every day in the week, and mostly twice a day. The grand subject of conversation was Mr. Whitefield, and the whole business of the town to run from place to place to hear him preach. And as he preached under such uncommon advantages, being high in the opinion of the people and having the body of the ministers hanging on his lips, he soon insinuated himself still further into the affections of multitudes, insomuch that it became dangerous to mention his name without saying something in commendation of him. . . .

I deny not but there might be here and there a person stopped from going on in a course of sin; and some might be made really better. But so far as I could judge upon the nicest observation, the town, in general, was not much mended in those things wherein a reformation was greatly needed. I could not discern myself, nor many others whom I have talked with and challenged on this head, but that there was the same pride and vanity, the same luxury and intemperance, the same lying and tricking and cheating as before this gentleman came among us.

There was certainly no remarkable difference as to these things, and 'tis vain in any to pretend there was. This I am sure of, there was raised such a spirit of bitter, censorious, uncharitable judging as was not known before; and is, wherever it reigns, a scandal to all who call themselves Christians. Nor was it ever evident to me but that the greatest friends to Mr. Whitefield were as much puffed up with conceit and pride as any of their neighbors; and as to some of them, and the more eminent too, I verily believe they possess a worse spirit than before they heard of his name, and it had been as well for them if they had never seen his face.

Source: "A Letter from a Gentleman in Boston to Mr. George Wishart," in *The Clarendon Historical Society's Reprints*, Series 1 (Edinburgh: Clarendon Historical Society, 1883), 5–7.

DOCUMENT 4.10

Dr. Squintum's Exaltation or the Reformation, 1763

The engraving shown here satirizes George Whitefield and his followers, with the title highlighting an eye disease that left Whitefield cross-eyed. The image shows an imp and "Fame" hovering on either side of Whitefield's head, while the Devil rakes in money below his podium. On the left, Whitefield's followers are seen with a prostitute, while other followers are shown shoving a mother and child and taking food from a poor woman.

Interpret the Evidence

1. How do these documents reflect debates over emotionalism and intellectualism in religious life?

2. What are Tennent's accusations against Old Light ministers in his sermon "The Danger of an Unconverted Ministry" (Document 4.7)?

3. What aspects of the Great Awakening did Old Light ministers find threatening?

4. How do Chauncy's letter (Document 4.9) and the engraving of Dr. Squintum (Document 4.10) criticize Whitefield? How are his followers portrayed?

5. Why did James Davenport (Document 4.8) encourage his followers to burn religious books by traditional ministers like Chauncy, and how did the Boston newspaper respond to the resulting bonfires?

Put It in Context

● How do these documents help explain the appeal of the Great Awakening to American colonists, particularly non-elites? What legacies—ideas or practices—remained after the revivals ended?

Private Collection/Phillips, Fine Art Auctioneers, New York, USA/The Bridgeman Art Library

The Granger Collection, New York

The death of General James Wolfe, commander of British forces against the French at Quebec in 1759.

Paul Revere's engraving of British troops in Boston Harbor, 1774.

5
Wars and Empires
1750–1774

Sketch of Boston Tea Party, 1773.

AMERICAN HISTORIES

Although best known as the founding father of the United States, George Washington grew to adulthood as a loyal British subject. He was born in 1732 to a prosperous farm family in eastern Virginia. When George's father died in 1743, he became the ward of his half-brother Lawrence and moved to Lawrence's Mount Vernon estate. Lawrence's father-in-law, William Fairfax, was an agent for Lord Fairfax, one of the chief proprietors of the colony. When George was sixteen, William hired him as an assistant to a party surveying Lord Fairfax's land on Virginia's western frontier.

Although less well educated and less well positioned than the sons of Virginia's largest planters, George shared their ambitions. As a surveyor, he journeyed west, coming into contact with Indians, both friendly and hostile, as well as other colonists seeking land. George himself began investing in western properties. But when Lawrence Washington died in 1752, twenty-year-old George suddenly became head of a large estate. He gradually expanded Mount Vernon's boundaries and increased its profitability, in part by adding to Mount Vernon's enslaved workforce. He now had the resources to speculate more heavily in western lands.

George was soon appointed an officer in the Virginia militia, and in the fall of 1753 Virginia's governor sent him to warn the French stationed near Lake Erie against encroaching on British territory in the Ohio River valley. The French commander rebuffed Washington and within six months gained control of a British post near present-day Pittsburgh, Pennsylvania, and named it Fort Duquesne. With help from Indians hostile to the French, Lieutenant Colonel Washington launched a surprise attack on Fort Duquesne in May 1754. The initial attack was successful and led the governors of Virginia and North Carolina to send in more troops under the command of the newly promoted Colonel Washington. The French then responded with a much larger force that repelled the British troops, and Washington was forced to surrender.

Colonel Washington gained valuable experience through both successful surveying expeditions and failed military ventures. As a landowner in Virginia and on the western frontier, he had also gained property to defend. Washington's fortunes and his family increased when he married the wealthy widow Martha Dandridge Custis in 1759 and became stepfather to her two children. An increasingly successful planter, Washington sought to extend Britain's North American empire westward as a way to create opportunities for an expanding population as well as a protective buffer against European and Indian foes.

Like Washington, Herman Husband hoped to improve his lot through hard work and the opportunities offered by the frontier. Born to a modest farm family in Maryland in 1724, he was swept up by the Great Awakening in the early 1740s. He became a New Light Presbyterian but later joined the Society of Friends, or Quakers. In 1754, as Washington headed to the Ohio valley, Husband explored prospects on the North Carolina frontier and decided to settle with his family at Sandy Creek.

Husband proved a successful farmer, but he denounced wealthy landowners and speculators who made it difficult for small farmers to obtain sufficient land. He also challenged established leaders in the Quaker meeting and was among a number of worshippers disowned from the Cane Creek Friends Meeting in 1764. Disputes within radical Protestant congregations were not unusual in this period as members with deep religious convictions chose the liberty of their individual conscience over church authority.

In 1766 a number of Quaker and Baptist farmers joined Husband in organizing the Sandy Creek Association. The group hoped to increase farmers' political clout as a way to combat corruption among local officials. The association disbanded after two years, but its ideas lived on in a group called the Regulation, which brought together frontier farmers who sought to "regulate" government abuse. Husband quickly emerged as one of the organization's chief spokesmen. The Regulators first tried to achieve reform through legal means. They petitioned the North Carolina Assembly and Royal Governor William Tryon, demanding legislative reforms and suing local officials for extorting labor, land, or money from poorer residents.

Husband wrote pamphlets articulating the demands of the Regulators and wielding religious principles to justify resistance to existing laws and customs. In certain ways, his ideas echoed those of colonial leaders like Governor Tryon, who had launched protests in 1765 against British efforts to impose taxes on the colonies. Tryon, however, viewed the Regulators as political foes who threatened the colony's peace and order. In 1768 he had Husband and other Regulators arrested, which confirmed the Regulators' belief that they could not receive fair treatment at the hands of colonial officials. They then turned to extralegal methods to assert their rights, such as taking over courthouses so that legal proceedings against debt-ridden farmers could not proceed. This led the Regulators into open conflict with colonial officials. •

THE AMERICAN HISTORIES of Washington and Husband were shaped by both opportunities and conflicts. Mid-eighteenth-century colonial America offered greater opportunities for social advancement and personal expression than anywhere in Europe, but the efforts of individuals to take advantage of these opportunities often led to tension and discord. The conflicts on the frontiers of Virginia, Pennsylvania, and North Carolina foreshadowed a broader struggle for land and power within the American colonies. Religious and economic as well as political discord intensified in the mid-eighteenth century as conflicts within the colonies increasingly occurred alongside challenges to

British authority. Individual men and women made difficult choices about where their loyalties lay. Whatever their grievances, most worked hard to reform systems they considered unfair or abusive before resorting to more radical means of instituting change. Some, such as Washington, became revered leaders. Others, like Husband, gained local support but were viewed by those in authority as extremists who threatened to subvert the religious, economic, and political order.

A War for Empire, 1754–1763

The war that erupted in the Ohio valley in 1754 sparked an enormous shift in political and economic relations in colonial North America. What began as a small-scale, regional conflict expanded into a brutal and lengthy global war. Known as the French and Indian War in North America and the Seven Years' War in Great Britain and Europe, the conflict led to a dramatic expansion of British territory in North America, but also to increasing demands from American colonists for more control over their own lives.

The Opening Battles

Even before Washington and his troops were defeated in July 1754, the British sought to protect the colonies against threats from the French and the Indians. To limit such threats, the British were especially interested in cementing an alliance with the powerful Iroquois Confederacy, composed of six northeastern tribes. Thus the British invited an official delegation from the Iroquois to a meeting in June 1754 in Albany, New York, with representatives from the New England colonies, New York, Pennsylvania, and Maryland. Benjamin Franklin of Philadelphia had drawn up a Plan of Union that would establish a council of representatives from the various colonial assemblies to debate issues of frontier defense, trade, and territorial expansion and to recommend terms mutually agreeable to colonists and Indians. Their deliberations were to be overseen by a president-general appointed and supported by the British crown.

The **Albany Congress** created new bonds among a small circle of colonial leaders, but it failed to establish a firmer alliance with the Iroquois or resolve problems of colonial governance. The British government worried that the proposed council would prove too powerful, undermining the authority of the royal government. At the same time, the individual colonies were unwilling to give up any of their autonomy in military, trade, and political matters to some centralized body. Moreover, excluded from Franklin's Plan of Union, the Iroquois delegates at the Albany Congress broke off talks with the British in early July. The Iroquois became more suspicious and resentful when colonial land agents and fur traders used the Albany meeting as an opportunity to make side deals with individual Indian leaders.

Yet if war was going to erupt between the British and the French, the Iroquois and other Indian tribes could not afford to have the outcome decided by imperial powers alone. For most Indians, contests among European nations for land and power offered them the best chance of survival in the eighteenth century. They gained leverage as long as various imperial powers needed their trade items, military support, and political alliances. This leverage would be far more limited if one European nation controlled most of North America.

The various Indian tribes adopted different strategies. The Delaware, Huron, Miami, and Shawnee nations, for example, allied themselves with the French, hoping that a French victory would stop the far more numerous British colonists from invading their settlements in the Ohio valley.

Join, or Die

Benjamin Franklin created the first political cartoon in American history to accompany an editorial he wrote in the *Pennsylvania Gazette* in 1754. Franklin's cartoon urged the mainland British colonies to unite politically during the French and Indian War. Legend had it that a snake could come back to life if its severed sections were attached before dusk. Library of Congress

Members of the Iroquois Confederacy, on the other hand, tried to play one power against the other, hoping to win concessions from the British in return for their military support. The Creek, Choctaw, and Cherokee nations also sought to perpetuate the existing stalemate among European powers by bargaining alternately with the British in Georgia and the Carolinas, the French in Louisiana, and the Spaniards in Florida.

Faced with incursions into their lands, some Indian tribes launched preemptive attacks on colonial settlements. Along the northern border of Massachusetts, for example, in present-day New Hampshire, Abenaki Indians attacked British settlements in August 1754, taking settlers captive and marching them north to Canada. There they traded them to the French, who later held the colonists for ransom or exchanged them for their own prisoners of war with the British.

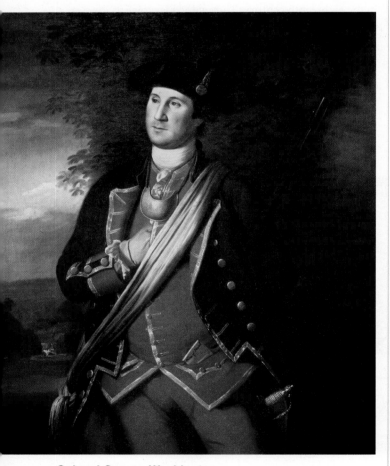

Colonel George Washington

This 1772 oil painting by Charles Willson Peale portrays George Washington as a colonel in the Virginia militia. Washington commanded this militia during the French and Indian War following the death of General Braddock. After the war, Washington prospered as a planter and land speculator.   The Granger Collection, New York

The British government soon decided it had to send additional troops to defend its American colonies against attacks from Indians and intrusions from the French. General Edward Braddock and two regiments arrived in 1755 to expel the French from Fort Duquesne. At the same time, colonial militia units were sent to battle the French and their Indian allies along the New York and New England frontiers. Colonel Washington joined Braddock as his personal aide-de-camp. Within months, however, Braddock's forces were ambushed, bludgeoned by French and Indian forces, and Braddock was killed. Washington was appointed commander of the Virginia troops, but with limited forces and meager financial support from the Virginia legislature, he had little hope of victory.

Other British forces fared little better during the next three years. Despite having far fewer colonists in North America than the British, the French had established extensive trade networks that helped them sustain a protracted war with support from numerous Indian nations. They also benefited from the help of European and Canadian soldiers as well as Irish conscripts who happily fought their British conquerors. Alternating guerrilla tactics with conventional warfare, the French captured several important forts, built a new one on Lake Champlain, and moved troops deep into British territory. The ineffectiveness of the British and colonial armies also encouraged Indian tribes along the New England and Appalachian frontiers to reclaim land from colonists. Bloody raids devastated many outlying settlements, leading to the death and capture of hundreds of Britain's colonial subjects.

A Shift to Global War

As the British faced defeat after defeat in North America, European nations began to contest imperial claims elsewhere in the world. In 1756 France and Great Britain officially declared war against each other. Eventually Austria, Russia, Sweden, most of the German states, and Spain allied with France, while Portugal and Prussia sided with Great Britain. Naval warfare erupted in the Mediterranean Sea and the Atlantic and Indian Oceans. Battles were also fought in Europe, the West Indies, India, and the Philippines. By the end of 1757, Britain and its allies had been defeated in nearly every part of the globe. The war appeared to be nearing its end, with France in control.

Then in the summer of 1757, William Pitt took charge of the British war effort and transformed the political and military landscape. A man of formidable talents and grand vision, Pitt redirected British efforts toward victory in North America, while Prussian forces held the line in Europe. Pouring more soldiers and arms into the North

American campaign along with young and ambitious officers, Pitt energized colonial and British troops.

By the summer of 1758, the tide began to turn. In July, British generals recaptured the fort at Louisburg on Cape Breton Island, a key to France's defense of Canada. Then British troops with George Washington's aid seized Fort Duquesne, which was renamed Pittsburgh. Other British forces captured Fort Frontenac along the St. Lawrence River, while Prussia defeated French, Austrian, and Russian forces in Europe and Britain gained key victories in India (Map 5.1). In 1759 General Jeffrey Amherst captured Forts Ticonderoga and Crown Point on Lake Champlain. Then General James Wolfe, with only four thousand men, attacked a much larger French force in Quebec. Despite heavy casualties, including Wolfe himself, the British won Quebec and control of Canada.

The Costs of Victory

Despite Wolfe's dramatic victory, the war dragged on in North America, Europe, India, and the West Indies for three more years. By then, however, King George III had tired of Pitt's grand, and expensive, strategy and dismissed him. He then opened peace negotiations with France and agreed to give up a number of conquered territories in order to finalize the **Peace of Paris** in 1763. Other countries

MAP 5.1 The French and Indian War, 1754–1763

Clashes between colonial militia units and French and Indian forces erupted in North America in 1754. The conflict helped launch a wider war that engulfed Europe as well as the West Indies and India. In the aftermath of this first global war, Britain gained control of present-day Canada and India, but France retained its West Indies colonies.

134 **CHAPTER 5** Wars and Empires   1750–1774

were ready to negotiate as well. To regain control of Cuba and the Philippines, Spain ceded Florida to Great Britain. Meanwhile France rewarded Spain for its support by granting it Louisiana and all French lands west of the Mississippi River. Despite these concessions, the British empire reigned supreme, regaining control of India as well as North America east of the Mississippi, all of Canada, and a number of Caribbean islands.

The wars that erupted between 1754 and 1763 reshaped European empires, transformed patterns of global trade, and initially seemed to tighten bonds between North American residents and the mother country. English colonists in North America as well as their Scottish, Irish, German, and Dutch neighbors celebrated the British victory. Yet the Peace of Paris did not resolve many of the problems that had plagued the colonies before the war, and it created new ones as well.

The incredible cost of the war raised particularly difficult problems. Over the course of the war, the national debt of Great Britain had more than doubled. At the same time, as the North American colonies grew and conflicts erupted along their frontiers, the costs of administering these colonies increased fivefold. With an empire that stretched around the globe, the British crown and Parliament were forced to consider how to pay off war debts, raise funds to administer old and new territories, and keep sufficient currency in circulation for expanding international trade. Just as important, the Peace of Paris ignored the claims of the Iroquois, Shawnee, Creek, and other Indian tribes to the territories that France and Spain turned over to Great Britain. Nor did the treaty settle contested claims among the colonies themselves over lands in the Ohio valley and elsewhere along British North America's new frontiers.

Battles and Boundaries on the Frontier

The sweeping character of the British victory encouraged thousands of colonists to move farther west, into lands once controlled by France. This exacerbated tensions on the southern and western frontiers of British North America, tensions that escalated in the final years of the war and continued long after the Peace of Paris was signed.

In late 1759, for example, the Cherokee nation, reacting to repeated incursions on their hunting grounds, dissolved their long-term trade agreement with South Carolina. Cherokee warriors attacked backcountry farms and homes, leading to counterattacks by British troops. The fighting continued into 1761, when Cherokees on the Virginia frontier launched raids on colonists there. General Jeffrey Amherst then sent 2,800 troops to invade Cherokee territory and end the conflict. The soldiers sacked fifteen villages; killed men, women, and children; and burned acres of fields.

Although British raids diminished the Cherokees' ability to mount a substantial attack, sporadic assaults on frontier settlements continued for years. These conflicts fueled resentments among backcountry settlers against political leaders in more settled regions of the colonies who rarely provided sufficient funds or soldiers for frontier defense. The raids also intensified hostility toward Indians.

A more serious conflict erupted in the Ohio valley when Indians there realized the consequences of Britain's victory in Quebec. As the British took over French forts along the Great Lakes and in the Ohio valley in 1760, they immediately antagonized local Indian groups by hunting and fishing on tribal lands and depriving villages of much-needed food. British traders also defrauded Indians on numerous occasions and ignored traditional obligations of gift giving. They refused to provide kettles, gunpowder, or weapons to the Indians and thereby caused near starvation among many tribes that depended on hunting and trade.

The harsh realities of the British regime led some Indians to seek a return to ways of life that preceded the arrival of white men. An Indian visionary named Neolin, known to the British as the Delaware Prophet, preached that Indians had been corrupted by contact with Europeans and urged them to purify themselves by returning to their ancient traditions, abandoning white ways, and reclaiming their lands. Neolin was a prophet, not a warrior, but his message inspired others, including an Ottawa leader named Pontiac.

When news arrived in early 1763 that France was about to cede all of its North American lands to Britain and Spain, Pontiac convened a council of more than four hundred Ottawa, Potawatomi, and Huron leaders near Fort Detroit. Drawing on Neolin's vision, he mobilized support to drive out the British. In May 1763, Pontiac's forces laid siege to Detroit and soon gained the support of eighteen Indian nations. They then attacked Fort Pitt and other British frontier outposts and attacked white settlements along the Virginia and Pennsylvania frontier.

> **Explore**
>
> Read part of Pontiac's speech to a council of Indian tribes in Document 5.1.

Accounts of violent encounters with Indians on the frontier circulated throughout the colonies and sparked resentment among local colonists as well as British troops. Many colonists did not bother to distinguish between friendly and hostile Indians, and General Amherst claimed that all Indians deserved extermination "for the good of

DOCUMENT 5.1

Pontiac | Speech to Ottawa, Potawatomi, and Huron Leaders, 1763

Following Great Britain's victory in the French and Indian War, many American Indian leaders grew discontented with British settlements in the former French territories. In the Great Lakes region, this dissatisfaction turned to open rebellion when Pontiac, an Ottawa leader, convened a council of local tribes who then laid siege to Fort Detroit. Pontiac's speech at that council is excerpted here. Though the siege was ultimately unsuccessful, Pontiac's uprising soon spread beyond the Detroit region and lasted until the summer of 1766, when the British negotiated a peace with Pontiac and other Indian leaders.

Explore

It is important, my brothers, that we should exterminate from our land this nation, whose only object is our death. You must be all sensible, as well as myself, that we can no longer supply our wants in the way we were accustomed to do with our Fathers the French. They [the English] sell us their goods at double the price that the French made us pay, and yet their merchandise is good for nothing; for no sooner have we bought a blanket or other thing to cover us than it is necessary to procure others against the time of departing for our wintering ground. Neither will they let us have them on credit, as our brothers the French used to do. When I visit the English chief, and inform him of the death of any of our comrades, instead of lamenting, as our brothers the French used to do, they make game of us. If I ask him for any thing for our sick, he refuses, and tells us he does not want us, from which it is apparent he seeks our death. We must therefore, in return, destroy them without delay; there is nothing to prevent us: there are but few of them, and we shall easily overcome them—why should we not attack them? Are we not men? Have I not shown you the belts [beaded belts symbolizing a treaty] I received from our Great Father the King of France? He tells us to strike—why should we not listen to his words? What do you fear? The time has arrived.

Source: Francis Parkman, *The Conspiracy of Pontiac and the Indian Wars after the Conquest of Canada* (Boston: Little, Brown, 1884), 330.

Interpret the Evidence

- How would you explain Chief Pontiac's decision to emphasize the differences between the French and the British?
- What action against the British does he advocate, and why?

Put It in Context

How does Pontiac's speech reflect larger tensions between British officials and colonists and various Indian nations?

mankind." A group of men from Paxton Creek, Pennsylvania, agreed. In December 1763, they raided families of peaceful, Christian Conestoga Indians near Lancaster, killing thirty. Protests from eastern colonists infuriated the Paxton Boys, who then marched on Philadelphia demanding protection from "savages" on the frontier.

Although violence on the frontier slowly subsided, neither side had achieved victory. Without French support, Pontiac and his followers ran out of guns and ammunition and had to retreat. About the same time, Benjamin Franklin negotiated a truce between the Paxton Boys and the Pennsylvania authorities, but it did not settle the fundamental issues over protection of western settlers. These conflicts convinced the British that the government could not endure further costly frontier clashes. So in October 1763, the crown issued a proclamation forbidding colonial settlement west of a line running down the Appalachian Mountains to create a buffer between Indians and colonists (Map 5.2).

The **Proclamation Line of 1763** denied colonists the right to settle west of the Appalachian Mountains. Instituted just months after the Peace of Paris was signed, the Proclamation Line frustrated colonists who sought the economic benefits won by a long and bloody war. Small

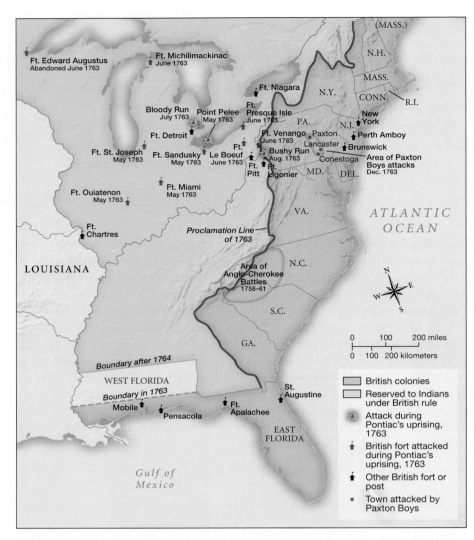

MAP 5.2   British Conflicts with Indians, 1758–1763, and the Proclamation Line
The entrance of British troops into former French territory in the Ohio River valley following the French and Indian War fueled conflicts with Indian nations. Colonists in Pennsylvania and the Carolinas also battled with Indians, including tribes who were allies or remained neutral during the war. Parliament established the Proclamation Line to limit westward expansion and thereby diminish such hostilities.

before the war, and these struggles continued into the 1760s. New clashes also occurred in the Carolinas as pioneer settlers like Herman Husband clashed with landlords and speculators there.

Even before the French and Indian War ended, the owners of large estates along the Hudson River in New York State raised rents and reduced the rights of tenants. These enormous estates had been granted in two periods. In 1629 the Dutch government established a patroon system by which men who provided fifty adult settlers to New Amsterdam were granted vast estates. Then in the early 1680s, the newly installed English governor Thomas Dongan granted lands to a select group of Englishmen. Some of these estates encompassed nearly 400 square miles, far larger than the island of Manhattan. In the early eighteenth century, the titles to some of these estates were challenged by small landowners and tenants, but even where legitimate titles existed, tenants declared a moral right to own the land they had long farmed. The manors and estates of the Hudson valley, they claimed, were more appropriate to a feudal government than to an enlightened empire.

Farmers in neighboring New

farmers, backcountry settlers, and squatters had hoped to improve their lot by acquiring rich farmlands, and wealthy land speculators like Washington had staked claims to property no longer threatened by the French or their Indian allies. Now both groups were told to stay put.

Conflicts over Land and Labor Escalate

Conflicts among colonists and with Britain were not confined to frontier regions. Land riots directed against the leasing policies of landlords and the greed of speculators had plagued New York's Hudson valley and New Jersey

Hampshire were drawn into battles over land when the king's Privy Council in London decided in 1764 that the Green Mountains belonged to New York rather than New Hampshire. Landlords along the Hudson River hoped to expand eastward into this region, but the farmers already living there claimed they had bought the land in good faith and deserved to keep it.

Following the Privy Council's decision, groups of farmers in New Hampshire waged guerrilla warfare against New York authorities, large landowners, and New York farmers who now claimed land that others had already cleared and settled. These Green Mountain Boys,

Catamount Tavern

This nineteenth-century photograph shows the Catamount Tavern, located in present-day Bennington, Vermont. Here Ethan Allen founded the Green Mountain Boys and used the tavern as a meeting place. After British authorities ruled that the Green Mountains belonged to New York rather than New Hampshire, Allen and his troops battled outsiders seeking land, a struggle that lasted through the American Revolution.   Courtesy, Vermont Historical Society

led by Ethan Allen, refused to recognize New York authorities as legitimate in the region and established their own local governments and popular courts.

Inspired by the Green Mountain Boys and earlier uprisings in New Jersey, tenants in the Hudson valley banded together in 1765–1766. Under the leadership of William Prendergast, a group of tenants calling themselves Levellers refused to pay rent and instead claimed freehold title to the land they farmed. New York tenants petitioned the colonial assembly and sought redress in a variety of ways. But landowners refused to negotiate, and Prendergast concluded that "there was no law for poor men."

In many ways, the beliefs of Allen, Prendergast, and their followers echoed those of Herman Husband and the North Carolina **Regulators**. All of these groups developed visible, well-organized networks of supporters, targeted specific landlords, sought redress first through colonial courts and assemblies, and then established popular militias and other institutions to govern themselves and to challenge those in authority. These challenges included attacks on property: Burning barns, attacking livestock, and pulling down fences were common practices among irate farmers.

Conflicts in North Carolina escalated when the colonial assembly, dominated by the eastern slaveholding elite, passed a measure to build a stately mansion for Governor Tryon with public funds. Outraged frontier farmers, many already in debt and paying high taxes, withheld their taxes, took over courthouses, and harassed corrupt local officials. By the spring of 1771, faced with what he viewed as open rebellion on his western frontier, Governor Tryon recruited a thousand militiamen to

confront the Regulators. In May, armed conflict erupted. The Regulators were defeated, and half a dozen leaders were publicly hanged. Herman Husband managed to escape and headed to the Pennsylvania frontier to establish a new homestead for his family. There, too, he met frontier farmers angered by their lack of political representation, economic opportunity, and protection from Indians.

REVIEW & RELATE

How did the French and Indian War and the subsequent peace treaty affect relations between Britain and its North American subjects?

How did the French and Indian War and the increasing power of large landowners contribute to conflict between average colonists and colonial elites?

LEARNINGCurve bedfordstmartins.com/hewittlawson/LC

Postwar British Policies and Colonial Unity

Throughout the 1750s and 1760s, ordinary colonists challenged the authority of economic and political elites to impose their will on local communities and individual residents. Before and during the French and Indian War, most of these challenges involved conflicts among colonists themselves. Yet in the decade following the war, from

1764 to 1774, common grievances against Britain united colonists on the frontier and along the eastern seaboard, allowing them to launch effective protests against the British government. British policies, like the Proclamation Line of 1763, inspired widespread dissent as poor farmers, large landowners, and speculators sought to expand westward. A second policy, impressment, by which the Royal Navy forced young colonial men into military service, also aroused anger across regions and classes. At the same time, the Great Awakening, for all the upheaval it had engendered, provided colonists with shared ideas about moral principles and new techniques for mass communication. Finally, Britain's efforts to repay its war debts by taxing colonists and its plan to continue quartering troops in North America led colonists to forge intercolonial protest movements.

Common Grievances

Like the Proclamation Line, which denied all colonists the right to settle beyond the Appalachian Mountains,

the policy of impressment affected port city residents of all classes. British agents, desperate for seamen during the extended European wars of the eighteenth century, periodically impressed sailors and other poor men from British ports around the world, including seaboard cities in North America, and from merchant ships at sea. Impressment had been employed for decades by the time of the French and Indian War. Increasingly, however, merchants and other well-to-do American colonists joined common folk in demanding an end to this practice.

Seamen and dockworkers had good reason to fight off impressment agents. Men in the Royal Navy faced low wages, bad food, harsh punishment, rampant disease, and high mortality. As the practice escalated with each new war, the efforts of British naval officers and impressment agents to capture new "recruits" met violent resistance, especially in the North American colonies. At times, whole communities joined in the battle—relatives and friends, blacks and whites, women and men.

In 1757, in the midst of the French and Indian War, some 3,000 British soldiers cordoned off New York City

Impressment by the British
This eighteenth-century engraving depicts the harsh impressment of men into the British navy. Set in England, this illustration shows that impressment was widely practiced at home. Thus the British government did not single out colonists for special mistreatment.   © Mary Evans/The Image Works

and visited "the Taverns and other houses, where sailors usually resorted." According to printer Hugh Gaines, "All kinds of Tradesmen and Negroes" were in by British press gangs. Local residents rioted along the docks the next day, but of the 800 men picked up the night before, some 400 were "retained in the service." With impressment robbing colonial seaports of much-needed laborers, some merchants and colonial officials began to petition Parliament for redress. But Parliament, seeing no reason why the British in America should avoid the fate of their counterparts in Great Britain, ignored the petitions.

In the aftermath of the French and Indian War, more serious impressment riots erupted in Boston, New York City, and Newport, Rhode Island. Increasingly, poor colonial seamen and dockworkers made common cause with owners of merchant ships and mercantile houses in protesting British policy. Colonial officials—mayors, governors, and custom agents—were caught in the middle. Some insisted on upholding the Royal Navy's right of impressment; others tried to placate both naval officers and local residents; and still others resisted what they saw as an oppressive imposition on the rights of colonists. Both those who resisted British authority and those who sought a compromise had to gain the support of the lower and middling classes to succeed.

Employers and politicians who opposed impressment gained an important advantage if they could direct the anger of colonists away from themselves and toward British officials and policies. The decision of British officials to continue quartering troops in the colonies gave local leaders another opportunity to join forces with ordinary colonists. Colonial towns and cities were required to quarter (that is, house and support) British troops even after the Peace of Paris was signed. While the troops were intended to protect the colonies against disgruntled Indians and French on their borders, they also provided reinforcements for impressment agents and surveillance over other illegal activities like smuggling and domestic manufacturing. Thus a range of issues and policies began to bind colonists together through common grievances against the British Parliament.

Forging Ties across the Colonies

The ties forged between poorer and wealthier colonists over issues of westward expansion, impressment, and quartering grew stronger in the 1760s, but they tended to be localized in seaport cities or in specific areas of the frontier. Creating bonds across the colonies required considerably more effort in a period when communication and transportation beyond local areas were limited. The Albany Congress of 1754 had been one of the first attempts to develop

intercolonial bonds, but it had not been very successful. Means had to be found to disseminate information and create a sense of common purpose if the colonists were going to persuade Parliament to take their complaints seriously. One important model for such intercolonial communication was the Great Awakening.

By the 1750s, the Great Awakening seemed to be marked more by dissension than by unity as new denominations continued to split from traditional churches. For example, in the Sandy Creek region of North Carolina, home to Herman Husband, radical Protestants formed the Separate Baptists (named for their separation from traditional Baptists) in order to proclaim a message of absolute spiritual equality. From the late 1750s through the 1770s, Separate Baptists converted thousands of small farmers, poor whites, and enslaved women and men and established churches throughout Virginia, Georgia, and the Carolinas.

Methodists, Dunkards, Moravians, and Quakers joined Separate Baptists in offering southern residents religious experiences that highlighted spiritual equality. Appealing to blacks and whites, women and men, they challenged the social order, especially in frontier regions that were beyond the reach of many established institutions. Some dissenting preachers invited slaves and free blacks to attend their services alongside local white farmers and laborers. Slaveholders and other elite southerners considered such practices outrageous and a challenge to the political as well as the social order.

Most women and men who converted to Separate Baptism, Methodism, or other forms of radical Protestantism did not link their religious conversion directly to politics. Those who did, including many Regulators, suggested that religion was a force for division rather than unity in the colonies. But as more and more ordinary colonists and colonial leaders voiced their anger at offensive British policies, evangelical techniques used to rouse the masses to salvation became important for mobilizing colonists to protest.

Thus even though the Great Awakening had spent its religious passion in most parts of North America by the 1760s, the techniques of mass communication and critiques of opulence and corruption it initiated provided emotional and practical ways of forging ties among widely dispersed colonists. Many evangelical preachers had condemned the lavish lifestyles of colonial elites and the spiritual corruption of local officials who failed to consider the needs of their less well-to-do neighbors. Now in the context of conflicts with Great Britain, colonial leaders could turn such rhetoric against new targets of resentment by painting Parliament and British officials as aristocrats with little faith and less compassion.

During the Great Awakening, preachers also honed techniques of popular appeal that proved useful in uniting colonists to voice opposition to British policies. The public sermons and mass rallies meant to inspire loyalty to a greater moral cause could all be translated into forms applicable to political protest. These techniques challenged established forms of authority, which certainly gave pause to some colonial leaders. Nonetheless, casting aside deference to king and Parliament was necessary if colonists were going to gain rights within the British empire that met the needs of elites and laborers alike. The efforts of Great Britain to assert greater control over its North American colonies provided colonial dissidents an opportunity to test out these new ways to forge intercolonial ties.

Great Britain Seeks Greater Control

Until the French and Indian War, British officials and their colonial subjects coexisted in relative harmony. Economic growth led Britain to ignore much of the smuggling and domestic manufacturing that took place in the colonies. Although the system of mercantilism (see chapter 3) assumed that the colonies supplied raw materials and the mother country manufactured goods, a bit of manufacturing for local needs did not significantly disrupt British industry. Similarly, although the king and Parliament held ultimate political sovereignty, or final authority, over the American colonies, it was easier to allow some local government control over decisions, given the communication challenges created by distance.

This pattern of **benign** (or "salutary") **neglect** led some American colonists to view themselves as more independent of British control than they really were. Impressment offers a good example. The Royal Navy had the right to impress men when needed, yet even in the midst of the French and Indian War, American colonists viewed impressment as an unwarranted infringement on their rights as British subjects. Many colonists had also begun to see smuggling, domestic manufacturing, and local self-governance as rights rather than privileges. Thus when British officials decided to assert greater control, many colonists protested.

To King George III and to Parliament, asserting control over the colonies was both right and necessary. In 1763 King George appointed George Grenville to lead the British government. As prime minister and chancellor of the Exchequer, Grenville faced an economic depression in England, rebellious farmers opposed to a new tax on domestic cider, and growing numbers of unemployed soldiers returning from the war. He believed that regaining political and economic control in the colonies abroad could help resolve these crises at home.

Eighteenth-century wars, especially the French and Indian War, cost a fortune. British subjects in England paid taxes to help offset the nation's debts, even though few of them benefited as directly from the British victory as did their counterparts in the American colonies. The colonies would cost the British treasury more if the crown could not control colonists' movement into Indian territories, limit smuggling and domestic manufacturing, and house British troops in the colonies cheaply. With more British troops and officials stationed in or visiting the colonies during the French and Indian War, they had greater opportunities to observe colonial life. Many of these observers voiced concern about the extent of criminality in the colonies and the rebellious spirit that existed among many servants, seamen, frontiersmen, tenants, and even women and slaves. Others feared that the religious enthusiasm of the Great Awakening had nurtured disdain for established authority among the colonists. Clearly it was time to impose a true imperial order.

To establish order, Parliament launched a three-prong program. First, it sought stricter enforcement of existing laws and established a Board of Trade to centralize policies and ensure their implementation. The **Navigation Acts**, which prohibited smuggling, established guidelines for legal commerce, and set duties on trade items, were the most important laws to be enforced. Second, Parliament extended wartime policies into peacetime. For example, the Quartering Act of 1765 ensured that British troops would remain in the colonies to enforce imperial policy. Colonial governments were expected to support them by allowing them to use vacant buildings and providing them with food and supplies.

The third part of Grenville's colonial program was the most important. It called for the passage of new laws to raise funds and reestablish the sovereignty of British rule. The first revenue act passed by Parliament was the American Duties Act of 1764, known as the **Sugar Act**. It imposed an **import duty**, or tax, on sugar, coffee, wines, and other luxury items. The act also reduced the import tax on foreign molasses but insisted that the duty be collected, a shock to the many colonial merchants and rum distillers who relied on cheap molasses smuggled in from the French and Spanish Caribbean. The crackdown on smuggling increased the power of customs officers and established the first vice-admiralty courts in North America to ensure that the Sugar Act raised money for the crown. That same year, Parliament passed the Currency Act, which prohibited colonial assemblies from printing paper money or bills of credit. Taken together, these provisions meant that colonists would pay more money into the British treasury even as the supply of money (and illegal goods) diminished in the colonies.

294 SAMUEL A. OTIS

Has juſt imported, and is determined to ſell at the loweſt
Advance, at Store No. 5. South Side of the Town-
Dock, by Wholeſale and Retail,

CHoice Jamaica Sugars by the Hogſhead, Barrel, or ſingle C.wt.	3-4, ⅞ and yard wide Linnens
Weſt-India and New-England-Rum.	Iriſh Linnens
Cotton Wool	Cotton Checks
Pepper	Pins of all Numbers
Pipes Wool Cards	Gun Powder
Spices of all Kinds	Ticklinburgs & Oznabrigs
Ruſſia and Ravens Duck	Kilmarnock Caps
Codlines	Belladine Sewing Silk
Junk	London Scythes
Frying Pans	Seeming Twine——&c.
Iron Pots and Kettles.	Cotton Cards
White Beans	Roll Brimſtone
	Copperas
	Allum

✕✕✕✕✕✕✕✕✕✕✕✕✕✕✕✕✕✕✕✕✕✕✕

Beſt Sperma Ceti Candles,

Warranted Pure,

MADE AND SOLD by JOHN LANGDON in
Fleet-Street, above HANCOCK's Wharf, near
the Old North Meeting Houſe. He alſo ſells the beſt
Refin'd Sperma Ceti Oil by the Barrel. Beſt Tal-
low Candles mould and dipp'd, and Bayberry Wax
Candles. ALL as low as they can be had at any
Place in Town.

※✕✕✕✕✕✕✕✕✕✕✕✕✕✕✕✕✕✕✕✕✕

To be Sold this Fall or next Spring.

A collection
of an Hundred of the
beſt Sorts of young
Grafted and Inocula-
ted Engliſh Fruit
Trees—of Apples—
Pears-Plumbs—Cher-
ries—Peaches—Apri-
cots—Nectons—Quin-
ces—Lime-Trees——

Engliſh Elms—and Mulberry Trees for Silk Worms——
Grape Vines of all Sorts—Red and White Dutch Cur-
rant Buſhes—Engliſh Gooſeberry Buſhes of all Sorts—
Aſparagus Plants of the large Early Sort—and Box for
Edgings of Walks—Alſo, Garlick—Shalots—and Horſe
Radiſh 5ſ. Old Tenor a Pound.—All ſorts of Dried
Sweet Herbs.

N. B. Garden Seeds ſaved here moſt ſuitable for the
Weſt-Indies than any Imported, and warranted Good, &c.
all at the very loweſt Price for Caſh, &c.—By William
Davidſon, Gardiner, in Seven-Star Lane, Boſton.

TO BE SOLD,

By Joſeph Dennie,

In Union-Street, oppoſite Mr. James Jackſon's,

BOHEA TEA by the Cheſt or Hundred, Nutmegs,
Pepper by the Bag or Hundred.

✕✕✕✕✕✕✕✕✕✕✕✕✕✕✕✕✕✕✕✕✕✕✕

Boston Advertisements

Advertisements from the *Boston Gazette and Country Journal* show the array of consumer goods brought in to Boston Harbor. Among the items listed were rum, tea, and English cloth, all of which were subject to import duties and trade restrictions. As boycotts developed in the colonies, Bostonians would have to choose which of these items to continue buying.   Courtesy of the Massachusetts Historical Society

Some colonial leaders protested the Sugar Act through speeches, pamphlets, and petitions, and Massachusetts established a **committee of correspondence** to circulate concerns to leaders in other colonies. However, dissent remained disorganized and ineffective. Nonetheless, the passage of the Sugar and Currency Acts caused anxiety among many colonists, which was heightened by passage of the Quartering Act the next year. Colonial responses to these developments marked the first steps in an escalating conflict between British officials and their colonial subjects.

REVIEW & RELATE

How did Britain's postwar policies lead to the emergence of unified colonial protests?

Why did British policymakers believe they were justified in seeking to gain greater control over Britain's North American colonies?

✔ *LEARNINGCurve* bedfordstmartins.com/hewittlawson/LC

Resistance to Britain Intensifies

Over the next decade, between 1764 and 1774, the British Parliament sought to extend its political and economic control over the American colonies, and the colonists periodically resisted. With each instance of resistance, Parliament demanded further submission to royal authority. With each demand for submission, colonists responded with greater assertions of their rights and autonomy. Yet no one—neither colonists nor British officials—could have imagined in 1764, or even in 1774, that a revolution was in the making.

The Stamp Act Inspires Coordinated Resistance

Grenville decided that his next step would be to impose a stamp tax on the colonies similar to that long used in England. The stamp tax required that a revenue stamp be affixed to all transactions involving paper items, from newspapers and contracts to playing cards and diplomas. Grenville announced his plans in 1764, a full year before Parliament enacted the **Stamp Act** in the spring of 1765. The tax was to be collected by colonists appointed for the purpose, and the money was to be spent within the colonies at the direction of Parliament for "defending, protecting and securing the colonies." To Grenville and a majority in Parliament, the Stamp Act seemed completely fair. After all,

Englishmen paid on average 26 shillings in tax annually, while Bostonians averaged just 1 shilling. Moreover, the act was purposely written to benefit the American colonies.

The colonists viewed it in a more threatening light. The Stamp Act differed from earlier parliamentary laws in three important ways. First, by the time of its passage, the colonies were experiencing rising unemployment, falling wages, and a downturn in trade. All of these developments were exacerbated by the Sugar, Currency, and Quartering Acts passed by Parliament the previous year. Indeed, in cities like Boston, British soldiers often competed with colonists for scarce jobs in order to supplement their low wages. Second, critics viewed the Stamp Act as an attempt to control the *internal* affairs of the colonies. It was not an indirect tax on trade, paid by importers and exporters, but a direct tax on daily business: getting a marriage certificate, selling land, and publishing or buying a newspaper or an almanac. Third, such a direct intervention in the economic affairs of the colonies unleashed the concerns of leading colonial officials, merchants, lawyers, shopkeepers, and ministers that Parliament was taxing colonists who had no representation in its debates and decisions. Their arguments resonated with ordinary women and men, who were affected far more by the stamp tax than by an import duty on sugar, molasses, or wine.

By announcing the Stamp Act a year before its passage, Grenville assured that colonists had plenty of time to organize their opposition. In New York City, Boston, and other cities, merchants, traders, and artisans formed groups dedicated to the repeal of the Stamp Act. Soon Sons of Liberty, Daughters of Liberty, Sons of Neptune, Vox Populi, and similar organizations emerged to challenge the imposition of the Stamp Act. Even before the act was implemented, angry mobs throughout the colonies attacked stamp distributors. Some were beaten, others tarred and feathered, and all were forced to take an oath never to sell stamps again.

Colonists lodged more formal protests with the British government as well. The Virginia House of Burgesses, led by Patrick Henry, acted first. It passed five resolutions, which it sent to Parliament, denouncing taxation without representation. The Virginia Resolves were reprinted in many colonial newspapers and repeated by orators to eager audiences in Massachusetts and elsewhere. At the same time, the Massachusetts House adopted a circular letter—a written protest circulated to the other colonial assemblies—calling for a congress to be held in New York City in October 1765 to consider the threat posed by the Stamp Act.

In the meantime, popular protests multiplied. The protests turned violent in Boston, where **Sons of Liberty** leaders like Samuel Adams organized mass demonstrations. Adams modeled his oratory on that of itinerant preachers,

but with a political twist. Sons of Liberty also spread anti-British sentiment through newspapers and handbills that they posted on trees and buildings throughout the city and in surrounding towns. At dawn on August 14, 1765, the Boston Sons of Liberty hung an effigy of stamp distributor Andrew Oliver on a tree and called for his resignation. A mock funeral procession, joined by farmers, artisans, apprentices, and the poor, marched to Boston Common. The crowd, led by twenty-seven-year-old Ebenezer Mackintosh—a shoemaker, a veteran of the French and Indian War, and a popular working-class leader—carried the fake corpse to the Boston stamp office and destroyed the building. Demonstrators saved pieces of lumber, "stamped" them, and set them on fire outside Oliver's house. Oliver, wisely, had already left town.

Oliver's brother-in-law, Lieutenant Governor Thomas Hutchinson, arrived at the scene and tried to quiet the crowd, but he only angered them further. They soon destroyed Oliver's stable house, coach, and carriage, which the crowd saw as signs of aristocratic opulence. Twelve days later, demonstrators attacked the homes of Judge William Story, customs officer Benjamin Hallowell, and Lieutenant Governor Hutchinson.

The battle against the Stamp Act unfolded across the colonies with riots, beatings, and resignations reported from Newport, Rhode Island, to New Brunswick, New Jersey, to Charles Town (later Charleston), South Carolina. In Charleston, slave trader and stamp agent Henry Laurens was attacked by white artisans who hanged him in effigy and then by white workers and finally by slaves who harassed him with chants of "Liberty! Liberty!!" On November 1, 1765, when the Stamp Act officially took effect, not a single stamp agent remained in his post in the colonies.

Protesters carefully chose their targets: stamp agents, sheriffs, judges, and colonial officials. Even when violence erupted, it remained focused, with most crowds destroying stamps and stamp offices first and then turning to the private property of Stamp Act supporters. These protests made a mockery of notions of deference toward British rule. But they also revealed growing autonomy on the part of middling- and working-class colonists who attacked men of wealth and power, sometimes choosing artisans rather than wealthier men as their leaders. However, this was not primarily a class conflict because many wealthier colonists made common cause with artisans, small farmers, and the poor. Indeed, colonial elites considered themselves the leaders, inspiring popular uprisings through the power of their political arguments and oratorical skills, although they refused to support actions they considered too radical. For example, when Levellers in the Hudson valley proclaimed themselves Sons of Liberty and sought assistance from

Stamp Act rebels in New York City, the merchants, judges, and large landowners who led the protests there refused to help them.

It was these more affluent protesters who dominated the Stamp Act Congress in New York City in October 1765, which brought together twenty-seven delegates from nine colonies. The delegates petitioned Parliament to repeal the Stamp Act, arguing that taxation without representation was tyranny and that such laws "have a manifest Tendency to subvert the Rights and Liberties of the Colonists." Delegates then urged colonists to boycott British goods and refuse to pay the stamp tax. Yet they still proclaimed their loyalty to king and country.

The question of representation became a mainstay of colonial protests. Whereas the British accepted the notion of "virtual representation," by which members of Parliament gave voice to the views of particular classes and interests, the North American colonies had developed a system of representation based on locality. According to colonial leaders, only members of Parliament elected by colonists could represent their interests.

Even as delegates at the Stamp Act Congress declared themselves disaffected but loyal British subjects, they participated in the process of developing a common identity in the American colonies. Christopher Gadsden of South Carolina expressed the feeling most directly. "We should stand upon the broad common ground of natural rights," he argued. "There should be no New England man, no New-Yorker, known on the continent, but all of us Americans."

Eventually the British Parliament was forced to respond to colonial protests and even more to rising complaints from English merchants and traders whose business had been damaged by the colonists' boycott. Parliament repealed the Stamp Act in March 1766, and King George III granted his approval a month later. When news reached the colonies in May, crowds celebrated in the streets, church bells rang, and fireworks and muskets saluted the victory. Colonists now looked forward to a new and better relationship between themselves and the British government.

From the colonists' perspective, the crisis triggered by the passage of the Stamp Act demonstrated the limits of parliamentary control. Colonists had organized effectively and forced Parliament to repeal the hated legislation. Protests had raged across the colonies and attracted support from a wide range of colonists, including young and old, men and women, merchants, lawyers, artisans, and farmers. Individual leaders, like Patrick Henry of Virginia and Samuel Adams of Massachusetts, became more widely known through their fiery oratory and their success in appealing to the masses. The Stamp Act agitation also demonstrated the growing influence of ordinary citizens who led parades and demonstrations and joined in attacks on stamp agents and the homes of British officials. And the protests revealed the growing power of the written word and printed images in disseminating ideas among colonists. Broadsides, political cartoons, handbills, newspapers, and pamphlets circulated widely, reinforcing discussions and proclamations at taverns, rallies, demonstrations, and more formal political assemblies.

Explore

See Documents 5.2 and 5.3 for two different types of dissent.

For all the success of the Stamp Act protests, American colonists still could not imagine in 1765 that protest would ever lead to open revolt against British sovereignty. More well-to-do colonists were concerned that a revolution against British authority might fuel a dual revolution in which small farmers, tenants, servants, slaves, and laborers would rise up against their political and economic superiors in the colonies. Even most middling- and working-class protesters believed that the best solution to the colonies' problems was to gain greater economic and political rights within the British empire, not to break from it. After all, Great Britain was the most powerful nation in the world, and the colonies could only benefit from their place in its far-reaching empire.

The Townshend Act and the Boston Massacre

The repeal of the Stamp Act in March 1766 led directly to Parliament's passage of the Declaratory Act. That act declared that Parliament had the authority to pass any law "to bind the colonies and peoples of North America" closer to Britain. No new tax or policy was established; Parliament simply wanted to proclaim Great Britain's political supremacy in the aftermath of the successful stamp tax protests.

Following this direct assertion of British sovereignty, relative harmony prevailed in the colonies for more than a year. Having rid themselves of the burden of parliamentary taxation, colonists were content to abide by less offensive restrictions on smuggling, domestic manufacturing, and similar matters. Then in June 1767, a new chancellor of the Exchequer, Charles Townshend, rose to power in England. He persuaded Parliament to return to the model offered by the earlier Sugar Act. The **Townshend Act**, like the Sugar Act, instituted an import tax on a range of items sent to the colonies, including glass, lead, paint, paper, and tea.

Now, however, even an indirect tax led to immediate protests and calls for a boycott of the items subject to the tax. In February 1768, Samuel Adams wrote a circular letter reminding colonists of the importance of the boycott, and the

Protesting the Stamp Act: Two Views

The announcement of the Stamp Act in 1764 ignited widespread protests throughout the colonies. Colonial governments petitioned Parliament for its repeal, crowds attacked stamp agents and distributors, broadsides and newspapers denounced "taxation without representation," and boycotts and mass demonstrations were organized in major cities, some of which turned violent. Protests were not limited to the colonists, however, as shown in the petition to Parliament from London merchants, who argued that they were losing revenue because of colonial boycotts of British goods. The second document celebrates the repeal of the Stamp Act by depicting a funeral for the act led by its supporters. Dr. William Scott, who published letters supporting the Stamp Act in a London newspaper, leads the procession.

Explore

5.2 London Merchants Petition to Repeal the Stamp Act, 1766

And that, in consequence of the trade between the colonies and the mother country, as established and permitted for many years, and of the experience which the petitioners have had of the readiness of the Americans to make their just remittances to the utmost of their real ability, they have been induced to make and venture such large exportations of British manufactures, as to leave the colonies indebted to the merchants of Great Britain in the sum of several millions sterling; at that at this time the colonists, when pressed for payment, appeal to past experience, in proof of their willingness; but declare it is not in their power, at present, to make good their engagements, alleging, that the taxes and restrictions laid upon them, and the extension of the jurisdiction of vice admiralty courts established by some late acts of parliament, particularly . . . by an act passed in the fifth year of his present Majesty, for granting and applying certain stamp duties, and other duties, in the British colonies and plantations in America, with several regulations and restraints, which, if founded in acts of parliament for defined purposes, are represented to have been extended in such a manner as to disturb legal commerce and harass the fair trader, have so far interrupted the usual and former most fruitful branches of their commerce, restrained the sale of their produce, thrown the state of the several provinces into confusion, and brought on so great a number of actual bankruptcies, that the former opportunities and means of remittances and payments are utterly lost and taken from them; and that the petitioners are, by these unhappy events, reduced to the necessity of applying to the House, in order to secure themselves and their families from impending ruin; to prevent a multitude of manufacturers from becoming a burthen to the community, or else seeking their bread in other countries, to the irretrievable loss of this kingdom; and to preserve the strength of this nation entire.

Source: Guy Steven Callender, *Selections from the Economic History of the United States, 1765–1860* (Boston: Ginn, 1909), 146–47.

Explore

5.3 **The Repeal, 1766**

Interpret the Evidence

- How do both the petition and the cartoon emphasize the economic arguments against the Stamp Act? What role, if any, do arguments about political representation play in these documents?
- Who do you think was the intended audience for each of these documents? What evidence can you find in each document to support your answer?

Put It in Context

What do these documents suggest about the more general relations among the colonies, British merchants, and Parliament in 1766?

Massachusetts Assembly disseminated it to other colonial assemblies. In response, Parliament posted two more British army regiments in Boston and New York City to enforce the law, including the Townshend Act. Angry colonists did not retreat when confronted by this show of military force. Instead, a group of outspoken colonial leaders demanded that colonists refuse to import goods of any kind from Britain.

Explore

See Document 5.4 for one colonist's objection to the Townshend Act.

This boycott depended especially on the support of women, who were often in charge of the day-to-day purchase of household items that appeared on the boycott list. Women were expected to boycott a wide array of British goods—gloves, hats, shoes, cloth, sugar, and tea among them. Single women and widows who supported themselves as shopkeepers were expected to join male merchants and store owners in refusing to sell British goods. To make up for the boycotted goods, wives, mothers, and daughters produced homespun shirts and dresses and brewed herbal teas to replace British products.

Despite the hardships, many colonial women embraced the boycott. Twenty-two-year-old Charity Clarke voiced the feelings of many colonists when she wrote to a friend in England, "If you English folks won't give us the liberty we ask . . . I will try to gather a number of ladies armed with spinning wheels [along with men] who shall learn to weave & keep sheep, and will retire beyond the reach of arbitrary power." Women organized spinning bees in which dozens of participants produced yards and yards of homespun cloth. By 1770 wearing homespun came to symbolize women's commitment to the colonial cause.

Refusing to drink tea offered another way for women to show their support of protests against parliamentary taxation. In February 1770, more than "300 Mistresses of Families, in which number the Ladies of the Highest Rank and Influence," signed a petition in Boston and pledged to abstain from drinking tea, and dozens of women from less prosperous families signed their own boycott agreement.

Boston women's refusal to drink tea and their participation in spinning bees were part of a highly publicized effort to make their city the center of opposition to the Townshend Act. Printed propaganda, demonstrations, rallies, and broadsides announced to the world that Bostonians rejected Parliament's right to impose its will, or at least its taxes, on the American colonies. Throughout the winter of 1769–1770, boys and young men confronted British soldiers stationed in Boston. Although they were angry over Parliament's taxation policies, Boston men also considered the soldiers, who moonlighted for extra pay, as economic competitors. The taunts and tension soon escalated into violence.

By March 1770, 1,700 British troops were stationed in Boston, a city of 18,000 people. On the evening of March 5, boys began throwing snowballs and insults at the lone soldier guarding the Boston Customs House. An angry crowd began milling about, now joined by a group of sailors led by Crispus Attucks, an ex-slave of mixed African and Indian ancestry. The nervous guard called for help, and Captain Thomas Preston arrived at the scene with seven British soldiers. He appealed to the "gentlemen" present to disperse the crowd. Instead, the harangues of the crowd continued, and snowballs, stones, and other projectiles flew in greater numbers. Then a gun fired, and soon more shooting erupted. Eleven men in the crowd were hit, and four were "killed on the Spot," including Crispus Attucks.

Despite confusion about who, if anyone, gave the order to fire, colonists expressed outrage at the shooting of ordinary men on the streets of Boston. Samuel Adams and other Sons of Liberty, though horrified by the turn of events, recognized the incredible potential for anti-British propaganda. Adams organized a mass funeral for those killed, and thousands watched the caskets being paraded through the city. Newspaper editors and broadsides printed by the Sons of Liberty labeled the shooting a "massacre." When the accused soldiers were tried in Boston for the so-called **Boston Massacre** and the jury acquitted six of the eight of any crime, colonial leaders became more convinced that British rule had become tyrannical and that such tyranny must be opposed. **See Document Project 5: The Boston Massacre, page 153**.

To ensure that colonists throughout North America learned about the Boston Massacre, committees of correspondence formed once again to spread the news. These committees became important pipelines for sending information about plans and protests across the colonies, connecting seaport cities with one another and with like-minded colonists in the countryside. They also circulated an engraving by Bostonian Paul Revere that suggested the soldiers purposely shot at a peaceful crowd.

In the aftermath of the shootings, public pressure increased on Parliament to repeal the Townshend duties. Merchants in England and North America pleaded with Parliament to reconsider policies that had resulted in economic losses on both sides of the Atlantic. In response, Parliament repealed all of the Townshend duties except the import tax on tea. Parliament retained the tea tax to prove its political authority to do so.

Continuing Conflicts at Home

As colonists in Boston and other seaport cities rallied to protest British taxation, other residents of the thirteen colonies continued to challenge authorities closer to home. In the same years as the Stamp Act and Townshend Act

DOCUMENT 5.4

John Dickinson | Letter from a Farmer, 1768

In 1767 the British Parliament passed a series of taxes on the American colonies to raise revenue and gain greater control of colonial government and trade. The Townshend duties, as they were called, outraged many colonists. John Dickinson, a prominent Pennsylvania attorney who had been a representative at the Stamp Act Congress, wrote the most famous attacks on the Townshend Act. Published under the pseudonym "A Farmer," Dickinson's letters criticized British taxation policies and called for peaceful resistance to them.

Explore

I hope to demonstrate before these letters are concluded, yet even in such a supposed case, these colonies ought to regard the act with abhorrence. For who are a free people? Not those over whom government is reasonably and equitably exercised but those who live under a government, so *constitutionally checked* and *controuled*, that proper provision is made against its being otherwise exercised. The late act is founded on the destruction of this constitutional security.

If the parliament have a right to lay a duty of four shillings and eight pence on a hundred weight of glass, or a ream of paper, they have a right to lay a duty of any other sum on either. They may raise the duty, as the author before quoted says has been done in some countries, till it "exceeds seventeen or eighteen times the value of the commodity." In short, if they have a right to levy a tax of *one penny* upon us, they have a right to levy a *million* upon us: For where does their right stop? At any given number of pence, shillings, or pounds? To attempt to limit their right, after granting it to exist at all, is

as contrary to reason, as granting it to exist at all is contrary to justice. If they have any right to tax us, then, whether our own money shall continue in our own pockets, or not, depends no longer on *us*, but on *them*. "There is nothing which we can call our own," or to use the words of Mr. Locke, "What property have we in that, which another may, by right, take, when he pleases, to himself?"

These duties, which will inevitably be levied upon us, and which are now levying upon us, are expressly laid for the sole purpose of taking money. This is the true definition of taxes. They are therefore taxes. This money is to be taken from us. We are therefore taxed. Those who are taxed without their own consent, given by themselves, or their representatives, are slaves. We are taxed without our own consent given by ourselves, or our representatives. We are therefore—I speak it with grief—I speak it with indignation—we are slaves.

Source: John Dickinson, *Letters from a Farmer in Pennsylvania to the Inhabitants of the British Colonies* (New York: The Outlook Company, 1903), 75–78.

Interpret the Evidence

- Is Dickinson's main criticism of the Townshend duties that they are an economic burden, or is it broader than that?
- What is Dickinson's definition of a just government?

Put It in Context

What does Dickinson's complaint about colonists being treated as slaves suggest about the limits of his political vision?

protests, tenants in New Jersey and the Hudson valley continued their campaign for economic justice. So, too, did Herman Husband and the Sandy Creek Association. Governor Tryon of North Carolina had been among those who claimed that Parliament had abused its power in taxing the colonies, but he did not recognize such abuses in his own colony. Instead, he viewed the Regulators, formed during the

campaign against the Townshend Act, as traitors. The Regulators, however, insisted that they were simply trying to protect farmers and laborers from deceitful speculators, corrupt politicians, and greedy employers. A year after the Boston Massacre, Governor Tryon sent troops to quell what he viewed as open rebellion on the Carolina frontier. The Regulators amassed two thousand farmers to defend

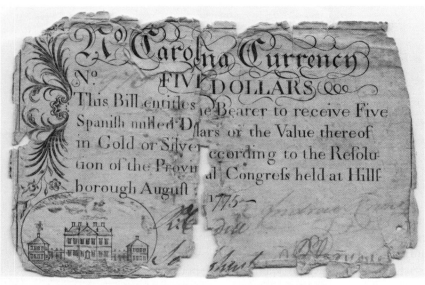

The Regulators and Governor William Tryon

When the Regulators rebelled against the Townshend duties in 1771 along the North Carolina frontier, Governor Tryon, who also questioned British tax policies, nevertheless dispatched colonial troops and crushed the rebellion. Tryon's lavish palace in New Bern appears in the lower left corner of this $5 bill, issued in 1775 on the eve of the American Revolution. North Carolina Collection, University of North Carolina at Chapel Hill

themselves, although Husband, a pacifist, was not among them. But when twenty Regulators were killed and more than a hundred wounded at the Battle of Alamance Creek in May 1771, he surely knew many of the fallen. Six Regulators were hanged a month later in front of Governor Tryon, local officials, and hundreds of neighboring farm families. Although North Carolina Regulators did not proclaim this the Alamance Massacre, many local residents harbored deep resentments against colonial officials for what they viewed as the slaughter of honest, hardworking men. Herman Husband fled the Carolina frontier and headed north.

Resentments against colonial leaders were not confined to North Carolina. An independent Regulator movement emerged in South Carolina in 1767. Far more effective than their North Carolina counterparts, South Carolina Regulators seized control of the western regions of the colony, took up arms, and established their own system of frontier justice. By 1769 the South Carolina Assembly negotiated a settlement with the Regulators, establishing new parishes in the colony's interior that ensured greater representation for frontier areas and extending colonial political institutions, such as courts and sheriffs, to the region.

Tea and Widening Resistance

For a brief period after the Boston Massacre, conflicts within the colonies generally overshadowed protests against British policies. During this period, the tea tax was collected, the increased funds ensured that British officials in

the colonies were less dependent on local assemblies to carry out their duties, and general prosperity seemed to lessen the antagonism between colonists and royal authorities. In May 1773, however, all that changed. That month Parliament passed a new act that granted the East India Company a monopoly on shipping and selling tea in the colonies. Although this did not add any new tax or raise the price of tea, it did fuel a new round of protests.

Founded in the early seventeenth century, the East India Company had been one of the major trading companies in the British empire and a symbol of British commercial supremacy for more than 150 years. By the 1770s, however, it was on the verge of economic collapse and asked for a monopoly on the tea trade and the right to sell tea through its own agents rather than through independent shopkeepers and merchants in the colonies. Many members of Parliament had invested in the East India Company, so their decision to grant it a monopoly on tea involved financial as well as political considerations. Still, the decision was not seen as especially controversial since East India Company tea sold by company agents cost less, even with the tax, than smuggled Dutch or French tea.

Samuel Adams, Patrick Henry, Christopher Gadsden, and other radicals had continued to view the tea tax as an illegal imposition on colonists and refused to pay it as a matter of principle. They had established committees of correspondence to keep up the pressure for a colony-wide boycott, and Adams published and circulated "Rights of the Colonies," a pamphlet that listed a range of grievances against British policies. Their concerns became the basis for a new round of protests when Parliament granted the East India Company its monopoly. By eliminating colonial merchants from the profits to be made on tea and implementing a monopoly for a single favored company, Parliament pushed merchants into joining with radicals to demand redress.

Committees of correspondence quickly organized another colony-wide boycott. In some cities, like Charleston, South Carolina, tea was unloaded from East India Company ships but never sold. In others, like New York, the ships were turned back at the port. Only in Boston, however, did violence erupt as ships loaded with tea, and protected by British troops, sat anchored in the harbor. On the night of December 16, 1773, the Sons of Liberty organized a "tea party." After a massive rally against British policy, a group of about fifty men disguised as Indians boarded the British ships and dumped forty-five tons of tea into the sea.

Although hundreds of spectators knew who had boarded the ship, witnesses refused to provide names or other information to British officials investigating the incident. The Boston Tea Party was a direct challenge to British authority and resulted in massive destruction of valuable property.

Parliament responded immediately with a show of force. The **Coercive Acts**, passed in 1774, closed the port of Boston until residents paid for the tea, moved Massachusetts court cases against royal officials back to England, and revoked the colony's charter in order to strengthen the authority of royal officials and weaken that of the colonial assembly. The British government also approved a new Quartering Act, which forced Boston residents to accommodate more soldiers in their own homes or build more barracks.

The royal government passed the Coercive Acts to punish Massachusetts and to discourage similar protests in other colonies. Instead, the legislation, which colonists called the **Intolerable Acts**, spurred a militant reaction. Committees of correspondence spread news of the fate of Boston and the entire colony of Massachusetts. Colonial leaders, who increasingly identified themselves as patriots, soon formed committees of safety—armed groups of colonists who gathered weapons and munitions and vowed to protect themselves against British encroachments on their rights and institutions. Other colonies sent support, both political and material, to Massachusetts and instituted a boycott of British goods. All ranks of people—merchants, laborers, farmers, housewives—throughout the colonies joined the boycott.

Explore

See Document 5.5 for a British reaction to colonial women's efforts to boycott tea.

At the same time, a group of patriots meeting in Williamsburg, Virginia, in the spring of 1774 called for colonies to send representatives to a **Continental Congress** to meet in Philadelphia the following September to discuss relations between the North American colonies and Great Britain.

By passing the Coercive Acts, Parliament had hoped to dampen the long-smoldering conflict with the colonies. Instead, it flared even brighter, with radical leaders committing themselves to the use of violence, moderate merchants and shopkeepers making common cause with radicals, and ordinary women and men embracing a boycott of all British goods.

The Continental Congress and Colonial Unity

When the Continental Congress convened in Philadelphia's Carpenter Hall in September 1774, fifty-six delegates

First Continental Congress

This 1783 French engraving depicts the meeting of the first Continental Congress, held in Philadelphia in September 1774. Fifty-six delegates attended from every colony but Georgia. After spending most of the first day debating whether to start the meeting off with a prayer, the congress got down to the business of petitioning King George III to remedy the colonists' grievances.   The Granger Collection, New York

represented every colony but Georgia. Many of these men—and they were all men—had met before. Some had worked together in the Stamp Act Congress in 1765; others had joined forces in the intervening years on committees of correspondence or in petitions to Parliament. Still, the representatives disagreed on many fronts. Some were radicals like Samuel Adams, Patrick Henry, and Christopher Gadsden. Others held moderate views, including George Washington of Virginia and John Dickinson of Pennsylvania. And a few, like John Jay of New York, voiced more conservative positions.

Despite their differences, all the delegates agreed that the colonies must resist further parliamentary encroachments on their liberties. They did not talk of independence, but rather of reestablishing the freedoms that colonists had enjoyed in an earlier period: freedom from British taxes and from the presence of British troops and the right to control local economic and political affairs. Washington voiced the sentiments of many. Although opposed to the idea of independence, he echoed John Locke by refusing to submit "to the loss of those valuable rights and privileges, which are essential to the happiness of every free State, and without which life, liberty, and property are rendered totally insecure."

DOCUMENT 5.5

The Edenton Proclamation, 1774

When colonial leaders called for a boycott of tea following the 1773 Tea Act, women throughout the colonies joined in the campaign. In Edenton, North Carolina, a group of women published a proclamation stating their allegiance to the cause of liberty by refusing to serve or drink British tea. Their public statement received much attention in both the American and the British press. The following political cartoon, which satirizes the Edenton women who signed the public declaration, appeared in several London newspapers.

Explore

What is the significance of the female slave holding the inkstand?

How are the women portrayed in this cartoon?

What is the presence of the infant and dog on the floor meant to suggest about the character of female petitioners?

A SOCIETY of PATRIOTIC LADIES,
AT
EDENTON in NORTH CAROLINA.

Plate V.

Library of Congress

Put It in Context

How does the cartoon use contemporary understandings of women's role in society to undermine their actions?

To demonstrate their unified resistance to the Coercive Acts, delegates called on colonists to continue the boycott of British goods and to end all colonial exports to Great Britain. Committees were established in all of the colonies to coordinate and enforce these actions. Delegates also insisted that Americans were "entitled to a free and exclusive power of legislation in their several provincial legislatures." By 1774 a growing number of colonists supported these measures and the ideas on which they were based.

The delegates at the Continental Congress could not address all the colonists' grievances, and most had no interest in challenging race and class relations within the colonies themselves. Nonetheless, it was a significant event because the congress drew power away from individual colonies—most notably Massachusetts—and local organizations like the Sons of Liberty and placed the emphasis instead on colony-wide plans and actions. To some extent, the delegates shifted leadership of colonial protests away from more radical artisans, like Ebenezer Mackintosh, and put planning back in the hands of men of wealth and standing. Moreover, even as they denounced Parliament, many representatives felt a special loyalty to the king and sought his intervention to rectify relations between the mother country and the colonies.

REVIEW & RELATE

How and why did colonial resistance to British policies escalate in the decade following the conclusion of the French and Indian War?	How did internal social and economic divisions shape the colonial response to British policies?

✓ *LEARNINGCurve* **bedfordstmartins.com/hewittlawson/LC**

Conclusion: Liberty within Empire

From the Sugar Act in 1764 to the Continental Congress in 1774, colonists reacted strongly to parliamentary efforts to impose greater control over the colonies. Their protests grew increasingly effective as colonists developed organizations, systems of communication, and arguments to buttress their position. Residents of seacoast cities like Boston and New York City developed especially visible and effective challenges, in large part because they generally had the most to lose if Britain implemented new economic, military, and legislative policies.

In frontier areas, such as the southern backcountry, the Hudson valley, and northern New England, complaints against British tyranny vied with those against colonial land

speculators and officials throughout the 1760s and 1770s. Still, few of these agitators questioned the right of white colonists to claim Indian lands or enslave African labor. In this sense, at least, most frontier settlers made common cause with more elite colonists who challenged British authority, including the many planters and large landowners who attended the Continental Congress.

One other tie bound the colonists together in 1774. No matter how radical the rhetoric, the aim continued to be resistance to particular policies, not independence from the British empire. Colonists sought greater liberty within the empire, focusing on parliamentary policies concerning taxation, troops, and local political control. Only on rare occasions did a colonist question the fundamental framework of imperial governance, and even then, the questions did not lead to a radical reformulation of economic or political relations. And despite some colonists' opposition to certain parliamentary acts, many others supported British policies. While royal officials and many of their well-to-do neighbors were horrified by the new spirit of lawlessness that had erupted in the colonies, the majority of colonists did not participate in the Sons or Daughters of Liberty, the colonial congresses, or the petition campaigns. Small farmers and backcountry settlers were often far removed from centers of protest activity, while poor families in seaport cities who purchased few items to begin with had little interest in boycotts of British goods. Finally, some colonists still hesitated to consider open revolt against British rule for fear of a revolution from below. The activities of land rioters, Regulators, evangelical preachers, female petitioners, and African American converts to Christianity reminded more well-established settlers that the colonies harbored their own tensions and conflicts.

The fates of George Washington and Herman Husband suggest the uncertainties that still plagued the colonies and individual colonists in 1774. As Washington returned to his Virginia estate from the Continental Congress, he began to devote more time to military affairs. He took command of the volunteer militia companies in the colonies and chaired the committee on safety in his home county. Although still opposed to rebellion, he was nonetheless preparing for it. Herman Husband, on the other hand, had already watched his rebellion against oppressive government fail at the Battle of Alamance Creek. When the Continental Congress met in Philadelphia, he was living on the Pennsylvania frontier, trying to reestablish his farm and family there. Whether ruled by Great Britain or eastern colonial elites, he was most concerned with the rights of poor and working people. Yet he and Washington would have agreed with the great British parliamentarian Edmund Burke, who, on hearing of events in the American colonies in 1774, lamented, "Clouds, indeed, and darkness, rest upon the future."

Chapter Review

Online Study Guide ▶ bedfordstmartins.com/hewittlawson

KEY TERMS

Albany Congress (p. 131)
Peace of Paris (p. 133)
Proclamation Line of 1763 (p. 135)
Regulators (p. 137)
benign neglect (p. 140)
Navigation Acts (p. 140)
Sugar Act (p. 140)
import duty (p. 140)
committee of correspondence (p. 141)
Stamp Act (p. 141)
Sons of Liberty (p. 142)
Townshend Act (p. 143)
Boston Massacre (p. 146)
Coercive Acts (Intolerable Acts) (p. 149)
Continental Congress (p. 149)

REVIEW & RELATE

1. How did the French and Indian War and the subsequent peace treaty affect relations between Britain and its North American subjects?

2. How did the French and Indian War and the increasing power of large landowners contribute to conflict between average colonists and colonial elites?

3. How did Britain's postwar policies lead to the emergence of unified colonial protests?

4. Why did British policymakers believe they were justified in seeking to gain greater control over Britain's North American colonies?

5. How and why did colonial resistance to British policies escalate in the decade following the conclusion of the French and Indian War?

6. How did internal social and economic divisions shape the colonial response to British policies?

TIMELINE OF EVENTS

1754–1763	French and Indian War
1754	George Washington launches surprise attack on Fort Duquesne
	Albany Congress convenes
1757	William Pitt takes charge of British war effort
May 1763	Pontiac launches pan-Indian revolt to drive out British
June 1763	Peace of Paris
October 1763	British establish Proclamation Line of 1763
December 1763	Paxton Boys attack Conestoga Indians
1764	Green Mountain Boys resist New York authorities
	Sugar Act passed
1765	Stamp Act passed
	Stamp Act Congress convenes
1766	Sandy Creek Association formed
	Stamp Act repealed and Declaratory Act passed
1767	Townshend Act passed
1770	Boston Massacre
1771	Battle of Alamance Creek, North Carolina
1773	Boston Tea Party
1774	Coercive Acts passed
	Continental Congress convenes in Philadelphia

DOCUMENT PROJECT 5

The Boston Massacre

The Boston Massacre was a critical episode in the American independence movement. The origins of this skirmish between Bostonians and British troops lie in the passage of the Townshend Act in 1767, three years before the so-called massacre.

There was widespread resistance to the Townshend duties, including public demonstrations, petitions to King George and Parliament, and boycotts against British goods. Boston was the scene of numerous disturbances, and the situation in Boston was so tense that four thousand British troops were brought in to enforce the Townshend Act. Then in late February 1770, a British sympathizer, Ebenezer Richardson, tore down an anti-British poster. When an angry mob threw stones at Richardson's house and hit his wife, Ebenezer fired into the crowd and killed an eleven-year-old boy. A mass funeral for the boy set the stage for the events of March 5, 1770.

On that chilly evening, an exchange between a local tradesman and a British officer outside the Customs House escalated when companions on both sides joined in the dispute. Church bells were rung, bringing more colonists to the scene (Document 5.6). Captain Thomas Preston, the officer in charge that day, tried to gain control of the situation by calling in reinforcements (Document 5.9). In the ensuing melee, Bostonians overwhelmed the British regulars, who sought to protect themselves. Someone fired his gun, and a number of British soldiers then followed suit, killing three men immediately and fatally injuring two others (Documents 5.6 and 5.9).

Within the month, Preston and eight British soldiers were indicted for murder and tried in fall 1770. Unable to find attorneys willing to defend himself and his troops, Preston appealed directly to patriot John Adams, who agreed to take the case to ensure a fair trial. Preston was tried separately and was acquitted. Six other soldiers were also acquitted, but two were found guilty of murder, a charge later reduced to manslaughter. Parliament repealed all of the Townshend duties except for the tax on tea.

The following documents reveal the chaos of that night from the differing perspectives of Bostonians and British soldiers. They also illustrate the ways that colonial leaders used the event to promote the patriot cause (Documents 5.7, 5.8, and 5.10).

DOCUMENT 5.6

Deposition of William Wyatt, March 7, 1770

Just two days after the Boston Massacre, city officials began deposing dozens of witnesses to the event. They later published these descriptions as part of a pamphlet that criticized the event as a "Horrid Massacre." The following selection is from the testimony of William Wyatt and describes his version of the scene just as British soldiers were loading their weapons.

That last Monday evening, being the fifth day of March current, I was in Boston, down on Treat's wharf, where my vessel was lying, and hearing the bells ring, supposed there was a fire in the town, whereupon I hastened up to the Town-house, on the south side of it, where I saw an officer of the army lead out of the guard-house there seven or eight soldiers of the army, and lead them down in seeming haste, to the Custom-house on the north side of King street, where I followed them, and when the officer had got there with the men, he bid them face about. I stood just below them on the left wing, and the said officer ordered his men to load, which they did accordingly, with the utmost dispatch, then they remained about six minutes, with their firelocks rested and bayonets fixed, but not standing in exact order. I observed a considerable number of young lads, and here and there a man amongst them, about the middle of the street, facing the soldiers, but not within ten or twelve feet distance from them; I observed some of them, viz., the lads, etc., had sticks in their hands, laughing, shouting, huzzaing, and crying fire; but could not observe that any of them threw anything at the soldiers, or threatened any of them. Then the said officer retired from before the soldiers and stepping behind them, towards the right wing, bid the soldiers fire; they not firing, he presently again bid 'em fire, they not yet firing, he stamped and said, "Damn your bloods, fire, be the consequence what it will"; then the second man on the left wing fired off his gun, then, after a very short pause, they fired one after another as quick as possible, beginning on the right wing; the last man's gun on the left wing flashed in the pan, then he primed again, and the people being withdrawn from before the soldiers, most of them further down the street, he turned his gun toward them and fired upon them. Immediately after the principal firing, I saw three of the people fall down in the street; presently after the last gun was fired off, the said officer, who had commanded the soldiers (as above) to fire, sprung before them, waving his sword or stick, said, "Damn ye, rascals, what did ye fire for?" and struck up the gun of one of the soldiers who was loading again, whereupon they seemed confounded and fired no more.

Source: *A Short Narrative of the Horrid Massacre in Boston Perpetrated in the Evening of the Fifth Day of March, 1770, by the Soldiers of the 29th Regiment* (Boston, 1770), republished with additional material by John Doggett Jr. (New York, 1849), 72.

DOCUMENT 5.7

Account of Boston Massacre Funeral Procession, March 12, 1770

One week after the Boston Massacre, a massive public funeral was held for the four victims who had already died: Samuel Gray, Samuel Maverick, James Caldwell, and Crispus Attucks. In the scene described here, shops were closed and church bells marked the event in Boston and also in nearby Charlestown and Roxbury. Note that the article mentions that Bostonians from all ranks attended the funeral.

Last Thursday, agreeable to a general request of the inhabitants, and by the consent of parents and friends, were carried to their grave in succession, the bodies of Samuel Gray, Samuel Maverick, James Caldwell, and Crispus Attucks, the unhappy victims who fell in the bloody massacre of the Monday evening preceding!

On this occasion most of the shops in town were shut, all the bells were ordered to toll a solemn peal, as were also those in the neighboring towns of Charlestown, Roxbury, etc. The procession began to move between the hours of 4 and 5 in the afternoon; two of the unfortunate sufferers, Messrs. James Caldwell and Crispus Attucks, who were strangers [not residents of Boston], borne from Faneuil Hall, attended by a numerous train of persons of all ranks; and the other two, Mr. Samuel Gray, from the house of Mr. Benjamin Gray (his brother), on the north side of the Exchange, and Mr. Maverick, from the house of his distressed mother, Mrs. Mary Maverick, in Union Street, each followed by their respective relations and friends: The several hearses forming a junction in King Street, the theatre of the inhuman tragedy! proceeded from thence through the Main Street, lengthened by an immense concourse of people, so numerous as to be obliged to follow in ranks of six, and brought up by a long train of carriages belonging to the principal gentry of the town. The bodies were deposited in one vault in the middle burying ground. The aggravated circumstances of their death, the distress and sorrow visible in every countenance, together with the peculiar solemnity with which the whole funeral was conducted, surpass description.

Source: *Boston Gazette and Country Journal*, March 12, 1770.

DOCUMENT 5.8

Paul Revere | Etching of the Boston Massacre, 1770

Published three weeks after the Boston Massacre, Paul Revere's famous etching of the event stirred anti-British sentiment among the colonists. Revere was not at the Customs House on March 5 and largely copied this image from the engraving of another artist, Henry Pelham. Revere's etching depicts an organized line of British soldiers firing into a crowd of unarmed colonists. At the time of the Boston Massacre, Revere was a prominent silversmith and a member of the Sons of Liberty.

DOCUMENT 5.9
Account of Captain Thomas Preston, June 25, 1770

Seven months after the Boston Massacre, British troops involved in the event went on trial. Captain Thomas Preston was the officer in charge the night of March 5, and he was tried separately from the other soldiers. His trial centered on whether or not he had ordered his men to fire on the crowd. Assuming that defendants in criminal trials would perjure themselves to gain an acquittal, English legal custom prohibited them from testifying. But Preston had presented his version of events to British authorities just a week after the event. While imprisoned in Boston, he released this account of events, which was published in the *Boston Gazette* on March 12, 1770. In April, it appeared in London papers and was republished in the *Boston Evening-Post* on June 25, 1770. Thus it is likely that jurors in his trial knew that he strenuously denied the charges against him.

ON MONDAY NIGHT about Eight o' Clock two Soldiers were attacked and beat. But the Party of the Towns-People, in order to carry Matters to the utmost Length, broke into two Meeting-Houses, and rang the Alarm Bells, which I supposed was for Fire as usual, but was soon undeceived. About Nine some of the Guard came to and informed me, the Town-Inhabitants were assembling to attack the Troops, and that the Bells were ringing as the Signal for that Purpose, and not for Fire, and the Beacon intended to be fired to bring in the distant People of the Country. This, as I was Captain of the Day, occasioned my repairing immediately to the Main-Guard. In my Way there I saw the People in great Commotion, and heard them use the most cruel and horrid Threats against the Troops. In a few Minutes after I reached the Guard, about an hundred People passed it, and went towards the Custom-House, where the King's Money is lodged. They immediately surrounded the Sentinel posted there, and with Clubs and other Weapons threatened to execute their Vengeance on him. I was soon informed by a Townsman, their Intention was to carry off the Soldier from his Post, and probably murder him. On which I desired him to return for further Intelligence; and he soon came back and assured me he heard the Mob declare they would murder him. This I feared might be a Prelude to their plundering the King's Chest. I immediately sent a non-commissioned Officer and twelve Men to protect both the Sentinel and the King's-Money, and very soon followed myself, to prevent (if possible) all Disorder; fearing lest the Officer and Soldiery by the Insults and Provocations of the Rioters, should be thrown off their Guard and commit some rash Act. They soon rushed through the People, and, by charging their Bayonets in half Circle, kept them at a little Distance. Nay, so far was I from intending the Death of any Person, that I suffered the Troops to go to the Spot where the unhappy Affair took Place, without any Loading in their Pieces, nor did I ever give Orders for loading them. This remiss Conduct in me perhaps merits Censure; yet it is Evidence, resulting from the Nature of Things, which is the best and surest that can be offered, that my Intention was not to act

(continued on page 158)

offensively, but the contrary Part, and that not without Compulsion. The mob still increased, and were more outrageous, striking their clubs or bludgeons one against another, and calling out, "Come on you rascals, you bloody backs, you lobster scoundrels, fire if you dare, G–d damn you, fire and be damned; we know you dare not"; and much more such language was used. At this time I was between the soldiers and the mob, parleying with and endeavouring all in my power to persuade them to retire peaceably; but to no purpose. They advanced to the points of the bayonets, struck some of them, and even the muzzles of the pieces, and seemed to be endeavouring to close with the soldiers. On which some well-behaved persons asked me if the guns were charged. I replied, yes. They then asked me if I intended to order the men to fire. I answered no, by no means; observing to them that I was advanced before the muzzles of the men's pieces, and must fall a sacrifice if they fired; that the soldiers were upon the half-cock and charged bayonets, and my giving the word fire under those circumstances would prove me no officer. While I was thus speaking, one of the soldiers, having received a severe blow with a stick, stepped a little on one side and instantly fired, on which turning to and asking him why he fired without orders, I was struck with a club on my arm, which for some time deprived me of the use of it, which blow, had it been placed on my head, most probably would have destroyed me. On this a general attack was made on the men by a great number of heavy clubs, and snowballs being thrown at them, by which all our lives were in imminent danger; some persons at the same time from behind calling out, "Damn your bloods, why don't you fire?" Instantly three or four of the soldiers fired, one after another, and directly after three more in the same confusion and hurry.

The mob then ran away, except three unhappy men who instantly expired, in which number was Mr. Gray, at whose rope-walk the prior quarrel took place; one more is since dead, three others are dangerously, and four slightly wounded. The whole of this melancholy affair was transacted in almost 20 minutes. On my asking the soldiers why they fired without orders, they said they heard the word "Fire" and supposed it came from me. This might be the case, as many of the mob called out "Fire, fire," but I assured the men that I gave no such order, that my words were, "Don't fire, stop your firing."

Source: *Supplement to the Boston Evening-Post*, June 25, 1770.

DOCUMENT 5.10

John Hancock | Oration on the Boston Massacre, 1774

In the years following the Boston Massacre, the city of Boston held an annual Massacre Day commemoration on March 5. On the fourth anniversary of the event, John Hancock delivered an emotional speech to the crowd. His tribute tied the Boston Massacre to the growing independence movement and demonstrated that the event remained a source of inspiration for years afterward. The last Massacre Day memorial was celebrated with the end of the American Revolutionary War in 1783.

Some boast of being friends to government; I am a friend to righteous government, to a government founded upon the principles of reason and justice; but I glory in publicly avowing my eternal enmity to tyranny. Is the present system, which the British administration have adopted for the government of the colonies, a righteous government—or is it tyranny? Here suffer me to ask (and would to heaven there could be an answer), what tenderness, what regard, respect or consideration has Great Britain shown, in their late transactions, for the security of the persons or properties of the inhabitants of the colonies? Or rather what have they omitted doing to destroy that security?

They have declared that they have ever had, and of right ought ever to have, full power to make laws of sufficient validity to bind the colonies in all cases whatever. They have exercised this pretended right by imposing a tax upon us without our consent; and lest we should show some reluctance at parting with our property, her fleets and armies are sent to enforce their mad pretensions. . . .

But I forbear, and come reluctantly to the transactions of that dismal night when in such quick succession we felt the extremes of grief, astonishment, and rage; when heaven in anger, for a dreadful moment, suffered hell to take the reins; when Satan with his chosen band opened the sluices of New England's blood, and sacrilegiously polluted our land with the dead bodies of her guiltless sons!

Let this sad tale of death never be told without a tear; let not the heaving bosom cease to burn with a manly indignation at the barbarous story through the long tracts of future time: let every parent tell the shameful story to his listening children until tears of pity glisten in their eyes and boiling passions shake their tender frames; and whilst the anniversary of that ill-fated night is kept a jubilee in the grim court of pandemonium, let all America join in one common prayer to heaven that the inhuman, unprovoked murders of the 5th of March, 1770, planned by Hillsborough and a knot of treacherous knaves in Boston, and executed by the cruel hand of Preston and his sanguinary coadjutors, may ever stand on history without a parallel. . . .

We have all one common cause; let it, therefore, be our only contest who shall most contribute to the security of the liberties of America. And may the same kind Providence which has watched over this country from her infant state still enable us to defeat our enemies.

Source: Mayo Williamson Hazeltine, ed., *Orations from Homer to McKinley* (New York: P. F. Collier and Sons, 1903), 7:2628–29, 2631, 2637.

Interpret the Evidence

1. How accurate is Paul Revere's etching of the Boston Massacre (Document 5.8)? Why would he have chosen to depict the scene as he did?

2. Compare Revere's portrayal of the event with the testimonies of William Wyatt (Document 5.6) and Captain Preston (Document 5.9).

3. Why did the funeral procession (described in Document 5.7) further incite popular sentiment against the British?

4. In what ways does William Wyatt's deposition (Document 5.6) support the colonists' view of the event? In what ways might it support the British view? Where does it overlap with Captain Preston's account (Document 5.9)?

5. How does John Hancock (Document 5.10) connect the Boston Massacre with the ongoing struggle for American independence?

Put It in Context

- What events had occurred between March 1770 and March 1774 that made the Boston Massacre a touchstone of resistance?

- How might the deaths of the five colonists and the outcome of the trial have changed the way patriots and ordinary colonists viewed the British authorities?

background photos: pages 155 and 158, The Granger Collection, New York

akg-images

Library of Congress

The Battle of Bunker Hill, June 17, 1775.

Slaves destroy a statue of King George III in New York City on July 9, 1776.

6
Revolutions
1775–1783

Everett Collection

African American slave James Armistead worked as a spy for the Americans during the Revolutionary War.

AMERICAN HISTORIES

On November 30, 1774, Thomas Paine arrived in Philadelphia aboard a ship from London. At age thirty-seven, Paine had failed at several occupations and two marriages. But he was an impassioned writer. A pamphlet he wrote caught the eye of Benjamin Franklin, who helped him secure a job on *The Pennsylvania Magazine* just as tensions between the colonies and Great Britain neared open conflict.

Born in 1737, Paine was raised in an English market town by parents who owned a small grocery store and made whalebone corsets. The Paines managed to send him to school for a few years before his father introduced him to the trade of corset-making. Over the next dozen years, Paine also worked as a seaman, a preacher, a teacher, and an excise (or tax) collector. He drank heavily and beat both his wives. Yet despite his personal vices, Paine tried to improve himself and the lot of other British workers. He taught working-class children how to read and write and attended lectures on science and politics in London. As an excise collector in 1762, he wrote a pamphlet that argued for better pay and working conditions for tax collectors. He was fired from his job, but Franklin convinced Paine to try his luck in Philadelphia.

Paine quickly gained in-depth political knowledge of the conflicts between the colonies and Great Britain and gained patrons among Philadelphia's economic and political elite. When armed conflict with British troops erupted in April 1775, colonial debates over whether to declare independence intensified. Pamphlets were a popular means of influencing these debates, and Paine hoped to write one that would tip the balance in favor of independence.

In January 1776, his pamphlet *Common Sense* did just that.

An instant success, *Common Sense* provided a rationale for independence and an emotional plea for creating a new democratic republic. Paine urged colonists not only to separate from England but also to establish a political structure that would ensure liberty and equality for all Americans: "A government of our own is our natural right," he concluded. " 'Tis time to part."

When *Common Sense* was published in 1776, sixteen-year-old Deborah Sampson was working as a servant to Jeremiah and Susanna Thomas in Marlborough, Massachusetts. Indentured at the age of ten, she looked after the Thomases' five sons and worked hard in both the house and the fields. Jeremiah Thomas thought education was above the lot of servant girls, but Sampson insisted on reading whatever books she could find. However, her commitment to American independence likely developed less from reading and more from the fighting that raged in Massachusetts and drew male servants and the Thomas sons into the Continental Army in the 1770s.

When Deborah Sampson's term of service ended in 1778, she sought work as a weaver and then a teacher. In March 1782, she disguised herself as a man and enlisted in the Continental Army, which was then desperate for recruits. Her height and muscular frame allowed her to fool local recruiters, and she accepted the bounty paid to those who enlisted. But Deborah never reported for duty, and when her charade was discovered, she was forced to return the money.

In May 1782, Sampson enlisted a second time under the name Robert Shurtliff. To explain the absence of facial hair, she told the recruiter that she was only seventeen years old. For the next year, Sampson, disguised as Shurtliff, marched, fought, and lived with her Massachusetts regiment. Her ability to carry off the deception was helped by lax standards of hygiene: Soldiers rarely undressed fully to bathe, and most slept in their uniforms.

Even after the formal end of the war in March 1783, Sampson/Shurtliff continued to serve in the Continental Army. In the fall of 1783, she was sent to Philadelphia to help quash a mutiny by Continental soldiers angered over the army's failure to provide back pay. While there, Sampson/Shurtliff fell ill with a raging fever, and a doctor at a local army hospital discovered that "he" was a woman. He reported the news to General John Paterson, and Sampson was honorably discharged, having served the army faithfully for more than a year. •

AS THE AMERICAN HISTORIES of Thomas Paine and Deborah Sampson demonstrate, the American Revolution transformed individual lives as well as the political life of the nation. Paine had failed financially and personally in England but gained fame in the colonies through his skills as a patriot pamphleteer. Sampson, who was forced into an early independence by her troubled family, excelled as a soldier. Still, while the American Revolution offered opportunities for some colonists, it promised hardship for others. Most Americans had to choose sides long before it was clear whether the colonists could defeat Great Britain, and the long years of conflict (1775–1783) took a toll on families and communities across the thirteen colonies. Over the course of a long and difficult war, could the patriots attract enough Tom Paines and Deborah Sampsons to secure independence and establish a new nation?

The Question of Independence

The Continental Congress that met to protest the Coercive Acts (see chapter 5) adjourned in October 1774, but delegates reconvened in May 1775. During the intervening months, patriot leaders honed their arguments for resisting British tyranny, and committees of correspondence circulated the latest news and debates. While leading patriots began to advocate resistance in the strongest possible terms, the eruption of armed clashes between British soldiers and local farmers fueled the argument for independence. It also led the Continental Congress to establish a Continental Army in June 1775. A year later, in July 1776, as the fighting continued, the congress finally declared independence.

Armed Conflict Erupts

As debates over independence intensified, the Sons of Liberty and other patriot groups not only spread propaganda against the British but also gathered and stored weapons and organized and trained local militia companies. Female patriots continued the boycott of British goods but began to manufacture bandages and bullets as well. Some northern colonists freed enslaved African Americans who agreed to enlist in the militia. Others kept close watch on the movements of British troops.

On April 18, 1775, Boston patriots observed British soldiers boarding boats in the harbor. The British were headed to Lexington, intending to confiscate guns and ammunition hidden there and in neighboring Concord and perhaps arrest patriot leaders. Hoping to warn his fellow patriots of the approaching soldiers, Paul Revere beat them to Lexington but was stopped on the road to Concord by the British. By that time, however, a network of riders was spreading the alarm. One of them alerted Concord residents of the impending danger.

Early in the morning of April 19, the first shots rang out on the village green of Lexington. After a brief exchange between British soldiers and local militiamen—known as minutemen for the speed with which they assembled—eight colonists lay dead. The British troops then moved on to Concord, where they uncovered and burned colonial

The Battle of Lexington
On April 19, 1775, British soldiers fought local militias, killing eight Lexington minutemen before marching off to Concord. Two visitors from Connecticut witnessed the battle on the village green in Lexington: Amos Doolittle, a silversmith, and Ralph Earl, a portraitist. From Earle's sketches, Doolittle engraved the militiamen scrambling for safety, while the main redcoat column advances from the north.
Superstock/Everett Collection

supplies. However, patriots in nearby towns had now been alerted. Borrowing guerrilla tactics from American Indians, colonists hid behind trees, walls, and barns and battered the British soldiers as they marched back to Boston, killing 73 and wounding 200.

Word of the conflict traveled quickly. Outraged Bostonians attacked British troops and forced them to retreat to ships in the harbor. The victory was short-lived, however, and the British soon regained control of Boston. But colonial forces entrenched themselves on hills just north of the city. Then in May, Ethan Allen and his Green Mountain Boys from Vermont joined militias from Connecticut and Massachusetts to capture the British garrison at Fort Ticonderoga, New York. The battle for North America had begun.

When the **Second Continental Congress** convened in Philadelphia on May 10, 1775, the most critical question for delegates like Pennsylvania patriot John Dickinson was how to ensure time for discussion and negotiation. Armed conflict had erupted, but did that mean that independence should, or must, follow? Other delegates insisted that independence was the only appropriate response to armed attacks on colonial residents. Patrick Henry of Virginia declared, "Gentlemen may cry 'peace, peace' but there is no peace. The war is actually begun!"

Less than a month later, on June 16, British forces under General Sir William Howe attacked patriot fortifications on Breed's Hill and Bunker Hill, north of the city. The British won the day when patriots ran out of ammunition. But the redcoats—so called because of their bright red uniforms—suffered more than 1,000 casualties, while only half that number of patriots were killed or wounded. This costly victory allowed the British to maintain control of Boston for nine more months, but the heavy losses emboldened patriot militiamen.

Building a Continental Army

The Battle of Bunker Hill convinced the congress to establish an army for the defense of the colonies and appoint forty-three-year-old Brigadier General George Washington as commander in chief. More comfortable leading troops than debating politics, Washington gave up his seat at the Continental Congress and on June 23 headed to Cambridge, Massachusetts, to take command of ten companies of frontier marksmen along with militia companies already engaged in battle.

Since the Continental Congress had not yet proclaimed itself a national government, Washington depended largely on the willingness of local militia companies to accept his command and of individual colonies to supply soldiers, arms, and ammunition. Throughout the summer of 1775,

Washington wrote dozens of letters to patriot political leaders, including delegates at the Continental Congress, detailing the army's urgent need for men, supplies, and discipline. He sought to remove incompetent officers and improve order among the troops, who spent too much time drinking, gambling, visiting prostitutes, and fighting with militiamen from other locales.

As he sought to forge a disciplined army, Washington and his officers developed a twofold military strategy.

Militiamen

This 1784 German illustration shows a uniform worn by a sharpshooter (left) and a Pennsylvania regular infantryman (right). Patriot soldiers often dressed in the uniforms of their local militia, which gave the Continental Army a very diverse appearance. Many Germans (Hessians) who fought as mercenaries for the British would have seen these uniforms. Anne S. K. Brown Military Collection, Brown University Library

Concerned about British forces and their Indian allies in Canada and New York, they sought to drive the British out of Boston and to secure the colonies from attack by enemy forces farther north. In November 1775, American troops under General Richard Montgomery captured Montreal. However, the difficult trek in cold weather decimated the patriot reinforcements led by General Benedict Arnold, and American troops failed to dislodge the British from Quebec. Smallpox ravaged many of the survivors.

Despite the disastrous outcome of the invasion of Canada, the Continental Army secured important victories in the winter of 1775–1776. To improve Washington's position in eastern Massachusetts, General Henry Knox retrieved weapons captured at Fort Ticonderoga. In March, Washington positioned the forty-three cannons on Dorchester Heights and surprised the British with a bombardment that drove them from Boston. General Howe was forced to retreat with his troops to Nova Scotia.

Reasons for Caution and for Action

As the British retreated from Boston, the war had already spread into Virginia. In the spring of 1775, local militias had forced Lord Dunmore, Virginia's royal governor, to take refuge on British ships in Norfolk harbor. Dunmore encouraged white servants and black slaves to join him there, and thousands did so. When Dunmore led his army back into Virginia in November 1775, hundreds of black men fought with British troops at the Battle of Great Bridge. Once he reclaimed the governor's mansion in Williamsburg, Dunmore issued an official proclamation that declared "all indent[ur]ed Servants, Negroes or others (appertaining to Rebels)" to be free if they were "able and willing to bear Arms" for the British.

Dunmore's Proclamation, which offered freedom to slaves willing to fight for the crown, heightened concerns among patriot leaders about the consequences of declaring independence. Although they wanted liberty for themselves, most did not want to disrupt the plantation economy or the existing social hierarchy. Could the colonies throw off the shackles of British tyranny without loosening other bonds at the same time? Given these concerns, many delegates at the Continental Congress, which included large planters, successful merchants, and professional men, hesitated to act.

Moreover, some still hoped for a negotiated settlement. But the king and Parliament refused to compromise in any way with colonies that they considered to be in rebellion. Instead, in December 1775, the king prohibited any negotiation or trade with the colonies, adding further weight to the claims of radicals that independence was a necessity. The January 1776 publication of Tom Paine's **Common Sense**, which sold more than 120,000 copies in three months, helped turn the tide toward independence as well.

Paine rooted his arguments both in biblical stories familiar to American readers and in newer scientific analogies, such as Isaac Newton's theory of gravity. It was Paine's ability to wield both religious and scientific ideas—appealing to the spirit and the intellect—that made *Common Sense* attractive to diverse groups of colonists. Within weeks of its publication, George Washington wrote to a friend that "the sound Doctrine and unanswerable reasoning contain[in] Common Sense" would convince colonists of the "Propriety of a Separation." Farmers and artisans also applauded *Common Sense*, debating its claims at taverns and coffeehouses, which had become increasingly popular venues for political discussion in the 1760s and 1770s.

Explore

Read Paine's words and a rebuttal in Documents 6.1 and 6.2.

By the spring of 1776, a growing number of patriots believed that independence was necessary. Colonies began to take control of their legislatures and instruct their delegates to the Continental Congress to support independence. The congress also sent an agent to France to request economic and military assistance for the patriot cause. And in May, the congress advised colonies that had not yet done so to establish independent governments.

Declaring Independence

Taken together, the spread of armed conflict and the rationale offered in *Common Sense* convinced patriots that the time to declare independence was at hand. In early June 1776, Richard Henry Lee of Virginia introduced a motion to the Continental Congress, resolving that "these United Colonies are, and of right ought to be, Free and Independent States." A heated debate followed in which Lee and John Adams argued passionately for independence. Eventually, even more cautious delegates, like Robert Livingston of New York, were convinced. Livingston concluded that "they should yield to the torrent if they hoped to direct it." He then joined Adams, Thomas Jefferson, Benjamin Franklin, and Roger Sherman on a committee to draft a formal statement justifying independence.

The thirty-three-year-old Jefferson took the lead in preparing the declaration. Building on ideas expressed by Paine, Adams, Lee, and George Mason, he drew on language used in the dozens of local "declarations" written earlier by town meetings, county officials, and colonial assemblies. The Virginia Declaration of Rights drafted by Mason in May 1776, for example, claimed that "all men are

DOCUMENTS 6.1 AND 6.2

Debating Independence: Two Views

Thomas Paine's *Common Sense* was the most widely read pamphlet supporting American independence. Paine's plain style and use of biblical allusions appealed to ordinary people and ignited the Revolutionary movement. But not all colonists were convinced. Charles Inglis, rector of Trinity Church in New York City, published loyalist pamphlets, though often anonymously and from the safety of the British-occupied city. His 1776 pamphlet *The True Interest of America Impartially Stated* provided one of the most influential loyalist arguments.

Explore

6.1 Thomas Paine | *Common Sense*, January 1776

In England a King hath little more to do than to make war and give away places; which, in plain terms, is to impoverish the nation, and set it together by the ears. A pretty business, indeed, for a man to be allowed eight hundred thousand sterling a year for, and worshipped into the bargain! Of more worth is one honest man to society, and in the sight of God, than all the crowned ruffians that ever lived. . . .

But where, say some, is the King of America? I will tell you, friend, he reigns above, and does not make havock of mankind like the royal brute of Great Britain. Yet that we may not appear to be defective even in earthly honors, let a day be solemnly set apart for proclaiming the charter; let it be brought forth, placed on the divine law, the word of God: let a crown be placed thereon, by which the world may know that so far we approve of monarchy, that in America, THE LAW IS KING. For as in absolute governments the King is law, so in free countries the Law *ought* to be King; and there ought to be no other. But lest any ill use should afterwards arise, let the crown, at the conclusion of the ceremony, be demolished, and scattered among the people whose right it is.

A government of our own is our natural right; and when a man seriously reflects on the precariousness of his human affairs, he will become convinced, that it is infinitely wiser and safer, to form a constitution of our own in a cool deliberate manner, while we have it in our power, than to trust such an interesting event to time and chance.

Source: Thomas Paine, *Common Sense; Addressed to the Inhabitants of America* (London: H. D. Symonds, 1792), 11, 20.

---

born equally free and independent, and have certain inherent natural Rights." Central to many of these documents was the contract theory of government proposed by the seventeenth-century British philosopher John Locke. He argued that sovereignty resided in the people, who submitted voluntarily to laws and authorities in exchange for protection of their life, liberty, and property. The people could therefore reconstitute or overthrow a government that abused its powers. Jefferson summarized this argument and then listed the abuses and crimes perpetrated by King George III against the colonies, which justified patriots' decision to break their contract with British authorities.

Once prepared, the **Declaration of Independence** was then debated and revised. In the final version, all references to slavery were removed. But delegates agreed to list among the abuses suffered by the colonies the fact that the king "excited domestic insurrections amongst us," referring to the threat posed by Dunmore to the institution of slavery. On July 2, 1776, delegates from twelve colonies approved the Declaration, with only New York abstaining. Independence was publicly proclaimed on July 4 when the Declaration was published as a broadside to be circulated throughout the colonies, although such an act was tantamount to treason.

REVIEW & RELATE

- What challenges did Washington face when he was given command of the Continental Army?

- How and why did proponents of independence prevail in the debates that preceded the publication of the Declaration of Independence?

 LEARNINGCurve bedfordstmartins.com/hewittlawson/LC

Explore

6.2 Charles Inglis | The True Interest of America Impartially Stated, March 1776

Suppose we were to revolt from Great Britain, declare ourselves independent, and set up a republic of our own—what would be the consequence? I stand aghast at the prospect; my blood runs chill when I think of the calamities, the complicated evils that must ensue, and may be clearly foreseen—it is impossible for any man to foresee them all. . . .

The Americans are properly Britons. They have the same manners, habits, and ideas of Britons; and have been accustomed to a similar form of government. But Britons never could bear the extremes, either of monarchy or republicanism. Some of their kings have aimed at despotism, but always failed. Repeated efforts have been made toward democracy, and they equally failed. Once, indeed, republicanism triumphed over the constitution; the despotism of one person ensued; both were finally expelled. . . . Limited monarchy is the form of government which is most favorable to liberty, which is best adapted to the genius and temper of Britons; although here and there among us a crackbrained zealot for democracy or absolute monarchy may be sometimes found.

Source: The Reverend Charles Inglis, *The True Interest of America Impartially Stated* (Philadelphia, 1776).

Interpret the Evidence

- How do Paine and Inglis differ in what they consider the proper form of government for the Americas?
- Why might Inglis have chosen to attack Paine's argument in *Common Sense* so vehemently?

Put It in Context

Why did the pamphlet emerge as a popular form of political discourse during the Revolutionary era?

Choosing Sides

Probably no more than half of American colonists actively supported the patriots. Perhaps a fifth actively supported the British, including many merchants and most officials appointed by the king and Parliament. The rest tried to stay neutral or were largely indifferent unless the war came to their doorstep. Both patriots and loyalists included men and women from all classes and races and from both rural and urban areas.

Recruiting Supporters

Men who took up arms against the British before independence was declared and the women who supported them clearly demonstrated their commitment to the patriot cause. In some colonies, patriots had organized local committees, courts, and assemblies to assume governance should British officials lose their authority. White servants and enslaved blacks in Virginia who fled to British ships or marched with Lord Dunmore made their loyalties known as well. Some Indians, too, declared their allegiance early in the conflict. In May 1775, Guy Johnson, the British superintendent for Indian affairs for the northern colonies, left Albany, New York, and sought refuge in Canada. He was accompanied by 120 British loyalists and 90 Mohawk warriors. The latter were led by the mission-educated chief of the Mohawks, Joseph Brant (Thayendanegea), who had translated the Anglican prayer book into Mohawk and who had fought with the British in the French and Indian War.

The Continental Congress, like Johnson, recognized the importance of Indians to the outcome of any colonial war. It appointed commissioners from the "United Colonies" to meet with representatives of the six nations of the Iroquois Confederacy in August 1775. While Brant's group of Mohawk warriors had already committed to supporting the British, some Oneida Indians, influenced by missionary and patriot sympathizer Samuel Kirkland, wanted to support the colonies. Others, however, urged neutrality, at least for the moment.

> **Explore**
>
> See Document 6.3 for one Oneida leader's reasons for remaining neutral.

Once independence was declared, there was far more pressure on all groups to choose sides. The stance of political and military leaders and soldiers was clear. But to win against Great Britain required the support of a large portion of the civilian population as well. As battle lines shifted back and forth across New England, the Middle Atlantic region, and the South, many civilians caught up in the fighting were faced with difficult choices.

DOCUMENT 6.3

Oneida Address to Connecticut Governor Jonathan Trumbull, June 1775

American Indians faced a potentially perilous choice once the Revolutionary War began. Like the undecided colonists, Indians had to determine whether to align with the patriots or with the loyalists. The members of the Oneida tribe in Connecticut sought a middle course, hoping to stake out neutral ground between the opposing sides. The following statement from the chief warriors of the Oneida to the governor of Connecticut outlines the tribe's reasoning. The Oneidas eventually did take a side; unlike most tribes, they fought alongside the colonists.

Explore

BROTHERS: We have heard of the unhappy differences and great contention between you and Old England. We wonder greatly, and are troubled in our minds.

BROTHERS: Possess your minds in peace respecting us Indians. We cannot intermeddle in this dispute between two brothers. The quarrel seems to be unnatural. You are *two brothers of one blood*. We are unwilling to join on either side in such a contest, for we bear an equal affection to both you Old and New England. Should the great king of England apply to us for aid, we shall deny him; if the Colonies apply, we shall refuse. The present situation of you two brothers is new and strange to us. We Indians cannot find, nor recollect in the traditions of our ancestors, the like case, or a similar instance.

BROTHERS: For these reasons possess your minds in peace, and take no umbrage that we Indians refuse joining in the contest. We are for peace.

BROTHERS: Was it an alien, a foreign nation, who had struck you, we should look into the matter. We hope, through the wise government and good pleasure of God, your distresses may soon be removed and the dark clouds be dispersed.

BROTHERS: As we have declared for peace, we desire you will not apply to our Indian brethren in New England for their assistance. Let us Indians be all of one mind, and live with one another; and you white people settle your own disputes between yourselves.

Source: William Leete Stone, *Life of Joseph Brant—Thayendanegea* (New York: Anderson V. Blake, 1838), 1:62–63.

Interpret the Evidence

- Why does the Oneida chief address his audience as "brothers"?
- How does the chief justify the Oneidas' neutral stance?

Put It in Context

Why was it difficult, if not impossible, for Indians and colonists to remain neutral once the fighting started?

Many colonists who remained loyal to the king found safe haven in cities like New York, Newport, and Charleston, which remained under British control throughout much of the war. **Loyalist** men were welcomed as reinforcements to the British army. Still, those who made their loyalist sympathies clear risked a good deal. When British troops were forced out of cities or towns they had temporarily occupied, many loyalists faced harsh reprisals. Patriots had no qualms about invading the homes of loyalists, punishing women and children, and destroying or confiscating property. Grace Galloway was denounced by former friends and evicted from her Philadelphia home after her loyalist husband, Joseph, fled to New York City in 1777.

Many loyalists were members of the economic and political elite, but others came from ordinary backgrounds. Tenants, small farmers, and slaves joined the loyalist cause in defiance of their landlords, their owners, and wealthy planters. The Hudson valley was home to many poorer loyalists, whose sympathy for the British was heightened by the patriot commitments of their wealthy landlords. When the fighting moved south, many former Regulators (see chapter 5) also supported the British as a result of their hostility to patriot leaders among North Carolina's eastern elite.

Perhaps most importantly, the majority of Indian nations ultimately sided with the British. The Mohawk, Seneca, and Cayuga nations in the North and the Cherokee and Creek nations in the South were among Great Britain's leading allies. Although British efforts to limit colonial migration, such as the Proclamation Line of 1763, had failed, most Indian nations still believed that a British victory offered the only hope of ending further encroachments on their territory.

Choosing Neutrality

Early in the war, many Indian nations proclaimed their neutrality. The Delaware and Shawnee nations, caught between British and American forces in the Ohio River valley, were especially eager to stay out of the fighting. The Shawnee chief Cornstalk worked tirelessly to maintain his nation's neutrality, but American soldiers killed him under a flag of truce in 1777. Eventually the Shawnees, like the Delawares, chose to ally with the British side after patriot forces refused to accept their claims of neutrality.

Colonists who sought to remain neutral during the war also faced hostility and danger. Some 80,000 Quakers, Mennonites, Amish, Shakers, and Moravians considered war immoral and embraced neutrality. These men refused to bear arms, hire substitutes, or pay taxes to new state governments. The largest number of religious pacifists lived in Pennsylvania. Despite Quakerism's deep roots there, pacifists were treated as suspect by both patriots and loyalists.

In June 1778, Pennsylvania authorities jailed nine Mennonite farmers who refused to take an oath of allegiance to the revolutionary government. Their worldly goods were sold by the state, leaving their wives and children destitute. Quakers were routinely fined and imprisoned for refusing to support the patriot cause and harassed by British authorities in the areas they controlled. At the same time, Quaker meetings regularly disciplined members who offered aid to either side, disowning more than 1,700 members during the Revolution. Betsy Ross was among those disciplined when her husband joined the patriot forces and she sewed flags for the Continental Army.

Committing to Independence

After July 4, 1776, the decision to support independence took on new meaning. If the United States failed to win the war, all those who actively supported the cause could be considered traitors. The families of Continental soldiers faced especially difficult decisions as the conflict spread across the colonies and soldiers moved farther and farther from home. Men too old or too young to fight proved their patriotism by gathering arms and ammunition and patrolling local communities.

Meanwhile some female patriots accompanied their husbands or fiancés as camp followers, providing food, laundry, sewing, and other material resources to needy soldiers. Most patriot women remained at home, however, and demonstrated their commitment to independence by raising funds, gathering information, and sending clothes, bedding, and other goods to soldiers at the front. The Continental Army was desperately short of supplies from the beginning of the war. Northern women were urged to increase cloth production, while farm women in the South were asked to plant crops to feed the soldiers. The response was overwhelming. Women in Hartford, Connecticut, produced 1,000 coats and vests and 1,600 shirts in 1776 alone. Mary Fraier of Chester County, Pennsylvania, was one of many women who collected clothing door-to-door and then washed and mended it before delivering it to troops stationed nearby. Other women opened their homes to soldiers wounded in battle or ill with fevers, dysentery, and other diseases.

Some African American women also became ardent patriots. Phillis Wheatley of Boston, whose owners taught her to read and write, published a collection of poems in

1776 and sent a copy to General Washington. She urged readers to recognize Africans as children of God:

> Remember Christians, Negroes, black as Cain,
> May be refin'd, and join th' angelic train

Rewarded with freedom by her master, Wheatley was among a small number of blacks who actively supported the patriot cause. Of course, the majority of black Americans labored as slaves in the South. While some joined the British in hopes of gaining their freedom, most were not free to choose sides.

REVIEW & RELATE

How did colonists choose sides during the Revolutionary War? What factors influenced their decisions?

Why did so many Indian tribes try to stay neutral during the conflict? Why was it so difficult for Indians to remain neutral?

 LEARNINGCurve bedfordstmartins.com/hewittlawson/LC

Fighting for Independence

After July 4, 1776, battles between British and colonial troops intensified, and the patriots suffered a series of military defeats that must have made some wonder about the wisdom of undertaking a revolution. It was more than five months after independence was declared before patriots celebrated a military victory against the British. In 1777, however, the tide turned for the Continental Army, although British forces remained formidable. A year later, it was clear that victory would not be easily won and that each side needed support from women on the home front as well as men on the battlefront.

British Troops Gain Early Victories

In the summer of 1776, when General Washington tried to lead his army out of Boston to confront British troops en route to New York City, many soldiers deserted and returned home. They believed that New York men should defend New York. Among the soldiers who remained with Washington, many were landless laborers whose wives and sisters followed the troops as their only means of support. Although Washington deemed these "camp followers" undesirable, the few hundred women provided critical services to ordinary soldiers. Ultimately, Washington arrived in New York with 19,000 men, many of whom were

poorly armed and poorly trained and some of whom were coerced into service by local committees of safety.

The ragtag Continental force faced a formidable foe with a powerful navy and a far larger and better-trained army. Throughout the summer, British ships sailed into New York harbor or anchored off the coast of Long Island. General Howe, hoping to overwhelm the colonists, ordered 10,000 troops to march into the city in the weeks immediately after the Declaration of Independence was signed. But the Continental Congress rejected Howe's offer of peace and a royal pardon.

So Howe prepared to take control of New York City by force and then march up the Hudson valley, isolating New York and New England from the rest of the rebellious colonies. He was aided by some 8,000 Hessian mercenaries (German soldiers being paid to fight for the British) and naval reinforcements under the command of Admiral Richard Howe. On August 27, 1776, British forces clashed with a far smaller contingent of Continentals on Long Island. More than 1,500 patriots were killed or wounded in the fierce fighting, diminishing the army's strength even further.

By November, the British had captured Fort Lee in New Jersey and attacked the Continental Army at Fort Washington, north of New York City. The large community of loyalists in the New York/New Jersey region served as ready hosts for General Howe and his officers, and ordinary redcoats survived by looting the stores, farms, and homes of patriots. Meanwhile Washington led his weary troops and camp followers into Pennsylvania, while the Continental Congress, fearing a British attack on Philadelphia, fled to Baltimore.

Although General Howe might have ended the patriot threat right then by a more aggressive campaign, he was interested primarily in wearing down the Continental Army so that the colonies would plead for peace. Neither he nor Washington engaged in full-scale frontal assaults. Washington did not have the troops or arms to do so, but he also hoped that the British would accept American independence once they saw the enormous effort it would take to defeat the colonies.

Patriots Prevail in New Jersey

The Continental Army had not gained a single military victory between July 1776, when the colonies declared independence, and December. Fortunately for Washington, Howe followed the European tradition of waiting out the winter months and returning to combat after the spring thaw. This tactic gave the patriots the opportunity to regroup, repair weapons and wagons, and recruit soldiers. Yet Washington was not eager to face the cold and discomfort of the winter with troops discouraged by repeated defeats and retreats.

Camped in eastern Pennsylvania, Washington discovered that General Howe had sent Hessian troops to occupy

The British Burn New York City, 1776

This print by François Xavier Haberman shows several buildings along a New York City street set ablaze by the British troops of General William Howe on September 19, 1776. It also depicts citizens being beaten by redcoats while African slaves engage in looting. The British promised slaves their freedom if they opposed the patriots.   Library of Congress

the city of Trenton, New Jersey, just across the Delaware River. On Christmas Eve, Washington crossed the river with some 2,500 soldiers and attacked Trenton. The Continentals quickly routed the surprised Hessians. Then they marched on Princeton, where they battled three regiments of regular British troops, defeating them on January 3, 1777. The British army retreated from New Jersey, settling back into New York City, and the Continental Congress returned to Philadelphia. By January 1777, it seemed clear to both sides that the conflict would indeed be harder, more costly, and more deadly than anyone had imagined in the spring of 1775.

A Critical Year of Warfare

The British and Continental armies emerged from their winter camps in the spring of 1777. The British forces, including regular army units, American loyalists, Indian allies, Hessians, and naval men-of-war, were concentrated largely in New York City and Canada. The Continental forces, numbering fewer than 5,000 men, were entrenched near Morristown, New Jersey, far from the patriot centers of New England and from the coastal areas controlled by the British army and navy. Although the Continental Congress had returned to Philadelphia, it feared that the British would seek to capture the city and split the United States in two.

General Howe also believed that the key to victory was capturing Philadelphia, and he hoped that success there might lead the patriots to surrender. Washington's force was too small to defeat Howe's army, but it delayed his advance on the capital city by attacks along the way. En route, Howe learned that he was still expected to reinforce General John Burgoyne's soldiers, who were advancing south from Canada. Too late to redirect his efforts, Howe continued to Philadelphia and captured it in September 1777. Meanwhile Burgoyne and his 7,200 troops had regained control of Fort Ticonderoga on July 7. He continued south along the Hudson valley, but by late July his forces stalled as they waited for supplies from Canada and reinforcements from Howe and General Barry St. Leger.

In July, St. Leger had marched east through New York State while Joseph Brant and his sister Molly Brant, a powerful Indian leader in her own right, gathered a force of Mohawk, Seneca, and Cayuga warriors to support the British forces. But on August 6, they suffered a stunning defeat. At Oriskany, New York, a band of German American farmers led by General Nicholas Herkimer held off the British advance, allowing General Arnold to reach nearby Fort Stanwix with reinforcements. On August 23, the British and Indian troops were forced to retreat to Canada (Map 6.1).

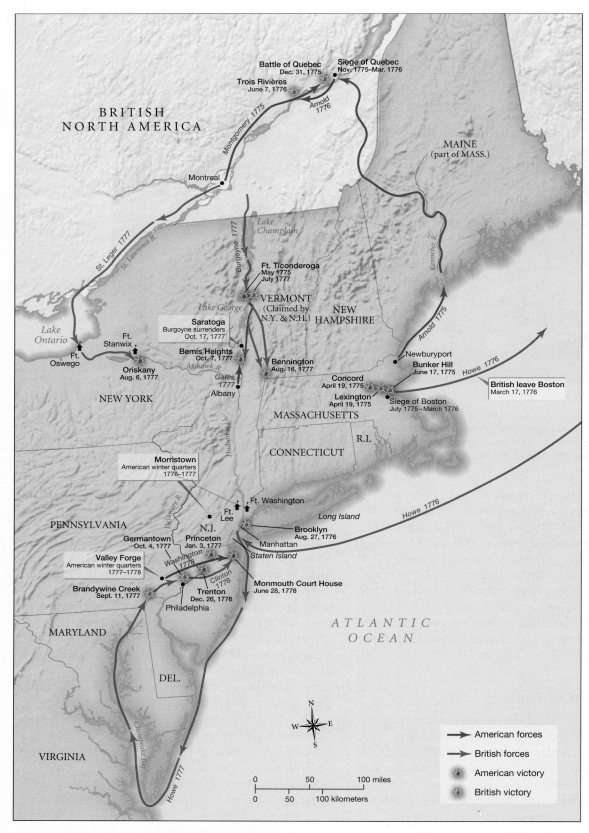

MAP 6.1   The War in the North, 1775–1778

After early battles in Massachusetts, patriots invaded Canada but failed to capture Quebec. The British army captured New York City in 1776 and Philadelphia in 1777, but New Jersey remained a battle zone through 1778. Meanwhile General Burgoyne secured Canada for Britain and then headed south, but his forces were defeated by patriots at the crucial Battle of Saratoga.

General Howe's reinforcements never materialized, and Burgoyne now faced a brutal onslaught from patriot militiamen. Vermont's Green Mountain Boys, Continental soldiers under the command of Generals Horatio Gates and Benedict Arnold, and their Oneida allies also poured into the region. In September, patriots defeated the British at Freeman's Farm, with the British suffering twice the casualties of the Continentals. Fighting intensified in early October, when Burgoyne lost a second battle at Freeman's Farm. Ten days later, he surrendered his remaining army of 5,800 men to General Gates at nearby Saratoga, New York.

The Continental Army's victory in the **Battle of Saratoga** stunned the British and strengthened the patriots. It undercut the significance of Howe's victory at Philadelphia and indicated the general's misunderstanding of the character of the patriot cause and the nature of the war he was fighting. The patriot victory gave hope to General Washington as his troops dug in at Valley Forge for another long winter and to members of the Continental Congress who had temporarily retreated to York, Pennsylvania. It also gave Benjamin Franklin greater leverage to convince French officials to support the American cause.

Patriots Gain Critical Assistance

Despite significant victories in the fall of 1777, the following winter proved especially difficult for Continental forces. The quarters at **Valley Forge** were again marked by bitter cold, poor food, inadequate clothing, and scarce supplies. Discipline deteriorated, and many recent recruits were poorly trained. Critical assistance arrived through the voluntary efforts of Baron Friedrich von Steuben, a Prussian officer recruited by Benjamin Franklin, who took charge of drilling soldiers. Other officers experienced in European warfare also joined the patriot cause during the winter of 1777–1778: the Marquis de Lafayette of France, Johann Baron de Kalb of Bavaria, and Thaddeus Kosciusko and Casimir Count Pulaski, both of Poland. The Continental Army continued to be plagued by problems of recruitment, discipline, wages, and supplies. But the contributions of Steuben, Lafayette, and other foreign volunteers, along with the leadership of Washington and his officers, sustained the military effort.

Patriots on the home front were also plagued by problems in 1777–1778. Families living in battlefield areas were especially vulnerable to the shifting fortunes of war. When British troops captured Philadelphia in the fall of 1777, a British officer commandeered the house of Elizabeth Drinker, a well-to-do Quaker matron. An angry Drinker reported that the officer moved in with "3 Horses 2 Cows 2 Sheep and 3 Turkeys" along with "3 Servants 2 White Men and one Negro Boy." Meanwhile women who lived far from the conflict were forced to fend for themselves as soldiers moved wherever the Continental Army took them. The wives of political leaders also faced long years alone while their husbands remained at their posts. To hasten the end, many women formed voluntary associations, like the Ladies Association of Philadelphia, to provide critical resources for the army and thus aid the patriot cause. **See Document Project 6: Women in the Revolution, page 185.**

While most women worked tirelessly on the home front, some cast their fate with the army. Camp followers continued to provide critical services to the military, including cooking, washing, sewing, and nursing. They suffered along with the troops in the face of scarce supplies and harsh weather and depended like the soldiers on food, clothing, and bedding supplied by female volunteers in Philadelphia, Boston, Baltimore, and other cities.

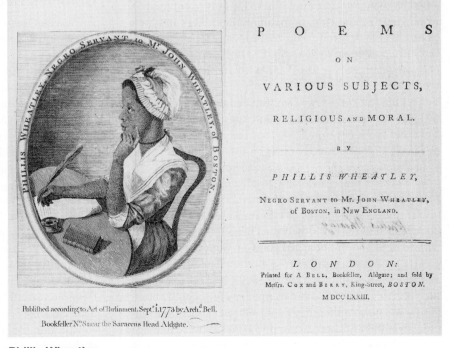

Phillis Wheatley

This portrait of Phillis Wheatley appears on the title page of her book of poems, printed in London in 1773. Like Deborah Sampson, Phillis Wheatley sided with the patriots, but as a writer, not a soldier. She won her personal freedom as a result of her efforts.   The Pierpont Morgan Library/Art Resource, NY

Women with sufficient courage and resources served as spies and couriers for British and Continental forces. Lydia Darragh, a wealthy Philadelphian, eavesdropped on conversations among the British officers who occupied her house and then carried detailed notes to Washington hidden in the folds of her dress. Some women, like Nancy Hart Morgan of Georgia, took more direct action. Morgan protected her backcountry home from half a dozen British soldiers by lulling them into a sense of security at dinner, hiding their guns, and shooting two before neighbors came to hang the rest.

Some patriot women took up arms on the battlefield. A few, such as Margaret Corbin, accompanied their husbands to the front lines and were thrust into battle. When her husband was killed in battle at Fort Washington in November 1776, Corbin took his place loading and firing cannons until the fort fell to the British. In addition, a small number of women, like Deborah Sampson, disguised themselves as men and enlisted as soldiers.

Surviving on the Home Front

Whether black or white, enslaved or free, women and children faced hardship, uncertainty, loneliness, and fear as a result of the war. Even those who did not directly engage enemy troops took on enormous burdens during the conflict. Farm wives had to take on the tasks of plowing or planting in addition to their normal domestic duties. In cities, women worked ceaselessly to find sufficient food, wood, candles, and cloth to maintain themselves and their children. One desperate wife, Mary Donnelly, wrote, "[I was] afraid to open my Eyes on the Daylight [lest] I should hear my infant cry for Bread and not have it in my power to relieve him."

As the war spread, women watched as Continental and British forces slaughtered cattle and hogs for food, stole corn and other crops or burned them to keep the enemy from obtaining supplies, looted houses and shops, and kidnapped or liberated slaves and servants. Some home invasions turned savage. Both patriot and loyalist papers in New York, Philadelphia, and Charleston reported cases of rape.

Despite the desperate circumstances, most women knew they had to act on their own behalf to survive. Faced with merchants who hoarded goods in hopes of making greater profits when prices rose, housewives raided stores and warehouses and took coffee, sugar, and other items they needed. Others learned as much as they could about family finances so that they could submit reports to local officials if their houses, farms, or businesses were damaged or looted. Growing numbers of women banded together to assist one another, to help more impoverished families, and to supply troops badly in need of clothes, food, bandages, and bullets.

How did the patriot forces fare in 1776? How and why did the tide of war turn in 1777?

What role did colonial women and foreign men play in the conflict in the early years of the war?

LEARNINGCurve bedfordstmartins.com/hewittlawson/LC

Governing in Revolutionary Times

Amid the constant upheavals of war, patriot leaders established governments to replace those abolished by declaring independence. At the national level, responsibilities ranged from coordinating and funding military operations to developing diplomatic relations with foreign countries and Indian nations. At the state level, constitutions had to be drafted and approved, laws enforced, and military needs assessed and met. Whether state or national, new governments had to assure their followers that they were not simply replacing old forms of oppression with new ones. Yet few states moved to eliminate the most oppressive institution in the nation, slavery.

Colonies Become States

For most of the war, the Continental Congress acted in lieu of a national government while the delegates worked to devise a more permanent structure. But the congress had little authority of its own and depended mainly on states for funds and manpower. Delegates did draft the **Articles of Confederation** in 1777 and submitted them to the states for approval. Eight of the thirteen states ratified the plan for a national government by mid-1778. But nearly three more years passed before the last state, Maryland, approved the Articles. The lack of a central government meant that state governments played a critical role throughout the war.

Even before the Continental Congress declared American independence, some colonies had forced royal officials to flee and established new state governments. Some states abided by the regulations in their colonial charters or by English common law. Others, including Delaware, South Carolina, Virginia, New Jersey, and Pennsylvania, created new governments based on a written constitution. Because the earliest constitutions were written in the midst of war, they were often completed in haste, sometimes by legislative bodies without any specific authorization and without popular approval of the final document.

These constitutions reflected the fear of centralized power that emerged from the struggle against British tyranny. In Pennsylvania, radical patriots influenced by Tom Paine developed one of the most democratic constitutions, enhancing the power of voters and legislators and limiting the power of the executive branch. The constitution established only one legislative house, elected by popular vote, and the governor was replaced by an executive council. Those elected to the legislature could not serve for more than four in any seven years to discourage the formation of a political aristocracy in the state. Although Pennsylvania's constitution was among the most radical, all states limited centralized power in some way.

Finally, most states, building on the model offered by Virginia, included in their constitutions a bill of rights that ensured citizens freedom of the press, freedom of elections, speedy trials by one's peers, humane punishments, and the right to form militias. Some state constitutions expanded these rights to include freedom of speech and assembly, the right to petition and to bear arms, and equal protection of the laws. The New Jersey constitution, written in 1776, enfranchised all free inhabitants who met the property qualifications, thereby allowing some single or widowed women and free blacks to vote in local and state elections. This surprising decision was apparently made with little debate or dissent.

Patriots Divide over Slavery

Although state constitutions were revolutionary in many respects, few of them addressed the issue of slavery. Only Vermont abolished slavery in its 1777 constitution. Legislators in Pennsylvania approved a gradual abolition law by which slaves born after 1780 could claim their freedom at age twenty-eight. In Massachusetts, two slaves sued for their freedom in county courts in 1780–1781. Quock Walker, who had been promised his freedom by a former master, sued his current master to gain manumission (release from slavery). About the same time, an enslaved woman, Mumbet, who was the widow of a Revolutionary soldier, initiated a similar case. Mumbet won her case and changed her name to Elizabeth Freeman. When Walker's owner appealed the local court's decision to free his slave, the Massachusetts Supreme Court cited the Mumbet case and ruled that slavery conflicted with the state constitution, which declared "all men . . . free and equal." Walker, too, was freed.

In southern states, however, slaves had little recourse to the law. No state south of Pennsylvania abolished the institution of slavery. And southerners held about 400,000 of the nation's 450,000 slaves. In states such as Virginia, the Carolinas, and Georgia, life for enslaved women and men

Elizabeth "Mumbet" Freeman

This watercolor portrait of Elizabeth "Mumbet" Freeman was painted on ivory by Susan Anne Ridley Sedgwick in 1811 when Freeman was sixty-nine. The first slave to be freed in Massachusetts as a result of a court case, she later worked as a domestic servant for her attorney, Theodore Sedgwick, Susan Ridley Sedgwick's father-in-law.   © Massachusetts Historical Society, Boston/The Bridgeman Art Library

grew increasingly harsh during the war. Because British forces promised freedom to blacks who fought with them, slave owners and patriot armies in the South did everything possible to ensure that African Americans did not make it behind British lines. The thousands who did manage to flee to British-controlled areas were often left to defend themselves when the redcoats retreated. There were exceptions. Lord Dunmore took a few thousand blacks with him when he fled Virginia in 1776, and British forces under General Sir Henry Clinton carried some 20,000 African Americans aboard ships retreating from Charleston and Savannah in 1781.

Despite the uncertain prospects for African Americans, the American Revolution dealt a blow to the institution of slavery. For many blacks, Revolutionary ideals required the end of slavery. Northern free black communities grew rapidly during and after the war, especially in seaport cities like New York, Philadelphia, and Boston where labor was in high demand. In the South, too, thousands of slaves gained freedom during the war, either by joining the British or by fleeing in the midst of battlefield chaos. As many as one-quarter of South Carolina's slaves had emancipated themselves by the end of the Revolution. Yet as the Continental Congress worked toward developing a framework for a national government, few delegates considered slavery or its abolition a significant issue.

France Allies with the Patriots

The Continental Congress considered an alliance with France far more critical to patriot success than the issue of slavery. French financial and military support could aid the patriots immensely, and France's traditional rivalry with Great Britain made an alliance plausible.

For France, defeat of the British would mean increased trade with North America and redressing the balance of power in Europe, where Great Britain had gained the upper hand since France's defeat in the French and Indian War. Indeed, in 1775 the French government had secretly provided funds to smuggle military supplies to the colonies. In December 1776, the Continental Congress sent Benjamin Franklin to Paris to serve as an unofficial liaison for the newly independent United States. Franklin was enormously successful, securing supplies and becoming a favorite among the French aristocracy and ordinary citizens alike.

But the French were initially unwilling to forge a formal compact with the upstart patriots. Only when the Continental Army defeated General Burgoyne at Saratoga in October 1777 did King Louis XVI agree to an official alliance. By February 1778, Franklin had secured an agreement that approved trading rights between the United States and all French possessions. France then recognized the United States as an independent nation, relinquished French territorial claims on mainland North America, and sent troops to reinforce the Continental Army. In return, the United States promised to defend French holdings in the Caribbean. A year later, Spain allied itself with France to protect its own North American holdings.

British leaders, infuriated by the alliance, declared war on France. Yet doing so ensured that military conflicts would spread well beyond North America as French forces attacked British outposts in Gibraltar, the Bay of Bengal, Senegal in West Africa, and Grenada in the West Indies. British military expenditures skyrocketed from £4 million in 1775 to £20 million in 1782. Meanwhile, in addition to their attacks on British outposts, the French supplied the United States with military officers, weapons, funds, and critical naval resources. Spain contributed by capturing British forts in West Florida and using New Orleans as a base for privateering expeditions against British ships.

Explore

To read one French volunteer soldier's experience, see Document 6.4.

Washington's French Allies

This late-eighteenth-century painting by James Peale the Elder shows Washington and his generals at Yorktown, site of the final major battle of the Revolutionary War. Among Washington's generals were the Frenchmen the Marquis de Lafayette and the Comte de Rochambeau. Peale was not at Yorktown, but he fought in the Continental Army for three years. Private Collection/Photo © Christie's Images/The Bridgeman Art Library

Faced with this new alliance, Britain's prime minister, Lord North (1771–1782), decided to concentrate British forces in New York City. This tactic forced the British army to abandon Philadelphia and return the city to patriot control in the summer of 1778. For the remainder of the war, New York City provided the sole British stronghold in the North, serving as a supply center and prisoner-of-war camp. At the same time, the American cause gained the support of the French navy, a critical addition given the limited state of American naval forces.

DOCUMENT 6.4

Chevalier de Pontgibaud | A French Volunteer at Valley Forge, 1828

After a string of defeats in the fall of 1777, the Continental Army needed an encampment to wait out the winter and prepare for the fighting to resume in the spring. General George Washington chose to station his men in Valley Forge, Pennsylvania. The conditions proved formidable; more than 2,000 men died from disease, exacerbated by poor housing and scant supplies. In the following selection, from a memoir written in 1828, Chevalier de Pontgibaud, a French volunteer in the Continental Army, describes his arrival at Valley Forge in December 1777.

Explore

What problems seem particularly troublesome to Pontgibaud?

What is the significance of the woolen coats worn by Continental officers?

Why does Pontgibaud believe the colonial cause was eventually successful?

Soon I came in sight of the camp. My imagination had pictured an army with uniforms, the glitter of arms, standards, etc., in short, military pomp of all sorts. Instead of the imposing spectacle I expected, I saw, grouped together or standing alone, a few militia men, poorly clad, and for the most part without shoes; many of them badly armed, but all well supplied with provisions, and I noticed that tea and sugar formed part of their rations. I did not then know that this was not unusual, and I laughed, for it made me think of the recruiting sergeants on the Quai de la Ferraille at Paris, who say to the yokels, "You will want for nothing when you are in the regiment, but if bread should run short you must not mind eating cakes." Here the soldiers had tea and sugar. In passing through the camp I also noticed soldiers wearing cotton night-caps under their hats, and some having for cloaks or great-coats, coarse woollen blankets, exactly like those provided for the patients in our French hospitals. I learned afterwards that these were the officers and generals.

Such, in strict truth, was—at the time I came amongst them—the appearance of this armed mob, the leader of whom was the man who has rendered the name of Washington famous; such were the colonists—unskilled warriors who learned in a few years how to conquer the finest troops that England could send against them. Such also—at the beginning of the War of Independence—was the state of want in the insurgent army, and such was the scarcity of money, and the poverty of that government, now so rich, powerful, and prosperous, that its notes, called Continental Paper Money, were nearly valueless.

Source: Chevalier de Pontgibaud, *A French Volunteer of the War for Independence*, ed. and trans. Robert Douglas (New York: J. W. Bouton, 1897), 40–41.

Put It in Context

How did the Continental Army differ from the military forces of European nations?

Raising Armies and Funds

The French alliance did create one unintended problem for the Continental Army. When Americans heard that France was sending troops, fewer men volunteered for military service, even when bounties were offered. Others took the bounty and then failed to report for duty. Local officials had the authority to draft men into the army or to accept substitutes for draftees. By the late 1770s, some draftees forced enslaved men to take their place; others hired landless laborers, the handicapped, or the mentally unfit as substitutes.

As the war spread south and west in 1778–1779, Continental forces were stretched thin, and enlistments faltered further. Soldiers faced injuries, disease, and shortages of food and ammunition. Soldiers also risked capture by the British, one of the worst fates to befall a Continental. Most patriot prisoners were held in jails in New York City or on ships in the harbor under abusive, unsanitary conditions. Colonel Ethan Allen, a captive for two and a half years, described the filthy accommodations, inadequate water, and horrid stench of the British prisons and noted the "hellish delight and triumph of the tories . . . exulting over the dead bodies of their murdered country-men." A few brave women like Elizabeth Burgin carried food and other supplies to patriot prisoners of war. Alto-gether, between 8,000 and 11,500 patriots died in British prisons in New York—more than died in battle.

The Continental Congress could do little to aid prisoners or their families, given the financial problems it faced. With no authority to impose taxes on American citizens, the congress had to find other ways to meet its financial responsibilities. It borrowed money from wealthy patriots, accepted loans from France and the Netherlands, and printed money of its own—some $200 million by 1780. However, money printed by the states was still used far more widely than were Continental dollars. "Continentals" depreciated so quickly that by late 1780 it took one hundred continentals to buy one silver dollar's worth of goods.

The situation in Philadelphia, the seat of national government, demonstrated the difficulties caused by inflation. In January 1779, housewives, sailors, and artisans gathered on the cold streets to protest high prices and low wages. Although officials tried to regulate prices, riots erupted and flour merchants were especially targeted by mobs of women and young people. By October, Philadel-phia militiamen joined the protests, marching on the house of James Wilson, a Philadelphia lawyer who sided with merchants accused of hoarding goods. Hours of rioting followed, and eventually fifteen militiamen were arrested and fined. But in the following days, city officials distrib-uted much-needed food to the poor. The Fort Wilson riot echoed events in towns and cities across the young nation.

The congress finally improved its financial standing slightly by using a $6 million loan from France to back certificates issued to wealthy patriots. Meanwhile states raised money through taxes to provide funds for govern-ment operations, backing for its paper money, and other expenses. Most residents found such taxes incredibly burdensome given wartime inflation, and even the most patriotic began to protest further efforts to squeeze money out of them. Thus the financial status of the new nation remained precarious.

Indian Affairs and Land Claims

The congress also sought to settle land claims in the western regions of the nation and build alliances with additional Indian nations. The two issues were intertwined, and both were difficult to resolve. Most Indian nations had long-standing complaints against colonists who intruded on their lands, and many patriot leaders made it clear that indepen-dence would mean further expansion into western lands.

In the late 1770s, British forces and their Indian allies fought bitter battles against patriot militias and Continental forces all along the frontier. Each side destroyed property, ruined crops, and killed civilians. In the summer and fall of 1778, Indian and American civilians suffered through a series of brutal attacks in Wyoming, Pennsylvania; Ono-quaga, New York (Brant's home community); and Cherry Valley, New York. Patriots and Indians also battled along the Virginia frontier after pioneer and militia leader Daniel Boone established a fort there in 1775.

In the South, 6,000 patriot troops laid waste to Cherokee villages in the Appalachian Mountains in retaliation for the killing of white intruders along the Watauga River by a renegade Cherokee warrior, Dragging Canoe. Yet a cousin of Dragging Canoe, Nancy Ward (Nanye-hi), who had married a white trader, remained sympathetic to the patriot cause. During the Revolution, she warned patriots of pending attacks by pro-British Cherokee warriors in 1776 and 1780, allowing the patriots to launch their own attacks. Ward apparently believed that white settlement was inevitable and that winning the friendship of patriots was the best way to ensure the survival of the Cherokee nation. Hers, however, was a minority voice among frontier Indians.

Much western land had already been claimed by individual states like Virginia, Massachusetts, Connecticut, New York, and Georgia. States with western claims hoped to use the lands to reward soldiers and expand their settlements. Maryland spoke for states without such claims, arguing that if such lands were "wrested from the common enemy by the blood and treasure of the thirteen States," they should be considered "common property, subject to be parcelled out by Congress into free and independent governments." In 1780 New York State finally ceded its western claims to the Continental Congress, and Connecti-cut and Massachusetts followed suit.

With land disputes settled, Maryland ratified the Articles of Confederation in March 1781, and a new national government was finally formed. But the congress's guarantee that western lands would be "disposed of for the common benefit of the United States" ensured continued conflicts with Indians.

REVIEW & RELATE

What values and concerns shaped state governments during the Revolutionary War?

What issues and challenges did the Continental Congress face even after the French joined the patriot side?

 LEARNINGCurve bedfordstmartins.com/hewittlawson/LC

Winning the War and the Peace

From 1778 to 1781, the battlefront in the Revolution moved south and west. As conflicts with Britain and its Indian allies intensified along the western frontier, British troops reinforced by African American fugitives fought patriots in the Carolinas and Georgia. In the final years of the war, the patriots' ability to achieve victory rested on a combination of superb strategy, alliances with France and Spain, and the continued material support of affluent men and women. However, even after Britain's surrender in October 1781, the war dragged on while peace terms were negotiated. The celebrations of victory following the signing of a peace treaty were tempered by protests among Continental soldiers demanding back pay and by the realization of the new nation's looming problems.

Fighting in the West

While the congress debated the fate of western land claims, battles continued in the Ohio and Mississippi River valleys. British commanders at Fort Michilimackinac on Lake Huron recruited Sioux, Chippewa, and Sauk warriors to attack Spanish forces along the Mississippi, while soldiers at Fort Detroit armed Ottawa, Fox, and Miami warriors to assault American settlers flooding into the Ohio River valley. British forces from Fort Detroit also moved deeper into this region, establishing a post at Vincennes on the Wabash River.

The response to these British forays was effective, if not well coordinated. In 1778 a young patriot surveyor, George Rogers Clark of Virginia, organized a patriot expedition to counter Indian raids in the west and to reinforce Spanish and French allies in the upper Mississippi valley. He fought successfully against British and Indian forces at Kaskaskia

and Cahokia on the Mississippi River. Then Clark marched his troops through the bitter February cold and launched a surprise attack on British forces at Vincennes. Although Detroit remained in British hands, Spanish troops defeated British-allied Indian forces that attacked St. Louis, giving the patriots greater control in the Ohio valley (Map 6.2).

In the summer of 1779, General John Sullivan led 4,000 patriot troops on a campaign to wipe out Mohawk, Seneca, Cayuga, and Onondaga villages in central and western New York. He succeeded in ending most attacks by Britain's Iroquois allies and disrupting the supplies being sent by British forces at Fort Niagara. Patriot attacks in Ohio also continued. In one of the worst atrocities fomented by patriots, Pennsylvania militiamen massacred more than one hundred Delaware men, women, and children near present-day Canton, Ohio, even though the Delawares had converted to Christianity and declared their neutrality.

Battles between Indian nations and American settlers did not end with the American Revolution. For the moment, however, patriot militia units and Continental forces supported by French and Spanish allies had defeated British and Indian efforts to control the Mississippi and Ohio River valleys.

War Rages in the South

Meanwhile British troops sought to regain control of southern states from Georgia to Virginia. British troops captured Savannah, Georgia, in 1778 and soon extended their control over the entire state. When General Clinton was called north in late 1778 to lead British troops against Washington's Continentals in New Jersey, he left the southern campaign in the hands of Lord Charles Cornwallis.

In May 1780, General Cornwallis reclaimed Charleston, South Carolina, and accepted the surrender of 5,000 Continental soldiers, the largest surrender of patriot troops during the war. He then evicted patriots from the city, purged them from the state government, gained military control of the state, and imposed loyalty oaths on all Carolinians able to fight. To aid his efforts, local loyalists organized militias to battle patriots in the interior. Banastre Tarleton led one especially vicious company of loyalists who slaughtered civilians and murdered many who surrendered. In retaliation, planter and merchant Thomas Sumter organized 800 men who showed a similar disregard for regular army procedures, raiding largely defenseless loyalist settlements near Hanging Rock, South Carolina, in August 1780.

Conflicts between patriots and loyalists raged across the South until the war's end (see Map 6.2). As retaliatory violence erupted in the interior of South Carolina, General Gates marched his Continental troops south to join 2,000 militiamen from Virginia and North Carolina. But his

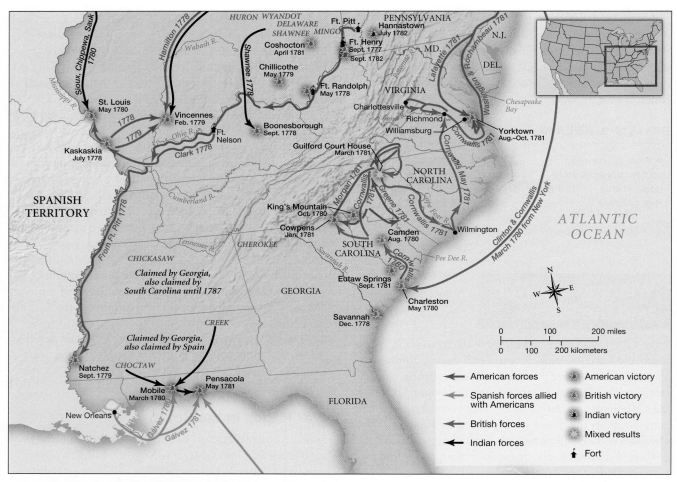

MAP 6.2 The War in the West and the South, 1777–1782
Between 1780 and 1781, major battles between Continental and British troops took place in Virginia and the Carolinas, and the British general Cornwallis finally surrendered at Yorktown, Virginia, in October 1781. But patriot forces also battled British troops and their Indian allies from 1777 to 1782 in the Ohio River valley, the lower Mississippi River, and the Gulf coast.

troops were exhausted and short of food, and on August 16 Cornwallis won a smashing victory against the combined patriot forces at Camden, South Carolina. Soon after news of Gates's defeat reached General Washington, he heard that Benedict Arnold, commander at West Point, had defected to the British. Indeed, he had been passing information to the British for some time.

Suddenly, British chances for victory seemed more hopeful. Clinton had moved the bulk of northern troops into New York City and could send units south from there to bolster Cornwallis. Cornwallis was in control of Georgia and South Carolina, and local loyalists were eager to gain control of the southern countryside. Meanwhile Continental soldiers in the North mutinied in early 1780 over terms of enlistment and pay. Patriot morale was low, funds were scarce, and civilians were growing weary of the war.

Yet somehow the patriots prevailed. A combination of luck, strong leadership, and French support turned the tide.

In October 1780, when Continental hopes looked especially bleak, a group of 800 frontier sharpshooters routed Major Patrick Ferguson's loyalist troops at King's Mountain in South Carolina. The victory kept Cornwallis from advancing into North Carolina and gave the Continentals a chance to regroup.

Shortly after the battle at King's Mountain, Washington sent General Nathanael Greene of Rhode Island to replace Gates as head of southern operations. Taking advice from local militia leaders like Daniel Morgan and Francis Marion, Greene divided his limited force into even smaller units. Marion and Morgan each led 300 Continental soldiers into the South Carolina backcountry, picking up hundreds of local militiamen along the way. At the village of Cowpens, Morgan drew Tarleton's much larger force into a circle of sharpshooters backed by Continentals and an armed cavalry. While Tarleton escaped, 100 of his men died and 800 were captured.

Cornwallis, enraged at the patriot victory, pursued Continental forces as they retreated. But Cornwallis's troops had outrun their cannons, and Greene circled back and attacked them at Guilford Court House. Although Cornwallis eventually forced the Continentals to withdraw from the battlefield, his troops suffered enormous losses. In August 1781, frustrated at the ease with which patriot forces still found local support in the South, he hunkered down in Yorktown on the Virginia coast and waited for Clinton to send reinforcements from New York.

Washington now coordinated strategy with his French allies. Comte de Rochambeau marched his 5,000 troops south from Rhode Island to Virginia as General Lafayette led his troops south along Virginia's eastern shore. At the same time, French naval ships headed north from the West Indies. One unit cut off a British fleet trying to resupply Cornwallis by sea. Another joined up with American privateers to bombard Cornwallis's forces. By mid-October, British supplies had run out, and it was clear that Clinton was not going to send reinforcements. On October 19, 1781, the British army admitted defeat.

Francis Marion

Francis Marion, known as "the Swamp Fox," and his militia waged guerrilla warfare against the British in South Carolina. Marion wreaked havoc by avoiding frontal assaults, instead conducting quick surprise attacks. This print from an 1836 painting by John Blake White shows Marion in striking headgear inviting a British officer to share a meal, while Marion's slave Oscar kneels by the table.   Anne S. K. Brown Military Collection, Brown University Library

An Uncertain Peace

The Continental Army had managed the impossible. It had defeated the British army and won the colonies' independence. Yet even with the surrender at **Yorktown**, the war continued in fits and starts. Peace negotiations in Paris dragged on as French, Spanish, British, and American representatives sought to settle a host of issues. Meanwhile British forces challenged Continental troops in and around New York City even as American recruiters found it nearly impossible to find new enlistments.

Some Continental soldiers continued to fight, but others focused on the long-festering issue of overdue wages. When the congress decided in June 1783 to discharge the remaining troops without providing back pay, a near mutiny erupted in Pennsylvania. Nearly 300 soldiers marched on the congress in Philadelphia. Washington sent troops, including Deborah Sampson/Robert Shurtliff, to put down the mutiny, and bloodshed was avoided when the Pennsylvania soldiers agreed to accept half pay and certificates for the remainder. Despite this compromise, the issue of back pay would continue to plague the nation over the next decade.

Meanwhile patriot representatives in Paris—Benjamin Franklin, John Adams, and John Jay—continued to negotiate peace terms. Rising antiwar sentiment on the British home front, especially after the surrender at Yorktown, forced the government's hand. But the Comte de Vergennes, the French foreign minister, opposed the Americans' republican principles and refused to consider the American delegates as his political equals. Given the importance of the French to the American victory, the congress had instructed its delegates to defer to French wishes. This blocked the American representatives from signing a separate peace with the British.

Eventually, however, U.S. delegates finalized a treaty that secured substantial benefits for the young nation. The United States gained control of all lands south of Canada and north of Louisiana and Florida stretching to the Mississippi River. In addition, the treaty recognized the United States to be "free Sovereign and independent states." Spain signed a separate treaty with Great Britain in which it regained control of Florida. Despite their role in the war, none of the Indian nations that occupied the lands under negotiation were consulted.

When the **Treaty of Paris** was finally signed on September 2, 1783, thousands of British troops and their supporters left the colonies for Canada, the West Indies, or England. British soldiers on the western frontier were supposed to be withdrawn at the same time, but they remained for many years and continued to foment hostilities between Indians in the region and U.S. settlers along the frontier.

The evacuation of the British also entailed the exodus of thousands of African Americans who had fought against the patriots. At the end of the war, British officials granted certificates of manumission to more than 1,300 men, 900 women, and 700 children. The largest number of these freed blacks settled in Nova Scotia, where they received small allotments of land from the British. Most, however, lacked the money, tools, or livestock to make such homesteads profitable. Despite these obstacles, some created a small Afro-Canadian community in Nova Scotia, while others migrated to areas considered more hospitable to black residents, such as Sierra Leone. Although thousands gained their freedom by taking up arms for the British, few were well rewarded for their efforts.

Explore

See Document 6.5 for a black loyalist's petition to the British cabinet.

A Surprising Victory

Americans had managed to defeat one of the most powerful military forces in the world. That victory resulted from the convergence of many circumstances. Certainly Americans benefited from fighting on their own soil. Their knowledge of the land and its resources as well as earlier experiences fighting against Indians and the French helped prepare them for battles against the British.

Just as important, British troops and officers were far removed from centers of decision making and supplies. Even supplies housed in Canada could not be easily transported the relatively short distance into New York. British commanders were often hesitant to make decisions independently, but awaiting instructions from England proved costly on several occasions, especially since strategists in London often had little sense of conditions on the ground in America.

Both sides depended on outsiders for assistance, but here, too, Americans gained the advantage. While the British army certainly outnumbered its Continental adversary, it relied heavily on German mercenaries, Indian allies, and freed blacks to bolster its regular troops. In victory, such "foreign" forces were relatively reliable, but in defeat, many of them chose to look out for their own interests. The patriots meanwhile marched with French and Spanish armies well prepared to challenge British troops and motivated to gain advantages for France and Spain if Britain was defeated.

Perhaps most importantly, a British victory was nearly impossible without conquering the American colonies one by one. Because a large percentage of colonists supported the patriot cause, British troops had to contend not only with Continental soldiers but also with an aroused citizenry fighting for its independence.

REVIEW & RELATE

How and why did the Americans win the Revolutionary War?

What uncertainties and challenges did the new nation face in the immediate aftermath of victory?

LEARNINGCurve bedfordstmartins.com/hewittlawson/LC

Conclusion: Legacies of the Revolution

After the approval of the Declaration of Independence, Thomas Hutchinson, the British official who had gained fame during the Stamp Act upheavals in Boston, charged that patriot leaders had "sought independence from the beginning." But the gradual and almost reluctant move from resistance to revolution in the American colonies suggests otherwise. When faced with threats from British troops, a sufficient number of colonists took up arms to create the reality of war, and this surge of hostilities finally gave the advantage to those political leaders urging independence.

The victory over Great Britain won that independence but left the United States confronting difficult problems. Most soldiers simply wanted to return home and reestablish their former lives. But the government's inability to pay back wages and the huge debt the nation owed to private citizens and state and foreign governments hinted at difficult economic times ahead.

Like many soldiers, Deborah Sampson embraced a conventional life after the war. But times were hard. A decade after she was discharged, Massachusetts finally granted her a small pension for her wartime service. In 1804 Paul Revere successfully appealed to the U.S. Congress to grant her a federal pension. When Sampson died in 1827, a special congressional act awarded her children additional money. Many men also waited years to receive compensation for their wartime service while they struggled to reestablish farms and businesses and pay off the debts that accrued while they were fighting for independence.

Political leaders tried to address the concerns of former soldiers and ordinary citizens while they developed a governmental structure to manage an expansive and diverse nation. Within a few years of achieving independence, financial distress among small farmers and tensions with Indians on the western frontier intensified concerns about the ability of the

DOCUMENT 6.5

Thomas Peters | Petition to the British Cabinet, 1790

During the war, thousands of African Americans fled from slavery to join the British. Former slave Thomas Peters escaped from his owner in North Carolina and became a sergeant in a British regiment called the Black Pioneers. Like other loyalists, he settled in Nova Scotia after the war. He soon realized that even in Canada blacks were treated unequally. In 1790 he went to London to present the following petition to the British cabinet on behalf of other black loyalists. Faced with persistent inequality, Peters and many other ex-slaves eventually migrated to Sierra Leone.

Explore

The humble Memorial and Petition of Thomas Peters a free Negro and late a Serjt. [sergeant] in the Regiment of Guides and Pioneers serving in North America under the command of Genl. Sir Henry Clinton on Behalf of himself and others the Black Pioneers and loyal Black Refugees hereinafter described

Sheweth

That your Memorialist and the said other Black Pioneers having served in North America as aforesaid for the Space of seven years and upwards, during the War, afterwards went to Nova Scotia under the Promise of obtaining the usual Grant of Lands and Provision.

That notwithstanding they have made repeated Applications to all Persons in that Country who they conceived likely to put them in Possession of the due Allotments, the said Pioneers with their Wives and Children amounting together in the whole to the Number of 102 People now remain at Annapolis Royal have not yet obtained their Allotments of Land except one single Acre of land each for a Town Lot and tho' a further Proportion of 20 Acres each Private man (viz) about a 5th part of the Allowance of Land that is due to them was actually laid out and located for them agreeable to the Governor's Order it was afterwards taken from them on Pretense that it had been included in some former Grant and they have never yet obtained other Lands in Lieu thereof and remain destitute and helpless.

Source: Great Britain, Public Record Office, Colonial Office file CO217/63fol. 63, reprinted in David Northrup, *Crosscurrents in the Black Atlantic* (Boston: Bedford/St. Martin's, 2008), 39–40.

Interpret the Evidence

- On what grounds do Peters and his supporters base their claims to land in Nova Scotia?
- How were they rewarded for their service in the British military?

Put It in Context

What was required to make freedom meaningful for ex-slaves living in the United States or abroad?

confederation government to secure order and prosperity. In response, some patriots demanded a new political compact to strengthen the national government. But others feared that such a change would simply replicate British tyranny.

Leading revolutionaries engaged in heated debates over the best means to unify and stabilize the United States in the decade following the Revolution. However, some key leaders lived abroad in this period. Although Thomas Paine was awarded land and money by Pennsylvania and the U.S. Congress, in 1791 he moved to France, where he wrote pamphlets advocating revolution there. His increasingly radical political views and attacks on organized religion led many Americans to malign the former hero. He returned to

the United States in 1802, but his death in New York City in 1809 was mentioned only briefly in most newspapers. Other patriot leaders remained celebrated figures, but Thomas Jefferson, Benjamin Franklin, and John Adams all spent significant amounts of time in England and France as ambassadors for the young nation. There they played key roles in building ties to European powers, thus ensuring U.S. security.

The legacies of the Revolution seemed far from clear in the decade following the American victory. As problems escalated, Americans were challenged to reimagine their political future while holding on to the republican impulses that drove them to revolution.

Chapter Review

Online Study Guide ▶ bedfordstmartins.com/hewittlawson

KEY TERMS

Second Continental Congress (p. 164)
Dunmore's Proclamation (p. 165)
Common Sense (p. 165)
Declaration of Independence (p. 166)
loyalist (p. 169)
Battle of Saratoga (p. 173)
Valley Forge (p. 173)
Articles of Confederation (p. 174)
Yorktown (p. 181)
Treaty of Paris (p. 182)

REVIEW & RELATE

1. What challenges did Washington face when he was given command of the Continental Army?

2. How and why did proponents of independence prevail in the debates that preceded the publication of the Declaration of Independence?

3. How did colonists choose sides during the Revolutionary War? What factors influenced their decisions?

4. Why did so many Indian tribes try to stay neutral during the conflict? Why was it so difficult for Indians to remain neutral?

5. How did the patriot forces fare in 1776? How and why did the tide of war turn in 1777?

6. What role did colonial women and foreign men play in the conflict in the early years of the war?

7. What values and concerns shaped state governments during the Revolutionary War?

8. What issues and challenges did the Continental Congress face even after the French joined the patriot side?

9. How and why did the Americans win the Revolutionary War?

10. What uncertainties and challenges did the new nation face in the immediate aftermath of victory?

TIMELINE OF EVENTS

April 19, 1775	Battles of Lexington and Concord
June 1775	Continental Congress establishes Continental Army
June 16, 1775	Battle of Bunker Hill
August 1775	Representatives of the Continental Congress meet with representatives of the six nations of the Iroquois Confederacy
November 1775	Dunmore issues his proclamation
1776	New Jersey constitution enfranchises all free inhabitants, including women and free blacks, who meet property qualifications
January 1776	Thomas Paine publishes *Common Sense*
July 4, 1776	Continental Congress publicly declares independence
July 1776– mid-December 1776	British forces defeat Continental Army and force retreat
December 1776– January 1777	Patriot victories at Trenton and Princeton, New Jersey
October 1777	Patriot victory at Saratoga
Winter 1777–1778	Continental Army encamps at Valley Forge, Pennsylvania
1778	Articles of Confederation ratified by eight states
February 1778	France enters into formal alliance with the United States
Summer 1779	Patriot forces wipe out Iroquois Confederacy villages on New York frontier
1780–1781	Quock Walker and Elizabeth "Mumbet" Freeman successfully sue for their freedom in Massachusetts
March 1781	Articles of Confederation ratified
October 19, 1781	British surrender at Yorktown, Virginia
May 1782	Deborah Sampson enlists in Continental Army under the name Robert Shurtliff
September 2, 1783	Treaty of Paris signed

DOCUMENT PROJECT **6**

Women in the Revolution

The Revolutionary War had a tremendous impact on the lives of women, just as women helped shape the course of that conflict. As in all wars, women faced the fear and hardships brought on by absent men, inadequate supplies, roaming enemy soldiers, and nearby battles. But at a time when women were supposed to limit their activities to domestic concerns, the war also opened up new opportunities. On the home front, they ran family farms and shops, raised money, and produced homespun goods for the Continental Army, and they defended themselves and their homes. Women also spied on enemy encampments, provided medical care for soldiers, and even fought alongside men on the battlefield. Women gained new skills, felt pride in their independence and abilities, and, like their male counterparts, gained satisfaction and sometimes fame in supporting the cause in which they believed. They cast their everyday responsibilities in a political light, even as the war generally failed to expand women's legal or political rights.

The women represented in the following documents demonstrate a variety of experiences during the war. Some women, like Christian Barnes (Document 6.6), remained loyal to Great Britain and suffered attacks by patriot neighbors and soldiers. As a Seneca, Mary Jemison (Document 6.10) sought to remain neutral during the war, but she also faced hardships brought on by pillaging colonial soldiers. The other documents offer a window into the lives of patriot women who worked to defend their new country and their families during the war. Even here, there were differences between the activities of wealthy women (Documents 6.7 and 6.9) and those of ordinary women (Document 6.8). In reading these documents, think about the extent to which being a woman shaped how they experienced the war. Almost all women faced new challenges, but some were also offered new opportunities. Still, even the innovative roles women played were often justified in domestic or familial terms.

185

DOCUMENT 6.6

Christian Barnes | Letter to Elizabeth Inman, April 29, 1775

As the conflict intensified between Great Britain and America, colonists were forced to choose sides. Whether patriots or loyalists, women were often terrorized by enemy soldiers. One such woman was Christian Barnes, the wife of a well-known loyalist who fled to Marlborough, Massachusetts, to avoid capture by the colonial government. The following selection is from a letter written by Barnes in the spring of 1775, in which she describes a frightening visit by a colonial soldier.

I T IS NOW A WEEK since I had a line from my dear Mrs. Inman, in which time I have had some severe trials, but the greatest terror I was ever thrown into was on Sunday last. A man came up to the gate and loaded his musket, and before I could determine which way to run he entered the house and demanded a dinner. I sent him the best I had upon the table. He was not contented, but insisted upon bringing in his gun and dining with me; this terrified the young folks, and they ran out of the house. I went in and endeavored to pacify him by every method in my power, but I found it was to no purpose. He still continued to abuse me, and said that when he had eat his dinner he should want a horse and if I did not let him have one he would blow my brains out. He pretended to have an order from the General for one of my horses, but did not produce it. His language was so dreadful and his looks so frightful that I could not remain in the house, but fled to the store and locked myself in. He followed me and declared he would break the door open. Some people very luckily passing to meeting prevented his doing any mischief and staid by me until he was out of sight, but I did not recover from my fright for several days. The sound of drum or the sight of a gun put me into such a tremor that I could not command myself. I have met with but little molestation since this affair, which I attribute to the protection sent me by Col. Putnam and Col. Whitcomb. I returned them a card of thanks for their goodness tho' I knew it was thro' your interest I obtained this favor. . . . The people here are weary at his [Mr. Barnes's] absence, but at the same time give it as their opinion that he could not pass the guards. . . . I do not doubt but upon a proper remonstrance I might procure a pass for him through the Camp from our two good Colonels. . . . I know he must be very unhappy in Boston. It was never his intention to quit the family.

Source: Nina M. Tiffany, ed., *Letters of James Murray, Loyalist* (Boston, 1901), 187–88.

DOCUMENT 6.7

Deborah Champion | Letter to Patience, October 2, 1775

Deborah Champion was the daughter of Henry Champion, a high-ranking officer in the Continental Army. In the fall of 1775, she traveled from Connecticut to Boston to deliver secret messages from her father to George Washington. Accompanied by a family slave named Aristarchus, she was stopped by British troops several times during her journey. Several days after her return home, she described the adventure in a letter to a friend, excerpted here.

FATHER LAID HIS HAND on my shoulder, (a most unusual caress with him) and said almost solemnly, "Deborah I have need of thee. Hast thee the courage to go out and ride, it may be even in the dark and as fast as may be, till thou comest to Boston town?" He continued, "I do not believe Deborah, that there will be actual danger to threaten thee, else I would not ask it of thee, but the way is long, and in part lonely. I shall send Aristarchus with thee and shall explain to him the urgency of the business. Though he is a slave, he understands the mighty matters at stake, and I shall instruct him yet further. There are reasons why it is better for you a woman to take the despatches I would send than for me to entrust them to a man; else I should send your brother Henry. Dare you go? . . ."

Everywhere we heard the same thing, love for the Mother Country, but stronger than that, that she must *must* give us our rights, that we were fighting not for independence, though that might come and would be the war-cry if the oppression of unjust taxation was not removed. Nowhere was a cup of imported tea offered us. It was a glass of milk, or a cup of "hyperion" the name they gave to a tea made of raspberry leaves. We heard that it would be almost impossible to avoid the British, unless by going so far out of the way that too much time would be lost, so plucked up what courage I could as darkness began to come on at the close of the second day. I secreted the papers in a small pocket in a saddle bag under some eatables that mother had put up. We decided to ride all night. Providentially the moon just past full, rose about 8 o'clock and it was not unpleasant, for the roads were better. I confess that I began to be weary. It was late at night or rather very early in the morning, that I heard a sentry call and knew that if at all the danger point was reached. I pulled my calash [a large hood] as far over my face as I could, thanking my wise mother's forethought, and went on with what boldness I could muster. I really believed I heard Aristarchus' teeth chatter as he rode to my side and whispered "De British missus for sure." Suddenly I was ordered to *halt*. As I could not help myself I did so. A soldier in a red coat appeared and suggested that I go to headquarters for examination. I told him "It was early to wake his Captain and to please let me pass for I had been sent in urgent haste to see a friend in need," which was true, if a little ambiguous. To my joy he let me go saying "Well, you are only an old woman any way." Evidently as glad to be rid of me as I of him.

Source: Deborah Champion to Patience, 2 October 1775, in *Women's Letters: America from the Revolutionary War to the Present*, ed. Lisa Grunwald and Stephen J. Adler (New York: Dial Press, 2005), 25–28.

DOCUMENT 6.8

Abigail Adams | Letter to John Adams, July 13, 1777

Food shortages among colonial militias during the Revolutionary War are well documented, but civilian populations also struggled with high prices and scarce resources. Because women were responsible for their family budgets, they dealt with these problems on a daily basis during the war, just as they had during the prewar boycotts. In July 1777, some women in Boston found an unusual solution, which Abigail Adams describes in a letter to her husband, John.

I have nothing new to entertain you with, unless it is an account of a new set of mobility [popular uprising], which has lately taken the lead in Boston. You must know that there is a great scarcity of sugar and coffee, articles which the female part of the state is very loth to give up, especially whilst they consider the scarcity occasioned by the merchants having secreted a large quantity. There had been much rout and noise in the town for several weeks. Some stores had been opened by a number of people, and the coffee and sugar carried into the market, and dealt out by pounds. It was rumored that an eminent, wealthy, stingy merchant (who is a bachelor) had a hogshead of coffee in his store, which he refused to sell to the committee under six shillings per pound. A number of females, some say a hundred, some say more, assembled with a cart and trucks, marched down to the warehouse, and demanded the keys, which he refused to deliver. Upon which, one of them seized him by his neck, and tossed him into the cart. Upon his finding no quarter, he delivered the keys, when they tipped up the cart and discharged him; then opened the warehouse, hoisted out the coffee themselves, put it into the truck, and drove off.

It was reported, that he has personal chastisement [physical beating] among them; but this, I believe was not true. A large concourse of men stood amazed, silent spectators of the whole transaction.

Source: Charles F. Adams, ed., *Letters of Mrs. Adams, the Wife of John Adams*, 4th ed. (Boston: Wilkins, Carter, 1848), 84–85.

DOCUMENT 6.9

Esther De Berdt Reed | The Sentiments of an American Woman, 1780

Esther De Berdt Reed was born and raised in England, moving to Philadelphia only after her marriage to merchant Joseph Reed in 1770. Joseph was a leading patriot and was elected president (governor) of Pennsylvania during the war. In June 1780, Esther Reed, the mother of five young children and recently recovered from smallpox, called on women in Philadelphia to aid the Continental Army. Her broadside "The Sentiments of an American Woman" was the foundation of the Ladies Association of Philadelphia, which raised large sums by going door-to-door and soliciting contributions from women. Reed's goal was to give money directly to the soldiers, but at George Washington's request the money was instead used to make clothing for the troops.

WHO KNOWS IF PERSONS DISPOSED TO censure, and sometimes too severely with regard to us, may not disapprove our appearing acquainted even with the actions of which our sex boasts? We are at least certain, that he cannot be a good citizen who will not applaud our efforts for the relief of the armies which defend our lives, our possessions, our liberty? . . .

We know that at a distance from the theatre of war, if we enjoy any tranquility, it is the fruit of your watchings, your labours, your dangers. If I live happy in the midst of my family; if my husband cultivates his field, and reaps his harvest in peace; if, surrounded with my children, I myself nourish the youngest, and press it to my bosom, without being affraid of seeing myself separated from it, by a ferocious enemy; if the house in which we dwell; if our barns, our orchards are safe at the present time from the hands of those incendiaries, it is to you that we owe it. And shall we hesitate to evidence to you our gratitude? Shall we hesitate to wear a cloathing more simple; hair dressed less elegant, while at the price of this small privation, we shall deserve your benedictions. Who, amongst us, will not renounce with the highest pleasure, those vain ornaments, when she shall consider that the valiant defenders of America will be able to draw some advantage from the money which she may have laid out in these; that they will be better defended from the rigours of the seasons, that after their painful toils, they will receive some extraordinary and unexpected relief; that these presents will perhaps be valued by them at a greater price, when they will have it in their power to say: *This is the offering of the Ladies.* The time is arrived to display the same sentiments which animated us at the beginning of the Revolution, when we renounced the use of teas, however agreeable to our taste, rather than receive them from our persecutors; when we made it appear to them that we placed former necessaries in the rank of superfluities, when our liberty was interested; when our republican and laborious hands spun the flax, prepared the linen intended for the use of our soldiers; when exiles and fugitives we supported with courage all the evils which are the concomitants of war. Let us not lose a moment; let us be engaged to offer the homage of our gratitude at the altar of military valour, and you, our brave deliverers, while mercenary slaves combat to cause you to share with them, the irons with which they are loaded, receive with a free hand our offering, the purest which can be presented to your virtue,

BY AN AMERICAN WOMAN

Source: Esther De Berdt Reed, "The Sentiments of an American Woman" (Philadelphia: John Dunlop, 1780).

Mary Jemison | The War's Impact on Native Americans, 1823

Many Indian communities chose to aid either the British or the colonists, but even those who sought to remain neutral were often affected by the war. In the following passage, Mary Jemison describes the impact of the war on her Seneca community. Jemison, an Irish immigrant to the Americas, had been captured in 1758 at the age of fifteen by Shawnee Indians. Though most of her family was killed in the attack, she was spared and eventually given to the Seneca tribe. She married a Seneca man and had six children. In 1823 she recounted her capture and life among the Senecas in *Life of Mrs. Mary Jemison*, which became one of the best-selling books of the 1820s.

In one or two days after the skirmish at Conesus Lake, Sullivan and his army arrived at Genesee River, where they destroyed every article of the food kind that they could lay their hands on. A part of our corn they burnt, and threw the remainder into the river. They burnt our houses, killed what few cattle and horses they could find, destroyed our fruit-trees, and left nothing but the bare soil and timber. But the Indians had eloped, and were not to be found.

Having crossed and recrossed the river, and finished the work of destruction, the army marched off to the east. Our Indians saw them move off, but, suspecting it was Sullivan's intention to watch our return, and then to take us by surprise, resolved that the main body of our tribe should hunt where *we* then were, till Sullivan had gone so far that there would be no danger of his returning to molest us.

This being agreed to, we hunted continually till the Indians concluded that there could be no risk in our once more taking possession of our lands. Accordingly, we all returned; but what were our feelings when we found that there was not a mouthful of any kind of sustenance left—not even enough to keep a child one day from perishing with hunger.

The weather by this time had become cold and stormy; and as we were destitute of houses, and food, too, I immediately resolved to take my children, and look out for myself, without delay. With this intention, I took two of my little ones on my back, bade the other three follow, and traveled up the river to Gardeau Flats, where I arrived that night.

At that time, two negroes, who had run away from their masters some time before, were the only inhabitants of those flats. They lived in a small cabin, and had planted and raised a large field of corn, which they had not yet harvested. As they were in want of help to secure their crop, I hired them to husk corn till the whole harvest arrived. . . .

The next summer after Sullivan's campaign, our Indians, highly incensed at the whites for the treatment they had received, and the sufferings which they had consequently endured, determined to obtain some redress, by destroying their frontier settlements.

Source: James E. Seaver, ed., *Life of Mrs. Mary Jemison*, 4th ed. (New York: Miller, Orton, and Mulligan, 1856), 123–24; 126.

Interpret the Evidence

1. What types of activities did female patriots undertake in the service of the colonies? What evidence is offered about how men responded to these activities?

2. In addition to carrying secret messages to General Washington, how else does Deborah Champion reveal her support for the colonial cause (Document 6.7)?

3. What unique dangers did women face during the war, whether loyalist, neutral, or patriot? In what ways did being female offer new opportunities during a time of war?

4. Although many women had participated actively in pre-Revolutionary boycotts and protests, they were still confined largely to the domestic sphere. How did these women justify their public and political actions (Documents 6.7, 6.8, and 6.9)?

5. How did the different social and economic backgrounds of the women represented here affect their experiences during the war?

6. What groups of women are not represented in the documents? How might historians study the lives of these women?

Put It in Context

● What were women's main contributions to the war effort? How did their efforts shape the outcome of the war and the lives of their families?

LEARNINGCurve
Check what you know.
bedfordstmartins.com/hewittlawson/LC

© Chicago History Museum, USA/The Bridgeman Art Library

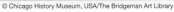

The Treaty of Greenville, 1785.

The Granger Collection, New York

Portrait of Catherine Brass Yates, 1794.

7
Political Cultures
1783–1800

Farmer plowing near Moravian settlement of Salem, North Carolina, 1787.

AMERICAN HISTORIES

Like many young farmers in Massachusetts, Daniel Shays enlisted in a local militia company in the early 1770s. Born to Irish parents in Hopkinton, Massachusetts, in 1747 and one of six children, Daniel received little formal education. In 1772 he married, had a child, and settled into farming. But in April 1775, he, his father, and his brother grabbed muskets and raced toward Concord to meet the British forces. By June, he was among the patriots defending Breed's Hill and Bunker Hill.

After distinguished service in the Continental Army, Shays resigned from service in 1780 and purchased a farm in Pelham, Massachusetts. He hoped to return to a normal life, but in the years following the Revolution, the nation entered a period of economic turmoil. Farmers in western Massachusetts, many deeply in debt, were especially hard hit. Debtors, including former soldiers and their families, lost their land, tools, livestock, clothes, and furniture, and many were also imprisoned. Although Shays managed to keep his farm, many of his neighbors faced eviction. Shays was chosen to represent his town at county conventions that petitioned the state government for economic relief. However, the Massachusetts legislature, sitting in Boston, largely ignored their concerns.

Angered by the legislature's failure to act, armed groups of farmers attacked courthouses throughout western Massachusetts in 1786. Although Shays was reluctant to lead the movement, he soon headed the largest contingent of farmer-soldiers, a band that eventually numbered more than a thousand men. After a series of small skirmishes against local militias, Massachusetts governor James Bowdoin moved to quash the rebellion. In January 1787, Shays and his men headed to the federal arsenal at Springfield, Massachusetts, to seize guns and ammunition. The farmers were routed by state militia and pursued by the governor's army. Many rebel leaders were captured; others, including Shays, escaped to Vermont and later New York State. Four were convicted and two were hanged before Bowdoin granted amnesty to the rest of the rebels, in hopes of avoiding further conflict.

This uprising, known as Shays's Rebellion, fueled grave concern on the part of many state and national leaders. They feared that the U.S. government was too weak to put down such insurgencies and advocated amending or replacing the Articles of Confederation to create a new political structure that would strengthen federal power. Among those outraged by the rebels was Alexander Hamilton, a young New York politician with an admirable record of military service. Hamilton was born illegitimate and impoverished in the British West Indies. Orphaned at eleven, he was apprenticed to a firm of merchants, where his gift for commerce and finance quickly became clear. The firm sent him for schooling to the American colonies, where he was drawn into the activities of radical patriots. Hamilton joined the Continental Army in 1776 and gained a reputation as courageous, even reckless, in the pursuit of military glory.

During the war, Hamilton fell in love with Elizabeth Schuyler, who came from a wealthy New York family, and they married in December 1780. After the American victory, Hamilton used military and marital contacts to establish himself as a lawyer and financier in New York City. In 1786 he focused his efforts on improving the state of the nation's finances. He was elected to the New York State legislature that spring and by fall was serving as a delegate to a convention on interstate commerce held in Annapolis, Maryland. Hamilton was among a small group of delegates who sought to strengthen the central government. They pushed through a resolution calling for a second convention "to render the constitution of the Federal Government adequate to the exigencies of the Union."

Although the initial response to the call was lukewarm, the eruption of Shays's Rebellion and the federal government's financial problems soon convinced many in the congress and the states that change was required. Although Hamilton played only a small role in the 1787 convention in Philadelphia, he worked tirelessly for ratification of the Constitution drafted there. Once the new federal government was established, in the fall of 1789 Hamilton accepted appointment to the job he most deeply desired, secretary of the treasury. ●

photos: The Granger Collection, New York; Library of Congress

AS ALEXANDER HAMILTON took charge of the nation's economic policy, Daniel Shays retreated to a modest living on the frontiers of New York State. Despite the suppression of Shays's Rebellion, the grievances that fueled the uprising persisted, and other problems confronted the new nation as well. Moreover, Hamilton's efforts to stabilize and strengthen the national economy, although deemed successful by many political and economic elites, sparked controversy and conflicts in the years ahead. As the American histories of Daniel Shays and Alexander Hamilton demonstrate, Americans may have come together to win the Revolutionary War, but not all Americans shared a common vision of the independent nation that military victory made possible.

Postwar Problems

The United States faced serious financial instability in its formative years. Other issues also threatened the emerging nation. Indians, with support from British allies, continued to launch raids against frontier settlements. Western migrants fueled these conflicts and forced the confederation government to take a more active role in governing its frontier territories. Meanwhile Spain closed the port of New Orleans to U.S. trade as states struggled to regulate commerce within the nation and abroad. Another threat to American trade arose off the coast of North Africa, where Barbary pirates attacked U.S. merchant ships. Issues of trade and piracy required diplomacy with European powers, but diplomatic relations were plagued with uncertainty given America's outstanding war debts and the relative weakness of the confederation government.

Officers Threaten Mutiny

As the American Revolution ground to an end, issues of military pay and government finances sparked conflict. Uprisings by ordinary soldiers were common but successfully put down. Threats by Continental officers, however, posed a greater problem. In March 1783, some five hundred officers were still encamped at Newburgh, New York. Many officers came from wealthy families and had served without pay during the war. In 1780 they had extracted a promise from the Continental Congress for half pay for life but had received no compensation since.

Some confederation leaders were sympathetic to the officers' plight and hoped to use pressure from this formidable group to enhance the powers of the congress. Hamilton was among the leaders pressing state governments to grant the confederation congress a new duty of 5 percent on imported goods. The federal government would thereby gain an independent source of revenue by which it could begin paying off its debts and ensure the loyalty of wealthy Americans who had helped finance the war. Perhaps the actions of the officers at Newburgh could convince states like New York to agree to the collection of this import duty.

Quietly encouraged by these supporters, dissident officers circulated petitions that included veiled threats of a military takeover. When the officers met on March 15, however, they were confronted by General George Washington, who urged the officers to respect civilian control of the government and to allow the fragile U.S. government time to prove itself. Most of the Newburgh officers quickly retreated from the "infamous propositions" circulated earlier. At the same time, congressional leaders, fearing a mutiny, promised the officers full pay for five years. Within weeks, news arrived that a peace treaty was near completion in Paris, and over the next three months the officers headed home.

Indians, Land, and the Northwest Ordinance

One anonymous petitioner at Newburgh suggested that the officers move as a group to "some unsettled country" and let the confederation fend for itself. In reality, no such unsettled country existed beyond the thirteen states. Numerous Indian nations and American settlers claimed control of these western lands, and more American settlers were arriving all the time. In 1784 some two hundred Indian leaders from the Iroquois, Shawnee, Creek,

George Washington's Headquarters
Hasbrouck House, the Revolutionary War headquarters of George Washington, was located near Newburgh, New York, sixty miles north of New York City. In operation from April 1782 to August 1783, this base housed a group of affluent officers who considered a military takeover of the government. Washington convinced them to abandon the idea.   Ivy Close Images/Landov

Cherokee, and other nations gathered in St. Louis, where they complained to the Spanish governor that the Americans were "extending themselves like a plague of locusts."

Despite the continued presence of British and Spanish troops in the Ohio River valley, the United States hoped to convince Indian nations—both friendly and hostile—that it controlled the territory. The confederation congress sought to strengthen these claims by signing treaties with the vanquished nations. In the fall of 1784, U.S. commissioners met with Iroquois delegates at Fort Stanwix, New York, and demanded land cessions that covered all of western New York and Pennsylvania as well as areas farther west. They backed up their demands with the threat of force. Although the six Indian nations in the council later refused to ratify the treaty, the U.S. government acted as though the treaty was valid. With a similar mix of negotiation and coercion, U.S. commissioners signed treaties at Fort McIntosh, Pennsylvania (1785), and Fort Finney, Ohio (1786), and claimed lands held by the Wyandots, Delawares, Shawnees, and others.

As more and more eastern Indians were pushed into the Ohio River valley, they crowded onto lands already claimed by other nations. Initially, these migrations increased conflict among Indians, but eventually some leaders used this forced intimacy to launch pan-Indian movements against further American encroachment on their land.

DOCUMENTS 7.1 AND 7.2

Conflicts over Western Lands: Two Views

Following the Revolutionary War, one of the most pressing issues that the confederation government faced was the disposition of western lands. To resolve these issues, the U.S. government negotiated with a number of Indian tribes to gain clear title to western lands, but it backed these negotiations with the threat of force. The following documents offer very different views of these negotiations. The first selection is from the journal of General Richard Butler, who had fought against Indians in the region. In 1786, he was appointed to negotiate with the Shawnee tribe, a British ally during the Revolutionary War. In his exchange with an Indian representative, Butler mentions a "string," which refers to a wampum belt. A black belt was a sign of war, and a white belt represented peace. The second selection comes from a speech given at a pan-Indian council meeting. The speech was addressed to the U.S. Congress and expressed the Indians' united stance and their hopes for fair and open dealings with the United States.

Explore

7.1 General Richard Butler | Fort Finney Treaty Negotiations, 1786

It rests now with you, the destruction of your women and children, or their future happiness, depends on your present choice. Peace or war is in your power; make your choice like men, and judge for yourselves. We shall only add this: had you judged as it is your interest to do, you would have considered us as your friends, and followed our counsel; but if you choose to follow the opinion which you have expressed, you are guided either by evil counsel or rashness, and are blinded. We plainly tell you that this country belongs to the United States—their blood hath defended it, and will forever protect it. Their proposals are liberal and just; and you instead of acting as you have done, and instead of persisting in your folly, should be thankful for the forgiveness and offers of kindness of the United States, instead of the sentiments which this string imparts, and the manner in which you have delivered it. . . .

. . . Kekewepellethe [the Indian representative] then arose and spoke as follows:

. . . Brethren, our people are sensible of the truths you have told them. You have every thing in your power—you are great, and we see you own all the country; we therefore hope, as you have every thing in your power, that you will take pity on our women and children.

Source: Neville B. Craig, ed., *The Olden Time* (Pittsburgh, 1848), 2:524.

Explore

See Documents 7.1 and 7.2 for two perspectives on
U.S.-Indian interactions.

Indians and U.S. political leaders did share one concern over western lands: the vast numbers of squatters, mainly white men and women, who moved onto land to which they had no legal claim. In the fall of 1784, George Washington traveled with family members and slaves to survey nearly thirty thousand acres of western territory he had been granted as a reward for military service. He found much of the land occupied by squatters who refused to purchase their homesteads or pay rent to Washington. Unable to impose his will on the squatters, he became more deeply concerned about the weaknesses of the confederation government.

Washington feared that the federal government was not strong enough to protect his and others' property rights. Indeed, the confederation congress struggled just to convince the remaining states with western land claims to cede that territory to federal control. Slowly, however, between 1783 and 1785, the congress convinced the two remaining states with the largest western land claims, Virginia and Massachusetts, to relinquish all territory north of the Ohio River (Map 7.1).

Explore

7.2 United Indian Nations Council | Message to Congress, 1786

To the Congress of the United States of America:

Brethren of the United States of America: It is now more than three years since peace was made between the King of Great Britain and you, but we, the Indians, were disappointed, finding ourselves not included in that peace, according to our expectations: for we thought that its conclusion would have promoted a friendship between the United States and Indians, and that we might enjoy that happiness that formerly subsisted between us and our elder brethren. . . . In the course of our councils, we imagined we hit upon an expedient that would promote a lasting peace between us.

Brothers: We are still of the same opinion as to the means which may tend to reconcile us to each other; and we are sorry to find, although we had the best thoughts in our minds, during the beforementioned period, mischief has, nevertheless, happened between you and us. We are still anxious of putting our plan of accommodation into execution, and we shall briefly inform you of the means that seem most probable to us of effecting a firm and lasting peace and reconciliation: the first step towards which should, in our opinion, be, that all treaties carried on with the United States, on our parts, should be with the general voice of the whole confederacy, and carried on in the most open manner, without any restraint on either side; and especially as landed matters are often the subject of our councils with you, a matter of the greatest importance and of general concern to us, in this case we hold it indispensably necessary that any cession of our lands should be made in the most public manner, and by the united voice of the confederacy; holding all partial treaties as void and of no effect.

Source: *American State Papers, Class II: Indian Affairs* (Washington, 1832), 1:8.

Interpret the Evidence

- What does Butler's journal reveal about his view of U.S.-Indian relations? How does he see the power dynamic between the two groups?
- Does the United Indian Nations Council frame U.S.-Indian relations as between dominant and dependent peoples or as between two separate and equal nations? How do the Indians' views compare with those of Butler?
- Why do you think the Indians emphasize the importance of the entire confederacy's participation in treaty negotiations?

Put It in Context

How did the United States use divisions among Indians to its advantage?

MAP 7.1   Cessions of Western Land, 1782–1802

Beginning with the congress established under the Articles of Confederation, political leaders sought to resolve competing state claims to western territory based on colonial charters. The confederation congress and, after ratification of the Constitution, the U.S. Congress gradually persuaded all states to cede their claims and create a "national domain," part of which was then organized as the Northwest Territory.

To regulate this vast territory, Thomas Jefferson drafted the **Northwest Land Ordinance** in 1785. It provided that the territory be surveyed and divided into adjoining townships of thirty-six sections, each 1 square mile (640 acres) in area. He hoped to carve fourteen small states out of the region to enhance the representation of western farmers and to ensure the continued dominance of agrarian views in the national government. The congress revised his proposal, however, stipulating that only three to five states be created from the vast territory.

The population of the territory grew rapidly, with speculators buying up huge tracts of land and selling smaller parcels to eager settlers. In response, congressional leaders modified the original Northwest Ordinance in 1787 and clarified the process by which territories could become states. The congress appointed territorial officials and guaranteed residents the basic rights of U.S. citizens. After a territory's population reached 5,000, residents could choose an assembly, but the territorial governor retained the power to veto all legislation. When a prospective state reached a population of 60,000, it could apply for admission to the United States on an equal basis with the existing states. Thus the congress established an orderly system by which territories became states in the Union.

The 1787 ordinance also addressed concerns about race and political power in the region, though with mixed results. It encouraged fair treatment of Indian nations, although it did not include any means of enforcing such treatment and failed to resolve Indian land claims. It abolished slavery throughout the territory, but the law included a clause that mandated the return of fugitive slaves to their owners to forestall a flood of fugitives into the Northwest Territory. By restricting the number of states established in the territory, the ordinance also sought to limit the future clout of western settlers in the federal government.

Meanwhile, ownership of the region south of the Ohio River and west of the original thirteen states remained in dispute. By 1785 thirty thousand Americans had settled in Kentucky, and thousands more streamed into Tennessee. Spanish officials claimed rights to this land and signed treaties with Creek, Choctaw, and Chickasaw tribes in the area. Supplied with weapons by Spanish traders, these Indians along with Cherokees harassed Anglo-American settlers in the lower Mississippi valley. The region would remain an arena of conflict for decades to come.

Depression and Debt

Disputes over western lands were deeply intertwined with the economic difficulties that plagued the new nation. Victory in the Revolution was followed by years of economic depression and mushrooming debt. The war had fueled the demand for domestic goods and ensured high employment. However, after the peace settlement, both the demand and the jobs declined. In addition, international trade was slow to recover from a decade of disruption. Meanwhile, the nation was saddled with a huge war debt. Individuals, the states, and the federal government each viewed western lands as a solution to their problems. Farm families could move west and start over on "unclaimed" land; states could distribute land in lieu of cash payments to veterans or creditors; and the congress could sell land to fund its debts. Yet there was never enough land to meet these conflicting needs, nor did the United States hold secure title to the territory.

Some national leaders, including Hamilton, focused on other ways of repaying the war debt. Fearing that wealthy creditors would lose faith in the new nation if it could not repay its debts, they wanted to grant the federal government the right to collect a percentage of import duties as a way to increase its revenue. Meanwhile, legislators in a number of states, including Massachusetts, passed hard-money laws that required debts to be repaid in gold or silver rather than in paper currency. Creditors—mainly well-to-do merchants and professionals—favored hard-money measures to ensure repayment in full. Artisans and small farmers, including many veterans who had borrowed paper money during the war, were now asked to repay loans in hard currency as the money supply shrank. Taxes, too, were rising as states sought to cover the interest on wartime bonds held by affluent investors.

Revolutionary War Currency

In 1779 the Continental Congress authorized the issuance of paper currency, including this $4 bill. The congress backed up these notes with either gold or silver to encourage their acceptance. The insignia on the front shows a wild boar charging into a spear with the motto *Aut mors aut vita decora* (Either death or an honorable life).   Reproduced from the original held by the Department of Special Collections of the University Libraries of Notre Dame

Failures of American diplomacy weakened the nation's economy further. In 1783 the British Parliament denied the United States the right to trade with the British West Indies, and New England merchants lost lucrative markets for fish, grain, and lumber. The following year, Spain, unhappy with Americans' insistence on pushing into disputed western territories, prohibited U.S. ships from accessing the port of New Orleans. This embargo closed off a primary trade route for western settlers. Spain and Great Britain also threatened U.S. sovereignty by conspiring with American citizens on the frontier and promising them protection from Indians. At the same time, British troops that had refused to abandon forts in the western United States urged Indians to harass frontier settlers.

The United States fared better in its relations with France and Holland. Both nations granted American ships the right to trade with their West Indies colonies. Yet the continuation of America's wartime alliance with France also ensured continued conflicts with Great Britain.

REVIEW & RELATE

What challenges did the new nation face in the immediate aftermath of the Revolutionary War?

How and why did the conflict between America and Great Britain continue after the war ended?

 LEARNINGCurve bedfordstmartins.com/hewittlawson/LC

On the Political Margins

In the aftermath of the Revolution, the United States was forced to the political margins in international affairs. At the same time, as the new Republic moved from war to peace to nationhood, some groups within the nation were marginalized as well. Small farmers were among those who suffered in the postwar period, but they were not alone. Church leaders who had enjoyed government support in the colonial period now had to compete for members and funds. African Americans, whose hopes for freedom had been raised by the Revolution, continued to fight for full-fledged citizenship and an end to slavery. Women, too, faced challenges as they sought to claim a greater voice in the nation.

Separating Church and State

Government support of churches largely ended with the establishment of the United States. Anglican churches had long benefited from British support and collected taxes to support their ministry during the Revolution. Then in 1786

the Virginia Assembly approved the Statute of Religious Freedom, which was drafted earlier by Thomas Jefferson and made church attendance and support voluntary and eliminated many Anglican privileges. Other states soon followed suit, affecting all churches that had previously counted on government support.

Most states did require that officeholders be Christians, or even Protestants. But by the 1780s, that designation included a wide array of denominations. Especially in frontier areas, Baptists and Methodists, the latter of which broke off from the Anglican Church in 1784, gained thousands of converts. The Society of Friends, or Quakers, and the Presbyterians also gained new adherents in this period, while Catholics and Jews experienced greater tolerance than in the colonial era. In fact, in 1790 the Vatican appointed John Carroll the first Roman Catholic bishop of the United States. As a result of this diversity, no single religious voice or perspective dominated in the new nation. Instead, all denominations competed for members, money, and political influence.

Many Protestant churches were also challenged from within by free blacks who sought a greater role in church governance. In 1794 Richard Allen, a preacher who had been born a slave, led a small group of Philadelphia blacks who founded the first African American church in the United States. The Bethel African-American Methodist Church initially remained within the larger Methodist fold. By the early 1800s, however, Allen's church would serve as the basis for the first independent black denomination, the African Methodist Episcopal Church.

African Americans Struggle for Rights

Black churches provided one arena in which African Americans could demonstrate their independence. It was no accident that the Bethel African-American Methodist Church was founded in Philadelphia, which attracted large numbers of free blacks after passage of the state's gradual emancipation law in 1780. Although the northern states with the largest enslaved populations—New York and New Jersey—did not pass such laws until 1799 and 1804, the size of the free black population increased throughout the region.

Many of these free blacks were migrants from the South, where tens of thousands of enslaved women and men gained their freedom during or immediately following the Revolution (see chapter 6). A few slave owners took Revolutionary ideals to heart and emancipated their slaves following the war. Many others emancipated slaves in their wills. In addition, several states prohibited the importation of slaves from Africa during or immediately following the Revolution, including Delaware, Pennsylvania, Virginia, and Maryland. Despite these emancipations and prohibitions, the number of individuals enslaved in the United States in 1800 was far greater than in 1776, and the enslaved population continued to grow rapidly thereafter. Now, however, slavery was increasingly confined to the South. As northern states passed gradual abolition laws, southern states moved in the opposite direction, making it more difficult for owners to free their slaves and for free blacks to remain in the South.

The limits on emancipation in the South nurtured the growth of free black communities in the North, especially in seaport cities like Philadelphia, New York, Boston, and New Bedford, Massachusetts. In these areas, most African Americans focused on establishing families, finding jobs, and securing the freedom of relatives still enslaved. Others, like Richard Allen, sought to build black communities by establishing churches, schools, and voluntary societies and demanding a political voice. Some northern states, such as New Jersey, granted property-owning blacks the right to vote. Others, such as Pennsylvania, did not specifically exclude them. Records suggest that few black men partici-pated in elections in the early Republic, yet many petitioned state and local governments—in the North and the South—to provide African American communities with schooling, burial grounds, and other forms of assistance.

Explore

To read a petition from free blacks, see Document 7.3.

Although blacks gained little support from most white Americans, they did have some allies. The Society of Friends, the only religious denomination to oppose slavery in the colonial period, became more adamant in its stance in the post-Revolutionary period. Many affluent Quakers finally freed their slaves and withdrew from the slave trade. Anthony Benezet, a Quaker writer and educator, advocated tirelessly for the abolition of slavery within the Society of Friends and directed the Negro School in Philadelphia, which he had founded in 1770.

Women Seek Wider Roles

Quaker women as well as men testified against slavery in the 1780s, writing statements on the topic in separate women's meetings. Although few other women experienced such spiritual autonomy, many gained a new sense of economic and political independence during the Revolution. Once peace was achieved, should they demand rights based on their wartime service or create new roles for themselves in the new Republic? Differences of age, wealth, region, race, and religion shaped women's responses to these questions.

The most famous Revolutionary claim for women's rights was penned by Abigail Adams in 1776 when she warned her husband, John, that "if particular care and attention is not paid to the Ladies we are determined to foment a Rebelion [*sic*], and will not hold ourselves bound by any Laws in which we have no voice, or Representation." Adams and other elite women sought a more public voice following the Revolution as well. Only in New Jersey could women—widowed or single, property-owning women—vote, and many cast ballots in state and local elections by the early nineteenth century.

The vast majority of women, however, could shape political decisions only by influencing their husbands, sons, and brothers. Fortunately, many leaders of the early Republic viewed virtuous wives and mothers as necessary to the development of a strong nation. In 1787 Benjamin Rush, a signer of the Declaration of Independence, published his *Essay on Female Education*. He believed that women could best shape political ideas and relations by "instructing their sons in principles of liberty and government" and rewarding husbands engaged in public service with "approbation and applause." To prepare young women for this enhanced domestic role, Rush suggested educating them in literature, music, composition, geography, history, and bookkeeping.

A more radical approach to women's education was presented by Judith Sargent Murray. Murray argued that "girls should be enabled to procure for themselves the necessaries of life; independence should be placed within their grasp." In addition to such practical instruction, Murray also advocated an education for girls that included science, mathematics, Latin, and Greek. She argued that at age two, boys and girls were intellectually equal. But from then on, "the one is taught to aspire, and the other is early confined and limited." A few American women in the late eighteenth century did receive broad educations, and some ran successful businesses; wrote plays, poems, and histories; and established urban salons where women and men discussed the issues of the day. In 1789 Massachusetts became the first state to institute free elementary education for all children, and female academies also multiplied in this period. Still, most girls' education was focused on preparing them for domesticity, and most women wielded what influence they had as an extension of their domestic responsibilities.

While women's influence was praised in the post-Revolutionary era, state laws rarely expanded women's rights. All states limited women's economic autonomy, although a few allowed married women to enter into business. Divorce was also legalized in many states but was still available only to the wealthy and well connected. Meanwhile women were excluded from juries and legal training and with rare exceptions from voting rights.

African American and Indian women lived under even more severe restraints than white women did. By the 1790s, the number of enslaved women began to increase rapidly once again. Even black women who gained their freedom

DOCUMENT 7.3

Petition from Free Blacks of Charleston, 1791

Although most African Americans in the early Republic were slaves, small free black communities existed in both the North and the South. However, their civil and political rights were often significantly curtailed. In South Carolina, free blacks lived under the harsh rules of the Negro Act of 1740, passed in the wake of the Stono rebellion, which restricted their freedom of movement and assembly, among other constraints. In 1791 free blacks in Charleston petitioned the state legislature for increased judicial rights.

Explore

How do free blacks in Charleston view their citizenship status?

What are these petitioners asking for?

On what grounds do the petitioners base their claims?

That in the enumeration of free citizens by the Constitution of the United States for the purpose of representation of the Southern states in Congress your memorialists [petitioners] have been considered under that description as part of the citizens of this state.

Although by the fourteenth and twenty-ninth clauses in an Act of Assembly made in the year 1740 . . . commonly called the Negro Act, now in force, your memorialists are deprived of the rights and privileges of citizens by not having it in their power to give testimony on oath in prosecutions on behalf of the state; from which cause many culprits have escaped the punishment due to their atrocious crimes, nor can they give their testimony in recovering debts due to them, or in establishing agreements made by them within the meaning of the Statutes of Frauds and Perjuries in force in this state except in cases where persons of color are concerned, whereby they are subject to great losses and repeated injuries without any means of redress.

That by the said clauses in the said Act, they are debarred of the rights of free citizens by being subject to a trial without the benefit of a jury and subject to prosecution by testimony of slaves without oath by which they are placed on the same footing.

Your memorialists show that they have at all times since the independence of the United States contributed and do now contribute to the support of the government by cheerfully paying their taxes proportionable to their property with others who have been during such period, and now are, in full enjoyment of the rights and immunities of citizens, inhabitants of a free independent state.

Source: Petition of Thomas Cole, Peter Bassnett Matthewes, and Matthew Webb to the South Carolina Senate, January 1, 1791, Records of the General Assembly, no. 181.

Put It in Context

What does this petition reveal about life for free blacks in the early Republic?

could find jobs only as domestic servants or agricultural workers. Indian women also faced a difficult future. Years of warfare had enhanced men's role as warriors and diplomats while restricting women's political influence. Furthermore, American officials and missionaries encouraged Indians to embrace gender roles that mirrored those of Anglo-American culture by giving men hoes and women spinning wheels. When forced to move farther west, Indian women also lost political and economic authority that was linked to their traditional control over land, crops, and households.

Indebted Farmers Fuel Political Crises

Although many Americans struggled economically in the 1780s, ordinary men did gain a greater voice in politics. Under constitutions written during the Revolution, most state governments broadened the electorate, allowing men with less property (or in some cases no property) to vote and hold office. They also increased representation from western areas. Although most elected officials still came from the wealthier classes, many felt some responsibility to address the claims of the less fortunate.

Still, the economic interests of poor farmers and of wealthy merchants and landowners diverged sharply. As conflicts between rich and poor, debtors and creditors, escalated between 1783 and 1787, state governments came down firmly on the side of those with money. When petitions and elections failed, impoverished workers and farmers mounted protests. In New Hampshire, debt-ridden farmers marched on the original state capital at Exeter to demand reform. They were confronted by cavalry units, who quickly seized and imprisoned their leaders.

In addition to rebellions by farmers and debtors, many political and economic leaders were worried about the continued efforts of Great Britain and Spain to undercut U.S. sovereignty, ongoing struggles with Indian nations, and attacks on private property by squatters. When James Madison and Alexander Hamilton attended the 1785 convention in Annapolis to address problems related to interstate commerce, they discovered that their concerns about the weakness of the confederation were shared by many large landowners, planters, and merchants. Despite these concerns, state legislatures were reluctant to give up the powers conferred on them under the Articles.

Shays's Rebellion, the 1786 armed uprising by disgruntled, indebted farmers in western Massachusetts, turned the tide by crystallizing fears among prominent patriots about the limits of the confederation model. On December 26, 1786, Washington wrote Henry Knox to express his concerns about the rebellion and other upheavals along the frontier: "If the powers [of the central government] are inadequate, amend or alter them; but do not let us sink into the lowest states of humiliation and contempt." Hamilton, too, believed that Shays's Rebellion marked "almost the last stage of national humiliation." Speaking of the confederation government, he claimed that this "frail and toddering edifice seems ready to fall upon our heads and crush us beneath its ruins."

Daniel Shays

This sketch is the only eighteenth-century illustration in existence of Daniel Shays (on the left in this detail). In it he stands with Jacob Shattuck, another anti-government leader. The picture appeared in a pro-Constitution Boston almanac, which ridiculed the two rebels by showing them in fancy uniforms and holding swords, in contrast to what would have been their usual homespun appearance.   National Portrait Gallery, Smithsonian Institution/Art Resource, NY

REVIEW & RELATE

How did America's experience of the Revolutionary War change the lives of African Americans and women?

What do uprisings by farmers and debtors tell us about social and economic divisions in the early Republic?

✓ *LEARNINGCurve* bedfordstmartins.com/hewittlawson/LC

Reframing the American Government

The delegates who met in Philadelphia in 1787 did not agree on the best way to reform the government. Some delegates, like James Monroe of Virginia, hoped to strengthen the existing government by amending the Articles of Confederation. Others joined with Madison and Hamilton, who argued for nothing less than a new structure for governing the United States. Once representatives agreed to draft a new constitution, they still disagreed over questions of representation, the relations between state and national governments, and the limits of popular democracy.

Even after the ratification of the Constitution and the election of George Washington as president, there was much to do. The Senate, House of Representatives, and Supreme Court had to be organized. The president had to select administrators to help him implement policies and programs. A system for levying, collecting, and distributing funds had to be put in place, and a host of economic problems had to be addressed. Foreign powers and Indian nations needed to be assured that treaties would be honored and diplomatic relations reestablished. A bill of rights, demanded in so many ratifying conventions, had to be drafted and approved. Finally, both proponents and opponents of the Constitution had to be convinced that the U.S. government could respond to the varied needs of its citizens.

The Philadelphia Convention of 1787

The fifty-five delegates who attended the Philadelphia convention were composed of white, educated men of property, mainly lawyers, merchants, and planters. Although many delegates had played important roles in the Revolution, only eight had signed the Declaration of Independence two decades earlier. The elite status of the delegates and the paucity of leading patriots raised concern among those who saw the convention as a threat to the rights of states and of citizens. Whatever changes they imagined, all the delegates realized that discussions about restructuring the U.S. government could alarm many

Americans, and thus they agreed to meet in secret until they had concluded their business.

On May 25, the convention opened, and delegates quickly turned to the key question: Was the convention going to revise the Articles of Confederation or draft an entirely new framework of governance? The majority of men came to Philadelphia with the intention of amending the Articles. However, a core group of federalists, who sought a more powerful central government, met in the weeks before the convention and drafted a plan to replace the Articles. This **Virginia Plan** proposed a strong centralized state, including a bicameral (two-house) legislature in which representation was to be based on population. Members of the two houses would select the national executive and the national judiciary. The new Congress would retain all the powers held by the confederation, and it would gain the power to settle disputes between states and veto legislation passed by an individual state. According to the Virginia Plan, Congress would not have the power to tax citizens or to regulate interstate or international commerce. Although most delegates opposed the Virginia Plan, it launched discussions in which strengthening the central government was assumed to be the goal.

Discussions of the Virginia Plan raised another issue that nearly paralyzed the convention: the question of representation. Heated debates pitted large states against small states even though political interests were not necessarily determined by size. Yet delegates held on to size as the critical issue in determining representation. In mid-June, William Patterson of New Jersey introduced a "small-state" plan in which Congress would consist of only one house, with each state having equal representation. Although Patterson's congressional plan was doomed to failure, he also articulated ideas of constitutional supremacy and judicial review that became key elements in the American legal system.

With few signs of compromise, the convention finally appointed a special committee of one delegate from each state to hammer out the problem of representation. Their report broke the logjam. Members of the House of Representatives were to be elected by voters in each state; members of the Senate would be appointed by state legislatures. Representation in the House would be determined by population—counted every ten years in a national census—and each state, regardless of size, would have equal representation in the Senate. The Senate could approve treaties and presidential appointments, try cases of impeachment, and initiate certain kinds of legislation. The House, however, had the singular authority to introduce all funding bills.

Included within this compromise was one of the few considerations of slavery at the Philadelphia convention. With little apparent debate, the committee decided that

James Madison

James Madison of Virginia was one of the framers of the Constitution and one of the authors of *The Federalist Papers*, which supported its ratification. This striking portrait of Madison was painted around 1792 by the artist Charles Willson Peale, who had served during the Revolutionary War in the Pennsylvania militia and attained the rank of captain.   Independence National Historical Park

representation in the House of Representatives was to be based on an enumeration of the entire free population and three-fifths of "all other persons," that is, slaves. If delegates had moral scruples about this **three-fifths compromise**, most found them outweighed by the urgency of settling the troublesome question of representation.

Still, slavery was on the minds of delegates. In the same week that the Philadelphia convention tacitly accepted the institution of slavery, the confederation congress meeting in New York City outlawed slavery in the Northwest Territory. It was perhaps news of that decision that inspired representatives from Georgia and South Carolina to insist that the Constitution protect the slave trade. Delegates in Philadelphia agreed that "the migration or importation of such persons as any of the states now existing shall think proper to admit" would not be interfered with for twenty years. At the same time, northern delegates insisted that the three-fifths

formula be used in assessing taxation as well as representation, ensuring that the South paid for the increased size of its congressional delegation with increased taxes.

Two other issues provoked considerable debate in the following weeks: the balance of power between states and the central government, and the degree of popular participation in selecting national leaders. The delegates supported federalism, a system in which states and the central government share power. But the new Constitution increased the powers of the central government significantly over those granted by the Articles of Confederation. The new Congress was granted the right to raise revenue by levying and collecting taxes and tariffs and coining money; to raise armies; to regulate interstate commerce; to settle disputes between the states; to establish uniform rules for the naturalization of immigrants; and to make treaties with foreign nations and Indians. But Congress could veto state laws only when those laws challenged "the supreme law of the land," and states retained all rights that were not specifically granted to the federal government.

One of the important powers retained by the states was the right to determine who was eligible to vote, but delegates in Philadelphia decided how much influence eligible voters would have in national elections. Members of the House of Representatives were to be elected directly by popular vote for two-year terms. Senators—two from each state—were to be selected by state legislatures for a term of six years. Voters were also involved only indirectly in the selection of the president. The president would be selected for a four-year term by an electoral college, members of which were appointed by state legislatures and equal to the whole number of senators and representatives to which the state was entitled. Finally, the federal judicial system was to be wholly removed from popular influence. Justices on the Supreme Court were to be appointed by the president and approved by the Senate. Once approved, they served for life to protect their judgments from the pressure of popular opinion.

With the final debates concluded, delegates agreed that approval by nine states, rather than all thirteen, would make the Constitution the law of the land. Some delegates sought formal reassurance that the powers granted the federal government would not be abused and urged inclusion of a bill of rights, modeled on the Virginia Declaration of Rights. But weary men eager to finish their business voted down the proposal. On September 17, 1787, the Constitution was approved and sent to the states for ratification.

Americans Battle over Ratification

Although the confederation congress neither approved nor rejected the Constitution, it did circulate the document to state legislatures and asked them to call conventions to consider ratification. At the same time, printers published thousands of copies of the Constitution in newspapers and as broadsides. Soon Americans were proclaiming their opinions from pulpits, papers, and other public platforms. In homes, churches, and taverns, ordinary citizens debated the wisdom of abolishing the confederation and establishing a stronger central government.

There were many opinions on the Constitution, but the states were not allowed to modify the document, only to accept or reject it in whole. Fairly quickly then, two sides emerged. The **Federalists**, who supported ratification, came mainly from urban and commercial backgrounds and lived in towns and cities along the Atlantic coast. They viewed a stronger central government as essential to the economic and political stability of the nation. Their opponents, who were generally more rural, less wealthy, and more likely to live in interior or frontier regions, opposed increasing the powers of the central government. Known more for what they stood against than what they stood for, opponents were labeled **Antifederalists**.

The pro-Constitution position was most fully expressed in a series of eighty-five editorials that appeared in New York newspapers in 1787–1788 and were published collectively as *The Federalist Papers.* Written by James Madison, John Jay, and Alexander Hamilton, these brilliant essays articulated broad principles embraced by most supporters of the Constitution. Most notably, in *Federalist* No. 10, Madison countered the common wisdom that small units of government were most effective in representing the interests of their citizens and avoiding factionalism. Recognizing that factions were inevitable, he argued that in a large political body, groups with competing interests had to collaborate and compromise in order to rule. This check on the "tyranny of the majority" protected the rights and freedoms of all. Although these editorials did not have a profound impact on delegates during the ratification process, they had a major influence in shaping the government that emerged after ratification.

Antifederalists continued to view a large and powerful central government as leading to tyranny, invoking the actions of the British king and Parliament to illustrate their point. Small farmers worried that a strong central government filled with merchants, lawyers, and planters might place the interests of creditors above those of ordinary (and indebted) Americans. Some wealthy patriots, like Mercy Otis Warren of Boston, feared that the Constitution would hand over power to a few individuals who remained isolated from the "true interests of the people." Finally, many Americans were concerned about the absence of a bill of rights.

Explore

See Document 7.4 for one farmer's concerns about a strong central government.

Federalists worked in each state to soften their critics by persuasive arguments, flattering hospitality, and timely compromises regarding a bill of rights. They also gained strength from a few states that ratified the Constitution quickly. By January 1788, Delaware, Pennsylvania, New Jersey, Georgia, and Connecticut had all approved the Constitution. Federalists also gained the support of the most influential newspapers, which were based in eastern cities and tied to commercial interests.

Despite the Federalists' successes, the contest in many states became heated. In Massachusetts, Antifederalists, including some leaders of Shays's Rebellion, gained the majority among convention delegates. Many were deeply opposed to the centralization of power established by the Constitution. Federalists worked hard to overcome the objections of their opponents, drafting a bill of rights to be proposed for adoption following the Constitution's ratification. Finally, on February 6, the Massachusetts delegates voted 187 to 168 in favor of ratification. Maryland and South Carolina followed in April and May. A month later, New Hampshire Federalists won a close vote, making it the ninth state to ratify the Constitution.

Two of the most populous and powerful states, New York and Virginia, had not yet ratified. Passionate debates erupted in both states. Finally, after promising that a bill of rights would be added quickly, Virginia Federalists won the day by a few votes. A month later, New York also approved the Constitution by a narrow margin. The divided nature of the votes, and the fact that two states (North Carolina and Rhode Island) had still not ratified, meant that the new government would have to prove itself quickly (Table 7.1).

TABLE 7.1   Votes of State-Ratifying Conventions

State	Date	For	Against
Delaware	December 1787	30	0
Pennsylvania	December 1787	46	23
New Jersey	December 1787	38	0
Georgia	January 1788	26	0
Connecticut	January 1788	128	40
Massachusetts	February 1788	187	168
Maryland	April 1788	63	11
South Carolina	May 1788	149	73
New Hampshire	June 1788	57	47
Virginia	June 1788	89	79
New York	July 1788	30	27
North Carolina	November 1788	194	77
Rhode Island	May 1790	34	32

DOCUMENT 7.4

Amos Singletary | Speech to the Massachusetts Ratifying Convention, 1788

By the time of the Massachusetts ratifying convention in January 1788, five of the nine required states had already ratified the federal Constitution. But the debates in Massachusetts were fierce, with the memory of Shays's Rebellion still fresh in the delegates' minds. Amos Singletary, a farmer and a convention delegate, claimed to represent the "little folk" when he addressed the convention. He sided with the Antifederalists and framed the debate about the Constitution in class terms and in the context of the pre-Revolutionary struggle between Britain and the colonists.

Explore

We contended with Great Britain—some said for a threepenny duty on tea; but it was not that—it was because they claimed a right to tax us and bind us in all cases whatever. And does not this constitution do the same? Does it not take away all we have—all our property? Does it not lay all taxes, duties, imposts, and excises? And what more have we to give? . . . These lawyers, and men of learning, and monied men, that talk so finely and gloss over matters so smoothly, to make us poor illiterate people swallow down the pill, expect to get into Congress themselves; they expect to be the managers of this constitution, and get all the power and all the money into their own hands, and then they will swallow up all us little folks, like the great Leviathan, Mr. President; yes, just as the whale swallowed up Jonah.

Source: Albert Bushell Hart, ed., *American Patriots and Statesmen from Washington to Lincoln*, vol. 2, 1775–1789 (New York: P. F. Collier and Sons, 1916), 335–36.

Interpret the Evidence

- What can we infer from this speech about Singletary's understanding of the causes of the Revolution?
- What connections does Singletary seem to make among education, money, and power? What motives does he ascribe to supporters of the Constitution?

Put It in Context

What light does this speech shed on Singletary's view of social and economic relations in the early Republic?

Organizing the Federal Government

Most political leaders hoped that the partisanship of the Federalist/Antifederalist struggle would fade away with the ratification of the Constitution. The electoral college's unanimous decision to name George Washington the first president helped calm some of this political turmoil. John Adams was selected as vice president. On April 30, 1789, Washington and Adams were sworn in at the nation's capital in New York City.

Washington quickly established four departments—State, War, Treasury, and Justice—to bring order to his administration. Thomas Jefferson was named secretary of state; Henry Knox, secretary of war; Alexander Hamilton, secretary of the treasury; and Edmund Randolph, attorney general, head of the Department of Justice. These men had been major figures in the Revolution and helped draft the Constitution.

Congress was also busy in the spring of 1789. The Constitution called for a Supreme Court, but it offered little guidance on its practical organization. The Judiciary Act of 1789 established a Supreme Court composed of six justices along with thirteen district courts and three circuit courts to hear cases appealed from the states. Congress also worked quickly to establish a bill of rights. Representative James Madison gathered more than two hundred resolutions passed by state ratifying conventions and honed them down to twelve amendments, which Congress approved and submitted to the states for ratification. In 1791 ten of the amendments were ratified by the necessary three-fourths of the states, and these became the **Bill of Rights**. It guaranteed the rights of individuals and states in the face of a more powerful central government, including freedom of speech, the press, religion, and the right to petition.

Federal Hall

This drawing shows Federal Hall, located on Wall Street in New York City. Originally built in 1700 as City Hall, the building housed the Stamp Act Congress in 1765 and the confederation congress from 1785 to 1788. In 1789 it became the seat of Congress under the new Constitution and the site of President Washington's first inauguration.   New York Public Library/Art Resource, NY

Hamilton Forges an Economic Agenda

Even as the new government was being organized, its leaders recognized that without a stable economy, the best political structure could falter. Thus Washington's appointment of Alexander Hamilton as secretary of the treasury was especially significant. In formulating the nation's economic policy, Hamilton's main goal was to establish the nation's credit. This would strengthen the United States in the eyes of the world and tie wealthy Americans more firmly to the federal government.

Hamilton formulated a policy that involved funding the national debt at face value and assuming the remaining state debts as part of the national debt. To pay for this policy, he planned to raise revenue through government bonds, an excise tax on goods traded within the United States, and tariffs on imported goods. Hamilton also called for the establishment of a central bank to carry out the financial operations of the United States. His ideas were bold and controversial, but he had the support of

Washington and key Federalists in Congress. Hamilton also had the charm and intellectual ability to persuade skeptics of the utility of his proposals and the wisdom to compromise when necessary. In three major reports to Congress—on public credit and a national bank in 1790 and on manufactures in 1791—he laid out a system of state-assisted economic development.

Hamilton's proposal to repay at face value the millions of dollars in securities issued by the confederation to foreign and domestic creditors was particularly controversial. Thousands of soldiers, farmers, artisans, and shop owners had been paid with these securities during the war, but most had long ago sold them for a fraction of their value to speculators. Thus speculators would make enormous profits if the securities were paid off at face value. Madison argued that the original owners of the securities should be rewarded in some way. Others, such as Patrick Henry, claimed that Hamilton's policy was intended "to erect, and concentrate, and perpetuate a large monied interest" that would prove "fatal to the existence of American liberty." Despite the passion of his opponents, Hamilton won the day.

The federal government's assumption of the remaining state war debts also faced fierce opposition, especially from southern states like Virginia that had already paid off their debt. Hamilton again won his case, though this time by agreeing to "redeem" (that is, reimburse) the money spent by states that had repaid their debts. In addition, Hamilton and his supporters had to agree to move the nation's capital from Philadelphia to a more central location along the Potomac River.

Funding the national debt, assuming the remaining state debts, and reimbursing states for debts already paid would cost $75.6 million (about $1.5 billion today). Rather than paying off the entire debt, Hamilton proposed the establishment of a Bank of the United States, funded by $10 million in stock to be sold to private stockholders and the national government. The bank would serve as a repository for income generated by taxes and tariffs and would grant loans and sell bills of credit to merchants and investors, thereby creating a permanent national debt. This, he argued, would bind investors to the United States, turning the national debt into a "national blessing."

Not everyone agreed with Hamilton's plans. Jefferson and Madison argued vehemently against the Bank of the United States, noting that there was no constitutional sanction for a federal bank. The secretary of the treasury fought back, arguing that Congress had the right to make "all Laws which shall be necessary and proper" for carrying out the provisions of the Constitution. Once again, Hamilton prevailed. Congress chartered the bank for a period of twenty years, and Washington signed the legislation into law.

The final piece of Hamilton's plan focused on raising revenue. Congress quickly passed tariffs on a range of imported goods. Tariffs generated some $4 million to $5 million annually for the federal government. Excise taxes placed on the consumption of wine, tea, coffee, and distilled spirits and on the sale of whiskey generated another $1 million each year. Some congressmen viewed these tariffs as a way to protect new industries in the United States, such as the furniture, tobacco, upholstery, hatmaking, and shoemaking industries. Hamilton was most concerned with generating income for the Treasury, but he also supported industrial development.

Hamilton's financial policies proved enormously successful in stabilizing the American economy, repaying outstanding debts, and tying men of wealth to the new government. The federal bank functioned effectively to collect and distribute the nation's resources. Commerce flourished, revenues rose, and confidence revived among foreign and domestic investors. Hamilton's support for "infant industries," expressed in his 1791 *Report on Manufactures*, also

proved prescient even as farmers remained the backbone of the economy for decades to come.

REVIEW & RELATE

What issues attracted the most intense debate during the drafting and ratification of the Constitution? Why?

What role did Hamilton imagine the federal government playing in the American economy? Why were his proposals controversial?

LEARNINGCurve bedfordstmartins.com/hewittlawson/LC

Years of Crisis, 1792–1796

By 1792 Hamilton had succeeded in implementing his plan for U.S. economic development. Yet as Washington began his second term in the spring of 1793, signs of strain appeared throughout the nation. The French Revolution, which had begun to dissolve into chaos and terror, posed challenges to foreign trade and diplomacy. Reduced prices for western land fueled migration to the frontier, intensified conflicts between Indians and white settlers, and increased hostilities between the United States and Great Britain. Finally, the excise tax on whiskey inspired discontent among frontier farmers. This cluster of crises reinforced disagreements among Federalists, splitting them into warring factions during Washington's second term.

Foreign Trade and Foreign Wars

Jefferson and Madison led the faction opposed to Hamilton's policies. Their supporters were mainly southern Federalists who envisioned the country's future rooted in agriculture, not the commerce and industry supported by Hamilton and his allies. Jefferson agreed with the Scottish economist Adam Smith that an international division of labor could best provide for the world's people. Americans could supply Europe with food and raw materials in exchange for clothes and other items manufactured in Europe. When wars in Europe, including a revolution in France, disrupted European agriculture in the 1790s, Jefferson's views were reinforced.

The French Revolution (1789–1799) had broader implications for U.S. politics than simply increasing the profits from American wheat. The efforts of French revolutionaries to overthrow the monarchy, end feudal practices, and institute a republic gained enthusiastic support from many Americans, especially the followers of Jefferson and Madison. They formed Republican societies, modeled on the of the royal family in the Reign of Terror, wealthy Federalists grew more anxious. The beheading of King Louis XVI horrified them, as did the revolution's condemnation of Christianity. When France declared war against Prussia, Austria, and finally Great Britain, merchants worried about the impact on trade, and Hamilton feared a loss of valuable revenue from tariffs. In response, Congress passed the **Neutrality Act** in 1793, prohibiting ships of belligerent nations—including France or Great Britain—from using American ports. This act overrode a 1778 treaty, signed in the midst of the American Revolution, in which the United States had agreed to defend France in any war with Britain.

The immediate effect of the Neutrality Act was positive for American merchants. They eagerly increased trade with colonies in the British and French West Indies, and U.S. ships captured much of the lucrative sugar trade. Employment rose, and a building boom transformed seacoast cities as affluent residents hired carpenters, masons, and other craftsmen to construct fashionable homes in the "Federal" style. At the same time, farmers in the Chesapeake and Middle Atlantic regions benefited from European demand for grain, and the price of American wheat soared.

Yet these benefits did not bring about a political reconciliation. Instead, tensions escalated in the spring of 1793 when the French diplomat Edmond Genêt visited the United States. Republican clubs poured out to hear Citizen Genêt speak, and their members donated generously to support the French Revolution. Thousands of young Americans enlisted as volunteers on privateering vessels that harassed British and Spanish shipping in the Caribbean. At the same time, the British navy began stopping U.S. ships carrying French sugar and seized more than 250 vessels. American merchants were outraged and demanded that the government intervene to protect the "free trade" guaranteed by the Neutrality Act.

President Washington sent John Jay to England to negotiate a settlement with the British. In the meantime, Genêt's popularity began to fade as he sought to pull the United States into the war. Pro-British Federalists were more adamant than Republicans in their disapproval, arguing that Genêt was seeking to provoke conflict. Finally, in August 1793, just as yellow fever erupted in the nation's capital, Washington demanded Genêt's recall to France. Jay returned from England in 1794 with a treaty negotiated

A Connecticut Merchant

This 1789 portrait of Elijah Boardman by Ralph Earl depicts a successful merchant in his Connecticut dry goods store. Boardman served in the Continental Army and became a political supporter of Thomas Jefferson. The Neutrality Act of 1793 increased commercial opportunities abroad, especially in the West Indies, allowing affluent merchants to expand their businesses, hire skilled craftsmen, and build elegant homes.   Image copyright © The Metropolitan Museum of Art. Image source: Art Resource, NY

Sons of Liberty, to keep tabs on Federalist encroachments on American rights. Many members adopted the French term *citizen* when addressing each other. Moreover, the strong presence of workers and farmers among France's revolutionary forces sparked further critiques of the "monied power" that drove Federalist policies.

In late 1792, as French revolutionary leaders began executing thousands of priests, aristocrats, and members with the British, although many congressmen thought he had given away too much and were hesitant to ratify it. The treaty, for instance, did not include an agreement by the British to stop impressing American seamen.

The Whiskey Rebellion

Despite these foreign crises, it was the effect of Federalist policies on the American frontier that crystallized Republican opposition and led to the development of a **Democratic-Republican Party**. In the early 1790s, Republican societies from Maine to Georgia had demanded the removal of British and Spanish troops from frontier areas, while frontier farmers lashed out at Federalist enforcement of the so-called whiskey tax. Many farmers on the frontier grew corn and turned it into whiskey to make it easier to transport and more profitable to sell. The whiskey tax hurt these farmers, who considered themselves "industrious citizens" and "friends of liberty." Hundreds of them in Pennsylvania, North Carolina, and Kentucky petitioned the federal government for relief.

Much like their counterparts in Massachusetts in the 1780s, western Pennsylvania farmers rallied in 1792 and 1793 to protest the tax and those who enforced it. Former North Carolina Regulator Herman Husband was one of the most outspoken critics of the excise tax (see chapter 5). They burned sheriffs in effigy, marched on courthouses, assaulted tax collectors, and petitioned the federal government. Washington and his advisers failed to respond, paralyzed by a yellow fever epidemic in Philadelphia that ground government operations to a halt. By 1794 an all-out rebellion erupted, with protesters adopting slogans from Stamp Act protests, Shays's Rebellion, and even the French Revolution.

President Washington and his advisers worried that the rebellion could spread and feared that uprisings by white settlers might encourage Indians to rise up as well. Furthermore, Spanish and British soldiers were eager to foment trouble along the frontier, and the **Whiskey Rebellion** might spark intervention by either Spain or Great Britain. Federalists suspected that pro-French immigrants from Scotland and Ireland were behind the insurgency.

When Shays's Rebellion had erupted in 1787, the confederation government had had no power to intervene. Now, however, the United States could raise an army to quash such insurgencies. In August 1794, Washington federalized militias from four states, calling up nearly thirteen thousand soldiers. The president asked Hamilton, author of the whiskey tax, to accompany the troops into battle. The army that marched into western Pennsylvania in September vastly outnumbered the "whiskey rebels"

and easily suppressed the uprising. Having gained victory, only two of the leaders were tried and convicted, and they were later pardoned by Washington. **See Document Project 7: The Whiskey Rebellion, page 218.**

Washington proved that the Constitution provided the necessary powers to put down internal threats. Yet in doing so, the administration horrified many Americans who viewed the force used against the farmers as excessive. Jefferson, who had resigned as secretary of state in 1793, joined Madison in his outrage at the government's action. Despite a strong aversion to partisan politics among leaders of the Revolutionary generation, the divisions inspired by Hamilton's policies convinced Jefferson and Madison to launch an opposition party known as the Democratic-Republican Party.

Further Conflicts on the Frontier

In one area, Federalists and Democratic-Republicans voiced common concerns: the continued threats to U.S. sovereignty by Indian, British, and Spanish forces. In 1790 Congress had passed the Indian Trade and Intercourse Act to regulate Indian-white relations on the frontier and to ensure fair and equitable dealings. However, the act was widely ignored. Traders regularly cheated Indians, settlers launched private expeditions to claim Indian lands illegally, and government agents approved sham treaties. Federal troops sent to the Northwest Territory to enforce the law ended up fighting against the Indians.

The government's failure to stem the flood of settlers into the Ohio and Mississippi River valleys proved costly. In 1790 Little Turtle, a war chief of the Miami nation, gathered a large force of Shawnee, Delaware, Ottawa, Chippewa, Sauk, Fox, and other Indians. This pan-Indian alliance successfully attacked federal troops in the Ohio valley that fall. A year later, the allied Indian warriors defeated a large force under General Arthur St. Clair, governor of the Northwest Territory (Map 7.2). The stunning defeat shocked Americans, who continued to blame British forces encamped in forts on U.S. soil for encouraging Little Turtle and his warriors. In the meantime, Spanish authorities negotiated with Creeks and Cherokees to attack U.S. settlements on the southern frontier.

Washington decided to deal with problems in the Northwest Territory first, sending 2,000 men under the command of General Anthony Wayne into the Ohio frontier. In the spring of 1794, Wayne's troops built Fort Defiance in the heart of Ohio territory. Augmented by several hundred mounted Kentucky riflemen, Wayne's forces then attacked some 1,500 to 2,000 Indians gathered at a nearby British fort. In the Battle of Fallen Timbers, the

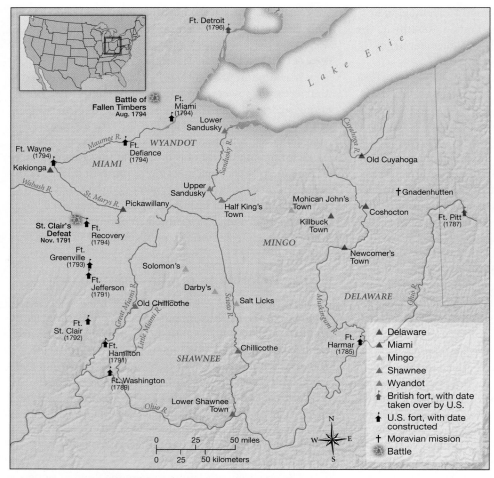

MAP 7.2   American Indians in the Ohio River Valley, c. 1785–1795

In the early to mid-eighteenth century, despite periodic conflicts, Indian tribes in the Ohio River valley forged trade and diplomatic relations with various colonial powers. But once the United States established the Northwest Territory in 1785, conflicts between Indians and U.S. settlers and soldiers escalated dramatically. As tribes forged pan-Indian alliances, the United States constructed numerous forts in the region.

pan-Indian forces, led by Little Turtle, suffered a bitter defeat. A year later, the warring Indians in the Northwest Territory signed the Treaty of Greenville, granting the United States vast tracks of land.

Amid this turmoil, in November 1794 the Senate finally approved the **Jay Treaty** with Great Britain, which required the withdrawal of British forces from U.S. soil by 1796. But it also required Americans to make "full and complete compensation" to British firms for debts outstanding at the time of the American Revolution and limited U.S. trade with the British West Indies. Before Jay's controversial treaty took effect, Spain agreed to negotiate an end to hostilities on the southern frontier of the United States. Envoy Thomas Pinckney, a South Carolina planter,

negotiated the treaty, which recognized the thirty-first parallel as the boundary between U.S. and Spanish territory in the South and opened the Mississippi River and the port of New Orleans to U.S. shipping. The **Pinckney Treaty**, ratified in 1796, advanced the interests of the South, while the Jay Treaty promoted those of the North.

REVIEW & RELATE

How did events overseas shape domestic American politics in the 1790s?

What common concerns underlay the Whiskey Rebellion and Shays's Rebellion? How did the U.S. government deal differently with each?

 LEARNINGCurve bedfordstmartins.com/hewittlawson/LC

The First Party System

In 1796 executive power was placed in the hands of politicians who represented opposing factions in the national government: John Adams (a Federalist) became president and Thomas Jefferson (a Democratic-Republican) vice president. The two disagreed fundamentally on a wide range of issues, and events soon heightened these divisions. Foreign crises once again fueled political antagonisms as fear of war with Britain or France intensified. In response to the increasingly passionate debates over foreign policy, Federalists in Congress passed two acts in 1798 relating to aliens (immigrants) and to sedition (activities that promote civil disorder). Instead of resolving tensions, however, these laws exacerbated opposition to Federalist rule. By 1800, as the nation's fourth presidential election approached, partisan debates had crystallized into opposing factions, and the Democratic-Republicans threatened to oust the Federalists from power.

The Adams Presidency

The election of 1796 was the first to be contested by candidates identified with opposing factions. After private consultations among party leaders, Federalists supported John Adams for president and Thomas Pinckney for vice president. Though less well organized, Democratic-Republicans chose Thomas Jefferson and Aaron Burr of New York to represent their interests. When the electoral college was established, political parties did not exist and, in fact, were seen as promoting conflict. Thus electors were asked to choose the best individuals to serve, regardless of their views. In 1796 they picked Adams for president and Jefferson for vice president, perhaps hoping to lessen partisan divisions by forcing men of different views to work together. Instead, the effects of an administration divided against itself were nearly disastrous, and opposing interests became even more thoroughly entrenched.

Adams and Jefferson had disagreed on almost every major policy issue during Washington's administration. Not surprisingly, the new president rarely took advice from his vice president, who continued to lead the opposition. At the same time, Adams retained most of Washington's appointees, who repeatedly sought advice from Hamilton, which further undercut Adams's authority. Worse still, the new president had poor political instincts and faced numerous challenges.

At first, foreign disputes enhanced the authority of the Adams administration. The Federalists remained pro-British, and French seizures of U.S. ships threatened to provoke war.

In 1798 Adams tried to negotiate compensation for the losses suffered by merchants. When an American delegation arrived in Paris, however, three French agents demanded a bribe to initiate talks.

The Democratic-Republicans in Congress believed that Adams was exaggerating the issue to undermine U.S.-French relations. Adams then made public secret correspondence from the French agents, whose names were listed only as X, Y, and Z. Americans, including Democratic-Republicans, expressed outrage at this French insult to U.S. integrity, which became known as the **XYZ affair**. Congress quickly approved an embargo act that prohibited trade with France and permitted privateering against French ships. In May 1798, Congress allocated funds to build up the navy and defend the American coastline against attack. For the next two years, the United States fought an undeclared war with France.

Despite widespread support for his handling of the XYZ affair, Adams feared dissent from opponents at home and abroad. Consequently, the Federalist majority in Congress passed a series of security acts in 1798. The Alien Act allowed the president to order the imprisonment or deportation of noncitizens and was directed primarily at Irish and Scottish dissenters who criticized the government's pro-British policies. Congress also approved the Naturalization Act, which raised the residency requirement for citizenship from five to fourteen years. Finally, Federalists pushed through the Sedition Act, which outlawed "false, scandalous, or malicious statements against President or Congress" and penalized those who incited hatred of the government.

The First Amendment stated that Congress "shall make no law . . . abridging the freedom of speech, or of the press." However, as a Federalist newspaper explained, in the current situation, "All who are against us are at war." No opposition to Federalist policies would be tolerated. Over the next several months, nearly two dozen Democratic-Republican editors and legislators were arrested for sedition, and some were fined and imprisoned.

Democratic-Republicans were, understandably, infuriated by the **Alien and Sedition Acts**. They considered the attack on immigrants an attempt to limit the votes of farmers, artisans, and frontiersmen, who formed the core of their supporters. The Sedition Act also challenged the party since it was Republican critics who faced arrest. Jefferson and Madison encouraged states to pass resolutions that would counter this violation of the Bill of Rights. Accepting resolutions drafted by Jefferson and Madison, legislators in Virginia and Kentucky declared the Alien and Sedition Acts "void and of no force." Virginia went even further, claiming that states had a right to nullify any powers exercised by the federal government that were not explicitly granted to it.

Matthew Lyon and Roger Griswold
This political cartoon depicts a fight on the floor of the House of Representatives in February 1798 between Representatives Matthew Lyon of Vermont, a Democratic-Republican brandishing tongs, and Roger Griswold of Connecticut, a Federalist waving a cane. A newspaper editor and a critic of the Alien and Sedition Acts, Lyon was later convicted of sedition but won reelection while in jail. Library of Congress

Although the Alien and Sedition Acts curbed dissent in the short run, they reinforced popular concerns about the power wielded by the Federalists. Combined with the ongoing war with France, continuing disputes over taxes, and relentless partisan attacks and denunciations in the press, these acts set the stage for the presidential election of 1800.

The Election of 1800

By 1800 Adams had negotiated a peaceful settlement of U.S. conflicts with France, considering it one of the greatest achievements of his administration. However, other Federalists, including Hamilton, disagreed, continuing to seek open warfare and an all-out victory. Thus the Federalists faced the election of 1800 deeply divided. Democratic-Republicans meanwhile, although more loosely organized than the Federalists, united behind Jefferson. They portrayed the Federalists as the "new British," tyrants who abused their power and violated the rights guaranteed ordinary citizens.

For the first time, congressional caucuses selected candidates for each party. The Federalists agreed on Adams and Charles Cotesworth Pinckney of South Carolina. The Democratic-Republicans again chose Jefferson and Burr as their candidates. The campaign quickly escalated into a series of bitter accusations, with advocates for each side denouncing the other.

In the first highly contested presidential election, the different methods states used to record voters' preferences gained more attention. Only five states determined members of the electoral college by popular vote. In the rest of the states, legislatures appointed electors. In some states, voters orally declared their preference for president; in other states, voters submitted paper ballots. In addition, because the idea of party tickets was new, the members of the electoral college were not prepared for the situation

Monumental Inscription.

" *That life is long which answers Life's great end*"

YESTERDAY EXPIRED,
Deeply regretted by MILLIONS of grateful Americans,
And by *all* GOOD MEN,
The FEDERAL ADMINISTRATION
Of the
GOVERNMENT of the *United States* :
Animated by
A WASHINGTON, an ADAMS ;—a
HAMILTON, KNOX, PICKERING, WOL-
COTT, M'HENRY, MARSHALL,
STODDERT and DEXTER.
Æt. 12 years.

Its death was occasioned by the
Secret Arts, and Open Violence
Of Foreign and Domestic Demagogues :
Notwithstanding its whole Life
Was devoted to the Performance of every Duty
to promote
The UNION, CREDIT, PEACE, PROSPER-
ITY, HONOR, and
FELICITY OF ITS COUNTRY.

At its birth it found
The Union of the States dissolving like a Rope of snow ;
It hath left it
Stronger than the Threefold cord.

It found the United States
Bankrupts in Estate and Reputation ;
It hath left them
Unbounded in Credit ; and respected throughout
the World.

The Election of 1800

The election of 1800 marked the first transfer of political power in the United States from one party to another. The Democratic-Republican candidate for president, Thomas Jefferson, defeated the Federalist Party incumbent, John Adams. On March 4, 1801, the *Columbian Centinel*, a Federalist newspaper in Boston, viewed Jefferson's inauguration as the end of the peace, prosperity, and honor achieved under the Federalists.   The Granger Collection, New York

they faced in January 1801, when Jefferson and Burr received exactly the same number of votes. After considerable political maneuvering, Jefferson, the intended presidential candidate, emerged victorious.

Jefferson labeled his election a revolution achieved not "by the sword" but by "the suffrage of the people." The election of 1800 was hardly a popular revolution, given the restrictions on suffrage (of some 5.3 million Americans, only about 550,000 could vote) and the limited participation of voters in selecting the electoral college. Still, partisan factions had been transformed into opposing parties, and the United States had managed a peaceful

transition from one party in power to another, which was a development few other nations could claim in 1800.

REVIEW & RELATE

What were the main issues dividing the Federalists and the Democratic-Republicans?

What do the Alien and Sedition Acts tell us about attitudes toward political partisanship in late-eighteenth-century America?

 LEARNINGCurve bedfordstmartins.com/hewittlawson/LC

Conclusion: A Young Nation Comes of Age

In the 1780s and 1790s, the United States faced numerous obstacles to securing its place as a nation. Financial hardship, massive debts, hostile Indians, and shifting European alliances and conflicts had to be addressed by a federal government that, under the Articles of Confederation, was relatively weak. Yet despite these challenges, the confederation congress did initiate diplomatic relations with European and Indian nations and successfully organized the vast Northwest Territory. Nonetheless, by 1787 concerns about national security, fueled by rebellious farmers and frontier conflicts, led to the drafting of a new constitution. After a fierce battle in many states, the Constitution was ratified, and the federal government's power to raise money, raise armies, and regulate interstate commerce was enhanced.

George Washington served as the first American president, and his administration implemented policies that enhanced U.S. power at home and abroad. Most important, Secretary of the Treasury Alexander Hamilton implemented a series of measures to stabilize the American economy, pay off Revolutionary War debts, and promote trade and industry. Yet these policies also aroused opposition among political leaders like Jefferson and Madison, who viewed agriculture as the foundation of the American nation. And specific acts like the whiskey tax also fueled antagonism among ordinary farmers and frontiersmen. Although the Federalists continued to support Hamilton's economic policies and pro-British diplomacy, they faced growing opposition from agrarian and pro-French Democratic-Republicans.

In 1798 the Federalist-controlled Congress passed the Alien and Sedition Acts, further unifying Democratic-Republicans. By 1800 the Democratic-Republicans had created an opposition party that was less solid in its structure than the Federalists but sufficiently powerful to win control of Congress and the presidency. This peaceful transition in power boded well for the young United States.

Despite political setbacks, the Federalist legacy remained powerful. Many of Hamilton's policies would continue to shape national economic growth, and the Federalists retained their political power in the Northeast for years to come. Hamilton himself retreated from public service following Jefferson's election. Marginalized by the defeat of the Federalists and tainted after admitting to an adulterous affair, he focused on his law practice. Yet he could not stay entirely clear of politics. In 1804 Aaron Burr was passed over as the vice presidential candidate by the Democratic-Republicans and decided to seek the governorship of New York instead. Hamilton worked tirelessly to defeat Burr, and when the vice president lost, he challenged his nemesis to a duel. On July 11, 1804, Burr fatally shot Hamilton. Even in death, though, Hamilton retained his stature as the architect of the nation's first economic policy.

Meanwhile Democratic-Republicans, many of whom were small farmers and frontiersmen, often fared worse than their Federalist counterparts, at least economically, even after Jefferson's election. We do not know whether Daniel Shays voted in 1800, but he likely supported Jefferson. The rebellion Shays led in 1787 had helped convince many political leaders of the need for a new constitution, yet his role in creating the new nation was largely forgotten. Indeed, Shays, like many ordinary Continental soldiers, spent the rest of his life in relative obscurity. Having moved with his family to eastern New York in 1788, he finally received a federal military pension in 1818, just seven years before he died.

Shays's pension was granted by a U.S. Congress still controlled by Democratic-Republicans. The Democratic-Republican Party would not be seriously challenged for national power until 1824, giving it nearly a quarter century to implement its vision of the United States. Yet developing a vision in opposition to that of the Federalists proved far easier than implementing that vision once the Democratic-Republicans—a heterogeneous group—held the power of the central government in their own hands.

LEARNINGCurve
Check what you know.
bedfordstmartins.com/hewittlawson/LC

Chapter Review

Online Study Guide ▶ bedfordstmartins.com/hewittlawson

KEY TERMS

Northwest Land Ordinance (1785 and 1787) (p. 198)
Shays's Rebellion (p. 203)
Virginia Plan (p. 204)
three-fifths compromise (p. 205)
Federalists (p. 206)
Antifederalists (p. 206)
Bill of Rights (p. 207)
Neutrality Act (p. 210)
Democratic-Republican Party (p. 211)
Whiskey Rebellion (p. 211)
Jay Treaty (p. 212)
Pinckney Treaty (p. 212)
XYZ affair (p. 213)
Alien and Sedition Acts (p. 213)

REVIEW & RELATE

1. What challenges did the new nation face in the immediate aftermath of the Revolutionary War?

2. How and why did the conflict between America and Great Britain continue after the war ended?

3. How did America's experience of the Revolutionary War change the lives of African Americans and women?

4. What do uprisings by farmers and debtors tell us about social and economic divisions in the early Republic?

5. What issues attracted the most intense debate during the drafting and ratification of the Constitution? Why?

6. What role did Hamilton imagine the federal government playing in the American economy? Why were his proposals controversial?

7. How did events overseas shape domestic American politics in the 1790s?

8. What common concerns underlay the Whiskey Rebellion and Shays's Rebellion? How did the U.S. government deal differently with each?

9. What were the main issues dividing the Federalists and the Democratic-Republicans?

10. What do the Alien and Sedition Acts tell us about attitudes toward political partisanship in late-eighteenth-century America?

TIMELINE OF EVENTS

1780–1804	Northern states pass gradual emancipation laws
March 1783	Officers encamped at Newburgh, New York, threaten to mutiny
1784	U.S. commissioners meet with Iroquois delegates at Fort Stanwix, New York
1785	Northwest Land Ordinance passed
	Annapolis Convention
1786–1787	Shays's Rebellion
1787	Constitutional Convention in Philadelphia
	Northwest Land Ordinance revised
June 1788	U.S. Constitution ratified
1789	Alexander Hamilton named secretary of the treasury
	Judiciary Act of 1789 passed
1789–1799	French Revolution
1790–1794	Little Turtle leads pan-Indian alliance against American settlements in the Ohio valley
1791	Bill of Rights ratified
1793	Neutrality Act passed
July–October 1793	Yellow fever epidemic paralyzes Philadelphia
1794	Whiskey Rebellion
	Bethel African-American Methodist Church in Philadelphia founded
1796	Jay Treaty and Pinckney Treaty ratified
	Democratic-Republicans and Federalists contest presidential election
1798	Alien and Sedition Acts passed

The Whiskey Rebellion

In 1791 Alexander Hamilton, the first secretary of the treasury, sought a way to reduce the national debt, and he convinced Congress to pass the first internal revenue tax in the form of an excise tax on distilled spirits. This direct tax angered many Americans, especially farmers who turned their excess grain into whiskey, a lucrative and easily transported product. Their resentment increased because of provisions that taxed smaller producers at almost twice the rate as large producers and required that all stills be federally registered.

Farmers in western Pennsylvania were particularly resistant to the new tax. Many refused to pay the tax, and towns sent petitions to state and federal officials asking that the tax be repealed (see Document 7.5). When this did not work, angry farmers resorted to violence. By the summer of 1794, the Whiskey Rebellion, as it became known, reached a crisis state. Tax collectors were tarred and feathered, groups of farmers burned the homes of tax officials in western counties, and armed rebels attacked neighbors who supported the whiskey tax. Sympathetic residents in towns like Pittsburgh offered their support as farmers prepared for an armed confrontation (Document 7.6).

Washington and his cabinet feared that the revolt would become another Shays's Rebellion, and Hamilton described the rebels accordingly (Documents 7.8 and 7.9). When the "whiskey rebels" refused to negotiate with government representatives, Washington placed the militias of four states under federal control (Document 7.7). When this force of 13,000 men arrived in Pennsylvania, however, most of the rebels had dispersed. The leaders were arrested and tried for treason, but only two leaders were convicted. Washington eventually pardoned all those involved in the revolt.

The Whiskey Rebellion was Washington's most serious domestic crisis and a test of the federal government's powers under the Constitution (Document 7.9). Washington successfully defeated the rebels, but many Americans were outraged that force had been used against their fellow citizens. In response, Thomas Jefferson and James Madison, dissatisfied with this and other Federalist policies, formed the Democratic-Republican political party (Document 7.10).

DOCUMENT 7.5

Resolution to the Pennsylvania Legislature, 1791

Throughout the summer of 1791, farmers in Pennsylvania met to discuss and protest the excise tax on whiskey. In September, representatives from several western counties, including the former North Carolina Regulator Herman Husband, met in Pittsburgh (see chapter 5). There they drafted a resolution to be printed in the *Pittsburgh Gazette* and sent to the U.S. Congress and the Pennsylvania legislature. The following selection highlights the farmers' objections to the whiskey tax.

Resolved, That the said law is deservedly obnoxious to the feelings and interests of the people in general, as being attended with infringements on liberty, partial in its operations, attended with great expense in the collection, and liable to much abuse. It operates on a domestic manufacture, a manufacture not equal through the States. It is insulting to the feelings of the people to have their vessels marked, houses painted and ransacked, to be subject to informers, gaining by the occasional delinquency of others. It is a bad precedent tending to introduce the excise laws of Great Britain and of countries where the liberty, property, and even the morals of the people are sported with, to gratify particular men in their ambitious and interested measures.

Resolved, That in the opinion of this committee, the duties imposed by the said act on spirits distilled from the produce of the soil of the United States, will eventually discourage agriculture, and a manufacture highly beneficial in the present state of the country, that those duties which fall heavy, especially upon the western parts of the United States, which are, for the most part, newly settled, and where the aggregate of the citizens is of the laborious and poorer class, who have not the means of procuring the wines, spirituous liquors, etc., imported from foreign countries.

Source: Pennsylvania Archives, 2nd Series, 4:21.

DOCUMENT 7.6

The Pittsburgh Resolution, 1794

As the Whiskey Rebellion reached a climax in the summer of 1794, its leaders called on armed volunteers to meet at Braddock's Field near Pittsburgh. At the same time, towns across western Pennsylvania held meetings to consider how best to support the rebels. Pittsburgh residents met on July 31 and drafted their own resolution to support the protesters, a portion of which follows.

In consequence of certain letters sent by the last mail, certain persons were discovered as advocates of the excise law, and enemies to the interests of the country, and that a certain Edward Day, James Brison, and Abraham Kirkpatrick, were particularly obnoxious, and that it was expected by the country that they should be dismissed without delay; whereupon, it was resolved it should be so done, and a committee of twenty-one were appointed to see this resolution carried into effect.

Also, that, whereas it is a part of the message from the gentlemen of Washington, that a great body of the people of the country will meet to-morrow at Braddock's Field, in order to carry into effect measures that may seem to them advisable with respect to the excise law, and the advocates of it.

Resolved, That the above committee shall, at an early hour, wait upon the people on the ground, and assure the people that the above resolution, with respect to the proscribed persons, has been carried into effect.

Resolved, also, That the inhabitants of the town shall march out and join the people on Braddock's Field, as brethren, to carry into effect with them any measure that may seem to them advisable for the common cause.

Resolved, also, That we shall be watchful among ourselves of all characters that, by word or act, may be unfriendly to the common cause; and, when discovered, will not suffer them to live amongst us, but they shall instantly depart the town.

Resolved, That the town committee shall exist as a committee of information and correspondence, as an organ of our sentiments until our next town meeting. And that *whereas,* a general meeting of delegates from the townships of the country, on the west of the mountains, will be held at Parkinson's Ferry, on the Monongahela, on the 14th of August next.

Resolved, That delegates shall be appointed to that meeting, and that the 9th August next be appointed for a town meeting to elect such delegates.

Source: Pennsylvania Archives, 2nd Series, 4:21, 80–81.

DOCUMENT 7.7

George Washington | Proclamation against the Rebels, 1794

In August 1794, President Washington met with his cabinet and the governor of Pennsylvania in order to formulate a response to the rebels' growing threat. Washington then issued a proclamation that called on the rebels and anyone "aiding, abetting, or comforting" them to end their revolt and return home. In the proclamation, Washington also utilized the Militia Act of 1792 to call up troops from Maryland, New Jersey, Pennsylvania, and Virginia to put down the rebellion.

And whereas, By a law of the United States, intitled "An Act to provide for calling forth the Militia to execute the laws of the Union; suppress insurrections and repel invasions," it is enacted that whenever the laws of the United States shall be opposed, or the execution thereof obstructed in any State by combinations too powerful to be suppressed by the ordinary course of judicial proceedings, or by the powers vested in the Marshal by that act, the same being notified by an associate Justice or a district Judge, it shall be lawful for the President of the United States to call forth the Militia of such State to suppress such combinations, and to cause the laws to be duly executed. And if the Militia of a State where such combinations may happen, shall refuse or be insufficient to suppress the same, it shall be lawful for the President, if the Legislature shall not be in session, to call forth and employ such numbers of the Militia of any other State or States most convenient thereto, as may be necessary; and the use of the militia so to be called forth may be continued, if necessary, until the expiration of thirty days after the commencement of the ensuing session: *Provided, always,* That whenever it may be necessary, in the judgment of the President, to use the Militia force hereby directed to be called forth, the President shall forthwith, and previous thereto, by Proclamation, command such insurgents to disperse and retire peaceably to their respective abodes within the limited time: . . .

And whereas, it is, in my judgment, necessary under the circumstances of the case to take measures for calling forth the militia in order to suppress the combinations aforesaid, and to cause the laws to be duly executed, and I have accordingly determined so to do, feeling the deepest regret for the occasion, but withal the most solemn conviction that the essential interest of the Union demand it, that the very existence of the government and the fundamental principles of social order are materially involved in the issue, and that the patriotism and firmness of all good citizens are seriously called upon as occasion may require, to aid in the suppression of so fatal a spirit;

Wherefore, and in pursuance of the proviso above recited, I, George Washington, President of the United States, do hereby command all persons, being insurgents, as aforesaid, and all others whom it may concern, on or before the first day of September next to disperse and retire peaceably to their respective abodes. And I do moreover warn all persons whomsoever against aiding, abetting, or comforting the perpetrators of the aforesaid treasonable acts; and do require all officers and other citizens, according to their respective duties and the laws of the land, to exert their utmost endeavors to prevent and suppress such dangerous proceedings.

Source: Pennsylvania Archives, 2nd Series, 4:21, 125–27.

DOCUMENT 7.8

Alexander Hamilton | Letter to George Washington, August 5, 1794

Washington's military preparations resulted in large part from the increasing violence occurring in western Pennsylvania. Tax collectors in particular faced the wrath of angry farmers and other citizens sympathetic to their plight. In the following letter, Alexander Hamilton relays to Washington reports of the violence that had occurred since the rebellion began. He also offers his own explanation of the types of people responsible for attacking not only government officials but also anyone who offered any support for the whiskey tax.

Sometime in October 1791, an unhappy man of the name of Wilson, a stranger in the county and manifestly disordered in his intellects, imagining himself to be a collector of the revenue, or invested with some trust in relation to it, was so unlucky as to make inquiries concerning distillers who had entered their stills, giving out that he was to travel through the United States to ascertain and report to Congress the number of stills, etc. This man was pursued by a party in disguise, taken out of his bed, carried about five miles back to a smith's shop, stripped of his clothes, which were afterwards burnt, and having been himself inhumanly burnt in several places with a heated iron, was tarred and feathered and about day-light dismissed naked, wounded and otherwise in a very suffering condition. These particulars are communicated in a letter from the inspector of the revenue of the 17th of November, who declares that he had then himself seen the unfortunate maniac, the abuse of whom, as he expresses it, exceeded description and was sufficient to make human nature shudder. The affair is the more extraordinary as persons of weight and consideration in that county are understood to have been actors in it, and as the symptoms of insanity were, during the whole time of inflicting the punishment, apparent; the unhappy sufferer displaying the heroic fortitude of a man who conceived himself to be a martyr to the discharge of some important duty.

Not long after a person of the name of Roseberry underwent the humiliating punishment of tarring and feathering with some aggravations for having in conversation hazarded the very natural and just but unpalatable remark that the inhabitants of that county could not reasonably expect protection from a government whose laws they so strenuously opposed.

The audacity of the perpetrators of these excesses was so great that an armed banditti ventured to seize and carry off two persons who were witnesses against the rioters in the case of Wilson in order to prevent their giving testimony of the riot to a court then sitting or about to sit.

Designs of personal violence against the inspector of the revenue himself, to force him to a resignation, were repeatedly attempted to be put in execution by armed parties, but, by different circumstances, were frustrated.

Source: Pennsylvania Archives, 2nd Series, 4:21, 88–89.

DOCUMENT 7.9

Alexander Hamilton | Tully's Pamphlet, 1794

Many Americans criticized Washington's decision to organize troops against the whiskey rebels. Fearful that public sentiment would make it impossible to find enough militia recruits, Alexander Hamilton (using the pen name Tully) wrote a series of pamphlets in support of the government. These pamphlets, one of which is excerpted here, were so compelling that militias had to turn away volunteers.

Fellow citizens: You are told that it will be intemperate to urge the execution of the laws which are resisted. What? Will it be indeed intemperate in your Chief Magistrate, sworn to maintain the Constitution, charged faithfully to execute the laws, and authorized to employ for that purpose force, when the ordinary means fail—will it be intemperate in him to exert that force, when the Constitution and the laws are opposed by force? Can he answer it to his conscience, to you, not to exert it?

Yes, it is said; because the execution of it will produce civil war—the consummation of human evil.

Fellow citizens: Civil war is, undoubtedly, a great evil. It is one that every good man would wish to avoid, and will deplore if inevitable. But it is incomparably a less evil than the destruction of government. The first brings with it serious but temporary and partial ills: the last undermines the foundations of our security and happiness; and where should we be if it were once to grow into a maxim that force is not to be used against the seditious combinations of parts of the community to resist the laws? This would be to give a carte blanche to ambition, to licentiousness, to foreign intrigue, to make you the prey of the gold of other nations—the sport of the passions and vices of individuals among yourselves. The hydra Anarchy would rear its head in every quarter. The goodly fabric you have established would be rent asunder and precipitated into the dust. You knew how to encounter civil war rather than surrender your liberty to foreign domination; you will not hesitate now to brave it rather than to surrender your sovereignty to the tyranny of a faction; you will be as deaf to the apostles of anarchy now as you were to the emissaries of despotism then. Your love of liberty will guide you now as it did then; you know that the power of the majority and liberty are inseparable. Destroy that, and this perishes. But, in truth, that which properly can be called civil war is not to be apprehended—unless from the act of those who endeavor to fan the flame, by rendering the Government odious. A civil war is a contest between two great parts of the same empire. The exertion of the strength of the nation to suppress resistance to its laws, by a sixtieth part of itself, is not of that description.

Source: John C. Hamilton, ed., *The Works of Alexander Hamilton* (New York: Charles F. Francis, 1851), 7:166–67.

Y ou will learn from the newspapers and official communications the unfortunate scene in the Western parts of Pennsylvania which unfolded itself during the recess. The history of its remote and immediate causes, the measures produced by it, and the manner in which it has been closed, does not fall within the compass of a letter. It is probable, also, that many explanatory circumstances are yet but imperfectly known. I can only refer to the printed accounts, which you will receive from the Department of State, and the comments which your memory will assist you in making on them. The event was, in several respects, a critical one for the cause of liberty, and the real authors of it, if not in the service, were, in the most effectual manner, doing the business of Despotism. You well know the general tendency of insurrections to increase the momentum of power. You will recollect the particular effect of what happened some years ago in Massachusetts. Precisely the same calamity was to be dreaded on a larger scale in this case. There were enough, as you may well suppose, ready to give the same turn to the crisis, and to propagate the same impressions from it. It happened most auspiciously, however, that, with a spirit truly Republican, the people every where, and of every description, condemned the resistance to the will of the majority, and obeyed with alacrity the call to vindicate the authority of the laws. You will see, in the answer of the House of Representatives to the President's speech, that the most was made of this circumstance, as an antidote to the poisonous influence to which Republicanism was exposed. If the insurrection had not been crushed in the manner it was, I have no doubt that a formidable attempt would have been made to establish the principle that a standing army was necessary for *enforcing the laws*. When I first came to this City, about the middle of October, this was the fashionable language. Nor am I sure that the attempt would not have been made, if the President could have been embarked in it, and particularly if the temper of New England had not been dreaded on this point. I hope we are over that danger for the present. You will readily understand the business detailed in the newspapers relating to the denunciation of the "self-created Societies." The introduction of it by the President was, perhaps,

DOCUMENT 7.10

James Madison | Letter to James Monroe, December 4, 1794

James Madison and Thomas Jefferson were the leading critics of the Federalist policies of George Washington and Alexander Hamilton. Washington's decision to raise an army to put down the western Pennsylvania rebels confirmed Madison's fears that the national government had become too strong. In his letter to James Monroe, then serving as U.S. minister to France, Madison expresses his concern about Washington's use of military force and the dangers of a standing army. He also criticizes Federalist efforts to link rebellious farmers with the Republican societies (also sometimes called Democratic societies) established in support of the French Revolution and the emerging political opposition in the United States.

the greatest error of his political life. For his sake, as well as for a variety of obvious reasons, I wished it might be passed over in silence by the House of Representatives. The answer was penned with that view, and so reported. This moderate course would not satisfy those who hoped to draw a party advantage out of the President's popularity. The game was to connect the Democratic Societies with the odium of the insurrection; to connect the Republicans in Congress with those Societies; to put the President ostensibly at the head of the other party, in opposition to both, and by these means prolong the illusions in the North, and try a new experiment on the South. To favor the project, the answer of the Senate was accelerated, and so framed as to draw the President into the most pointed reply on the subject of the Societies. At the same time, the answer of the House of Representatives was procrastinated, till the example of the Senate and the commitment of the President could have their full operation. You will see how nicely the House was divided, and how the matter went off. As yet, the discussion has not been revived by the newspaper combatants. If it should, and equal talents be opposed, the result cannot fail to wound the President's popularity more than anything that has yet happened. It must be seen that no two principles can be either more indefensible in reason, or more dangerous in practice, than that—1. Arbitrary denunciations may punish what the law permits, and what the Legislature has no right by law to prohibit; and that, 2. The Government may stifle all censure whatever on its misdoings; for if it be itself the Judge, it will never allow any censures to be just; and if it can suppress censures flowing from one lawful source, it may those flowing from any other—from the press and from individuals, as well as from Societies, &c.

The elections for the House of Representatives are over in New England and Pennsylvania. In Massachusetts, they have been contested so generally as to rouse the people compleatly from their lethargy, though not sufficiently to eradicate the errors which have prevailed there. The principal members have been all severely pushed; several changes have taken place, rather for the better, and *not one* for the worse.

Interpret the Evidence

1. What are the chief complaints of the whiskey rebels and their supporters (Documents 7.5 and 7.6)? Are they opposed only to the economic burden of a tax? Which of their arguments do you find the most convincing?

2. What arguments do Washington and Hamilton make in favor of government action against the rebels (Documents 7.7 and 7.9)? Which do you find most convincing?

3. According to Hamilton's letter (Document 7.8), who was responsible for carrying out the violence of the Whiskey Rebellion? How does Hamilton characterize the attackers and the victims? How can we evaluate his claims?

4. Why do you think Hamilton's pamphlets elicited such overwhelming support for the government and militia (Document 7.9)? Why did he write them under a pen name?

5. On what basis does James Madison criticize President Washington's actions in response to the rebellion? Why does he believe that the Federalists' response to the rebellion is of greater concern than the rebellion itself (Document 7.10)?

6. Washington justified his use of force to put down the revolt by pointing to the violence employed by the rebels. What other strategies did the rebels use to protest the tax? How else might the federal government have responded to armed rebellion among its citizens?

Put It in Context

- What role did the Whiskey Rebellion play in the formation of a new political party?

- What Democratic-Republican ideas are represented in the documents written by the whiskey rebels and their supporters, including James Madison?

Private Collection/Peter Newark American Pictures/The Bridgeman Art Library

Private Collection/The Bridgeman Art Library

Eli Whitney's cotton gin operated by black slaves, 1793.

Portrait of Meriwether Lewis, 1815.

8
New Frontiers
1790–1820

The Granger Collection, New York

Birthplace of Abigail Adams, Weymouth, Massachusetts.

When Parker Cleaveland graduated from Harvard University in 1799, his well-to-do family might have expected him to pursue a career in medicine, law, or the ministry. Instead, he turned to teaching. In 1805 Cleaveland secured a position in Brunswick, Maine, a territory that was then part of the state of Massachusetts, as the first professor of mathematics and natural philosophy at Bowdoin College.

In 1806 he married Martha Bush, who joined him on the Maine frontier. The Cleavelands emerged as leading citizens of Brunswick, a community of some three thousand residents. Most local families supported themselves in the lumbering or shipbuilding trades, but the recently opened college attracted middle-class professionals, whose intellectual interests and consumption habits transformed Brunswick into a more cosmopolitan town.

Over the next twenty years, the Cleavelands raised eight children, boarded and fed dozens of students, entertained faculty and visiting scholars, and corresponded with professors at other institutions. The busy couple served as a model of new ideals of companionate marriage, in which husbands and wives shared interests, friendship, and affection. They also instilled republican virtue and scientific principles in their charges. While Parker taught the students math and science, Martha trained them in manners and morals.

Professor Cleaveland believed in using scientific research to benefit society. Thus when local workers asked him to identify colored rocks found in the river, Parker began studying geology and chemistry. In 1816 he published his *Elementary Treatise on Mineralogy and*

Geology, which served as a text for college students and a handbook for travelers interested in the topic. He also lectured throughout New England, displaying mineral samples and performing chemical experiments.

The Cleavelands viewed Bowdoin College and the surrounding community as a laboratory in which distinctly American values and ideas could be taught and sustained. So, too, did the residents of other college towns. Although less than 1 percent of men in the United States and no women attended universities at the time, frontier colleges were considered important vehicles for bringing republican virtue—especially the desire to act for the public good rather than for personal gain—to the far reaches of the young nation. Yet these colleges were also enmeshed in the country's racial history. Several were constructed with the aid of slave labor, and all were built on land purchased or confiscated from Indians. In Maine, the Penobscot nation lost considerable territory to whites following the American Revolution, much of it under the direction of Massachusetts governor John Bowdoin II, the college's namesake. Moreover, the Indians' displacement continued as the success of colleges like Bowdoin attracted more white families to frontier regions.

The purchase of the Louisiana Territory by President Thomas Jefferson in 1803 marked out a new American frontier and ensured further encroachments on native lands. This vast territory covered 828,000 square miles and stretched from the Mississippi River to the Rocky Mountains and from New Orleans to present-day Montana. The area was home to tens of thousands of Indian inhabitants.

In the late 1780s, a baby girl, later named Sacagawea, was born to a family of Shoshone Indians who lived in an area later included in the Louisiana Purchase. In 1800 she was on a berry-picking expedition when her group was attacked by a Hidatsa raiding party that killed several Shoshones and took a number of women and children captive. Sacagawea and her fellow captives were marched some five hundred miles to a Hidatsa-Mandan village near present-day Bismarck, North Dakota. Eventually Sacagawea was sold to a French fur trader, Toussaint Charbonneau, along with another young Shoshone woman, and both became his wives.

In November 1804, an expedition led by Meriwether Lewis and William Clark set up winter camp near the village where Sacagawea lived. Lewis and Clark had been hired by the U.S. government to lead an exploring party through the newly acquired Louisiana Territory. Both Charbonneau, who spoke French and Hidatsa, and Sacagawea joined the expedition as interpreters in April 1805.

The only woman in the party, Sacagawea traveled with her infant son strapped to her back. Her presence was crucial, as Clark noted in his journal: "The Wife of Chabono our interpreter we find reconsiles all the Indians, as to our friendly intentions. A woman with a party of men is a token of peace." •

BOTH CLEAVELAND AND SACAGAWEA forged new identities on the frontiers of the United States. Yet while Cleaveland gained fame as "the father of American mineralogy," Sacagawea was rarely mentioned in accounts of the journey over the following decades. The American histories of both Sacagawea and Cleaveland were shaped by the efforts of political leaders and ordinary citizens to extend the boundaries of the emerging nation. Their different fates make clear that the young United States was marked by stark racial, class, and gender divisions—divisions that were more often deepened than bridged by the nation's expansion westward.

Creating an American Identity

In his inaugural address in March 1801, President Thomas Jefferson noted that the United States was "kindly separated by nature and a wide ocean from the exterminating havoc of one quarter of the globe," that is, Europe. He believed that the distance allowed Americans to develop their own unique culture and institutions. Jefferson also viewed the nation's extensive frontiers as a boon to its development, providing room for "our descendants to the thousandth and thousandth generation."

For many Americans, education offered one means of ensuring a distinctive national identity. Public schools could train American children in republican values, while the wealthiest among them could attend private academies and colleges. Written works such as newspapers, sermons, books, and magazines helped forge a common identity among the nation's far-flung citizens. Even the presence of Indians and Africans contributed to art and literature that were uniquely American. In addition, the construction of a new capital city to house the federal government offered a potent symbol of nationhood.

Yet these developments also illuminated underlying conflicts that defined the young nation. The decision to move the U.S. capital south from Philadelphia was prompted by concerns among southern politicians about the power of northern economic and political elites. The very construction of the capital, in which enslaved and free workers labored side by side, highlighted racial and class differences in the nation. Educational opportunities differed by race and class as well as by sex. The question thus remained: Could a singular notion of American identity be forged in a country where differences of race, class, and sex loomed so large?

Education for a New Nation

The desire to create a specifically American culture began as soon as the Revolution ended. In 1783 Noah Webster, a schoolmaster, declared that "America must be as independent in *literature* as in *Politics*, as famous for *arts* as for *arms*." To this end, the twenty-five-year-old Webster published the *American Spelling Book*, which by 1810 had become the second best-selling book in the United States (the Bible was the first). In 1828 Webster produced his *American Dictionary of the English Language*.

Webster's books were widely used in the nation's expanding network of schools and academies and led to more standardized spelling and pronunciation of commonly used words. Before the Revolution, public education for children, which focused on basic reading and writing skills, was widely available in New England and the Middle Atlantic region. In the South, only those who could afford private schooling—perhaps a quarter of the boys and 10 percent of the girls—received any formal instruction. Few young people enrolled in high school in any part of the colonies, and far fewer attended college.

New England Grammar School

In this New England grammar school in the 1790s, boys and girls gather for instruction by their schoolmaster. They likely used one of Noah Webster's spellers or readers. The schoolmaster surely taught lessons in geography, as can be seen by the wall map and the two globes at the rear of the room.   The Granger Collection, New York

Following the Revolution, state and national leaders proposed ambitious plans for public education. In 1789 Massachusetts became the first state to institute free public elementary education for all children, and private academies and boarding schools proliferated throughout the nation.

Before 1790, the American colonies boasted nine colleges that provided further education for young men, including Harvard, Yale, King's College (Columbia), Queen's College (Rutgers), and the College of William and Mary. After independence, many Americans worried that these institutions were tainted by British and aristocratic influences. Situated in urban centers or crowded college towns, they were also criticized as centers of vice where youth might be corrupted by "scenes of dissipation and amusement." New colleges based on republican ideals needed to be founded.

Frontier towns offered opportunities for colleges to enrich the community and benefit the nation. Located in isolated villages, these colleges assured parents that students would focus on education. The young nation benefited as well, albeit at the expense of Indians and their lands. The founders of Franklin College in Athens, Georgia, encouraged white settlement in the state's interior, an area still largely populated by Creeks and Cherokees. And frontier colleges provided opportunities for ethnic and religious groups outside the Anglo-American main-stream—like Scots-Irish Presbyterians—to cement their place in American society.

Frontier colleges were organized as community institutions in which extended families—composed of administrators and faculty, their wives and children, servants and slaves, and students—played the central role. The familial character of these colleges—and their lower tuition fees—was also attractive to parents. Women were viewed as exemplars of virtue in the new nation, and the wives of professors were thus especially important in maintaining a refined atmosphere. They held salons where students could learn proper deportment and social skills. They also served as maternal figures for young adults living away from home. In some towns, students in local female academies joined college men on field trips and picnics to cultivate proper relations between the sexes.

Literary and Cultural Developments

While frontier colleges expanded educational and cultural opportunities, older universities also contributed to the development of a national identity. A group known as the Hartford Wits, most of them graduates of Yale, gave birth to a new literary tradition. This circle of poets, playwrights,

and essayists expressed distinctly American (though largely Federalist) perspectives. Members of the Hartford Wits published paeans to democracy, satires about Shays's Rebellion, and plays about specifically American dilemmas, such as the proper role of the central government in a republican nation.

The young nation also produced a number of novel-ists. Advances in printing and the production of paper increased the circulation of novels, a literary genre developed in Britain and continental Europe at the turn of the eighteenth century. At the same time, improvements in girls' education produced a growing audience among women, who were thought to be the genre's most avid readers. Novelists like Susanna Rowson and Charles Brockden Brown sought to educate readers about virtuous action by placing ordinary women and men in moments of high drama that tested their moral character. They also emphasized new marital ideals, by which husbands and wives became partners and companions in building a home and family.

Explore

See Document 8.1 for a dramatic warning to young women from novelist Susanna Rowson.

Among the most important American literary figures to emerge in the early nineteenth century was Washington Irving. While living in Europe in the 1810s, he wrote a series of short stories and essays, including "The Legend of Sleepy Hollow" and "Rip Van Winkle," that were published in his *Sketchbook* in 1820. These popular folktales drew on the Dutch culture of the Hudson valley region in New York and often poked fun at more celebra-tory tales of early American history. But Irving also wrote serious essays. One challenged colonial accounts of Indian-English conflicts, which he argued ignored courageous actions by Indians while applauding atrocities committed by whites.

While Irving achieved fame by making fun of roman-ticized versions of American history, books that glorified the nation's past were also enormously popular. Among the most influential were a three-volume *History of the Revolution* (1805) written by Mercy Otis Warren and the *Life of Washington* (1806), a celebratory if somewhat fanciful biography by an Anglican clergyman, Mason "Parson" Weems. The influence of American authors increased as residents in both urban and rural areas purchased growing numbers of books. By 1820–1821, for instance, an astonishing 80 percent of households of middling wealth in Chester County, Pennsylvania, owned books.

DOCUMENT 8.1

Susanna Rowson | *Charlotte Temple*, 1791

The English-born novelist Susanna Rowson lived much of her life in Massachusetts, where she was educated mainly by private tutors. She based her plots on historical events and in 1791 published *Charlotte Temple*, which enjoyed enormous popularity in the United States. This sentimental (and, for its time, racy) story focused on the seduction and betrayal of a young woman by a British naval officer.

Explore

In affairs of love, a young heart is never in more danger than when attempted by a handsome young soldier. A man of an indifferent appearance will, when arrayed in a military habit, show to advantage, but when beauty of person, elegance of manner, and an easy method of paying compliments are united to the scarlet coat, smart cockade, and military sash, ah! well-a-day for the poor girl who gazes on him: she is in imminent danger; but if she listens to him with pleasure, 'tis all over with her, and from that moment she has neither eyes nor ears for any other object.

. . . I mean no more by what I have here advanced than to ridicule those romantic girls who foolishly imagine a red coat and silver epaulet constitute the fine gentleman; and should that fine gentleman make half a dozen fine speeches to them they will imagine themselves so much in love as to fancy it a meritorious action to jump out of a two-pair of stairs window, abandon their friends, and trust entirely to the honor of a man who, perhaps, hardly knows the meaning of the word, and if he does, will be too much the modern man of refinement to practise it in their favor. . . .

Oh, my dear girls—for to such only am I writing—listen not to the voice of love, unless sanctioned by paternal approbation: be assured, it is now past the days of romance: no woman can be run away with contrary to her own inclination: then kneel down each morning and request kind Heaven to keep you free from temptation, or should it please to suffer you to be tried, pray for fortitude to resist the impulse of inclination when it runs counter to the precepts of religion and virtue.

Source: Susanna Haswell Rowson, *Charlotte Temple: A Tale of Truth* (New York: Funk and Wagnalls, 1905), 51–54.

Interpret the Evidence

- How would you describe Rowson's literary style?
- What was Rowson's advice to her readers? How did she use this story to help elevate the moral character of women?

Put It in Context

Why do you think *Charlotte Temple* became so popular in the early 1790s? Who might have viewed the book as controversial?

Artists, too, devoted considerable attention to historical themes. Charles Willson Peale painted Revolutionary generals while serving in the Continental Army and became best known for his portraits of George Washington. Samuel Jennings offered a more radical perspective on the nation's character when he presented *Liberty Displaying the Arts and Sciences* (1792) to the Philadelphia Library Company. Many of the library's directors opposed slavery, and Jennings portrayed Lady Liberty offering a book to a group of attentive African Americans. Engravings, which were less expensive than paintings, circulated widely, and many also highlighted national symbols like flags, eagles, and Lady Liberty.

Engravings of nature were especially popular. Books like Cleaveland's *Elementary Treatise on Mineralogy and Geology* included plates that illustrated rocks and geological formations. William Bartram's *Travels* (1791), based on his journey through the southeastern United States and Florida, illustrated plants and animals, such as the alligator, previously unknown to Anglo-American scientists.

Illustration by William Bartram, Naturalist

William Bartram was a naturalist from Pennsylvania who traveled through the South during the 1770s. He visited Indian villages and sketched plant and animal life, including alligators and other animals that most Americans had never seen. This drawing of a great yellow bream was among many illustrations that he published in his *Travels* (1791), a popular compendium of his work. HarperCollins Publishers/The Art Archive at Art Resource, NY

In the 1780s, Benjamin Franklin helped found the American Philosophical Society in Philadelphia to promote American literature and science. Like-minded gentlemen in Boston and Salem established the American Academy of Arts and Sciences. Colleges like Bowdoin, Franklin, and Dickinson advanced scientific research in frontier regions, while the University of Pennsylvania in Philadelphia established the nation's first medical school. As in the arts, American scientists built on developments in continental Europe and Great Britain, but the young nation prided itself on contributing its own expertise.

The Racial Limits of American Culture

One subject that received significant attention from writers and scientists in the United States was the American Indian. White Americans in the late eighteenth century often wielded native names and symbols as they worked to create a distinct national identity. In long-settled regions along the Atlantic seaboard, where Indian nations no longer posed a significant threat, some Americans followed in the tradition of the Boston Tea Party, dressing as Indians to protest economic and political tyranny. Antirent rioters in the Hudson valley, participants in the Whiskey Rebellion, and squatters in the backcountry of Maine disguised themselves as Indians before attacking landlords, tax collectors, and land speculators. More well-to-do whites also embraced Indian names, costumes, and symbols. Tammany societies, for example, which were named after a mythical Delaware chief called Tammend, promoted patriotism and republicanism in the late eighteenth century and attracted large numbers of skilled artisans, lawyers, and merchants.

Poets, too, focused on American Indians. In his 1787 poem "Indian Burying Ground," Philip Freneau offered a sentimental portrait that highlighted the lost heritage of a nearly extinct native culture in New England. The theme of lost cultures and heroic (if still savage) Indians became even more pronounced in American poetry in the following decades.

Such sentimental portraits of American Indians were less popular along the nation's frontier, where Indians still posed a threat. Even a woman like Sacagawea, who aided the efforts of Lewis and Clark, did not become the object of literary or artistic efforts for several generations. Sympathetic depictions of Africans and African Americans by white artists and authors appeared with even less frequency. Most were produced in the North and were intended, like Jennings's *Liberty*, for the rare patrons who opposed slavery. Typical images of blacks and Indians were far more demeaning. Especially when describing Indians in frontier regions, authors, artists, politicians, and soldiers tended to focus on their savagery, their duplicity, or both. Most images of Africans and African Americans highlighted their innate inferiority and exaggerated their perceived physical and intellectual differences from white Americans.

Whether their depiction was realistic, sentimental, or derogatory, Africans, African Americans, and American Indians were almost always presented to the American public through the eyes of whites. Few blacks or Indians had access to English-language schools, books, or newspapers, and few whites were willing to publish or purchase works by those who did. Educated African Americans like the Reverend Richard Allen of Philadelphia or the Reverend Thomas Paul of Boston generally wrote for black audiences or corresponded privately with sympathetic whites. Similarly, cultural leaders among American Indians worked mainly within their own nation either to maintain traditional languages and customs or to introduce their people to Anglo-American ideas and beliefs.

White Americans who demanded improved education generally ignored or excluded blacks and Indians. Most southern planters had little desire to teach their slaves to read and write. Even in the North, states did not generally incorporate black children into their plans for public education. It was African Americans in cities with large free black populations who established the most long-lived schools for their race. The Reverend Allen opened a Sunday school for children in 1795 at his African Methodist Church, and other free blacks formed literary and debating societies for young people and adults. Still, only a small percentage of African Americans received an education equivalent to that available to whites in the new Republic.

U.S. political leaders were more interested in the education of American Indians, but government officials never proposed any systematic method of providing them with schools. Instead, various religious groups sent missionaries to the Seneca, Cherokee, and other tribes. A few of the most successful students were then sent to American colleges to be trained as ministers or teachers for their own people. However, just as with African Americans, only a small percentage of American Indians were taught to read or write in English, and whites made almost no efforts to teach Indians the languages and histories of their own nations.

The divergent approaches that whites took to Indian and African American education demonstrated broader assumptions about the two groups rooted in geographical expansion and slave labor. Most white Americans believed that Indians were untamed and uncivilized, but not innately different from Europeans. Africans and African Americans, on the other hand, were assumed to be inferior, and most whites believed that no amount of education could make blacks their intellectual or moral equals. As U.S. frontiers expanded, white Americans considered ways to "civilize" Indians and incorporate them into the nation. But the requirements of slavery made it much more difficult for whites to imagine African Americans as anything more than lowly laborers, despite free blacks who clearly demonstrated otherwise. **See Document Project 8: Race Relations in the Early Republic, page 250.**

Emigration and Colonization

Some African Americans did question the benefits of remaining in the United States. In the late 1780s, the Newport African Union Society in Rhode Island developed a plan to establish a community for American blacks in Africa.

Many whites, too, viewed the settlement of blacks in Africa as the only way to solve the nation's racial dilemma. William Thornton, a Quaker physician who had inherited his father's sugar plantation in the West Indies, joined a group in London who tried to establish a free black commonwealth on the west coast of Africa. He traveled to the United States to promote what he called colonization. But when Thornton presented his plans to the Free African Society in Philadelphia in 1787, local leaders opposed the effort.

Over the next three decades, the idea of emigration (as blacks viewed it) or colonization (as whites saw it) received widespread attention. Those who opposed slavery hoped to persuade slave owners to free or sell their human property on the condition that they be shipped to Africa. Others assumed that free blacks could find opportunities for economic, religious, and political leadership in Africa that did not exist in the United States. Still others simply wanted to rid the nation of its race problem by ridding it of blacks. In 1817 a group of southern slave owners and northern merchants formed the **American Colonization Society (ACS)** to carry "civilization" and Christianity to the African continent and establish colonies of freed slaves and free-born American blacks there. Although some African Americans supported this scheme, northern free blacks generally opposed it, viewing colonization as an effort originating "more immediately from prejudice than philanthropy."

Ultimately the plans of the ACS proved impractical. Particularly as cotton production expanded from the 1790s on, few slave owners were willing to emancipate their workers. Indeed, even in the supposedly enlightened communities where higher education flourished, slavery was widely accepted. In southern colleges, in particular, slaves cleared land, constructed buildings, cleaned rooms, did laundry, and prepared meals.

Building a National Capital

The construction of Washington City, the nation's new capital, depended on the labor of slaves as well. The capital was situated along the Potomac River in an area surrounded by farms and plantations. More than 300,000 slaves lived in Virginia and Maryland, the states that provided the land for the federal district, and the commissioners appointed to oversee the city's construction held almost 100 slaves themselves. Between 1792 and 1809, dozens of enslaved men were hired out by their owners, who were paid $50 to $70 annually for their slaves' labor on the city. Most enslaved men cleared land, built roads, and constructed the White House and the Capitol. Some performed skilled labor as carpenters and sawyers (who cut trees and lumber) or as assistants to stonemasons and

MEETING OF THE AMERICAN COLONIZATION SOCIETY AT WASHINGTON—MR. EVERETT'S ADDRESS

American Colonization Society Meeting, Washington, D.C.
Formed in 1817, the American Colonization Society consisted of northern merchants and southern plant-
ers who sought to resolve the race problem in the United States by shipping free and enslaved blacks to
Africa. Although the society helped found Liberia, most African Americans opposed the venture, and as
slave labor became increasingly profitable, few slaveholders allowed their enslaved workers to emigrate.
© Bettman/CORBIS

surveyors. A few enslaved women were hired as cooks, nurses, and washerwomen.

Free blacks also participated in the development of Washington, working in many of the same positions as slaves did. One of the most noteworthy African Americans involved in the project was Benjamin Banneker, a self-taught clock maker, astronomer, and surveyor. He was hired as an assistant to the surveyor, Major Andrew Ellicott, in 1791, helping to plot the 100-square-mile area on which the capital was to be built.

African Americans worked alongside whites, including many Irish immigrants, whose wages were kept in check by the availability of slave labor. Most workers, regardless of race, faced poor housing, sparse meals, and limited medical care as well as malarial fevers. Despite these obstacles, in less than a decade, a system of roads was laid out and cleared, the Executive Mansion was built, and the north wing of the Capitol was completed.

Although Washington City was considered a symbol of the nation, it was experts from abroad who created the U.S.

capital. The streets were laid out according to plans developed by the French engineer Pierre L'Enfant, the Executive Mansion was designed by the Irish-born James Hoban, and the Capitol building was envisioned by the West Indian physician turned architect (and colonizationist) William Thornton. The Capitol's construction was directed by the English architect Benjamin Latrobe, and African Americans and immigrants made up the majority of the labor force. What was perhaps most "American" about the nation's capital were the diverse races and nationalities that designed and built it.

Washington's founders envisioned the city as a beacon to the world, proclaiming the advantages of republican principles. But its location on a slow-moving river and its clay soil left the area hot, humid, and dusty in the summer and muddy and damp in the winter and spring. When John Adams and his administration moved to Washington in June 1800, they considered themselves on the frontiers of civilization. The mile-long road from the Capitol to the Executive Mansion was filled with tree stumps and was nearly impossible to navigate in a carriage. On rainy days, when roads proved impassable, officials walked or rode horses to work. That November, when Abigail Adams moved into the Executive Mansion, she complained that the roof leaked, the huge house was hard to heat, and firewood was difficult to obtain. Abigail Adams was not alone in criticizing the capital city. Although the founders considered it "an experiment in republican simplicity," most residents painted Washington in harsh tones. New Hampshire representative Ebenezer Matroon wrote a friend, "If I wished to punish a culprit, I would send him to do penance in this place . . . this swamp—this lonesome dreary swamp, secluded from every delightful or pleasing thing." Others described the city as a "fever-stricken morass."

Despite the drawbacks, the new capital played an important role in the social and political world of American elites, drawing wealthy and influential Americans to this center of federal power. From January through March, the height of the social season, the wives of congressmen, judges, and other officials created a lively schedule of teas, parties, and balls in the new capital city. When Thomas Jefferson became president, he opened the White House to visitors on a regular basis, a style that seemed appropriate for the man who had drafted the Declaration of Independence. This, too, helped reshape the Washington social scene. Yet for all his republican principles, Jefferson moved into the Executive Mansion with a retinue of slaves.

In decades to come, Washington City would become Washington, D.C., a city with broad boulevards decorated with beautiful monuments to the American political experiment. And the Executive Mansion would become the White House, a proud symbol of republican government.

The United States Capitol

This watercolor by William Russell Birch presents a view of the Capitol in Washington, D.C., before it was burned down by the British during the War of 1812. Birch had emigrated from England in 1794 and lived in Philadelphia. As this painting suggests, neither the Capitol nor the city was as yet a vibrant center of republican achievements.   Library of Congress

Still, Washington was characterized by wide disparities in wealth, status, and power, which were especially visible when Jefferson occupied the Executive Mansion and slaves labored in its kitchen, laundry, and yard. Moreover, President Jefferson's efforts to incorporate new territories into the United States only exacerbated these divisions by providing more economic opportunities for planters, investors, and white farmers while ensuring the expansion of slavery and the decimation of American Indians.

REVIEW & RELATE

How did developments in education, literature, and the arts contribute to the emergence of a distinctly American identity?

What place did blacks and American Indians inhabit in the predominant white view of American society and culture?

 LEARNINGCurve bedfordstmartins.com/hewittlawson/LC

Extending U.S. Borders

Thomas Jefferson, like other leading Democratic-Republicans, favored limited government, imagining a nation made up of small, independent farmers who had little need and less desire for an expansive federal government (see chapter 7). Initially, the president was successful in imposing his vision on the young government. By the middle of his first term, however, developments in international affairs converged with Supreme Court rulings to expand federal power. Jefferson contributed directly to this expansion by purchasing the Louisiana Territory from France. In turn, the development of this vast territory raised new questions about the place of Indians and African Americans in a republican society.

A New Administration Faces Challenges

In 1801 Democratic-Republicans worked quickly to implement their vision of limited federal power. Holding the majority in Congress, they repealed the hated whiskey tax and let the Alien and Sedition Acts expire. The Senate also approved Jefferson's appointment of Albert Gallatin, who served as a lawyer for the whiskey rebels, as secretary of the treasury. The president significantly reduced government expenditures, and he and Gallatin immediately set about slashing the national debt, cutting it nearly in half by the end of Jefferson's second term. Democratic-Republicans also worked to curb the powers granted to the Bank of the United States and the federal court system.

Soon, however, international upheavals forced Jefferson to make fuller use of his presidential powers. The U.S. government had paid tribute to the Barbary States of North Africa during the 1790s to gain protection for American merchant ships. The new president opposed this practice and in 1801 refused to continue the payments. The Barbary pirates quickly resumed attacks on American ships, and Jefferson was forced to send the U.S. navy and Marine Corps to retaliate. Although the combined American and Arab mercenary force did not achieve their objective of capturing Tripoli, the Ottoman viceroy agreed to negotiate a new agreement with the United States. Seeking to avoid all-out war, Congress accepted a treaty with the Barbary States that reduced the tribute payment.

Jefferson had also followed the developing crisis in the West Indies during the 1790s. In 1791 slaves on the sugar-rich island of Saint Domingue launched a revolt against French rule. The **Haitian Revolution** escalated into a complicated conflict in which free people of color, white slave owners, and slaves formed competing alliances with British and Spanish forces as well as with leaders of the French Revolution. Finally, in December 1799, Toussaint L'Ouverture, a former slave and military leader, claimed the presidency of the new Republic of Haiti. But Napoleon Bonaparte seized power in France that same year and sent thousands of troops to reclaim the island. Although Toussaint was shipped off to France, where he died in prison, other Haitian rebels continued the fight. As the struggle intensified, thousands of Haitian refugees, black and white, fled to the United States. However, by November 1803, prolonged fighting, yellow fever, and the loss of sixty thousand soldiers forced Napoleon to admit defeat. Haiti became the first independent black-led nation in the Americas.

Explore

See Document 8.2 for a vivid description of the uprising in Haiti.

Incorporating the Louisiana Territory

Thomas Jefferson had enthusiastically supported the American and French revolutions, but he was not sympathetic to an independent black nation. Nonetheless, in France's defeat he saw an opportunity to gain navigation rights on the Mississippi River, which the French controlled. This was a matter of crucial concern to Americans living west of the Appalachian Mountains. Jefferson sent fellow Virginian James Monroe to France to offer Napoleon $2 million to ensure Americans the right of navigation and deposit (that is, offloading cargo from ships) on the Mississippi. To Jefferson's surprise, Napoleon offered instead to sell the entire **Louisiana Territory** for $15 million.

DOCUMENT 8.2

Mary Hassal | *Secret History*, 1808

The Haitian Revolution elicited a range of emotions from Americans who read or heard about the island's violent slave uprising. Unlike most people in the United States, however, Mary Hassal of Philadelphia was in Haiti during the historic event. She relayed her firsthand interpretation of the revolution in a series of letters to her uncle, Vice President Aaron Burr. The following excerpt describes the grim fate of three black rebels.

Explore

Cape Francois

What did these slaves do to receive such severe punishment?

How does Hassal describe the men's reactions to their deaths?

What effect did the executions have on the people of Cape Francois, white and black?

Ah, my dear friend, where shall I find expressions to convey to you an idea of the horror that fills my soul; how describe scenes at which I tremble even now with terror?

Three negroes were caught setting fire to a plantation near the town. They were sentenced to be burnt alive; and the sentence was actually executed. When they were tied to the stake and the fire kindled, one of them, I understand, held his head over the smoke and was suffocated immediately. The second made horrible contortions, and howled dreadfully. The third, looking at him contemptuously said, Peace! Do you not know how to die? and preserved an unalterable firmness till the devouring flames consumed him. This cruel act has been blamed by everybody as giving a bad example to the negroes, who will not fail to retaliate on the first prisoners they take. But it has been succeeded by a deed which has absolutely chilled the hearts of the people. Everyone trembles for his own safety, and silent horror reigns throughout the place.

Source: Mary Hassal, *Secret History; or, The Horrors of Santo Domingo* (Philadelphia: Bradford and Inskeep, 1808), 99–100.

Put It in Context

How might reports like this one have contributed to American slaveholders' fear of slave revolts?

The president agonized over the constitutionality of such a purchase. Since the Constitution contained no provisions for buying land from foreign nations, a strict interpretation would not allow the purchase. In the end, though, the opportunity proved too tempting, and in late 1803 the president finally agreed to buy the Louisiana Territory based on a loose interpretation of the Constitution. Because the acquisition of the vast territory proved enormously popular among both politicians and ordinary Americans, few cared that it expanded presidential and congressional powers.

Congress soon appropriated funds for an exploratory expedition known as the **Corps of Discovery** to map the terrain. This effort, which Sacagawea and her husband joined, was led by Captain Meriwether Lewis, who had served as Jefferson's personal secretary, and William Clark, an army officer. Beginning on May 14, 1804, Lewis, Clark, and three dozen men traveled thousands of miles up the Missouri River, through the northern plains, over the Rocky Mountains, and beyond the Louisiana Territory to the Pacific coast. Members of the expedition meticulously recorded observations about local plants and animals as well as Indian residents, providing valuable evidence for young scientists like Parker Cleaveland and fascinating information for ordinary Americans.

Sacagawea was the only Indian to travel as a permanent member of the expedition, but other native women and men assisted the Corps when it journeyed near their villages. They provided food and lodging for the travelers, hauled baggage up steep mountain trails, and offered food, horses, and other trade items. The one African American on the expedition, a slave named York, also helped negotiate trade with local Indians. York recognized his value as a trader, hunter, and scout and asked Clark for his freedom when the expedition ended in 1806. York did eventually become a free man, but it is not clear whether it was by Clark's choice or because York escaped.

Other expeditions followed Lewis and Clark's successful venture. In 1806 Lieutenant Zebulon Pike led a group to explore the southern portion of the Louisiana Territory (Map 8.1). After traveling from St. Louis to the Rocky Mountains, the expedition traveled into Mexican territory. In early 1807, Pike and his men were captured by Mexican forces. They were returned to the United States at the Louisiana border that July. Pike had learned a great deal about lands that would eventually become part of the United States and about Mexican desires to overthrow Spanish rule, information that proved valuable over the next two decades.

Early in this series of expeditions, in November 1804, Jefferson stood for reelection, winning an easy victory. His popularity among farmers, already high, increased when Congress passed an act that reduced the minimum allotment for federal land sales from 320 to 160 acres. This act allowed more farmers to purchase land on their own rather than via speculators. Yet by the time of his second inauguration in March 1805, the president's vision of limiting the powers of the federal government had been shattered by his own actions and those of the Supreme Court.

The Supreme Court Extends Its Reach

The Supreme Court, the last bastion of Federalist power, extended its reach during Jefferson's presidency. In 1801, just before the Federalist-dominated Congress turned over

MAP 8.1   Lewis and Clark and Zebulon Pike Expeditions, 1804–1807

The expeditions led by Meriwether Lewis, William Clark, and Zebulon Pike illustrate the vast regions explored in just four years after the purchase of the Louisiana Territory by the United States. Lewis and Clark as well as Pike journeyed through and beyond the borders of that territory, gathering important information about Indian nations, plants, animals, and the natural terrain throughout the West.

power to the Democratic-Republicans, it passed a new **Judiciary Act**. The act created six additional circuit courts and sixteen new judgeships, which President Adams filled with Federalist "midnight appointments" before he left office. Jefferson accused the Federalists of having "retired into the judiciary" and worried that "from that battery all the works of Republicanism are to be beaten down and destroyed." Meanwhile John Marshall, who sat as the chief justice of the Supreme Court (1801–1835), insisted that the powers of the Court must be equal to and balance those of the executive and legislative branches.

One of the first cases to test the Court's authority involved a dispute over President Adams's midnight appointments. Jefferson's newly appointed secretary of state, James Madison, refused to deliver the appointment papers to several of these appointees, including William Marbury. Marbury and three others sued Madison to receive their commissions. In *Marbury v. Madison* (1803), the Supreme Court ruled that it was not empowered to force the executive branch to give Marbury his commission. But in his decision, Chief Justice Marshall declared that the Supreme Court did have the duty "to say what the law is." He thus asserted a fundamental constitutional point: that the Supreme Court had the authority to decide what federal laws were constitutional. The following year, the Court also claimed the right to rule on the constitutionality of state laws. In doing so, the Court rejected the view of Democratic-Republicans who claimed that state legislatures had the power to repudiate federal law.

Over the next dozen years, the Supreme Court continued to assert Federalist principles. In 1810, to strengthen its claims for judicial review, the nation's highest court insisted that it was the proper and sole arena for determining matters of constitutional interpretation. In another case, *McCulloch v. Maryland* (1819), the Federalist-dominated Court reinforced its loose interpretation of the Constitution's implied powers clause. This clause gave the federal government the right to "make all laws which shall be necessary and proper" for carrying out the explicit powers granted to it by the Constitution. Federalists had used this clause to establish the first national bank. Despite Democratic-Republicans' early opposition to a national bank, Congress chartered the Second Bank of the United States in 1816. Its branch banks issued notes that circulated widely in local business communities. Legislators in Maryland, believing that these banks had gained excessive power, approved a tax on their operations. Marshall's Court ruled that the establishment of the bank was "necessary and proper" for the functioning of the national government and rejected Maryland's right to tax the branch bank, claiming that "the power to tax involves the power to destroy."

By 1820 the Supreme Court, under the forceful direction of John Marshall, had established the power of judicial review—the authority of the nation's highest court to rule on cases involving states as well as the nation. From the Court's perspective, the judiciary was as important an institution in framing and preserving a national agenda as Congress or the president.

Democratic-Republicans Expand Federal Powers

Although Democratic-Republicans generally opposed Marshall's rulings, they, too, continued to expand federal power. Once again, international developments drove the Jefferson administration's political agenda. By 1805 the security of the United States was threatened by continued conflicts between France and Great Britain. Both sought alliances with the young nation, and both ignored U.S. claims of neutrality. Indeed, each nation sought to punish Americans for trading with the other. Britain began stopping American ships carrying sugar and molasses from the French West Indies on the pretense of searching them for British deserters. Between 1802 and 1811, the Royal Navy impressed (forced into service) more than eight thousand sailors taken from such ships, including many American citizens. Remembering similar abuses during the colonial period, Americans demanded action. Yet the United States was in no position to launch a war against Great Britain. France claimed a similar right to stop American ships if they continued to trade with Great Britain.

Unable to convince foreign powers to recognize U.S. neutrality, Jefferson and Madison pushed for congressional passage of an embargo that they hoped would, like colonial boycotts, force Great Britain's hand. In 1807 Congress passed the **Embargo Act**, which prohibited U.S. ships from leaving their home ports until Britain and France repealed their restrictions on American trade. Although the act kept the United States out of war, it had a devastating impact on national commerce.

New England merchants immediately voiced their outrage. Some merchants began sending items to Europe via Canada. In response, Congress passed the Force Act, granting extraordinary powers to customs officials to end such smuggling. The economic pain spread well beyond the merchant class. Young professionals like Parker Cleaveland were affected by the embargo-fueled recession; he was forced to sell his home to the Bowdoin trustees and become their tenant in 1807. Farmers and planters also suffered the embargo's effects, as did urban workers, especially in port cities where sailors and dockworkers faced escalating unemployment. The recession raised deep concerns about the expansion of federal power.

Opposition to the Embargo Act

Although Congress repealed the Embargo Act in 1809, lawmakers still barred the United States from trading with Great Britain and France, both of which attacked American shipping in violation of American neutrality. This political cartoon by Alexander Anderson criticizes the embargo, which proved costly to merchants, sailors, and dockworkers. Here a merchant carrying a barrel of goods curses the snapping turtle "Ograbme," which is *embargo* spelled backward.   The Granger Collection, New York

Congress and the president had not simply regulated international trade; they had brought it to a halt.

In Jefferson's first inaugural address, he acknowledged that "it will rarely fall to the lot of imperfect man to retire from this station [the presidency] with the reputation and the favor which bring him into it." Not only had Jefferson failed to contain the powers of the federal government, but the Embargo Act also threatened the livelihood of those who had once seen him as their champion. At the end of his second term, a Philadelphia seaman wrote to him, claiming that because of the Embargo Act he had lost what little he owned and threatening to "throttle his honored neck."

Despite such sentiments, many Americans still viewed Jefferson favorably. He had devoted his adult life to the creation of the American Republic, and he had purchased the Louisiana Territory, opening up vast lands to American exploration and development. This geographical boon had encouraged inventors and artisans to pursue ideas that would help the young nation take full advantage of its resources and recover from its current economic plight.

REVIEW & RELATE

How did Jefferson and the Democratic-Republicans contribute to the expansion of the role of the federal government in American life?	How did the conflict between France and Great Britain in the late eighteenth and early nineteenth centuries lead to domestic problems in the United States?

Remaking the U.S. Economy

As the United States expanded geographically, technological ingenuity became a highly valued commodity. The spread of U.S. settlements into new territories necessitated improved forms of transportation and increased the need for muskets and other weapons to protect the nation's frontier. The growing population also fueled improvements in agriculture and manufacturing to meet demands for clothing, food, and farm equipment. Continued conflicts with Great Britain and France also highlighted the need to develop the nation's natural resources and technological capabilities. Still, the daily lives of most Americans changed only slowly. And some workers, especially enslaved women and men, found that technological advances just added to their burdens.

The U.S. Population Grows and Migrates

Although Democratic-Republicans initially hoped to limit the powers of the national government, the rapid growth of the United States pulled in the opposite direction. An increased population, combined with the exhaustion of farmland along the eastern seaboard, fueled migration to the west as well as the growth of cities. By 1820 one-quarter of non-Indian Americans lived west of the Appalachian Mountains. These developments heightened conflicts with Indians and over slavery, but they also encouraged advances in transportation and communication and improvements in agriculture and manufacturing.

Sacagawea must have realized that the expedition she accompanied was a harbinger of white expansion, but many Indians only gradually came to realize that the few dozen men who joined Lewis and Clark heralded the arrival of hundreds and then thousands of migrants from the East. As white Americans encroached farther and farther on lands long settled by native peoples, Indian tribes in the eastern United States and the midsection of the nation were forced westward. As early as 1800, groups like the Shoshones, who originally inhabited the Great Plains, had been forced into the Rocky Mountains by Indians moving into the plains from the Mississippi and Ohio valleys (Map 8.2).

At the same time, although the vast majority of Americans continued to live in rural areas, a growing number moved to cities (defined as places with 8,000 or more inhabitants). New York City and Philadelphia both counted more than 100,000 residents by 1810. In New York, immigrants, most of them Irish, made up about 10 percent of the population in 1820 and twice that percentage five years later. During this time, the number of African Americans in New York City increased to more than 10,000. New cities began to emerge along the nation's frontier as well. After the United States acquired the Louisiana Territory, New Orleans grew rapidly, and western migration fueled the development of Cincinnati. Even smaller frontier towns served important functions for migrants traveling west. Trading posts appeared across the Mississippi valley, which eased the migration of thousands headed farther west. They served as sites of exchange between Indians and white Americans and created the foundations for later cities (Table 8.1).

Most Americans who headed west hoped to benefit from the increasingly liberal terms offered by the federal government for purchasing land. Yeomen farmers sought sufficient acreage to support their families and grow some additional crops for sale. They were eager to settle in western sections of the

original thirteen states, in the Ohio River valley, or in newly opened territories along the Missouri and Kansas Rivers. In the South, small farmers had to compete with slave-owning planters who headed west in the early nineteenth century. Migrants to the Mississippi valley also had to contend with a sizable population of long-settled Spanish residents and French planters who had taken refuge from Saint Domingue with their slaves, as well as Chickasaw and Creek Indians in the South and Shawnee, Chippewa, Sauk, and Fox Indians farther north.

The development of roads and turnpikes hastened the movement of people and the transportation of goods. Frontier farmers required methods to get their produce to eastern markets quickly and cheaply. Before completion of the Lancaster Turnpike in Pennsylvania, it cost as much to carry wheat and other items overland the sixty-two miles to Philadelphia as it did to ship them by sea from Philadelphia to London. Those who lived farther west faced

MAP 8.2　Indian Land Cessions, 1790–1820

With the ratification of the Constitution, the federal government gained greater control over Indian relations, including land cessions. At the same time, large numbers of white settlers poured into regions west of the Appalachian Mountains. The U.S. government gained most Indian land by purchase or treaty, but these agreements were often the consequence of military victories by the U.S. army.

TABLE 8.1 Prices at George Davenport's Trading Post, Rock Island, Illinois, c. 1820

Item	Price	Item	Price
Ax	$6.00	Large copper kettle	$30.00
Beaver trap	$8.00	Lead	$0.20 per pound
Black silk handkerchief	$2.00	Lead shot for guns	$1.00 per 5 pounds
Breechcloth	$3.00	Medium copper kettle	$10.00
Bridles	$2.00–$10.00	Muskrat spear	$2.00
Chain for staking down traps	$0.75 per 6 feet	Muskrat trap	$5.00
Combs	$1.00 per pair	Muslin or calico shirt	$3.00
File (for sharpening axes)	$2.00	Ordinary butcher knife	$0.50
Flannel	$1.00 per yard	Sheet iron kettle	$10.00
Flannel mantle	$3.00	Small copper kettle	$3.00
Gunflints	$1.00 per 15	Spurs	$6.00 per pair
Hand-size mirrors	$0.25	Tin kettle	$14.00
Heavy wool cloth	$10.00 per yard	Tomahawk	$1.50
Hoe	$2.00	Trade gun	$20.00–$25.00
Horn of gunpowder	$1.50	Wool blanket	$4.00
Horses	$35.00–$50.00	Wool mantle (short cloak or shawl)	$4.00

Source: Will Leinicke, Marion Lardner, and Ferrel Anderson, *Two Nations, One Land* (Rock Island, IL: Citizens to Preserve Black Hawk Park, 1981).

even greater challenges. With the admission of Kentucky (1792), Tennessee (1796), and Ohio (1803) to the Union, demands for congressional assistance in building transportation routes grew louder. By 1819 five more states were admitted along the Mississippi River, from Louisiana to Illinois.

During Jefferson's administration, Albert Gallatin urged Congress to fund internal improvements—that is, roads and canals—to enhance the economic development of the nation. Legislatures chartered and sometimes helped fund improved transportation in their own states, but Gallatin focused on transportation across regions. He advocated a "great turnpike road" along the Atlantic seaboard from Maine to Georgia as well as roads to connect the four main rivers that flowed from the Appalachians to the Atlantic Ocean. In 1815 Congress approved funds for one such project, the **National Road** from western Maryland through southwestern Pennsylvania to Wheeling, West Virginia. This so-called Cumberland Road was completed in 1818, and in the following decades it was extended into Ohio and Illinois.

Carrying people and goods by water was even faster and cheaper than transporting them over land, but rivers ran mainly north and south. In addition, although loads could be delivered quickly downstream, the return voyage was long and slow. While politicians advocated the construction of canals along east-west routes to link river systems, inventors and mechanics focused on building boats powered by steam to overcome the problems of sending goods upriver.

Oliver Evans, a machinist in Philadelphia, developed a steam-powered gristmill—to produce flour from grain—in 1788. Then in 1804 he invented a high-pressure steam engine attached to a dredge that cleaned the silt around the docks in Philadelphia harbor. He had insufficient funds, however, to pursue work on a steam-powered boat.

In New York State, Robert Fulton sought to improve on Evans's efforts, using the low-pressure steam engine developed in England. Fulton had moved to Paris in the early nineteenth century to train as a painter. While there, he met the wealthy ambassador Robert Livingston, who helped negotiate the Louisiana Purchase. Livingston convinced Fulton to focus on engineering and provided funds for him to do so. In 1807 Fulton launched the first successful steamboat, the *Clermont*, which traveled up the Hudson River from New York City to Albany in only thirty-two hours. The powerful Mississippi River proved a greater challenge, but by combining Evans's high-pressure steam engine with a flat-bottom hull that avoided the river's sandbars, mechanics who worked along the frontier improved Fulton's original design and launched the steamboat era in the West.

Technology Reshapes Agriculture and Industry

Advances in agricultural and industrial technology paralleled the development of roads and steamboats. Here, too, a single invention spurred others, inducing a **multiplier effect** that inspired additional dramatic changes during the decades following the Revolution. Two inventions—the cotton gin and the spinning machine—were especially notable in transforming southern agriculture and northern industry, transformations that were deeply intertwined.

American developments were also closely tied to the earlier rise of industry in Great Britain. By the 1770s, British manufacturers had built spinning mills in which steam-powered machines spun raw cotton into yarn. Importing cotton from Britain's colonies, British manufacturers thrived. Eager to maintain their monopoly on industrial technology, the British made it illegal for engineers to emigrate. They could not, however, keep everyone who worked in a cotton mill from leaving the country. At age fourteen, Samuel Slater was hired as an apprentice in an English mill that used a yarn-spinning machine designed by Richard Arkwright. Slater was promoted to supervisor of the factory, but at age twenty-one he sought greater opportunities in America. While working in New York City, he learned that Moses Brown, a wealthy Rhode Island merchant, was seeking help in developing a machine like Arkwright's. Funded by Rhode Island investors and assisted by local craftsmen, Slater designed and built a spinning mill in Pawtucket.

The mill opened in December 1790 and began producing yarn, which was then woven into cloth in private shops and homes. By 1815 a series of cotton mills, most built to look like New England meetinghouses in order to limit hostility from local farmers, dotted the Pawtucket River. These factories promised a steady income for workers in the mills, most of whom were the wives and children of farmers, and ensured employment for weavers in the countryside. They also increased the demand for cotton in New England just as British manufacturers sought new sources of the crop as well.

Ensuring a steady supply of cotton, however, required another technological innovation, this one created by Eli Whitney. After graduating from Yale at age twenty-seven, Whitney agreed to serve as a private tutor for a planter family in South Carolina. On the ship carrying him to his new position, Whitney met Catherine Greene, widow of the Revolutionary War general Nathanael Greene. He ended up staying on her Mulberry Plantation near Savannah, Georgia, where local planters complained to him about the difficulty of making a profit on cotton in the area. Long-staple cotton, grown in the Sea Islands, yielded enormous profits, but the soil in most of the South could sustain only the short-staple variety, which required hours of intensive labor to separate its sticky green seeds from the cotton fiber.

The Cotton Gin
Invented by Eli Whitney in 1793, the cotton gin, which separated cotton fibers from seed, transformed American industry and agriculture. As presented in this engraving, which was likely part of the patent application, Whitney's invention was a relatively simple device that had an enormous impact on the South and the nation at large.   Culver Pictures/The Art Archive at Art Resource, NY

In 1793, in as little as ten days, Eli Whitney built a machine that could ease the labor of deseeding short-staple cotton. His **cotton gin** consisted of a wooden box with a mesh screen, rollers, brushes, and wire hooks. The cotton boll was drawn through the mesh, where wire hooks caught the seeds and the rotating brushes then swept the cotton lint into a tray. Whitney's gin could clean as much cotton fiber in one hour as several workers could clean in a day. Recognizing the gin's value, Whitney received a U.S. patent, but because the machine was easy to duplicate, he never profited from his invention.

Fortunately, Whitney had other ideas that proved more profitable. In June 1798, amid U.S. fears of a war with France, the U.S. government granted him an extraordinary contract to produce 4,000 rifles in eighteen months. Rifles were then produced individually by highly trained artisans, but the inventor claimed he could devise a machine to manufacture guns in large quantities. By January 1801, having produced only 500 rifles, Whitney met with national political leaders to reassure them that success was near. Adapting the plan of Honoré Blanc, a French mechanic who devised a musket with interchangeable parts, Whitney demonstrated the potential for using machines to produce various parts of a musket, which could then be assembled in mass quantities. With Jefferson's enthusiastic support, the federal government extended Whitney's contract, and by 1809 his New Haven factory was turning out 7,500 guns annually.

Whitney's factory became a model for the **American system of manufacturing**, in which water-powered machinery and the division of production into many small tasks allowed less skilled workers to produce mass quantities of a particular item, like guns or shoes. Whitney viewed this system as a boon to men and women who were unable or unwilling to obtain apprenticeships in skilled crafts. In factories, they could be trained quickly to do a particular task and thereby support themselves or supplement family earnings from farming.

The factories developed by Whitney and Slater became training grounds for younger mechanics and inventors who devised improvements in machinery or set out to solve new technological puzzles. Their efforts also transformed the lives of generations of workers—enslaved and free—who planted and picked the cotton, spun the yarn, wove the cloth, and sewed the clothes that cotton gins and spinning mills made possible.

Transforming Household Production

Slater and Whitney were among the most influential American inventors, but both required the assistance and collaboration of other inventors, machinists, and artisans to implement their ideas. The achievement of these enterprising individuals was seen by many Americans as part of a larger spirit of inventiveness and technological ingenuity that marked the United States as a young

---

DOCUMENTS 8.3 AND 8.4

Industrial Beginnings in Massachusetts: Two Views

American industry began in earnest in New England, and Massachusetts mills garnered great attention from interested observers at home and abroad, many of whom assessed the success and potential of American industry. In the first document, Henry Wansey, a retired clothier from England who visited New England's mills in 1794 to determine whether they would provide competition for his home country, describes his visit. In the second document, Timothy Dwight, the president of Yale College, surveys the mills in Worcester, Massachusetts.

Explore

8.3 Henry Wansey | An Excursion to the United States, 1794

Near Boston are the following manufactories established, according to the accounts given me by a considerable merchant there: A cotton and carpet manufactory at Worcester, carried on by Peter Stowell and Co. with a good capital; and one of woollen, by Thomas Stowell; at Newbury Port, Joseph Brown, a clothier, makes a variety of woollen goods of the coarse kinds. . . . But all these I judge rather the seeds of manufactories, than any large or permanent establishments. That energy which is created in our country by necessity and difficulty of living cannot take place there for many years; nor need England fear a rivalship there, or in any other country. France, when disburdened of her present military government, will be many years in recovering her manufactories.

When we consider that the United States, with scarcely four million inhabitants, import annually of our manufactures more than twelve million dollars in value, it follows that when her inhabitants are increased to eight million, she will want manufactures to the annual amount of twenty-four million dollars. From hence I conclude that her population and prosperity are an advantage to Great Britain. I am convinced that the ability of the United States to manufacture cannot keep pace by any means with her increasing population; at least for a century. It therefore follows, that she must increase her demand for foreign manufactures; and the Americans generally acknowledge that no country can supply them so well as Great Britain.

Source: Henry Wansey, *An Excursion to the United States of North America, in the Summer of 1794* (London: Salisbury, 1798), 29–30.

nation. That spirit led to a cascade of inventions between 1790 and 1820.

Cotton gins and steam engines, steamboats and interchangeable parts, gristmills and spinning mills—each of these items and processes was improved upon over time and led to myriad other inventions. For instance, in 1811 Francis Cabot invented a power loom for weaving, a necessary step once spinning mills began producing more yarn than hand weavers could use. Similarly, Jethro Wood perfected the cast-iron plow in 1819, ensuring that western farmers could provide adequate food for the small but rising population of city dwellers and factory workers.

Despite these rapid technological advances, the changes that occurred in the early nineteenth century were more evolutionary than revolutionary. Most political leaders and social commentators viewed gradual improvement as a blessing. For many Americans, the ideal situation consisted of either small mills scattered through the countryside or household enterprises that could supply neighbors with finer cloth, wool cards, or other items that improved home production.

Explore

For two distinct views on the progress of manufacturing in early New England, see Documents 8.3 and 8.4.

The importance of domestic manufacturing increased after passage of the Embargo Act as imports of cloth and other items fell dramatically. Small factories, like those along the Pawtucket River, increased their output, and so did ordinary housewives. Blacksmiths, carpenters, and

Explore

8.4 Timothy Dwight | Travels in New England, 1821

Few towns in New-England exhibit so uniform an appearance of neatness and taste or contain so great a proportion of good buildings, and so small a proportion of those which are indifferent, as Worcester. There is probably more wealth in it also than in any other, which does not exceed it in dimensions and number of inhabitants. Its trade, considering its inland situation, is believed to be extensive and profitable. . . .

There are in Worcester four grist-mills, four saw-mills, two fulling-mills, and a large paper-mill. The proprietors of the fulling-mills carry on the Clothiers' business to a great extent; and with skill supposed not to be excelled in the State. Scarlet and blue have for some time been dyed here in a superiour manner.

On the subject of *mills* I wish you to observe, once for all, that I shall rarely mention them. There is scarcely a township in New-England which has not a complete set of grist-mills and saw-mills. . . . There is, probably, no country in the world where mill-streams are so numerously and universally dispersed, or grist-mills and saw-mills so universally erected as in New-England. Conveniences of this kind may be said, almost if not quite literally, to be furnished in abundance to every Parish in the Country. To reiterate this fact would be to take very effectual means for wearing out your patience.

Source: Timothy Dwight, *Travels; in New-England and New-York* (New Haven: Timothy Dwight, 1821), 366–67.

Interpret the Evidence

- According to Wansey, would the mills in Worcester and other Massachusetts towns be able to compete with their British counterparts? Why or why not?
- How does Dwight characterize Worcester? Do you think he would agree with Wansey's assessment of America's industrial prospects?

Put It in Context

What do these reports reveal about the industrial innovations occurring in the United States in the late eighteenth and early nineteenth centuries?

wheelwrights busily repaired and improved the spindles, looms, and other equipment that allowed family members to produce more and better cloth from wool, flax, and cotton. New ideas about companionate marriage, which emphasized affection and mutual obligations between spouses, may have encouraged husbands and wives to work more closely in these domestic enterprises. While husbands generally carried out the heavier or more skilled parts of home manufacturing, like weaving, wives spun yarn and sewed together sections of cloth into finished goods.

At the same time, daughters, neighbors, and servants remained critical to the production of household items. In Hallowell, Maine, in the early nineteenth century, the midwife Martha Ballard worked alongside her daughters and a niece, producing the goods necessary to survive on the northern frontier, even as she supplemented her husband's income as a surveyor. In more populated areas, older forms of mutuality continued alongside newer patterns of companionate marriage. Neighbors shared tools and equipment while those with specialized skills assisted neighbors—threading a loom, for instance—in exchange for items they needed. Yet young couples who joined in these activities no doubt imagined themselves embarking on more egalitarian marriages than those of their parents. If they ended up living on the southern frontier, however, they might well discover that traditional patterns of hierarchical marriage prevailed there, shaping both household production and social life.

In wealthy households, whatever the contours of marriage, servants and slaves took on a greater share of domestic labor by the late eighteenth and early nineteenth centuries. Most female servants in the North were young and unmarried. Some arrived with children in tow or became pregnant while on the job, a mark of the rising rate of out-of-wedlock births following the Revolution. Planters' wives in the South had fewer worries in this regard because if household slaves became pregnant, their children added to the slave owner's labor supply. And on larger planta- tions, owners increasingly assigned a few enslaved women to spin, cook, wash clothes, make candles, and wait on table. Plantation mistresses also hired the wives of small farmers and landless laborers to turn cotton into yarn, weave yarn into cloth, and sew clothing for slaves and children. While mistresses in both regions continued to engage in household production, they also expanded their roles as domestic managers.

Still, at the turn of the nineteenth century, most people continued to live on family farms; to produce or trade locally for food, clothing, and other basic needs; and to use techniques handed down for generations to produce candles and soap, prepare meals, and deliver

babies. Yet by 1820, their lives, like those of wealthier Americans, were transformed by the expanding market economy. More and more families sewed clothes with machine-spun thread made from cotton ginned in the American South, worked their fields with cast-iron plows, and varied their diet by adding items shipped from other regions by steamboats.

Technology, Cotton, and Slaves

Some of the most dramatic technological changes occurred in agriculture, and none was more significant than the cotton gin, which led to the vast expansion of agricultural production in the South. This in turn fueled regional specialization, ensuring that residents in one area of the nation—the North, South, or West—depended on those in other areas. Southern planters relied on a growing demand for cotton from northern merchants and manufacturers. At the same time, planters, merchants, manufacturers, and factory workers became more dependent on western farmers to produce the grain and livestock needed to feed the nation.

As cotton gins spread across the South, any thoughts of abolishing slavery in the region disappeared. Instead, cotton and slavery expanded into the interior of many southern states as well as into the lower Mississippi valley. Cotton was not the only crop produced in the South—in Louisiana, planters made their fortunes on sugar and in South Carolina on rice—but it quickly became the most important. In 1790 southern farms and plantations produced about 3,000 bales of cotton, each weighing about 300 pounds. By 1820, with the aid of the cotton gin, the South produced more than 330,000 bales annually (Table 8.2). For southern blacks, increased production meant increased burdens. Because seeds could be separated from raw cotton with much greater efficiency, farmers could plant vastly larger quantities of the crop. On small farms, the work was still performed primarily by family members, neighbors, or hired hands. But planters could purchase additional slaves, particularly as cotton prices rose in the early nineteenth century.

The dramatic increase in the amount of cotton planted and harvested each year was paralleled by a jump in the size of the slave population. Thus even as northern states began to abolish the institution and the international slave trade ended (in 1808), southern planters significantly increased the number of slaves they held. Some smuggled in women and men from Africa and the Caribbean. Most planters, however, depended on enslaved women to bear more children, increasing the size of their labor force through natural reproduction. In addition, planters in the Deep South—from Georgia and the Carolinas west to

TABLE 8.2 **Growth of Cotton Production in the United States, 1790–1830**

Year	Production in Bales
1790	3,135
1795	16,719
1800	73,145
1805	146,290
1810	177,638
1815	208,986
1820	334,378
1825	532,915
1830	731,452

Source: Lewis Cecil Gray, *History of Agriculture in the Southern United States to 1860*, vol. 2 (Gloucester, MA: Peter Smith, 1958).

Louisiana—began buying slaves from farmers in Maryland and Virginia, where cotton and slavery were less profitable.

In 1790 there were fewer than 700,000 slaves in the United States. By 1820 there were nearly 1.5 million. Still, because of the increased competition for field hands to plant, maintain, and harvest the cotton crop, the price of slaves increased, roughly doubling between 1795 and 1805. The dramatic growth of slave markets in Charleston and New Orleans was one measure of the continued importance of the slave trade as cotton lands moved west.

In the early nineteenth century, most white southerners believed that there was enough land to go around. And the rising price of cotton allowed small farmers to imagine they would someday be planters. Some southern Indians also placed their hopes in cotton. Cherokee and Creek Indians cultivated the crop, even purchasing black slaves to increase production. Some Indian villages now welcomed ministers to their communities, hoping that embracing Protestantism and "American" culture might allow them to retain their current lands. Yet other native residents foresaw the increased pressure for land that cotton cultivation produced and organized to defend themselves from whites invading their territory. Regardless of the policies adopted by Indians, cotton and slavery expanded rapidly into Cherokee- and Creek-controlled lands in the interior of Georgia and South Carolina. And the admission of the states of Louisiana, Mississippi, and Alabama between 1812 and 1819 marked the rapid spread of southern agriculture farther westward.

Enslaved men and women played critical roles in the South's geographical expansion. Without their labor, neither cotton nor sugar could have become mainstays of the South's economy. Because clearing new cotton fields and planting and harvesting sugarcane involved heavy labor, most planters selected young slave men and women to move west, breaking apart families in the process. Some slaves resisted their removal to new plantations. If forced to go, they could still use their role in the labor process to limit owners' control. Slaves worked slowly, broke tools, and feigned illness or injury. Enslaved women and men hid out temporarily as a respite from brutal work regimes or harsh punishments. Others ran to areas controlled by Indians, hoping for better treatment, or to regions where slavery was no longer legal.

Still, given the power and resources wielded by whites, most slaves had to find ways to improve their lives within the system of bondage. The end of the international slave trade helped blacks in this regard since planters then had to depend more on natural reproduction to increase their labor supply. To ensure that slaves lived longer and healthier lives, planters were forced to provide sturdier housing, better clothing, and increased food allotments. Some slaves gained leverage to fish, hunt, or maintain small gardens in order to improve their diet. With the birth of more children, southern blacks also developed more extensive kinship networks, ensuring that family members could care for children if their parents were compelled to move west. Enslavement was still brutal, but slaves made small gains that improved their chances of survival.

Southern slaves also established their own religious ceremonies, often held in the woods or swamps at night. African Americans were swept up as well in the religious revivals that burned across the southern frontier beginning in the 1790s. Itinerant preachers, or circuit riders, held camp meetings that tapped into deep emotional wells of spirituality. Baptist and Methodist clergy drew free and enslaved blacks as well as white frontier families to their gatherings. They encouraged physical displays of spiritual rebirth, from trembling and quaking to calling out and dancing, offering release from the oppressive burdens of daily life for poor whites and blacks alike.

Evangelical religion, combined with revolutionary ideals promoted in the United States and Haiti, proved a potent mix, and planters rarely lost sight of the potential dangers this posed to the system of bondage. Outright rebellions occurred only rarely, yet the successful revolt of blacks in Haiti reminded slaves and owners alike that uprisings were possible. In 1800 Gabriel, an enslaved blacksmith in Richmond, Virginia, plotted such a rebellion. His supporters rallied around the demand for "Death or Liberty." Gabriel's plan to kill all whites except those who opposed slavery failed when informants betrayed him to local authorities. Nonetheless, news of the plot traveled across the South and terrified white residents, reminding them that the promise of new frontiers could not be separated from the dangers embedded in the nation's oppressive racial history.

REVIEW & RELATE

| How did new inventions and infrastructure improvements contribute to the development of the American economy? | Why did slavery expand rapidly and become more deeply entrenched in southern society in the early nineteenth century? |

 LEARNINGCurve bedfordstmartins.com/hewittlawson/LC

Conclusion: New Frontiers and New Challenges

The geographical and economic expansion that marked the period from 1790 to 1820 inspired scientific and technological advances as well as literary and artistic paeans to a distinctly American identity. For young, ambitious men like Parker Cleaveland, Eli Whitney, Washington Irving, and Meriwether Lewis, the frontiers that opened in education, science, literature, and exploration offered opportunities for fame and financial success. Though his name is unfamiliar today, Cleaveland was offered prestigious professorships as well as the presidency of Bowdoin College during the early decades of the nineteenth century. He chose, however, to live out his life as a professor of mathematics, chemistry, and mineralogy in Brunswick, Maine, where he died in 1858.

Of course, not all white men had the luxury of a college education or the resources to invest in commercial enterprises or technological improvements. Many sought opportunities on the frontier, hoping to find fertile land, abundant wildlife, or opportunities for trade. In some cases, they and their families faced Indians angered by the constant encroachment of white Americans on their lands. In other cases, land speculators and planters bought up western lands, raising prices and pushing the frontier farther west.

The same developments that provided opportunities for enterprising white men also transformed the lives of white women. Those of elite or middling status benefited from improved educational opportunities and new ideals that highlighted mothers' role in raising children and

marriage based on companionship and mutual responsibilities. Yet these changes occurred gradually and unevenly, and many men expected their wives to fulfill all their traditional household obligations while also providing their husband with greater affection and attention. At the same time, domesticity itself changed as the market economy allowed some women to purchase goods they had once produced at home. Such changes increased expectations regarding the quality of domestic life, even though many women still had to supply most of their needs through intensive household labor.

Transformations in white society introduced even more difficult challenges for African Americans. While blacks in the North had greater hopes of gaining their freedom, most remained enslaved until the 1820s or later. Southern slaves faced far worse prospects. As cotton cultivation expanded into new territories, many slaves were forced to move west and to labor on bigger farms and plantations. There they honed means of survival and resistance that became even more crucial in the decades ahead.

At the same time, all along the expanding U.S. frontier, American Indians faced continued pressure to embrace white culture, leave their lands, or both. In 1810 Sacagawea, Charbonneau, and their son Baptiste apparently traveled to St. Louis at the invitation of William Clark, who offered to pay for Baptiste's education. The next spring, Charbonneau and his wife returned to their village, leaving Baptiste in Clark's care. It is not clear whether Sacagawea ever saw her son again, but William Clark penned the phrase "Se car ja we au Dead" on the cover of his cash book for 1825–1828, suggesting that she died during those years. By then, the Shoshone and Hidatsa nations where she was raised had begun to face the onslaught of white settlement. They, along with Indians living in older areas like Georgia, the Carolinas, and Tennessee, resisted the claims of the United States on their ancestral lands and struggled to control the embattled frontier.

Thus even as the young nation conquered new frontiers in education, technology, and the arts, it was forced to defend itself against attacks both internal and external. In the 1810s and 1820s, new conflicts erupted over slavery and against Indians. But the United States also faced its first major economic crisis, while Great Britain and France challenged American sovereignty. New frontiers created new opportunities but also intensified older challenges and conflicts.

LEARNING*Curve*
Check what you know.
bedfordstmartins.com/hewittlawson/LC

Chapter Review

Online Study Guide ▶ bedfordstmartins.com/hewittlawson

KEY TERMS

American Colonization Society (ACS) (p. 233)
Haitian Revolution (p. 236)
Louisiana Territory (p. 236)
Corps of Discovery (p. 237)
Judiciary Act of 1801 (p. 239)
Marbury v. Madison (p. 239)
McCulloch v. Maryland (p. 239)
Embargo Act (p. 239)
National Road (p. 242)
multiplier effect (p. 242)
cotton gin (p. 243)
American system of manufacturing (p. 244)

REVIEW & RELATE

1. How did developments in education, literature, and the arts contribute to the emergence of a distinctly American identity?

2. What place did blacks and American Indians inhabit in the predominant white view of American society and culture?

3. How did Jefferson and the Democratic-Republicans contribute to the expansion of the role of the federal government in American life?

4. How did the conflict between France and Great Britain in the late eighteenth and early nineteenth centuries lead to domestic problems in the United States?

5. How did new inventions and infrastructure improvements contribute to the development of the American economy?

6. Why did slavery expand rapidly and become more deeply entrenched in southern society in the early nineteenth century?

TIMELINE OF EVENTS

1789	Massachusetts institutes free public elementary education for all children
1790	Spinning mill designed and built by Samuel Slater opens
1790–1820	Cotton production in the South increases from 3,000 to 330,000 bales annually
	U.S. slave population more than doubles from 700,000 to 1.5 million
1791–1803	Free and enslaved blacks revolt against French rule in Saint Domingue
1792–1809	New capital of Washington City constructed
1793	Eli Whitney invents cotton gin
1801	Federalists pass new Judiciary Act
	Jefferson sends U.S. force to challenge Barbary pirates
1803	United States purchases Louisiana Territory from France
	Haiti established as the first independent black-led nation in the Americas
	Marbury v. Madison
1804–1806	Corps of Discovery explores Louisiana Territory
April 1805	Sacagawea joins Corps of Discovery
1807	Robert Fulton launches first successful steamboat
	Embargo Act passed
1810	Population of both New York and Philadelphia exceeds 100,000
1816	Parker Cleaveland publishes *Elementary Treatise on Mineralogy and Geology*
1817	American Colonization Society founded
1819	*McCulloch v. Maryland*
1820	One-quarter of non-Indian Americans live west of the Appalachian Mountains
	Washington Irving publishes *Sketchbook*
1828	Noah Webster publishes *American Dictionary of the English Language*

249

Race Relations in the Early Republic

In the late eighteenth century, the United States was far from extending the promises of equality and democracy championed in the Revolutionary War to all Americans. African Americans and Indians in particular were denied most civil and political rights. Indeed, Thomas Jefferson (Document 8.5) and many others were uncertain about whether the two groups could be fully incorporated into white society. When Jefferson bought the Louisiana Territory in 1803, he acquired lands inhabited by numerous Indian communities. In Document 8.6, Meriwether Lewis describes his encounter with Indians in the region. Despite promises of aid, Indian nations in the West fared no better than those in the eastern United States as white settlers, backed by government force, gradually took over Indian lands.

The majority of African Americans in the early Republic era were enslaved, and eight of the first ten presidents were slaveholders. As cotton production expanded in the South, slavery did as well, and the slave population increased dramatically after 1790. With the end of the international slave trade in 1808, owners grew even more reluctant to free their slaves. As Andrew Jackson's 1804 ad for a runaway slave demonstrates (Document 8.8), slavery was a brutal system. The English Quaker Robert Sutcliff noted this physical brutality in his travels to Virginia and Pennsylvania (Document 8.9). While slave revolts were rare, those that occurred involved extensive planning, as suggested by the confession of a slave involved in one plot (Document 8.7).

Even free blacks lacked political and civil rights and suffered severe discrimination. However, some free blacks managed to create vibrant communities, as in Philadelphia. There African Americans agitated publicly against racism despite being denied the formal rights of citizenship (Document 8.10). The following documents reveal popular white perceptions of African Americans and Indians. They also suggest how blacks and Indians sought to carve out a place for themselves in the early Republic.

DOCUMENT 8.5

Thomas Jefferson | Letter to the Marquis de Chastellux, 1785

Thomas Jefferson sent copies of the first edition of his *Notes on the State of Virginia* to several friends in Europe, including the Marquis de Chastellux. In this book, he defended America against the claims of those who thought that human beings, plants, and animals degenerated in the New World. In a letter to the marquis, which is excerpted here, Jefferson repeats some of his arguments in the book, including his opinions about American Indians in relation to whites. He also hazards a tentative view about African Americans in relation to Indians.

AND I AM SAFE in affirming, that the proofs of genius given by the Indians of North America place them on a level with whites in the same uncultivated state. The North of Europe furnishes subjects enough for comparison with them, and for a proof of their equality. I have seen some thousands myself, and conversed much with them, and have found in them a masculine, sound understanding. I have had much information from men who had lived among them, and whose veracity and good sense were so far known to me, as to establish a reliance on their information. They have all agreed in bearing witness in favor of the genius of this people. As to their bodily strength, their manners rendering it disgraceful to labor, those muscles employed in labor will be weaker with them, than with the European laborer; but those which are exerted in the chase, and those faculties which are employed in the tracing an enemy or a wild beast, in contriving ambuscades [ambushes] for him, and in carrying them through their execution, are much stronger than with us, because they are more exercised. I believe the Indian, then, to be, in body and mind, equal to the white man. I have supposed the black man, in his present state, might not be so; but it would be hazardous to affirm, that, equally cultivated for a few generations, he would not become so.

Source: Willson Whitman, ed., *Jefferson's Letters* (Eau Claire, WI: Hale, 1900), 23.

DOCUMENT 8.6

Meriwether Lewis | Journal Entry, 1805

Throughout the Lewis and Clark expedition, both men kept journals and extensive notes on the plants, animals, terrain, and people they encountered. The following journal entry, in which Meriwether Lewis describes his encounter with Sacagawea's tribe, the Shoshone, was written fifteen months into the journey in what is today Idaho.

I can discover that these people are by no means friendly to the Spaniards. Their complaint is, that the Spaniards will not let them have fire arms and amunition, that they put them off by telling them that if they suffer them to have guns they will kill each other, thus leaving them defenceless and an easy prey to their bloodthirsty neighbours to the East of them, who being in possession of fire arms hunt them up and murder them without rispect to sex or age and plunder them of their horses on all occasions. They told me that to avoid their enemies who were eternally harrassing them that they were obliged to remain in the interior of these mountains at least two thirds of the year where the[y] suffered as we then saw great heardships for the want of food sometimes living for weeks without meat and only a little fish roots and berries. But this added Câmeahwait [a Shoshone leader], with his ferce eyes and lank jaws grown meager for the want of food, would not be the case if we had guns, we could then live in the country of buffaloe and eat as our enimies do and not be compelled to hide ourselves in these mountains and live on roots and berries as the bear do. We do not fear our enimies when placed on an equal footing with them. I told them that the Minnetares Mandans & Recares [other native tribes] of the Missouri had promised us to desist from making war on them & that we would indevour to find the means of making the Minnetares of fort d Prarie or as they call them Pahkees desist from waging war against them also. That after our finally returning to our homes towards the rising sun whitemen would come to them with an abundance of guns and every other article necessary to their defence and comfort, and that they would be enabled to supply themselves with these articles on reasonable terms in exchange for the skins of the beaver Otter and Ermin [long-tailed weasel] so abundant in their country. They expressed great pleasure at this information and said they had been long anxious to see the whitemen that traded guns; and that we might rest assured of their friendship and that they would do whatever we wished them.

Source: Reuben Gold Thwaites, ed., *Original Journals of the Lewis and Clark Expedition, 1804–1808* (New York: Dodd, Mead, 1904), 383–84.

DOCUMENT 8.7

Confession of Solomon, September 1800

Gabriel's Conspiracy was a plan for a massive slave rebellion in Virginia during the summer of 1800. The revolt's leader, Gabriel, was a slave and blacksmith on a tobacco plantation near Richmond who was often hired out to businesses in Richmond, where he recruited others to his plan. Gabriel was strongly influenced by the ideals of liberty advocated by participants in the American and Haitian revolutions. When some of the slaves involved confessed the plan to their masters before the revolt began, Governor James Monroe ordered the state militia to round up the leaders of the conspiracy. Gabriel's brother Solomon was caught in the initial patrols and gave his confession, excerpted here, while several leaders were still at large. Gabriel was caught several weeks later, and Gabriel, Solomon, and twenty-five other slaves were executed for the conspiracy.

My brother Gabriel was the person who influenced me to join him and others in order that (as he said) we might conquer the white people and possess ourselves of their property. I enquired how we were to effect it. He said by falling upon them (the whites) in the dead of night, at which time they would be unguarded and unsuspicious. I then enquired who was at the head of the plan. He said Jack, alias Jack Bowler. I asked him if Jack Bowler knew anything about carrying on war. He replied he did not. I then enquired who he was going to employ. He said a man from Caroline who was at the siege of Yorktown, and who was to meet him (Gabriel) at the Brook and proceed on to Richmond, take, and then fortify it. This man from Caroline was to be commander and manager the first day, and then, after exercising the soldiers, the command was to be resigned to Gabriel. If Richmond was taken without the loss of many men they were to continue there some time, but if they sustained any considerable loss they were to bend their course for Hanover Town or York, they were not decided to which, and continue at that place as long as they found they were able to defend it, but in the event of a defeat or loss at those places they were to endeavor to form a junction with some negroes which, they had understood from Mr. Gregory's overseer, were in rebellion in some quarter of the country. This information which they had gotten from the overseer, made Gabriel anxious, upon which he applied to me to make scythe-swords, which I did to the number of twelve. Every Sunday he came to Richmond to provide ammunition and to find where the military stores were deposited. Gabriel informed me, in case of success, that they intended to subdue the whole of the country where slavery was permitted, but no further.

The first places Gabriel intended to attack in Richmond were, the Capitol, the Magazine, the Penitentiary, the Governor's house and his person. The inhabitants were to be massacred, save those who begged for quarter and agreed to serve as soldiers with them. The reason why the insurrection was to be made at this particular time was, the discharge of the number of soldiers, one or two months ago, which induced Gabriel to believe the plan would be more easily executed.

Source: H. W. Flournoy, ed., *Calendar of Virginia State Papers and Other Manuscripts from January 1, 1799, to December 31, 1807* (Richmond, 1890), 9:147.

DOCUMENT 8.8

Andrew Jackson | Runaway Slave Advertisement, 1804

STOP THE RUNAWAY.
FIFTY DOLLARS REWARD.

Eloped from the subscriber, living near Nashville, on the 25th of June last, a Mulatto Man Slave, about thirty years old, six feet and an inch high, stout made and active, talks sensible, stoops in his walk, and has a remarkably large foot, broad across the root of the toes—will pass for a free man, as I am informed he has obtained by some means, certificates as such—took with him a drab great-coat, dark mixed body coat, a ruffled shirt, cotton home spun shirts, and overalls. He will make for Detroit, through the states of Kentucky and Ohio, or the upper part of Louisiana. The above reward will be given any person that will take him and deliver him to me or secure him in jail so that I can get him. If taken out of the state, the above reward, and all reasonable expenses paid— and ten dollars extra for every hundred lashes any person will give him to the amount of three hundred.

Andrew Jackson, near Nashville, State of Tennessee

Source: *Tennessee Gazette*, November 7, 1804.

Future president Andrew Jackson bought his first slaves in 1794 and by 1804 owned 9 slave men and women. In that same year, he bought the Hermitage, a Tennessee cotton plantation, and slowly increased the size of his property and its slave population. By the time he was president, he owned 100 slaves and would own more than 160 before his death in 1845. Although Jackson was known to provide adequate food and housing for his slaves, he was not above employing corporal punishment, as is evidenced by the following advertisement he placed for a runaway slave in 1804.

DOCUMENT 8.9

Robert Sutcliff, *Travels in Some Parts of North America*, 1812

Robert Sutcliff, an English Quaker, arrived in the United States on a business trip in 1804. Over the next three years, he recorded his travels in the country and published his experiences as a book in 1812. In the following excerpts, Sutcliff describes his encounters with the institution of slavery in the area around Richmond, Virginia, which include a reference to Gabriel's Conspiracy, and then in the last segment, near Philadelphia, Pennsylvania.

9th Month, 25th [1804].

I pursued my way to Richmond in the mail stage, through a beautiful country, but clouded and debased by Negro slavery. At the house where I breakfasted, which is called the Bowling-green, I was told that the owner had in his possession 200 slaves. In one field near the house, planted with tobacco, I counted nearly 20 women and children, employed in picking grubs from the plant. In the afternoon I passed by a field in which several poor slaves had lately been executed, on the charge of having an intention to rise against their masters. A lawyer who was present at their trials at Richmond, informed me that on one of them being asked what he had to say to the court on his defence, he replied in a manly tone of voice: "I have nothing more to offer than what General Washington would have had to offer, had he been taken by the British and put to trial by them. I have adventured my life in endeavouring to obtain the liberty of my countrymen, and am a willing sacrifice in their cause: and I beg, as a favour, that I may be immediately led to execution. I know that you have pre-determined to shed my blood, why then all this mockery of a trial?" . . .

8th Month, 15th [1805].

I spent this day at Richmond. In the evening I walked to Manchester, over the bridge at James's River, which at this place is nearly half a mile wide. From my own observations, and the information I received from an inhabitant, Richmond appears to be a place of great dissipation; chiefly arising from the loose and debauched conduct of the white people with their black female slaves. It sometimes happens here, as in other places, that the white inhabitants, in selling the offspring of these poor debased females, sell their own sons and daughters with as much indifference as they would sell their cattle. By such means, every tender sentiment of the human breast is laid waste, and men become so degraded that their feelings rank but little above those of the beasts in the field. In their treatment of their offspring, how far do some of the brute creation surpass them! . . .

1st Month, 25th [1806].

In crossing the Schuylkill [River, at Philadelphia] on the floating bridge at the upper ferry, I passed a Negro boy apparently about 12 years of age. Round his neck an iron collar was locked, and from each side of it an iron bow passed over his head. His dress was a light linsey jacket and trowsers, without hat, shoes, or stockings. Soon after passing the boy, whom I supposed to be a runaway slave, I met a person of whom I inquired the reason of the boy's having so much iron about him. The man replied that the boy was his, and was so often running away that he had used that method to prevent him.

Source: Robert Sutcliff, *Travels in Some Parts of North America, in the Years 1804, 1805, and 1806* (Philadelphia: B&T Kite, 1812), 50, 94, 181.

Resolved unanimously, That the following address, signed on behalf of the meeting by the Chairman and Secretary, be published and circulated.

To the humane and benevolent Inhabitants of the city and county of Philadelphia.

The free people of color, assembled together, under circumstances of deep interest to their happiness and welfare, humbly and respectfully lay before you this expression of their feelings and apprehensions.

Relieved from the miseries of slavery, many of us by your aid, possessing the benefits which industry and integrity in this prosperous country assure to all its inhabitants, enjoying the rich blessings of religion, by opportunities of worshipping the only true God, under the light of Christianity, each of us according to his understanding; and having afforded to us and to our children the means of education and improvement; we have no wish to separate from our present homes for any purpose whatever. Contented with our present situation and condition, we are not desirous of increasing their prosperity but by honest efforts, and by the use of those opportunities for their improvement, which the constitution and laws allow to all. It is therefore with painful solicitude and sorrowing regret we have seen a plan for colonizing the free people of color of the United States on the coast of Africa brought forward under the auspices and sanction of gentlemen whose names give value to all they recommend, and who certainly are among the wisest, the best, and the most benevolent of men in this great nation.

If the plan of colonizing is intended for our benefit and those who now promote it will never seek our injury; we humbly and respectfully urge that it is not asked for by us nor will it be required by any circumstances, in our present or future condition; as long as we shall be permitted to share the protection of the excellent laws and just government which we now enjoy, in common with every individual of the community.

DOCUMENT 8.10

Free Blacks in Philadelphia Oppose Colonization, 1817

Many African Americans fiercely resisted the idea of colonization—that free blacks and slaves should be returned to their ancestral homeland of Africa. The following document lists the resolutions of a group of prominent free blacks who met in Philadelphia in 1817 to express opposition to the American Colonization Society. The chair of the committee, sailmaker James Forten, was one of the wealthiest African Americans in the country.

We, therefore, a portion of those who are the objects of this plan, and among those whose happiness, with that of others of our color, it is intended to promote; with humble and grateful acknowledgements to those who have devised it, renounce and disclaim every connexion with it; and respectfully but firmly declare our determination not to participate in any part of it.

If this plan of colonization now proposed, is intended to provide a refuge and a dwelling for a portion of our brethren, who are now held in slavery in the south, we have other and stronger objections to it, and we entreat your consideration of them.

The ultimate and final abolition of slavery in the United States, by the operation of various causes, is, under the guidance and protection of a just God, progressing. Every year witnesses the release of numbers of the victims of oppression, and affords new and safe assurances that the freedom of all will be in the end accomplished. As they are thus by degrees relieved from bondage, our brothers have opportunities for instruction and improvement; and thus they become in some measure fitted for their liberty. Every year, many of us have restored to us by the gradual, but certain march of the cause of abolition—parents, from whom we have long been separated—wives and children whom we had left in servitude—and brothers, in blood as well as in early sufferings, from whom we had been long parted.

But if the emancipation of our kindred shall, when the plan of colonization shall go into effect, be attended with transportation to a distant land, and shall be granted on no other condition; the consolation for our past sufferings and of those of our color who are in slavery, which have hitherto been, and under the present situation of things would continue to be, afforded to us and to them, will cease for ever. The cords, which now connect them with us, will be stretched by the distance to which their ends will be carried, until they break; and all the sources of happiness, which affection and connexion and blood bestow, will be ours and theirs no more.

Source: William Lloyd Garrison, *Thoughts on African Colonization; or, An Impartial Exhibition of the Doctrines, Principles, and Purposes of the American Colonization Society, together with the Resolutions, Addresses, and Remonstrances of the Free People of Color* (Boston: Garrison and Knapp, 1832), part 2, 10–11.

Interpret the Evidence

1. What do Thomas Jefferson's letter (Document 8.5) and Meriwether Lewis's journal entry (Document 8.6) tell us about how American Indians were perceived in the early Republic? How would you compare their opinions of Indians?

2. What encouraged slaves to revolt (Documents 8.7 and 8.9)? What do these documents reveal about slavery in Richmond and in Virginia more generally?

3. What does the runaway slave advertisement in Document 8.8 tell us about Andrew Jackson as a slave owner? Does the fact that it was written by a future president shape how you view it? Why or why not?

4. What does Robert Sutcliff's report (Document 8.9) reveal about the treatment that slaves in the North and in the South endured? Judging from his writing, how does Sutcliff's English and Quaker background affect his views of slavery?

5. Given the horrors of slavery in the North and the South and the near impossibility of overthrowing the institution, why did free blacks in Philadelphia oppose colonization (Document 8.10)? What language did they use to address their audience?

Put It in Context

- According to these documents, how did race relations in the United States change between 1785 and 1817 as slavery expanded along with white Americans' movement into new western territories?

LEARNING*Curve*
Check what you know.
bedfordstmartins.com/hewittlawson/LC

The Granger Collection, New York

The Granger Collection, New York

● View of Broadway in New York City, c. 1830s.

● Portrait presumed to be Tecumseh by an unknown artist.

9

Defending and Redefining the Nation

1809–1832

© Collection of the New-York Historical Society, USA/The Bridgeman Art Library

Junction of Erie and Northern Canals, c. 1830–1832.

AMERICAN HISTORIES

Dolley Payne, a future First Lady, was raised on a Virginia plantation. But her Quaker parents, moved by the Society of Friends' growing antislavery sentiment, decided to free their slaves. In 1783, when Dolley was fifteen, the Paynes moved to Philadelphia. There, Dolley's father suffered heavy economic losses, and Dolley lost her first husband and her younger son to yellow fever. In 1794 the young widow met and married Virginia congressman James Madison. The two made a perfect political couple. James was brilliant but reserved, while Dolley, witty and charming, loved entertaining. When the newly elected president Thomas Jefferson appointed James secretary of state in 1801, the couple moved to Washington.

Since Jefferson and his vice president, Aaron Burr, were widowers, Dolley Madison served as hostess for White House affairs. When James Madison succeeded Jefferson as president in 1809, he, too, depended on his wife's social skills and networks. Dolley held lively informal receptions to which she invited Federalists, Democratic-Republicans, diplomats, cabinet officers, and their wives. These social events helped bridge the ideological differences that continued to divide Congress and proved crucial in creating a unified front when Congress declared war on Great Britain in 1812.

During the War of 1812, British forces attacked Washington City and burned the Executive Mansion. With the president away, his wife was left to secure important state papers, emerging as a symbol of national courage at a critical moment in the war. When peace came the following year, Dolley Madison quickly reestablished a busy social calendar to help mend conflicts that had erupted during the war.

In 1817, at the end of the president's second term, the Madisons left Washington for Virginia just as a young Scots-Cherokee trader named John Ross entered the political arena. Born in 1790 in the Cherokee nation, John (also known as Guwisguwi) was the son of a Scottish trader and his wife, who was both Cherokee and Scottish. John Ross was raised in an Anglo-Indian world in eastern Tennessee where he played with Cherokee children and attended tribal ceremonies and festivals but was educated by private tutors and in Protestant missionary schools. At age twenty, Ross was appointed as a U.S. Indian agent among the Cherokees and during the War of 1812 served as an adjutant (or administrative assistant) in a Cherokee regiment.

After the war, Ross focused on business ventures in Tennessee, including the establishment of a plantation. He also became increasingly involved in Cherokee political affairs, using his bilingual skills and Protestant training to represent Indian interests to government officials. In 1819 Ross was elected president of the Cherokee legislature. In the 1820s, he moved to Georgia, near the Cherokee capital of New Echota, where he served as president of the Cherokee constitutional convention in 1827. Having overseen the first written constitution produced by an Indian nation, Ross was then elected principal chief in 1828. Over the next decade, he battled to retain the Cherokee homeland in Georgia, North Carolina, and Tennessee against the pressures of white planters and politicians. ●

AMERICAN POLITICS IN the early nineteenth century was a white man's world, but, as the American histories of Dolley Madison and John Ross demonstrate, it was possible for some of those on the political margins to influence national developments. Both Madison and Ross sought to defend and expand the democratic ideals that defined the young nation. The First Lady helped forge social networks and nurture a nascent political culture in Washington that included women as well as men. At the same time, she struggled with the issue of slavery on her husband's Montpelier plantation. Ross encouraged the Cherokee people to embrace Anglo-American religion, language, and political ideals in the hopes of providing them with a path to inclusion in the United States. Yet ultimately, given the nation's economic growth, he could not overcome the power of white planters and politicians to wrest territory from even the most Americanized Indians. Although Ross most directly confronted the limits of American democracy, Dolley Madison also grappled with the dilemmas posed to the nation's democratic ideals by the expansion of slavery and the limits of citizenship.

Conflicts at Home and Abroad

When Thomas Jefferson completed his second term as president in March 1809, he was succeeded by his friend and ally James Madison. Madison was the principal author of the Constitution; coauthor of *The Federalist Papers*, which ensured its ratification; and secretary of state in Jefferson's administration. Like Jefferson, he sought to end foreign interference in American affairs and to resolve conflicts between Indians and white residents on the nation's frontier. Congress itself was divided over how best to address these problems. By 1815 the United States had weathered a series of domestic and foreign crises, including another war with Britain, but American sovereignty remained fragile. At the same time, even though Madison (like Jefferson) believed in a national government with limited powers, he found himself expanding federal authority.

Tensions at Sea and on the Frontier

When President Madison took office, Great Britain and France remained embroiled in the Napoleonic Wars in Europe and refused to modify their policies toward American shipping or to recognize U.S. neutrality. American ships were subject to seizure by both nations, and British authorities continued to impress "deserters" into the Royal Navy. In response, the new president convinced Congress to pass the **Non-Intercourse Act** in 1809, which allowed Americans to trade with every nation except France and Britain. When that act failed to satisfy the warring nations or improve the economy, Congress approved a bill that opened trade with both Great Britain and France but allowed the president to reimpose an embargo on one nation if the other lifted its restrictions. When Napoleon promised to lift all restrictions on U.S. shipping, Madison stalled, giving British officials time to match France's policy. Britain refused.

In the midst of these crises, Madison also faced difficulties in the Northwest Territory. In 1794 General "Mad Anthony" Wayne had won a decisive victory against a multitribe coalition led by the Shawnees at the Battle of Fallen Timbers. But this victory inspired two forceful native leaders to create a pan-Indian alliance in the Ohio River valley. The Shawnee prophet Tenskwatawa and his half-brother Tecumseh, a warrior, encouraged native peoples to resist white encroachments on their territory and to give up all aspects of white society and culture, including clothing, liquor, and other popular trade goods. They imagined an Indian nation that stretched from the Canadian border to the Gulf of Mexico.

Although powerful Creek and Choctaw nations in the lower Mississippi valley refused to join the alliance, bands of Indians in the upper Midwest, frustrated with continuing white encroachments, rallied around the brothers. In 1808 Tenskwatawa and Tecumseh established Prophet Town along the Tippecanoe River in Indiana Territory. The next year, William Henry Harrison, the territorial governor, plied several Indian leaders with liquor and persuaded them to sign a treaty selling three million acres of land to the United States for only $7,600. Tecumseh was enraged by Harrison's methods and dismissed the treaty, claiming the land belonged to all the Indians together.

Explore

Read part of Tecumseh's response to Harrison in Document 9.1.

In November 1811, fearing the growing power of the Shawnee leaders, President Madison ordered Harrison to attack Prophet Town. With more troops and superior weapons, the U.S. army defeated the Shawnees, and soldiers then burned Prophet Town to the ground. The rout damaged Tenskwatawa's stature as a prophet, and he and his supporters fled to Canada. Skirmishes continued between Indians and U.S. troops along the Canadian border, but federal officials now returned their attention to conflicts with Great Britain.

War Erupts with Britain

Convinced that British officials in Canada fueled Indian resistance, supporters of war with Great Britain demanded an end to British intervention on the western frontier. They were even more concerned about British interference with transatlantic trade. Yet merchants in the Northeast, who depended on trade with Great Britain and the British West Indies, feared the commercial disruptions that war entailed. Once staunch supporters of expanding the power of the national government, New England Federalists now adamantly opposed a declaration of war.

For months, Madison avoided taking a clear stand for or against war. On June 1, 1812, however, having exhausted diplomatic efforts and seeing no end to these conflicts as long as the Napoleonic Wars raged across Europe, Madison sent a secret message to Congress outlining American grievances against Great Britain. Within weeks, Congress declared war by a sharply divided vote of 79 to 49 in the House of Representatives and 19 to 13 in the Senate.

Supporters claimed that a victory over Great Britain would end threats to U.S. sovereignty and raise Americans' stature in Europe, but the nation was ill prepared to launch a major offensive against such an imposing foe. Cuts in federal spending and falling tax revenues over the previous decade had diminished military resources. Democratic-Republicans had also failed to renew the charter of the Bank of the United States when it expired in 1811, so the nation lacked a vital source of credit. Nonetheless, many in Congress believed that Britain would be too distracted and overcommitted by the ongoing conflict with France to attack North America.

Meanwhile U.S. commanders devised plans to attack Canada. The most enthusiastic advocates of war imagined that the United States could defeat Britain and gain control of all of North America. Initially, however, the U.S. army and navy proved no match for Great Britain and its Indian allies. Tecumseh, who was appointed a brigadier general in the British army, helped capture Detroit. Joint British and Indian forces also launched successful attacks on Fort Dearborn, Fort Mackinac, and other points along the U.S.-Canadian border.

Even as U.S. forces faced defeat after defeat in the summer and fall of 1812, American voters reelected James

DOCUMENT 9.1

Tecumseh | Speech to William Henry Harrison, 1810

In 1809 William Henry Harrison, governor of the Indiana Territory, negotiated a treaty with a coalition of native peoples to cede three million acres to the United States. Unhappy with this treaty, two Shawnee brothers, Tecumseh and Tenskwatawa, united with other Indian nations to resist American settlement of the region. In August 1810, Tecumseh confronted Harrison and delivered a speech, excerpted here, urging him to return the land. Harrison refused, and in the fall of 1811 U.S. troops attacked and defeated the Shawnees at Prophet Town.

Explore

Brother. Since the peace was made you have kill'd some of the Shawanese, Winebagoes, Delawares, and Miamies and you have taken our lands from us, and I do not see how we can remain at peace with you if you continue to do so. You have given goods to the Kickapoos for the sale of their lands . . . which has been the cause of many deaths among them. You have promised us assistance but I do not see that you have given us any.

You try to force the red people to do some injury. It is you that is pushing them on to do mischief. You endeavor to make distinctions, you wish to prevent the Indians to do as we wish them: to unite and let them consider their land as the common property of the whole.

You take tribes aside and advise them not to come into this measure [coalition] and untill our design is accomplished we do not wish to accept of your invitation to go and visit the President.

The reason I tell you this is you want by your distinctions of Indian tribes in allotting to each a particular track of land to make them to war with each other. You never see an Indian come and endeavour to make the white people do so. You are continually driving the red people when at last you will drive them into the great Lake where they can't eather stand or work.

Source: Logan Esarey, ed., *Messages and Letters of William Henry Harrison* (Indianapolis: Indiana Historical Commission, 1922), 1:465.

Interpret the Evidence

- How does Tecumseh's view of Indian land differ from that negotiated in the treaty?
- What blame does he place on other Indians? Why does Tecumseh consider white Americans untrustworthy?

Put It in Context

What does this document reveal about the relationship between American Indians and the U.S. government by the 1810s?

Madison as president. His narrow victory demonstrated the geographical divisions caused by the war. Madison won most of the western and southern states, where the war was most popular, and was defeated in New England and New York, where Federalist opponents held sway.

After a year of fighting, U.S. forces—with the aid of crucial naval victories on the Great Lakes—finally drove the British back into Canada (Map 9.1). Tecumseh was killed in Canada at the Battle of the Thames, and U.S. forces burned York (present-day Toronto). Yet just as U.S. prospects in the war improved, New England Federalists demanded retreat. In the fall of 1813, state legislatures in New England

withdrew their support for any invasions of "foreign British soil," and Federalists in Congress sought to block appropriations for the war and challenge the deployment of local militia units into the U.S. army.

New England Federalists did not have sufficient power to change national policy, but they called a meeting at Hartford, Connecticut, in 1814 to consider their options. Some participants at the **Hartford Convention** called for New England's secession from the United States. Most, however, supported amendments to the U.S. Constitution that would limit presidents to a single term and ensure that presidents were elected from diverse states (so that Virginia planters could not dominate the executive branch). Other amendments would limit embargoes to sixty days and require a two-thirds majority in Congress to declare war, prohibit trade, or admit new states.

The ideas debated at Hartford gained increased attention as British forces once again launched attacks into the United States and British warships blockaded U.S. ports. In August 1814, the British sailed up the Chesapeake. As American troops retreated, Dolley Madison and a family slave, Peter Jennings, gathered up government papers and valuable belongings before fleeing the city. The redcoats then burned and sacked Washington City. The invasion of the U.S. capital was humiliating, but American troops quickly rallied to defeat the British in Maryland and expel them from Washington and New York.

Meanwhile news arrived from the South that in March 1814 militiamen from Tennessee led by Andrew Jackson had defeated a force of Creek Indians, important allies of the British. Cherokee warriors (and adjutant John Ross), longtime foes of the Creeks, joined the fight as well. At the Battle of Horseshoe Bend, in present-day Alabama, the combined U.S.-Cherokee forces slaughtered some eight hundred Creek warriors. Jackson then demanded punitive terms, and in the resulting treaty the Creek nation lost two-thirds of its tribal domain.

Despite sporadic U.S. victories, America was no closer to winning the war. In June 1814, the British finally defeated Napoleon, ending the war in Europe. And in December of that year, the British fleet landed thousands of seasoned troops at New Orleans, threatening U.S. control of that crucial port city. But exhausted from twenty years of European warfare, the British were losing steam as well. As a result, representatives of the two countries met in Ghent, Belgium, to negotiate a peace settlement. On Christmas Eve 1814, the Treaty of Ghent was signed, returning to each nation the lands it controlled before the war.

Although the war had officially ended, it took time for the news to reach the United States. In January 1815, American troops under General Andrew Jackson attacked and routed the British army at New Orleans. The victory

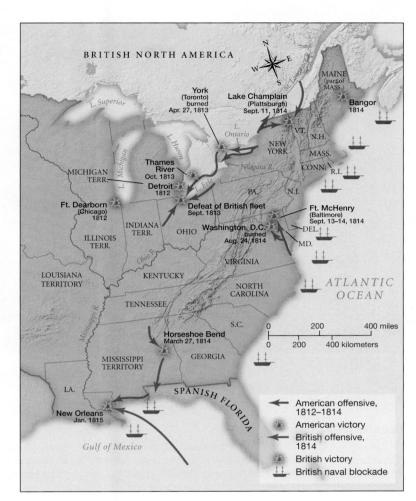

MAP 9.1   The War of 1812

Most conflicts in this war occurred in the Great Lakes region or around Washington, D.C. Yet two of the most significant victories were achieved by General Andrew Jackson in the South. At Horseshoe Bend, his troops defeated Creek allies of the British, and at New Orleans they beat British forces two weeks after a peace agreement was signed in Europe.

cheered Americans, who did not know that peace had already been achieved, and Jackson became a national hero.

Although the War of 1812 achieved no official territorial gains, Jackson's late victory in the Battle of New Orleans made it appear that American forces had vanquished Great Britain. The war did represent an important defense of U.S. sovereignty and garnered international prestige for the young nation. In addition, Indians on the western frontier lost a powerful ally when British representatives at Ghent failed to act as advocates for their allies. Thus, in practical terms, the U.S. government gained greater control over vast expanses of land in the Ohio and Mississippi River valleys held by these Indian nations.

Battle of New Orleans

On January 8, 1815, General Andrew Jackson's troops launched grapeshot and canister bombs against British forces in New Orleans in this final battle of the War of 1812. Jackson's troops included Indian allies, backcountry immigrants, and French-speaking black soldiers. This engraving by Francisco Scacki shows the slain British commander, Major General Sir Edward Pakenham, in the center foreground.

The Granger Collection, New York

REVIEW & RELATE

How were conflicts with Indians in the West connected to ongoing tensions between the United States and Great Britain on land and at sea?

What were the long-term consequences of the War of 1812?

✓ *LEARNINGCurve* bedfordstmartins.com/hewittlawson/LC

Expanding the Economy and the Nation

By further expanding federal powers, the War of 1812 reinforced political changes that had been under way for more than a decade. At the Hartford Convention, Federalists who had once advocated broad national powers called for restrictions on federal authority. By contrast, the Democratic-Republicans, who gained support in 1800 by demanding restraints on federal power, now applauded its expansion. Indeed, Democratic-Republicans in Congress sought to use federal authority to settle boundary disputes in the West, make investments in transportation, and reestablish a national bank. Increasingly, many ordinary Americans viewed such federal assistance as critical to the continued development of industry and agriculture.

Governments Fuel Economic Growth

At the nation's founding, Alexander Hamilton led a coalition that advocated the use of federal power to fuel commercial development. Over the following decade, this coalition's efforts to expand federal authority in the interest of commerce and industry inspired opposition within Federalist ranks. In 1800 Thomas Jefferson captured the presidency by advocating a reduction in federal powers and a renewed emphasis on the needs of small farmers and working men. Once in power, however, Jefferson and his Democratic-Republican supporters faced a series of economic and political developments that led many of them to embrace Hamilton's loose interpretation of the U.S. Constitution and support federal efforts to aid economic growth (see chapter 8). In the 1810s, for example, Democratic-Republican representative Henry Clay of Kentucky sketched out a plan called the **American System**, which combined federally funded internal improvements to aid farmers with federal tariffs to protect U.S. manufacturing and a national bank to oversee economic development.

Western expansion helped fuel the demand for federally funded internal improvements. The non-Indian population west of the Appalachian Mountains more than doubled between 1810 and 1820, from 1,080,000 to 2,234,000. The new residents included veterans of the War of 1812, many of whom received 160-acre parcels of land between the Illinois and Mississippi Rivers. They and their families established farms, shops, and communities throughout the territory. Four frontier states were admitted to the Union in just four years: Indiana (1816), Mississippi (1817), Illinois (1818), and Alabama (1819).

Population growth and commercial expansion moved hand in hand. In 1811 the first steamboat traveled down the Mississippi from the Ohio River to New Orleans; over the next decade, steamboat traffic expanded, and freight charges dropped precipitously. This development helped western and southern residents but hurt trade on overland routes between northeastern seaports and the Ohio River valley. The Cumberland Road, a federally funded highway linking Maryland and Ohio, reestablished this connection, and Congress passed bills to fund more ambitious federal transportation projects. But President Madison vetoed much of this legislation, believing that it overstepped even a loose interpretation of the Constitution.

Congress also developed new trade routes by negotiating treaties with Indian nations. For instance, an ancient trail from Missouri to Santa Fe, a town in northern Mexico, cut across territory claimed by the Osage Indians. White traders began using the trail in 1821, and four years later Congress approved a treaty with the Osage nation to guarantee right of way for U.S. merchants. In the following decade, the Santa Fe Trail became a critical route for commerce between the United States and Mexico.

East of the Appalachian Mountains, most internal improvement projects were funded by individual states. The most significant of these was New York's **Erie Canal**, a 363-mile waterway stretching from the Mohawk River to Buffalo that was completed in 1825. Tolls on the Erie Canal quickly repaid the tremendous cost of its construction. Freight charges and shipping times plunged. In 1820 transporting a ton of grain by land from Buffalo to New York City cost $100 and took 20 days; in 1825 shipping a ton of grain by canal between those two cities cost only $9 and took 6 days. And by linking western farmers to the Hudson River, the Erie Canal ensured that New York City became the nation's premier seaport (Map 9.2).

The Erie Canal's success inspired hundreds of similar projects in other states. Canals carried manufactured goods from New England and the Middle Atlantic states to rural households in the Ohio River valley. Western farmers, in turn, shipped hogs, hemp, flour, whiskey, and other farm products back east. Just as important, canals linked smaller cities within Pennsylvania and Ohio, facilitating the rise of commercial and manufacturing centers like Harrisburg, Pittsburgh,

ENTERPISE ON HER FAST TRIP TO LOUISVILLE, 1815.

Steamboat *Enterprise*

In 1814 the steamboat *Enterprise* made its maiden voyage, traveling six hundred miles from Louisville to Pittsburgh. The voyage showed that steamboats could overcome the strong currents of the Ohio River. Later that year, the *Enterprise* departed from Pittsburgh carrying arms to supply General Jackson's troops at New Orleans, proving it could also navigate the waters of the mighty Mississippi River. Beinecke Rare Book and Manuscript Library, Yale University

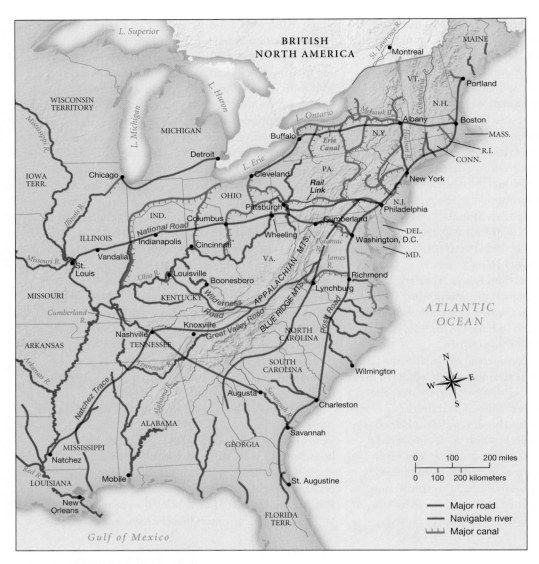

MAP 9.2   Roads and Canals to 1837

During the 1820s and 1830s, state and local governments as well as private companies built roads and canals to foster migration and commercial development. The Erie Canal, completed in 1825, was the most significant of these projects. But many other states, particularly in the Northeast and the old Northwest, sought to duplicate that canal's success over the following decade.

Cincinnati, and Toledo. Canals also allowed vast quantities of coal to be transported out of the Allegheny Mountains, fueling industrial development throughout the Northeast.

Americans Expand the Nation's Borders

In 1816, in the midst of the nation's economic resurgence, James Monroe, a Democratic-Republican from Virginia, won an easy victory in the presidential election over Rufus King, a New York Federalist. Monroe, who had served as secretary of state under Madison, hoped to use improved relations with Great Britain to resolve Indian problems on the frontier. Believing that hostile Indians would "lose their terror" once

the British no longer encouraged them, he sent John Quincy Adams to London to negotiate treaties that limited U.S. and British naval forces on the Great Lakes, set the U.S.-Canadian border at the forty-ninth parallel, and provided for joint British-U.S. occupation of the Oregon Territory. In 1817 and 1818, the Senate approved these treaties, which further limited Indian rights and power in the North.

President Monroe harbored grave concerns about the nation's southern boundary as well. He sought to limit Spain's power in North America and stop Seminole Indians in western Florida and Alabama from claiming lands ceded to the United States by the defeated Creeks. Shifting from diplomacy to military force, in 1817 the president sent

General Andrew Jackson and his Tennessee militia to force the Seminoles back into Florida. Nonetheless, he ordered Jackson to avoid direct conflict with Spanish forces for fear of igniting another war. But in the spring of 1818, having chased the Seminoles deep into Florida, Jackson attacked two Spanish forts, hanged two Seminole chiefs, and executed two British citizens allied with local Indians.

Jackson's attacks spurred outrage among Spanish and British officials and many members of Congress. Indeed, the threat of conflict with Britain, Spain, and hostile Indians prompted President Monroe to establish the nation's first peacetime army in 1818. In the end, however, the British chose to ignore the execution of citizens engaged in "unauthorized" activities, while Spain decided to sell the Florida Territory to the United States rather than fight to retain it. In the Adams-Onís Treaty (1819), negotiated by John Quincy Adams, Spain ceded all its lands east of the Mississippi to the United States along with ancient claims to the Oregon Territory.

Success in acquiring Florida encouraged the administration to look for other opportunities to limit European influence in the Western Hemisphere. By 1822 Argentina, Chile, Peru, Colombia, and Mexico had all overthrown Spanish rule. In March of that year, President Monroe recognized the independence of these southern neighbors, and Congress quickly established diplomatic relations with the new nations. Yet Monroe also secretly attempted to survey Mexican lands in hopes of gaining more territory for the United States. The following year, President Monroe added a codicil to a treaty with Russia that claimed that the Western Hemisphere was part of the U.S. sphere of influence. Although the United States did not have sufficient power to enforce what later became known as the **Monroe Doctrine**, it had quietly declared its intention to challenge Europeans for authority in the Atlantic world.

By the late 1820s, U.S. residents were moving to and trading with newly independent Mexican territories. Southern whites began occupying Mexican lands in east Texas, while midwestern traders traveled the Santa Fe Trail. Meanwhile New England manufacturers and merchants had begun shipping their wares via clipper ships to another Mexican territory, Alta California, whose residents eagerly purchased U.S.-made shoes, cloth, and tools.

Some Americans looked even farther afield. U.S. merchants had begun trading with China in the late eighteenth century, and by the early nineteenth century, ships from eastern ports carried otter pelts and other merchandise across the Pacific, returning with Chinese porcelains and silks. In the 1810s and 1820s, the Alta California and China trades converged, expanding the reach of U.S. merchants and the demand for U.S. manufactured goods. The desire to expand trade also led some Americans to look to the Pacific, especially Hawaii and Samoa, for additional markets and land.

Extended trade routes along with wartime disruptions of European imports fueled the expansion of U.S. manufacturing. By 1813 the area around Providence, Rhode Island, boasted seventy-six spinning mills with more than 51,000 spindles. Two years later, Philadelphia claimed pride of place as the nation's top industrial city, turning out glass, chemicals, metalwork, leather goods, and dozens of other products. Workers in factories, artisans' shops, and homes as well as in prisons and poorhouses contributed to an economic boom that seemed boundless.

Regional Economic Development

Clay's American System was intended to bind the various regions of the United States together. Yet even as roads, rivers, canals, and steamboats helped unify a growing nation, they also reinforced the development of regional economies. Although regional ties remained fluid, between 1815 and 1830 increasingly distinct economies developed that promoted the rise of particular labor systems and political priorities.

In the South, for instance, the defeat of the Creek nation, vast Indian land cessions, and the acquisition of Florida ensured the growth of cotton cultivation, which had been initiated by the invention of the cotton gin (see chapter 8). Although the foreign slave trade had ended in 1808, planters extended slavery into new lands to produce cash crops like cotton, sugar, and rice. They used profits from these goods to buy food from the West and shoes and cloth from the North. Small farmers, too, sought to benefit from rising cotton prices, planting as much of their land in cotton as they could. Because continuous cultivation drained nutrients from the soil, planters and small farmers constantly sought more fertile fields, leading to further pressure on those Indians who still controlled large areas of rich southern soil.

When James and Dolley Madison returned to Montpelier in 1817, they experienced the new possibilities and problems of southern agriculture. Plantation homes in long-settled areas like the Virginia piedmont became more fashionable as they incorporated luxury goods imported from China and Europe. The Madisons entertained hundreds of guests, hosted dinners and dances, and provided beds and meals for three dozen people at a time. But soil exhaustion in the region limited the profits from tobacco and made a shift to cotton impossible. While some Virginia planters made money by selling slaves to other planters farther south, James Madison refused to break up slave families who had worked the plantation for decades. With no desire to leave for lands farther west, he and Dolley were forced to reduce their standard of living.

Other white Americans, however, benefited from the expansion of southern agriculture. Of course, many cotton farmers made substantial profits in the 1810s. So did western farmers, who shipped vast quantities of food and other farm products to the South. Towns like Cincinnati, located across the Ohio River from Kentucky, sprang up as regional centers of commerce. In 1811 Cincinnati settlers still confronted Indians along the nearby White Water River. Eight years later, the booming town was incorporated as a city with nearly ten thousand residents.

Americans living in the Northeast increased their commercial connections with the South as well. Northern merchants became more deeply engaged in the southern cotton trade, opening warehouses in port cities like Savannah and Charleston and sending cotton factors, or agents, into the countryside to broker deals with planters. Meanwhile the southern cotton boom fueled industrial expansion. Indeed, factory owners in New England shipped growing amounts of yarn, thread, and cloth along with shoes, tools, and leather goods to the South. As merchants in New England and New York focused on the cotton trade, those in Philadelphia and Pittsburgh built ties to western farmers, exchanging manufactured goods for agricultural products across the Appalachian Mountains.

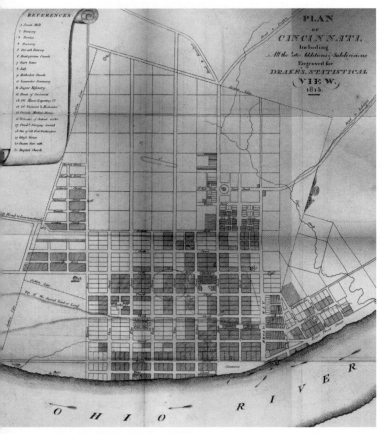

Plan of Cincinnati, 1815

This map, drawn four years before Cincinnati was incorporated as a city, illustrates the importance of the Ohio River to the city's development. Nestled along the riverbank, the village of Cincinnati was laid out in a grid pattern. The map lists a steam mill; two breweries; ferries; a potash factory, sugar refinery, and sawmill; churches; banks; and other important locations.   Courtesy Archives & Rare Books Library, University of Cincinnati

REVIEW & RELATE

What role did government play in early-nineteenth-century economic development?

How and why did economic development contribute to regional differences and shape regional ties?

LEARNINGCurve bedfordstmartins.com/hewittlawson/LC

Economic and Political Crises

As America's regions developed distinct economies in the 1810s, they became more, not less, dependent on each other. Western farmers needed manufactured goods from the North; northern manufacturers needed raw cotton from the South; southern planters needed food crops from the West. The growth in trade required the expansion of commercial institutions such as banks, which forged economic links across the United States. This economic integration stimulated the economy, but interdependence also made the nation more vulnerable when financial crises hit. The panic of 1819, the nation's first severe recession, brought economic growth to an abrupt halt. At the same time, when Missouri applied for statehood in 1819, it set off the first serious national debate over slavery.

The Panic of 1819

The **panic of 1819** resulted primarily from irresponsible banking practices in the United States and was deepened by the declining overseas demand for American goods, especially cotton. Beginning in 1816, American banks, including the Second Bank of the United States (BUS), loaned out huge sums to settlers seeking land on the frontier and to merchants and manufacturers expanding their businesses. Many of these loans were not backed by sufficient collateral. Banks, meanwhile, issued notes without adequate hard currency as European governments, fearful of growing turmoil in South America, hoarded gold and silver. State and local banks and their clients were betting on continued economic growth to ensure repayment. Western banks were especially reckless in offering discounted loans. Then, as agricultural production in Europe revived with the end of the Napoleonic Wars, the demand for American foodstuffs dropped sharply. Farm income plummeted by roughly one-third in the late 1810s.

In 1818 the directors of the Second Bank, fearing a continued expansion of the money supply, tightened the credit it provided to branch banks. This sudden effort to curtail credit led to economic panic. Some branch banks failed immediately. Others survived by calling in loans to companies and individuals, who in turn demanded repayment from those to whom they had extended credit. The chain of indebtedness pushed more people to the brink of economic ruin just as factory owners cut their workforce and merchants limited orders for new goods. Both individuals and enterprises faced bankruptcy and foreclosures on mortgages. In New York State, property values fell from a total of $315 million in 1818 to $256 million in 1820. In Richmond, Virginia, property values fell by half during the panic.

Bankruptcies, foreclosures, unemployment, and poverty spread like a plague across the country. Cotton farmers were especially hard hit by declining exports and falling prices. Planters who had gone into debt to purchase land in Alabama and Mississippi were unable to pay their mortgages. Many western residents, who had invested all they had in new farms, lost their land or simply stopped paying their mortgages. This put further strains on state banks, some of which simply collapsed, leaving the Second Bank holding mortgages on vast amounts of western territory. At the same time, public land sales plummeted from $13.6 million in 1818 to $1.3 million in 1821.

Many Americans viewed banks as the cause of the panic. Some states defied the Constitution and the Supreme Court by trying to tax BUS branches or printing state banknotes with no specie (gold or silver) to back them. Some Americans called for government relief, but there was no system to provide the kinds of assistance needed. Meanwhile Congress debated how to reignite the nation's economic engines. Northern manufacturers called for even higher tariffs to protect U.S. products from foreign competition, but southern planters argued that high tariffs raised the price of manufactured goods even as agricultural profits declined. And working men, small farmers, and frontier settlers feared that their economic needs were being ignored by politicians with ties to bankers, planters, manufacturers, and merchants.

By 1823 the panic had largely dissipated, but the prolonged economic crisis had shaken national confidence, and citizens became more skeptical of federal authority and more suspicious of banks. From 1819 until the Civil War, one of the greatest limitations on national expansion remained the cycle of economic expansion and contraction, which was tied ever more closely to unregulated national and international markets. **See Document Project 9: The Panic of 1819, page 284**.

Slavery in Missouri

The spread of slavery fueled a second national crisis. In February 1819, the Missouri Territory applied for statehood. New York congressman James Tallmadge Jr. proposed that it be admitted only if it banned further importation of slaves and passed a gradual emancipation law modeled on those in many northern states. With the support of southern

congressmen, however, whites in the territory defeated Tallmadge's proposals. The northern majority in the House of Representatives then rejected Missouri's admission.

Southern politicians were outraged, claiming that since the Missouri Territory allowed slavery, so should the state of Missouri. Although the region bordered the Northwest Territory, where slavery was outlawed in 1787, it also bordered the slave states of Kentucky and Tennessee. With cotton production moving ever westward, southern congressmen wanted to ensure the availability of new lands. They also wanted to ensure the South's power in Congress. Because the northern population had grown more rapidly than that in the South, by 1819 northern politicians controlled the House of Representatives. The Senate, however, was evenly divided, with two senators representing each state: eleven slave and eleven free. If northerners could block the admission of slave states like Missouri while allowing the admission of free states, the balance of power in the Senate would tip in the North's favor. Thus southern senators blocked the admission of Maine, which sought to separate itself from Massachusetts and become a free state.

For southern planters, the decision on Missouri defined the future of slavery. With foreign trade in slaves outlawed, planters relied on natural increase and trading slaves from older to newer areas of cultivation to meet the demand for labor. Moreover, with free blacks packing the congressional galleries in Washington to listen to congressmen debate Missouri statehood, supporters of slavery worried that divisions among whites could fuel resistance to slavery and even open revolt. Two rebellions had occurred in recent memory. In 1811 some four hundred slaves in Louisiana had killed two whites and burned several plantations. Their advance on New Orleans was stopped only when U.S. troops killed more than sixty rebels. Even more immediately, several hundred fugitive slaves had joined forces with Seminole Indians in 1817, raiding Georgia plantations and establishing autonomous communities in central Florida. Andrew Jackson's 1818 attack halted their activities, but most of the fugitive blacks escaped deep into Florida.

In 1820 Representative Henry Clay of Kentucky forged a compromise that resolved the immediate issues and promised a long-term solution. Maine was to be admitted as a free state and Missouri as a slave state, thereby maintaining the balance between North and South in the U.S. Senate (Map 9.3). At the same time, Congress agreed that the southern border of Missouri—latitude 36°30′—was to serve as the boundary between slave and free states throughout the Louisiana Territory.

Explore

Compare two critiques of the Missouri Compromise in Documents 9.2 and 9.3.

DOCUMENTS 9.2 AND 9.3

Protesting the Missouri Compromise: Two Views

Missouri's statehood application sparked a crisis over the future of slavery in America, and the resulting Missouri Compromise did little to ease the fears of Americans who wanted to contain its spread. Timothy Claimright and Thomas Jefferson both opposed the Missouri Compromise, but they offered different reasons for doing so. Claimright of Brunswick, Maine, argues in a poem published as a broadside that his home state should not join the Union if it means inviting the admission of Missouri as a slave state. Thomas Jefferson predicts in a letter that the temporary solution of the compromise will only lead to a future tragedy.

Explore

9.2 Timothy Claimright | Maine Not to Be Coupled with the Missouri Question, 1820

If the South will not yield, to the West be it known,
That Maine will declare for a *King* of her own;
And *three hundred thousand* of freemen demand
The justice bestow'd on each State in the land.
Free whites of the East are not blacks of the West,
And Republican souls on this principle rest,
That if no respect to their rights can be shown,
They know how to vindicate what are their own. . . .

They are founded on freedom, humanity's right,
Ordained by God against slavery to fight.
And Heaven born liberty sooner than yield,
The whites of Missouri shall dress their own field.
We are hardy and healthy, can till our own soil,
In labour delight; make a pleasure of toil. . . .
They too lazy to work, drive slaves, whom they fear;
We school our own children, and brew our own beer.
We do a day's work and go fearless to bed;
Tho' lock'd up, they dream of slaves, whom they dread. . . .
They may boast of their blacks; we boast of our plenty,
And swear to be free, eighteen hundred and twenty.
South and West, now be honest, to MAINE give her due,
If you call her a child, she's an Hercules too.
A Sister in Union admit her, as free;
To be coupled with slaves, she will never agree.

Source: Timothy Claimright, *Maine Not to Be Coupled with the Missouri Question* (Brunswick, ME, 1820), Library of Congress Ephemera Collection.

9.3 Thomas Jefferson | Letter to John Holmes, 1820

Monticello, April 22, 1820

I thank you, dear Sir, for the copy you have been so kind as to send me of the letter to your constituents on the Missouri question. It is a perfect justification to them. I had for a long time ceased to read newspapers, or pay any attention to public affairs, confident they were in good hands, and content to be a passenger in our bark [ship] to the shore from which I am not distant. But this momentous question, like a fire-bell in the night, awakened and filled me with terror. I considered it at once as the knell of the Union. It is hushed, indeed, for the moment. But this is a reprieve only, not a final sentence. A geographical line, coinciding with a marked principle, moral and political, once conceived and held up to the angry passions of men, will never be obliterated; and every new irritation will mark it deeper and deeper. I can say, with conscious truth, that there is not a man on earth who would sacrifice more than I would to relieve us from this heavy reproach, in any *practicable* way. The cession of that kind of property [slavery], for so it is misnamed, is a bagatelle [an insignificant thing] which would not cost me a second thought, if, in that way, a general emancipation and *expatriation* could be effected; and, gradually, and with due sacrifices, I think it might be. But as it is, we have the wolf by the ears, and we can neither hold him, nor safely let him go. Justice is in one scale, and self-preservation in the other. Of one thing I am certain, that as the passage of slaves from one State to another, would not make a slave of a single human being who would not be so without it, so their diffusion over a greater surface would make them individually happier, and proportionally facilitate the accomplishment of their emancipation, by dividing the burthen on a greater number of coadjutors.

Source: Thomas Jefferson Randolph, ed., *Memoirs, Correspondence, and Private Papers of Thomas Jefferson* (London: Henry Colburn and Richard Bentley, 1829), 4:332.

Interpret the Evidence

- Why does Claimright oppose the Missouri Compromise? How does he differentiate Maine and other northern states from the slave societies of the South?
- Why does Jefferson believe that the Missouri Compromise would exacerbate the conflict over slavery? Does he offer a solution to the slavery issue in the United States?

Put It in Context

How might supporters of the Missouri Compromise have responded to the arguments of Claimright and Jefferson?

MAP 9.3 The Missouri Compromise and Westward Expansion, 1820s

The debate over the Missouri Compromise occurred just as the United States began expanding farther westward. Within a few years of its adoption, the growth of U.S. settlements in eastern Texas and increased trade with a newly independent Mexico suggested the importance of drawing a clear boundary between slave and free states.

The **Missouri Compromise** gained the support of a majority of representatives and senators and ended the crisis for the moment. Still, the debates made clear how quickly a disagreement over slavery could escalate into clashes that threatened the survival of the nation.

REVIEW & RELATE

What were the political consequences of the panic of 1819?

What regional divisions did the conflict over slavery in Missouri reveal?

LEARNINGCurve bedfordstmartins.com/hewittlawson/LC

Redefining American Democracy

With the frontier moving ever westward and the panic of 1819 shaking many Americans' faith in traditional political and economic leaders, the nation was ripe for change. Working men, small farmers, and frontier settlers, who had long been locked out of the electoral system by property qualifications and eastern elites, demanded the right to vote. They also looked for a different kind of candidate to champion their cause. Frontier heroes like Andrew Jackson, with few ties to banks, business, and eastern power brokers, appealed to this new constituency. The resulting political movement widened voting rights in the United States and brought more diverse groups of men into the electorate. Yet the new democratic movement advanced the interests only of white men. During the 1820s, African Americans lost political and civil rights in most northern and western states. Indians, too, fared poorly under the new political regime. While some white women gained greater access to political activities as a result of the expanded voting rights of fathers and husbands, they did not achieve independent political rights. Finally, during the 1820s and 1830s, ongoing conflicts over slavery, tariffs, and the rights of Indian nations transformed party alignments as a wave of new voters entered the political fray.

Expanding Voting Rights

Between 1788 and 1820, the U.S. presidency was dominated by Virginia elites and after 1800 by Democratic-Republicans. With little serious political opposition at the national level, few people bothered to vote in presidential elections. Far more people engaged in partisan and popular political activities at the state and local level. Many towns held public celebrations on the Fourth of July and election days, and politicians of every stripe invited women to participate. Female participants often sewed symbols of their partisan loyalties on their clothes and joined in parades and feasts organized by men.

This popular political activity stimulated interest in presidential elections following the panic of 1819, when, as Scottish traveler James Flint noted, "the faith of the people was shaken." Laboring men, who were especially vulnerable to economic downturns, demanded the right to vote as a means of forcing politicians to respond to their concerns.

In New York State, Martin Van Buren, a rising star in the Democratic-Republican Party, led the fight to eliminate property qualifications for voting. At the state constitutional convention of 1821, the committee on suffrage reflected his views, arguing that the only qualification for voting should be "the virtue and morality of the people." By the word *people*, Van Buren and the committee meant white men, but even this limited demand aroused heated opposition. A year earlier, attorney Daniel Webster had been elected to the Massachusetts constitutional convention, where he argued vociferously that "political power naturally and necessarily goes into the hands which hold the property."

Although many wealthy conservatives supported Webster's views, he lost the debate, and both Massachusetts and New York instituted universal white male suffrage. By 1825 most states along the Atlantic seaboard had lowered or eliminated property qualifications on

Election Day in Philadelphia, 1815

John Lewis Krimmel, a recent German immigrant, painted this image of an election day celebration in Philadelphia in 1815. The image highlights the widespread popular participation of men, women, and children in political events even before the expansion of voting rights for white men in the 1820s.   Courtesy, Winterthur Museum white male voters. Meanwhile states along the frontier that had joined the Union in the 1810s established universal white male suffrage from the beginning. And by 1824 three-quarters of the states (18 of 24) allowed voters, rather than state legislatures, to elect members of the electoral college.

Yet as white men gained political rights in the 1820s, democracy did not spread to other groups. Indian nations were considered sovereign entities, so Indians voted in their own nations, not in U.S. elections. Women were excluded from voting because of their perceived dependence on men. New Jersey had granted single or widowed property-owning women the right to vote during the Revolution, but in 1807 the state legislature rescinded that right—along with suffrage for African American men—when small numbers of female and black voters proved they could make a difference in contested elections.

African American men faced challenges to their rights well beyond New Jersey. No southern legislature had ever granted blacks the right to vote, and in the 1820s northern states began to disfranchise African Americans. In many cases, expanded voting rights for white men went hand in hand with new restrictions on black men. In New York State, for example, the constitution of 1821, which eliminated property qualifications for white men, raised property qualifications for African American voters, disfranchising most African Americans in the state in the process.

When African American men protested their disfranchisement in northern states, some whites spoke out on their behalf. They claimed that denying rights to men who had in no way abused the privilege of voting set "an ominous and dangerous precedent." In response, opponents of black suffrage offered explicitly racist justifications. Some worried that blacks might eventually secure seats in state legislatures, on juries, and in Congress. Some argued that black voting would lead to interracial socializing, even marriage. However, the growing population of free blacks in northern cities posed the greatest threat. Once again, white politicians feared that black voters might hold the balance of power in close elections, forcing white civic leaders to accede to their demands. Gradually, racist arguments won the day, and by 1840, 93 percent of free blacks in the North were excluded from voting.

Racial Restrictions and Antiblack Violence

Restrictions on voting followed other constraints on African American men and women. As early as 1790, Congress limited naturalization (the process of becoming a citizen) to white aliens, or immigrants. It also excluded blacks from enrolling in federal militias. In 1820 Congress authorized city officials in Washington, D.C., to adopt a separate legal code governing free blacks and slaves. This federal legislation encouraged states to add their own restrictions, including segregation of public schools, public transportation, and public accommodations like churches and theaters. Such laws were passed in the North as well as in the South. Some northern legislatures even denied African Americans the right to settle in their state.

In addition, blacks faced mob and state-sanctioned violence across the country. In 1822 officials in Charleston, South Carolina, accused Denmark Vesey of following the revolutionary leader Toussaint L'Ouverture's lead and plotting a conspiracy to free the city's slaves. One of 1,500 free blacks residing in the city, Vesey had helped to organize churches, mutual aid societies, and other black institutions. Whites viewed these efforts as a threat to the future of slavery because such accomplishments challenged assumptions about black inferiority. Vesey may have organized a plan to free slaves in the city, but it is also possible that white officials concocted the plot in order to terrorize free blacks and slaves in the area and to shore up the power of ruling white elites. Despite scant evidence, Vesey and 34 of his alleged co-conspirators were found guilty and hanged. Another 18 were exiled outside the United States. The African Methodist Episcopal church where they supposedly planned the insurrection was torn down.

Northern blacks also suffered from violent attacks by whites. Assaults on individual African Americans often went unrecorded, but race riots received greater attention. For example, in 1829 white residents of Cincinnati attacked black neighborhoods, and more than half of the city's black residents fled. Many of them resettled in Ontario, Canada. They were soon joined by Philadelphia blacks who had been attacked by groups of white residents in 1832. Such attacks continued in northern cities throughout the 1830s.

Political Realignments

Restrictions on black political and civil rights converged with the decline of the Federalists in the North. Federalist majorities in New York State had approved the gradual abolition law of 1799. In 1821 New York Federalists advocated equal rights for black and white voters as long as property qualifications limited suffrage to respectable citizens. But Federalists were losing power by this time, and the concerns of African Americans were low on the Democratic-Republican agenda.

Struggles among Democratic-Republicans in the 1820s turned to a large extent on the same issue that had earlier divided them from Federalists: the limits of federal power. After nearly a quarter century in power, many Democratic-Republicans embraced a more expansive view of federal authority and a looser interpretation of the U.S.

Constitution. Yet others in the party argued forcefully for a return to Jeffersonian principles of limited federal power and a strict construction of the Constitution. At the same time, rising young politicians—like Martin Van Buren and Andrew Jackson—and newly enfranchised voters sought to seize control of the party from its longtime leaders.

The election of 1824 brought these conflicts to a head, splitting the Democratic-Republicans into rival factions that by 1828 had coalesced into two distinct entities: the **Democrats** and the **National Republicans**. Unable to agree on a single presidential candidate in 1824, the Democratic-Republican congressional caucus fractured into four camps backing separate candidates: John Quincy Adams, Andrew Jackson, Henry Clay, and Secretary of the Treasury William Crawford. John C. Calhoun, Monroe's secretary of war, eventually threw his support behind Jackson and sought the vice presidency.

As the race developed, Adams and Jackson emerged as the two strongest candidates. John Quincy Adams's stature rested on his diplomatic achievements and the reputation of his father, former president John Adams. Like Clay, he favored internal improvements and protective tariffs that would bolster northern industry and commerce. Jackson, on the other hand, relied largely on his fame as a war hero and Indian fighter to inspire popular support. Like Crawford, he advocated limited federal power.

As a candidate who appealed to ordinary voters, Jackson held a decided edge. Jackson, outgoing and boisterous, claimed to support "good old Jeffersonian Democratic republican principles" and organized a campaign that took his case to the people. Emphasizing his humble origins, he appealed to small farmers and northern workers who hoped to emulate his success as a self-made man. Just as important, Jackson gained the support of Van Buren, who also wanted to expand the political clout of the "common [white] man" and limit the reach of a central government that was becoming too powerful.

The four presidential candidates created a truly competitive race. With more white men eligible to vote and more states allowing voters to choose members of the electoral college, turnout at the polls increased to more than a quarter of eligible voters. Jackson won the popular vote by carrying Pennsylvania, New Jersey, the Carolinas, and much of the West and led in the electoral college with 99 electors. But with no candidate gaining an absolute majority in the electoral college, the Constitution called for the House of Representatives to choose the president from the three leading contenders—Jackson, Adams, and Crawford. Clay, who came in fourth, asked his supporters to back Adams, ensuring his election. Once in office, President Adams appointed Clay his secretary of state. Jackson claimed that the two had engineered a "corrupt bargain" that denied the will of the people. Yet the decisions of Clay and Adams involved a logical alliance between two candidates who agreed on the need to increase federal investment in internal improvements, raise tariffs, and expand the powers of the BUS.

But when President Adams sought to implement his agenda, he ran into vigorous opposition in Congress led by Van Buren. Calhoun, who had been elected vice president, also opposed his policies. Van Buren argued against federal funding for internal improvements since New York State had financed the Erie Canal with its own monies. Calhoun, meanwhile, joined other southern politicians in opposing any expansion of federal power for fear it would then be used to restrict the spread of slavery.

The most serious battle in Congress, however, involved tariffs. The tariff of 1816 had excluded most cheap English cotton cloth from the United States, thereby allowing New England textile manufacturers to gain control of the domestic market. In 1824 the tariff was extended to more expensive cotton and woolen cloth and to iron goods. During the presidential campaign, Adams and Clay appealed to northern voters by advocating even higher duties on these items. When Adams introduced tariff legislation that extended duties to raw materials like wool, hemp, and molasses, he gained support from both Jackson and Van Buren, who considered these tariffs beneficial to farmers on the frontier. Despite the opposition of Vice President Calhoun and congressmen from older southern states, the tariff of 1828 was approved, raising duties on imports to an average of 62 percent.

The tariff of 1828, however, was Adams's only notable legislative victory. His foreign policy was also stymied by a hostile Congress. Moreover, Jackson's supporters gained a majority in the midterm elections of 1826, intensifying conflicts among Democratic-Republicans. Adams thus entered the 1828 election campaign with little to show in the way of domestic or foreign achievements, and Jackson and his supporters took full advantage of the president's political vulnerability.

The Presidential Election of 1828

The election of 1828 tested the power of the two major factions in the Democratic-Republican Party. President Adams followed the traditional approach of "standing" for office. He told supporters, "If my country wants my services, she must ask for them." Jackson and his supporters, who deeply distrusted established political leaders, chose instead to "run" for office. They took their case directly to the voters, introducing innovative techniques to create enthusiasm among the electorate.

Van Buren managed the first truly national political campaign in U.S. history, seeking to re-create the original Democratic-Republican coalition among farmers, northern artisans, and southern planters while adding a sizable constituency of frontier voters. He was aided in the effort by Calhoun, who again ran for vice president and supported the Tennessee war hero despite their disagreement over tariffs. Jackson's supporters organized state party conventions to nominate him for president rather than relying on the congressional caucus. They established local Jackson committees in critical states such as Virginia and New York. They organized newspaper campaigns and developed a logo, the hickory leaf, based on the candidate's nickname "Old Hickory."

Jackson traveled the country to build loyalty to himself as well as to his party. His Tennessee background, rise to great wealth, and reputation as an Indian fighter ensured his popularity among southern and western voters. He also reassured southerners that he advocated "judicious" duties on imports, suggesting that he might try to lower the rates imposed in 1828. At the same time, his support of the tariff of 1828 and his military credentials created enthusiasm among northern working men and frontier farmers.

President Adams's supporters demeaned the "dissolute" and "rowdy" men who poured out for Jackson rallies, and they also launched personal attacks on the candidate.

Dragging politicians' private lives into public view was nothing new, but opposition papers focused their venom this time on the candidate's wife, Rachel. They questioned the timing of her divorce from her first husband and remarriage to Jackson, suggesting she was an adulterer and a bigamist. Rachel Jackson felt humiliated, but her husband refused to be intimidated by scandal.

Adams distanced himself from his own campaign. He sought to demonstrate his statesmanlike gentility by letting others speak for him. This strategy worked well when only men of wealth and property could vote. But with an enlarged electorate and an astonishing turnout of more than 50 percent of eligible voters, Adams's approach failed and Jackson became president. Jackson won handily in the South and the West and carried most of the Middle Atlantic states as well as New York. Adams dominated only in New England (Figure 9.1).

The election of 1828 formalized a new party alignment. During the campaign, Jackson and his supporters referred to themselves as "the Democracy" and forged a new national Democratic Party. In response, Adams's supporters called themselves National Republicans. The competition between Democrats and National Republicans heightened interest in national politics among ordinary voters and ensured that the innovative techniques introduced by Jackson would be widely adopted in future campaigns.

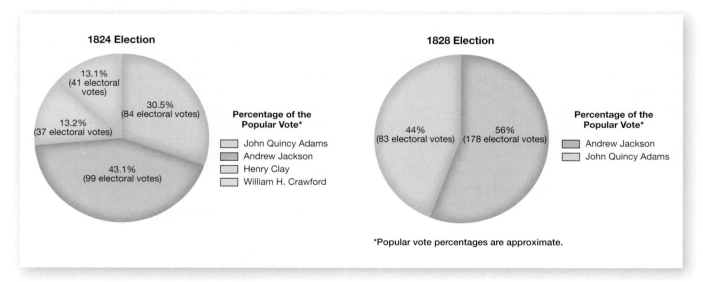

FIGURE 9.1 The Elections of 1824 and 1828
Andrew Jackson lost the 1824 election to John Quincy Adams when the decision was thrown into the House of Representatives. In 1828 Jackson launched the first popular campaign for president, mobilizing working-class white men who were newly enfranchised. Three times as many men—more than one million voters—cast ballots in 1828 than in 1824, ensuring Jackson's election as president.

REVIEW & RELATE

| How and why did the composition of the electorate change in the 1820s? | How did Jackson's 1828 campaign represent a significant departure from earlier patterns in American politics? |

✓ *LEARNINGCurve* bedfordstmartins.com/hewittlawson/LC

Jacksonian Democracy in Action

Many ordinary Americans held high expectations for Jackson's presidency, and Jackson hoped to make government more responsive to the "common man." But the president's notion of democracy, while inclusive of white men regardless of wealth or property, did not extend to Indians or African Americans. During his presidency, Indian nations would actively resist his efforts to take more of their land, and blacks would continue to resist their enslavement. Of more immediate importance, since President Jackson had to take clear positions on tariffs and other controversial issues, he could not please all of his constituents. He also confronted experienced adversaries like Clay, Webster, and John Quincy Adams, who was elected to the House of Representatives from Massachusetts in 1830. The president thus faced considerable difficulty in translating popular support into public policy.

A Democratic Spirit?

On March 4, 1829, crowds of ordinary citizens came to see their hero's inauguration. Jackson's wife Rachel had died less than three months earlier, leaving her husband devastated. Now Jackson, dressed in a plain black suit, walked alone to the Capitol as vast throngs of supporters waved and cheered. Wealthy planters were jammed shoulder to shoulder with frontier farmers and working men and

President Andrew Jackson's First Inauguration, 1829
This illustration by the British artist Robert Cruikshank, entitled *President's Levee, or All Creation Going to the White House*, depicts crowds in front of the White House during Andrew Jackson's first inaugural reception in 1829. The crowds of ordinary people were so enthusiastic and unrestrained that President Jackson had to flee out the back of the White House to escape injury.   The Granger Collection, New York

women. Local African Americans also turned out for the spectacle. A somber Jackson read a brief inaugural address, took the oath of office, and then rode his horse through the crowds to the White House.

The size and enthusiasm of the crowds soon shattered the decorum of the inauguration. Author Margaret Bayard Smith reported mobs "scrambling, fighting, [and] romping" through the White House reception. Jackson was nearly crushed to death by "rabble" eager to shake his hand. Tubs of punch laced with rum, brandy, and champagne were finally placed on the lawn to draw the crowds outdoors.

Nonetheless, Jackson and his supporters viewed the event as a symbol of a new democratic spirit. Others were less optimistic. Bayard Smith warned against putting too much faith in "the people," who "have been found in all ages and countries where they get power in their hands, that of all tyrants, they are the most ferocious, cruel, and despotic." She and other conservative political leaders also saw echoes of the French Revolution in the unruly behavior of the masses. Supreme Court justice Joseph Story, too, feared "the reign of King 'Mob.'"

Tensions between the president and the capital's traditional leaders intensified in the first months of his administration. Jackson's appointment of Tennessee senator John Eaton as secretary of war added to the rancor. Eaton had had an affair with a woman thought to be of questionable character and later married her. When Jackson announced his plans to appoint Eaton to his cabinet, congressional leaders urged him to reconsider. When the president appointed Eaton anyway, the wives of Washington's leading politicians snubbed Mrs. Eaton and refused to accept her social calls. This time Jackson was outmaneuvered in what became known as the **Petticoat Affair**, and Eaton was eventually forced from office.

From the days of Dolley Madison, political wives had wielded considerable influence in Washington. In 1831 they pressured Eaton to resign. But the Petticoat Affair also led Jackson's entire cabinet to resign, after which his legislative agenda stalled in Congress and National Republicans regained the momentum lost after Adams's defeat. The Eaton appointment had reinforced concerns that the president used his authority to reward his friends. So, too, did his reliance on an informal group of advisers, known as the Kitchen Cabinet, rather than his official cabinet. While his administration opened up government posts to a wider range of individuals, ensuring more democratic access, he often selected appointees based on personal ties. The resulting **spoils system**—introduced by Jackson and continued by future administrations—assigned federal posts as gifts for partisan loyalty rather than as jobs that required experience or expertise.

Confrontations over Tariffs and the Bank

The Democratic Party that emerged in the late 1820s was built on an unstable foundation. The coalition that formed around Jackson included northern workers who benefited from high tariffs as well as southern farmers and planters who did not. It brought together western voters who sought federal support for internal improvements and strict constructionists who believed that such expenditures were unconstitutional. Weakened by conflicts over appointments, Jackson had to decide which factions to reward. In 1830 Congress passed four internal improvement bills with strong support from National Republicans. Jackson vetoed each one, claiming that the "voice of the people" demanded careful spending. These vetoes worried his frontier supporters but pleased his southern constituency.

Southern congressmen, however, were more interested in his stand on tariffs. The tariff of 1828 still enraged many southern planters and politicians, but most believed that once Jackson reached the White House, he would reverse course and reduce this "Tariff of Abominations." Instead, he avoided the issue, and southern agriculture continued to suffer. Agricultural productivity in Virginia, South Carolina, and other states of the Old South was declining from soil exhaustion, while prices for staples like cotton and rice had not fully recovered after the panic of 1819. At the same time, higher duties on manufactured items meant that southerners had to pay more for the goods they bought.

Even as Calhoun campaigned with Jackson in 1828, the South Carolinian developed a philosophical argument to negate the effects of high tariffs on his state. Like opponents of the War of 1812, Calhoun drew on states' rights doctrines outlined in the Kentucky and Virginia Resolutions of 1798 (see chapter 7). In *The South Carolina Exposition and Protest*, published anonymously in 1828, Calhoun argued that states should have the ultimate power to determine the constitutionality of laws passed by Congress. When Jackson, after taking office, realized that his vice president advocated **nullification**—the right of individual states to declare individual laws void within their borders—it further damaged their relationship, which was already frayed by the Eaton affair.

When Congress debated the tariff issue in 1830, South Carolina senator Robert Hayne defended nullification. He claimed that the North intended to crush the South economically and that only the right of states to nullify federal legislation could protect southern society. In response, Daniel Webster denounced nullification and the states' rights doctrine on which it was built. At a banquet held after the Hayne-Webster debate, Jackson further antagonized southern political leaders by supporting Webster's position.

Matters worsened in 1832 when northern and western congressmen ignored their southern counterparts and confirmed the high duties set four years earlier. Jackson signed the 1832 tariff into law. In response, South Carolina held a special convention that approved an Ordinance of Nullification. It stated that duties on imports would not be collected in the state after February 1, 1833, and threatened secession if federal authorities tried to collect them. Many of the state's residents believed armed conflict was at hand, and some planters raised regiments to secure their property and defend what they viewed as the state's rights.

The tariff crisis thus escalated in the fall of 1832 just as Jackson faced reelection. The tariff debates had angered many southerners, and Calhoun refused to run again as his vice president. Fortunately for Jackson, however, opponents in Congress had provided him with another issue that could unite his supporters and highlight his commitment to the common man: the renewal of the BUS charter.

Clay and Webster persuaded Nicholas Biddle, head of the BUS, to request an early recharter of the bank. Jackson's opponents in Congress knew they had the votes to pass a new charter in the summer of 1832, and they hoped Jackson would veto the bill and thereby split the Democratic Party just before the fall elections. The Second Bank was a political quagmire. Although a private institution, it was chartered, or granted the right to operate, by the federal government, which owned 20 percent of its stock. The bank had stabilized the economy during the 1820s by regularly demanding specie (gold or silver) payments from state-chartered banks. This kept those banks from issuing too much paper money and thereby prevented inflation and higher prices. The Second Bank's tight-money policies also kept banks from expanding too rapidly in the western states. Bankers, merchants, and entrepreneurs in eastern cities as well as most planters applauded the bank's efforts, but its tight-money policies aroused hostility among the wider public. When state-chartered banks closed because of lack of specie, ordinary Americans were often stuck with worthless paper money. Tight-money policies also made it more difficult for individuals to get credit to purchase land, homes, or farm equipment.

As the president's opponents had hoped, Congress approved the new charter, and Jackson vetoed it. Yet rather than dividing the Democrats, Jackson's veto gained enormous support from voters across the country. In justifying his action, the president cast the Second Bank as a "monster" that was "dangerous to the liberties of the people"—particularly farmers, mechanics, and laborers— and promoted "the advancement of the few." Finally, Jackson noted that wealthy Britons owned substantial shares of the bank's stock and that national pride demanded ending the Second Bank's reign over the U.S. economy. Jackson rode the enthusiasm for his bank veto to

reelection over National Republican candidate Henry Clay. Within a year, the Second Bank was dead, deprived of government deposits by Jackson.

Explore

For a satirical view of Jackson's attack on the BUS, see Document 9.4.

Soon after his reelection, however, the president faced a grave political crisis related to the tariff issue. Jackson now supported lower tariffs, but he was adamant in his opposition to nullification. In early 1833, he persuaded Congress to pass a Force Bill, which gave him authority to use the military to enforce national laws in South Carolina. At the same time, Jackson made clear that he would work with Congress to reduce tariffs, allowing South Carolina to rescind its nullification ordinance without losing face. Open conflict was averted, but the question of nullification was not resolved.

Contesting Indian Removal

On another long-standing issue—the acquisition of Indian land—Jackson gained the support of white southerners and most frontier settlers. Yet not all Americans agreed with his effort to remove or exterminate Indians. In the 1820s, nations like the Cherokee that sought to maintain their homelands gained the support of Protestant missionaries who hoped to "civilize" Indians by converting them to Christianity and "American" ways. In 1819 Congress had granted these groups federal funds to establish schools and churches to help acculturate and convert Indian men and women. Presidents James Monroe and John Quincy Adams supported the rights of Indians to maintain their sovereignty if they embraced missionary goals. Jackson was much less supportive of efforts to incorporate Indians into the United States and sided with political leaders who sought to force eastern Indians to accept homelands west of the Mississippi River.

In 1825, three years before Jackson was elected president, Creek Indians in Georgia and Alabama were forcibly removed to Unorganized Territory (previously part of Arkansas Territory and later called Indian Territory) based on a fraudulent treaty. Jackson supported this policy. When he became president, politicians and settlers in Georgia, Florida, the Carolinas, and Illinois demanded federal assistance to force Indian communities out of their states.

The largest Indian nations vehemently protested their removal. The Cherokees, who had fought against the Creeks alongside Jackson at Horseshoe Bend, adopted a republican form of government in 1827 based on the U.S. Constitution. John Ross served as the president of the Cherokee constitutional convention, and a year later he was

General Jackson Slaying the Many Headed Monster, 1836

Few issues exposed the differences between the Democrats and the National Republicans more clearly than the battle over the national bank. This political cartoon depicts President Andrew Jackson, holding a cane marked "Veto," with his ally Vice President Martin Van Buren and a character named Major Jack Downing. The three attempt to slay "the many headed monster." The American humorist Seba Smith created the fictional Downing to represent a provincial Maine "down-easterner" who used a very broad dialect. He was presented as a close chum of Andrew Jackson to satirize the goings-on in Washington. The hydra features the faces of Nicholas Biddle, the president of the Bank of the United States, and other men who represent the banks of the various states. Biddle wears a hat that says "Penn" and "$35,000,000," which refers to the state of Pennsylvania's effort to recharter the BUS in defiance of Jackson's efforts to destroy it.

 Explore

How does the artist characterize Jackson, Van Buren, and Downing?

How does Jackson intend to eliminate the bank?

Why do you think the artist portrayed the banks as a hydra?

GENERAL JACKSON SLAYING THE MANY HEADED MONSTER.

Private Collection/Peter Newark American Pictures/The Bridgeman Art Library

Put It in Context

What do you think the artist believes about the feasibility of the Jackson administration's efforts to destroy the bank?

Cherokee Phoenix
As U.S. officials pressured the Cherokee nation to relocate west of the Mississippi River, Cherokee leaders sought to convince them that the tribe had become Americanized. Elias Boudinot, whose Cherokee name was Galagina Uwatie, attended Christian mission schools and married a white woman. In 1828 he published the bilingual *Phoenix* to build internal unity and gather support against Cherokee removal.   Library of Congress

chosen principal chief in the first constitutional election. He and the other chiefs then declared themselves a sovereign nation within the borders of the United States. The Georgia legislature rejected the Cherokee claims of independence and argued that Indians were simply guests of the state. When Ross appealed to Jackson to recognize Cherokee sovereignty, the president refused. Instead, Jackson proclaimed that Georgia, like other states, was "sovereign over the people within its borders." At his urging, Congress passed the **Indian Removal Act** in 1830, by which the Cherokee and other Indian nations would be forced to exchange ancient claims on lands in the Southeast for a "clear title forever" on territory west of the Mississippi River. Still, the majority of Cherokees refused to accept these terms and worked assiduously to maintain control of their existing territory.

As the dispute between the Cherokee nation and Georgia unfolded, Jackson made clear his intention to implement the Indian Removal Act. In 1832 he sent federal troops into western Illinois to force Sauk and Fox peoples to move farther west. Instead, whole villages, led by Chief

Black Hawk, fled to the Wisconsin Territory. Black Hawk and a thousand warriors confronted U.S. troops at Bad Axe, but the Sauk and Fox warriors were decimated in a brutal daylong battle. The survivors were forced to move west. Meanwhile the Seminole Indians, who had fought against Jackson when he invaded Florida in 1818, prepared for another pitched battle to protect their territory, while John Ross pursued legal means to resist removal through state and federal courts. The contest for Indian lands would continue well past Jackson's presidency, but the president's desire to force indigenous nations westward would ultimately prevail.

REVIEW & RELATE

What did President Jackson's response to the Eaton affair and Indian removal reveal about his vision of democracy?

To what extent did Jackson's policies favor the South? Which policies benefited or antagonized which groups of Southerners?

 LEARNINGCurve bedfordstmartins.com/hewittlawson/LC

Conclusion: The Nation Faces New Challenges

From the 1810s through the early 1830s, the United States was buffeted by a series of crises. The War of 1812 threatened the stability of the nation, not only due to attacks on its recently constructed capital city but also because New Englanders so deeply opposed the conflict that some considered seceding from the Union. The panic of 1819 then threw the nation into economic turmoil and led to demands for expanded voting rights for white men. It also heightened disputes over banks and tariffs as residents of various regions and classes sought to ensure their own financial security. The admission of Missouri similarly intensified debates over slavery as white southerners saw themselves losing out in population growth and political representation to the North. At the same time, the western expansion that allowed territories like Missouri to claim statehood also escalated struggles over Indian rights. By the 1820s, those struggles involved a diverse array of Indian nations as well as deep differences among white Americans over the future of native peoples who had embraced Christianity and other forms of "civilization."

In navigating these difficult issues, some Americans sought to find a middle ground. Dolley Madison worked to overcome partisan divisions through social networking. After the death of her husband, James, in 1836, she returned to Washington where her house on Lafayette Street became a center of social activity for politicians, ambassadors, and their wives. Although her son's misman-agement of Montpelier forced her to sell the beloved estate, Dolley secured her old age when Congress purchased President James Madison's papers from her. Similarly, John Ross wielded his biracial heritage to seek rights for Indians within a white-dominated world. He served as both a lobbyist for Cherokee interests in Washington and an advocate of acculturation to Anglo-American ways among the Cherokee. Still, congressional passage of the Indian Removal Act in 1830 challenged Ross's efforts to maintain his tribe's sovereignty and homeland. When Henry Clay was reelected to the U.S. Senate in November 1831, he spoke out against Cherokee removal. But Clay was more widely known for helping to forge key compromises on the admission of Missouri and on tariffs. In each case, he hoped to bring a deeply divided Congress together and provide time for the nation's political leaders to develop more permanent solutions.

Yet despite the efforts of Madison, Ross, Clay and others, differences often led to division in the 1820s and 1830s. Indeed, Henry Clay provided the final push that ensured John Quincy Adams's selection as president in 1824. In the aftermath of that election, two distinct political parties emerged out of the once-united Democratic-Republicans: the Democrats and the National Republicans. In the context of the political, military, and economic upheaval that marked the early Republic, it is not surprising that a charismatic but divisive figure like Andrew Jackson emerged to lead the new Democratic Party. Transforming the process of political campaigning, he gave voice to the "common man," but he also introduced the spoils system to government, smashed the Second Bank of the United States, and forced thousands of Indians off their lands. The extermination and removal of Indians then fostered the geographical expansion of American settle-ments southward and westward, ensuring the growth of slavery.

Dolley Madison, who lived into the late 1840s, and John Ross, who survived the Civil War, observed the continuing conflicts created by geographical expansion and partisan agendas. Madison remained a beloved figure in Washington, escorted through the Executive Mansion by President James K. Polk in February 1849, just months before her death. Ross, however, faced much more difficult circumstances as the Cherokee nation divided over whether to accept removal. Ross fought to delay removal as long as possible but eventually oversaw the forced march west of thousands of Cherokees. In their new homes, Cherokees continued to fight each other and the U.S. government. Indeed, Ross died in 1866 in Washington, D.C., while trying to negotiate a new treaty with the federal government.

Despite the dramatically different backgrounds and careers of Madison and Ross, both worked to bridge differences in the young nation, and both defended it against attack. Both harbored democratic ideals of a nation that could incorporate women as well as men, Indians as well as whites. Ultimately, however, neither had the power to overcome the partisan rivalries and economic crises that shaped the young nation or to halt the rising tensions over Indian lands and slave labor that would continue to plague Americans in the decades to come.

LEARNINGCurve
Check what you know.
bedfordstmartins.com/hewittlawson/LC

Chapter Review

Online Study Guide ▶ bedfordstmartins.com/hewittlawson

KEY TERMS

Non-Intercourse Act (p. 261)
Hartford Convention (p. 262)
American System (p. 265)
Erie Canal (p. 265)
Monroe Doctrine (p. 267)
panic of 1819 (p. 268)
Missouri Compromise (p. 272)
Democrats and National Republicans (p. 275)
Petticoat Affair (p. 278)
spoils system (p. 278)
nullification (p. 278)
Indian Removal Act (p. 281)

REVIEW & RELATE

1. How were conflicts with Indians in the West connected to ongoing tensions between the United States and Great Britain on land and at sea?

2. What were the long-term consequences of the War of 1812?

3. What role did government play in early-nineteenth-century economic development?

4. How and why did economic development contribute to regional differences and shape regional ties?

5. What were the political consequences of the panic of 1819?

6. What regional divisions did the conflict over slavery in Missouri reveal?

7. How and why did the composition of the electorate change in the 1820s?

8. How did Jackson's 1828 campaign represent a significant departure from earlier patterns in American politics?

9. What did President Jackson's response to the Eaton affair and Indian removal reveal about his vision of democracy?

10. To what extent did Jackson's policies favor the South? Which policies benefited or antagonized which groups of Southerners?

TIMELINE OF EVENTS

1809	Non-Intercourse Act passed
1811	First steamboat travels down the Mississippi to New Orleans
	William Henry Harrison defeats Shawnees at Prophet Town
June 1812	War of 1812 begins
1814	Hartford Convention
March 1814	Battle of Horseshoe Bend
August 1814	British burn Washington City
December 1814	Treaty of Ghent
1815	Battle of New Orleans
1817–1818	Andrew Jackson fights Spanish and Seminole forces in Florida
1818	Great Britain and U.S. agree to joint occupation of Oregon Territory
1819	Spain cedes Florida to U.S.; establishes boundary between U.S. and Spanish territory through the Adams-Onís Treaty
	Panic of 1819 sparks severe recession that lasts until 1823
1820	Missouri Compromise
1821	White traders begin using Santa Fe Trail
1822	Denmark Vesey accused of organizing a slave uprising
1823	Monroe Doctrine articulated
1825	Erie Canal completed
1828	Tariff of 1828 passed
	John Ross elected principal chief of the Cherokee nation
1829	Petticoat Affair
1830	Indian Removal Act passed
1832	South Carolina passes Ordinance of Nullification
1833	Force Bill passed

DOCUMENT PROJECT 9

The Panic of 1819

The panic of 1819 lasted more than four years and was the first serious economic recession faced by the United States. It resulted primarily from irresponsible banking practices and the declining demand for cotton, foodstuffs, and other American goods in Europe. This combination prompted farm foreclosures, factory layoffs, bank failures, and widespread personal and business bankruptcies. In every region of the country, people were left jobless, homeless, and destitute, and thousands auctioned off their household goods or were thrown into debtors' prisons (Documents 9.5 and 9.6). Private charities were overwhelmed, and most could not meet the demand for clothes, housing, and food.

In the midst of this tremendous suffering, the public focused its blame on bankers and government officials. There was much disagreement, however, about the proper remedy for the economic recession. Some sought permanent restriction of bank credit, whereas others believed that cheaper credit would enable the economy to grow. Proposals were put forward to give direct government relief to debtors, abolish debtors' prisons, and start public works projects. Debates over whether to increase protective tariffs revealed the sectional differences emerging in the United States. In 1816 Congress had passed a tariff raising duties on foreign imports, and during the panic northern manufacturers wanted this tariff increased to further protect the U.S. market from foreign competition. Southern planters, on the other hand, blamed tariffs for raising the costs of manufactured goods and felt they benefited the North at the expense of the South (Document 9.7). The panic also led to calls for political reforms, especially by those who felt the government was not responsive to the needs of the laboring classes. Many states considered lowering or even abolishing property qualifications for eligible voters. Documents 9.8 and 9.9 demonstrate both sides of this debate as it was taken up at the New York constitutional convention in 1821. By 1823 the panic had ended, but the economic and political changes it engendered reshaped American society and politics and would influence future responses to economic crises.

DOCUMENT 9.5

Auction in Chatham Square, 1820

Cities throughout the United States were hit hard by the panic, and in the first year of the crisis the number of paupers in New York City increased from 8,000 to 13,000. Widespread unemployment resulted in evictions and homelessness for thousands of families. The following image of Chatham Square in lower Manhattan, painted in 1843, reveals a common scene in urban areas—the public auction of goods from an evicted family. Artist E. Didier depicted Chatham Square as it was in 1820, the last year auctions were held there as the area became increasingly residential.

DOCUMENT 9.6

James Flint | Account of the Panic, 1820

The Scottish traveler James Flint was touring America when the panic hit. In his letters home, he described the impact of the economic recession on banks, factories, and merchants. The following passage is from a letter he wrote from Jeffersonville, Indiana, describing the impossible conditions that many American workers faced.

Merchants in Cincinnati, as elsewhere, have got into debt, by buying property, or by building houses, but are now secure in the possession. Such people, notwithstanding complain of the badness of the times, finding that the trade of buying without paying cannot be continued. Those who have not already secured an independence for life, may soon be willing to have trade and fair dealing as formerly. Property laws deprive creditors of the debts now due to them; but they cannot force them to give credit as they were wont to do.

Agriculture languishes—farmers cannot find profit in hiring labourers. The increase of produce in the United States is greater than any increase of consumpt that may be pointed out elsewhere. To increase the quantity of provisions, then, without enlarging the numbers of those who eat them, will be only diminishing the price farther. Land in these circumstances can be of no value to the capitalist who would employ his funds in farming. The spare capital of farmers is here chiefly laid out in the purchase of lands.

Labourers and mechanics are in want of employment. I think I have seen upwards of 1500 men in quest of work within eleven months past, and many of these declared, that they had no money. Newspapers and private letters agree in stating, that wages are so low as eighteen and three-fourth cents (about ten-pence) per day, with board, at Philadelphia, and some other places. Great numbers of strangers lately camped in the open field near Baltimore, depending on the contributions of the charitable for subsistence. You have no doubt heard of emigrants returning to Europe without finding the prospect of a livelihood in America. Some who have come out to this part of the country do not succeed well. Labourers' wages are at present a dollar and an eighth part per day. Board costs them two three-fourths or three dollars per week, and washing three-fourths of a dollar for a dozen of pieces. On these terms, it is plain that they cannot live two days by the labour of one, with the other deductions which are to be taken from their wages. Clothing, for example, will cost about three times its price in Britain: and the poor labourer is almost certain of being paid in depreciated money; perhaps from thirty to fifty per cent. under par. I have seen several men turned out of boarding houses, where their money would not be taken. They had no other resource left but to lodge in the woods, without any covering except their clothes. They set fire to a decayed log, spread some boards alongside of it for a bed, laid a block of timber across for a pillow, and pursued their labour by day as usual. . . .

Employers are also in the habit of deceiving their workmen, by telling them that it is not convenient to pay wages in money, and that they run accounts with the storekeeper, the tailor, and the shoemaker, and that from them they may have all the necessities they want very cheap. The workman who consents to this mode of payment procures orders from the employer, on one or more of these citizens, and is charged a higher price for the goods than the employer actually pays for them. This is called *paying in trade.* . . .

In the district of Jeffersonville, there has been an apparent interruption of the prosperity of the settlers. Upwards of two hundred quarter sections of land are by law forfeited to the government, for non-payment of part of the purchase money due more than a year ago. A year's indulgence was granted by Congress, but unless farther accommodation is immediately allowed, the lands will soon be offered a second time for sale. Settlers seeing the danger of losing their possessions are now offering to transfer their rights for less sums than have already been paid; it being still in the power of purchasers to retain the lands on paying up the arrears due in the land office. This marks the difficulty that individuals at present have in procuring small sums of money in this particular district.

Source: Reuben Gold Thwaites, ed., *Early Western Travels, 1748–1846* (Cleveland: Arthur H. Clark, 1904), 9:226–28; 236.

DOCUMENT 9.7

Virginia Agricultural Society | Antitariff Petition, 1820

As political debates raged on whether to raise the protective tariff on imported goods, many groups around the country wrote Congress to support or protest the tariff. Most southern planters and farmers spoke out against the tariff, including the Virginia Agricultural Society of Fredericksburg. In January 1820, the organization sent a petition to Congress, from which the following selection is taken. In the aftermath of the panic, Congress passed the tariff of 1824, which raised duties on foreign imports.

THAT HOSTILITY, resulting from true republican principles, to partial taxation, exclusive privileges, and monopolies created by law, was the primary cause of our glorious and ever-memorable revolution.

That, although most of us are only the descendants of those patriots who achieved that revolution, by the lavish expenditure of their treasure and their blood, yet that we inherit enough of their spirit to feel equal aversion to similar oppressions; at the same time, we confidently trust that neither we, nor our sons after us, will ever be found backward or reluctant in offering up at the shrine of national good and national happiness any sacrifices, however great, which *their* promotion and preservation may obviously and necessarily require. But we have been taught to believe that a parental Government—a Government founded upon the immutable and sacred principles of truth, justice, and liberty—if she required sacrifices at all from those whom she is so solemnly bound to protect, would make them such as should operate equally upon every member of the community.

That we view with great concern, both nationally and individually, certain late attempts, on the part of various descriptions of domestic manufacturers, to induce your honorable body to increase the duties upon imports, already so high as to amount, upon many articles, nearly to a prohibition. This increased cost upon some of these may truly be designated a tax upon knowledge, if not a bounty to ignorance; such, for example, as the duty upon books in foreign languages, and upon philosophical, mathematical, surgical, and chemical instruments.

That, although these attempts are sustained under the plausible pretext of "promoting national industry," they are calculated (we will not say in *design*, but certainly in *effect*) to produce a tax highly impolitic in its nature, partial in its operation, and oppressive in its effects: a tax, in fact, to be levied principally on the great body of agriculturists, who constitute a large majority of the whole American people, and who are the chief consumers of all foreign imports.

That such a tax would be a flagrant violation of the soundest and most important principles of political economy, amongst which we deem the following to be incontrovertibly true: that, as the interests of dealers and consumers necessarily conflict with each other, the first always aiming to *narrow*, whilst the latter, who form the majority of every nation, as constantly endeavor to *enlarge* competition; by which enlargement alone extravagant prices and exorbitant profits are prevented, it is the duty of every wise and just government to secure the consumers against both exorbitant profits and extravagant prices by leaving competition as free and open as possible.

Source: "Remonstrance against Increase of Duties on Imports," House of Representatives, January 17, 1820, no. 570, 16th Cong., 1st sess., *American State Papers: Finance*, 3:447–48.

DOCUMENT 9.8

James Kent | Arguments against Expanding Male Voting Rights, 1821

The economic crisis spawned debates throughout the country about the political system and its responsiveness to all classes of American citizens. The New York constitutional convention of 1821 included a committee that reviewed the state's voting laws and considered implementing "universal suffrage," that is, granting voting rights to all white men regardless of wealth or property. The committee heard testimony from supporters and opponents of property qualifications for voting. Chief Justice and Chancellor James Kent of New York argued in favor of property qualifications.

I have reflected upon the report of the select committee with attention and with anxiety. We appear to be disregarding the principles of the constitution, under which we have so long and so happily lived, and to be changing some of its essential institutions. . . .

The tendency of universal suffrage is to jeopardize the rights of property and the principles of liberty. . . .

The notion that every man that works a day on the road, or serves an idle hour in the militia, is entitled as of right to an equal participation in the whole power of the government is most unreasonable and has no foundation in justice. We had better at once discard from the report such a nominal test of merit. If such persons have an equal share in one branch of the legislature, it is surely as much as they can in justice or policy demand. Society is an association for the protection of property as well as of life, and the individual who contributes only one cent to the common stock ought not to have the same power and influence in directing the property concerns of the partnership as he who contributes his thousands. He will not have the same inducements to care, and diligence, and fidelity. His inducements and his temptation would be to divide the whole capital upon the principles of agrarian law [to ensure a more equal distribution of land to all classes].

Liberty, rightly understood, is an inestimable blessing, but liberty without wisdom, and without justice, is no better than wild and savage licentiousness. The danger which we have hereafter to apprehend, is not the want, but the abuse, of liberty. We have to apprehend the oppression of minorities, and a disposition to encroach on private right—to disturb chartered privileges—and to weaken, degrade, and overawe the administration of justice; we have to apprehend the establishment of unequal, and consequently, unjust systems of taxation, and all the mischiefs of a crude and mutable legislation. A stable senate, exempted from the influence of universal suffrage, will powerfully check these dangerous propensities.

Source: *Report of the Proceedings and Debates of the Convention of 1821* (Albany, 1821), 219, 221–22.

DOCUMENT 9.9

Nathan Sanford | Arguments for Expanding Male Voting Rights, 1821

Nathan Sanford, a former U.S. senator and a delegate to the New York constitutional convention, argued in favor of removing property qualifications. Sanford and his supporters won the debate, and property qualifications were removed for white male voters. However, property qualifications were increased for black male voters, thus denying most African Americans the right to vote in the state.

The question before us is the right of suffrage—who shall, or who shall not, have the right to vote. The committee have presented the scheme they thought best; to abolish all existing distinctions and make the right of voting uniform. Is this not right? Where did these distinctions arise? They arose from British precedents. In England, they have their three estates, which must always have their separate interests represented. Here there is but one estate—the people. To me, the only qualifications seem to be the virtue and morality of the people; and if they may be safely entrusted to vote for one class of our rulers, why not for all? In my opinion, these distinctions are fallacious. We have the experience of almost all the other states against them. The principle of the scheme now proposed is that those who bear the burthens of the state should choose those that rule it. There is no privilege given to property, as such; but those who contribute to the public support, we consider as entitled to share in the election of rulers. . . .

. . . But how is the extension of the right of suffrage unfavourable to property? Will not our laws continue the same? Will not the administration of justice continue the same? And if so, how is private property to suffer? Unless these are changed, and upon them rest the rights and security of property, I am unable to perceive how property is to suffer by the extension of the right of suffrage. But we have abundant experience on this point in other states. Now, sir, in many states the right of suffrage has no restriction; every male inhabitant votes. Yet what harm has been done in those states? What evil has resulted to them from this cause? The course of things in this country is for the extension and not the restriction of popular rights. I do not know that in Ohio or Pennsylvania, where the right of suffrage is universal, there is not the same security for private rights and private happiness as elsewhere.

Source: *Report of the Proceedings and Debates of the Convention of 1821* (Albany, 1821), 178–79.

Interpret the Evidence

1. How might images such as the one of the public auction (Document 9.5) have shaped public opinion about the panic?

2. How does James Flint (Document 9.6) describe the panic, and what comparisons does he make between American society and conditions in Europe?

3. On what grounds does the Virginia Agricultural Society of Fredericksburg protest the tariff (Document 9.7)? How does it place its struggles within the context of American history?

4. Compare the arguments of James Kent (Document 9.8) and Nathan Sanford (Document 9.9) in the debate over voting rights in New York. How do they conceptualize the principles of justice, rights, and equality? Which arguments do you find the most convincing, and why?

5. Do you think the members of the Virginia Agricultural Society would agree more with Nathan Sanford or with James Kent? What about James Flint or the creator of the public auction image?

Put It in Context

- How did the devastating impact of the panic of 1819 shape state and national-level debates over economic policies and political rights?

- How did the policies implemented during and immediately after the panic of 1819—particularly voting rights and tariff laws—change the U.S. political and economic landscape over the following decade?

The Granger Collection, New York

Private Collection/Peter Newark Western Americana/The Bridgeman Art Library

The storming of the Alamo, 1836.

Painting of a Sioux village, by George Catlin.

10
Slavery Expands South and West

1830–1850

The Granger Collection, New York

A planter's home near New Orleans, Louisiana.

AMERICAN HISTORIES

Although James Henry Hammond became one of the richest plantation owners in South Carolina, he began life more modestly. Born in 1807 near Newberry, South Carolina, he was the only one of six siblings to earn a college degree. Certain that a legal career would lead to wealth and power, James opened a law practice in Columbia, the state capital, in 1828. Two years later, bored by his profession, he established a newspaper, the *Southern Times*. Writing bold editorials that supported nullification of the "Tariff of Abominations," Hammond quickly gained attention and acclaim.

While launching his journalistic career, James courted Catherine Fitzsimmons, the daughter of a wealthy, politically connected family. When they married in June 1831, James became master of Silver Bluff, a 7,500-acre plantation worked by 147 slaves. Giving up his editorial career to focus on managing the estate, he quickly gained prominence as an agricultural reformer and was elected to the U.S. House of Representatives in 1834.

Hammond's political career was erratic. In 1836 he led a campaign that resulted in congressional passage of the so-called gag rule, ensuring that antislavery petitions would be tabled rather than read on the floor of the House. Soon afterward, he took ill and resigned from Congress, but he returned to politics in 1842 as governor of South Carolina. His ambitions were stymied once more, however, when Catherine discovered that James had made sexual advances on his four nieces, aged thirteen to sixteen. Fearing public exposure, Hammond withdrew from politics, but he soon joined southern intellectuals in arguing that slavery was a positive good rather than a necessary evil.

This proslavery argument intensified in the late 1840s as northern reformers sought to halt the spread of slavery into newly acquired lands in the West. In the early nineteenth century, a thriving trade in enslaved workers had developed between the Upper South and more fertile areas in the Lower South. It bolstered the economy in both regions but also highlighted the brutalities of bondage. With westward expansion, this internal trade in slaves burgeoned.

Solomon Northrup was among tens of thousands of African Americans who endured the ravages of the internal slave trade. Unlike the vast majority, however, Northrup was born free in Minerva, New York, in 1808. His father, Mintus, had been born into slavery but was freed by his owner's will. Once free, Mintus acquired sufficient property to qualify to vote, an impressive achievement for a former slave.

After his marriage to Anne Hampton at the age of twenty-one, Solomon found employment transporting goods along the region's waterways. He was also hired as a fiddle player for local dances, while Anne worked as a cook in neighborhood taverns. In 1834 the couple moved to Saratoga Springs, a tourist haven that provided more job opportunities. There they raised their three children until tragedy struck.

In March 1841, Solomon met two white circus performers who hired him to play fiddle for them on tour. They paid his wages up front and told him to obtain documents proving his free status. After reaching Washington, D.C., however, Northrup was drugged, chained, and sold to James Birch, a notorious slave trader. Northrup was resold in New Orleans to William Ford, whom he later described as a "kind, noble, candid Christian man" who was nonetheless blind "to the inherent wrong at the bottom of the system of Slavery." Ford gave Northrup a new name, Platt, and put him to work as a raftsman while Northrup tried unsuccessfully to get word to his wife.

In 1842 Ford sold "Platt" to a neighbor, John Tibeats, who whipped and abused his workers. When Tibeats attacked his newly acquired slave with an ax, Northrup fought back and fled to Ford's house. His former owner shielded him from Tibeats's wrath and arranged his sale to Edwin Epps, who owned a large cotton plantation. For the next ten years, Northrup worked the fields and played the fiddle at local dances.

Finally, in 1852 Samuel Bass, a Canadian carpenter who openly acknowledged his antislavery views, came to work on Epps's house. Northrup persuaded Bass to send a letter to his wife in Saratoga Springs. Anne Northrup, astonished to hear from her husband after more than a decade, took the letter to lawyer Henry Northrup, the son of Mintus's former owner. After months of legal efforts, Henry traveled to Louisiana and, with the help of a local judge, freed Solomon Northrup in January 1853. ●

both photos: Courtesy of Documenting the American South, The University of North Carolina at Chapel Hill Libraries

THE AMERICAN HISTORIES of Solomon Northrup and James Henry Hammond were both intertwined in the struggle over slavery. By 1850 slave labor had become central to the South's and the nation's economic success, even as slave ownership became concentrated in the hands of a smaller proportion of wealthy white families. The concentration of more slaves on each plantation created a stronger sense of community and a truly African American culture, although it did not negate the brutality of the institution. At the same time, the volatility of the cotton market fueled economic instability, which planters claimed could be resolved only by cultivating more cotton. In response, sympathetic administrations in Washington forcibly removed Indians from the Southeast, supported independence for Texas, and proclaimed war on Mexico. But these policies led to growing conflicts with western Indian nations and heightened political conflicts over slavery and the nation's future.

Planters Expand the Slave System

The cotton gin, developed in the 1790s, ensured the growth of southern agriculture into the 1840s (see chapter 8). As the cotton kingdom spread west, planters forged a distinctive culture around the institution of slavery. But slavery limited the development of cities, technology, and educational institutions, leaving the South increasingly dependent on the North and West for food, industrial goods, commercial resources, books and magazines, and even

higher education. In addition, westward expansion extended the trade in slaves within the South, shattering black families. Still, southern planters viewed themselves as national leaders, both the repository of traditional American values and the engine of economic progress.

A Plantation Society Develops in the South

Plantation slavery existed throughout the Americas in the early nineteenth century. British, French, Dutch, Portuguese, and Spanish colonies in the West Indies and South America all housed large numbers of slaves and extensive plantations. In the U.S. South, however, the volatile cotton market and a scarcity of fertile land kept most plantations relatively small before 1830. But from the early 1840s on, territorial expansion and profits from cotton, as well as from rice and sugar, fueled a period of conspicuous consumption. Successful southern planters now built grand houses and purchased a variety of luxury goods.

South Carolina Plantation

This wood engraving from the mid-nineteenth century depicts a planter's residence on the Cumbee River, South Carolina. When cotton prices began to rise after 1843, leading planters invested more of their profits in fancy houses and luxurious furnishings. They bought expensive clothing and jewelry for their wives and daughters and traveled abroad with their families.   The Granger Collection, New York

As plantations grew, especially in states like South Carolina and Mississippi where slaves outnumbered whites, a wealthy aristocracy sought to ensure productivity by employing harsh methods of discipline. Masters whipped slaves for a variety of offenses, from not picking enough cotton to breaking tools or running away. Although James Henry Hammond imagined himself a progressive master, he used the whip liberally, hoping thereby to ensure that his estate generated sufficient profits to purchase fancy furnishings, trips to Europe, fashionable clothing, and fine jewelry.

Increased attention to comfort and luxury helped make the heavy workload of plantation mistresses tolerable. Although mistresses were idealized for their beauty, piety, and grace, they took on considerable managerial responsibilities. They directed the domestic slaves as well as the feeding, clothing, and medical care of the entire labor force. They were expected to organize and preside over lavish social events, host relatives and friends for extended stays, and direct the plantation in their husband's absence. When James was traveling, Catherine Hammond struggled to manage the estate while caring for their seven children.

Of course, plantation mistresses were relieved of the most arduous labor by enslaved women, who cooked, cleaned, and washed for the family, cared for the children, and even nursed the babies. Wealthy white women benefited from the best education, the greatest access to music and literature, and the finest clothes and furnishings to be had in the region. Yet the pedestal on which plantation mistresses stood was shaky, built on a patriarchal system in which husbands and fathers held substantial power. For example, most wives were forced to ignore the sexual relations that husbands initiated with female slaves. As Mary Boykin Chesnut explained in her diary, "Every lady tells you who is the father of all the Mulatto children in everybody's household, but those in her own, she seems to think drop from the clouds or pretends to think so." In 1850, when Catherine Hammond discovered James's sexual relations with an enslaved mother and daughter, she moved to Charleston with her two youngest daughters. Most wives, however, stayed put, and some took out their anger and frustration on slave women already victimized by their husbands. Moreover, some mistresses owned slaves themselves, traded them on the slave market, and gave them as gifts or bequests to family members and friends.

Not all slaveholders were wealthy planters like the Hammonds, with fifty or more slaves and extensive landholdings. Far more planters in the 1830s and 1840s owned between twenty and fifty slaves, and an even larger number of farmers owned just three to six slaves. These small planters and farmers could not afford to emulate the lives of the largest slave owners. Still, as Hammond wrote a friend in 1847, "The planters here are essentially what the nobility are in other countries. They stand at the head of society & politics."

Urban Life in the Slave South

The insistence on the supremacy of slave owners had broad repercussions. The richest men in the South invested in slaves, land, and household goods, with little left to develop industry, technology, or urban institutions. The largest factory in the South, the Tredegar Iron Works in Richmond, Virginia, was constructed in 1833, and by 1850 it employed several hundred free and enslaved African Americans. Most southern industrialists, however, like South Carolina textile manufacturer William Gregg, employed poor white women and children. But neither Tredegar nor a scattering of textile mills fundamentally reshaped the region's economy.

The South also fell behind in urban development. The main exception was port cities, which boasted fine shops, a growing professional class, and ready access to national and international news. Yet even in Baltimore, Charleston, and Savannah, commerce was often directed by northern agents, especially cotton brokers. In addition, nearly one-third of southern whites had no access to cash and instead bartered goods and services, further restricting the urban economy. In the South, only Baltimore and New Orleans reached a population of 100,000 by 1850.

Despite their relative scarcity, southern cities attracted many free blacks, providing them with the best hope of finding employment and distancing themselves from hostile planters. The growing demand for cheap domestic labor in urban areas and planters' greater willingness to emancipate less valuable single female slaves meant that free black women generally outnumbered men in southern cities. These women worked mainly as washerwomen, cooks, and general domestics, while free black men labored as skilled artisans, dockworkers, or sailors in southern seaports. In these jobs, free blacks competed with slaves and with growing numbers of Irish, German, and Jewish immigrants who flocked to southern cities in the 1840s and 1850s. The presence of immigrants and free blacks and the reputation of ports as escape hatches for runaway slaves ensured that cities remained suspect in the South.

The scarcity of cities and industry also curtailed the development of transportation. State governments and private citizens invested little in roads, canals, and railroads. Most small farmers traded goods locally, and planters used the South's extensive river system to ship goods to commercial hubs. Where rivers did not meet this need, rail lines were sometimes built. However, only Virginia and Maryland, with their proximity to the nation's capital, developed extensive rail networks.

New Orleans, 1841

New Orleans was one of the few major urban areas in the South and, like Baltimore and Charleston, prospered through its seaport. Not only did the port of New Orleans attract sailing ships engaged in foreign commerce, but it was also the destination for steamships carrying goods along the Mississippi River.   Eileen Tweedy/The Art Archive at Art Resource, NY

The Consequences of Slavery's Expansion

Outside the South, industry and agriculture increasingly benefited from technological innovation. Indeed, the booming textile industry in New England fueled the demand for cotton and drove up prices during the 1840s and 1850s. Planters, however, continued to rely on intensive manual labor. Even reform-minded planters focused on fertilizer and crop rotation rather than machines to enhance productivity. The limited use of new technologies—such as iron plows or seed drills—resulted from a lack of investment capital and planters' attitudes toward African American laborers. Believing them to be inherently lazy, ignorant, and untrustworthy, planters refused to purchase expensive equipment that might be broken or purposely sabotaged. Instead, they relied on continually expanding the acreage under cultivation.

One result of these practices was that a declining percentage of white Southerners came to control vast estates with large numbers of enslaved laborers. Between 1830 and 1850, the absolute number of both slaves and owners grew. But slave owners became a smaller proportion of all white Southerners because the white population grew faster than the number of slave owners. At the same time, distinctions among wealthy planters, small slaveholders, and whites who owned no slaves also increased.

The concern with productivity and profits and the concentration of more slaves on large plantations did have some benefits for black women and men. The end of the international slave trade in 1808 forced planters to rely more heavily on natural reproduction to increase their labor force. Thus many planters thought more carefully about how they treated their slaves, who were increasingly viewed as "valuable property." It was no longer good business to work slaves to death, cripple them with severe whippings, or cut off fingers, ears, or other body parts.

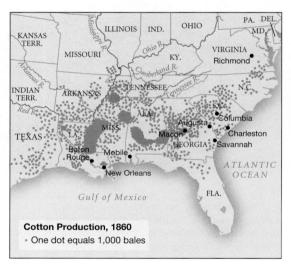

MAP 10.1 The Spread of Slavery and Cotton, 1820–1860

While tobacco, rice, and sugar remained important crops in a few states, cotton became the South's and the nation's major export. The need to find more fertile fields led planters to migrate to Alabama, Mississippi, and Louisiana. As a result of cotton's success, the number of enslaved people increased dramatically, the internal slave trade expanded, and labor demands intensified.

Nonetheless, owners continued to whip slaves with regularity and made paltry investments in diet and health care for enslaved workers. Most slaves lived in small houses with dirt floors and minimal furniture and were given three or four suits of clothes a year despite laboring six days a week. They ate a diet high in calories, especially fats and carbohydrates, but with little meat, fish, fresh vegetables, or fruits. The high mortality rate among slave infants and children—more than twice that of white children to age five—reflected the limits of planters' care.

The spread of slavery into Mississippi, Louisiana, Alabama, Missouri, and Texas affected both white and black families, though again not equally. The younger sons of wealthy planters were often forced to move to the frontier, and their families generally lived in rough quarters on isolated plantations. Such moves were far more difficult for slaves, however. Between 1830 and 1850, more than 440,000 slaves were forced to move from the Upper South to the Lower South (Map 10.1). On the southern frontier, they endured especially harsh conditions as they carved out new cotton fields and rice paddies or planted and harvested sugarcane. Many of these frontier slaves had been torn away from their families and communities.

Explore

See Document 10.1 for one visitor's description of a slave pen in Washington, D.C.

By the 1830s, slave markets blossomed in Richmond, Charleston, Savannah, Natchez, New Orleans, and Washington, D.C. Solomon Northrup described one in Washington, D.C., in 1841 where a woman named Eliza watched as her son Randall was "won" by a planter from Baton Rouge. She promised "to be the most faithful slave that ever lived" if he would also buy her and her daughter. The slave trader threatened the desperate mother with a hundred lashes, but neither his threats nor her tears could change the outcome. As slavery spread westward, such scenes were repeated thousands of times.

DOCUMENT 10.1

Edward Strutt Abdy | Description of Washington, D.C., Slave Pen, 1833

Slavery and the slave trade had always been legal in Washington, D.C., and enslaved laborers cleared land and constructed buildings. As the debate over slavery increased in the nineteenth century, abolitionists often highlighted the incongruence of slavery in the capital city of American democracy. Visitors wrote with disgust about slave auctions held within sight of the Capitol steps. In the 1830s, the English writer Edward Strutt Abdy toured the United States and described the scene at a slave pen.

Explore

How does Abdy describe the construction of the slave pen and its relation to the U.S. Capitol?

How are whites and blacks described?

How might northern and southern audiences have reacted to this description of a slave pen? How might readers in Great Britain, where slavery had just been abolished, have responded?

One day I went to see the "slaves' pen"—a wretched hovel, "right against" the Capitol, from which it is distant about half a mile, with no house intervening. The outside alone is accessible to the eye of a visitor; what passes within being reserved for the exclusive observation of its owner (a man of the name of Robey) and his unfortunate victims. It is surrounded by a wooden paling fourteen or fifteen feet in height, with the posts outside to prevent escape, and separated from the building by a space too narrow to admit of a free circulation of air. At a small window above, which was unglazed and exposed alike to the heat of summer and the cold of winter, so trying to the constitution, two or three sable faces appeared, looking out wistfully to while away the time and catch a refreshing breeze; the weather being extremely hot. In this wretched hovel, all colors, except white—the only guilty one—both sexes, and all ages, are confined, exposed indiscriminately to all the contamination which may be expected in such society and under such seclusion. The inmates of the gaol, of this class I mean, are even worse treated; some of them, if my informants are to be believed, having been actually frozen to death, during the inclement winters which often prevail in the country. While I was in the city, Robey had got possession of a woman, whose term of slavery was limited to six years. It was expected that she would be sold before the expiration of that period, and sent away to a distance, where the assertion of her claim would subject her to ill-usage. Cases of this kind are very common.

Source: Edward Strutt Abdy, *Journal of a Residence and Tour in the United States of North America, from April, 1833, to October, 1834* (London: John Murray, 1835), 2:96–97.

Put It in Context

How did the gradual elimination of slavery in the northern United States and in other parts of the world affect views of slavery in the American South?

REVIEW & RELATE

What role did the planter elite play in southern society and politics?

What were the consequences of the dominant position of slave-based plantation agriculture in the southern economy?

✔ *LEARNINGCurve* bedfordstmartins.com/hewittlawson/LC

Slave Society and Culture

Because slave labor formed the backbone of the southern economy, enslaved workers gained some leverage against owners and overseers. But these women and men did not simply define themselves in relation to whites. They also developed relationships and identities within the slave quarters. By maintaining aspects of African culture, creating strong kinship networks, and embracing religion, southern blacks found ways to lighten their bondage. Many also found small ways to resist their enslavement on an everyday basis. Others resisted more openly, and a small number organized rebellions against their masters.

Slaves Fuel the Southern Economy

The labor of enslaved blacks drove the nation's economy as well as the South's. In 1820 the South produced some 500,000 bales of cotton, much of it exported to England. By 1850 the region produced nearly 3 million bales, feeding textile mills in New England and abroad. A decade later, cotton accounted for nearly two-thirds of the U.S. export trade and added nearly $200 million a year to the American economy.

Carpenters, blacksmiths, and other skilled slaves were sometimes hired out and allowed to keep a small amount of the money they earned. They traveled to nearby households, compared their circumstances to those on other plantations, and sometimes made contact with free blacks. Some skilled slaves also learned to read and write and had access to tools and knowledge denied to field hands. And they were less likely to be sold to slave traders. Still, they were constantly hounded by whites who demanded travel passes and deference, were more acutely aware of alternatives to slavery, and were often suspected of involvement in rebellions.

Household slaves sometimes received old clothes and bedding or leftover food from their owners. Yet they were under the constant surveillance of whites, and women especially were vulnerable to sexual abuse. Moreover, the work they performed was physically demanding. Enslaved women chopped wood, hauled water, baked food, and washed clothes. Fugitive slave James Curry recalled that his mother, a cook in North Carolina, rose early each morning to milk fourteen cows, bake bread, and churn butter. She was responsible for meals for her owners and the slaves. In summer, she cooked her last meal around eight o'clock, after which she milked the cows again. Then she returned to her

HAULING THE WHOLE WEEKS PICKING

Plantation Slaves at Work

Slaves performed a wide variety of labor, such as planting and harvesting crops, domestic work, and carpentry and blacksmithing. These two panels painted by William Henry Brown in about 1842 illustrate slaves hauling a week's worth of picking. Although most tasks were physically demanding, workers who carried goods to market at least had the chance to briefly leave the plantation. The Historic New Orleans Collection, accession no. 1975.93.1 and 1975.93.2

quarters, put her children to bed, and often fell asleep while mending clothes.

Field hands often left their youngest children in the care of cooks and washerwomen. But once slaves reached the age of eleven or twelve, they were put to work full-time. Although field labor was defined by its relentless pace and drudgery, it also brought together large numbers of slaves for the entire day and thus helped forge bonds among laborers on the same plantation. Songs provided a rhythm for their work and offered slaves the chance to communicate their frustrations or their hopes.

Field labor was generally organized by task or by gang. Under the task system, typical on rice plantations, a slave could return to his or her quarters once the day's task was completed. This left time for some slaves to cultivate gardens, fish for supper, make quilts, or repair furniture. In the gang system, widely used on cotton plantations, men and women worked in groups under the supervision of a driver and swept across fields hoeing, planting, or picking.

Developing an African American Culture

Amid hard work and harsh treatment, slaves created social bonds and a rich culture of their own. Thus blacks in America continued to employ African names, like Cuffee and Binah, generations after their enslavement. Even if masters gave them English names, they might use African names in the slave quarters to sustain family and community networks and memories. Some also retained elements of West African languages. Along the South Carolina and Georgia coast, enslaved workers spoke Gullah, a dialect that combined African words and speech patterns with English. Agricultural techniques, medical practices, forms of dress, folktales, songs and musical instruments, dances, and courtship rituals—all demonstrated the continued importance of West African and Caribbean culture to African Americans. This **syncretic culture**, which combined elements from Africa and the Caribbean with those from the United States, was disseminated as slaves hauled cotton to market, forged families across plantation boundaries, or were sold farther south. It was also handed down across generations through storytelling, music, rituals, and religious services.

Religious practices offer an important example of syncretic cultural forms. Africans from Muslim communities often continued to pray to Allah even if they were also required to attend Protestant churches. Black preachers who embraced Christianity developed rituals that combined African and American elements. In the early nineteenth century, slaves eagerly embraced the evangelical teachings offered by Baptist and Methodist preachers, which echoed some of the expressive spiritual forms in West Africa. By midcentury, African Americans made up one-third of Baptist and perhaps one-quarter of Methodist church membership. On Sunday mornings, slaves might listen to white ministers proclaim that slavery was God's will; that evening, they might gather in the woods to hear their own preachers tell of God's love and the possibilities of black liberation, at least in the hereafter. Slaves often incorporated drums, conch shells, dancing, or other West African elements into these worship services.

Although most black preachers were men, a few women gained a spiritual following in slave communities. Many female slaves embraced religion enthusiastically, hoping that Christian baptism might substitute for West African rituals that protected newborn babies. Enslaved women also called on church authorities to intervene when white owners or overseers or even enslaved men abused them. They also considered the church one means of sanctifying slave marriages that were not recognized legally.

Slaves also generally provided health care for their community. Most slave births were attended by black midwives, and African American healers often turned to herbal medicines, having discovered southern equivalents to cures used in West Africa. Forced to labor in the fields, gather branches and roots in the forest, and supplement their meager rations with local plants, slaves were far more attuned to the natural world than were their owners.

Resistance and Rebellion

Many owners worried that black preachers and West African folktales inspired blacks to resist enslavement. Fearing defiance, planters went to incredible lengths to control seemingly powerless slaves. Although they were largely successful in quelling open revolts, they were unable to eliminate more subtle forms of opposition, like slowing the pace of work, feigning illness, and damaging white-owned equipment, food, and clothing. Even slaves' ability to sustain a distinct African American culture was viewed by some planters as undermining the institution of bondage. More overt forms of resistance—such as truancy and running away, which disrupted work and lowered profits—also proved impossible to stamp out.

The forms of everyday resistance slaves employed varied in part on their location and resources. Skilled artisans, mostly men, could do more substantial damage because they used more expensive tools, but they were less able to protect themselves through pleas of ignorance. Field laborers could damage only hoes and a few cotton

Nat Turner's Rebellion

This woodcut depicts the rebellion in the top panel and the capture of rebels below. It was published in 1831 by Samuel Warner, a New York publisher who based his lurid account on eyewitness testimony and the supposed confessions of participants. He linked the Turner rebellion to the Haitian Revolution and to suspected (though unproven) conspiracies elsewhere in the South.   Library of Congress

plants, but they could do so on a regular basis without exciting suspicion. House slaves could burn dinners, scorch shirts, break china and glassware, and even poison owners or burn down houses. Often considered the most loyal slaves, they were also among the most feared because of their intimate contact with white families. Single male slaves were the most likely to run away, planning their escape carefully to get as far as possible before their owners noticed they were missing. Women who fled plantations were more likely to hide out for short periods in the local area and return at night to get food and visit family. Eventually, isolation, hunger, or concern for children led most of these truants to return if slave patrols did not find them first.

Despite their rarity, efforts to organize slave uprisings, such as that planned by Gabriel (see chapter 8) and the one supposedly hatched by Denmark Vesey (see chapter 9) in the early nineteenth century, continued to haunt southern whites. Rebellions in the West Indies, especially the one in Saint Domingue, also echoed through the early nineteenth century. Then in 1831 a seemingly obedient slave named Nat Turner organized a revolt in rural Virginia that stunned whites across the South. Turner was a self-styled preacher and religious visionary who believed that God had given him a mission. On the night of August 21, he and his followers killed their owners, the Travis family, and then headed to nearby plantations in Southampton County. The bloody insurrection led to the deaths of 57 white men, women, and children and liberated more than 50 slaves. But on August 22, outraged white militiamen burst on the scene and eventually captured the black rebels. Turner managed to hide out for two months but was eventually caught. Tried and convicted on November 5, he was hanged six days later. Virginia executed 55 other African Americans suspected of assisting Turner. White mobs also beat, tortured, or killed some 200 more blacks with no connection to the rebellion.

Nat Turner's rebellion instilled panic among white Southerners, who now worried they might be killed in their sleep by a seemingly submissive slave. News of the uprising traveled through slave communities as well, inspiring both pride and anxiety. The execution of Turner and his followers reminded African Americans how far whites would go to protect the institution of slavery.

REVIEW & RELATE

How did enslaved African Americans create ties of family, community, and culture?

How did enslaved African Americans resist efforts to control and exploit their labor?

LEARNINGCurve bedfordstmartins.com/hewittlawson/LC

Planters Tighten Control

Fears of rebellion led to stricter regulations of black life, and actual uprisings temporarily reinforced white solidarity. Yet yeomen farmers, poor whites, and middle-class professionals all voiced some doubts about the ways in which human bondage affected southern society. To unite these disparate groups, planters wielded their economic and political authority, highlighted bonds of kinship and religious fellowship, and promoted an ideology of white supremacy. Their efforts intensified as northern states and other nations began eradicating slavery.

Harsher Treatment for Southern Blacks

Slave revolts led many southern states to impose harsher controls; however, Nat Turner's rebellion led some white Virginians to question slavery itself. In December 1831, the state Assembly established a special committee to consider the crisis. Representatives from western counties, where slavery was never profitable, argued for the gradual abolition of slavery and the colonization of the state's black population in Africa. Hundreds of women in the region sent petitions to the Virginia legislature supporting these positions. But slaveholders from eastern districts claimed that even discussing emancipation might encourage blacks who observed the Assembly's debates to rebel.

Advocates of colonization gained significant support, but the state's leading intellectuals spoke out adamantly for the benefits of slavery. Professor Thomas Dew, president of the College of William and Mary, emphasized the advantages for planters and slaves alike. Dew claimed that slaveholders performed godly work in raising Africans from the status of brute beast to civilized Christian. Dew's proslavery argument turned the tide, and in the fall of 1832 the Virginia legislature rejected gradual emancipation and imposed new restrictions on slaves and free blacks.

Explore

See Documents 10.2 and 10.3 for opposing views on abolition in Virginia.

From the 1820s to the 1840s, more stringent codes were passed across the South. Most southern legislatures prohibited owners from manumitting their slaves, made it illegal for whites to teach slaves to read or write, limited the size and number of independent black churches, abolished slaves' already-limited access to courts, outlawed slave marriage, banned antislavery literature as obscene, defined rape as a crime only against white women, and outlawed assemblies of more than three blacks without a white person present.

States also regulated the lives of free blacks. Some prohibited free blacks from residing within their borders, others required large bonds to ensure good behavior, and most forbade free blacks who left the state from returning. The homes of free blacks could be raided at any time on suspicion of possessing stolen goods or harboring runaways, and the children of free black women were subject to stringent apprenticeship laws that kept many in virtual slavery.

Planters, aided by state legislatures and local authorities, proved largely successful in controlling slaves, but there was a price to pay. Laws to regulate black life tended to restrict education, mobility, and urban development for southern whites as well. Such laws also characterized the region's primary labor force as savage, heathen, and lazy,

hardly a basis for sustained economic development. And the regulations increased tensions between poorer whites, who were often responsible for enforcement, and wealthy whites, who benefited most clearly from their imposition.

White Southerners without Slaves

Yeomen farmers, independent landowners who did not own any slaves, had a complex relationship with the South's plantation economy. Many were related to slave owners, and they often depended on planters to ship their crops to market. Some hoped to rise into the ranks of slaveholders one day, and others made extra money by hiring themselves out to planters. Yet yeomen farmers also recognized that their economic interests often diverged from those of planters. As growing numbers gained the right to vote in the 1820s and 1830s, they voiced their concerns in county and state legislatures.

Most yeomen farmers believed in slavery, but they sometimes challenged planters' authority and assumptions. In the Virginia slavery debates, small farmers from western districts advocated gradual abolition. In other states, they advocated more liberal policies toward debtors and the protection of fishing rights. Yeomen farmers also questioned certain ideals embraced by elites. Although plantation mistresses considered manual labor beneath them, the wives and daughters of many small farmers had to work in the fields, haul water, chop wood, and perform other arduous tasks. Still, yeomen farmers' ability to diminish planter control was limited by the continued importance of cotton to the southern economy.

In their daily life, however, many small farmers depended more on friends and neighbors than on the planter class. Barn raisings, corn shuckings, quilting bees, and other collective endeavors offered them the chance to combine labor with sociability. Church services and church socials also brought communities together. Farmers lost such ties when they sought better land on the frontier. There, families struggled to establish new crops and new lives in relative isolation but hoped that fertile fields might offer the best chance to rise within the South's rigid class hierarchy.

One step below the yeomen farmers were the even larger numbers of white Southerners who owned no property at all. These poor whites depended on hunting and fishing in frontier areas, performing day labor on farms and plantations, or working on docks or as servants in southern cities. Poor whites competed with free blacks and slaves for employment and often harbored resentments as a result. Yet they also built alliances based on their shared economic plight. Poor immigrants from Ireland, Wales, and Scotland were especially hostile to American planters, who reminded them of English landlords.

DOCUMENTS 10.2 AND 10.3

Debating Slavery: Two Views

Nat Turner's rebellion in Southampton, Virginia, sparked discussions about slavery nationwide. In Virginia, the General Assembly debated whether to gradually abolish slavery in the state. Arguments for and against abolition flooded the legislature. Although they never mentioned Nat Turner by name, women in Augusta County indicated the ways in which his revolt had intensified their fears, and they concluded that eliminating slavery was the only way to ensure their safety. Slavery proponents had no more forceful advocate than Thomas Dew, president of the College of William and Mary, who argued that slavery was beneficial for slaves and their owners. The Virginia legislature took no action on the issue of emancipation and instead passed laws that further restricted free and enslaved blacks in Virginia.

Explore

10.2 Memorial of the Ladies of Augusta to the Virginia General Assembly, January 19, 1832

We pretend not to conceal from [you], our fathers & brothers, our protectors . . . , the fears which agitate our bosoms, and the dangers which await us, as revealed to us by recent tragical deeds; our fears, we admit, [are] great, but we do not concede that they are the effects of blind & unreflecting cowardice: we do not concede that they spring from the superstitious timidity of our sex. Alas! . . . we appeal to your manly reason, to your more matured wisdom, to attest the justice & propriety of our fears, when we call to your remembrance the late slaughter of our sisters & their little ones in certain parts of our land, & the strong probability, that that slaughter was but a partial execution of a widely projected scheme of carnage. We know not, we cannot know the right, nor the unguarded moments, by day or by night, which is pregnant with our destruction & that of our husbands & brothers, & sisters & children; but we do know that we are at every moment, exposed to the means of our own excision & of all that is dear to us in life. The bloody monster which threatens us is warmed & cherished on our own hearths. O hear our prayer & remove it, ye protectors of our persons, ye guardians of our peace!

Our fears teach us to reflect & reason: and our reflections & reasonings have taught us that the peace of our homes, the welfare of society, the prosperity of future generations call aloud & imperatively for some decisive & efficient measure—and that measure cannot, we believe, be decisively efficient, or of much benefit if it have not, for its ultimate object, the extinction of slavery from amongst us.

Source: Virginia General Assembly, Legislative Petitions: Petition of the Females of Augusta County, 19 January 1832, Accession 36121, State Records Collection, The Library of Virginia, Richmond, Virginia.

Some poor whites remained in the same community for decades, establishing themselves on the margins of society. They attended church regularly, performed day labor for affluent families, and taught their children to defer to their betters. In Savannah and other southern cities, wealthy families organized benevolent associations and more affluent immigrants established mutual aid societies to help poorer members of their community in hard times. It was the most respectable among this downtrodden class who had the best chance of securing assistance.

Other poor whites moved frequently and survived by combining legal and illegal ventures. Some rejected laws and customs established by elites and joined forces with blacks or other poor whites. These men and women often had few ties to local communities, little religious training or education, and settled scores with violence. Although poor whites unnerved southern elites by flouting the law and sometimes befriending poor blacks, they could not mount any significant challenge to planter control.

Explore

10.3 Thomas Dew | The Proslavery Argument, 1832

Every one acquainted with southern slaves knows that the slave rejoices in the elevation and prosperity of his master; and the heart of no one is more gladdened at the successful debut of young master or miss on the great theatre of the world than that of either the young slave who has grown up with them and shared in all their sports, and even partaken of all their delicacies—or the aged one who has looked on and watched them from birth to manhood, with the kindest and most affectionate solicitude, and has ever met from them all the kind treatment and generous sympathies of feeling, tender hearts. Judge Smith, in his able speech on Foote's Resolutions in the Senate, said, in an emergency, he would rely upon his own slaves for his defence—he would put arms into their hands, and he had no doubt they would defend him faithfully. In the late Southampton insurrection, we know that many actually convened their slaves and armed them for defence, although slaves were here the cause of the evil which was to be repelled.

Source: William Harper, James Henry Hammond, William Gilmore Simms, and Thomas Roderick Dew, *The Pro-Slavery Argument* (Philadelphia: Lippincott, Grambo, 1853), 457–58.

Interpret the Evidence

- On what grounds do the women of Augusta County argue for an end to slavery, and how does their petition reflect their status as women?
- Why does Dew argue that slavery is beneficial for slaves? How do you think the Augusta women would respond to Dew's arguments?

Put It in Context

What do these statements convey about the divide over slavery in Virginia following Nat Turner's rebellion?

Unlike poor whites, the South's small but growing middle class sought stability and respectability. These middle-class Southerners, who worked as doctors, lawyers, journalists, teachers, and shopkeepers, often looked to the North for models to emulate. Many were educated in northern schools and developed ties with their commercial or professional counterparts in northern cities. They were avid readers of newspapers, religious tracts, and literary periodicals published in the North. And like middle-class Northerners, southern businessmen often depended on their wives' social and financial skills to succeed.

Nonetheless, middle-class southern men shared many of the social attitudes and political priorities of slave owners. They participated alongside planters in benevolent associations, literary and temperance (antialcohol) societies, and agricultural reform organizations. Most middle-class Southerners also adamantly supported slavery and benefited from planters' demands for goods and services. In

Gentlemen's Fashions

The owner of Welch's clothing store was among Charleston's well-known entrepreneurs. With this ad he appealed to middle-class men visiting the city on business as well as local residents, who he assumed shared a common sense of proper dress. The ad declares that Danskin's Pattern shirts received the "commendation of gentlemen in all parts of the United States." Courtesy, David M. Rubenstein Rare Book & Manuscript Library, Duke University, Durham, North Carolina

fact, some suggested that bound labor might be as useful to industry as it was to agriculture, and they sought to expand the institution further. Despite the emergence of a small middle class, however, the gap between rich and poor continued to expand in the South.

Planters Seek to Unify Southern Whites

Planters faced another challenge as nations in Europe and South America began to abolish slavery. Antislavery views, first expressed by a few Enlightenment thinkers and Quakers, gained growing support among evangelical

Protestants in Great Britain and the United States and among political radicals in Europe. Slave rebellions in Saint Domingue (Haiti) and the British West Indies in the early nineteenth century intensified these efforts. In 1807 the British Parliament forbade the sale of slaves within its empire and in 1834 emancipated all those who remained enslaved. France followed suit in 1848. As Spanish colonies such as Mexico and Nicaragua gained their independence in the 1820s and 1830s, they, too, eradicated the institution. Meanwhile gradual abolition laws in the northern United States slowly eliminated slavery there. Although slavery continued in Brazil and in Spanish colonies such as Cuba and serfdom remained in Russia, international attitudes toward human bondage were shifting.

In response, planters wielded their political and economic power to forge tighter bonds among white Southerners. According to the three-fifths compromise in the U.S. Constitution, areas with large slave populations gained more representatives in Congress than those without. The pattern held for state elections, too. In addition, well-educated planters and their allies were the likeliest candidates for office and the most successful. Planters also used their resources to provide credit for those in need, offer seasonal employment for poorer whites, transport crops to market for yeomen farmers, and contribute food, clothing, and other goods in times of crisis. Few poorer whites could afford to antagonize these affluent benefactors.

Wealthy planters also emphasized ties of family and faith. James Hammond, for example, assisted his siblings and other family members financially throughout their lives. Many slave owners also worshipped alongside their less well-to-do neighbors, and both the pastor and the congregation benefited from maintaining good relations with the wealthiest congregants. Many church members, like many relatives and neighbors, genuinely admired and respected planter elites who looked out for them.

Still, planters did not take white solidarity for granted. From the 1830s on, they relied on the ideology of white supremacy to cement the belief that all whites, regardless of class or education, were superior to all blacks. Following on Thomas Dew, southern elites argued with growing vehemence that the moral and intellectual failings of blacks meant that slavery was not just a necessary evil but actually a positive good. At the same time, they insisted that blacks harbored deep animosity toward whites, which could be controlled only by regulating every aspect of their lives. Combining racial fear and racial pride, planters forged bonds with poor and middling whites to guarantee their continued dominance. They also sought support from officials in the nation's capital.

REVIEW & RELATE

- What groups made up white southern society? How did their interests overlap? How did they diverge?

- How and why did the planter elite seek to reinforce white solidarity?

✓ *LEARNINGCurve* bedfordstmartins.com/hewittlawson/LC

Democrats Face Political and Economic Crises

Southern planters depended on federal power to expand and sustain the system of slavery. Although President Andrew Jackson disappointed slave owners on issues such as the tariff and states' rights, he stood with them on the policies of Indian removal and independence for Texas. Jackson's successor in the White House, Martin Van Buren, continued his predecessor's Indian policies and his support for the Republic of Texas. But Van Buren faced a more well-organized opposition in the **Whig Party**, which formed in the 1830s, while Texas rebels faced powerful resistance from Mexican and Comanche forces. Then in 1837 a prolonged and severe economic panic gripped the nation, creating an opportunity for the Whigs to end Democratic control of the federal government.

Continued Conflicts over Indian Lands

In 1830 Congress had passed the Indian Removal Act in hopes of settling the powerful Cherokee and Seminole tribes on land west of the Mississippi River. Not all Indian peoples went peacefully. As federal authorities forcibly removed the majority of Seminoles to Indian Territory between 1832 and 1835, a minority fought back. Jackson and his military commanders expected that this **Second Seminole War** would be short-lived. However, they misjudged the Seminoles' strength; the power of their charismatic leader, Osceola; and the resistance of African American fugitives living among the Seminoles. Hundreds of southern slaves had fled to Florida in the early nineteenth century seeking freedom. Some married Seminole women, while others were reenslaved by Seminole Indians. But the Seminoles treated slaves with more leniency than did southern whites, allowing them to live on small farms with their own families and enjoy

many of the rights of full members of the tribe. Thus free and enslaved blacks fought fiercely against Seminole removal.

The war continued long after Jackson left the presidency. During the seven-year guerrilla war, 1,600 U.S. troops died and the government spent more than $30 million. U.S. military forces defeated the Seminoles in 1842 only by luring Osceola into an army camp with false promises of a peace settlement. Instead, officers took him captive, finally breaking the back of the resistance. Still, to end the conflict, the U.S. government had to allow fugitive slaves living among the Seminoles to accompany the tribe to Indian Territory.

Members of the Cherokee nation also resisted removal, but they fought their battles in the arena of public opinion and in the courts. Throughout the early nineteenth century, growing numbers of Cherokees had embraced "Americanization" programs offered by white missionaries, educators, and government agents. John Ross and other Indian leaders urged Cherokee people to accommodate to white ways, believing it was the best means to ensure the continued control of their own communities. When Georgia officials sought to impose new regulations on the Cherokees living within the state's borders, tribal leaders took them to court and sought to use evidence of their Christianity, domesticity, and republican government to maintain their rights.

In 1831 *Cherokee Nation v. Georgia* reached the Supreme Court, where Indian leaders demanded recognition as a separate nation as stipulated in the U.S. Constitution. Chief Justice John Marshall spoke for the majority when he ruled that all Indians in the United States were "domestic dependent nations" rather than fully sovereign governments. The Court thus denied a central part of the Cherokees' claim. Yet the following year, in *Worcester v. Georgia*, Marshall and the Court declared that the state of Georgia could not impose *state* laws on the Cherokees, for they had "territorial boundaries, within which their authority is exclusive," and that both their land and their rights were protected by the federal government.

President Jackson held a distinctly different view. He argued that only the removal of the Cherokees west of the Mississippi River could ensure their "physical comfort," "political advancement," and "moral improvement." Most southern whites agreed because they sought to expand cotton production into fertile Cherokee fields. But Protestant women and men in the North launched a massive petition campaign in 1830 supporting the Cherokees' right to their land. The Cherokees themselves forestalled action through Jackson's second term, but many federal and state officials continued to press for the tribe's removal.

Explore

Read a petition from Cherokee women resisting their removal in Document 10.4.

DOCUMENT 10.4

Petition of the Women's Councils to the Cherokee National Council, 1831

Throughout the early nineteenth century, Cherokee women fought against land cessions and removal and argued for communal land use rather than individual allotments. Traditionally, land and political authority passed through the mother's line, but as the Cherokee people adopted Anglo-American ways, patrilineal descent and men's authority replaced this matrilineal system. Despite this change, Cherokee women continued to petition the Cherokee National Council, urging the council to resist land cessions and removal. The following excerpt comes from an 1831 petition.

Explore

To the Committee and Council,

We the females, residing in Salequoree and Pine Log, believing that the present difficulties and embarrassments under which this nation is placed demands a full expression of the mind of every individual, on the subject of emigrating to Arkansas, would take upon ourselves to address you. Although it is not common for our sex to take part in public measures, we nevertheless feel justified in expressing our sentiments on any subject where our interest is as much at stake as any other part of the community.

We believe the present plan of the General Government to effect our removal West of the Mississippi, and thus obtain our lands for the use of the State of Georgia, to be highly oppressive, cruel, and unjust. And we sincerely hope there is no consideration which can induce our citizens to forsake the land of our fathers of which they have been in possession from time immemorial, and thus compel us, against our will, to undergo the toils and difficulties of removing with our helpless families hundreds of miles to unhealthy and unproductive country. We hope therefore the Committee and Council will take into deep consideration our deplorable situation, and do everything in their power to avert such a state of things. And we trust by a prudent course their transactions with the General Government will enlist in our behalf the sympathies of the good people of the United States.

Source: *Cherokee Phoenix*, November 12, 1831, in *The Cherokee Removal: A Brief History with Documents*, 2nd ed., ed. Theda Purdue and Michael Green (Boston: Bedford/St. Martin's, 2005), 134.

Interpret the Evidence

- On what grounds did the women protest Cherokee removal?
- How did the women use references to their gender to inspire sympathy and support from council members?

Put It in Context

What light does the petition shed on the women's understanding of the politics and government of the United States?

In December 1835, U.S. officials convinced a small group of Cherokee men—without tribal sanction—to sign the **Treaty of New Echota**. It proposed the exchange of 100 million acres of Cherokee land in the Southeast for $68 million and 32 million acres in Indian Territory. Cherokee leaders, including John Ross, lobbied Congress to reject the treaty, but to no avail. In May 1836, Congress approved the treaty by a single vote and set the date for final removal two years later. Although most of the

17,000 Cherokees resisted this plan, they had few means left to defy the U.S. government (Map 10.2).

In May 1838, the U.S. army began to forcibly remove any Cherokee who had not yet resettled in Indian Territory. General Winfield Scott, assisted by 7,000 U.S. soldiers, forced some 15,000 Cherokees into forts and military camps that June. The Cherokees spent the next several months without sufficient food, water, sanitation, or medicine. The situation went from bad to worse. In

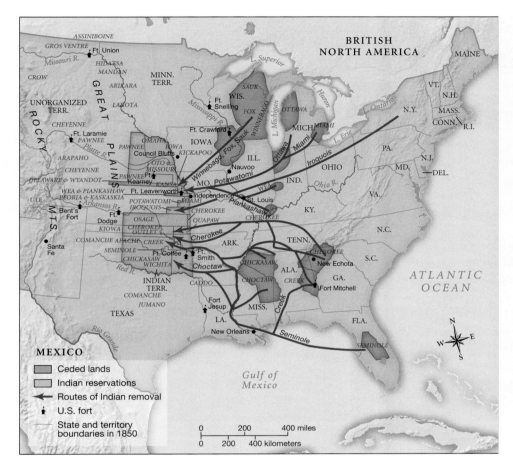

MAP 10.2   Indian Removals and Relocations, 1820s–1850s

In the 1820s and 1830s, the federal government used a variety of tactics, including military force, to expel Indian nations residing east of the Mississippi River. As these tribes resettled in the West, white migration along the Oregon and other trails began to increase. The result, by 1850, was the forced relocation of many western Indian nations as well.

October, when the Cherokees began the march west, torrential rains were followed by snow. Although the U.S. army planned for a trip of less than three months, the journey actually took five months. As supplies ran short, many Indians, weakened by disease and hunger, died, including Ross's wife. The remaining Cherokees completed this **Trail of Tears**, as it became known, in March 1839. But thousands remained near starvation a year later.

The Battle for Texas

While whites in Georgia sought Cherokee land, those on the frontier looked toward Texas. Some Southerners had moved into Texas in the early nineteenth century, but the Adams-Onís Treaty of 1819 guaranteed Spanish control of the territory. Then in 1821 Mexicans overthrew Spanish rule and claimed Texas as part of the new Republic of Mexico. But Mexicans, like the Spaniards before them, faced serious competition from Comanche Indians, who controlled vast areas to the north and west and launched raids into Texas for horses and other livestock.

Eager to increase settlement in the area and to create a buffer against the Comanches, the Mexican government granted U.S. migrants some of the best land in eastern Texas. It hoped these settlers—many of whom brought slaves to cultivate cotton—would eventually spread into the interior, where Comanche raids had devastated Mexican communities. To entice more Southerners, the Mexican government negotiated a special exemption for U.S. planters when it outlawed slavery in 1829. But rather than spreading into the interior, U.S. farmers and planters stayed east of the Colorado River, out of reach of Comanche raiders and close to U.S. markets in Louisiana.

While the Mexican residents of Texas developed a vibrant Tejano culture that combined Catholicism, Spanish language and culture, and indigenous customs, U.S. settlers resisted acculturation. Instead, they continued to worship as Protestants, speak English, send their children to separate schools, and trade mainly with the United States. By 1835 the 27,000 white Southerners and their 3,000 slaves far outnumbered the 3,000 Mexicans living in eastern Texas.

Comanche Lodge
George Catlin's painting of a buffalo-skin lodge in the mid-1830s shows Little Spaniard, of mixed Spanish and Indian heritage, arriving in camp. The introduction of horses on the Great Plains allowed nomadic hunters like the Comanches, who had relied on dogs to transport the poles and covers of their tepees, to live in much bigger and heavier shelters.   Smithsonian American Art Museum, Washington, DC/Art Resource, NY

Forming a majority of the east Texas population and eager to expand their plantations and trade networks, growing numbers of U.S. settlers demanded independence. **See Document Project 10: Claiming Texas, page 319**. Then in 1836 Mexicans elected a strong nationalist leader, General Antonio López de Santa Anna, as president. He sought to rein in **Tejanos** angered over their vulnerability to Comanche attacks and to curb American settlers seeking further concessions. When Santa Anna appointed a military commander to rule Texas, independence-minded U.S. migrants organized a rebellion. On March 2, they declared eastern Texas an independent republic and adopted a constitution that legalized slavery. Some elite Tejanos, long neglected by authorities in Mexico City, sided with the rebels. The rebellion appeared to be short-lived, however. On March 6, 1836, General Santa Anna crushed settlers defending the **Alamo** in San Antonio. His troops killed all 250 men at the fort but freed the women and children. Soon thereafter, Santa Anna captured the U.S. settlement at Goliad.

Although Santa Anna's troops suffered more than 1,500 casualties, several times those of the rebel forces, the general was convinced that the uprising was over. But the U.S. government, despite its claims of neutrality, aided the rebels with funds and army officers. Newspapers in New Orleans and New York picked up the story of the Alamo and published dramatic accounts of the battle, describing the Mexican fighters as brutal butchers bent on saving Texas for the pope. These stories, though more fable than fact, increased popular support for the war at a time when many Americans were growing increasingly hostile to Catholic immigrants in the United States.

As hundreds of armed volunteers headed to Texas, General Sam Houston led rebel forces in a critical victory at San Jacinto in April 1836. While the Mexican government refused to recognize rebel claims, it did not try to regain the lost ground in east Texas. Few of the U.S. volunteers arrived in time to participate in the fighting, but some settled in the newly liberated region. Still, the failure of Santa Anna to recognize Texan independence kept the

U.S. government from granting the territory statehood for fear it would lead to war with Mexico. Fortunately for the rebels, the Comanche nation did recognize the Republic of Texas and developed trade relations with residents to gain access to the vast U.S. market.

Meanwhile President Jackson worried that admitting a new slave state might split the national Democratic Party just before the fall elections. To limit debate on the issue, Congress passed a **gag rule** in March 1836 that tabled all antislavery petitions without being read. Nevertheless, thousands of women and men from Ohio to Massachusetts still flooded the House of Representatives with petitions opposing the annexation of Texas.

Van Buren and the Panic of 1837

With Jackson suffering from tuberculosis, the Democratic convention chose Vice President Martin Van Buren to run for president in 1836. The Whigs hoped to defeat Van Buren by bringing together diverse supporters: financiers and commercial farmers who advocated internal improvements and protective tariffs; merchants and manufacturers who favored a national bank; evangelical Protestants who objected to Jackson's Indian policy; and Southerners who were antagonized by the president's heavy-handed use of federal authority. But these disparate interests led the Whigs to nominate three different men for president, and this lack of unity allowed Democrats to fend off an increasingly powerful opposition. Although Van Buren won the popular vote by only a small margin (50.9 percent), he secured an easy majority in the electoral college.

Inaugurated on March 4, 1837, President Van Buren soon faced another crisis that threatened the Democrats' hold on power. The **panic of 1837** started in the South and was rooted in the changing fortunes of American cotton in Great Britain. During the 1830s, the British invested heavily in cotton plantations and brokerage firms, and southern planters used the funds to expand cotton production and improve shipping facilities. British banks also lent large sums to states such as New York to fund internal improvements. This infusion of British money into the U.S. economy fueled inflation, and in February 1837 rising prices prompted protests by farmers and workers. But worse problems lay ahead.

In late 1836, the Bank of England, faced with bad harvests and declining demand for textiles, had tightened credit to limit the flow of money out of the country. This forced British investors to call in their loans and drove up interest rates in the United States just as cotton prices started to fall. Some of the largest American cotton merchants were forced to declare bankruptcy. The banks

where they held accounts then failed—ninety-eight of them in March and April 1837 alone.

The economic crisis hit the South hard. Cotton prices fell by nearly half in less than a year. Land values declined dramatically, many southern whites lost farms and homes, port cities came to a standstill, and cotton communities on the southern frontier collapsed. The damage soon radiated throughout the United States. Northern brokers, shippers, and merchants were devastated by losses in the cotton trade, and northern banks were hit by unpaid debts incurred for canals and other internal improvements. Entrepreneurs who borrowed money to expand their businesses defaulted in large numbers. Shopkeepers, artisans, and farmers in the North and Midwest suffered unemployment and foreclosures.

Many Americans, especially in the North and West, blamed Jackson's war against the Bank of the United States for precipitating the panic. They were also outraged at Van Buren's refusal to intervene in the crisis. Probably no federal policy could have resolved the problems created by the "credit bubble," which had been brought on by the ready availability of British money. Still, the president's apparent disinterest in the plight of the people inspired harsh criticisms from ordinary citizens as well as political opponents. Worse, despite brief signs of recovery in 1838, the depression deepened in 1839 and continued for four more years.

The Whigs Win the White House

Van Buren was clearly vulnerable as he faced reelection in 1840. Eager to exploit the Democrats' weakness, the Whig Party organized its first national convention that fall and united behind military hero William Henry Harrison (see chapter 9). Harrison was born to a wealthy planter family in Virginia, but the sixty-eight-year-old soldier was portrayed as a self-made man who lived in a simple log cabin in Indiana. His running mate, John Tyler, another Virginia gentleman and a onetime Democrat, joined the Whigs because of his opposition to Jackson's stand on nullification. Whig leaders hoped he would attract southern voters. Taking their cue from the Democrats, the Whigs organized rallies, barbecues, parades, and mass meetings. They turned the tables on their foe by portraying Van Buren as an aristocrat who enjoyed fine wines and expensive clothes and Harrison as the hero of the common man. Reminding voters that Harrison had defeated Tenskwatawa at the Battle of Tippecanoe, the Whigs adopted the slogan "Tippecanoe and Tyler Too."

Explore

See Document 10.5 for a poster from Harrison's "log cabin" campaign.

DOCUMENT 10.5

William Henry Harrison Campaign Poster, 1840

The 1840 presidential campaign pitted the incumbent Martin Van Buren against William Henry Harrison. Harrison, the Whig Party candidate, was portrayed as a man from humble origins even though he was the son of a wealthy Virginia planter. His campaign slogan "Tippecanoe and Tyler Too" highlighted his military background and leadership in the defeat of Tenskwatawa at the Battle of Tippecanoe. The campaign was a rousing success, and Harrison and his running mate, John Tyler, handily defeated Van Buren with 53 percent of the popular vote.

Explore

Library of Congress

Interpret the Evidence

• What impression of Harrison and his background was the poster meant to convey?
• What characteristics does the poster associate with the "common man" and, by extension, Harrison?

Put It in Context

How does this poster illustrate the democratization of American politics in the first half of the nineteenth century?

The Whigs also welcomed women into the campaign. By 1840 thousands of women had circulated petitions against Cherokee removal, organized temperance societies, promoted religious revivals, and joined charitable associations. They embodied the kind of moral force that the Whig Party claimed to represent. In October 1840, Whig senator Daniel Webster spoke to a gathering of 1,200 women. He praised women's moral virtues and asked audience members to encourage their brothers and husbands to vote for Harrison.

The Whig strategy paid off handsomely on election day when some 80 percent of eligible voters cast ballots. Harrison won easily, and the Whigs gained a majority in Congress. Yet the election's promise was shattered when "old Tippecanoe" died of pneumonia a month after his inauguration. Whigs in Congress now had to deal with John Tyler, whose sentiments were largely southern and Democratic. Frustrating Whig plans for reform with vetoes, Tyler allowed the Democratic Party to regroup and set the stage for close elections in 1844 and 1848.

REVIEW & RELATE

How and why did Indian nations in the Southeast resist removal to the West while some Indians in the West forged ties with U.S. markets?

What events and developments led to a Whig victory in the election of 1840?

 LEARNINGCurve bedfordstmartins.com/hewittlawson/LC

The National Government Looks to the West

Despite the Whig victory in 1840, planters wielded considerable clout in Washington, D.C., because of the importance of cotton to the U.S. economy. In turn, Southerners needed federal support to expand into more fertile areas. The presidential election of 1844 turned on this issue, with Democratic candidate James K. Polk demanding continued expansion into Oregon and Mexico. Once Polk was in office, his claims were contested not only by Britain and Mexico but also by the Comanches, who controlled the southern plains. After the United States won vast Mexican territories in 1848, conflicts with Indians and debates over slavery only intensified.

Expanding to Oregon and Texas

Southerners eager to expand the plantation economy looked not only to the West for additional lands but also

to Cuba and Nicaragua in the 1830s and 1840s. Although efforts to capture these areas failed, planters continued to press for expansion. Yet expansion was not merely a southern strategy. Northerners demanded that the United States renounce its joint occupation of the Oregon Country with Great Britain. And some northern politicians and businessmen believed that acquisition of lands in Hawaii and Samoa could benefit U.S. trade. In 1844 the Democratic Party built on these expansionist dreams to recapture the White House.

Initially, Democrats could not agree on a candidate, but they ultimately nominated a Tennessee congressman and governor, James K. Polk. The Whigs, unwilling to nominate Tyler for president, chose the well-known Kentucky senator Henry Clay. Polk ran on a platform that proclaimed the "Reoccupation of Oregon and the Annexation of Texas." Clay, meanwhile, remained uncommitted on the issue of Texas. This proved his undoing when the small but growing Liberty Party, adamantly opposed to slavery, denounced annexation. Liberty Party candidate James G. Birney captured just enough votes in New York State to throw the state and the election to Polk.

In February 1845, a month before Polk took office, Congress passed a joint resolution annexing the Republic of Texas. The day before Polk's inauguration, Florida was also admitted to statehood. That summer, John L. O'Sullivan, editor of the *Democratic Review*, captured the American mood by declaring that nothing must interfere with "the fulfillment of our manifest destiny to overspread the continent allotted by Providence for the free development of our yearly multiplying millions." This vision of **manifest destiny**—of the nation's God-given right to expand its borders—defined Polk's presidency.

With the Florida and Texas questions seemingly resolved, President Polk turned his attention to Oregon, which stretched from the forty-second parallel to latitude 54°40′ and was jointly occupied by Great Britain and the United States. Residents of either nation could settle anywhere in the region, but most of the British lived north of the Columbia River, while most Americans settled to the south.

In 1842, three years before Polk took office, settlers' glowing reports of the mild climate and fertile soil around Puget Sound had inspired thousands of farmers and traders to migrate to Oregon. Americans flooded into the Willamette valley, and merchants involved in the China trade imagined a thriving U.S. trading post on the Oregon coast. Alarmed by this "Oregon fever," the British tried to confine Americans to areas south of the Columbia River. But American settlers demanded access to the entire territory, proclaiming "Fifty-four forty or fight!" As president, Polk encouraged migration into Oregon, but he was unwilling to risk war with

Astoria, Oregon, 1848
In 1845 the British army sent Lieutenant Henry Warre to the Oregon Country to gather intelligence on American settlements in case of war with the United States. Warre sketched Astoria, which lies at the mouth of the Columbia River. The first permanent settlement in the Oregon Country, it was established by John Jacob Astor's Pacific Fur Company in 1811.   The Granger Collection, New York

Great Britain. Instead, diplomats negotiated a treaty in 1846 that extended the border with British Canada (the forty-ninth parallel) to the Pacific Ocean. Over the next two years, Congress admitted Iowa and Wisconsin to statehood, reassuring northern residents that expansion benefited all regions of the nation.

Many of the lands newly claimed by the U.S. government were home to vast numbers of Indians. Indeed, the West had become more crowded as the U.S. government forced eastern tribes to move west of the Mississippi (see Map 10.2). When the Cherokee and other southeastern tribes were removed to Indian Territory, for example, they confronted local tribes such as the Osage. Pushed into the Southwest, the Osages came into conflict with the Comanches, who had earlier fought the Apaches for control of the southern plains. Other Indian nations were pushed onto the northern plains from the Old Northwest. There the Sioux became the dominant tribe by the 1830s after seizing hunting grounds from the Omahas, Iowas, and Cheyennes, who resettled farther south and west.

The flood of U.S. migrants into Texas and the southern plains transformed relations among Indian nations as well as with Mexico. In the face of Spanish and then Mexican claims on their lands, for example, the Comanches forged alliances with former foes like the Wichitas and the Osages. The Comanches also developed commercial ties with tribes in Indian Territory and with Mexican and Anglo-American traders on the frontiers of their respective nations. In these ways, they hoped to benefit from the imperial ambitions of the United States and Mexico while strengthening bonds among Indians in the region.

Comanche expansion was especially problematic for Mexico once it achieved independence in 1821. The young nation did not have sufficient resources to sustain the level of gift giving that Spanish authorities used to maintain peace. As a result, Comanche warriors launched continual raids against Tejano settlements in Texas. But the Comanches also developed commercial relations with residents of New Mexico, who flaunted trade regulations promulgated in Mexico City in order to maintain peace with neighboring

Indians. By 1846 Comanche trade and diplomatic relations with New Mexican settlements had seriously weakened the hold of Mexican authorities on their northern provinces.

Pursuing War with Mexico

At the same time, with Texas now a state, Mexico faced growing tensions with the United States. Conflicts centered on Texas's western border. Mexico insisted on the Nueces River as the boundary line, while Americans claimed all the land to the Rio Grande. In January 1846, Polk secretly sent emissary John Slidell to negotiate with Mexico, offering

President José Herrera $30 million for New Mexico and California after securing the Rio Grande boundary. But Polk also sent U.S. troops under General Zachary Taylor across the Nueces River. Mexican officials refused to see Slidell and instead sent their own troops across the Rio Grande. Meanwhile U.S. naval commanders prepared to seize San Francisco Bay if war was declared. The Mexican government responded to these hostile overtures by sending more troops into the disputed Texas territory.

When fighting erupted near the Rio Grande in May 1846 (Map 10.3), Polk claimed that "American blood had been shed on American soil" and declared a state of war.

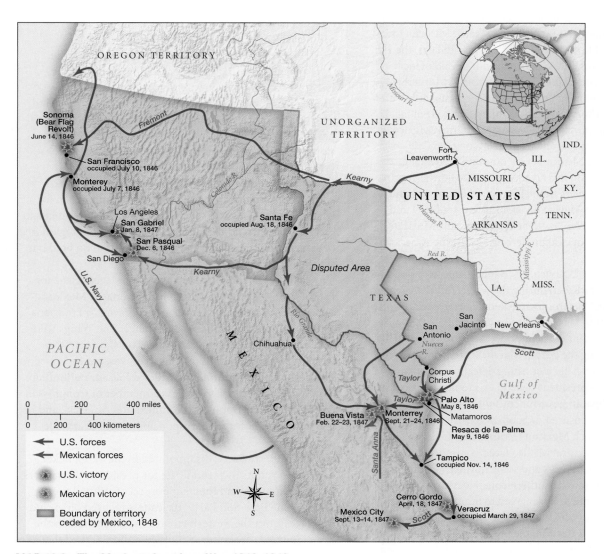

MAP 10.3   The Mexican-American War, 1846–1848

Although a dispute over territory between the Nueces River and the Rio Grande initiated the Mexican-American War, most of the fighting occurred between the Rio Grande and Mexico City. In addition, U.S. forces in California launched battles to claim independence for that region even before gold was discovered there.

Many Whigs in Congress protested, arguing that the president had provoked the conflict. Congressman Abraham Lincoln of Illinois demanded that Polk "show me the spot" where U.S. blood was shed. However, antiwar Whigs failed to convince the Democratic majority, and Congress voted to finance the war.

The South was solidly behind the war. As the Charleston, South Carolina, *Courier* declared: "Every battle fought in Mexico and every dollar spent there, but insures the acquisition of territory which must widen the field of Southern enterprise and power in the future." Most Northerners also supported the war. Although ardent opponents of slavery protested, most Americans considered westward expansion a boon (see Map 10.3).

Once the war began, battles erupted in a variety of locations. In May 1846, U.S. troops defeated Mexican forces in Palo Alto and Resaca de la Palma. A month later, the U.S. army captured Sonoma, California, with the aid of local settlers. John Frémont then led U.S. forces to Monterey, California, where the navy launched a successful attack and declared the territory part of the United States. That fall, U.S. troops gained important victories at Monterrey, Mexico, just west of the Rio Grande, and Tampico, along the Gulf coast.

Although the Mexican army outnumbered U.S. forces, it failed to capitalize on this advantage. In the northern provinces, Mexican soldiers were ill equipped for major battles, and in the heart of Mexico divisions among political and military leaders limited battlefield success. Still, Mexican soldiers and residents fought fiercely against the American invaders.

Despite major U.S. victories, Santa Anna, who reclaimed the presidency of Mexico during the war, refused to give up. In February 1847, his troops attacked General Taylor's forces at Buena Vista and nearly secured a victory. Polk then agreed to send General Winfield Scott to Veracruz with 14,000 soldiers. Capturing the port in March, Scott's army marched on to Mexico City. After a crushing defeat of Santa Anna at Cerro Gordo, the president-general was removed from power, and the new Mexican government sought peace.

With victory ensured, U.S. officials faced a difficult decision: How much Mexican territory should they claim? The U.S. army in central Mexico faced continued guerrilla attacks. Meanwhile Whigs and some northern Democrats denounced the war as a southern conspiracy to expand slavery. In this context, Polk agreed to limit U.S. claims to the northern regions of Mexico. Eager to unite the Democratic Party before the fall election, the president signed the **Treaty of Guadalupe Hidalgo** in February 1848, and the U.S. Senate ratified it in March. The treaty committed the United States to pay Mexico $15 million in return for control over Texas north and east of the Rio Grande plus California and the New Mexico territory.

Debates over Slavery Intensify

News of the U.S. victory traveled quickly across the United States. In the South, planters imagined slavery spreading into the lands acquired from Mexico. Northerners, too, applauded the expansion of U.S. territory but focused on California as a center for agriculture and commerce. Yet the acquisition of new territory only heightened sectional conflicts. Debates over slavery had erupted during the war, with a few northern Democrats joining Whigs in denouncing "the power of SLAVERY" to "govern the country, its Constitutions and laws." In August 1846, Democratic congressman David Wilmot of Pennsylvania proposed outlawing slavery in all territory acquired from Mexico so that the South could not profit from the war. The **Wilmot Proviso** passed in the House, but in the Senate, Southerners and proslavery northern Democrats killed it.

The presidential election of 1848 opened with the unresolved question of whether to allow slavery in the territories acquired from Mexico. Polk, exhausted by the war effort and divisions among Democrats, refused to run for a second term. In his place, Democrats nominated Lewis Cass, a senator from Michigan and an ardent expansionist. He had suggested that the United States purchase Cuba from Spain in 1848 and advocated seizing all of Oregon and more of Mexico. Hoping to keep northern antislavery Democrats in the party, Cass campaigned for what he called "squatter sovereignty," by which residents in each territory would decide whether to make the region free or slave. This strategy put the slavery question on hold but satisfied almost no one.

The Whigs, too, hoped to avoid the slavery issue for fear of losing southern votes. They nominated Mexican-American War hero General Zachary Taylor, a Louisiana slaveholder with no political experience. The Whigs were pleased that he had not taken a stand on slavery in the western territories. But they sought to reassure their northern wing by nominating Millard Fillmore of Buffalo, New York, for vice president. As a member of Congress in the 1830s, he had opposed the annexation of Texas, and he had a reputation for fiscal responsibility and charitable endeavors.

The Liberty Party, disappointed in the Whig ticket, decided to run its own candidate for president. But leaders who hoped to expand their support reconstituted themselves as the Free-Soil Party. Its leaders focused on excluding slaves from the western territories rather than on the moral injustice of slavery. Still, Free-Soilers argued that slavery empowered "aristocratic men" and threatened the rights of "the great mass of the people." The party nominated former president Martin Van Buren and appealed to small farmers and urban workers who hoped to benefit from western expansion.

Once again, the presence of a third party affected the outcome of the election. While Whigs and Democrats tried to avoid the slavery issue, Free-Soilers demanded attention to it. By focusing on the exclusion of slavery in western territories rather than its abolition, the Free-Soil Party won more adherents in northern states. Indeed, Van Buren won enough northern Democrats so that Cass lost New York State and the 1848 election. Zachary Taylor and the Whigs won, but only by placing a southern slaveholder in the White House.

REVIEW & RELATE

- How did western expansion both benefit Americans and exacerbate conflicts among them?

- How did the Mexican-American War reshape national politics and intensify debates over slavery?

 LEARNINGCurve bedfordstmartins.com/hewittlawson/LC

Conclusion: Geographical Expansion and Political Division

By the mid-nineteenth century, the United States stood at a crossroads. Most Americans considered expansion advantageous and critical to revitalizing the economy.

Planters believed it was vital to slavery's success. While most white Northerners were willing to leave slavery alone where it already existed, many hoped to keep it out of newly acquired territories. The vast lands gained from Mexico in 1848 intensified these debates. Between 1830 and 1850, small but growing numbers of Northerners joined slaves, American Indians, and Mexicans in protesting U.S. expansion. Even some yeomen farmers and middle-class professionals in the South questioned whether extending slavery benefited the region economically and politically. But these challenges remained limited until 1848, when the fight over slavery in the territories fractured the Democratic Party, created a crisis for the Whigs, and inspired the growth of the Free-Soil Party.

Political realignments continued over the next decade, fueled by growing antislavery sentiment in the North and proslavery ideology in the South. In 1853 Solomon Northrup horrified thousands of antislavery readers with his book *Twelve Years a Slave*, which vividly described his life in bondage. Such writings alarmed planters like James Henry Hammond, who continued to believe that slavery was "the greatest of all the great blessings which Providence has bestowed upon our glorious region." Yet in insisting on the benefits of slave labor, the planter elite inspired further conflict with Northerners, whose lives were increasingly shaped by commercial and industrial developments and the expansion of free labor.

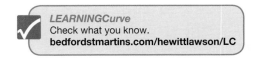

LEARNINGCurve
Check what you know.
bedfordstmartins.com/hewittlawson/LC

Chapter Review

Online Study Guide ▶ bedfordstmartins.com/hewittlawson

KEY TERMS

syncretic culture (p. 301)
Nat Turner's rebellion (p. 302)
yeomen farmers (p. 303)
Whig Party (p. 307)
Second Seminole War (p. 307)
Treaty of New Echota (p. 308)
Trail of Tears (p. 309)
Tejanos (p. 310)
Alamo (p. 310)
gag rule (p. 311)
panic of 1837 (p. 311)
manifest destiny (p. 313)
Treaty of Guadalupe Hidalgo (p. 316)
Wilmot Proviso (p. 316)

REVIEW & RELATE

1. What role did the planter elite play in southern society and politics?

2. What were the consequences of the dominant position of slave-based plantation agriculture in the southern economy?

3. How did enslaved African Americans create ties of family, community, and culture?

4. How did enslaved African Americans resist efforts to control and exploit their labor?

5. What groups made up white southern society? How did their interests overlap? How did they diverge?

6. How and why did the planter elite seek to reinforce white solidarity?

7. How and why did Indian nations in the Southeast resist removal to the West while some Indians in the West forged ties with U.S. markets?

8. What events and developments led to a Whig victory in the election of 1840?

9. How did western expansion both benefit Americans and exacerbate conflicts among them?

10. How did the Mexican-American War reshape national politics and intensify debates over slavery?

TIMELINE OF EVENTS

1820–1850	Southern cotton production increases from about 500,000 bales to 3 million bales
1821	Mexico overthrows Spanish rule and encourages U.S. settlement in Texas
1830–1850	440,000 slaves from the Upper South sold to owners in the Lower South
1831	*Cherokee Nation v. Georgia*
August 1831	Nat Turner leads slave uprising in Virginia
December 1831	Virginia's Assembly establishes special committee on slavery
1832	*Worcester v. Georgia*
1833	Tredegar Iron Works established
1834	Britain abolishes slavery
1835–1842	Second Seminole War
1836	Treaty of New Echota
March 2, 1836	U.S. settlers declare eastern Texas an independent republic
March 6, 1836	General Santa Anna crushes U.S. rebels at the Alamo
March 1836	James Hammond leads campaign that results in congressional gag rule
1837	Panic of 1837 triggers recession
October 1838– March 1839	Trail of Tears
1840	Whigs win the presidency and gain control of Congress
1841	Solomon Northrup kidnapped and sold into slavery
1845	U.S. annexes Texas
1846	U.S. settles dispute with Great Britain over Oregon
May 1846– February 1848	Mexican-American War
August 1846	David Wilmot proposes Wilmot Proviso
March 1848	Treaty of Guadalupe Hidalgo
1853	Solomon Northrup publishes *Twelve Years a Slave*

Claiming Texas

When Mexico overthrew Spanish control in 1821, the newly formed Mexican government encouraged more U.S. residents to move into Texas, hoping to expand settlement on its northern frontier. Some families, like the one led by Moses Austin, acquired huge tracts of land and then resold land titles to other American families. These settlers were mostly interested in the rich farmland they found, and they brought their slaves with them to cultivate cotton and other plantation-style crops (Document 10.6). Throughout the 1830s, conflicts erupted between these recent settlers and the Mexican government over control of the region. By 1836 open rebellion broke out in east Texas, and in March of that year U.S.-born Texans declared their region an independent republic (Document 10.7). But after declaring independence, rebels at the Alamo in San Antonio were overrun by Mexican forces, who killed all 250 men stationed there. Stories of the heroic efforts of Americans at the Alamo reached the eastern United States, including letters such as the one from Colonel William Travis (Document 10.8), who pleaded for reinforcements in a desperate attempt to hold the fort. Although reinforcements arrived too late to save the Alamo, hundreds of volunteers flocked to Texas from the United States. They helped General Sam Houston win a decisive victory against Mexican forces just a month later at the Battle of San Jacinto. Still the Mexican government refused to recognize Texas as an independent republic, and the U.S. government refused to annex Texas, fearing it would lead to war with Mexico.

As an independent republic, Texas had to resolve both the issue of slavery and relations with Indians. Leaders drafted a constitution in 1836 that legalized slavery, and many new settlers supported the provision. In response, abolitionists in the United States opposed statehood for Texas. Documents 10.9 and 10.10 demonstrate opposing sides of this debate, one that continued even after Texas was admitted as a state in 1845. At the same time, Texas sought to ensure its stability by sometimes seeking peace with and at other times making war on the numerous Indian tribes on its borders. Likewise, Comanche, Caddo, Shawnee, and other Indian nations alternately traded with and raided the Texas settlements. After years of broken treaties, hostage taking, and warfare, Texas officials and Indian chiefs finalized a treaty in October 1844 to ensure peace and improve trade in the region (Document 10.11).

DOCUMENT 10.6

Mary Austin Holley | Letter to Charles Austin, 1831

In 1831 Mary Holley visited her cousin Stephen Austin at his home in Texas. It was her first visit to the region, and her letters home were filled with vivid, if idealized, descriptions of the people and land she encountered there. Her letters were published in 1833, and she later wrote the first English-language history of Texas. Although she never permanently settled in Texas, Holley's writings attracted many others to the region.

Bolivar, Texas, December, 1831

One's feelings in Texas are unique and original, and very like a dream or youthful vision realized. Here, as in Eden, man feels alone with the God of nature, and seems, in a peculiar manner, to enjoy the rich bounties of heaven, in common with all created things, The animals, which do not fly from him; the profound stillness; the genial sun and soft air—all are impressive, and are calculated both to delight the imagination and to fill the heart with religious emotions.

With regard to the state of society here, as is natural to expect, there are many incongruities. It will take some time for people gathered from the north and from the south, from the east, and from the west to assimilate and adapt themselves to new situations. The people are universally kind and hospitable, which are redeeming qualities. Everybody's house is open and table spread to accommodate the traveller. There are no poor people here, and none rich; that is, none who have much money. The poor and the rich, to use the correlatives, where distinction, there is none, get the same quantity of land on arrival, and if they do not continue equal, it is for want of good management on the one part, or superior industry and sagacity on the other. All are happy because busy; and none meddle with the affairs of their neighbours because they have enough to do to take care of their own. They are bound together by a common interest, by sameness of purpose and hopes. As far as I could learn, they have no envyings, no jealousies, no bickerings, through politics or fanaticism. . . .

. . . I should say, industrious farmers will certainly do well, and cannot fail of success; that is to say, if abundant crops and a ready market with high prices will satisfy them. Substantial planters with capital and hands may enlarge their operations here to any extent and with enormous profits. One gentleman, for instance, whom I visited, has ninety-three acres under cultivation by seven hands. His crop this year consists of eighty bales of cotton, two thousand bushels of corn, five hundred bushels of sweet potatoes, besides other articles of minor importance.

Source: Mary Austin Holley, *Texas: Observations, Historical, Geographical, and Descriptive, in a Series of Letters, Written during a Visit to Austin's Colony, with a View of a Permanent Settlement in That Country, in the Autumn of 1831* (Baltimore: Armstrong & Plaskitt, 1833), 127–29.

DOCUMENT 10.7

Colonel Gregorio Gomez | Call to Arms against the Texans, 1835

In the early 1830s, more and more settlers from the United States moved to Texas. They viewed Mexican/Tejano culture and Catholicism with suspicion, while Mexicans considered these "Texian colonists" as outsiders with little claim to the land. By 1835 these tensions erupted in armed conflict. In the following selection, Colonel Gregorio Gomez calls on Mexicans to defend their nation against U.S. invaders. The next month, Gomez waged a successful battle at Tampico under the leadership of Mexican exile José Antonio Mexia.

October 17, 1835

Gregorio Gomez, colonel of the battalion Tres Villas, and commandant of this town, to his brothers in arms and to the inhabitants.

Friends: It is now proved that the fears of all good Mexicans have been too well founded. The hypocritical and false promises of the Texian colonists have not deceived the enlightened part of the nation: These ungrateful traitors, these unnatural guests, in return for the liberality and the favors shown them by our country, are attempting now to plunge a murderous poignard [knife] in her bosom. The crisis in which the republic is now involved has favored their plans. They have openly declared their rebellion; and attempt no less than dismembering that rich part of our territory, where they have been received with such liberal hospitality. By the last official accounts we have learned that they have already begun to act. The weak garrison stationed at Bahia del Espiritu Santo has been captured by the rebels, who have taken military possession of the place. What will be the consequence of such wanton proceedings, if not the complete annihilation of those usurpers? Is there a Mexican who would not be fired with indignation at beholding the national honor and integrity of territory violated by a gang of lawless foreigners? Foreigners they are certainly by birth and principles; and by their treacherous conduct they have forfeited all the privileges and immunities granted to them by our too generous country.

It is now [not?] an internal question, when the members of the same family may be involved in domestic quarrels; but it is a question where adventurous foreigners are preying upon us, to rob us of one of our most precious gems, whilst we are deliberating on the ways and means to regulate properly the whole of our public concerns. Thousand curses on the Mexican who should be dastardly enough to join the murderous and anti-national plot! His name should be branded with infamy; and his crime never forgotten by his brethren. Let us then appeal to arms, let us rally round the government, and, with the native bravery of Mexicans, let us rush on these gangs of perfidious foreigners. Let us dispel them as the wind doth a flying cloud; and let us avenge her [the country's] honor, sullied in so atrocious a manner. Such are the sentiments of your brother in arms, and of your comrade who is ever ready to sacrifice his life in defence of such a noble cause.

Source: *Niles' Weekly Register*, November 21, 1835, 188.

DOCUMENT 10.8

Colonel William Travis | Appeal for Reinforcements, March 3, 1836

In February 1836, a small group of Texian colonists gathered at the Alamo in San Antonio to defend their settlements against Mexican forces. The rebels held out for thirteen days, during which time one of the co-commanders, twenty-six-year-old William Travis, wrote several letters appealing to supporters in the United States for reinforcements, including his last appeal, which was sent on March 3.

I hope your honorable body will hasten on reinforcements, ammunition, and provisions to our aid, as soon as possible. We have provisions for twenty days for the men we have: our supply of ammunition is limited. At least five hundred pounds of cannon powder, and two hundred rounds of six, nine, twelve, and eighteen pound balls—ten kegs of rifle powder, and a supply of lead, should be sent to this place without delay, under a sufficient guard.

If these things are promptly sent and large reinforcements are hastened to this frontier, this neighborhood will be the great and decisive battle ground. The power of Santa Ana is to be met here, or in the colonies; we had better meet them here, than to suffer a war of desolation to rage in our settlements. A blood-red banner waves from the church of Bejar, and in the camp above us, in token that the war is one of vengeance against rebels; they have declared us such, and demanded that we should surrender at discretion, or that this garrison should be put to the sword. Their threats have had no influence on me, or my men, but to make all fight with desperation, and that high souled courage which characterizes the patriot, who is willing to die in defence of his country's liberty and his own honor.

The citizens of this municipality are all our enemies except those who have joined us heretofore; we have but three Mexicans now in the fort: those who have not joined us in this extremity, should be declared public enemies, and their property should aid in paying the expenses of the war.

The bearer of this will give your honorable body a statement more in detail should he escape through the enemies lines.

God and Texas—Victory or Death!!

Your obedient ser't
W. Barrett Travis, Lieut. Col. Comm.

P.S. The enemies troops are still arriving and the reinforcement will probably amount to two or three thousand.

Source: *Telegraph and Texas Register*, March 12, 1836, 3.

DOCUMENT 10.9

Benjamin Lundy | The War in Texas, 1836

As battles raged in Texas, many Americans outside the territory debated whether or not the United States should annex it. Slavery was at the heart of this debate, with abolitionists fearing that the added Texas territory would strengthen the power of slaveholders. Benjamin Lundy, a Quaker and an ardent abolitionist who published several antislavery newspapers, was well known for his 1836 publication *The War in Texas*, in which he argued against the annexation of Texas.

It is generally admitted that the war in Texas has assumed a character which must seriously affect both the interests and honor of this nation. It implicates the conduct of a large number of our citizens, and even the policy and measures of the government are deeply involved in it. The subject, as now presented to our view, is indeed one of vital importance to the people of the United States; and it particularly invites the attention—the most solemn and deliberate consideration—of all who profess to be guided by the true principles of justice and philanthropy. It is not only to be viewed as a matter of interest, at the present day. The great fundamental principles of universal liberty—the perpetuity of our free republican institutions—the prosperity, the welfare, and the happiness of future generations—are measurably connected with the prospective issue of this fierce and bloody conflict.

But the prime cause and the real objects of this war are not distinctly understood by a large portion of the honest, disinterested, and well-meaning citizens of the United States. Their means of obtaining correct information upon the subject have been necessarily limited; and many of them have been deceived and misled by the misrepresentations of those concerned in it, and especially by hireling writers for the newspaper press. They have been induced to believe that the inhabitants of Texas were engaged in a legitimate contest for the maintenance of the sacred principles of Liberty, and the natural, inalienable Rights of Man: whereas, the motives of

its instigators, and their chief incentives to action, have been, from the commencement, of a directly opposite character and tendency. It is susceptible of the clearest demonstration, that the immediate cause and the leading object of this contest originated in a settled design, among the slaveholders of this country (with land speculators and slave-traders), to wrest the large and valuable territory of Texas from the Mexican Republic, in order to re-establish the SYSTEM OF SLAVERY; to open a vast and profitable SLAVE-MARKET therein; and, ultimately, to annex it to the United States. And further, it is evident—nay, it is very generally acknowledged—that the insurrectionists are principally citizens of the United States, who have proceeded thither for the purpose of revolutionizing the country; and that they are dependent upon this nation, for both the physical and pecuniary means, to carry the design into effect. We have a still more important view of the subject. The Slaveholding Interest is now paramount in the Executive branch of our national government; and its influence operates, indirectly, yet powerfully, through that medium, in favor of this Grand Scheme of Oppression and Tyrannical Usurpation. Whether the national Legislature will join hands with the Executive, and lend its aid to this most unwarrantable, aggressive attempt, will depend on the VOICE OF THE PEOPLE, expressed in their primary assemblies, by their petitions, and through the ballot-boxes.

Source: Benjamin Lundy, *The War in Texas* (Philadelphia: Merrihew and Gunn, 1837), 3.

DOCUMENT 10.10

Southerners Support Texas Settlers, 1837

Throughout the South, slaveholders and politicians urged support for American settlers in Texas and sought annexation of the territory. The southern press defended Texas slavery and bitterly denounced northern and abolitionist resistance to annexation. The following selection from the *Charleston Mercury* outlined the prevailing southern opinion on Texas and the "slavery question."

That Texas will be the cause of a severe sectional struggle is almost certain. Either the establishment of her independence as a separate state, or her admission into the Union, would tend greatly to strengthen the South, and ensure the stability and security of Southern institutions, placing the question of slavery beyond the reach of Northern agitation; and it is a grave question for the South and one of difficult decision, whether we should prefer that Texas should be a powerful and independent slave holding state upon our borders, untrammelled by Northern connections, or that she should become a member of the Union. That either her admission, or the acknowledgment of her Independence, will be opposed by a powerful Northern party, there is no doubt. But we fear not for the result. When the question arises, we can say to the North, now make good your oft repeated pledges—make the South forever safe on the subject of Slavery. Set our minds at rest by perpetuating Slavery. The North may be blind enough to wish to refuse, but the West is becoming every day more aware of the value of its connection with this section, and our just demand will be complied with. The North may then choose between the Union with Texian Independence—with the establishment of Slavery above the reach of fanaticism—and no Union; and when they are compelled to choose, we have no fear of their abhorrence of Slavery driving them to disunion. Until then the South and South West will rally upon Texas, which is already de facto an independent state, and will never want the means to maintain her Independence, while there are rifles in our back woods.

Source: *Charleston Mercury*, as reprinted in *Telegraph and Texas Register*, January 11, 1837, 3.

DOCUMENT 10.11

Treaty of Tehuacana Creek, October 9, 1844

For eight years following the achievement of independence, Texas residents and Comanches and other local Indian nations engaged in sporadic warfare and almost constant raids on each other's settlements. Men, women, and children were killed and taken hostage on both sides, and barns, fields, and villages were devastated. In 1840, following a smallpox epidemic, Comanche chiefs sought peace and sent a large group to San Antonio to negotiate terms. Instead, white officials and San Antonio residents murdered thirty-five of them. A year later, Sam Houston, a leader of the Texas rebellion but an advocate of fair treatment for Indians, was elected president of the Republic of Texas. After numerous discussions, Texas officials and the Comanches, along with nine other Indian tribes, signed the Treaty of Tehuacana Creek.

The commissioners of the Republic of Texas, and the Chiefs and head men of the before mentioned tribes of Indians, being met in council at Tehuacana Creek on the ninth day of October, in the Year 1844, have concluded, accepted, and agreed to and signed the following articles of treaty:

Article I. Both parties agree and declare, that they will forever live in peace, and always meet as friends and brothers. The tomahawk shall be buried, and no more blood appear in the path between them now made white. The Great Spirit will look with delight upon their friendship, and will frown in anger upon their enmity.

Article II. They further agree and declare, that the Government of Texas shall permit no bad men to cross the line into the hunting grounds of the Indians; and that if the Indians should find any such among them, they will bring him or them to some one of the agents, but not do any harm to his or their person or property. . . .

Article V. They further agree and declare, that the Indians shall no more steal horses or other property from the whites; and if any property should be stolen, or other mischief done by the bad men among the tribes, that they will punish those who do so and restore the property taken to some one of the agents. . . .

Article VII. They further agree and declare, that the Government of Texas shall establish trading houses for the convenience and benefit of the Indians, and such articles shall be kept for the Indian trade as they may need for their support and comfort.

Article VIII. They further agree and declare, that when peace is fully established between the white and the red people, and no more war or trouble exists, the Indians shall be supplied with powder, lead, guns, spears, and other arms to enable them to kill game and live in plenty. . . .

Article XV. They further agree and declare, that the President may send among the Indians such blacksmiths and other mechanics, as he may think best, for their benefit: and also that he may send schoolmasters and families for the purpose of instructing them in a Knowledge of the English language and Christian Religion, as well as other persons to teach them how to cultivate the soil and raise corn. . . .

Article XIX. They further agree and declare, that they will mutually surrender and deliver up all the prisoners which they have of the other party for their own prisoners; and that they will not be friendly with any people or nation, or enter into treaty with them, who will take prisoners from Texas, or do its citizens any injury. . . .

Source: Dorman H. Winfrey and James M. Day, eds., *The Indian Papers of Texas and the Southwest, 1825–1916* (Austin, TX: Pembroke Publishers, 1966), 2:114–19.

Interpret the Evidence

1. How does Mary Austin Holley (Document 10.6) describe Texas as a unique place for settlers? What accounts for its distinctiveness?

2. How does Gregorio Gomez's description of Americans in Texas (Document 10.7) compare to Holley's? How do you explain the differences? On what grounds does Gomez attempt to gain support for the fight against "Texian colonists" from the United States?

3. According to William Travis (Document 10.8), why was defending the Alamo important? Why do you think the defeat of Americans there gained so much attention in the United States?

4. Compare the discussions of Texas found in Benjamin Lundy's *The War in Texas* (Document 10.9) and the article from the *Charleston Mercury* (Document 10.10). How is slavery described, and how do the attitudes expressed in the documents affect each author's view about the fighting in Texas? What do the two documents reveal about the differences between the North and the South in the 1830s?

5. What does the Treaty of Tehuacana Creek (Document 10.11) suggest about what Indians hoped to gain from negotiating peace with the Republic of Texas? What do the specific articles in the treaty suggest about the issues that mattered most to white Texans?

Put It in Context

- What do the various documents presented here suggest about the ongoing debates over statehood for Texas in the United States?

- How would the United States benefit from adding Texas to the Union, and what problems might admitting Texas create?

background photo: pages 320–321, The Granger Collection, New York

The Granger Collection, New York

View of New York from Brooklyn Heights, 1849.

Library of Congress

Portrait of Jarena Lee, the first female preacher of the African
Methodist Episcopal Church, 1844.

11

Social and Cultural Ferment in the North

1820–1850

From *Memoir of Samuel Slater, the Father of American Manufactures*, 1836

Engraving of a textile mill from the memoir of the English-American industrialist Samuel Slater, 1836.

AMERICAN HISTORIES

Charles Grandison Finney, one of the greatest preachers of the nineteenth century, was born in 1792 and raised in rural New York State. As a young man, Finney studied the law. But in 1821, like many others of his generation, he experienced a powerful religious conversion. No longer interested in a legal career, he turned to the ministry instead.

After being ordained in the Presbyterian Church, Finney joined "New School" ministers who rejected the more conservative traditions of the Presbyterian Church and embraced a vigorous evangelicalism. In the early 1830s, while his wife, Lydia, remained at home with their growing family, the Reverend Finney traveled throughout New York State preaching about Christ's place in a changing America. He held massive revivals in cities along the Erie Canal, most notably in Rochester, and then moved on to New York City. He achieved his greatest success in places experiencing rapid economic development and an influx of migrants and immigrants, where the clash of cultures and classes fueled fears of moral decay. Spiritual renewal could rescue the young nation from sin and depravity.

Finney urged Christians to actively seek salvation. Once individuals reformed themselves, he said, they should work to abolish poverty, intemperance, prostitution, and slavery. He expected women to participate in revivals and good works but advised them to balance these efforts with their domestic responsibilities, an ideal modeled by his own wife.

327

In many ways, Amy Kirby Post fit Finney's ideal. She raised five children while devoting herself to spiritual and social reform. However, Amy Kirby was born into a large, close-knit Quaker family in the farming community of Jericho, New York. While most Quakers believed in quiet piety rather than evangelical revivals, their faith also provided solace in times of sorrow. In 1823, at age twenty-one, Amy became engaged to a fellow Quaker in central New York, where her sister Hannah lived with her husband, Isaac Post. But her fiancé died in June 1825 just before their wedding. Hannah took sick a year later, and Amy nursed her until her death in April 1827. She stayed on to care for Hannah's two young children and two years later married Isaac Post.

Amy experienced these personal upheavals in the midst of heated religious controversies among Quakers. In the 1820s, Elias Hicks claimed that the Society of Friends had abandoned its spiritual roots and become too much like a traditional church. His followers, called Hicksites, insisted that Friends should reduce their dependence on disciplinary rules, elders, and preachers and rely instead on the "Inner Light"—the spirit of God dwelling within each individual. When the Society of Friends divided into Hicksite and Orthodox branches in 1827, Amy Kirby and Isaac Post joined the Hicksites.

In 1836 Amy Post moved with her husband and four children to Rochester, New York. In a city marked by the spirit of Finney's revivals, Quakers emphasized quiet contemplation rather than fiery sermons and emotional conversions. But the Society of Friends allowed women to preach when moved by the spirit. Quaker women also held separate meetings to discipline female congregants, evaluate marriage proposals, and write testimonies on important religious issues.

Amy Post's spiritual journey was increasingly shaped by the rising tide of abolition. Committed to ending slavery, she joined non-Quakers in signing an 1837 antislavery petition. Five years later, she helped found the Western New York Anti-Slavery Society, which included Quakers and evangelicals, women and men, and blacks and whites. Post's growing commitment to abolition caused tensions in the Hicksite Meeting since some members opposed working in "worldly" organizations alongside non-Quakers. By 1848 Post and other radical Friends had withdrawn from the Hicksite Meeting and invited like-minded people to join them in the newly established Congregational Friends. Their meetings attracted abolitionists, advocates of Indian rights and women's rights, and peace activists, all causes Post embraced. ●

THE AMERICAN HISTORIES of Charles Finney and Amy Post were shaped by the dynamic religious, social, and economic developments in the early-nineteenth-century United States. Finney changed the face of American religion, aided by masses of evangelical Protestants. The rise of cities and the expansion of industry in the northern United States made problems like poverty, unemployment, alcohol abuse, crime, and prostitution more visible, drawing people to Finney's message. Other Americans brought their own religious traditions to bear on the problems of the day. Some, like Post, were so outraged by the moral stain of slavery that they burst traditional religious bonds and reconsidered what it meant to do God's work. For both Finney and Post, Rochester—the fastest-growing city in the nation between 1825 and 1835—exemplified the problems and the possibilities created by urban expansion and social change.

The Growth of Cities

Commercial and industrial development, immigration from Europe, and migration from rural areas led to the rapid growth of U.S. cities from 1820 on. Urbanization stimulated economic expansion but also created social upheaval. Cultural divisions intensified in urban areas where Catholics and Protestants, workers and the well-to-do, immigrants, African Americans, and native-born whites lived side by side. The emergence of a middle class of shopkeepers, professionals, and clerks might have bridged these divides, but most middle-class Americans highlighted their distinctiveness from both the wealthy few at the top and the mass of workers and the poor at the bottom.

The Lure of Urban Life

Across the North, urban populations boomed. As centers of national and international commerce, seaports like New York and Philadelphia gained the greatest population in the early to mid-nineteenth century. But boomtowns also emerged along inland waterways. Rochester, New York, first settled in 1812, was flooded by goods and people once the Erie Canal was completed in 1825. Between 1820 and 1850, the number of cities with 100,000 inhabitants grew from two to six. In the Northeast, some farm communities doubled or tripled in size and were incorporated into neighboring cities such as Philadelphia. By 1850, among the nation's ten most populous urban centers, only two—Baltimore and New Orleans—were located in the South.

Cities increased not only in size but also in the diversity of their residents. During the 1820s, some 150,000 European immigrants entered the United States; during the 1830s, nearly 600,000; and during the 1840s, more than 1,700,000. This surge of immigrants included more Irish and German settlers than ever before as well as large numbers of Scandinavians. Many settled along the eastern seaboard, but others added to the growth of frontier cities such as Cincinnati, St. Louis, and Chicago.

Irish families had settled in North America early on, most of them Scots-Irish Presbyterians. Then in the 1830s and 1840s, the Irish countryside was plagued by bad weather, a potato blight, and harsh economic policies imposed by the English government. In 1845–1846 a full-blown famine forced thousands of Irish farm families—most of them Catholic—to emigrate. Young Irish women emigrated in especially large numbers, working as seamstresses and domestics to help fund passage to the United States for other family members. Poor harvests, droughts, failed revolutions, and repressive landlords convinced large numbers of Germans and Scandinavians to flee their homelands as well. By 1850 the Irish made up about 40 percent of immigrants to the United States, and Germans nearly a quarter (Figure 11.1).

Commerce and industry attracted immigrants to northern cities. These newcomers provided an expanding pool of cheap labor that further fueled economic growth. Banks, mercantile houses, and dry goods stores multiplied. Industrial enterprises in cities such as New York and Philadelphia included mechanized factories as well as traditional workshops in which master craftsmen oversaw the labor of apprentices. Credit and insurance agencies were created to aid entrepreneurs in their ventures. The increase in business also drove the demand for ships, newspapers catering to merchants and businessmen, warehouses, and other trade necessities, which created a surge in jobs and attracted even more people.

Businesses that focused on leisure also flourished. In the 1830s, theater became affordable to working-class families, who attended comedies, musical revues, and morality plays. They also joined middle- and upper-class

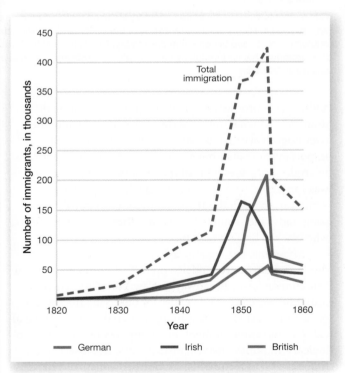

FIGURE 11.1　Immigration to the United States, 1820–1860

Famine, economic upheaval, and political persecution led masses of people from Ireland, Germany, and Britain to migrate to the United States from the 1820s through the 1850s. The vast majority settled in cities and factory towns in the North or on farms in the Midwest. An economic recession in the late 1850s finally slowed immigration, though only temporarily.

Leisure Pursuits

City residents who lived a more sedentary life used their leisure time to keep fit. This 1850 lithograph advertising Dr. Rich's Institute for Physical Education shows newly developed exercises and gymnastic equipment that have become standard today. Dr. Rich's Institute was one of many urban gymnasiums that promoted health through systematic physical training.   © Museum of the City of New York, USA/The Bridgeman Art Library

audiences at productions of Shakespeare and nationalistic dramas in which strong and clever Americans triumphed over English aristocrats. Minstrel shows mocked self-important capitalists but also portrayed African Americans in crude caricatures. One of the most popular characters was Jim Crow, who appeared originally in an African American song. In the 1820s, he was incorporated into a song-and-dance routine by Thomas Rice, a white performer who blacked his face with burnt cork.

Museums, too, became a favorite destination for city dwellers. Many were modeled on P. T. Barnum's American Museum on lower Broadway in New York City. These museums were not staid venues for observing the fine arts or historical artifacts. Instead, they offered an abundance of exhibits and entertainment, including wax figures, archaeo-logical antiquities, medical instruments, and insect collec-tions, as well as fortune-tellers, bearded ladies, and snake charmers.

The lures of urban life were especially attractive to the young. Single men and women and newly married couples flocked to cities. By 1850 half the residents of New York City, Philadelphia, and other seaport cities were under sixteen years old. Young men sought work in construction, in the maritime trades, or in banks and commercial houses, while young women competed for jobs as seamstresses and domestic servants.

The Roots of Urban Disorder

In addition to stimulating economic growth by providing the labor that made industrial development possible, immigrants also transformed the urban landscape in the nineteenth century. They filled factories and workshops, crowded into houses and apartments, and built ethnic institutions, including synagogues and convents—visible indicators of the growing diversity of the American city.

Such marks of difference aroused growing concern among native-born Protestants. Crude stereotypes of immigrant groups appeared more frequently, and anti-Catholicism and anti-Semitism flourished in the 1830s and 1840s. Jews, who were long denied admission to skilled crafts and professions in Europe, had little choice but to pursue commercial ventures. Yet they were portrayed not as well-educated businessmen but as manipulative money-lenders. Similarly, many Irishmen enjoyed a beer with friends after laboring at difficult and low-paid jobs. But rather than being viewed as hardworking comrades, they were often pictured as habitual drunkards.

Rural Americans, seeking better jobs and new social experiences, added to urban diversity. Native-born white men often set out on their own, but most white women settled in cities under the supervision of a husband, a landlady, or an employer. African Americans, too, sought greater opportunities in urban areas. In the 1830s, more blacks joined Philadelphia's vibrant African American community, attracted by its churches, schools, and mutual aid and literary societies. New Bedford, Massachusetts, a thriving whaling center, provided employment for black men, including growing numbers of fugitive slaves, as well as for American Indians from the region. Although relative racial tolerance prevailed in New Bedford, in most urban areas racial minorities faced hostility and discrimination that limited their opportunities.

Even as cities promised better lives for many immigrants and migrants, they also posed dangers. Battles erupted between immigrant and native-born residents, Protestant and Catholic gangs, and white and black workers. Robberies, gambling, prostitution, and other criminal activities flourished. Diseases spread quickly through densely populated neighborhoods. When innovations in transportation made it possible for more affluent residents to distance themselves from crowded inner cities, they leaped at the chance. The first horse-drawn streetcar line was built in New York City in 1832, and as lines multiplied there and elsewhere, wealthy families moved to less crowded neighborhoods away from the urban center.

Violence increased as economic competition intensified in the 1840s. Native-born white workers and employers pushed Irish immigrants to the bottom of the economic ladder, where they competed with African Americans. Yet Irish workers insisted that their whiteness gave them a higher status than skilled blacks. When black temperance reformers organized a parade in Philadelphia in August 1842, white onlookers—mostly Irish laborers—attacked the marchers. Blacks fought back, and the conflict escalated into a riot.

Americans who lived in small towns and rural areas regularly read news of urban riots, murders, robberies, and vice. Improvements in printing created vastly more and cheaper newspapers. Tabloids wooed readers by publishing sensational stories of crime, sex, and scandal. Even more respectable newspapers carried stories about urban mayhem, and religious periodicals warned their parishioners against the city's moral temptations. After Congress funded construction of the first telegraph line in 1844 between Baltimore and Washington, D.C., news could travel even more quickly. In response to both a real increase in crime and a heightened perception of urban dangers, cities—beginning with Boston in

1845—replaced voluntary night watchmen with police forces. Fire companies, too, became established parts of city government, and city and county jails expanded with the population.

The New Middle Class

Members of the emerging middle class were among the most avid readers of the burgeoning numbers of newspapers and magazines. They included ambitious businessmen, successful shopkeepers, doctors, and lawyers as well as teachers, journalists, ministers, and other salaried employees. In Britain, the middle class emerged at the turn of the nineteenth century. In the United States, it was still a class in the making, rather than a stable entity, in the first half of the nineteenth century. At the top rungs, wealthy entrepreneurs and professionals adopted luxurious lifestyles. At the lower rungs, a growing cohort of salaried clerks and managers hoped that their hard work, honesty, and thrift would be rewarded with upward mobility.

Education, religious affiliation, and sobriety were important indicators of middle-class status. A well-read man who attended a well-established church and drank in strict moderation was marked as belonging to this new rank. A middle-class man was also expected to own a comfortable home, marry a pious woman, and raise well-behaved children. Entrance to the middle class required the efforts of wives as well as husbands, and so couples adopted new ideas about marriage and family. They believed that marital relationships should be based on affection and companionship rather than the husband's supreme authority. As partners for life, the husband focused on achieving financial security while the wife managed the household. The French traveler Alexis de Tocqueville captured this development in *Democracy in America* (1835). "In no country," he wrote, "has such constant care been taken . . . to trace two clearly distinct lines of action for the two sexes." The millions of women who toiled on farms and plantations or as mill workers and domestic servants certainly challenged this notion of **separate spheres** for men and women, but it captured the middle-class ideal.

The rise of the middle class inspired a flood of advice books, ladies' magazines, religious periodicals, and novels that advocated new ideals of womanhood, ideals that emphasized the centrality of child rearing and homemaking to women's identities. This cult of domesticity seemed to restrict wives to home and hearth, where they provided their husbands with respite from the cares and corruptions of the world. But wives were also expected to cement social and economic bonds by visiting the wives of business

Middle-Class Shoppers
Although middle-class women did most of the daily shopping for the family, this 1847 lithograph shows that men were involved as well. This store on Main Street in Worcester, Massachusetts, sold goods from the West Indies, no doubt including rum, which attracted a male clientele. The store hired young boys to help load the purchased items.   The Granger Collection, New York

associates, serving in local charitable societies, and attending prayer circles. In carrying out these duties, the ideal woman bolstered her family's status by performing public as well as private roles.

Middle-class families also played a crucial role in the growing market economy. Although wives and daughters were not expected to work for wages, they were responsible for much of the family's consumption. They purchased factory-produced shoes and cloth, handcrafted clocks and cast-iron stoves, fine European crystal, and porcelain figures imported from China. Some middling housewives also bought basic goods once made at home, such as butter and candles. And middle-class children required books, pianos, and dancing lessons.

Although increasingly recognized for their ability to consume wisely, middle-class women still performed significant domestic labor. Only upper-middle-class women could afford servants. Most middle-class women, aided by daughters or temporary "help," cut and sewed garments, cultivated gardens, canned fruits and vegetables, plucked chickens, cooked meals, and washed and ironed clothes. As houses expanded in size and clothes became fancier, these chores continued to be laborious and time-consuming. But they were also increasingly invisible, focused inwardly on the family rather than outwardly as part of the market economy.

Middle-class men contributed to the consumer economy as well. Most directly, they created and invested in industrial and commercial ventures. But in carrying out their business and professional obligations, they supported new leisure pursuits. Many joined colleagues at restaurants, the theater, or sporting events. They also attended plays and lectures with their wives, visited museums, and took their children to the circus.

REVIEW & RELATE

Why did American cities become larger and more diverse in the first half of the nineteenth century?

What values and beliefs did the emerging American middle class embrace?

LEARNINGCurve bedfordstmartins.com/hewittlawson/LC

The Rise of Industry

Although the percentage of Americans employed in manufacturing never rose above 10 percent of the laboring population in the mid-nineteenth century, industrial enterprises in the Northeast transformed the nation's economy. In the 1830s and 1840s, factories grew considerably in size, and some investors, especially in textiles, constructed factory towns. Textile mills now relied heavily on the labor of girls and young women recruited from rural areas, while urban workshops hired varied groups of workers, including children, young women and men, and older adults. As industry expanded, however, working men's access to highly skilled jobs declined. The panic of 1837 exacerbated this trend and also increased tensions within the working class, especially among workers from different ethnic and racial backgrounds.

Factory Towns and Women Workers

In the late 1820s, investors and manufacturers joined forces to create factory towns in the New England countryside, the most famous of which was constructed in Lowell, Massachusetts, along the Merrimack River. Funded by the Boston Associates, a group of investors from eastern Massachusetts, the Lowell mills were based on an earlier experiment in nearby Waltham. In the Waltham system, every step of the production process was mechanized. The factories were far larger than earlier ones and were built as part of a planned community that included boardinghouses, government offices, and churches. Agents for the Waltham system traveled throughout New England to recruit the daughters of farm families as workers. They assured parents that their daughters would be watched over by managers and foremen as well as by landladies. The young women were required to attend church and observe curfews, and their labor was regulated by clocks and bells to ensure discipline and productivity.

Textile towns allowed young women to contribute to family finances while living in a well-ordered environment. Farm families needed more cash because of the growing market economy, and daughters could save money for the clothes and linens required for married life. Factory jobs also provided an alternative to marriage as young New England men moved west and left a surplus of women behind. The boardinghouses provided a relatively safe, all-female environment for the young workers, and sisters and neighbors often lived together. Despite constant regulation and supervision, many rural women viewed factory work as an adventure. They could send money home and still set aside a bit for themselves, and they could attend lectures and concerts, meet new people, and acquire a wider view of the world.

Initially, factory towns offered many benefits to young women and their families, but by the 1830s working conditions began to deteriorate. Factory owners cut wages, lengthened hours, and sped up machines, forcing women to produce more cloth in less time for lower pay. Many boardinghouses became overcrowded, and company officials regulated both rents and expenses, so higher prices

for lodging did not necessarily mean better food or furnishings. Factory workers launched numerous strikes in the 1830s against longer hours, wage cuts, and speedups in factory production. The solidarity required to sustain these strikes was forged in boardinghouses and at church socials as well as on the factory floor.

Explore

See Documents 11.1 and 11.2 for firsthand accounts of life in the mills.

Despite the mill workers' solidarity, it was not easy to overcome the economic power wielded by manufacturers. Working women's efforts at collective action were generally short-lived, lasting only as long as the strike itself. Then employees returned to their jobs until the next crisis hit. And as competition increasingly cut into profits, owners resisted mill workers' demands more vehemently. When the panic of 1837 intensified fears of job loss, women's organizing activities were doomed until the economy recovered.

Deskilling and the Response of Working Men

While the construction of factory towns expanded economic opportunities for young women, the gradual decline of time-honored crafts narrowed the prospects for working men. As craft workshops increased in size, they hired fewer skilled workers and more men who learned only a single aspect of production—cutting barrel staves or attaching soles to shoes. Like mill operatives, these workers performed distinct tasks, many of which were mechanized over the course of the nineteenth century. The final product was less distinctive than an item crafted by a skilled artisan, but it was also less expensive and available in mass quantities.

The shift from craft work to factory work threatened to undermine working men's skills, pay, and labor conditions. Soon masters hired foremen to regulate the workforce and installed bells and clocks to regulate the workday. Artisans were offended by the new regime, which treated them as wage-earning dependents rather than as independent craftsmen. As the process of **deskilling** transformed shoemaking, printing, bookbinding, tailoring, and other trades, laboring men fought to maintain their status.

Some workers formed mutual aid societies to provide assistance in times of illness, injury, or unemployment. Others participated in religious revivals or joined fraternal orders, such as the Masons and the Red Men, to find the camaraderie they once enjoyed at work. The expansion of voting rights in the 1820s offered another avenue for action. The first workingmen's political party was founded in Philadelphia in 1827, and soon white farmers, mechanics,

DOCUMENTS 11.1 AND 11.2

Life in the Mills: Two Views

In the 1820s, the textile mills of Lowell, Massachusetts, provided the daughters of local farmers a way to contribute to their family incomes and experience some adventure. Soon, however, a slowing economy led to reduced wages, longer hours, and demands for increased productivity. The Lowell workers organized to protest these changes and went on strike several times during the late 1820s and the 1830s. The first selection below is from an 1844 edition of *The Lowell Offering*, a magazine to which mill workers contributed stories and poems. Factory owners controlled the content of the magazine to ensure an idealized vision of life in the mills. Still, the letter from "Susan" below does highlight the physical toll of industrial labor. Susan was a pseudonym for Harriet Farley, a weaver and the editor of *The Lowell Offering*. The selection at right is by Harriet Robinson, who entered the mills at age ten in 1834. She published a memoir in 1898 in which she recalls the growing dissatisfaction of the women workers and her critical role in a strike in 1836.

Explore

11.1 Letter from a Lowell Factory Worker, 1844

It makes my feet ache and swell to stand so much, but I suppose I shall get accustomed to that too. The girls generally wear old shoes about their work, and you know nothing is easier; but they almost all say that when they have worked here a year or two they have to procure shoes a size or two larger than before they came. The right hand, which is the one used in stopping and starting the loom, becomes larger than the left; but in other respects the factory is not detrimental to a young girl's appearance. Here they look delicate, but not sickly; they laugh at those who are much exposed, and get pretty brown; but I, for one, had rather be brown than pure white. I never saw so many pretty looking girls as there are

here. Though the number of men is small in proportion there are many marriages here, and a great deal of courting. I will tell you of this last sometime. . . .

You ask if the work is not disagreeable. Not when one is accustomed to it. It tried my patience sadly at first, and does now when it does not run well; but, in general, I like it very much. It is easy to do, and does not require very violent exertion, as much of our farm work does.

You also ask how I get along with the girls here. Very well indeed.

Source: Harriet Farley, "Letters from Susan, Second Letter," *The Lowell Offering*, June 1844, 170–71.

and workingmen started joining forces throughout the North to advocate for principles of liberty and equality. Self-educated artisans like Thomas Skidmore of New York City argued for the redistribution of property and the abolition of inheritance to equalize wealth in the nation. However, most workingmen's parties focused on more practical proposals: government distribution of free land in the West, the abolition of compulsory militia service and imprisonment for debt, public funding for education, and the regulation of banks and corporations. Although the

success of these parties at the polls was modest, by the 1830s Democrats and Whigs adopted many of their proposals.

Workingmen, like workingwomen, also formed unions to demand better wages and working conditions. In the 1820s and 1830s, skilled journeymen held mass meetings to protest employers' efforts to extend the workday from ten to eleven hours, merge smaller workshops into larger factories, and cut wages. In New York City in 1834, labor activists formed a citywide federation, the General Trades Union, which provided support for striking workers. The National

Explore

11.2 Harriet Robinson | Reflections on the 1836 Lowell Mills Strike, 1898

My own recollection of this first strike (or "turn out" as it was called) is very vivid. I worked in a lower room, where I had heard the proposed strike fully, if not vehemently, discussed; I had been an ardent listener to what was said against this attempt at "oppression" on the part of the corporation, and naturally I took sides with the strikers. When the day came on which the girls were to turn out, those in the upper rooms started first, and so many of them left that our mill was at once shut down. Then, when the girls in my room stood irresolute, uncertain what to do, asking each other, "Would you?" or "Shall we turn out?" and not one of them having the courage to lead off, *I*, who began to think they would not go out, after all their talk, became impatient, and started on ahead, saying, with childish bravado, "I don't care what you do, I am going to turn out, whether any one else does or not"; and I marched out, and was followed by the others.

As I looked back at the long line that followed me, I was more proud than I have ever been since at any success I may have achieved, and more proud than I shall ever be again until my own beloved State gives to its women citizens the right of suffrage.

The agent of the corporation where I then worked took some small revenges on the supposed ringleaders; on the principle of sending the weaker to the wall, my mother [a landlady] was turned away from her boarding-house, that functionary saying, "Mrs. Hanson, you could not prevent the older girls from turning out, but your daughter is a child, and *her* you could control."

It is hardly necessary to say that so far as results were concerned this strike did no good. The dissatisfaction of the operatives subsided, or burned itself out, and though the authorities did not accede to their demands, the majority returned to their work, and the corporation went on cutting down the wages.

Source: Harriet H. Robinson, *Loom and Spindle; or, Life among the Early Mill Girls* (New York: Thomas Y. Crowell, 1898), 84–86.

Interpret the Evidence

- How did life on the farm differ from life in the factory? How does "Susan" describe her own adjustment to industrial work?
- What connections does Robinson make between the strike and the larger social and political context of 1830s Massachusetts? How does she see herself and her actions?

Put It in Context

Were "Susan" and Robinson typical factory workers in this period? Why or why not?

Trades Union was established later that year, with delegates representing more than twenty-five thousand workers across the North. These organizations aided skilled workers but refused admission to women and unskilled men.

Broad labor organizations proved difficult to sustain because of differences in skill and ethnicity as well as in age and marital status among members. Even workingmen's parties, which recruited men across occupations and ages, refused to recruit laborers who could not vote—women, new immigrants, and most blacks. With the onset of the panic of 1837, the common plight of workers became clearer. But the economic crisis made unified action nearly impossible as individuals sought to hold on to what little they had by any means available.

The Panic of 1837 in the North

The panic of 1837 began in the South, but it hit northern cotton merchants hard (see chapter 10). Textile factories drastically cut production, metal foundries that supplied

Hat Manufacturing, 1850

This 1850 lithograph advertises Charles Oakford's hat factory in Philadelphia. Like many industries, hat making became increasingly mechanized in the 1840s. Here Oakford talks with a client in the center of the room, across from his steam-powered lathe, while workers stand at stations shaping and stacking hats. A boy packs the merchandise into a box ready for shipping. © Philadelphia History Museum at the Atwater Kent/The Bridgeman Art Library

their machinery were wiped out, workers lost their jobs, and merchants and investors went broke. Those who kept their jobs saw their wages cut in half. As with the panic of 1819, hunger plagued urban residents while crops rotted in the Midwest because farmers could not afford to harvest them. In Rochester, the Posts were among hundreds who lost their homes to foreclosure. Petty crime, prostitution, and violence also rose as men and women struggled to make ends meet.

In Lowell and other textile towns, hours increased and wages fell. Just as important, the process of deskilling intensified. Factory owners considered mechanization one way to improve their economic situation. In the 1830s and 1840s, the sewing machine was invented and

improved. When it came into widespread use in the 1850s, factories began to mass-produce inexpensive clothing, employing women who worked for low wages. Mechanical reapers, steam boilers, and the steam press transformed other occupations as manufacturers invested more of their resources in machines. At the same time, the rising tide of immigrants provided a ready supply of relatively cheap labor. Artisans tried to maintain their traditional skills and status, but in many trades they were fighting a losing battle.

By the early 1840s, when the panic subsided, new technologies did spur new jobs. Factories demanded more workers to handle new machines that ran at a faster pace. The ease of harvesting wheat inspired changes in flour milling that required engineers to design machines and mechanics to build and repair them. The steam press allowed publication of more newspapers and magazines, creating positions for editors, publishers, printers, engravers, reporters, and sales agents. Advertising became an occupation unto itself.

Following the panic, new labor organizations also emerged to address workers' changing circumstances. Many of these unions were made up of a particular trade or ethnic group, and almost all continued to address primarily the needs of skilled male workers. Textile operatives remained the one important group of organized female workers. In the 1840s, workingwomen joined with workingmen in New England to fight for a ten-hour day. Slowly, however, farmers' daughters abandoned the fight and left the mills as Irish immigrants flooded the labor market and agreed to accept lower pay and longer hours.

For most women in need, charitable organizations offered more support than unions did. Organizations like Philadelphia's Female Association for the Relief of Women and Children in Reduced Circumstances provided a critical safety net for many poor families since public monies for such purposes were limited. Although nearly every town and city provided some form of public assistance in this period, municipalities never had sufficient resources to meet the needs of growing populations, much less the extraordinary demands posed by hard times. Despite financial constraints, towns and cities continued to expand almshouses and workhouses, offer some financial assistance, and provide land and supplemental funds for private benevolent ventures like orphan asylums.

Rising Class and Cultural Tensions

By the 1840s, leaders of both public and private charitable endeavors linked relief to the moral character of those in need and generally measured that character by the standards of affluent Protestants. Upper-class Americans had long debated whether the poor would learn habits of industry and thrift if they were simply given aid without working for it. Concern over the "idle poor"—those who were physically able to work but did not—intensified as more and more immigrants joined the ranks of the needy. The debate was deeply gendered. Women and children were considered the worthiest recipients of aid, and middle- and upper-class women the appropriate dispensers of charity. Successful men, meanwhile, often linked poverty to weakness and considered giving pennies to a beggar an unmanly act that indulged the worst traits of the poor. They focused on building workhouses or expanding almshouses, though preferably at little expense to city residents.

The panic of 1837 convinced some benevolent leaders that public workhouses and almshouses offered the best hope for helping the poor. Alternatively, charitable societies sought to improve the environment in an effort to change the conditions that produced poverty. In the 1840s and 1850s, they built orphan asylums, schools, hospitals, and homes for working women to provide vulnerable residents with housing, education, domestic skills, and advice.

The "undeserving" poor faced grimmer choices. They received public assistance only through the workhouse or the local jail. Rowdy men who gambled away what little they earned, prostitutes who tempted respectable men into vice, and immigrants who preferred idle poverty to virtuous labor figured in newspaper articles, investigative reports, and novels. In fictional portrayals, naive girls were often the victims of immoral men or unfortunate circumstance. One of the first mass-produced books in the United States, Nathaniel Hawthorne's *The Scarlet Letter* (1850) was set in Puritan New England but addressed contemporary concerns about the seduction of innocents. It illustrated the social ostracism and poverty suffered by a woman who bore a child out of wedlock.

Other fictional tales placed the blame for fallen women on foreigners, especially Catholics. Such works drew vivid portraits of young nuns ravished by priests and then thrown out pregnant and penniless. These stories attracted tens of thousands of readers in the United States and heightened anti-Catholic sentiment, which periodically boiled over into attacks on Catholic homes, schools, churches, and convents.

Economic competition further intensified conflicts between immigrants and native-born Americans. By the 1840s, Americans who opposed immigration took the name **nativists** and launched public campaigns against foreigners, especially Irish Catholics. In May 1844, nativists clashed with Irishmen in Philadelphia after shots were fired from a firehouse. A dozen nativists and one Irishmen were killed the first day. The next night, nativists looted and burned Irish businesses and Catholic churches.

Explore

See Document 11.3 for an example of nativist sentiment from a well-known inventor.

Most native-born workers distanced themselves from immigrants, but others believed that class solidarity was crucial to overcoming the power wielded by employers. Nevertheless, only highly skilled immigrants were likely to gain entrance to labor organizations. Although immigrants with sufficient resources to open businesses or establish themselves in professions might

DOCUMENT 11.3

Samuel F. B. Morse | The Dangers of Foreign Immigration, 1835

Samuel Morse is best remembered as a painter and the inventor of the telegraph, but he was also a leader in the nativist movement of the mid-nineteenth century, and he wrote and spoke out against immigration throughout his life. He viewed Catholicism in particular as a grave threat to American democracy and advocated strict restriction of immigration from countries with large Catholic populations. The following passage is from an anti-immigration book Morse wrote in 1835.

Explore

Let us examine this point a little more minutely. These materials are the *varieties of Foreigners* of the same Creed, the Roman Catholic, over all of whom the Bishops or Vicars General hold, as a matter of course, ecclesiastical rule; and we well know what is the nature of Roman Catholic ecclesiastical rule—it is the double refined spirit of despotism, which, after arrogating to itself the prerogatives of Deity, and so claiming to bind or loose the *soul* eternally, makes it, in the comparison, but a mere trifle to exercise absolute sway in all that relates to the body. The notorious ignorance in which the great mass of these emigrants have been all their lives sunk, until their minds are dead, makes them but senseless machines; they obey orders mechanically, for it is the habit of their education, in the despotic countries of their birth. And can it be for a moment supposed by any one that by the act of coming to this country, and being naturalized, their darkened intellects can suddenly be illuminated to discern the nice boundary where their *ecclesiastical obedience* to their priests *ends*, and their *civil independence* of them *begins*? The very supposition is absurd. They obey their priests as demigods, from the habit of their whole lives; they have been taught from infancy that their priests are infallible in the greatest matters, and can they, by mere importation to this country, be suddenly imbued with the knowledge that in civil matters their priests may err, and that they are not in these also their infallible guides? Who will teach them this? Will their priests? Let common sense answer this question. Must not the priests, as a matter almost of *certainty*, control the opinions of their ignorant flock in civil as well as religious matters? and do they not do it?

Source: Samuel F. B. Morse, *Imminent Dangers to the United States through Foreign Immigration* (New York: E. B. Clayton, 1835), 13.

Interpret the Evidence

- Why does Morse single out Catholicism as a threat to the United States?
- Why does Morse believe most immigrants are incapable of becoming good citizens?

Put It in Context

What is the relationship among Morse's hostility to Catholic immigrants, the growth and increasing diversity of cities, and rising class tensions in this period?

gain middle-class status, only pious immigrants from Protestant backgrounds were likely to be truly accepted into middle-class society.

REVIEW & RELATE

How and why did American manufacturing change over the course of the first half of the nineteenth century?

How did Northerners respond to the hard times that followed the panic of 1837? How did responses to the crisis vary by class, ethnicity, and religion?

✓ *LEARNINGCurve* **bedfordstmartins.com/hewittlawson/LC**

Saving the Nation from Sin

Americans had established Bible societies, prayer circles, and urban missions as early as the 1810s. These efforts were infused with new energy as evangelical fires—lit by southern camp meetings in the early nineteenth century—swept across the North. Men and women of all classes and races embraced this **Second Great Awakening** to express deeply held beliefs and reclaim a sense of the nation's godly mission. Yet evangelical Protestantism was not the only religious tradition to thrive in the 1830s and 1840s. The Quaker and Unitarian faiths also grew in this period. Catholic churches and Jewish synagogues expanded along with immigration, and new religious groups—including Mormons and Millerites—attracted thousands of followers. At the same time, transcendentalists sought deeper engagements with nature as another path to spiritual renewal.

The Second Great Awakening

Although diverse religious traditions flourished in the United States, evangelical Protestantism proved the most powerful in the 1820s and 1830s. Evangelical churches hosted revivals, encouraged conversions, and organized prayer and missionary societies. This second wave of religious revivals began in Cane Ridge, Kentucky, in 1801, took root across the South, and then spread northward. Although revivals had diminished by the late 1830s, they erupted periodically through the 1850s and again during the Civil War. But it was the revivals of the 1830s that transformed Protestant churches and the social fabric of northern life.

Northern ministers like Charles Grandison Finney adopted techniques first wielded by southern Methodists and Baptists: plain speaking, powerful images, and mass meetings. But Finney molded these techniques for a more

affluent audience and held his "camp meetings" in established churches. Northern evangelicals also insisted that religious fervor demanded social responsibility and that good works were a sign of salvation.

In the late 1820s, boomtown growth along the Erie Canal aroused deep concerns about the rising tide of sin. In September 1830, the Reverend Finney arrived in Rochester and began preaching in the city's Presbyterian churches. Arguing that "nothing is more calculated to beget a spirit of prayer, than to unite in social prayer with one who has the spirit himself," Finney led prayer meetings that lasted late into the night. Individual supplicants walked to special benches designated for anxious sinners, who were prayed over in public. Female parishioners played crucial roles, encouraging their husbands, sons, friends, and neighbors to submit to God.

Thousands of Rochester residents joined in the evangelical experience as Finney's powerful message spilled over into other denominations (Map 11.1). But the significance of the Rochester revivals went far beyond a mere increase in church membership. Finney had converted "the great mass of the most influential people" in the city: merchants, lawyers, doctors, master craftsmen, and

MAP 11.1 Religious Movements in the Burned-Over District, 1831–1848

Western and central New York State were burned over by the fires of religious revivalism in the 1830s and 1840s. But numerous other religious groups also formed or flourished in the region at the same time, including radical Quakers, Mormons, and Millerites. In the 1840s, Fourierist phalanxes, the Oneida community, and other utopian experiments also flourished here. Source: Whitney R. Cross, *The Burned-Over District: The Social and Intellectual History of Enthusiastic Religion in Western New York, 1800–1850* (1950).

shopkeepers. Equally important, he proclaimed that if Christians were "united all over the world the Millennium [Christ's Second Coming] might be brought about in three months." Local preachers in Rochester and the surrounding towns took up his call, and converts committed themselves to preparing the world for Christ's arrival.

Lyman Beecher, a powerful Presbyterian minister in Boston, declared that the spiritual renewal of the early 1830s was the greatest revival of religion the world had ever seen. Middle-class and wealthy Americans were swept into Presbyterian, Congregational, and Episcopalian churches, while Baptists and Methodists ministered mainly to laboring women and men. Black Baptists and Methodists evangelized in their own communities, where independent black churches combined powerful preaching with haunting spirituals. In Philadelphia, African Americans built fifteen churches between 1799 and 1830. Over the next two decades, a few black women, such as Jarena Lee, joined men in evangelizing among African American Methodists and Baptists.

Tens of thousands of Christian converts both black and white embraced evangelicals' message of moral outreach. They formed Bible, missionary, and charitable societies; Sunday schools; and reform organizations. No movement gained greater impetus from the revivals than did **temperance**, which sought to moderate and then ban the sale and consumption of alcohol. In the 1820s, Americans fifteen years and older consumed six to seven gallons of distilled alcohol per person per year (about double the amount consumed today). Middle-class evangelicals, who once accepted moderate drinking as healthful and proper, now insisted on eliminating alcohol consumption in the United States.

New Spirits Rising

Although enthusiasm for temperance and other reforms waned during the panic of 1837 and many churches lost members, the Second Great Awakening revived following the panic. Increasingly, however, evangelical ministers competed for souls with a variety of other religious groups. In the 1840s, diverse religious groups flourished, many of which supported good works and social reform. The Society of Friends, or Quakers, the first religious group to refuse fellowship to slaveholders, grew throughout the early and mid-nineteenth century. Having divided in 1827 and then again in 1848, the Society of Friends continued to grow. So, too, did its influence in reform movements as activists like Amy Post carried Quaker testimonies against alcohol, war, and slavery into the wider society. Unitarians also combined religious worship with social reform. Their primary difference from other Christians was their belief in a single unified higher spirit rather than the Trinity of the Father,

the Son, and the Holy Spirit. First established in Boston in 1787, Unitarian societies spread across New England in the 1820s, emerging mainly out of Congregational churches. Opposed to evangelical revivalism, Unitarians nonetheless spread west and south in the 1830s and 1840s, attracting well-to-do merchants and manufacturers as well as small farmers, shopkeepers, and laborers. Dedicated to a rational approach to understanding the divine, Unitarian church members included prominent literary figures such as Ralph Waldo Emerson and Harvard luminaries such as William Ellery Channing.

Other churches grew as a result of immigration. Dozens of Catholic churches were established to meet the needs of many Irish and some German immigrants. With the rapid increase in the number of Catholic churches, more Irish priests were ordained in the United States, and women's religious orders also became increasingly Irish in the 1840s and 1850s. By 1860 the Irish numbered 1.6 million of the 2.2 million Catholics in the United States. Meanwhile synagogues, Hebrew schools, and Hebrew aid societies signaled the growing presence of Jews in the United States. They came chiefly from Germany, though Jews were far fewer in number than Catholics.

Entirely new religious groups also flourished in the 1840s. One of the most important was the Church of Jesus Christ of Latter-Day Saints, or Mormons, founded by Joseph Smith. Smith claimed that he began to receive visions from God at age fifteen and was directed to dig up gold plates inscribed with instructions for redeeming the Lost Tribes of Israel. *The Book of Mormon* (1830), supposedly based on these inscriptions, granted spiritual authority to the unlearned and mercy to the needy while it castigated the pride and wealth of those who oppressed the humble and the poor. At the same time, Smith founded the Church of Jesus Christ of Latter-Day Saints, which he led as the Prophet. Although seeking converts, the church did not admit African Americans to worship.

Smith founded not only a church but a theocracy (a community governed by religious leaders). In the mid-1830s, Mormons established a settlement at Nauvoo, Illinois, built homes and churches, and recruited followers from the eastern United States and from England. But after Smith received revelations sanctioning polygamy, local authorities arrested him and his brother, and a mob lynched them. Brigham Young, a successful missionary, took over as Prophet and in 1846 led 12,000 followers west, 5,000 of whom built a thriving theocracy near the Great Salt Lake, in what would become the Utah Territory in 1850.

New religious groups also formed by separating from established denominations, just as Unitarians had split from Congregationalists. William Miller, a prosperous farmer and Baptist preacher, led one such movement.

Religious Fervor

This broadside depicts the rapture that Baptist minister William Miller predicted would occur when Jesus Christ returned between March 21, 1843, and March 21, 1844. Although the failure of this and later predictions caused many Americans to satirize Miller and his followers, some Millerites continued to believe the Second Coming was imminent and formed the Seventh-Day Adventists. The New-York Historical Society

He claimed that the Bible proved that the Second Coming of Jesus Christ would occur in 1843. Thousands of Americans read Millerite pamphlets and newsletters and attended sermons by Millerite preachers. When various dates for Christ's Second Coming passed without incident, however, Millerites developed competing interpretations for the failure and divided into distinct groups. The most influential group formed the Seventh-Day Adventist Church in the 1840s.

Transcendentalism

Another important movement for spiritual renewal was rooted in the transcendent power of nature. The founder of this transcendentalist school of thought was Ralph Waldo Emerson, a Unitarian pastor who gave up his post to travel and read. In 1836 he published an essay entitled "Nature"

that expressed his newfound belief in a Universal Being. This Being existed as an ideal reality beyond the material world and was accessible through nature. The natural world Emerson described was distinctly American and offered hope that moral perfection could be achieved in the United States despite the corruptions of civil society and man-made governments. Emerson expressed his ideas in widely read essays and books and in popular lectures to packed houses.

From the 1830s on, Emerson's town of Concord, Massachusetts, served as a haven for writers, poets, intellectuals, and reformers who embraced his views. Many Unitarians and other liberal Protestants in the Boston area were drawn to **transcendentalism** as well. In 1840 Margaret Fuller, a close friend of Emerson, became the first editor of *The Dial*, a journal dedicated to transcendental thought. In 1844 she moved to New York City, where the editor Horace Greeley hired her as a critic at the *New York Tribune*. While in New York, she published her ideas about the conflict between women's assigned roles and their innate abilities in *Woman in the Nineteenth Century* (1845), which combined transcendental ideas with arguments for women's rights.

Henry David Thoreau also followed the transcendentalist path. He grew up in Concord and read "Nature" while a student at Harvard. In July 1845, Thoreau moved to a cabin near Walden Pond and launched an experiment in simple living. A year later, he was imprisoned overnight for refusing to pay his taxes as a protest against slavery and the Mexican-American War. In the anonymous *Civil Disobedience* (1846), he argued that individuals of conscience had the right to resist government policies they believed to be immoral. Five years later, Thoreau published *Walden*, which offered a classic statement of the interplay among a simple lifestyle, natural harmony, and social justice.

Emerson also urged Americans to break their cultural dependence on Europe, and American artists agreed. Led by Thomas Cole, members of the Hudson River School painted romanticized landscapes from New York's Catskill and Adirondack Mountains. The sweeping vistas tied the nation's power to its natural beauty. Western vistas inspired artistic efforts as well. George Catlin portrayed the dramatic scenery of western mountains, gorges, and waterfalls and offered moving portraits of Plains Indians, who, he feared, faced extinction. Other artists captured birds, plants, and animals distinctive to the West. Although relatively few Americans had yet visited the region, many hung copies of frontier paintings on their walls or marveled at them in books and magazines. Clearly the hand of God must be at work in such glorious landscapes.

REVIEW & RELATE

What impact did the Second Great Awakening have in the North?	What new religious organizations and viewpoints emerged in the first half of the nineteenth century, *outside* of Protestant evangelical denominations?

 LEARNINGCurve bedfordstmartins.com/hewittlawson/LC

Organizing for Change

Both religious commitments and secular problems spurred social activism in the 1830s and 1840s. In cities, small towns, and rural communities, Northerners founded organizations, launched campaigns, and established institutions to better the world around them. Yet even those

Americans who agreed that society needed to be reformed did not share a common sense of priorities or solutions. Moreover, while some activists worked to persuade Americans to follow their lead, others insisted that change would occur only if imposed by law.

Varieties of Reform

Middle-class Protestant women and men formed the core of many reform movements in the early to mid-nineteenth century. They had more time and money to devote to social reform than did their working-class counterparts and were less tied to traditional ways than were their wealthy neighbors. Nonetheless, workers and farmers, African Americans and immigrants, Catholics and Jews also participated in efforts to improve society. The array of causes reformers pursued was astonishing: charity to the poor and sick; establishing religious missions; prison reform, health reform, dress reform, and educational reform; eradicating prostitution; aid to orphans, the deaf, the blind, the mentally ill, and immigrants; the exclusion of immigrants; the rights of workers, of women, and of Indians; ending alcohol and tobacco abuse; abolishing capital punishment; racial justice; and the abolition of slavery.

Explore

See Document 11.4 for an illustration of the dangers of alcohol.

Reformers used different techniques to pursue their goals. Since women could not vote, for example, they were excluded from direct political participation. Instead, they established charitable associations, distributed food and medicine, constructed asylums, circulated petitions, organized boycotts, arranged meetings and lectures, and published newspapers and pamphlets. Other groups with limited political rights—African Americans and immigrants, for instance—embraced similar modes of action. White men wielded these forms of activism but also organized political campaigns and lobbied legislators. The techniques employed were also affected by the goals of a particular movement. Moral suasion worked best with families, churches, and local communities, while legislation was more likely to succeed if the goal involved transforming people's behavior across a whole state or region.

Reformers often used a variety of tactics to support a single cause, and many changed their approach over time. For instance, reformers who sought to eradicate prostitution began by praying in front of urban brothels and attempting to rescue "fallen" women. They soon

DOCUMENT 11.4

Drunkard's Home, 1850

Temperance societies undertook a variety of activities to publicize the dangers of alcohol. Public lectures, ceremonies, and parades were popular venues, as were newspapers and books. This engraved illustration is from *The National Temperance Offering*, an 1850 publication of the Sons of Temperance of North America. Founded in New York City in 1842, the Sons of Temperance was one of the oldest temperance organizations in the United States. It was also a mutual aid society that offered members life insurance, funeral benefits, and assistance if they were injured or ill.

Explore

How does the father's drinking seem to affect the family's economic situation?

In this illustration, what is the source of the father's violence?

How does alcohol affect each member of this family?

The National Temperance Offering, and Sons and Daughters of Temperance Gift (PS1265.N3 1850), University of Virginia Library

Put It in Context

What moral arguments did members of the temperance movement use to support their cause?

launched *The Advocate of Moral Reform*, a newspaper that published morality tales, advice to mothers, and the names of men who visited brothels. Moral reform societies in small towns and rural areas worked to alert young women and men to the dangers of city life. Those in cities opened Homes for Virtuous and Friendless Females in the 1840s to provide safe havens for vulnerable women. But moral reformers also started to petition state legislators to make punishments for men who hired prostitutes as harsh as those for prostitutes themselves.

The Temperance Movement

Many moral reformers also advocated temperance. Organized temperance work began in 1826 with the founding of the American Temperance Society, an all-male organization led by clergy and businessmen who focused on alcohol abuse among working-class men. Religious revivals then inspired the establishment of some 5,000 local chapters with more than 100,000 members. Over time, the temperance movement changed the goal from moderation to total abstinence, targeted middle-class and elite as well as working-class men, and welcomed women's support. Wives and mothers were expected to persuade family members to stop drinking, sign a temperance pledge, and commit their newly sober souls to God. To promote this work, women founded dozens of female temperance societies in the 1830s. African Americans, too, created their own temperance organizations.

Some white working men viewed temperance as a way to gain dignity and respect. For Protestants, in particular, embracing temperance distinguished them from Irish Catholic workers, who were caricatured as happy drunkards. Some working-class temperance advocates also criticized liquor dealers, whom they considered to be greedy capitalists overseeing "the vilest, meanest, most earth-cursing and hell-filling business ever followed."

Despite the rapid growth of temperance organizations, moral suasion failed to reduce alcohol consumption significantly. As a result, many temperance advocates turned to legal reform in the 1840s, hoping to legislate where they could not persuade. In 1851 Maine passed legislation that prohibited the sale of all alcoholic beverages. By 1855 twelve states had joined Maine in restricting the manufacture or sale of alcohol. Yet these stringent measures inspired a backlash. Hostile to the imposition of middle-class Protestant standards on the population at large, Irish workers in Maine organized the Portland Rum Riot in 1855. It led to the law's repeal the next year.

Legal strategies generally complemented rather than replaced moral arguments. Temperance advocates

continued to publish short stories, magazine articles, sermons, and novels alerting Americans to the dangers of "demon rum." Working-class families were often the subjects of didactic tales written by and for the middle class. But laboring men and women had their own ideas about how to deal with alcohol abuse. Small groups of men who abused alcohol gathered together in the 1840s and formed Washingtonian societies—named in honor of the nation's founder—to help each other stop drinking. Martha Washington societies appeared shortly thereafter, composed not of female alcoholics but of the wives, mothers, and sisters of male alcoholics.

Temperance advocates thus used various strategies to limit alcohol abuse and its consequences. Over the course of the nineteenth century, these efforts gradually reduced the consumption of beer, wine, and spirits, although they did not eliminate the problem.

Utopian Communities

While most reformers reached out to the wider society to implement change, some activists withdrew into self-contained communities that they hoped would serve as models for other groups. The architects of these **utopian societies** turned to European intellectuals and reformers for inspiration as well as to American religious and republican ideals.

In the 1820s, Scottish and Welsh labor radicals such as Frances Wright, Robert Owen, and his son Robert Dale Owen established utopian communities in the United States. They believed that a young nation founded on republican principles would be particularly open to experiments in communal labor, gender equality, and (in Wright's case) racial justice. Their efforts ultimately failed, but they did arouse impassioned debate. After founding the community of New Harmony, Indiana, in 1828 with his father, Robert Dale Owen returned briefly to Europe. He then joined Wright in New York City, where they established a reform newspaper, reading room, and medical dispensary. Resettling in New Harmony in 1833, Owen continued to advocate for workers' rights, birth control, and the abolition of slavery. But he also embraced Jacksonian democracy and won election to the Indiana House of Representatives and then the U.S. Congress. Owen thus pursued both utopian communalism and political activism in the larger society.

Former Unitarian minister George Ripley also sought to bridge a critical divide—between physical and intellectual labor. He established a transcendentalist community at Brook Farm in Massachusetts in 1841. In 1845 the farm was reconfigured according to the principles of the French socialist Charles Fourier, who believed that cooperation across classes was necessary to temper the conflicts inherent in capitalist society. He developed a plan for communities, called phalanxes, where residents chose jobs based on their individual interests and were paid according to the contribution of each job to the community's well-being. Fourier also advocated equality for women. More than forty Fourierist phalanxes were founded in the northern United States during the 1840s.

A more uniquely American experiment, the Oneida community, was established in central New York by John Humphrey Noyes in 1848. He and his followers believed that Christ's Second Coming had already occurred and embraced the communalism of the early Christian church. But Noyes also advocated sexual freedom and developed a plan for "complex marriage" in which women were liberated from male domination and constant childbearing. Divorce and remarriage were permitted, children were raised communally, and a form of birth control was instituted. Despite the public outrage provoked by Oneida's sexual practices, the community recruited several hundred residents and thrived for more than three decades.

Explore

See Document 11.5, in which Ripley invites Ralph Waldo Emerson to join Brook Farm.

DOCUMENT 11.5

George Ripley | Letter to Ralph Waldo Emerson, November 9, 1840

George Ripley was a Unitarian minister and an avid reformer. In 1840 he wrote to Ralph Waldo Emerson, the well-known transcendentalist, inviting him to join his planned utopian community, Brook Farm. Although Emerson rejected the invitation, Brook Farm began operations in 1841 in West Roxbury, Massachusetts. The Brook Farmers lived and dined communally and divided their time between farm work and artistic and scholarly pursuits. The community could not sustain itself financially, however, and a year after a devastating fire in 1846, the experiment ended. In the following excerpt, Ripley explains his ideas about the importance of combining physical and mental labor.

Explore

Our objects, as you know, are to insure a more natural union between intellectual and manual labor than now exists; to combine the thinker and the worker, as far as possible, in the same individual; to guarantee the highest mental freedom, by providing all with labor, adapted to their tastes and talents, and securing to them the fruits of their industry; to do away [with] the necessity of menial services, by opening the benefits of education and the profits of labor to all; and thus to prepare a society of liberal, intelligent, and cultivated persons, whose relations with each other would permit a more simple and wholesome life, than can be led amidst the pressure of our competitive institutions.

To accomplish these objects, we propose to take a small tract of land, which, under skillful husbandry, uniting the garden and the farm, will be adequate to the subsistence of the families; and to connect with this a school or college, in which the most complete instruction shall be given, from the first rudiments to the highest culture. Our farm would be a place for improving the race of men that lived on it; thought would preside over the operations of labor, and labor would contribute to the expansion of thought; we should have industry without drudgery, and true equality without its vulgarity.

Source: Octavius Brooks Frothingham, *George Ripley* (Boston: Houghton Mifflin, 1882), 307–8.

Interpret the Evidence

- How does Ripley describe the benefits of combining physical and mental labor at Brook Farm?
- Why might George Ripley be interested in persuading Ralph Waldo Emerson to join the Brook Farm community?

Put It in Context

How does Ripley's plan for his utopian community fit with the visions of social reformers more generally in this period?

REVIEW & RELATE

How did the temperance movement reflect the range of tactics and participants involved in reform during the 1830s and 1840s?

What connections can you identify between utopian communities and mainstream reform movements in the first half of the nineteenth century?

 LEARNINGCurve bedfordstmartins.com/hewittlawson/LC

Abolitionism Expands and Divides

For a small percentage of Northerners, slavery was the ultimate injustice. While most Northerners applauded themselves for ridding their region of the institution, antislavery advocates urged them to recognize the North's continued complicity in human bondage. After all, slaves labored under brutal conditions to provide cotton for New England factories, sugar and molasses for northern tables, and profits for urban traders. Free blacks were among the most vocal advocates of abolition. Yet their leadership became a source of conflict as more whites joined the movement in the 1830s. The place of the church, of women, and of politics in antislavery efforts also caused controversy. In addition, abolitionists disagreed over whether to focus on abolishing slavery in the South or simply preventing its extension into western territories. Although these debates often weakened individual organizations, they expanded the number and range of antislavery associations and campaigns.

The Beginnings of the Antislavery Movement

In the 1820s, African Americans and a few white Quaker allies led the fight to abolish slavery. They published pamphlets, lectured to small audiences, and helped runaway slaves escape. In 1829 David Walker wrote the most militant statement of black abolitionist sentiment, *Appeal . . . to the Colored Citizens*. The free son of an enslaved father, Walker left his North Carolina home for Boston in the 1820s. There he became an agent and a writer for *Freedom's Journal*, the country's first newspaper published by African Americans. In his *Appeal*, Walker criticized the false promises of African colonization and warned that slaves would claim their freedom by force if whites did not agree to emancipate them. Quaker abolitionists, such as Benjamin Lundy, the editor of the *Genius of Universal Emancipation*, admired Walker's courage but rejected his call for violence.

William Lloyd Garrison, a white Bostonian who worked on Lundy's Baltimore newspaper, was inspired by Walker's radical stance. In 1831 he returned to Boston and launched his own abolitionist newspaper, the *Liberator*, urging white antislavery activists to embrace the black perspective. White reformers, he claimed, worried more about the moral and practical problems that slavery posed for whites than about the wrongs it imposed on blacks. From blacks' perspective, Garrison claimed, the goal must be immediate, uncompensated emancipation.

The *Liberator* demanded that whites take an absolute stand against slavery where it existed and halt its spread. With the aid of like-minded reformers in Boston, Philadelphia, and New York City, Garrison organized the **American Anti-Slavery Society (AASS)** in 1833. By the end of the decade, the AASS boasted branches in dozens of towns and cities, from Boston to Salem, Ohio. Members supported lecturers and petition drives, criticized churches that refused to denounce slavery, and proclaimed that the U.S. Constitution was a proslavery document. Some Garrisonians also participated in the work of the **underground railroad**, a secret network of activists who assisted fugitives fleeing enslavement.

In 1835 Sarah and Angelina Grimké joined the AASS and soon began lecturing for the organization. Daughters of a prominent South Carolina planter, they had moved to Philadelphia and converted to Quakerism. As Southerners, their denunciations of slavery carried particular weight. Yet as women, their public presence aroused fierce opposition. In 1837 Congregationalist ministers in Massachusetts decried their presence in front of "promiscuous" audiences of men and women.

The Grimkés were not the first women to speak out against slavery. Maria Stewart, a free black widow, lectured in Boston in 1831–1832. She demanded that northern blacks take more responsibility for ending slavery in the South and for fighting racial discrimination everywhere. In 1833 free black and white Quaker women formed an interracial organization, the Philadelphia Female Anti-Slavery Society. The organization built on the earlier efforts of white Quakers and free blacks in Philadelphia to boycott slave-produced goods such as cotton and sugar.

The abolitionist movement and the AASS quickly expanded to the frontier, and by 1836 Ohio claimed more antislavery groups than any other state. That year, Ohio women initiated a petition to abolish slavery in the District of Columbia, which was circulated from Rhode Island to Illinois. The petition campaign inspired the first national meeting of women abolitionists, held in New York City in 1837. But in Ohio and the rest of the Midwest, female and male abolitionists worked side by side, claiming it was their Christian duty "to *unite* our efforts for the accomplishment of the holy object of our association."

Death of Capt. Ferrer, the Captain of the Amistad, July, 1839.

The *Amistad* Revolt, 1839
This illustration depicts the mutiny of forty-nine African slaves led by Cinqué on board the Spanish ship *Amistad* off the coast of Cuba. After the rebels killed Captain Ramón Ferrer, they sailed to Long Island, New York. In subsequent judicial proceedings, the federal courts ruled that the slaves were entitled to their freedom, and they were returned to Africa.   Beinecke Rare Book and Manuscript Library, Yale University

Abolition Gains Ground and Enemies

The abolitionist movement shocked many Northerners, and in the late 1830s violence often erupted in response to antislavery agitation. Mobs threatened participants at the 1838 Antislavery Convention of American Women at Pennsylvania Hall in Philadelphia. After black and white women left the meeting arm in arm, the hall was burned to the ground. From 1834 to 1838, mobs routinely attacked antislavery meetings, lecturers, and presses as AASS agents crisscrossed the North recruiting followers and organizing local societies.

The massive petition campaigns in 1836 and 1837 generated both support and opposition. Thousands of women and men, including Amy Post and her husband Isaac, signed their names to petitions to ban slavery in the District of Columbia, end the internal slave trade, and oppose the annexation of Texas. While some evangelical women considered such efforts part of their Christian duty, evangelical ministers (including the Reverend Finney) condemned antislavery work as outside women's sphere. Many female evangelicals retreated in the face of clerical disapproval, but others continued their efforts alongside their nonevangelical sisters. **See Document Project 11: The Second Great Awakening and Women's Activism, page 352**. Many politicians were also opposed to mass petitioning, whether by women or men, so in 1836 Congress passed the gag rule (see chapter 10).

But gag rules did not silence abolitionists. In the 1840s, fugitive slaves helped alert Northerners to the horrors of slavery. The most important of the fugitive abolitionists was Frederick Douglass, a Maryland-born slave who fled to New Bedford, Massachusetts, in 1838. He met Garrison in 1841, joined the AASS, and four years later published his life story, *Narrative of the Life of Frederick Douglass, as Told by Himself*. Having revealed his identity as a fugitive slave, Douglass sailed for England, where he launched a successful two-year lecture tour. He then returned to the United States; moved to Rochester, New York; and began publishing his own antislavery newspaper, the *North Star*. Amy Post befriended Douglass, and the Western New York Anti-Slavery Society raised funds and subscribers to support his work.

While eager to have fugitive slaves tell their dramatic stories, many abolitionist leaders did not match Post's vigorous support of African American activists asserting an independent voice. Although these abolitionists opposed slavery, they still believed that blacks were inferior to whites. Thus several affiliates of the AASS refused to accept black members. Those that did often faced resignations from members who opposed the innovation. Ultimately, the independent efforts of black activists such as Douglass helped to expand the antislavery movement even as they made clear the limits of white abolitionist ideals.

Conflicts also arose over the responsibility of churches to challenge slavery. The major Protestant denominations included southern as well as northern churches. If mainstream churches such as Presbyterians, Baptists, or Methodists refused communion to slave owners, their southern branches would certainly secede. Still, from the 1830s on, abolitionists pressured their churches to take Christian obligations seriously and denounce human bondage.

Abolitionism and Women's Rights

Women were increasingly active in the AASS and the "come outer" movement, but their growing participation aroused opposition even among abolitionists. By 1836–1837, female societies formed the backbone of antislavery petition campaigns. More women also joined the lecture circuit, including Abby Kelley, a fiery Quaker orator who demanded that women be granted an equal role in the movement. But when Garrison and his supporters appointed Kelley to the AASS business committee in the spring of 1839, they triggered a crisis. At the AASS annual convention that May, debates erupted over the propriety of women participating "in closed meetings with men." Of the 1,000 abolitionists in attendance, some 300 walked out in protest. The opposition came mainly from the evangelical wing of the movement and included Lewis Tappan, one of the chief financiers of the AASS. The dissidents soon formed a new organization, the American and Foreign Anti-Slavery Society, which excluded women from public lecturing and officeholding but encouraged them to support men's efforts.

The Garrisonians responded by expanding the roles of women in the AASS. In 1840 local chapters appointed a handful of female delegates, including Lucretia Mott, to the World Anti-Slavery Convention in London. The majority of men at the meeting, however, rejected the female delegates' credentials. Women were then forced to watch the proceedings from a separate section of the hall, confirming for some that women could be effective in

Antislavery Meeting

This daguerreotype (an early form of photograph) shows the abolitionist Frederick Douglass seated at a table beside a Quaker woman, with two other former slaves from Washington, D.C., Mary and Emily Edmondson, standing behind him. The open-air meeting in Cazenovia, New York, was held on August 22, 1850, to protest the impending passage of the Fugitive Slave Act, which penalized individuals who aided escaped slaves.   The Granger Collection, New York

Individual churches responded, but aside from the Society of Friends, larger denominations failed to follow suit.

In response, abolitionists urged individual Christians to break with churches that continued to accept slaveholders. Antislavery preachers and parishioners pushed the issue, and some worshippers "came out" from mainstream churches to form antislavery congregations. Union churches, composed of evangelical "come outers" from various denominations, were founded in New York State and New England. White Wesleyan Methodists and Free Will Baptists joined African American Methodists and Baptists in insisting that congregants oppose slavery in order to gain membership. Although these churches remained small, they served as constant reminders to mainstream denominations of their continued ties to slavery.

campaigns against slavery only if they gained more rights for themselves.

Finally, in July 1848, a small circle of women, including Lucretia Mott and a young American she met in London, Elizabeth Cady Stanton, organized the first convention focused explicitly on women's rights. Held in Stanton's hometown of Seneca Falls, New York, the convention attracted three hundred women and men, including Garrisonian abolitionists, radical Quakers, and members of the antislavery Liberty Party. James Mott presided over part of the convention and Frederick Douglass spoke, but women dominated the proceedings. One hundred participants signed a **Declaration of Sentiments** that called for women's equality in everything from education and employment to legal rights and voting. Two weeks later, a second convention in Rochester, New York, took the radical action of electing a woman, Abigail Bush, to preside. Here, too, Douglass and other black abolitionists as well as local working women participated.

Although abolitionism provided much of the impetus for the women's rights movement, it was not the only influence. Strikes by seamstresses and mill workers in the 1830s and 1840s highlighted women's economic needs. Utopian communities experimented with gender equality, and temperance reformers focused attention on domestic violence against women and called for changes in divorce laws. A diverse coalition advocated for married women's property rights. Women's rights were also debated among the Seneca Indians in western New York. Like the Cherokees, Seneca women had lost traditional rights over land and tribal policy as their nation adopted more Anglo-American ways. In the summer of 1848, the creation of a written constitution threatened to enshrine these losses in writing. The Seneca constitution did strip women of their role in selecting chiefs but protected their right to vote on any decision to sell tribal lands. Earlier in 1848, revolutions had erupted against repressive regimes in France and elsewhere in Europe. Antislavery papers like the *North Star* covered developments in detail, including European women's demands for political and civil recognition. French rebels such as Jeanne Deroin and German revolutionaries such as Mathilde Anneke were especially noted for their advocacy of women's rights. The meetings in Seneca Falls and Rochester drew on these ideas and influences even as they attended primarily to the rights of white American women.

The Rise of Antislavery Parties

As women's rights conventions began calling for female suffrage, debates over the role of partisan politics in the antislavery campaign intensified. Keeping slavery out of western territories depended on the actions of Congress, as did abolishing slavery in the nation's capital and ending the internal slave trade. Moral suasion had seemingly done little to change minds in Congress or in the South. To force abolition onto the national political agenda, the **Liberty Party** was formed in 1840. Many Garrisonians were appalled at the idea of participating in what they considered a proslavery government, but the Liberty Party gained significant support among abolitionists in New York, the Middle Atlantic states, and the Midwest.

The Whigs and Democrats sought to avoid the antislavery issue in order to keep their southern and northern wings intact, but that strategy became much more difficult once the Liberty Party entered campaigns. In 1840 the party won less than 1 percent of the popular vote but

Campaign Ribbon from the Election of 1844

The Liberty Party, though fiercely opposed to the proslavery presidential candidate James K. Polk, helped turn the 1844 election in Polk's favor by taking votes away from the Whig contender, Henry Clay, who compromised on slavery. This Whig campaign ribbon from the fourth ward in Lynn, Massachusetts, proclaims "Clay, the Union and Liberty."   © David J. and Jane L. Frent Collection/CORBIS organized large rallies that attracted men, women, and children. In sparsely settled regions like Illinois, Garrisonians even joined Liberty Party supporters to get out the antislavery message. In 1844 the party won a little more than 2 percent of the vote, but this time its presence in the race was enough to ensure a victory for James K. Polk over the Whig candidate, Henry Clay (see chapter 10).

When President Polk led the United States into war with Mexico, interest in an antislavery political party surged. In 1848 the Liberty Party gained the support of antislavery Whigs, also called Conscience Whigs; northern Democrats who opposed the extension of slavery into the territories; and African American leaders like Frederick Douglass, who broke with Garrison on the issue of electoral politics. Seeing a political opportunity, more practically minded political abolitionists founded the Free-Soil Party, which quickly subsumed the Liberty Party. Free-Soilers focused less on the moral wrongs of slavery than on the benefits of keeping western territories free for northern whites. The Free-Soil Party nominated Martin Van Buren, a former Democrat, for president in 1848 and won 10 percent of the popular vote. Once again, the result was to send a slaveholder to the White House— Zachary Taylor, who had led U.S. troops in the war with Mexico. Nonetheless, the Free-Soil Party had expanded beyond the Liberty Party, raising fears in the South and in the two major parties that the battle over slavery could no longer be contained.

REVIEW & RELATE

| How did the American Anti-Slavery Society differ from earlier abolitionist organizations? | How did conflicts over gender and race shape the development of the abolitionist movement in the 1830s and 1840s? |

LEARNINGCurve bedfordstmartins.com/hewittlawson/LC

Conclusion: From the North to the Nation

Charles Grandison Finney followed these developments from Oberlin College, where he served as president in the 1840s. Resistant to women's growing demands for rights and skeptical that politics could transform society, he continued to view individual conversions as the wellspring of change. As the nation expanded westward, he trained ministers to travel the frontier converting American Indians to Christianity and reminding Christian pioneers of their religious obligations. After the discovery of gold in California in 1848, religious leaders of every faith feared that the desire for material gain would once again lead Americans to neglect spiritual responsibilities.

Amy Post watched close friends leave for California with husbands struck by gold fever. Other friends and coworkers moved to Ohio, Michigan, and Kansas. Those who remained in Rochester became even more immersed in abolitionist campaigns but continued to clash over the best strategies for achieving their goals. Amy Post, like most Quakers, rejected participation in a government that accepted slavery and fomented war, causing a rift with Frederick Douglass. The disagreement caused her deep personal anguish, but the debates revitalized the movement, creating new opportunities for action.

Finney and Post were among tens of thousands of Northerners inspired by religious and reform movements between 1820 and 1850. Driven by urban and industrial development, immigration, and moral concerns, activists focused on a wide range of causes. But abolitionism carried the most powerful national implications. The addition of vast new territories at the end of the Mexican-American War in 1848 ensured that those concerns would become even more pressing in the decade ahead.

Chapter Review

Online Study Guide ▶ bedfordstmartins.com/hewittlawson

KEY TERMS

separate spheres (p. 331)
deskilling (p. 333)
nativists (p. 337)
Second Great Awakening (p. 339)
temperance (p. 340)
transcendentalism (p. 341)
utopian societies (p. 344)
Appeal . . . to the Colored Citizens (p. 346)
Liberator (p. 346)
American Anti-Slavery Society (AASS) (p. 346)
underground railroad (p. 346)
Declaration of Sentiments (p. 348)
Liberty Party (p. 349)

REVIEW & RELATE

1. Why did American cities become larger and more diverse in the first half of the nineteenth century?

2. What values and beliefs did the emerging American middle class embrace?

3. How and why did American manufacturing change over the course of the first half of the nineteenth century?

4. How did Northerners respond to the hard times that followed the panic of 1837? How did responses to the crisis vary by class, ethnicity, and religion?

5. What impact did the Second Great Awakening have in the North?

6. What new religious organizations and viewpoints emerged in the first half of the nineteenth century, *outside* of Protestant evangelical denominations?

7. How did the temperance movement reflect the range of tactics and participants involved in reform during the 1830s and 1840s?

8. What connections can you identify between utopian communities and mainstream reform movements in the first half of the nineteenth century?

9. How did the American Anti-Slavery Society differ from earlier abolitionist organizations?

10. How did conflicts over gender and race shape the development of the abolitionist movement in the 1830s and 1840s?

TIMELINE OF EVENTS

1820–1850	Size, number, and diversity of northern cities grow; immigration surges
1823	Textile factory town built in Lowell, Massachusetts
1826	American Temperance Society founded
1827	First workingmen's political party founded
1829	David Walker publishes *Appeal . . . to the Colored Citizens*
1830	Joseph Smith publishes *The Book of Mormon*
September 1830	Charles Grandison Finney brings Second Great Awakening to Rochester, New York
1833	William Lloyd Garrison founds American Anti-Slavery Society (AASS)
1837–1842	Panic of 1837
1839	American Anti-Slavery Society splits over the role of women in the society
1840	Liberty Party formed
	World Anti-Slavery Convention, London
1842	Amy Post helps found the Western New York Anti-Slavery Society
1843	William Miller predicts Second Coming of Christ
1844	Congress funds construction of the first telegraph line
May 1844	Anti-immigrant violence rocks Philadelphia
1845	Frederick Douglass publishes *Narrative of the Life of Frederick Douglass*
	Margaret Fuller publishes *Woman in the Nineteenth Century*
1845–1846	Irish potato famine
1846	Henry David Thoreau publishes *Civil Disobedience*
1848	Free-Soil Party formed
	Frederick Douglass publishes the *North Star*
July 1848	Seneca Falls Woman's Rights Convention
1851	Maine prohibits the sale of alcoholic beverages

The Second Great Awakening and Women's Activism

From the 1790s through the 1830s, a religious movement known as the Second Great Awakening swept through communities across the United States. Revivals and camp meetings transformed many denominations, and evangelical Protestant churches were especially affected by this religious fervor, which not only altered the nature of church services but also led to a surge in church membership. In Documents 11.6 and 11.7, evangelist Charles Grandison Finney and the English traveler Frances Trollope describe the character of revivals in quite different terms.

The Second Great Awakening's social impact extended beyond church membership, and many of the newly converted sought to put their religious beliefs into action through good works. Especially in the North, this meant joining movements designed to rid American society of what they believed were the consequences of sin. Temperance societies, charitable organizations, antiprostitution campaigns, and the abolitionist movement all benefited from this commitment to social reform.

Women formed the backbone of the Second Great Awakening, bringing their husbands, sons, and brothers to mass meetings. It was natural, then, that they also sought to extend their beliefs into reform activities. As women slowly took on a more public role in reform efforts, their actions generated passionate and heated debates over the proper place for women in American society. Several of the documents that follow explore these debates through the lens of the abolitionist movement. Document 11.9, the pastoral letter from Congregationalist ministers, is an example of the criticism directed at women when they engaged in public antislavery work. The female abolitionists in Documents 11.8 and 11.10 defend themselves by appealing to religious doctrines and also the principles of American democracy. Women's reform impulse eventually led some to argue for an expansion of women's rights. While small numbers of abolitionist, temperance, and moral reform activists initiated the women's rights movement of the mid-nineteenth century, many of them came from Quaker and Unitarian rather than evangelical backgrounds.

DOCUMENT 11.6

Charles Grandison Finney | What Revival Is, 1835

In 1835 Charles Finney moved from New York City to Ohio, where he became a professor at Oberlin College and Theological Seminary. In Ohio, Finney continued to preach and also trained new generations of ministers to carry on his theological message. He reached out to an even wider audience through the publication of *Lectures on Revivals of Religion*. Originally a series of sermons printed in the *New York Evangelist*, Finney's book was enormously popular and sold twelve thousand copies in three months. The following selection is from the first lecture, "What Revival Is."

A REVIVAL ALWAYS INCLUDES conviction of sin on the part of the church. Backslidden professors cannot wake up and begin right away in the service of God, without deep searchings of heart. The fountains of sin need to be broken up. In a true revival, Christians are always brought under such convictions; they see their sins in such a light, that often they find it impossible to maintain a hope of their acceptance with God. It does not always go to that extent; but there are always, in a genuine revival, deep convictions of sin, and often cases of abandoning all hope.

Backslidden Christians will be brought to repentance. A revival is nothing else than a new beginning of obedience to God. Just as in the case of a converted sinner, the first step is a deep repentance, a breaking down of heart, a getting down into the dust before God, with deep humility, and forsaking of sin.

Christians will have their faith renewed. While they are in their backslidden state they are blind to the state of sinners. Their hearts are as hard as marble. The truths of the Bible only appear like a dream. They admit it to be all true; their conscience and their judgment assent to it; but their faith does not see it standing out in bold relief, in all the burning realities of eternity. But when they enter into a revival, they no longer see men as trees walking, but they see things in that strong light which will renew the love of God in their hearts. This will lead them to labor zealously to bring others to him. They will feel grieved that others do not love God, when they love him so much. And they will set themselves feelingly to persuade their neighbors to give him their hearts. So their love to men will be renewed. They will be filled with a tender and burning love for souls. They will have a longing desire for the salvation of the whole world. They will be in an agony for individuals whom they want to have saved; their friends, relations, enemies. They will not only be urging them to give their hearts to God, but they will carry them to God in the arms of faith, and with strong crying and tears beseech God to have mercy on them, and save their souls from endless burnings.

A revival breaks the power of the world and of sin over Christians. It brings them to such vantage ground that they get a fresh impulse towards heaven. They have a new foretaste of heaven, and new desires after union with God; and the charm of the world is broken, and the power of sin overcome.

When the churches are thus awakened and reformed, the reformation and salvation of sinners will follow, going through the same stages of conviction, repentance, and reformation. Their hearts will be broken down and changed. Very often the most abandoned profligates are among the subjects. Harlots, and drunkards, and infidels, and all sorts of abandoned characters, are awakened and converted. The worst part of human society are softened and reclaimed, and made to appear as lovely specimens of the beauty of holiness.

Source: Charles G. Finney, *Lectures on Revivals of Religion* (New York: Leavitt, Lord, 1835), 14–15.

DOCUMENT 11.7

Frances Trollope | Description of a Revival Meeting, 1832

Frances Trollope was an English author who toured the United States and lived briefly in Cincinnati in the early 1830s. In 1832 she published *Domestic Manners of the Americans*, a critical and often biting account of American society. The book was a best seller in the United States and Europe, and Trollope was both widely praised and criticized for the work. She discussed a variety of topics and aimed much of her criticism at the influence of the Second Great Awakening and evangelicalism on Americans. In the following selection, she describes a revival meeting in Indiana.

Four high frames, constructed in the form of altars, were placed at the four corners of the inclosure; on these were supported layers of earth and sod, on which burned immense fires of blazing pine-wood. On one side a rude platform was erected to accommodate the preachers, fifteen of whom attended this meeting, and with very short intervals for necessary refreshment and private devotion, preached in rotation, day and night, from Tuesday to Saturday.

When we arrived, the preachers were silent; but we heard issuing from nearly every tent mingled sounds of praying, preaching, singing, and lamentation. The curtains in front of each tent were dropped, and the faint light that gleamed through the white drapery, backed as it was by the dark forest, had a beautiful and mysterious effect, that set the imagination at work; and had the sounds which vibrated around us been less discordant, harsh, and unnatural, I should have enjoyed it; but listening at the corner of a tent, which poured forth more than its proportion of clamour, in a few moments chased every feeling derived from imagination, and furnished realities that could neither be mistaken nor forgotten. . . .

At midnight, a horn sounded through the camp, which, we were told, was to call the people from private to public worship; and we presently saw them flocking from all sides to the front of the preachers' stand. Mrs. B. and I contrived to place ourselves with our backs supported against the lower part of this structure, and we were thus enabled to witness the scene which followed without personal danger. There were about two thousand persons assembled.

One of the preachers began in a low nasal tone, and, like all other Methodist preachers, assured us of the enormous depravity of man as he comes from the hands of his Maker, and of his perfect sanctification after he had wrestled sufficiently with the Lord to get hold of him, *et cætera*. The admiration of the crowd was evinced by almost constant cries of "Amen! Amen!" "Jesus! Jesus!" "Glory! Glory!" and the like. . . .

. . . Above a hundred persons, nearly all females, came forward, uttering howlings and groans so terrible that I shall never cease to shudder when I recall them. They appeared to drag each other forward, and on the word being given, "let us pray," they all fell on their knees; but this posture was soon changed for others that permitted greater scope for the convulsive movements of their limbs; and they were soon all lying on the ground in an indescribable confusion of heads and legs. They threw about their limbs with such incessant and violent motion, that I was every instant expecting some serious accident to occur.

But how am I to describe the sounds that proceeded from this strange mass of human beings? I know no words which can convey an idea of it. Hysterical sobbings, convulsive groans, shrieks and screams the most appalling, burst forth on all sides. I felt sick with horror. As if their hoarse and overstrained voices failed to make noise enough, they soon began to clap their hands violently. . . .

Many of these wretched creatures were beautiful young females. The preachers moved about among them, at once exciting and soothing their agonies. I heard the muttered "Sister! dear sister!" I saw the insidious lips approach the cheeks of the unhappy girls; I heard the murmured confessions of the poor victims, and I watched their tormentors, breathing into their ears consolations that tinged the pale cheek with red. Had I been a man, I am sure I would have been guilty of some rash act of interference. . . .

One woman near us continued to "call on the Lord," as it is termed, in the loudest possible tone, and without a moment's interval, for the two hours that we kept our dreadful station. She became frightfully hoarse, and her face so red as to make me expect she would burst a blood-vessel. Among the rest of her rant, she said, "I will hold fast to Jesus, I never will let him go; if they take me to hell, I will still hold him fast, fast, fast!"

The stunning noise was sometimes varied by the preachers' beginning to sing; but the convulsive movements of the poor maniacs only became more violent. At length the atrocious wickedness of this horrible scene increased to a degree of grossness and drove us from our station; we returned to the carriage at about three o'clock in the morning, and passed the remainder of the night listening to the ever-increasing tumult at the pen. To sleep was impossible.

Source: Frances Trollope, *Domestic Manners of the Americans* (London: Whittaker, Treacher, 1832), 140, 142–45.

DOCUMENT 11.8

Elizabeth Emery and Mary P. Abbott | Letter to the *Liberator*, 1836

Many women's experiences in the religious revivals of the Second Great Awakening moved them to engage in social activism. Abolitionism attracted female activists who believed they were called to rid America of a grave sin. Like many women across the country, women in Andover, Massachusetts, organized a Female Antislavery Society. Elizabeth Emery and Mary Abbott, two leaders in the society, wrote a letter to the antislavery newspaper the *Liberator*, expressing their belief that women had a moral responsibility to work to end slavery.

Mr. Editor:

In these days of women's doings, it may not be amiss to report the proceedings of some ladies in Andover. The story is now and then told of a new thing done here, as the opening of a railroad, or the building of a factory, but we have news better than all—it is the formation of a "Female Antislavery Society."

The call of our female friends across the waters—the energetic appeal of those untiring sisters in the work of emancipation in Boston—above all, the sighs, the groans, the deathlike struggles of scourged sisters in the South—these have moved our hearts, our hands. We feel that woman has a place in this Godlike work, for woman's woes, and woman's wrongs, are borne to us on every breeze that flows from the South; woman has a place, for she forms a part in God's created intelligent instrumentality to reform the world. God never made her to be inactive nor in all cases to follow in the wake of man. When man proves recreant to his duty and faithless to his Maker, woman, with her feeling heart, should rouse him—should start his sympathies—should cry in his ear, and raise such a storm of generous sentiment, as shall never let him sleep again. We believe God gave woman a heart to feel—an eye to weep—a hand to work—a tongue to speak. Now let her use that tongue to speak on slavery. Is it not a curse—a heaven-daring abomination? Let her employ that hand, to labor for the slave. Does not her sister in bonds, labor night and day without reward? Let her heart grieve, and her eye fill with tears, in view of a female's body dishonored—a female's mind debased—a female's soul forever ruined! Woman nothing to do with slavery! Abhorred the thought!! We will pray to abhor it more and more. Is not woman abused—woman trampled upon—woman spoiled of her virtue, her probity, her influence, her joy! And this, not in India—not in China—not in Turkey—not in Africa but in America—in the United States of America, in the birthplace of Washington, the father of freedom, the protector of woman, the friend of equality and human rights!

Woman out of her place, in feeling, praying, and acting for the slave! Impious idea! Her oppressed sister cries aloud for help. She tries to lift her manacled hand—to turn her bruised face—to raise her tearful eye, and by all these, to plead a remembrance in our prayers—an interest in our labors. . . . As Christian women, we will do a Christian woman's duty. . . .

Our preamble gives our creed:

"We believe American Slavery is a sin against God—at war with the dictates of humanity, and subversive of the principles of freedom, because it regards rational beings as goods and chattel; robs them of compensation for their toil—denies to them the protection of law—disregards the relation of husband and wife, brother and sister, parent and child; shuts out from the intellect the light of knowledge; overwhelms hope in despair and ruins the soul—thus sinking to the level of brutes, more than one million of American females, who are created in God's image, a little lower than the angels', and consigns them over to degradation, physical, social, intellectual, and moral: consequently, every slaveholder is bound instantly to cease from all participation in such a system. We believe that we should have no fellowship with these works of darkness, but rather reprove them—and that the truth spoken in love, is mighty to the removal of slavery, as of all other sins." . . .

May fearful foreboding lead the slave holder to timely repentance.

Source: Elizabeth Emery and Mary P. Abbott, "Letter to *The Liberator*," *The Liberator*, August 27, 1836, 138.

DOCUMENT 11.9

Pastoral Letter to the *Liberator*, 1837

As women's involvement in abolitionism became more public, it generated controversy from inside and outside of the movement. In August 1837, ministers from the Congregational Church wrote a letter to the *Liberator* denouncing women's public abolitionist efforts. Their immediate concern was the work of Angelina and Sarah Grimké, sisters and speakers on the abolitionist lecture circuit. The lectures the Grimkés presented to mixed-sex audiences infuriated these Congregationalist ministers, whose letter broadly condemned all women's public activism.

We invite your attention to the dangers which at present seem to threaten the female character with wide-spread and permanent injury. The appropriate duties and influence of woman are clearly stated in the New Testament. Those duties and that influence are unobtrusive and private, but the source of mighty power. When the mild, dependent, softening influence of woman upon the sternness of man's opinions is fully exercised, society feels the effects of it in a thousand ways. The power of woman is in her dependence, flowing from the consciousness of that weakness which God has given her for her protection, and which keeps her in those departments of life that form the character of individuals and of the nation. There are social influences which females use in promoting piety and the great objects of Christian benevolence which we cannot too highly commend. We appreciate the unostentatious prayers and efforts of woman in advancing the cause of religion at home and abroad; in Sabbath-schools; in leading religious inquirers to the pastors for instruction; and in all such associated effort as becomes the modesty of her sex; and earnestly hope that she may abound more and more in these labors of piety and love.

But when she assumes the place and tone of man as a public reformer, our care and protection of her seem unnecessary; we put ourselves in self-defence against her; she yields the power which God has given her for protection, and her character becomes unnatural. If the vine, whose strength and beauty is to lean upon the trellis-work and half conceal its clusters, thinks to assume the independence and the over-shadowing nature of the elm, it will not only cease to bear fruit, but fall in shame and dishonor into the dust. We cannot, therefore, but regret the mistaken conduct of those who encourage females to bear an obtrusive and ostentatious part in measures of reform, and countenance any of that sex who so far forget themselves as to incinerate in the character of public lecturers and teachers. . . . We especially deplore the intimate acquaintance and promiscuous conversation of females with regard to things "which ought not to be named"; by which that modesty and delicacy which is the charm of domestic life, and which constitutes the true influence of woman in society, is consumed, and the way opened, as we apprehend, for degeneracy and ruin. We say these things, not to discourage proper influences against sin, but to secure such reformation as we believe is Scriptural, and will be permanent.

Source: "Pastoral Letter of the General Association of Massachusetts to the Congregational Churches under Their Care," *The Liberator*, August 11, 1837.

DOCUMENT 11.10

Sarah Grimké | Response to the Pastoral Letter, 1837

In response to the ministers' criticism, Sarah Grimké wrote her own letter to the *Liberator*, which defended her work and that of her sister, Angelina. Daughters of a slave owner in South Carolina, the Grimké sisters had moved to Philadelphia in the 1820s. Their conversion to Quakerism strengthened their belief in the evils of slavery, and by 1837 they were nationally known abolitionist activists. Their work included public lectures on behalf of the American Anti-Slavery Society. Criticisms of this work led the sisters to develop arguments in support of women's rights.

Dear Friend,

When I last addressed thee, I had not seen the Pastoral Letter of the General Association. It has since fallen into my hands, and I must digress from my intention of exhibiting the condition of women in different parts of the world, in order to make some remarks on this extraordinary document. I am persuaded that when the minds of men and women become emancipated from the thraldom [bondage] of superstition and "traditions of men," the sentiments contained in the Pastoral Letter will be recurred to with as much astonishment as the opinions of Cotton Mather and other distinguished men of his day, on the subject of witchcraft; nor will it be deemed less wonderful, that a body of divines should gravely assemble and endeavor to prove that woman has no right to "open her mouth for the dumb," than it now is that judges should have sat on the trials of witches, and solemnly condemned nineteen persons and one dog to death for witchcraft.

But to the letter. It says, "We invite your attention to the dangers which at present seem to threaten the female character with wide-spread and permanent injury." I rejoice that they have called the attention of my sex to this subject, because I believe if woman investigates it, she will soon discover that danger is impending, though from a totally different source from that which the Association apprehends—danger from those who, having long held the reins of *usurped* authority, are unwilling to permit us to fill that sphere which God created us to move in, and who have entered into league to crush the immortal mind of woman. I rejoice, because I am persuaded that the rights of woman, like the rights of slaves, need only be examined to be understood and asserted, even by some of those who are now endeavoring to smother the irrepressible desire for mental and spiritual freedom which glows in the breast of many who hardly dare to speak their sentiments.

"The appropriate duties and influence of women are clearly stated in the New Testament. Those duties are unobtrusive and private, but the sources of *mighty power*. When the mild, *dependent*, softening influence of woman upon the sternness of man's opinions is fully exercised, society feels the effects of it in a thousand ways." No one can desire more earnestly than I do, that woman may move exactly in the sphere which her Creator has assigned her; and I believe her having been displaced from that sphere has introduced confusion into the world. It is, therefore, of vast importance to herself and to all the rational creation, that she should ascertain what are her duties and her privileges as a responsible and immortal being. . . .

But the influence of woman, says the Association, is to be private and unobtrusive; her light is not to shine before man like that of her brethren; but she is passively to let the lords of the creation, as they call themselves, put the bushel over it, lest peradventure [perhaps] it might appear that the world has been benefitted by the rays of *her* candle. So that her quenched light, according to their judgment, will be of more use than if it were set on the candlestick. "Her influence is the source of mighty power." This has ever been the flattering language of man since he laid aside the whip as a means to keep woman in subjection. He spares her body; but the war he has waged against her mind, her heart, and her soul, has been no less destructive to her as a moral being. How monstrous, how anti-christian, is the doctrine that woman is to be dependent on man! Where, in all the sacred Scriptures, is this taught? Alas! she has too well learned the lesson, which MAN has labored to teach her. She has surrendered her dearest RIGHTS, and been satisfied with the privileges which man has assumed to grant her; she has been amused with the show of power, whilst man has absorbed all the reality into himself. He has adorned the creature whom God gave him as a companion, with baubles and gew-gaws [showy things], turned her attention to personal attractions, offered incense to her vanity, and made her the instrument of his selfish gratification, a plaything to please his eye and amuse his hours of leisure. . . .

. . . We are told, "the power of woman is in her dependence, flowing from a consciousness of that weakness which God has given her for her protection." If physical weakness is alluded to, I cheerfully concede the supe-riority; if brute force is what my brethren are claiming, I am willing to let them have all the honor they desire; but if they mean to intimate, that mental or moral weakness belongs to woman, more than to man, I utterly disclaim the charge. Our powers of mind have been crushed, as far as man could do it, our sense of morality has been impaired by his interpretation of our duties; but no where does God say that he made any distinc-tion between us, as moral and intelligent beings.

. . . As to the pretty simile, introduced into the Pastoral Letter, "If the vine whose strength and beauty is to lean upon the trellis work, and half conceal its clusters, thinks to assume the independence and the overshad-owing nature of the elm," etc. I shall only remark that it might well suit the poet's fancy, who sings of spar-kling eyes and coral lips, and knights in armor clad; but it seems to me utterly inconsistent with the dignity of a Christian body, to endeavor to draw such an anti-scriptural distinction between men and women. Ah! how many of my sex feel in the dominion, thus unrighteously exercised over them, under the gentle appellation of *protection*, that what they have leaned upon has proved a broken reed at best, and oft a spear.

Source: Sarah Grimké, *Letters on the Equality of the Sexes and the Condition of Woman* (Boston: Isaac Knapp, 1838), 14–18, 21.

Interpret the Evidence

1. What ideas in Charles Finney's *Lectures on Revivals of Religion* (Document 11.6) might have strengthened the connection between the Second Great Awakening and the social reform movements of the nineteenth century?

2. What seem to be Frances Trollope's main criticisms of the camp meeting in Indiana (Document 11.7)? How might Finney and other ministers have responded to those criticisms?

3. Since Trollope's *Domestic Manners of the Americans* was so popular within the United States, how might her views of women and revivalism have shaped public opinion?

4. How do the criticisms of female activism in the pastoral letter of 1837 (Document 11.9) compare with Trollope's criticism of women at revivals?

5. How do both Elizabeth Emery and Mary Abbott (Document 11.8) and Sarah Grimké (Document 11.10) use religious principles to support women's public role in the abolitionist movement?

Put It in Context

- How do the arguments of Emery, Abbott, and Grimké affirm mid-nineteenth-century beliefs about the differences between men and women? In what ways do they challenge those beliefs?

background photos: pages 354–355 and 357, Library of Congress

Library of Congress

Peter Newark American Pictures/The Bridgeman Art Library

Emigrant party headed to California, 1850.

Slaves fleeing Maryland coast to Delaware, 1850.

12

Imperial Ambitions and Sectional Crises

1848–1861

© Collection of the New-York Historical Society, USA/The Bridgeman Art Library

California town, 1855.

AMERICAN HISTORIES

John C. Frémont, a noted explorer and military leader and the first presidential nominee of the Republican Party, rose from humble beginnings. He was the illegitimate child of Anne Beverley Whiting Pryor of Savannah, Georgia, who abandoned her wealthy husband and ran off with a French immigrant, Jean Charles Fremon. As a young man, John changed his last name to Frémont, either reclaiming the original spelling or seeking to create a more aristocratic one. He attended the College of Charleston, where he excelled at mathematics, but was eventually expelled for neglecting his studies. Frémont was hired to teach aboard a navy ship in 1833 through the help of an influential South Carolina politician. He then obtained a surveying position to map new railroad lines and Cherokee lands in Georgia and was finally appointed a second lieutenant in the Corps of Topographical Engineers.

In 1840 Lieutenant Frémont traveled to Washington, D.C., to assist in publishing maps and reports from an expedition along the upper Mississippi River. The following year, the twenty-eight-year-old explorer eloped with Jessie Benton, the seventeen-year-old daughter of Missouri senator Thomas Hart Benton. Despite the scandal, Senator Benton supported his son-in-law's selection for a federally funded expedition to the West. In 1842 Frémont and his guide, Kit Carson, led twenty-three men along the emerging Oregon Trail. Two years later, John returned to Washington, where he and his wife Jessie wrote a vivid report on the Oregon Territory and California. Congress published the report, which inspired a wave of hopeful migrants to head west.

John Frémont shared many Americans' imperial ambitions, but his success was tainted by a quest for personal glory. On a federal mapping expedition in 1845, he left his post and headed to California. Arriving in the Sacramento valley in the winter of 1846, he stirred support among U.S. settlers for war with Mexico. His brash behavior nearly provoked a battle that would have wiped out his small company. Frémont then fled to the Oregon Territory, where he and Kit Carson became involved in conflicts with Modoc Indians. Then, as the nation moved closer to war with Mexico, Frémont returned to California, where he supported Anglo-American settlers' efforts to declare the region an independent republic. Although Frémont was denied the republic's governorship, he worked tirelessly for California's admission to the Union and served as one of the state's first senators. With his wife's encouragement, he also embraced abolition and in 1856 was nominated for president by the new Republican Party.

Dred Scott also traveled the frontier in the 1830s and 1840s, but not of his own free will. Born a slave in Southampton, Virginia, around 1800, he and his master, Peter Blow, moved west to Alabama in 1818 and then relocated to St. Louis, Missouri, in 1830. Three years later, short of funds, Blow sold Scott to Dr. John Emerson, an assistant surgeon in the U.S. army. In 1836 Emerson took Scott to Fort Snelling in the Wisconsin Territory, a free territory that offered glimpses of a different life. There Scott met Harriet Robinson, a young African American woman who was enslaved to the local Indian agent. Her master was also a justice of the peace and agreed to marry the couple in 1837 and transfer ownership of Harriet to Dr. Emerson. When Emerson was transferred back to St. Louis, the Scotts returned with him. After his death in 1843, the couple was hired out to local residents in St. Louis by Emerson's widow.

In April 1846, the Scotts initiated lawsuits in the Missouri courts seeking their freedom. The Missouri Supreme Court had ruled in earlier cases that slaves who resided for any time in free territory must be freed, and the Scotts had lived and married in Wisconsin. Dred Scott's former owners, the Blows, supported his suit, and in 1850 the Missouri Circuit Court ruled in the Scotts' favor. However, the Emerson family appealed the decision to the state Supreme Court, with Harriet's case to follow the outcome of her husband's. Two years later, that court ruled against all precedent and overturned the lower court's decision. Dred Scott then appealed to the U.S. Supreme Court, but it, too, ultimately ruled against the Scotts, leaving them enslaved. •

both photos: Library of Congress

THE AMERICAN HISTORIES of John Frémont and Dred Scott were shaped by the explosive combination of westward expansion and the growing regional division over the issue of slavery. Whereas Frémont joined expeditions to map and conquer the West, Scott followed the migrations of slave owners and soldiers. Both Frémont and Scott found strength through marriage. Jessie Frémont served as her husband's confidante and coauthor, providing both practical and emotional support through nearly fifty years of marriage. Harriet Scott joined her husband in the prolonged litigation to win their freedom. Frémont also opposed slavery, but he focused on legislative means to end it. From their different positions, these two men reflected the dramatic changes that occurred as westward expansion pushed the issues of empire and slavery to the center of national debate.

Wagon Train, 1860

This early photograph, taken in 1860, shows a train of covered wagons, oxen, and men on horseback setting out from Manhattan, Kansas.   Kansas State Historical Society

Claiming the West

During the 1830s and 1840s, national debates over slavery intensified. The most important battles now centered on western territories gained through victory in the war with Mexico. Before 1848, government-sponsored expeditions had opened up vast new lands for American pioneers seeking opportunity. Eastern migrants, along with immigrants from Germany and Scandinavia, moved west in growing numbers. Then, following the Mexican-American War and the discovery of gold in California, tens of thousands of men rushed to the Pacific coast seeking riches. But the West was already home to a diverse population that included Indians, Mexicans, Mormons, and missionaries. Eager pioneers converged, and often clashed, with these groups.

Traveling the Overland Trail

In the 1830s, a few white families had ventured to the western frontier. Some traveled around the southern tip of South America by ship or across the Isthmus of Panama by boat and mule train. But a growing number followed overland trails to the far West. In 1836 Narcissa Whitman and Eliza Spaulding joined a group traveling to the Oregon Territory, the first white women to make the trip. They accompanied their husbands, both Presbyterian ministers, who hoped to convert the region's Indians. Their letters to friends and associates back east described the rich lands and needy souls in the Walla Walla valley and encouraged further migration.

The panic of 1837 also prompted Americans to head west as thousands of U.S. migrants and European immigrants sought new opportunities in the 1840s. They were drawn to Oregon, the Rocky Mountain region, and the eastern plains. The Utah Territory, not yet officially part of the United States, attracted large numbers of Mormons. Some pioneers opened trading posts in the West where Indians exchanged goods with Anglo-American settlers or with merchants back east. Small settlements developed around these posts and near the expanding system of forts that dotted the region.

For many pioneers, the journey on the **Oregon Trail** began at St. Louis. From there, they traveled by wagon train across the Great Plains and the Rocky Mountains to the Pacific coast. By 1860 some 350,000 Americans had made the journey, claimed land from the Mississippi to the Pacific, and transformed the United States into an expanding empire.

Because the trip to the West required funds for wagons and supplies, most pioneers were of middling status. The three- to six-month journey was also physically demanding, and most pioneers traveled with family members to help share the labor and provide support, though men outnumbered women and children, comprising some 60 percent of western migrants.

Explore

See Document 12.1 for one account of the journey west.

DOCUMENT 12.1

Elizabeth Smith Geer | Oregon Trail Diary, 1847

Like thousands of families, Elizabeth and Cornelius Smith and their seven children set out for the Oregon Territory in the spring of 1847. They fared well through the summer, but in the fall heavy rains made things difficult, as Elizabeth describes in the following diary entry, and by November Cornelius had become sick. The Smiths continued on to Oregon, arriving in Portland by Thanksgiving, where Cornelius died two months later. In 1849 Elizabeth married Joseph Geer, the father of ten children whose wife died after making the rough journey on the Oregon Trail.

Explore

November 18.

It rains and snows. We start around the falls this morning with our wagons. We have five miles to go. I carry my babe and lead, or rather carry another, through snow, mud, and water almost to my knees. It is the worst road a team could possibly travel. I went ahead with my children and I was afraid to look behind me for fear of seeing the wagons overturn into the mud and water with everything in them. My children gave out with cold and fatigue and could not travel, and the boys had to unhitch the oxen and bring them and carry the children on to camp. I was so cold and numb that I could not tell by the feeling that I had any feet. We started this morning at sunrise and did not camp until after dark, and there was not one dry thread on one of us—not even on the babe. I had carried my babe and I was so fatigued that I could scarcely speak or step. When I got here I found my husband lying in Welch's wagon very sick. He had brought Mrs. Polk down the day before and was taken sick. We had to stay up all night for our wagons were left halfway back. I have not told half we suffered. I am not adequate to the task.

Source: Theodore Thurston Geer, *Fifty Years in Oregon* (New York: Neale, 1912), 146.

Interpret the Evidence

- This diary entry reflects common experiences of women, and especially mothers, on the Oregon Trail. Why do you think so many women were willing to make the journey?
- What does this diary reveal about how women experienced the trip differently from how men did?

Put It in Context

Despite widespread fear of Indian attacks on the trail, what were the most serious dangers that pioneers faced on the journey west?

Early in the journey, women and men generally followed their customary roles: Men hunted, fished, and drove the wagons, while women cooked, washed, and watched the children. But traditional roles often broke down on the trail, and even conventional domestic tasks posed novel problems. Women had to cook unfamiliar food over open fires in all kinds of weather and with only a handful of pots and utensils. They washed laundry in rivers or streams, and on the plains they had to haul water for cooking or cleaning from great distances. Wood, too, was scarce on the plains, and women and children gathered buffalo dung (called "chips") for fuel. Men frequently had to gather food rather than hunt and fish, or they had to learn to catch strange (and sometimes dangerous) animals, such as jack rabbits and rattlesnakes. Few men were prepared for the arduous work of pulling wagons out of ditches or floating them across rivers with powerful currents. Nor were many of them expert in shoeing horses or fixing wagon wheels, tasks that were performed by skilled artisans at home.

Expectations changed dramatically when men took ill or died on the journey. Then wives drove the wagon, gathered or hunted for food, and learned to repair axles and other wagon parts. When large numbers of men were injured or ill, women might serve as scouts and guides or pick up guns to defend wagons under attack by Indians or wild animals. Yet despite the growing burdens on pioneer women, they gained little power over decision making. Moreover, the addition of men's jobs to women's responsibilities was rarely reciprocated. Few men cooked, did laundry, or cared for children on the trail. Single men generally paid women on the trail to perform such chores for them, and a husband who lost his wife on the journey generally relied on "neighbor" women as he would at home.

In one area, however, relative equality reigned. Men and women were equally susceptible to disease, injury, and death on the trail. Accidents, gunshot wounds, drowning, broken bones, and infections affected individuals on every wagon train. Some groups were struck as well by influenza, cholera, measles, mumps, or scarlet fever—all deadly in the early nineteenth century. In addition, about 20 percent of women on the overland trail became pregnant, which posed even greater dangers than at home given rough roads, a lack of water, the abundance of dirt, and the frequent absence of midwives and doctors. Some 20 percent of women lost children or spouses on the trip west, though most had little time to mourn. Wagon trains usually stopped only briefly to bury the dead, leaving a cross or a pile of stones to mark the grave, and then moved on. Overall, about one in ten to fifteen migrants died on the western journey, leaving some 65,000 graves along the trails west.

The Gold Rush

Despite the hazards, more and more Americans traveled the Oregon Trail, the Santa Fe Trail, and other paths to the Pacific coast. Initially only a few thousand Americans settled in California. Some were agents sent by New England merchants to purchase fine leather made from the hides of Spanish cattle raised in the area. Several of these agents married into families of elite Mexican ranchers, known as Californios, and adopted their culture, even converting to Catholicism.

However, the Anglo-American presence in California changed dramatically after 1848 when gold was discovered at Sutter's Mill in northeastern California. News of the discovery brought tens of thousands of new settlers from the eastern United States, South America, Europe, and Asia. In the **gold rush**, "forty-niners" raced to claim riches in the California mountains, and men vastly outnumbered women. Single men came with brothers, neighbors, or friends. Married men left wives and children behind, promising to send for them once they struck gold. Some 80,000 arrived in 1849 alone.

The rapid influx of gold seekers heightened tensions between newly arrived whites, local Indians, and Californios. Forty-niners confiscated land owned by Californios, shattered the fragile ecosystem in the California mountains, and

Gold Rush Miner, 1849
This prospector was one of some 80,000 who arrived in northeast California in 1849 after gold was discovered at Sutter's Mill. Photographed fully equipped with the tools of his trade—pickax, hoe, and pan—he, like other miners, was capable of digging out only surface gold. Armed with two pistols, the prospector in this photograph also suggests the dangers miners faced. Private Collection/ Peter Newark American Pictures/The Bridgeman Art Library

forced Mexican and Indian men to labor for low wages or a promised share in uncertain profits. New conflicts erupted when foreign-born migrants joined the search for wealth. Forty-niners from the United States regularly stole from and assaulted foreign-born competitors—whether Asian, European, or South American. With the limited number of sheriffs and judges in the region, most criminals knew they were unlikely to be arrested, much less tried and convicted.

The gold rush also led to conflicts over gender roles as thousands of male migrants demanded food, shelter, laundry, and medical care. Some women in the region earned a good living by renting rooms, cooking meals, washing clothes, or working as prostitutes. But many faced heightened forms of exploitation. Indian and Mexican women were especially vulnerable to sexual harassment and rape, while Chinese women were imported specifically to provide sexual services for male miners.

Chinese men were also victims of abuse by whites, as evidenced by Chinese workers who were hired by a

British mining company and then run off their claim by Anglo-American gold seekers. Yet some Chinese men used the skills traditionally assigned them in their homeland—cooking and washing clothes—to earn a far steadier income than prospecting for gold could provide. Other men also took advantage of the demand for goods and services. Levi Strauss, a twenty-four-year-old German Jewish immigrant, moved from New York to San Francisco to open a dry goods store in 1853. He was soon producing canvas and then denim pants that could withstand harsh weather and long wear. These blue jeans made Strauss far richer than any forty-niner seeking gold.

A Crowded Land

While U.S. promoters of migration continued to depict the West as an open territory waiting to be tamed and cultivated, it was in fact the site of competing imperial ambitions in the late 1840s. Despite granting statehood to Texas in 1845 and winning the war against Mexico in 1848, the United States had to compete with Comanche, Sioux, and other powerful Indian nations for control of the Great Plains (see chapter 10). As the U.S. government sought to secure land for railroads and forts and as American migrants and European immigrants carved out farms and villages, they had to contend with a range of Indian nations that refused to relinquish control (Map 12.1).

Although attacks on wagon trains were rare, Indians did threaten frontier settlements throughout the 1840s and 1850s. Settlers often retaliated, and U.S. army troops joined them in efforts to push Indians back from areas newly claimed by whites. Yet in many parts of the West, Indians were as powerful as whites, and they did not cede territory without a fight. For example, the Reverend Marcus Whitman and his wife Narcissa became victims of their success in promoting western settlement. In 1843 Marcus returned east and led one thousand Christian emigrants on a "Great Migration" to the Oregon Territory. The settlers were enthusiastic about their new homes, but the arrival of more whites proved disastrous for local Indians. The pioneers brought a deadly measles epidemic to the region, killing thousands of Cayuse and Nez Percé Indians. In 1847, convinced that whites brought disease but no useful medicine, a group of Cayuse Indians killed the Whitmans and ten other white settlers.

Yet violence against whites could not stop the flood of migrants into the Oregon Territory. Indeed, attacks by one Indian tribe were often used to justify assaults on any Indian tribe. For example, John Frémont and Kit Carson, whose party had been attacked by a group of Modoc Indians in Oregon in 1846, took their revenge by destroying a Klamath Indian village and killing men, women,

and children there. The defeat of Mexico and the discovery of gold in California in 1848 only intensified these conflicts.

Although Indians and white Americans were the main players in many battles, Indian nations also competed with each other. In the southern plains, drought and disease exacerbated those conflicts in the late 1840s and dramatically changed the balance of power in the region. In 1845 the southern plains were struck by a dry spell, which lasted on and off until the mid-1860s. Three years later, smallpox ravaged Comanche villages, and then forty-niners heading to California introduced a virulent strain of cholera that killed prominent Comanche leaders as well as hundreds of their followers. In the late 1840s, the Comanches were the largest Indian nation, with about twenty thousand members; by the mid-1850s, less than half that number remained.

Yet the collapse of the Comanche empire was not simply the result of outside forces. As the Comanches expanded their trade networks and incorporated smaller Indian nations into their orbit, they overextended their reach. Most important, they allowed too many bison to be killed in order to meet the needs of their Indian allies and the demand for bison robes by Anglo-American and European traders. The Comanches also herded growing numbers of horses, which required expansive grazing lands and winter havens in the river valleys and pushed the bison onto more marginal lands. Opening up the Santa Fe Trail to commerce multiplied the problems by destroying vegetation, polluting springs, and thus damaging some of the last refuges for bison. The prolonged drought then completed the depopulation of the bison on the southern plains. Without bison, the Comanches lost one of their most critical trade items; by the late 1850s, they were left without the goods or leverage to sustain their commercial and political networks. As the Comanche empire collapsed, former Indian allies sought to advance their own interests. These two developments reignited Indian wars on the southern plains as tens of thousands of Anglo-Americans and European immigrants poured through the region.

African Americans also participated in these western struggles. Many were held as slaves by southeastern tribes forced into Indian Territory, while others were freed and married Seminole or Cherokee spouses. The Creeks proved harsh masters, prompting some slaves to escape north to free states or south to Mexican or Comanche territory. Yet as southern officers in the U.S. army moved to frontier outposts to secure American dominance, they carried more slaves into the region. Many, including Dr. Emerson, changed posts frequently, taking slaves like Dred Scott into western territories that

MAP 12.1 Western Trails and Indian Nations, c. 1850

As wagon trains and traders journeyed west in rapidly growing numbers during the 1830s and 1840s, the United States established forts along the most well-traveled routes. At the same time, Indians claimed or were forced into new areas through the pressure of Indian removals, white settlement, and the demands of hunting, trade, and agriculture.

were alternately slave and free. Still, it was white planters who brought the greatest numbers of African Americans into Texas, Missouri, and Kansas, pushing the frontier of slavery ever westward. At the same time, some free blacks joined the migration voluntarily in hopes of finding better economic opportunities and less overt racism on the frontier.

REVIEW & RELATE

- Why did Americans go west in the 1830s and 1840s, and what was the journey like?

- What groups competed for land and resources in the West? How did competition lead to violence?

Expansion and the Politics of Slavery

The place of African Americans and of slavery in the West aroused intense political debates as territories in the region began to seek statehood. Debates over the eradication of slavery and limits on its expansion had shaped the highly contested presidential election of 1848 (see chapters 10 and 11). After the Mexican-American War, the battle between proponents and opponents of slavery intensified and focused more specifically on its westward expansion. Each time a territory achieved the requirements for statehood, a new crisis erupted. To resolve these crises required strong presidential and congressional leadership, judicial moderation, and a spirit of compromise among the people as well as their representatives. None of these conditions prevailed. Instead, passage of the Fugitive Slave Act in 1850 aroused deeper hostilities, and President Franklin Pierce (1853–1857) encouraged further expansion but failed to address the crises that ensued.

California and the Compromise of 1850

In the winter of 1849, just before Zachary Taylor's March inauguration, California applied for admission to the Union as a free state. Some California political leaders opposed slavery on principle. Others wanted to "save" the state for whites by outlawing slavery, discouraging free blacks from migrating to the state, and restricting the rights of American Indian, Mexican, and Chinese residents. Yet the internal debates among Californians were not uppermost in the minds of those in Congress. Southerners were concerned about the impact of California's free-state status on the sectional balance in Congress, while northern Whigs were shocked when President Taylor suggested that slavery should be allowed anywhere in the West.

Other debates percolated in Congress at the same time. Many Northerners were horrified by the spectacle of slavery and slave trading in the nation's capital and argued that it damaged America's international reputation. Southerners, meanwhile, complained that the Fugitive Slave Act of 1793 was being widely ignored in the North, as abolitionists aided runaways seeking freedom. A boundary dispute between Texas and New Mexico irritated western legislators, and Texas continued to claim that debts it accrued while an independent republic and during the Mexican-American War should be assumed by the federal government.

Senator Henry Clay of Kentucky, the Whig leader who had hammered out the Missouri Compromise in 1819–1820, again tried to resolve the many conflicts that stalled congressional action. He offered a compromise by which California would be admitted as a free state; the remaining land acquired from Mexico would be divided into two territories—New Mexico and Utah—and slavery there would be decided by popular sovereignty; the border dispute between New Mexico and Texas would be decided in favor of New Mexico, but the federal government would assume Texas's war debts; the slave trade (but not slavery) would be abolished in the District of Columbia; and a new and more effective fugitive slave law would be approved. Although Clay's compromise offered something to everyone, his colleagues did not immediately embrace it.

By March 1850, after months of debate, the sides remained sharply divided, with senators on both sides of the issue opposing the measure. John C. Calhoun, a proslavery senator from South Carolina, refused to support any compromise that allowed Congress to decide the fate of slavery in the western territories. Meanwhile William H. Seward, an antislavery Whig senator from New York, proclaimed that in all good conscience he could not support a compromise that forced Northerners to help hunt down fugitives from slavery. Daniel Webster, a Massachusetts Whig and an elder statesman, appealed to his fellow senators to support the compromise in order to preserve the Union, but Congress adjourned with the fate of California undecided.

Explore

See Document 12.2 for Calhoun's final attempt to reject a compromise.

Before the Senate reconvened in the fall of 1850, however, the political landscape changed in unexpected ways. Henry Clay retired in the spring of 1850, leaving the Capitol with his last great legislative effort unfinished. On March 31, Calhoun died; his absence from the Senate made compromise more likely. In July, President Taylor died unexpectedly, and his vice president, Millard Fillmore of Buffalo, New York, was elevated to the presidency. Fillmore then appointed Webster as secretary of state, removing him from the Senate as well.

In September 1850, with President Fillmore's support, a younger cohort of senators and representatives steered the **Compromise of 1850** through Congress, one clause at a time, thereby allowing legislators to support only those parts of the compromise they found palatable. In the end, all the provisions passed, and Fillmore quickly signed the bills into law. California entered the Union as a free state, and John C. Frémont entered Congress as one of that state's first two senators. The Compromise of 1850, like the Missouri Compromise thirty years earlier, fended off a sectional crisis, but it also signaled future problems. Would popular sovereignty prevail when later territories sought admission to the Union, and would Northerners abide by a fugitive slave law that called on them to aid directly in the capture of runaway slaves?

The Fugitive Slave Act Inspires Northern Protest

The fugitive slave laws of 1793 and 1824 mandated that all states aid in apprehending and returning runaway slaves to their owners. The **Fugitive Slave Act of 1850** was different in two important respects. First, it eliminated jury trials for alleged fugitives. Second, the law required individual citizens, not just state officials, to help return runaways or

DOCUMENT 12.2

John C. Calhoun | On the Compromise of 1850, 1850

California's application for statehood in 1849 prompted another crisis over slavery. Southerners feared that admitting California as a free state would tip the balance in Congress against them. Senator Henry Clay tried to broker a compromise that would admit California as a free state but toughen the fugitive slave law. Amid vigorous congressional debate, South Carolina senator John C. Calhoun insisted that slavery be preserved. A colleague read Calhoun's address for the aging and ill senator. Calhoun's death a few weeks later helped pave the way for final passage of the Compromise of 1850.

Explore

How can the Union be saved? To this I answer, there is but one way by which it can be, and that is, by adopting such measures as will satisfy the States belonging to the Southern section that they can remain in the Union consistently with their honor and their safety. . . .

. . . The South asks for justice, simple justice, and less she ought not to take. She has no compromise to offer but the Constitution, and no concession or surrender to make. She has already surrendered so much that she has little left to surrender. Such a settlement would go to the root of the evil, and remove all cause of discontent, by satisfying the South that she could remain honorably and safely in the Union, and thereby restore the harmony and fraternal feelings between the sections which existed anterior to the Missouri agitation. . . .

But can this be done? Yes, easily; not by the weaker party, for it can of itself do nothing—not even protect itself—but by the stronger. The North has only to will it to accomplish it—to do justice by conceding to the South an equal right in the acquired territory, and to do her duty by causing the stipulations relative to fugitive slaves to be faithfully fulfilled—to cease the agitation of the slave question, and to provide for the insertion of a provision in the Constitution, by an amendment, which will restore to the South in substance the power she possessed of protecting herself, before the equilibrium between the sections was destroyed by the action of this Government. There will be no difficulty in devising such a provision—one that will protect the South, and which at the same time will improve and strengthen the Government, instead of impairing and weakening it.

Source: *The Congressional Globe*, 31st Cong., 2nd Sess. (1850), 453, 455.

Interpret the Evidence

- Calhoun objects to the Compromise of 1850 because it does not sufficiently protect southern rights. Which rights does he think need protection, and why does he think those rights are in jeopardy?
- Calhoun wants to regain the "harmony and fraternal feelings" between the sections that existed before "the Missouri agitation." Why does he pinpoint the Missouri Compromise as the moment when sectional divisions took hold?

Put It in Context

What developments in the 1840s led Calhoun and other southern leaders to fear that the South was becoming weaker, at least politically, compared to the North? Would northern senators have agreed?

else risk being fined or imprisoned. The act angered many Northerners who believed that the federal government had gone too far in protecting the rights of slaveholders and thereby aroused sympathy for the abolitionist cause.

Before 1850, the most well-known individuals aiding fugitives were free blacks such as David Ruggles in New

York City; Jermaine Loguen in Syracuse, New York; and, after his own successful escape, Frederick Douglass in Rochester, New York. Their main allies in this work were white Quakers such as Amy and Isaac Post in Rochester; Thomas Garrett in Chester County, Pennsylvania; and Levi and Catherine Coffin in Newport, Indiana. The work was dangerous. Charles Turner Torrey, a white Congregationalist minister, may have aided as many as four hundred fugitives, but he was eventually caught and imprisoned. He died of tuberculosis in a Baltimore jail in 1846.

Following passage of the Fugitive Slave Act, the number of slave owners and hired slave catchers pursuing fugitives increased dramatically. But so, too, did the number of northern abolitionists helping blacks escape. Enslaved women and men followed various paths northward from rural plantations and southern cities. Once they crossed into free territory, most fugitives contacted free blacks or individuals known to be sympathetic to their cause. They then began the often slow progress along the underground railroad, from house to house or barn to barn, until they found safe haven. A small number of fortunate slaves were led north by fugitives like Harriet Tubman, who returned south repeatedly to free dozens of family members and other enslaved men and women. Fugitives followed disparate paths through the Midwest, Pennsylvania, New York, and New England, and there was little coordination among the "conductors" from one region or state to another. But the underground railroad was nonetheless an important resource for fugitives, some of whom sought refuge in Canada while others hoped to blend into free black communities in the United States.

Free blacks were endangered by the claim that slaves hid themselves in their midst. In Chester County, Pennsylvania, on the Maryland border, newspapers reported on at least a dozen free blacks who were kidnapped or arrested as runaways in the first three months of 1851. One provision of the Fugitive Slave Act encouraged such arrests: Commissioners were paid $10 for each slave sent back but only $5 if a slave was not returned. Without the right to a trial, a free black could easily be sent south as a fugitive. It was this fear that prompted hundreds of African Americans, both free and enslaved, to flee to Canada.

At the same time, a growing number of Northerners challenged the federal government's right to enforce the law. Blacks and whites organized protest meetings throughout the free states. At a meeting in Boston in 1851, abolitionist William Lloyd Garrison denounced the law: "We execrate it, we spit upon it, we trample it under our feet." Abolitionists also joined forces to rescue fugitives who had been arrested. In Syracuse, New York, in October 1851, Jermaine Loguen, Samuel Ward, and the Reverend Samuel J. May led a well-organized crowd as it broke into a Syracuse courthouse to rescue a fugitive slave known as Jerry. They successfully hid him from authorities and then spirited him to Canada. As such incidents increased across the North, Daniel Webster bemoaned the lack of respect for federal law, and President Fillmore lamented the rise of "mob rule." But northern abolitionists gained growing sympathy from their neighbors and became bolder in denouncing both the Fugitive Slave Act and "the bloodhound kidnappers" who sought to enforce it.

Meanwhile members of Congress continued to debate the law's effects. Senator Frémont was among the legislators who helped defeat a bill that would have imposed harsher

Rescue of Fugitive Slaves

This 1872 illustration portrays the dramatic rescue of the North Carolina slave Jane Johnson and her two children aboard a Philadelphia ferry in 1855 as they accompanied their owner on a trip through the free state of Pennsylvania. They were liberated by members of the Pennsylvania Anti-Slavery Society, led by the black abolitionist William Still, who boarded the boat and removed them to safety.   Photo Researchers, Inc.

penalties on those who assisted runaways. And Congress felt growing pressure to calm the situation, including from foreign officials who were horrified by the violence required to sustain slavery in the United States. Abolitionist speakers like Frederick Douglass, who spent six months denouncing the Fugitive Slave Act across Canada, Ireland, and England, intensified foreign concern over the law. Great Britain and France had already abolished slavery in their West Indian colonies and found it hard to support what they saw as extreme policies to keep the institution alive in the United States. Yet neither southern slaveholders nor northern abolitionists were willing to compromise any further.

Pierce Encourages U.S. Expansion

In the presidential election of 1852, the Whigs and the Democrats tried once again to appeal to voters across the North-South divide by running candidates who either skirted the critical issues of the day or held ambiguous views. The Democrats, who had great difficulty choosing a candidate, finally nominated Franklin Pierce. A successful New Hampshire lawyer who opposed abolition, Pierce had served in Congress from 1833 to 1842 and in the U.S. army during the Mexican-American War. The Whigs rejected Vice President Millard Fillmore, who had angered many in the party by supporting popular sovereignty and vigorous enforcement of the Fugitive Slave Act. The Whig Party turned instead to another military leader, General Winfield Scott of Virginia, to head the ticket. General Scott had served with distinction in the war against Mexico, but he had not expressed any proslavery views. The Whigs thus hoped to gain southern support while maintaining their northern base. The Free-Soil Party, too, hoped to expand its appeal, given northern hostility to the Fugitive Slave Act. But Free-Soilers were unable to take advantage of the moment, nominating John P. Hale, a relatively unknown former Democratic senator from New Hampshire.

Franklin Pierce's eventual victory left the Whigs and the Free-Soilers in disarray. A third of southern Whigs threw their support to the Democrats, seeking a truly proslavery party. Many Democrats who had supported Free-Soilers in 1848, like Martin Van Buren, were driven to vote for Pierce by their enthusiasm over the admission of California as a free state. But despite the Democratic triumph, that party also remained fragile. The nation now faced some of its gravest challenges under a president with limited political experience and no firm base of support. His cabinet included men of widely differing views, part of an effort to appease the various factions of the Democratic Party. But when confronted with difficult decisions, Pierce often received contradictory advice and generally pursued his own expansionist vision.

Early in his administration, Pierce focused on expanding U.S. trade and extending the "civilizing" power of U.S. institutions to other parts of the world. Inspired by the promise of new markets, Pierce and his supporters sought to shift Americans' attention outward. Trade with China had declined in the 1840s, but the United States had begun commercial negotiations with Japan in 1846. These came to fruition in 1854, when U.S. emissary Commodore Matthew C. Perry obtained the first formal treaty with Japan that allowed for mutual trading. Within four years, Pierce and his agent, international trader Townsend Harris, succeeded in expanding commercial ties and enhancing diplomatic relations with Japan, in large part by ensuring U.S. support for the island nation against its traditional enemies in China, Russia, and Europe.

Although the president rejected Commodore Perry's offer to take military possession of Formosa and other territories near Japan, Pierce was willing to consider conquests in the Caribbean and Central America. For decades, U.S. politicians, particularly Southerners, had looked to gain control of Cuba, Mexico, and Nicaragua. A "Young America" movement within the Democratic Party imagined manifest destiny reaching southward as well as westward. In hopes of stirring up rebellious Cubans against Spanish rule, some Democrats joined with private adventurers to send three expeditions, known as *filibusters*, to invade Cuba under the leadership of Cuban exile General Narciso Lopez. In 1854 the capture of one of the filibustering ships led to an international incident. Spanish officials confiscated the ship, while Democrats eager to add Cuba to the United States urged Pierce to seek an apology and redress from Spain. But many northern Democrats rejected any effort to obtain another slave state, and Pierce was forced to withdraw even tacit federal approval for the filibusters.

Other politicians still pressured Spain to sell Cuba to the United States. These included Pierce's secretary of state, William Marcy, and the U.S. ambassador to Great Britain, James Buchanan, as well as the ministers to France and Spain. In October 1854, these ministers met in Ostend, Belgium, and sent a letter to Pierce: "If we possess the power, [the United States is justified] by every law, human and Divine" in taking Cuba by force. When this Ostend Manifesto was leaked to the press, Northerners were outraged. They viewed the whole episode as "a dirty plot" to gain more slave territory and forced Pierce to give up any plans to obtain Cuba. In 1855 a private adventurer named William Walker, who had organized four filibusters to Nicaragua, invaded that country and set himself up as ruler. He then invited southern planters to take up vast lands he had confiscated from local farmers and to reintroduce slavery in Nicaragua. Pierce and many Democrats endorsed his plan, but neighboring Hondurans forced Walker from power in 1857 and executed him by firing squad three years later. Although Pierce's expansionist dreams failed, his efforts heightened sectional tensions.

REVIEW & RELATE

What steps did legislators take in the 1840s and early 1850s to resolve the issue of the expansion of slavery?

How were slavery and American imperialist ambitions intertwined in the 1840s and 1850s?

 LEARNINGCurve bedfordstmartins.com/hewittlawson/LC

Sectional Crises Intensify

The political crises that divided Americans in the 1850s infused cultural as well as political life, leading to a lively trade in antislavery literature. This cultural turmoil, combined with the weakness and fragmentation of the existing political parties, helped give rise to the Republican Party in 1854. Although it spoke almost solely for Northerners who opposed the continued expansion of slavery, the Republican Party soon absorbed enough Free-Soilers, Whigs, and northern Democrats to become a major political force. The events that drove these cultural and political developments included continued challenges to the Fugitive Slave Act, a battle over the admission of Kansas to the Union, and a Supreme Court ruling in the *Dred Scott* case.

Popularizing Antislavery Sentiment

The Fugitive Slave Act had forced Northerners to reconsider their role in sustaining the institution of slavery. In 1852, just months before Franklin Pierce was elected president, their concerns were heightened by the publication of the novel **Uncle Tom's Cabin** by Harriet Beecher Stowe. Stowe's father, Lyman Beecher, and brother Henry were among the nation's leading evangelical clergy, and her sister Catharine had opposed Cherokee removal and promoted women's education. Stowe was inspired to write *Uncle Tom's Cabin* by passage of the Fugitive Slave Act in 1850, and the story originally ran as a forty-installment serial in an abolitionist periodical, the *National Era*. Once published in book form, the novel sold more than 350,000 copies in a matter of months.

Uncle Tom's Cabin built on accounts by former slaves as well as tales gathered by abolitionist lecturers and writers. During the 1850s, tales of life in bondage received growing attention in the North in both abolitionist circles and the mainstream press. The autobiographies of

Frederick Douglass (1845), Josiah Henson (1849), and Henry Bibb (1849) set the stage for Stowe's novel. So, too, did the expansion of the antislavery press, which by the 1850s included dozens of newspapers across the North, the Midwest, and eastern Canada. Antislavery poems and songs also circulated widely and were performed at abolitionist conventions and fund-raising fairs.

Still, nothing captured the public's attention as did *Uncle Tom's Cabin*. Read by millions in the United States and England and translated into French and German, the book reached a mass audience, far exceeding the reach of other abolitionist literature. Its sentimental portrait of saintly slaves and its vivid depiction of cruel masters and overseers offered white Northerners a way to identify with enslaved blacks. Although some African Americans were frustrated by its demeaning portraits of northern free blacks, they recognized that it helped to fuel anger at the Fugitive Slave Act and at efforts to expand slavery into new territories. Its success and its limitations also convinced other fugitives, including Harriet Jacobs, to publish their real-life stories.

Explore

See Documents 12.3 and 12.4 for two contrasting literary depictions of slavery.

In some cases, the real-life stories of fugitive slaves surpassed their fictional counterparts for emotional impact. In May 1854, abolitionists sought to free fugitive slave Anthony Burns from a Boston courthouse, where his master was attempting to reclaim him. They failed to secure his release, and Burns was soon marched to the docks to be shipped south. Twenty-two companies of state militia held back tens of thousands of Bostonians who lined the streets, hissing and shouting "Kidnappers!" at the soldiers and police. A year later, supporters purchased Burns's freedom from his master, but the incident raised anguished questions among local residents. In a city that was home to intellectual, religious, and antislavery leaders such as Ralph Waldo Emerson, the Reverend Theodore Parker, and William Lloyd Garrison, Bostonians wondered how they had come so far in aiding and abetting slavery.

The Kansas-Nebraska Act Stirs Dissent

Kansas provided the first test of the effects of *Uncle Tom's Cabin* on northern sentiments toward slavery's expansion. As white Americans slowly displaced Indian nations from their homelands, large and diverse groups of Indians settled in the northern half of the Louisiana Territory. This unorganized region had once been considered beyond the reach of white settlement, but Senator Stephen Douglas of

Illinois was eager to have a transcontinental railroad run through his home state. He needed the federal government to gain control of land along the route he proposed, and therefore he argued for the establishment of a vast Nebraska Territory. But to support his plan, Douglas also needed to convince southern congressmen, who sought a route through their own region. Much of the unorganized territory lay too far north to support plantation slavery, but a small portion lay directly west of Missouri, the northernmost slave state. According to the Missouri Compromise, states lying above the southern border of Missouri were automatically free. To gain southern support, Douglas sought to reopen the question of slavery in the territories. Pointing to the Compromise of 1850, by which territories acquired from Mexico would decide the fate of slavery by popular sovereignty, he argued that the same standard should apply to all new territories.

In January 1854, Douglas introduced the **Kansas-Nebraska Act** to Congress. The act extinguished Indians' long-held treaty rights in the region and repealed the Missouri Compromise. Two new territories—Kansas and Nebraska— would be carved out of the unorganized lands, and each would determine whether to enter the nation as a slave or a free state by a referendum of eligible voters (Map 12.2). The act spurred intense opposition from most Whigs and some northern Democrats who wanted to retain the Missouri Compromise line. Months of fierce debate followed. Finally, on May 25, Douglas's proposed act passed by a comfortable majority when most Democrats followed the party line to vote yes. President Pierce quickly signed the bill into law.

Passage of the Kansas-Nebraska Act enraged many Northerners, who considered the dismantling of the Missouri Compromise a sign of the rising power of the South. They were infuriated that the South—or what some now called the Slave Power Conspiracy—had once again benefited from northern politicians' willingness to compromise. Although few of these opponents considered the impact of the law on Indians, the act also shattered treaty provisions that had protected the Arapaho, Cheyenne, Ponco, Pawnee, and Sioux nations. These Plains Indians lost half the land they had held by treaty as thousands of settlers swarmed into the newly organized territories. In the fall of 1855, conflicts between white settlers and Indians erupted across the southern and central plains. The U.S. army then sent six hundred troops to retaliate against a Sioux village, killing eighty-five residents of Blue Water in the Nebraska Territory and triggering continued violence throughout the region.

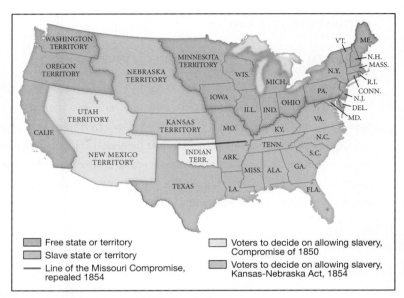

MAP 12.2   **Kansas-Nebraska Territory**

From 1820 on, Congress attempted to limit sectional conflict. But the Missouri Compromise (1820) and the Compromise of 1850 failed to resolve disagreements over slavery's expansion. The creation of the Kansas and Nebraska territories in 1854 also heightened sectional conflict and ensured increased hostilities with Indians in the region.

As tensions escalated across the nation, Americans faced the 1854 congressional elections. The Democrats, increasingly viewed as supporting the priorities of slaveholders, lost badly in the North. But the Whig Party also proved weak, having failed to stop the Slave Power from extending its leverage over federal policies. A third party, the American Party, was founded in the early 1850s and attracted native-born workers and Protestant farmers who were drawn to its anti-immigrant and anti-Catholic message (see chapter 11). Responding to these political realignments, another new party—the Republicans—was founded in the spring of 1854. Led by antislavery Whigs, the **Republican Party** slowly attracted former Free-Soilers to its ranks. Among its early members was a Whig politician from Illinois, Abraham Lincoln.

Born in Kentucky in 1809, Lincoln moved north to Illinois with his family and worked as a farmhand and surveyor. He also taught himself the rudiments of the law and was elected to the state legislature in 1834. In 1842 he married Mary Todd, the daughter of a wealthy banker, and established a lucrative law practice. Four years later, Lincoln was elected as a Whig to the House of Representatives. Serving his two-year term during the crisis over war with Mexico, he challenged Polk's claim that the first blood had been shed on U.S. soil (see chapter 11). After resuming his Springfield law practice, Lincoln joined the new Republican Party in 1856.

DOCUMENTS 12.3 AND 12.4

Slavery in Literature: Two Views

The 1852 publication of *Uncle Tom's Cabin* by Harriet Beecher Stowe helped mobilize northern antislavery sentiment but provoked a hostile reaction among Southerners, who said she misrepresented their way of life. Written in response to Stowe's work, Caroline Hentz's novel *The Planter's Northern Bride* argued that slaves' lives were better than those of working-class and poor Northerners. Hentz defended southern values and traditions, including slavery. The following excerpt from *Uncle Tom's Cabin* depicts a scene in which the overseer Simon Legree punishes Tom for helping another slave. In the second selection, from *The Planter's Northern Bride*, Hentz's main character, Eulalia Moreland, describes meeting the slaves on her husband's plantation.

Explore

12.3 Harriet Beecher Stowe | *Uncle Tom's Cabin*, 1852

"Well, here's a pious dog, at last, let down among us sinners!—a saint, a gentleman, and no less, to talk to us sinners about our sins! Powerful holy critter, he must be! Here, you rascal, you make believe to be so pious—didn't you never hear, out of yer Bible, 'Servants, obey yer masters'? An't I yer master? Didn't I pay down twelve hundred dollars, cash, for all there is inside yer old cussed black shell? An't yer mine, now, body and soul?" he said, giving Tom a violent kick with his heavy boot; "tell me!"

In the very depth of physical suffering, bowed by brutal oppression, this question shot a gleam of joy and triumph through Tom's soul. He suddenly stretched himself up, and, looking earnestly to heaven, while the tears and blood that flowed down his face mingled, he exclaimed,

"No! no! no! my soul an't yours, Mas'r! You haven't bought it—ye can't buy it! It's been bought and paid for, by one that is able to keep it—no matter, no matter, you can't harm me!"

Original Cover of *Uncle Tom's Cabin*
Newberry Library, Chicago, Illinois, USA/ The Bridgeman Art Library

"I can't!" said Legree, with a sneer; "we'll see— we'll see! Here, Sambo, Quimbo, give this dog such a breakin' in as he won't get over this month!"

Source: Harriet Beecher Stowe, *Uncle Tom's Cabin; or, Life among the Lowly* (Boston: John P. Jewett, 1852), 197.

Although established only months before the fall 1854 elections, the Republican Party gained significant support in the Midwest, particularly in state and local campaigns. Meanwhile the American Party gained control of the Massachusetts legislature and nearly captured New York as well. These victories marked the demise of the Whigs as a national party. Although the American Party dissolved as a political force by 1856, the Republicans continued to gain strength. They replaced the Whig Party—which was built on a national constituency—with a party rooted solely in the North. Like Free-Soilers, the Republicans argued that slavery

12.4 Caroline Hentz | *The Planter's Northern Bride*, 1854

Soon, returning in grand march from the fields, came the negroes, poising on their heads immense baskets, brimming with the light and flaky cotton. . . . Eulalia . . . recollected all the horrible stories she had heard of negro insurrections, and thought what an awful thing it was to be at the mercy of so many slaves, on that lonely plantation. When she saw her husband going out among them, and they all closed round, shutting him in as with a thick cloud, she asked herself if he were really safe. Safe. . . . They gathered round him, eager to get within reach of his hand, the sound of his voice, the glance of his kind, protecting, yet commanding eye. More like a father welcomed by his children . . . he stood, the centre of that sable ring. . . . He appeared to her in a new character. She had known him as the fond, devoted bridegroom; now he was invested with the authority and responsibility of a master. And she must share that responsibility, assist him in his duties, and make the welfare, comfort, and happiness of these dependent beings the great object of her life. . . .

   Never before had she made an elaborate comparison between the white and the black man. She had so often heard her father say that they were born equal . . . that she had believed it. . . . But as she

Illustration from *The Planter's Northern Bride*
Image courtesy of Documenting the American South, The University of North Carolina at Chapel Hill Libraries

looked at her husband, standing in their midst, the representative of the fair sons of Japheth [son of the biblical Noah], wearing on his brow the signet of a loftier, nobler destiny, every lineament and feature expressive of intellect and power, and then at each of that dark, lowly throng, she felt a conviction that freedom, in its broadest latitude, education, with its most exalted privileges, could never make them equal to him.

Source: Caroline Lee Hentz, *The Planter's Northern Bride* (Philadelphia: T. B. Peterson and Brothers, 1854), 331–33.

Interpret the Evidence

● What do these passages reveal about northern and southern opinions about slaves and slavery?
● Compare the attitudes of Simon Legree and Mr. Moreland toward their slaves. How might these characterizations have affected northern and southern readers?

Put It in Context

What do these different characterizations suggest about mid-nineteenth-century responses to the Fugitive Slave Act?

should not be extended into new territories. But the Republicans also advocated a program of commercial and industrial development and internal improvements. With this platform, the party attracted a broader base than did earlier antislavery political coalitions. The Republican Party included both ardent abolitionists

and men whose only concern was keeping western territories open to free white men. This latter group was more than willing to accept slavery where it already existed and to exclude black migrants, who might compete for jobs and land, from western states and territories.

Bleeding Kansas and the Election of 1856

The 1854 congressional elections exacerbated sectional tensions by bringing representatives from a strictly northern party—the Republicans—into Congress, where Democrats and Southerners, by virtue of their seniority, controlled most of the powerful committee assignments. But the conflicts over slavery reached far beyond the nation's capital. After passage of the Kansas-Nebraska Act, advocates and opponents of slavery poured into Kansas in anticipation of a vote on whether the state would enter the Union slave or free. Southerners flooded in from Missouri, while emigrant aid societies in the North funded antislavery settlers willing to relocate to Kansas.

As Kansas prepared to hold its referendum, settlers continued to arrive daily, making it difficult to determine who was eligible to vote. In 1855 Southerners installed a proslavery government at Shawnee Mission, while abolitionists established a stronghold in Lawrence. Violence erupted when proslavery settlers invaded Lawrence, killing one resident, demolishing newspaper offices, and plundering shops and homes. Fearing that the southern settlers who had come to Kansas were better armed than the antislavery Northerners in the territory, eastern abolitionists raised funds to ship rifles to Kansas. The Reverend Henry Ward Beecher of Brooklyn, a popular preacher and leading abolitionist, advocated armed self-defense. As cases of Sharps rifles arrived in Kansas, they came to be known as Beecher's Bibles.

Longtime abolitionist John Brown took more direct action. He joined four of his sons already living in Kansas and, with two friends, kidnapped five proslavery advocates from their homes along Pottawatomie Creek and hacked them to death. The so-called Pottawatomie Massacre infuriated southern settlers; in response, they drew up the Lecompton Constitution, which declared Kansas a slave state. President Pierce made his support of the proslavery government clear, but Congress remained divided. While Congress deliberated, armed battles continued. In the first six months of 1856, another two hundred settlers were killed in what became known as **Bleeding Kansas**.

Fighting also broke out on the floor of Congress. Republican senator Charles Sumner of Massachusetts delivered an impassioned speech against the continued expansion of what he termed the Slave Power. He launched scathing verbal attacks on planter politicians like South Carolina senator Andrew Butler, who supported the admission of Kansas as a slave state. Butler's nephew, Preston Brooks, a Democratic member of the House of Representatives, felt compelled to redress his family's honor. He assaulted Sumner in the Senate chamber, beating him senseless with a cane. Sumner, who never fully recovered from his injuries, was considered a martyr in the North. Meanwhile Brooks was feted across the state of South Carolina.

Clarina Howard Nichols

An abolitionist, a journalist, and a women's rights advocate in Vermont, Clarina Howard Nichols joined the New England Emigrant Aid Society in 1854. The next year, she moved with her family to the Kansas Territory, where this photograph was taken. Nichols advocated women's legal rights through lectures and editorials and was the only woman to participate in the Kansas constitutional convention of 1859.   Kansas State Historical Society

Explore

See Document 12.5 for one cartoonist's portrayal of the Kansas-Nebraska Act.

The presidential election of 1856 began amid an atmosphere poisoned by violence and recrimination. The Democratic Party nominated James Buchanan, a proslavery advocate and longtime party stalwart from Pennsylvania. The young Republican Party ticket was headed by John C. Frémont. The American Party, in its final presidential contest, selected former president Millard Fillmore as its candidate. The strength of nativism in politics was waning, however, and Fillmore won only the state of Maryland. Frémont attracted cheering throngs as he traveled across the nation. Large numbers of women turned out to see Jessie Frémont, the first national candidate's wife to play a

DOCUMENT 12.5

John Magee | Forcing Slavery down the Throat of a Freesoiler, 1856

The passage of the Kansas-Nebraska Act deepened the conflict over slavery. The act repealed the Missouri Compromise and allowed voters in Kansas and Nebraska to decide whether their territories would enter the Union as free or slave states. Advocates and opponents of slavery poured into Kansas, leading to open violence throughout the state. The following antislavery cartoon shows presidential candidate James Buchanan and Democratic senator Lewis Cass holding down a free-soiler while Franklin Pierce and Stephen Douglas force a black man down his throat.

Explore

Whom does Magee hold responsible for the violence in Kansas?

MURDER !!! help — neighbors help, O my poor Wife and Children.

FORCING SLAVERY DOWN THE THROAT OF A FREESOILER

Library of Congress

What is the significance of binding the free-soiler to the Democratic Platform?

What argument is Magee making by putting Central America, Cuba, and Kansas on the Democratic Platform?

Put It in Context

What does this cartoon suggest about the role of northern Democratic Party leaders in the ongoing conflicts over the expansion of slavery?

significant role in a campaign. Frémont carried most of the North and the West, establishing the Republican Party's dominance in those regions. Buchanan, claiming that he alone could preserve the Union, captured the South along with Pennsylvania, Indiana, and Illinois. Although Buchanan won only 45.2 percent of the popular vote, he received a comfortable majority in the electoral college, securing his victory. But even as the nation was becoming increasingly divided along sectional lines, President Buchanan did little to resolve these differences.

The *Dred Scott* Decision

Just two days after Buchanan's inauguration, the Supreme Court finally announced its decision in the *Dred Scott* case. Led by Chief Justice Roger Taney, a proslavery Southerner, the majority ruled that a slave was not a citizen and therefore could not sue in court. Indeed, Taney claimed that black men had no rights that a white man was bound to respect. The ruling annulled Scott's suit and meant that he and his wife remained enslaved. But the ruling went further. The ***Dred Scott* decision** declared that Congress had no constitutional authority to exclude slavery from any territory, thereby nullifying the Missouri Compromise and any future effort to restrict slavery's expansion. Buchanan was happy to have the fate of slavery taken out of the hands of Congress, hoping it would alleviate sectional tensions. His hopes proved unfounded. Instead of quieting the debate over slavery, the ruling further outraged many Northerners, who were now convinced that a Slave Power conspiracy had taken hold of the federal government.

In 1858, when Stephen Douglas faced reelection to the U.S. Senate, the Republican Party nominated Abraham Lincoln to oppose him. The candidates participated in seven debates in which they explained their positions on slavery in the wake of the *Dred Scott* decision. Pointing to the landmark ruling, Lincoln asked Douglas how he could favor popular sovereignty, which allowed residents to keep slavery out of a territory, and yet support the *Dred Scott* decision, which protected slavery in all territories. Douglas devised a clever response, known as the Freeport Doctrine. He claimed that if residents did not adopt local legislation to protect slaveholders' property, they could thereby exclude slavery for all practical purposes. At the same time, he accused Lincoln of advocating "negro equality," a position that went well beyond his opponent's views. Lincoln did support economic opportunity for free blacks, but not political or social equality. Still, the Republican candidate did declare that "this government cannot endure permanently half slave and half free. . . . It will become all one thing or all the other."

The Lincoln-Douglas debates attracted national attention, but the Illinois legislature selected the state's senator. Narrowly controlled by Democrats, it returned Douglas to Washington. Although the senator retained his seat, he was chastened by how far the Democratic Party had tilted toward the South. So when President Buchanan tried to push the Lecompton Constitution through Congress, legitimating the proslavery government in Kansas, Douglas opposed him. The two struggled over control of the party, with Douglas winning a symbolic victory in January 1861 when Kansas was admitted as a free state. By then, however, the Democratic Party had split into southern and northern wings, and the nation was on the verge of civil war.

Dred and Harriet Scott

This illustration of Dred Scott and his wife Harriet appeared in the June 27, 1857, issue of *Frank Leslie's Illustrated Newspaper*, four months after the Supreme Court ruled that the Scotts were not legally entitled to their freedom. In the 1830s, Dred and Harriet had received permission from their owners to marry, and they had two children.
Library of Congress

REVIEW & RELATE

What factors contributed to the spread of antislavery sentiment in the North beyond committed abolitionists?

How did the violence in Kansas in the mid-1850s reflect and intensify the growing sectional divide within the nation?

 LEARNINGCurve bedfordstmartins.com/hewittlawson/LC

From Sectional Crisis to War

During the 1850s, a profusion of abolitionist lectures, conventions, and literature increased antislavery sentiment in the North. Mainstream as well as antislavery newspapers now covered rescues of fugitives, the *Dred Scott* case, and the bloody crisis in Kansas. Republican candidates in state and local elections also kept concerns about slavery's expansion and southern power alive. Nothing, however, riveted the nation's attention as much as John Brown's raid on the federal arsenal at Harpers Ferry, Virginia, in 1859. Less than a year later, Republican Abraham Lincoln captured the White House. In the wake of his election, South Carolina seceded from the Union, agreeing with the president-elect that the nation could no longer exist half slave and half free.

John Brown's Raid

John Brown was committed not only to the abolition of slavery but also to complete equality between whites and blacks. A friend to many abolitionist leaders, Brown held views quite similar to those of David Walker, whose 1829 *Appeal* (see chapter 11) warned that slaves would eventually rise up and claim their freedom by force of arms. By 1859, following the bloody battles in Kansas, Brown believed strongly that direct action was the only answer. Deeply religious, he saw himself as the instrument of God's plan to liberate the enslaved.

Brown focused his efforts on the federal arsenal in **Harpers Ferry, Virginia**. With 18 followers—including 5 African Americans and 13 whites, including 3 of his sons—Brown planned to capture the arsenal and distribute the arms stored there to slaves in the surrounding area. He hoped this action would ignite a rebellion that would take down the plantation system. He tried to convince Frederick Douglass to join the venture, but Douglass, who admired Brown, considered it a foolhardy plan. However, the passionate rebel Brown did manage to persuade a small circle of white abolitionists to bankroll the effort.

On the night of October 16, 1859, Brown and his men successfully kidnapped some leading townsmen and seized the arsenal. Local residents were stunned but managed to alert authorities, and state militia swarmed into Harpers Ferry. The next day, federal troops arrived, led by Colonel Robert E. Lee. The rebels had failed to consider how they would alert slaves to the arsenal's capture so that slaves could gain access to the town and the weapons. With state and federal troops flooding into Harpers Ferry, Brown and his men were soon under siege, trapped in the arsenal. Fourteen rebels were killed, including two of Brown's sons. On October 18, Brown and three others were captured.

As word of the daring raid spread, Brown was hailed as a hero by devoted abolitionists and depicted as a madman by southern planters. Southern whites were sure he was part of a widespread conspiracy led by power-hungry abolitionists. Federal authorities moved quickly to quell slaveholders' fears and end the episode. Brown rejected his lawyer's advice to plead insanity, and a local jury found him guilty of murder, criminal conspiracy, and treason on October 31. He was hanged on December 2, 1859.

John Brown's execution unleashed a massive outpouring of grief, anger, and uncertainty across the North. Abolitionists organized parades, demonstrations, bonfires, and tributes to the newest abolitionist martyr. Even many Quakers and other pacifists viewed John Brown as a hero for giving his life in the cause of emancipation. But most northern politicians and editors condemned the raid as a rash act that could only intensify sectional tensions. **See Document Project 12: Visions of John Brown, page 384.**

Among southern whites, fear and panic greeted the raid on Harpers Ferry, and the execution of John Brown did little to quiet the outrage they felt at having their peculiar institution once again threatened with violence. Southern intellectuals had developed a sophisticated proslavery argument that they believed demonstrated the benefits of bondage for African Americans and its superiority to the northern system of wage labor. Yet neither that argument nor any federal law or Supreme Court decision seemed able to deter antislavery activism. Not surprisingly, Americans on both sides of the sectional divide considered the 1860 presidential election critical to the nation's future.

The Election of 1860

Brown's hanging set the tone for the 1860 presidential campaign. The Republicans met in Chicago in May 1860 and made clear that they sought national prominence by distancing themselves from the more radical wing of the abolitionist movement. The party platform condemned

Republican Party Presidential Ticket, 1860

This campaign banner for the Republican ticket of Abraham Lincoln and Hannibal Hamlin highlighted Lincoln's backwoods origins by including rustic bentwood frames and a rail fence. The images of industrial growth and protection sought to appeal to laborers and manufacturers, while the motto "Free Speech, Free Homes, Free Territory" indicated the candidates' support for small farmers and their opposition to the extension of slavery.   Library of Congress

John Brown along with southern "Border Ruffians" who initiated the violence in Kansas. The platform accepted slavery where it already existed, but continued to advocate its exclusion from western territories. Finally, the party platform argued forcefully for internal improvements and protective tariffs. On the third ballot, Republicans nominated Abraham Lincoln as their candidate for president. Recognizing the impossibility of gaining significant votes in the South, the party focused instead on winning large majorities in the Northeast and Midwest.

The Democrats met in Charleston, South Carolina. Although Stephen Douglas was the leading candidate, he could not assuage southern delegates who were still angry that Kansas had been admitted as a free state. Mississippi senator Jefferson Davis then introduced a resolution to protect slavery in the territories, but Douglas's northern supporters rejected it. When President Buchanan came out against Douglas, the Democratic convention ended without choosing a candidate. Instead, various factions held their own conventions. A group of largely northern Democrats met in Baltimore and nominated Douglas. Southern or "cotton" Democrats selected John Breckinridge, the current vice president and a Kentucky slaveholder, on a platform that included the extension of slavery and the annexation of Cuba. The Constitutional Union Party, comprised mainly of former southern Whigs, advocated "no political principle other than the Constitution of the country, the union of the states, and the enforcement of the laws." Its members nominated Senator John Bell of Tennessee, a onetime Whig.

Although Lincoln won barely 40 percent of the popular vote, he carried a clear majority in the electoral college. With the admission of Minnesota and Oregon to the Union in 1858 and 1859, free states now outnumbered slave states eighteen to fifteen, and Lincoln won all but one

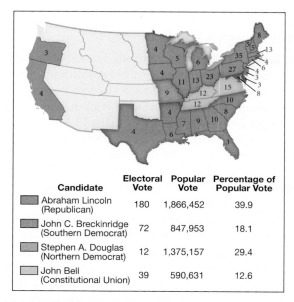

Candidate	Electoral Vote	Popular Vote	Percentage of Popular Vote
Abraham Lincoln (Republican)	180	1,866,452	39.9
John C. Breckinridge (Southern Democrat)	72	847,953	18.1
Stephen A. Douglas (Northern Democrat)	12	1,375,157	29.4
John Bell (Constitutional Union)	39	590,631	12.6

MAP 12.3   The Election of 1860

Four candidates vied for the presidency in 1860, and the voters split along clearly sectional lines. Although Stephen Douglas ran a vigorous campaign and gained votes in all regions of the country, he won a majority only in Missouri. Lincoln triumphed in the North and far West, and Breckinridge in most of the South.

of them. Moreover, free states in the Middle Atlantic and Midwest were among the most populous in the nation and therefore had a large number of electoral votes. Douglas ran second to Lincoln in the popular vote, but Bell and Breckinridge captured more electoral votes than Douglas did. Despite a deeply divided electorate, Lincoln became president (Map 12.3).

Although many abolitionists were wary of the Republicans' position on slavery, especially their willingness to leave slavery alone where it already existed, most were nonetheless relieved at Lincoln's victory and hoped he would become more sympathetic to their views once in office. Meanwhile, southern whites, especially those in the deep South, were furious that a Republican had won the White House without carrying a single southern state.

The Lower South Secedes

On December 20, 1860, six weeks after Lincoln's election, the legislature of South Carolina announced that because "a sectional party" had engineered "the election of a man to the high office of President of the United States whose opinions and purposes are hostile to slavery, [the people of South Carolina dissolve their union with] the other states of North America." The first southern state had seceded from the Union, and its leaders now worked to convince neighboring states to join them. In early 1861, Mississippi, Florida, Alabama, Georgia, Louisiana, and Texas followed suit. Representatives from these states met on February 8 in Montgomery, Alabama, where they adopted a provisional constitution, elected Mississippi senator and slaveholder

Jefferson Davis as their president, and established the **Confederate States of America** (Map 12.4).

Although President Buchanan was aware of developments in the South, he did nothing. His cabinet included three secessionists and two unionists, one of whom resigned in mid-December in frustration over Buchanan's failure to act. But Washington, D.C., was filled with southern sympathizers, who urged caution on an already timid president. Although some Northerners were shocked by the decision of South Carolina and its allies, many others supported their right to leave or believed they would return to the Union when they realized they could not survive economically on their own. Moreover, with Virginia, Maryland, and other Upper South slave states still part of the nation, the secession movement seemed both limited and unlikely to succeed.

Buchanan did urge Congress to find a compromise, and Kentucky senator John Crittenden proposed a plan that gained significant support. Indeed, Congress approved the first part of his plan, which called for a constitutional amendment to protect slavery from federal interference in any state where it already existed. But the second part of Crittenden's plan failed to pass after Republicans voiced their unanimous opposition. It would have extended the Missouri Compromise line (latitude 36°30′) to the California border and barred slavery north of that line. South of that line, however, slavery would be protected, including in any territories "acquired hereafter." Fearing that passage would encourage southern planters to once again seek territory in Cuba, Mexico, or Central America, Lincoln and the Republicans rejected the proposal. Despite the hopes of

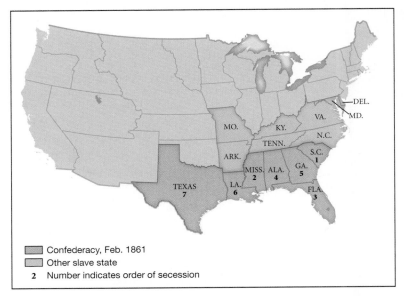

MAP 12.4 The Original Confederacy

Seven states in the Lower South seceded from the United States and formed the Confederate States of America in February 1861. While the original Confederacy was too limited in population and resources to defend itself against the U.S. government, its leaders hoped that other slave states would soon join them.

Confederacy, Feb. 1861
Other slave state
2 Number indicates order of secession

the Buchanan administration, it was becoming apparent that compromise was impossible. The Confederacy was not a fleeting disruption of the national order. It was the beginning of the Civil War.

REVIEW & RELATE

How and why did John Brown's raid on Harpers Ferry move the country closer to civil war?

Why did many in the South believe that the election of Abraham Lincoln was cause for secession?

 LEARNINGCurve bedfordstmartins.com/hewittlawson/LC

Conclusion: The Coming of the Civil War

Dred Scott did not live to see Abraham Lincoln take the oath of office in March 1861. Following the Supreme Court's 1857 ruling, Scott was returned to Irene Emerson, who had married abolitionist Calvin Chaffee while awaiting the Supreme Court ruling. When that ruling was announced, Chaffee found himself the owner of the most well-known slave in America. He quickly returned Dred Scott and his family to his original owners, the Blow family. On May 26, 1857, the Blows freed the Scotts, so Dred Scott spent the last year and a half of his life as a free man. His wife Harriet and his daughters survived to see Lincoln inaugurated, the Confederacy defeated, and slavery abolished throughout the nation. Although they had to face a brutal civil war, they could take comfort from the fact that the *Dred Scott* case had helped to solidify northern support for both Lincoln and abolition.

John C. Frémont, like almost all slavery opponents, was outraged at the *Dred Scott* decision. He had helped to open

the far West to settlement and bring California into the Union as a free state. Yet these achievements led to the demise of large numbers of Indians and fueled the battle over slavery. Despite the efforts of the Comanche and other Indian nations to fend off white encroachment, the U.S. government and eastern settlers claimed more and more territory in the 1840s and 1850s. By 1860, however, most white Americans thought less and less about Indian policy as they focused more and more on slavery.

Some Confederate planters imagined a nation that included Cuba, Nicaragua, and other slave territories. Meanwhile Northerners proved they would fight back. Those outraged by the Fugitive Slave Act had launched rescues of fugitives, and those appalled by Bleeding Kansas applauded John Brown's raid. These more militant activists were joined by thousands of more moderate Northerners who voted for Lincoln in the fall of 1860. By the time Abraham Lincoln took office in March 1861, the ever-widening political chasm brought the United States face-to-face with civil war.

Yet even as war erupted, the issue of slavery remained unresolved. When Frémont was appointed major general in charge of the Department of the West in 1861, he faced a chaotic situation as proslavery forces tried to wrest Missouri from Union control. In response to a Confederate military victory in August 1861 at Wilson's Creek in southwest Missouri, Frémont issued a limited emancipation proclamation, freeing the slaves of Missourians who supported the Confederacy. But the order flew in the face of Lincoln's efforts to keep Missouri from joining the Confederacy and was soon rescinded. Southern states had seceded and were willing to wage war to maintain slavery. Was the North willing to face prolonged battles and high casualties to reunite the nation and abolish human bondage once and for all?

Chapter Review

Online Study Guide ▶ bedfordstmartins.com/hewittlawson

KEY TERMS

Oregon Trail (p. 363)
gold rush (p. 365)
Compromise of 1850 (p. 368)
Fugitive Slave Act of 1850 (p. 368)
Uncle Tom's Cabin (p. 372)
Kansas-Nebraska Act (p. 373)
Republican Party (p. 373)
Bleeding Kansas (p. 376)
Dred Scott decision (p. 378)
Harpers Ferry, Virginia (p. 379)
Confederate States of America (p. 381)

REVIEW AND RELATE

1. Why did Americans go west in the 1830s and 1840s, and what was the journey like?

2. What groups competed for land and resources in the West? How did competition lead to violence?

3. What steps did legislators take in the 1840s and early 1850s to resolve the issue of the expansion of slavery?

4. How were slavery and American imperialist ambitions intertwined in the 1840s and 1850s?

5. What factors contributed to the spread of antislavery sentiment in the North beyond committed abolitionists?

6. How did the violence in Kansas in the mid-1850s reflect and intensify the growing sectional divide within the nation?

7. How and why did John Brown's raid on Harpers Ferry move the country closer to civil war?

8. Why did many in the South believe that the election of Abraham Lincoln was cause for secession?

TIMELINE OF EVENTS

1842	John C. Frémont leads expedition along the Oregon Trail
1843	Marcus and Narcissa Whitman lead 1,000 Christian emigrants to the Oregon Territory
1845	Texas granted statehood
1846	Dred Scott and his family sue for their freedom
1848	Gold discovered at Sutter's Mill in California
1850	Compromise of 1850
	Fugitive Slave Act passed
1852	Harriet Beecher Stowe publishes *Uncle Tom's Cabin*
1854	U.S.-Japanese treaty allows for mutual trading
	Republican Party founded
May 1854	Fugitive slave Anthony Burns returned to his owner
	Kansas-Nebraska Act passed
1854–1858	Period of violence in Bleeding Kansas
1857	Supreme Court ruling in *Dred Scott* case
1858	Lincoln-Douglas debates
October 16, 1859	John Brown's raid on Harpers Ferry, Virginia
December 2, 1859	John Brown executed
November 1860	Abraham Lincoln elected president
December 20, 1860	South Carolina secedes from the Union
January 1861	Mississippi, Florida, Alabama, Georgia, Louisiana, and Texas secede
February 1861	Confederate States of America established
March 1861	Lincoln inaugurated as president

DOCUMENT PROJECT **12**

Visions of John Brown

On October 16, 1859, John Brown led a group of eighteen men on a raid on the federal arsenal at Harpers Ferry, Virginia. The plan failed, and Brown and his surviving accomplices were captured and put on trial. On December 2, a mere seven weeks after the raid began, Brown was executed by hanging.

The raid shocked the nation, not least because John Brown was a white man leading an uprising to free enslaved blacks. Brown's quick trial and execution were designed to calm southern fears and minimize northern support for his actions. Neither goal was accomplished. Although the northern press and political establishment denounced the raid, many tempered their observations with an equally powerful condemnation of slavery. Abolitionists held demonstrations, wrote tributes and poems to Brown, and organized a "Day of Mourning" to coincide with his execution (Documents 12.7 and 12.9). Southerners and some northern Democrats labeled Brown a terrorist and a traitor and believed he was part of a vast abolitionist conspiracy to violently overthrow their way of life (Documents 12.6 and 12.10). The raid on Harpers Ferry may have ended quickly, but it intensified the sectional dispute over slavery and gave both sides a focal point for their anger. The following sources highlight some of the varying attitudes about John Brown—painting him as a hero, a saint, a stooge, a brute, and a fanatic. In addition, a letter John Brown writes from prison captures his state of mind shortly after his capture, and an 1863 painting makes clear the continued importance of his legacy (Documents 12.8 and 12.11). The differing representations tell us as much about the authors of the sources as they do about Brown himself. As you examine them, consider what they reveal about America on the eve of the Civil War.

DOCUMENT 12.6

State Register (Springfield, Illinois) | The Irrepressible Conflict, 1859

While many Northerners shared Brown's antislavery beliefs, most disagreed with his violent approach to abolition. The following passage from an editorial in the *State Register* (Springfield, Illinois) reflects the outrage felt throughout the nation. The *State Register* was known as a supporter of the Democratic Party, and it blamed the Harpers Ferry raid on the Republican Party. The editorial singles out William Seward and Abraham Lincoln for condemnation because of earlier speeches in which they identified the differences between the North and South as, in Seward's words, an "irrepressible conflict."

The telegraphic dispatches yesterday morning startled the public with an account of one of the most monstrous villainies ever attempted in this country. It was no less than an effort on the part of a party of abolitionists and negroes to take possession of one of the national arsenals, at Harper's Ferry, with the military stores and the public money there deposited. Under the lead of the most infamous of the Kansas crew of black republican marauders, Ossawatomie Brown, the insurgents, to the number of five or six hundred, attacked and took possession of the whole town of Harper's Ferry, including the government buildings and stores, stopped the mails, imprisoned peaceable citizens, and, before they were dislodged, numbers were killed and wounded on both sides.

It was scarcely credible, when the first dispatch was received yesterday, that the object of the ruffians could be other than plunder, but late dispatches, including those we publish this morning, show, conclusively, that the movement was a most extensive one, having for its object the uprising of the negroes throughout the south, a servile war, and its consequences— murder, rapine, and robbery.

The leader chosen was just the man to initiate the work. Bankrupt in fortune and character, an outlaw and an outcast, he was just the man to commence the work which ultra Abolitionism, through its diligent Parkers and Garrisons, hope to reach the millennium of their traitorous designs. Their open-mouthed treason, which culminates in precisely such outrages as that at Harper's Ferry, is but the logical sequence of the teachings of Wm. H. Seward and Abraham Lincoln—the one boldly proclaiming an "irrepressible conflict" between certain states of the Union, because of their local institutions, and the other declaring from stump and hustings, the country round, that the Union cannot continue as the fathers made it—part slave and part free states. When such men, by specious demagogism, in the name of freedom and liberty, daily labor to weaken the bonds of our glorious governmental fabric, the work of sages and patriots, themselves the holders of black men as slaves, is it to be wondered at that ignorant, unprincipled, and reckless camp followers of the party for which these leaders speak, attempt, practically, to illustrate the doctrines which they preach, and in advocacy of which they seek to obtain control of the national government.

Brown, though a blood-stained ruffian, is a bold man. As a black republican he practices what his leaders preach. As it is urged by statesmen (save the mark!) of his party that there is an "irrepressible conflict," he wants it in tangible, material shape. He believes in blows, not words, and the Harper's Ferry villainy is the first in his line of performance.

Who is so blind as not to see the inevitable tendency of black republican teaching? Now we have a bloody, glaring, ghastly fact before us. The "conflict" by blows has commenced. The proofs of an extensive and ramified organization is disclosed, the object of which is to stir the southern slaves to bathe their hands in the blood of the whites of the south. Traitorous scoundrels, with white faces, but black hearts, lead them, and the country is stunned with their deeds of infamy, treason, and blood.

Such is the ripening of the black republican harvest. Can an intelligent people doubt that to such ends the maudlin philanthropy, the hypocritical cant, the blatant demagogism, of black republicanism, tends? "By their fruits shall ye know them." Disunion and bloody anarchy.

Source: "The 'Irrepressible Conflict' Fruits of the Lincoln-Seward Doctrine," *State Register* (Springfield, Illinois), October 20, 1859.

DOCUMENT 12.7

Henry David Thoreau | A Plea for Captain John Brown, 1859

Although most abolitionists were quick to condemn John Brown, Henry David Thoreau rushed to his defense. A prominent author, reformer, and transcendentalist, Thoreau had been introduced to Brown several years earlier by Franklin Sanborn, who helped finance the Harpers Ferry raid. A few weeks after the raid, Thoreau wrote an essay, "A Plea for Captain John Brown," and delivered it in front of a public gathering in Concord, Massachusetts. Thoreau's essay was widely circulated and helped establish Brown as a martyr for the abolitionist cause.

I do not wish to force my thoughts upon you, but I feel forced myself. Little as I know of Captain Brown, I would fain [willingly] do my part to correct the tone and the statements of the newspapers, and of my countrymen generally, respecting his character and actions. It costs us nothing to be just. We can at least express our sympathy with, and admiration of, him and his companions, and that is what I now propose to do. . . .

. . . He was a superior man. He did not value his bodily life in comparison with ideal things. He did not recognize unjust human laws, but resisted them as he was bid. For once we are lifted out of the trivialness and dust of politics into the region of truth and manhood. No man in America has ever stood up so persistently and effectively for the dignity of human nature, knowing himself for a man, and the equal of any and all governments. In that sense he was the most American of us all. He needed no babbling lawyer, making false issues, to defend him. He was more than a match for all the judges that American voters, or office-holders of whatever grade, can create. He could not have been tried by a jury of his peers, because his peers did not exist. When a man stands up serenely against the condemnation and vengeance of mankind, rising above them literally *by a whole body*—even though he were of late the vilest murderer, who has settled that matter with himself—the spectacle is a sublime one—didn't ye know it, ye Liberators, ye Tribunes, ye Republicans? [various newspapers]—and we become criminal in comparison. Do yourselves the honor to recognize him. He needs none of your respect. . . .

It was his peculiar doctrine that a man has a perfect right to interfere by force with the slaveholder, in order to rescue the slave. I agree with him. They who are continually shocked by slavery have some right to be shocked by the violent death of the slaveholder, but no others. Such will be more shocked by his life than by his death. I shall not be forward to think him mistaken in his method who quickest succeeds to liberate the slave. I speak for the slave when I say, that I prefer the philanthropy of Captain Brown to that philanthropy which neither shoots me nor liberates me. At any rate, I do not think it is quite sane for one to spend his whole life in talking or writing about this matter, unless he is continually inspired, and I have not done so. A man may have other affairs to attend to. I do not wish to kill nor to be killed, but I can foresee circumstances in which both these things would be by me unavoidable. We preserve the so-called peace of our community by deeds of petty violence every day. Look at the policeman's billy and handcuffs! Look at the jail! Look at the gallows! Look at the chaplain of the regiment! We are hoping only to live safely on the outskirts of *this* provisional army. So we defend ourselves and our hen-roosts, and maintain slavery. I know that the mass of my countrymen think that the only righteous use that can be made of Sharpe's rifles and revolvers is to fight duels with them, when we are insulted by other nations, or to hunt Indians, or shoot fugitive slaves with them, or the like. I think that for once the Sharpe's rifles and revolvers were employed in a righteous cause. The tools were in the hands of one who could use them.

The same indignation that is said to have cleared the temple once will clear it again. The question is not about the weapon, but the spirit in which you use it. No man has appeared in America, as yet, who loved his fellow-man so well, and treated him so tenderly. He lived for him. He took up his life and he laid it down for him. What sort of violence is that which is encouraged, not by soldiers but by peaceable citizens, not so much by laymen as by ministers of the gospel, not so much by the fighting sects as by the Quakers, and not so much by Quaker men as by Quaker women? . . .

I am here to plead his cause with you. I plead not for his life, but for his character—his immortal life; and so it becomes your cause wholly, and is not his in the least. Some eighteen hundred years ago Christ was crucified; this morning, perchance, Captain Brown was hung. These are the two ends of a chain which is not without its links. He is not Old Brown any longer; he is an angel of light.

I see now that it was necessary that the bravest and humanest man in all the country should be hung. Perhaps he saw it himself. I *almost fear* that I may yet hear of his deliverance, doubting if a prolonged life, if *any* life, can do as much good as his death.

"Misguided"! "Garrulous"! "Insane"! "Vindictive"! So ye write in your easy chairs, and thus he wounded responds from the floor of the Armory, clear as a cloudless sky, true as the voice of nature is: "No man sent me here; it was my own prompting and that of my Maker. I acknowledge no master in human form." . . .

I foresee the time when the painter will paint that scene, no longer going to Rome for a subject; the poet will sing it; the historian record it; and, with the Landing of the Pilgrims and the Declaration of Independence, it will be the ornament of some future national gallery, when at least the present form of Slavery shall be no more here. We shall then be at liberty to weep for Captain Brown. Then, and not till then, we will take our revenge.

Source: James Redpath, *Echoes of Harper's Ferry* (Boston: Thayer and Eldridge, 1860), 2, 30, 37–38, 41–42.

DOCUMENT 12.8

John Brown | Letter to E.B. from Jail, November 1, 1859

John Brown's actions raised especially difficult questions for Quaker abolitionists, who as pacifists did not support violence. A Quaker woman (E.B.) from Newport, Rhode Island, wrote Brown on October 27, expressing her admiration for his motives even though she opposed the means he employed. John Brown replied, offering a religious rationale for his raid. He also urged this letter writer, and many others, to worry less about him and more about his wife Mary, his daughters-in-law, and other widows of those who died during the raid. Although Brown's family received financial assistance, they found it difficult to escape the notoriety of Harpers Ferry and eventually resettled in California.

CHARLESTOWN, JEFFERSON COUNTY, VA., NOV. 1, 1859

My dear Friend E.B. of R.I.,

Your most cheering letter of the 27th of October is received; and may the Lord reward you a thousandfold for the kind feeling you express toward me; but more especially for your fidelity to the "poor that cry, and those that have no help." For this I am a prisoner in bonds. It is solely my own fault, in a military point of view, that we met with our disaster. I mean that I mingled with our prisoners and so far sympathized with them and their families that I neglected my duty in other respects. But God's will, not mine, be done.

You know that Christ once armed Peter. So also in my case I think he put a sword into my hand, and there continued it so long as he saw best, and then kindly took it from me. I mean when I first went to Kansas. I wish you could know with what cheerfulness I am now wielding the "sword of the Spirit" on the right hand and on the left. I bless God that it proves "mighty to the pulling down of strongholds." I always loved my Quaker friends, and I commend to their kind regard my poor bereaved widowed wife and my daughters and daughters-in-law, whose husbands fell at my side. One is a mother and the other likely to become so soon. They, as well as my own sorrow-stricken daughters, are left very poor, and have much greater need of sympathy than I, who, through Infinite Grace and the kindness of strangers, am "joyful in all my tribulations."

Dear sister, write them at North Elba, Essex County, N.Y., to comfort their sad hearts. Direct to Mary A. Brown, wife of John Brown. There is also another—a widow, wife of Thompson, who fell with my poor boys in the affair at Harper's Ferry—at the same place.

I do not feel conscious of guilt in taking up arms; and had it been in behalf of the rich and powerful, the intelligent, the great (as men count greatness), or those who form enactments to suit themselves and corrupt others, or some of their friends, that I interfered, suffered, sacrificed, and fell, it would have been doing very well. But enough of this. These light afflictions, which endure for a moment, shall but work for me "a far more exceeding and eternal weight of glory." I would be very grateful for another letter from you. My wounds are healing. Farewell. God will surely attend to his own cause in the best possible way and time, and he will not forget the work of his own hands.

Your friend,
John Brown

Source: F. B. Sanborn, *The Life and Letters of John Brown* (Boston: Roberts Brothers, 1891), 582–83.

DOCUMENT 12.9

Reverend J. Sella Martin | Day of Mourning Speech, December 2, 1859

On the day of John Brown's execution, abolitionists and African Americans around the country held a "Day of Mourning" in his honor. In Boston, four thousand people gathered at the Tremont Temple to celebrate Brown's life and to grieve over his passing. The Reverend J. Sella Martin, a former slave and the pastor of the Joy Street Baptist Church in Boston, addressed the crowd.

KNOW THAT JOHN BROWN, in thus rebuking our public sin, in thus facing the monarch, has had to bear just what John the Baptist bore. His head today, by Virginia—that guilty maid of a more guilty mother, the American Government—has been cut off, and it has been presented to the ferocious and insatiable hunger, the terrible and inhuman appetite, of this corrupt government. Today, by the telegraph, we have received the intelligence that John Brown has forfeited his life—all this honesty, all this straight-forwardness, all this self-sacrifice, which has been manifested in Harper's Ferry. . . .

I know that there is some quibbling, some querulousness, some fear, in reference to an out-and-out endorsement of his course. Men of peace principles object to it, in consequence of their religious conviction; politicians in the North object to it, because they are afraid that it will injure their party; pro-slavery men in the South object to it, because it has touched their dearest idol; but I am prepared, my friends (and permit me to say, this is not the language of rage), I am prepared, in the light of all human history, to approve of the *means*; in the light of all Christian principle, to approve of the *end*. (Applause.) I say this is not the language of rage, because I remember that our Fourth-of-July orators sanction the same thing; because I remember that Concord, and Bunker Hill, and every historic battlefield in this country, and the celebration of those events, all go to approve the means that John Brown has used; the only difference being, that in our battles, in America, means have been used for *white* men and that John Brown has used his means for *black* men. (Applause.) And I say, that so far as principle is concerned, so far as the sanctions of the Gospel are concerned, I am prepared to endorse his end; and I endorse it because God Almighty has told us that we should feel with them that are in bonds as being bound with them. I endorse his end, because every single instinct of our nature rises and tells us that it is right. I find an endorsement of John Brown's course in the large assembly gathered here this evening; I find an endorsement of the principles that governed him in going to Virginia, in the presence of the men and women who have come here to listen to his eulogy, and sympathize with his suffering family. . . .

Now, I bring this question down to the simple test of the Gospel; and, agreeing with those men who say the sword should not be used, agreeing with them in that principle, and recognizing its binding obligation upon us all, yet I believe in that homeopathic principle which operates by mercury when mercury is in the system, and that that which is supported by the sword should be overthrown by the sword. I look at this question as a peace man. I say, in accordance with the principles of peace, that I do not believe the sword should be unsheathed. I do not believe the dagger should be drawn, until there is in the system to be assailed such terrible evidences of corruption, that it becomes the *dernier* [last] *resort*. And my friends, we are not to blame the application of the instrument, we are to blame the disease itself. When a physician cuts out a cancer from my face, I am not to blame the physician for the use of the knife; but the impure blood, the obstructed veins, the disordered system, that have caused the cancer, and rendered the use of the instrument necessary.

Source: *The Liberator*, December 9, 1859, in *Blacks on John Brown*, ed. Benjamin Quarles (Urbana: University of Illinois Press, 1972), 26–27.

DOCUMENT 12.10

A Southern Paper Reacts to Brown's Execution, December 3, 1859

The following article appeared in a North Carolina newspaper the day after Brown's execution. It predicts that the North will make Brown a martyr and ridicules the Day of Mourning held in his honor. The article singles out the celebration in Boston, at which J. Sella Martin gave a speech (Document 12.9), for particular condemnation and labels those who attended as treasonous.

The chances are ninety-nine in a hundred, that before this paper reaches our subscribers John Brown will have paid the penalty of his crimes on the gallows, and gone to render an account of his life to that Being who says "thou shalt do no murder."

While we have not the slightest fear that any attempt has been made to rescue Old Brown, we are not without painful apprehensions that among such a large body of inexperienced and excited soldiery, mischief has happened from the incautious use of fire arms.

It is to be hoped, with Brown's exit from the world, the excitement at the North will subside. But we must confess that this hope is but of the faintest character. Fanaticism at the North is rampant, and overrides every thing. On yesterday, the godly city of Boston, built up and sustained by the products of negro slave labor, went into mourning, fasting, and prayer, over the condign [deserved] punishment of a negro stealer, murderer, and traitor, and from fifty pulpits the Praise-God-Bare-bones belched forth volumes of blasphemy and treason.

In all the Noo England towns and villages, we may expect to hear that mock funerals have been celebrated, and all kinds of non-sensically lugubrious displays made. (It is a pity that they haven't a witch or two to drown or burn, by way of variety.) We hope that Gov. Wise [governor of Virginia] will have the gallows on which Brown was hung burned, and give notice of the fact. Our reasons for this wish is this: The Yankees have no objection to mingling money making with their grief, and they will, unless Brown's gallows is known to have been burned, set to work and make all kinds of jim-cracks and notions out of what they will call parts of Old John Brown's gallows and sell them. Let the rope which choked him, too, be burned and the fact advertised, or we shall see vast quantities of breast pins, lockets, and bracelets, containing bits of the "rope which hung Old Brown" for sale. [P. T.] Barnum is already in the market for Old Brown's old clothes, and hopes and expects to make [a good] speculation out of them.

Source: "Execution of John Brown," *Register* (Raleigh, North Carolina), December 3, 1859.

DOCUMENT 12.11

Currier and Ives | John Brown on His Way to Execution, 1863

In the weeks after Brown's death, newspapers were filled with accounts of his final days and execution. The *New York Tribune* published a story claiming that Brown had kissed a slave child he encountered on his way to the gallows. Although this story was untrue, it was widely repeated and became the subject of a painting by Louis Ransom. This 1863 Currier and Ives lithograph based on Ransom's painting further cemented the legend.

Library of Congress

Interpret the Evidence

1. How do these different sources describe Brown? What language and imagery do they use? How is religious imagery employed in the various documents?

2. In what ways do Brown's admirers, such as Henry David Thoreau (Document 12.7) and J. Sella Martin (Document 12.9), attempt to support Brown without praising the violence of his raid?

3. Those who condemned Brown often used his raid as a way to criticize the North and abolitionists. On what grounds did they make these more generalized claims of northern guilt (Documents 12.6 and 12.10)?

4. What is John Brown's state of mind after his conviction (Document 12.8)? How does he describe his actions?

5. What images and messages are used in the Currier and Ives illustration (Document 12.11) to portray Brown as a martyr?

Put It in Context

● How do the varied reactions to John Brown's 1859 raid on Harpers Ferry illuminate the conflicts that led to Abraham Lincoln's election as president in 1860 and South Carolina's secession in 1861?

background photos: page 387, Library of Congress; page 390, Peter Newark American Pictures/The Bridgeman Art Library

Library of Congress

Library of Congress

Confederate officer with wife and child.

Cabin interior with African American women and children, Spotsylvania Court House, Virginia, 1864.

13
Civil War
1861–1865

Library of Congress

Union family in camp of Thirty-first Pennsylvania Infantry near Washington, D.C., 1862.

AMERICAN HISTORIES

Though born into slavery in 1818, by 1860 Frederick Douglass had become a celebrated orator, editor, and abolitionist. He ensured his fame in 1845 with publication of the *Narrative of the Life of Frederick Douglass*. In it, he described his experiences of slavery in Maryland, his defiance against his masters, and his eventual escape to New York in September 1838 with the help of Anna Murray, a free black servant.

Frederick and Anna married in New York and then moved to New Bedford, Massachusetts, and changed their last name to Douglass to avoid capture. But in 1841 Frederick began lecturing for the American Anti-Slavery Society, offering stirring accounts of his enslavement and escape. By publishing his *Narrative* four years later, Douglass made his capture even more likely, so in August 1845 he left for England, where wildly enthusiastic audiences attended his lectures and supporters raised funds to purchase his freedom. Douglass returned to Massachusetts in 1847, a truly free man.

A year later, Frederick moved to Rochester, New York, with Anna and their five children to launch his abolitionist paper, the *North Star*. Over the next decade, he became the most famous black abolitionist in the United States and an outspoken advocate of women's rights. He also broke with the Garrisonian branch of abolitionists by joining the Liberty Party and later the Free-Soil and Republican parties. He was thus well placed when war erupted in April 1861 to lobby President Lincoln to make emancipation a war aim and enlist African Americans in the Union army.

Douglass embraced electoral politics and the use of military force to end slavery. His greatest fear was that Lincoln was more committed to reconstituting the Union than to abolishing slavery. But after the president issued the Emancipation Proclamation in January 1863, Douglass spoke enthusiastically on its behalf. At the same time, he continued to believe that military service was essential for black men to demonstrate their patriotism. His stirring editorial "Men of Color, to Arms" was turned into a recruiting poster, and he urged his own sons to join the Massachusetts Fifty-fourth Colored Infantry, one of the first African American regiments. But Douglass also protested discrimination against black troops and lobbied for federal protections of black civil rights.

Like Douglass, Rose O'Neal was born on a Maryland plantation, but she was white and free. Her father was likely John O'Neal, a planter who was slain by a slave in 1817, when Rose was four years old. In early adolescence, she moved to Washington, D.C., with her older sister. They lived with an aunt who ran a fashionable boardinghouse near Capitol Hill. The boarders included John C. Calhoun, whose states' rights views Rose eagerly embraced. Intrigued by the lively political debates that marked the Jacksonian era, she was also schooled in the social graces. Charming and beautiful, Rose was welcomed into elite social circles, including invitations from Dolley Madison. In 1835 she married Robert Greenhow, a cultivated Virginian who worked for the State Department.

Rose O'Neal Greenhow quickly became a favorite Washington hostess. Like Dolley Madison, she entertained

congressmen, cabinet ministers, and foreign diplomats with a wide range of views. In the midst of this social and political whirl, Rose gave birth to four daughters. Yet she also remained deeply invested in her husband's career. She assisted Robert in the 1840s as he researched U.S. land claims in the Pacific Northwest. Ardent proslavery expansionists, the Greenhows supported efforts to acquire Cuba, and in 1850 they traveled to Mexico City to study California land claims. When Robert died in 1854, Rose moved into a smaller house in Washington but continued to entertain political leaders and sustained friendships with powerful men like President James Buchanan.

In May 1861, just as the Civil War commenced, a U.S. army captain about to join the Confederate cause recruited Greenhow to head an espionage ring in Washington, D.C. With her close ties to southern sympathizers working in government offices and her extensive social network, Greenhow gathered important intelligence on Union political and military plans. Although she initially avoided suspicion, by August Greenhow was investigated and placed under house arrest. When she continued to smuggle out letters, embarrassing Union officials, she was sent to the Old Capitol Prison in January 1862. Once again, Greenhow managed to transmit information and riled up the other prisoners. In June, she was exiled to Richmond, where Confederate president Jefferson Davis hailed her as a hero and awarded her $2,500. •

THE AMERICAN HISTORIES of Frederick Douglass and Rose O'Neal Greenhow were shaped by the sectional conflict over slavery that culminated in the Civil War. Both were born on Maryland plantations, one as a slave and the other a daughter of slave owners. Both

honed their innate talents, one as an orator and a writer, the other as a hostess and gatherer of intelligence. And both embraced the Civil War as the last best hope for national salvation, one on the side of union and emancipation, the other on the side of secession and slavery. They were among hundreds of thousands of Americans—men and women, black and white, North and South—who saw the war as a means to achieve their goals: a free nation, a haven for slavery, or a reunited country.

The Nation Goes to War

When Abraham Lincoln took office, seven states in the Lower South had already formed the Confederate States of America, and the threat of more secessions remained. Lincoln had promised not to interfere with slavery where it already existed, but many southern whites were unconvinced by such assurances. By seceding, the southern slaveholding class also proclaimed its unwillingness to become a permanent minority in the nation. Still, not all slave states were yet willing to cut their ties to the nation, and Northerners, too, disagreed about the consequences of secession and the appropriate response to it. Once fighting erupted, however, preparations for war became the primary focus in both the North and the South.

The South Embraces Secession

Confederate president Davis joined other planters in arguing that Lincoln's victory jeopardized the future of slavery and that secession was, therefore, a necessity. Advocates of secession contended that the federal government had failed to implement fully the Fugitive Slave Act and the *Dred Scott* decision. With Republicans in power, they were convinced that the administration would do even less to support southern interests. White Southerners also feared that a Republican administration might inspire a massive uprising of slaves. In the aftermath of John Brown's raid on Harpers Ferry, one southern newspaper warned that the region was "slumbering over a volcano, whose smoldering fires may, at any quiet starry midnight, blacken the social sky with the smoke of desolation and death." Secession would allow whites to maintain greater control over the South's black population.

Slaveholders were also anxious about the loyalty of white Southerners who did not own slaves. "I mistrust our own people more than I fear all of the efforts of the Abolitionists," claimed a South Carolina politician in 1859. He went on to argue that by denouncing social and economic inequality, Republicans might recruit nonslaveholders to their party and thereby create a "contest for slavery . . . in the South between people of the South." Secession would effectively isolate southern yeomen from potential Republican allies.

When Lincoln was inaugurated, legislators in the Upper South still hoped a compromise could be reached. Although many Northerners believed that the secessionists needed to be punished, Lincoln sought to bring the Confederates back into the Union without using military force. Yet he also sought to demonstrate Union strength to curtail further secessions. He focused on **Fort Sumter** in South Carolina's Charleston harbor, where a small Union garrison was running low on food and medicine. On April 8, 1861, Lincoln dispatched ships to the fort but promised to use force only if the Confederates blocked his peaceful effort to send supplies.

Lincoln's action presented the Confederate government with a choice. It could attack the Union vessels and bear responsibility for starting a war, or it could permit a "foreign power" to maintain a fort in its territory. President Davis and his advisers chose the aggressive course, demanding the unconditional surrender of Fort Sumter before supplies arrived. The commanding officer refused, and on April 12 Confederate guns opened fire. Two days later, Fort Sumter surrendered. On April 15, Lincoln called for 75,000 volunteers to put down the southern insurrection.

The declaration of war led whites in the Upper South to reconsider secession. Some small farmers and landless whites in the region were drawn to Republican promises of free labor and free soil and remained suspicious of the goals and power of secessionist planters. Moreover, their land sat in the direct path of military engagement. Yet the vast majority of southern whites, rich and poor, defined their liberty in relation to black bondage. They feared that Republicans would free the slaves and introduce racial amalgamation in the South.

Explore

See Documents 13.1 and 13.2 for two sides of the secession debate in Georgia.

Fearing more secessions, Lincoln used the powers of his office to keep the border states that allowed slavery—Maryland, Delaware, Missouri, and Kentucky—in the Union. He waived the right of habeas corpus (which protects citizens against arbitrary arrest and detention), jailed secessionists, arrested state legislators, and limited freedom of the press. Despite these measures, four more slave states—North Carolina, Virginia, Tennessee, and Arkansas—seceded. Of these, Virginia was by far the most significant. It was strategically located near the nation's capital. Richmond was also home to the South's largest iron manufacturer, which could produce weapons and munitions. By June 1861, the Confederacy had moved its capital to Richmond in recognition of Virginia's importance.

DOCUMENTS 13.1 AND 13.2

Debating Secession in Georgia: Two Views

Immediately after Abraham Lincoln's election, several southern states began to discuss secession. Georgia called a special convention to debate the issue on November 13–14, 1860. Two of the principal speakers were Robert Toombs and Alexander Stephens, close friends who had met in Washington, D.C., as U.S. congressmen from Georgia. In the following selections from their speeches, Toombs argues in favor of secession, and Stephens urges a more cautious approach. In January 1861, Georgia became the fifth state to secede, two months before Lincoln took office. In February, Stephens was elected vice president of the Confederacy.

Explore

13.1 Robert Toombs | For Secession, 1860

The stern, steady march of events has brought us in conflict with our non-slaveholding confederates upon the fundamental principles of our compact of Union. We have not sought this conflict; we have sought too long to avoid it. . . . The door of conciliation and compromise is finally closed by our adversaries, and it remains only to us to meet the conflict with the dignity and firmness of men worthy of freedom. . . .

. . . The South at all times demanded nothing but equality in the common territories, equal enjoyment of them with their property, to that extended to Northern citizens and their property—nothing more. . . . In 1790 we had less than eight hundred thousand slaves. Under our mild and humane administration of the system they have increased above four millions. The country has expanded to meet this growing want, and Florida, Alabama, Mississippi, Louisiana, Texas, Arkansas, Kentucky, Tennessee, and Missouri have received this increasing tide of African labor; before the end of this century, at precisely the same rate of increase, the Africans among us in a subordinate condition will amount to eleven millions of persons. What shall be done with them? We must expand or perish. . . . The North understand it better—they have told us for twenty years that their object was to pen up slavery within its present limits—surround it with a border of free States, and like the scorpion surrounded with fire, they will make it sting itself to death.

Source: Frank Moore, ed., *The Rebellion Record: A Diary of American Events* (New York: G. P. Putnam and Henry Holt, 1864), 1:362–63, 365.

When the first seven states seceded, outrage and anxiety escalated in the North. Textile manufacturers feared the permanent loss of the southern cotton crop, and bankers worried whether Confederates would repay their loans. In northeastern cities, stock prices plummeted, banks shut their doors, factories laid off workers, and unsold goods piled up on docks. But the firing on Fort Sumter prompted many Northerners to line up behind Lincoln's call for war. Manufacturers and merchants, once intent upon maintaining economic links with the South, now rushed to support the president, while northern workers, including immigrants, responded to Lincoln's call for volunteers. They assumed that the Union, with its greater resources and manpower, could quickly set the nation right. New York editor Horace Greeley proclaimed, "Jeff Davis and Co. will be swingin' from the battlements at Washington at least by the 4th of July." A Philadelphia newspaper echoed, "This much-ado about nothing will end in a month." Greeley and his fellow journalists were sadly mistaken.

Both Sides Prepare for War

At the onset of the war, the Union held a decided advantage in resources and population. The Union states held more than 60 percent of the U.S. population, while the Confederate states held less than 40 percent. And the Confederacy included several million slaves who would not be armed for

13.2 Alexander Stephens | Against Secession, 1860

The first question that presents itself is, Shall the people of the South secede from the Union in consequence of the election of Mr. Lincoln to the Presidency of the United States? My countrymen, I tell you frankly, candidly, and earnestly, that I do not think they ought. . . . To make a point of resistance to the Government, to withdraw from it because a man has been constitutionally elected, puts us in the wrong. We are pledged to maintain the Constitution. Many of us have sworn to support it. Can we, therefore, for the mere election of a man to the Presidency, and that too in accordance with the prescribed forms of the Constitution, make a point of resistance to the Government, without becoming the breakers of that sacred instrument ourselves by withdrawing ourselves from it? Would we not be in the wrong? . . .

The Northern States, on entering into the Federal compact, pledged themselves [under the 1793 Fugitive Slave Law] to surrender such fugitives; and it is in disregard of their constitutional obligations that they have passed laws which even tend to hinder or inhibit the fulfillment of that obligation. . . . What ought we to do in view of this? . . . By the law of nations, you would have a right to demand the carrying out of this article of agreement, and I do not see that it should be otherwise with respect to the States of this Union; and in case it be not done, we would, by these principles, have the right to commit acts of reprisal on these faithless governments, and seize upon their property, or that of their citizens, wherever found. The States of this Union stand upon the same footing with foreign nations in this respect. But by the law of nations we are equally bound, before proceeding to violent measures, to set forth our grievances before the offending government, to give them an opportunity to redress the wrong. Has our State yet done this? I think not.

Source: Richard Malcolm Johnston and William Hand Browne, *Life of Alexander H. Stephens* (Philadelphia: J. B. Lippincott, 1878), 565–66, 575.

Interpret the Evidence

- What type of language does each man use to describe the North and the South?
- On what issues do they focus, and how do they describe the relationship of the South to the United States as a whole?

Put It in Context

Explain the importance of the issue of slavery to the arguments regarding secession that Toombs and Stephens make.

combat. The Union also outstripped the Confederacy in manufacturing and even led the South in agricultural production. The North's many miles of railroad track ensured greater ease in moving troops and supplies. And the Union could launch far more ships to blockade southern ports (Figure 13.1).

Yet Union forces were less prepared for war than were the Confederates, who had been organizing troops and gathering munitions for months. To match their efforts, Winfield Scott, general in chief of the U.S. army, told Lincoln he would need at least 300,000 men committed to serve for two or three years. But the president, who feared unnerving Northerners, asked for only 75,000 volunteers for three months. Recruits poured into state militias, and

thousands more offered their services directly to the federal government. Yet rather than forming a powerful national army led by seasoned officers, Lincoln left recruitment, organization, and training largely to the states. The result was disorganization and the appointment of new officers based more on political connections than on military expertise.

Confederate leaders also initially relied on state militia units and volunteers, but they prepared for a prolonged war from the start. Before the firing on Fort Sumter, President Davis signed up 100,000 volunteers for a year's service. The labor provided by slaves allowed a large proportion of white working-age men to volunteer for military service. And Southerners knew they were likely to be fighting mainly on

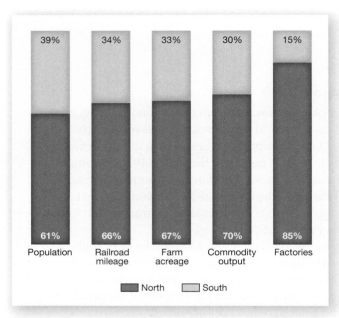

FIGURE 13.1   Economies of the North and South, 1860

This figure provides graphic testimony to the enormous advantages in resources the North held on the eve of the Civil War. Perhaps most surprisingly, the North led the South in farm acreage as well as factories and commodity output. Over four years of war, the North's significantly larger population would also prove crucial. Source: Data from Stanley Engerman, "The Economic Impact of the Civil War," in *The Reinterpretation of American Economic History*, ed. Robert W. Fogel and Stanley Engerman (New York: Harper and Row).

home territory, where they had expert knowledge of the terrain. When the final four states joined the Confederacy, the southern army also gained important military leadership. It ultimately recruited 280 West Point graduates, including Robert E. Lee, Thomas "Stonewall" Jackson, James Longstreet, and others who had proved their mettle in the Mexican-American War.

The South's advantages were apparent in the first major battle of the war. But Confederate troops were also aided by information on Union plans sent by Rose Greenhow. Confederate forces were thus well prepared when 30,000 Union troops marched on northern Virginia on July 21, 1861. At the Battle of Bull Run (or Manassas), 22,000 Confederates repelled the Union attack. During the fighting, 800 men lost their lives, giving Americans their first taste of the carnage that lay ahead. Civilians from Washington who traveled to the battle site to view the combat had to flee for their lives to escape Confederate artillery.

Despite Union defeats at Bull Run and Wilson's Creek, Missouri, in August 1861, the Confederate army did not follow up with major strikes against Union forces. Meanwhile the Union navy began blockading the South's deepwater ports. When the armies settled into winter camps in 1861–1862, both sides recognized that the war was likely to be a long struggle demanding a far greater commitment of men and resources than anyone had imagined just months earlier.

Battle of Wilson's Creek

This illustration depicts the First Iowa Regiment, led by General Nathaniel Lyon, charging Confederate forces at the Battle of Wilson's Creek, near Springfield, Missouri, on August 10, 1861. Lyon was shot in the head and killed, becoming the first Union general to die in the war. The Confederates won the battle, marking their second victory together with Bull Run.   Library of Congress

REVIEW & RELATE

What steps did Lincoln take to prevent war? Why were they ineffective?

What advantages and disadvantages did each side have at the onset of the war?

LEARNINGCurve bedfordstmartins.com/hewittlawson/LC

Fighting for Union or against Slavery?

The Union and the Confederacy faced very different tasks in the war. The South had to defend its territory and force the federal government to halt military action. The North had to bring the Confederacy to its knees by invading the South and isolating it from potential allies abroad. While most northern leaders believed that the nation could be reunited without challenging the institution of slavery, enslaved Southerners immediately looked for ways to loosen their bonds. Meanwhile northern abolitionists worked to convince Lincoln and Congress that only emancipation could resolve the problems that had led to war.

Debating the Role of African Americans

The outbreak of war intensified debates over abolition. Some 225,000 African Americans lived in the free states, and many offered their services in the hopes that victory would lead to the emancipation of southern slaves. At a recruitment meeting in Cleveland, African American leaders proclaimed, "Today, as in the times of '76, we are ready to go forth and do battle in the common cause of our country." But Secretary of War Simon Cameron had no intention of calling up black soldiers, and some local officials prohibited African American recruitment meetings.

Northern optimism about a quick victory contributed to the rejection of black soldiers. Union leaders also feared that whites would not enlist if they had to serve alongside blacks. In addition, Lincoln and his advisers were initially wary of letting a war to preserve the Union become a war against slavery, and they feared that any further threat to slavery might drive the four slave states that remained in the Union into the Confederacy. African Americans and their supporters nevertheless believed that the war opened a door to freedom and that continued pressure might convince Union leaders to change their minds. As activist Amy Post proclaimed, "The abolitionists surely have a job to do now in influencing and directing the bloody struggle, that it may end in Emancipation."

For their part, southern slaves quickly realized that the presence of Union troops made freedom a distinct possibility. Enslaved workers living near battle sites circulated information on Union troop movements. Then, as slaveholders in Virginia began to send male slaves to more distant plantations for fear of losing them, some slaves chose to flee. Those who could headed to Union camps, where they provided labor as well as knowledge of the local terrain and the location of Confederate forces. Slave owners, in turn, followed fugitives into Union camps and demanded their return. Some Union commanders denied slaves entrance or returned them to their masters, but a few Union officers saw the value of embracing these fugitives.

On the night of May 23, 1861, for example, three Virginia slaves paddled upriver to the Union outpost at Fort Monroe, requesting sanctuary from General Benjamin Butler. Butler was no abolitionist, but he realized that slaves were valuable assets to the Union cause and so offered them military protection. He claimed fugitive slaves as **contraband** of war: property forfeited by the act of rebellion. As news of Butler's decision spread, more runaways sought refuge at Fort Monroe. Within four days, another sixty-seven slaves had arrived at "Freedom Fort."

Explore

See Document 13.3 for an account of life among freedpeople on the Sea Islands.

Lincoln endorsed Butler's policy as a legitimate tactic of war because it allowed the Union to strike at the institution of slavery without proclaiming a general emancipation that might prompt the border states with slaves to secede. Congress expanded Butler's policy. On August 6, 1861, it passed a confiscation act, proclaiming that any slave owner whose bondsmen were used by the Confederate army would lose all claim to those slaves. Although it was far from a clear-cut declaration of freedom, the act spurred the hopes of abolitionists.

Fighting for the Right to Fight

From the start, the Union army recruited a wide array of Americans. Indeed, nearly every ethnic and racial group served in Union ranks except African Americans. German and Irish immigrants; Catholic, Protestant, and Jewish Americans; native-born whites from the Northeast and Midwest; and Mexican American soldiers in the West all fought with the Union army. In an effort to eliminate this one exception, abolitionists had long argued that African Americans would make excellent soldiers, and Radical

---

Charlotte Forten | Life on the Sea Islands, 1864

As Union forces began receiving former slaves as "contraband," many were settled in the Sea Islands of South Carolina, which were controlled by the Union army. Northern abolitionists sent teachers to these camps to help educate the former slaves. Charlotte Forten, who came from a prominent free African American family in Philadelphia, was a well-known abolitionist and the first black teacher to arrive in the camps in 1864. Forten's impressions of the newly freed slaves appeared in an article she wrote for the *Atlantic Monthly*, a progressive literary and cultural magazine.

Explore

It was on the afternoon of a warm, murky day late in October that our steamer, the *United States*, touched the landing at Hilton Head. A motley assemblage had collected on the wharf—officers, soldiers, and "contrabands" of every size and hue: black was, however, the prevailing color. . . .

Little colored children of every hue were playing about the streets, looking as merry and happy as children ought to look—now that the evil shadow of Slavery no longer hangs over them. . . .

. . . The school was opened in September. Many of the children had, however, received instruction during the summer. It was evident that they had made very rapid improvement, and we noticed with pleasure how bright and eager to learn many of them seemed. . . .

These people are exceedingly polite in their manner towards each other, each new arrival bowing, scraping his feet, and shaking hands

with the others, while there are constant greetings, such as, "Huddy? How's yer lady?" ("How d' ye do? How's your wife?"). The hand-shaking is performed with the greatest possible solemnity. There is never the faintest shadow of a smile on anybody's face during this performance. The children, too, are taught to be very polite to their elders, and it is the rarest thing to hear a disrespectful word from a child to his parent, or to any grown person. They have really what the New-Englanders call "beautiful manners." . . .

Daily the long-oppressed people of these islands are demonstrating their capacity for improvement in learning and labor. What they have accomplished in one short year exceeds our utmost expectations. . . . An old freedman said to me one day, "De Lord make me suffer long time. . . . But now we's free. He bring us all out right at las'."

Source: Charlotte Forten, "Life on the Sea Islands," *The Atlantic Monthly*, May–June 1864, 587, 589, 592, 676.

Interpret the Evidence

- How does Forten describe the former slaves? What aspects of their behavior seem to strike her most forcefully?
- How is Forten trying to shape northern opinion about former slaves in this article?

Put It in Context

What resources could northern abolitionists and teachers provide for newly freed slaves?

Republicans in Congress emphasized the military advantages of allowing black enlistment. As Massachusetts senator Charles Sumner explained, "You will observe that I propose no crusade for abolition. [Emancipation] is to be presented strictly as a measure of military necessity." Meanwhile American Indians fought on both sides. The Comanches negotiated with both Union and Confederate agents while raiding the Texas frontier for horses and cattle. The Confederacy gained the greatest support from slaveholding Indians who had earlier been removed from the Southeast. The Cherokee general Stand Watie led a pan-Indian force that battled alongside white Confederate troops on the western frontier. However, most members of the Cherokee and other southeastern tribes, along with Osage, Delaware, and Seneca Indians, sided with the Union. Ely Parker, a Seneca sachem and engineer, rose to become a lieutenant colonel in the Union army, serving with General Ulysses S. Grant.

While some Indian regiments were rejected by state officials, African Americans were barred from enlisting by federal authority. In 1862, however, a series of military defeats helped transform northern attitudes. Although Union forces gained ground along the southern Mississippi River, they lost important battles farther north. In the spring of 1862, Confederate troops led by Stonewall Jackson won a series of stunning victories against three Union armies in Virginia's Shenandoah Valley. That June and July,

General Robert E. Lee fought General George B. McClellan to a standstill in the Seven Days Battle near Richmond. Then in August, Lee, Jackson, and General James Longstreet joined forces to defeat Union troops at the Second Battle of Bull Run (Map 13.1).

As the war turned against the North, the North turned against slavery. In April 1862, Congress approved a measure to abolish slavery in the District of Columbia, symbolizing a significant shift in Union sentiment. During that bloody summer, Congress passed a second confiscation act, declaring that the slaves of anyone who supported the Confederacy should be "forever free of their servitude, and not again held as slaves." Finally, Congress passed a militia act that allowed

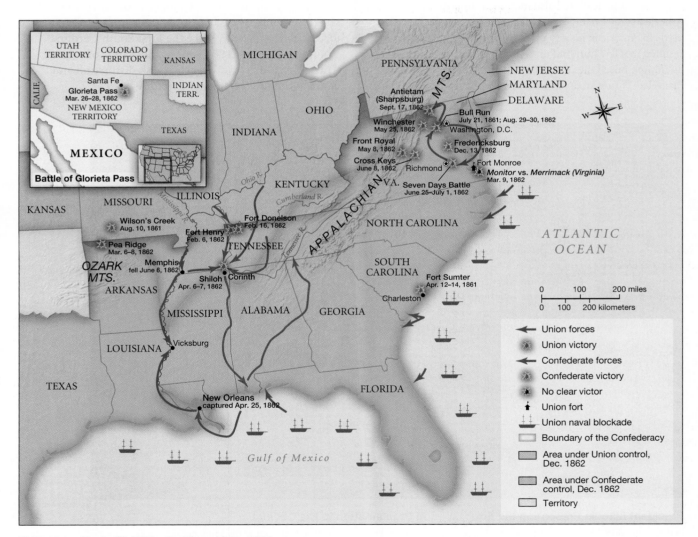

MAP 13.1   Early Civil War Battles, 1861–1862

In 1861 and 1862, the Confederate army stunned Union forces with a series of dramatic victories in Virginia and Missouri. However, the Union army won a crucial victory at Antietam (Sharpsburg); gained control of Confederate territory in Tennessee, Arkansas, and Mississippi; fended off Confederate efforts to gain New Mexico Territory; and established a successful naval blockade of Confederate ports.

"persons of African descent" to be employed in "any military or naval service for which they may be found competent." Lincoln quickly signed these acts into law.

Yet support for the 1862 militia act also built on Union victories. In April 1862, a Union blockade led to the capture of New Orleans, while the **Battle of Shiloh** in Tennessee provided the army entrée to the Mississippi valley. There Union troops came face-to-face with slavery. Few of these soldiers were abolitionists, but many were shocked by what they saw. At some captured plantations, soldiers discovered instruments used to torture slaves. One Union soldier reported he had seen "enough of the horror of slavery to make one an Abolitionist forever." Local blacks also provided valuable intelligence to Union officers.

The rising death toll also increased support for African American enlistment. The Battle of Shiloh was the bloodiest battle in American history up to that point. Earlier battles had resulted in a few hundred or even a few thousand casualties, but Shiloh raised the carnage to a new level. General Grant marveled, "I saw an open field . . . so covered with dead that it

would have been possible to walk across the clearing, in any direction, stepping only on dead bodies without a foot touching the ground." As the war continued, such deadly battles became routine. The Union army would need every available man to sustain its effort against the Confederates.

Amid the roller coaster of victory and defeat, African Americans gave practical force to the 1862 militia act. In October 1862, a group of African American soldiers in the First Kansas Colored Volunteers repulsed Confederates at a battle in Missouri. Early the next year, another black regiment—the Massachusetts Fifty-fourth—attracted recruits from across the North. Frederick Douglass helped recruit a hundred men from New York State, including his three sons—Charles, Lewis, and Frederick Jr. In the South, Colonel Thomas Wentworth Higginson and other abolitionist officers organized former slaves into units like the First South Carolina Volunteers. By late 1863, tens of thousands of African American soldiers were serving with distinction and contributing to key northern victories.

President Lincoln Presenting the Emancipation Proclamation to His Cabinet

In this engraving, based on a painting by Francis B. Carpenter, Lincoln reads the first draft of his Emancipation Proclamation to his cabinet on September 22, 1862. To the left of Lincoln are Secretary of War Edwin Stanton (seated) and Secretary of the Treasury Salmon P. Chase, the two strongest supporters of the Proclamation. To the right of Lincoln are Secretary of the Navy Gideon Welles (seated), Secretary of the Interior Caleb B. Smith, Secretary of State William Seward (seated), Postmaster General Montgomery Blair, and Attorney General Edward Bates (seated). Bates and Blair opposed the plan.   Library of Congress

Union Politicians Consider Emancipation

By the fall of 1862, African Americans and abolitionists had gained widespread support for emancipation as a necessary goal of the war. In making a final decision, Lincoln and his cabinet had to consider numerous factors. Embracing abolition as a war aim would likely prevent international recognition of southern independence, a significant advantage; but it might also arouse deep animosity in the slaveholding border states and drive them from the Union.

International recognition was critical to the Confederacy. Support from European nations might persuade the North to accept southern independence. More immediately, recognition would ensure markets for southern agriculture and access to manufactured goods and war materiel. Confederate officials were especially focused on Britain, the leading market for cotton and a potentially important supplier of industrial products. President Davis considered sending Rose Greenhow to England to promote the Confederate cause among British textile workers and government officials, who were concerned about disruptions to their economy caused by the Union blockade.

Fearing that the British might capitulate to Confederate pressure, abolitionist lecturers toured Britain, reminding residents of their early leadership in the antislavery cause. The abolitionists recognized that the Union's formal commitment to emancipation could give the North an edge in the battle for public opinion and prevent diplomatic recognition of the Confederacy. By the summer of 1862, Lincoln agreed. But he wanted to proclaim emancipation as a sign of Union strength, not weakness, so he waited for a victory before making a formal announcement.

A series of Union defeats in the summer of 1862 had allowed Lee to march his army into Union territory in Maryland. On September 17, Longstreet joined Lee in a fierce battle along Antietam Creek as Union troops brought the Confederate advance to a standstill near the town of Sharpsburg. Union forces suffered more than 12,000 casualties and the Confederates more than 10,000, the bloodiest single day in U.S. warfare. Yet because Lee and his army were forced to retreat, Lincoln claimed Antietam as a great victory. Five days later, the president announced his preliminary **Emancipation Proclamation** to the assembled cabinet. He held firm despite a bloody defeat at Fredericksburg, Virginia, that December, when Confederate troops inflicted nearly 13,000 Union casualties while suffering only 5,000 of their own.

On January 1, 1863, Lincoln signed the final edict, proclaiming that slaves in areas still in rebellion were "forever free" and inviting them to enlist in the Union army. In many ways, the proclamation was a conservative document, applying only to slaves largely beyond the reach of federal power. Its provisions exempted from emancipation the 450,000 slaves in the loyal border states, 275,000 slaves in Union-occupied Tennessee, and tens of thousands more in Louisiana and Virginia. The proclamation also justified the abolition of southern slavery on military, not moral, grounds.

Despite its limits, the Emancipation Proclamation prompted joyous "Watch Meetings" as abolitionists and free blacks met to give thanks as the edict took effect. At black churches across the North, crowds sang "Glory Hallelujah," "John Brown's Body," and "Marching On." If the Union proved victorious, the Emancipation Proclamation promised a total transformation of southern society.

REVIEW & RELATE

What arguments did each side make in the debate over African American enlistment in the Union army?

How and why did the Civil War become a war to end slavery?

LEARNINGCurve **bedfordstmartins.com/hewittlawson/LC**

War Transforms the North and the South

For soldiers caught in the midst of battle, for civilians caught between warring armies, and for ordinary families seeking to survive the upheaval, political pronouncements did little to alleviate the dangers they faced. The extraordinary death tolls in Civil War battles shocked Americans on both sides. On the home front, the war created labor shortages and severe inflation in both the North and the South. It initially disrupted industrial and agricultural production as men were called to service, but the North recovered fairly quickly by building on its prewar industrial base and technological know-how. In the South, manufacturing increased, with some enslaved laborers pressed into service as industrial workers. But pulling slaves away from agricultural work only created more problems on plantations, which were already suffering labor shortages. These changing circumstances required women to take on new responsibilities on the home front and the battlefront. But the dramatic transformations also inspired dissent and protest as rising death tolls and rising prices made the costs of war ever clearer.

Life and Death on the Battlefield

Few soldiers entered the conflict knowing what to expect. A young private wrote home that his idea of combat had

Civil War Soldiers

The Civil War was the first major war to be photographed extensively. Photographers recorded many images of the aftermath of battle and the daily lives of soldiers. Soldiers also had portraits taken to send to loved ones. These images of a black and a white soldier suggest the pride that these men felt in their uniforms and their weapons.   both photos: Library of Congress

been that the soldiers "would all be in line, all standing in a nice level field fighting, a number of ladies taking care of the wounded, etc., etc., but it isn't so." **See Document Project 13: Civil War Letters, page 417.** Even where traditional forms of engagement did occur, improved weaponry turned them into scenes of carnage. Although individual soldiers could fire only a few times a minute, their Enfield and Springfield rifles were murderously effective at a quarter-mile distance. New conical bullets that expanded to fit the grooves of rifles proved far more accurate and more deadly than older round bullets. Minié balls that exploded on impact also increased fatalities. By mid-1863, the rival armies relied on heavy fortifications, elaborate trenches, and distant mortar and artillery fire when they could, but the casualties continued to rise, especially since the trenches proved to be a breeding ground for disease.

The hardships and discomforts of war extended beyond combat itself. As General Lee complained before the fighting at Antietam, many soldiers went into battle in ragged uniforms and without shoes. In the First Battle of Bull Run, a Georgia major reported that more than one

hundred of his men were barefoot, "many of whom left bloody foot-prints among the thorns and briars through which they rushed." Rations, too, ran short. Food was dispensed sporadically and was often spoiled. Many Union troops survived primarily on an unleavened biscuit called hardtack as well as small amounts of meat and beans and enormous quantities of coffee. At least their diet improved over the course of the war as the Union supply system grew more efficient. Confederate troops, however, subsisted increasingly on cornmeal and fatty meat. As early as 1862, Confederate soldiers were gathering food from the haversacks of Union dead.

"There is more dies by sickness than gets killed," a recruit from New York complained in 1861. Indeed, for every soldier who died as a result of combat, three died of disease. Measles, dysentery, typhoid, and malaria killed thousands who drank contaminated water, ate tainted food, and were exposed to the elements. Prisoner-of-war camps were especially deadly locales. Debilitating fevers in a camp near Danville, Virginia, spread to the town, killing civilians as well as soldiers. In the fall of 1862, yellow fever and malaria killed nearly five hundred in

Wilmington, Delaware, as infected soldiers built fortifications along the beaches.

African American troops fared worst of all. The death rate from disease for black Union soldiers was nearly three times greater than that for white Union soldiers, reflecting their generally poorer health upon enlistment, the hard labor they performed, and the minimal medical care they received in the field. Those who began their army careers in contraband camps fared even worse, with a camp near Nashville losing a quarter of its residents to death in just three months in 1864.

Even for white soldiers, medical assistance was primitive. Antibiotics did not exist, antiseptics were still unknown, and a perennial shortage of anesthetics meant that amputations were frequently conducted without it. Union soldiers did gain some access to better medical care from the **U.S. Sanitary Commission**, which was established by the federal government in June 1861 to improve and coordinate the medical care of Union soldiers. Nonetheless, a commentator accurately described most field hospitals as "dirty dens of butchery and horror."

The need to bury the dead after battle was also a gruesome task. Early in the war, officers and enlisted men tried to recover and bury individual remains, but this practice proved unfeasible given the vast numbers killed. Instead, mass graves provided the final resting place for many soldiers on both sides. As the horrors of battle sank in and enlisted men discovered the inadequacies of food, sanitation, and medical care, large numbers of soldiers deserted. As the number of volunteers declined and the number of deserters rose, both the Confederate and the Union governments were eventually forced to institute conscription laws to draft men into service.

Explore

See Document 13.4 for an example of how photography brought the horrors of war home to civilians.

The Northern Economy Booms

As the war dragged on, the North's economic advantages became more apparent. The Union could provide more arms, food, and clothing to its troops and more of the necessities of life for families back home. Indeed, the Civil War quickened the industrial development of the North that had begun in the early nineteenth century. By 1860 manufacturing establishments in the region outnumbered those in the South six to one, with 1.3 million industrial workers in the North compared with only 110,000 in the South. Northern factories flourished as they turned out weapons, ammunition, blankets, clothing, and shoes, and shipyards built the fleets that blockaded southern ports.

Initially, the effects of the war on northern industry were little short of disastrous. Raw cotton for textiles was no longer available, southern planters stopped ordering shoes, and trade fell off precipitously in seaport cities. By 1863, however, the economic picture had improved dramatically. Coal mining and iron production boomed in Pennsylvania. In New England, woolen manufacturing replaced cotton, and the shoe industry thrived on orders from the army. Merchants dealing in war materiel made particularly handsome profits.

The economic boom was linked to a vast expansion in the federal government's activities. Direct orders from the War Office for blankets, firearms, boots, and other goods fueled the industrial surge. The government also granted large contracts to northern railroads to carry troops and supplies. With southern Democrats out of federal office, Congress increased the protection of northern industries by passing a steep tariff on imported manufactured goods. The government also hired thousands of "sewing women," who worked under contract in their homes (often in crowded tenements) to make uniforms for Union soldiers. Other women joined the federal labor force as clerical workers, who sustained the expanding bureaucracy by handling the increasing amounts of government-generated paperwork.

That paperwork multiplied exponentially when the federal government created a national currency and a national banking system. Before the Civil War, private banks (chartered by the states) issued their own banknotes, which were used in most economic transactions. During the war, Congress revolutionized this system, giving the federal government the power to create currency, issue federal charters to banks, and take on national debt (which totaled $2 billion by the war's end). The government used its new powers to flood the nation with treasury bills, commonly called **greenbacks**. The federal budget mushroomed as well—from $63 million in 1860 to nearly $1.3 billion in 1865. By the end of the war, the federal bureaucracy had grown to be the nation's largest single employer.

These federal initiatives provided a tremendous stimulus to industry, and northern manufacturers greeted them, on the whole, with enthusiasm. But they faced one daunting problem: a shortage of labor. Over half a million workers left their jobs to serve in the Union army, and others were hired by the expanding federal bureaucracy. Manufacturers dealt with the labor shortage primarily by mechanizing more tasks and by increasing the employment of native-born women and children and recently arrived immigrants. Mechanization advanced quickly in the clothing and shoe industries, allowing more jobs to be filled by unskilled or semiskilled workers. Industrialists also formed organizations such as the Boston Foreign

DOCUMENT 13.4

Timothy H. O'Sullivan | Burial of Federal Dead, Fredericksburg, Virginia, May 1864

As the first war to be photographed extensively, the Civil War offered civilians new perspectives on the horrors of battle. Exhibited in the studios of photographers such as Mathew Brady in New York City, urban residents could view the carnage of war in stunning detail. This image was taken by Timothy H. O'Sullivan, an Irish-born photographer who worked with Brady after serving in the Union army. It captures a Union burial team near Fredericksburg during a period of intense fighting in northern Virginia.

Explore

Why were black Union soldiers, like those pictured here, often assigned to bury the dead?

How does this photo-graph represent the boundary between the battlefront and the home front?

What does this image suggest about the different experiences of officers and enlisted men even after death?

Library of Congress

Put It in Context

How might images such as this one affect civilian attitudes toward the war?

Emigrant Aid Society to encourage European migration, which had fallen off sharply in the first two years of the war. By 1863 the number of immigrants—mostly Irish, German, and British—had reached pre-1860 levels and continued to increase. Combining the lower wages paid to women and immigrants with production speedups, manufacturers improved their profits while advancing the Union cause.

Urbanization and Industrialization in the South

Although Southerners had gone to war to protect an essentially rural lifestyle, several factors encouraged the growth of industry and cities during the war. The creation of a large governmental and military bureaucracy brought thousands of Southerners to the Confederate capital of Richmond. Refugees merely trickled into cities during the early years of the war, but by 1863 they were flooding Atlanta, Savannah, and Mobile.

Industrialization also contributed to urban growth. Military necessity spurred southern industrialization. At the beginning of the war, the South contained only 15 percent of the factories in the United States. But unable to buy industrial goods from the North and limited in its trade with Europe, the South was forced to industrialize. By January 1863, the huge Tredegar Iron Works in Richmond employed more than 2,500 men, black and white. A factory to produce cannons opened in Selma, Alabama, where more than 10,000 people worked in war industries. According to a local newspaper, clothing and shoe factories had "sprung up almost like magic" in Natchez and Jackson, Mississippi. War widows and orphans, enslaved blacks, and white men too old or injured to fight were recruited for industrial labor in many cities.

The vast expansion of the South's cities and industry enhanced class consciousness during the war. When Virginia legislators introduced a bill in the fall of 1863 to control food prices, Richmond workers hailed it by voicing their resentment toward the rich. "From the fact that he consumes all and produces nothing," they proclaimed, "we know that without [our] labor and production the man with money could not exist." Workers also criticized lavish balls hosted by the wives of wealthy industrialists, planters, and politicians during the war. Women like Mary Boykin Chesnut, a planter's wife, insisted that such events were necessary to maintain morale and demonstrate that the South was far from defeated. But the *Richmond Enquirer* captured the views of the laboring class, arguing that these events were "shameful displays of indifference to national calamity . . . a mockery of the misery and desolation that covers the land."

Women Aid the War Effort

Women of all classes contributed to the Union and Confederate war effort in numerous ways. Thousands filled jobs in agriculture, industry, and the government that were traditionally held by men. Others sought to assist the war effort more directly, by serving as nurses, spies, couriers, or soldiers; gathering supplies; and lobbying to influence government policies. Although Rose Greenhow and a few other women were recruited as spies early in the conflict, most military and political officials initially opposed women's direct engagement in the war. Yet so many women organized relief efforts early on that the federal government organized the U.S. Sanitary Commission to coordinate their efforts. By 1862 tens of thousands of women had volunteered funds and assistance through hundreds of local chapters across the North and Midwest. They hosted fund-raising fairs, coordinated sewing and knitting circles, rolled bandages, and sent supplies to the front lines. With critical shortages of medical staff, some female nurses and doctors eventually gained acceptance in northern hospitals and field camps. Led by such memorable figures as Clara Barton, Mary Ann "Mother" Bickerdyke, and Dr. Mary Walker, northern women almost entirely replaced men as military nurses by the end of the war.

In the South, too, much of the medical care was performed by women. But without a government-sanctioned body to coordinate efforts and lobby for resources, women were left largely to their own devices, and nursing was never recognized as a legitimate profession for them. As a result, a Confederate soldier's chances of dying from wounds or disease were even greater than those of his Union counterpart. Nonetheless, southern women worked tirelessly to supply soldiers with clothes, blankets, munitions, and food. But this work, too, was often performed locally and by individuals rather than as part of a coordinated Confederate effort. For example, Ann Cobb, the wife of a Georgia officer, went door-to-door among neighbors to gather provisions for her husband's eighty-man unit.

Some Union and Confederate women played even more unusual roles in the war. A few dozen women joined Greenhow in gathering information for military and political authorities. One of the most effective on the Union side was the former fugitive Harriet Tubman. She worked as a spy in South Carolina from 1862 to 1864 and regularly secured military intelligence from slaves living behind Confederate lines. Even more women served as couriers, carrying messages across battle lines to alert officers of critical changes in military orders or in the opponent's position. In addition, at least four hundred women disguised themselves as men and fought as soldiers; the identities of many were discovered only after they were wounded in battle.

Dr. Mary E. Walker

Dr. Mary E. Walker received her medical degree from Syracuse Medical College and became the first female army surgeon. Wearing bloomers (pants under a skirt), she assisted soldiers and civilians in numerous battlefield areas. Captured by Confederate troops in 1864, Walker soon returned to Union ranks. She was the first woman awarded the Medal of Honor for military service.   Library of Congress

Finally, abolitionist women sought to influence federal wartime policies. Following the Emancipation Proclamation, Elizabeth Cady Stanton, Susan B. Anthony, and Lucy Stone founded the **Women's National Loyal League** and launched a massive petition drive to broaden Lincoln's policy. Collecting 260,000 signatures, two-thirds of them from women, the League demanded a congressional act "emancipating all persons of African descent" everywhere in the nation.

Dissent and Protest in the Midst of War

While the Women's National Loyal League lobbied Congress for universal emancipation, other Northerners wondered whether defeating the Confederacy was worth

the cost. Families were hard hit as wages fell and prices rose, and many Northerners cared more about the safe return of their husbands and sons than the fate of slavery. As the war dragged on, these concerns led to a rising tide of dissent and protest.

Despite the expanding economy, northern farmers and workers suffered tremendously during the war. Women, children, and old men took over much of the field labor in the Midwest, trying to feed their families and produce sufficient surplus to supply the army and pay their mortgages and other expenses. In the East, too, inflation eroded the earnings of factory workers, servants, and day laborers. As federal greenbacks flooded the market and military production took priority over consumer goods, prices climbed about 20 percent faster than wages. While industrialists garnered huge profits, railroad stocks leaped to unheard-of prices, and government contractors made huge gains, ordinary workers suffered. A group of Cincinnati seamstresses complained to President Lincoln in 1864 about employers "who fatten on their contracts by grinding immense profits out of the labor of their operatives." Although Republicans pledged to protect the rights of workers, employers successfully lobbied a number of state legislatures to pass laws prohibiting strikes. The federal government, too, proved a better friend to business than to labor. When workers at the Parrott arms factory in Cold Spring, New York, struck for higher wages in 1864, the government sent in troops, declared martial law, and arrested the strike leaders.

Discontent intensified when the Republican Congress passed a draft law in March 1863. The **Enrollment Act** provided for draftees to be selected by an impartial lottery, but a loophole allowed a person with $300 to pay the government in place of serving or to hire another man as a substitute. Many workers deeply resented the draft law's profound inequality. Some also opposed the emancipation of slaves who, they assumed, would compete for scarce jobs once the war ended.

Dissent turned to violence in July 1863 when the new draft law went into effect. Riots broke out in cities across the North. In New York City, where inflation caused tremendous suffering and a large immigrant population solidly supported the Democratic machine, implementation of the draft triggered four days of the worst rioting Americans had ever seen. Women and men—many of them Irish and German immigrants—attacked Protestant missionaries, Republican draft officials, and wealthy businessmen. Homes in wealthy neighborhoods were looted, but the free black community became the rioters' main target. Rioters lynched at least a dozen African Americans and looted and burned the city's Colored Orphan Asylum. The violence ended only when Union troops put down the riot by force. By then, more than one hundred New Yorkers lay dead.

A more prolonged battle raged in Missouri, where Confederate sympathizers never reconciled themselves to living in a Union state. From the beginning of this "inner civil war," prosouthern residents formed militias and staged guerrilla attacks on Union supporters. The militias, with the tacit support of Confederate officials, claimed thousands of lives and forced the Union army to station troops in the area. The militia members hoped that Midwesterners, weary of the conflicts, would elect peace Democrats and end the war.

Northern Democrats saw the widening unrest as a political opportunity. Although some Democratic leaders supported the war effort, many others—whom opponents called **Copperheads**, after the poisonous snake—rallied behind Ohio politician Clement L. Vallandigham in opposing the war. Presenting themselves as the "peace party," these Democrats enjoyed considerable success in eastern cities where inflation was rampant and immigrant workers were caught between low wages and military service. The party was also strong in parts of the Midwest where sympathy for the southern cause and antipathy to African Americans ran deep.

In the South, too, some whites expressed growing dissatisfaction with the war. In April 1862, Jefferson Davis had signed the first conscription act in U.S. history, inciting widespread opposition. The concept of a national draft undermined the southern tradition of states' rights. As in the North, men could hire a substitute if they had enough money, and an October 1862 law exempted men owning twenty or more slaves from military service. Although the exemption was supposedly a response to growing

unruliness among slaves in the absence of masters, in practice it meant that large planters, many of whom served in the Confederate legislature, had exempted themselves from fighting. As one Alabama farmer fumed, "All they want is to get you pumpt up and go to fight for their infernal negroes, and after you do their fighting you may kiss their hine parts for all they care."

Small farmers were also hard hit by policies that allowed the Confederate army to take whatever supplies it needed. The army's forced acquisition of farm produce intensified food shortages that had been building since early in the war. The southern economy was rooted in cash crops rather than foodstuffs. Quantities of grain and livestock were produced in South Carolina, central Virginia, and central Tennessee, but by 1863 the latter two areas had fallen under Union control. The Union blockade of port cities and the lack of an extensive railroad or canal system in the South limited the distribution of what food was available. Hungry residents of the Shenandoah Valley discovered that despite military victories there, food shortages worsened as Confederate troops ravaged the countryside.

Food shortages drove up prices on basic items like bread and corn, while the Union blockade and the focus on military needs dramatically increased the price of other consumer goods. As the Confederate government issued more and more treasury notes to finance the war, inflation soared 2,600 percent in less than three years. Food riots, often led by women, broke out in cities across the South, including the Confederate capital of Richmond.

Conscription, food shortages, and inflation took their toll on support for the Confederacy. The devastation of the war itself added to these grievances. Most battles were fought in the Upper South or along the Confederacy's western frontier, where small farmers saw their crops, animals, and fields destroyed. A phrase that had seemed cynical in 1862—"A rich man's war and a poor man's fight"—became the rallying cry of the southern peace movement in 1864. The Washington Constitutional Union, a secret peace society with a large following among farmers, elected several members to the Confederate Congress. Another secret organization centered in North Carolina took more drastic measures, providing Union forces with information on southern troop movements and encouraging desertion by Confederates. In mountainous regions of the South, draft evaders and deserters formed guerrilla groups that attacked draft officials and actively impeded the war effort. In western North Carolina, some women hid deserters, raided grain depots, and burned the property of Confederate officials.

When slaveholders led the South out of the Union in 1861, they had assumed the loyalty of yeomen farmers, the deference of southern ladies, and the privileges of the southern way of life. Far from preserving social harmony and social order, however, the war undermined ties between elite and poor Southerners, between planters and small farmers, and between women and men. Although most white Southerners still supported the Confederacy in 1864 and internal dissent alone did not lead to defeat, it did weaken the ties that bound soldiers to their posts in the final two years of the war.

REVIEW & RELATE

What were the short- and long-term economic effects of the war on the North?

How did the war change the southern economy? What social tensions did the war create in the South?

✔ *LEARNINGCurve* bedfordstmartins.com/hewittlawson/LC

The Tide of War Turns

In the spring of 1863, Lee's army defeated a Union force twice its size at Chancellorsville, Virginia, setting the stage for a Confederate thrust into Pennsylvania. Yet Lee's decision to go on the offensive ultimately proved the Confederacy's undoing. Even as draft riots erupted across the North in July 1863, the Union won two decisive military victories: at Gettysburg, Pennsylvania, and Vicksburg, Mississippi. These victories improved northern morale while devastating Confederate hopes. At the same time, the flood of African Americans, including former slaves, into the Union army transformed the very meaning of the war. In late 1864 and early 1865, the momentum favored the Union, and the South was forced to consider prospects for peace.

Key Victories for the Union

In mid-1863, Confederate commanders believed the tide was turning in their favor. Following victories at Fredericksburg and Chancellorsville, General Lee launched an invasion of northern territory. While the Union army maneuvered to protect Washington, D.C., from Lee's advance, General Joseph Hooker resigned as head of the Union army. When Lincoln appointed George A. Meade as the new Union commander, the general immediately faced a major engagement at **Gettysburg**, Pennsylvania. If Confederates won a victory there, European countries might finally recognize the southern nation and force the North to accept peace.

Neither Lee nor Meade set out to launch a battle in this small Pennsylvania town. But Lee was afraid of outrunning his supply lines, and Meade wanted to keep Confederates from gaining control of the roads that crossed at Gettysburg. So on July 1, fighting commenced, with Lee pushing Union forces to the south of town. The Union vanguard managed to hold the ground along Cemetery Ridge until more troops arrived the following day. Although Confederate troops suffered heavy losses on July 2, Lee believed that Union forces were spread thin and ordered General George Pickett to launch a frontal assault on July 3 (Map 13.2). But Pickett's men were mowed down as they crossed an open field. The battle was a disaster for the South: More than 4,700 Confederates were killed, including a large number of officers; another 18,000 were wounded, captured, or missing. Although the Union suffered similar casualties, it had more men to lose, and it could claim victory.

As a grieving Lee retreated to Virginia, the South suffered another devastating defeat. Troops under General Ulysses S. Grant had been pounding Vicksburg, Mississippi, for months. In May 1863, Grant sent his men in a wide arc around the city and attacked from the east, setting the stage for a six-week siege. Although civilians refused to leave and even hid out in caves to outlast the Union barrage, Confederate troops were forced to surrender the city on July 4. This victory was even more important strategically than Gettysburg (Map 13.2). Combined with a victory five days later at Port Hudson, Louisiana, the Union army now controlled the entire Mississippi valley, the richest plantation region in the South. This series of victories also effectively cut off the Confederacy from Louisiana, Arkansas, and Texas, ensuring Union control of the West. In

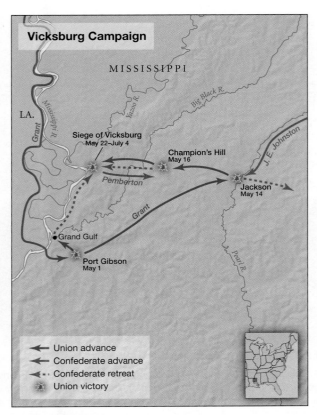

MAP 13.2   Battles of Gettysburg and Vicksburg, 1863

The three-day battle in Gettysburg and the six-week siege of Vicksburg led to critical victories for the Union. Together, these victories forced General Lee's troops back into Confederate territory and gave the Union control of the Mississippi River. Still, the war was far from over. Confederate troops controlled the southern heartland, and Northerners wearied of the ever-increasing casualties.

November 1863, Grant's troops achieved a major victory at Chattanooga, opening up much of the South's remaining territory to invasion. Thousands of slaves deserted their plantations, and many joined the Union war effort.

As 1864 dawned, the Union had twice as many forces in the field as the Confederacy, whose soldiers were suffering from low morale, high mortality, and dwindling supplies. Although some difficult battles still lay ahead, the war of attrition (in which the larger, better-supplied Union forces slowly wore down their Confederate opponents) had begun to pay dividends.

The changing Union fortunes increased support for Lincoln and his congressional allies. Union victories and the Emancipation Proclamation also convinced Great Britain not to recognize the Confederacy as an independent nation. And the heroics of African American soldiers, who in 1863 engaged in direct and often brutal combat against southern troops, encouraged wider support for emancipation. Republicans, who now fully embraced abolition as a war aim, were nearly assured the presidency and a congressional majority in the 1864 elections.

Northern Democrats still campaigned for peace and the readmission of Confederate states with slavery intact. They nominated George B. McClellan, the onetime Union commander, as their candidate for president. McClellan attracted working-class and immigrant voters who traditionally supported the Democrats and who bore the heaviest burdens of the war. But Democratic hopes for victory in November were crushed when Union general William Tecumseh Sherman captured Atlanta, Georgia, just two months before the election. Lincoln and the Republicans won easily, giving the party a clear mandate to continue the war to its conclusion.

African Americans Contribute to Victory

Lincoln's election secured the eventual downfall of slavery. Yet neither the president nor Congress eradicated human bondage on their own. From the fall of 1862 on, African Americans enlisted in the Union army and helped ensure that nothing short of universal emancipation would be the outcome of the war. By the spring of 1865, nearly 200,000

The 107th U.S. Colored Infantry Band

The 107th U.S. Colored Infantry Band was photographed at Fort Corcoran in Arlington, Virginia. These 20 African American soldiers with their musical instruments were among the nearly 200,000 black men who volunteered for military service and served as soldiers and sailors to prove their manhood and their worthiness for full citizenship. Some 37,000 black soldiers died during the Civil War.   Library of Congress

African Americans were serving in the Union army and navy. Private Thomas Long, a former slave serving with the First South Carolina Volunteers, explained the connection between African American enlistment and emancipation: "If we hadn't become sojers, all might have gone back as it was before; our freedom might have slipped through de two houses of Congress and President Linkum's four years might have passed by and notin' been done for us. But now tings can neber go back, because we have showed our energy and our courage and our naturally manhood."

In the border states, which were exempt from the Emancipation Proclamation, enslaved men were adamant about enlisting since those who served in the Union army were granted their freedom. Because of this provision, slaveholders in the border states did everything in their power to prevent their slaves from joining the army, including assault and even murder. Despite these efforts, between 25 and 60 percent of military-age enslaved men in the four border states joined the Union army and quickly distinguished themselves in battle. By the end of the war, approximately 37,000 black soldiers had given their lives for freedom and the Union.

Yet despite their courage and commitment, black soldiers felt the sting of racism. They were segregated in camps, given the most menial jobs, and often treated as inferiors by white recruits and officers. Many blacks, for instance, were assigned the gruesome and exhausting task of burying the dead after grueling battles in which they had fought alongside whites. Particularly galling was the Union policy of paying black soldiers less than whites were paid. African American soldiers openly protested this discrimination even after a black sergeant who voiced his views was charged with mutiny and executed by firing squad in February 1864. An African American corporal wrote to Lincoln, describing the blood black troops had shed for the Union and asking, "We have done a Soldier's Duty. Why can't we have a Soldier's pay?" The War Department finally equalized wages in June 1864.

One of African American soldiers' primary concerns was to liberate slaves as Union armies moved deeper into the South. During 1863 and 1864, thousands more slaves headed for Union lines, joining the "contraband" who had escaped earlier in the war. Even those forced to remain on plantations realized that Union troops and freedom were headed their way. In areas close to Union lines, they talked openly of the advancing army. "Now they gradually threw off the mask," a slave remembered of this moment, "and were not afraid to let it be known that the 'freedom' in their songs meant freedom of the body in this world."

The Final Battles and the Promise of Peace

In the spring of 1864, the war entered its final stage. That March, Lincoln placed General Grant in charge of all Union forces, and he embarked on a strategy of **total war**, including attacks against civilian as well as military targets. Grant was willing to accept huge casualties in order to achieve victory. Over the next year, he led his troops overland through western Virginia in an effort to take Richmond. At the same time, he ordered General Sherman to head south through Georgia, destroying the remnants of the plantation system.

Grant's troops headed toward Richmond, where Lee's army controlled strong defensive positions. The Confederates won narrow victories in May 1864 at the Battles of the Wilderness and Spotsylvania Court House. In June, 7,000 Union soldiers were killed in one hour during a frontal assault at Cold Harbor, Virginia, where Confederates once again turned back the Union army. But Grant continued to push forward. Although Lee lost fewer men (31,000 casualties at Cold Harbor versus 55,000 for the Union), his army was melting away with each so-called victory.

The battles took a terrible toll on soldiers on both sides. Union troops and civilians called Grant "the butcher" for his seeming lack of regard for human life. Grant, however, was not deterred. He laid siege to Petersburg in June 1864, where both sides lived in trenches and tunnels for months on end. That August, Sherman also laid siege to Atlanta, but on September 2 he ordered his troops out of the trenches, swept around the city, and destroyed the roads and rails that connected it to the rest of the Confederacy. When General John B. Hood and his southern troops abandoned their posts, Sherman telegraphed Lincoln: "Atlanta is ours, and fairly won." The victory cut the South in two.

Sherman then led his troops on a 300-mile march to the Atlantic coast and north through the Carolinas. Embracing the strategy of total war, his troops cut a path of destruction 50 miles wide during their "March to the Sea," destroying crops, livestock, and houses before they reached Savannah in late December. Nearly 18,000 enslaved men, women, and children left the ruined plantations and sought to join Sherman's victorious troops. To the fleeing slaves' dismay, soldiers refused to take them along. Worse, some Union soldiers abused African American men, raped black women, or stole their few possessions. Angry Confederates captured many of those who were turned away, killing some and reenslaving others.

Richmond in Ruins, April 1865

This photograph captures the devastation the war brought to the Richmond and Petersburg Railroad Depot after General Grant drove General Lee's troops out of the Confederate capital in April 1865. This defining moment marked the end of the Civil War and the defeat of the South. During the next decade, the North and South struggled over reconfiguring the Union.   Library of Congress

Explore

See Document 13.5 for a description of the destruction of Columbia, South Carolina.

Sherman's callous actions caused a scandal in Washington. In January 1865, Lincoln dispatched Secretary of War Edwin Stanton to Georgia to investigate the charges. At an extraordinary meeting in Savannah, Stanton and Sherman met with black ministers to hear their complaints and to ask what newly emancipated African Americans wanted. The ministers spoke movingly of the war lifting "the yoke of bondage." Freed blacks, they argued, "could reap the fruit of their own labor" and, if given land, "take care of ourselves, and assist the Government in maintaining our freedom." In response, Sherman issued **Field Order Number 15**, setting aside more than 400,000 acres of captured Confederate land to be divided into small plots for former slaves. Although

Sherman's order proved highly controversial, it suggested that the Civil War might, in the end, be a revolutionary force for change.

As defeat loomed, even Confederate leaders began to talk of emancipating the slaves. Jefferson Davis called for recruiting slaves into the army, with their payment to include freedom for themselves and their families. The Confederate Congress passed such a law in early 1865, but it was too late to make any difference. Still, the very idea suggested that the Civil War had turned southern society upside down.

In early April 1865, with Sherman heading toward Raleigh, North Carolina, Grant captured Petersburg and then drove Lee and his forces out of Richmond. In one of the war's most dramatic moments, seasoned African American troops led the final assault on the city and were among the first Union soldiers to enter the Confederate capital. On April 9, after a brief engagement at

---

DOCUMENT 13.5

Eleanor Cohen Seixas | Journal Entry, February 1865

In February 1865, General Sherman and his men reached Columbia, South Carolina, intent on destroying as much property as possible. Thousands of residents fled the Columbia fires, including Philip and Cordelia Cohen and their daughter, Eleanor. Philip was a pharmacist, slave owner, and part of the state's small Jewish population. During the war, he moved his family to Columbia to find safety in the city. Eleanor recorded the trials of wartime and her hopes for southern victory in her journal. In this selection, she describes the arrival of Sherman's troops.

Explore

The fire raged fearfully all night, but on Saturday perfect quiet reigned. The vile Yankees took from us clothing, food, jewels, all our cows, horses, carriages, etc., and left us in a deplorable condition after stealing from us. Sherman, with great generosity, presented the citizens with 500 cattle, so poor they could hardly stand up. No words of mine can give any idea of the brutality of the ruffians. They swore, they cussed, plundered, and committed every excess. No age or sex was safe from them. Sometimes, after saving some valueless token, it was ruthlessly

snatched from our hands by some of their horde. Our noble women were insulted by words, and some, I have heard of, in deeds, but none came under my knowledge, for I myself, God be praised, I received no rude word from any of them. I did not speak . . . to them at all. The fire burned eighty-four squares, and nothing can tell the quantity of plunder they carried off as on Monday they left us, and though we feared starvation, yet we were glad to be rid of them.

Source: Jacob R. Marcus, ed., *Memoirs of American Jews, 1775–1885* (Philadelphia: Jewish Publication Society of America, 1955), 3:363.

Interpret the Evidence

● What does this journal entry reveal about how Southerners viewed the Union army?

● What insight does it provide into how Union soldiers felt about the South?

Put It in Context

What impact did Sherman's march have on Southerners' morale?

Appomattox Court House, Virginia, Lee surrendered to Grant with fewer than 30,000 soldiers remaining under his command. Within hours, his troops began heading home. Although Confederate soldiers continued to engage Union forces in North Carolina and west of the Mississippi, the Civil War, for all intents and purposes, had come to an end.

The legal abolition of slavery was initiated in Washington a few months before Lee's surrender. Following on the petitions submitted by the Women's National Loyal League, Congress passed the **Thirteenth Amendment** to the U.S. Constitution on January 31, 1865, prohibiting slavery and involuntary servitude anywhere in the United States. Although it still required approval by three-quarters of the states, wartime experiences made ratification likely. Some states and cities had already enacted laws to ease racial inequities. Ohio, California, and Illinois repealed statutes barring blacks from testifying in court and serving on juries. San Francisco, Cincinnati, Cleveland, and New York City desegregated their streetcars. In May 1865, Massachusetts passed the first comprehensive public-accommodations law in U.S. history, ensuring equal treatment in theaters, stores, schools, and other social spaces. With the final surrender of the Confederacy, many Northerners were hopeful that the nation reunited would be stronger and more just.

REVIEW & RELATE

What role did African Americans play in the defeat of the South?

How did the Union win the war? How did attitudes toward African Americans change in the final year of the war?

 LEARNINGCurve bedfordstmartins.com/hewittlawson/LC

Conclusion: An Uncertain Future

Jubilation in the North did not last long. On April 14, less than a week after Lee's surrender, Abraham Lincoln was shot at Ford's Theatre by a Confederate fanatic named John Wilkes Booth. The president died the next day, leading to an outpouring of grief across the North and leaving the entire nation in shock.

Lincoln left behind an incredible legacy. He had led the Union to victory in a devastating civil war, promulgated the Emancipation Proclamation, and resolved the conflict between competing systems based on slavery and free labor. More than 600,000 Americans died in the war, but nearly 4 million Americans who had been born enslaved were now

free. At the same time, northern and southern women had entered the labor force and the public arena in numbers never before imagined. Soldiers returned to their families, jobs, and communities with experiences and knowledge, but also with physical and emotional wounds that transformed their lives. And the federal government had extended its reach into more and more areas of daily life. The war had dramatically accelerated the pace of economic, political, and social change, transforming American society both during the war and afterward.

Still, the legacies of the war were far from certain in 1865. Defeated Southerners looked for heroes, and most considered Confederate generals the greatest representatives of the "Lost Cause." They honored Lee and his officers with statues, portraits, poems, and parades. Confederate women worked endlessly to preserve the memory of both military leaders and ordinary soldiers. They formed memorial associations to decorate cemeteries and promoted a southern perspective on the war in schools and history books. They also joined in paying tribute to heroines like Rose O'Neal Greenhow. Greenhow had traveled to England and France in 1863, promoting Confederate bond issues and publishing a book about her imprisonment under "abolition rule." On her return in August 1864, the British vessel she was on was pursued by federal ships blockading the harbor. Fearing capture, Greenhow insisted that she be rowed ashore carrying a bag of gold coins, the profits from her book. But the boat overturned in high seas, and Greenhow drowned. She was buried with full military honors in Wilmington, North Carolina.

Victorious Northerners had far more reason to celebrate, but they knew that much still needed to be done. Frederick Douglass was thrilled that slavery had been abolished, but he argued vehemently that "the work of Abolitionists is not done." He was deeply committed to the enfranchisement of African American men as the means to secure the rights of former slaves, for he had no illusions about the lengths to which many whites would go to protect their traditional privileges. Although Douglass considered the Republican Party the best hope for reconstructing the nation, not everyone shared his agenda. Some white abolitionists argued that their work was done; some women's rights advocates thought they were as entitled to voting rights as were black men; some militant blacks viewed the Republican Party as too moderate. Moreover, many northern whites were exhausted by four years of war and hoped to leave the problems of slavery and secession behind. Others wanted to rebuild the South quickly in order to ensure the nation's economic recovery. These competing visions—between Northerners and Southerners and within each group—would shape the promises of peace in ways few could imagine at the end of the war.

LEARNINGCurve
Check what you know.
bedfordstmartins.com/hewittlawson/LC

Chapter Review

Online Study Guide ▶ bedfordstmartins.com/hewittlawson

KEY TERMS

Fort Sumter (p. 395)
contraband (p. 399)
Battle of Shiloh (p. 402)
Emancipation Proclamation (p. 403)
U.S. Sanitary Commission (p. 405)
greenbacks (p. 405)
Women's National Loyal League (p. 408)
Enrollment Act (p. 408)
Copperheads (p. 409)
Gettysburg (p. 410)
total war (p. 413)
Field Order Number 15 (p. 414)
Thirteenth Amendment (p. 415)

REVIEW AND RELATE

1. What steps did Lincoln take to prevent war? Why were they ineffective?

2. What advantages and disadvantages did each side have at the onset of the war?

3. What arguments did each side make in the debate over African American enlistment in the Union army?

4. How and why did the Civil War become a war to end slavery?

5. What were the short- and long-term economic effects of the war on the North?

6. How did the war change the southern economy? What social tensions did the war create in the South?

7. What role did African Americans play in the defeat of the South?

8. How did the Union win the war? How did attitudes toward African Americans change in the final year of the war?

TIMELINE OF EVENTS

1845	Frederick Douglass publishes *Narrative of the Life of Frederick Douglass*
April 14, 1861	Fort Sumter surrenders to Confederate forces
May 23, 1861	General Benjamin Butler declares escaped slaves "contraband"
June 1861	U.S. Sanitary Commission established
July 21, 1861	First Battle of Bull Run (Manassas)
August 6, 1861	Confiscation Act passed
April 1862	Slavery abolished in the District of Columbia
	Battle of Shiloh
	Jefferson Davis signs conscription act
June 1862	Rose O'Neal Greenhow exiled to the South
September 1862	Battle of Antietam
	Lincoln issues preliminary Emancipation Proclamation
January 1, 1863	Lincoln signs Emancipation Proclamation
March 1863	Enrollment Act passed in North
July 1863	Draft riots in New York City
	Battle of Gettysburg
	Battle of Vicksburg
September 2, 1864	Atlanta falls; Sherman begins "March to the Sea"
1865	200,000 African Americans serving in the Union army and navy
January 1865	Sherman issues Field Order Number 15
January 31, 1865	Congress passes Thirteenth Amendment
April 9, 1865	General Lee surrenders to General Grant at Appomattox Court House
April 14, 1865	Assassination of President Abraham Lincoln

Civil War Letters

Throughout the Civil War, many soldiers and their families kept in close touch by writing letters. The volume of wartime correspondence was immense, with ninety thousand letters a day processed in the Union alone. Letters from soldiers often described the boredom of encampments, the excitement or horrors of battle, and worries about their families back home (Document 13.7). Soldiers' letters also expressed their views on the causes of the war and sometimes their changing understandings of the war's meaning (Documents 13.6 and 13.10). Nurses provided another dramatic perspective on the war (Document 13.9), and letters from families revealed the experiences, as well as frustrations, of life on the home front. While many parents, spouses, and children of soldiers wrote letters to bolster the spirits of men at the front, they also expressed the heartbreak of separation and the problems experienced by families and local communities, including shortages of food and labor and spiraling inflation (Document 13.8). Regardless of the content, correspondence helped families maintain connections during soldiers' lengthy tours of duty. For historians, these letters are a unique window into the everyday lives of soldiers and their families during the Civil War.

The letters reprinted here, from both Northerners and Southerners, represent an array of experiences, including those of soldiers and civilians, women and men, blacks and whites. Written between April 1861 (Document 13.6) and November 1864 (Document 13.8), they also help us trace transformations in the North and South over the course of the war. As you read them, think about the usefulness of letters as primary sources. What common themes emerge in these letters? How do the letter writers feel about the larger significance of the Civil War? How do their feelings about the war change over time? What can we learn about the war from these letters?

DOCUMENT 13.6

Fred Spooner | Letter to His Brother Henry, April 30, 1861

At the start of the war, many Northerners expected a quick victory, as evidenced in this letter written by Fred Spooner to his older brother Henry. A native of Providence, Rhode Island, Fred believed the South was weakened by its reliance on slavery. Perhaps inspired by these same beliefs, Henry enlisted in the Union army in 1862. Henry later practiced law in Rhode Island and served in the U.S. House of Representatives.

Dear Henry,

Your letter was received, and I now sit down in my shirt sleeves (as it is warm) to write in return.

For the last few weeks there has been great excitement here, and nothing has been thought of scarcely except that one subject which now received the undivided attention of the whole loyal North—war.

And well may war, so hideous and disgusting in itself receive such attention when carried on for such noble and just principles as in the present case.

Traitors have begun the conflict, let us continue and end it. Let us settle it now, once and for all.

Let us settle it, even if the whole South has to be made one common graveyard, and their cotton soaked in blood. Let us do it *now* while the whole North is aroused from the inactivity and apparent laziness in which it has been so long.

There are plenty of men, an abundance of money, and a military enthusiasm never before known in the annals of history, all of which combined will do the work nice and clean, and if need be will wipe out that palmetto, pelican, rattlesnake region entirely. The holy cause in which our volunteers are enlisted will urge them on to almost super-human exertions. The South *may* be courageous but I doubt it, they can *gas* and *hag* [complain and bluster] first rate; they can lie and steal to perfection, but I really do believe that they cannot fight—"Barking dogs never bite." Southern senators can bluster, bully, and blackguard [verbally abuse], but I believe them to be cowards at heart. . . .

Besides the very nature of their country and their manner of living, have a tendency, I think, to make them otherwise than brave.

But granting them to be brave (which I don't believe can be proven) they have no chance to overturn this government. They haven't the resources, the "almighty dollar," that powerful ally, or formidable enemy—is against them. They have no money—their property has legs and will be continually disappearing.

They have prospered dealing in human flesh—let them now take the results of it.

They have had what *they* consider the *blessings* of slavery—let them now receive the *curses* of it.

They must be put down, conquered, and thoroughly subdued if need be. They have no earthly hope of overcoming this government. The fifteen weak states of the South can stand no chance against the nineteen powerful states of the North. . . .

When I began I did not intend to give a lecture or write a composition on the "crisis," and I had not as Mayor Knight [mayor of Providence] would say "made preparations for a speech," but unconsciously I got on the all-absorbing topic at the very commencement, and it was hard work to let go of it.

There hasn't been much studying lately, and it is very hard work to think or write concerning any other subject than that on which I've paused so long.

So therefore excuse my "crisis" beginning.

Source: Nina Silber and Mary Beth Sievens, eds., *Yankee Correspondence: Civil War Letters between New England Soldiers and the Home Front* (Charlottesville: University Press of Virginia, 1996), 55–56.

DOCUMENT 13.7

John Hines | Letter to His Parents, April 22, 1862

Confederate soldier John Hines describes the Battle of Shiloh in southwestern Tennessee in this letter written to his parents back home in Kentucky. The bloodiest battle up to that point in the war, Shiloh was also Hines's first combat experience. As was common for most soldiers on both sides of the conflict, Hines's early enthusiasm for the war and his opinion of the enemy changed with his first taste of battle.

Dear Ma and G. Pa

. . . I was in the battle of Shiloh from beginning to end. It is said to have been the hardest fought battle ever fought on this continent. Persons who were in the battles of Manassas and Ft. Donelson say they were skirmishes in comparison. . . .

Our squadron was ordered close to the federal lines on Saturday evening. We stopped close enough to hear their drums beating. We were very tired and hungry. Some of the men not having et [eaten] for 36 hours. I gave a teamster 50 cents for a biscuit. Tied my horse close to me and laid down without taking off boots or pistols and slept soundly until just at dawn the loud peal of some half dozen cannons aroused us. In a few moments we were in our saddles, overcoats and extra equipment lashed to our saddles. In our shirt sleeves, we sat on our horses examining our arms, ready for the coming fray, for we knew we would give the enemy battle if they would stand.

The increased roaring of artillery and an occasional ambulance bearing off wounded soldiers told that, as we say in camp, the ball was open. Before the sun was up we were marching to the scene of action, which was perhaps a mile off. We had not marched very far before we came upon our line of infantry. For three miles in one unbroken line stood our troops, their fixed bayonets glistening in the new sunbeams, for the sun was just coming over the top of a small elevation.

Almost every hill now on both sides looked like a volcano, for the deep mouthed cannon were roaring on every side. Soon the rattle of musketry announced that our vanguard had found the foe. The dark line of men now moved quickly in. After minutes more the volleys of musketry announced that they too had entered the bloody arena. It was really a grand scene now: you could not distinguish a musket shot now, it was one continual roar like the rushing of a storm. The thundering of the artillery at regular intervals alone disturbed the continual sounds. A shell or cannonball would tear some of your comrades to pieces and a person could not tell whose turn it might be next.

Being mounted and ordered to different places during the day, I had an opportunity to see everything that happened almost and I can assure you that a battlefield is far from being a pleasant place, laying aside the dangers of being hurt, because you can't get out of hearing the groans of the dying or out of sight of the dead. It seemed to me like my acquaintances were always lying in the most auspicious places. Turn what way we might I could find some ghastly looking face that perhaps an hour ago I had seen rushing to the contest with a smile on his face. I could not enumerate a hundredth part of the incidents of note that occurred during both days. . . .

We have again returned to camp which is now outside of the former federal [Union] lines and are resting quietly. I've a good slice of cheese and a can of oysters which I took out of a federal tent before setting fire to it. I have nothing to do but think over what has happened in the last few days. . . .

Your affectionate son,
J. H. Hines

Source: Rod Gragg, ed., *The Illustrated Confederate Reader* (New York: HarperCollins, 1989), 99–100.

DOCUMENT 13.8

Ginnie Ott | Letter to Enos Ott, November 21, 1864

The Ott family were longtime residents of Augusta County, Virginia. Union and Confederate forces had fought grueling battles in the region in 1862, but by the fall of 1864 the area was under firm Confederate control. However, the Confederate army regularly sent soldiers to confiscate crops, cattle, and other goods as the southern economy unraveled under the strain of war. In this letter, Ginnie Ott tells her husband Enos, stationed at Camp Lee in Richmond, about shortages in the area and encourages him to stay where he is rather than seek a transfer to a company closer to home.

Nov 21st 1864

My Dear Husband

I seat myself this morning to drop you a few lines, in answer to yours of the 15th. I was not at Pa's when they got the letter but they sent it to me the same day. I was glad to hear that you were well and hope when these few lines reach you, you may still be enjoying the best of health. Henry came home last night on a seven days furlough to gather up some provisions for the company he belongs to & to take down his cattle. Frank McNutt came with him. Henry has a bad cold & sore throat. Mag and Sister went to Staunton last Friday. I would have written and sent the letter by them but I sent with them for some things I was obliged to have and I thought I would not write until they would get back and see whether they could get the things or not. They got all I wanted except white flanel & I wish if you can get any in Richmond you would send me 4 or 5 yds. The calico you sent me came to hand all right; it is very pretty indeed. Mr. Row is at home now. He says he cannot make your boots without your measure. You will have to send it soon or he cannot make them atal [at all] as he expects to go to the army the ninth of next month. Mag went out last week to hunt the brandy & could not find it. She wishes to know where it is though I suppose she will say something about it in her letter. Sister wants to know what black calico is selling at down there. She wants to get a dress and there was but one peice in Staunton and it was very coarse. She says if [it] is not too dear she would [like] for you to get her a dress & she will pay you in silver if you wish it. There was three men here gathering the tithe corn [the 10 percent of crops requisitioned by the Confederate government] out of the field last week, and four men here yesterday trying to get wheat, and there are two wagons here now for the hay. I have not heard from Mr Newton yet whether he can let you have a hat or not. Pa will see about it and I will let you know. We will send you the things you wrote for as soon as we can. You spoke about getting before the board but I think if you have to stay in service you are as safe there as any place else. The men in the Valley have had some very hard marching to do lately. I believe I have no news to write. We are all well. Nothing more at present.

your affectionate Wife
Ginnie Ott

Source: Ginnie Ott to Enos Ott, November 21, 1864, The Valley of the Shadow: Augusta County, Virginia, Personal Papers, University of Virginia Library, http://valley.lib.virginia.edu/papers/A2909.

DOCUMENT 13.9

Katharine Prescott Wormeley | Letter to Her Mother, May 26, 1862

In 1861 the federal government created the U.S. Sanitary Commission to coordinate the efforts of female relief organizations and provide better medical care to Union soldiers. Throughout the North, women volunteered to collect and send money, medical supplies, and food to soldiers at the front. The commission also sent nurses to army camps, including volunteers such as British-born Katharine Prescott Wormeley, who lived in Rhode Island. In 1862 she worked as a nurse for the commission, transporting and caring for Union soldiers during the military campaign in Virginia. In this letter to her mother, she describes some of the difficulties of her work aboard hospital boats.

The boat had a little shelter-cabin. As we were laying mattresses on the floor, while the doctors were finding the men, the captain stopped us, refusing to let us put typhoid fever cases below the deck—on account of the crew, he said—and threatening to push off at once from the shore. Mrs. Griffin and I looked at him. I did the terrible, and she the pathetic; and he abandoned the contest. The return passage was rather an anxious one. The river is much obstructed with sunken ships and trees, and we had to feel our way, slackening speed every ten minutes. If we had been alone, it would not have mattered; but to have fifty men upon our hands unable to move was too heavy a responsibility not to make us anxious. The captain and pilot said the boat was leaking (we heard the water gurgling under our feet), and they remarked casually that the river was "four fathoms deep about there"; but we saw their motive, and were not scared. We were safe alongside the "Spaulding" by midnight; but Mr. Olmsted's tone of voice as he said, "You don't know how glad I am to see you," showed how much he had been worried. And yet it was the best thing we could have done, for three, perhaps five, of the men would have been dead before morning. We transferred the deck-men (who were not very ill) at once to the "Elm City," and kept the others on board the tug till the next morning (Sunday), when they were taken on board the "Spaulding," all living, and likely to live. Later in the day the "Spaulding" filled up to three hundred and fifty very sick men.

No one who has not shared them can form any idea of the hurry—unless it is kept down by extreme quiet of manner—and the solid hard work caused by this sudden influx of bad cases. Dr. Grymes taught me a valuable lesson the night I was at Yorktown on the "Webster." A man with a ghastly wound—the first I ever saw—asked for something; I turned hastily to get it, with some sort of exclamation. Dr. Grymes stopped me and said: "Never do that again; never be hurried or excited, or you are not fit to be here"; and I've thanked him for that lesson ever since. It is a piteous sight to see these men; no one knows what war is until they see this black side of it. We may all

(continued on page 422)

sentimentalize over its possibilities as we see the regiments go off, or when we hear of a battle; but it is as far from the reality as to read of pain is far from feeling it. We who are here, however, dare not let our minds, much less our imaginations, rest on suffering; while *you* must rely on your imagination to project you into the state of things here. . . .

I can give you *no* idea of the work thus accumulated into one day. But there were cheerful things in it after all. One thing I specially remember. A man very low with typhoid fever had been brought on board early in the afternoon, and begged me piteously to keep the bunk next him for his brother—his twin brother—from whom he had never been parted in his life, not even now in sickness; for his brother was sick too, and had come down on the same train. But, alas! in shipping the poor helpless fellows they had got separated. Of course I kept the next bunk empty, even taking out of it a man who had been put in during my absence; and all day long the painful look in the anxious eyes distressed me. Late at night, as the last men were coming off the "Elm City," and I was standing at the gangway by Dr. Draper, receiving his orders as he looked at the men when they came on board, I heard him read off the name of the brother! You may be sure I asked for that man; and the pleasure of putting him beside his brother cheered even that black night.

Source: Katharine Prescott Wormeley, *The Other Side of the War with the Army of the Potomac* (Boston: Ticknor, 1889), 75–80.

Mourning at Stonewall Jackson's Gravesite, 1866

Many Northerners were concerned that the defeat of the Confederacy did not lessen white Southerners' devotion to the "Lost Cause" of a society based on the domination of African Americans. Women, who led the efforts to memorialize Confederate soldiers, are shown at the gravesite of General Stonewall Jackson in Lexington, Virginia. Virginia Military Institute Archives

had been for if the South admitted no mistakes, was led by the same people, and continued to oppress its black inhabitants. The *Chicago Tribune* declared that Northerners would not allow the black codes to "disgrace one foot of soil in which the bones of our soldiers sleep and over which the flag of freedom waves." **See Document Project 14: Testing and Contesting Freedom, page 449.**

Johnson and Congressional Resistance

Faced with growing opposition in the North, Johnson stubbornly held his ground. He insisted that the southern states had followed his plan and were entitled to resume their representation in Congress. Republicans objected, and in December 1865 they barred the admission of southern lawmakers, an action that Johnson denounced as illegitimate. Up to this point, it was still possible for Johnson and Congress to work together, if Johnson had been willing to compromise. He was not. Instead, Johnson pushed moderates into the Radical camp with a series of legislative vetoes that challenged the fundamental tenets of Republican policies toward African Americans and the South. In January 1866, the president

refused to sign a bill passed by Congress to extend the life of the Freedmen's Bureau for another two years. A few months later, he vetoed the Civil Rights Act, which Congress had passed to protect freedpeople in the South from the restrictions placed on them by the black codes. These bills represented a consensus among moderate and Radical Republicans on the government's responsibility toward former slaves.

Explore

See Documents 14.1 and 14.2 for two perspectives on the Freedmen's Bureau.

Johnson justified his vetoes on both constitutional and personal grounds. Along with Democrats, he contended that so long as Congress refused to admit southern representatives, it could not legally pass laws affecting the South. The chief executive also condemned the Freedmen's Bureau bill because it infringed on the rights of states to handle their internal affairs concerning education and economic matters. Johnson's vetoes exposed his racism and his lifelong belief that the evil of slavery lay in the harm it did to poor white Southerners, not to enslaved blacks. Johnson

DOCUMENTS 14.1 AND 14.2

Debating the Freedmen's Bureau: Two Views

From the start, the Freedmen's Bureau generated controversy. To its Republican supporters, it helped southern blacks make the transition from slavery to freedom. For most white Southerners and many northern Democrats, however, the bureau was little more than an expensive social welfare program that rewarded idleness in blacks. Both points of view are represented in the following documents. In a report written to the Congressional Joint Committee on Reconstruction, Colonel Eliphalet Whittlesey, the assistant head of the Freedmen's Bureau in North Carolina, outlined the bureau's initial accomplishments. The anti-bureau cartoon reprinted here was created during the height of the conflict over Reconstruction between the Republican Congress and President Andrew Johnson; it was intended to support the election of a Democratic candidate for governor of Pennsylvania, an ally of Johnson.

Explore

14.1 Colonel Eliphalet Whittlesey | Report on the Freedmen's Bureau, 1865

All officers of the bureau are instructed—

To aid the destitute, yet in such a way as not to encourage dependence.

To protect freedmen from injustice.

To assist freedmen in obtaining employment and fair wages for their labor.

To encourage education, intellectual and moral. Under these four divisions the operations of the bureau can best be presented. . . .

The statistical reports prepared by Captain Almy, commissary of subsistence, forwarded herewith, will show a steady and healthy decrease of the number of dependents from month to month.

July there were issued 215,285 rations, valued at $44,994.56; August there were issued 156,289 rations, valued at $32,664.40; September there were issued 137,350 rations, valued at $28,706.15.

Should no unforeseen trouble arise, the number will be still further reduced. But we have in our camps at Roanoke island and Newbern, many women and children, families of soldiers who have died in the service, and refugees from the interior during the war, for whom permanent provision must be made. . . . The reports prepared by Surgeon Hogan will show the condition of freedmen hospitals. In the early part of the summer much suffering and mortality occurred for want of medical attendance and supplies. This evil is now being remedied by the employment of surgeons by contract. . . .

Contrary to the fears and predictions of many, the great mass of colored people have remained quietly at work upon the plantations of their former masters during the entire summer. The crowds seen about the towns in the early part of the season had followed in the wake of the Union army, to escape from slavery. After hostilities ceased these refugees returned to their homes, so that but few vagrants can now be found. In truth, a much larger amount of vagrancy exists among the whites than among the blacks. It is the almost uniform report of officers of the bureau that freedmen are industrious.

The report is confirmed by the fact that out of a colored population of nearly 350,000 in the State, only about 5,000 are now receiving support from the government. Probably some others are receiving aid from kind-hearted men who have enjoyed the benefit of their services from childhood. To the general quiet and industry of this people there can be no doubt that the efforts of the bureau have contributed greatly.

Source: *The Reports of the Committees of the House of Representatives Made during the First Session, Thirty-ninth Congress, 1865–1866* (Washington, D.C.: Government Printing Office, 1866), 186–87, 189.

14.2 Democratic Flier Opposing the Freedmen's Bureau Bill, 1866

Library of Congress

Interpret the Evidence

- Why was there a need for the Freedmen's Bureau? How did Colonel Whittlesey measure its success?
- How is the Freedmen's Bureau portrayed in the poster? Why might its argument have appealed to some northern whites?

Put It in Context

How did prevailing racial assumptions shape both the cartoon and the report?

argued that these congressional bills discriminated against whites, who would receive no benefits under them, and put whites at a disadvantage with blacks who received government assistance. Johnson's private secretary recorded in his diary, "The president has at times exhibited a morbid distress and feeling against the Negroes," including those like Jefferson Long, who spoke out for their full civil rights.

Johnson's actions united moderates and Radicals against him. In April 1866, Congress repassed both the Freedmen's Bureau extension and Civil Rights Act over the president's vetoes. In June, lawmakers adopted the **Fourteenth Amendment**, which incorporated many of the provisions of the Civil Rights Act, and submitted it to the states for ratification (see Appendix). Reflecting its confrontational dealings with the president, Congress wanted to ensure more permanent protection for African Americans than simple legislation could provide. Lawmakers also wanted to act quickly, as the situation in the South seemed to be deteriorating rapidly. The previous month, a race riot had broken out in Memphis, Tennessee. For a day and a half, white mobs, egged on by local police, went on a rampage, during which they terrorized black residents of

the city and burned their houses and churches. "The late riots in our city," the editor of a Memphis newspaper asserted, "have satisfied all of one thing, that the *southern man* will not be ruled by the *negro*."

The Fourteenth Amendment defined citizenship to include African Americans, thereby nullifying the ruling in the *Dred Scott* case of 1857, which declared that blacks were not citizens. It extended equal protection and due process of law to all persons and not only citizens. The amendment repudiated Confederate debts, which some state governments had refused to do, and it barred Confederate officeholders from holding elective office unless Congress removed this provision by a two-thirds vote. Although most Republicans were upset with Johnson's behavior, at this point they were not willing to embrace the Radical position entirely. Rather than granting the right to vote to black males at least twenty-one years of age, the Fourteenth Amendment gave the states the option of excluding blacks and accepting a reduction in congressional representation if they did so.

Johnson remained inflexible. Instead of counseling the southern states to accept the Fourteenth Amendment, which would have sped up their readmission to the Union,

Memphis Race Riot

A skirmish between white policemen and black Union veterans on May 1, 1866, resulted in three days of rioting by white mobs that attacked the black community of Memphis, Tennessee. Before federal troops restored peace, numerous women had been raped, and forty-six African Americans and two whites had been killed. This illustration from *Harper's Weekly* depicts the carnage.   Courtesy of the Tennessee State Library and Archives

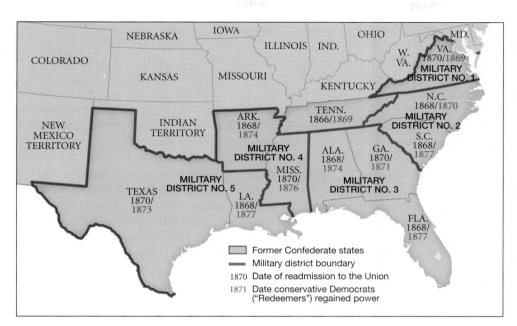

MAP 14.1   Reconstruction in the South

In 1867, Congress enacted legislation dividing the former Confederate states into five military districts. All the states were readmitted to the Union by 1870 and white, conservative Democrats (Redeemers) had replaced Republicans in most states by 1875. Only in Florida, Louisiana, and South Carolina did federal troops remain until 1877.

he encouraged them to reject it. Ironically, Johnson's home state of Tennessee ratified the amendment, but the other states refused. In the fall of 1866, Johnson decided to take his case directly to northern voters before the midterm congressional elections. Campaigning for candidates who shared his views, he embarked on a swing through the Midwest. Clearly out of touch with northern public opinion, Johnson attacked Republican lawmakers and engaged in shouting matches with audiences. On election day, Republicans increased their majorities in Congress and now controlled two-thirds of the seats, providing them with greater power to override presidential vetoes.

Congressional Reconstruction

When the Fortieth Congress convened in 1867, Republican lawmakers charted a new course for Reconstruction. With moderates and Radicals united against the president, Congress intended to force the former Confederate states not only to protect the basic civil rights of African Americans but also to grant them the vote. Moderates now agreed with Radicals that unless blacks had access to the ballot, they would not be able to sustain their freedom. Extending the suffrage to African Americans also aided the fortunes of the Republican Party in the South by adding significant numbers of new black voters. By the end of March, Congress enacted three Military Reconstruction Acts. Together they divided ten southern states into five military districts, each under the supervision of a Union general and his troops (Map 14.1). The male voters of each state, regardless of race, were to elect delegates to a constitutional convention; only former Confederate officials were disfranchised.

The conventions were required to draft constitutions that guaranteed black suffrage and ratified the Fourteenth Amendment. Within a year, North Carolina, South Carolina, Florida, Alabama, Louisiana, and Arkansas had fulfilled these obligations and reentered the Union.

Having ensured congressional Reconstruction in the South, Republican lawmakers turned their attention to disciplining the president. Johnson continued to resist congressional policy and used his power as commander in chief to order generals in the military districts to soften the intent of congressional Reconstruction. In response, Congress passed the Command of the Army Act in 1867, which required the president to issue all orders to army commanders in the field through the General of the Army in Washington, D.C., Ulysses S. Grant. The Radicals had won over Grant and knew they could count on him to carry out their policies. Even more threatening to presidential power, Congress passed the **Tenure of Office Act**, which prevented Johnson from firing cabinet officers sympathetic to congressional Reconstruction. This measure barred the chief executive from removing from office any appointee that the Senate had ratified previously without returning to the Senate for approval.

Johnson sincerely believed that the Tenure of Office Act violated his presidential prerogative to remove subordinates he considered disloyal or incompetent. He may have had a legitimate constitutional point. However, the quick-tempered Johnson chose to confront the Radical Republicans directly rather than find a way to maneuver around a congressional showdown. In February 1868, Johnson fired Secretary of War Edwin Stanton, a Lincoln appointee and a Radical sympathizer, without Senate approval. In response, congressional Radicals prepared articles of impeachment on eleven counts of misconduct, including willful violation of the Tenure of Office Act.

In late February, the House voted 126 to 47 to impeach Johnson, the first president ever to be impeached, or charged with unlawful activity. The case then went to trial in the Senate, where the chief justice of the Supreme Court presided and a two-thirds vote was necessary for conviction and removal from office. After a six-week hearing, the Senate fell one vote short of convicting Johnson. Most crucial for Johnson's fate were the votes of seven moderate Republicans who refused to find the president guilty of violating his oath to uphold the Constitution, convinced that Johnson's actions were insufficient to merit the enormously significant step of removing a president from office. Although Johnson narrowly remained in office, Congress effectively ended his power to shape Reconstruction policy.

Not only did the Republicans restrain Johnson but they also won the presidency in 1868. Ulysses S. Grant, the popular Civil War Union general, ran against Horatio Seymour, the Democratic governor of New York. Although an ally of the Radical Republicans, Grant called for reconciliation with the South. He easily defeated Seymour, winning nearly 53 percent of the popular vote and 73 percent of the electoral vote.

The Struggle for Universal Suffrage

In February 1869, Congress passed the **Fifteenth Amendment** to protect black suffrage, which had initially been guaranteed by the Military Reconstruction Acts. A compromise between moderate and Radical Republicans, the amendment prohibited voting discrimination based on race, but it did not deny states the power to impose qualifications based on literacy, payment of taxes, moral character, or any other standard that did not directly relate to race. Subsequently, the wording of the amendment provided loopholes for white leaders to disfranchise African Americans and any other "undesirable" elements. The amendment did, however, cover the entire nation, including the North, where several states, such as Connecticut, Kansas, Michigan, New York, Ohio, and Wisconsin, still excluded blacks from voting.

The Fifteenth Amendment sparked serious conflicts not only within the South but also among old abolitionist allies. The American Anti-Slavery Society disbanded with abolition, but many members believed that important work still remained to be done to guarantee the rights of freedpeople. They formed the **American Equal Rights Association** immediately following the war. Members of this group divided over the Fifteenth Amendment.

Women's rights advocates, such as Elizabeth Cady Stanton and Susan B. Anthony, had earlier objected to the Fourteenth Amendment because it inserted the word *male* into the Constitution for the first time when describing citizens. Although they had been ardent abolitionists before the war, Stanton and Anthony worried that postwar policies intended to enhance the rights of southern black men would further limit the rights of women. Some African American activists also voiced concern. At a meeting of the Equal Rights Association in 1867, Sojourner Truth noted, "There is quite a stir about colored men getting their rights, but not a word about colored women."

The Fifteenth Amendment ignored women. At the 1869 meeting of the Equal Rights Association, differences over supporting the measure erupted into open conflict. Stanton and Anthony denounced suffrage for black men only, and Stanton now supported her position on racial grounds. She claimed that the "dregs of China, Germany, England, Ireland, and Africa" were degrading the U.S. polity and argued that white, educated women should certainly have the same rights as immigrant and African American men. Black and white supporters of the Fifteenth Amendment, including Frances Ellen Watkins Harper, Wendell Phillips, Abby Kelley, and Frederick Douglass, denounced Stanton's bigotry. Believing that southern black men urgently needed suffrage to protect their newly won freedom, they argued that the ratification of black men's suffrage would speed progress toward the achievement of suffrage for black and white women.

> **Explore**
>
> See Document 14.3 for one activist's views on ratifying suffrage for black men.

This conflict led to the formation of competing organizations committed to women's suffrage. The **National Woman Suffrage Association**, established by Stanton and Anthony, allowed only women as members and opposed ratification of the Fifteenth Amendment. The **American Woman Suffrage Association**, which attracted the support of women and men, white and black, supported ratification. Less than a year later, in the spring of 1870, the Fifteenth Amendment was ratified and went into effect. However, the amendment did not grant the vote to either white or black women. As a result, women suffragists turned to the Fourteenth Amendment to achieve their goal. In 1875 Virginia Minor, who had been denied the ballot in Missouri, argued that the right to vote was one of the "privileges and immunities" granted to all citizens under the Fourteenth Amendment. In *Minor v. Happersatt*, the Supreme Court ruled against her.

REVIEW & RELATE

What was President Johnson's plan for reconstruction? How were his views out of step with those of most Republicans?

What characterized congressional Reconstruction? What priorities were reflected in congressional Reconstruction legislation?

DOCUMENT 14.3

Frances Ellen Watkins Harper | On Suffrage, 1869

Born a free person of color in Baltimore, Maryland, Frances Ellen Watkins Harper distinguished herself as a poet, a teacher, and an abolitionist. After the Civil War, she became a staunch advocate of women's suffrage and a supporter of the Fifteenth Amendment, which set her at odds with the suffragists Susan B. Anthony and Elizabeth Cady Stanton. In this discussion at the May 1869 American Equal Rights Association meeting, she argues for ratification of the Fifteenth Amendment.

Explore

When it was a question of race, she [black women] let the lesser question of sex go. But the white women all go for sex, letting race occupy a minor position. She liked the idea of working women, but she would like to know if it was broad enough to take colored women? . . . [When I] was at Boston there were sixty women who left work because one colored woman went to gain a livelihood in their midst. If the nation could only handle one question, I would not have the black women put a single straw in the way, if only the men of the race could obtain what they wanted.

Source: Susan B. Anthony, Elizabeth Cady Stanton, and Matilda Joslyn Gage, eds., *History of Women's Suffrage, 1861–1876* (Rochester, NY: Susan B. Anthony, 1882), 2:391–92.

Frances Ellen Watkins Harper   Image courtesy of Documenting the American South, The University of North Carolina at Chapel Hill Libraries

Interpret the Evidence

- According to Frances Harper, why do black and white women differ on support for black male suffrage?
- How does Harper's experience in Boston influence her opinion?

Put It in Context

Why was it important for black men to gain the right to vote even if it meant delaying women's suffrage?

Remaking the South

With President Johnson's power effectively curtailed, reconstruction of the South moved quickly. However, despite the fears of southern whites and their supporters in the North, the results were neither extreme nor revolutionary. Although African Americans for the first time participated extensively in electoral politics and made unprecedented gains, whites retained control of the majority of the region's wealth and political power. In contrast to revolutions and civil wars in other countries, only one rebel was executed for war crimes (the commandant of Andersonville Prison in Georgia); only one high-ranking official went to prison (Jefferson Davis); no official was forced into exile, though some fled voluntarily; very little land was confiscated and redistributed; and most rebels regained voting rights and the ability to hold office within seven years after the end of the rebellion.

Whites Reconstruct the South

During the first years of congressional Reconstruction, two groups of whites occupied the majority of elective offices in the South. A significant number of native-born Southerners joined Republicans in forming postwar constitutions and governments. Before the war, some had belonged to the Whig Party and opposed secession from the Union. Many mountain dwellers in Alabama, Georgia, North Carolina, and Tennessee had demonstrated a fiercely independent strain and had remained loyal to the Union. As a white resident of the Georgia mountains commented, "Now is the time for every man to come out and speak his principles publickly and vote for liberty as we have been in bondage long enough." Small merchants and farmers who detested large plantation owners also threw their lot in with the Republicans. Even a few ex-Confederates, such as General James A. Longstreet, decided that the South must change and allied with the Republicans. The majority of whites who continued to support the Democratic Party viewed these whites as traitors. They showed their distaste by calling them **scalawags**, an unflattering term meaning "scoundrels."

At the same time, northern whites came south to support Republican Reconstruction. They had varied reasons for making the journey, but most considered the South a new frontier to be conquered culturally, politically, and economically. Some had served in the Union army during the war, liked what they saw of the region, and decided to settle there. Some came to help provide education and assist the freedpeople in adjusting to a new way of life. As a relatively underdeveloped area, the South also beckoned fortune seekers and adventurers who saw in the South an opportunity to get rich building railroads, establishing factories, and selling consumer goods. Southern Democrats denounced such northern interlopers as **carpetbaggers**, suggesting that they invaded the region with all their possessions in a satchel, seeking to plunder it and then leave. This characterization applied to some, but it did not accurately describe the motivations of most transplanted Northerners. While they did seek economic opportunity, they were acting as Americans always had in settling new frontiers and pursuing dreams of success. In dismissing them as carpetbaggers, their political enemies employed a double standard because they did not apply this demeaning label to those who traveled west—from both the North and the South—in search of economic opportunity at the expense of Indians and Mexicans settled there. Much of the negative feelings directed toward carpetbaggers resulted primarily from their attempts to ally with African Americans in reshaping the South.

Black Political Participation and Economic Opportunities

As much as the majority of southern whites detested scalawags and carpetbaggers, the primary targets of white hostility were African Americans who attempted to exercise their hard-won freedom. Blacks constituted a majority of voters in five states—Alabama, Florida, South Carolina, Mississippi, and Louisiana—while in Georgia, North Carolina, Texas, and Virginia they fell short of a majority. They did not use their ballots to impose black rule on the South as many white Southerners feared. Only in South Carolina did African Americans control the state legislature, and in no state did they manage to elect a governor. Nevertheless, for the first time in American history, blacks won a wide variety of elected positions. More than six hundred blacks served in state legislatures; another sixteen, including Jefferson F. Long, held seats in the U.S. House of Representatives; and two from Mississippi were chosen to serve in the U.S. Senate.

Officeholding alone does not indicate the enthusiasm that former slaves had for politics. African Americans considered politics a community responsibility, and in addition to casting ballots, they held rallies and mass meetings to discuss issues and choose candidates. Although they could not vote, women attended these gatherings and helped influence their outcome. Covering a Republican convention in Richmond in October 1867, held in the African First Baptist Church, the *New York Times* reported that "the entire colored population of Richmond" attended. Freedpeople also formed associations to promote education, economic advancement, and social welfare programs, all of which they saw as deeply intertwined with politics. These included organizations like Richmond's Mutual Benefit Society, a group formed by single mothers, and the Independent Order of St. Luke, a mutual aid society for black women and men. African American women led both.

The efforts of southern blacks to bolster their freedom included building alliances with sympathetic whites. The resulting interracial political coalitions produced considerable reform in the South. These coalitions created a public school system where none had existed before the war; provided funds for social services, such as poor relief and state hospitals; upgraded prisons; and rebuilt the South's transportation system by supporting railroads and construction projects. Moreover, the state constitutions that the Republicans wrote brought a greater measure of political democracy and equality to the South by extending the right to vote to poor white men as well as black men. Some states allowed married women greater control over their property and liberalized the criminal justice system. In effect, these Reconstruction governments brought the South into the nineteenth century.

Obtaining political representation was one way in which African Americans defined freedom. Economic independence constituted a second. Without government-sponsored land redistribution, however, the options for southern blacks remained limited. Lacking capital to start farms, they entered into various forms of tenant contracts with large landowners. **Sharecropping** proved the most common arrangement. Blacks and poor whites became sharecroppers for much the same economic reasons. They received tools and supplies from landowners and farmed their own plots of land on the plantation. In exchange, sharecroppers turned over a portion of their harvest to the owner and kept some for themselves. Crop divisions varied but were usually explained in detail on written agreements. To make this system profitable, sharecroppers concentrated on producing staple crops such as cotton and tobacco that they could sell for cash.

The benefits of sharecropping proved more valuable to black farmers in theory than in practice. To tide them over during the growing season, croppers had to purchase household provisions on credit from a local merchant, who was often also the farmers' landlord. At the mercy of store owners who kept the books and charged high interest rates, tenants usually found themselves in considerable debt at the end of the year. To satisfy the debt, merchants devised a crop lien system in which tenants pledged a portion of their yearly crop to satisfy what they owed. Most indebted tenants found themselves bound to the landlord because falling prices in agricultural staples during this period meant that they did not receive sufficient return on their produce to get out of debt. For many African Americans, sharecropping turned into a form of virtual slavery.

Explore

See Document 14.4 for an example of a sharecropping agreement.

The picture for black farmers was not all bleak, however. About 20 percent of black farmers managed to buy their own land. Through careful management and extremely hard work, black families planted gardens for household consumption and raised chickens for eggs and food. Despite its pitfalls, sharecropping provided a limited measure of labor independence and allowed some blacks to accumulate small amounts of cash.

Following the war's devastation, many of the South's white, small farmers known as yeomen also fell into sharecropping. Yet planters, too, had changed. Many sons of planters abandoned farming and became lawyers, bankers, and merchants. Despite these changes, one thing remained the same: White elites ruled over blacks and poor whites, and they kept these two economically exploited groups from uniting by fanning the flames of racial prejudice.

Economic hardship and racial bigotry drove many blacks to leave the South. In 1879 former slaves pooled their resources to create land companies and purchase property in Kansas on which to settle. They created black towns that attracted some 25,000 African American migrants from the South, known as **Exodusters**. Kansas was ruled by the Republican Party and had been home to the great antislavery martyr John Brown. As one hopeful freedman from Louisiana wrote to the Kansas governor in 1879, "I am anxious to reach your state . . . because of the sacredness of her soil washed in the blood of humanitarians for the cause of black freedom." Exodusters did not find the Promised Land, however, as poor-quality land and unpredictable weather made farming on the Great Plains a hard and often unrewarding experience. Nevertheless, for many African American migrants, the chance to own their own land and escape the oppression of the South was worth the hardships. In 1880 the census counted 40,000 blacks living in Kansas.

White Resistance to Congressional Reconstruction

Despite the Republican record of accomplishment during Reconstruction, white Southerners did not accept its legitimacy. They accused interracial governments of conducting a spending spree that raised taxes and encouraged corruption. Indeed, taxes did rise significantly, but mainly because of the need to provide new educational

DOCUMENT 14.4

Sharecropping Agreement, 1870

Because Congress did not generally provide freedpeople with land, African Americans lacked the capital to start their own farms. At the same time, plantation owners needed labor to plant and harvest their crops for market. Out of mutual necessity, white plantation owners entered into sharecropping contracts with blacks to work their farms in exchange for a portion of the crop, such as the following contract between Willis P. Bocock and several of his former slaves. Bocock owned Waldwick Plantation in Marengo County, Alabama.

Explore

What are the farmers' responsibilities?

Why would Bocock want to clarify that his laborers would work equally hard throughout the year?

How might putting a lien on crops for debts owed create difficulties for the black farmer?

Contract made the 3rd day of January in the year 1870 between us the free people who have signed this paper of one part, and our employer, Willis P. Bocock, of the other part. We agree to take charge of and cultivate for the year 1870, a portion of land, say [left blank] acres or thereabouts, to be laid off to us by our employer on his plantation, and to tend the same well in the usual crops, in such proportions as we and he may agree upon. We are to furnish the necessary labor, say an average hand to every 15 acres in the crops, making in all average hands; and are to have all proper work done, ditching, fencing, repairing, etc., as well as cultivating and saving the crops of all kinds, so as to put and keep the land we occupy and tend in good order for cropping, and to make a good crop ourselves; and to do our fair share of job work about the place. . . . We are to be responsible for the good conduct of ourselves, our hands, and families, and agree that all shall be respectful to employer, owners, and manager, honest, industrious, and careful about every thing, and shall not interrupt any thing about the place, working as industriously the last part of the year as the first; and then our employer agrees that he and his manager shall treat us kindly, and help us to study our interest and do our duty. If any hand or family proves to be of bad character, or dishonest, or lazy, or disobedient, or any way unsuitable our employer or manager has the right, and we have the right, to have such turned off. . . .

For the labor and services of ourselves and hands rendered as above stated, we are to have one third part of all the crops, or their net-proceeds, made and secured, or prepared for market by our force. . . .

We are to be furnished by our employer through his manager with provisions if we call for them: not over one peck of meal or corn, and $3\frac{1}{2}$ pounds of meat or its equivalent per week, for every 15 acres of land or average hand, to be charged to us at fair market prices.

And whatever may be due by us, or our hands to our employer for provisions or any thing else, during the year, is to be a lien on our share of the crops, and is to be retained by him out of the same before we receive our part.

Source: Waldwick Plantation Records, 1834–1971, LPR174, box 1, folder 9, Alabama Department of Archives and History.

Put It in Context

Why would free blacks and poor whites be willing to enter into such a contract?

Exodusters

This photograph of two black couples standing on their homestead was taken around 1880 in Nicodemus, Kansas. These settlers, known as Exodusters, had migrated to northwest Kansas following the end of Reconstruction. They sought economic opportunity free from the racial repression sweeping the South.   Library of Congress

and social services. Corruption, where building projects and railroad construction were concerned, was common during this time. Still, it is unfair to single out Reconstruction governments and especially black legislators as inherently depraved, as their Democratic opponents did. Economic scandals were part of American life after the Civil War. As enormous business opportunities arose and the pent-up energies that had gone into battles over slavery exploded into desires to accumulate wealth, many business leaders and politicians made unlawful deals to enrich themselves.

Most Reconstruction governments had only limited opportunities to transform the South. By the end of 1870, civilian rule had returned to all of the former Confederate states, and they had reentered the Union. Republican rule did not continue past 1870 in Virginia, North Carolina, and Tennessee and did not extend beyond 1871 in Georgia and 1873 in Texas. In 1874 Democrats deposed Republicans in Arkansas and Alabama; two years later, Democrats triumphed in Mississippi. In only three

states—Louisiana, Florida, and South Carolina—did Reconstruction last until 1877.

The Democrats who replaced Republicans trumpeted their victories as bringing "redemption" to the South. Of course, these so-called **Redeemers** were referring to the white South. For black Republicans and their white allies, redemption meant defeat, not resurrection. Democratic victories came at the ballot boxes, but violence, intimidation, and fraud usually paved the way. It was not enough for Democrats to attack Republican policies. They also used racist appeals to divide poor whites from blacks and backed them up with force. In 1865 in Pulaski, Tennessee, General Nathan Bedford Forrest organized Confederate veterans into a social club called the **Knights of the Ku Klux Klan (KKK)**. The name came from the Greek word *kuklos*, meaning "circle." Spreading throughout the South, the KKK did not function as an ordinary social association; its followers donned robes and masks to hide their identities and terrify their victims. Ku Kluxers wielded rifles and guns and rode on horseback to the homes and

Visit of the Ku Klux Klan
This 1872 wood engraving by the noted magazine illustrator Frank Bellew appeared at the height of Ku Klux Klan violence against freed blacks in the South. This image depicts a black family seemingly secure in their home in the evening while masked Klansmen stand in their doorway ready to attack with rifles. Library of Congress

churches of black and white Republicans to keep them from voting. When threats did not work, they murdered their victims. In 1871, for example, 150 African Americans were killed in Jackson County in the Florida Panhandle. A black clergyman lamented, "That is where Satan has his seat." Here and elsewhere, many of the individuals targeted had managed to buy property, gain political leadership, or in other ways defy white stereotypes of African American inferiority. Local rifle clubs, hunting groups, and other white supremacist organizations joined the Klan in waging a reign of terror. During the 1875 election in Mississippi, which toppled the Republican government, armed terrorists killed hundreds of Republicans and scared many more away from the polls.

To combat the terror unleashed by the Klan and its allies, Congress passed three Force Acts in 1870 and 1871. These measures empowered the president to dispatch officials into the South to supervise elections and prevent voting interference. Directed specifically at the KKK, one law barred secret organizations from using force to violate equal protection of the laws. In 1872 Congress established a joint committee to probe Klan tactics, and its investigations produced thirteen volumes of vivid testimony about the horrors perpetrated by the Klan. Elias Hill, a freedman

from South Carolina who had become a Baptist preacher and teacher, was one of those who appeared before Congress. He and his brother lived next door to each other. The Klansmen went first to his brother's house, where, as Hill testified, they "broke open the door and attacked his wife, and I heard her screaming and mourning [moaning]. . . . At last I heard them have [rape] her in the yard. She was crying and the Ku-Klux were whipping her to make her tell where I lived." When Klansmen finally discovered Elias Hill, they dragged him out of his house, accused him of preaching against the Klan, beat and whipped him, and threatened to kill him. On the basis of such testimony, the federal government prosecuted some 3,000 Klansmen. Only 600 were convicted, however. As the Klan disbanded in the wake of federal prosecutions, other vigilante organizations arose to take its place.

REVIEW & RELATE

What role did black people play in remaking southern society during Reconstruction?

How did southern whites fight back against Reconstruction? What role did terrorism and political violence play in this effort?

LEARNING*Curve* bedfordstmartins.com/hewittlawson/LC

The Unmaking of Reconstruction

The violence, intimidation, and fraud perpetrated by Redeemers against black and white Republicans in the South does not fully explain the unmaking of Reconstruction. Although Republicans in Congress enacted legislation combating the KKK and racial discrimination in public facilities, by the early 1870s white Northerners had grown weary of the struggle to protect the rights of freedpeople. In the minds of many, white Northerners had done more than enough for black Southerners, and it was time to focus on other issues. Growing economic problems intensified this feeling. More and more northern whites came to believe that any debt owed to black people for northern complicity in the sin of slavery had been wiped out by the blood shed during the Civil War. By the early 1870s, burying and memorializing the Civil War dead emerged as a common concern among white Americans, in both the North and the South. White America was once again united, if only in the shared belief that it was time to move on, consigning the issues of slavery and civil rights to history.

The Republican Retreat

Most northern whites shared the racial views of their counterparts in the South. Although they had supported protection of black civil rights and suffrage, they still believed that African Americans were inferior to whites, and social integration was no more tolerable to them than it was to white Southerners. They began to sympathize with racist complaints voiced from the South that blacks were not capable of governing honestly and effectively.

In 1872 a group calling themselves **Liberal Republicans** challenged the reelection of President Grant, the Civil War general who had won the presidency on the Republican ticket in 1868. Financial scandals had racked the Grant administration. This high-level corruption reflected the get-rich-quick schemes connected to economic speculation and development following the Civil War. Outraged by these misdeeds and the rising level of immoral behavior in government and business, Liberal Republicans nominated Horace Greeley, editor of the *New York Tribune*, to run against Grant. They linked government corruption to the expansion of federal power that accompanied Reconstruction, and called for the removal of troops from the South and amnesty for former Confederates. They also campaigned for civil service reform in order to establish a merit system for government employment and for abolition of the "spoils system"—in which the party in power rewarded loyal supporters with political

appointments—that had been in place since the administration of Andrew Jackson.

The Democratic Party believed that Liberal Republicans offered the best chance to defeat Grant, and it endorsed Greeley. Despite the scandals that surrounded him, Grant remained popular. Moreover, the main body of Republicans "waved the bloody shirt," reminding northern voters that a ballot cast for the opposition tarnished the memory of brave Union soldiers who had died during the war. With the newly created national cemeteries, particularly the one established in Arlington, Virginia, providing a vivid reminder of the hundreds of thousands of soldiers killed, the "bloody shirt" remained a potent symbol. The president won reelection with an even greater margin than he had four years earlier. Nevertheless, the attacks against Grant foreshadowed the Republican retreat on Reconstruction. Among the Democrats sniping at Grant was Andrew Johnson. Johnson had returned to Tennessee, and in 1874 the state legislature chose the former president to serve in the U.S. Senate. He continued to speak out against the presence of federal troops in the South until his death in 1875.

Congressional and Judicial Retreat

By the time Grant began his second term, Congress was already considering bills to restore officeholding rights to former Confederates who had not yet sworn allegiance to the Union. Black representatives, such as Georgia congressman Jefferson Long, as well as some white lawmakers, remained opposed to such measures, but in 1872 Congress removed the penalties placed on former Confederates by the Fourteenth Amendment and permitted nearly all rebel leaders the right to vote and hold office. Two years later, for the first time since the start of the Civil War, the Democrats gained a majority in the House of Representatives and prepared to remove the remaining troops from the South.

Economic concerns increasingly replaced racial considerations as the top priority for northern Republican leaders. Northerners and Southerners began calling more loudly for national unity and reconciliation. In 1873 a financial panic resulting from the collapse of the Northern Pacific Railroad triggered a severe economic depression lasting late into the decade. Tens of thousands of unemployed workers across the country worried more about finding jobs than they did about blacks in the South. Businessmen, too, were plagued with widespread bankruptcy. As workers looked to labor unions for support, business leaders looked to the federal government for assistance. When strikes erupted across the country in 1877, most notably the Great Railway Strike, employers asked the U.S. government to remove troops from the

South and dispatch them against strikers in the North and the West.

While Northerners sought a way to extricate themselves from Reconstruction, the Supreme Court weakened enforcement of the civil rights acts. In 1873 the *Slaughterhouse* cases defined the rights that African Americans were entitled to under the Fourteenth Amendment very narrowly. Reflecting the shift from moral to economic concerns, the justices interpreted the amendment as extending greater protection to corporations in conducting business than that extended to blacks. As a result, blacks had to depend on southern state governments to protect their civil rights, the same state authorities that had deprived them of their rights in the first place. In *United States v. Cruikshank* (1876), the high court narrowed the Fourteenth Amendment further, ruling that it protected blacks against abuses only by state officials and agencies, not by private groups such as the Ku Klux Klan. Seven years later, the Court struck down the Civil Rights Act of 1875, which had extended "full and equal treatment" in public accommodations for persons of all races.

The Presidential Compromise of 1876

The presidential election of 1876 set in motion events that officially brought Reconstruction to an end. The Republicans nominated Rutherford B. Hayes, a Civil War officer and governor of Ohio. A supporter of civil service reform, Hayes was chosen, in part, because he was untainted by the corruption that plagued the Grant administration. The Democrats selected their own crusader against bribery and graft, Governor Samuel J. Tilden of New York, who had prosecuted political corruption in New York City.

The outcome of the election depended on twenty disputed electoral votes, nineteen from the South and one from Oregon. Tilden won 51 percent of the popular vote, but Reconstruction political battles in Florida, Louisiana, and South Carolina put the election up for grabs. In each of these states, the outgoing Republican administration certified Hayes as the winner, while the incoming Democratic regime declared for Tilden.

The Constitution assigns Congress the task of counting and certifying the electoral votes submitted by the states. Normally, this is merely a formality, but 1876 was different. Democrats controlled the House, Republicans controlled the Senate, and neither branch would budge on which votes to count. Hayes needed all twenty for victory; Tilden needed only one. To break the logjam, Congress created a fifteen-member **Joint Electoral Commission**, composed of seven Democrats, seven Republicans, and one independent (five members of the House, five U.S. senators, and five Supreme Court justices). As it turned out, the independent commissioner, Justice David Davis,

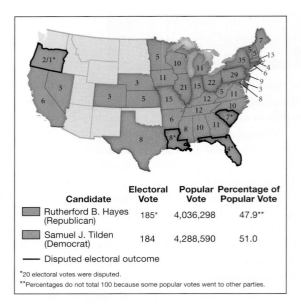

MAP 14.2   The Election of 1876

The presidential election of 1876 got swept up in Reconstruction politics. Democrats defeated Republicans in Florida, Louisiana, and South Carolina, but both parties claimed the electoral votes for their candidates. A federal electoral commission set up to investigate the twenty disputed votes, including one from Oregon, awarded the votes and the election to the Republican, Rutherford B. Hayes.

resigned, and his replacement, Justice Joseph P. Bradley, voted with the Republicans to count all twenty votes for Hayes, making him president (Map 14.2).

Still, Congress had to ratify this count, and disgruntled southern Democrats in the Senate threatened a filibuster—unlimited debate—to block certification of Hayes. With the March 4, 1877, date for the presidential inauguration creeping perilously close and no winner officially declared, behind-the-scenes negotiations finally helped settle the controversy. A series of meetings between Hayes supporters and southern Democrats led to a bargain. According to the agreement, Democrats would support Hayes in exchange for the president appointing a Southerner to his cabinet, withdrawing the last federal troops from the South, and endorsing construction of a transcontinental railroad through the South. This **compromise of 1877** averted a crisis over presidential succession, underscored increased southern Democratic influence within Congress, and marked the end to strong federal protection for African Americans in the South.

REVIEW & RELATE

Why did northern interest in Reconstruction wane in the 1870s?

What common values and beliefs among white Americans were reflected in the compromise of 1877?

Conclusion: The Legacies of Reconstruction

Reconstruction was, in many ways, profoundly limited. African Americans did not receive the landownership that would have provided them with the economic independence to bolster their freedom from the racist assaults of white Southerners. The civil and political rights that the federal government conferred did not withstand Redeemers' efforts to disfranchise and deprive the freedpeople of equal rights. The Republican Party shifted its priorities elsewhere, and Democrats gained enough political power nationally to short-circuit federal intervention, while numerous problems remained unresolved in the South. Northern support for racial equality did not run very deep, so white Northerners, who shared many of the prejudices of white Southerners, were happy to extricate themselves from further intervention in southern racial matters. Nor was there sufficient support to give women, white and black, the right to vote. Finally, federal courts, with growing concerns over economic rather than social issues, sanctioned Northerners' retreat by providing constitutional legitimacy for abandoning black Southerners and rejecting women's suffrage in court decisions that narrowed the interpretation of the Fourteenth and Fifteenth Amendments.

Despite all of this, Reconstruction did transform the country. As a result of Reconstruction, slavery was abolished, and the legal basis for freedom was enshrined in the Constitution. Indeed, blacks exercised a measure of political and economic freedom during Reconstruction that never entirely disappeared over the decades to come. In many areas, freedpeople, as exemplified by Congressman Jefferson Franklin Long among many others, asserted what they could never have during slavery—control over their lives, their churches, their labor, and their families. What they could not practice during their own time because of racial discrimination, their descendants would one day revive through the promises codified in the Fourteenth and Fifteenth Amendments.

African Americans transformed not only themselves; they transformed the nation. The Constitution became much more democratic and egalitarian through inclusion of the Reconstruction amendments. Reconstruction lawmakers took an important step toward making the United States the "more perfect union" that the nation's Founders had pledged to create. Reconstruction established a model for expanding the power of the federal government to resolve domestic crises that lay beyond the abilities of states and ordinary citizens. It remained a powerful legacy for those elected officials in the future who dared to invoke it. And Reconstruction transformed the South to its everlasting benefit. It modernized state constitutions, expanded educational and social welfare systems, and unleashed the repressed potential for industrialization and economic development that the preservation of slavery had restrained. Ironically, Reconstruction did as much for white Southerners as it did for black Southerners in liberating them from the past.

LEARNINGCurve
Check what you know.
bedfordstmartins.com/hewittlawson/LC

Chapter Review   Online Study Guide ▶ bedfordstmartins.com/hewittlawson

KEY TERMS

Freedmen's Bureau (p. 427)
Proclamation of Amnesty and Reconstruction (p. 431)
Thirteenth Amendment (p. 431)
black codes (p. 432)
Fourteenth Amendment (p. 436)
Tenure of Office Act (p. 437)
Fifteenth Amendment (p. 438)
American Equal Rights Association (p. 438)
National Woman Suffrage Association (p. 438)

American Woman Suffrage Association (p. 438)
scalawags (p. 440)
carpetbaggers (p. 440)
sharecropping (p. 441)
Exodusters (p. 441)
Redeemers (p. 443)
Knights of the Ku Klux Klan (KKK) (p. 443)
Liberal Republicans (p. 445)
Joint Electoral Commission (p. 446)
compromise of 1877 (p. 446)

REVIEW & RELATE

1. What were freedpeople's highest priorities in the years immediately following the Civil War? Why?

2. How did freedpeople define freedom? What steps did they take to make freedom real for themselves and their children?

3. What was President Johnson's plan for reconstruction? How were his views out of step with those of most Republicans?

4. What characterized congressional Reconstruction? What priorities were reflected in congressional Reconstruction legislation?

5. What role did black people play in remaking southern society during Reconstruction?

6. How did southern whites fight back against Reconstruction? What role did terrorism and political violence play in this effort?

7. Why did northern interest in Reconstruction wane in the 1870s?

8. What common values and beliefs among white Americans were reflected in the compromise of 1877?

TIMELINE OF EVENTS

1863	Lincoln issues Proclamation of Amnesty and Reconstruction
1865	Ku Klux Klan formed
	Freedmen's Bureau established
	Congress passes Thirteenth Amendment
April 1865	Lincoln assassinated; Andrew Johnson becomes president
May–December 1865	Presidential Reconstruction under Andrew Johnson
1866	Congress passes extension of Freedmen's Bureau and Civil Rights Act over Johnson's presidential veto
	Congress passes Fourteenth Amendment
1867	Military Reconstruction Acts divide the South into military districts
	Congress passes Command of the Army and Tenure of Office Acts
1868	Andrew Johnson impeached
1869	Congress passes Fifteenth Amendment
	Women's suffrage movement splits over support of Fifteenth Amendment
1870	250,000 blacks attend schools established by the Freedmen's Bureau
	Civilian rule reestablished in all former Confederate states
1870–1871	Jefferson Long serves as a Republican congressman from Georgia
1870–1872	Congress takes steps to curb KKK violence in the South
1872	Liberal Republicans challenge reelection of President Grant
1873	Financial panic sparks depression lasting until the late 1870s
1873–1883	Supreme Court limits rights of African Americans
1875	Congress passes Civil Rights Act outlawing discrimination in public accommodations, which the Supreme Court rules unconstitutional in 1883
1877	Republicans and southern Democrats reach compromise resulting in the election of Rutherford B. Hayes as president and the end of Reconstruction
1879	Black Exodusters migrate from South to Kansas

Testing and Contesting Freedom

Nine months after the Civil War ended in April 1865, twenty-seven states ratified the Thirteenth Amendment, abolishing slavery throughout the United States. Freedom, however, did not guarantee equal rights or the absence of racial discrimination. Immediately following the North's victory, white southern leaders enacted black codes, which aimed to prevent the former slaves from improving their social and economic status. Although Lincoln's successor, Andrew Johnson, himself a Southerner, did not support the codes, he did nothing to overturn them. An advocate of limited government, Johnson clashed repeatedly with Congress over Reconstruction, vetoing renewal of the Freedmen's Bureau bill and opposing ratification of the Fourteenth Amendment. In 1867 the Republican majority in Congress passed the Military Reconstruction Acts, which placed the South under military rule and forced it to extend equal political and civil rights to African Americans.

The Military Reconstruction Acts, followed by the ratification of the Fifteenth Amendment in 1870, extended suffrage to black men. In alliance with white Republicans, blacks won election to a variety of public offices, including seats on local and state governmental bodies. When these interracial legislatures provided funds for public education of blacks—for the first time in the South—and for black hospitals and other social services, their opponents attacked them for fraud, corruption, wasteful spending, and imposing "Black Rule." Opponents also created vigilante groups like the Ku Klux Klan to intimidate black and white Republicans through scare tactics backed up by violence and bloodshed. By 1877 the attempt of white southern Democrats, or Redeemers, had succeeded, leaving African Americans struggling to retain the freedom they had enjoyed during Reconstruction.

As you read the following documents, consider these general questions: How did blacks and whites view freedom? How essential was it for the federal government to supervise the movement from slavery to freedom? Why didn't southern whites accept the extension of civil rights for blacks, if only in a limited way? How did views about Reconstruction change over time?

DOCUMENT 14.5

Mississippi Black Code, 1865

Southern legislatures created black codes primarily to limit the rights of free blacks after emancipation and return them to a condition as close as possible to slavery. Mississippi was one of the first states to enact a black code. Although its laws did legalize marriage for blacks and allowed them to own property and testify in court, its primary intent was to limit freedpeople's mobility and economic opportunities. New vagrancy laws required blacks to provide written proof of residency and employment or else risk arrest, while other sections limited where they could live, restricted the terms of their employment, and banned intermarriage.

An Act to Confer Civil Rights on Freedmen, and for other Purposes

SECTION 1. All freedmen, free negroes and mulattoes may sue and be sued . . . in all the courts of law and equity of this State, and may acquire personal property, and choses in action [right to bring a lawsuit to recover chattels, money, or a debt], by descent or purchase, and may dispose of the same in the same manner and to the same extent that white persons may: Provided, That the provisions of this section shall not be so construed as to allow any freedman, free negro or mulatto to rent or lease any lands or tenements except in incorporated cities or towns, in which places the corporate authorities shall control the same.

SECTION 2. All freedmen, free negroes and mulattoes may intermarry with each other, in the same manner and under the same regulations that are provided by law for white persons: Provided, that the clerk of probate shall keep separate records of the same.

SECTION 3. All freedmen, free negroes or mulattoes who do now and have herebefore lived and cohabited together as husband and wife shall be taken and held in law as legally married, and the issue shall be taken and held as legitimate for all purposes; and it shall not be lawful for any freedman, free negro or mulatto to intermarry with any white person; nor for any person to intermarry with any freedman, free negro or mulatto; and any person who shall so intermarry shall be deemed guilty of felony, and on conviction thereof shall be confined in the State penitentiary for life; and those shall be deemed freedmen, free negroes and mulattoes who are of pure negro blood, and those descended from a negro to the third generation, inclusive, though one ancestor in each generation may have been a white person.

SECTION 4. In addition to cases in which freedmen, free negroes and mulattoes are now by law competent witnesses, freedmen, free negroes or mulattoes shall be competent in civil cases, when a party or parties to the suit, either plaintiff or plaintiffs, defendant or defendants; also in cases where freedmen, free negroes and mulattoes is or are either plaintiff or plaintiffs, defendant or defendants. They shall also be competent witnesses in all criminal prosecutions where the crime charged is alleged to have been committed by a white person upon or against the person or property of a freedman, free negro or mulatto. . . .

SECTION 5. Every freedman, free negro and mulatto shall, on the second Monday of January, one thousand eight hundred and sixty-six, and annually thereafter, have a lawful home or employment, and shall have written evidence thereof as follows, to wit: if living in any incorporated city, town, or village, a license from that mayor thereof; and if living outside of an incorporated city, town, or village, from the member of the board of police of his beat, authorizing him or her to do irregular and job work; or a written contract, as provided in SECTION 6 in this act; which license may be revoked for cause at any time by the authority granting the same.

Section 6. All contracts for labor made with freedmen, free negroes and mulattoes for a longer period than one month shall be in writing, and a duplicate, attested and read to said freedman, free negro or mulatto by a beat, city or county officer, or two disinterested white persons of the county in which the labor is to [be] performed, of which each party shall have one: and said contracts shall be taken and held as entire contracts, and if the laborer shall quit the service of the employer before the expiration of his term of service, without good cause, he shall forfeit his wages for that year up to the time of quitting. . . .

An Act to Amend the Vagrant Laws of the State . . .

Section 2. All freedmen, free negroes and mulattoes in this State, over the age of eighteen years, found on the second Monday in January, 1866, or thereafter, with no lawful employment or business, or found unlawful[ly] assembling themselves together, either in the day or night time, and all white persons assembling themselves with freedmen, free negroes or mulattoes, or usually associating with freedmen, free negroes or mulattoes, on terms of equality, or living in adultery or fornication with a freed woman, freed negro or mulatto, shall be deemed vagrants, and on conviction thereof shall be fined in a sum not exceeding, in the case of a freedman, free negro or mulatto, fifty dollars, and a white man two hundred dollars, and imprisonment at the discretion of the court, the free negro not exceeding ten days, and the white man not exceeding six months. . . .

Section 6. The same duties and liabilities existing among white persons of this State shall attach to freedmen, free negroes or mulattoes, to support their indigent families and all colored paupers; and that in order to secure a support for such indigent freedmen, free negroes, or mulattoes, it shall be lawful, and is hereby made the duty of the county police of each county in this State, to levy a poll or capitation tax on each and every freedman, free negro, or mulatto, between the ages of eighteen and sixty years, not to exceed the sum of one dollar annually to each person so taxed, which tax, when collected, shall be paid into the county treasurer's hands, and constitute a fund to be called the Freedman's Pauper Fund, which shall be applied by the commissioners of the poor for the maintenance of the poor of the freedmen, free negroes and mulattoes of this State, under such regulations as may be established by the boards of county police in the respective counties of this State.

Source: *Laws of the State of Mississippi, Passed at a Regular Session of the Mississippi Legislature, Held in the City of Jackson, October, November, and December, 1865* (Jackson, MS, 1866), 82–86, 165–67.

DOCUMENT 14.6

Richard H. Cain | Federal Aid for Land Purchase, 1868

Richard H. Cain, a free black minister raised in Ohio, went to South Carolina after the war and served as a Republican member of the U.S. House of Representatives for two terms in the 1870s. The following excerpt comes from a speech Cain made in 1868 as a representative to the South Carolina constitutional convention. Cain proposed that the convention petition Congress for a $1 million loan to purchase land that could be resold to freedmen at a reasonable price.

I BELIEVE THE BEST MEASURE to be adopted is to bring capital to the State, and instead of causing revenge and unpleasantness, I am for even-handed justice. I am for allowing the parties who own lands to bring them into the market and sell them upon such terms as will be satisfactory to both sides. I believe a measure of this kind has a double effect: first, it brings capital, what the people want; second, it puts the people to work; it gives homesteads, what we need; it relieves the Government and takes away its responsibility of feeding the people; it inspires every man with a noble manfulness, and by the thought that he is the possessor of something in the State; it adds also to the revenue of the country. By these means men become interested in the country as they never were before. It was said that five and one-seventh acres were not enough to live on. If South Carolina, in its sovereign power, can devise any plan for the purchase of the large plantations in this State now lying idle, divide and sell them out at a reasonable price, it will give so many people work. I will guarantee to find persons to work every five acres. I will also guarantee that after one year's time, the Freedman's Bureau will not have to give any man having one acre of land anything to eat. This country has a genial clime, rich soil, and can be worked to advantage. The man who can not earn a living on five acres, will not do so on twenty-five.

I regret that another position taken by gentlemen in the opposition, is that they do not believe that we will get what we ask for. I believe that the party now in power in the Congress of the United States, will do whatever they can for the welfare of the people of this State and of the South. I believe that the noble men who have maintained the rights of the freedmen before and since their liberation, will continue to do everything possible to forward these great interests. I am exceedingly anxious, if possible, to allay all unpleasant feeling—I would not have any unpleasant feeling among ourselves.

I would not have any unpleasant feelings between the races. If we give each family in the State an opportunity of purchasing a home, I think they will all be better satisfied.

But it is also said that it will disturb all the agricultural operations in the State. I do not believe if the Congress of the United States shall advance one million of dollars to make purchase of lands, the laborers will abandon their engagement and run off. I have more confidence in the people I represent. I believe all who have made contracts will fulfill those contracts, and when their contracts have expired, they will go on their own lands, as all freemen ought to go.

Source: *Proceedings of the South Carolina Constitutional Convention of 1868* (Charleston, SC, 1868), 420–21.

DOCUMENT 14.7

Ellen Parton | Testimony on Klan Violence, 1871

In March 1871, white mobs killed some thirty African Americans in Meridian, Mississippi. Later that month, a joint committee of the Mississippi legislature held hearings on the violence, which included the following testimony by Ellen Parton of Mississippi, a former slave and domestic worker. The Klan suspected that Parton's husband was involved in the Union League, a southern affiliate of the Republican Party. Congress also conducted hearings on the vigilante violence against blacks throughout the South.

Ellen Parton, being sworn, states:

I reside in Meridian; have resided here nine years; occupation, washing and ironing and scouring; Wednesday night was the last night they came to my house; by "they" I mean bodies or companies of men; they came on Monday, Tuesday, and Wednesday. On Monday night they said that they came to do us no harm. On Tuesday night they said they came for the arms; I told them there was none, and they said they would take my word for it. On Wednesday night they came and broke open the wardrobe and trunks, and committed rape upon me; there were eight of them in the house; I do not know how many there were outside; they were white men; there was a light in the house; I was living in Marshal Ware's house; there were three lights burning. Mr. Ware has been one of the policemen of this town. He was concealed at the time they came; they took the claw hammer and broke open the pantry where he was lying; he was concealed in the pantry under some plunder, covered up well; I guess he covered himself up. A man said "here is Marshal's hat, where is Marshal?" I told him "I did not know"; they went then into everything in the house, and broke open the wardrobe; I called upon Mr. Mike Slamon, who was one of the crowd, for protection; I said to him "please protect me tonight, you have known me for a long time." This man covered up his head then; he had a hold of me at this time; Mr. Slamon had an oil-cloth and put it before his face, trying to conceal himself, and the man that had hold of me told me not to call Mr. Slamon's name any more. He then took me in the dining room, and told me that I had to do just what he said: I told him I could do nothing of that sort; that was not my way, and he replied "by God, you have got to," and then threw me down. This man had a black eye, where some one had beaten him; he had a black velvet cap on. After he got through with me he came through the house, and said that he was after the Union Leagues; I yielded to him because he had a pistol drawn; when he took me down he hurt me of course; I yielded to him on that account.

Source: *Report of the Joint Select Committee [of Congress] to Inquire into the Condition of Affairs in the Late Insurrectionary States, Mississippi* (Washington, D.C.: Government Printing Office, 1872), 1:38–39.

DOCUMENT 14.8

The Force Act, 1871

As testimony of antiblack violence mounted, Congress passed the Force Act (also known as the Ku Klux Klan Act) in April 1871. A federal response to stop the terror and intimidation of southern black and white Republicans by their opponents, the act provided both civil relief for damages and criminal penalties. It was rooted in the Fourteenth Amendment's guarantees of the rights and privileges of U.S. citizenship. The federal government dispatched troops to enforce the law and prosecuted hundreds of Klan members, often before predominantly black juries, resulting in the breakup of the Klan within a few years.

B e it enacted . . . That any person who, under color of any law, statute, ordinance, regulation, custom, or usage of any State, shall subject, or cause to be subjected, any person within the jurisdiction of the United States to the deprivation of any rights, privileges, or immunities secured by the Constitution of the United States, shall, any such law, statute, ordinance, regulation, custom, or usage of the State to the contrary notwithstanding, be liable to the party injured in any action at law, suit in equity, or other proper proceeding for redress; such proceeding to be prosecuted in the several district or circuit courts of the United States, with and subject to the same rights of appeal, review upon error, and other remedies provided in like cases in such courts, under the provisions of the [Civil Rights Act of 1866], and the other remedial laws of the United States which are in their nature applicable in such cases. . . .

Sec. 3. That in all cases where insurrection, domestic violence, unlawful combinations, or conspiracies in any State shall so obstruct or hinder the execution of the laws thereof, and of the United States, as to deprive any portion or class of the people of such State of any of the rights, privileges, or immunities, or protection, named in the Constitution and secured by this act, and the constituted authorities of such State shall either be unable to protect, or shall, from any cause, fail in or refuse protection of the people in such rights, such facts shall be deemed a denial by such State of the equal protection of the laws to which they are entitled under the Constitution of the United States; and in all such cases, or whenever any such insurrection, violence, unlawful combination, or conspiracy shall oppose or obstruct the laws of the United States or the due execution thereof, or impede or obstruct the due course of justice under the same, it shall be lawful for the President, and it shall be his duty to take such measures, by the employment of the militia or the land and naval forces of the United States, or of either, or by other means, as he may deem necessary for the suppression of such insurrection, domestic violence, or combinations. . . .

Sec. 6. That any person or persons, having knowledge that any of the wrongs conspired to be done and mentioned in the second section of this act are about to be committed, and having power to prevent or aid in preventing the same, shall neglect or refuse to do so, and such wrongful act shall be committed, such person or persons shall be liable to the person injured, or his legal representatives, for all damages caused by any such wrongful act which such first-named person or persons by reasonable diligence could have prevented.

Source: George P. Sanger, ed., *Statutes at Large and Proclamations of the United States of America from March 1871 to March 1873* (Boston: Little, Brown, 1873), 13–15.

DOCUMENT 14.9

Thomas Nast | Colored Rule in a Reconstructed (?) State, 1874

COLORED RULE IN A RECONSTRUCTED (?) STATE.—[See Page 242.]
(THE MEMBERS CALL EACH OTHER THIEVES, LIARS, RASCALS, AND COWARDS.)
COLUMBIA. "You are Aping the lowest Whites. If you disgrace your Race in this way you had better take Back Seats."

Thomas Nast began drawing for the popular magazine *Harper's Weekly* in 1859. Nast initially used his illustrations to rouse northern public sentiment for the plight of blacks in the South after the Civil War. By 1874, however, many Northerners had become disillusioned with federal efforts to enforce Reconstruction. Like them, Nash accepted the white southern point of view that "Black Reconstruction" was a recipe for corruption and immorality. This cartoon imagines a raucous scene in the South Carolina legislature, where black legislators have taken over the floor and call each other "thieves, liars, rascals, and cowards." Note the figure of Columbia (at the top right), who represents the nation, chastising black lawmakers with a switch. Nast highlights Columbia's message in the caption: "You are Aping the lowest Whites. If you disgrace your Race in this way you had better take Back Seats."

DOCUMENT 14.10

What the Centennial Ought to Accomplish, 1875

The following editorial appeared in the northern periodical *Scribner's Journal*. A year before the celebration of the nation's centennial, Northerners as well as Southerners were calling for national unity and reconciliation, and thus a true end to Reconstruction. Rather than dwelling on the "Lost Cause," the magazine's editors remind southern readers of the glories of the old nation as celebrated by former Confederate president Jefferson Davis in recalling the national unity during the victorious Mexican-American War.

WE ARE TO HAVE grand doings next year. There is to be an Exposition. There are to be speeches, and songs, and processions, and elaborate ceremonies and general rejoicings. Cannon are to be fired, flags are to be floated, and the eagle is expected to scream while he dips the tip of either pinion in the Atlantic and the Pacific, and sprinkles the land with a new baptism of freedom. . . .

. . . Before we begin our celebration of this event, would it not be well for us to inquire whether we have a nation? In a large number of the States of this country there exists not only a belief that the United States do not constitute a nation, but a theory of State rights which forbids that they ever shall become one. We hear about the perturbed condition of the Southern mind. We hear it said that multitudes there are just as disloyal as they were during the civil war. This, we believe, we are justified in denying. . . . They are not actively in rebellion, and they do not propose to be. They do not hope for the re-establishment of slavery. They fought bravely and well to establish their theory, but the majority was against them; and if the result of the war emphasized any fact, it was that *en masse* the people of the United States constitute a nation—indivisible in constituents, in interest, in destiny. The result of the war was without significance, if it did not mean that the United States constitute a nation which cannot be divided; which will not permit itself to be divided; which is integral, indissoluble, indestructible. . . . The great point with them is to recognize the fact that, for richer or poorer, in sickness and health, until death do us part, these United States constitute a nation; that we are to live, grow, prosper, and suffer together, united by bands that cannot be sundered.

Unless this fact is fully recognized throughout the Union, our Centennial will be but a hollow mockery. If we are to celebrate anything worth celebrating, it is the birth of a nation. If we are to celebrate anything worth celebrating, it should be by the whole heart and united voice of the nation. If we can make the Centennial an occasion for emphasizing the great lesson of the war, and universally assenting to the results of the war, it will, indeed, be worth all the money expended upon and the time devoted to it. . . .

A few weeks ago, Mr. Jefferson Davis, the ex-President of the Confederacy, was reported to have exhorted an audience to which he was speaking to be as loyal to the old flag of the Union now as they were during the Mexican War. If the South could know what music there was in these words to Northern ears—how grateful we were to their old chief for them—it would appreciate the strength of our longing for a complete restoration of the national feeling that existed when Northern and Southern blood mingled in common sacrifice on Mexican soil. This national feeling, this national pride, this brotherly sympathy *must be restored*; and accursed be any Northern or Southern man, whether in power or out of power, whether politician, theorizer, carpet-bagger, president-maker, or plunderer, who puts obstacles in the way of such a restoration. Men of the South, we want you. Men of the South, we long for the restoration of your peace and your prosperity. We would see your cities thriving, your homes happy, your plantations teeming with plenteous harvests, your schools overflowing, your wisest statesmen leading you, and all causes and all memories of discord wiped out forever. You do not believe this? Then you do not know the heart of the North. Have you cause of complaint against the politicians? Alas! so have we. Help us, as loving and loyal American citizens, to make our politicians better. Only remember and believe that there is nothing that the North wants so much to-day, as your recognition of the fact that the old relations between you and us are forever restored—that your hope, your pride, your policy, and your destiny are one with ours. Our children will grow up to despise our childishness, if we cannot do away with our personal hates so far, that in the cause of an established nationality we may join hands under the old flag.

To bring about this reunion of the two sections of the country in the old fellowship, should be the leading object of the approaching Centennial. A celebration of the national birth, begun, carried on, and finished by a section, would be a mockery and a shame. The nations of the world might well point at it the finger of scorn. The money expended upon it were better sunk in the sea, or devoted to repairing the waste places of the war. Men of the South, it is for you to say whether your magnanimity is equal to your valor—whether you are as reasonable as you are brave, and whether, like your old chief, you accept that definite and irreversible result of the war which makes you and yours forever members of the great American nation with us. Let us see to it, North and South, that the Centennial heals all the old wounds, reconciles all the old differences, and furnishes the occasion for such a reunion of the great American nationality, as shall make our celebration an expression of fraternal good-will among all sections and all States, and a corner-stone over which shall be reared a new temple to national freedom, concord, peace, and prosperity.

Source: "What the Centennial Ought to Accomplish," *Scribner's Monthly*, August 1875, 509–10.

Interpret the Evidence

1. How did the black codes (Document 14.5) attempt to reimpose bondage on former slaves?

2. Why did African Americans consider property holding a fundamental right (see Document 14.6)?

3. Under what circumstances did the Force Act (Document 14.8) authorize federal prosecutions?

4. Contrast the image of South Carolina's black politicians as presented in Richard Cain's speech (Document 14.6) and Thomas Nast's cartoon (Document 14.9).

5. Despite Ku Klux Klan intimidation and the fear it produced in African Americans, what does the testimony of Ellen Parton (Document 14.7) reveal about black attempts to resist it?

6. What sources of unity existed between the North and the South that would bring Reconstruction to an end (see Document 14.10)?

Put It in Context

- How much did Reconstruction transform the South and the nation? What were its limitations?

Private Collection/Peter Newark American Pictures/The Bridgeman Art Library

Library of Congress

Railroad construction crew, 1886.

Lone Wolf and his wife Etla, Kiowa Indians, c. 1860.

15
Frontier Encounters
1865–1896

Library of Congress

Nebraska family in front of sod house with cow on the hillside that forms the roof, 1887.

AMERICAN HISTORIES

As an adult, Phoebe Ann Moses embodied the excitement and adventure of the mythical American West. Her childhood, however, was one of poverty and hardship. Born in 1860, Phoebe Ann grew up east of the Mississippi, seventy miles north of Cincinnati, Ohio. One of seven surviving children, she was sent to an orphanage at the age of nine, after her father died and her mother could not care for all her children. After working for a farm family, she ran away at the age of twelve and found a new home with a recently remarried widow. Over the next four years, Phoebe Ann learned to ride and hunt and became an expert shot with a rifle. At fifteen, she entered a shooting contest and defeated a professional marksman, Frank Butler. The competition sparked a romance, and the two married in 1876. Phoebe Ann changed her professional name to "Annie Oakley," and she and Butler went on tour throughout the Midwest in an act that featured precision shooting.

In 1884 Oakley and Butler met William F. "Buffalo Bill" Cody in New Orleans. Cody had been a buffalo hunter on the Great Plains and an army scout during the Indian wars of the 1870s. In 1883, as the western frontier began to recede and the U.S. government relocated Native Americans who lived there, Cody attempted to recapture and reinvent the frontier experience by staging "Wild West" shows. A year later, he hired Oakley, with Butler serving as her manager. For the next fifteen years, the diminutive Oakley was the star of the show. Wearing a fringed skirt, an embroidered blouse, and a broad felt hat emblazoned with a star, she stood atop her horse and shot the lights out of a revolving wheel of lit candles and took dead aim at other targets tossed in the air. Oakley toured Europe and fascinated heads of state and audiences alike with her version of "western authenticity." Fans at home and overseas displayed great nostalgia for a fast-diminishing era. When the census of 1890 reported that no open land was left to settle and thus no western frontier was left to conquer, Oakley's popularity soared. She continued performing in Wild West shows until her death in 1926.

While Annie Oakley portrayed the Wild West, Geronimo had lived it. Born to a Chiricahua Apache family in what was then northern Mexico (present-day Arizona and New Mexico), Geronimo led Apaches in a constant struggle against Spain, Mexico, and the United States. Driven to the hills of Arizona and New Mexico by Spanish conquistadors centuries before Geronimo was born, Apaches raided settlements to support themselves. In 1851 a band of Mexicans raided an Apache camp, murdering Geronimo's mother, wife, and three children. After fighting Mexicans, Geronimo clashed with U.S. troops and evaded capture until 1877, when an Indian agent arrested him in New Mexico. Sent to a reservation, Geronimo escaped and for eight years engaged in daring raids against his foes. In 1886 two Chiricahua scouts recruited by General Nelson Miles led the military to Geronimo. Against an army of five thousand soldiers, the Apache warrior, with a band of eighteen fighters and some women and children, finally surrendered and was eventually relocated by the U.S. government to Fort Sill, Oklahoma.

The once-elusive warrior decided to take advantage of his legendary reputation. With Buffalo Bill cashing in on America's fascination with the mythic West and "savage" Indians, Geronimo, like Annie Oakley, exploited this appeal. He sold photos of himself and pieces of his clothing; he appeared at the 1904 World's Fair in St. Louis, selling bows and arrows and autographs; and in 1905 he rode in President Theodore Roosevelt's inaugural parade as an example of a "tamed" Indian. Although he converted to Christianity, Geronimo, ever the rebel, was later expelled from his church for gambling. Crass commercialism and religious conversion aside, Geronimo never gave up the idea of returning to his birthplace. As long as the U.S. government prohibited him from going back to his ancestral lands in the Southwest, he considered himself a "prisoner of war." And so he remained until his death in 1909. •

AS PROFOUNDLY DIFFERENT as Annie Oakley's and Geronimo's individual histories were, they both contributed to the creation of a shared story, the myth of the American West. The West has great fascination in American culture. Stories about the frontier have romanticized both cowboys and Indians. These stories have also glorified individualism, self-help, and American ingenuity and minimized cooperation, organization, and the role of foreign influence in developing the West. As the American histories of Annie Oakley and Geronimo make clear, reality presents a more complicated picture of a diverse region initially inhabited by native peoples who were pushed aside by the arrival of white settlers and immigrants. In the areas known as the Great Plains and the far West, women took on new roles, and new cities emerged to accommodate the influx of miners, ranchers, and farmers.

Opening the West

The lands west of the Mississippi were not hospitable to farmers and other adventurers lured by the appeal of cheap land and a fresh start. These pioneers faced many challenges with rugged determination; however, they could not have settled the West on their own. Federal policy and foreign investment played a large role in encouraging and financing the development of the West. Railroads were essential in transforming the region (Map 15.1).

The Great Plains

In the mid-nineteenth century, the western frontier lay in the **Great Plains**. This region spreads through present-day North and South Dakota, Nebraska, Kansas, Oklahoma, Texas, Montana, Wyoming, Colorado, New Mexico, Idaho, Utah, Arizona, and Nevada. Lying on both sides of the Rocky Mountains, the Great Plains plateau was a semiarid territory with an average yearly rainfall of twenty inches, enough to sustain short grasslands but not many trees. Bison, pronghorn antelope, jack rabbits, and prairie dogs roamed over great distances to nourish themselves on the sparse vegetation that grew in this delicate ecosystem.

Grasshoppers and locusts periodically swarmed into the area. Indian hunters in the very dry central and southern plains—Apache, Arapaho, Cheyenne, Comanche, Kiowa—opened up these lands to human habitation and survived by hunting and cultivating the grasslands.

Prospects for sedentary farmers in this dry region did not appear promising. In 1878 geologist John Wesley Powell issued a report that questioned whether the land beyond the easternmost portion of the Great Plains could support small farming. Lack of rainfall, he argued, would make it difficult or even impossible for homesteaders to support themselves on family farms of 160 acres. Instead, he recommended that for the plains to prove economically sustainable, settlers would have to work much larger stretches of land, around 2,560 acres (4 square miles). This would provide ample room to raise livestock under dry conditions.

Powell's words of caution did little to diminish Americans' conviction, dating back to Thomas Jefferson, that small farmers would populate the territories brought under U.S. jurisdiction and renew democratic values as they ventured forth. Charles Dana Wilber, a booster of settlement in Nebraska, summed up the view of those who saw no barriers to the expansion of small farmers in the plains. Rejecting the idea that either a Divine Creator or nature had determined that these lands should remain a "perpetual desert," Wilber asserted that "in reality

MAP 15.1   The American West, 1860–1900

Railroads played a key role in the expansion and settlement of the American West. The network of railroads running throughout the West opened the way for extensive migration from the East and for the development of a national market. None of this would have been possible without the land grants provided to the railroads by the U.S. government.

there is no desert anywhere except by man's permission or neglect." Along with millions of others, he had great faith in Americans' ability to turn the Great Plains into a place where Jefferson's republican vision could take root and prosper.

Federal Policy and Foreign Investment

Despite the popular association of the West with individual initiative and self-sufficiency, the federal government played a huge role in facilitating the settlement of the West. National lawmakers enacted legislation offering free or cheap land to settlers and to mining, lumber, and railroad companies. The U.S. government also provided subsidies for transporting mail and military supplies, recruited soldiers to subdue the Indians who stood in the way of expansion, and appointed officials to govern the territories.

Along with federal policy, foreign investment helped fuel development of the West. Lacking sufficient funds of its own, the United States turned to Europe to finance the sale of public bonds and private securities. European financial houses held a majority ownership in the United States Mortgage Company and the Equitable Trust Company of New York, both of which bought and sold mortgages. European firms also invested in American mines, with the British leading the way. In 1872 an Englishman wrote that mines in Nevada were "more British than American." The development of the western cattle range—the symbol of the American frontier and the heroic cowboy—was also funded by overseas financiers. At the height of the cattle boom in the 1880s, British firms supplied some $45 million to underwrite ranch operations.

The largest share of money that flowed from Europe to the United States came with the expansion of the railroads, the most important ingredient in opening the West (Figure 15.1). The economist Joseph Schumpeter concluded that it was "primarily English (and other European) capital which took the responsibility for a great part of the $2 billion which are said to have been expended on American railroads from 1867 to 1873."

The **transcontinental railroad** became the gateway to the West. In 1862 the Republican-led Congress appropriated vast areas of land that railroad companies could use to lay their tracks or sell to raise funds for construction. The Central Pacific Company built from west to east, starting in Sacramento, California. The construction project attracted thousands of Chinese railroad workers, boosting the sparse population of the western territory. From the opposite direction, the Union Pacific Company began laying track in Council Bluffs, Iowa, and hired primarily Irish workers. In May 1869, the

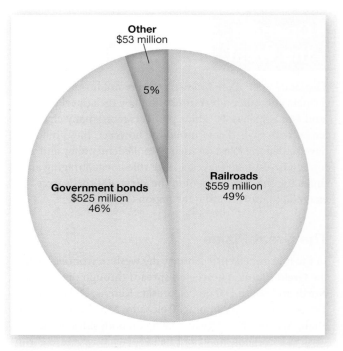

FIGURE 15.1   British Foreign Investment in the United States, 1876

British investment was an important source of funding for westward expansion following the Civil War. Nearly half of all British loans went toward financing railroad construction, which required large capital expenditures. The British also invested heavily in government bonds and to a lesser extent in cattle ranching and mining enterprises.

Source: Data from Mina Wilkins, *The History of Foreign Investment in the United States to 1914* (Cambridge, MA: Harvard University Press, 1989), 164.

Central Pacific and Union Pacific crews met at Promontory Point, Utah, amid great celebration. Workmen from the two companies drove a golden spike to complete the connection. For many Americans recovering from four years of brutal civil war and still embroiled in southern reconstruction (see chapter 14), the completion of the transcontinental railroad renewed their faith in the nation's ingenuity and destiny. A wagon train had once taken six to eight weeks to travel across the West. That trip could now be completed by rail in seven days. The railroad allowed both people and goods to move faster and in greater numbers than before. The West was now open not just to rugged pioneers but to anyone who could afford a railroad ticket.

The building of the railroads fostered corruption. Union Pacific promoters created a fake construction company called the Crédit Mobilier, which they used to funnel government bond and contract money into their own pockets. They also bribed congressmen to avoid investigation into their sordid dealings. Despite these efforts, in 1872 Congress exposed these wrongdoings.

Railroad Construction Crew
Chinese and other immigrant groups were instrumental in the construction of the transcontinental railroad. This Union Pacific construction crew includes a Chinese laborer standing in the center next to African American workers and a white foreman in the front left. The boulders in the rear show the massive rock formations and rugged terrain they had to blast through.   Denver Public Library, Western History Collection, E. & H. T. Anthony, Call Number Z-3335

REVIEW & RELATE

What role did the federal government play in opening the West to settlement and economic exploitation?

Explain the determination of Americans to settle in land west of the Mississippi River despite the challenges the region presented.

 LEARNINGCurve bedfordstmartins.com/hewittlawson/LC

Conquest of the Frontier

American pioneers may have thought they were moving into a wilderness, but the West was home to large numbers of American Indians. Before pioneers and entrepreneurs could go west to pursue their economic dreams, the U.S. government would have to remove this unwelcome obstacle to American expansion. Through treaties—most of which Americans broke—and war, white Americans conquered the Indian tribes inhabiting the Great Plains during the nineteenth century. After the native population was largely subdued, those who wanted to reform Indian policy focused on carving up tribal lands and forcing Indians to assimilate into American society.

Indian Civilizations

Long before white settlers appeared, the frontier was already home to diverse peoples. The many native groups who inhabited the West spoke distinct languages, engaged in different economic activities, and competed with one another for power and resources. The descendants of Spanish conquistadors had also lived in the Southwest and California since the late sixteenth century, pushing the boundaries of the Spanish empire northward from Mexico. Indeed, Spaniards established the city of Santa Fe as the territorial capital of New Mexico years before the English landed at Jamestown, Virginia, in 1607. The United States then acquired the New Mexican and California territories as spoils of the Mexican-American War in 1848.

By the end of the Civil War, around 350,000 Indians were living west of the Mississippi. They constituted the surviving remnants of the 1 million people who had occupied the land for thousands of years before Europeans set foot in America. Nez Percé, Ute, and Shoshone Indians lived in the Northwest and the Rocky Mountain region; Lakota, Cheyenne, Blackfoot, Crow, and Arapaho tribes occupied the vast expanse of the central and northern plains; and Apaches, Comanches, Kiowas, Navajos, and Pueblos made up the bulk of the population in the Southwest. Some of the tribes, such as the Cherokee, Creek, and Shawnee, had been forcibly removed from the East during Andrew

Jackson's presidency in the 1830s. The tribes each adapted in unique ways to the geography and climate of their home territories, spoke their own language, and had their own history and traditions. Some were hunters, others farmers; some nomadic, others sedentary. In New Mexico, the Apaches, including Geronimo, were expert horsemen and fierce warriors, while the Pueblo Indians built homes out of adobe and developed a flourishing system of agriculture. The lives of all Indian peoples were affected by the arrival of Europeans, but the consequences of cross-cultural contact varied considerably depending on the history and circumstances of each tribe (Map 15.2).

Given the rich assortment of Indian tribes, it is difficult to generalize about Indian culture and society. Pueblo Indians cultivated the land through methods of irrigation that foreshadowed modern practices. The Pawnees

periodically set fire to the land to improve game hunting and the growth of vegetation. Indians on the southern plains gradually became enmeshed in the market economy for bison robes, which they sold to American traders. Indians were not pacifists, and they engaged in warfare with their enemies in disputes over hunting grounds, horses, and honor. However, the introduction of guns by European and American traders had transformed Indian warfare into a much more deadly affair than had existed previously. And by the mid-nineteenth century, some tribes had become so deeply engaged in the commercial fur trade with whites that they had depleted their own hunting grounds.

Native Americans had their own approach toward nature and the land they inhabited. Most tribes did not accept private ownership of land, as white pioneers did. Indians recognized the concept of private property in

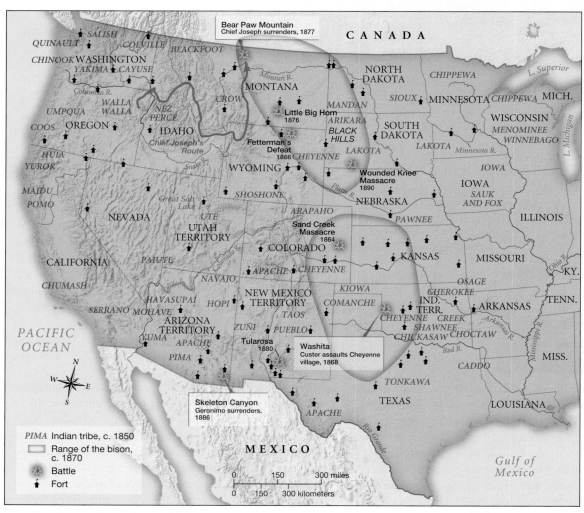

MAP 15.2   The Indian Frontier, 1870

Western migration posed a threat to the dozens of Indian tribes and the immense herds of bison in the region. The tribes had signed treaties with the U.S. government recognizing the right to live on their lands. The presence of U.S. forts did not protect the Indians from settlers who invaded their territories.

ownership of their horses, weapons, tools, and shelters, but they viewed the land as the common domain of their tribe, for use by all members. "The White man knows how to make everything," the Hunkpapa Lakota chieftain Sitting Bull remarked, "but he does not know how to distribute it." This communitarian outlook also reflected native attitudes toward the environment. They considered human beings not as superior to the rest of nature's creations, but rather as part of an interconnected world of animals, plants, and natural elements. Chief Joseph, leader of the Nez Percé Indians, explained to whites who tried to encroach on his land: "The country was made without lines of demarcation, and it's no man's business to divide it. . . . I see whites all over the country gaining wealth, and see their desire to give us lands that are worthless. . . . The earth and myself are of one mind. The measure of the land and the measure of our bodies are the same." According to this view, all plants and animals were part of a larger spirit world, which flowed from the power of the sun, the sky, and the earth.

The bison played a central role in Indian religion and society. By the mid-nineteenth century, approximately thirty million bison (commonly known as buffalo) grazed on the Great Plains. Before acquiring guns, Indians used a variety of means to hunt their prey, including bows and arrows and spears. Some rode their horses to chase bison and stampede them over cliffs. The meat from the buffalo provided food; its hide provided material to construct tepees and make blankets and clothes; bones were crafted into tools, knives, and weapons; even bison dung served a purpose—after it dried and hardened, "buffalo chips" became an excellent source of fuel. It is therefore not surprising that the Plains Indians dressed up in colorful outfits, painted their bodies, and danced to the almighty power of the buffalo and the spiritual presence within it.

Indian hunting societies contained gender distinctions, primarily around the use of horses to pursue bison. The task of riding horses to hunt bison became men's work; women waited for the hunters to return and then prepared the buffalo hides. Nevertheless, women refused to think of their role as passive: They saw themselves as sharing in the work of providing food, shelter, and clothing for the members of their tribe. Similarly, the religious belief that the spiritual world touched every aspect of the material world gave women an opportunity to experience this transcendent power without the mediation of male leaders, including the revered medicine men.

Changing Federal Policy toward Indians

The U.S. government started out by treating western Indians as autonomous nations, thereby recognizing their stewardship over the land they occupied. In 1851 the **Treaty of Fort Laramie** confined tribes on the northern plains to designated areas in an attempt to keep white

Buffalo Hunting

This pictograph from around 1875 depicts a Shoshone man on a buffalo hunt, affirming the personal connection between Indians and the buffalo. The successful hunter shows his skill as a horseman in this drawing made on his buffalo skin robe. The garment also includes a brightly ornamented quillwork strip at the top.   © Werner Forman/TopFoto/The Image Works

settlers from encroaching on their land. A treaty two years later applied these terms to tribes on the southern plains. Indians kept their part of the agreement, but white miners racing to strike it rich did not. They roamed through Indian hunting grounds in search of ore and faced little government enforcement of the existing treaties. In fact, the U.S. military made matters considerably worse. On November 29, 1864, a peaceful band of 700 Cheyennes and Arapahos under the leadership of Chief Black Kettle gathered at Sand Creek, Colorado, supposedly under guarantees of U.S. protection. Instead, Colonel John M. Chivington and his troops launched an attack, despite a white flag of surrender hoisted by the Indians, and brutally scalped and killed some 270 Indians, mainly women and children. A congressional investigation later determined that the victims "were mutilated in the most horrible manner." Although there was considerable public outcry over the incident, as evidenced by the congressional investigation, the government did nothing to increase enforcement of its treaty obligations. In almost all disputes between white settlers and Indians, the government sided with the whites, regardless of the Indians' legal rights.

The duplicity of the U.S. government was not without consequences. The Sand Creek massacre unleashed Indian wars throughout the central plains, where the Lakota Sioux led the resistance from 1865 to 1868. In 1866 they killed eighty soldiers under the command of Captain William J. Fetterman in Wyoming. After two years of fierce fighting, both sides signed a second Treaty of Fort Laramie, which gave northern tribes control over the "Great Reservation" set aside in parts of present-day Montana, Wyoming, North Dakota, and South Dakota. Another treaty placed the southern tribes in a reservation carved out of western Oklahoma.

One of the tribes that wound up in Oklahoma was the Nez Percé. Originally settled in the corner where Washington, Oregon, and Idaho meet, the tribe was forced to sign a treaty ceding most of its land to the United States and to relocate onto a reservation. In 1877 Chief Joseph led the Nez Percé out of the Pacific Northwest, directing his people in an excruciating but daring march of 1,400 miles over mountains into Montana and Wyoming as federal troops pursued them. Intending to flee to Canada, the Nez Percé were finally intercepted in the mountains of northern Montana, just thirty miles from the border. Exhausted by the incredible journey, they surrendered. Subsequently, the government relocated these northwestern Indians to the southwestern territory of Oklahoma. In 1879 Chief Joseph pleaded with lawmakers in Congress to return his people to their home and urged the U.S. government to live up to the original intent of the treaties. His words carried some weight, and the Nez Percé returned under armed escort to a reservation in Washington.

The treaties did not produce a lasting peace. Though most of the tribes relocated onto reservations, some refused. The Apache chief Victorio explained why he would not resettle his people on a reservation. "We prefer to die in our own land under the tall cool pines," he declared. "We will leave our bones with those of our people. It is better to die fighting than to starve." General William Tecumseh Sherman, commander of the military forces against the Indians, issued orders to "push his measures for the utter destruction and subjugation of all who are outside the reservations in a hostile attitude." He went on to propose that the army "shall prosecute the war with vindictive earnestness against all hostile Indians till they are obliterated or beg for mercy." In November 1868, Lieutenant Colonel George Armstrong Custer took Sherman at his word and assaulted a Cheyenne village, killing more than one hundred Indians. Nearly a decade later, in 1876, the Indians, this time Lakota Sioux, exacted revenge by killing Custer and his troops at the **Battle of the Little Big Horn** in Montana. Yet this proved to be the final victory for the Lakota nation, as the army mounted an extensive and fierce offensive against them that shattered their resistance.

Among the troops that battled the Indians were African Americans. Known as "**buffalo soldiers**," a name given to them by the Indians but whose origin is unclear, they represented a cross section of the postwar black population looking for new opportunities that were now available after their emancipation. One enlisted man recalled: "I got tired of looking mules in the face from sunrise to sunset. Thought there must be a better livin' in this world." Some blacks enlisted to learn how to read and write; others sought to avoid unpleasant situations back home. Cooks, waiters, painters, bakers, teamsters, and farmers signed up for a five-year stint in the army at $13 a month. A few gained more glory than money. In May 1880, Sergeant George Jordan of the Ninth Cavalry led troops under his command to fend off Apache raids in Tularosa, New Mexico, for which he was awarded the Congressional Medal of Honor.

Indian Defeat

By the late 1870s, Indians had largely succumbed to U.S. military supremacy. The tribes, as their many victories demonstrated, contained agile horsemen and skilled warriors, but the U.S. army was backed by the power of an increasingly industrial economy. Telegraph lines and railroads provided logistical advantages in the swift deployment of U.S. troops and the ability of the central command to communicate with field officers. Although Indians had acquired firearms over the years from American traders as well as from defeated enemies on the battlefield, the army boasted an essentially unlimited supply of superior weapons. The diversity of Indians and historic rivalries among tribes also made it difficult for them to unite against their common enemy. The federal government exploited these divisions by hiring Indians to serve as army scouts against their traditional tribal foes.

In addition to federal efforts to subdue Indians, other disasters devastated native peoples in the second half of the nineteenth century. Even before the Civil War, many Indians had died of diseases such as smallpox, cholera, scarlet fever, and measles, for which they lacked the immunity that Europeans and white Americans had acquired. Moreover, Indian policy was fundamentally flawed by cultural misunderstanding. Even the most sensitive white administrators of Indian affairs considered Indians a degraded race, in accordance with the scientific thinking of the time. At most, whites believed that Indians could be lifted to a higher level of civilization, which in practice meant a withering away of their traditional culture and heritage. See Document Project 15: American Indians and Whites on the Frontier, page 484.

The wholesale destruction of the bison was the final blow to Indian independence. As railroads pushed their tracks beyond the Mississippi, they cleared bison from their path by sending in professional hunters with high-powered rifles to shoot the animals. Buffalo Bill Cody built his reputation by working as a crack sharpshooter for the Kansas Pacific Railroad. At the same time, buffalo products such as shoes, coats, and hats became fashionable in the East. By the mid-1880s, hunters had killed more than thirteen million bison. As a result of the relentless move of white Americans westward and conspicuous consumption back east, bison herds were almost annihilated.

Faced with decimation of the bison, broken treaties, and their opponents' superior military technology, Native Americans' capacity to wage war collapsed. Indians had little choice but to settle on shrinking reservations that the government established for them. The absence of war, however, did not necessarily bring them security. In the late 1870s, gold discoveries in the Black Hills of North Dakota ignited another furious rush by miners who swooped into the sacred lands supposedly guaranteed to the Lakota people. Rather than honoring its treaties, the U.S. government forced the tribes to relinquish still more land. Government officials continued to encourage western expansion by white settlers despite previous agreements with the Indians. General Custer's Seventh Cavalry was part of the military force trying to push Indians out of this mining region, when it was annihilated at the Little Big Horn in 1876. Elsewhere, Congress opened up a portion of western Oklahoma to white homesteaders in 1889. Although this land had not been assigned to specific tribes relocated in Indian Territory, more than eighty thousand Indians from various tribes lived there. This government-sanctioned land rush only added to the pressure from homesteaders and others to acquire more land at the expense of the Indians. A decade later, Congress officially ended Indian control of Indian Territory.

Reforming Indian Policy

As reservations continued to shrink under expansionist assault and government acquiescence, a movement arose to reform Indian policy. Largely centered in the East where few Indians lived, reformers came to believe that the future welfare of Indians lay not in sovereignty but in assimilation. In 1881 Helen Hunt Jackson published *A Century of Dishonor*, her exposé of the unjust treatment the Indians had received, including broken promises and fraudulent activities by government agents. Roused by this depiction of the Indians' plight, groups such as the Women's National Indian Association joined with ministers and philanthropists to advocate the transformation of native peoples into full-fledged Americans.

From today's vantage point, these well-intentioned reformers could be viewed as contributing to the demise of

the Indians by trying to eradicate their cultural heritage. Judged by the standards of their own time, however, they truly wanted to save the Indians from the brutality and corrupt behavior they had endured, and they honestly believed they were acting in the Indians' best interests. The most advanced thinking among anthropologists at the time offered an approach that supported assimilation as the only alternative to extinction. The influential Lewis Morgan, author of *Ancient Society* (1877), concluded that all cultures evolved through three stages: savagery, barbarism, and civilization. Indians occupied the lower rungs, but reformers argued that by adopting white values they could become civilized. In effect, this would mean the cultural extermination of the Indians, but reformers such as Richard Henry Pratt, the founder of the Carlisle Indian School, stressed salvation as their motive. "Do not feed America to the Indian, which is tribalizing and not an Americanizing process," he wrote, "but feed the Indian to America, and America will do the assimilating and annihilate the problem."

Reformers such as Pratt faced opposition from white Americans who doubted that Indian assimilation was possible. For many Americans, secure in their sense of their own superiority, the decline and eventual extinction of the Indian peoples was an inevitable consequence of what they saw as Indians' innate inferiority. For example, a Wyoming newspaper predicted: "The same inscrutable Arbiter that decreed the downfall of Rome has pronounced the doom of extinction upon the red men of America." And it warned: "To pretend to defer this by mawkish sentimentalism . . . is unworthy of the age."

Reformers found their legislative spokesman in Senator Henry Dawes of Massachusetts. As legislative director of the Boston Indian Citizenship Association, Dawes shared Christian reformers' belief that becoming a true American would save both the Indians and the soul of the nation. "Soon I trust," Dawes remarked, "we will wipe out the disgrace of our past treatment and lift the [Indian] up into citizenship and manhood and cooperation with us to the glory of the country." A Republican who had served in Congress since the Civil War, Dawes had the same paternalistic attitude toward Indians as he had toward freed slaves. He believed that if both degraded groups worked hard and practiced thrift and individual initiative in the spirit of Dawes's New England Puritan forebears, they would succeed. The key for Dawes was private ownership of land.

Passed in 1887, the **Dawes Act** ended tribal rule and divided Indian lands into 160-acre parcels. The act allocated one parcel to each family head. The government held the lands in trust for the Indians for twenty-five years; at the end of this period, the Indians would receive American citizenship. In return, the Indians had to abandon their religious and cultural rites and practices, including storytelling and the use of medicine men. Whatever lands remained after this reallocation—and the amount was considerable—would be sold on the open market, and the profits from the sales would be placed in an educational fund for Indians.

Unfortunately, like most of the policies it replaced, the Dawes Act proved detrimental to Native Americans. Indian families received inferior farmlands and inadequate tools to cultivate them, while speculators reaped profits from the sale of the "excess" Indian lands. A little more than a decade after the Dawes Act went into effect, Indians controlled 77 million acres of land, down sharply from the 155 million acres they held in 1881. Additional legislation in 1891 forced Indian parents to send their children to boarding schools or else face arrest. At these educational institutions, Indian children were given "American" names, had their long hair cut, and wore uniforms in place of their native dress. The program for boys provided manual and vocational training and that for girls taught domestic skills, so that they could emulate the gender roles in middle-class American families. However, this schooling offered few skills of use in an economic world undergoing industrial transformation. The students "found themselves in a twilight world," one historian claimed. "They were not equipped or allowed to enter American society as equals, yet they had been subjected to sufficient change as to make returning to the reservations difficult and sometimes traumatic."

Indian Assimilation and Resistance

Not all Indians conformed to the government's attempt at forced acculturation. Some refused to abandon their traditional social practices, and others rejected the white man's version of private property and civilization. Many displayed more complicated approaches to survival in a world that continued to view Indians with prejudice. Geronimo and Sitting Bull participated in pageants and Wild West shows but refused to disavow their heritage. Ohiyesa, a Lakota also known as Charles Eastman, went to boarding school, graduated from Dartmouth College, and earned a medical degree from Boston University. He supported passage of the Dawes Act, believed in the virtues of an American education, and worked for the Bureau of Indian Affairs. At the same time, he spoke out against government corruption and fraud perpetrated against Indians. Reviewing his life in his later years, Eastman/Ohiyesa reflected: "I am an Indian and while I have learned much from civilization . . . I have never lost my Indian sense of right and justice."

Disaster loomed for those who resisted assimilation and held on too tightly to the old ways. In 1888 the prophet Wovoka, a member of the Paiute tribe in western Nevada, had a vision that Indians would one day regain control of the world and that whites would disappear. He believed that the

Creator had provided him with a **Ghost Dance** that would make this happen. The dance spread to thousands of Lakota Sioux in the northern plains. Seeing the Ghost Dance as a sign of renewed Indian resistance, the army attempted to put a stop to the revival. On December 29, 1890, the Seventh Cavalry, Custer's old regiment, chased three hundred ghost dancers to Wounded Knee Creek on the Pine Ridge Reservation in present-day South Dakota. In a confrontation with the Lakota leader Big Foot, a gunshot accidentally rang out during a struggle with one of his followers. The cavalry then turned the full force of their weaponry on the Indians. When the hail of bullets ceased, about 250 Native Americans, many of them women and children, lay dead.

The message of the massacre at Wounded Knee was clear for those who raised their voices against Americanization. As Black Elk, a spiritual leader of the Oglala Lakota tribe, asserted: "A people's dream died there. . . . There is no center any longer, and the sacred tree is dead." It may not have been the policy of the U.S. government to exterminate the Indians as a people, but it was certainly U.S. policy to destroy Indian culture and society once and for all.

REVIEW & RELATE

How and why did federal Indian policy change during the nineteenth century?

Describe some of the ways that Indian peoples responded to federal policies. Which response do you think offered their greatest chance for survival?

✓ *LEARNINGCurve* bedfordstmartins.com/hewittlawson/LC

The Mining Frontier

Among the settlers pouring into Indian Territory in the Rocky Mountains were miners in search of gold and silver. These prospectors envisioned instant riches that would come from a lucky strike. The vast majority found only backbreaking work, danger, and frustration. Miners continued to face hardship and danger as industrial mining operations took over from individual prospectors, despite the efforts of some miners to fight for better wages and working conditions. By 1900 the mining rush had peaked, and many of the boomtowns that had cropped up around the mining industry had emptied out.

The Business of Mining

The discovery of gold in California in 1848 had set this mining frenzy in motion. Over the next thirty years, successive waves of gold and silver strikes in Colorado, Nevada,

Washington, Idaho, Montana, and the Dakotas lured individual prospectors with shovels and wash pans. One of the biggest finds came with the **Comstock Lode** in the Sierra Nevada. All told, miners extracted around $350 million worth of silver from this source. Two of those who came to share in the wealth were Samuel Clemens and his brother Orion. Writing from Carson City, Nevada, Samuel described his new surroundings to his family: "The country is fabulously rich in gold, silver, copper, lead . . . thieves, murderers, desperadoes, ladies . . . lawyers, Christians, Indians, Chinamen, Spaniards, gamblers, sharpers, coyotes . . . poets, preachers, and jackass rabbits." He did not find his fortune in Nevada and soon turned his attention to writing, finally achieving success as the author called Mark Twain.

Like Twain, many of those who flocked to the Comstock Lode and other mining frontiers were men. Nearly half were foreign-born, many of them coming from Mexico or China. Using pans and shovels, prospectors could find only the ore that lay near the surface of the earth and water. Once these initial discoveries were played out, individual prospectors could not afford to buy the equipment needed to dig out the vast deposits of gold and silver buried deep in the earth. As a result, western mining operations became big businesses run by men with the financial resources necessary to purchase industrial mining equipment.

Explore

See Document 15.1 for a description of a gold rush town.

When mining became an industry, prospectors became wageworkers. In Virginia City, Nevada, miners labored for $4 a day, which was a decent wage for the time, but one that barely covered the monthly expenses of life in a mining boomtown. Moreover, the work was extremely dangerous. Mine shafts extended down more than a thousand feet, and working temperatures regularly exceeded 100 degrees Fahrenheit. Noxious fumes, fires, and floods of scalding water flowing through the shafts posed a constant threat. Between 1863 and 1880, at least three hundred miners died on the job, and accidents were a daily occurrence, leaving many men disabled and out of work with no compensation.

Struggling with low pay and dangerous work conditions, western miners sought to organize. In the mid-1860s, unions formed in the Comstock Lode areas of Virginia City and Gold Hill, Nevada. Although these unions had some success, they also provoked a violent backlash from mining companies determined to resist union demands. Companies hired private police forces to help break strikes. Such forces were often assisted by state militias deployed by elected officials with close ties to the companies. For example, in 1892 the governor of Idaho crushed an unruly strike by calling up the National Guard, a confrontation that resulted in the deaths of seven strikers. A year later, mine workers

formed one of the most militant labor organizations in the nation, the Western Federation of Miners. Within a decade, it had attracted fifty thousand members. However, union solidarity did not extend to all races and ethnicities. The union was made up of members from Irish, English, Italian, Slavic, and Greek backgrounds but excluded Chinese, Mexican, and Indian workers from its ranks.

Life in the Mining Towns

Men worked the mines, but women flocked to the area as well. In Storey County, Nevada, the heart of the Comstock Lode, the 1875 census showed that women made up about half the population. Most employed women worked long hours as domestics in boardinghouses, hotels, and private homes. Prostitution, which was legal, accounted for the single largest segment of the female workforce. Most prostitutes were between the ages of nineteen and twenty-four, and they entered this occupation because few other well-paying jobs were available to them. The demand for their services remained high among the large population of unmarried men. Yet prostitutes faced constant danger, and many were victims of physical abuse, robbery, and murder.

Boomtowns like Virginia City sported a wild assortment of miners. They sought relief in taverns, brothels, and opium

Prostitution on the Frontier

Prostitution was one of the main sources of employment for women in frontier mining towns. A legal enterprise, it paid better than other work such as domestic service and teaching. In 1875 in the Comstock region of Nevada, 307 women plied their trade in brothels and saloons similar to the saloon shown here.

The Art Archive/Bill Manns/Art Resource, NY

DOCUMENT 15.1

Granville Stuart | Gold Rush Days, 1925

When the gold rush began in the West, Granville Stuart and his brother were among those who flooded into Montana in 1863 and struck it rich. News of their discovery set off a stampede of prospectors seeking their fortune. A second Virginia City sprang up in Montana to house the miners and the assortment of business people who served them. Gold dust, valued at $18 an ounce, became the medium of exchange. Stuart published his journals and reminiscences from his gold rush days sixty-two years later in 1925.

Explore

About the middle of January, 1864, a regular stampede craze struck Virginia City. The weather had been quite cold and work in the mines was temporarily suspended. A large number of idle men were about town and it required no more than one man with an imaginative mind to start half the population off on a wild goose chase. Somebody would say that somebody said, that somebody had found a good thing and without further inquiry a hundred or more men would start out for the reported diggings. . . .

Late in the evening on January 22, a rumor started that a big discovery had been made on Wisconsin creek, a distance of thirty miles from Virginia City. The report said that as much as one hundred dollars to the pan had been found; and away the people flew all anxious to be first on the ground, where they could "just shovel up gold." Virginia City was almost deserted: men did not stop for horses, blankets, or provisions, the sole aim was to get there first and begin to shovel it out at the rate of one hundred to the pan. Fortunately the distance was not great and the weather was mild. Robert Dempsey had a ranch nearby and the stampeders got a supply of beef from him to last them back to town. It is needless to say that they found no diggings and all returned to Virginia [City] in a few days.

Source: Granville Stuart, *Forty Years on the Frontier as Seen in the Journals and Reminiscences of Granville Stuart, Gold-Miner, Trader, Merchant, Rancher, and Politician*, ed. Paul C. Phillips (Cleveland: Arthur H. Clark, 1925), 1:270–71.

Interpret the Evidence

- How did the expectations of newly arrived prospectors differ from reality?
- How would you characterize Stuart's attitude toward the scenes he describes?

Put It in Context

As western towns grew more crowded and the mining process became more complex, who profited from the frenzied atmosphere of mining regions?

dens. In Butte, Montana, miners frequented bars with such colorful names as "Bucket of Blood," "The Cesspool," and "Graveyard." They boarded in houses run by characters nicknamed "Mag the Rag," "Take-Five Annie," "Ellen the Elephant," and "The Racehorse." A folk tune described Butte's annual gala event, the "Hopheads' [drug addicts'] Ball":

All the junkies were invited
Yes every gink [skinny man] and muff [prostitute]
Not a single one was slighted
If they were on the stuff [opium].

Invitations were presented
To every hustler and her man.
They even sent up invites
To the hopheads in the can [jail].

As early as the 1880s, gold and silver discoveries had played out in the Comstock Lode. Boomtowns, which had sprung up almost overnight, now became ghost towns as gold and silver deposits dwindled. Even more substantial places like Virginia City, Nevada, experienced a severe decline as the veins of ore ran out. One revealing sign of the city's plummeting fortunes was the drop in the number of prostitutes, which declined by more than half by 1880. The mining frontier then shifted from gold and silver to copper, lead, and zinc, centered in Montana and Idaho. As with the early prospectors in California and Nevada, these miners eventually became wageworkers for giant consolidated mining companies. By the end of the nineteenth century, the Amalgamated Copper Company and the American Smelting and Refining Company dominated the industry.

Mining towns that survived, like Butte, became only slightly less rowdy places, but they did settle into more complex patterns of urban living. Though the population remained predominantly young and male, the young men were increasingly likely to get married and raise families. Residents lived in neighborhoods divided by class and ethnicity. For example, in Butte the west side of town became home to the middle and upper classes. Mine workers lived on the east side in homes subdivided into apartments and in boardinghouses. "The houses were almost skin to skin," one resident described the area, "and boy, there were kids all over in the neighborhood." The Irish lived in one section; Finns, Swedes, Serbs, Croatians, and Slovenes in other sections. Each group formed its own social, fraternal, and religious organizations to relieve the harsh conditions of overcrowding, poor sanitation, and discrimination. Residents of the east side relied on one another for support and frowned on those who deviated from their code of solidarity. "They didn't try to outdo the other one," one neighborhood woman remarked. "If you did, you got into trouble. . . . If they thought you were a little richer than they were, they wouldn't associate with you." Although western mining towns retained distinctive qualities, in their social and ethnic divisions they came to resemble older cities east of the Mississippi River.

REVIEW & RELATE

How and why did the nature of mining in the West change during the second half of the nineteenth century?

How did miners and residents of mining towns reshape the frontier landscape?

☑ *LEARNINGCurve* bedfordstmartins.com/hewittlawson/LC

Ranching and Farming Frontiers

Ranchers and farmers heading west also faced harsh realities. Cowboys worked long hours in tough but boring conditions on the open range. Farmers endured great hardships in trying to raise crops in an often inhospitable climate. Women played a critical role as pioneers, often setting out to acquire their own land or helping to run the family farm. Falling crop prices, however, led to soaring debt and forced many farmers into bankruptcy and off their land. Despite difficult physical and economic conditions, many of these women and men showed grit and determination not only in surviving but in improving their lives as well.

The Life of the Cowboy

There is no greater symbol of the frontier West than the cowboy. As portrayed in novels and film, the cowboy hero was the essence of manhood, an independent figure who fought for justice and defended the honor and virtue of women. Never the aggressor, he fought to protect law-abiding residents of frontier communities. Having helped tame some wild western town, the cowboy rode off into the sunset in search of new frontiers to challenge him.

This romantic image excited generations of American readers and later movie and television audiences. In reality, cowboys' lives were much more mundane. Cowpunchers worked for paltry monthly wages, put in long days herding cattle, and spent part of the night guarding them on the open range. Their major task was to make the 1,500-mile **Long Drive** along the Chisholm Trail. Beginning in the late 1860s, cowboys moved cattle from ranches in Texas through Oklahoma to rail depots in Kansas towns such as Abilene and Dodge City; from there, cattle were shipped by train eastward to slaughterhouses in Chicago. Life along the trail was monotonous, and riders had to contend with bad weather, dangerous work, and disease.

Numbering around forty thousand and averaging twenty-four years of age, the cowboys who rode through the Great Plains from Texas to Kansas came from diverse backgrounds. The majority, about 66 percent, were white, predominantly southerners who had fought for the South during the Civil War. Most of the rest were divided evenly between Mexicans, who had first tended cattle during Spanish rule in the Southwest, and African Americans, some of whom were former slaves and others Union veterans of the Civil War.

Explore

See Documents 15.2 and 15.3 for two depictions of cowboy life.

Besides experiencing rugged life on the range, black and Mexican cowboys faced racial discrimination. Jim Perry, an African American who rode for the three-million-acre XIT

DOCUMENTS 15.2 AND 15.3

Cowboy Myths and Realities: Two Views

William F. Cody, known as "Buffalo Bill," had been a real-life bison hunter in the American West and an army scout in the Indian wars of the 1860s and 1870s. Drawing on his authentic adventures and his heroism, Cody helped romanticize the figures that populated the American frontier, especially the cowboys, through his Wild West shows, a poster from which is shown here. The diary entries of George C. Duffield present a more mundane description of cowboy life. Duffield drove cattle on the open range in 1866 from Texas, where they were bred, to Iowa, where they went to market.

Explore

15.2
Buffalo Bill's Wild West Show, 1893

15.3 George C. Duffield |
Diary of a Real Cowboy, 1866

12th

Hard Rain & Wind. Big stampede & here we are among the Indians with 150 head of Cattle gone. Hunted all day & the Rain pouring down with but poor success. Dark days are these to me. Nothing but Bread & Coffee. Hands all Growling & Swearing—everything wet & cold. Beeves [steers] gone. Rode all day & gathered all but 35 mixed with 8 other Herds. Last Night 5000 Beeves stampeded at this place & a general mix up was the result.

13th

finished separating our Cattle & Moved up 4 miles. Very warm day—

14th

Last night there was a terrible storm. Rain poured in torrents *all* night & up to 12 AM today. Our Beeves left us in the night but for *once* on the whole trip we found them *all* together near camp at day break. *All* the other droves as far as I can hear are scattered to the four winds. Our Other Herd was all gone. We are now 25 Miles from Ark River & it is Very High. We are water bound by two creeks & but Beef & Flour to eat, am not Homesick but Heart sick. . . .

16th

Last night was a dark Gloomey night but we made it all right. Today it is raining & we have crossed Honey creek & am informed that there is another creek 6 miles ahead swimming. Twelve o clock today it rained one Hour so hard that a creek close by rose 20 ft in the afternoon. All wet.

Source: George C. Duffield, "Driving Cattle from Texas to Iowa, 1866," *Annals of Iowa* 14, no. 4 (1924): 253–54.

Interpret the Evidence

- What does the placement of Cody's portrait in the poster suggest about the role of white men in the West?
- How does Duffield's experience of the West differ from that conveyed in the poster?

Put It in Context

Why do you think Americans remember Buffalo Bill's version of the West rather than Duffield's?

Ranch in Texas for more than twenty years, complained: "If it weren't for my damned old black face I'd have been boss of one of these divisions long ago." Mexican *vaqueros*, or cowboys, earned one-third to one-half the wages of whites, whereas blacks were usually paid on a par with whites. Because the cattle kingdoms first flourished during Reconstruction, racial discrimination and segregation carried over into the Southwest. On one drive along the route to Kansas, a white boss insisted that a black cowboy eat and sleep separately from whites and shot at him when he refused to heed this order. Another white trail driver admitted that blacks "were usually called on to do the hardest work around the outfit." Nevertheless, the close proximity in which cowboys worked and the need for cooperation to overcome the pitfalls of the long drive made it difficult to enforce rigid racial divisions on the open range.

Large ranchers benefited the most from the cowboys' grueling work. Spaniards had originally imported cattle into the Southwest, and by the late nineteenth century some 5 million Texas longhorn steers grazed in the area. Cattle that could be purchased in Texas for $3 to $7 fetched a price of $30 to $40 in Kansas. The extension of railroads across the West opened up a quickly growing market for beef in the East. The development of refrigerated railroad cars guaranteed that slaughtered meat could reach eastern consumers without spoiling. With money to be made, the cattle industry rose to meet the demand. Fewer than 40 ranchers owned more than 20 million acres of land. One ranch in Texas spanned 200 miles and stocked 150,000 steers annually. Easterners and Europeans joined the boom and invested money in giant ranches. By the mid-1880s, approximately 7.5 million head of cattle roamed the western ranges, and large cattle ranchers became rich. Cattle ranching had become fully integrated into the national commercial economy.

Then the bubble burst. Ranchers who were already raising more cattle than the market could handle increasingly faced competition from cattle producers in Canada and Argentina. Prices spiraled downward. Another source of competition came from homesteaders who moved into the plains and fenced in their farms with barbed wire, thereby reducing the size of the open range. Yet the greatest disaster occurred from 1885 to 1887. Two frigid winters, together with a torrid summer drought, destroyed 90 percent of the cattle on the northern plains of the Dakotas, Montana, Colorado, and Wyoming. Under these conditions, outside capital to support ranching diminished, and many of the great cattle barons went into bankruptcy. This economic collapse consolidated the remaining cattle industry into even fewer hands. Some of those forced out of business turned to raising sheep, which require less water and grass than cattle to survive. The cowboy, never more than a hired hand, became a laborer for large corporations.

Farmers Head West

The federal government played a major role in opening up the Great Plains to the farmers who eventually clashed with cattlemen. The Republican Party of Abraham Lincoln had opposed the expansion of slavery in order to promote the virtues of free soil and free labor for white men and their families. During the Civil War, preoccupation with battlefield losses did not stop the Republican-controlled Congress from passing the **Homestead Act**. As an incentive for western migration, the act established procedures for distributing 160-acre lots to western settlers, on condition that they develop and farm their land. What most would-be settlers did not know, however, was that lots of 160 acres were not suitable to conditions on the Great Plains. As geologist John Wesley Powell would demonstrate, the intensive techniques needed to farm 160-acre plots simply would not work in the harsh, dry climate of the Great Plains.

Reality did not deter pioneers and adventurers. In fact, weather conditions in the region temporarily fooled them. The decade after 1878 witnessed an exceptional amount of rainfall west of the Mississippi. Though not precisely predictable, this cycle of abundance and drought had been going on for millennia. One settler, convinced that Providence was smiling on Americans, remarked about the sudden burst of rain: "The Lord knowed we needed more land an' He's gone and changed the climate." In addition, innovation and technology bolstered dreams of success. Farmers planted heartier strains of wheat imported from Russia that survived the fluctuations of dry and wet and hot and cold weather. Machines produced by industrial laborers in northern factories to the east allowed farmers to plow tough land and harvest its yield. Steel-tipped plows, threshers, combines, and harvesters expanded production greatly, and windmills and pumping equipment provided sources of power and access to scarce water.

The people who accepted the challenge of carving out a new life were a diverse lot. The Great Plains attracted a large number of immigrants from Europe, some two million by 1900. Minnesota and the Dakotas welcomed communities of settlers from Sweden and Norway. Nebraska housed a considerable population of Germans, Swedes, Danes, and Czechs. About one-third of the people who migrated to the northern plains came directly from a foreign country. Many of the rest, both native-born and foreign-born, had lived in towns and villages along the Mississippi River before they decided to seek new opportunities farther west.

Railroads and land companies lured settlers to the plains with tales of the fabulous possibilities that awaited their arrival. The federal government had given railroads generous grants of public land on which to build their tracks as well as parcels surrounding the tracks that they could sell off to raise revenue for construction. Western railroads advertised in both the United States and Europe, proclaiming that migrants to the plains would find "the garden spot of the world." The land "will grow anything that any other country will grow, and with less work," the Rock Island Railroad announced, "because it rains here more than any other place, and at just the right time."

Having lured prospective settlers with exaggerated claims, railroads offered bargain rates to transport them to their new homes. Families and friends often journeyed together and rented an entire car on the train, known as "the immigrant car," in which they loaded their possessions, supplies, and even livestock. Often migrants came to the end of the rail line before reaching their destination. They completed the trip by wagon or stagecoach.

Commercial advertising alone did not account for the desire to journey westward. Settlers who had made the trip successfully wrote to relatives and neighbors back east and in the old country about the chance to start fresh. Linda Slaughter, the wife of an army doctor in the Dakotas, gushed: "The farms which have been opened in the vicinity of Bismarck have proven highly productive, the soil being kept moist by frequent rains. Vegetables of all kinds are grown with but little trouble." Descriptions of abundance, combined with a spirit of adventure, inspired Lucy Goldthorpe to claim a homestead near Epping in the Dakota Territory. "Even if you hadn't inherited a bit of restlessness and a pioneering spirit from your ancestors," she asserted, "it would have been difficult to ward off the excitement of the boom which, like the atmosphere, involved every conversation."

Those who took the chance shared a faith in the future and a willingness to work hard and endure misfortune. They found their optimism and spirits sorely tested. Despite the company of family members and friends, settlers faced a lonely existence on the vast expanse of the plains. Homesteads were spread out, and a feeling of isolation became a routine part of daily life.

With few trees around, early settlers constructed sod houses. These structures let in little light but a good deal of moisture, keeping them gloomy and damp. A Nebraskan who lived in this type of house jokingly remarked: "There was running water in our sod house. It ran through the

Women Homesteaders in Nebraska

The Chrisman sisters—Lizzie, Lutie, Jennie Ruth, and Hattie—are shown outside their sod house in 1886. They are among the thousands of homesteaders who moved west in the late nineteenth century and built homes from the only natural resource the Great Plains had in abundance: sod.　AP Photo roof." Bugs, insects, and rodents, like the rain, often found their way inside to make living in such shelters even more uncomfortable.

If these dwellings were bleak, the climate posed even greater challenges. The plains did experience an unusual amount of rainfall in the late 1870s and early 1880s, but severe drought quickly followed. A plague of grasshoppers ravaged the northern plains in the late 1870s, destroying fruit trees and plants. Intense heat in the summer alternated with frigid temperatures in the winter. The Norwegian American writer O. E. Rolvaag, in *Giants in the Earth* (1927), his epic novel about Norwegian settlement in the Great Plains, described the extreme hardships that accompanied the fierce weather: "Blizzards from out of the northwest raged, swooped down and stirred up a greyish-white fury, impenetrable to human eyes. As soon as these monsters tired, storms from the northeast were sure to come, bringing more snow."

Women Homesteaders

The women of the family were responsible for making these houses more bearable. Mothers and daughters were in charge of household duties, cooking the meals, canning fruits and vegetables, and washing and ironing clothing. Despite the drudgery of this work, women contributed significantly to the economic well-being of the family by occasionally taking in boarders and selling milk, butter, and eggs.

In addition, a surprisingly large number of single women staked out homestead claims by themselves. Some were young, unmarried women seeking, like their male counterparts, economic opportunity. Others were widows attempting to take care of their children after their husband's death. One such widow, Anne Furnberg, settled a homestead in the Dakota Territory in 1871. Born in Norway, she had lived with her husband and son in Minnesota. After her husband's death, the thirty-four-year-old Furnberg moved with her son near Fargo and eventually settled on eighty acres of land. She farmed, raised chickens and a cow, and sold butter and eggs in town. The majority of women who settled in the Dakotas were between the ages of twenty-one and twenty-five, most had never been married, and a majority were native-born children of immigrant parents. A sample of nine counties in the Dakotas shows that more than 4,400 women became landowners. Nora Pfundheler, a single woman, explained her motivation: "Well I was 21 and had no prospects of doing anything. The land was there, so I took it."

Explore

See Document 15.4 for a description of one Norwegian homesteader's experience.

Once families settled in and towns began to develop, women, married and single, directed some of their energies to moral reform and extending democracy on the frontier. Because of loneliness and grueling work, some men turned to alcohol for relief. Law enforcement in newly established communities was often no match for the saloons that catered to a raucous and drunken crowd. In their roles as wives, mothers, and sisters, many women tried to remove the source of alcohol-induced violence that disrupted both family relationships and public decorum. In Kansas in the late 1870s, women flocked to the state's Woman's Christian Temperance Union, founded by Amanda M. Way. Although they did not yet have the vote, in 1880 these women vigorously campaigned for a constitutional amendment that banned the sale of liquor.

Temperance women also threw their weight behind the issue of women's suffrage. In 1884 Kansas women established the statewide Equal Suffrage Association, which delivered to the state legislature a petition with seven thousand signatures in support of women's suffrage. Their attempt failed, but in 1887 women won the right to vote and run for office in all Kansas municipal elections. By the end of the nineteenth century, fifteen women had held city offices throughout the state. Julia Robinson, who campaigned for women's suffrage in Kansas, recalled the positive role that some men played: "My father had always said his family of girls had just as much right to help the government as if we were boys, and mother and he had always taught us to expect Woman Suffrage in our day." Kansas did not grant equal voting rights in state and national elections until 1912, but women obtained full suffrage before then in many western states.

Farming on the Great Plains

Surviving loneliness, drudgery, and the weather still did not guarantee financial success for homesteaders. In fact, the economic realities of farming on the plains proved formidable. Despite the image of yeomen farmers—individuals engaged in subsistence farming with the aid of wives and children—most agriculture was geared to commercial transactions. Few farmers were independent or self-reliant. Farmers depended on barter and short-term credit. They borrowed from banks to purchase the additional land necessary to make agriculture economically feasible in the semiarid climate. They also needed loans to buy machinery to help increase production and to sustain their families while they waited for the harvest.

Instead of raising crops solely for their own use, farmers concentrated on the cash crops of corn and wheat.

DOCUMENT 15.4

Gro Svendsen | Letter from a Homesteader, 1863

Many of the settlers who moved to Minnesota and the Dakotas migrated from northern Europe. Most did not speak English, left behind family members, and experienced geographical and emotional isolation. Women played a significant role in running farms, as shown in the following letter that Gro Svendsen wrote to her family in Norway about her life as a homesteader in Minnesota in 1863. Svendsen offers a typical account of the challenges many settlers faced.

Explore

Dear Parents, Sisters, and Brothers (always in my thoughts):

I have often thought that I ought to tell you about life here in the New World. Everything is so totally different from what it was in our beloved Norway. You never will really know what it's like, although you no doubt try to imagine what it might be. Your pictures would be all wrong, just as mine were.

What emotions does Svendsen express about her life in America?

I only wish that I could be with you to tell you all about it. Even if I were to write you countless pages, I still could not tell you everything.

I remember I used to wonder when I heard that it would be impossible to keep the milk here as we did at home. Now I have learned that it is indeed impossible because of the heat here in the summertime. One can't make cheese out of the milk because of flies, bugs, and other insects. I don't know the names of all these insects, but this I do know: If one were to make cheese here in the summertime, the cheese itself would be alive with bugs. Toward late autumn it should be possible to keep the milk. The people who have more milk than they need simply feed it to the hogs.

It's difficult, too, to preserve the butter. One must pour brine over it or salt it; otherwise it gets full of maggots. Therefore it is best, if one is not too far from town, to sell the butter at once. This summer we have been getting from eight to ten cents a pound. Not a great profit. For this reason people around here do not have many cows—just enough to supply the milk needed for the household. It's

What differences between life in Norway and life on the Great Plains does this letter indicate?

not wise to have more than enough milk, because the flies are everywhere. Even the bacon must be preserved in brine, and so there are different ways of doing everything. . . .

Why would Svendsen's relatives think she might be exaggerating?

I could tell you even more, but possibly many who read this letter may think I am exaggerating. I assure you that all that I have told you I have experienced myself. If they do not believe me, they should come over and find out for themselves.

Source: Gro Svendsen, *Frontier Mother: The Letters of Gro Svendsen*, ed. Pauline Farseth and Theodore Blegen (Northfield, MN: Norwegian-American Historical Association, 1950), 39–40.

Put It in Context

What particular challenges did homesteaders who emigrated from other countries face?

The price of these commodities depended on the impersonal economic forces of an international market that connected American farmers to growers and consumers throughout the world. When supply expanded and demand remained relatively stable during the 1880s and 1890s, prices fell. This deflation made it more difficult for farmers to pay back their loans, and banks moved to foreclose. Corn growers had a hedge against falling prices. By withholding some of their corn from market, they could feed it to their hogs, fatten them up, and sell them at higher prices. The reduction in the supply of corn caused prices to rise until it was worth selling corn again.

This "corn-hog cycle," however, did not benefit wheat growers. When prices plummeted, they had little choice but to raise more wheat in the hope that increased volume would yield more income. Instead, the expansion in supply, coming as it did from so many farmers, merely depressed prices further, leaving wheat farmers with debts they could not repay. Under these circumstances, almost half of the homesteaders in the Great Plains picked up and moved either to another farm or to a nearby city. Large operators bought up the farms they left behind and ran them like big businesses. As had been the case in mining and ranching, western agriculture was increasingly commercialized and consolidated over the course of the second half of the nineteenth century.

The federal government unwittingly aided this process of commercialization and consolidation, to the benefit of large companies. The government sought to make bigger plots of land available in regions where small farming had proven impractical. The Desert Land Act (1877) offered 640 acres to settlers who would irrigate the land, but it brought small relief for farmers because the land was too dry. These properties soon fell out of the hands of homesteaders and into those of cattle ranchers. The Timber and Stone Act (1878) allowed homesteaders to buy 160 acres of forestland at $2.50 an acre. Lumber companies hired "dummy entrymen" to file claims and then quickly transferred the titles and added the parcels to their growing tracts of woodland.

REVIEW & RELATE

| How did market forces contribute to the boom and bust of the cattle ranching industry? | How did women homesteaders on the Great Plains in the late nineteenth century respond to frontier challenges? |

LEARNINGCurve bedfordstmartins.com/hewittlawson/LC

Pushing Farther West

Some pioneers settled on the Great Plains or moved west for reasons beyond purely economic motives. The Mormons, for example, settled in Utah to find a religious home. The West Coast states of Washington, Oregon, and especially California, with their abundant resources and favorable climates, beckoned adventurers to travel beyond the Rockies and settle along the Pacific Ocean. The far West attracted many white settlers and foreign immigrants—especially Chinese—who encountered Spaniards and Mexicans already inhabiting the region. This encounter among diverse cultural groups sparked clashes that produced more oppression than opportunity for nonwhites.

Mormons Head West

Unlike miners, cowboys, and farmers, **Mormons** sought refuge in the West for religious reasons. By 1870 the migration of Mormons (members of the Church of Jesus Christ of Latter-Day Saints) into the Utah Territory had attracted more than 85,000 settlers, most notably in Salt Lake City. Originally traveling to Utah under the leadership of Brigham Young in the late 1840s, Mormons had come under attack from opponents of their religion and the federal government for several reasons. Most important, Mormons believed in polygamy (the practice of having more than one wife at a time), which violated traditional Christian standards of morality. Far from seeing the practice as immoral, Mormon doctrine held polygamy as a blessing that would guarantee both husbands and wives an exalted place in the afterlife. Non-Mormons denounced polygamy as a form of involuntary servitude, similar to African American slavery. In reality, only a small minority of Mormon men had multiple wives, and most of these polygamists had only two wives.

Mormons also departed from the mainstream American belief in private property. The church considered farming a communal enterprise. To this end, church elders divided land among their followers, so that, as Brigham Young explained, "each person perform[ed] his several duties for the good of the whole more than for individual aggrandizement." Mormon communities also displayed a tolerant attitude toward the Native American tribes they encountered, learning their languages in order to convert rather than destroy them.

In the 1870s, the federal government took increased measures to control Mormon practices. In *Reynolds v. United States* (1879), the Supreme Court upheld the criminal conviction of a polygamist Mormon man. Previously in 1862 and 1874, Congress had banned plural marriages in the Utah Territory, and the justices ruled that despite their religious convictions, Mormons possessed no constitutional right to violate federal law. Congress went further in 1882 by passing the Edmunds Act, which disfranchised men engaging in polygamy. In 1887 Congress aimed to slash the economic power of the church by limiting Mormon assets to $50,000 and seizing the rest for the federal Treasury. A few years later, under this considerable pressure, the Mormons officially abandoned polygamy.

Related to the attack on polygamy was the question of women's suffrage. In 1870 voters in Utah endorsed a referendum granting women the right to vote, which enfranchised more than seventeen thousand women. Emmeline B. Wells, a Mormon woman who defended both women's rights and polygamy, argued that women "should be recognized as . . . responsible being[s]," capable of choosing plural marriage of their own free will. Opponents of enfranchisement contended that as long as polygamy existed, extending the vote to "enslaved" Mormon women would only perpetuate the practice because they would vote the way their husbands did. This point of view prevailed, and the Edmunds-Tucker Act (1887) rescinded the right to vote for women in the territory. Only with the rejection of polygamy did Congress accept statehood for Utah in 1896. The following year, the state extended the ballot to women.

Californios

As with the nation's other frontiers, migrants to the West Coast did not find uninhabited territory. Besides Indians, the largest group that lived in California consisted of Spaniards and Mexicans. Since the eighteenth century, these *Californios* had established themselves as farmers and ranchers. The 1848 Treaty of Guadalupe Hidalgo, which ended the Mexican-American War, supposedly guaranteed the property rights of Californios and granted them U.S. citizenship, but reality proved different. Mexican American miners had to pay a "foreign miners tax," and Californio landowners lost their holdings to squatters, settlers, and local officials. Anglo politicians argued that the descendants of the original owners of Spanish land grants did not use them efficiently, and clever lawyers used the courts to deprive Californios of much of their property. By the end of the nineteenth century, about two-thirds of all land originally owned by Spanish-speaking residents had fallen into the hands of Euro-American settlers. By this time, many of these once proud and wealthy Californios had been forced into poverty and the low-wage labor force. The loss of land was matched by a diminished role in the region's government, as economic decline, ethnic bias, and the continuing

influx of white migrants combined to greatly reduce the political influence of the Californio population.

Spaniards and Mexicans living in the Southwest met the same fate as the Californios. Although they battled to keep their landholdings, they did not receive the first-class citizenship promised by the Treaty of Guadalupe-Hidalgo. When Anglo cattle ranchers began forcing Mexican Americans off their land near Las Vegas, New Mexico, a rancher named Juan Jose Herrera assembled a band of masked night riders known as *Las Gorras Blancas* (The White Caps). In 1889 and 1890, as many as seven hundred White Caps burned Anglo fences, haystacks, barns, and homes. They also set fire to thousands of railroad ties when the Atchison, Topeka, and Santa Fe Railroad refused to increase wages for Hispanic workers. In the end, however, Spanish-speaking inhabitants could not prevent the growing number of whites from pouring onto their lands and isolating them politically, economically, and culturally.

Explore

See Document 15.5 for a list of demands from the White Caps.

The Chinese in the Far West

California and the far West also attracted a large number of Chinese immigrants. Migration to California and the West Coast was part of a larger movement in the nineteenth century out of Asia that brought impoverished Chinese to Australia, Hawaii, Latin America, and the United States. The Chinese migrated for several reasons in the decades after 1840. Internal conflicts in China sent them in search of refuge. Economic dislocation related to the British Opium Wars (1839–1842 and 1856–1860), along with bloody family feuds and a decade of peasant rebellion from 1854 to 1864, propelled migration. Faced with unemployment and starvation, the Chinese sought economic opportunity overseas. One man recounted the hardships that drove him to emigrate: "Sometimes we went hungry for days. My mother and [I] would go over the harvested rice fields of the peasants to pick the grains they dropped. . . . We had only salt and water to eat with the rice."

Chinese immigrants were attracted first by the 1848 gold rush and then by jobs building the transcontinental railroad. By 1880 the Chinese population had grown to 200,000, most of whom lived in the West. San Francisco became the center of the transplanted Chinese population, which congregated in the city's Chinatown. Under the leadership of a handful of businessmen, Chinese residents found jobs, lodging, meals, and social, cultural, and recreational outlets. Most of those who came were young unmarried men who intended to earn

DOCUMENT 15.5

White Caps Flier, 1890

Before the United States acquired California and the territories of Arizona and New Mexico in 1848, most of the people living in the area were of Spanish heritage. In New Mexico, Hispanic villagers farmed on communal land. In the 1880s, Anglo authorities enclosed the communal land with barbed wire to promote individual farming. In response, a group of frustrated residents known as *Las Gorras Blancas*, or "White Caps," burned barns and destroyed the fences of ranchers who enclosed common lands. In 1890 the White Caps posted fliers in the town of Las Vegas, New Mexico, in which they described a range of grievances.

Explore

NUESTRA PLATFORMA— [Our Platform]

Our purpose is to protect the rights and interests of the people in general and especially those of the helpless classes.

We want the Las Vegas Grant settled to the benefit of all concerned, and this we hold is the entire community within the Grant.

We want no "land grabbers" or obstructionists of any sort to interfere. We will watch them.

We are not down on lawyers as a class, but the usual knavery and unfair treatment of the people must be stopped.

Our judiciary hereafter must understand that we will sustain it only when "Justice" is its watchword.

We are down on race issues, and will watch race agitators.

We favor irrigation enterprises, but will fight any scheme that tends to monopolize the supply of water sources to the detriment of residents living on lands watered by the same streams.

The people are suffering from the effects of partisan "bossism" and these bosses had better quietly hold their peace. The people have been persecuted and hauled about in every which way to satisfy their caprices.

We must have a free ballot and fair court and the will of the Majority shall be respected.

We have no grudge against any person in particular, but we are the enemies of bulldozers and tyrants.

If the old system should continue, death would be a relief to our suffering. And for our rights our lives are the least we can pledge.

If the fact that we are law-abiding citizens is questioned, come out to our houses and see the hunger and desolation we are suffering; and "this" is the result of the deceitful and corrupt methods of "bossism."

The White Caps 1,500 Strong and Gaining Daily

Source: *Las Vegas Daily Optic*, March 12, 1890, reprinted in *Foreigners in Their Native Land: Historical Roots of the Mexican Americans*, ed. David J. Weber (Albuquerque: University of New Mexico Press, 1973), 235–36.

Interpret the Evidence

- Whom do the White Caps claim to represent, and what are their grievances?
- How did the White Caps support their claim to be law-abiding citizens? How might Anglo authorities have responded to their claims?

Put It in Context

What kinds of difficulties did nonwhites face as white Americans moved westward during the nineteenth century?

enough money to return to China and start anew. The relatively few women who immigrated came as servants or prostitutes.

For many Chinese, the West proved unwelcoming. When California's economy slumped in the mid-1870s, many whites looked to the Chinese as scapegoats. White workingmen believed that the plentiful supply of Chinese laborers in the mines and railroads undercut their demands for higher wages. They contended that Chinese would work for less because they were racially inferior people who lived degraded lives. Anti-Chinese clubs mushroomed in California during the 1870s, and they soon became a substantial political force in the state. The Workingmen's Party advocated laws that restricted Chinese labor, and it initiated boycotts of goods made by Chinese people. Vigilantes attacked Chinese in the streets and set fire to factories that employed Asians. The Workingmen's Party and the Democratic Party joined forces in 1879 to craft a new state constitution that blatantly discriminated against Chinese residents. In many ways, these laws resembled the Jim Crow laws passed in the South that deprived African Americans of their freedom following Reconstruction (discussed in chapter 16).

Pressured by anti-Chinese sentiment on the West Coast, the U.S. government enacted drastic legislation to prevent any further influx of Chinese. The **Chinese Exclusion Act** of 1882 banned Chinese immigration into the United States and prohibited those Chinese already in the country from becoming naturalized American citizens. As a result, the Chinese remained a predominantly male, aging, and isolated population until World War II. The exclusion act, however, did not stop anti-Chinese assaults. In the mid-1880s, white mobs drove Chinese out of Eureka, California; Seattle and Tacoma, Washington; and Rock Springs, Wyoming.

Rock Springs Massacre

This engraving depicts the Rock Springs massacre in Wyoming. On September 3, 1885, a mob of white coal miners killed at least 28 Chinese miners, injured 15, and burned 75 homes of Chinese residents. The violence came after years of anti-Chinese sentiment in the western United States. White miners blamed the Chinese for working for lower wages and taking their jobs.   The Granger Collection, New York

REVIEW & RELATE

What migrant groups were attracted to the far West? What drew them there?

Explain the rising hostility to the Chinese and other minority groups in the late-nineteenth-century far West.

 LEARNINGCurve bedfordstmartins.com/hewittlawson/LC

Conclusion: The Ambiguous Legacy of the Frontier

The legacy of the pioneering generation of Americans has proven mixed. Men and women pioneers left their old lives behind and boldly pushed into uncharted territory to reinvent themselves. They encountered numerous obstacles posed by difficult terrain, forbidding climate, and unfamiliar inhabitants of the land they sought to harness. They built their homes, tilled the soil to raise crops, and mined the earth to remove the metals it contained. They developed cities that would one day rival those back east: San Francisco, Los Angeles, Seattle, and Denver. These pioneers served as the advance guard of America's expanding national and international commercial markets. As producers of staple crops and livestock and consumers of manufactured goods, they contributed to the expansion of America's factories, railroads, and telegraph communication system. The nation would memorialize their spirit as a model of individualism and self-reliance.

In fact, settlement of the West required more than individual initiative and self-determination. Without the direct involvement of the federal government, settlers would not have received free or inexpensive homesteads and military protection to clear native inhabitants out of their way. Without territorial governors and judges appointed by Washington to preside over new settlements, there would have been even less law, order, and justice than appeared in the rough-and-tumble environment that attracted outlaws, con artists, and speculators. Railroads, mining, and cattle ventures all relied heavily on foreign investors. Moreover, all the individualism and self-reliance that pioneers brought would not have saved them from the harsh conditions and disasters they faced without banding together as a community and pitching in to create institutions that helped them collectively. Despite their desire to achieve success, various pioneers—farmers, prospectors, cowboys—mostly found it difficult to make it on their own and began working for larger farming, mining, and ranching enterprises, with many of them becoming wageworkers. And for an experience that has been portrayed as a predominantly male phenomenon, settlement of the West depended largely on women.

Pioneers did not fully understand the land and people they encountered. More from ignorance than design, settlers engaged in agricultural, mining, and ranching practices that depleted fragile grasses, eroded hillsides, and polluted rivers and streams with runoff wastes. The settlement of the West nearly wiped out the bison and left Native Americans psychologically demoralized, culturally endangered, and economically impoverished. Some Indians willingly adopted white ways, but most of them fiercely resisted acculturation. Other nonwhite minorities in the West, such as Mexicans and Chinese, experienced less extreme treatment, but they suffered nonetheless.

Panoramic landscape paintings often depicted glorious scenes of the Wild West, but the truth was more nuanced. Annie Oakley pleased audiences with daring exploits that glorified a West she had not experienced. Geronimo surrendered and spent the rest of his life exiled from his native lands. He, too, tried to follow the path of Oakley, but his public appearances could not hide the devastation that he and other Native Americans had experienced. The western frontier represented both opportunity and loss.

Chapter Review

Online Study Guide ▶ bedfordstmartins.com/hewittlawson

KEY TERMS

Great Plains (p. 461)
transcontinental railroad (p. 462)
Treaty of Fort Laramie (p. 465)
Battle of the Little Big Horn (p. 466)
buffalo soldiers (p. 466)
Dawes Act (p. 467)
Ghost Dance (p. 468)
Comstock Lode (p. 469)
Long Drive (p. 471)
Homestead Act (p. 474)
Mormons (p. 478)
Californios (p. 479)
Chinese Exclusion Act (p. 481)

REVIEW & RELATE

1. What role did the federal government play in opening the West to settlement and economic exploitation?

2. Explain the determination of Americans to settle in land west of the Mississippi River despite the challenges the region presented.

3. How and why did federal Indian policy change during the nineteenth century?

4. Describe some of the ways that Indian peoples responded to federal policies. Which response do you think offered their greatest chance for survival?

5. How and why did the nature of mining in the West change during the second half of the nineteenth century?

6. How did miners and residents of mining towns reshape the frontier landscape?

7. How did market forces contribute to the boom and bust of the cattle ranching industry?

8. How did women homesteaders on the Great Plains in the late nineteenth century respond to frontier challenges?

9. What migrant groups were attracted to the far West? What drew them there?

10. Explain the rising hostility to the Chinese and other minority groups in the late-nineteenth-century far West.

TIMELINE OF EVENTS

1848	Gold discovered in California
1851	First Treaty of Fort Laramie
1862	Homestead Act passed
1864	Sand Creek massacre
1865–1868	Lakota Sioux lead Indian resistance
Late 1860s	Large-scale cattle drives begin
1868	Second Treaty of Fort Laramie
1869	Transcontinental railroad completed
1870s	Gold discovered in Black Hills of North Dakota
1876	Battle of the Little Big Horn
1877	Desert Land Act
1878	John Wesley Powell questions suitability of Great Plains for small-scale farming
	Timber and Stone Act
1881	Helen Hunt Jackson publishes *Century of Dishonor*
1882	Edmunds Act passed
	Chinese Exclusion Act passed
1884	Annie Oakley joins William Cody's Wild West show
1885–1887	Cattle industry collapses
1886	Geronimo captured
1887	Dawes Act passed
	Kansas women win right to vote and run for office in municipal elections
1889–1890	Mexican American White Caps attack Anglo property
1890	Massacre at Wounded Knee
1893	Western Federation of Miners formed

American Indians and Whites on the Frontier

Views on the relationship between whites and American Indians varied widely in the late-nineteenth-century West. Some white Americans advocated exterminating the Indians, whereas others sought to assimilate them. These attitudes differed significantly by region. Whites who were most likely to encounter Indians were generally the least sympathetic. Government officials were also divided. The most notable differences were between civilians in the Interior Department who favored peaceful solutions and those in the War Department who were inclined to use military force to resolve conflicts. However, even white reformers did not always understand Indian culture; as a result, they developed policies that led to the decline of Indian tribal societies. On the other side, Indian attitudes ranged from fierce resistance to accommodation and, in rare cases, assimilation. Even those who eventually adapted to white society and gained a measure of fame within it, like Zitkala-Ša (Document 15.9), never fully abandoned their pride in Indian traditions.

The following documents speak to important recurring questions in American history: How do white Americans and their leaders deal with differences among people rooted in race and nationality? How do those considered minorities forge strategies to gain political and economic access while maintaining their own identities and heritage? And how well did the U.S. government in the late nineteenth century balance its commitment to the competing values of continental expansion and equal justice under the law?

DOCUMENT 15.6

James Michael Cavanaugh | Support for Indian Extermination, 1868

James Michael Cavanaugh was originally from Springfield, Massachusetts, but moved to Minnesota in 1854, where he served in Congress for one term. He subsequently moved to Colorado and then Montana and served in the House of Representatives as a Democrat from 1867 to 1871. In the following congressional speech, Cavanaugh explains his attitude toward Indians in a discussion about Indian appropriations with Republican representative Benjamin Butler of Massachusetts.

WILL SAY THAT I like an Indian better dead than living. I have never in my life seen a good Indian (and I have seen thousands) except when I have seen a dead Indian. I believe in the Indian policy pursued by New England in years long gone. I believe in the Indian policy which was taught by the great chieftain of Massachusetts, Miles Standish. I believe in the policy that exterminates the Indians, drives them outside the boundaries of civilization, because you cannot civilize them. Gentlemen may call this very harsh language; but perhaps they would not think so if they had had my experience in Minnesota and Colorado. In Minnesota the almost living babe has been torn from its mother's womb; and I have seen the child, with its young heart palpitating, nailed to the window-sill. I have seen women who were scalped, disfigured, outraged. In Denver, Colorado Territory, I have seen women and children brought in scalped. Scalped why? Simply because the Indian was "upon the war-path," to satisfy his devilish and barbarous propensities. You have made your treaties with the Indians, but they have not been observed. General [William Tecumseh] Sherman went out a year ago to Colorado Territory. He made a treaty; and in less than twenty-four hours after the treaty was made the Indians were again "upon the war-path." The Indian will make a treaty in the fall, and in the spring he is again "upon the war-path." The torch, the scalping-knife, plunder, and desolation follow wherever the Indian goes.

But, Mr. Chairman, I will answer the gentleman's question more directly. My friend from Massachusetts [Mr. Butler] has never passed the barrier of the frontier. All he knows about Indians (the gentleman will pardon me for saying it) may have been gathered, I presume, from the brilliant pages of the author of "The Last of the Mohicans," or from the lines of the poet Longfellow in "Hiawatha." The gentleman has never yet seen the Indian upon the war-path. He has never been chased, as I have been, by these red devils—who seem to be the pets of the eastern philanthropists.

Mr. Chairman, I regret that I have not prepared myself with statistics as to Indian atrocities. I desire to answer the gentleman from Massachusetts fairly. I repeat that the Indian policy of the Government from beginning to end is wrong. If the management of the Indians is to continue as a part of the civil service, then there ought to be a bureau of Indian affairs, under the charge of a Cabinet officer, who should be responsible for all matters connected with the management of the Indians.

Source: United States Congress, *The Congressional Globe: Containing the Debates and Proceedings of the Second Session of the Fortieth Congress*, May 28, 1868, 2638.

DOCUMENT 15.7

Thomas Nast | "Patience until the Indian Is Civilized—So to Speak," 1878

Through his cartoons, artist Thomas Nast crusaded against political corruption and mistreatment of freedpeople in the South. Although generally sympathetic to the rights of American Indians, in this illustration he raises questions about what the federal government should do regarding conflicts between white settlers and Indians in the West. Nast depicts Secretary of the Interior Carl Schurz (left), an Indian reformer, counseling patience to western settlers.

Library of Congress

DOCUMENT 15.8

Helen Hunt Jackson | Challenges to Indian Policy, 1881

Helen Hunt Jackson's book *A Century of Dishonor* severely criticized U.S. policy toward Indians. Jackson sent a copy of her book to every member of Congress. Her handwritten inscription, intended to move lawmakers to action, contained the words of Benjamin Franklin: "Look upon your hands! They are stained with the blood of your relations." Despite her attack on the government's treatment of Indians and her advocacy of reform, Jackson believed that American Indians could not become citizens until they received proper training from enlightened white teachers.

There is not among these three hundred bands of Indians one which has not suffered cruelly at the hands either of the Government or of white settlers. The poorer, the more insignificant, the more helpless the band, the more certain the cruelty and outrage to which they have been subjected. This is especially true of the bands on the Pacific slope. These Indians found themselves of a sudden surrounded by and caught up in the great influx of gold-seeking settlers, as helpless creatures on a shore are caught up in a tidal wave. There was not time for the Government to make treaties; not even time for communities to make laws. The tale of the wrongs, the oppressions, the murders of the Pacific-slope Indians in the last thirty years would be a volume by itself, and is too monstrous to be believed.

It makes little difference, however, where one opens the record of the history of the Indians; every page and every year has its dark stain. The story of one tribe is the story of all, varied only by differences of time and place; but neither time nor place makes any difference in the main facts. Colorado is as greedy and unjust in 1880 as was Georgia in 1830, and Ohio in 1795; and the United States Government breaks promises now as deftly as then, and with an added ingenuity from long practice.

One of its strongest supports in so doing is the wide-spread sentiment among the people of dislike to the Indian, of impatience with his presence as a "barrier to civilization," and distrust of it as a possible danger. The old tales of the frontier life, with its horrors of Indian warfare, have gradually, by two or three generations' telling, produced in the average mind something like an hereditary instinct of unquestioning and unreasoning aversion which it is almost impossible to dislodge or soften. . . .

To assume that it would be easy, or by any one sudden stroke of legislative policy possible, to undo the mischief and hurt of the long past, set the Indian policy of the country right for the future, and make the Indians at once safe and happy, is the blunder of a hasty and uninformed judgment. The notion which seems to be growing more prevalent, that simply to make all Indians at once citizens of the United States would be a sovereign and instantaneous panacea for all their ills and all the Government's perplexities, is a very inconsiderate one. To administer complete citizenship of a sudden, all round, to all Indians, barbarous and civilized alike, would be as grotesque a blunder as to dose them all round with any one medicine, irrespective of the symptoms and needs of their diseases. It would kill more than it would cure. Nevertheless, it is true, as was well stated by one of the superintendents of Indian Affairs in 1857, that, "so long as they are not citizens of the United States, their rights of property must remain insecure against invasion. The doors of the federal tribunals being barred against them while wards and dependents, they can only partially exercise the rights of free government, or give to those who make, execute, and construe the few laws they are allowed to enact, dignity sufficient to make them respectable. While they continue individually to gather the crumbs that fall from the table of the United States, idleness, improvidence, and indebtedness will be the rule, and industry, thrift, and freedom from debt the exception. The utter absence of individual title to particular lands deprives every one among them of the chief incentive to labor and exertion—the very mainspring on which the prosperity of a people depends."

(continued on page 488)

All judicious plans and measures for their safety and salvation must embody provisions for their becoming citizens as fast as they are fit, and must protect them till then in every right and particular in which our laws protect other "persons" who are not citizens. . . .

Cheating, robbing, breaking promises—these three are clearly things which must cease to be done. One more thing, also, and that is the refusal of the protection of the law to the Indian's rights of property, "of life, liberty, and the pursuit of happiness."

When these four things have ceased to be done, time, statesmanship, philanthropy, and Christianity can slowly and surely do the rest. Till these four things have ceased to be done, statesmanship and philanthropy alike must work in vain, and even Christianity can reap but small harvest.

Source: Helen Hunt Jackson, *A Century of Dishonor: A Sketch of the United States Government's Dealings with Some of the Indian Tribes* (New York: Harper and Brothers, 1881), 337–38, 340–42.

DOCUMENT 15.9

Zitkala-Ša | Life at an Indian Boarding School, 1921

Gertrude Simmons Bonnin, who later took the Indian name Zitkala-Ša, lived on the Yankton Reservation in South Dakota, with her mother and brother until 1884, when missionaries recruited her to attend school so that she would become assimilated into Anglo-American culture. After attending a Quaker school in Wabash, Indiana, Zitkala-Ša briefly attended Earlham College and then taught at the Carlisle Indian Industrial School in Pennsylvania for two years. During that time, she experienced a reawakening of her American Indian heritage and consciousness and began publishing autobiographical accounts criticizing the educational practices of the schools she attended and at which she taught. In 1921 she recounted her own experiences in these Indian schools, including the incident she describes in the following selection.

THE FIRST DAY IN THE LAND of apples was a bitter-cold one; for the snow still covered the ground, and the trees were bare. A large bell rang for breakfast, its loud metallic voice crashing through the belfry overhead and into our sensitive ears. The annoying clatter of shoes on bare floors gave us no peace. The constant clash of harsh noises, with an undercurrent of many voices murmuring an unknown tongue, made a bedlam within which I was securely tied. And though my spirit tore itself in struggling for its lost freedom, all was useless.

A paleface woman, with white hair, came up after us. We were placed in a line of girls who were marching into the dining room. These were Indian girls, in stiff shoes and closely clinging dresses. The small girls wore sleeved aprons and shingled hair [haircut with the hair cut short from the back of the head to the nape of the neck]. As I walked noiselessly in my soft moccasins, I felt like sinking to the floor, for my blanket had been stripped from my shoulders. I looked hard at the Indian girls, who seemed not to care that they were even more immodestly dressed than I, in their tightly fitting clothes. While we marched in, the boys entered at an opposite door. I watched for the three young braves who came in our party. I spied them in the rear ranks, looking as uncomfortable as I felt.

A small bell was tapped, and each of the pupils drew a chair from under the table. Supposing this act meant they were to be seated, I pulled out mine and at once slipped into it from one side. But when I turned my head, I saw that I was the only one seated, and all the rest at our table remained standing. Just as I began to rise, looking shyly around to see how chairs were to be used, a second bell was sounded. All were seated at last, and I had to crawl back into my chair again. I heard a man's voice at one end of the hall, and I looked around to see him. But all the others hung their heads over their plates. As I glanced at the long chain of tables, I caught the eyes of a paleface woman upon me. Immediately I dropped my eyes, wondering why I was so keenly watched by the strange woman. The man ceased his mutterings, and then a third bell was tapped. Every one picked up his knife and fork and began eating. I began crying instead, for by this time I was afraid to venture anything more.

But this eating by formula was not the hardest trial in that first day. Late in the morning, my friend Judéwin gave me a terrible warning. Judéwin knew a few words of English; and she had overheard the paleface woman talk about cutting our long, heavy hair. Our mothers had taught us that only unskilled warriors who were captured had their hair shingled by the enemy. Among our people, short hair was worn by mourners, and shingled hair by cowards!

We discussed our fate some moments, and when Judéwin said, "We have to submit, because they are strong," I rebelled.

"No, I will not submit! I will struggle first!" I answered.

I watched my chance, and when no one noticed I disappeared. I crept up the stairs as quietly as I could in my squeaking shoes—my moccasins had been exchanged for shoes. Along the hall I passed, without knowing whither I was going. Turning aside to an open door, I found a large room with three white beds in it. The windows were covered with dark green curtains, which made the room very dim. Thankful that no one was there, I directed my steps toward the corner farthest from the door. On my hands and knees I crawled under the bed, and cuddled myself in the dark corner.

From my hiding place I peered out, shuddering with fear whenever I heard footsteps near by. Though in the hall loud voices were calling my name, and I knew that even Judéwin was searching for me, I did not open my mouth to answer. Then the steps were quickened and the voices became excited. The sounds came nearer and nearer. Women and girls entered the room. I held my breath and watched them open closet doors and peep behind large trunks. Some one threw up the curtains, and the room was filled with sudden light. What caused them to stoop and look under the bed I do not know. I remember being dragged out, though I resisted by kicking and scratching wildly. In spite of myself, I was carried downstairs and tied fast in a chair.

I cried aloud, shaking my head all the while until I felt the cold blades of the scissors against my neck, and heard them gnaw off one of my thick braids. Then I lost my spirit. Since the day I was taken from my mother I had suffered extreme indignities. People had stared at me. I had been tossed about in the air like a wooden puppet. And now my long hair was shingled like a coward's! In my anguish I moaned for my mother, but no one came to comfort me. Not a soul reasoned quietly with me, as my own mother used to do; for now I was only one of many little animals driven by a herder.

Source: Zitkala-Ša (Gertrude Bonnin), *American Indian Stories* (Washington, D.C.: Hayworth, 1921), 52–56.

DOCUMENT 15.10

Chief Joseph | Views on Indian Affairs, 1879

In 1877, following a string of treaties broken by the U.S. government, Chief Joseph led the Nez Percé on a 1,300-mile march from their tribal land in Oregon to Canada, in search of a home. Thirty miles from the Canadian border, they were surrounded by U.S. troops. Explaining "I am tired of fighting. . . . I will fight no more forever," Joseph was forced into negotiations with U.S. army general Nelson Miles. After his capture, Chief Joseph was taken to Washington, D.C., where he addressed a gathering of cabinet members and congressmen and tried to convince them to return tribal lands to the Nez Percé.

AT LAST I WAS GRANTED permission to come to Washington and bring my friend Yellow Bull and our interpreter with me. I am glad we came. I have shaken hands with a great many friends, but there are some things I want to know which no one seems able to explain. I can not understand how the Government sends a man out to fight us, as it did General Miles, and then breaks his word. Such a government has something wrong about it. I can not understand why so many chiefs are allowed to talk so many different ways, and promise so many different things. I have seen the Great Father Chief [President Rutherford B. Hayes], the next Great Chief [Secretary of the Interior], the Commissioner Chief [E. A. Hayt, Commissioner of Indian Affairs], the Law Chief [Congressman Benjamin Butler], and many other law chiefs [congressmen], and they all say they are my friends, and that I shall have justice, but while their mouths all talk right I do not understand why nothing is done for my people. I have heard talk and talk, but nothing is done. Good words do not last long unless they amount to something. Words do not pay for my dead people. They do not pay for my country, now overrun by white men. They do not protect my father's grave. They do not pay for all my horses and cattle. Good words will not give me back my children. Good words will not make good the promise of your War Chief General Miles. Good words will not give my people good health and stop them from dying. Good words will not get my people a home where they can live in peace and take care of themselves. I am tired of talk that comes to nothing. It makes my heart sick when I remember all the good words and all the broken promises. There has been too much talking by men who had no right to talk. Too many misrepresentations have been made, too many misunderstandings have come up between the white men about the Indians. If the white man wants to live in peace with the Indian he can live in peace. There need be no trouble. Treat all men alike. Give them all the same law. Give them all an even chance to live and grow. All men were made by the same Great Spirit Chief. They are all brothers. The earth is the mother of all people, and all people should have equal rights upon it. You might as well expect the rivers to run backward as that any man who was born a free man should be contented when penned up and denied liberty to go where he pleases. If you tie a horse to a stake, do you expect he will grow fat? If you pen an Indian up on a small spot of earth, and compel him to stay there, he will not be contented, nor will he grow and prosper. I have asked some of the great white chiefs where they get their authority to say to the Indian that he shall stay in one place, while he sees white men going where they please. They can not tell me.

I only ask of the Government to be treated as all other men are treated. If I can not go to my own home, let me have a home in some country where my people will not die so fast. I would like to go to Bitter Root Valley. There my people would be healthy; where they are now they are dying. Three have died since I left my camp to come to Washington.

When I think of our condition, my heart is heavy. I see men of my race treated as outlaws and driven from country to country, or shot down like animals.

I know that my race must change. We can not hold our own with the white men as we are. We only ask an even chance to live as other men live. We ask to be recognized as men. We ask that the same law shall work alike on all men. If the Indian breaks the law, punish him by the law. If the white man breaks the law, punish him also.

Let me be a free man—free to travel, free to stop, free to work, free to trade where I choose, free to choose my own teachers, free to follow the religion of my fathers, free to think and talk and act for myself—and I will obey every law, or submit to the penalty.

Whenever the white man treats the Indian as they treat each other, then we shall have no more wars. We shall all be alike—brothers of one father and one mother, with one sky above us and one country around us, and one government for all. Then the Great Spirit Chief who rules above will smile upon this land, and send rain to wash out the bloody spots made by brothers' hands from the face of the earth. For this time the Indian race are waiting and praying. I hope that no more groans of wounded men and women will ever go to the ear of the Great Spirit Chief above, and that all people may be one people.

Source: "An Indian's View of Indian Affairs," *North American Review*, April 1879, 431–33.

Interpret the Evidence

1. On what basis does James Michael Cavanaugh (Document 15.6) claim to be in a better position than Benjamin Butler to judge the best way to deal with Indians?

2. How does Thomas Nast's illustration (Document 15.7) compare with the arguments made by Congressman Cavanaugh?

3. What assumptions about Indians and their culture underlay the policy of assimilation advocated by reformers such as Helen Hunt Jackson (Document 15.8)?

4. What options did Indians have when confronted with white determination to eradicate their culture? What choice did Zitkala-Ša (Document 15.9) make? Why?

5. How did Chief Joseph's experience (Document 15.10) reflect the fundamental contradiction of federal policy toward Indians?

Put It in Context

- Imagine that you are an American president in the second half of the nineteenth century and can design Indian policy. Based on what you have read, what would you do, and why? What challenges might you face as you attempted to implement your policy?

The Granger Collection, New York

The Granger Collection, New York

Sawmill in Terraville, South Dakota, 1888.

Shoe-factory worker in Lynn, Massachusetts, 1895.

16

American Industry in the Age of Organization

1877–1900

The Granger Collection, New York

Duryea's Glen Cove Starch Works Factory, Glen Cove, New York.

In 1848 Will and Margaret Carnegie left Scotland and sailed to America, hoping to find a better life for themselves and their two children. Once settled in Pittsburgh, Pennsylvania, the family went to work, including thirteen-year-old Andrew, who found a job in a textile mill. For $1.25 per week, he dipped spools into an oil bath and fired the factory furnace—tasks that left him nauseated by the smell of oil and frightened by the boiler. Nevertheless, like the hero of the rags-to-riches stories that were so popular in his era, Andrew Carnegie persevered, rising from poverty to great wealth through a series of jobs and clever investments. As a teenager, he worked as a messenger in a telegraph office and was soon promoted to telegraph operator. A superintendent of the Pennsylvania Railroad Company noticed Andrew's aptitude and made him his personal assistant and telegrapher. While in this position, Carnegie learned about the fast-developing railroad industry and purchased stock in a sleeping car company; the returns from that investment tripled his annual salary. Carnegie then became a railroad superintendent in western Pennsylvania, and by the time he was thirty-five, he had earned handsome returns on his investments in various industrial companies, as well as from oil investments he made just as that industry was emerging.

Andrew Carnegie eventually founded the greatest steel company in the world and became one of the wealthiest men of his time. In an era before personal and corporate income taxes, Carnegie earned hundreds of millions of dollars. He also became one of the era's greatest philanthropists, fulfilling his sense of community obligation by giving away a great deal of his fortune.

John Sherman also believed in public service, but for him it would come through politics. Sherman was born in Lancaster, Ohio, in 1823, a quarter of a century before the Carnegies set sail for the United States. Sherman became a lawyer like his father, an Ohio Supreme Court judge, and in 1844 he set up a practice with his older brother, William Tecumseh Sherman, the future Civil War general and Indian fighter (see chapter 15). Like Carnegie, Sherman made shrewd investments that made him a wealthy man, although not on the same scale as Carnegie.

Sherman decided to enter politics and in 1854 won election from Ohio to the House of Representatives as a member of the newly created Republican Party. He rose up the leadership ranks as Republicans came to national power with the election of Abraham Lincoln to the presidency in 1860. From 1861 to 1896, Sherman held a variety of major political positions, including U.S. senator from Ohio and secretary of the treasury under President Rutherford B. Hayes. After his term as treasury secretary ended, he returned to the Senate and wielded power as one of the top Republican Party leaders. Sherman, who had joined the Radical Republicans during Reconstruction (see chapter 14), did not hesitate to move with the Republican Party as its interests shifted from racial equality to promoting business and industry. With his background as chair of the Senate Finance Committee and as secretary of the treasury, Sherman was the most respected Republican of his time in dealing with monetary and financial affairs. Marcus Alonzo Hanna, a wealthy industrialist, considered the Ohio senator "our main dependence in the Senate for the protection of our business interests." Like Hanna, Sherman believed that government should serve business. His most famous accomplishment, the Sherman Antitrust Act, which authorized the government to break up organizations that restrained competition, embodied this belief. It enacted limited reforms without harming powerful business interests. ●

both photos: Library of Congress

WHILE THE AMERICAN HISTORIES of Andrew Carnegie and John Sherman began very differently, both men played a prominent role in developing the government-business partnership that was crucial to the rapid industrialization of the United States. Carnegie's organization and management skills helped shape the formation of large-scale business. At the same time, Sherman and his fellow lawmakers provided support for that enterprise, using the power of government to reduce risks for businessmen and to increase incentives for economic expansion. In the view of men like Carnegie and Sherman, government's primary purpose was, in fact, to advance the agenda and interests of the business community—an agenda they were certain was in the best interests of the country as a whole.

The emphasis Carnegie and Sherman placed on the government-business alliance was, in part, a reaction to the extreme economic volatility of the late nineteenth century. The economy experienced painful depressions in the 1870s, 1880s, and 1890s, each accompanied by business failures and mass unemployment. Though recovery came in every instance and industrial output continued to soar, these financial fluctuations left businessmen ever more intent on stabilizing profits, wages, and prices. When faced with harsh economic realities and swift change, businessmen chose organization, cooperation, and government support as strategies to deal with the challenges they confronted.

America Industrializes

In this Age of Organization between 1870 and 1900, the United States grew into a global industrial power. Transcontinental railroads spurred this breathtaking transformation, linking regional markets into a national market for manufactured goods; at the same time, railroads themselves served as a massive new market for raw materials, new technologies, and, perhaps most important, steel. Building on advantages developed over the course of the nineteenth century, the Northeast and the Midwest led the way in the new economy, while efforts to industrialize the South met with uneven success. Men like Andrew Carnegie became both the heroes and the villains of their age. They engaged in ruthless practices that would lead some to label the new industrialists "robber barons," but they also created ingenious systems of industrial organization and corporate management that altered the economic landscape of the country and changed the place of the United States in the world.

The New Industrial Economy

The industrial revolution of the late nineteenth century originated in Europe. Great Britain was the world's first industrial power, but by the 1870s Germany had emerged as a major challenger for industrial dominance, increasing its steel production at a rapid rate and leading the way in the chemical and electrical industries. The dynamic economic growth stimulated by industrial competition quickly crossed the Atlantic. Eager and ambitious American entrepreneurs and engineers soon began applying the latest industrial innovations to U.S. enterprises.

Industrialization transformed the American economy. As industrialization took hold, the U.S. gross domestic product, the output of all goods and services produced annually, quadrupled—from $9 billion in 1860 to $37 billion in 1890. During this same period, the number of Americans employed by industry doubled, as American workers moved from farms to factories and immigrants flooded in from overseas to fill newly created industrial jobs. Moreover, the nature of industry itself changed, as small factories catering to local markets were displaced by large-scale firms producing for national and international markets. The midwestern cities of Chicago, Cincinnati, and St. Louis joined Boston, New York, and Philadelphia as centers of factory production, while the exploitation of the natural resources in the West took on an increasingly industrial character. Trains, telegraphs, and telephones connected the country in ways never before possible. In 1889 the respected economist David A. Wells marveled at

what had occurred over the past two decades: "An almost total revolution has taken place, and is yet in progress, in every branch and in every relation of the world's industrial and commercial system."

Wells did not exaggerate. From 1870 to 1913, the United States experienced an extraordinary rate of growth in industrial output: In 1870 American industries turned out 23.3 percent of the world's manufacturing production; by 1913 this figure had jumped to 35.8 percent. In fact, U.S. output in 1913 almost equaled the combined total for Europe's three leading industrial powers: Germany, the United Kingdom, and France. Of these European countries, only Germany experienced a slight rise in output from 1870 to 1913 (2.5 percent), while Britain's output dropped a precipitous 17.8 percent and France's declined 3.9 percent. By the end of the nineteenth century, the United States was surging ahead of northern Europe as the manufacturing center of the world.

At the heart of the American industrial transformation was the railroad. Large-scale business enterprises would not have developed without a national market for raw materials and finished products. A consolidated system of railroads crisscrossing the nation facilitated the creation of such a market (Figure 16.1). In addition, railroads were direct consumers of industrial products, stimulating the growth of a number of industries through their consumption of steel, wood, coal, glass, rubber, brass, and iron. For example, late-nineteenth-century railroads purchased more than 90 percent of the steel produced in U.S. factories. Finally, railroads contributed to economic growth by increasing the speed and efficiency with which products and materials were transported. One observer guessed that in 1890 if the country had to rely only on roads and waterways instead of trains to ship agricultural and industrial goods, the nation would have lost approximately $560 million, or 5 percent, of its gross national product.

Before railroads could create a national market, they had to overcome several critical problems. In 1877 railroad lines dotted the country in haphazard fashion. They primarily served local markets and remained unconnected at key points. This lack of coordination stemmed mainly from the fact that each railroad had its own track gauge (the width between the tracks), making shared track use impossible and long-distance travel extremely difficult.

The consolidation of railroads solved many of these problems. In 1886 railroad companies finally agreed to adopt a standard gauge. Railroads also standardized time zones, thus eliminating confusion in train schedules. During the 1870s, towns and cities each set their own time zone, a practice that created discrepancies among them. In 1882 the time in New York City and in Boston varied by 11 minutes and 45 seconds. The following year, railroads

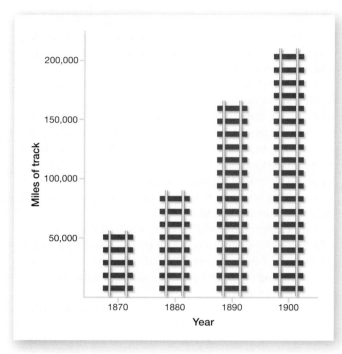

FIGURE 16.1   Expansion of the Railroad System, 1870–1900

The great expansion of the railroads in the late nineteenth century fueled the industrial revolution and the growth of big business. Connecting the nation from East Coast to West Coast, transcontinental railroads created a national market for natural resources and manufactured goods. The biggest surge in railroad construction occurred west of the Mississippi River and in the South.

agreed to coordinate times and divided the country into four standard time zones. Most cities soon cooperated, but not until 1918 did the federal government legislate the standard time zones that the railroads had first adopted.

Innovation and Inventions

As important as railroads were, they were not the only engine of industrialization. American technological innovation created new industries, while expanding the efficiency and productivity of old ones. Inventor Thomas Alva Edison began his career by devising ways to improve the telegraph and expand its uses. In 1866 a transatlantic telegraph cable connected the United States and Europe, allowing businessmen on both sides of the ocean to pursue profitable commercial ventures. New inventions also allowed business offices to run more smoothly: Typewriters were invented in 1868, carbon paper in 1872, adding machines in 1891, and mimeograph machines in 1892. As businesses grew, they needed more space for their operations. The construction of towering skyscrapers in the 1880s in cities such as Chicago and New York was made possible

by two innovations: structural steel, which had the strength to support tall buildings; and elevators, equipped with a safety device invented by Elisha Graves Otis in the 1850s.

Among the thousands of patents filed each year, Alexander Graham Bell's telephone revolutionized communications. By 1880 fifty-five cities offered local service and catered to a total of 50,000 subscribers, most of them business customers. A decade later, long-distance service connected New York, Boston, and Chicago, and by 1900 around 1.5 million telephones were in operation. Bell profited handsomely from his invention, created his own firm, and in 1885 established the giant American Telephone and Telegraph Company (AT&T).

Perhaps the greatest technological innovations that advanced industrial development in the late nineteenth century came in steel manufacturing. In 1859 Henry Bessemer, a British inventor, designed a furnace that burned the impurities out of melted iron and converted it into steel. The open-hearth process, devised by another Englishman, William Siemens, further improved the quality of steel by removing additional impurities from the iron. Railroads replaced iron rails with steel because it was lighter, stronger, and more durable than iron. Steel became the major building block of industry, furnishing girders and cables to construct manufacturing plants and office structures. As production became cheaper and more efficient, steel output soared from 13,000 tons in 1860 to 28 million tons in the first decade of the twentieth century.

Factory machinery needed constant lubrication, and the growing petroleum industry made this possible. A new drilling technique devised in 1859 tapped into pools of petroleum located deep below the earth's surface. In the post–Civil War era, new distilling techniques transformed this thick, smelly liquid into lubricating oil for factory machinery. This process of "cracking" crude oil also generated lucrative by-products for the home, such as kerosene and paraffin for heating and lighting. Robert A. Chesebrough discovered that a sticky oil residue could soothe cuts and burns, and in 1870 he began manufacturing a product he would soon trademark as Vaseline Petroleum Jelly. After 1900, the development of the gasoline-powered, internal combustion engine for automobiles opened up an even richer market for the oil industry.

Railroads also benefited from innovations in technology. Improvements included air brakes and automatic coupling devices to attach train cars to each other. Elijah McCoy, a trained engineer and the son of former slaves, was forced because of racial discrimination to work at menial railroad jobs shoveling coal and lubricating train parts every few miles to keep the gears from overheating. This grueling experience encouraged him to invent and patent an automatic lubricating device to improve efficiency.

Early innovations resulted from the genius of individual inventors, but by the late nineteenth century technological progress was increasingly an organized, collaborative effort. Thomas Edison and his team served as the model. In 1876 Edison set up a research laboratory in Menlo Park, New Jersey. Housed in a two-story, white frame building, Edison's "invention factory" was staffed by a team of inventors and craftsmen. Edison believed that "genius was 1 percent inspiration and 99 percent perspiration," and he devoted nearly every waking hour, often ignoring his family, to coordinating the invention process. In 1887 Edison opened another laboratory, ten times bigger than the one at Menlo Park, in nearby Orange, New Jersey. These facilities pioneered the research laboratories that would become a standard feature of American industrial development in the twentieth century.

Edison expected his research factories to produce "a minor invention every ten days and a big thing every six months or so." Edison and his crew largely succeeded. During his lifetime, Edison filed 1,093 U.S. patents; although he has received most of the credit, a good number of his inventions were the result of collaborative research. Out of his laboratory flowed inventions that revolutionized American business and culture. The phonograph and motion pictures changed the way people spent their leisure time. The electric lightbulb illuminated people's homes and made them safer by eliminating the need for candles and gas lamps, which were fire hazards. It also brightened city streets, making them available for outdoor evening activities, and lit up factories so that they could operate all night long.

Like his contemporaries who were building America's huge industrial empires, Edison cashed in on his workers' inventions. He joined forces with the Wall Street banker J. P. Morgan to finance the Edison Electric Illuminating Company, which in 1882 provided lighting to customers in New York City. Goods produced by electric equipment jumped in value from $1.9 million in 1879 to $21.8 million in 1890. In 1892, Morgan helped Edison merge his companies with several competitors and reorganized them as the General Electric Corporation, which became the industry leader.

Building a New South

Although the largely rural South lagged behind the North and the Midwest in manufacturing, industrial expansion did not bypass the region. Well aware of global economic trends and eager for the South to achieve its economic potential, southern business leaders and newspaper editors, especially the *Atlanta Constitution*'s editor Henry Grady, saw industrial development as the key to the creation of a **New South**. Attributing the Confederate defeat in the Civil War to the North's superior manufacturing output and

railroad supply lines, New South proponents hoped to modernize their economy in a similar fashion. One of those boosters was Richard H. Edmonds, the Virginia-born editor of the *Manufacturers' Record*. He extolled the virtues of the "real South" of the 1880s, characterized by "the music of progress—the whirr of the spindle, the buzz of the saw, the roar of the furnace, the throb of the locomotive." The South of Edmonds's vision would move beyond the regional separatism of the past and become fully integrated into the national economy.

Railroads were the key to achieving such economic integration, so after the Civil War new railroad tracks were laid throughout the South. Not only did this expanded railroad system create direct connections between the North and the South, but it also facilitated the growth of the southern textile industry. Seeking to take advantage of plentiful cotton, cheap labor, and the improved transportation system, investors built textile mills throughout the South, especially in the Carolinas and Georgia. Victims of falling prices and saddled with debt, sharecroppers and tenant farmers moved into mill towns in search of better employment. Mill owners preferred to hire girls and young women, who worked for low wages, to spin cotton and weave it on the looms. To do so, however, owners had to employ their entire family, for mothers and fathers would not let their daughters relocate without their supervision. Whatever attraction the mills offered applied only to whites. The pattern of white supremacy emerging in the post-Reconstruction South kept African Americans out of all but the most menial jobs.

Blacks contributed greatly to the construction of railroads in the New South, but they did not do so as free men. Convicts, most of whom were African American, performed the exhausting work of laying tracks through hills and swamps. Southern states used the **convict lease** system, in which blacks, usually imprisoned for minor offenses, were hired out to private companies to serve their time or pay off their fine. The convict lease system brought additional income to the state and supplied cheap labor to the railroads and planters, but it left African American convict laborers impoverished and virtually enslaved.

The South attracted a number of industries besides textile manufacturing. In the 1880s, James B. Duke established a cigarette manufacturing empire in Durham, North Carolina. Nearby tobacco fields provided the raw material that black workers prepared for white workers, who then rolled the cigarettes by machine. Acres of timber pines in the Carolinas, Florida, and Alabama sustained a lucrative lumber industry, one of the few to employ whites and blacks equally. Rich supplies of coal and iron in Alabama fostered the growth of the steel industry in Birmingham, which produced more than a million tons of steel at the turn of the twentieth century (Map 16.1).

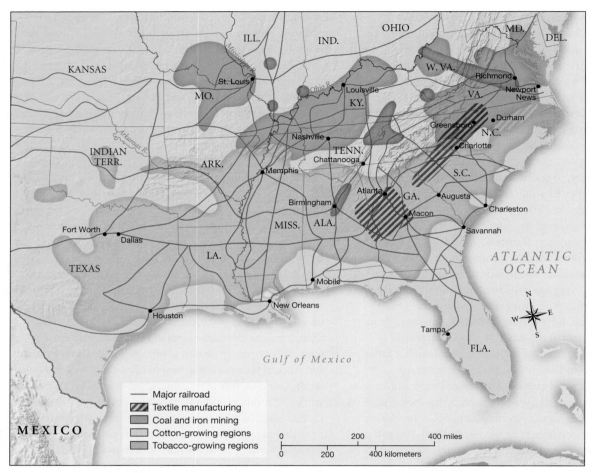

MAP 16.1   The New South, 1900
Although the South remained largely agricultural by 1900, it had made great strides toward building industries in the region. This so-called New South boasted an extensive railway network that
provided a national market for its raw materials and manufactured goods, including coal, iron, steel,
and textiles. Still, the southern economy in 1900 depended primarily on raising cotton and tobacco.

Despite this frenzy of industrial activity, the New
South in many ways resembled the Old South. Southern
entrepreneurs still depended on northern investors to
supply much of the capital for investment. Investors were
attracted by the low wages that prevailed in the South, but
low wages also meant that southern workers remained
poor and, in many cases, unable to buy the manufactured
goods produced by industry. Efforts to diversify agriculture beyond tobacco and cotton were constrained by a
sharecropping system based on small, inefficient plots. In
fact, even though industrialization did make considerable
headway in the South, the economy remained overwhelmingly agricultural. This suited many white southerners
who wanted to hold on to the individualistic, agrarian
values they associated with the Old South. In this way,

they sought to remain distinct from what they considered
the acquisitive North. Yoked to old ideologies and a system of forced labor, modernization in the South could go
only so far.

Industrial Consolidation

In both the North and the South, nineteenth-century
industrialists strove to minimize or eliminate competition. To gain competitive advantages and increase profits,
industrial entrepreneurs concentrated on reducing production costs, charging lower prices, and outselling the
competition. Successful firms could then acquire rival
companies that could no longer afford to compete, creating
an industrial empire in the process.

Building such industrial empires was not easy, however, and posed creative challenges for business ventures. Heavy investment in machinery resulted in very high fixed costs (or overhead) that did not change much over time. Because overhead costs remained stable, manufacturers could reduce the per-unit cost of production by increasing the output of a product—what economists call "economy of scale." Manufacturers thus aimed to raise the volume of production and find ways to cut variable costs—for labor and materials, for example. Shaving off even a few pennies from the cost of making each unit could save millions of dollars on the total cost of production. Through such savings, a factory owner could sell his product more cheaply than his competitors and gain a larger share of the market.

A major organizational technique for reducing costs and underselling the competition was **vertical integration**. "Captains of industry," as their admirers called them, did not just build a business; they created a system—a network of firms, each contributing to the final product. Men like Andrew Carnegie controlled the various phases of production from top to bottom (vertical), extracting the raw materials, transporting them to the factories, manufacturing the finished products, and shipping them to market. In 1881, when Carnegie combined his operations with those of Henry Clay Frick of Pennsylvania, he gained not only a talented factory manager but also access to Frick's coal business. By using vertical integration, Carnegie eliminated middlemen and guaranteed regular and cheap access to supplies. He also avoided duplications in machinery, lowered inventories, and gained increased flexibility by shifting segments of the labor force to areas where they were most needed. This integrated system demanded close and careful management of the overall operation, which Carnegie provided. He manufactured steel with improved efficiency and cut costs. His credo became "Watch the costs and the profits will take care of themselves."

Businessmen also employed another type of integration—**horizontal integration**. This approach focused on gaining greater control over the market by acquiring firms that sold the same products. John D. Rockefeller, the founder of the mammoth Standard Oil Company, specialized in this technique. In the mid-1870s, he brought a number of key oil refiners into an alliance with Standard Oil to control four-fifths of the industry. At the same time, the oil baron ruthlessly drove out or bought up marginal firms that could not afford to compete with him. One such competitor testified to a congressional committee in 1879 about how Standard Oil had squeezed him out: "[Rockefeller] said that he had facilities for freighting and that the coal-oil business belonged to them; and any concern that would start in that business, they had sufficient money to lay aside a fund and wipe them out."

Horizontal integration was also a major feature in the telegraph industry. By 1861 Western Union had strung 76,000 miles of telegraph line throughout the nation. Founded in 1851, the company had thrived during the Civil War by obtaining most of the federal government's telegraph business. The firm had 12,600 offices housed in railroad depots throughout the country and strung its lines adjacent to the railroads. In the eight years before Cornelius Vanderbilt bought Western Union in 1869, the value of its stock jumped from $3 million to $41 million. Seeing an opportunity to make money, Wall Street tycoon Jay Gould set out to acquire Western Union. In the mid-1870s, Gould, who had obtained control over the Union Pacific Railway, financed companies to compete with the giant telegraph outfit. Gould did not succeed until 1881, when he engineered a takeover of Western Union by combining it with his American Union Telegraph Company. Gould made a profit of $30 million on the deal. On February 15, the day after the agreement, the *New York Herald Tribune* reported: "The country finds itself this morning at the feet of a telegraphic monopoly," a business that controlled the market and destroyed competition.

Bankers played a huge role in engineering industrial consolidation. No one did it more skillfully than John Pierpont Morgan. In the 1850s, Morgan started his career working for a prominent American-owned banking firm in London, and in 1861 he created his own investment company in New York City. Unlike the United States, Great Britain had a surplus of capital that bankers sought to invest abroad. Morgan played the central role in channeling funds from Britain to support the construction of major American railroads. During the 1880s and 1890s, Morgan orchestrated the refinancing of several ailing railroads, including the Baltimore & Ohio and the Southern Railroad. To maintain control over these enterprises, the Wall Street financier placed his allies on their boards of directors and selected the companies' chief operating officers. Morgan then turned his talents for organization to the steel industry. In 1901 he was instrumental in merging Carnegie's company with several competitors in which he had a financial interest. United States Steel, Morgan's creation, became the world's largest industrial corporation, worth $1.4 billion. By the end of the first decade of the twentieth century, Morgan's investment house held more than 340 directorships in 112 corporations, amounting to more than $22 billion in assets, the equivalent of $608 billion in 2012, all at a time when there was no income tax.

The Growth of Corporations

With economic consolidation came the expansion of **corporations**. Before the age of large-scale enterprise, the predominant form of business ownership was the partnership. Unlike partnerships, corporations provided investors with "limited liability." This meant that if the corporation went bankrupt, shareholders could not lose more than they had invested. Limited liability encouraged investment by keeping the shareholders' investment in the corporation separate from their other assets. In addition, corporations provided "perpetual life." Partnerships dissolved on the death of a partner, whereas corporations continued to function despite the death of any single owner. This form of ownership brought stability and order to financing, building, and perpetuating what was otherwise a highly volatile and complex business endeavor.

Capitalists devised new corporate structures to gain greater control over their industries. Rockefeller's Standard Oil Company led the way by creating the trust, a monopoly formed through consolidation. To evade state laws against monopolies, Rockefeller created a petroleum trust. He combined other oil firms across the country with Standard Oil and placed their owners on a nine-member board of trustees that ran the company. Subsequently, Rockefeller fashioned another method of bringing rival businesses together. Through a holding company, he obtained stock in a number of other oil companies and held them under his control.

The movement to create trusts, Rockefeller boasted, "was the origin of the whole system of modern economic administration." Statistics backed up his assessment. Between 1880 and 1905, more than three hundred mergers occurred in 80 percent of the nation's manufacturing firms. Great wealth became heavily concentrated in the hands of a relatively small number of businessmen. Around two thousand businesses, a tiny fraction of the total number, dominated 40 percent of the nation's economy.

Explore

See Document 16.1 for one cartoonist's interpretation of Rockefeller's power.

In their drive to consolidate economic power and shield themselves from risk, corporate titans generally had the courts on their side. In *Santa Clara County v. Southern Pacific Railroad Company* (1886), the Supreme Court decided that under the Fourteenth Amendment, which originally dealt with the issue of federal protection of African Americans' civil rights, a corporation was considered a "person." In effect, this ruling gave corporations the same right of due process that the framers of the amendment had meant to give to former slaves. In the 1890s, a majority of the Supreme Court embraced this interpretation. The right of due process shielded corporations from prohibitive government regulation of the workplace, including the passage of legislation reducing the number of hours in the workday.

Yet trusts did not go unopposed. In 1890 Congress passed Senator Sherman's Antitrust Act, which outlawed monopolies that prevented free competition in interstate commerce. The bill passed easily with bipartisan support because it merely codified legal principles that already existed. Sherman and his colleagues never intended to stifle large corporations, which through efficient business practices came to dominate the market. Rather, the lawmakers attempted to limit underhanded actions that destroyed competition. The judicial system further bailed out corporate leaders. In *United States v. E.C. Knight Company* (1895), a case against the "sugar trust," the Supreme Court rendered the Sherman Act virtually toothless by ruling that manufacturing was a local activity within a state and that, even if it was a monopoly, it was not subject to congressional regulation. This ruling left most trusts in the manufacturing sector beyond the jurisdiction of the **Sherman Antitrust Act**.

The introduction of managerial specialists, already present in European firms, proved the most critical innovation for integrating industry. With many operations controlled under one roof, large-scale businesses required a corps of experts to oversee and coordinate the various steps of production. Comptrollers and accountants pored over financial records to keep track of every penny spent and dollar earned. Traffic managers directed the movement of raw materials into plants and finished products out for distribution. Marketing executives were in charge of advertising goods and finding new markets. Efficiency experts sought to cut labor costs and make the production process operate more smoothly. Frederick W. Taylor, a Philadelphia engineer and businessman, developed the principles of scientific management. Based on his concept of reducing manual labor to its simplest components and eliminating independent action on the part of workers, managers introduced time-and-motion studies. Using a stopwatch, they calculated how to break down a job into simple tasks that could be performed in the least amount of time. From this perspective, workers were no different from the machines they operated.

Another vital factor in creating large-scale industry was the establishment of retail outlets that could sell the enormous volume of goods pouring out of factories. As consumer goods became less expensive, retail outlets sprang up to serve the growing market for household items, including watches, jewelry, sewing machines, cameras, and an assortment of rugs and furniture. Customers could shop at department stores—such as Macy's in New York City, Filene's in Boston, Marshall Field's in Chicago, Nordstrom's in Seattle, Gump's in San Francisco, Nieman Marcus in Dallas, Jacome's in Tucson, Rich's in Atlanta, and Burdine's in Miami—where they were waited on by a

DOCUMENT 16.1

Horace Taylor | What a Funny Little Government, 1900

As large firms merged with competitors to form giant companies that dominated the marketplace, opponents of such trusts decried the power that these enterprises wielded over the economy and the political system. Responding to such concerns, Congress passed the Sherman Antitrust Act in 1890, but the law proved weak and was loosely enforced. In the following illustration, cartoonist Horace Taylor, a Democrat, sought to make trusts an issue in the 1900 election by attacking John D. Rockefeller, whose Standard Oil Company embodied the evils of trusts for many critics.

Explore

How are the Capitol and Treasury depicted?

How does this illustration of Rockefeller emphasize the cartoonist's antitrust position?

Collection of the New-York Historical Society

What is Rockefeller holding in his hand?

Put It in Context

What does this cartoon suggest about the relationship between big business and the federal government at the start of the twentieth century?

1899 Sears, Roebuck Catalog

The expansion of industrialization and completion of the transcontinental railroad created a national market for manufactured goods and led to the growth of consumer culture. The Chicago-based Sears, Roebuck used its mail-order catalog to attract customers throughout the United States and, as its cover suggests, the world. This colorful 1899 catalog offers the latest items in carpets, furniture, china, fashions, and photographic equipment and supplies.   The Granger Collection, New York

growing army of salesclerks. Or they could buy the cheaper items in Frank W. Woolworth's five and ten cent stores, which opened in towns and cities nationwide. Chain supermarkets—such as the Great Atlantic and Pacific Tea Company (A&P), founded in 1869—sold fruits and vegetables packed in tin cans. They also sold foods from the meatpacking firms of Gustavus Swift and Philip Armour, which shipped them on refrigerated railroad cars. Mail-order catalogs allowed Americans in all parts of the country to buy consumer goods without leaving their home. The catalogs of Montgomery Ward (established in 1872) and Sears, Roebuck (founded in 1886) offered tens of thousands of items. Rural free delivery (RFD), instituted by the U.S.

Post Office in 1891, made it even easier for farmers and others living in the countryside to obtain these catalogs and buy their merchandise without having to travel miles to the nearest post office. By the end of the nineteenth century, the industrial economy had left its mark on almost all aspects of life in almost every corner of America.

REVIEW & RELATE

What were the key factors behind the acceleration of industrial development in late-nineteenth-century America?

How did industrialization change the way American businessmen thought about their companies and the people who worked for them?

Free Markets and Rugged Individuals

American industrialization developed as rapidly as it did in large part because it was reinforced by traditional ideas and values. The notion that hard work and diligence would result in success meant that individuals felt justified, even duty-bound, to strive to achieve upward mobility and accumulate wealth. Churches, schools, intellectuals, and popular writers combined to buttress this doctrine of success. Those who succeeded believed that they had done so because they were more talented, industrious, and resourceful than others. Thus prosperous businessmen regarded competition and the free market as essential to the health of an economic world they saw based on merit. Yet these same businessmen also created trusts that destroyed competition, and they depended on the government for resources and protection. This obvious contradiction, along with the profoundly unequal distribution of wealth that characterized the late-nineteenth-century economy, generated a good deal of criticism of business tycoons and their beliefs.

The Doctrine of Success

Those at the top of the new industrial order justified their great wealth in a manner that most Americans could understand. The ideas of the Scottish economist Adam Smith, in *The Wealth of Nations* (1776), had gained popularity during the American Revolution. Advocating **laissez-faire** ("let things alone"), Smith contended that an "Invisible Hand," guided by natural law, guaranteed the greatest economic success if the government let individuals pursue their own self-interest unhindered by outside and artificial influences. In the late nineteenth century, businessmen and their conservative allies on the Supreme Court used Smith's doctrines to argue against restrictive government regulation. They equated their right to own and manage property with the personal liberty protected by the Fourteenth Amendment. Thus the Declaration of Independence, with its defense of "life, liberty, and the pursuit of happiness," and the Constitution, which enshrined citizens' political freedom, became instruments to guarantee unfettered economic opportunity and safeguard private property.

The view that success depended on individual initiative was reinforced in schools and churches. The McGuffey Readers, widely used to educate children, taught moral lessons of hard work, individual initiative, reliability, and thrift. The popular dime novels of Horatio Alger portrayed the story of young men, such as Ragged Dick, who rose through pluck and luck from "rags to riches." Americans could also hear success stories in houses of worship. Russell Conwell,

pastor of the Grace Baptist Church in Philadelphia, delivered a widely printed sermon entitled "Acres of Diamonds," which equated godliness with riches and argued that ordinary people had an obligation to strive for material wealth. "I say that you ought to get rich, and it is your duty to get rich," Conwell declared, "because to make money honestly is to preach the gospel." Conwell followed his own advice and became wealthy from the fees he earned delivering his popular sermon.

If economic success was a matter of personal merit, it followed that economic failure was as well. The British philosopher Herbert Spencer proposed a theory of social evolution based on this premise in his book *Social Statics* (1851). Imagining a future utopia, Spencer wrote, "Man was not created with an instinct for his own degradation, but from the lower he has risen to the higher forms. Nor is there any conceivable end to his march to perfection." In his view, those at the top of the economic ladder were closer

McGuffey Reader

Beginning in the mid-nineteenth century, McGuffey Readers became the most popular textbook for teaching elementary school pupils how to read. As this page from an edition first published in 1881 shows, the book included exercises that taught students moral lessons along with their readings. In emphasizing hard work and obedience, the readers instructed children in middle-class virtues.

to perfection than were those at the bottom. Any effort to aid the unfortunate would only slow the march of progress for society as a whole. Spencer's book proved extremely popular, selling nearly 400,000 copies in the United States by 1900. In recalling how Spencer's ideas influenced him, Carnegie wrote, "I remember that light came as in a flood and all was clear." Publication of Charles Darwin's landmark *On the Origin of Species* (1859) appeared to provide some scientific legitimacy for Spencer's view. The British naturalist argued that plants, animals, and humans progressed or declined because of their ability or inability to adapt favorably to the environment and transmit these characteristics to future generations. The connection between the two men's ideas has led some to label Spencer and his supporters "Social Darwinists." However, few defenders of laissez-faire principles in the late nineteenth century had actually read Darwin or referred to themselves as Social Darwinists, a term that came into widespread use only in the twentieth century.

Doctrines of success gained favor because they helped Americans explain the rapid economic changes that were disrupting their lives. Although most ordinary people would not climb out of poverty to middle-class respectability, let alone affluence, they clung to ideas that promised hope. After all, if a man like Carnegie could rise from poverty to become a multimillionaire, why not them? It mattered little that most of those who achieved extraordinary wealth did not emerge from the working class but rather came from the middle class. Ideas such as Spencer's that linked success with progress provided a way for those who did not do well to understand their failure and blame themselves for their own inadequacies. At the same time, the notion that economic success derived from personal merit legitimized the fabulous wealth of those who did rise to the top.

Capitalists such as Carnegie found a way to soften both the message of extreme competition and its impact on the American public. Denying that the government should help the poor, they proclaimed that men of wealth had a duty to furnish some assistance. In his famous essay **"The Gospel of Wealth"** (1889), Carnegie declared that "a man who died rich died disgraced." He argued that the rich should act as stewards of the wealth they earned. As trustees, they should administer their surplus income for the benefit of the community. Carnegie distinguished between charity (direct handouts to individuals), which he deplored, and philanthropy (building institutions that would raise educational and cultural standards), which he advocated. For example, Carnegie, Rockefeller, and railroad tycoons Leland Stanford and Cornelius Vanderbilt all gave endowments (and their names) to universities to provide education for those who worked hard to achieve it. Russell Conwell also gave away his fortune to various philanthropic enterprises, most

notably the founding of Temple University in Philadelphia, which opened its doors to poor men seeking a higher education. Carnegie was particularly generous in funding libraries (he provided the buildings but not the books) because they allowed people to gain knowledge through their own efforts.

Capitalists may have sung the praises of individualism and laissez-faire, but their actions contradicted their words. Successful industrialists in the late nineteenth century sought to destroy competition, not perpetuate it. Their efforts over the course of several decades produced giant corporations that measured the worth of individuals by calculating their value to the organization. As John D. Rockefeller, the master of consolidation, proclaimed, "The day of individual competition in large affairs is past and gone." **See Document Project 16: Debates about Laissez-Faire, page 517**.

Nor did capitalists strictly oppose government involvement. Although industrialists did not want the federal government to take any action that *retarded* their economic efforts, they did favor the use of the government's power to *promote* their enterprises and to stimulate entrepreneurial energies. Thus manufacturers pushed for congressional passage of high tariffs to protect goods from foreign competition and to foster development of the national marketplace. Industrialists demanded that federal and state governments dispatch troops when labor strikes threatened their businesses. They persuaded Washington to provide land grants for railroad construction and to send the army to clear Native Americans and bison from their tracks. They argued for state and federal courts to interpret constitutional and statutory law in a way that shielded property rights against attacks from workers. In large measure, capitalists succeeded not in spite of governmental support but because of it.

Challenges to Laissez-Faire

Proponents of government restraint and unbridled individualism did not go unchallenged. Critics of laissez-faire created an alternative ideology for those who sought to organize workers and expand the role of government as ways of restricting capitalists' power over labor and ordinary citizens.

Lester Frank Ward attacked laissez-faire in his book *Dynamic Sociology* (1883). A largely self-taught man who worked as a civil servant for the federal government, Ward did not disparage individualism but viewed the main function of society as "the organization of happiness." Contradicting Herbert Spencer, Ward maintained that societies progressed when government directly intervened to help citizens—even the unfortunate. Indeed, society could initiate "the systematic realization of its own interests, in the same manner that an intelligent and keen-sighted individual pursues his life-purposes." Rejecting laissez-faire, Ward argued that what people "really need is more government in its primary sense, greater protection from the rapacity of the favored few."

Some academics supported Ward's ideas. Most notably, economist Richard T. Ely applied Christian ethics to his scholarly assessment of capital and labor. He condemned the railroads for dragging "their slimy length over our country, and every turn in their progress is marked by a progeny of evils." In his book *The Labor Movement* (1886), Ely suggested that the ultimate solution for social ills resulting from industrialization lay in "the union of capital and labor in the same hands, in grand, wide-reaching, co-operative enterprises."

Two popular writers, Henry George and Edward Bellamy, added to the critique of materialism and greed. In *Progress and Poverty* (1879), George lamented: "Amid the greatest accumulations of wealth, men die of starvation." He blamed the problem on rent, which he viewed as an unjustifiable payment on the increase in the value of land, what he called "unearned increment." His remedy was to have government confiscate rent earned on land by levying a single tax on landownership. Though he advocated government intervention, he did not envision an enduring role for the state once it had imposed the single tax. By contrast, Bellamy imagined a powerful central government. In his novel *Looking Backward, 2000–1887* (1888), Bellamy scorned the "imbecility of private enterprise" and attacked industrialists who "maim and slaughter workers by thousands." In his view, the federal government should take over large-scale firms, administer them as workers' collectives, and redistribute wealth equally among all citizens.

Neither Bellamy, George, Ward, nor Ely endorsed the militant socialism of Karl Marx. The German philosopher predicted that capitalism would be overthrown and replaced by a revolutionary movement of industrial workers that would control the means of economic production and establish an egalitarian society. Although his ideas gained popularity among European labor leaders, they were not widely accepted in the United States during this period. George referred to Marx as "the prince of muddleheads." George and other critics believed that the American political system could be reformed without resorting to the extreme solution of a socialist revolution. They favored a cooperative commonwealth of capital and labor, with the government acting as an umpire between the two.

REVIEW & RELATE

In the late nineteenth century, how did many Americans explain individual economic success and failure?

How did the business community view the role of government in the economy at the end of the nineteenth century?

☑ *LEARNINGCurve* bedfordstmartins.com/hewittlawson/LC

Society and Culture in the Gilded Age

Wealthy people in the late nineteenth century used their fortunes to support lavish, indulgent lifestyles. For many of them, especially those with recent wealth, opulence rather than good taste was the standard of adornment. This tendency inspired writer Mark Twain and his collaborator Charles Dudley Warner to describe this era of wealth creation and vast inequality as the **Gilded Age**.

Twain and Warner had the very wealthy in mind when they coined the phrase, but others further down the social ladder found ways to participate in the culture of consumption. The rapidly expanding middle class enjoyed modest homes furnished with mass-produced consumer goods. Women played the central role in running the household, as most wives remained at home to raise children. Women and men often spent their free time attending meetings and other events sponsored by the many social, cultural, and political organizations that flourished during this era. Such prosperity was, however, largely limited to whites. For the majority of African Americans still living in the South, life proved much harder. In response to black aspirations for social and economic advancement, white politicians imposed a rigid system of racial segregation on the South. Although whites championed the cause of individual upward mobility, they restricted opportunities to achieve success to whites only.

Wealthy and Middle-Class Pleasures

In Chicago's Gold Coast, Boston's Back Bay, Philadelphia's Rittenhouse Square, San Francisco's Nob Hill, Denver's Quality Hill, and Cincinnati's Hilltop, urban elites lived lives of incredible material opulence. J. P. Morgan and John D. Rockefeller built lavish homes in New York City. William Vanderbilt constructed luxurious mansions along Fifth Avenue in Manhattan. High-rise apartment buildings also catered to the wealthy. Overlooking Central Park, the nine-story Dakota Apartments boasted fifty-eight suites, a banquet hall, and a wine cellar. Famous architects designed some of the finest of these stately homes, which their millionaire residents furnished with an eclectic mix of priceless art objects and furniture in a jumble of diverse styles. The rich and famous established private social clubs, sent their children to exclusive prep schools and colleges, and worshipped in the most fashionable churches.

Second homes, usually for use in the summer, were no less expensively constructed and decorated. Besides residences in Manhattan and Newport, Rhode Island, the Vanderbilts constructed a "home away from home" in the mountains of Asheville, North Carolina. The Biltmore, as they named it, contained 250 rooms, 40 master bedrooms, and an indoor swimming pool. Edward Julius Berwind of Philadelphia, who made his fortune in coal, constructed a magnificent summer residence in Newport. Modeled after a mid-eighteenth-century French chateau, The Elms cost $1.4 million (approximately $38.6 million in 2012) and was furnished with an assortment of Renaissance ceramics and French and Venetian paintings.

The wealthy also built and frequented opera houses, concert halls, museums, and historical societies as testimonies to their taste and sophistication. For example, the Vanderbilts, Rockefellers, Goulds, and Morgans financed the completion of the Metropolitan Opera House in New York City in 1883. When the facility opened, a local newspaper commented about the well-heeled audience: "The Goulds and the Vanderbilts and people of that ilk perfumed the air with the odor of crisp greenbacks." Upper-class women often traveled abroad to visit the great European cities and ancient Mediterranean sites.

Industrialization and the rise of corporate capitalism also brought an array of **white-collar workers** in managerial,

clerical, and technical positions. These workers formed a new, expanded middle class and joined the businesspeople, doctors, lawyers, teachers, and clergy who constituted the old middle class. More than three million white-collar workers were employed in 1910, nearly three times as many as in 1870.

Middle-class families decorated their residences with comfortable, mass-produced furniture, musical instruments, family photographs, books, periodicals, and a variety of memorabilia collected in their leisure time. They could relax in their parlors and browse through mass-circulation magazines like *Ladies' Home Journal* and *The Delineator*, a fashion and arts journal. They might also read a wide variety of popular newspapers that competed with one another with sensationalist stories. Or they could read some of the era's outpouring of fiction, including romances, dime novels, westerns, humor, and social realism, an art form that depicted working-class life.

> **Explore**
>
> See Document 16.2 for the cover of a popular women's magazine from 1900.

In the face of rapid economic changes, middle-class women and men joined a variety of social and professional organizations that were arising to deal with the problems accompanying industrialization (Table 16.1). During the 1880s, charitable organizations such as the American Red Cross were established to provide disaster relief. In 1892 the General Federation of Women's Clubs was founded to improve women's educational and cultural lives. Four years later, the National Association of Colored Women organized to help relieve suffering among the black poor, defend black women, and promote the interests of the black race. Many scholarly organizations were formed during this decade, including the American Historical Association, the Modern Language Association, and the American Mathematical Society.

During these swiftly changing times, adults became increasingly concerned about the nation's youth and sought to create organizations that catered to young people. Formed before the Civil War in England and expanded to the United States, the Young Men's Christian Association (YMCA) grew briskly during the 1880s as it erected buildings where young men could socialize, build moral character, and engage in healthy physical exercise. The Young Women's Christian Association (YWCA) provided similar

TABLE 16.1 An Age of Organizations, 1876–1896

Category	Year of Founding	Organization
Charitable	1881	American Red Cross
	1887	Charity Organization Society
	1889	Educational Alliance
	1893	National Council of Jewish Women
Sports/Fraternal	1876	National League of Baseball
	1882	Knights of Columbus
	1888	National Council of Women
	1892	General Federation of Women's Clubs
	1896	National Association of Colored Women
Professional	1883	Modern Language Association
	1884	American Historical Association
	1885	American Economic Association
	1888	American Mathematical Society

DOCUMENT 16.2

The Delineator, 1900

By 1900 *The Delineator* had become one of America's foremost women's magazines. On the surface, it appeared to cater to traditional gender norms, each month featuring stories on fashion, sewing, leisure, and home design. But the editors of *The Delineator* also called for women's rights and broader social reform. In 1907, for example, editor Theodore Dreiser organized a successful outreach program to find homes for abandoned and orphaned children.

Explore

VOL.XLVI N°1   JULY, 1900.

THE DELINEATOR

In Guise of Summer

PARIS, LONDON, NEW YORK

PUBLISHED MONTHLY BY THE BUTTERICK PUBLISHING CO. (LTD.)

SUBSCRIPTION PRICE, $1.00.   SINGLE COPY, 15 CENTS.

ENTERED AT THE POST-OFFICE, N. Y., AS SECOND-CLASS MAIL MATTER

© Sarah Fabian-Baddiel/Heritage-Images/The Image Works

Interpret the Evidence

- What does this woman's clothing and activity suggest about her background?
- Who do you think was the target audience for this magazine?

Put It in Context

What social and political trends during the late nineteenth century might account for the popularity of magazines like *The Delineator*?

opportunities for women. African Americans also participated in "Y" activities through the creation of racially
separate branches.

Changing Gender Roles

Middle-class wives generally remained at home, caring for
the house and children, often with the aid of a servant.
Whereas in the past farmers and artisans had worked
from the home, now most men and women accepted as
natural the separation of the workplace and the home
caused by industrialization and urbanization. Although
the birthrate and marriage rates among the middle class
dropped during the late nineteenth century, wives were
still expected to care for their husbands and family first
to fulfill their feminine duties. Even though daughters
increasingly attended colleges reserved for women, such
as Smith, Radcliffe, Wellesley, and Mount Holyoke, their
families viewed education as a means of providing
refinement rather than a career. One physician aptly
summed up the prevailing view that women could only
use their brains "but little and in trivial matters" and
should concentrate on serving as "the companion or
ornamental appendage to man."

Middle-class women were now confronted with the
new consumer culture. Department stores, chain stores,
ready-made clothes, and packaged goods, from Jell-O and
Kellogg's Corn Flakes to cake mixes, competed for the
money and loyalty of female consumers. Hairdressers,
cosmetic companies, and department stores offered a
growing and ever-changing assortment of styles, even as
they also provided new jobs to those unable to afford the
latest fashions without a weekly paycheck. The expanding array of consumer goods did not, however, decrease
women's domestic workload. They had more furniture to
dust, fancier meals to prepare, changing fashions to keep
up with, higher standards of cleanliness to maintain, and
more time to devote to entertaining. Yet the availability of
mass-produced goods to assist the housewife in her chores
made her role as consumer highly visible, while making her
role as worker nearly invisible.

For the more socially and economically independent
young women—those who attended college or beauty and
secretarial schools—new worlds of leisure opened up.
Bicycling, tennis, and croquet became popular sports for
women in the late nineteenth century. So, too, did playing
basketball, both in colleges and through industrial leagues.
Indeed, women's colleges made sports a requirement, to offset
the stress of intellectual life and produce
a more well-rounded woman. Young
women who sought an air of sophistication dressed according to the image of the
Gibson Girl, the creation of illustrator
Charles Dana Gibson. In the 1890s, the
Gibson Girl became the model for the
energetic, athletic "new woman," with
her upswept hair, fancy hats, long skirts,
flowing blouses, and disposable income.

Middle-class men enjoyed their
leisure by joining fraternal organizations.
Writing in the *North American Review*
in 1897, W. G. Harwood commented
that the late nineteenth century was the
"Golden Age of Fraternity." Five and a
half million men (of some 19 million
adult men in the United States) joined
fraternal orders, such as the Odd
Fellows, Masons, Knights of Pythias, and
Elks. These groups offered middle-class
men a network of business contacts and
gave them a chance to enjoy a communal, masculine social environment
otherwise lacking in their lives.

In fact, historians have referred
to a "crisis of masculinity" afflicting a
segment of middle- and upper-class men

Shopping in a Department Store

In cities around the country, department stores offered a variety of items appealing to
middle-class consumers, especially women. In this photograph from 1893, shoppers
interested in purchasing gloves receive personal attention from well-dressed salesclerks
behind the counter of Rike's Department Store in Dayton, Ohio.   © Bettmann/CORBIS

in the late nineteenth and early twentieth centuries. Middle-class occupations whittled away the sense of autonomy that men had experienced in an earlier era when they worked for themselves. The emergence of corporate capitalism had swelled the ranks of the middle class with organization men, who held salaried jobs in managerial departments. At the same time, the push for women's rights, especially the right to vote, and women's increasing involvement in civic associations threatened to reduce absolute male control over the public sphere.

Responding to this gender crisis, middle-class men sought ways to exert their masculinity and keep from becoming frail and effeminate. Psychologists like G. Stanley Hall warned that unless men returned to a primitive state of manhood, they risked becoming feminized and spiritually paralyzed. To avoid this, they should build up their bodies and engage in strenuous activities to improve their physical fitness. Edgar Rice Burroughs's *Tarzan of the Apes* (1912) extolled primitive manhood and contrasted its natural virtues with the vices of becoming overcivilized.

Men turned to sports to cultivate their masculinity. Besides playing baseball and football, they could attend various sporting events. Baseball became the national pastime, and men could root for their home team and establish a community with the thousands of male spectators who filled up newly constructed ballparks. These fields of dirt and grass were situated amid urban businesses, apartment buildings, and traffic and served as a metaphor for the preservation of an older, pastoral life alongside the hubbub of modern technology. Baseball, which had started as a game played by elites in New York City in the 1840s, soon became a commercially popular sport. It spread across the country as baseball clubs in different cities competed with each other. The sport came into its own with the creation of the professional National League in 1876 and the introduction of the World Series in 1903 between the winners of the National League and the American League pennant races.

Boxing also became a popular spectator sport in the late nineteenth century. Bare-knuckle fighting—without the protection of gloves—epitomized the craze to display pure masculinity. A boxing match lasted until one of the fighters was knocked out, leaving both fighters bloody and battered.

During the late nineteenth century, middle-class women and men also had increased opportunities to engage in different forms of sociability and sexuality. Gay men and lesbians could find safe havens in New York City's Greenwich Village and Chicago's North Side for their own entertainment. Although treated by medical experts as sexual "inverts" who might be cured by an infusion of "normal" heterosocial contact, gays and

lesbians began to emerge from the shadows of Victorian-era sexual constraints around the turn of the twentieth century. "Boston marriages" constituted another form of relationship between women. The term apparently came from Henry James's book *The Bostonians* (1886), which described a female couple living together in a monogamous, long-term relationship. This conjugal-style association appealed to financially independent women who did not want to get married. Many of these relationships were sexual, but some were not. In either case, they offered women of a certain class an alternative to traditional, heterosexual marriage.

Black America and Jim Crow

While wealthy and middle-class whites experimented with new forms of social behavior, African Americans faced greater challenges to preserving their freedom and dignity. In the South, where the overwhelming majority of blacks lived, post-Reconstruction southern governments adopted various techniques to keep blacks from voting. To circumvent the Fifteenth Amendment, southern states devised suffrage qualifications that they claimed were racially neutral, and the Supreme Court ruled in their favor. They instituted the poll tax, a tax that each person had to pay in order to cast a ballot. Poll taxes fell hardest on the poor, a disproportionate number of whom were African American. Disfranchisement reached its peak in the 1890s, as white southern governments managed to deny the vote to most of the black electorate (Map 16.2). Literacy tests officially barred the uneducated of both races, but they were administered in a manner that discriminated against blacks while allowing illiterate whites to satisfy the requirement. Many literacy tests contained a loophole called a "grandfather clause." Under this exception, men whose father or grandfather had voted in 1860—a time when white men but not black men, most of whom were slaves, could vote in the South—were excused from taking the test.

In the 1890s, white southerners also imposed legally sanctioned racial segregation on the region's black citizens. Commonly known as **Jim Crow** laws (named for a character in a minstrel show, where whites performed in blackface), these new statutes denied African Americans equal access to public facilities and ensured that blacks lived apart from whites. In 1883, when the Supreme Court struck down the 1875 Civil Rights Act (see chapter 14), it gave southern states the freedom to adopt measures confining blacks to separate schools, public accommodations, seats on transportation, beds in hospitals, and sections of graveyards. In 1896 the Supreme Court sanctioned Jim Crow, constructing the constitutional rationale for legally keeping the races apart. In *Plessy v. Ferguson*, the high court ruled

MAP 16.2   Black Disfranchisement in the South, 1889–1908

After Reconstruction, black voters posed a threat to the ruling Democrats by occasionally joining with third-party insurgents. To repel these challenges, Democratic Party leaders made racial appeals to divide poor whites and blacks. Chiefly in the 1890s and early twentieth century, white leaders succeeded in disfranchising black voters (and some poor whites), mainly by adopting poll tax and literacy requirements.

that a Louisiana law providing for "equal but separate" accommodations for "whites" and "coloreds" on railroad cars did not violate the equal protection clause of the Fourteenth Amendment. In its decision, the Court concluded that civil rights laws could not change racial destiny. "If one race be inferior to the other socially," the justices explained, "the Constitution of the United States cannot put them on the same plane." In practice, however, white southerners obeyed the "separate" part of the equation but never provided equal services. If blacks tried to overstep the bounds of Jim Crow in any way that whites found unacceptable, they risked their lives. Between 1884 and 1900, nearly 1,700 blacks were lynched in the South. Victims were often subjected to brutal forms of torture before they were hanged or shot.

In everyday life, African Americans carried on as best they could. Segregation provided many African Americans with opportunities to build their own businesses, control their own churches, develop their own schools staffed by black teachers, and form their own civic associations and fraternal organizations. Segregation, though harsh and unequal, did foster a sense of black community, promoted a rising middle class, and created social networks that enhanced racial pride. Founded in 1898, the North Carolina Life Insurance Company, one of the leading black-owned and black-operated businesses, employed many African Americans in managerial and sales positions. Burial societies ensured that their members received a proper funeral when they died. As with whites, black men joined lodges such as the Colored Masons and the Colored Odd Fellows, while women participated in the YWCA and the National Association of Colored Women. A small

percentage of southern blacks resisted Jim Crow by migrating to the North, where blacks still exercised the right to vote, more jobs were open to them, and segregation was less strictly enforced.

REVIEW & RELATE

What role did consumption play in the society and culture of the Gilded Age?

How did industrialization contribute to heightened anxieties about gender roles and race?

✔ *LEARNINGCurve* bedfordstmartins.com/hewittlawson/LC

National Politics in the Era of Industrialization

Politicians such as John Sherman played an important role in the expanding industrial economy that provided new opportunities for the wealthy and the expanding middle class. For growing companies and corporations to succeed, they needed a favorable political climate that would support their interests. Businessmen frequently looked to Washington for assistance at a time when politicians were held in low repute. During this era, the office of the president was a weak and largely administrative post, and corporate leaders were unconcerned with the quality of the mind and character of presidents, legislators, and judges so long as these officials furthered their economic objectives. For much of this period, the two national political parties battled to a standoff, which resulted in congressional gridlock with little accomplished. Yet spurred by fierce partisan competition, political participation grew among the electorate.

Why Great Men Did Not Become President

James Bryce, a British observer of American politics, devoted a chapter of his book *The American Commonwealth* (1888) to "why great men are not chosen presidents." He acknowledged that the office of president "is raised far above all other offices [and] offers too great a stimulation to ambition." Yet he believed that the White House attracted mediocre occupants because the president functioned mainly as an executor. The stature of the office had shrunk following the impeachment of Andrew Johnson and the reassertion of congressional power during Reconstruction (see chapter 14). Presidents considered themselves mainly as the nation's top administrator. They did not see their roles as formulating policy or intervening on behalf of legislative objectives. Presidents had only a small White House staff to assist them, which reflected the meager demands placed on their office, especially in times of peace, which prevailed until 1898. The Civil Service Act of 1883 had reduced even further the political patronage the president had at his disposal. With the office held in such low regard, Bryce asserted, "most of the ablest men for thought, planning, and execution in America, go into the business of developing the national resources of the country." During the Age of Organization, great men became corporate leaders, not presidents.

Perhaps aware that they could expect little in the way of assistance or imagination from national leaders, voters refused to give either Democrats or Republicans solid support. No president between Ulysses S. Grant and William McKinley won back-to-back elections or received a majority of the popular vote. The only two-time winner, the Democrat Grover Cleveland, lost his bid for reelection in 1888 before triumphing again in 1892. Republicans scored victories in four out of six presidential contests from 1876 to 1896, but the vote tallies were extremely close.

Explore

See Documents 16.3 and 16.4 for two views on presidential greatness.

Nevertheless, the presidency attracted accomplished individuals. Rutherford B. Hayes (1877–1881), James A. Garfield (1881), and Benjamin Harrison (1889–1893) all had served ably in the Union army as commanding officers during the Civil War and had prior political experience.

The nation greatly mourned Garfield following his assassination in 1881 by Charles Guiteau, a disgruntled applicant for federal patronage. Upon Garfield's death, Chester A. Arthur (1881–1885) became president. He had served as a quartermaster general during the Civil War, had a reputation as sympathetic to African American civil rights, and had run the New York City Customs House effectively. Grover Cleveland (1885–1889, 1893–1897) first served as mayor of Buffalo and then as governor of New York. All of these men, as even Bryce admitted, worked hard, possessed common sense, and were honest. However, they were uninspiring individuals who lacked qualities of leadership that would arouse others to action.

Congressional Inaction

Character alone did not diminish the power of the president. More important was the structure of Congress, which prevented the president from providing vigorous leadership. Throughout most of this period, Congress remained narrowly divided. Majorities continually shifted from one party to the other. For all but two terms, Democrats controlled the House of Representatives, while Republicans held the majority in the Senate. Divided government meant that during his term in office no late-nineteenth-century president had a majority of his party in both houses of Congress. Turnover among congressmen in the House of Representatives, who were elected every two years, was quite high, and there was little power of incumbency. For example, of the twenty-one congressmen from Ohio elected in 1882, only ten had served in the previous session, and only four of the ten won reelection two years later. The Senate, however, provided more continuity and allowed senators, with six-year terms of office, to amass greater power than congressmen could, as evidenced by John Sherman serving six terms in the upper chamber.

For all the power that Congress wielded, it failed to govern effectively or efficiently. Contemporary observers lamented the dismal state of affairs in the nation's capital. A cabinet officer in 1869 complained: "You can't use tact with a Congressman! A Congressman is a hog! You must take a stick and hit him on the snout!"

Although both the House and the Senate contained men of great talent, fine speaking ability, and clever legislative minds, the rules of each body turned orderly procedure into chaos. In the House, measures did not receive adequate attention on the floor because the Speaker did not have the power to control the flow of systematic debate. Committee chairmen held a tight rein over the introduction and consideration of legislation and competed with one another for influence in the chamber. Congressmen showed little decorum as they conducted business on

DOCUMENTS 16.3 AND 16.4

The Making of a Great President: Two Views

The British traveler James Bryce admired the United States and toured the country in the late 1880s. His book *The American Commonwealth* (1888), though flattering of U.S. traditions and accomplishments, found its political leaders lacking in greatness—an opinion that many subsequent historians have shared, although Bryce and more recent historians might differ in their definition of greatness. In the following passage from his book, Bryce comments on the ordinariness of most American presidents. Contrast Bryce's assessment with the excerpt from the obituary of President Grover Cleveland published in the *New York Times*.

Explore

16.3 James Bryce | Why Great Men Are Not Chosen Presidents, 1888

Europeans often ask, and Americans do not always explain, how it happens that this great office, the greatest in the world, unless we except the Papacy, to which any man can rise by his own merits, is not more frequently filled by great and striking men? In America, which is beyond all other countries the country of a "career open to talents," a country, moreover, in which political life is unusually keen and political ambition widely diffused, it might be expected that the highest place would always be won by a man of brilliant gifts. But since the heroes of the Revolution died out with Jefferson and Adams and Madison some sixty years ago, no person except General Grant has reached the chair whose name would have been remembered had he not been President, and no President except Abraham Lincoln has displayed rare or striking qualities in the chair. Who now knows or cares to know anything about the personality of James K. Polk or Franklin Pierce? The only thing remarkable about them is that being so commonplace they should have climbed so high. . . .

. . . Besides, the ordinary American voter does not object to mediocrity. He has a lower conception of the qualities requisite to make a statesman than those who direct public opinion in Europe have. He likes his candidate to be sensible, vigorous, and, above all, what he calls "magnetic," and does not value, because he sees no need for, originality or profundity, a fine culture or a wide knowledge. Candidates are selected to be run for nomination by knots of persons who, however expert as party tacticians, are usually commonplace men; and the choice between those selected for nomination is made by a very large body, an assembly of over eight hundred delegates from the local party organizations over the country, who are certainly no better than ordinary citizens.

Source: James Bryce, *The American Commonwealth* (London: Macmillan, 1888), 1:100, 102–3.

---

the House floor. Representatives chatted with each other, their voices drowning out the speakers at the podium, or they ignored the business at hand and instead answered correspondence and read newspapers.

The Senate, though more manageable in size and more stable in membership (only one-third of its membership stood for reelection every two years), did not function much more smoothly. Despite party affiliations, senators thought very highly of their own judgments and very little of the value of party unity. The position of majority leader, someone who could impose discipline on his colleagues and design a coherent legislative agenda, had not yet been created. An exasperated Woodrow Wilson, who favored the British system of parliamentary government, attributed the problem to the failure to place trust in somebody "to assume final responsibility and blame." Wilson, the author of *Congressional Government* (1885) and a future president, concluded: "Our government is defective as it parcels out power and confuses responsibility." Under these circumstances, neither the

16.4 Obituary of Grover Cleveland, 1908

As a public man, considering the splendid record that he made, he will be put in the same class with Washington and Lincoln—one of the three great Presidents that this country has had. His greatness was justified by his exceptionally strong character and his many intellectual gifts. He was a man of great moral strength, and having the advantage of a fine intellect he thought seriously and deeply upon all subjects, and, having reached a conclusion, particularly as to a principle of morals or religion, or public weal [welfare], he was uncompromising. He agreed with David Crockett that the first thing was to determine what was right and then to do that thing.

What he was in public life he was equally in private life; strong in his views, tolerant in method, but uncompromising in principle. Most of his time was spent in promoting education and philanthropy—work which entailed sacrifices of his time and personal convenience, without fee or hope of reward beyond the desire to do that which was useful and good. These occupied, when not in public life, most of his time, so that when we look over his career, though he reached the proverbial three score and ten years, it is not to be measured by years alone, but by his splendid deeds and lofty ideals which affected all who came within the range of his influence.

Source: "All Washington Mourns, All Flags at Half Staff in Tribute to Dead Statesman," *New York Times*, June 25, 1908, 5.

Interpret the Evidence

- What qualities was Bryce surprised to find missing in American presidents? How might Bryce have characterized the values and beliefs of the typical American voter?
- What does the obituary of Grover Cleveland tell you about the qualities many Americans associated with "greatness"? What qualities do you think make a president "great"?

Put It in Context

What role did late-nineteenth-century presidents play in the great economic growth of the United States?

president nor Congress governed efficiently or responsibly.

An Energized and Entertained Electorate

Despite all the difficulties of the legislative process, political candidates eagerly pursued office and conducted extremely heated campaigns. The electorate considered politics a form of entertainment. Political parties did not stand for clearly stated issues or offer innovative solutions; instead, campaigns took on the qualities of carefully staged performances. Candidates crafted their oratory to arouse the passions and prejudices of their audiences, and their managers handed out buttons, badges, and ceramic and glass plates stamped with the candidates' faces and slogans.

Partisanship helped fuel high political participation. During this period, voter turnout in presidential elections was much higher than at any time in the twentieth century. Region, as well as historical and cultural allegiances,

1892 Presidential Campaign Plate

Before radio, television, and the Internet, political parties advertised candidates in a variety of colorful ways, including banners, buttons, ribbons, and ceramic and glass plates. Voters, who turned out in record numbers during the late nineteenth century, coveted these items. This plate shows the 1892 Democratic presidential ticket of Grover Cleveland and Adlai Stevenson, who lost the election.   Collection of Steven F. Lawson

could be shaped to eradicate ignorance and vice. These Protestants were more likely to cast their ballots for Republicans, except in the South, where regional loyalty to the Democratic Party trumped religious affiliation.

Some people went to the polls because they fiercely disliked members of the opposition party. Northern white workers in New York City or Cincinnati, Ohio, for example, might vote against the Republican Party because they viewed it as the party of African Americans. Other voters cast their ballots against Democrats because they identified them as the party of Irish Catholics, intemperance, and secession.

Although political parties commanded fierce loyalties, the parties remained divided internally. For example, the Republicans pitted "Stalwarts" against "Half Breeds." Led by Senators Roscoe Conkling and Chester Arthur of New York, Zachariah Chandler of Michigan, and John Logan of Illinois, the Stalwarts presented themselves as the "Old Guard" of the Republican Party, what they called the "Grand Old Party" (GOP). The Half Breeds, a snide name given to them by the Stalwarts, tended to be younger Republicans and were represented by Senators James G. Blaine, John Sherman, and James A. Garfield of Ohio and George Frisbie Hoar of Massachusetts. This faction claimed to be more open to new ideas and less wedded to the old causes that the Republican Party promoted, such as racial equality. In the end, however, the differences between the two groups had less to do with ideas than with which faction would have greater power within the Republican Party.

Overall, the continuing strength of party loyalties produced equilibrium as voters cast their ballots primarily along strict party lines. The outcome of presidential elections depended on key "undecided" districts in several states in the Midwest and in New York and nearby states, which swung the balance of power in the electoral college. Indeed, from 1876 to 1896 all winning candidates for president and vice president came from Ohio, Indiana, Illinois, New York, and New Jersey.

replaced ideology as the key to party affiliation. The wrenching experience of the Civil War had cemented voting loyalties for many Americans. After Reconstruction, white southerners tended to vote Democratic; northerners and newly enfranchised southern blacks generally voted Republican. However, geographic region alone did not shape political loyalties; a sizable contingent of Democratic voters remained in the North, and southern whites and blacks periodically abandoned both the Democratic and Republican parties to vote for third parties.

Religion played an important role in shaping party loyalties during this period of intense partisanship. The Democratic Party tended to attract Protestants of certain sects, such as German Lutherans and Episcopalians, as well as Catholics. These faiths emphasized religious ritual and the acceptance of personal sin. They believed that the government should not interfere in matters of morality, which should remain the province of Christian supervision on Earth and divine judgment in the hereafter. By contrast, other Protestant denominations, such as Baptists, Congregationalists, Methodists, and Presbyterians, highlighted the importance of individual will and believed that the law

REVIEW & RELATE

| What accounted for the inefficiency and ineffectiveness of the federal government in the late nineteenth century? | How would you explain the high rates of voter turnout and political participation in an era of uninspiring politicians and governmental inaction? |

Conclusion: Industry in the Age of Organization

From 1877 to 1900, American businessmen demonstrated a zeal for organization. Prompted by new technology that opened up national markets of commerce and communication, business entrepreneurs created large-scale corporations that promoted industrial expansion. Borrowing from European investors and importing and improving on European technology, by 1900 U.S. industrialists had surpassed their overseas counterparts.

Capitalists made great fortunes and lived luxurious lifestyles, emulating the fashions of European elites. Most corporate leaders did not rise from poverty but instead came from the upper middle class and had access to education and connections. Those like Andrew Carnegie, who rose from rags to riches, were the exceptions. The wealthy explained their success as the result of individual effort and hard work. This idea was reinforced in schoolbooks such as the McGuffey Readers, the novels of Horatio Alger, and religious sermons, like those of Russell Conwell.

Although most working Americans did not achieve much wealth in the Age of Organization, they had faith in the possibility of improving their economic position. Members of the middle class lived less extravagantly than did the wealthy; nonetheless, they enjoyed the comforts of the growing consumer economy. Although Jim Crow restricted the black middle class and a heightened sense of masculinity inhibited opportunities available to white women, both groups managed to carve out ways to lift themselves economically and socially.

In gaining success, the wealthy exchanged individualism for organization, competition for consolidation, and laissez-faire for government support. Without pro-business policies from Washington lawmakers and favorable decisions from the Supreme Court, big business would not have developed as rapidly as it did in this era. To prosper, corporations needed sympathetic politicians—whether to furnish free land for railroad expansion, enact tariffs to protect manufacturers, or protect private property. Even when a public outcry led to the regulation of trusts, the pro-business senator John Sherman shaped the legislation so as to minimize damage to corporate interests. In general, national politicians avoided engaging in fierce ideological conflicts, but they, too, organized. The political parties they fashioned encouraged a high level of political participation among voters.

It remained for those who did not share in the glittering wealth of the Gilded Age to find ways to resist corporate domination. The next chapter explores the efforts of workers and farmers to remedy the economic, social, and political ills that accompanied industrialization.

Chapter Review

Online Study Guide ▶ bedfordstmartins.com/hewittlawson

KEY TERMS

New South (p. 497)
convict lease (p. 497)
vertical integration (p. 499)
horizontal integration (p. 499)
corporation (p. 499)
Sherman Antitrust Act (p. 500)
laissez-faire (p. 503)
"The Gospel of Wealth" (p. 504)
Gilded Age (p. 505)
white-collar workers (p. 506)
Jim Crow (p. 509)
Plessy v. Ferguson (p. 509)

REVIEW & RELATE

1. What were the key factors behind the acceleration of industrial development in late-nineteenth-century America?

2. How did industrialization change the way American businessmen thought about their companies and the people who worked for them?

3. In the late nineteenth century, how did many Americans explain individual economic success and failure?

4. How did the business community view the role of government in the economy at the end of the nineteenth century?

5. What role did consumption play in the society and culture of the Gilded Age?

6. How did industrialization contribute to heightened anxieties about gender roles and race?

7. What accounted for the inefficiency and ineffectiveness of the federal government in the late nineteenth century?

8. How would you explain the high rates of voter turnout and political participation in an era of uninspiring politicians and governmental inaction?

TIMELINE OF EVENTS

1859	Charles Darwin publishes *On the Origin of Species*
	Henry Bessemer improves steel production process
1860–1890	U.S. gross domestic product quadruples
1866	Transatlantic telegraph cable completed
1868	Typewriter invented
1870–1900	U.S. becomes a global industrial power
1870–1910	Number of U.S. white-collar workers triples
1870s	John D. Rockefeller takes control of oil refining business
1872	Montgomery Ward established
1876	Thomas Edison establishes research laboratory in Menlo Park, New Jersey
1881	James Garfield assassinated
1883	Civil Service Act passed
1884–1900	1,700 blacks lynched in the South
1885	Alexander Graham Bell founds American Telephone and Telegraph
1886	U.S. railroads adopt standard gauge
	Santa Clara County v. Southern Pacific Railroad Company
1889	Andrew Carnegie publishes "The Gospel of Wealth"
1890	Sherman Antitrust Act passed
1890s	African Americans disfranchised in the South
1891	Rural free delivery (RFD) begins
1895	*United States v. E.C. Knight Company*
1896	*Plessy v. Ferguson*
1901	United States Steel established

Debates about Laissez-Faire

From the nation's founding, the pursuit of individual opportunity has held a central place among American values. The Declaration of Independence extolled the "pursuit of happiness," which has increasingly been interpreted as the chance to accumulate material wealth. The Bill of Rights, adopted after the Constitution was ratified, protected personal liberties from interference by the federal government. Early Supreme Court decisions upheld the binding nature of contracts. The immigrants who came to the United States in the eighteenth and nineteenth centuries assumed that they would have the opportunity to achieve whatever success their talents and hard work would bring.

In the late nineteenth century, as big business consolidated and giant trusts came to dominate whole industries, defenders of unfettered big business argued that individual effort and initiative were still the central engine of the American economy. Championing Adam Smith's notion of laissez-faire—the idea that the marketplace should be left to regulate itself—they argued that government should do nothing to constrain the development of industry. Yet as poverty expanded while a small number of industrialists and financiers accumulated great wealth, reformers questioned whether individualism undermined community, and contended that the government should regulate the free market to promote the greater public welfare. With the gap between rich and poor growing, even industrialists realized that if they did not help the poor in some way, the working classes would rise up against them. Nevertheless, they continued to resist government interference.

Defenders of the status quo argued that individualism must be preserved as the natural order of society. Critics countered that cooperation rather than individual competition made social progress possible and that the government should protect ordinary people from the harm done by greedy capitalists. As you read the following documents, which provide contrasting views of the meaning of success, consider these questions: How does each author define success? How do these authors intend to promote success? And what can be done to relieve the plight of those who do not succeed?

DOCUMENT 16.5

William Graham Sumner | A Defense of Laissez-Faire, 1883

Yale professor William Graham Sumner believed that millionaires deserved their wealth, a notion that appealed to successful industrialists. Men like Andrew Carnegie, he declared, "may fairly be regarded as the naturally selected agents of society." The poor, he argued, also justly deserved their fate. Sumner and other defenders of economic inequality maintained that if the government tried to help these unfortunate losers in the competitive struggle, progress would be halted and civilization would decay.

There is no possible definition of "a poor man." A pauper is a person who cannot earn his living; whose producing powers have fallen positively below his necessary consumption; who cannot, therefore, pay his way. A human society needs the active co-operation and productive energy of every person in it. A man who is present as a consumer, yet who does not contribute either by land, labor, or capital to the work of society, is a burden. On no sound political theory ought such a person to share in the political power of the State. He drops out of the ranks of workers and producers. Society must support him. It accepts the burden, but he must be cancelled from the ranks of the rulers likewise. So much for the pauper. About him no more need be said. But he is not the "poor man." The "poor man" is an elastic term, under which any number of social fallacies may be hidden.

Neither is there any possible definition of "the weak." Some are weak in one way, and some in another; and those who are weak in one sense are strong in another. In general, however, it may be said that those whom humanitarians and philanthropists call the weak are the ones through whom the productive and conservative forces of society are wasted. They constantly neutralize and destroy the finest efforts of the wise and industrious, and are a dead-weight on the society in all its struggles to realize any better things. Whether the people who mean no harm, but are weak in the essential powers necessary to the performance of one's duties in life, or those who are malicious and vicious, do the more mischief, is a question not easy to answer.

Under the names of the poor and the weak, the negligent, shiftless, inefficient, silly, and imprudent are fastened upon the industrious and prudent as a responsibility and a duty. On the one side, the terms are extended to cover the idle, intemperate, and vicious, who, by the combination, gain credit which they do not deserve, and which they could not get if they stood alone. On the other hand, the terms are extended to include wage-receivers of the humblest rank, who are degraded by the combination. The reader who desires to guard himself against fallacies should always scrutinize the terms "poor" and "weak" as used, so as to see which or how many of these classes they are made to cover.

The humanitarians, philanthropists, and reformers, looking at the facts of life as they present themselves, find enough which is sad and unpromising in the condition of many members of society. They see wealth and poverty side by side. They note great inequality of social position and social chances. They eagerly set about the attempt to account for what they see, and to devise schemes for remedying what they do not like. In their eagerness to recommend the less fortunate classes to pity and consideration they forget all about the rights of other classes; they gloss over all the faults of the classes in question, and they exaggerate their misfortunes and their virtues. They invent new theories of property, distorting rights and perpetrating injustice, as any one is sure to do who sets about the re-adjustment of social relations with the interests of one group distinctly before his mind, and the interests of all other groups thrown into the background. When I have read certain of these discussions I have thought that it must be quite disreputable to be respectable, quite dishonest to own property, quite unjust to go one's own way and earn one's own living, and that the only really admirable person was the good-for-nothing. The man who by his own effort raises himself above poverty appears, in these discussions, to be of no account. The man who has done nothing to raise himself above poverty finds that the social doctors flock about him, bringing the capital which they have collected from the other class, and promising him the aid of the State to give him what the other had to work for. In all these schemes and projects the organized intervention of society through the State is either planned or hoped for, and the State is thus made to become the protector and guardian of certain classes. The agents who are to direct the State action are, of course, the reformers and philanthropists. . . . Here it may suffice to observe that, on the theories of the social philosophers to whom I have referred, we should get a new maxim of judicious living: Poverty is the best policy. If you get wealth, you will have to support other people; if you do not get wealth, it will be the duty of other people to support you.

Source: William Graham Sumner, *What the Social Classes Owe Each Other* (New York: Harper and Brothers, 1883), 19–24.

DOCUMENT 16.6

Edward Bellamy | *Looking Backward, 2000–1887*, 1888

Edward Bellamy's best-selling novel *Looking Backward, 2000–1887* offered utopian socialist solutions to the problems facing the rapidly industrializing United States. After falling into a medically induced sleep, Bellamy's narrator, Julian West, awakens in the year 2000 to find that many of the social inequities of the late nineteenth century have been resolved. In the following passage, Dr. Leete, who has revived West, attempts to explain the dramatic change in U.S. society. The passage begins with Leete asking West questions about his era.

"What should you name as the most prominent feature of the labor troubles of your day?"

"Why, the strikes, of course," I replied.

"Exactly; but what made the strikes so formidable?"

"The great labor organizations."

"And what was the motive of these great organizations?"

"The workmen claimed they had to organize to get their rights from the big corporations," I replied.

"That is just it," said Dr. Leete, "the organization of labor and the strikes were an effect, merely, of the concentration of capital in greater masses than had ever been known before. Before this concentration began, while as yet commerce and industry were conducted by innumerable petty concerns with small capital, instead of a small number of great concerns with vast capital, the individual workman was relatively important and independent in his relations to the employer. Moreover, when a little capital or a new idea was enough to start a man in business for himself, workingmen were constantly becoming employers and there was no hard and fast line between the two classes. Labor unions were needless then, and general strikes out of the question. But when the era of small concerns with small capital was succeeded by that of the great aggregations of capital, all this was changed. The individual laborer who had been relatively important to the small employer was reduced to insignificance and powerlessness over against the great corporation, while, at the same time, the way upward to the grade of employer was closed to him. Self-defence drove him to union with his fellows.

"The records of the period show that the outcry against the concentration of capital was furious. Men believed that it threatened society with a form of tyranny more abhorrent than it had ever endured. They believed that the great corporations were preparing for them the yoke of a baser servitude than had ever been imposed on the race, servitude not to men but to soulless machines incapable of any motive but insatiable greed. Looking back, we cannot wonder at their desperation, for certainly humanity was never confronted with a fate more sordid and hideous than would have been the era of corporate tyranny which they anticipated.

"Meanwhile, without being in the smallest degree checked by the clamor against it, the absorption of business by ever larger monopolies continued. In the United States, where this tendency was later in developing than in Europe, there was not, after the beginning of the last quarter of the century, any opportunity whatever for individual enterprise in any important field of industry, unless backed by a great capital. During the last decade of the century, such small businesses as still remained were fast failing survivals of a past epoch, or mere parasites on the great corporations, or else existed in fields too small to attract the great capitalists. Small businesses, as far as they still remained, were reduced to the condition of rats and mice, living in holes and corners, and counting on evading notice for the enjoyment of existence. The railroads had gone on combining till a few great syndicates controlled every rail in the land. In manufactories, every important staple was controlled by a syndicate. These syndicates, pools, trusts, or whatever their name, fixed prices and crushed all competition except when combinations as vast as themselves arose. Then a struggle, resulting in a still greater consolidation, ensued. The great city bazar crushed its country rivals with branch stores, and in the city itself absorbed its smaller rivals till the business of a whole quarter was concentrated under one roof with a hundred former proprietors of shops serving as clerks. Having no business of his own to put his money in, the small capitalist, at the same time that he took service under the corporation, found no other investment for his money but its stocks and bonds, thus becoming doubly dependent upon it.

"The fact that the desperate popular opposition to the consolidation of business in a few powerful hands had no effect to check it, proves that there must have been a strong economical reason for it. The small capitalists, with their innumerable petty concerns, had, in fact, yielded the field to the great aggregations of capital, because they belonged to a day of small things and were totally incompetent to the demands of an age of steam and telegraphs and the gigantic scale of its enterprises. To restore the former order of things, even if possible, would have involved returning to the day of stage-coaches. Oppressive and intolerable as was the regime of the great consolidations of capital, even its victims, while they cursed it, were forced to admit the prodigious increase of efficiency which had been imparted to the national industries, the vast economies effected by concentration of management and unity of organization, and to confess that since the new system had taken the place of the old, the wealth of the world had increased at a rate before undreamed of. To be sure this vast increase had gone chiefly to make the rich richer, increasing the gap between them and the poor; but the fact remained that, as a means merely of producing wealth, capital had been proved efficient in proportion to its consolidation. The restoration of the old system with the subdivision of capital, if it were possible, might indeed bring back a greater equality of conditions with more individual dignity and freedom, but it would be at the price of general poverty and the arrest of material progress. . . .

"Early in the last century the evolution was completed by the final consolidation of the entire capital of the nation. The industry and commerce of the country, ceasing to be conducted by a set of irresponsible corporations and syndicates of private persons at their caprice and for their profit, were intrusted to a single syndicate representing the people, to be conducted in the common interest for the common profit. The nation, that is to say, organized as the one great business corporation in which all other corporations were absorbed; it became the one capitalist in the place of all other capitalists, the sole employer, the final monopoly in which all previous and lesser monopolies were swallowed up, a monopoly in the profits and economies of which all citizens shared."

Source: Edward Bellamy, *Looking Backward, 2000–1887* (Boston: Ticknor, 1888), 71–78.

DOCUMENT 16.7

Andrew Carnegie | The Gospel of Wealth, 1889

Andrew Carnegie, who immigrated to the United States and experienced poverty as a young boy, made his fortune in the steel industry and became one of the richest men in the United States. Recognizing the dangers of widespread poverty among the mass of American workers, Carnegie sought to use philanthropy to provide opportunities for individuals to help themselves, as he explains in the following essay, which is usually referred to as "The Gospel of Wealth." As you read, note the distinction that Carnegie makes between charity and philanthropy.

THE BEST USES to which surplus wealth can be put have already been indicated. Those who would administer wisely must, indeed, be wise; for one of the serious obstacles to the improvement of our race is indiscriminate charity. It were better for mankind that the millions of the rich were thrown into the sea than so spent as to encourage the slothful, the drunken, the unworthy. Of every thousand dollars spent in so-called charity today, it is probable that nine hundred and fifty dollars is unwisely spent—so spent, indeed, as to produce the very evils which it hopes to mitigate or cure. . . .

In bestowing charity, the main consideration should be to help those who will help themselves; to provide part of the means by which those who desire to improve may do so; to give those who desire to rise the aids by which they may rise; to assist, but rarely or never to do all. Neither the individual nor the race is improved by almsgiving. Those worthy of assistance, except in rare cases, seldom require assistance. The really valuable men of the race never do, except in case of accident or sudden change. Every one has, of course, cases of individuals brought to his own knowledge where temporary assistance can do genuine good, and these he will not overlook. But the amount which can be wisely given by the individual for individuals is necessarily limited by his lack of knowledge of the circumstances connected with each. He is the only true reformer who is as careful and as anxious not to aid the unworthy as he is to aid the worthy, and, perhaps, even more so, for in almsgiving more injury is probably done by rewarding vice than by relieving virtue.

The rich man is thus almost restricted to following the examples of Peter Cooper, Enoch Pratt of Baltimore, Mr. Pratt of Brooklyn, Senator Stanford [noted philanthropists], and others, who know that the best means of benefiting the community is to place within its reach the ladders upon which the aspiring can rise—free libraries, parks, and means of recreation, by which men are helped in body and mind; works of art, certain to give pleasure and improve the public taste; and public institutions of various kinds, which will improve the general condition of the people; in this manner returning their surplus wealth to the mass of their fellows in the forms best calculated to do them lasting good.

Thus is the problem of rich and poor to be solved. The laws of accumulation will be left free, the laws of distribution free. Individualism will continue, but the millionaire will be but a trustee for the poor, intrusted for a season with a great part of the increased wealth of the community, but administering it for the community far better than it could or would have done for itself. The best minds will thus have reached a stage in the development of the race in which it is clearly seen that there is no mode of disposing of surplus wealth creditable to thoughtful and earnest men into whose hands it flows, save by using it year by year for the general good. This day already dawns. Men may die without incurring the pity of their fellows, still sharers in great business enterprises from which their capital cannot be or has not been withdrawn, and which is left chiefly at death for public uses; yet the day is not far distant when the man who dies leaving behind him millions of available wealth, which was free for him to administer during life, will pass away "unwept, unhonored, and unsung," no matter to what uses he leaves the dross which he cannot take with him. Of such as these the public verdict will then be: "The man who dies thus rich dies disgraced."

Such, in my opinion, is the true gospel concerning wealth, obedience to which is destined some day to solve the problem of the rich and the poor, and to bring "Peace on earth, among men good will."

Source: Andrew Carnegie, *The Gospel of Wealth and Other Timely Essays* (New York: Century, 1901), 16–19.

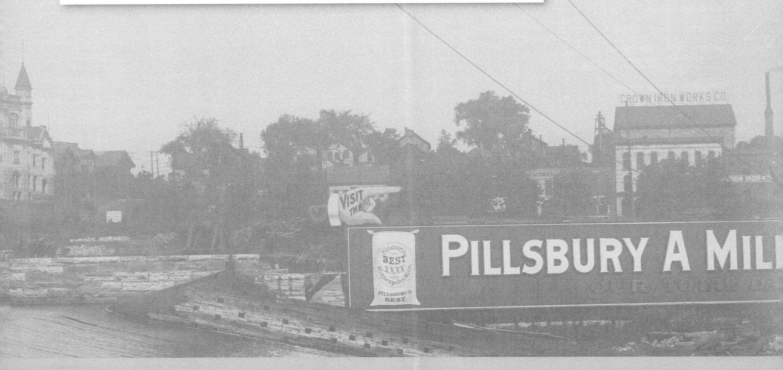

DOCUMENT 16.8

Henry Demarest Lloyd | Critique of Wealth, 1894

Many academics and writers attacked industrial capitalists, claiming that their excessive wealth came at the expense of workers and the general public. Lawyer and journalist Henry Demarest Lloyd wrote numerous articles for the *Chicago Tribune* exposing corruption in business and politics. A reformer influenced by British socialists, Lloyd supported legislation to ban child labor and to allow women to vote. In his 1894 book *Wealth against Commonwealth*, he denounced ruthless and unsavory competitive practices by industrialists who created monopolies that exploited working people. In the following excerpt, Lloyd raises questions about the fundamental value of industrial capitalism and its threat to social progress.

IF OUR CIVILIZATION IS DESTROYED, . . . it will not be by . . . barbarians from below. Our barbarians come from above. Our great money-makers have sprung in one generation into seats of power kings do not know.

The forces and the wealth are new, and have been the opportunity of new men. Without restraints of culture, experience, the pride, or even the inherited caution of class or rank, these men, intoxicated, think they are the wave instead of the float, and that they have created the business which has created them. To them science is but a never-ending repertoire of investments stored up by nature for the syndicates, government but a fountain of franchises, the nations but customers in squads, and a million the unit of a new arithmetic of wealth written for them. They claim a power without control, exercised through forms which make it secret, anonymous, and perpetual. The possibilities of its gratification have been widening before them without interruption since they began, and even at a thousand millions they will feel no satiation and will see no place to stop. They are gluttons of luxury and power, rough, unsocialized, believing that mankind must be kept terrorized. Powers of pity die out of them, because they work through agents and die in their agents, because what they do is not for themselves. . . .

. . . In casting about for the cause of our industrial evils, public opinion has successively found it in "competition," "combination," the "corporations," "conspiracies," "trusts." But competition has ended in combination, and our new wealth takes as it chooses the form of corporation or trust, or corporation again, and with every change grows greater and worse. Under these kaleidoscopic masks we begin at last to see progressing to its terminus a steady consolidation, the end of which is one-man power. The conspiracy ends in one, and one cannot conspire with himself. When this solidification of many into one has been reached, we shall be at last face to face with the naked truth that it is not only the form but the fact of arbitrary power, of control without consent, of rule without representation that concerns us.

Business motived by the self-interest of the individual runs into monopoly at every point it touches the social life—land monopoly, transportation monopoly, trade monopoly, political monopoly in all its forms, from contraction of the currency to corruption in office. The society in which in half a lifetime a man without a penny can become a hundred times a millionaire is as over-ripe, industrially, as was, politically, the Rome in which the most popular bully could lift himself from the ranks of the legion on to the throne of the Caesars. Our rising issue is with business. Monopoly is business at the end of its journey. It has got there. The irrepressible conflict is now as distinctly with business as the issue so lately met was with slavery. Slavery went first only because it was the cruder form of business. . . .

Our system, so fair in its theory and so fertile in its happiness and prosperity in its first century, is now, following the fate of systems, becoming artificial, technical, corrupt; and, as always happens in human institutions, after noon, power is stealing from the many to the few. Believing wealth to be good, the people believed the wealthy to be good. But, again in history, power has intoxicated and hardened its possessors, and Pharaohs are bred in counting-rooms as they were in palaces. Their furniture must be banished to the world-garret [attic], where lie the out-worn trappings of the guilds and slavery and other old lumber of human institutions.

Source: Henry Demarest Lloyd, *Wealth against Commonwealth* (New York: Harper and Brothers, 1902), 510–12, 515.

Interpret the Evidence

1. According to William Graham Sumner (Document 16.5), how are reformers mistaken in their attempts to help the poor?

2. Do Sumner (Document 16.5) and Andrew Carnegie (Document 16.7) agree on whether the wealthy have a responsibility to help the poor?

3. According to Edward Bellamy's *Looking Backward* (Document 16.6), why should the federal government intervene to halt the expansion of big business?

4. How do wealthy Americans maintain their power at the expense of everyone else, according to Henry Demarest Lloyd (Document 16.8)?

5. What might Bellamy and Lloyd see as the greatest obstacles to the realization of America's potential? What about Sumner and Carnegie? What changes in U.S. society and government might each man suggest to eliminate those obstacles?

Put It in Context

- Despite their different philosophies, what do these men think about the growth of organizations during the late nineteenth century?

background photos: pages 518–19 and 522–23, Library of Congress

The Granger Collection, New York

The Granger Collection, New York

Striking coal miners' wives protest the arrival of Pinkerton detectives in Buchtel, Ohio, 1884.

Horse-drawn harvester and binder invented by Cyrus Hall McCormick.

17
Workers and Farmers in the Age of Organization

1877–1900

Pioneer Ada McColl of Kearny County in western Kansas collects buffalo chips for fuel, 1893.

AMERICAN HISTORIES

John McLuckie worked at the Edgar Thompson Steel Works, Andrew Carnegie's plant in Homestead, Pennsylvania. A former miner, McLuckie earned $65 a month as an assistant steel roller. In this town of some eleven thousand residents, where nearly everyone worked for Carnegie, the popular McLuckie was twice elected mayor and headed the Amalgamated Association of Iron and Steel Workers, one of the largest unions in the country. Although McLuckie earned a relatively decent income for that time, steelworkers and other industrial laborers had little power over the terms and conditions under which they worked. Visiting fraternal lodges and saloons, where steelworkers congregated after grueling twelve-hour shifts, he spread the message of standing up to corporate leaders. "The constitution of this country," McLuckie declared, "guarantees all men the right to live, but in order to live we must keep up a continuous struggle."

In 1892 McLuckie faced the fight of his life when he battled with Carnegie and his plant manager, Henry Clay Frick, over wages and working conditions at the Homestead plant. Like Carnegie, the owners of a host of industries—including railroads, petroleum, textiles, cigarettes, communications, and electric power—had created giant organizations that produced great wealth but also reshaped the working conditions of ordinary Americans. Toward the end of the nineteenth century, workers who labored for these industrial giants sought greater control over their employment by organizing unions to increase their power to negotiate with their employers. The events that unfolded in Homestead in

1892 revealed that workers were vastly outmatched in their struggle with management.

Mary Elizabeth Clyens was the daughter of Irish Catholic parents who came to the United States as part of the great wave of Irish immigration that began in the 1840s. The sixth of eight children, Mary was raised in western Pennsylvania but moved to Kansas in 1870 to teach at a Catholic girls' school. There she met and married Charles L. Lease, a pharmacist turned farmer. The couple, however, could not support themselves and their four children through farming, and in 1883 the Leases moved to Wichita, where Charles returned to his original profession. In Wichita, Mary found a much wider scope to express her interests and beliefs than she had on the farm. She joined a variety of organizations and worked in support of Irish independence, women's suffrage, and movements to advance the cause of industrial workers and farmers exploited by big business, railroads, and banks.

Lease entered state and national politics through the Populist Party, which formed in 1890 to challenge the power of large corporations and their political allies, promote the interests of small farmers, and create an alliance between farmers and industrial workers. A mesmerizing speaker, she urged her audiences, according to reporters, to "raise less corn and more hell." In her book *The Problem of Civilization Solved* (1895), Lease offered a variety of remedies for late-nineteenth-century America's economic and political ills, including nationalizing railroad and telegraph lines, increasing the currency supply, and expanding popular democracy. She briefly served as president of the Kansas State Board of Charities when the Populists came to power in 1893, but her tendency to "raise hell" with elected officials in her party led to her removal from office. Following the collapse of the Populist Party in 1896, Lease and her family moved to New York City. She worked as a journalist, divorced her husband, and remained active as a speaker for educational reform and birth control until her death in 1931. •

bottom photo: Kansas State Historical Society

THE AMERICAN HISTORIES of John McLuckie and Mary Elizabeth Lease were linked by the economic and political forces that shaped the lives of both factory workers and farmers in industrialized America. Even though the culture of rural America was quite different from that of the nation's industrial towns and cities, farmers and workers faced many of the same problems. Over the course of the late nineteenth century, both groups had seen control over the nature and terms of their work pass from the individual worker or farmer to large corporations and financial institutions. Both groups felt marginalized, dependent, and devalued. McLuckie and Lease were part of a larger effort by laborers and farmers to fight for their own interests against the concentrated economic and political power of big business and to regain control of their lives and their work.

Working People Organize

Industrialists were not the only ones who built organizations to promote their economic interests. Like their employers, working men and women also saw the benefits of organizing to increase their political and economic leverage. Determined to secure decent wages and working conditions, workers joined labor unions, formed political parties, and engaged in a variety of collective actions, including strikes. However, because workers' organizations were beset by internal conflicts over occupational status, race, ethnicity, and gender and were no match for the powerful alliance between corporations and the federal government, they failed to become a lasting national political force. Workers fared better in their own communities, where family, neighbors, and local businesses were more likely to come to their aid.

The Industrialization of Labor

The industrialization of the United States described in chapter 16 transformed the workplace, bringing together large numbers of laborers under difficult conditions. In 1870 few factories employed 500 or more workers. Thirty years later, more than 1,500 companies had workforces of this size, including General Electric, International Harvester, Pullman Palace Car Company, and U.S. Steel. Just after the Civil War, manufacturing employed 5.3 million workers; thirty years later, the figure soared to more than 15.1 million. Most of these new industrial workers came from two main sources. First, farmers like the Leases who could not make a decent living from the soil moved to nearby cities in search of factory jobs. Although mostly white, this group also included blacks who sought to escape the oppressive conditions of sharecropping. Between 1870 and 1890, some 80,000 African Americans journeyed from the rural South to cities in the South and the North to search for employment. Second, the economic opportunities in America drew millions of immigrants from Europe over the course of the nineteenth century. Immigrant workers initially came from northern Europe, mainly from England, Ireland, Germany, and Scandinavia. However, by the end of the nineteenth century, the number of immigrants from southern and eastern European countries, such as Austria-Hungary, Greece, Italy, and Russia, had surpassed those coming from northern Europe.

Inside factories, **unskilled workers**, those with no particular skill or expertise, encountered a system undergoing critical changes, as small-scale manufacturing gave way to larger and more mechanized operations. Immigrants, who made up the bulk of unskilled laborers, had to adjust both to a new country and to unfamiliar, unpleasant, and often dangerous industrial work. A traveler from Hungary who visited a steel mill in Pittsburgh that employed many Hungarian immigrants compared the factories to penitentiaries. "In making a tour of these prisons," he wrote, "wherever the heat is most insupportable, the flames most choking, there we are certain to find compatriots bent and wasted with toil." Nor were any government benefits—such as workers' compensation or unemployment insurance—available to industrial laborers who were hurt in accidents or laid off from their jobs.

Skilled workers, who had particular training or abilities and were more difficult to replace, were not immune to the changes brought about by industrialization and the creation of large-scale business enterprises. In the early days of manufacturing, skilled laborers operated as independent craftsmen. They provided their own tools, worked at their own pace, and controlled their production output. This approach to work enhanced their sense of personal dignity, reflected their notion of themselves as free citizens, and distinguished them from the mass of unskilled laborers. Mechanization, however, undercut their autonomy by dictating both the nature and the speed of production through practices of scientific management (see chapter 16). Instead of producing goods, skilled workers increasingly applied their craft to servicing machinery and keeping it running smoothly. One example of workers' resistance to this loss of independence on the shop floor occurred in Lowell, Massachusetts. Responding to a new regulation requiring all employees to report to their jobs in work clothes at the opening bell and to remain there with the door locked until the closing bell, a machinist promptly packed his tools, quit, and told his boss that he had not "been brought up under a system of slavery." While owners reaped the benefits of the mechanization and regimentation of the industrial workplace, many skilled workers saw such "improvements" as a threat to their freedom.

Explore

See Document 17.1 for one worker's opinion on mechanization.

Still, most workers did not oppose the technology that increased their productivity and resulted in higher wages. Compared to their mid-nineteenth-century counterparts, industrial laborers now made up a larger share of the general population, earned more money, and worked fewer hours. During the 1870s and 1880s, the average industrial worker's real wages (actual buying power) increased by 20 percent. At the same time, the average workday declined from ten and a half hours to ten hours. From 1870 to 1890, the general price index dropped 30 percent, allowing consumers to benefit from lower prices.

Yet workers were far from content, and the lives of industrial workers remained extremely difficult. Although workers as a group saw improvements in wages and hours, they did not earn enough income to support their families adequately. Also, there were widespread disparities based on job status, race, ethnicity, sex, and region. Skilled workers earned more than unskilled workers. Whites were paid more than African Americans, who were mainly shut out of better jobs. Immigrants from northern Europe, who had settled in the United States before southern Europeans, tended to hold higher-paying skilled positions. Southern factory workers, whether in textiles, steel, or armaments, earned less than their northern counterparts. And women, an increasingly important component of the industrial workforce, earned less than men. On average, women earned only 25 percent of what men did.

Between 1870 and 1900, the number of female wage-workers grew by 66 percent, accounting for about one-quarter

DOCUMENT 17.1

John Morrison | Testimony on the Impact of Mechanization, 1883

Like other skilled laborers, New York City machinist John Morrison saw the introduction of machinery that accompanied industrialization as a threat to his identity as a craftsman. Though highly paid compared with unskilled workers, craftsmen led the way in organizing unions and engaging in strikes against big business. In the following excerpt from his testimony before a U.S. Senate committee investigating conflicts between capital and labor, Morrison discusses the source of many skilled workingmen's discontent.

Explore

Question: Is there any difference between the conditions under which machinery is made now and those which existed ten years ago?

Answer: A great deal of difference.

Question: State the differences as well as you can.

Answer: Well, the trade has been subdivided and those subdivisions have been again subdivided, so that a man never learns the machinist's trade now. Ten years ago he learned, not the whole of the trade, but a fair portion of it. Also, there is more machinery used in the business, which again makes machinery. In the case of making the sewing-machine, for instance, you find that the trade is so subdivided that a man is not considered a machinist at all. Hence it is merely laborers' work and it is laborers that work at that branch of our trade. The different branches of the trade are divided and subdivided so that one man may make just a particular part of a machine and may not know anything whatever about another part of the same machine. In that way machinery is produced a great deal cheaper than it used to be formerly, and in fact, through this system of work,

100 men are able to do now what it took 300 or 400 men to do fifteen years ago. By the use of machinery and the subdivision of the trade they so simplify the work that it is made a great deal easier and put together a great deal faster. There is no system of apprenticeship, I may say, in the business. You simply go in and learn whatever branch you are put at, and you stay at that unless you are changed to another. . . .

Question: Are the machinists here generally contented, or are they in a state of discontent and unrest?

Answer: There is mostly a general feeling of discontent, and you will find among the machinists the most radical workingmen, with the most revolutionary ideas. You will find that they don't so much give their thoughts simply to trade unions and other efforts of that kind, but they go far beyond that; they only look for relief through the ballot or through a revolution, a forcible revolution.

Source: *Report of the Committee of the Senate upon the Relations between Labor and Capital*, 48th Cong. (1885), 755–59.

Interpret the Evidence

- How does Morrison explain the subdivision of labor in the modern factory?
- How does Morrison characterize the mood of skilled laborers?

Put It in Context

How did the introduction of machinery affect skilled workers?

of all nonfarm laborers. The majority of employed women, including those working in factories, were single and between the ages of sixteen and twenty-four. Overall, only 5 percent of married women worked outside the home, although 30 percent of African American wives were employed. Women workers were concentrated in several areas. White and black women continued to serve as maids and domestics. Others took over jobs that were once occupied by men. They

became teachers, nurses, clerical workers, telephone operators, and department store salesclerks. Although these jobs were initially seen as opening up new opportunities for women, they soon became identified as "women's work," which meant lower pay and less potential for professional advancement. Other women toiled in manufacturing jobs requiring fine eye-hand coordination, such as cigar rolling and work in the needle trades and textile industry.

Women also turned their homes into workplaces. In crowded apartments, they sewed furs onto garments, made straw hats, prepared artificial flowers, and fashioned jewelry. Earnings from piecework (work that pays at a set rate per unit) were even lower than factory wages, but they allowed married women with young children to contribute to the family income. When sufficient space was available, families rented rooms to boarders, and women provided meals and house-keeping for the lodgers. Some female workers found other ways to balance work with the needs and constraints of family life. To gain greater autonomy in their work, black laundresses began cleaning clothes in their own homes, rather than their white employers' homes, so that they could control their own work hours. In 1881 black washerwomen in Atlanta conducted a two-week strike to secure higher fees from white customers.

Manufacturing also employed many child workers. By 1900 about 10 percent of girls and 20 percent of boys between the ages of ten and fifteen worked, and at least 1.7 million children under the age of sixteen held jobs. Employers often exposed children to dangerous and unsanitary conditions. Although some children got fresh air working as newsboys, shining shoes, and collecting junk, most worked long, hard hours breathing in dust and fumes as they labored in textile mills, tobacco plants, print shops, and coal mines. In Indiana, young boys worked the night shift in dark, windowless glass factories. One of the adults working in a Rhode Island textile mill lamented: "Poor, puny weak little children are kept at work the entire year without intermission or even a month for schooling." Children under the age of ten, known as "breaker boys," climbed onto filthy coal heaps and picked out unprocessed material. Working up to twelve-hour days, these children received less than a dollar a day.

Women and children worked because the average male head of household could not support his family on his own pay, despite the increase in real wages. As Carroll D. Wright, director of the Massachusetts Bureau of the Statistics of Labor, reported in 1882, "A family of workers can always live well, but the man with a family of small children to support, unless his wife works also, has a small chance of living properly." For example, in 1883 in Joliet, Illinois, a railroad brakeman tried to support his wife and eight children on $360 a year. They rented a three-room house for $5 per month and ate mainly bread and potatoes. A state investigator described the way they lived: "Clothes ragged, children half dressed and dirty. They all sleep in one room regardless of sex. The house is devoid of furniture, and the entire concern is as wretched as could be imagined." Although not all laborers lived in such squalor, many wageworkers barely lived at subsistence level.

Although the average number of working hours dropped during this era, many laborers put in more than 10 hours a day on the job. In 1890 bakers worked more than 65 hours a week, steelworkers more than 66, and canners 77. In the steel industry, blast-furnace operators toiled 12 hours a day, 7 days a week. They received a day off every 2 weeks, but only if they worked a 24-hour shift. Given the long hours and backbreaking work, it is not surprising that accidents were a regular feature of industrial life. Each year tens of thousands were injured on the job, and thousands died as a result of mine cave-ins, train wrecks, explosions in industrial plants, and fires at textile mills and garment factories. Railroad employment was especially unsafe—accidents ended the careers of one in six workers.

Agricultural refugees who flocked to cotton mills in the South also faced dangerous working conditions. Working twelve-hour days breathing the lint-filled air from the processed cotton posed health hazards, especially for the very young and the elderly. Textile workers also had to place their hands into heavy machinery to disentangle threads, making them extremely vulnerable to serious injury. Wages scarcely covered necessities, and on many occasions families did not know where their next meal was coming from. North Carolina textile worker J. W. Mehaffry complained that the mill owners "were slave drivers" who "work their employees, women, and children from 6 a.m. to 7 p.m. with a half hour for lunch." The company supplied houses, but the occupants had "very little furniture, just a couple of beds.

Chinese American Telephone Operator

The invention of the telephone brought jobs to many Americans, especially women. Yet not all operators were women, as this photograph shows. San Francisco's Chinatown employed workers from its own community, and in this photo a Chinese man works as a telephone operator while a child in a school uniform and an adult stand by him. © CORBIS

Just enough to get by on is about all we had." Their meals usually consisted of potatoes, cornbread, and dried beans cooked in fat. This diet, without dairy products and fresh meat, led to outbreaks of pellagra, a debilitating disease caused by niacin (vitamin B3) deficiency.

Although wages and working hours improved slightly for some workers, employers kept the largest share of the increased profits that resulted from industrialization. In 1877 John D. Rockefeller collected dividends at the rate of at least $720 an hour, roughly double what his average employee earned in a year. Despite some success stories, prospects for upward mobility for most American workers remained limited. Unskilled workers might climb up the economic ladder during their lifetime, but usually not more than one rung. A manual worker might rise into the ranks of the semiskilled but would not make it into the middle class. And to achieve even this small upward mobility required putting the entire family to work and engaging in rigorous economizing, what one historian called "ruthless underconsumption." The Horatio Alger "rags to riches" stories (see chapter 16) proved a myth for nearly all workers. Despite their best efforts, most Americans remained part of the working class.

Organizing Unions

Faced with improving but inadequate wages and hazardous working conditions, industrial laborers sought to counter the concentrated power of corporate capitalists by joining forces. They attempted to organize **unions**—groups of workers seeking rights and benefits from their employers through their collective efforts. Union organizing was prompted by attitudes that were common among employers. Most employers were convinced that they and their employees shared identical interests, and they believed that they were morally and financially entitled to establish policies on their workers' behalf. They refused to engage in negotiations with labor unions (a process known as **collective bargaining**) and rejected unions as illegitimate organizations. Although owners appreciated the advantages of companies banding together to eliminate competition or to lobby for favorable regulations, similar collective efforts by workers struck them as unfair, even immoral. It was up to the men who supplied the money and the machines—rather than the workers—to determine what was a fair wage and what were satisfactory working conditions. In 1877 William H. Vanderbilt, the son of transportation tycoon Cornelius Vanderbilt, explained this way of thinking: "Our men feel that although I . . . may have my millions and they the rewards of their daily toil, still we are about equal in the end. If they suffer, I suffer, and if I suffer they cannot escape." Needless to say, many workers disagreed. One of labor's central demands was the institution of the eight-hour workday. The idea came from Great Britain, which had industrialized earlier in the nineteenth century. In 1817 the British socialist Robert Owen had summarized this demand as "Eight hours labor, Eight hours recreation, Eight hours rest." This goal had not yet been achieved in Britain or the rest of industrial Europe when American labor activists picked it up in the 1860s, spreading the message through parades and rallies sponsored by Eight-Hour Leagues.

A growing number of working people failed to see the relationship between employer and employee as mutually beneficial. Increasingly, they considered labor unions to be the best vehicle for communication and negotiation between workers and owners. Though not the first national workers' organization, the **Noble Order of the Knights of Labor**, founded by Uriah Stephens in 1869, initiated the most extensive and successful campaign after the Civil War to unite workers and

Women in the Knights of Labor

Under the leadership of Terence Powderly, the Knights of Labor admitted women in 1881. Four years later, the Knights established the Women's Work Department, directed by Leonora Barry, a married garment worker in Philadelphia. This photograph shows women delegates to the 1886 Knights of Labor convention, one of whom holds her infant child. © Bettmann/CORBIS challenge the power of corporate capitalists. "There is no mutuality of interests . . . [between] capital and labor," the Massachusetts chapter of the Knights proclaimed. "It is the iron heel of a soulless monopoly, crushing the manhood out of sovereign citizens." In fact, the essential premise of the Knights was that *all* workers shared common interests that were very different from those of owners. Thus the union excluded only those it believed preyed on citizens both economically and morally—lawyers, bankers, saloon-keepers, and professional gamblers.

The Knights did not enjoy immediate success. Their participation in the Great Railroad Strike of 1877 (see chapter 14) drew some attention to the union, but the Knights did not really begin to flourish until Terence V. Powderly replaced Stephens as Grand Master of the organization in 1879. Powderly advocated the eight-hour workday, the abolition of child labor, and equal pay for women. Under his leadership, the Knights accepted African Americans, immigrants, and women as members, though they excluded Chinese immigrant workers, as did other labor unions. As a result, the Knights experienced a surge in membership from 9,000 in 1879 to nearly a million in 1885 (including John McLuckie), about 10 percent of the industrial workforce.

Rapid growth proved to be a mixed blessing. As membership grew, Powderly and the national organization exercised less and less control over local chapters. In fact, local chapters often defied the central organization by engaging in strikes, a labor tactic Powderly had officially disavowed. Nonetheless, with Powderly standing mainly on the sidelines, members of the Knights struck successfully against the Union Pacific Railroad and the Missouri Pacific Railroad in 1885. The following year, on May 1, 1886, local assemblies of the Knights joined a nationwide strike to press for an eight-hour workday, again without Powderly's approval. However, this strike was soon overshadowed by events in Chicago that would prove to be the undoing of the Knights (Figure 17.1).

For months before the general strike, the McCormick Harvester plant in Chicago had been at the center of an often violent conflict over wages and work conditions. On May 3, 1886, police killed two strikers in a clash between union members and strikebreakers who tried to cross the picket lines. In response, a group of anarchists led by the German-born activist August Spies called for a rally in **Haymarket Square** to protest police violence. Consisting mainly of foreign-born radicals, anarchists believed that government represented the interests of capitalists and stifled freedom for workers. Anarchists differed among themselves, but they generally advocated tearing down government authority, restoring personal freedom, and forming worker

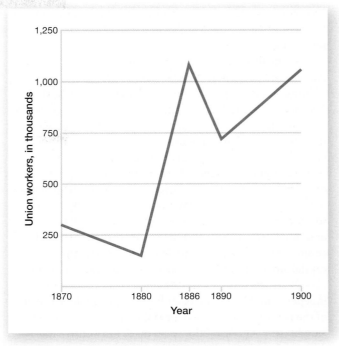

FIGURE 17.1   Union Membership, 1870–1900
Union membership fluctuated widely in the late nineteenth century. After reaching a low point in 1880, the number of union members rebounded after organizing by the Knights of Labor. Membership plummeted in the years after the Haymarket Square incident of 1886 but soared again in the 1890s through the efforts of the American Federation of Labor and western miners.   Source: Data from Richard B. Freeman, "Spurts in Union Growth: Defining Moments and Social Processes" (working paper 6012, National Bureau of Economic Research, Cambridge, MA, 1997).

communes to replace capitalism. To achieve their goals, anarchists like Spies advocated the violent overthrow of government.

The Haymarket rally began at 8:30 in the evening of May 4 and attracted no more than 1,500 people, who listened to a series of speeches as rain fell. By 10:30 p.m., when the crowd had dwindled to some 300 people, 180 policemen decided to break it up. As police moved into the square, someone set off a bomb. The police fired back, and when the smoke cleared, seven policemen and four protesters lay dead. Most of the fatalities and injuries resulted not from the bomb but from the police crossfire after the explosion. A subsequent trial convicted eight anarchists of murder, though there was no evidence that any of them had planted a bomb or used weapons; four of them, including August Spies, were executed. Although Powderly and other union leaders denounced the anarchists and the bombing, the incident greatly tarnished the labor movement. Capitalists and their allies in the press attacked labor unionists as radicals prone to violence and denounced strikes as un-American. Following the Haymarket incident, the membership rolls of the Knights plunged to below 500,000. By the mid-1890s, the Knights had fewer than 20,000 members.

As the fortunes of the Knights of Labor faded, the **American Federation of Labor (AFL)** grew in prominence, offering an alternative vision of unionization. Instead of one giant industrial union that included all workers, skilled and unskilled, the AFL organized only skilled craftsmen—the labor elite—into trade unions. In 1886 Samuel Gompers, a British-born cigar maker, became president of the AFL. Gompers considered trade unions "the business organizations of the wage earners to attend to the business of the wage earners" and favored the use of strikes. No social reformer, the AFL president concentrated on obtaining better wages and hours for workers so that they could share in the prosperity generated by industrial capitalism. By 1900 the AFL had around a million members. It achieved these numbers by recruiting the most independent, highest-paid, and least replaceable segment of the labor force—white male skilled workers. Unlike the Knights, the AFL had little or no place for women and African Americans in its ranks.

As impressive as the AFL's achievement was, the union movement as a whole experienced only limited success in the late nineteenth century. Only about one in fifteen industrial workers belonged to a union in 1900. Union membership was low for a variety of reasons. First, the political and economic power of corporations and the prospects of retaliation made the decision to sign up for union membership a risky venture. Second, the diversity of workers made organizing a difficult task. Foreign-born laborers came from many countries and were divided by language, religion, ethnicity, and history. Moreover, European immigrants quickly adopted native-born whites' racial prejudices against African Americans. Third, despite severe limitations in social mobility, American workers generally retained their faith in the benefits of the capitalist system. The pervasive doctrine of success defined workers not as laborers locked into the lower class but as businessmen on the rise, each with the potential to become a Rockefeller or a Carnegie. Finally, the government used its legal and military authority to side with employers and suppress militant workers.

Southern workers were the most resistant to union organizing. The agricultural background of mill workers left them with a heightened sense of individualism and isolation. In addition, their continued connection to family and friends in the countryside offered a potential escape route from industrial labor. Finally, employers' willingness to use racial tensions to divide working-class blacks and whites prevented them from joining together to further their common economic interests.

Clashes between Workers and Owners

Despite the difficulties of organizing workers, labor challenged some of the nation's largest industries in the late nineteenth century. Faced with owners' refusal to recognize or negotiate with unions, workers marshaled their greatest source of power: withholding their labor and going on strike. Employers in turn had powerful weapons at their command to break strikes. They could recruit strikebreakers and mobilize private and public security forces to protect their businesses. That workers went on strike against such odds testified to their desperation and courage.

Workers in the United States were not alone in their efforts to combat industrial exploitation. In England, laborers organized for better wages and working conditions. In 1888 in London, young women who worked as matchmakers staged a walkout to protest the exorbitant fines that employers imposed on them for arriving even one minute late to work. With community support, they won their demands. From 1888 to 1890, the number of strikes throughout Europe grew from 188 to 289. In 1890 thousands of workers in Budapest, Hungary, rose up to protest unsafe working conditions. European workers also campaigned for the right to vote, which unlike white male American workers, they were denied on economic grounds.

In the United States in the 1890s, labor mounted several highly publicized strikes. Perhaps the most famous was the 1892 **Homestead strike**. Steelworkers at Carnegie's Homestead, Pennsylvania, factory lived seven miles east of Pittsburgh and, like John McLuckie, played an active role in local politics and civic affairs. Residents generally believed that Andrew Carnegie's corporation paid decent wages that allowed them to support their families and buy their own homes. In 1892 craftsmen earned $180 a month, and they appeared to have Carnegie's respect. Others, like McLuckie, earned less than half that amount, and unskilled workers made even less.

In 1892, with steel prices falling, Carnegie decided to replace some of his skilled craftsmen with machinery, cut wages, save on labor costs, and bust McLuckie's union, the Amalgamated Association of Iron and Steel Workers, with which he had voluntarily negotiated in the past. Knowing that his actions would provoke a strike and seeking to avoid the negative publicity that would result, Carnegie left the country and went to Scotland, leaving his plant manager, Henry Clay Frick, in charge.

Fiercely anti-union, Frick prepared for the strike by building a three-mile, fifteen-foot-high fence, capped with barbed wire and equipped with searchlights, around three sides of the Homestead factory. A hated symbol of the manager's hostility, the fence became known as "Fort Frick." Along the fourth side of the factory flowed the Monongahela

River. Frick had no intention of negotiating seriously with the union on a new contract, and on July 1 he ordered a lockout. Only employees who rejected the union and accepted lower wages could return to work. The small town rallied around the workers, and the union members won a temporary victory. On July 6, barge-loads of armed Pinkerton detectives, hired by Frick to protect the plant, set sail toward the factory entrance alongside the Monongahela. McLuckie, the head of the Amalgamated, denounced the Pinkertons as "a band of cutthroats, thieves, and murderers in the employ of unscrupulous capital for the oppression of honest labor." From the shore, union men shot at the barges and set fire to a boat they pushed toward the Pinkertons. When the smoke cleared, the Pinkertons surrendered and hastily retreated onshore as women and men chased after them.

This triumph proved costly for the union. The battle left nine strikers and three Pinkerton detectives dead. Although community officials were on the workers' side, Frick convinced the governor of Pennsylvania to send in state troops to protect the factory and the strikebreakers. On July 23, Alexander Berkman, an anarchist who had no connection with the union, entered Frick's office and shot the steel executive in the neck, leaving him wounded but alive. The resulting unfavorable publicity, together with the state's prosecution of the union, broke the strike. Subsequently, steel companies blacklisted the union leaders for life, and McLuckie fled Pennsylvania and wound up nearly penniless in Arizona. Ever the philanthropist, when Carnegie heard of McLuckie's plight in 1900, he tried to give his former adversary some money anonymously. The proud and still defiant McLuckie declined the offer, but a friend of Carnegie's arranged for an Arizona railroad to hire him as a machinery-repair superintendent.

Explore

See Document 17.2 for an anarchist's account of the Homestead strike.

Like Andrew Carnegie, George Pullman considered himself an enlightened employer who took good care of the men who worked in his luxury sleeping railcar factory outside Chicago. However, also like the steel titan, Pullman placed profits over personnel. In 1893 a severe economic depression prompted Pullman to cut wages without correspondingly reducing the rents that his employees paid for living in company houses. This dual blow to worker income and purchasing power led to a fierce strike the following year. The Pullman workers belonged to the American Railway Union, headed by Eugene V. Debs, who believed that labor organizing was an integral part of a worker's rights of political and economic citizenship. After George Pullman refused to negotiate, the union voted to go on strike.

In the end, the **Pullman strike** was broken not by the Pullman company but by the federal government. The railroad managers association persuaded President Grover Cleveland's attorney general, Richard Olney, a former railroad lawyer, that strikers were interfering with delivery of the U.S. mail transported by train. Cleveland ordered federal troops to get the railroads operating, but the workers still refused to capitulate. Olney then obtained an injunction (a court order) from the federal courts to restrain Debs and other union leaders from continuing the strike. The government used the Sherman Antitrust Act to punish unions for conspiring to restrain trade, something it had rarely done with respect to large corporations. Refusing to comply, Debs and other union officials were charged with contempt, convicted under the Sherman Antitrust Act, and sent to jail. The strike collapsed. **See Document Project 17: The Pullman Strike of 1894, page 550.**

Debs remained unrepentant. After serving his jail sentence, he became even more radical. In 1901 he helped establish the Socialist Party of America. German exiles who came to the United States following revolutions in Europe in 1848 had brought with them the revolutionary ideas of the German philosopher Karl Marx. Marx argued that capital and labor were engaged in a class struggle that would end in a victory for the proletariat, the abolition of private property, and socialist rule. This revolution would come about through the violent overthrow of capitalist government and its replacement by communism. Marxist ideas attracted a small following in the United States, mainly among the foreign-born population. By contrast, other types of European socialists, including the German Social Democratic Party, which Marx denounced, appealed for working-class support by advocating the creation of a more just and humane economic system through the ballot box, not by violent revolution. Debs, born and raised in Terre Haute, Indiana, favored this nonviolent, democratic brand of socialism and managed to attract a broader base of supporters by articulating socialist doctrines in the language of cooperation and citizenship that many Americans shared. Debsian socialism appealed not only to industrial workers but also to dispossessed farmers and miners in the Southwest and Midwest.

Western miners had a history of labor activism, and by the 1890s they were ready to listen to radical ideas. Shortly after the Homestead strike ended in 1892, silver miners in Coeur d'Alene, Idaho, walked out after owners slashed their wages by 15 percent. Employers refused to recognize any union, obtained an injunction against the strike, imported strikebreakers to run the mines, and persuaded Idaho's governor to impose martial law, in which the military took over the normal operation of civilian affairs. The work stoppage lasted four months, resulting in the arrest of six hundred strikers, including their leader, Ed Boyce.

DOCUMENT 17.2

Emma Goldman | Reflections on the Homestead Strike, 1931

Emma Goldman was one of the most prominent radicals of the late nineteenth and early twentieth centuries. Goldman argued for sexual freedom and women's liberation. In addition, as an anarchist, she initially advocated the overthrow of capitalism through violent attacks. To this end, during the Homestead strike Goldman's lover, Alexander Berkman, attempted unsuccessfully to assassinate Henry Clay Frick, the manager of Carnegie's steel plant. In this passage from her autobiography, Goldman describes the events that led to the assassination attempt.

Explore

A few days after our return to New York the news was flashed across the country of the slaughter of steel-workers by Pinkertons. Frick had fortified the Homestead mills, built a high fence around them. Then, in the dead of night, a barge packed with strike-breakers, under protection of heavily armed Pinkerton thugs, quietly stole up the Monongahela River. The steel-men had learned of Frick's move. They stationed themselves along the shore, determined to drive back Frick's hirelings. When the barge got within range, the Pinkertons had opened fire, without warning, killing a number of Homestead men on the shore, among them a little boy, and wounding scores of others.

The wanton murders aroused even the daily papers. Several came out in strong editorials, severely criticizing Frick. He had gone too far; he had added fuel to the fire in the labour ranks and would have himself to blame for any desperate acts that might come.

We were stunned. We saw at once that the time for our manifesto had passed. Words had lost their meaning in the face of the innocent blood spilled on the banks of the Monongahela. Intuitively each felt what was surging in the heart of the others. Sasha [Alexander Berkman] broke the silence. "Frick is the responsible factor in this crime," he said; "he must be made to stand the consequences." It was the psychological moment for an *Attentat* [political violence]; the whole country was aroused, everybody was considering Frick the perpetrator of a cold-blooded murder. A blow aimed at Frick would re-echo in the poorest hovel, would call the attention of the whole world to the real cause behind the Homestead struggle. It would also strike terror in the enemy's ranks and make them realize that the proletariat of America had its avengers.

Source: Emma Goldman, *Living My Life* (New York: Alfred Knopf, 1931), 86–87.

Interpret the Evidence

- How does Goldman characterize the Pinkerton detectives?
- What did Goldman think the assassination of Frick would achieve?

Put It in Context

Why do you think public perception turned against militant labor activism in the aftermath of Homestead and other strikes during the late nineteenth century?

Although the workers lost, the following year they succeeded in forming the Western Federation of Miners, a radical union that continued their fight.

The **Industrial Workers of the World (IWW)**, which emerged largely through the efforts of the Western Federation of Miners, sought to raise wages, improve working conditions, and gain union recognition for the most exploited segments of American labor. The IWW, or "Wobblies" as they were popularly known, offered an alternative to Samuel Gompers's American Federation of Labor by attempting to unite all skilled and unskilled workers in an effort to overthrow capitalism. The

Wobblies favored strikes and direct-action protests rather than collective bargaining or mediation. At their rallies and strikes, they often encountered government force and corporation-inspired mob violence. Nevertheless, the IWW had substantial appeal among lumberjacks in the Northwest, dockworkers in port cities, miners in the West, farmers in the Great Plains, and textile workers in the Northeast. Of their 150 strikes, the most successful ones involved miners in Goldfield, Nevada (1906–1907); textile workers in Lawrence, Massachusetts (1912); and silk workers in Paterson, New Jersey (1913).

Even though industrialists usually had state and federal governments as well as the media on their side, workers continued to press for their rights. Workers used strikes as a last resort when business owners refused to negotiate or recognize their demands to organize themselves into unions. Although most late-nineteenth-century strikes failed, striking unionists nonetheless called for collective bargaining, higher wages, shorter hours, and improved working conditions—an agenda that unions and their political allies would build on in the future.

Working-Class Leisure in Industrial America

Despite the economic hardships and political repression that industrial laborers faced in the late nineteenth century, workers carved out recreational spaces over which they had control and that offered relief from their backbreaking toil. Time clocks, often viewed as an annoying part of scientific management, nevertheless clearly emphasized the difference between working and nonworking hours. For many, Sunday became a day of rest that took on a secular flavor.

Working-class leisure patterns varied by gender, race, and region. Women did not generally attend spectator sporting events, such as baseball and boxing matches, which catered to men. Nor did they find themselves comfortable in union halls and saloons, where men found solace in drink. Working-class wives preferred to gather to prepare for births, weddings, and funerals or to assist neighbors who lost their homes because of fire, death, or greedy landlords.

Once employed, working-class daughters found a greater measure of independence and free time by living in rooming houses on their own. Women's wages were only a small fraction of men's earnings, so working women rarely made enough money to support a regular social life along with paying for rent, food, and clothes. Still, they found ways to enjoy their free time. Some single

women went out in groups, hoping to meet men who would pay for drinks, food, or a vaudeville show. Others dated so that they knew they would be taken care of for the evening. Some of the men who "treated" on a date assumed a right to sexual favors in return, and some of these women then expected men to provide them with housing and gifts in exchange for an ongoing sexual relationship. Thus emotional and economic relationships became intertwined in complicated ways.

Around the turn of the twentieth century, dance halls flourished as one of the mainstays of working-class communities throughout the nation. Huge dance palaces that held three thousand to five thousand people were built in the entertainment districts of most large cities. They made their money by offering music with lengthy intermissions for the sale of drinks and refreshments. Women and men also attended cabarets, some of which were racially integrated. In so-called red-light districts of the city, prostitutes earned money entertaining their clients with a variety of sexual pleasures.

Not all forms of leisure were strictly segregated along class lines. A number of forms of cheap entertainment appealed not only to working-class women and men but also to their middle-class counterparts. By the turn of the twentieth century, most large American cities featured amusement parks. Brooklyn's Coney Island stood out as the most spectacular of these sprawling playgrounds of fun and excitement. In 1884 the world's first roller coaster was built at Coney Island, providing thrills to those brave enough to ride it. Chicago residents could enjoy the Ferris wheel, which appeared at the 1893 World's Columbian Exposition. Designed by George Ferris, who operated a firm specializing in structural steel, the wheel rose 250 feet in the air, was propelled by two 1,000-horsepower steam engines, and accommodated 1,440 riders at a time.

Vaudeville houses—with their minstrel shows (whites in blackface) and comedians, singers, and dancers—brought howls of laughter to working-class audiences. Nickelodeons charged five cents to watch short films. Live theater generally attracted more wealthy patrons; however, the Yiddish theater, which flourished on New York's Lower East Side, and other immigrant-oriented stage productions appealed mainly to working-class audiences.

Southern workers also enjoyed music in their leisure time. Cheap banjoes and fiddles were mass-produced by the end of the nineteenth century. Pianos also became readily available, and one mountain boy, on hearing a piano for the first time, commented that it was the "beautifullest thing he had ever heard."

Itinerant musicians entertained audiences throughout the South. Lumber camps, which employed mainly

Trocadero Music Hall, 1893

The Trocadero Music Hall in Chicago opened in 1893 to attract people attending the city's upcoming World's Fair. It provided a mix of classical music and exotic European variety acts, as shown above, but drew really huge audiences with the appearance of Eugene Sandow, a body builder who exhibited feats of great physical strength.   Library of Congress

African American men, offered a popular destination for these musicians. Each camp contained a "barrelhouse," also called a "honky tonk" or a "juke joint." Besides showcasing music, the barrelhouse also gave workers the opportunity to "shoot craps, dice, drink whiskey, dance, every modern devilment you can do," as one musician who played there recalled. From the Mississippi delta emerged a new form of music—the blues. W. C. Handy, "the father of the blues," discovered this music in his travels through the delta, where he observed that southern blacks "sang about everything. Trains, steamboats, steam whistles, sledge hammers, fast women, mean bosses, stubborn mules." They performed these songs of woe accompanying themselves with anything that would make a "musical sound or rhythmical effect, anything from a harmonica to a washboard." Meanwhile in New Orleans, an amalgam of black musical forms evolved into jazz. Musicians such as "Jelly Roll" Morton experimented

with a variety of sounds, putting together African and Caribbean rhythms with European music, mixing pianos with clarinets, trumpets, and drums. Blues and jazz spread throughout the South, appearing in juke joints in Atlanta and Memphis, where men and women danced the night away.

In mountain valley mill towns, southern white residents preferred "old time" music, but with a twist. Originally enjoyed by British settlers, traditional ballads and folk songs concerned the deeds of kings and princes; rural southerners modified the lyrics to extol the exploits of outlaws and adventurers. Country music, which combined romantic ballads and folk tunes to the accompaniment of guitars, banjos, and organs, emerged as a distinct brand of music by the twentieth century. As with African Americans, in the late nineteenth century working-class and rural whites found new and exciting types of music to entertain them in their leisure. Religious music

538

also appealed to both white and black audiences and drew crowds to evangelical revivals held in tents on acres of grass fields.

Mill workers also amused themselves by engaging in social, recreational, and religious activities. Women visited each other and exchanged confidences, gossip, advice on child rearing, and folk remedies. Men from various factories organized baseball teams that competed in leagues with one another. Managers of a mill in Charlotte, North Carolina, admitted that they "frequently hired men better known for their batting averages than their work records."

REVIEW & RELATE

How did industrialization change the American workplace? What challenges did it create for American workers?

How did workers resist the concentrated power of industrial capitalists in the late nineteenth century, and why did such efforts have only limited success?

 LEARNINGCurve bedfordstmartins.com/hewittlawson/LC

Farmers Organize

Like industrial workers, farmers experienced severe economic hardships and a loss of political power in the face of rapid industrialization. The introduction of new machinery such as the combine harvester, introduced in 1878, led to substantial increases in the productivity of American farms. Soaring production, however, led to a decline in agricultural prices in the late nineteenth century, a trend that was accelerated by increased agricultural production around the world. Faced with an economic crisis caused by falling prices and escalating debt, farmers fought back, creating new organizations to champion their collective economic and political interests.

Farmers Unite

From the end of the Civil War to the mid-1890s, increased production of wheat and cotton, two of the most important American crops, led to a precipitous drop in the price these crops fetched on the open market. Falling prices created a debt crisis for many farmers. Most American farmers were independent businessmen who borrowed money to pay for land, seed, and equipment. When their crops were harvested and sold, they repaid their debts with the proceeds. As prices fell, farmers increased production in an effort to cover their

debts. This tactic led to a greater supply of farm produce in the marketplace and even lower prices. Unable to pay back loans, many farmers lost their property in foreclosures to the banks that held their mortgages and furnished them credit.

To make matters worse, farmers lived isolated lives. Spread out across vast acres of rural territory, farmers had few social and cultural diversions to enliven the long, hard days they worked from sunup to sundown. As the farm economy declined, more and more of their children left the monotony of rural America behind and headed for cities in search of new opportunities and a better life.

Early efforts to organize farmers were motivated by a desire to counteract the isolation of rural life by creating new forms of social interaction and cultural engagement. In 1867, Oliver H. Kelly, who worked as a clerk in the Department of Agriculture, founded the Patrons of Husbandry to brighten the lonely existence of rural Americans through educational and social activities, including lectures, agricultural fairs, and picnics. Known as **Grangers** (from the French word for "granary"), the association grew rapidly in the early 1870s, especially in the Midwest and the South. Between 1872 and 1874, approximately fourteen thousand new Grange chapters were established.

In addition to helping to alleviate rural isolation, Grangers formed farm cooperatives to sell their crops at higher prices and pool their purchasing power to buy finished goods at wholesale prices. The Grangers' interest in promoting the collective economic interests of farmers led to their increasing involvement in politics. Rather than forming a separate political party, Grangers endorsed candidates who favored their cause. Perhaps their most important objective was the regulation of shipping and grain storage prices. In many areas, individual railroads had monopolies on both of these services and, as a result, were able to charge farmers higher-than-usual rates to store and ship their crops. By electing sympathetic state legislators, Grangers managed to obtain regulations that placed a ceiling on the prices railroads and grain elevators could charge. The Supreme Court temporarily upheld these victories in *Munn v. Illinois* (1877) by affirming the constitutionality of state regulation of private property that benefited the public interest. In 1886, however, in *Wabash v. Illinois* the Supreme Court reversed itself and struck down these state regulatory laws as hindering the free flow of interstate commerce.

Another apparent victory for regulation came in 1887 when Congress passed the Interstate Commerce Act, establishing the **Interstate Commerce Commission (ICC)** to regulate railroads. Although big businessmen could not prevent occasional government regulation, they

Granger Movement, 1876

As the farmer's central placement in this lithograph implies, farmers were the heart of the Granger movement. The title is a variation on the movement's motto, "I Pay for All." A farmer with a plough and two horses stands at the center of the scene providing food for all, while other occupational types positioned around him echo a similar refrain based on their profession. Note the attitude toward the broker implied by the label "I Fleece You All."   Library of Congress

managed to render it largely ineffective. Large railroad lines found it easier to influence decisions of the ICC than those of agencies at the state level, which were more inclined to support local farmers and other shippers. In time, railroad advocates came to dominate the ICC and enforced the law in favor of the railway lines rather than the shippers. Implementation of the Sherman Antitrust Act (see chapter 16) also favored big business. From the standpoint of most late-nineteenth-century capitalists, national regulations often turned out to be more of help than a hindrance.

By the late 1880s, the Grangers had abandoned electoral politics and once again devoted themselves strictly to social and cultural activities. A number of factors explain the Grangers' return to their original mission. First, prices began to rise for some crops, particularly corn, relieving the economic pressure on midwestern farmers. Second, the passage of regulatory

legislation in a number of states convinced some Grangers that their political goals had been achieved. Finally, a lack of marketing and business experience led to the collapse of many agricultural collectives.

The withdrawal of the Grangers from politics did not, however, signal the end of efforts by farmers to form organizations to advance their economic interests. While farmers in the midwestern corn belt experienced some political success and an economic upturn, farmers farther west in the Great Plains and in the Lower South fell more deeply into debt, as the price of wheat and cotton on the international market continued to drop. In both of these regions, farmers organized **Farmers' Alliances**. In the 1880s, Milton George formed the Northwestern Farmers' Alliance. At the same time, Dr. Charles W. Macune organized the much larger Southern Farmers' Alliance, which boasted more than 4 million members. Southern black farmers, excluded from the

Southern Farmers' Alliance by prevailing white suprem-acist sentiment, created a parallel Colored Farmers' Alliance, which attracted approximately a quarter of a million supporters. The Alliances formed a network of recruiters to sign up new members. No recruiter was more effective than Mary Elizabeth Lease, who excited farm audiences with her forceful and colorful rhetoric, delivering 160 speeches in the summer of 1890 alone. Not only did Lease urge farmers and workers to unite against capitalist exploitation, but she also agitated for women's rights and voiced her determination "to place the mothers of this nation on an equality with the fathers."

The Southern Farmers' Alliance advocated a sophisticated plan to solve the farmers' problem of mounting debt. Macune devised a proposal for a **sub-treasury system**. Under this plan, the federal govern-ment would locate offices near warehouses in which farmers could store nonperishable commodities. In return, farmers would receive federal loans for 80 percent of the current market value of their produce. In theory, temporarily taking crops off the market would decrease supply and, assuming demand remained stable, lead to increased prices. Once prices rose, farmers would return to the warehouses, redeem their crops, sell them at the higher price, repay the government loan, and leave with a profit. Of the many recommendations proposed by the Alliances, the subtreasury system came closest to suggesting a realistic solution to the problem of chronic farm debt.

The first step toward creating a nationwide farmers' organization came in 1889, when the Northwestern and Southern Farmers' Alliances agreed to merge. Alliance leaders, including Lease, saw workers as fellow victims of industrialization, and they invited the Knights of Labor to join them. They also attempted to lower prevailing racial barriers by bringing the Colored Farmers' Alliance into the coalition. The following year, the National Farmers' Alliance and Industrial Union held its conven-tion in Ocala, Florida. The group adopted resolutions endorsing the subtreasury system, as well as recommen-dations that would promote the economic welfare of farmers and extend political democracy to "the plain people." These proposals included tariff reduction, government ownership of banks and railroads, a con-stitutional amendment creating direct election of U.S. senators, adoption of the secret ballot, and provisions for state and local referenda to allow voters to initiate and decide public issues.

Finally, the Alliance pressed the government to increase the money supply by expanding the amount of silver coinage in circulation. In the Alliance's view, such

a move would have two positive, and related, conse-quences. First, the resulting inflation would lead to higher prices for agricultural commodities, putting more money in farmers' pockets. Second, the real value of farmers' debts would decrease, since the debts were contracted in pre-inflation dollars and would be paid back with inflated currency. Naturally, the eastern bankers who supplied farmers with credit opposed such a policy. In fact, in 1873 Congress, under the leadership of Senator John Sherman, had halted the purchase of silver by the Treasury Department, a measure that helped reduce the money supply. Investment bankers, such as J. P. Morgan, opposed a bimetallic monetary standard that added silver to gold coinage. They believed that only the use of gold would preserve the faith that foreign investors had in U.S. currency. Under the Sherman Silver Purchase Act (1890), the government resumed buying silver, but the act placed limits on its purchase and did not guarantee the creation of silver coinage by the Treasury. In the past, some members of the Alliance, including Lease, had favored expanding the money supply with greenbacks (paper money). However, to attract support from western silver miners, Alliance delegates emphasized the free and unlimited coinage of silver. Alliance supporters met with bitter disappoint-ment, though, as neither the Republican nor the Demo-cratic Party embraced their demands. Rebuffed, farmers took an independent course and became more directly involved in national politics through the formation of the Populist Party.

Populists Rise Up

In 1892 the National Farmers' Alliance moved into the electoral arena as a third political party. The People's Party of America, known as the **Populists**, held its first nominating convention in Omaha, Nebraska, in 1892. In addition to incorporating the Alliance's Ocala planks into their platform, they adopted recommendations to broaden the party's appeal to industrial workers. Popu-lists endorsed a graduated income tax, which would impose higher tax rates on higher income levels. They also favored the eight-hour workday, a ban on using Pinkerton "mercenaries" in labor disputes, and immigra-tion restriction, which stemmed from the unions' desire to keep unskilled workers from glutting the market and depressing wages. Reflecting the influence of women such as Mary Lease, the party endorsed women's suf-frage. Although African Americans contributed to the founding of the Populists, the party did not offer specific proposals to prohibit racial discrimination or segrega-tion. Rather, the party focused on remedies to relieve the economic plight of impoverished white and black farmers in general.

Explore

See Documents 17.3 and 17.4 to compare the central tenets of the Grange and the Populists.

In 1892 the Populists nominated for president former Union Civil War general James B. Weaver. Although Weaver came in third behind the Democratic victor, Grover Cleveland, and the Republican incumbent, Benjamin Harrison, he managed to win more than one million popular votes and 22 electoral votes. For a third

DOCUMENTS 17.3 AND 17.4

Farmers and Workers Organize: Two Views

Farmers in the Midwest and the South organized to address the problems they faced as a result of industrialization and the growth of big business. The Patrons of Husbandry (the Grange) in the 1860s and 1870s and the Populists in the 1880s and 1890s both tried to deal with various social and economic issues. Compare the following pronouncement of the Grange with an excerpt from the Populist Party platform, adopted on July 4, 1892, in Omaha, Nebraska.

Explore

17.3 The Ten Commandments of the Grange, 1874

1. Thou shalt love the Grange with all thy heart and with all thy soul and thou shalt love thy brother granger as thyself.
2. Thou shalt not suffer the name of the Grange to be evil spoken of, but shall severely chastise the wretch who speaks of it with contempt.
3. Remember that Saturday is Grange day. On it thou shalt set aside thy hoe and rake, and sewing machine, and wash thyself, and appear before the Master in the Grange with smiles and songs, and hearty cheer. On the fourth week thou shalt not appear empty handed, but shalt thereby bring a pair of ducks, a turkey roasted by fire, a cake baked in the oven, and pies and fruits in abundance for the Harvest Feast. So shalt thou eat and be merry, and "frights and fears" shall be remembered no more.
4. Honor thy Master, and all who sit in authority over thee, that the days of the Granges may be long in the land which Uncle Sam hath given thee.
5. Thou shalt not go to law[yers].
6. Thou shalt do no business on tick [time]. Pay as thou goest, as much as in thee lieth.
7. Thou shalt not leave thy straw but shalt surely stack it for thy cattle in the winter.
8. Thou shalt support the Granger's store for thus it becometh thee to fulfill the laws of business.
9. Thou shalt by all means have thy life insured in the Grange Life Insurance Company, that thy wife and little ones may have friends when thou art cremated and gathered unto thy fathers.
10. Thou shalt . . . surely charter thine own ships, and sell thine own produce, and use thine own brains.

This is the last and best commandment. On this hang all the law, and profits, and if there be any others they are these.

Choke monopolies, break up rings, vote for honest men, fear God and make money. So shalt thou prosper and sorrow and hard times shall flee away.

Source: "The Ten Commandments of the Grange," *Oshkosh Weekly Times*, December 16, 1874, reprinted in *Rich Harvest: A History of the Grange, 1876–1900*, by D. Sven Nordin (Jackson: University Press of Mississippi, 1974), 240.

party competing for the presidency for the first time, this was a noteworthy accomplishment.

At the state level, Populists performed even better. They elected 10 congressional representatives, 5 U.S. senators, 3 governors, and 1,500 state legislators. Two years later, the party made even greater strides by increasing its total vote by 42 percent and achieving its greatest strength in the South. This electoral momentum positioned the Populists to make an even stronger run in the next presidential election. The economic depression that began in 1893 and the political discontent it generated further enhanced Populist chances for success.

Explore

17.4 Populist Party Platform, 1892

FINANCE—We demand a national currency, safe, sound, and flexible issued by the general government. . . .

1. We demand free and unlimited coinage of silver and gold at the present legal ratio of 16 to 1. . . .
3. We demand a graduated income tax.
4. We believe that the money of the country should be kept as much as possible in the hands of the people, and hence we demand that all State and national revenues shall be limited to the necessary expenses of the government, economically and honestly administered. . . .

TRANSPORTATION—Transportation being a means of exchange and a public necessity, the government should own and operate the railroads in the interest of the people. The telegraph and telephone . . . should be owned and operated by the government in the interest of the people.

LAND—The land, including all the natural sources of wealth, is the heritage of the people, and should not be monopolized for speculative purposes, and alien ownership of land should be prohibited. All land now held by railroads and other corporations in excess of their actual needs, and all lands now owned by aliens should be reclaimed by the government and held for actual settlers only.

EXPRESSION OF SENTIMENTS

1. Resolved, That we demand a free ballot, and a fair count in all elections . . . without Federal intervention, through the adoption by the States of the . . . secret ballot system.
2. Resolved, That the revenue derived from a graduated income tax should be applied to the reduction of the burden of taxation now levied upon the domestic industries of this country. . . .
4. Resolved, That we condemn the fallacy of protecting American labor under the present system, which opens our ports to [immigrants including] the pauper and the criminal classes of the world and crowds out our [American] wage-earners; and we . . . demand the further restriction of undesirable immigration.
5. Resolved, That we cordially sympathize with the efforts of organized workingmen to shorten the hours of labor. . . .
6. Resolved, That we regard the maintenance of a large standing army of mercenaries, known as the Pinkerton system, as a menace to our liberties, and we demand its abolition. . . .
9. Resolved, That we oppose any subsidy or national aid to any private corporation for any purpose.

Source: "People's Party Platform," *Omaha Morning World-Herald*, July 5, 1892.

Interpret the Evidence

- What do the language and tone of these two documents tell you about the organizations that created them?
- What measures did the Populists propose that the Grangers did not? What issues did both address?

Put It in Context

How did both the Grangers and the Populists respond to the shifts in economic and political power that occurred at the end of the nineteenth century?

REVIEW & RELATE

• Why was life so difficult for American farmers in the late nineteenth century?

• What were the similarities and differences between farmers' and industrial workers' efforts to organize in the late nineteenth century?

✓ *LEARNINGCurve* bedfordstmartins.com/hewittlawson/LC

The Depression of the 1890s

When the Philadelphia and Reading Railroad went bankrupt in early 1893, it set off a chain reaction that pushed one-quarter of American railroads into insolvency. As a result, on May 5, 1893, "Black Friday," the stock market collapsed in a panic, triggering the **depression of 1893**. Making this situation worse, England and the rest of industrial Europe had experienced an economic downturn several years earlier. As a result, in the early 1890s foreign investors began selling off their American stocks, leading to a flow of gold coin out of the country and further damage to the banking system. Hundreds of banks failed, which hurt the business people and farmers who relied on a steady flow of bank credit to keep their enterprises afloat. By the end of 1894, some 3 million people, nearly 12 percent of the American workforce, remained unemployed. Tens of thousands of homeless people wandered the streets of major American cities. The depression became the chief political issue of the mid-1890s and resulted in a realignment of power between the two major parties. Rather than capitalizing on depression discontent, however, the Populist Party split apart and collapsed.

Depression Politics

President Grover Cleveland's handling of the depression only made a bad situation worse. Railroad executive James J. Hill warned the president, "Business is at a standstill and the people are becoming thoroughly aroused. Their feeling is finding expression about as it did during the War of the Rebellion [Civil War]." With talk of civil war in the air, the Cleveland administration faced protest marches and labor strife. In the spring of 1894, Jacob Coxey, a wealthy businessman and Populist reformer from Ohio, and his associate, Carl Browne, led a march on Washington, D.C., demanding that Cleveland and Congress initiate a federal public works program to provide jobs for the unemployed. Coxey had previously supported the Greenback Party, which advocated inflating

the money supply with paper currency to stimulate the economy and help those in distress. Though highly critical of the favored few who dominated the federal government, Coxey had faith that if "the people . . . come in a body like this, peaceably to discuss their grievances and demanding immediate relief, Congress . . . will heed them and do it quickly." For him, "relief" meant both creating jobs and increasing the money supply. After traveling for a month from Ohio, Coxey led a parade of some five hundred unemployed people into the nation's capital. Attracting thousands of spectators, **Coxey's army** attempted to mount their protest on the grounds of the Capitol building. In response, police broke up the demonstration and arrested Coxey for trespassing. Cleveland turned a deaf ear to Coxey's demands for federal relief and also disregarded protesters participating in nearly twenty other marches on Washington.

In the coming months, Cleveland's political stock plummeted further. He responded to the Pullman strike in the summer of 1894 by obtaining a federal injunction against the strikers and dispatching federal troops to Illinois when the workers disobeyed it. The president's action won him high praise from the railroads and conservative business interests, but it showed millions of American workers that the Cleveland administration did not have a solution for ending the suffering caused by the depression. From the outset of his term, the president had made his intentions about government assistance clear: "While the people should patriotically and cheerfully support their Government, its functions do not include the support of the people." In normal times, these words reflected the prevailing philosophy of self-help that most Americans shared, but in the midst of a severe depression they sounded heartless.

Making matters worse, Cleveland convinced Congress to repeal the Sherman Silver Purchase Act. This angered western miners, who relied on strong silver prices, along with farmers in the South and Great Plains who were swamped by mounting debt. At the same time, the removal of silver as a backing for currency caused private investors to withdraw their gold deposits from the U.S. Treasury. To keep the government financially solvent, Cleveland worked out an agreement with a syndicate led by J. P. Morgan to help sell government bonds, a deal that netted the businessmen a huge profit. In the midst of economic suffering, this deal looked like a corrupt bargain between government and the rich designed to ensure that the rich got richer as the poor got poorer.

Explore

See Document 17.5 for one cartoonist's depiction of the debt crisis.

DOCUMENT 17.5

Walter Huston | "Here Lies Prosperity," 1895

The "money question" became a focus of American politics in the first half of the 1890s and was exacerbated by the depression of 1893. Those who supported the gold standard believed that it provided the basis for a sound and stable economy. Proponents of the unlimited coinage of silver, especially Populists and Democrats such as William Jennings Bryan, asserted that expansion of the money supply would liberate farmers and workers from debt and bring prosperity to more Americans. The following cartoon illustrates the "free silver" point of view.

Explore

Why does the cartoonist use the phrases "enslaved," "stabbed in the back," "assassinated," and "traitors"? Whom does he accuse of these misdeeds?

According to this cartoon, what is the cause of poverty?

What burden keeps the working man in chains?

"The Situation: The Result of Interest Bearing Bonds and Sherman," in *Sound Money* (Massillon, OH), August 22, 1895. Reproduced from Worth Robert Miller, *Populist Cartoons: An Illustrated History of the Third Party Movement in the 1890s* (Kirksville, MO: Truman State University Press, 2011).

Put It in Context

How did the depression of 1893 affect the economic situation of farmers and working people? Whom did debt affect more?

In 1894 Congress also passed the Wilson-Gorman Act, which raised tariffs on imported goods. Intended to protect American businesses by keeping the price of imported goods high, it also deprived foreigners of the necessary income with which to buy American exports. This drop in exports did not help economic recovery. The Wilson-Gorman Act did include a provision that the Populists and other reformers endorsed: a progressive income tax of 2 percent on all annual earnings over $4,000. No federal income tax existed at this time, so even this mild levy elicited cries of "socialism" from conservative critics, who challenged the tax in the courts. They found a receptive audience in the Supreme Court. In *Pollack v. Farmers Loan and Trust* (1895), the justices, who had already struck down a number of attempts to regulate business, declared the income tax unconstitutional and denounced it as the opening wedge in "a war of the poor against the rich; a war constantly growing in intensity and bitterness."

With Cleveland's legislative program in shambles and his inability to solve the depression abundantly clear, the Democrats suffered a crushing blow at the polls. In the congressional elections of 1894, the party lost an astonishing 120 seats in the House. This defeat offered a preview of the political shakeup that loomed ahead.

Political Realignment in the Election of 1896

The presidential election of 1896 marked a turning point in the political history of the nation, one that would shape national politics for the next thirty-six years. Democrats nominated William Jennings Bryan of Nebraska, a farmers' advocate who favored silver coinage. When he vowed that he would not see Republicans "crucify mankind on a cross of gold," the Populists endorsed him as well. Bryan was the first major party nominee for the White House since 1868 who did not come from Ohio, Indiana, or New York.

Republicans nominated William McKinley, the governor of Ohio and a supporter of the gold standard and high tariffs on manufactured and other goods. While Bryan barnstormed around the country, McKinley remained at his home in Canton, Ohio, to conduct his campaign from his front porch. His campaign manager, Marcus Alonzo Hanna, an ally of Ohio senator John Sherman, raised an unprecedented amount of money, about $16 million, mainly from wealthy industrialists who feared that the free and unlimited coinage of silver would debase the U.S. currency. Hanna saturated the country with pamphlets, leaflets, and posters, many of them written in the native languages of immigrant groups. He also hired a platoon of speakers to fan out across the country

denouncing Bryan's free silver cause as financial madness. Republican Theodore Roosevelt, who would later become president himself, remarked that Hanna advertised McKinley "as if he were patent medicine." By contrast, Bryan raised about $1 million and had to travel around the country making personal appearances, in part to compensate for his campaign's lack of funds.

The outcome of the election transformed the Republicans into the majority party in the United States. McKinley won 51 percent of the popular vote and 61 percent of the electoral vote, making him the first president since Grant in 1872 to win a majority of the popular vote. More important than this specific contest, however, was that the election proved critical in realigning the two parties. Voting patterns shifted with the 1896 election, giving Republicans the edge in party affiliation among the electorate not only in this contest but also in presidential elections over the next three decades (Map 17.1).

What happened to produce this critical realignment in electoral power? The main ingredient was Republicans' success in fashioning a coalition that included both corporate capitalists and their workers. Although Bryan made sincere appeals for the votes of urban dwellers and industrial workers along class lines, they generally fell on deaf ears. Many of these voters took out their anger on Cleveland's Democratic Party and Bryan as its standard-bearer for failing to end the depression. In addition, Bryan, who hailed from Nebraska and reflected

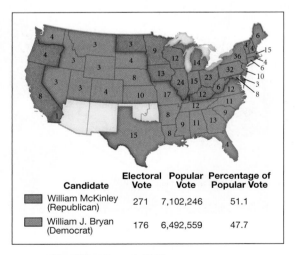

Candidate	Electoral Vote	Popular Vote	Percentage of Popular Vote
William McKinley (Republican)	271	7,102,246	51.1
William J. Bryan (Democrat)	176	6,492,559	47.7

MAP 17.1 The Election of 1896

William McKinley's election in 1896 resulted in a realignment of political power in the United States that lasted until 1932. Republicans became the nation's majority party by forging a coalition of big business and urban industrial workers from the Northeast and Midwest. Democratic strength was confined to the South and small towns and rural areas of the Great Plains and Mountain states.

small-town agricultural America and its values, could not win over the swelling numbers of urban immigrants who considered Bryan's world alien to their experience. A great orator, Bryan nevertheless sounded anti-urban, and his defeat signaled the decline of rural America in presidential politics. His campaign was the last serious effort to win the White House with mostly farm and small-town votes.

The election of 1896 broke the political stalemate in the Age of Organization. The core of Republican backing came from industrial cities of the Northeast and Midwest. Republicans won support from their traditional constituencies of Union veterans, businessmen, and African Americans and added to it the votes of a large number of urban wageworkers. The campaign persuaded voters that the Democratic Party represented the party of depression and that Republicans stood for prosperity and progress. Another factor helping the Republicans was that in 1897 the depression finally ended, largely as a result of gold discoveries in Alaska, which helped increase the money supply, and foreign crop failures, which raised American farm prices. Democrats managed to hold on to the South as their solitary political base.

The Decline of the Populists

The year 1896 also marked the end of the Populists as a national force, as the party was torn apart by internal divisions over policy priorities and electoral strategy. Populist leaders such as Tom Watson of Georgia did not want the Populist Party to emphasize free silver above the rest of its reform program. Other northern Populists, who either had fought on the Union side during the Civil War or had close relatives who did, such as Mary Lease, could not bring themselves to join the Democrats, the party of the old Confederacy. Nevertheless, the Populist Party officially backed Bryan, but to retain its identity, the party nominated Watson for vice president on its own ticket. After McKinley's victory, the Populist Party collapsed.

Losing the presidential election alone did not account for the disintegration of the Populists. Several problems plagued the third party. The nation's recovery from the depression removed one of the Populists' prime sources of electoral attraction. Despite appealing to industrial workers, the Populists were unable to capture their support. The free silver plank attracted silver miners in Idaho and Colorado, but the majority of workers failed to identify with a party composed mainly of farmers. As consumers of agricultural products, industrial laborers did not see any benefit in raising farm prices. Populists also failed to create a stable, biracial

coalition of dispossessed farmers. Most southern white Populists did not truly accept African Americans as equal partners, even though both groups had mutual economic interests. Southern white Populists framed their arguments around class as the central issue driving the exploitation of farmers and workers by wealthy planters and industrialists. However, in the end, they succumbed to racial prejudice.

To eliminate Populism's insurgent political threat, southern opponents found ways to disfranchise black and poor white voters. During the 1890s, southern states inserted into their constitutions voting requirements that virtually eliminated the black electorate and greatly diminished the white electorate. Seeking to circumvent the Fifteenth Amendment's prohibition against racial discrimination in the right to vote, conservative white lawmakers adopted regulations based on wealth and education because blacks were disproportionately poor and had lower literacy rates. They instituted poll taxes, which imposed a fee for voting, and literacy tests, which asked tricky questions designed to trip up would-be black voters (see chapter 16). In 1898 the Supreme Court upheld the constitutionality of these voter qualifications in *Williams v. Mississippi*. Recognizing the power of white supremacy, the Populists surrendered to its appeals.

Tom Watson provides a case in point. He started out by encouraging racial unity but then switched to divisive politics. In 1896 the Populist vice presidential candidate, who had assisted embattled black farmers in his home state of Georgia, called on citizens of both races to vote against the crushing power of corporations and railroads. By whipping up racial antagonism against blacks, his Democratic opponents appealed to the racial pride of poor whites to keep them from defecting to the Populists. Chastened by the outcome of the 1896 election and learning from the tactics of his political foes, Watson embarked on a vicious campaign to exclude blacks from voting. "What does civilization owe the Negro?" he bitterly asked. "Nothing! Nothing! NOTHING!!!" Only by disfranchising African Americans and maintaining white supremacy, Watson and other white reformers reasoned, would poor whites have the courage to vote against rich whites.

Nevertheless, even in defeat the Populists left an enduring legacy. Many of their political and economic reforms—direct election of senators, the graduated income tax, government regulation of business and banking, and a version of the subtreasury system (called the Commodity Credit Corporation, created in the 1930s)—became features of reform in the twentieth century. Populists also foreshadowed other attempts at

SMITH WANTS FAIR DIVISION OF PIE!

(OVER)

DEBATE IN THE LEGISLATURE ON THE ELECTION LAW.

Isaac Smith, Republican Leader, to C. H. Johnson, Populist Leader—"That's the way you Populists have done my race. We have elected them to good fat offices; we've made them Governor, and now you turn and tell us we ought never to have been allowed to vote, anyhow."

Populists and Race

The relationship between the Populists and African Americans was complex, but after 1896 the political connection between the two shattered. In this cartoon, Isaac Smith, a black Republican, chides C. H. Johnson, a Populist leader, for supporting a North Carolina election law that disfranchised blacks. Smith reminds Johnson that Populists had campaigned for African American votes in the past, and accuses him of walking off without sharing any of the pie. North Carolina Collection, University of North Carolina Library at Chapel Hill

creating farmer-labor parties in the 1920s and 1930s. Perhaps their greatest contribution, however, came in showing farmers that their old individualist ways would not succeed in the modern industrial era. Rather than re-creating an independent political party, most farmers looked to organized interest groups, such as the Farm Bureau, to lobby on behalf of their interests. Whatever their approach, farmers both reflected and contributed to the Age of Organization.

REVIEW & RELATE

How did the federal government respond to the depression of 1893?

What were the long-term political consequences of the depression of 1893?

✓ *LEARNINGCurve* bedfordstmartins.com/hewittlawson/LC

Conclusion: A Passion for Organization

From 1877 to 1900, industrial workers and farmers joined the march toward organization led by the likes of Carnegie, Rockefeller, and Morgan. These wealthy titans of industry and finance had created the large corporations that transformed the rhythms and meanings of factory labor and farm life. Working people such as John McLuckie met

the challenges of the new industrial order by organizing unions. Lacking the power of giant companies, which was reinforced by the federal government, labor unions nevertheless carved out sufficient space for workers to join together in their own defense to resist absolute corporate rule. At the same time, farmers, perhaps the most individualistic workers, and their advocates, such as Mary Elizabeth Lease, created organizations that proposed some of the most forward-looking solutions to remedy the ills accompanying industrialization. Though the political fortunes of the Grangers and Populists declined, their message persisted: Resourceful and determined workers and farmers could, and should, join together to ensure survival not just of the fittest but of the neediest as well.

Under the pressure of increased turmoil surrounding industrialization and a brutal economic depression, the political system reached a crisis in the 1890s. Despite the historic shift in party loyalties brought about by the election of William McKinley, it remained to be seen whether political party realignment could furnish the necessary leadership to address the problems of workers and farmers. Industrialization had proven painful and disorienting for millions of Americans. The events of the 1890s convinced many Americans, including many in the middle class, that the hands-off approach to social and economic problems that had prevailed in the past was no longer acceptable. In cities and states across the country, men and women took up the cause of reform. They had to wait for national leaders to catch up to them.

LEARNINGCurve
Check what you know.
bedfordstmartins.com/hewittlawson/LC

Chapter Review

Online Study Guide ▶ bedfordstmartins.com/hewittlawson

KEY TERMS

unskilled workers (p. 529)
skilled workers (p. 529)
unions (p. 532)
collective bargaining (p. 532)
Noble Order of the Knights of Labor (p. 532)
Haymarket Square (p. 533)
American Federation of Labor (AFL) (p. 534)
Homestead strike (p. 534)
Pullman strike (p. 535)
Industrial Workers of the World (IWW) (p. 536)
Grangers (p. 539)
Interstate Commerce Commission (ICC) (p. 539)
Farmers' Alliances (p. 540)
subtreasury system (p. 541)
Populists (p. 541)
depression of 1893 (p. 544)
Coxey's army (p. 544)

REVIEW & RELATE

1. How did industrialization change the American workplace? What challenges did it create for American workers?

2. How did workers resist the concentrated power of industrial capitalists in the late nineteenth century, and why did such efforts have only limited success?

3. Why was life so difficult for American farmers in the late nineteenth century?

4. What were the similarities and differences between farmers' and industrial workers' efforts to organize in the late nineteenth century?

5. How did the federal government respond to the depression of 1893?

6. What were the long-term political consequences of the depression of 1893?

TIMELINE OF EVENTS

1865–1895	U.S. manufacturing jobs jump from 5.3 million to 15.1 million
1867	Patrons of Husbandry (Grange) founded
1869	Noble Order of the Knights of Labor founded
1870–1900	Number of female wageworkers increases by 66 percent
1877	Great Railroad Strike
1879	Terence Powderly becomes leader of Knights of Labor
1880s	Northwestern, Southern, and Colored Farmers' Alliances formed
1886	Haymarket Square violence
American Federation of Labor founded
1887	Interstate Commerce Act passed
1889	Northwestern and Southern Farmers' Alliances merge
1890	Sherman Silver Purchase Act passed
1890s	Southern states strip blacks of the right to vote
1892	Homestead steelworkers' strike
Populist Party established
1893	Depression triggered by stock market collapse
1894	Pullman strike
Coxey's army marches to Washington
Sherman Silver Purchase Act repealed
1896	Populists back William Jennings Bryan for president
1897	Depression ends
Populist Party declines
1901	Eugene Debs establishes Socialist Party of America

The Pullman Strike of 1894

Late-nineteenth-century industrialists exercised massive power over workers and the conditions of labor. Yet this power was not absolute. Workers organized into unions to secure higher wages, shorter hours, improved safety, and a fairer measure of control of the labor process. Even those corporate owners who were considered sympathetic to the needs of laborers and their families, such as railcar magnate George Pullman, assumed the right to manage their businesses as they saw fit. Though Pullman had constructed a model town with clean housing and parks for his employees, he refused to heed workers' economic complaints after the depression of 1893 began.

When the American Railway Union (ARU), headed by Eugene V. Debs, launched a nationwide strike against the Pullman company in May 1894 to improve economic conditions and gain recognition for the union, Pullman refused to negotiate. Rebuffed by Pullman, the union coordinated strike activities across the country from its headquarters in Chicago. Workers refused to operate trains with Pullman cars attached, and when the railroads hired strikebreakers, some 260,000 strikers brought rail traffic to a halt. In response, U.S. Attorney General Richard Olney, a member of many railroad boards, obtained a federal injunction ordering strikers back to work, but without success. At Olney's recommendation, President Grover Cleveland ordered federal troops into Chicago to enforce the injunction. Their clash with strikers resulted in thirteen deaths, more than fifty injuries, hundreds of thousands of dollars in property damages, and the spread of violence to twenty-six states. After the government arrested union leaders, including Debs, for disobeying the injunction, the strike collapsed in July 1894, and the Supreme Court upheld Debs's imprisonment.

The following documents reveal the points of view from four major combatants in the labor struggle. As you read these documents, consider the larger questions raised by this episode: Why have organizations been essential to advancing the rights of individuals in an industrialized society? Why was organized labor not more successful in gaining a larger share of power from capital? How did gender influence labor conflict and organizing? And what role should the government play in shaping the outcome of conflicts between labor and capital?

DOCUMENT 17.6

George Pullman | Testimony before the U.S. Strike Commission, 1894

In July 1894, President Grover Cleveland appointed a Commission to Investigate the Chicago (Pullman) Strike. Although the Cleveland administration played a major role in ending the strike to the detriment of the American Railway Union, the president selected Carroll D. Wright, the U.S. commissioner of labor, to chair the commission. Wright had significant experience investigating labor conditions and collecting statistical data, and he was sympathetic to the plight of workers. George Pullman appeared before the commission to explain his position on the strike.

COMMISSIONER WRIGHT . . . State generally what the idea was of establishing the town [of Pullman] in connection with your manufacturing plant. . . .

PULLMAN [reading from a statement] The object in building Pullman was the establishment of a great manufacturing business on the most substantial basis possible, recognizing, as we did, and do now, that the working people are the most important element which enters into the successful operation of any manufacturing enterprise. We decided to build, in close proximity to the shops, homes for workingmen of such character and surroundings as would prove so attractive as to cause the best class of mechanics to seek that place for employment in preference to others. We also desired to establish the place on such a basis as would exclude all baneful [harmful] influences, believing that such a policy would result in the greatest measure of success, both from a commercial point of view, and also, what was equally important, or perhaps of greater importance, in a tendency toward continued elevation and improvement of the conditions not only of the working people themselves, but of their children growing up about them. . . .

If any lots had been sold in Pullman it would have permitted the introduction of the baneful elements which it was the chief purpose to exclude from the immediate neighborhood of the shops, and from the homes to be erected about them. The plan was to provide homes in the first place for all people who should desire to work in the shops, at reasonable rentals, with the expectation that as they became able and should desire to do so, they would purchase lots and erect homes for themselves within convenient distances, or avail themselves of the opportunity to rent homes from other people who should build in that vicinity. As a matter of fact, at the time of the strike 563 of the shop employees owned their homes, and 461 of that number are now employed in the shops; 560 others at the time of the strike lived outside; and, in addition, an estimated number from 200 to 300 others employed at Pullman were owners of their homes. . . .

Due attention was paid to the convenience and general well-being of the residents by the erection of stores and markets, a church, public schools, a library, and public halls for lectures and amusements; also a hotel and boarding houses. The basis on which rents were fixed was to make a return of 6 percent on the actual investment, which at that time, 1881, was a reasonable return to be expected from such an investment; and in calculating what, for such a purpose, was the actual investment in the dwellings on the one hand and the other buildings on the other, an allowance was made for the cost of the streets and other public improvements, just as it has to be considered in the valuation of any property for renting anywhere, all public improvements having to be paid for by the owner of a lot, either directly or by special assessment, and by him considered in the valuation. The actual operations have never shown a net return of 6 percent, the amount originally contemplated. The investment for several years returned a net revenue of about 4½ percent, but during the last two years additional taxes and heavier repairs have brought the net revenue down to 3.82 percent. . . .

(continued on page 552)

COMMISSIONER NICOLAS WORTHINGTON I wanted to know what you had in mind at the time you made the statement that "it was very clear that no prudent man could submit to arbitration in this matter" when you were referring to your daily losses as a reason why any prudent man could not submit to arbitration?

PULLMAN The amount of the losses would not cut any figure; it was the principle involved, not the amount that would affect my views as to arbitration.

WORTHINGTON Then it was not the amount of losses that the company was then sustaining, but it was the fact that a continuance of the business at the rates that had been paid would entail loss upon the company?

PULLMAN It was the principle that that should not be submitted to a third party. That was a matter that the company should decide for itself. . . .

WORTHINGTON Now, let me ask you if, taking all the revenues of the Pullman company for the last year, so far as you are advised, if the company has lost money or made money during the last year?

PULLMAN The company has made money during the last year.

Source: *Executive Documents of the Senate of the United States*, 53rd Cong. (1894–1895), 529–30, 553.

DOCUMENT 17.7
Eugene V. Debs | On Radicalism, 1902

American Railway Union leader Eugene Debs served six months in jail after leading the Pullman strike. This experience moved him in more radical directions politically, and he established the Socialist Party. He ran as the party's presidential candidate five times, and in 1905 Debs helped form the Industrial Workers of the World, an organization interested in uniting all workers and challenging the capitalist system. In 1902 he described to the readers of the *Comrade*, a New York socialist newspaper, his thoughts on the Pullman strike and how he became a socialist.

In 1894 the American Railway Union was organized and a braver body of men never fought the battle of the working class.

Up to this time I had heard but little of Socialism, knew practically nothing about the movement, and what little I did know was not calculated to impress me in its favor. I was bent on thorough and complete organization of the railroad men and ultimately the whole working class, and all my time and energy were given to that end. My supreme conviction was that if they were only organized in every branch of the service and all acted together in concert they could redress their wrongs and regulate the conditions of their employment. The stockholders of the corporation acted as one, why not the men? It was such a plain proposition—simply to follow the example set before their eyes by their masters—surely they could not fail to see it, act as one, and solve the problem. . . .

Next followed the final shock—the Pullman strike—and the American Railway Union again won, clear and complete. The combined corporations were paralyzed and helpless. At this juncture there [was] delivered, from wholly unexpected quarters, a swift succession of blows that blinded me for an instant and then opened wide my eyes—and in the gleam of every bayonet and the flash of every rifle *the class struggle was revealed.* This was my first practical lesson in Socialism, though wholly unaware that it was called by that name.

An army of detectives, thugs, and murderers [was] equipped with badge and beer and bludgeon and turned loose; old hulks of cars were fired; the alarm bells tolled; the people were terrified; the most startling rumors were set afloat; the press volleyed and thundered, and over all the wires sped the news that Chicago's white throat was in the clutch of a red mob; injunctions flew thick and fast, arrests followed, and our office and headquarters, the heart of the strike, was sacked, torn out, and nailed up by the "lawful" authorities of the federal government; and when in company with my loyal comrades I found myself in Cook county jail at Chicago, with the whole press screaming conspiracy, treason, and murder. . . .

Acting upon the advice of friends we sought to employ John Harlan, son of the Supreme Justice, to assist in our defense— a defense memorable to me chiefly because of the skill and fidelity of our lawyers, among whom were the brilliant Clarence Darrow and the venerable Judge Lyman Trumbull, author of the thirteenth amendment to the Constitution, abolishing slavery in the United States.

Mr. Harlan wanted to think of the matter over night; and the next morning gravely informed us that he could not afford to be identified with the case, "for," said he, "you will be tried upon the same theory as were the anarchists, with probably the same result." That day, I remember, the jailer, by way of consolation, I suppose, showed us the blood-stained rope used at the last execution and explained in minutest detail, as he exhibited the gruesome relic, just how the monstrous crime of lawful murder is committed.

But the tempest gradually subsided and with it the blood-thirstiness of the press and "public sentiment." We were not sentenced to the gallows, nor even to the penitentiary—though put on trial for conspiracy—for reasons that will make another story.

The Chicago jail sentences were followed by six months at Woodstock [the Illinois jail where Debs was imprisoned] and it was here that Socialism gradually laid hold of me in its own irresistible fashion. Books and pamphlets and letters from socialists came by every mail and I began to read and think and dissect the anatomy of the system in which workingmen, however organized, could be shattered and battered and splintered at a single stroke. . . .

The American Railway Union was defeated but not conquered—overwhelmed but not destroyed. It lives and pulsates in the Socialist movement, and its defeat but blazed the way to economic freedom and hastened the dawn of human brotherhood.

Source: Eugene V. Debs, *Debs: His Life, Writings, and Speeches* (Chicago: Charles Kerr, 1908), 81–84.

DOCUMENT 17.8

Jennie Curtis | Testimony before the U.S. Strike Commission, 1894

During the Pullman strike, seamstress Jennie Curtis was president of the American Railway Union Local 269, known as the "girls' union." Following a stirring speech by Curtis at an ARU convention, the union agreed to support workers striking against Pullman. In the following excerpt, Curtis explains to Carroll D. Wright, chairman of the congressional commission that later investigated the strike, the dire economic situation employees faced as the company cut back wages and raised rents.

COMMISSIONER WRIGHT   State your name, residence, and occupation.

CURTIS   Jennie Curtis; reside at Pullman; have been a seamstress for the Pullman company in the repair shops sewing room; worked for them five years.

WRIGHT   Are you a member of any labor organization?

CURTIS   Yes, sir; I am a member of the American Railway Union.

WRIGHT   How long have you been a member of that union?

CURTIS   Since about the 8th day of last May.

WRIGHT   Do you hold any position in the union?

CURTIS   I am president of the girls' union, local, No. 269, at Pullman.

WRIGHT   Did you have anything to do with the strike at Pullman, which occurred on the 11th of May, 1894?

CURTIS   No, sir.

WRIGHT   Had you anything to do with any of the efforts to avoid the strike, or to settle the difficulties?

CURTIS   I had not, further than being on a committee which called to see Mr. Pullman and Mr. Wickes, the general manager of the company, to ask for more wages, asking to arbitrate, and such as that.

WRIGHT   Were you on those committees, or some of them?

CURTIS   Yes, sir; I was.

WRIGHT   State briefly what you did as a member serving upon those committees.

CURTIS   I was on a committee that went from Pullman to speak for the girls in May before the strike, to ask for more wages. . . .

WRIGHT   State what took place at the first interview.

CURTIS   We went there and asked, as the men did, for more wages; we were cut lower than any of the men's departments throughout the works; in 1893 we were able to make 22 cents per hour, or $2.25 per day, in my department, and on the day of the strike we could only earn, on an average, working as hard as we possibly could, from 70 to 80 cents a day.

COMMISSIONER JOHN D. KERNAN   Can you give us how the wages changed from month to month?

CURTIS   Whenever the men were cut in their wages the girls also received a cut. We were cut twice inside of a week in November, 1893, and in January our wages were cut again; that was the last cut we received, and we worked as hard as we possibly could and doing all we could, too. The most experienced of us could only make 80 cents per day, and a great many of the girls could only average 40 to 50 cents per day. . . .

WRIGHT   Do you pay rent in Pullman?

CURTIS   No, sir; not now.

WRIGHT   You pay board?

CURTIS   Yes, sir. My father worked for the Pullman company for thirteen years. He died last September, and I paid the rent to the Pullman company up to the time he died; I was boarding at the time of my father's death. He being laid off and sick for three months, owed the Pullman company $60 at the time of his death for back rent, and the company made me, out of my small earnings, pay that rent due from my father.

KERNAN   How did they make you do it?

CURTIS   The contract was that I should pay $3 on the back rent every pay day; out of my small earnings I could not give them $3 every pay day, and when I did not do so I was insulted and almost put out of the bank by the clerk for not being able to pay it to them. My wages were cut so low that I could not pay my board and give them $3 on the back rent, but if I had $2 or so over my board I would leave it at the bank on the rent. On the day of the strike I still owed them $15, which I am afraid they never will give me a chance to pay back.

Source: *Executive Documents of the Senate of the United States*, 53rd Cong. (1894–1895).

DOCUMENT 17.9

Report from the Commission to Investigate the Chicago Strike, 1895

The commission appointed by President Grover Cleveland to investigate the Pullman strike concluded that strikes were wasteful, disruptive, and unlawful. Blaming both capital and labor for the strike, the commission believed that the Pullman trouble originated because neither the public nor the government had taken adequate measures to control monopolies and corporations and had failed "to reasonably protect the rights of labor and redress its wrongs."

Committee Recommendations Following Investigation of the Chicago Strike

I.

(1) That there be a permanent United States strike commission of three members, with duties and powers of investigation and recommendation as to disputes between railroads and their employees similar to those vested in the Interstate Commerce Commission as to rates, etc.

a. That, as in the interstate commerce act, power be given to the United States courts to compel railroads to obey the decisions of the commission, after summary hearing unattended by technicalities, and that no delays in obeying the decisions of the commission be allowed pending appeals.

b. That, whenever the parties to a controversy in a matter within the jurisdiction of the commission are one or more railroads upon one side and one or more national trade unions, incorporated under chapter 567 of the United States Statutes of 1885–86, or under State statutes, upon the other, each side shall have the right to select a representative, who shall be appointed by the President to serve as a temporary member of the commission in hearing, adjusting, and determining the particular controversy. . . .

c. That, during the pendency of a proceeding before the commission inaugurated by national trade unions, or by an incorporation of employees, it shall not be lawful for the railroads to discharge employees belonging thereto except for inefficiency, violation of law, or neglect of duty; nor for such unions or incorporation during such pendency to order, unite in, aid, or abet strikes or boycotts against the railroads complained of; nor, for a period of six months after a decision, for such railroads to discharge any such employees in whose places others shall be employed, except for the causes aforesaid; nor for any such employees, during a like period, to quit the service without giving thirty days' written notice of intention to do so, nor for any such union or incorporation to order, counsel, or advise otherwise. . . .

II.

(1) The commission would suggest the consideration by the States of the adoption of some system of conciliation and arbitration like that, for instance, in use in the Commonwealth of Massachusetts. That system might be reenforced by additional provisions giving the board of arbitration more power to investigate all strikes, whether requested so to do or not, and the question might be considered as to giving labor organizations a standing before the law, as heretofore suggested for national trade unions.

(2) Contracts requiring men to agree not to join labor organizations or to leave them, as conditions of employment, should be made illegal, as is already done in some of our States.

III.

(1) The commission urges employers to recognize labor organizations; that such organizations be dealt with through representatives, with special reference to conciliation and arbitration when difficulties are threatened or arise. It is satisfied that employers should come in closer touch with labor and should recognize that, while the interests of labor and capital are not identical, they are reciprocal.

(2) The commission is satisfied that if employers everywhere will endeavor to act in concert with labor; that if when wages can be raised under economic conditions they be raised voluntarily, and that if when there are reductions reasons be given for the reduction, much friction can be avoided. It is also satisfied that if employers will consider employees as thoroughly essential to industrial success as capital, and thus take labor into consultation at proper times, much of the severity of strikes can be tempered and their number reduced.

Source: *Report on the Chicago Strike of June–July, 1894 by the United States Strike Commission* (Washington, D.C.: Government Printing Office, 1895), LII–LIV.

DOCUMENT 17.10

Grover Cleveland | Reflections on the Pullman Strike, 1904

After Grover Cleveland left the White House in 1897, he became a trustee of Princeton University. He delivered several addresses as part of a lecture series on public affairs that was established in his honor. In 1904, a decade after the Pullman strike, he discussed his administration's role in dealing with the strike in an article in the popular magazine *McClure's*.

N THE LAST DAYS OF JUNE, 1894, a very determined and ugly labor disturbance broke out in the City of Chicago. Almost in a night it grew to full proportions of malevolence and danger. Rioting and violence were its early accompaniments; and it spread so swiftly that within a few days it had reached nearly the entire Western and Southwestern sections of our country. Railroad transportation was especially involved in its attacks. The carriage of United States mails was interrupted, interstate commerce was obstructed, and railroad property was riotously destroyed.

This disturbance is often called "The Chicago Strike." It is true that its beginning was in that city; and the headquarters of those who inaugurated it and directed its operations were located there; but the name thus given to it is an entire misnomer so far as it applies to the scope and reach of the trouble. Railroad operations were more or less affected in twenty-seven states and territories; and in all these the interposition of the General Government was to a greater or less extent invoked. . . .

The employees of the Pullman Palace Car Company could not on any reasonable and consistent theory be regarded as eligible to membership in an organization devoted to the interests of railway employees; and yet, during the months of March, April, and May, 1894, it appears that nearly 4,000 of these employees were enrolled in the American Railway Union. This, to say the least of it, was an exceedingly unfortunate proceeding, since it created a situation which implicated in a comparatively insignificant quarrel between the managers of an industrial establishment and their workmen, the large army of the Railway Union. It was the membership of these workmen in the Railway Union and the Union's consequent assumption of their quarrel, that gave it the proportions of a tremendous disturbance, paralyzing the most important business interests, obstructing the functions of the Government, and disturbing social peace and order. . . .

I shall not enter upon an enumeration of all the disorders and violence, the defiance of law and authority, and the obstructions of national functions and duties, which occurred in many localities as a consequence of this labor contention, thus tremendously reinforced and completely under way. It is my especial purpose to review the action taken by the Government for the maintenance of its own authority and the protection of the special interests intrusted to its keeping, so far as they were endangered by this disturbance; and I do not intend to especially deal with the incidents of the strike except in so far as a reference to them may be necessary to show conditions which not only justified but actually obliged the Government to resort to stern and unusual measures in the assertion of its prerogatives. . . .

Owing to the enforced relationship of Chicago to the strike which started within its borders, and because of its importance as a center of railway traffic, Government officials at Washington were not surprised by the early and persistent complaints of mail and interstate commerce obstructions which reached them from that city. It was from the first anticipated that this would be the seat of the most serious complications, and the place where the strong arm of the law would be most needed. In these circumstances it would have been a criminal neglect of duty if those charged with the protection of Governmental agencies and the enforcement of orderly obedience and submission to Federal authority, had been remiss in preparations for any emergency in that quarter.

. . . The Attorney-General, in making suggestions concerning legal proceedings, wrote: "It has seemed to me that if the rights of the United States were vigorously asserted in Chicago, the origin and center of the demonstration, the result would be to make it a failure everywhere else, and to prevent its spread over the entire country," and in that connection he indicated that it might be advisable, instead of relying entirely upon warrants issued under criminal statutes, against persons actually guilty of the offense of obstructing United States mails, that the courts should be asked to grant injunctions which would restrain and prevent any attempt to commit such offense.

Source: "The Government in the Chicago Strike of 1894," *McClure's Magazine*, July 1904, 227–29, 231–32.

Interpret the Evidence

1. Why does George Pullman (Document 17.6) think he has treated his workers fairly? Why might workers have disagreed with him?

2. According to Eugene V. Debs (Document 17.7), what was the purpose of labor activism? How did the Pullman strike teach Debs about socialism?

3. How did being a woman affect Jennie Curtis's experiences as a Pullman worker (see Document 17.8)?

4. How do you think Pullman and Debs would have responded to the report on the Pullman strike issued by the Commission to Investigate the Chicago Strike (Document 17.9)?

5. What do you think of Grover Cleveland's belief that the Pullman employees had no business joining the American Railway Union (see Document 17.10)?

Put It in Context

- What do these documents reveal about the complex relationship among labor, management, and government at the close of the nineteenth century?

background photos: pages 555 and 556–57, Library of Congress

LEARNINGCurve
Check what you know.
bedfordstmartins.com/hewittlawson/LC

The Granger Collection, New York

Private Collection/Peter Newark American Pictures/The Bridgeman Art Library

The Woolworth Building under construction, New York City, 1912.

An Italian family on the ferry from Ellis Island to New York City, 1905.

18

Cities, Immigrants, and the Nation

1880–1914

Baseball team, Franklin, Virginia.

AMERICAN HISTORIES

In the fall of 1905, Beryl Lassin faced a difficult choice. Living in the *shtetl* (a Jewish town) of Borrisnov in western Russia, Lassin had few if any opportunities as a young locksmith. Beryl and his wife, Lena, lived at a dangerous time in Russia. Jews were subject to periodic pogroms, state-sanctioned outbreaks of anti-Jewish violence carried out by local Christians. Beryl also faced a discriminatory military draft that required conscripted Jews to serve twenty-year terms in the army, far longer than their Christian countrymen. His wife's brother had already left Russia for the United States, and the couple decided that Beryl should follow his brother-in-law's example before the draft caught up with him. The couple couldn't afford two steamship tickets, so with the understanding that his wife would follow as soon as possible, Beryl set sail for America alone on the steamship *Zeeland*, which sailed from Antwerp, Belgium, on October 7, 1905. He was crammed into the steerage belowdecks with hundreds of other passengers, most of them fellow Jews. Ten days later, his ship chugged into New York harbor, where Beryl found a less than hospitable greeting. Disembarking at Ellis Island, the processing center for immigrants, he stood in long lines and underwent a strenuous medical examination, including a painful eye inspection, to ensure that he was fit to enter the country. He also had to prove that he had someplace to go, in his case the apartment of his brother-in-law on New York City's Lower East Side. With no money, Beryl boarded a ferry across the Hudson that took him to a new life in the United States.

**Beryl Lassin and
Maria Vik Takacs**

Less than a year later, Lena joined her husband. Over the next decade, the couple had five children. Shortly after the youngest girl was born, Lena died of cancer. Her death threw the family into turmoil, as Beryl, now called Ben, had to place two of the three youngest children in the Hebrew Children's Home and the other in foster care. The children were reunited with their father when Ben remarried, but life was still difficult. Ben was injured at his job as a mechanic and did not work full-time again. To make ends meet, his three eldest boys dropped out of school and went to work. Still, like many other immigrants, Ben's family managed to leave the crowded Lower East Side, following a trail blazed by earlier Jewish immigrants to Harlem and then the Bronx. Ben preferred to speak in Yiddish and never learned to read English. Nor did he become an American citizen, and after World War I, as an alien, he had to register annually with the federal government. His children, however, were all citizens because they had been born in the United States.

On June 8, 1912, another immigrant followed a similar route that took her on a different journey. Seventeen years old and unmarried, Maria Vik decided to leave her home in the small village of Kiestyderocz, Hungary. As a Catholic, Maria did not experience the religious persecution that Beryl did. Like many other Hungarians who ventured to the United States at this time, Maria, the oldest daughter, left to help support her family back in the old country. She had an aunt living in the United States, and she came across with a Hungarian couple who escorted young women for domestic service in America. Her sea voyage began in Hamburg, Germany, aboard the ship *Amerika*, and unlike Beryl she had a cabin in second class.

Maria, too, landed at Ellis Island and passed the rigorous entry exams. Soon she boarded a train for Rochester in western New York. There she worked as a cook for a German physician, learned English, and led an active social life within the local Hungarian community. In Rochester, she met and fell in love with Karoly (Charles) Takacs, a cabinetmaker from Hungary, who,

like Beryl Lassin, had come to avoid the military draft. Charles became a citizen in May 1916. By marrying him, Mary, as she was now called, became a citizen as well.

The couple moved forty-five miles west of Rochester to Middleport and purchased a small farm in a neighborhood filled with Hungarian immigrants. Because so many Hungarians lived in the area, Mary spoke mainly Hungarian and began to speak more English only when the oldest of her four children entered kindergarten.

The American histories of Beryl Lassin and Maria Vik Takacs took one to the urban bustle of New York City, the other to a quiet, rural village in western New York State. The Lassins, who rented walk-up apartments in five-story buildings and whose children had to drop out of school, did not fare as well economically as did the Takacses, who owned property and sent their three daughters to college. However, as different as their lives in America were, neither Beryl nor Maria regretted their choice to leave Europe for the United States. Like millions of other immigrants at the turn of the twentieth century, they had come to America to build better lives for themselves and their families, and both saw their children and grandchildren succeed in ways that they could have only dreamed of in their native countries. Indeed, Ben Lassin changed his surname to Lawson, and his son Murray married Ceil Puchowitzky (Parker), the daughter of another Russian-Jewish immigrant. Mary and Charles's daughter Irene married Robert Hewitt, whose family arrived from northern Europe in the nineteenth century. Murray's son, Steven F. Lawson, and Irene's daughter, Nancy A. Hewitt—the grandchildren of Beryl and Maria, respectively—became historians, got married, and wrote this textbook. The experiences of the Lawson and Hewitt families, like countless others, reflect the complicated ways that immigrants were transformed into Americans at the same time that the United States was forever changed by the new additions to its population. ●

photos: top photo courtesy of Steven F. Lawson; bottom photo courtesy of Irene Hewitt

THE LASSINS AND the Viks were part of a flood of immigrants who entered the United States from 1880 to the outbreak of World War I in 1914. Unlike the majority of earlier immigrants, who had come from northern Europe, most of the more than 20 million people who arrived during this period came from southern and eastern Europe. They entered the United States mainly through seaports in the Northeast, but some came through ports in New Orleans, Louisiana, and Key West and Tampa, Florida, in the South; across the Texas and California borders from Mexico; and through ports in San Francisco and Seattle on the West Coast. Though many moved to small towns and rural villages, most remained in cities, which experienced enormous population growth as a result. In these large urban areas, impoverished immigrants entered the political mainstream of American life, welcomed by political bosses and their machines, who saw in them a chance to gain the allegiance of millions of new voters. At the same time, their coming upset many middle- and upper-class city dwellers who blamed these new arrivals for lowering the quality of urban life.

A New Wave of Immigrants

For more than three hundred years following the settlement of the North American colonies, the majority of white immigrants to America were northern European Protestants. Black Americans were brought forcibly from Africa, mainly by way of the West Indies and the Caribbean. Although African Americans originally followed their own religious practices, most eventually converted to Protestantism. By the end of the nineteenth century, however, a new pattern of immigration had emerged, one that included much greater ethnic and religious diversity. These new immigrants often encountered hostility from those whose ancestors had arrived generations earlier, and faced the difficult challenge of retaining their cultural identities while becoming assimilated as Americans.

Immigrants Arrive from Many Lands

Immigration to the United States was part of a worldwide phenomenon. In addition to the United States, European immigrants also journeyed to other countries in the Western Hemisphere, especially Canada, Argentina, Brazil, and Cuba. Others left China, Japan, and India and migrated to Southeast Asia and Hawaii. From England and Ireland, migrants ventured to other parts of the British empire, including Australia, New Zealand, and South Africa. As with those who came to the United States, these immigrants left their homelands to find new job opportunities or to obtain land to start their own farms. In countries like Australia, New Zealand, and South Africa, white settlers often pushed aside native peoples—Aborigines in Australia, Maori in New Zealand, and blacks in South Africa—to make communities for themselves. Whereas most immigrants chose to relocate voluntarily, some made the move bound by labor contracts that limited their movement during the terms of the agreement. Chinese, Mexican, and Italian workers made up a large portion of this group.

The late nineteenth century saw a shift in the country of origin of immigrants to the United States: Instead of coming from northern and western Europe, many now came from southern and eastern European countries, most notably Italy, Greece, Austria-Hungary, Poland, and Russia. In 1882 around 789,000 immigrants entered the United States, 87 percent of whom came from northern and western Europe. By contrast, twenty-five years later in 1907,

SS *Zeeland*

The SS *Zeeland* was a British and Belgian ocean liner first launched in 1901. Four years later, like thousands of other immigrants, Beryl Lassin made the journey from Russia to Antwerp, where he boarded this ship, and finally landed at Ellis Island. Traveling in steerage, the cheapest fare, he ate poor meals and suffered from overcrowding and poor sanitation. Photograph courtesy of the Peabody Essex Museum, image no. 204962 of the 1,285,000 newcomers who journeyed to America, 81 percent originated from southern and eastern Europe.

Most of those settling on American shores after 1880 were Catholic or Jewish and hardly knew a word of English. They tended to be even poorer than immigrants who had arrived before them, coming mainly from rural areas and lacking suitable skills for a rapidly expanding industrial society. In the words of one historian, who could easily have been describing Beryl Lassin's life: "Jewish poverty [in Russia] is a kind of marvel for . . . it has origins in fathers and grandfathers who have been wretchedly poor since time immemorial." Even after relocating to a new land and a new society, such immigrants struggled to break patterns of poverty that were, in many cases, centuries in the making.

Immigrants came from other parts of the world as well. From 1860 to 1924, some 450,000 Mexicans migrated to the U.S. Southwest. Many traveled to El Paso, Texas, near the Mexican border, and from there hopped aboard one of three railroad lines to jobs on farms and in mines, mills, and construction. Cubans, Spaniards, and Bahamians traveled to the Florida cities of Key West and Tampa, where they established and worked in cigar factories. Tampa grew from a tiny village of a few hundred people in 1880 to a city of 16,000 in 1900. Although Congress had excluded Chinese immigration after 1882, it did not close the door to migrants from Japan. Unlike the Chinese, the Japanese had not competed with white workers for jobs on railroad and other construction projects. Moreover, Japan had emerged as a major world power in the late nineteenth century and gained some grudging respect from American leaders by defeating Russia in the Russo-Japanese War of 1904–1905. Some 260,000 Japanese arrived in the United States during the first two decades of the twentieth century. Many of them first settled in Hawaii and then moved to the West Coast states of California, Oregon, and Washington, where they worked as farm laborers and gardeners and established

businesses catering to a Japanese clientele. Nevertheless, like the Chinese before them, Japanese immigrants were considered part of an inferior "yellow race" and encountered discrimination in their West Coast settlements.

This wave of immigration changed the composition of the American population. By 1910 one-third of the population was foreign-born or had at least one parent who came from abroad. Foreigners and their children made up more than three-quarters of the population of New York City, Detroit, Chicago, Milwaukee, Cleveland, Minneapolis, and San Francisco. Immigration, though not as extensive in the South as in the North, also altered the character of southern cities. About one-third of the population of Tampa, Miami, and New Orleans consisted of foreigners and their descendants. The borderland states of Texas, New Mexico, Arizona, and southern California contained similar percentages of immigrants, most of whom came from Mexico.

These immigrants came to the United States largely for economic, political, and religious reasons. Nearly all were poor and expected to find ways to make money in America. U.S. railroads and steamship companies advertised in Europe and recruited passengers by emphasizing economic opportunities in the United States. Early immigrants wrote to relatives back home extolling the virtues of what they had found, perhaps exaggerating their success. However, for people barely making a living, or for those subject to religious discrimination and political repression, what did it matter if they arrived in America and the streets were not paved in gold, as legend had it? In fact, if many of the streets were not paved at all, at least the immigrants could get jobs paving them!

The importance of economic incentives in luring immigrants is underscored by the fact that millions returned to their home countries after they had earned sufficient money to establish a more comfortable lifestyle. Of the more than 27 million immigrants from 1875 to 1919, 11 million returned home (Table 18.1). One immigrant from Canton, China, accumulated a small fortune as a merchant on Mott Street, in New York City's Chinatown. According to residents of his hometown in China, "[Having] made his wealth among the barbarians this man had faithfully returned to pour it out among his tribesmen, and he is living in our village now very happy." Jews, Mexicans, Czechs, and Japanese had the lowest rates of return. Immigrant groups facing religious or political persecution in their homeland were the least likely to return. It is highly doubtful that a poor Jewish immigrant like Beryl Lassin would have received a warm welcome home in his native Russia, if he had been allowed to return at all.

TABLE 18.1 **Percentage of Immigrant Departures versus Arrivals, 1875–1914**

Year	Arrivals	Departures	Percentage of Departures to Arrivals
1875–1879	956,000	431,000	45%
1880–1884	3,210,000	327,000	10%
1885–1889	2,341,000	638,000	27%
1890–1894	2,590,000	838,000	32%
1895–1899	1,493,000	766,000	51%
1900–1904	3,575,000	1,454,000	41%
1905–1909	5,533,000	2,653,000	48%
1910–1914	6,075,000	2,759,000	45%

Creating Immigrant Communities

Immigrants were processed at their port of entry, and the government played no role in their relocation in America. New arrivals were left to search out transplanted relatives and other countrymen on their own. In cities such as New York, Boston, and Chicago, immigrants occupied neighborhoods that took on the distinct ethnic characteristics of the groups that inhabited them. A cacophony of different languages echoed in the streets as new residents continued to communicate in their mother tongues. The neighborhoods of immigrant groups often were clustered together, so residents were as likely to learn phrases in their neighbors' languages as they were to learn English.

The formation of **ghettos**—neighborhoods dominated by a single ethnic, racial, or class group—eased immigrants' transition into American society. Without government assistance or outside help, these communities assumed the burden of meeting some of the challenges that immigrants faced in adjusting to their new environment. Living within these ethnic enclaves made it easier for immigrants to find housing, hear about jobs, buy food, and seek help from those with whom they felt most comfortable. **Mutual aid societies** sprang up to provide social welfare benefits, including insurance payments and funeral rites. "A *landsman* died in the factory," a founder of one such Jewish association explained, and the worker was buried in an unmarked grave. When his Jewish neighbors heard about it, "his body [was] dug up, and the decision taken to start our organization with a cemetery." Group members established social centers where immigrants could play cards or dominoes, chat and gossip over tea or coffee, host dances and benefits, or just relax among people who shared a common heritage. In San Francisco's Chinatown, the largest Chinese community in California, such organizations usually consisted of people who had come from the same towns in China. These groups performed a variety of services, including finding jobs for their members, resolving disputes, campaigning against anti-Chinese discrimination, and sponsoring parades and other cultural activities. One society member explained: "We are strangers in a strange country. We must have an organization to control our country fellows and develop our friendship."

The same impulse to band together occurred in immigrant communities throughout the nation. On the West Coast, Japanese farmers joined *kenjinkai*, which not only provided social activities but also helped first-generation immigrants locate jobs and find housing. In Ybor City, Tampa's cigar-making section, mutual aid organizations rose to meet the needs of Spaniards, Cubans, Afro-Cubans, and Italians. El

El Centro Español

This 1912 postcard shows El Centro Español in Ybor City, the cigar-making district of Tampa, Florida. This facility served the Spanish community as a social club and mutual aid society. Immigrants attended dances, plays, and concerts and took English lessons, which eased their adaptation to a new homeland. Courtesy of the State Archives of Florida

Centro Español sponsored dances catering to Spaniards, only to be outdone by the rival El Centro Asturiano, which constructed a building that contained a 1,200-seat theater with a 27-by-80-foot stage, "$4,000 worth of modern lighting fixtures, a *cantina*, and a well stocked *biblioteca* (library)." Cubans constructed their own palatial $60,000 clubhouse, El Circulo Cubano, with lovely stained-glass windows, a pharmacy, a theater, and a ballroom. Less splendid and more economical, La Union Martí-Maceo became the home away from home for Tampa's Afro-Cubans. Besides the usual attractions, the club sponsored a baseball team that competed against other Latin teams. The establishment of such clubs and cultural centers speaks to the commitment of Tampa's immigrant groups to enhance their communities—a commitment backed up with significant financial expenditures.

Besides family and civic associations, churches and synagogues provided religious and social activities for ghetto dwellers. The number of Catholic churches nationwide more than tripled—from 3,000 in 1865 to 10,000 in 1900. Churches celebrated important landmarks in their parishioners' lives—births, baptisms, weddings, and deaths—in a far warmer and more personal manner than did clerks in city hall. Like mutual aid societies, churches offered food and clothing to those who were ill or unable to work and fielded sports teams to compete in recreational leagues. Immigrants altered the religious practices and rituals in their churches to meet their own needs and expectations, many times over the objections of their clergy. Various ethnic groups challenged the orthodox practices of the Catholic Church and insisted that their parishes adopt religious icons that they had worshipped in the old country. These included patron saints or protectresses from Old World towns, such as the Madonna del Carmine, whom Italian Catholics in New

York's East Harlem celebrated with an annual festival that their priests considered a pagan ritual. Women played the predominant role in running these street festivities. German Catholics challenged Vatican policy by insisting that each ethnic group have its own priests and parishes. Some Catholics, like Mary Vik, who lived in rural areas that did not have a Catholic church in the vicinity, attended services with local Christians from other denominations.

Religious worship also varied among Jews. German Jews had arrived in the United States in an earlier wave of immigration than their eastern European coreligionists. By the early twentieth century, they had achieved some measure of economic success and founded Reform Judaism, with Cincinnati, Ohio, as its center. This brand of Judaism relaxed strict standards of worship, including absolute fidelity to kosher dietary laws, and allowed prayers to be said in English. By contrast, eastern European Jews, like Beryl Lassin, observed the traditional faith and went to *shul* (synagogue) on a regular basis, maintained a kosher diet, and prayed in Hebrew.

With few immigrants literate in English, foreign-language newspapers proliferated to inform their readers of local, national, and international events. Between the mid-1880s and 1920, 3,500 new foreign-language newspapers came into existence. These newspapers helped sustain ethnic solidarity in the New World as well as maintain ties to the Old World. Newcomers could learn about social and cultural activities in their communities and keep abreast of news from their homeland. German-language tabloids dominated the field and featured such dailies as the *New Yorker Staatszeitung*, the *St. Louis Anzeiger des Westens*, the *Cincinnati Volkesblatt*, and the *Wisconsin Banner*.

Like other communities with poor, unskilled populations, immigrant neighborhoods bred crime. Young men joined gangs based on ethnic heritage and battled with those of other immigrant groups to protect their turf. Adults formed underworld organizations—some of them tied to international criminal syndicates, such as the Mafia—that trafficked in prostitution, gambling, robbery, and murder. Tongs (secret organizations) in New York City's and San Francisco's Chinatowns, which started out as mutual aid societies, peddled vice and controlled the opium trade, gambling, and prostitution in their communities. A survey of New York City police and municipal court records from 1898 concluded that Jews "are prominent in their commission of forgery, violation of corporation ordinance, as disorderly persons (failure to support wife or family), both grades of larceny, and of the lighter grade of assault."

Crime was not the only social problem that plagued immigrant communities. Newspapers and court records reported husbands abandoning their wife and children, engaging in drunken and disorderly conduct, or abusing

their family. Boarders whom immigrant families took into their homes for economic reasons also posed problems. Cramped spaces created a lack of privacy, and male boarders sometimes attempted to assault the woman of the house while her husband and children were out to work or in school. Finally, generational conflicts within families began to develop as American-born children of immigrants questioned their parents' values. Daughters born in America sought to loosen the tight restraints imposed by their parents. If they worked outside the home, young women were expected to turn their wages over to their parents. A young Italian woman, however, displayed her independence after receiving her first paycheck. "I just went downtown first and I spent a lot, more than half of my money," she admitted. "I just went hog wild." Thus the social organizations and mutual aid societies that immigrant groups established were more than a simple expression of ethnic solidarity and pride. They were also a response to the very real problems that challenged the health and stability of immigrant communities.

Explore

See Document 18.1 for a depiction of one immigrant family's intergenerational conflict.

Hostility toward Recent Immigrants

On October 28, 1886, the United States held a gala celebration for the opening of the Statue of Liberty in New York harbor, a short distance from Ellis Island. French sculptors Frédéric-Auguste Bartholdi and Alexandre-Gustave Eiffel had designed the 151-foot-tall monument, *Liberty Enlightening the World*, to appear at the Centennial Exposition in Philadelphia in 1876. Ten years overdue, the statue arrived in June 1885, but funds were still needed to finish construction of a base on which the sculpture would stand. Ordinary people dipped into their pockets for spare change, contributing to a campaign that raised $100,000 so that Lady Liberty could finally hold her uplifted torch for all to see. In 1903 the inspiring words of Emma Lazarus, a Jewish poet, were inscribed on the pedestal welcoming new generations of immigrants.

> Give me your tired, your poor,
> Your huddled masses yearning to breathe free,
> The wretched refuse of your teeming shore,
> Send these, the homeless, tempest-tossed to me,
> I lift my lamp beside the golden door!

Despite the welcoming inscription on the Statue of Liberty, many Americans whose families had arrived before the 1880s considered the influx of immigrants from southern and eastern Europe at best a necessary evil and at

DOCUMENT 18.1

Anzia Yerzierska | Immigrant Fathers and Daughters, 1925

Anzia Yerzierska, a Jewish immigrant who came to the United States from Poland around 1890, wrote about the struggles of immigrant families in adjusting to their new world. Her novel *Bread Givers* focuses on the conflict of a Jewish daughter, Sara Smolinski, patterned after herself, and the girl's father, Reb Smolinski, a Talmudic scholar. Intent on taking advantage of new opportunities in America, Sara resists her father's attempts to impose his Old World beliefs about the traditional duties of a subservient female.

Explore

As I came through the door with my bundle, Father caught sight of me. "What's this?" he asked. "Where are you going?"

"I'm going back to work, in New York."

"What? Wild-head! Without asking, without consulting your father, you get yourself ready to go? Do you yet know that I want you to work in New York? Let's first count out your carfare to come home every night. Maybe it will cost so much there wouldn't be anything left from your wages."

"But I'm not coming home!"

"What? A daughter of mine, only seventeen years old, not home at night?"

"I'll go to Bessie or Mashah."

"Mashah is starving poor, and you know how crowded it is by Bessie."

"If there's no place for me by my sisters, I'll find a place by strangers."

"A young girl, alone, among strangers? Do you know what's going on in the world? No girl can live without a father or a husband to look out for her. It says in the Torah, only through a man has a woman an existence. Only through a man can a woman enter Heaven."

"I'm smart enough to look out for myself. It's a new life now. In America, women don't need men to boss them."

"*Blut-und-Eisen!* ["blood and iron"] They ought to put you in a madhouse till you're cured of your crazy nonsense!" . . .

Wild with all that was choked in me since I was born, my eyes burned into my father's eyes. "My will is as strong as yours. I'm going to live my own life. Nobody can stop me. I'm not from the old country. I'm American!"

"You blasphemer!" His hand flung out and struck my cheek. "Denier of God! I'll teach you respect for the law!"

I leaped back and dashed for the door. The Old World had struck its last on me.

Source: Anzia Yerzierska, *Bread Givers* (New York: Persea Books, 1975), 136–38.

Interpret the Evidence

- How does Sara's father view the father-daughter relationship? How does Sara see it?
- Why does Sara's father object to her working in the city? What role does religion play in shaping his point of view?

Put It in Context

What values and beliefs does Sara associate with the Old World? What new values does she associate with America?

worst a menace. Industrialists counted on immigrants to provide the cheap labor that performed backbreaking work in their factories. Not surprisingly, existing industrial workers saw the newcomers as a threat to their economic livelihoods. In their view, the arrival of large numbers of immigrants could only result in greater competition for jobs and lower wages. Moreover, even though most immigrants came to America to find work and improve the lives of their families, a small portion antagonized and frightened capitalists and middle-class Americans with their radical calls for the reorganization of society and the overthrow of the government. Of course, the vast majority of immigrants were not radicals, but a large proportion of radicals were recent immigrants. During times of labor-management strife (see chapter 17), this fact made it easier for businessmen and their spokesmen in the press to advance the notion that anti-American radicalism was a chronic immigrant disease.

Anti-immigrant fears linked to ideas about race and ethnicity had a long history in the United States. In 1790 Congress passed a statute restricting citizenship to those deemed white:

> Any Alien being a free white person, who shall have resided within the limits and under the jurisdiction of the United States for the term of two years, may be admitted to become a citizen thereof on application to any common law Court of record in any one of the States wherein he shall have resided for the term of one year at least, and making proof to the satisfaction of such Court that he is a person of good character, and taking the oath or affirmation prescribed by law to support the Constitution of the United States.

This standard excluded American Indians, who were regarded as savages, and African Americans, most of whom were slaves at the time. In 1857 the Supreme Court ruled that even free blacks were not citizens. From the very beginning of the United States, largely Protestant lawmakers debated whether Catholics and Jews qualified as whites. Although lawmakers ultimately included Catholics and Jews within their definition of "white," over the next two centuries Americans viewed racial categories as not simply matters of skin color. Ethnicity (country or culture of origin) and religion became absorbed into and intertwined with racial categories. A sociological study of Homestead, Pennsylvania, published in 1910 broke down the community along the following constructed racial lines: "Slav, English-speaking European, native white, and colored." Russian Jewish immigrants such as Beryl Lassin were recorded as Hebrews rather than as Russians, suggesting that Jewishness was seen by Christian America as a racial identity.

Scores of races were presumed to exist based on perceived shades of skin color. In 1911 a congressional commission on immigration noted that Poles are "darker than the Lithuanians" and "lighter than the average Russian." These were not neutral judgments, however. Natural scientists and social scientists had given credence to the idea that some races and ethnic groups were superior and others were inferior. Based on Darwin's theory of evolution (see chapter 16), biologists and anthropologists constructed measures of racial hierarchies, placing descendants of northern Europeans with lighter complexions—Anglo-Saxons, Teutonics, and Nordics—at the top of the evolutionary scale. Those with darker skin were deemed inferior "races," with Africans and Native Americans at the bottom. Scholars attempting to

make disciplines such as history more "scientific" accepted these racial classifications. At Johns Hopkins University, the leading center of academic training in the social sciences in the 1880s, historian Herbert Baxter Adams argued that the influx of southern European immigrants threatened the capacity for self-government developed in the United States by early settlers originating from Great Britain and Germany. The prevailing sentiment of this era reflected demeaning images of many immigrant groups: Irish as drunkards, Chicanos and Cubans as lazy, Italians as criminals, Hungarians as ignorant peasants, Jews as cheap and greedy, and Chinese as drug addicts. These characteristics resulted supposedly from inherited biological traits, rather than from extreme poverty or other environmental conditions.

Newer immigrants, marked as racially inferior, became a convenient target of hostility. Skilled craftsmen born in the United States viewed largely unskilled workers from abroad who would work for low wages as a threat to their attempts to form unions and keep wages high. Middle-class city dwellers blamed urban problems on the rising tide of foreigners. In addition, Protestant purists felt threatened by Catholics and Jews and believed these "races" incapable or unworthy of assimilation into what they considered to be the superior white, Anglo-Saxon, and Protestant culture. In 1890 social scientist Richard Mayo Smith wrote, "It is scarcely probable that by taking the dregs of Europe, we shall produce a people of high social intelligence and morality."

Nativism—the belief that foreigners pose a serious danger to one's native society and culture—arose as a reactionary response to immigration. New England elites, such as Massachusetts senator Henry Cabot Lodge and writer John Fiske, argued that southern European, Semitic, and Slavic races did not fit into the "community of race" that had founded the United States. In 1893 Lodge and fellow Harvard graduates established the Immigration Restriction League and lobbied for federal legislation that would exclude adult immigrants unable to read in their own language. In 1887 Henry F. Bowers of Clinton, Iowa, founded a similar organization, the American Protective Association, which claimed a total membership of 2.5 million at its peak. The group proposed restricting Catholic immigration, making English a prerequisite to American citizenship, and prohibiting Catholics from teaching in public schools or holding public offices. Obsessed with the supposed threat posed by Catholics, Bowers directed the expansion of the organization throughout the Midwest.

Explore

See Document 18.2 for a nativist perspective on immigration.

DOCUMENT 18.2

"The Stranger at Our Gate," 1899

Critics of late-nineteenth-century immigration often relied on the germ theory of disease in their arguments for stricter immigration laws. However, nativist objections to immigrants went far beyond issues of public health. According to nativists, immigrants were sources of both biological and cultural "contamination." In the following cartoon, "The Stranger at Our Gate," the "germs" carried by immigrants are not limited to those associated with disease.

Explore

What do the inscription on the gate and the caption below the cartoon tell us about the specific policies the cartoon supports?

How would you interpret Uncle Sam's body language in facing the would-be immigrant?

What does the cartoon suggest about the role of religion in anti-immigrant sentiment?

What specific "threats" does the immigrant appear to pose to the United States?

THE STRANGER AT OUR GATE.

EMIGRANT.—Can I come in?   UNCLE SAM.—I 'spose you can; there's no law to keep you out.

The Ohio State University Billy Ireland Cartoon Library & Museum

Put It in Context

What does this cartoon tell us about prevailing attitudes toward immigration at the end of the nineteenth century?

Proposals to restrict immigration, however, did nothing to deal with the millions of foreigners already in America. To preserve their status and power and increase the size of the native-born population, nativists embraced the idea of **eugenics**—a pseudo-science that advocated "biological engineering"—and supported the selective breeding of "desirable" races to counter the rapid population growth of "useless" races. Accordingly, eugenicists promoted the institutionalization of people deemed "unfit," sterilization of those considered mentally impaired, and the licensing and regulation of marriages to promote better breeding. In pushing for such measures, eugenicists believed that they were following the dictates of modern science and acting in a humane fashion to prevent those deemed unfit from causing further harm to themselves and to society. Alexander Graham Bell (see chapter 16), the inventor of the telephone, was one of the early champions of eugenics and immigration restriction.

Others took a less harsh approach. As had been the case with American Indians (see chapter 15), reformers stressed the need for immigrants to assimilate into the dominant culture, embrace the values of individualism and self-help, adopt American styles of dress and grooming, and exhibit loyalty to the U.S. government. They encouraged immigrant children to attend public schools, where they would learn to speak English and adopt American cultural rituals by celebrating holidays such as Thanksgiving and Columbus Day. In 1892 schools adopted the pledge of allegiance, written by Francis Bellamy, which recited American ideals of "liberty and justice for all" and affirmed loyalty to the nation and its flag. Educators encouraged adult immigrants to attend night classes to learn English. Ben Lassin tried this approach sporadically, but he did not prove to be an apt pupil. Like many immigrants, he made only limited progress toward assimilation.

The Assimilation Dilemma

If immigrants were not completely assimilated, neither did they remain the same people who had lived on the farms and in the villages of Europe, Asia, Mexico, and the Caribbean. Some sought to become full-fledged Americans, like Mary Vik, or at least see that their children did so. Writer Israel Zangwill, an English American Jew, portrayed this goal and furnished the enduring image of assimilation in his 1908 play *The Melting-Pot*. Zangwill portrayed people from distinct backgrounds entering the cauldron of American life, mixing together, and emerging as citizens identical to their native-born counterparts. This representation of the **melting pot** became the ideal as depicted in popular cartoons, ceremonies adopted by business corporations, and lessons presented in school classrooms.

However, the melting pot worked better as an ideal than as a mirror of reality. Immigrants during this period never fully lost the social, cultural, religious, and political identities they had brought with them. Even if all immigrants had sought full assimilation, which they did not, the anti-immigrant sentiment of many native-born Americans reinforced their status as strangers and aliens. The same year that Zangwill's play was published, Alfred P. Schultz, a New York physician, provided a dim view of the prospects of assimilation in his book *Race or Mongrel*. Schultz dismissed the melting pot theory that public schools could change the children of all races into Americans, which he found absurd. **See Document Project 18: "Melting Pot" or "Vegetable Soup"?, page 582.**

Thus most immigrants faced the dilemma of assimilating while holding on to their heritage. Sociologist W. E. B. Du Bois summed up this predicament for one of the nation's earliest transported groups. In his monumental *The Souls of Black Folk* (1903), Du Bois wrote that African Americans felt a "two-ness," an identity carved out of their African heritage together with their lives as slaves and free people in America. This "double-consciousness . . . two souls, two thoughts, two unreconciled strivings" also applies to immigrants at the turn of the twentieth century. Immigrants who entered the country after 1880 were more like vegetable soup—an amalgam of distinct parts within a common broth—than a melting pot.

REVIEW & RELATE

What challenges did new immigrants to the United States face?

What steps did immigrants take to meet these challenges?

☑ *LEARNINGCurve* bedfordstmartins.com/hewittlawson/LC

Becoming an Urban Nation

In the half century after the Civil War, the population of the United States quadrupled, but the urban population soared sevenfold. In 1870 one in five Americans lived in cities with a population of 8,000 or more. By 1900 one in three resided in cities of this size. In 1870 only Philadelphia and New York had populations over half a million. Twenty years later, in addition to these two cities, Chicago's population exceeded 1 million; St. Louis, Boston, and Baltimore had more than 500,000 residents; and Cleveland, Buffalo, San Francisco, and Cincinnati boasted populations over 250,000. Urbanization was not confined to the Northeast and Midwest. Denver's population jumped from 4,700 in 1870 to more than 107,000 in 1890. During that same period, Los Angeles grew nearly fivefold, from 11,000 to 50,000, and Birmingham leaped from 3,000 to 26,000. "We live in the age of great cities," the Reverend Samuel Lane Loomis, a Massachusetts schoolteacher, remarked in 1886. "Each successive year finds a stronger and more irresistible current sweeping in towards the centers of life." This phenomenal urban growth also brought remarkable physical changes to the cities, as tall buildings reached toward the skies, electric lights brightened the nighttime hours, and water and gas pipes, sewers, and subways snaked below the ground.

The New Industrial City

Urban growth in America was part of a long-term global phenomenon. Between 1820 and 1920, some 60 million people globally moved from rural to urban areas. Most of them migrated after the 1870s, and as noted earlier, millions journeyed from towns and villages in Europe to American cities. Yet the number of Europeans who migrated internally was greater than those who went overseas. As in the United States, Europeans moved from the countryside to urban areas in search of jobs. Many migrated to the city on a seasonal basis, seeking winter employment in cities and then returning to the countryside at harvest time. Whether as permanent or temporary urban residents, these migrants took jobs as bricklayers, factory workers, and cabdrivers.

Before the Civil War, commerce was the engine of growth for American cities. Ports like New York, Boston, New Orleans, and San Francisco became distribution centers for imported goods or items manufactured in small shops in the surrounding countryside. Cities in the interior of the country located on or near major bodies of water, such as Chicago, St. Louis, Cincinnati, and Detroit, served similar functions. As the extension of railroad transportation led to the development of large-scale industry (see chapter 16), these cities and others became industrial centers as well.

Industrialization contributed to rapid urbanization in several ways. It drew those living on farms, who either could not earn a satisfactory living or were bored by the isolation of rural areas, into the city in search of better-paying jobs and excitement. One rural dweller in Massachusetts complained: "The lack of pleasant, public entertainments in this town has much to do with our young people feeling discontented with country life." In 1891, a year after graduating from Kansas State University, the future newspaper editor William Allen White headed to Kansas City, enticed, as he put it, by the "marvels" of "the gilded metropolis." In addition, while the mechanization of farming increased efficiency, it also reduced the demand for farm labor. In 1896 one person could plant, tend, and harvest as much wheat as it had taken eighteen farmworkers to do sixty years before.

Industrial technology also made cities more attractive and livable places. Electricity extended nighttime entertainment and powered streetcars to convey people around town. Improved water and sewage systems provided more sanitary conditions, especially given the demands of the rapidly expanding population. Structural steel and electric elevators made it possible to construct taller and taller buildings, which gave cities such as Chicago and New York their distinctive skylines. Scientists and physicians made significant progress in the fight against the spread of contagious diseases, which had become serious problems in crowded cities.

Although immigrants increasingly accounted for the influx into the cities, before 1890 the rise in urban population came mainly from Americans on the move. In addition to young men like William Allen White, young women left the farm to seek their fortune. The female protagonist of Theodore Dreiser's novel *Sister Carrie* (1900) abandons small-town Wisconsin for the lure of Chicago. In real life, mechanization created many "Sister Carries" by making farm women less valuable in the fields. The possibility of purchasing mass-produced goods from mail-order houses such as Sears, Roebuck also left young women less essential as homemakers because they no longer had to sew their own clothes and could buy labor-saving appliances from catalogs.

Similar factors drove rural black women and men into cities. Plagued by the same poverty and debt that white sharecroppers and tenants in the South faced, blacks suffered from the added burden of racial oppression and violence in the post-Reconstruction period. From 1870 to 1890, the African American population of Nashville, Tennessee, soared from just over 16,000 to more than 29,000. In Atlanta, Georgia, the number of blacks jumped from slightly above 16,000 to around 28,000. Richmond, Virginia, and Montgomery, Alabama, followed suit, though the increase was not quite as high.

Economic opportunities were more limited for black migrants than for their white counterparts. African American migrants found work as cooks, janitors, and domestic servants. Work in cotton mills remained off-limits to blacks, but many found employment as manual laborers in manufacturing companies—including tobacco factories, which employed women and men; tanneries; and cottonseed oil firms—and as dockworkers. In 1882 the Richmond Chamber of Commerce applauded black workers as "easily taught" and "most valuable hand[s]." Although the overwhelming majority of blacks worked as unskilled laborers for very low wages, others opened small businesses such as funeral parlors, barbershops, and construction companies or went into professions such as medicine, law, banking, and education that catered to residents of segregated black

African American Family, 1900

Despite the rigid racial segregation and oppression that African Americans faced in the late nineteenth century, some black families found ways to achieve economic success and upward mobility. With its piano and fine furniture, the home of this African American family reflects middle-class conventions of the period. The father is a graduate of Hampton Institute, a historically black university founded after the Civil War to educate freedpeople.　Library of Congress

in a railroad yard. "The colored women like this work," she explained, because "we make more money . . . and we do not have to work as hard as at housework," which required working sixteen-hour days, six days a week.

Although many blacks found they preferred their new lives to the ones they had led in the South, the North did not turn out to be the promised land of freedom. Black newcomers encountered discrimination in housing and employment. Residential segregation confined African Americans to racial ghettos, such as the South Side of Chicago and New York City's Harlem. Black workers found it difficult to obtain skilled employment despite their qualifications, and women and men most often toiled as domestics, janitors, and part-time laborers.

Nevertheless, African Americans in northern cities built their own communities that preserved and reshaped their southern culture and offered a degree of insulation against the harshness of racial discrimination. A small black middle class appeared in Washington, D.C., Philadelphia, Chicago, and New York City consisting of teachers, attorneys, and small business people. In 1888 African Americans organized the Capital Savings Bank of Washington, D.C. Ten years later, two black real estate agents in New York City were worth more than $150,000 each, and one agent in Cleveland owned $100,000 in property. The rising black middle class provided leadership in the formation of mutual aid societies, lodges, and women's clubs. Newspapers such as the *Chicago Defender* and *Pittsburgh Courier* furnished local news to their subscribers and reported national and international events affecting people of color. As was the case in the South, the church was at the center of black life in northern cities. More than just religious institutions, churches furnished space for social activities and the dissemination of political information. The Baptist Church attracted the largest following among blacks throughout the country, followed by the African Methodist Episcopal (AME) Church. By the first decade of the twentieth century, more than two dozen churches had sprung up in Chicago alone. Whether housed in newly constructed buildings or in storefronts, black churches provided worshippers freedom from white control. They also allowed members of the northern black middle class to demonstrate what they considered to be respectability and refinement.

neighborhoods. Despite considerable individual accomplishments, by the turn of the twentieth century most blacks in the urban South had few prospects for upward economic mobility.

In 1890, although 90 percent of African Americans lived in the South, a growing number were moving to Northern cities to seek employment and greater freedom. Boll weevil infestations during the 1890s decimated cotton production and forced sharecroppers and tenants off farms. At the same time, blacks saw significant erosion of their political and civil rights in the last decade of the nineteenth century. Most black citizens in the South were denied the right to vote and experienced rigid, legally sanctioned racial segregation in all aspects of public life (see chapter 16). Between 1890 and 1914 approximately 485,000 African Americans left the South. By 1914 New York, Chicago, and Philadelphia each counted more than 100,000 African Americans among their population, and another twenty-nine northern cities contained black populations of 10,000 or more. An African American woman expressed her enthusiasm about the employment she found in Chicago, where she earned $3 a day working

This meant discouraging enthusiastic displays of "old-time religion," which celebrated more exuberant forms of worship. As the Reverend W. A. Blackwell of Chicago's AME Zion Church declared, "Singing, shouting, and talking [were] the most useless ways of proving Christianity." This conflict over modes of religious expression reflected a larger process that was under way in black communities at the turn of the twentieth century. As black urban communities in the North grew and developed, tensions and divisions emerged within the increasingly diverse black community, as a variety of groups competed to shape and define black culture and identity.

Cities Expand Upward and Outward

As the urban population increased, cities expanded both out and up. Before 1860, the dominant form of brick and stone construction prevented buildings from rising more than four or five stories. As late as 1880, church steeples usually remained the tallest structures in cities. However, as cities became much more populous, land values soared. During the 1870s and 1880s, one piece of property in Chicago rose in value from $160 to $800. In Denver, the value of a city block leaped from $6,500 to $205,000, and in New York City a lot that sold for $80 in 1840 fetched $8,000 forty years later. Steep prices prompted architects to make the most of small, expensive plots of land by finding ways to build taller structures. Architects began using cast-iron columns instead of the thick, heavy walls of brick that limited floor space. The resulting "cloudscrapers" raised the urban skyline to ten stories. The development of structural steel, which was stronger and more durable than iron, turned cloudscrapers into **skyscrapers**, which stretched some thirty stories into the air. With the development of the electric elevator and the radiator, which replaced fireplaces with hot water circulated through pipes, even taller skyscrapers came to loom over downtown business districts in major cities.

Cities also expanded horizontally, as new transportation technology made it possible for residents to move around a much larger urban landscape. In the mid-nineteenth century in cities such as Boston and Philadelphia, pedestrians could still walk from one end of the city to the other within an hour. If residents preferred to ride public conveyances, they could pay a fare and hop on board a horse-drawn railcar. These vehicles moved slowly and left tons of horse manure in the streets. To avoid such problems, in 1873 San Francisco, followed by Seattle and Chicago, installed a system of cable-driven trolley cars. Still,

Chicago Skyscraper, 1898
Chicago's Marshall Field and Company building rose up twelve stories and became the second-tallest department store in the world. This granite skyscraper was constructed in sections between 1892 and 1914, and it was the first department store to install escalators. Courtesy Everett Collection

these trolleys proved slow and unreliable. By 1914, however, advances in transportation converted walking cities into riding cities.

Electricity provided the transportation breakthrough. In 1888 naval engineer Frank J. Sprague, who had once worked for inventor Thomas Edison, completed the first electric trolley line in Richmond, Virginia. Electric-powered streetcars traveled twice as fast as horses and left little mess on the streets. Subways could run underground without asphyxiating passengers and workmen with a steam engine's smoke and soot. Boston opened the first subway in 1897, followed by New York City in 1904.

Bridges spanning large rivers and waterways also helped extend the boundaries of the inner city. Railroad companies had originally worked out the details of constructing such bridges, but not until 1883 did they become the symbol of urban growth. In that year, the Brooklyn Bridge opened, connecting Manhattan with the city of Brooklyn. Designed and engineered by John Augustus Roebling, the bridge had taken thirteen years to complete and cost twenty men their lives. It stretched more than a mile across the East River and was broad enough for a footpath, two double carriage lanes, and two railroad lines. In addition, the bridge featured arches cut like giant cathedral windows. In looking up at its supporting cables, one observer marveled that they hung "like divine messages from above." During its first year in operation, more than 11 million people passed over the bridge; today, more than 51 million vehicles cross the bridge each year.

The electrification of public transportation and the construction of bridges made it feasible for some people to live considerable distances from their workplace. In the eighteenth and nineteenth centuries, middle- and upper-class merchants and professionals usually lived near their shops and offices in the heart of the city, surrounded by their employees. After 1880, the huge influx of immigration brought large numbers of impoverished workers to city centers. The resulting traffic congestion and overcrowded housing pushed wealthier residents to seek more open spaces in which to build houses. The new electric trolley lines allowed middle-class urbanites to move miles away from downtown areas. With an investment of $2,000 to $10,000, a considerable sum in those days, they built roomy homes filled with modern conveniences on leafy streets. In 1850 the Boston metropolis spread in a radius of two to three miles around the city and had a population of 200,000. In 1900 suburban Boston ringed the city in a ten-mile radius, with a population of more than 1 million. Increasingly, cities divided into two parts: an inner commercial and industrial core housing the working class, and outer communities occupied by a wealthier class of white, older-stock Americans.

How the Other Half Lived

As the middle and upper classes fled the industrial urban center for the suburbs, the working poor moved in to replace them. They lived in old factories and homes and in shanties and cellars. Because land values were higher in the city, the poorest people could least afford high rents. To make ends meet, families crowded into existing apartments, sometimes taking in boarders to help pay the rent. This led to increased population density and overcrowding in the urban areas where immigrants lived. On New York's Lower East Side, the population density was the highest in the world. In 1880, 47,000 people lived within the teeming area. Ten years later, the number had climbed to more than 57,000, a population density of 334,080 per square mile, about ten times the citywide average. Such overcrowding fostered communicable diseases and frustration, giving the area the nicknames "typhus ward" and "suicide ward."

Overcrowding combined with extreme poverty turned immigrant neighborhoods into slums, which were characterized by substandard housing. Impoverished immigrants typically lived in multiple-family apartment buildings called **tenements** (legally defined as containing more than three families). First constructed in 1850, these early dwellings often featured windowless rooms and little or no plumbing and heating. In 1879 a New York law reformed the building codes and required minimal plumbing facilities and that all bedrooms (but not all rooms) have a window. Constructed on narrow 25-by-100-foot lots, these five- and six-story buildings included four small apartments on a floor and had only two toilets off the hallway. Tenements stood right next to each other, with only an air shaft separating them. Although these dwellings marked some improvement in living conditions, they proved miserable places to live in—dark, damp, and foul smelling. In 1895 a federal government housing inspector observed that the air shafts provided "imperfect light and ventilation" and that "refuse matter or filth of one kind or another [was] very apt to accumulate at the bottom, giving rise to noxious odors." The air shafts also operated as a conduit for fires that moved swiftly from one tenement to another.

In fact, the density of late-nineteenth-century cities could turn individual fires into citywide disasters. The North Side of Chicago burned to the ground in 1871, and Boston and Baltimore suffered catastrophic fires as well. On April 18, 1906, an earthquake in San Francisco set the city ablaze, causing about 1,500 deaths and terrible destruction of businesses and homes. Such fires could, however, have long-term positive consequences. The great urban conflagrations encouraged construction of fireproof buildings made of brick and steel instead of wood. In addition, citizens organized fire watches and established municipal fire departments to replace volunteer companies. An unintended side effect, fires provided cities with a chance to rebuild. Chicago's skyscrapers and its system of urban parks were built on land cleared by fire.

Besides furnishing grossly inadequate housing, tenements stood out as eyesores, "scabs" on the landscape, especially for those who had lived in cities before the new wave of immigration began. In 1890 Jacob Riis, a Danish immigrant, newspaperman, and photographer, illustrated the brutal conditions endured by tenement families such as Beryl Lassin's on New York's Lower East Side. "In the stifling July nights," he wrote in *How the Other Half Lives*, "when the big barracks are like fiery furnaces, their very walls giving out absorbed heat, men and women lie in restless, sweltering rows, panting for air and sleep." Under these circumstances, Riis lamented, an epidemic "is excessively fatal among the children of the poor, by reason of the practical impossibility of isolating the patient in a tenement." Despite their obvious problems, tenements soon spread to other cities such as Cleveland, Cincinnati, and Boston, and one block might have ten of these buildings, housing as many as four thousand people.

With all the misery they spawned as places to live, tenements also functioned as workplaces. Czech immigrants made cigars in their apartments from six in the morning until nine at night, seven days a week, for about 6 cents an hour. By putting an entire family to work, they could make $15 a week and pay their rent of $12 a month. Clothing contractors in particular saw these tenement **sweatshops** as a cheap way to produce their products. By jamming two or three sewing machines into an apartment and paying workers a fixed amount for each item they produced, contractors kept their costs down and avoided factory regulations. Riis observed men, women, and children "bending over their machines, or ironing clothes at the window, half-naked. Proprieties do not count on the East Side."

Even when immigrants left sweatshop apartments and went to work in factories, they continued to face exploitation. The Jewish and Italian clothing workers who toiled in the **Triangle Shirtwaist Company**, located in New York City's Greenwich Village, worked long hours for little pay. In 1911 a fire broke out on the eighth story of the factory and quickly spread to the ninth and tenth floors. The fire engines' ladders could not reach that high, and one of the exits on the ninth floor was locked to keep workers from stealing material. More than 140 people died in the blaze—some by jumping out the windows, but most by getting trapped behind the closed exit door.

Explore

See Document 18.3 for one reaction to the Triangle Shirtwaist fire.

Slums compounded the potential for disease, poor sanitation, fire, congestion, and crime. Living on poor diets, slum dwellers proved particularly vulnerable to epidemics. Cholera and typhoid—as well as an outbreak of yellow fever in Memphis in the 1870s and in Tampa in the 1870s and 1880s—killed tens of thousands. Tuberculosis was even deadlier. An epidemic that began in a slum neighborhood could easily spread into more affluent areas of the city. Children suffered the most. Almost one-quarter of the children born in American cities in 1890 did not live to celebrate their first birthday.

Contributing to the outbreak of disease was faulty sewage disposal, a problem that vexed city leaders. Until the invention of the modern indoor flush toilet in the early twentieth century, people relied on outdoor toilets, with as

many as eight hundred people using a single facility. All too often, cities dumped human waste into rivers that also supplied drinking water. In 1881 the exasperated mayor of Cleveland called the Cuyahoga River "an open sewer through the center of the city." Two years later, a group of Philadelphians complained that their water was "not only distasteful and unwholesome for drinking, but offensive for bathing purposes." At the same time, the great demand for water caused by the population explosion resulted in lower water pressure. Consequently, residents in the upper floors of tenements had to carry buckets of water from the lower floors. Until cities overcame their water and sanitation challenges, epidemics would continue to plague urban dwellers.

Urban crowding created other problems as well. Traffic moved slowly through densely populated cities. Pedestrians and commuters had to navigate around throngs of people walking on sidewalks and streets, peddlers selling out of pushcarts, and piles of garbage cluttering the walkways. Streets remained in poor shape. In 1889 the majority of Cleveland's 440 miles of streets consisted of sand and gravel. Chicago did not fare much better. In 1890 most road surfaces were covered with wooden blocks, and three-quarters of the city's more than 2,000 miles of streets remained unpaved. Rainstorms quickly made matters worse by turning foul-smelling, manure-filled streets into mud. Washington, D.C., solved much of the problem of clogged roads by covering them with asphalt. For the most part, only smaller cities like New Haven, Connecticut, could afford to pave the streets.

Poverty and overcrowding contributed to increased crime. The U.S. murder rate quadrupled between 1880 and 1900, at a time when the murder rates in most European cities were declining. In New York City, crime thrived in slums with the apt names of "Bandit's Roost" and "Hell's Kitchen," and groups of young hoodlums, such as the "Sewer Rats" and "Rock Gang," preyed on unsuspecting citizens. Poverty forced some of the poor to turn to theft or prostitution. One twenty-year-old prostitute, who supported her sickly mother and four brothers and sisters, lamented: "Let God Almighty judge who's to blame most, I that was driven, or them that drove me to the pass I'm in." Rising criminality led to the formation of urban police departments, though many law officers supplemented their incomes by collecting graft (illegal payments) for ignoring criminal activities.

REVIEW & RELATE

What factors contributed to rapid urban growth in the late nineteenth century?

How did the American cities of 1850 differ from those of 1900? What factors account for these differences?

DOCUMENT 18.3

Rose Schneiderman | The Triangle Shirtwaist Fire, 1911

On March 25, 1911, fire erupted in the Triangle Shirtwaist factory in lower New York City. Most of the company's six hundred garment workers were immigrant women. The building had inadequate fire escapes and blocked exits, which resulted in the high death toll of 146 workers. This catastrophe aroused many New Yorkers to rally around factory reforms. In the aftermath of the fire, Rose Schneiderman, a Polish Jewish immigrant who had led a strike at the Triangle Shirtwaist Company in 1909, addressed a memorial gathering at the Metropolitan Opera House.

Explore

I would be a traitor to those poor burned bodies if I were to come here to talk good fellowship. We have tried you good people of the public—and we have found you wanting.

The old Inquisition had its rack and its thumbscrews and its instruments of torture with iron teeth. We know what these things are today: the iron teeth are our necessities, the thumbscrews are the high-powered and swift machinery close to which we must work, and the rack is here in the firetrap structures that will destroy us the minute they catch fire.

This is not the first time girls have been burned alive in this city. Every week I must learn of the untimely death of one of my sister workers. Every year thousands of us are maimed. The life of men and women is so cheap and property is so sacred! There are so many of us for one job, it matters little if 140-odd are burned to death.

We have tried you, citizens! We are trying you now and you have a couple of dollars for the sorrowing mothers and brothers and sisters by way of a charity gift. But every time the workers come out in the only way they know to protest against conditions which are unbearable, the strong hand of the law is allowed to press down heavily upon us.

Public officials have only words of warning for us—warning that we must be intensely orderly and

Victims of the Triangle Shirtwaist Company Fire, 1911   © Bettmann/CORBIS

must be intensely peaceable, and they have the workhouse just back of all their warnings. The strong hand of the law beats us back when we rise—back into the conditions that make life unbearable.

I can't talk fellowship to you who are gathered here. Too much blood has been spilled. I know from experience it is up to the working people to save themselves. And the only way is through a strong working-class movement.

Source: Leon Stein, *The Triangle Fire* (New York: Carroll & Graf, 1962), 144–45.

Interpret the Evidence

- Why did Schneiderman reject the possibility of an alliance between the middle class and the working class?
- In Schneiderman's view, what role did the government play in the oppression of working-class people?

Put It in Context

What does this speech convey about working conditions for female laborers at the start of the twentieth century?

Urban Politics at the Turn of the Century

The problems that booming cities faced in trying to absorb millions of immigrants proved formidable and at times seemed insurmountable. From a governmental standpoint, cities had limited authority over their own affairs. They were controlled by state legislatures and needed state approval to raise revenues and pass regulations. For the most part, there were no zoning laws to regulate housing construction. Private companies owned public utilities, and competition among them produced unnecessary duplication and waste. The government services that did exist operated on a segmented basis, with the emphasis on serving wealthier neighborhoods at the expense of the city at large. Missing was a vision of the city as a whole, one that would view the distinct sections as part of a larger tapestry. Cities had become so large and complex that no one could stand back and see the entire picture.

Political Machines and City Bosses

City government in the late nineteenth century was fragmented. Mayors usually did not have much power, and decisions involving public policies such as housing, transportation, and municipal services often rested in the hands of private developers. For instance, by 1890 Chicago had eleven branches of government that were constantly at odds with one another. Bringing some order out of this chaos, the **political machine** functioned to give cities the centralized authority and services that they otherwise lacked. At the head of the machine was the political **boss**. Although the boss himself (and they were all men) held some public office, his real authority came from leadership of the machine. These organizations maintained a tight network of loyalists throughout city wards (districts), each of which contained designated representatives responsible for catering to the needs of their constituents. Whether Democratic or Republican, political machines did not care about philosophical issues; they were concerned primarily with staying in power.

The strength of political machines rested in large measure on immigrants. The organization provided a kind of public welfare when private charity could not cope satisfactorily with the growing needs of the poor. Machines doled out turkeys on holidays, furnished a load of coal for the winter, provided jobs in public construction, arranged for shelter and meals if tenement houses burned down, and intervened with the police and the courts when a constituent got into trouble. Bosses sponsored baseball clubs, held barbecues and picnics, and attended christenings, bar

Philadelphia, 1897

This photograph shows the hustle and bustle of Philadelphia, which along with other cities grew enormously in the late nineteenth century. Urban politicians had to grapple with the challenges posed by the incredible pace of change, including the rapid influx of immigrants. The presence in this scene of carts, a horse, and a streetcar shows a city in transition.   Library of Congress

mitzvahs, weddings, and funerals, sometimes all in a single day. As George Washington Plunkitt, a boss in New York City's Tammany Hall machine, reflected, it was a "strenuous life." For enterprising members of immigrant groups—and this proved especially true for the Irish during this period—the machine offered upward mobility out of poverty as they rose through its ranks.

The poor were not the only group that benefited from connections to political machines. The machine and its functionaries helped businessmen maneuver through the maze of contradictory and overlapping codes regulating building and licenses that impeded their routine course of activities. In addition to assisting legitimate businessmen, the machine facilitated the underworld commerce of vice, prostitution, and gambling by acting as an arbiter to keep this trade within established boundaries—all for a cut of the illegal profits.

In return for these services, the machine received the votes of grateful immigrants and a plentiful supply of funds from businessmen. When challenged by reformers or other political rivals, the machine readily engaged in corrupt election practices to maintain its power. Mobilizing the "graveyard vote," bosses took names from tombstones to pad lists of registered voters. They also hired "repeaters" to vote more than once under phony names and did not flinch from dumping whole ballot boxes into the river or using hired thugs to scare opponents from the polls.

Bosses enriched themselves through graft and corruption. They secured protection money from both legitimate and illegitimate business interests in return for their services. Boss William Marcy Tweed, the head of Tammany Hall in the 1860s and 1870s, swindled New York City out of a fortune while supervising the construction of a lavish three-story courthouse in lower Manhattan. The original budget for the building was $250,000, but the city spent more than $13 million on the structure, making out checks to Tweed's phony associates "T. C. Cash" and "Philip F. Dummey." The building remained unfinished in 1873, when Tweed was convicted on fraud charges and went to jail. In later years, Tammany Hall's Plunkitt distinguished this kind of "dishonest graft" from the kind

of "honest graft" that he practiced. If he received inside information about a future sale of city property, Plunkitt reasoned, why shouldn't he get a head start, buy it at a low price, and then sell it at a higher figure? As he delighted in saying, "I seen my opportunities and I took 'em." What could be more American?

> **Explore**
>
> See Documents 18.4 and 18.5 for opposing perspectives on machine politics.

Yet the services of political machines came at a high cost. Corruption and graft led to higher taxes on middle-class residents. Moreover, the image of the political boss as a modern-day Robin Hood who stole from the rich and gave to the poor is greatly exaggerated. Much of the proceeds of machine activities went into the private coffers of machine bosses and other functionaries and did not go to worthy public ventures. Trafficking in vice might have run more smoothly under the coordination of the machine, but the

---

DOCUMENTS 18.4 AND 18.5

Political Machines: Two Views

At the turn of the twentieth century, investigative journalism exposed what many saw as glaring inequalities in industrializing America. In *The Shame of the Cities*, journalist Lincoln Steffens wrote about the need for significant political reform in the city of Philadelphia. Machine bosses such as New York City's George Washington Plunkitt, however, challenged Steffens's observations about the role of political machines in urban government, presenting themselves as much more effective representatives of the people's interests than the reformers.

> **Explore**

18.4 Lincoln Steffens | *The Shame of the Cities*, 1904

The honest citizens of Philadelphia have no more rights at the polls than the [N]egroes down South. Nor do they fight very hard for this basic privilege. You can arouse their Republican ire by talking about the black Republican votes lost in the Southern States by white Democratic intimidation, but if you remind the average Philadelphian that he is in the same position, he will look startled, then say, "That's so, that's literally true, only I never thought of it in just that way." And it is literally true.

The machine controls the whole process of voting, and practices fraud at every stage. The assessor's list is the voting list, and the assessor is the machine's man. . . . The assessor pads the list with the names of dead dogs, children, and non-existent persons. One newspaper printed the picture of a dog, another that of a little four-year-old [N]egro boy, down on such a list.

Source: Lincoln Steffens, *The Shame of the Cities* (New York: McClure, Phillips, 1904), 198–99.

safety and health of city residents hardly improved. Most importantly, although immigrants and the poor did benefit from an informal system of social welfare, the machine had no interest in resolving the underlying causes of their problems. As the dominant urban political party organization, the machine cared little about issues such as good housing, job safety, and sufficient wages. The British observer James Bryce, who toured America in the late 1880s and admired much of what he saw, nevertheless judged the machine-controlled municipal governments to be "the one conspicuous failure of the United States." It remained for others to provide alternative approaches to relieving the plight of the urban poor.

Urban Reformers

The men and women who criticized the political bosses and machines—and the corruption and vice they fostered—usually came from the ranks of the upper middle class and the wealthy. Their solutions to the urban crisis typically centered around toppling the political machine and replacing it with a civil service that would allow government to function on the basis of merit rather than influence peddling and cronyism. Both locally and nationally, they pushed for civil service reform. In 1883 Congress responded to this demand by passing the **Pendleton Civil Service Reform Act**, which required federal jobs to be awarded on the basis of merit, as determined by competitive examinations, rather than through political connections. As for the immigrants who supported machine politics, these reformers preferred to deal with them from afar and expected that through proper education they might change their lifestyles and adopt American ways.

Another group of Americans from upper- and middle-class backgrounds put aside whatever prejudices they might have held about working-class immigrants and dealt directly with newcomers to try to solve various social problems. These reformers—mostly young people, and many of them women and college graduates—took up residence in **settlement houses** located in urban slums. Settlement houses offered a variety of services to

---

Explore

18.5 George Washington Plunkitt | Confessions of a Political Boss, 1905

If a family is burned out I don't ask whether they are Republicans or Democrats, and I don't refer them to the Charity Organization Society, which would investigate their case in a month or two and decide they were worthy of help about the time they are dead from starvation. I just get quarters for them, buy clothes for them if their clothes were burned up, and fix them up till they get things runnin' again. It's philanthropy, but it's politics, too—mighty good politics. Who can tell how many votes one of these fires bring me? The poor are the most grateful people in the world, and, let me tell you, they have more friends in their neighborhoods than the rich have in theirs. . . .

I've been reading a book by Lincoln Steffens on *The Shame of the Cities*. Steffens means well but, like all reformers, he don't know how to make distinctions. He can't see no difference between honest graft and dishonest graft, and, consequent, he gets things all mixed up. There's the biggest kind of difference between political looters and politicians who make a fortune out of politics by keepin' their eyes wide open. The looter goes in for himself alone without considerin' his organization or his city. The politician looks after his own interests, the organization's interests, and the city's interests all at the same time.

Source: William L. Riordan, *Plunkitt of Tammany Hall* (New York: E. P. Dutton, 1963), 28–29.

Interpret the Evidence

- Why does Steffens claim that white urban voters are in a similar position as southern blacks?
- According to Plunkitt, what advantages does his form of community service have over that offered by reformers?

Put It in Context

What role did political machines play in the governance of cities?

community residents, including day care for children; cooking, sewing, and secretarial classes; neighborhood playgrounds; counseling sessions; and meeting rooms for labor unions. Settlement house organizers, pioneers of the social work profession, understood that immigrants gravitated to the political machine or congregated in the local tavern not because they were inherently immoral but because these institutions helped mitigate their suffering and, in some cases, offered concrete paths to advancement. Although settlement house workers wanted to Americanize immigrants, they also understood immigrants' need to hold on to remnants of their original culture.

By 1900 approximately one hundred settlement houses had been established in major American cities. Jane Addams, who founded Hull House in Chicago, contended that "the dependence of classes on each other is reciprocal" and insisted that "the things which make men alike are finer and better than the things that keep them apart." Other settlement houses reflecting a similar philosophy included the South End House in Boston, directed by Robert A. Woods, and the Henry Street Settlement in New York City, founded by Lillian Wald. Addams and Wald, as well as other social workers, preferred a hands-on approach. They actively mobilized neighborhood residents to engage in politics and to vote for candidates who understood their problems and would campaign for improved garbage collection, housing inspection, better schools, and other community improvements.

Religiously inspired reform provided similar support for slum dwellers. In contrast to clergy such as Russell Conwell (see chapter 16), who emphasized cash more than Christ, some Protestant ministers began to argue that immigrants' problems resulted not from chronic racial or ethnic failings but from their difficult environment. One of the best-known figures among this group was Washington Gladden, a minister who had lived in Springfield and Columbus, Ohio. Originally a defender of laissez-faire, by the mid-1880s Gladden had come to believe that unregulated private enterprise was "inequitable." He compared financial specula- tors to vampires "sucking the life-blood of our commerce." In books and from the pulpit, Gladden preached Christianity as a "social gospel," which included support for civil service reform, antimonopoly regulation, income tax legislation, factory inspection laws, and workers' right to strike.

Despite the efforts of social gospel advocates and the charitable organizations that arose to help relieve human misery, such as the Salvation Army, private attempts to combat the various urban ills, however well-meaning, proved insufficient. The problems were structural, not personal, and one group or even several operating together did not have the resources or power to make urban institutions more efficient, equitable, and humane. As Jane Addams noted, "Private beneficence is totally inadequate to deal with the vast numbers of the city's disinherited." If reformers were to succeed in tackling the most significant social problems and make lasting changes in American society and politics, they would have to enlist state and federal governments.

REVIEW & RELATE

What role did political machines play in late-nineteenth-century cities?

Who led the opposition to machine control of city politics, and what solutions and alternatives did they offer?

LEARNINGCurve bedfordstmartins.com/hewittlawson/LC

Conclusion: A Nation of Cities

Immigrants from southern and eastern Europe who came to the United States between the 1880s and 1914 survived numerous hardships as they strove to create a better life for their families. Like industrialists, workers, and farmers, they organized to advance collective interests. Immigrants joined together in neighborhood groups—houses of worship, fraternal organizations, burial societies, political machines, and settlement houses—to promote their own welfare. Some achieved success and returned to their homelands to live in relative splendor. Most of those who remained in the United States, like Mary Vik and Ben Lassin, struggled to earn a living but managed to pave the way for their children and grandchildren to obtain better education and jobs. Mary's granddaughter, Nancy A. Hewitt, earned a Ph.D. in history from the University of Pennsylvania, and Ben's grandson, Steven F. Lawson, earned a doctorate in history from Columbia University. They became university professors and in writing this book have tried to preserve their grandparents' legacy.

Immigrants were not the only group on the move in the late nineteenth century. African Americans migrated in search of political freedom and economic opportunity. They relocated from the rural South to the urban South and North, where they continued to encounter discrimination. Yet cities gave them more leeway to develop their own political, economic, cultural, and social institutions than they had before. Although they encountered segregation, African Americans in the North were allowed to vote, a tool they would use to gain equality in the future. Because of long-standing patterns of racism, supported by law, African Americans would struggle much longer than did white immigrants to obtain equality and justice.

Few public institutions attempted to aid immigrants or racial minorities as they made the difficult transition to urban and industrial life. Yet immigrants did participate in urban politics through the efforts of political bosses and their machines who sought immigrant votes. In return, political machines provided immigrants with rudimentary social and political services that they could rarely find anywhere else. Political machines, however, bred corruption, along with higher taxes to fund their extravagances. Dishonest government prompted middle- and upper-class urban dwellers to take up reform in order to sweep the political bosses out of office and diminish the power of their immigrant supporters, as we will see in the next chapter.

LEARNING*Curve*
Check what you know.
bedfordstmartins.com/hewittlawson/LC

Chapter Review

Online Study Guide ▶ bedfordstmartins.com/hewittlawson

KEY TERMS

ghettos (p. 565)
mutual aid societies (p. 565)
nativism (p. 568)
eugenics (p. 570)
melting pot (p. 570)
skyscrapers (p. 573)
tenements (p. 574)
sweatshops (p. 575)
Triangle Shirtwaist Company (p. 575)
political machine (p. 577)
boss (p. 577)
Pendleton Civil Service Reform Act (p. 579)
settlement houses (p. 579)

REVIEW & RELATE

1. What challenges did new immigrants to the United States face?

2. What steps did immigrants take to meet these challenges?

3. What factors contributed to rapid urban growth in the late nineteenth century?

4. How did the American cities of 1850 differ from those of 1900? What factors account for these differences?

5. What role did political machines play in late-nineteenth-century cities?

6. Who led the opposition to machine control of city politics, and what solutions and alternatives did they offer?

TIMELINE OF EVENTS

1880–1914	Period of significant immigration to United States
1882	Chinese Exclusion Act passed
1883	Pendleton Civil Service Reform Act requires that federal jobs be awarded on the basis of merit
	Brooklyn Bridge opens
1886	Statue of Liberty opens in New York City
1887	American Protective Association formed to restrict immigration
1892	U.S. schools adopt pledge of allegiance
1893	Immigration Restriction League founded
1897	Boston opens first subway system in the United States
1903	W. E. B. Du Bois publishes *The Souls of Black Folk*
1906	San Francisco earthquake
1908	Israel Zangwill publishes *The Melting-Pot*
1911	Triangle Shirtwaist Company fire in New York City

"Melting Pot" or "Vegetable Soup"?

In his play *The Melting-Pot* (1908), writer Israel Zangwill created what would become the dominant metaphor of immigrant assimilation. Zangwill portrayed people from different backgrounds entering American society, undergoing a process of assimilation, and becoming citizens virtually indistinguishable from their native-born counterparts. When the play premiered at the Columbia Theater in Washington, D.C., President Theodore Roosevelt, to whom the play was dedicated, was in the audience and reportedly cheered the production. The play went on to become a hit on Broadway the following year.

The reality of immigrant assimilation was more complicated than Zangwill's "melting pot" metaphor suggested (Document 18.6). There is some truth in Zangwill's metaphor: In the days before radio and television, immigrants absorbed new values, language, style of dress, taste in foods, and sense of humor from schools, newspapers, magazines, and silent movies. However, most of them also valued aspects of their cultural and social heritage and took pains to preserve cherished traditions and beliefs. Although immigrants saw the necessity of some degree of assimilation, many were unwilling to become "fully American" if that meant completely abandoning their previous cultural identity. Assimilation also varied by generation, with the children of immigrants becoming more Americanized than their parents.

While many native-born Americans saw assimilation as a requirement of true citizenship, others rejected the very possibility of assimilation, arguing that immigrants were inherently inferior and could not be absorbed into American society. Critics like Alfred Schultz (Document 18.8) and others believed that cultural differences would lead to the ruin of America. The following documents illustrate the debate at the turn of the twentieth century about immigrant assimilation from both supporters and opponents of assimilation.

DOCUMENT 18.6

Israel Zangwill | *The Melting-Pot*, 1908

The Melting-Pot explores the experiences of David Quixano, a Jewish immigrant and musician, as he writes a symphony that puts to music the racial and ethnic harmony created by the assimilation of immigrant groups in America at the turn of the twentieth century. In the following scene, David explains the process of assimilation to his love interest, Vera, and his Uncle Mendel.

VERA   So your music finds inspiration in America?

DAVID   Yes—in the seething of the Crucible.

VERA   The Crucible? I don't understand!

DAVID   Not understand! You, the Spirit of the Settlement! Not understand that America is God's Crucible, the great Melting-Pot where all the races of Europe are melting and re-forming! Here you stand, good folk, think I, when I see them at Ellis Island, here you stand in your fifty groups, with your fifty languages and histories, and your fifty blood hatreds and rivalries. But you won't be long like that, brothers, for these are the fires of God you've come to—these are the fires of God. A fig for your feuds and vendettas! Germans and Frenchmen, Irishmen and Englishmen, Jews and Russians—into the Crucible with you all! God is making the American.

MENDEL   I should have thought the American was made already—eighty millions of him.

DAVID   Eighty millions! Eighty millions! Over a continent! Why, that cockleshell of a Britain has forty millions! No, uncle, the real American has not yet arrived. He is only in the Crucible, I tell you—he will be the fusion of all races, the coming superman. Ah, what a glorious Finale for my symphony—if I can only write it.

Source: Israel Zangwill, *The Melting-Pot: Drama in Four Acts* (New York: Macmillan, 1909), 36–38.

DOCUMENT 18.7

"Be Just—Even to John Chinaman," 1893

The following cartoon appeared in the satirical magazine *Judge* the year after Congress renewed the Chinese Exclusion Act and added provisions requiring the Chinese already living in the United States to carry certificates of identity and residence. A caption (not shown) beneath the cartoon states: "Judge (to Miss Columbia)—'You allowed that boy to come into your school, it would be inhuman to throw him out now—it will be sufficient in the future to keep his brothers out.'" While the cartoon favors the Chinese Exclusion Act, it presents a more complex message. It accepts the presence of other immigrant groups and Native Americans, shown in stereotyped depictions, suggesting that schooling will turn them into true Americans. It also expresses some sympathy for the Chinese remaining in the country. The cartoon also proposes that some of these earlier immigrants harbored anti-Chinese feelings. Note the Irish American holding up a blackboard that says, "Kick Out the Heathen; He's Got No Vote."

BE JUST—EVEN TO JOHN CHINAMAN.

DOCUMENT 18.8

Alfred P. Schultz | The Mongrelization of America, 1908

Using the fall of Rome as his example, Alfred P. Schultz argued in *Race or Mongrel* that the mixing of races produced a mongrel civilization and inevitably led to the decay of a nation. As one reviewer noted at the time, the author's "apparent object is to check alien immigration into the United States." Like most opponents of the new immigrants, Schultz used arguments based on moral judgments and supposedly sound medical and scientific information.

The influx of these races cannot be without consequences. The surgeons at the ports of immigration observe that the present immigrants have a much higher percent of loathsome diseases, and that, in general physique, it is very much inferior to the immigration of thirty years ago. The history of the races now coming proves beyond doubt their mental inferiority to the races that immigrated before the advent of Slavs and Latins. If immigration is still a blessing, then the sturdy Northern races are in every way preferable to the Southern and Southeastern debris of races that have been. The free admission of these latter prevents the coming of the former, for if content to compete with Slavs and Latins, the Northerners need not migrate as far as the United States. Much more important than the economic effects of immigration are the racial effects of immigration. . . .

Up to the middle of the last century a distinct national character was developing in the United States, and certain distinctive traits were forming. The addition of millions of other races has caused a decomposition which prevented the endurance of these characteristics, and caused this development to cease. . . .

One cause only is sufficiently powerful to cause the decay of a nation. This cause is promiscuousness. A nation is decayed that consists of degenerates, and it consists of degenerates when it no longer constitutes a distinct race. A degenerated race is one that has no longer the same internal worth which it had of old, for the reason that incessant infusions of foreign blood have diluted and weakened the old blood. In other words, a nation is deteriorated that consists of individuals not at all related or very distantly related to the founders of the nation. . . .

The principle that all men are created equal is still considered the chief pillar of strength of the United States. It is a little declamatory phrase, and only one objection can be raised against it, that it does not contain one iota of truth. Every man knows that the phrase is a falsehood. The truth is that all men are created unequal. Even the men of one and the same race are unequal; the inequalities, however, are not greater than the inequalities existing between the individual leaves of one tree, for they are variations of one and the same type. The differences between individuals of distinct races are essential, and, as they are differences that exist between one species and another, they are lasting. The attempts at creating perfect man, man pure and simple, or "The American," by a fusion of all human beings, is similar to the attempt of creating the perfect dog by a fusion of all canine races. Every animal breeder knows that it cannot be done. . . .

The United States is not much less cosmopolitan today than imperial Rome was. The friends of universal uniformity and of eternal peace will say: "Well, as soon as we are equally worthless, we will not know it, and happiness and peace will prevail." The conclusion is false. The mongrels are equally worthless, but there is no harmony in the depraved lot. The instincts of the different races do not entirely disappear, but they cannot develop. The result is internal unhappiness as far as the individual is concerned, and discord, chronic civil war, as far as the state is concerned. Anarchy within the individual, anarchy in the state.

And why should promiscuousness in the United States have a different effect than it had in Rome and

(continued on page 586)

elsewhere? The opinion is advanced that the public schools change the children of all races into Americans. Put a Scandinavian, a German, and a Magyar boy in at one end, and they will come out Americans at the other end. Which is like saying, let a pointer, a setter, and a pug enter one end of a tunnel and they will come out three greyhounds at the other end.

Public schools are in our time not educational institutions, but information bureaus, and the cultivation of the memory predominates. The children of every race can be trained to the cultivation of memory, but they cannot all be educated alike. The instincts of the different races are too much out of harmony. It is for this reason that the schools give information, with very little education. Schools cannot accomplish the impossible. To express the same opinion biologically, "All animals cannot be fed with the same fodder." . . .

This is the truth: schools, political institutions, and environment are utterly incapable to produce anything. No man can ever become anything else than he is already potentially and essentially. Education and schools are favourable or detrimental to development. They cannot create. To express it differently, no man can ever learn anything or know anything that he does not know already potentially and essentially. . . . Biologically expressed, this sentence reads as follows: A young pug develops into nothing but an old pug, a young greyhound into nothing but an old greyhound; and never, in all the ages between the creation of the world and doomsday, does a pug develop into a greyhound, no matter what the education, the training, the political institutions, and the environment.

Source: Alfred P. Schultz, *Race or Mongrel* (Boston: L. C. Page, 1908), 254–55, 257–61, 266.

DOCUMENT 18.9

Randolph S. Bourne | Trans-national America, 1916

Not all Americans embraced the melting pot or disparaged immigrants. Randolph Bourne, a journalist and political activist, took a middle position on the issue dividing those calling for assimilation and those seeking to curtail immigration. In an essay that appeared in the *Atlantic Monthly*, Bourne argued for a "trans-national America," where instead of completely shedding their Old World cultures, immigrants retained the best of their cultural identities within the larger democratic American society.

We are all foreign-born or the descendants of foreign-born, and if distinctions are to be made between us they should rightly be on some other ground than indigenousness. The early colonists came over with motives no less colonial than the later. They did not come to be assimilated in an American melting-pot. They did not come to adopt the culture of the American Indian. They had not the smallest intention of "giving themselves without reservation" to the new country. They came to get freedom to live as they wanted to. They came to escape from the stifling air and chaos of the old world; they came to make their fortune in a new land. They invented no new social framework. Rather they brought over bodily the old ways to which they had been accustomed. Tightly concentrated on a hostile frontier, they were conservative beyond belief. Their pioneer daring was reserved for the objective conquest of material resources. In their folkways, in their social and political institutions, they were, like every colonial people, slavishly imitative of the mother-country. So that, in spite of the "Revolution," our whole legal and political system remained more English than the English, petrified and unchanging, while in England law developed to meet the needs of the changing times.

It is just this English-American conservatism that has been our chief obstacle to social advance. We have needed the new peoples—the order of the German and Scandinavian, the turbulence of the Slav and Hun—to save us from our own stagnation. I do not mean that the illiterate Slav is now the equal of the New Englander of pure descent. He is raw material to be educated, not into a New Englander, but into a socialized American along such lines as those thirty nationalities are being educated in the amazing schools of Gary [Indiana]. I do not believe that this process is to be one of decades of evolution. The spectacle of Japan's sudden jump from medievalism to post-modernism should have destroyed that superstition. We are not dealing with individuals who are to "evolve." We are dealing with their children, who, with that education we are about to have, will start level with all of us. Let us cease to think of ideals like democracy as magical qualities inherent in certain peoples. Let us speak, not of inferior races, but of inferior civilizations. We are all to educate and to be educated. These peoples in America are in a common enterprise. It is not what we are now that concerns us, but what this plastic next generation may become in the light of a new cosmopolitan ideal.

We are not dealing with static factors, but with fluid and dynamic generations. To contrast the older and the newer immigrants and see the one class as democratically motivated by love of liberty, and the other by mere money-getting, is not to illuminate the future. To think of earlier nationalities as culturally assimilated to America, while we picture the later as a sodden and resistive mass, makes only for bitterness and misunderstanding.

There may be a difference between these earlier and these later stocks, but it lies neither in motive for coming nor in strength of cultural allegiance to the homeland. . . .

What we emphatically do not want is that these distinctive qualities should be washed out into a tasteless, colorless fluid of uniformity. Already we have far too much of this insipidity—masses of people who are cultural half-breeds, neither assimilated Anglo-Saxons nor nationals of another culture. Each national colony in this country seems to retain in its foreign press, its vernacular literature, its schools, its intellectual and patriotic leaders, a central cultural nucleus. From this nucleus the colony extends out by imperceptible gradations to a fringe where national characteristics are all but lost. Our cities are filled with these half-breeds who retain their foreign names but have lost the foreign savor. This does not mean that they have actually been changed into New Englanders or Middle Westerners. It does not mean that they have been really Americanized. It means that, letting slip from them whatever native culture they had, they have substituted for it only the most rudimentary American—the American culture of the cheap newspaper, the "movies," the popular song, the ubiquitous automobile. The unthinking who survey this class call them assimilated, Americanized. The great American public school has done its work. With these people our institutions are safe. We may thrill with dread at the aggressive hyphenate [hyphenated American], but this tame flabbiness is accepted as Americanization. The same moulders of opinion whose ideal is to melt the different races into Anglo-Saxon gold hail this poor product as the satisfying result of their alchemy. . . .

. . . Let us face realistically the America we have around us. Let us work with the forces that are at work. Let us make something of this trans-national spirit instead of outlawing it. Already we are living this cosmopolitan America. What we need is everywhere a vivid consciousness of the new ideal. Deliberate headway must be made against the survivals of the melting-pot ideal for the promise of American life.

Source: Randolph S. Bourne, "Trans-national America," *Atlantic Monthly*, July 1916, 87–88, 90, 97.

DOCUMENT 18.10

Jacob Riis | The Color Line in New York, 1891

Jacob Riis is best known for writing about eastern European immigrants living in crowded tenements on New York's Lower East Side. However, his classic work of photojournalism, *How the Other Half Lives*, also provided a portrait of New York's African American residents, many of whom migrated from the South after the Civil War and lived on the Upper East Side of Manhattan in the neighborhoods of Yorkville and Harlem. As this passage demonstrates, Riis was a sharp observer of the forces of racial discrimination that placed blacks at a disadvantage compared to white immigrants.

The color line must be drawn through the tenements to give the picture its proper shading. The landlord does the drawing, does it with an absence of pretense, a frankness of despotism, that is nothing if not brutal. The Czar of all the Russias is not more absolute upon his own soil than the New York landlord in his dealings with colored tenants. Where he permits them to live, they go; where he shuts the door, stay out. By his grace they exist at all in certain localities; his ukase [order] banishes them from others. He accepts the responsibility, when laid at his door, with unruffled complacency. It is business, he will tell you. And it is. He makes the prejudice in which he traffics pay him well, and that, as he thinks it quite superfluous to tell you, is what he is there for. . . .

Cleanliness is the characteristic of the [N]egro in his new surroundings, as it was his virtue in the old. In this respect he is immensely the superior of the lowest of the whites, the Italians and the Polish Jews, below whom he has been classed in the past in the tenant scale. Nevertheless, he has always had to pay higher rents than even these for the poorest and most stinted rooms. The exceptions I have come across, in which the rents, though high, have seemed more nearly on a level with what was asked for the same number and size of rooms in the average tenement, were in the case of tumble-down rookeries in which no one else would live, and were always coupled with the condition that the landlord should "make no repairs." It can readily be seen that his profits were scarcely curtailed by his "humanity." The reason advanced for this systematic robbery is that white people will not live in the same house with colored tenants, or even in a house recently occupied by [N]egroes, and that consequently its selling value is injured. The prejudice undoubtedly exists, but it is not lessened by the house agents, who have set up the maxim "once a colored house, always a colored house."

There is method in the maxim, as shown by an inquiry made last year by the *Real Estate Record*. It proved agents to be practically unanimous in the endorsement of the [N]egro as a clean, orderly, and "profitable" tenant. Here is the testimony of one of the largest real estate firms in the city: "We would rather have [N]egro tenants in our poorest class of tenements than the lower grades of foreign white people. We find the former cleaner than the latter, and they do not destroy the property so much. We also get higher prices. We have a tenement on Nineteenth Street, where we get $10 for two rooms which we could not get more than $7.50 for from white tenants previously." . . .

[Riis cites several similar instances of higher rents charged to black tenants.]

I have quoted these cases at length in order to let in light on the quality of this landlord despotism that has purposely confused the public mind, and for its own selfish ends is propping up a waning prejudice. It will be cause for congratulation if indeed its time has come at last. Within a year, I am told by one of the most intelligent and best informed of our colored citizens, there has been evidence, simultaneous with the colored hegira [flight] from the low downtown tenements, of a movement toward less exorbitant rents.

Source: Jacob Riis, *How the Other Half Lives: Studies among the Tenements of New York* (New York: Charles Scribner's and Sons, 1914), 148, 150–52.

Interpret the Evidence

1. According to Israel Zangwill, how will immigrants become "real Americans" (Document 18.6)?

2. What is Alfred Schultz's view of the melting pot (Document 18.8)? In his estimation, why is assimilation an impossible goal for America?

3. Why might other immigrant groups have supported Chinese exclusion (see Document 18.7)?

4. How does Randolph Bourne's vision of America's future differ from that of Zangwill? On what points might the two men have agreed?

5. What explanation does Jacob Riis offer for the high rents and poor accommodations that African Americans were forced to accept (Document 18.10)? What differences between the experiences of white immigrants and African Americans does Riis's description suggest?

Put It in Context

- What are the limitations of the melting pot metaphor for immigrant assimilation? What metaphor would you employ to describe the assimilation process? Why?

background photo: page 588, Library of Congress

LEARNINGCurve
Check what you know.
bedfordstmartins.com/hewittlawson/LC

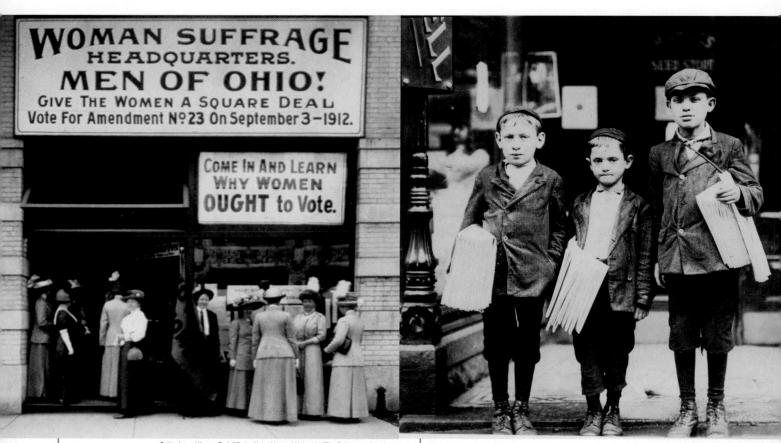

Schlesinger Library, Radcliffe Institute, Harvard University/The Bridgeman Art Library

Library of Congress

The women's suffrage organization headquarters of Ohio, 1912.

Newsboys in Philadelphia, 1910.

19

Progressivism and the Search for Order

1900–1917

Library of Congress

Sewing class at Haines Normal and Industrial Institute, Augusta, Georgia.

Gifford Pinchot grew up on a lavish Connecticut estate catered to by tutors and governesses and vacationing in rural areas, where Gifford learned to hunt, fish, and enjoy the splendor of nature. Yet Pinchot rejected a life of leisure and gentility. Like other affluent young men and women of his time, Pinchot sought to make his mark through public service, in his case by working to conserve and protect America's natural resources. In 1885, following his father's advice, Gifford entered Yale University to study forestry. However, the university did not offer a forestry program, reflecting the predominant view that the nation's natural resources were, for all practical purposes, unlimited. Pinchot cobbled together courses in various scientific fields at Yale, but he knew that after graduating his only option for further study was to travel to Europe, where forests were treated as crops that needed care and replenishing.

By the time Pinchot returned in 1890, many Americans had begun to see the need to conserve the nation's forests, waterways, and oil and mineral deposits and to protect its wild spaces. Drawing on his training as a scientist and his experiences in Europe, Pinchot advocated the use of natural resources by sportsmen and businesses under carefully regulated governmental authority. Appointed to head the Federal Division of Forestry in 1898, Pinchot found a vigorous ally in the White House when Theodore Roosevelt took office in 1901 after William McKinley's assassination. In 1907 Pinchot began to speak of the need for

591

conservation, which he defined as "the use of the natural resources now existing on this continent for the benefit of the people who live here now." This use of resources included responsible business practices in industries such as logging and mining.

Not all environmentalists agreed. In contrast to Pinchot, author and nature photographer Geneva (Gene) Stratton-Porter focused her energies on *preservation*, the protection of public land from any private development and the creation of national parks. Born in 1863 in Wabash County, Indiana, Stratton-Porter spent her childhood on a farm roaming through fields, watching birds, and observing "nature's rhythms." After marrying in 1886,

Stratton-Porter took up photography and hiked into the wilderness of Indiana to take pictures of wild birds.

Stratton-Porter built a reputation as a nature photographer. She also published a series of novels and children's books that revealed her vision of the harmony between human beings and nature. She urged readers to preserve the environment for plant life and wildlife so that men and women could lead a truly fulfilling existence on Earth and not destroy God's creation. Of all the preservationists, Stratton-Porter reached the widest audience. Five of her books sold more than a million copies, and several were made into movies. •

photos: Library of Congress; Indiana Historical Society P0391 (detail)

THE AMERICAN HISTORIES of Gifford Pinchot and Gene Stratton-Porter reveal the efforts of just two of the many individuals who searched for ways to control the damaging impact of modernization on the United States. From roughly 1900 to 1917, many Americans sought to bring some order out of the chaos accompanying rapid industrialization and urbanization. Despite the magnitude of the issues they targeted, those who believed in the need to combat the problems of industrial America possessed an optimistic faith—sometimes derived from religious principles, sometimes from a secular outlook—that they could relieve the stresses and strains that modern life brought. Such people were not bound together by a single, rigid ideology. Instead, they were united by faith in the notion that if people joined together and applied human intelligence to the task of improving the nation, progress was inevitable. So widespread was this hopeful conviction that we call this period the Progressive Era.

In pursuit of progress and stability, reformers tried to control the behavior of groups they considered a threat to the social order. Equating difference with disorder, many progressives tried to impose white middle-class standards of behavior on immigrant populations. Some

sought to eliminate the "problem" altogether by curtailing further immigration from southern and eastern Europe. Many white progressives, particularly in the South, supported segregation and disfranchisement, which limited opportunities for African Americans. At the same time, however, black progressives and their white allies created organizations dedicated to securing racial equality.

The Roots of Progressivism

At the turn of the twentieth century, many Americans believed that the nation was in dire need of reform. Two decades of westward expansion, industrialization, urbanization, and skyrocketing immigration had transformed the country in unsettling and, in the minds of many, dangerous ways. In the aftermath of the social and economic turmoil that accompanied the depression of the 1890s, many members of the middle and upper classes were convinced that unless they took remedial measures, the country would collapse under the weight of class conflict. Progressives advocated governmental intervention, yet they sought change without radically altering capitalism or the democratic political system. A progressive newspaper editor explained in 1912: "The world moves and we have to move with it. So with all that is going on with politics today. . . . It is evolution, and not revolution."

Progressive Origins

Progressives contended that old ways of governing and doing business did not address modern conditions. In one sense, they inherited the legacy of the Populist movement of the 1890s. Progressives attacked laissez-faire capitalism, and by regulating monopolies they aimed to limit the power of corporate trusts, which they saw as a threat to economic and political democracy. Like the Populists, progressive reformers advocated instituting an income tax as well as a variety of initiatives designed to give citizens a greater say in government. However, progressives differed from Populists in fundamental ways. Perhaps most important, progressives were interested primarily in urban and industrial America, while the Populist movement had emerged in direct response to the problems that plagued rural America in the late nineteenth century.

Progressives were heirs to the intellectual critics of the late nineteenth century who challenged laissez-faire and rejected Herbert Spencer's doctrine of the "survival of the fittest" (see chapter 16). **Pragmatism** greatly influenced progressives. Identified with Harvard psychologist and philosopher William James and philosopher John Dewey, pragmatists contended that the meaning of truth did not reside in some absolute doctrine but could only be discovered through experience. Ideas had to be measured by their practical consequences. From these critics, progressives derived a healthy skepticism toward rigid dogma and instead relied on human experience to guide social action.

Reformers also drew inspiration from the religious ideals of the **social gospel** (see chapter 18). In *Christianity and the Social Crisis* (1907), the Protestant clergyman Walter Rauschenbusch of Rochester, New York, urged Christians to embrace the teachings of Jesus on the ethical obligations for social justice and to put these teachings into action by working among the urban poor. Progressive leaders such as Theodore Roosevelt and Gifford Pinchot combined the moral fervor of the social gospel with the rationalism of the gospel of scientific efficiency.

Pragmatism and the social gospel appealed to members of the new middle class. Before the Civil War, the middle class had consisted largely of ministers, lawyers, physicians, and small proprietors. The growth of large-scale businesses during the second half of the nineteenth century expanded the middle class, which now included men whose professions grew out of industrialization, such as engineering, corporate management, and social work. The new middle class established organizations to promote their own professional goals and further the public interest. One of the most powerful groups, the American Medical Association (AMA), had originally formed in 1847 but grew rapidly at the turn of the century. The AMA raised qualifications to increase the level of education required to practice medicine, thus limiting access to the profession. Progressivism drew many of its most devoted adherents from this new middle class.

Muckrakers

The growing desire for reform at the turn of the century received a boost from investigative journalists known as **muckrakers**. Popular magazines such as *McClure's* and *Collier's* sought to increase their readership by publishing exposés of corruption in government and the shady operations of big business. Filled with details uncovered through

Ida M. Tarbell

Investigative journalist Ida Tarbell, shown in her home office in 1905, exposed the ruthless business practices that John D. Rockefeller used to create and run his Standard Oil Company. Tarbell was one of the Progressive Era's muckrakers, who published articles in popular magazines and wrote books that evoked public outrage and calls for reform. The Ida M. Tarbell Collection, Pelletier Library, Allegheny College intensive research, these articles had a sensationalist appeal that both informed and aroused their mainly middle-class readers. In 1902 journalist Ida Tarbell lambasted the ruthless and dishonest business practices of the Rockefeller family's Standard Oil Company, the model of corporate greed. Lincoln Steffens wrote about machine bosses' shameful rule in cities such as Chicago, Cincinnati, Cleveland, Minneapolis, New York, St. Louis, and Philadelphia. Ida B. Wells, a Memphis journalist, wrote scathing articles and pamphlets condemning the lynching of African Americans. Other muckrakers exposed fraudulent practices in insurance companies, child labor, drug abuse, and prostitution.

Ironically, President Theodore Roosevelt coined the term *muckraker* in 1906 not as a compliment but as a sign of disgust for journalists he thought were more interested in making sensationalist charges than in carefully documenting their stories. He compared them to the character in John Bunyan's novel *Pilgrim's Progress* who was so absorbed in looking at the filth (muck) on the ground that he did not see a beautiful gift offered to him. Roosevelt feared that if muckraking became too sensational and unrestrained, it would threaten moderate reform and encourage more radical alternatives. Yet muckrakers did succeed in raising middle-class awareness and generated wide support for the political reforms that Roosevelt and other progressives proposed.

REVIEW & RELATE

- What late-nineteenth-century trends and developments influenced the progressives?
- Why did the progressives focus on urban and industrial America?

 LEARNINGCurve bedfordstmartins.com/hewittlawson/LC

Humanitarian Reform

Humanitarian reformers focused on the plight of urban immigrants, African Americans, and the underprivileged. They tried mainly to improve housing and working conditions for impoverished city dwellers. Their motives were not always purely altruistic. Unless living standards improved, many reformers reasoned, immigrants and racial minorities would contaminate the cities' middle-class inhabitants with communicable diseases, escalating crime, and threats to traditional cultural norms. These reformers also supported suffrage for women, whose votes, they believed, would help purify electoral politics and elect candidates committed to social and moral reform.

Female Progressives and the Poor

Women played the leading role in efforts to improve the lives of the impoverished. Jane Addams, the daughter of a wealthy businessman, had toured Europe after graduating from a women's college in Illinois. The Toynbee Hall settlement house in London impressed her for its work in helping poor residents of the area. In 1889 Addams, after returning home to Chicago, and her friend Ellen Starr established **Hull House** as a center for social reform in the northwest neighborhood of the city. Hull House inspired a generation of young women to work directly in immigrant communities. Many were college-educated, professionally trained women who were shut out of jobs in male-dominated professions. Staffed mainly by women, settlement houses became all-purpose urban support centers. Not only did they provide recreational facilities, social activities, and educational classes for neighborhood residents, but they also became launching pads for campaigns aimed at improving living and working conditions for the urban poor. Calling on women to take up **civic housekeeping**, Addams maintained that women could protect their individual households from the chaos of industrialization and urbanization only by attacking the sources of that chaos in the community at large.

> **Explore**
>
> See Document 19.1 for a description of one civic housekeeping effort.

Settlement house and social workers occupied the front lines of humanitarian reform, but they found considerable support from women's clubs. Formed after the Civil War, these local groups provided protected spaces for middle-class women to meet, share ideas, and work on common projects. In 1890 these local associations were brought together under the umbrella of the General Federation of Women's Clubs, which by the end of the nineteenth century counted 495 chapters and 160,000 members. By 1900 these clubs—which had initially been devoted to discussions of religion, culture, and science—began to help the needy and lobby for social justice legislation. "Since men are more or less closely absorbed in business," one club woman remarked about this civic awakening, "it has come to pass that the initiative in civic matters has devolved largely upon women." Starting out in towns and cities, club women carried their message to state and federal governments and campaigned for legislation that would establish social welfare programs for working women and their children.

In an age of strict racial segregation, African American women formed their own clubs to undertake reform activities. They sponsored day care centers, kindergartens, and work and home training projects. The activities of black club women, like those of white club women,

DOCUMENT 19.1

Jane Addams | Civic Housekeeping, 1910

In the following excerpt from her memoir, *Twenty Years at Hull-House*, Jane Addams describes the activities of the Hull House Woman's Club, formed by the residents of the neighborhood served by the settlement house. In an effort to improve their surroundings, club women took it upon themselves to investigate the city's poor garbage collection service in their wards and its possible connection to high death rates in the area.

Explore

The Hull-House Woman's Club had been organized the year before by the resident kindergartner [teacher] who had first inaugurated a mothers' meeting. The new members came together, however, in quite a new way that summer when we discussed with them the high death rate so persistent in our ward. After several club meetings devoted to the subject, despite the fact that the death rate rose highest in the congested foreign colonies and not in the streets in which most of the Irish American club women lived, twelve of their number undertook in connection with the residents, to carefully investigate the condition of the alleys. During August and September the substantiated reports of violations of the law sent in from Hull-House to the health department were one thousand and thirty-seven. For the club woman who had finished a long day's work of washing or ironing followed by the cooking of a hot supper, it would have been much easier to sit on her doorstep during a summer evening than to go up and down ill-kept alleys and

get into trouble with her neighbors over the condition of their garbage boxes. It required both civic enterprise and moral conviction to be willing to do this three evenings a week during the hottest and most uncomfortable months of the year. Nevertheless, a certain number of women persisted, as did the residents, and three city inspectors in succession were transferred from the ward because of unsatisfactory services. Still the death rate remained high and the condition seemed little improved throughout the next winter. In sheer desperation, the following spring when the city contracts were awarded for the removal of garbage, with the backing of two well-known business men, I put in a bid for the garbage removal of the nineteenth ward. My paper was thrown out on a technicality but the incident induced the mayor to appoint me the garbage inspector of the ward.

Source: Jane Addams, *Twenty Years at Hull-House* (New York: Macmillan, 1910), 284–85.

Interpret the Evidence

- Why did Addams and the other club women decide to tackle the garbage problem in their neighborhood?
- What does this action suggest about the role that residents played in improving their own neighborhood?

Put It in Context

How does the women's investigation reflect the progressive notion of civic housekeeping?

reflected a class bias, and they tried to lift up poorer blacks to ideals of middle-class womanhood. In doing so, they challenged white supremacist notions that black women and men were incapable of raising healthy and strong families. By 1916 the National Association of Colored Women, whose motto was "lifting as we climb," boasted 1,000 clubs and 50,000 members.

White working-class women also organized, but because of employment discrimination there were few, if any, black female industrial workers to join them. Building on the settlement house movement and together with middle-class and wealthy women, working-class women founded the National Women's Trade Union League (WTUL) in 1903. The WTUL was dedicated to securing higher wages and

Children at Hull House, 1900

Child care was one of the many services that Hull House provided for immigrants on the west side of Chicago. Founded in 1889 by Jane Addams and Ellen Starr, Hull House also offered health care, job counseling, and English lessons. Settlement house workers also led campaigns to abolish child labor, support women's suffrage, and reform immigration.   Jane Addams Collection, Swarthmore College Peace Collection

Not all women believed in the idea of protective legislation for women. In 1898 Charlotte Perkins Gilman published *Women and Economics*, in which she argued against the notion that women were ideally suited for domesticity. She contended that women's accepted relationship to men was unnatural. "We are the only animal species in which the female depends on the male for food," Gilman wrote, "the only animal species in which the sex relation is also the economic relation." Emphasizing the need for economic independence, Gilman advocated the establishment of communal kitchens that would free women from household chores and allow them to compete on equal terms with men in the workplace. Emma Goldman, an anarchist critic of capitalism and middle-class sexual morality, also spoke out against the kind of marriage that made women "keep their mouths shut and their wombs open." She endorsed "free love," in which women and men enjoyed sex equally. These and a growing number of other women did not consider themselves reformers so much as radicals, and even feminists—women who aspire to reach their full potential and gain access to the same opportunities as men.

improved working conditions, and its slogan, "The Eight-Hour Day: A Living Wage; to Guard the Home," expressed its objectives. The WTUL recognized that many women needed to earn an income to help support their families, and it backed protective legislation based on women's specific needs.

Believing women to be physically weaker than men, most female reformers advocated special legislation to protect women in the workplace. They campaigned for state laws prescribing the maximum number of hours women could work, and they succeeded in 1908 when they won a landmark victory in the Supreme Court in *Muller v. Oregon*, which upheld an Oregon law establishing a ten-hour workday for women. These reformers also convinced lawmakers in forty states to establish pensions for mothers and widows. In 1912 their focus shifted to the federal government with the founding of the Children's Bureau in the Department of Commerce and Labor. Headed by Julia Lathrop, an Addams disciple from Illinois, the bureau attracted female reformers, collected sociological data, and devised a variety of publicly funded social welfare measures. In 1916 Congress enacted a law banning child labor under the age of fourteen (it was declared unconstitutional in 1918). In 1921 Congress passed the Shepherd-Towner Act, which allowed nurses to offer maternal and infant health care information to mothers.

Fighting for Women's Suffrage

Until 1910, women did not have the right to vote, except in a handful of western states (see chapter 15). The passage of the Fourteenth and Fifteenth Amendments had disappointed many campaigners for women's suffrage. Although the amendments extended citizenship to African Americans and protected the voting rights of black men, they left women, both white and black, ineligible to vote. The Fourteenth Amendment had underscored this distinction by specifically referring to "male inhabitants" in its provision dealing with voting for national officials (see chapter 14). Following Reconstruction, the two major organizations campaigning for women's suffrage at the state and national levels—Susan B. Anthony and Elizabeth Cady Stanton's National Woman Suffrage Association and Lucy Stone and Julia Ward Howe's American Woman Suffrage Association—failed to achieve major victories. In 1890 the two groups combined to form the National American Woman Suffrage Association, and by 1918 women could vote in fifteen states and the territory of Alaska (Map 19.1).

Suffragists included a broad coalition of supporters and based their campaign on a variety of arguments. Reformers such as Jane Addams stressed that suffrage for women would be an extension of "civic housekeeping." They attributed corruption in politics to the absence of women's maternal influence. In this way, mainstream suffragists couched their arguments within traditional conceptions of women as family nurturers. They claimed that men should not fear women's desire to vote; rather, they should see it as an expansion of traditional household duties into the public sphere. By contrast, suffragists such as Alice Paul rejected arguments stressing women's domesticity and their inherent difference from men. Paul, who had earned a Ph.D. from the University of Pennsylvania and two law degrees, asserted that women deserved the vote on the basis of their equality with men as citizens. She founded the National Woman's Party and in 1923 proposed that Congress adopt an Equal Rights Amendment to provide full legal equality to women.

Traditionalists, both male and female, fought against women's suffrage. They believed that women were best suited by nature to devote themselves to their families and leave the rough-and-tumble world of politics to men. Suffrage opponents insisted that extending the right to vote to women would destroy the home, lead to the moral degeneracy of children, and tear down the social fabric of the country.

Campaigns for women's suffrage did not apply to all women. White suffragists in the South often manipulated racial prejudice to support female enfranchisement. In the wake of the Populist Party's efforts to recruit black voters in the 1890s, most of the former Confederate states rewrote their constitutions or enacted statutes removing African Americans from the voter rolls through the use of poll taxes, literacy tests, and grandfather clause requirements (see chapter 17). Although they did not constitute a majority, outspoken white suffragists such as Rebecca Latimer Felton from Georgia, Belle Kearney from Mississippi, and Kate Gordon from Louisiana used white suprem-acist arguments to make a case for white women gaining the vote. As long as even a fraction of black men voted and the Fifteenth Amendment continued to exist, they contended that allowing southern white women to vote would preserve white supremacy by offsetting black men's votes. These arguments also had a class component. Poll taxes and literacy tests disfranchised poor, uneducated whites. Extending the vote to white women would benefit mainly those in the middle class who had some education and enough family income to satisfy restrictive literacy test and poll tax requirements.

Many middle-class women outside the South used similar reasoning, but they targeted newly arrived immigrants instead of African Americans. Many Protestant women and men viewed Catholics and Jews from southern and eastern Europe as racially inferior and spiritually

dangerous. They blamed such immigrants for the ills of the cities in which they congregated, and some suffragists believed that the vote of middle-class Protestant women would help clean up the mess the immigrants created. One supporter proclaimed that suffragists "had always recognized the usefulness of woman suffrage as a counterbalance to the foreign vote."

African American women challenged these racist arguments and mounted their own drive for female suffrage. If "white women needed the vote to acquire advantages and protection of their rights," Adella Hunt Logan of Tuskegee, Alabama, remarked, "then Black women needed the vote even more so." African American women had an additional incentive to press for enfran-chisement. As the target of white sexual predators during slavery and its aftermath, some black women saw the vote as a way to address this problem. Although they did not gain much support from the National American Woman Suffrage Association, by 1916 African American women worked through the National Association of Colored Women and formed suffrage clubs throughout the nation.

Explore

See Document 19.2 for an argument for suffrage for black women.

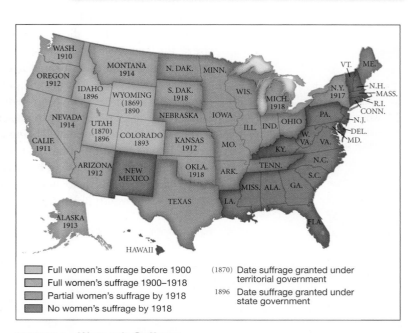

MAP 19.1　Women's Suffrage

Western states and territories were the first to approve women's suffrage. Yet even as western states enfranchised women, most placed restrictions on or excluded African American, American Indian, Mexican American, and Asian American women. States granting partial suffrage allowed women to vote only in certain contests, such as municipal or school board, primary, or presidential elections.

DOCUMENT 19.2

Nannie Helen Burroughs | Suffrage for Black Women, 1915

Nannie Helen Burroughs, a founder of the National Association of Colored Women, spoke out for black women's right to vote at a time when many white women's suffrage groups excluded African Americans. For Burroughs and other black suffragists, the right to vote was not just a civic duty but essential for eliminating racial discrimination and subservience. In the following excerpt that appeared in the *Crisis*, the magazine of the NAACP, Burroughs presents the case for suffrage for black women.

Explore

Why does Burroughs claim it is more important for black women than for black men to obtain and exercise the right to vote?

How does Burroughs characterize the role of black women in reform movements?

What does Burroughs mean when she says that the ballot is black women's "weapon of moral defense"?

When the ballot is put into the hands of the American woman the world is going to get a correct estimate of the Negro woman. It will find her a tower of strength of which poets have never sung, orators have never spoken, and scholars have never written.

Because the black man does not know the value of the ballot, and has bartered and sold his most valuable possession, it is no evidence that the Negro woman will do the same. The Negro woman, therefore, needs the ballot to get back, by the wise *use* of it, what the Negro man has lost by the *misuse* of it. She needs it to ransom her race. A fact worthy of note is that in every reform in which the Negro woman has taken part, during the past fifty years, she has been as aggressive, progressive, and dependable as those who inspired the reform or led it. The world has yet to learn that the Negro woman is quite superior in bearing moral responsibility. A comparison with the men of her race, in moral issues, is odious. She carries the burdens of the Church, and of the school and bears a great deal more than her economic share at home.

Another striking fact is that the Negro woman carries the moral destiny of two races in her hand. Had she not been the woman of unusual moral stamina that she is, the black race would have been made a great deal whiter, and the white race a great deal blacker during the past fifty years. She has been left a prey for the men of every race, but in spite of this, she has held the enemies of Negro female chastity at bay. The Negro woman is the white woman's as well as the white race's most needed ally in preserving an unmixed race.

The ballot, wisely used, will bring to her the respect and protection that she needs. It is her weapon of moral defense. Under present conditions, when she appears in court in defense of her virtue, she is looked upon with amused contempt. She needs the ballot to reckon with men who place no value upon her virtue, and to [mold] healthy public sentiment in favor of her own protection.

Source: Nannie Helen Burroughs, "Black Women and Reform," *The Crisis*, August 1915, 187.

Put It in Context

How do Burroughs's arguments differ from those of white suffragists?

The campaign for women's suffrage in the United States was part of an international movement. Victories in New Zealand (1893), Australia (1902), and Norway (1913) spurred on American suffragists. In the 1910s, radical American activists found inspiration in the militant tactics employed by some in the British suffrage movement. Activists such as Alice Paul conducted wide-ranging demonstrations in Washington, D.C., including chaining themselves to the gates of the White House. Although mainstream suffrage leaders denounced these new tactics, they gained much-needed publicity for the movement, which in turn aided the lobbying efforts of more moderate activists. In 1919 Congress passed the Nineteenth Amendment granting women the vote. The following year, the amendment was ratified by the states.

Progressivism and African Americans

As with the suffrage, social justice progressives faced huge barriers in the fight for racial equality. By 1900 white suprem- acists in the South had disfranchised almost all black voters and imposed a rigid system of segregation in education and all aspects of public life, and they enforced these measures with violence. From 1880 to 1900, white supremacists lynched thousands of African Americans, often because of perceived violations of racial norms. Antiblack violence also took the form of race riots that erupted in southern cities such as Wilmington, North Carolina, and Tampa, Florida, in 1898 and Atlanta in 1906. Farther north, in Springfield, Illinois, a riot broke out in 1908 when the local sheriff tried to protect two black prisoners, one accused of raping a white woman and the other charged with murdering a white man, from a would-be lynch mob. This confrontation triggered two days of white violence against blacks, some of whom fought back, leaving twenty-four businesses and forty homes destroyed and seven people (two blacks and five whites) dead.

As the situation for African Americans deteriorated, black leaders responded in several ways. Booker T. Wash- ington espoused an approach that his critics called accom- modation but that he defended as practical. Born a slave and emancipated at age nine, Washington attended Hampton Institute in his home state of Virginia. Run by sympathetic whites, the school considered moral training its top priority. In their view, because slavery had hindered black advancement, African Americans would first have to build up their character and accept the virtues of absti- nence, thrift, and industriousness before seeking a more intellectual education. In 1881 Washington founded **Tuskegee Institute** in Alabama, which he modeled on Hampton. In 1895 white business and civic leaders invited Washington to deliver an address at a cotton exposition held in Atlanta. The black educator received an enthusiastic reception for his message urging African Americans to remain in the South, accept racial segregation, concentrate on moral and economic development, and avoid politics. At the same time, he called on white leaders to fulfill their part of the bargain by protecting blacks from the growing violence directed at them.

White leaders in both the South and the North embraced Washington, and he became the most powerful African American of his generation. He secured philan- thropic contributions from white benefactors for Tuskegee and other schools he favored. He had considerable influence over leading black newspapers and in 1900 organized the National Negro Business League. Although he discouraged public protests against segregation, he emphasized racial pride and solidarity among African Americans. "We are a nation within a nation," he commented, and "[we must] see to it that in every wise and legitimate way our people are taught to patronize racial enterprises." Yet Washington was a complex figure, who secretly financed and supported court challenges to electoral disfranchisement, railroad segrega- tion, jury discrimination, and peonage (forced labor to repay debt).

Washington's enormous power did not discourage opposing views among African Americans. Ida B. Wells, like Washington, had been born a slave. In 1878, at age sixteen, Wells lost her parents in a yellow fever epidemic that swept through her hometown in Mississippi. To support her five siblings, she took a job in Memphis as a teacher. Six years later, Wells sued the Chesapeake & Ohio Railroad for moving her from the first-class "Ladies Coach" to the segregated smoking car because she was black. She won her case in the lower court, but her victory was reversed by the Tennessee Supreme Court. Undeterred, she began writing for the *Free Speech* newspaper, in which she owned a one-third interest. When her articles exposing injustices in the Memphis school system got her fired from teaching, she took up journalism full-time.

Unlike Washington, Wells believed that black leaders had to speak out vigorously against racial inequality and lynching. From 1885 to 1900, approximately 2,500 people were lynched, most of them southern blacks. One lynching took place in Memphis on March 9, 1892, when three black men were murdered by a white mob. The victims had operated a grocery store that had become the target of hostility from white competitors, who forcibly tried to put it out of business. In response, the black businessmen resisted an assault by armed whites and shot three of them in self-defense. Wells applauded the black store owners' actions. As she wrote, "When the white man . . . knows he runs as great a risk of biting the dust every time his Afro-American victim does, he will have greater respect for Afro-American life." Subsequently arrested for their armed resistance, the three men were snatched from jail and lynched.

In response to Wells's articles about the Memphis lynching, a white mob burned down her newspaper's building. She fled to Chicago, where she continued to investigate the issue of lynching. In a report she published, she refuted the myth that the rape of white women by black men was the leading cause of lynching and asserted that evidence of such crimes was scarce. She concluded that racists used this brand of extralegal violence to ensure that African Americans would not challenge white supremacy. Wells took her campaign throughout the North and to Europe, where she gave lectures condemning lynching. She also joined the drive for women's suffrage, which she hoped would give black women a chance to use their votes to help combat racial injustice.

W. E. B. Du Bois also rejected Washington's accommodationist stance and urged blacks to demand first-class citizenship. In contrast to Washington and Wells, Du Bois had not experienced slavery. His ancestors were free blacks, and he grew up in Great Barrington, Massachusetts. Educated at Fisk University, a black institution, he transferred to Harvard and earned a Ph.D. in history. In 1899 he published *The Philadelphia Negro*, the first scientific study of the plight of blacks in urban America—a scholarly counterpart to the emerging investigative literature that fueled progressive reform. Du Bois

DOCUMENTS 19.3 AND 19.4

Addressing Inequality: Two Views

By the end of the nineteenth century, the former Confederate states had stripped most blacks of the right to vote and instituted legal forms of segregation. In the face of violence, hostility, and widespread discrimination, African American leaders Booker T. Washington and W. E. B. Du Bois developed two of the most influential approaches to the problem of racial inequality. Washington emphasized black economic self-development and accommodation within the existing social and political system, whereas Du Bois insisted that blacks must resist second-class citizenship in all forms.

Explore

19.3 Booker T. Washington | The Atlanta Compromise, 1895

The wisest among my race understand that the agitation of questions of social equality is the extremest folly, and that progress in the enjoyment of all the privileges that will come to us must be the result of severe and constant struggle rather than of artificial forcing. No race that has anything to contribute to the markets of the world is long in any degree ostracized. It is important and right that all privileges of the law be ours, but it is vastly more important that we be prepared for the exercise of those privileges. The opportunity to earn a dollar in a factory just now is worth infinitely more than the opportunity to spend a dollar in an opera house.

In conclusion, may I repeat that nothing in thirty years has given us more hope and encouragement, and drawn us so near to you of the white race, as this opportunity offered by the Exposition [a cotton exhibition held in Atlanta]; and here bending, as it were, over the altar that represents the results of the struggles of your race and mine, both starting practically empty-handed three decades ago, I pledge that, in your effort to work out the great and intricate problem which God has laid at the doors of the South, you shall have at all times the patient, sympathetic help of my race; only let this be constantly in mind that, while from representations in these buildings of the product of field, of forest, of mine, of factory, letters, and art, much good will come, yet far above and beyond material benefits will be that higher good, that, let us pray God, will come, in a blotting out of sectional differences and racial animosities and suspicions, in a determination to administer absolute justice, in a willing obedience among all classes to the mandates of law. This, coupled with our material prosperity, will bring into our beloved South a new heaven and a new earth.

Source: Booker T. Washington, *The Story of My Life and Work* (Cincinnati: W. W. Ferguson, 1900), 170–71.

agreed with Washington about advocating self-help as a means for advancement, but he did not believe this effort would succeed without a proper education and equal voting rights. In *The Souls of Black Folk* (1903), Du Bois argued that African Americans needed a liberal arts education, in the tradition of Fisk and Harvard, rather than the manual training and industrial arts curriculum at Tuskegee. Du Bois contended that a classical, humanistic education would produce a cadre of leaders, the "Talented Tenth," who would guide African Americans to the next stage of their development. Rather than forgoing immediate political rights, as Washington advocated, African American leaders should demand the universal right to vote. Only then, Du Bois contended, would African Americans gain equality, self-respect, and dignity as a race.

Explore

See Documents 19.3 and 19.4 for Washington's and Du Bois's responses to inequality.

Du Bois was an intellectual who put his ideas into action. In 1905 he spearheaded the creation of the Niagara

Explore

19.4 W. E. B. Du Bois | Response to Washington, 1903

It has been claimed that the Negro can survive only through submission. Mr. Washington distinctly asks that black people give up, at least for the present, three things—

First, political power,

Second, insistence on civil rights,

Third, higher education of Negro youth—

and concentrate all their energies on industrial education, the accumulation of wealth, and the conciliation of the South. This policy has been courageously and insistently advocated for over fifteen years, and has been triumphant for perhaps ten years. As a result of this tender of the palm-branch, what has been the return? In these years there have occurred:

1. The disfranchisement of the Negro.
2. The legal creation of a distinct status of civil inferiority for the Negro.
3. The steady withdrawal of aid from institutions for the higher training of the Negro.

These movements are not, to be sure, direct results of Mr. Washington's teachings; but his propaganda has, without a shadow of doubt, helped their speedier accomplishment. The question then comes: Is it possible, and probable, that nine millions of men can make effective progress in economic lines if they are deprived of political rights, made a servile caste, and allowed only the most meagre chance for developing their exceptional men? If history and reason give any distinct answer to these questions, it is an emphatic *No.* And Mr. Washington thus faces the triple paradox of his career:

1. He is striving nobly to make Negro artisans, business men, and property-owners; but it is utterly impossible, under modern competitive methods, for workingmen and property-owners to defend their rights and exist without the right of suffrage.
2. He insists on thrift and self-respect, but at the same time counsels a silent submission to civic inferiority such as is bound to sap the manhood of any race in the long run.
3. He advocates common-school and industrial training, and depreciates institutions of higher learning; but neither the Negro common-schools, nor Tuskegee itself, could remain open a day were it not for teachers trained in Negro colleges, or trained by their graduates.

Source: W. E. B. Du Bois, *The Souls of Black Folk: Essays and Sketches* (Chicago: A. C. McClurg, 1907), 51–52.

Interpret the Evidence

- Why does Washington believe that economic development is the key to racial progress?
- How does Du Bois challenge Washington's agenda? Why does he insist that political and social reforms are essential to black economic progress?

Put It in Context

How do Washington and Du Bois reflect in different ways the status of African Americans in the United States at the turn of the twentieth century?

Movement, a group that first met on the Canadian side of Niagara Falls because participants could not find accommodations open to blacks in Buffalo, New York. The all-black organization demanded the vote and equal access to public facilities for African Americans. By 1909 internal squabbling and a shortage of funds had crippled the group. That same year, however, Du Bois became involved in the creation of an organization that would shape the fight for racial equality throughout the twentieth century: the **National Association for the Advancement of Colored People (NAACP)**. In addition to Du Bois, Ida B. Wells, and veterans of the Niagara Movement, white activists played leading roles in forming the organization. They included Jane Addams; Mary White Ovington, a settlement house worker in Brooklyn; and William English Walling, a social worker, socialist, and cofounder of the Women's Trade Union League. The descendants of white abolitionists also contributed significantly to the birth of the group. Of the fifty-two white signers of the document calling for the creation of the NAACP, fifteen were former abolitionists or their descendants. Beginning in 1910, the NAACP initiated court cases challenging racially discriminatory voting practices and other forms of bias in housing and criminal justice. Its first victory came in 1915, when its lawyers convinced the Supreme Court to strike down the grandfather clause that discriminated against black voters (*Guinn v. United States*).

African Americans also pursued social justice initiatives outside the realm of politics. Southern blacks remained committed to securing a quality education for their children after whites failed to live up to their responsibilities under *Plessy v. Ferguson*. Governor James K. Vardaman of Mississippi, who served from 1904 to 1908, expressed the prevailing racist sentiment: "Education only spoils a good field hand and makes a shyster lawyer or a fourth-rate teacher. It is money thrown away." Black schools remained inferior to white schools, and African Americans did not receive a fair return from their tax dollars; in fact, a large portion of their payments helped subsidize white schools. To raise money for books, buildings, and teacher salaries, blacks voluntarily taxed themselves in addition to the property taxes they were required to pay the county to support schools. Du Bois calculated that black Mississippians paid 113 percent of the costs of their own schools through double taxation.

Black women played a prominent role in promoting education. For example, Charlotte Hawkins Brown, born in North Carolina and educated in Massachusetts, returned to her home state in 1901 and set up the Palmer Memorial Institute outside of Greensboro. In these endeavors, black educators received financial assistance from northern philanthropists, white club women interested in moral uplift of the black race, and religious missionaries seeking

converts in the South. By 1910 more than 1.5 million black children went to school in the South, most of them taught by the region's 28,560 black teachers. Thirty-four black colleges existed, and more than 2,000 African Americans held college degrees.

REVIEW & RELATE

What role did women play in the early-twentieth-century fight for social justice?

How did social reformers challenge discrimination against women and minorities?

 LEARNINGCurve bedfordstmartins.com/hewittlawson/LC

Morality and Social Control

In many cases, progressive initiatives crossed over from social reform into social control. Convinced that the "immorality" of the poor was the cause of social disorder, some reformers sought to impose middle-class standards of behavior and morality on the lower classes. As with other forms of progressivism, progressives interested in social control were driven by a variety of motives. However, regardless of their motives, efforts to prohibit alcohol, fight prostitution, and combat juvenile delinquency often involved attempts to repress and control the poor. Some social control progressives went even further in their effort to impose their own morality, calling for restrictions on immigration, particularly from southern and eastern Europe and Asia. Anti-immigration advocates viewed cultural and religious differences as a threat and sought to prevent such people from becoming part of American society in the first place.

Prohibition

Prohibition campaigns began long before the Civil War but scored few important successes until after 1865. In 1869 anti-alcohol forces established the Prohibition Party, and in 1881 Kansas became the first state whose constitution banned the consumption of alcohol. Women spearheaded the prohibition movement by forming the **Woman's Christian Temperance Union (WCTU)** in 1874. Frances Willard headed the group from 1879 until her death in 1898. Willard held a broad view of temperance reform that grew from religious, moral, and social justice convictions. Under her direction, the WCTU and its nationwide chapters supported women's suffrage, laws to end child labor, and labor unions. Willard built the temperance movement around the need to protect the home. Husbands and fathers who drank excessively were also likely to abuse their wives and children and to drain the family finances. Prohibiting the consumption of alcohol would, therefore, help combat these evils. At the same time, the quality of family and public life would be improved if women received the right to vote and young children completed their education without having to go to work. Although Willard died before progressive reform had gained momentum, she influenced activists such as Jane Addams. However, with her death, WCTU leaders withdrew from supporting broad social reforms and concentrated instead on the single issue of temperance.

At the turn of the twentieth century, the Anti-Saloon League (ASL) became the dominant force in the prohibition movement. Established in 1893, the league grew out of evangelical Protestantism, with Baptists and Methodists leading the way. The group had particular appeal in the rural South, where Protestant fundamentalism flourished. Between 1906 and 1917, twenty-one states, mostly in the South and West, banned liquor sales. However, concern over alcohol was not confined to the South. Middle-class progressives in northern cities, who identified much of urban decay with the influx of immigrants, saw the tavern as a breeding ground for immoral activities. In 1913 the ASL convinced Congress to pass the Webb-Kenyon Act, which banned the transportation of alcoholic beverages into dry states. After the United States entered World War I in 1917, reformers argued that prohibition would help win the war by conserving grain used to make liquor and by saving soldiers from intoxication. The Eighteenth Amendment, ratified in 1919, made prohibition the law of the land.

The Crusade against Vice

Alarmed by the expansion in the number of brothels and "streetwalkers" that accompanied the growth of cities, progressives sought to eliminate prostitution. Some framed the issue in terms of public health, linking prostitution to the spread of sexually transmitted diseases. Others presented the crusade as an effort to protect female virtue. In 1907 the muckraking *McClure's Magazine*, reporting on the spread of prostitution in Chicago, contended that many of the women were victims of "white slavery" and had been forced into prostitution against their will. Such reformers were generally interested only in white women, who, unlike African American and Asian women in similar circumstances, were considered sexual innocents coerced into prostitution. Still others claimed that prostitutes themselves were to blame, seeing women who sold their sexual favors as inherently immoral.

Reformers offered two different approaches to the problem. Taking the moralistic solution, Representative

James R. Mann of Chicago steered through Congress the White Slave Trade Act in 1910, banning the transportation of women across state lines for immoral purposes. This legislation became known as the Mann Act after its sponsor. By contrast, the American Social Hygiene Association, founded in 1914, subsidized scientific research into sexually transmitted diseases, funded investigations to gather more information, and drafted model ordinances for cities to curb prostitution. By 1915 every state had laws making sexual solicitation a crime. The United States' entry into World War I further helped curtail prostitution; brothels near military bases were closed because reformers argued that soldiers' health was at risk.

Prosecutors used the Mann Act to enforce codes of traditional racial as well as sexual behavior. In 1910 Jack Johnson, an African American boxer, defeated the white

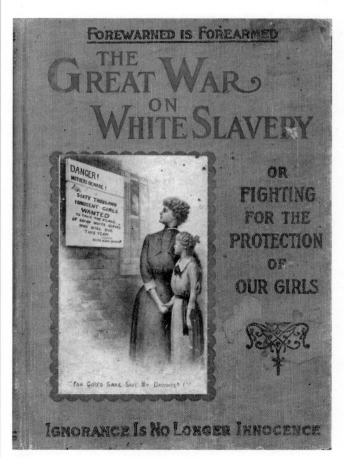

The Crusade against White Slavery
Published by Clifford B. Roe and B. S. Steadwell in 1911, *The Great War on White Slavery* campaigned against prostitution and the criminals who lured impoverished young women into what they called "the human stockyards . . . for girls." As an assistant state's attorney in Chicago, Roe prosecuted more than 150 cases against sex traffickers. He exemplified progressivism's moral reform impulse.   © Mary Evans Picture Library/The Image Works

heavyweight champion, Jim Jeffries. Black Americans took great pride in his triumph, while his victory upset some white men who were obsessed with preserving their racial dominance and masculine integrity. Johnson's relationships with white women further angered some whites, who eventually succeeded in bringing down the outspoken, black champion by prosecuting him on morals charges in 1913.

Moral crusaders also sought to eliminate the use and sale of narcotics. By 1900 approximately 250,000 people in the United States were addicted to opium, morphine, or cocaine—far fewer, however, than those who abused alcohol. Patent medicines, such as "Mrs. Winslow's Soothing Syrup," a remedy for crying babies, contained diluted amounts of opium, and cocaine was an ingredient in Coca-Cola until 1903. On the West Coast, immigration opponents associated opium smoking with the Chinese and tried to eliminate its use as part of their wider anti-Asian campaign. In alliance with the American Medical Association, which had a professional stake in the issue, reformers convinced Congress to pass the Harrison Narcotics Control Act of 1914, prohibiting the sale of narcotics except by a doctor's prescription.

Progressives also tried to combat juvenile delinquency. Led by women, these reformers lobbied for a juvenile court system that focused on rehabilitation rather than punishment for youthful offenders. Judge Ben Lindsay of Denver, Colorado, removed delinquents from dysfunctional homes and made them wards of the state. Despite progressives' sincerity, many youthful offenders doubted their intentions. Young women often appeared before a magistrate because their parents did not like their choice of friends, their sexual conduct, or their frequenting dance halls and saloons. These activities, which violated middle-class social norms, had now become criminalized, even if in a less coercive and punitive manner than that applied to adults.

Immigration Restriction

Moral reformers tended to perceive immigrants as innately predisposed to vice. As a result, some reformers sought to restrict immigration. Anti-immigrant sentiment often reflected racial and religious bigotry, as reformers concentrated on preventing Catholics, Jews, and all non-Europeans from entering the United States. Social scientists validated these prejudices by categorizing darker-skinned immigrants as inferior races. The harshest treatment was reserved for Asians. In 1882 Congress passed the Chinese Exclusion Act (see chapter 15), and in 1908 President Theodore Roosevelt entered into an executive agreement with Japan that reduced Japanese immigration to the United States. For many Californians, this agreement was not strict enough. In 1913

the state legislature passed a statute barring Japanese immigrants from buying land, a law that twelve other states subsequently enacted.

In 1917 reformers succeeded in further restricting immigration. Congress passed legislation to ban illiterates who could not read English or their native language from entering the country. The act also denied entry to other undesirables: "alcoholics," "feeble-minded persons," "epileptics," "people mentally or physically defective," "professional beggars," "anarchists," and "polygamists." In barring those considered unfit to enter the country, lawmakers intended to keep out those who could not support themselves and might become a public ward of the state and, in the case of anarchists and polygamists, people who threatened the nation's political and religious values. **See Document Project 19: Progressivism and Social Control, page 614**.

REVIEW & RELATE

What practices and behaviors of the poor did social control progressives find most alarming? Why?

What role did anti-immigrant sentiment play in motivating and shaping progressives' social control initiatives?

LEARNINGCurve **bedfordstmartins.com/hewittlawson/LC**

Good Government Progressivism

In an effort to diminish the power of corrupt urban political machines and unregulated corporations, progressives pushed for good government reforms, promoting initiatives they claimed would produce greater efficiency, openness, and accountability in government. Many of the progressives' proposed reforms appeared, at least on the surface, to give citizens more direct say in their government; however, a closer look reveals a more complicated picture.

Municipal and State Reform

Cities were at the forefront of government reform during the Progressive Era. Antiquated systems of municipal rule failed to keep up with the problems ushered in by immigration and accelerated urban growth. Political machines distributed city services to meet skyrocketing demands within a system bloated by corruption and graft (see chapter 18). Upper-middle-class businessmen and professionals fed up with wasteful and inefficient political machines sought to institute new forms of government that functioned more rationally and cost less.

The adoption of the commission form of government was a hallmark of urban reform. The idea originally came from the South in response to a hurricane in 1900 that destroyed the Texas Gulf coast city of Galveston and disabled its local government. Municipal leaders faced the crisis by establishing a commission composed of five men to operate the government. They replaced the old form of a mayor and city council with elected commissioners, each of whom ran a municipal department as if it were a business. By 1917 the commission form of government had spread to more than four hundred cities throughout the country. Governments with a mayor and city council also began to appoint city managers, who functioned as chief operating officers, to foster businesslike efficiency. The head of the National Cash Register Company, who helped bring the city manager system to Dayton, Ohio, praised it for resembling "a great business enterprise whose stockholders are the people."

To help overturn political machines, reformers adopted direct primaries so that voters could select candidates rather than allowing a handful of politicians to decide elections behind closed doors. Urban bosses had thrived on decentralized ward elections. To reverse the influence of immigrants clustered in ghettos who supported their own ethnic candidates and to topple the machines that catered to them, municipal reformers replaced district elections with citywide "at-large" elections. Ethnic enclaves lost not only their ward representatives but also a good deal of their influence because citywide election campaigns were expensive, shifting power to those who could afford to run. Good government progressives equated efficiency and honesty with democracy; however, rather than extending democracy to immigrant groups and racial minorities, these changes had the opposite effect. Working- and lower-class residents of cities still retained the right to vote, but their power was diluted.

In the South, where fewer immigrants lived, white supremacists employed these tactics to build on steps taken in the late nineteenth century to disfranchise African Americans. Southern lawmakers diminished whatever black political power remained by adopting at-large elections and commission governments. Throughout the South, direct primary contests (or "white primaries") were closed to blacks.

If urban progressivism fell short of putting democratic ideals into practice, it did produce a number of mayors who carried out genuine reforms. As Frederic C. Howe, a key adviser to Cleveland mayor Tom L. Johnson, observed, "The challenge of the city has become one of decent human existence." Elected in 1901, Johnson implemented measures to assess taxes more equitably, regulate utility companies, and reduce public transportation fares. Samuel "Golden Rule" Jones, who served as Toledo's mayor from 1897 to 1903, supported social justice measures by establishing an eight-hour workday for municipal employees, granting them paid vacations, and prohibiting child labor. Under Mayor Hazen Pingree, who served from 1889 to 1896, Detroit constructed additional schools and recreational facilities and put the unemployed to work on municipal projects during economic hard times.

Progressives also took action at the state level. Robert M. La Follette, Republican governor of Wisconsin from 1901 to 1906, led the way by initiating a range of reforms to improve the performance of state government and increase its accountability to constituents. During his tenure as governor, La Follette dismantled the statewide political machine by instituting direct party primaries, an expanded civil service, a law forbidding direct corporate contributions to political parties, a strengthened railroad regulatory commission, and a graduated income tax. In 1906 La Follette entered the U.S. Senate, where he battled for further reform.

Governors in other states picked up and expanded La Follette's progressive agenda. In New York, Governor Charles Evans Hughes implemented measures to regulate insurance companies and public utilities. In New Jersey, Governor Woodrow Wilson sought reforms similar to those in Wisconsin. On the West Coast, California's reform governor Hiram Johnson challenged the powerful Southern Pacific Railroad. In 1913 three-quarters of the states ratified the Seventeenth Amendment, which mandated that U.S. senators would be elected by popular vote, instead of being chosen by state legislatures. This constituted another effort to remove the influence of money from politics.

Conservation and Preservation of the Environment

The penchant for efficiency that characterized good government progressivism also shaped progressive efforts to conserve natural resources. As chief forester in the Department of Agriculture, Gifford Pinchot emphasized the efficient use of resources and sought ways to reconcile the public interest with private profit motives. His approach often won support from large lumber companies, which had a long-term interest in sustainable forests. Large companies also saw conservation as a way to drive their smaller competitors out of business, as large companies could better afford the additional costs associated with managing healthy forests.

Theodore Roosevelt and John Muir, 1903

Theodore Roosevelt (left) and John Muir, two leading conservationists of the Progressive Era, stand atop Glacier Point in Yosemite valley, California. Muir, who founded the Sierra Club, convinced Roosevelt to place Yosemite under federal control, which led to the establishment of a national park in 1906. Library of Congress

This gospel of efficiency faced a stiff test in California. After the devastating earthquake of 1906, San Francisco officials, coping with water and power shortages, asked the federal government to approve construction of a hydroelectric dam and reservoir in **Hetch Hetchy valley**, located in Yosemite National Park. The pragmatic Pinchot supported the project because he saw it as the best use of the land for the greatest number of people. The famed naturalist John Muir, who had spearheaded the establishment of Yosemite, strongly disagreed. He campaigned to save Hetch Hetchy from "ravaging commercialism" and warned against choosing economic gains over spiritual values. "Dam Hetch Hetchy!" Muir exclaimed. "As well dam for water-tanks the people's cathedrals and churches, for no holier temple has ever been consecrated by the heart of man." After a bruising seven-year battle, Pinchot (by this time a private citizen) triumphed. Still, this incursion into a national park, the first since the system was initiated in 1872 with Yellowstone National Park, helped spur the development of environmentalism as a political movement.

Besides the clash with preservationists, the Hetch Hetchy Dam project reveals another aspect of the progressive conservation movement. Like progressives who focused on urban and political issues, progressive conservationists had a racial bias. Conservationists such as Pinchot may have seen themselves as acting in the public interest, but their definition of "the public" did not include all Americans. In planning for the Hetch Hetchy Dam, progressives did not consult with the Mono Lake Paiutes who lived in Yosemite and who were most directly affected by the project. Conservation was meant to serve the interests of white San Franciscans and not those of the Indian inhabitants of Yosemite.

REVIEW & RELATE

Who gained and who lost political influence as a result of progressive reforms?

How did a commitment to greater efficiency shape progressives' political and environmental initiatives?

✓ *LEARNINGCurve* **bedfordstmartins.com/hewittlawson/LC**

Presidential Progressivism

The problems created by industrialization and the growth of big business were national in scope. No municipal or state government had the authority, power, and finances to address issues that transcended political boundaries and affected people throughout the country. Recognizing this fact, prominent progressives sought national leadership positions. Two of the three early-twentieth-century presidents, Theodore Roosevelt and Woodrow Wilson, instituted progressive reforms during their terms. In the process, they reinvigorated the presidency, an office that had declined in power and importance during the late nineteenth century.

Theodore Roosevelt and the Square Deal

Born into a moderately wealthy New York family, Theodore Roosevelt graduated from Harvard in 1880 and entered government service. Appointed by William McKinley as assistant secretary of the navy in 1897, Roosevelt left his post the following year to form a regiment of soldiers—the "Rough Riders"—and fought in Cuba against Spanish forces. In 1898 voters in New York sent the popular war hero to Albany as the new Republican governor. Elected as William McKinley's vice president in 1900,

Roosevelt became president after McKinley's assassination a year later.

Roosevelt brought an activist style to the presidency. Rather than seeing himself as merely administering the nation's business, he considered his office a **bully pulpit**— a platform from which to promote his programs and from which he could rally public opinion. To this end, he used his energetic and extroverted personality to establish an unprecedented rapport with the American people, providing newspaper reporters with a limitless supply of colorful stories about his life and exploits.

For all his exuberance and energy, President Roosevelt pursued a moderate domestic course. Like his progressive colleagues, he opposed ideological extremism in any form. Rather than promoting any particular cause, Roosevelt believed that as head of state he could serve as an impartial arbiter among competing factions and determine what was best for the public. Reform was, in his view, the best defense against revolution.

As president, Roosevelt sought to provide economic and political stability, what he referred to as a "Square Deal." He insisted that "a republic such as ours can exist only by virtue of the orderly liberty which comes through the equal domination of the law over all men alike." The coal strike that began in Pennsylvania in 1902 gave Roosevelt an opportunity to play the role of impartial mediator and defender of the public good. Miners had gone on strike for an eight-hour workday, a pay increase of 20 percent, and recognition of their union. Roosevelt sympathized with the plight of the workers, but he was more concerned that a prolonged strike would choke the supply of heating fuel to consumers as winter approached. Union representatives agreed to have the president create a panel to settle the dispute, but George F. Baer, president of the Reading Railroad, which also owned the mines, pledged that he would never agree to the workers' demands. Disturbed by what he considered the owners' "arrogant stupidity," Roosevelt threatened to dispatch federal troops to take over and run the mines. When the owners backed down, the president established a commission that hammered out a compromise giving the strikers a 10 percent wage hike and a reduction of the workday to nine hours, but not union recognition.

At the same time, Roosevelt used his executive authority to tackle the problems caused by giant business trusts. In February 1902, the president instructed the Justice Department to sue the Northern Securities Company under the Sherman Antitrust Act (see chapter 16), a law that had rarely been used against big business since its passage in 1890. Northern Securities held monopoly control of the northernmost transcontinental railway lines. The powerful financier behind Northern Securities, J. P. Morgan, believed that he could do business with Roosevelt as he had with previous presidents. "Send your man to my man and they can fix it up," Morgan informed Roosevelt. However, the president's man at the Justice Department responded: "We don't want to fix it up, we want to stop it." In 1904 the Supreme Court ordered that the Northern Securities Company be dissolved, ruling that the firm had restricted competition. With this victory, Roosevelt affirmed the federal government's power to regulate business trusts that violated the public interest. Overall, Roosevelt initiated twenty-five suits under the Sherman Antitrust Act, including litigation against the tobacco and beef trusts and the Standard Oil Company, actions that earned him the title of "trustbuster."

Roosevelt distinguished between "good" trusts, which acted responsibly, and "bad" trusts, which abused their power and hurt consumers. Railroads had earned an especially bad reputation with the public for charging higher rates to small shippers and those in remote regions while granting rebates to favored customers, such as Standard Oil. In 1903 Roosevelt helped persuade Congress to pass the Elkins Act, which outlawed railroad rebates. Three years later, the president increased the power of the Interstate Commerce Commission to set maximum railroad freight rates. In 1903 Roosevelt also secured passage of legislation that established the Department of Commerce and Labor. Within this cabinet agency, the Bureau of Corporations gathered information about large companies in an effort to promote fair business practices.

Soaring in popularity, Roosevelt ran for president in 1904 and easily defeated the Democratic nominee, Judge Alton B. Parker. During the next four years, the president applied antitrust laws even more vigorously than before. He steered through Congress various reforms concerning the railroads, such as the Hepburn Act (1906), which standardized shipping rates, and took a strong stand for conservation of public lands. Roosevelt charted a middle course between preservationists and conservationists. He reserved 150 million acres of timberland as part of the national forests, an action that delighted the preservationists. At the same time, he authorized the expenditure of more than $80 million in federal funds to construct dams, reservoirs, canals, and other conservation projects, largely in the West.

Not all reform came from Roosevelt's initiative. Congress passed two notable consumer laws in 1906 that reflected the multiple and sometimes contradictory forces that shaped progressivism. That year, Upton Sinclair published *The Jungle*, a muckraking novel that portrayed the impoverished lives of immigrant workers in Packingtown (Chicago) and the deplorable working conditions they endured. Outraged readers responded to the vivid description of the shoddy and filthy ways the meatpacking

"The Jungle"

Upton Sinclair's 1906 novel *The Jungle* exposed unsanitary conditions in the meat-packing industry and led to passage of the Meat Inspection Act and Pure Food and Drug Act that same year. In this photo from around 1905, workers at the Swift company process sausages as they roll off machines at ten feet per second.   Library of Congress

industry slaughtered animals and prepared beef for sale. The book revealed in grisly detail how the meat cut up for sausage "would be dosed with borax and glycerine, and dumped into hoppers, and made over again for home consumption." The largest and most efficient meatpacking firms had financial reasons to support reform as well. They were losing money because European importers refused to purchase tainted meat. Congress responded by passing the Meat Inspection Act, which benefited consumers and provided a way for large corporations to eliminate competition from smaller, marginal firms that could not afford to raise standards to meet the new federal meat-processing requirements.

In 1906 Congress also passed the Pure Food and Drug Act, which prohibited the sale of adulterated and fraudulently labeled food and drugs. The impetus for this law came from consumer groups, medical professionals, and government scientists. Dr. Harvey Wiley, a chemist in the Department of Agriculture, drove efforts for reform from within the government. He considered it part of his professional duty to eliminate harmful products (Table 19.1).

Roosevelt initially gave African Americans reason to believe that they, too, would get a square deal. In October 1901, at the outset of his first term, Roosevelt invited Booker T. Washington to a dinner at the White House. White supremacists in the South denounced the social gathering as a "damnable outrage." Though Roosevelt dismissed this criticism, he never invited another black guest. Also in his first term, Roosevelt supported the appointment of a few black Republicans to federal posts in the South. When segregationist whites chased Minnie Cox from her job as postmistress of Indianola, Mississippi, Roosevelt refused to accept her resignation and closed the post office.

Nevertheless, Roosevelt lacked a commitment to black equality and espoused the racist ideas of eugenics then in fashion (see chapter 18). He deplored the declining birthrate of native-born white Americans compared with that of eastern and southern European newcomers and African Americans, whom he considered inferior stock. He argued that unless Anglo-Saxon women produced more children, whites would end up committing "race suicide." "If the women flinch from breeding," Roosevelt worried, "the . . . death of the race takes place even quicker." Roosevelt never wavered in his belief in the superiority of the white race over people of color.

TABLE 19.1   National Progressive Legislation

1903	Department of Labor and Commerce established to promote fair business practices
1906	Pure Food and Drug Act
	Meat Inspection Act; Hepburn Act
1910	White Slave Trade Act
1913	Underwood Act reduces tariffs to benefit farmers
	Sixteenth Amendment (graduated income tax)
	Seventeenth Amendment (election of senators by popular vote)
	Federal Reserve System
1914	Harrison Narcotics Control Act
	Federal Trade Commission
	Clayton Antitrust Act
1916	Adamson Act provides eight-hour workday for railroad workers
	Keating-Owen Act outlaws child labor in firms engaged in interstate commerce
	Workmen's Compensation Act
1919	Eighteenth Amendment (prohibition)
1920	Nineteenth Amendment (women's suffrage)

Once he won reelection in 1904, Roosevelt had less political incentive to defy the white South. He stopped cooperating with southern black officeholders and maneuvered to build the Republican Party in the region with all-white support. However, his most reprehensible action involved an incident that occurred in Brownsville, Texas, in 1906. White residents of the town charged that black soldiers stationed at Fort Brown shot up the main street, killing one man and wounding another. Roosevelt ordered that unless the perpetrators stepped forward, the entire regiment would receive dishonorable discharges without a court-martial. Roosevelt never doubted the guilt of the black soldiers, and when no one admitted responsibility, he summarily dismissed 167 men from the military. Although the president spoke out against the brutality of lynching blacks in the South, he participated in this mass "legal lynching" of African American soldiers.

Taft Retreats from Progressivism

When Roosevelt decided not to seek another term as president in 1908, choosing instead to back William Howard Taft as his successor, he thought he was leaving his reform legacy in capable hands. A Roosevelt loyalist and an Ohio native, Taft had compiled a distinguished record as a federal judge, solicitor general of the United States, governor of the Philippines, and secretary of

war. Taft easily defeated the Democratic candidate, William Jennings Bryan, who was running for the presidency for the third and final time.

Taft's presidency did not proceed as Roosevelt and his progressive followers had hoped. Taft did not have the charisma or energy of his predecessor and appeared to move in slow motion compared with Roosevelt. More important, the new president, in contrast to Roosevelt, had a narrower view of the scope of his office and its power to shape public opinion. Taft proved a weak leader and frequently took stands opposite to those of progressives. After convening a special session of Congress in March 1909 to support lower tariffs, a progressive issue, the president retreated in the face of conservative Republican opposition in the Senate. That year, when lawmakers passed the Payne-Aldrich tariff, which raised duties on imports, Taft signed it into law, thereby alienating key progressive legislators such as Senator Robert M. La Follette. The president also remained aloof from the fight by House insurgents to curb the dictatorial powers of Speaker Joseph Cannon, a foe of reform.

The situation deteriorated even further in the field of conservation, which was close to Roosevelt's heart. When Pinchot criticized Taft's secretary of the interior, Richard Ballinger, for returning restricted Alaskan coal mines to private mining companies in 1910, Taft fired Pinchot. Taft did not oppose conservation—he transferred more land from private to public control than did Roosevelt—but his dismissal of Pinchot angered conservationists.

Even more harmful to Taft's political fortunes, Roosevelt turned against his handpicked successor. After returning from a hunting safari in Africa and a speaking tour of Europe in 1910, Roosevelt became increasingly troubled by Taft's missteps. The loss of the House of Representatives to the Democrats in the 1910 elections highlighted the split among Republicans that had developed under Taft. A year later, relations between the ex-president and the incumbent further deteriorated when Roosevelt attacked Taft for filing antitrust litigation against U.S. Steel for a deal that the Roosevelt administration had approved in 1907. Ironically, Roosevelt, known as a trustbuster, believed that filing more lawsuits under the Sherman Antitrust Act yielded diminishing returns, whereas Taft, the conservative, initiated more antitrust litigation than did Roosevelt.

The Election of 1912

Convinced that only he could heal the party breach, Roosevelt announced that he would run for the 1912 Republican presidential nomination. However, despite Roosevelt's widespread popularity among rank-and-file Republicans, Taft still controlled the party machinery and the majority of convention delegates. Losing to Taft on the first ballot, an embittered but optimistic Roosevelt formed a third party to sponsor his run for the presidency. Roosevelt excitedly told thousands of supporters gathered in Chicago, including Jane Addams and Gifford Pinchot, that he felt "as strong as a BULL MOOSE," which became the nickname for Roosevelt's new **Progressive Party**.

In accepting the nomination of his new party, Roosevelt articulated the philosophy of **New Nationalism**. He argued that the federal government should use its considerable power to fight against the forces of special privilege and for social justice for the majority of Americans. To this end, the Progressive Party platform advocated income and inheritance taxes, an eight-hour workday, the abolition of child labor, workers' compensation, fewer restrictions on labor unions, and women's suffrage. This last plank mobilized the efforts of women throughout the country who, like Jane Addams, supported the party that she said "pledged itself to the protection of children, to the care of the aged, to the relief of overworked girls, to the safeguarding of burdened men."

Roosevelt was not the only progressive candidate in the contest. The Democrats nominated Woodrow Wilson, the reform governor of New Jersey. The son of a Presbyterian minister, Wilson had the moral conviction of a pastor who knew what was best for his flock. As an alternative to Roosevelt's New Nationalism, Wilson offered his **New Freedom**. As a Democrat and a southerner (he was born in Virginia), Wilson had a more limited view of government than did the Republican Roosevelt. Wilson envisioned a society of small businesses, with the government's role confined to ensuring open competition among businesses and freedom for individuals to make the best use of their opportunities. Unlike Roosevelt's New Nationalism, Wilson's New Freedom did not embrace social reform and rejected federal action in support of women's suffrage and the elimination of child labor.

If voters considered either Roosevelt's or Wilson's brand of reform too mainstream, they could cast their ballots for Eugene V. Debs, the Socialist Party candidate who had been imprisoned for his leadership in the Pullman strike (see chapter 17). He favored overthrowing capitalism through peaceful, democratic methods and replacing it with government ownership of business and industry for the benefit of the working class.

The Republican Party split decided the outcome of the election. The final results gave Roosevelt 27 percent of the popular vote and Taft 23 percent. Together they had a majority, but because they were divided, Wilson became president, with 42 percent of the popular vote and 435 electoral votes. Finishing fourth, Debs did not win any electoral votes, but he garnered around a million popular votes (6 percent). Counting the votes for Wilson, Roosevelt, and Debs, the American electorate overwhelmingly cast their ballots for reform.

Woodrow Wilson and the New Freedom Agenda

Once in office, Wilson hurried to fulfill his New Freedom agenda. Even though he differed from Roosevelt about the scope of federal intervention, both men believed in a strong presidency. An admirer of the British parliamentary system, Wilson viewed the president as an active and strong leader whose job was to provide his party with a legislative program. The 1912 elections had given the Democrats control over Congress, and Wilson expected his party to support his New Freedom measures.

Tariff reduction came first. The Underwood Act of 1913 reduced import duties, a measure that appealed to southern and midwestern farmers who sought lower prices on the manufactured goods they bought that were subject to the tariff. The law also incorporated a reform that progressives had adopted from the Populists: the graduated income tax (tax rates that increase at higher levels of income). The ratification of the Sixteenth Amendment in 1913 provided the legal basis for the income tax after the Supreme Court had previously declared such a levy unconstitutional. The graduated income tax was meant to advance the cause of social justice by moderating income inequality. The need to recover revenues lost from lower tariffs provided an additional practical impetus for imposing the tax. Because the law exempted people earning less than $4,000 a year from paying the income tax, more than 90 percent of Americans owed no tax. Those with incomes exceeding this amount paid rates ranging from 1 percent to 6 percent on $500,000 or more.

Also in 1913, Wilson pressed Congress to consider banking reform. As chronic debtors who had to borrow against next year's crops, farmers favored a system supervised by the government that afforded them an ample supply of credit at low interest rates. Eastern bankers wanted reforms that would stabilize a system plagued by cyclical financial panics, the most recent in 1907, while keeping the banking system under the private control of bankers. The resulting compromise created the Federal Reserve System.

Woodrow Wilson and William Howard Taft

This photograph shows Woodrow Wilson (left) on inauguration day in 1913 with his predecessor, William Howard Taft. Taft, a Republican, had disappointed progressives, especially Theodore Roosevelt, during his one term in office. Wilson, a Democrat, would expand progressive reforms from 1913 to 1917. Not considered a jovial man, Wilson is seen here enjoying himself as he takes office.   Library of Congress

The act established twelve regional banks. These banks lent cash reserves to member banks in their districts at a "rediscount rate," a rate that could be adjusted according to the fluctuating demand for credit. Federal Reserve notes (paper money insured by the government) also became the medium of exchange and the foundation for a uniform currency. The Federal Reserve Board, appointed by the president and headquartered in Washington, D.C., supervised the system. Nevertheless, as with other progressive agencies, the experts selected to oversee the new banking system came from within the banking industry itself. Although farmers won a more rational and flexible credit supply, Wall Street bankers retained considerable power over the operation of the Federal Reserve System.

Next, President Wilson took two steps designed to help resolve the problem of economic concentration. First, in 1914 he persuaded Congress to create the Federal Trade Commission. Although the agency replaced Roosevelt's Bureau of Corporations, it pursued basically the same approach that Roosevelt had favored. The commission had the power to investigate corporate activities and prohibit "unfair" practices (which the law left undefined). Wilson's second measure directly attacked monopolies. Enacted in 1914, the Clayton Antitrust Law strengthened the Sherman Antitrust Act by banning certain corporate operations, such as price discrimination and overlapping membership on company boards, which undermined economic competition. The statute also exempted labor unions from

prosecution under antitrust legislation, reversing the policy initiated by the federal government in the wake of the Pullman strike (see chapter 17).

By the end of his second year in office, Wilson had achieved most of his New Freedom objectives. Political considerations, however, soon forced him to widen his progressive agenda and support measures he had previously rejected. With the Republican Party once again united after the electoral fiasco of 1912, Democrats lost a substantial number of seats in the 1914 congressional elections, though they still maintained a majority. Fearful for his prospects for reelection in 1916, Wilson resumed the campaign for progressive legislation. Wilson appealed to Roosevelt's constituency by supporting New Nationalism social justice measures. In 1916 he signed into law the Adamson Act, which provided an eight-hour workday and overtime pay for railroad workers; the Keating-Owen Act, outlawing child labor in firms that engaged in interstate commerce; and the Workmen's Compensation Act, which provided insurance for federal employees in case of injury. In supporting programs that required greater intervention by the federal government, Wilson had placed political expediency ahead of his professed principles. He would later show a similar flexibility when he lent his support to a women's suffrage amendment, a cause he had long opposed.

Despite facing a challenge from a united Republican Party led by progressive Charles Evans Hughes, a former governor of New York, Wilson won the 1916 election with slightly less than 50 percent of the vote. Wilson's reelection owed little to the support of African Americans. W. E. B. Du Bois, who backed Wilson in 1912 for pledging to "assist in advancing the interest of [the black] race," had become disillusioned with the president. Born in the South and with deep southern roots, Wilson surrounded himself with white appointees from the South, some of whom told racist jokes at cabinet meetings. Despite black protests, Wilson held a screening in the White House of the film *Birth of a Nation*, which glorified the Ku Klux Klan and denigrated African Americans. Making the situation worse, Wilson introduced racial segregation into government offices and dining facilities in the nation's capital, and blacks lost jobs in post offices and other federal agencies throughout the South. In Wilson's view, segregation and discrimination were in the "best interests" of African Americans.

Still, President Wilson achieved much of the progressive agenda—more, in fact, than he had intended to when he first came to office. By the beginning of his second term, the federal government had further extended regulation over the activities of corporations and banks. Big business and finance still wielded substantial power and maintained considerable leeway in conducting their own affairs, but Wilson had steered the government on a course that also benefited ordinary citizens, including passage of social justice measures he had originally opposed.

REVIEW & RELATE

How did the progressive agenda shape presidential politics in the first two decades of the twentieth century?

How and why did the role of the president in national politics change under Roosevelt, Taft, and Wilson?

LEARNINGCurve bedfordstmartins.com/hewittlawson/LC

Conclusion: The Progressive Legacy

By the end of the Progressive Era, Americans had come to expect more from their government. They were more confident that their food and medicine were safe, that children would not have to sacrifice their health and education by going to work, that women laborers would not be exploited, and that political officials would be more responsive to their wishes. As a result of the efforts of environmentalists as different as Gifford Pinchot and Gene Stratton-Porter, the nation expanded its efforts both to conserve and to preserve its natural resources. These and other reforms accomplished what Theodore Roosevelt,

Woodrow Wilson, and their fellow progressives wanted: to bring order out of chaos.

In challenging laissez-faire and championing governmental intervention, progressives did not intend to stamp out individualism or competition. These values were too embedded in the American political tradition, a system that held the allegiance of most reformers. Rather, progressives sought to balance individualism with social justice and social control. Despite cloaking many of their political reforms in democratic garb, middle- and upper-class progressives generally were more interested in augmenting their ability to advance their own agenda than in expanding opportunities for political participation for all Americans. Confident that they spoke for the "interests of the people," progressives had little doubt that increasing their own political power would be good for the nation as a whole.

Progressivism was not for whites only, but racial boundaries shaped the progressive movement. Blacks were active participants in progressivism, whether through extending educational opportunities, working in settlement houses, campaigning for women's suffrage, or establishing the NAACP. Nevertheless, racism was also a characteristic of progressivism. White southern reformers generally favored disfranchisement and segregation. Northern whites did not prove much more sympathetic, as Theodore Roosevelt's handling of the Brownsville incident shows. The southern-born Woodrow Wilson provided even more ample evidence of the racist dimensions of progressivism. Immigrants also found themselves unwelcome targets of moral outrage as progressives forced these newcomers to conform to middle-class standards of social behavior. Crusades for temperance, physical hygiene, and moral reform all shared a desire to mold people deemed inferior into proper citizens, uncontaminated by chronic vice and corruption.

Progressivism was not monolithic and included a range of disparate and overlapping efforts to reorder political, social, moral, and physical environments. Except for the brief existence of the Progressive Party in 1912, reformers did not have a tightly knit organization or a fixed agenda. Leaders were more likely to come from the middle class, but support came from the rich as well as the poor, depending on the issue. Of course, many Americans did not embrace progressive principles, as conservative opponents continued to hold power and to fight against reform. Nevertheless, by 1920 a combination of voluntary changes and government intervention had cleared the way to regulate corporations, increase governmental efficiency, and promote social justice. Progressives succeeded in ameliorating conditions that might have produced violent revolution and more disorder. In time, they would bring their ideas to reordering international affairs.

LEARNINGCurve
Check what you know.
bedfordstmartins.com/hewittlawson/LC

Chapter Review

Online Study Guide ▶ bedfordstmartins.com/hewittlawson

KEY TERMS

pragmatism (p. 593)
social gospel (p. 593)
muckrakers (p. 593)
Hull House (p. 594)
civic housekeeping (p. 594)
suffragists (p. 596)
Tuskegee Institute (p. 599)
National Association for the Advancement of Colored
   People (NAACP) (p. 602)
Woman's Christian Temperance Union (WCTU) (p. 602)
Hetch Hetchy valley (p. 606)
bully pulpit (p. 607)
Progressive Party (p. 610)
New Nationalism (p. 610)
New Freedom (p. 610)

REVIEW & RELATE

1. What late-nineteenth-century trends and developments influenced the progressives?

2. Why did the progressives focus on urban and industrial America?

3. What role did women play in the early-twentieth-century fight for social justice?

4. How did social reformers challenge discrimination against women and minorities?

5. What practices and behaviors of the poor did social control progressives find most alarming? Why?

6. What role did anti-immigrant sentiment play in motivating and shaping progressives' social control initiatives?

7. Who gained and who lost political influence as a result of progressive reforms?

8. How did a commitment to greater efficiency shape progressives' political and environmental initiatives?

9. How did the progressive agenda shape presidential politics in the first two decades of the twentieth century?

10. How and why did the role of the president in national politics change under Roosevelt, Taft, and Wilson?

TIMELINE OF EVENTS

1874	Woman's Christian Temperance Union (WCTU) founded
1889	Jane Addams and Ellen Starr establish Hull House
1890	National American Woman Suffrage Association formed
1895	Booker T. Washington delivers Atlanta address
1900	First commission form of government established in Galveston, Texas
1902	President Roosevelt settles coal strike
1903	National Women's Trade Union League founded
1906	Meat Inspection Act and Pure Food and Drug Act passed
1908	Race riot in Springfield, Illinois
1909	National Association for the Advancement of Colored People (NAACP) founded
1910	Gifford Pinchot is fired by President Taft
1912	Roosevelt forms Progressive Party
	Children's Bureau of the Department of Commerce and Labor established
1913	Sixteenth Amendment instituting a graduated income tax ratified
	Federal Reserve System created
1914	Harrison Narcotics Control Act passed
	Federal Trade Commission created
	Passage of Clayton Anti-Trust Act to benefit labor unions
1916	Keating-Owen Act outlaws child labor
	Workmen's Compensation Act provides disability insurance
1919	Eighteenth Amendment establishing prohibition ratified
1920	Nineteenth Amendment granting women the right to vote ratified

Progressivism and Social Control

At its core, progressivism was a response to the unsettling forces of rapid industrialization, corporate capitalism, urbanization, and immigration. Although the Populists of the 1890s addressed similar grievances, they focused more on the economic plight of rural Americans than did progressives. Progressivism emerged a decade later during relative prosperity and tended to originate in cities of the East and Midwest. Progressives shared common concerns as consumers, urban residents, and political citizens. In their search for political, economic, social, and cultural order, they supported a variety of reforms, including direct primary elections, conservation measures, the abolition of child labor, and the regulation of trusts, banks, and railroads.

Often forgotten in the history of these reforms is the extent to which progressives sought to control the behavior of people they considered morally deficient and a danger to civilization. Unlike governmental reforms that aimed to expand democracy and political participation, progressives' efforts to impose their moral values on the rest of the population ignored the wishes of ordinary people. Progressives favored policies that reflected their own brand of middle-class morality and targeted the behavior of immigrants, the working classes, women of questionable character, and nonwhites. What these progressives called moral reform—prohibition, antivice campaigns, immigration restriction— poor and working-class families often saw as an invasion of their privacy and a threat to their way of life. The eugenics movement, which sought to maintain white racial purity through selective breeding, represented the most sinister form of progressive reform. While some eugenicists advocated birth control for the poor, others favored sterilization for those deemed "undesirable." By 1931 more than thirty states had passed laws allowing the forced sterilization of people with mental or physical disabilities, as well as individuals from socially disadvantaged groups.

As you read the following documents, consider why progressives singled out these groups for attention. Why did many progressives think members of these groups posed a threat to society? What social and moral norms did the progressives who initiated these reforms hope to impose on society as a whole?

DOCUMENT 19.5

Frances Willard | On Behalf of Home Protection, 1884

Frances Willard was an educator and a dean of the Women's College of Northwestern University. She became president of the Woman's Christian Temperance Union (WCTU) in 1879 and served in that position until her death in 1898. Willard wrote a history of the WCTU that included reflections on how she became an advocate for both prohibition and women's suffrage at an early age.

LONGER AGO THAN I SHALL TELL, my father returned one night to the far-off Wisconsin home where I was reared; and, sitting by my mother's chair, with a child's attentive ear, I listened to their words. He told us of the news that day had brought about Neal Dow [mayor of Portland, Maine, who sponsored Maine's prohibition law] and the great fight for prohibition down in Maine, and then he said: "I wonder if poor, rum-cursed Wisconsin will ever get a law like that?" And mother rocked a while in silence in the dear old chair I love, and then she gently said: "Yes, Josiah, there'll be such a law all over the land some day, when women vote."

My father had never heard her say so much before. He was a great conservative; so he looked tremendously astonished, and replied, in his keen, sarcastic voice: "And pray how will you arrange it so that women shall vote?" Mother's chair went to and fro a little faster for a minute, and then, not looking into his face, but into the flickering flames of the grate, she slowly answered: "Well, I say to you, as the apostle Paul said to his jailor, 'You have put us into prison, we being Romans, and you must come and take us out.'"

That was a seed-thought in a girl's brain and heart. Years passed on, in which nothing more was said upon this dangerous theme. My brother grew to manhood, and soon after he was twenty-one years old he went with his father to vote. Standing by the window, a girl of sixteen years, a girl of simple, homely fancies, not at all strong-minded, and altogether ignorant of the world, I looked out as they drove away, my father and my brother, and as I looked I felt a strange ache in my heart, and tears sprang to my eyes. Turning to my sister Mary, who stood beside me, I saw that the dear little innocent seemed wonderfully sober, too. I said: "Don't you wish we could go with them when we are old enough? Don't we love our country just as well as they do?" and her little frightened voice piped out:

"Yes, of course we ought. Don't I know that? but you mustn't tell a soul—not mother, even; we should be called strong-minded."

In all the years since then I have kept these things, and many others like them, and pondered them in my heart; but two years of struggle in this temperance reform have shown me, as they have ten thousand other women, so clearly and so impressively, my duty, that I have passed the Rubicon [a limiting boundary] of silence, and am ready for any battle that shall be involved in this honest declaration of faith that is within me. . . .

I thought that women ought to have the ballot as I paid the hard-earned taxes upon my mother's cottage home—but I never said as much—somehow the motive did not command my heart. For my own sake, I had not the courage, but I have for thy sake, dear native land, for thy necessity is as much greater than mine as thy transcendent hope is greater than the personal interest of thy humble child. . . .

Ah, it is women who have given the costliest hostages to fortune. Out into the battle of life they have sent their best beloved, with fearful odds against them, with snares that men have legalized and set for them on every hand. Beyond the arms that held them long, their boys have gone forever. Oh! by the danger they have dared; by the hours of patient watching over beds where helpless children lay; by the incense of ten thousand prayers wafted from their gentle lips to Heaven, I charge you give them power to protect, along life's treacherous highway, those whom they have so loved. Let it no longer be that they must sit back among the shadows, hopelessly mourning over their strong staff broken, and their beautiful rod; but when the sons they love shall go forth to life's battle, still let their mothers walk beside them, sweet and serious, and clad in the garments of power.

Source: Frances Willard, *Women and Temperance; or, The Work and Workers of the Woman's Christian Temperance Union* (Hartford, CT: Park Publishing, 1884), 457–59.

DOCUMENT 19.6

Abstinence Poster, 1919

This 1919 poster is one of forty-eight produced by the U.S. Public Health Service for its "Keeping Fit" campaign, a sex education program aimed at adolescent boys that stressed moral and physical fitness. Here a fast-talking "wise guy" tries to persuade an innocent-looking youth to overlook the possibly serious consequences of sexual promiscuity.

DOCUMENT 19.7

Indiana Sterilization Law, 1907

Many progressives embraced eugenics—a pseudo-science that advocated selective breeding to improve the quality of human beings—as a way to combat social ills that they thought derived from hereditary factors. The popularity of eugenics among progressives at the turn of the twentieth century led to the passage of measures like Indiana's Compulsory Sterilization Law of 1907, which promoted forced sterilization to prevent people with mental and physical defects or other "undesirable" traits from procreating.

Whereas, Heredity plays a most important part in the transmission of crime, idiocy, and imbecility;

Penal Institutions—Surgical Operations.

Therefore, *Be it enacted by the general assembly of the State of Indiana*, That on and after the passage of this act it shall be compulsory for each and every institution in the state, entrusted with the care of confirmed criminals, idiots, rapists, and imbeciles, to appoint upon its staff, in addition to the regular institutional physician, two skilled surgeons of recognized ability, whose duty it shall be, in conjunction with the chief physician of the institution, to examine the mental and physical condition of such inmates as are recommended by the institutional physician and board of managers. If, in the judgment of this committee of experts and the board of managers, procreation is inadvisable and there is no probability of improvement of the mental condition of the inmate, it shall be lawful for the surgeons to perform such operation for the prevention of procreation as shall be decided safest and most effective. But this operation shall not be performed except in cases that have been pronounced unimprovable: *Provided*, That in no case shall the consultation fee be more than three dollars to each expert, to be paid out of the funds appropriated for the maintenance of such institution.

Source: *Acts 1907, Laws of the State of Indiana, Passed at the Sixty-fifth Regular Session of the General Assembly* (Indianapolis: William B. Burford, 1907), 377–78.

DOCUMENT 19.8

The Immigration Act of 1917

The wave of immigration from eastern and southern Europe between 1890 and 1914 prompted strenuous efforts to restrict immigration. Labor unions worried that an oversupply of cheap labor would drive down wages. Native-born whites, whose Protestant ancestors had arrived generations earlier, feared that the newer, primarily Jewish and Catholic immigrants endangered their moral and cultural values. In 1917 Congress enacted legislation to reduce the influx of foreigners. The new law included the following provisions outlining who should be denied entry.

SEC. 3. That the following classes of aliens shall be excluded from admission into the United States: All idiots, imbeciles, feeble-minded persons, epileptics, insane persons; persons who have had one or more attacks of insanity at any time previously; persons of constitutional psychopathic inferiority; persons with chronic alcoholism; paupers; professional beggars; vagrants; persons afflicted with tuberculosis in any form or with a loathsome or dangerous contagious disease; persons not comprehended within any of the foregoing excluded classes who are found to be and are certified by the examining surgeon as being mentally or physically defective, such physical defect being of a nature which may affect the ability of such alien to earn a living; persons who have been convicted of or admit having committed a felony or other crime or misdemeanor involving moral turpitude; polygamists, or persons who practice polygamy or believe in or advocate the practice of polygamy; anarchists, or persons who believe in or advocate the overthrow by force or violence of the Government of the United States, or of all forms of law, or who disbelieve in or are opposed to organized government, or who advocate the assassination of public officials, or who advocate or teach the unlawful destruction of property; persons who are members of or affiliated with any organization entertaining and teaching disbelief in or opposition to organized government, or who advocate or teach the duty, necessity, or propriety of the unlawful assaulting or killing of any officer or officers, either of specific individuals or of officers generally, of the Government of the United States or of any other organized government, because of his or their official character, or who advocate or teach the unlawful destruction of property; prostitutes, or persons coming into the United States for the purpose of prostitution or for any other immoral purpose; persons who directly or indirectly procure or attempt to procure or import prostitutes or persons for the purpose of prostitution or for any other immoral purpose; persons who are supported by or receive in whole or in part the proceeds of prostitution; persons hereinafter called contract laborers, who have been induced, assisted, encouraged, or solicited to migrate to this country by offers or promises of employment, whether such offers or promises are true or false, or in consequence of agreements, oral, written or printed, express or implied, to perform labor in this country of any kind, skilled or unskilled; persons who have come in consequence of advertisements for laborers printed, published, or distributed in a foreign country; persons likely to become a public charge; persons who have been deported under any of the provisions of this Act, and who may again seek admission within one year from the date of such deportation, unless prior to their reembarkation at a foreign port or their attempt to be admitted from foreign contiguous territory the Secretary of Labor shall have consented to their reapplying for admission; persons whose tickets or passage is paid for with the money of another, or who are assisted by others to come, unless it is affirmatively and satisfactorily shown that such persons do not belong to one of the foregoing excluded classes; persons whose ticket or passage is paid for by any corporation, association, society, municipality, or foreign Government, either directly or indirectly; stowaways, except that any such stowaway, if otherwise admissible, may be admitted in the discretion of the Secretary of Labor; all children under sixteen years of age, unaccompanied by or not coming to one or both of their parents, except that any such children may, in the discretion of the Secretary of Labor, be admitted if in his opinion they are not likely to become a public charge and are otherwise eligible.

Source: Immigration Act of 1917, 39 Stat. 875–76 (1917).

DOCUMENT 19.9

"Sanitary Precaution," c. 1914

Although progressives' interest in public health and sanitation was often motivated by a sincere desire to prevent the spread of disease, these concerns were often closely linked to racial and ethnic anxieties. Immigration opponents, for example, argued that certain immigrant groups, by virtue of an inherent disposition toward uncleanliness, posed a direct threat to public health. The cartoon here suggests a similar link between African American servants and the spread of disease.

Atlanta Journal-Constitution Historic Online Archives

Interpret the Evidence

1. What role does Frances Willard suggest women should play in controlling the behavior of men (Document 19.5)? What light does Willard's memoir shed on the role of motherhood in shaping progressive values?

2. What connection does the abstinence poster make between disease and vice (Document 19.6)? What do you make of the absence of a direct moral argument against promiscuity in the poster?

3. Why was eugenics so attractive to many progressive reformers (see Document 19.7)?

4. Who benefited and who lost from immigration restriction laws (Document 19.8), temperance laws, and antiprostitution laws?

5. What racial assumptions lie behind the cartoon on health threats (Document 19.9)?

Put It in Context

- How did the progressives' emphasis on disease reflect their larger vision of American society at the turn of the twentieth century?

- How did progressives' understanding of the sources of disease shape the kinds of "cures" they proposed for America's ills?

background photo: page 617, Library of Congress

Library of Congress

The Granger Collection, New York

Puck magazine cover showing Theodore Roosevelt admiring "imperialism" crown on display, 1904.

Alabama troops of the 167th Infantry in a trench near Ancerviller, France, 1918.

20
Empire and Wars
1898–1918

Library of Congress

Red Cross poster, 1917.

AMERICAN HISTORIES

Alfred Thayer Mahan came from a military family. Born in 1840, he grew up in West Point, New York, where his father served as dean of the faculty at the U.S. Military Academy. Seeking to emerge from his father's shadow, Alfred attended the U.S. Naval Academy, from which he graduated and received his commission in 1861, just as the Civil War was getting under way. His wartime experience convinced him that the navy, with its plodding, antiquated wooden vessels, needed a dramatic overhaul.

After the war, Mahan continued his naval career. Rather than making his mark on the high seas, Captain Mahan built his reputation as a military historian and strategist at the U.S. Naval War College. In 1890 he published *The Influence of Sea Power upon History*, in which he argued that the great imperial powers in modern history—Spain, the Netherlands, Great Britain, and France—had succeeded because they possessed strong navies and merchant marines. In his view, sea power had allowed these nations to defeat their enemies, conquer territories, and establish colonies from which they extracted raw materials and opened markets for finished goods. Appearing at a time when European nations were embarking on a new round of empire building, this book and subsequent writings had an enormous influence on American imperialists, including Theodore Roosevelt. Mahan's work reinforced the belief of men like Roosevelt that the long-term prospects of the United States depended on the acquisition of strategic outposts in Asia and the Caribbean that could guarantee American access to overseas markets.

**Alfred Thayer Mahan
and José Martí**

As the economic and strategic importance of the Caribbean grew in the minds of imperial strategists such as Mahan and Roosevelt, the Cuban freedom fighter José Martí developed a very different vision of the region's future. Born in 1853 to Spanish immigrants who had migrated to Cuba for economic reasons, Martí got involved in the fight for Cuban independence from Spain as a teenager. In 1869, at age seventeen, he was arrested for protest activities during a revolutionary uprising against Spain. Sentenced to six years of hard labor, Martí was released after six months and was forced into exile. He returned to Cuba in 1878, only to be arrested and deported again the following year.

Martí settled in the United States, where, along with other Cuban exiles, he continued to promote Cuban independence and the establishment of a democratic republic. He conceived of the idea of *Cuba Libre* (Free Cuba) not just as a struggle for political independence but also as a social revolution that would erase unfair distinctions based on race and class. "Our goal," Martí declared in 1892, "is not so much a mere political change as a good, sound, and just and equitable system." Martí united disparate elements in expatriate communities in the United States and the Caribbean under the banner of a single Cuban Revolutionary Party.

When Cubans once again rebelled against Spain in 1895, Martí returned to Cuba to fight alongside his comrades. On May 19, 1895, only three months after he had returned to Cuba, Martí died in battle. Cuba ultimately won its independence from Spain, but Martí's vision of *Cuba Libre* was only partially realized. In 1898 the United States intervened on the side of the Cuban rebels, guaranteeing their victory, but not their freedom. America entered the war to gain control over Cuba, not to help Cubans take control of their own country. •

both photos: Library of Congress

THE AMERICAN HISTORIES of Alfred Thayer Mahan and José Martí embodied disparate understandings of America's relationship with the rest of the world. Up until the late nineteenth century, most Americans associated colonialism with the European powers and saw overseas expansion as incompatible with American values of independence and self-determination. In this context, they shared Martí's point of view. The American imperialism espoused by Mahan and others, therefore, represented a reversal of traditional American attitudes. Supporters of American imperialism saw the acquisition and control of overseas territories, by force if necessary, as essential to the protection of American interests. This perspective would come to dominate American foreign policy in the early twentieth century. Theodore Roosevelt and Woodrow Wilson, progressive presidents who sanctioned increased federal regulation of economic and moral matters within the United States, also supported vigorous intervention in world affairs. Although Roosevelt and Wilson differed in style and approach, in foreign affairs they asserted America's right to

use its power to secure order and thwart revolution wherever American interests were seen to be threatened. Having become a major power on the world stage in the early twentieth century, the United States chose to enter World War I, in which rival European alliances battled for imperial domination. The end of the war heightened America's critical role in world affairs but brought neither lasting peace nor the dissolution of empire.

The Awakening of Imperialism

The United States became a modern imperial power relatively late. In the decades following the Civil War, the U.S. government concentrated most of its energies on settling the western territories, pushing Native Americans aside, and extracting the region's resources. Unlike Europe, the United States possessed a sparsely inhabited frontier that would furnish land for its growing population, as well as raw materials and markets for its industries. By the end of the nineteenth century, however, sweeping economic, cultural, and social changes led many Americans to conclude that the time had come for the country to assert its power beyond its borders. Convinced of the argument for empire advanced by Mahan and other imperialists, American officials embraced an expansionist foreign policy. In a burst of overseas expansion from 1898 to 1904, the United States acquired Guam, Hawaii, the Philippines, and Puerto Rico; established a protectorate in Cuba; and exercised force to build a canal through Panama. These gains paved the way for subsequent U.S. intervention in Haiti, the Dominican Republic, and Nicaragua.

The Economics of Expansion

The industrialization of America and the growth of corporate capitalism stimulated imperialist desires in the late nineteenth century. Throughout its early history, the United States had sought overseas markets for exports, particularly its agricultural products. However, the importance of exports to the American economy increased dramatically in the second half of the nineteenth century, as industrialization gained momentum. In 1870 American exports totaled $500 million. By 1905 the value of American exports had increased sixfold to $1.5 billion (Figure 20.1). John D. Rockefeller's Standard Oil Company led the way in selling products to European and Asian markets, and firms such as Coca-Cola, Kodak, and McCormick earned profits by exporting soft drinks, cameras, and farm machinery, respectively.

The bulk of American exports went to the developed markets of Europe and Canada, which had the greatest purchasing power. Although the less economically advanced nations of Latin America and Asia did not have the same ability to buy American products, businessmen still considered these regions—especially China, with a population of millions of potential consumers—as future markets for American industries.

The desire to expand foreign markets remained a steady feature of American business interests. The fear that the domestic market for manufactured goods was shrinking gave this expansionist hunger greater urgency. The fluctuating business cycle of boom and bust that characterized the economy in the 1870s and 1880s reached its peak in the depression of the 1890s, the most severe economic downturn up to that point in American history. The social unrest that accompanied this depression, including protest marches and strikes (see chapter 17), worried business and political leaders about the stability of the country. The way to sustain prosperity and contain radicalism, many businessmen agreed, was to find foreign markets for goods that

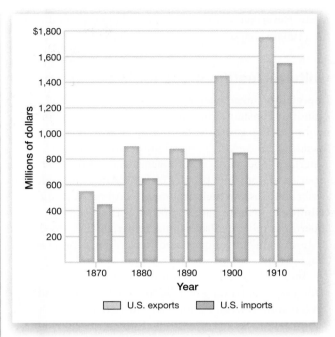

FIGURE 20.1   U.S. Exports and Imports, 1870–1910

As American industrial power increased at the end of the nineteenth century, exports increased dramatically. Between 1870 and 1910, U.S. exports more than tripled. Imports rose as well but were restrained by protective tariffs.

poured out of factories but could not be absorbed at home. Senator William Frye of Maine argued, "We must have the market [of China] or we shall have revolution."

Similar commercial ambitions led many Americans to see Hawaii as an imperial prize. Interest in the islands dated back to the early nineteenth century. American missionaries first visited the Hawaiian Islands in 1820. As missionaries tried to convert native islanders to Christianity, American businessmen sought to establish plantations on the islands, especially to grow sugarcane, as the market for sugar had grown rapidly during the 1870s and 1880s. In exchange for duty-free access to the U.S. sugar market, white Hawaiians signed an agreement in 1887 that granted the United States exclusive rights to a naval base at Pearl Harbor in Honolulu.

The growing influence of white sugar planters on the islands alarmed native Hawaiians. In 1891 Queen Liliuokalani, a strong nationalist leader who voiced the slogan "Hawaii for the Hawaiians," sought to increase the power of the indigenous peoples she governed, at the expense of the sugar growers. In 1893 white plantation owners, with the cooperation of the American ambassador to Hawaii and 150 U.S. marines, overthrew the queen's government. Once in command of the government, they entered into a treaty of annexation with the United States. However, President Grover Cleveland opposed annexation and withdrew the treaty. Nevertheless, planters remained in power and waited for a suitable opportunity to seek annexation.

Cultural Justifications for Imperialism

Imperialists linked overseas expansion to practical, economic considerations, but race was also a key component in their arguments for empire. Drawing on Herbert Spencer's concept of "survival of the fittest," many Americans and western Europeans declared themselves superior to nonwhite peoples of Latin America, Asia, and Africa. Buttressing their arguments with racist studies claiming to demonstrate scientifically the "racial" superiority of white Protestants, imperialists claimed a "natural right" of conquest and world domination (see chapter 19).

Imperialists added an ethical dimension to this ideology by contending that "higher civilizations" had a duty to uplift inferior nations. In *Our Country* (1885), the Congregationalist minister Josiah Strong proclaimed the superiority of the Anglo-Saxon, or white northern European, race and the responsibility of the United States to spread the "blessings" of its Christian way of life throughout the world. Secular intellectuals, such as historian John Fiske, praised the English race for settling the United States and predicted that "its language . . . its religion . . . its political habits, and . . . the blood of its people" would become "predominant" in the less civilized parts of the globe.

As in Hawaii, Christian missionaries served as foot soldiers for the advancing American commercial empire. In fact, there was often a clear connection between religious and commercial interests. For example, in 1895 industrialists John D. Rockefeller Jr. and Cyrus McCormick created the World Student Christian Federation, which dispatched more than five thousand young missionaries throughout the world, many of them women. Likewise, it was no coincidence that China, an enormous potential market for American products, became a magnet for American missionary activity. By 1920 missionaries in China were operating schools, hospitals, orphanages, leper colonies, churches, and seminaries, seeking to convert the "backward" Chinese to Christianity and the American way of life. Many Americans hoped that, under missionary supervision, the Chinese would become consumers of both American ideas and American products.

Gender and Empire

Gender anxieties provided an additional motivation for American imperialism. In the late nineteenth century, with the Civil War long over, many Americans worried that the rising generation of American men lacked opportunities to test and strengthen their manhood. For example, in 1897 Mississippi congressman John Sharp Williams lamented the waning of "the dominant spirit which controlled in this Republic [from 1776 to 1865] . . . one of honor, glory, chivalry, and patriotism." Such gender anxieties were not limited to elites. The depression of the 1890s hit working-class men hard, causing them to question their self-worth as they lost the ability to support their families. In this context, the poem "The White Man's Burden," written by the British writer and poet Rudyard Kipling in 1899, touched a nerve with American men. In the poem, Kipling urges white men to take up the "burden" of bringing civilization to non-Western peoples. By embracing the imperialist project, they would regain their manly honor.

Explore

See Document 20.1 for part of Kipling's famous poem.

The growing presence of women as political activists in campaigns for suffrage and moral, humanitarian, and governmental reforms was particularly troubling to male identity. Some men warned that dire consequences would result if women succeeded in feminizing politics. Alfred Thayer Mahan believed that women's suffrage would undermine the nation's military security because women lacked the will to use physical force. He asserted that giving the vote to women would destroy the "constant practice of the past ages by which to men are assigned the outdoor rough action of life and to women that indoor sphere which we call the family." As Mahan's comment shows, calling American men to action was often paired with a call for American women to leave the public arena and return to the home.

American males could reassert their manhood by adopting a militant spirit. An English verse from 1878 described this attitude: "We don't want to fight, yet by Jingo! If we do, we've got the ships, we've got the men, and got the money too." Known as **jingoists**, war enthusiasts such as Theodore Roosevelt could not contain their desire to find a war in which to prove their masculinity. "You and your generation have had your chance from 1861 to 1865," Roosevelt exclaimed to a Civil War veteran. "Now let us of this generation have ours!" Captain Mahan concurred. "No greater danger could befall civilization than the disappearance of the warlike spirit (I dare say *war*) among civilized men," he asserted. "There are too many barbarians still in the world." Mahan and Roosevelt echoed the British jingoists' pride in naval power. The Naval Act of 1890 authorized funding for construction of three battleships to join the two existing ones. These

DOCUMENT 20.1

Rudyard Kipling | "The White Man's Burden," 1899

The English writer Rudyard Kipling was a leading exponent of British imperialism. His famous poem "The White Man's Burden" originally appeared in the popular American magazine *McClure's* with the subtitle "The United States and the Philippine Islands." Given this subtitle, the poem can be seen as a direct appeal to American men to join their British counterparts in the global imperial project.

Explore

Take up the White Man's burden—
Send forth the best ye breed—
Go, bind your sons to exile
To serve your captives' need;
To wait, in heavy harness,
On fluttered folk and wild—
Your new-caught sullen peoples,
Half devil and half child. . . .

Take up the White Man's burden—
The savage wars of peace—
Fill full the mouth of Famine,
And bid the sickness cease;
And when your goal is nearest
(The end for others sought)
Watch sloth and heathen folly
Bring all your hope to nought. . . .

Take up the White Man's burden!
Have done with childish days—
The lightly-proffered laurel,
The easy ungrudged praise:
Comes now, to search your manhood
Through all the thankless years,
Cold, edged with dear-bought wisdom,
The judgment of your peers.

Source: Rudyard Kipling, "The White Man's Burden," *McClure's Magazine*, February 1899, 290–91.

Interpret the Evidence

- How does Kipling characterize the relationship between colonizers and the colonized?
- According to Kipling, why was it appropriate to describe imperialism as a "burden"?

Put It in Context

How was the notion of "the white man's burden" used to justify expansion and annexation?

warships would provide the foundation for a revitalized navy capable of safeguarding American interests in the Atlantic and Pacific Oceans. Ten years later, the U.S. fleet had grown to seventeen battleships and six armored cruisers, making it the third most powerful navy in the world, up from twelfth place in 1880. Having built a powerful navy, the United States would soon find opportunities to use it.

REVIEW & RELATE

- What role did economic developments play in prompting calls for an American empire? What role did social and cultural developments play?
- Why did the United States embark on building an empire in the 1890s and not decades earlier?

The War with Spain

The United States went to war with Spain in 1898 not to defend itself from attack but because American policymakers decided that Cuban independence from Spain was in America's national interest. American leaders had long coveted Cuba for its economic resources and strategic location in the Caribbean. When the Cubans revolted against Spain in the mid-1890s, the United States seized its chance. Victory over Spain, however, brought America much more than control over Cuba. In the peace negotiations following the war, the United States acquired a significant portion of Spain's overseas empire, turning the United States into a major imperial power.

Cuba Libre

The Cuban War for Independence began in 1895 around the concept of *Cubanidad*—pride of nation. José Martí envisioned that this war of national liberation from Spain would provide land to impoverished peasants and offer genuine racial equality for the large Afro-Cuban population that had been liberated from slavery less than a decade earlier, in 1886. Black Cubans, such as Antonio Maceo, flocked to the revolutionary cause and constituted a significant portion of the senior ranks in the rebel army.

The insurgents fought a brilliant guerrilla war. Facing some 200,000 Spanish troops, 50,000 rebels ground them down in a war of attrition. The Cuban insurgents burned crops, laid siege to land, and cut railroad lines to keep the Spaniards from using these vital resources. Within eighteen months, the rebellion had spread across the island and garnered the support of all segments of the Cuban population. The Spanish government's brutal attempts to crack down on the rebels only stiffened their resistance. By the end of 1897, the Spanish government recognized that the war was going poorly and offered the rebels a series of reforms that would give the island home rule within the empire but not independence. Sensing victory, the insurgents held out for total separation to realize their vision of **Cuba Libre**, an independent Cuba with greater social and racial equality.

The revolutionaries had every reason to feel confident as they wore down Spanish troops. First, they had help from the climate. One-quarter of Spanish soldiers had contracted yellow fever, malaria, and other tropical illnesses and remained confined to hospitals. The chief military commander of the rebel forces, General Maximo Gómez, bragged that his three best generals were "*Junio, Julio,* and *Agosto,*" referring to the months of June, July, and August, which ushered in the rainy season and increased the spread of disease. Second, mounting a successful counterinsurgency would have required far more troops than Spain

Cuban Revolutionary Soldiers
Under the command of General Maximo Gómez, these Cuban soldiers fought against Spanish forces in 1898. Gómez waged guerrilla warfare for Cuban independence from Spain before the United States entered the war. His army consisted of numerous Afro-Cubans, whose race troubled white American commanders when they occupied Cuba. The Granger Collection, New York

could spare. Its forces were spread too thin around the globe to keep the empire intact. In addition to Cuba, Spain stationed some 200,000 troops in Puerto Rico, the Philippines, and Africa. Finally, antiwar sentiment was mounting in Spain, and on January 12, 1898, Spanish troops mutinied in Havana. Speaking for many, a former president of Spain asserted: "Spain is exhausted. She must withdraw her troops and recognize Cuban independence before it is too late." U.S. Secretary of State John Sherman concurred: "Spain will lose Cuba. . . . She cannot continue the struggle."

The War of 1898

With the Cuban insurgents on the verge of victory, American policymakers, including President William McKinley, came to favor military intervention as a way to increase American control of postwar Cuba. By intervening before the Cubans won on their own, the United States staked its claim for determining the postwar relationship between the two countries and protecting its vital interests in the Caribbean, including the private property rights of American landowners in Cuba.

The American press, however, helped build support for American intervention not by focusing on economic interests and geopolitics but by framing the war as a matter of American honor. Most Americans followed the war through newspaper accounts. William Randolph Hearst's *New York Journal* competed with Joseph Pulitzer's *New York World* to see which could provide the most lurid coverage of Spanish atrocities. The two newspapers sent correspondents to Cuba to cover every grisly story they could find—and to make up stories, if necessary. Known disparagingly as **yellow journalism**, these sensationalist newspaper accounts aroused jingoistic outrage against Spain.

On February 9, 1898, the *Journal* printed a letter that had come into Hearst's possession. Under the headline "Worst Insult to the United States in History," the newspaper quoted a private letter from Enrique Depuy de Lôme, the Spanish minister in Washington, scorning President McKinley as a "weak" politician who pandered to "the crowd" to win public favor. Nearly a week later, on February 15, the battleship *Maine*, anchored in Havana harbor, exploded, killing 266 American sailors. American newspapers blamed Spain. The *World* shouted the rallying cry "Remember the *Maine*! To hell with Spain!" Assistant Secretary of the Navy Theodore Roosevelt seconded this sentiment by denouncing the explosion as a Spanish "act of treachery." Why the Spaniards would choose to blow up the *Maine* and provoke war with the United States while already losing to Cuba remained unanswered, but the incident was enough to turn American opinion toward war.

On April 11, 1898, McKinley asked Congress to declare war against Spain. The declaration included an amendment proposed by Senator Henry M. Teller of Colorado declaring that Cuba "ought to be free and independent." Yet the document left enough room for American maneuvering to satisfy the imperial ambitions of the McKinley administration. In endorsing independence, the war proclamation asserted the right of the United States to remain involved in Cuban affairs until it had achieved "pacification." On April 21, the United States officially went to war with Spain.

In going to war, McKinley embarked on an imperialistic course that had been building since the early 1890s. The president signaled the broader expansionist concerns behind the war when, shortly after it began, he successfully steered a Hawaiian annexation treaty through Congress. Businessmen joined imperialists in seizing the moment to create a commercial empire that would catch up to their European rivals.

It was fortunate for the United States that the Cuban insurgents had seriously weakened Spanish forces before the Americans arrived. The U.S. army, consisting of fewer than 30,000 men, lacked sufficient strength to conquer Cuba on its own, and McKinley had to mobilize some 200,000 National Guard troops and assorted volunteers. Theodore Roosevelt resigned from his post as assistant secretary of the navy and organized his own regiment, called "Rough Riders." American forces faced several problems: They lacked battle experience; supplies were inadequate; their uniforms were not suited for the hot, humid climate of a Cuban summer; and the soldiers did not have immunity from tropical diseases.

African American soldiers, who made up about one-quarter of the troops, encountered additional difficulties. As more and more black troops arrived in southern ports for deployment to Cuba, they faced increasingly hostile crowds, angered at the presence of armed African American men in uniform. In Tampa, Florida, where troops gathered from all over the country to be transported to Cuba, racial tensions exploded on the afternoon of June 8. Intoxicated white soldiers from Ohio grabbed a two-year-old black boy from his mother and used him for target practice, shooting a bullet through his shirtsleeve. In retaliation, African American soldiers stormed into the streets and exchanged gunfire with whites, leaving three whites and twenty-seven black soldiers wounded. Reporting the story of this "riot," the *Atlanta Constitution* denounced the "wild and demonic conduct of the [N]egro regulars," completely ignoring the behavior of the white troops that had prompted the fracas. Undaunted, black troops went on to distinguish themselves on Cuban battlefields.

Despite military inexperience, logistical problems, and racial tensions, the United States quickly defeated the weakened Spanish military, and the war was over four months after it began. During the war, 460 Americans died in combat, far fewer than the more than 5,000 who lost their lives to disease. It was not surprising, then, that Secretary of State John Hay referred to the hostilities as "a splendid little war." The subsequent peace treaty ended Spanish rule in Cuba, ceded Puerto Rico and the Pacific island of Guam to the United States, and recognized American occupation of the Philippines until the two countries could arrange a final settlement. As a result of the territorial gains in the war, American foreign-policy strategists could now begin to construct the empire that Mahan had envisioned.

A Not-So-Free Cuba

Although Congress had adopted the **Teller Amendment** in 1898 pledging Cuba's independence from Spain, President McKinley and his supporters insisted that Cuban self-rule would come only after pacification. Racial prejudice and cultural chauvinism blinded Americans to the contributions Cubans had made to defeat Spain. When white commanding officers arrived in Cuba, they expressed shock at the large number of blacks in the Cuban military, many of whom held leadership positions. One U.S. officer reported to the *New York Times:* "The typical Cuban I encountered was a treacherous, lying, cowardly, thieving, worthless half-breed mongrel, born of a mongrel spawn of [Spain], crossed upon the fetches of darkest Africa and aboriginal America." José Martí may have been fighting for racial equality, but the U.S. government certainly was not.

Because U.S. officials presumed that Cuba was unfit for immediate freedom, the island remained under U.S. military occupation until 1902. The highlight of Cuba's transition to self-rule came with the adoption of a governing document based on the U.S. Constitution. However, the Cuban constitution came with strings attached. In March 1901, Congress passed the **Platt Amendment**, introduced by Senator Orville Platt of Connecticut, which limited Cuban sovereignty. The amendment prohibited the Cuban government from signing treaties with other nations without U.S. consent, permitted the United States to intervene in Cuba to preserve independence and remove threats to economic stability, and leased Guantánamo Bay to the United States as a naval base, an arrangement that continues to this day. American officials pressured Cuban leaders to incorporate the Platt Amendment into their constitution. When U.S. occupation ended in 1902, Cuba was not fully independent. Instead, the United States established Cuba as a protectorate, paving the way for economic exploitation of the island and the return of American troops to safeguard investments.

The Philippine War

Even before invading Cuba, the United States had won a significant battle against Spain on the other side of the world. At the outset of the war, the U.S. Pacific Fleet, under the command of Commodore George Dewey, attacked Spanish forces in their colony of the Philippines. Dewey defeated the Spanish flotilla in Manila Bay on May 1, 1898, killing nearly four hundred Spanish sailors, while eight Americans suffered only minor injuries. Two and a half months later, American troops followed up with an invasion of Manila, and Spanish forces promptly surrendered (Map 20.1).

While pacifying Cuba, the U.S. government had to decide what to do with the Philippines. Imperialists viewed American control of the islands as an important step forward in the quest for entry into the China market. The Philippines could serve as a naval station for the merchant marine and the navy to safeguard potential trade with the Asian mainland. Moreover, President McKinley believed that if the United States did not act, another European power would take Spain's place, something he thought would be "bad business and deplorable."

With this in mind, McKinley decided to annex the Philippines. As with Cuba, McKinley and many other Americans believed that nonwhite Filipinos were not yet capable of self-government. Indiana senator Albert Beveridge commented: "We must never forget that in dealing with the Filipinos we deal with children." McKinley agreed and set out "to educate the Filipinos, and uplift and Christianize them." As was often the case with imperialism, assumptions of racial and cultural superiority provided a handy justification for the pursuit of economic and strategic advantage.

The president's plans, however, ran into vigorous opposition. Anti-imperialist lawmakers took a strong stand against annexing the Philippines. Despite the jingoist fervor surrounding the War of 1898, opponents of imperialism constituted a vocal group. Their cause drew support from such prominent Americans as industrialist Andrew Carnegie, social reformer Jane Addams, writer Mark Twain, and labor organizer Samuel Gompers, all of whom joined the **Anti-Imperialist League**, founded in November 1898. Some argued that the United States would violate its anticolonialist heritage by acquiring the islands. Union leaders feared that annexation would prompt the migration of cheap laborers into the country and undercut wages. Others worried about the financial costs of supporting military forces across the Pacific. Most anti-imperialists had

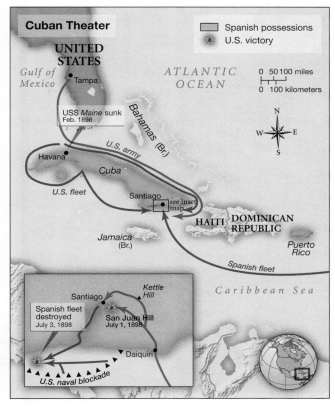

MAP 20.1   The War of 1898

The United States and Spain fought the War of 1898 on two fronts—the Philippines and Cuba. Naval forces led by Admiral George Dewey made the difference in the U.S. victory by first defeating the Spaniards in Manila Bay and then off the coast of Cuba. In Cuba, rebels had seriously weakened the Spanish military before U.S. ground troops secured victory.

racial reasons for rejecting the treaty. Like imperialists, they considered Asians to be inferior to Europeans. In fact, many anti-imperialists held an even dimmer view of the capabilities of people of color than did their opponents, rejecting the notion that Filipinos could be "civilized" under American tutelage. **See Document Project 20: Imperialism versus Anti-Imperialism, page 644**.

Despite this opposition, the imperialists won out. Approval of the treaty annexing the Philippines in 1898 marked the beginning of problems for the United States. As in Cuba, rebellion had preceded American occupation. At first, the rebels welcomed the Americans as liberators, but once it became clear that American rule would simply replace Spanish rule, the mood changed. Led by Emilio Aguinaldo, insurgent forces fought back against the 70,000 troops sent by this latest colonial power. "Either independence or death!" became the battle cry of Aguinaldo's rebel army. The rebels adopted guerrilla tactics and resorted to terrorist assaults against the U.S. army.

U.S. forces responded in kind, adopting harsh methods to suppress the uprising. General Jacob H.

Smithy ordered his troops to "kill and burn, and the more you kill and burn, the better you will please me." Racist sentiments inflamed passions against the dark-skinned Filipino insurgents. One American soldier wrote home saying that "he wanted to blow every nigger into nigger heaven." American counterinsurgency efforts, which indiscriminately targeted combatants and civilians alike, alienated the native population. An estimated 200,000 Filipino civilians died between 1899 and 1902.

The Americans' taste for war and sacrifice quickly waned. Nearly 5,000 Americans died in the Philippine war, far more combat deaths than in Cuba. With casualties mounting and reports growing of combat-related atrocities, antiwar sentiment spread in the United States. Dissenters turned imperialist arguments of manly American honor upside down. Reports of battlefield horrors inflicted on Filipino civilians prompted Senator George L. Wellington of Maryland to complain that the army had "step by step departed from the broad highway of honorable warfare . . . and [had] adopted methods of barbarism

Filipino Prisoners of War
After the United States annexed the Philippines in 1899, Filipino rebels continued their struggle for independence. The United States had a more difficult time subduing the rebels led by Emilio Aguinaldo than they had defeating Spain, but after three years American forces triumphed. In this photograph, Filipino prisoners of war are held in Manila. Library of Congress

and savagery such as the wild natives of the unconquered Philippine Islands could not approach." For many Americans, the "splendid little war" had turned into a sordid affair. Anti-imperialists claimed that the war had done nothing to affirm American manhood; rather, they charged, the United States acted as a bully, taking the position of "a strong man" fighting against "a weak and puny child."

Despite growing casualties on the battlefield and antiwar sentiment at home, the conflict ended with an American military victory. In March 1901, U.S. forces captured Aguinaldo and broke the back of the rebellion. Exhausted, the Filipino leader asked his comrades to lay down their arms. In July 1901, President McKinley appointed Judge William Howard Taft of Ohio as the first civilian governor to oversee the government of the Philippines. For the next forty-five years, except for a brief period of Japanese rule during World War II, the United States remained in control of the islands.

REVIEW & RELATE

Why did the United States go to war with Spain in 1898?

In what ways did the War of 1898 mark a turning point in the relationship between the United States and the rest of the world?

Extending U.S. Imperialism, 1899–1913

The War of 1898 turned the United States into an imperial nation. Once the war was over, and with its newly acquired empire in place, the United States sought to extend its influence, competing with its European rivals for even greater global power. President Theodore Roosevelt and his successors achieved Captain Mahan's dream of building a Central American canal and wielded American military and financial might in the Caribbean with little restraint. At the same time, the United States took a more active role in Asian affairs.

Theodore Roosevelt and "Big Stick" Diplomacy

After President McKinley was assassinated in 1901, Vice President Theodore Roosevelt succeeded him as president. As in domestic matters, Roosevelt believed in using power to protect American commercial and strategic interests as well as to preserve international order and stability. In his view, the United States required a strong military and the political will to use it. "It is contemptible for a nation, as for an individual," Roosevelt instructed Congress, "[to] proclaim its purposes, or to take positions which are ridiculous if unsupported by potential force, and then to refuse to provide this force." This Progressive Era interventionist, inspired by Captain Mahan's writings, welcomed his nation's new role as a major world power. From this point on, the United States would play the role of an international policeman, using force if necessary to keep the peace.

Explore

See Document 20.2 for Roosevelt's views on the virtue of exhibiting strength.

As the most important part of his international agenda, Roosevelt sought to demonstrate American might and preserve order in the Caribbean and Central and South America. The building of the Panama Canal provides a case in point. Mahan considered a canal across Central America as vital because it would provide faster access to Asian markets and improve the U.S. navy's ability to patrol two oceans effectively. The United States took a step toward realizing Mahan's goal in 1901, when it signed the Hay-Pauncefote Treaty with Britain, granting the United States the right to construct a canal connecting the Atlantic and Pacific Oceans. After first considering Nicaragua, Roosevelt settled on Panama as the prime location. A French company had already begun construction at this site and had completed two-fifths of the operation; however, when it ran out of money, it sold its holdings to the United States for the bargain price of $40 million.

Before the United States could resume building, it had to negotiate with the South American country of Colombia, which controlled Panama. Secretary of State Hay and Colombian representatives reached an agreement highly favorable to the Americans, which the Colombian government refused to ratify. When Colombia held out for a higher price, Roosevelt accused the Colombians of being "utterly incapable of keeping order" in Panama and declared that transit across Panama was vital to world commerce. In 1903 the president supported a pro-American uprising by sending warships into the harbor of Panama City, an action that prevented the Colombians from quashing the insurrection. Roosevelt quickly recognized the new government of Panama and signed a treaty with it granting the United States the right to build the canal and exercise "power and authority" over it. In 1914, under American control, the Panama Canal opened to sea traffic.

With the United States controlling Cuba, the Panama Canal, and Puerto Rico, President Roosevelt intended to deter any threats to America's power in the region. The economic instability of Central American and Caribbean nations provided Roosevelt with the opportunity to brandish what he called a "big stick" to keep these countries in check and prevent intervention by European powers also interested in the area. (The term comes from a proverb Roosevelt was fond of quoting: "Speak softly and carry a big stick.") Referring to neighboring countries to the south, the president grumbled: "These wretched republics cause me a great deal of trouble." In 1904, when the government of the Dominican Republic was teetering on the edge of bankruptcy and threatened to default on $22 million in European loans, Roosevelt sprang into action. He announced U.S. opposition to any foreign intervention to reclaim debts, a position that echoed the principles of the Monroe Doctrine, which in 1823 proclaimed that the United States would not tolerate outside intervention in the Western Hemisphere. However, the president went even further and added his own corollary to the Monroe Doctrine by affirming the right of the United States to intervene in the internal affairs of any country in Latin America or the Caribbean that displayed "chronic wrong-doing" and could not preserve order and manage its own affairs. The **Roosevelt Corollary** proclaimed what Cubans and Panamanians already knew: The United States considered the region south of its border to be within its sphere of influence. Retaining nominal independence, the countries of Central America and the Caribbean had to behave according to U.S. wishes or face American military invasion.

Opening the Door in China

Roosevelt displayed American power in other parts of the world. His major concern was protecting the **Open Door** policy in China that his predecessor McKinley had engineered to secure naval access to the China market. By 1900 European powers already dominated foreign access to Chinese markets, leaving scant room for newcomers. When the United States sent 2,500 troops to China in August 1900 to help quell a nationalist uprising against foreign involvement known as the Boxer uprising, European competitors in return were compelled to allow the United States free trade access to China.

In 1904 the Russian invasion of the southern Chinese province of Manchuria prompted the Japanese to attack the Russian fleet. Roosevelt held mixed emotions about the Japanese. The president admired Japanese military prowess, but he worried that if Japan succeeded in driving the Russians out of the area, it would cause "a real shifting of equilibrium as far as the white races are concerned." To prevent that from happening, Roosevelt convened a peace conference in Portsmouth, New Hampshire, in 1905. Under the agreement reached at the conference, Japan received

DOCUMENT 20.2

Theodore Roosevelt | The Strenuous Life, 1899

Imperialists often promoted U.S. overseas expansion as a way for overly civilized men to develop their virility. In the following passage, Theodore Roosevelt urges Americans to embrace a "strenuous life," one that includes an active role for the United States in international affairs.

Explore

How can men and women contribute to the health of the nation?

On what grounds does Roosevelt criticize men who oppose American imperialism? What fears does he express about American society?

In Roosevelt's view, what is the relationship between material prosperity and a strenuous life?

We of this generation do not have to face a task such as that our fathers faced, but we have our tasks, and woe to us if we fail to perform them! We can not, if we would, play the part of China, and be content to rot by inches in ignoble ease within our borders, taking no interest in what goes on beyond them, sunk in scrambling commercialism; heedless of the higher life, the life of aspiration, of toil and risk, busying ourselves only with the wants of our bodies for the day, until suddenly we should find, beyond a shadow of question, what China has already found, that in this world the nation that has trained itself into a career of unwarlike and isolated ease is bound, in the end, to go down before other nations which have not lost the manly and adventurous qualities. If we are to be a really great people, we must strive in good faith to play a great part in the world. We can not avoid meeting great issues. All that we can determine for ourselves is whether we shall meet them well or ill. . . .

We can not avoid the responsibilities that confront us in Hawaii, Cuba, Porto Rico, and the Philippines. All we can decide is whether we shall meet them in a way that will redound to the national credit, or whether we shall make of our dealings with these new problems a dark and shameful page in our history. . . . The timid man, the lazy man, the man who distrusts his country, the overcivilized man, who has lost the great fighting, masterful values, the ignorant man, and the man of dull mind, whose soul is incapable of feeling the mighty lift that thrills "stern men with empires in their brains"—all these, of course, shrink from seeing the nation undertake its new duties; shrink from seeing us build a navy and an army adequate to our needs; shrink from seeing us do our share of the world's work, by bringing order out of chaos in the great, fair tropic islands from which the valor of our soldiers and sailors has driven the Spanish flag. These are the men who fear the strenuous life, who fear the only national life which is really worth leading. They believe in that cloistered life which saps the hardy virtues in a nation, as it saps them in the individual; or else they are wedded to that base spirit of gain and greed which recognizes commercialism the be-all and end-all of national life, instead of realizing that, though an indispensable element, it is, after all, but one of the many elements that go to make up true national greatness.

Source: Theodore Roosevelt, *The Strenuous Life* (New York: The Review of Reviews, 1910), 7–9.

Put It in Context

How did concerns over masculinity encourage U.S. imperialism?

Boxer Uprising

In 1900 the Society of Righteous and Harmonious Fists, a Chinese militaristic and secret society known as the Boxers, attacked foreign diplomatic offices in Beijing to expel outsiders. This illustration from Hunan province portrays the Boxers killing foreigners and burning Christian books. The Boxers viewed Christian missionaries as cultural enemies. A coalition of multinational forces crushed the uprising. Kharbine-Tapabor/The Art Archive at Art Resource, NY

control over Korea and parts of Manchuria but pledged to support the United States' Open Door policy. In 1906, fresh from this achievement, the president sent sixteen American battleships on a trip around the globe in a show of force meant to demonstrate that the United States was serious about taking its place as a premier world power.

When Roosevelt's secretary of war, William Howard Taft, became president (1909–1913), he continued his predecessor's foreign policy with slight modification. Proclaiming that he would rather substitute "dollars for bullets," Taft encouraged private bankers to invest money in the Caribbean and Central America. Eager to embrace the president's policy of **dollar diplomacy**, the bankers doubled their investments in the region. Yet Taft did not rely on financial influence alone. He backed up American commercial investments by dispatching more than 2,000 U.S. troops to the region to guarantee economic stability. The president sought to extend his dollar diplomacy to China by trying to weaken Russia's and Japan's hold over Manchuria, but he succeeded only in drawing the two rivals closer together.

Taft's diplomacy also led to extensive intervention in Nicaragua. In 1909 American fruit and mining companies in Nicaragua helped install a regime sympathetic to their interests. When a group of rebels threatened this pro-American government, Taft invoked the Roosevelt Corollary and sent in American marines to police the country and deter further uprisings. They remained there for another twenty-five years.

Under the U.S. occupation, American bankers took control of the country's customs houses and paid off debts owed to foreign investors, a move meant to forestall outside intervention in a nation that was now under American "protection."

REVIEW & RELATE

How did the United States assert its influence and control over Latin America in the early twentieth century?

How did U.S. policies in Latin America mirror U.S. policies in Asia?

✓ *LEARNINGCurve* bedfordstmartins.com/hewittlawson/LC

Wilson and American Foreign Policy, 1912–1917

When Woodrow Wilson became president in 1913, he pledged to open a new chapter in America's relations with Latin America and the rest of the world. The United States would continue to support order, stability, and American access to overseas markets, but it would no longer "carry a big stick." Disdaining power politics and the use of force, Wilson vowed to place diplomacy and moral persuasion at the center of American foreign policy. Diplomacy, however, proved less effective than he had hoped. Despite Wilson's stated commitment to the peaceful resolution of international issues, during his presidency the American military intervened repeatedly in Latin American affairs, and American troops fought on European soil in the bloody global conflict that contemporaries called the Great War.

Diplomacy and War

Despite his stated preference for moral diplomacy, Wilson preserved the U.S. sphere of influence in the Caribbean using much the same methods as had Roosevelt and Taft. To protect American investments from political disturbances and economic crises, the president sent marines to Haiti in 1915, to the Dominican Republic in 1916, and to Cuba in 1917.

The most serious challenge to Wilson's diplomacy came in Mexico, where he found his ideals tempered by reality. The **Mexican revolution** in 1911 spawned a civil war among various insurgent factions. The resulting instability threatened U.S. interests in Mexico, particularly oil. When Mexicans refused to accept Wilson's demands to install leaders he considered "good men," Wilson withdrew diplomatic recognition from Mexico. In a disastrous attempt to influence Mexican politics, Wilson sent the U.S. navy to the port of Veracruz on April 22, 1914, leading to a bloody clash that killed 19 Americans and 126 Mexicans. The situation worsened after Wilson first supported and then turned against one of the rebel competitors for power in Mexico, General Francisco "Pancho" Villa. In response to this betrayal, Villa and 1,500 troops rode across the border and attacked the town of Columbus, New Mexico. In July 1916, Wilson ordered General John Pershing to send 10,000 army troops three hundred miles into Mexico in an attempt to capture Villa. The operation was a complete failure that only further angered Mexican leaders and confirmed their sense that Wilson had no respect for Mexican national sovereignty. In January 1917, Wilson ordered Pershing to withdraw his troops.

The president had little choice. At the same time as the situation in Mexico was deteriorating, a much more serious problem was developing in Europe. On June 28, 1914, an ardent Serbian nationalist, intending to strike a blow against Austria-Hungary, assassinated the Austrian archduke Franz Ferdinand in Sarajevo, the capital of the province of Bosnia. This terrorist attack plunged Europe into what would become a world war, fracturing the unsteady peace that had been maintained for the previous forty years. On August 4, 1914, the Central Powers—Germany, the Ottoman empire, and Austria-Hungary—officially declared war against the Allies—Great Britain, France, and Russia (Italy joined them in 1915).

As the most powerful neutral nation, the United States looked on from afar. For the first three years of the Great War, Wilson kept the United States neutral, though privately he believed that a British defeat would be "fatal to our form of Government and American ideals."

Nevertheless, the president urged Americans to remain "in fact as well as in name impartial in thought as well as action." Peace activists sought to keep Wilson to his word. In 1915 women reformers and suffragists such as Jane Addams and Carrie Chapman Catt organized the Women's Peace Party to keep the United States out of war. One of its leaders, Lucia True Ames Mead, called replacing war with law "the most pressing reform before civilization to-day." Yet even Mead showed how difficult it was to keep a neutral mind. "There can be no peace," she exclaimed, "until the military domination of [Germany] is destroyed."

Wilson faced two key problems in keeping the country out of war. First, America had closer and more important economic ties with the Allies than with the Central Powers, a disparity that would only grow as the war went on. The Allies purchased more than $750 million in American goods in 1914, a figure that quadrupled over the next three years. By contrast, the Germans bought approximately $350 million worth of American products in 1914; by 1917 the figure had shrunk to $30 million. Moreover, when the Allies did not have the funds to pay for American goods, they sought loans from private bankers. Initially, the Wilson administration followed the wishes of Secretary of State William Jennings Bryan, who argued that providing these loans would violate "the true spirit of neutrality." In 1915, however, Wilson reversed course. Concerned that failure to keep up the prewar level of commerce with the Allies would hurt the country economically, the president authorized private loans. The gap in financial transactions with the rival war powers grew even wider; by 1917 American bankers had loaned the Allies $2.2 billion, compared with just $27 million to Germany.

The second problem facing Wilson arose from Great Britain's and Germany's differing war strategies. As the superior naval power, Britain established a blockade of the North Sea to quarantine Germany and starve it into submission. The British navy violated international law by mining the waters to bottle up the German fleet and keep foreign ships from supplying Germany with food and medicines. The blockade even ensnared U.S. ships, despite the fact that the United States, as a neutral nation, had the right to ship non-war items to Germany. However, Britain extended the list of prohibited items and hauled American vessels into British ports. Although Wilson protested this treatment, he did so weakly. He believed that the British could pay compensation for such violations of international law after the war.

Confronting a strangling blockade, Germany depended on the newly developed U-boat (*Unterseeboot*, or submarine) to counter the British navy. In February 1915, Germany declared a blockade of the British Isles and warned citizens of neutral nations to stay off British ships in the area. U-boats, which were lighter and sleeker than British battleships and merchant marine ships, relied on surprise. This strategy violated the rules of engagement under international maritime law, which required belligerent ships to allow civilians to leave passenger liners and cargo ships before firing. The British complicated the situation for the Germans by flying flags of neutral countries on merchant vessels and arming them with small "defensive" weapons. Therefore, if U-boats played by the rules and surfaced before inspecting merchant ships, they risked being blown out of the water by disguised enemy guns.

Under these circumstances, American neutrality could not last long. On May 15, 1915, catastrophe struck. Without surfacing and identifying itself, a German submarine off the Irish coast attacked the British luxury liner *Lusitania*, which had departed from New York City en route to England. Although the ship's stated objective was to provide passengers with relaxation, sumptuous dining, and dancing, its cargo contained a large supply of ammunition for British weapons. The U-boat's torpedoes rapidly sank the ship, killing 1,198 people, including 128 Americans.

Outraged Americans called on the president to respond; some, including Theodore Roosevelt, advocated the immediate use of military force. Despite his pro-British sentiments, Wilson resisted going to war. Instead, he held the Germans in "strict accountability" for their action. Appalled by the loss of human life, Wilson demanded that Germany refrain from further attacks against passenger liners and offer a financial settlement to the *Lusitania*'s survivors. Unwilling to risk war with the United States, the Germans consented.

Wilson had, however, only delayed America's entry into the war. By pursuing a policy of neutrality that treated the combatants unequally and by insisting that Americans had a right to travel on the ships of belligerent nations, the president diminished the chance that the United States would stay out of the war. Recognizing this situation, Secretary of State Bryan resigned following the *Lusitania* affair over what he considered the president's one-sided understanding of "strict accountability." Wilson quickly replaced him with a more pro-British secretary of state, Robert Lansing, who endorsed Wilson's expansion of the loan program to Britain.

Throughout 1916, Wilson pursued two separate but interrelated policies that embodied the ambivalence that he and the American people shared about the war. On the one hand, with Germany alternating between continued U-boat attacks and apologies, the president sought to build the country's military preparedness in the event of war. He signed into law the National Defense Act, which increased the size of the army, navy, and National Guard. On the other hand, Wilson stressed his desire to remain neutral and stay out of the war. With American public opinion divided on the Great War, Wilson chose to run for reelection as a peace candidate. The president sent his personal emissary, Colonel Edward House, to Europe to negotiate an armistice and end the fighting, without success. The Democrats adopted the slogan "He kept us out of war" and also emphasized the president's substantial record of progressive reform. Wilson won a narrow victory

against Charles Evans Hughes, the former governor of New York, who wavered between advocating peace and criticizing Wilson for not sufficiently supporting the Allies.

Making the World Safe for Democracy

As 1917 dawned, the Great War headed toward its third bloody year. Neither side wanted a negotiated peace because each counted on victory to gain sufficient territory and financial compensation to justify the great sacrifices in human lives and materiel caused by the conflict. Nevertheless, Wilson tried to persuade the belligerents to abandon the battlefield for the bargaining table. On January 22, 1917, he declared that the world needed a "peace without victory," one based on self-determination, freedom of the seas, respect for international law, and the end of hostile alliances. It was a generous vision from a nation that had made few sacrifices.

Germany quickly rejected Wilson's proposal. America had never been truly neutral, and Germany's increasingly desperate leaders saw no reason to believe that the situation would change. In 1915 and again in 1916, to prevent the United States from entering the war, Germany had pledged to refrain from using its most potent weapon, the U-boat, against passenger ships and merchant ships. However, the Germans now chose to change course and resume unrestricted submarine warfare, calculating that they could defeat the Allies before the United States declared war and its troops could make a substantial difference. On February 1, 1917, Germany announced that it would attack all ships, including unarmed American merchant vessels that penetrated its blockade of Great Britain. In response, Wilson used his executive power to arm merchant ships, bringing the United States one step closer to war.

The country moved even closer to war after the **Zimmermann telegram** became public. On February 24, the British turned over to Wilson an intercepted message from Arthur Zimmermann, the German foreign minister, to the Mexican government. The decoded note revealed that Germany had offered Mexico an alliance in the event that the United States joined the Allies. If the Central Powers won, Mexico would receive the territory it had lost to the United States in the mid-nineteenth century—Texas, New Mexico, and Arizona. When U.S. newspapers broke the story several days later, it inflamed public opinion and provided the Wilson administration another reason to fear a German victory.

In late February and March, German U-boats sank several armed American merchant ships, and on April 2, 1917, President Wilson asked Congress to declare war against Germany and the other Central Powers. After four days of vigorous debate led by opponents of the war— including the first female elected representative, Jeanette P. Rankin from Montana—Congress voted to approve the war resolution. However, the United States underscored its historic commitment against "entangling alliances" by refusing to officially join the Allies, instead declaring itself an "Associated Power."

Explore

See Document 20.3 for one senator's argument against going to war.

President Wilson had not reached his decision lightly. For three years, he resisted calls for war. His policies had tended to favor the Allies, but the president understood that going to war would have grave consequences. He knew that he would be sending thousands of American men to their deaths and that the "spirit of ruthless brutality [would] enter the very fiber of our national life." In the end, however, Wilson decided that only by going to war would he be able to ensure that the United States played a role in shaping the peace. For the president, the security of the nation rested on respect for law, human rights, and extension of free governments. "The world must be made safe for democracy," he informed Congress in his war message, and he had concluded that the only way to

DOCUMENT 20.3

Robert La Follette | Antiwar Speech, 1917

Wisconsin senator Robert La Follette strongly opposed America's entry into World War I. He urged Congress to reject Wilson's request for a declaration of war against Germany. In his remarks to Congress, La Follette accused Wilson of hypocrisy for arguing that the autocratic nature of the German government made friendship between the United States and Germany impossible.

Explore

Just a word of comment more upon one of the points in the President's address. He says that this is a war "for the things which we have always carried nearest to our hearts—for democracy, for the right of those who submit to authority to have a voice in their own government." In many places throughout the address is this exalted sentiment given expression.

It is a sentiment peculiarly calculated to appeal to American hearts and, when accompanied by acts consistent with it, is certain to receive our support; but in this same connection, and strangely enough, the President says that we have become convinced that the German Government as it now exists— "Prussian autocracy" he calls it—can never again maintain friendly relations with us. His expression is that "Prussian autocracy was not and could never be our friend," and repeatedly throughout the address the suggestion is made that if the German people would overturn their Government it would probably be the way to peace. So true is this that the dispatches from London all hailed the message of the President as sounding the death knell of Germany's Government.

But the President proposes alliance with Great Britain, which, however liberty-loving its people, is a hereditary monarchy, with a hereditary ruler, with a hereditary House of Lords, with a hereditary landed system, with a limited and restricted suffrage for one class and a multiplied suffrage power for another, and with grinding industrial conditions for all the wageworkers. The President has not suggested that we make our support of Great Britain conditional to her granting home rule to Ireland, or Egypt, or India. We rejoice in the establishment of a democracy in Russia, but it will hardly be contended that if Russia was still an autocratic Government, we would not be asked to enter this alliance with her just the same.

Source: *Congressional Record*, April 4, 1917, 228.

Interpret the Evidence

- How does La Follette counter Wilson's claim that America is siding with the proponents of democracy?
- What are La Follette's chief criticisms of Great Britain?

Put It in Context

Under what circumstances do you think someone like La Follette might have supported America's entry into the war?

guarantee this outcome was by helping to defeat Germany.

It would take a while for Americans to live up to the lyrics of George M. Cohan's patriotic song "Over There," which announced that "the Yanks [were] coming" to rescue the Allies from defeat. First, the United States needed a large army, which it created through the draft. The Selective Service Act of 1917 conscripted 3 million men by war's end. Mobilizing such a large force required substantial time, and American troops on the battlefield did not make much of an impact until 1918. Before then, the U.S. navy made the greatest contribution. American warships joined the British in escorting merchant vessels, combating German submarines, and laying mines in the North Sea. The United States also provided crucial funding and supplies to the Allies as their reserves became depleted.

U.S. troops finally began to make an impact in Europe in May 1918. Allied forces were exhausted and weary, and in November 1917 they had suffered a further blow when the Russian Revolution installed a Bolshevik (Communist) regime that negotiated a separate peace with the Central Powers. Fresh recruits from the United States helped shift the war toward Allied victory. From May through September, more than 1 million American troops under the command of General Pershing helped the Allies repel German offensives in northern France near the Belgian border. One momentous battle in the Argonne Forest lasted two months until the Allies broke through enemy lines and pushed toward Germany. Nearly 50,000 American troops died in the fierce fighting, and another 230,000 were injured. Like their European counterparts, who suffered a staggering 8 to 10 million casualties, Americans experienced the horrors of war magnified by new technology. Dug into filthy trenches, soldiers dodged rapid machine-gun fire, heavy artillery explosions, and poison gas shells. In the end, however, American troops succeeded in tipping the balance in favor of the Allies. On November 11, 1918, an exhausted Germany surrendered.

Trench Warfare
Trench warfare was at the center of the fighting in World War I. Both sides constructed a network of trenches and dugout shelters, fortified by barbed wire, and fought from these trenches to wear the enemy down. In this photograph, members of the 369th Infantry, a segregated African American unit nicknamed the "Harlem Hellfighters," occupy trenches to repel a German offensive into France in 1918.   The Art Archive at Art Resource, NY

REVIEW & RELATE

| In what ways, if any, did President Wilson's approach to Latin American affairs differ from that of his predecessors? | Why did President Wilson find it so difficult to keep the United States out of World War I? |

Fighting the War at Home

Modern global warfare required full mobilization at home. With U.S. ground forces entering the fray late in the war, most Americans felt the effects of mobilization far more dramatically on the home front than on the battlefront. In preparing to support the war effort, the country drew on recent experience. The progressives' passion for organization, expertise, efficiency, and moralistic control was harnessed to the effort of placing the economy on a wartime footing and rallying the American people behind the war. In the process, the government gained unprecedented control over American life. At the same time, the war effort also produced unforeseen economic and political opportunities.

Government by Commission

Progressives had relied on government commissions to regulate business practices as well as health and safety standards, and in July 1917 the Wilson administration followed suit by establishing the **War Industries Board** (**WIB**) to supervise the purchase of military supplies and to gear up private enterprise to meet demand. However, the WIB was largely ineffective until March 1918, when the president found the right man to lead it. He chose Wall Street financier Bernard Baruch, who recruited staff from business enterprises that the board regulated. Baruch prodded businesses into compliance mainly by offering lucrative contracts rather than by coercion. Working for a token $1 a year (but still on their company payrolls), the members of this agency helped reduce the chaos of mobilization. Ultimately, these businessmen created a government partnership with the corporate sector that would last beyond the war.

Labor also experienced significant gains through government regulation. Shortages of workers and an outbreak of strikes—more than four thousand in 1917—hampered the war effort. In April 1918, Wilson created the **National War Labor Board (NWLB)** to settle labor disputes. The agency consisted of representatives from unions, corporations, and the public.

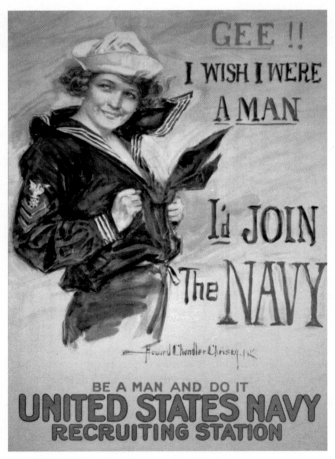

Recruitment Poster

Artist Howard Chandler Christy created this poster in 1917 to encourage enlistment in the U.S. navy. This illustration appealed to masculinity not just by showing an attractive woman but also by challenging potential recruits to "Be a Man and Do It."　Library of Congress

In exchange for obtaining a "no strike pledge" from organized labor, the NWLB supported an eight-hour workday with time-and-a-half pay for overtime, labor's right to collective bargaining, and equal pay for equal work by women.

The NWLB fell short of reaching this last goal, but the war employed more than a million women who had not held jobs before. As military and government services expanded, women found greater opportunities as telephone operators, nurses, and clerical workers. At the same time, the number of women employed as domestic servants declined. Women took over formerly male jobs driving streetcars, delivering ice, assembling airplane motors, operating drill presses, oiling railroad engines, and welding parts. Yet women's incomes continued to lag significantly behind those of men performing the same tasks.

Americans probably experienced the expanding scope of government intervention most directly through the efforts of three new agencies that regulated consumption and travel. Wilson appointed Herbert Hoover, a progressive mining engineer, to head the Food Administration. Hoover sought to increase the military and civilian food supply mainly through voluntary conservation measures. He generated a massive publicity campaign urging Americans to adopt "wheatless Mondays," "meatless Tuesdays," and "porkless Thursdays and Saturdays." Chicago housewives demonstrated their ingenuity in cooking leftovers, as evidenced by a sharp decline in the volume of raw garbage in the city. The government also mobilized schoolchildren to plant vegetable gardens to increase food production for the home front. Wilson considered children's work in the School Garden Army "just as real and patriotic an effort as the building of ships or the firing of cannon."

Consumers saved gas and oil under the prodding of the Fuel Administration. The agency encouraged fuel "holidays" along the line of Hoover's voluntary restrictions and created daylight saving time to conserve fuel by adding an extra hour of sunlight to the end of the workday. The Fuel Administration also offered higher prices to coal companies in order to increase productivity. Patterns of consumer travel changed under government regulation. The Railroad Administration acted more forcefully than most other agencies. Troop and supply shipments depended on the efficient operation of the railways. The administration controlled the railroads during the war, coordinating train schedules, overseeing terminals and regulating ticket prices, upgrading tracks, and raising workers' wages.

Winning Hearts and Minds

America's entry into the Great War did not immediately end the significant antiwar sentiment. Consequently, Wilson waged a campaign to rally support for his aims and to stimulate patriotic fervor. To generate enthusiasm and ensure loyalty, the president appointed Denver journalist George Creel to head the **Committee on Public Information (CPI)**, which focused on generating propaganda. Creel recruited a vast network of lecturers to speak throughout the country and spread patriotic messages. The committee coordinated rallies to sell bonds and raise money to fund the war. The CPI persuaded reporters to censor their war coverage, and most agreed in order to avoid government intervention. The agency helped produce films depicting the Allies as heroic saviors of humanity and the Central Powers as savage beasts. The CPI also distributed colorful and sometimes lurid posters emphasizing the depravity of the enemy and the nation's moral responsibility to defeat the Central Powers. All the talk of fighting for democracy encouraged groups with long-standing grievances because of their treatment at home to rally around the flag. W. E. B. Du Bois, one of the founders of the NAACP, backed Wilson's democratic aims in the hope that the war would lead to racial equality in the United States.

Explore

See Documents 20.4 and 20.5 for Du Bois's thoughts on supporting the war.

Propaganda did not, however, prove sufficient, and many Americans remained deeply divided about the war. To suppress dissent, Congress passed the Espionage Act in 1917 and the Sedition Act a year later. Both limited freedom of speech by criminalizing certain forms of expression. The **Espionage Act** prohibited antiwar activities, including interfering with the draft. It also banned the mailing of publications advocating forcible interference with any laws. The **Sedition Act** punished individuals who expressed beliefs disloyal or abusive to the American government, flag, or military uniform. Of the slightly more than two thousand prosecutions under these laws, only a handful concerned charges of actual sabotage or espionage. Most defendants brought to trial were critics who merely spoke out against the war. In 1918, for telling a crowd that the military draft was a form of slavery that turned inductees into "cannon fodder," the Socialist Party's Eugene V. Debs was tried, convicted, and sentenced to ten years under the Espionage Act. (President Warren G. Harding pardoned Debs in 1921.) The Justice Department also went after the Industrial Workers of the World (IWW), which continued to initiate labor strikes during the war. The government broke into the offices of the IWW, ransacked the Wobblies' files for evidence of disloyalty, and arrested more than 130 members, including their dynamic leader Big Bill Haywood, who subsequently fled to the Soviet Union to avoid jail.

Government efforts to promote national unity and punish those who did not conform prompted local communities to enforce "one hundred percent Americanism." Civic groups banned the playing of German music and operas from concert halls, and schools prohibited teaching the German language. Arbiters of culinary taste, prompted by patriotic enthusiasm, renamed foods with German origins—sauerkraut became "liberty cabbage," and hamburgers became "liberty sandwiches." Such sentiments were expressed in a more sinister fashion when mobs assaulted German Americans.

Prejudice toward German Americans was further inflamed by the formation of the **American Protective League (APL)**, a quasi-official association endorsed by the Justice Department. Consisting of 200,000 chapters throughout the country, the APL employed individuals to spy on German residents suspected of disloyal behavior. In cooperation with the Bureau of Investigation (later the FBI), APL members tried to uncover German spies, but most often they found little more than German immigrants who merely retained attachments to family and friends in their homeland. Gossip and rumor fueled many of the league's loyalty probes. In May 1918, the APL sent one of its agents to investigate the cook of a family living in Manhattan, because she allegedly had "a picture of the Kaiser in her room" and was "very pro-German and talks in favor of the Germans." The investigator found no photograph of the kaiser or any other evidence of suspicious behavior.

The repressive side of progressivism came to the fore in other ways as well. Anti-immigrant bias, shared by many reformers, flourished. The effort to conserve manpower and grain supplies bolstered the impulse to control standards of moral behavior, particularly those associated with immigrants, such as drinking. This anti-immigrant prejudice in part explains the ratification of the Eighteenth Amendment in 1919, prohibiting the sale of all alcoholic beverages. Yet not all the moral indignation unleashed by the war resulted in restriction of freedom. After considerable wartime protest and lobbying, women suffragists succeeded in securing the right to vote (see chapter 19).

Waging Peace

In January 1918, ten months before the war ended, President Wilson presented Congress with his plan for peace without rancor. Wilson centered his ideas around **Fourteen Points**, principles that he hoped would prevent future wars. Based on his assessment of the causes of the Great War, Wilson envisioned a generous peace treaty that included freedom of the seas, open diplomacy and the abolition of secret treaties, free trade, self-determination for colonial subjects, and a

DOCUMENTS 20.4 AND 20.5

African Americans and the War: Two Views

African Americans played an active role in the war effort; however, given their poor treatment by much of white America, it is not surprising that many blacks were ambivalent about their service. In a controversial editorial in the *Crisis*, the journal of the NAACP, W. E. B. Du Bois urged the black community to "close ranks" with the rest of American society to fight Germany. Du Bois hoped that their service would lead to greater acceptance for African Americans by white society. Less than a year later, Du Bois published a bitter attack against the treatment of African American soldiers and enduring American racism.

Explore

20.4 W. E. B. Du Bois | "Close Ranks," 1918

This is the crisis of the world. For all the long years to come men will point to the year 1918 as the great Day of Decision, the day when the world decided whether it would submit to military despotism and an endless armed peace—if peace it could be called—or whether they would put down the menace of German militarism and inaugurate the United States of the World.

We of the colored race have no ordinary interest in the outcome. That which the German power represents today spells death to the aspirations of Negroes and all darker races for equality, freedom, and democracy. Let us not hesitate. Let us, while this war lasts, forget our special grievances and close our ranks shoulder to shoulder with our own white fellow citizens and the allied nations that are fighting for democracy. We make no ordinary sacrifice, but we make it gladly and willingly with our eyes lifted to the hills.

Source: W. E. B. Du Bois, "Close Ranks," *The Crisis*, July 1918, 111.

reduction in military spending. More important than any specific measure, Wilson's proposal hinged on the creation of the **League of Nations**, a body of large and small nations that would guarantee peaceful resolution of disputes and back up decisions through collective action, including the use of military force as a last resort.

Following the armistice that ended the war on November 11, 1918, Wilson personally took his message to the Paris Peace Conference, the postwar meeting of the victorious Allied nations that would set the terms of the peace. The first sitting president to travel overseas, Wilson was greeted in Paris by joyous crowds when he arrived leading the American delegation.

For nearly six months, Wilson tried to convince reluctant Allied leaders to accept the central components of his plan. Having exhausted themselves financially and having suffered the loss of a generation of young men, the Allies intended to scoop up the spoils of victory and make the Central Powers pay dearly. The European Allies intended to hold on to their respective colonies regardless of Wilson's

call for self-determination, and as a nation that depended on a strong navy, Britain refused to limit its options by discussing freedom of the seas. Perhaps Georges Clemenceau, France's president, best expressed his colleagues' skepticism about Wilson's idealistic vision: "President Wilson and his Fourteen Points bore me. Even God Almighty has only ten!"

During the conference, Wilson was forced to compromise on a number of his principles in order to retain the cornerstone of his diplomacy—the establishment of the League of Nations. He abandoned his hope for peace without bitterness by agreeing to a "war guilt" clause that levied huge economic reparations on Germany for starting the war. He was willing to sacrifice some of his ideals because the league took on even greater importance in the wake of the Communist revolution in Russia. The president believed that capitalism, as regulated and reformed during the Progressive Era, would raise living conditions throughout the world as it had done in the United States, would prevent the spread of communism, and would benefit U.S. commerce by paving the way to free trade. Wilson needed the league to keep the peace so that war-ravaged and

Explore

20.5 W. E. B. Du Bois | "Returning Soldiers," 1919

We are returning from war! . . .

. . . We return from the slavery of uniform which the world's madness demanded us to don to the freedom of civil garb. We stand again to look America squarely in the face and call a spade a spade. We sing: This country of ours, despite all its better souls have done and dreamed, is yet a shameful land.

It *lynches*. . . .

It *disfranchises* its own *citizens*. . . .

It encourages *ignorance*. . . .

It *steals* from us. . . .

It *insults* us. . . .

This is the country to which we Soldiers of Democracy return. This is the fatherland for which we fought! But it is *our* fatherland. It was right for us to fight. The faults of *our* country are *our* faults. Under similar circumstances, we would fight again. But by the God of Heaven, we are cowards and jackasses if now that that war is over, we do not marshal every ounce of our brain and brawn to fight a sterner, longer, more unbending battle against the forces of hell in our own land.

We *return*.

We *return from fighting*.

We *return fighting*.

Make way for Democracy! We saved it in France, and by the Great Jehovah, we will save it in the United States of America, or know the reason why.

Source: W. E. B. Du Bois, "Returning Soldiers," *The Crisis*, May 1919, 13–14.

Interpret the Evidence

- In both articles, how does Du Bois explain why African Americans fought in World War I?
- What did Du Bois see as the greatest threat to the black community in 1918? What about in 1919? Why do you think Du Bois reversed his position?

Put It in Context

What do both these editorials reveal about the treatment of black Americans during World War I?

recovering nations had the opportunity to practice economic freedom and political democracy. In the end, the president won agreement for the establishment of his cherished League of Nations. The final treaty signed at the palace of Versailles, just outside Paris, authorized the league to combat aggression against any member nation through collective military action.

The Failure of Ratification

In July 1919, after enduring bruising battles in Paris, Wilson returned to Washington, D.C., only to face another wrenching struggle in the Senate over ratification of the Versailles treaty. The odds were stacked against Wilson from the start. The Republicans held a majority in the Senate, and Wilson needed the support of two-thirds of the Senate to secure ratification. Moreover, Henry Cabot Lodge, the Republican chairman of the Senate Foreign Relations Committee, opposed Article X of the League of Nations covenant, which sanctioned collective security arrangements against military aggression. Lodge argued that such an alliance compromised

the United States' independence in conducting its own foreign relations. The Massachusetts senator wanted the United States to preserve the possibility of unilateral action without being restrained by the league's policies. Lodge had at least thirty-nine senators behind him, more than enough to block ratification. Conceding the need to protect the country's national self-interest, the president agreed to modifications to the treaty so that the Monroe Doctrine and America's obligations in the Caribbean and Central America were kept intact. Lodge, who loathed Wilson, was not satisfied and insisted on adding fourteen "reservations" limiting compliance with the treaty, including strong language affirming Congress's right to declare war before agreeing to a League of Nations military action.

Wilson's stubbornness more than equaled Lodge's, and the president refused to compromise further over the league. Insisting that he was morally bound to honor the treaty he had negotiated in good faith, Wilson rejected additional changes demanded by Lodge and his supporters. Making matters worse, Wilson faced resistance from sixteen lawmakers dubbed "irreconcilables," who opposed the league under any circumstances. Mainly Republicans from the Midwest and West, they voiced the traditional American rejection of entangling alliances.

To break the logjam, the president attempted to rally public opinion behind him. In September 1919, he embarked on a nationwide speaking tour to carry his message directly to the American people. Over a three-week period, he traveled eight thousand miles by train, keeping a grueling schedule that exhausted him. After a stop in Pueblo, Colorado, on September 25, Wilson collapsed and canceled the rest of his trip. On October 2, Wilson suffered a massive stroke that nearly killed him. The effects of the stroke, which left him partially paralyzed, emotionally unstable, and mentally impaired, dimmed any remaining hopes of compromise. The full extent of his illness was kept from the public, and his wife, Edith, ran the White House for the next eighteen months.

On November 19, 1919, the Senate rejected the amended treaty. The following year, Wilson had one final chance to obtain ratification, but still he refused to accept reservations. He ignored leaders of his own party who were willing to vote for the Republican-sponsored amendments. "Let Lodge compromise," the president responded defiantly. In March 1920, treaty ratification failed one last time, falling just seven votes short of the required two-thirds majority. Had Wilson shown the same willingness to compromise that he had in Paris, the outcome might have been different. In the end, however, the United States never signed the Treaty of Versailles or joined the League of Nations, weakening the league and diminishing the prospects for long-term peace.

REVIEW & RELATE

What steps did the U.S. government take to control the economy and public opinion during World War I?

How did President Wilson's wartime policies and his efforts to shape the peace that followed reflect his progressive roots?

LEARNINGCurve bedfordstmartins.com/hewittlawson/LC

Conclusion: An American Empire

In the final decade of the nineteenth century, the United States transformed itself into an imperial power. Presidents McKinley and Roosevelt carried out the strategy outlined by Captain Alfred Thayer Mahan to enlarge the navy, construct a canal linking the Atlantic and Pacific Oceans, and acquire coaling stations and bases in the Pacific to service the fleet. U.S. officials disregarded the nationalistic aspirations of freedom fighters such as José Martí in Cuba and Emilio Aguinaldo in the Philippines in favor of the imperial spoils gained from winning the War of 1898. The United States justified intervention on moral grounds predicated on racist beliefs: As a fit and manly nation, the United States had the responsibility to uplift inferior peoples to "civilized" standards and make them capable of self-government. This justification quickly wore thin. To crush the rebellion in the Philippines, the military engaged in atrocities that called into question the honor and virtue of the United States. Once it achieved victory in the Philippines, the nation concentrated its efforts on maintaining territories primarily for commercial purposes. Within the few short years from 1898 to 1904, this commercial empire had fallen into place.

The progressive presidents, Roosevelt and Wilson, created and sustained an American empire. They disagreed significantly in approach—Roosevelt favoring force, Wilson preferring negotiations; Roosevelt a realist, Wilson a moralist—but in practice they shared a willingness to use military power to protect national interests. These two presidents helped construct the modern American state, an expanded federal government that officially sanctioned cooperation with responsible corporate leaders. This relationship reached its peak during World War I. In mobilizing the home front, the Wilson administration blurred the line between public and private business by expanding the reach of government over the economy and curtailed personal liberty.

In 1917, because of its heavy reliance on trade with foreign countries, especially in Europe, the United States confronted its first major international crisis of the twentieth century. Wilson reluctantly led the country into war to guarantee a world order in which reasonable nations attempted to resolve controversies through negotiation, not violence. The failure of the United States to join the League of Nations, for which the president was largely responsible, shattered that idealistic dream.

The United States retreated from joining an international body offering collective security, but it did not isolate itself from participation in the world. The country emerged from the war in excellent financial shape; it had become the leading foreign creditor, and its industrial capacity had greatly expanded. Tending its commercial empire in the Caribbean and Central America, the United States probed for new markets in Asia and the Middle East. It would take another two decades for policymakers to realize that the country's refusal to support a strong collective response to expansionist aggression posed serious dangers for American commerce and values.

LEARNINGCurve
Check what you know.
bedfordstmartins.com/hewittlawson/LC

Chapter Review

Online Study Guide ► bedfordstmartins.com/hewittlawson

KEY TERMS

jingoists (p. 624)
Cuba Libre (p. 626)
yellow journalism (p. 627)
Teller Amendment (p. 628)
Platt Amendment (p. 628)
Anti-Imperialist League (p. 628)
Roosevelt Corollary (p. 631)
Open Door (p. 631)
dollar diplomacy (p. 633)
Mexican revolution (p. 634)
Zimmermann telegram (p. 635)
War Industries Board (WIB) (p. 637)
National War Labor Board (NWLB) (p. 638)
Committee on Public Information (CPI) (p. 639)
Espionage Act (p. 639)
Sedition Act (p. 639)
American Protective League (APL) (p. 639)
Fourteen Points (p. 639)
League of Nations (p. 640)

REVIEW & RELATE

1. What role did economic developments play in prompting calls for an American empire? What role did social and cultural developments play?

2. Why did the United States embark on building an empire in the 1890s and not decades earlier?

3. Why did the United States go to war with Spain in 1898?

4. In what ways did the War of 1898 mark a turning point in the relationship between the United States and the rest of the world?

5. How did the United States assert its influence and control over Latin America in the early twentieth century?

6. How did U.S. policies in Latin America mirror U.S. policies in Asia?

7. In what ways, if any, did President Wilson's approach to Latin American affairs differ from that of his predecessors?

8. Why did President Wilson find it so difficult to keep the United States out of World War I?

9. What steps did the U.S. government take to control the economy and public opinion during World War I?

10. How did President Wilson's wartime policies and his efforts to shape the peace that followed reflect his progressive roots?

TIMELINE OF EVENTS

1880–1900	U.S. creates third most powerful navy in the world
1890	Alfred Mahan publishes *The Influence of Sea Power upon History*
1893	American plantation owners overthrow Queen Liliuokalani of Hawaii
1895	Cuban War for Independence begins
1898	U.S. battleship *Maine* explodes
	The War of 1898 begins
	Anti-Imperialist League founded
1899–1902	Philippine-American War
1901	Platt Amendment passed
1904	Roosevelt Corollary announced
1909	U.S. intervenes in Nicaragua on behalf of American fruit and mining companies
1914	Panama Canal opens under American control
	World War I begins
1915	German submarine sinks the *Lusitania*
1916	Wilson sends U.S. troops into Mexico to capture Pancho Villa
1917	Zimmermann telegram becomes public
	United States enters World War I
	Espionage Act passed
	War Industries Board established
	Committee on Public Information established
1918	Sedition Act passed
	National War Labor Board established
	Germany surrenders, ending World War I
1919	Wilson loses battle for ratification of Treaty of Versailles

DOCUMENT PROJECT 20

Imperialism versus Anti-Imperialism

On January 16, 1893, the USS *Boston* sailed into Honolulu harbor, in a show of support for American businessmen who were aligned against Queen Liliuokalani, Hawaii's ruling monarch. Liliuokalani sought to overturn the 1887 constitution that had been forced on King Kalākaua. This "Bayonet Constitution," as it came to be known, favored American and other foreign interests and limited the political power of native islanders, the poor, and the monarchy. The day after American forces landed, Liliuokalani abdicated and a provisional government, the Republic of Hawaii, was set up under the control of American sugar growers. Native Hawaiians continued to rebel against their American-dominated government, and in 1897 representatives from several political groups issued the Hawaiian Memorial (Document 20.6). This petition for self-rule failed, and Hawaii was formally annexed in 1898. In that same year, U.S. territorial acquisitions from the War of 1898 intensified the heated debate over American imperialism and the principles of self-governance and democracy.

The following documents reveal the viewpoints of imperialists, anti-imperialists, and colonized people. Those supporting imperialism could find no greater advocate than Senator Albert Beveridge of Indiana, who served from 1899 to 1911. His speech entitled "The March of the Flag," compared Philippine colonization to U.S. westward expansion across North America and argued that Filipinos were a childlike and savage race incapable of self-governance (Document 20.7). A different view of the Philippine conflict came from a New Hampshire woman who in 1899 wrote to her local newspaper to scold American women for failing to speak out against the "murderous, cowardly, dastardly war" in the Philippines (Document 20.9). Throughout this period—on the Senate floor and in town meeting halls, schoolrooms, national magazines, and local newspapers—Americans deliberated the significance and implications of international expansion.

DOCUMENT 20.6

The Hawaiian Memorial, 1897

Hawaiian political groups sent the following petition (also called a memorial) to the U.S. government as a formal request to remove the provisional government of the Hawaiian Islands, which they viewed as illegitimate. Although the U.S. Senate initially refused to ratify President McKinley's effort to annex Hawaii in 1897, the following year Congress adopted a joint resolution annexing Hawaii as a territory.

To the President, the Congress, and the People of the United States of America:

This Memorial respectfully represents as follows:

1. That your memorialists are residents of the Hawaiian Islands; that the majority of them are aboriginal Hawaiians; and that all of them possess the qualifications provided for electors of representatives in the Hawaiian Legislature by the Constitution and laws prevailing in the Hawaiian Islands at the date of the overthrow of the Hawaiian Constitutional Government, January 17, 1893.

2. That the supporters of the Hawaiian Constitution of 1887 have been, thence to the present time, in the year 1897, held in subjection by the armed forces of the Provisional Government of the Hawaiian Islands, and of its successor, the Republic of Hawaii, and have never yielded and do not acknowledge a spontaneous or willing allegiance or support to said Provisional Government, or to said Republic of Hawaii.

3. That the Government of the Republic of Hawaii has no warrant for its existence in the support of the people of these islands; that it was proclaimed and instituted and has hitherto existed and now exists without considering the rights and wishes of a great majority of the residents, native and foreign-born, of the Hawaiian Islands; and especially that said Government exists and maintains itself solely by force of arms, against the rights and wishes of almost the entire aboriginal population of these islands.

4. That said Republic is not and never has been founded or conducted upon a basis of popular government or republican principles; that its Constitution was adopted by a convention, a majority of whose members were self-appointed, and the balance of whose members were elected by a numerically insignificant minority of the white and aboriginal male citizens and residents of these islands. . . .

5. That the Constitution so adopted by said convention has never been submitted to a vote of the people of these islands, but was promulgated and established over the said islands, and has ever since been maintained only by force of arms, and with indifference to the will of practically the entire aboriginal population, and a vast majority of the whole population of these islands.

6. That the said Government, so existing under the title of the Republic of Hawaii, assumes and asserts the right to extinguish the Hawaiian nationality, heretofore existing, and to cede and convey all rights of sovereignty in and over the Hawaiian Islands and their dependencies to a foreign power, namely, to the United States of America.

7. That your memorialists have learned with grief and dismay that the President of the United States has entered into, and submitted for ratification by the United States Senate, a treaty with the Government of the Republic of Hawaii, whereby it is proposed to extinguish our existence as a nation, and to annex our territory to the United States. . . .

9. That your memorialists humbly but fervently protest against the consummation of this invasion of their political rights; and they earnestly appeal to the President, the Congress, and the people of the United States to refrain from further participating in the wrong so proposed; and they invoke in support of

(continued on page 646)

this memorial the spirit of that immortal instrument, the Declaration of American Independence; and especially the truth therein expressed, that governments derive their just powers from the consent of the governed—and here repeat that the consent of the people of the Hawaiian Islands to the forms of government imposed by the so-called Republic of Hawaii, and to said proposed treaty of annexation, has never been asked by and is not accorded, either to said government or to said project of annexation.

10. That the consummation of the project of annexation dealt with in said treaty would be subversive of the personal and political rights of these memorialists and of the Hawaiian people and nation. . . .

11. Wherefore your memorialists respectfully submit that they, no less than the citizens of any American Commonwealth, are entitled to select, ordain, and establish for themselves such forms of government as to them shall seem most likely to effect their safety and happiness. . . .

12. And your memorialists humbly pray the President, Congress, and the people of the United States that no further steps be taken toward the ratification of said treaty, or toward the extinguishment of the Hawaiian nationality, or toward the absorption of the Hawaiian people and territory into the body politic and territory of the United States of America, at least until the Hawaiian people, as represented by those citizens and residents of the Hawaiian Islands who, under the provisions of the Hawaiian Constitution, promulgated July 7, 1887, would be qualified to vote for representatives in the Legislature, shall have had the opportunity to express, at the ballot-box, their wishes as to whether such project of annexation shall be accepted or rejected.

13. And your memorialists, for themselves, and in behalf of the Hawaiian people and of the residents of the Hawaiian Islands, pledge their faith that if they shall be accorded the privilege of voting upon said questions, at a free and fair election to be held for that purpose, and if a fair count of the votes that shall be cast at such election shall show a majority in favor of such annexation, these memorialists and the Hawaiian people will yield a ready and cheerful acquiescence in said project.

Signed

J. Kalua Kahookano, Samuel K. Pua, F. J. Testa, C. B. Maile, Samuel K. Kamakaia, Citizens' Committee

James Keauiluna Kaulia, President of the Hawaiian Patriotic League

David Kalauokalani, President of the Hawaiian Political Association

Source: "The Hawaiian Memorial," *City and State*, December 2, 1897, 143.

DOCUMENT 20.7

Albert Beveridge | The March of the Flag, 1898

In September 1898, Albert Beveridge, who was campaigning to become U.S. senator from Indiana, gave a rousing speech supporting the annexation of Spain's former colonies. At the time of this address, the war with Spain had ended, but American troops still occupied the Philippines. Once in office, Beveridge was an ardent supporter of American imperial policies.

Hawaii is ours; Porto Rico is to be ours; at the prayer of her people Cuba finally will be ours; in the islands of the East, even to the gates of Asia, coaling stations are to be ours at the very least; the flag of a liberal government is to float over the Philippines, and may it be the banner that [Zachary] Taylor unfurled in Texas and [John] Fremont carried to the coast.

The Opposition tells us that we ought not to govern a people without their consent. I answer, the rule of liberty that all just government derives its authority from the consent of the governed, applies only to those who are capable of self-government. We govern the Indians without their consent, we govern our territories without their consent, we govern our children without their consent. How do they know [what] our government would be without their consent? Would not the people of the Philippines prefer the just, humane, civilizing government of this Republic to the savage, bloody rule of pillage and extortion from which we have rescued them?

And, regardless of this formula of words made only for enlightened, self-governing people, do we owe no duty to the world? Shall we turn these peoples back to the reeking hands from which we have taken them? Shall we abandon them, with Germany, England, Japan, hungering for them? Shall we save them from those nations, to give them a self-rule of tragedy?

They ask us how we shall govern these new possessions. I answer: Out of local conditions and the necessities of the case, methods of government will grow. If England can govern foreign lands, so can America. If Germany can govern foreign lands, so can America. If they can supervise protectorates, so can America. Why is it more difficult to administer Hawaii than New Mexico or California? Both had a savage and an alien population; both were more remote from the seat of government when they came under our dominion than the Philippines are today.

Will you say by your vote that American ability to govern has decayed; that a century's experience in self-rule has failed of a result? Will you affirm by your vote that you are an infidel to American power and practical sense? Or will you say that ours is the blood of government; ours the heart of dominion; ours the brain and genius of administration? Will you remember that we do but what our fathers did—we but pitch the tents of liberty farther westward, farther southward—we only continue the march of the flag?

The march of the flag! In 1789 the flag of the Republic waved over 4,000,000 souls in thirteen states, and their savage territory which stretched to the Mississippi, to Canada, to the Floridas. The timid minds of that day said that no new territory was needed, and, for the hour, they were right. But Jefferson, through whose intellect the centuries marched; Jefferson, who dreamed of Cuba as an American state; Jefferson, the first Imperialist of the Republic—Jefferson acquired that imperial territory which swept from the Mississippi to the mountains, from Texas to the British possessions, and the march of the flag began!

The infidels to the gospel of liberty raved, but the flag swept on! The title to that noble land out of which Oregon, Washington, Idaho, and Montana have been carved was uncertain; Jefferson, strict constructionist of constitutional power though he was, obeyed the Anglo-Saxon impulse within him, whose watchword then and whose watchword throughout the world today is, "Forward!": another empire was added to the Republic, and the march of the flag went on! . . .

(continued on page 648)

The ocean does not separate us from lands of our duty and desire—the oceans join us, rivers never to be dredged, canals never to be repaired. Steam joins us; electricity joins us—the very elements are in league with our destiny. Cuba not contiguous! Porto Rico not contiguous! Hawaii and the Philippines not contiguous! The oceans make them contiguous. And our navy will make them contiguous.

But the Opposition is right—there is a difference. We did not need the western Mississippi Valley when we acquired it, nor Florida, nor Texas, nor California, nor the royal provinces of the far northwest. We had no emigrants to people this imperial wilderness, no money to develop it, even no highways to cover it. No trade awaited us in its savage fastnesses [remote places]. Our productions were not greater than our trade. There was not one reason for the land-lust of our statesmen from Jefferson to Grant, other than the prophet and the Saxon within them. But, today, we are raising more than we can consume, making more than we can use. Therefore we must find new markets for our produce.

And so, while we did not need the territory taken during the past century at the time it was acquired, we do need what we have taken in 1898, and we need it now. The resources and the commerce of these immensely rich dominions will be increased as much as American energy is greater than Spanish sloth. In Cuba, alone, there are 15,000,000 acres of forest unacquainted with the ax, exhaustless mines of iron, priceless deposits of manganese, millions of dollars' worth of which we must buy, today, from the Black Sea districts. There are millions of acres yet unexplored.

The resources of Porto Rico have only been trifled with. The riches of the Philippines have hardly been touched by the fingertips of modern methods. And they produce what we consume, and consume what we produce—the very predestination of reciprocity—a reciprocity "not made with hands, eternal in the heavens." They sell hemp, sugar, cocoanuts, fruits of the tropics, timber of price like mahogany; they buy flour, clothing, tools, implements, machinery, and all that we can raise and make. Their trade will be ours in time. Do you indorse that policy with your vote?

Source: Albert J. Beveridge, *The Meaning of the Times and Other Speeches* (Indianapolis: Bobbs-Merrill, 1908), 48–50, 52–53.

DOCUMENT 20.8

"There's Plenty of Room at the Table," 1906

The satirical weekly magazine *Judge* was a strong supporter of President McKinley and the Republican Party. Its illustrations often depicted imperial expansion as good for the American public as well as for colonized nations.

THERE'S PLENTY OF ROOM AT THE TABLE. WHY NOT ASK THE HUNGRY LITTLE FELLOW TO SIT DOWN?

DOCUMENT 20.9

Anti-Imperialism Letter, 1899

What began in 1898 as a conflict to free the Philippines from Spanish control quickly became a struggle to subdue Filipino rebels intent on establishing their own government. The following letter was written to the *Springfield (Massachusetts) Republican* just one month after the new Philippine Republic declared war on the United States. The brutality of the fighting caused many Americans to question the motives and methods of American imperial aspirations.

To The Editor of the Republican:

I cannot longer hold my peace, though only a woman. I am thankful to see today that the business men (some of them, I should say) have started a plan for the cessation of this murderous, cowardly, dastardly war. Also I saw yesterday that Gamaliel Bradford [an American writer and poet] has volunteered to speak in the same just and holy cause wheresoever needed. This is the thing I have longed to see done weeks and weeks ago. The "peace" treaty never would have been ratified if the nation had been waked up to the meaning of its iniquity. Speaking everywhere is needed, such as we had at the beginning of the civil war, giving light to the thousands that now do not care. "It is no business of theirs." "Congress will take care," they say, reading the papers that hurrah for McKinley. What do they know about it? They don't feel the burden much yet. Taxes are bad enough, but those that must come with the McKinley policy long continued, they don't feel yet. It is healthy for all they see out there, none of theirs have died, and it's only the Filipinos mostly that are killed: and we are to be a "bigger country." What the whole country needs is to rouse the people, that they demand that this sin shall cease, that America's shame may be wiped out ere it is too late!

I blush for my sisters who call themselves "Colonial Dames," "Daughters of the Revolution," "Abraham Lincoln circle of the Ladies of the Grand Army," and such patriotic sounding titles, where is their claim to such? In all these months of anxiety and anguish never one word of protest have I heard of their breathing! They have gathered for various social reasons and held good times, but the solemn duties and responsibilities that should be their first concern seem to have been utterly ignored. Cannot they be induced to begin likewise an appeal in every place where their orders exist, signed by every woman who has at heart the love of her country and its true honor. Only that something should be done! While we wait the islanders are being murdered by hundreds and a price put on the head of their brave leader!

J. W. P.

Source: Letter to the editor, *Springfield Republican*, March 16, 1899.

DOCUMENT 20.10

"Civilization Begins at Home," 1898

Newspapers and magazines waged their own battles for and against U.S. expansion overseas. The *New York World* built its circulation through sensationalism and the extensive use of illustrations. This cartoon from the *World* questions the imperialist mission to spread the benefits of civilization to "uncivilized" parts of the world. While President McKinley contemplates a map of the Philippines, Lady Justice reveals racial problems at home.

"CIVILIZATION BEGINS AT HOME."   *THE WORLD — NEW YORK*

General Research Division, The New York Public Library, Astor, Lenox and Tilden Foundations

Interpret the Evidence

1. Why do the petitioners of the Hawaiian Memorial (Document 20.6) claim that the provisional government is illegitimate? How do they describe their government and people before annexation, and how do they characterize the United States?

2. Why does Albert Beveridge claim that it is the United States' duty to colonize the Philippines, and what does he think are the benefits to Americans and Filipinos (Document 20.7)? How does he respond to the anti-imperialist argument that America shouldn't govern a people without their consent?

3. What common arguments against American colonization connect the Hawaiian Memorial (Document 20.6), the letter from J. W. P. (Document 20.9), and the cartoon "Civilization Begins at Home" (Document 20.10)?

4. How do imperialists and anti-imperialists portray each other in these documents?

5. How are the sentiments of Rudyard Kipling (Document 20.1) and Theodore Roosevelt (Document 20.2) echoed in these imperialist arguments?

6. How did imperialists and anti-imperialists shape their arguments to appeal to either men or women?

Put It in Context

• Why did the arguments of the imperialists prevail over those of anti-imperialists from 1898 to 1904? In what ways do you think the anti-imperialist arguments might have contributed to reshaping the imperialist cause after that time?

background photo: page 648, Library of Congress

The Granger Collection, New York

The Granger Collection, New York

Three women strolling on Seventh Avenue in Harlem, 1927.

Cover of *Vanity Fair* magazine, December 1927.

21

An Anxious Affluence

1919–1929

Library of Congress

Prohibition agents pouring out liquor in New York City, c. 1921.

David Curtis (D. C.) Stephenson's relentless pursuit of the American dream kept him constantly on the move. Born in 1891 to Texas sharecroppers, Stephenson moved with his family to the Oklahoma Territory in 1901. After quitting school at age sixteen, he drifted around the state for more than a decade, working for a string of newspapers and gaining a reputation as a heavy drinker and a ladies' man. In 1915 he married and appeared to settle down; however, he soon lost his newspaper job, abandoned his pregnant wife, and hit the road working for one newspaper after another in between binges of drunkenness. His wife divorced him, and in 1917 Stephenson joined the army to fight in World War I. He was stationed stateside, but his service was marked by a series of drunken brawls and sexual misadventures. Nevertheless, he rose to the rank of second lieutenant and received an honorable discharge in 1919.

Stephenson remarried and settled in Indiana, where he finally found financial and political success. In 1920 he joined the Ku Klux Klan (KKK), the Reconstruction-era organization that had reemerged in 1915 in Georgia. The newly revived Klan spread beyond the South, targeting African Americans, recent immigrants, Jews, and Catholics as enemies of traditional Protestant family values. Stephenson directed Klan operations in twenty-three states, building a profitable empire on fear and prejudice as well as get-rich-quick schemes that appealed to the spirit of American adventure. A few years later, however, his old pattern of self-destruction led to his arrest and conviction on rape and second-degree murder charges and the end of his Klan career.

Ossian Sweet also pursued the American dream. Like Stephenson, he rose from humble beginnings, but he had far more to overcome. The descendant of slaves, Sweet was born in 1895 and grew up in the central Florida town of Bartow. Hoping to shield him from the violence that whites used to keep Bartow's blacks in their place, Sweet's parents sent him north when he was thirteen years old to get an education.

After attending Wilberforce University in Ohio and Howard Medical School in Washington, D.C., Sweet moved to Detroit in 1921 to open a medical practice in the city's ghetto known as "Black Bottom." He married, and in 1924 the Sweets decided to buy a house for their growing family, which now included an infant daughter, in a working-class neighborhood occupied exclusively by whites. Before the Sweets moved in, their white neighbors, with Klan backing, began organizing to keep them out.

When the Sweet family finally moved into their house on September 8, 1925, they encountered a hostile crowd in the street. Dr. Sweet had brought some backup with him, including two of his younger brothers and several friends. Armed in case the mob got out of hand, the Sweets and their defenders fired their weapons at the crowd after rocks smashed through the upstairs windows of the house. When the shooting stopped and the police restored calm, one white man lay dead and another wounded. Dr. Sweet, his wife Gladys, and the other nine occupants of his house went on trial on first-degree murder charges. The NAACP represented the eleven defendants and hired the famous criminal defense attorney Clarence Darrow. After two trials—the first ended in a hung jury—Darrow won an acquittal for his clients in 1926. •

photos: The Indianapolis Star; Courtesy of the Burton Historical Collection, Detroit Public Library

THE AMERICAN HISTORIES of Ossian Sweet and D. C. Stephenson illustrate the competing forces that shaped the 1920s. Both achieved a measure of financial success, but they did so in the post–World War I atmosphere of growing social friction and intense racial resentments. After serving in the war, many blacks and ethnic minorities had a greater sense of pride in themselves. When Sweet's parents decided to send him north to get an education, they were responding to the racial violence that plagued the South, but they were also demonstrating their belief that a better life was possible for their son. By contrast, Stephenson grew wealthy by tapping into the same racial tensions that shaped the Sweets' lives. Just as the census of 1890 had announced the end of the frontier, the census of 1920 indicated that the population of rural America had dwindled and that the majority of Americans now lived in cities with more than 2,500 people. Many who considered themselves "100 percent Americans," born and bred in small towns or living in

sections of cities with homogeneous populations, believed that racial and ethnic minorities threatened their power. Although the general prosperity of the period masked the tensions lying beneath the surface, it did not eliminate them. As the experiences of D. C. Stephenson and Ossian Sweet show, the decade following the end of World War I opened up fresh avenues for economic prosperity as well as new sites for cultural clashes exacerbated by the tensions of modern America.

Postwar Turmoil

The return of peace in 1918 brought with it problems that would persist into the 1920s. Government efforts to suppress opposition to U.S. involvement in World War I fostered an atmosphere of repression that continued after the war ended, culminating in a wave of anti-Communist actions known as the Red scare. An influenza epidemic that killed hundreds of thousands of Americans and millions of people around the world heightened the climate of fear. Finally, the abrupt and painful transition away from a wartime economy produced inflation, labor unrest, and escalating racial tensions. The 1920s would come to be known as a decade of prosperity, but in the years immediately following the war the prospects for growth and stability seemed bleak.

The Supreme Court and Civil Liberties

On March 3, 1919, the Supreme Court invoked the Espionage Act to uphold the conviction of Charles Schenck, the general secretary of the Socialist Party, for mailing thousands of leaflets opposing the military draft. Delivering the Court's unanimous opinion, Justice Oliver Wendell Holmes argued that during wartime Congress has the authority to prohibit individuals from using words that create "a clear and present danger" to the safety of the country. Although the trial record failed to show that Schenck's leaflets had convinced any young men to resist conscription, the Court upheld his conviction under Holmes's doctrine.

Later in 1919, the Supreme Court demonstrated what a slippery slope the "clear and present danger" test presented for freedom of speech in a case that concerned what many American leaders believed posed a great threat to the nation: the spread of worldwide communism, the system of government that challenged capitalism. The success of the Bolshevik Revolution in Russia in 1917 and the subsequent creation of the Union of Soviet Socialist Republics terrified officials of capitalist countries in western Europe and the United States. Their concerns escalated in 1918, when Russia, until then an Allied power, signed a separate treaty with Germany and pulled out of the war (see chapter 20). In response, President Woodrow Wilson ordered U.S. troops to assist anti-Communist Russian forces fighting against the Bolshevik regime.

Wilson's actions generated vocal opposition from American supporters of the Russian Revolution. In New York City, a small group of anarchists and socialists welcomed the fall of capitalism in Russia and the prospects of a worker-controlled state that would promote economic democracy. Many of these activists were immigrants who had fled from Russia to avoid czarist repression against political dissidents and Jews. In August 1918, a handful of anarchists, including Jacob Abrams, dropped leaflets off a building on the Lower East Side urging workers to protest "barbaric [American] intervention" and calling on them to engage in "a general strike" until the United States removed its troops from Russia. The government prosecuted six defendants, five men and one woman, for violating the Espionage and Sedition Acts; the jury found all of them

guilty. On November 10, 1919, in *Abrams v. United States*, the Supreme Court affirmed the trial verdict, finding the distribution of the incendiary leaflets in wartime illegal.
See Document Project 21: The *Abrams* Case and the Red Scare, page 677.

The Red Scare, 1919–1920

The conviction in the *Abrams* case reflected broader concern over the **Red scare**—the fear of Communist-inspired radicalism in the wake of the Russian Revolution. Though communism failed to gain a foothold in the United States, the actions of a tiny contingent of radicals kept the threat alive and played into the hands of ambitious politicians and business leaders who wanted to crush labor agitation, which they perceived as anti-American.

Immediate postwar economic problems further increased the anxiety of American citizens, reinforcing the position of officials who sought to restore order by suppressing radicals. Industries were slow to convert their plants from military to civilian production, and consumer goods therefore remained in short supply. The war had brought jobs and higher wages on the home front, and consumers who had been restrained by wartime rationing were eager to spend their savings. With demand greatly exceeding supply, however, prices soared by 77 percent, frustrating consumers. At the same time, farmers, who had benefited from wartime conditions, faced falling crop prices as European nations resumed agricultural production and the federal government ended price supports.

A series of widespread strikes launched by labor unions in 1919 contributed to the fear that the United States was under assault by sinister, radical forces. As skyrocketing inflation undercut wages and employers launched a new round of union-busting efforts, labor went on the offensive. In 1919 more than four million workers went on strike nationwide, including those in key industries such as steel, transportation, and shipbuilding. In September, striking Boston policemen left the city unguarded, resulting in widespread looting and violence. Massachusetts governor Calvin Coolidge sent in the National Guard to break the strike and restore order.

Public officials and newspapers decried the violence, but they also greatly exaggerated the peril. Communists and socialists did support some union activities; however, few of the millions of workers who struck for higher wages and better working conditions had ties to extremists or sought to overthrow capitalism. The major prewar radical organization, the Industrial Workers of the World, never recovered from the government harassment that had crippled it during World War I. Postwar Communist parties in the United States claimed fewer than seventy thousand followers. However, scattered acts of real violence allowed government and business leaders to stir up anxieties about the Communist threat. On May 1, 1919, radicals sent more than thirty incendiary devices through the mail to prominent Americans, though authorities defused them before the mail bombs reached their intended targets. The following month, bombs exploded in eight cities, including one at the doorstep of the home of A. Mitchell Palmer, the attorney general of the United States, who emerged shocked but uninjured.

After the attack on his home, Palmer launched a government crusade to root out and prosecute Communist extremists. Like many American officials, Palmer traced the source of radicalism to recent immigrants, mainly those from Russia and eastern and southern Europe. To track down what he called the "moral perverts and hysterical neurasthenic [neurotic] women who abound in communism," Palmer selected J. Edgar Hoover,

Emma Goldman

Emma Goldman was a Russian anarchist who immigrated to the United States in 1885. She challenged capitalism and led campaigns in support of industrial workers and women's sexual and political freedom. An outspoken critic of World War I and the military draft, "Red Emma" was deported to Russia in 1919 after a roundup of alien radicals by the Justice Department. The Granger Collection, New York

a young Washington, D.C., lawyer, to head the General Intelligence Division in the Department of Justice. In November 1919, based on Hoover's research and undercover activities, government agents in twelve cities rounded up and arrested hundreds of foreigners, including the anarchist and feminist Emma Goldman. Goldman, along with some 250 people caught in the government dragnet, were soon deported to Russia. Over the next few months, the **Palmer raids** continued in more than thirty cities. Authorities seized approximately six thousand suspected radicals from their homes and community centers, took them to police stations, interrogated them without the benefit of legal counsel, and held them incommunicado without stipulating the charges against them. Of the thousands arrested, the government found reason to deport 556. The raids failed to uncover extensive plots to overthrow the U.S. government, nor did they lead to the arrest of the bombers.

Initially, most American citizens supported the Palmer raids, but their enthusiasm quickly waned. Many came to see the violations of civil liberties that accompanied the raids as a greater threat to the nation's traditions than the existence of a handful of American Communists. In 1920 a group of pacifists, progressives, and constitutional lawyers formed the American Civil Liberties Union (ACLU) to monitor government abridgments of the Bill of Rights. Although the Palmer raids ended, the Red scare manifested itself in different forms throughout the 1920s. After J. Edgar Hoover became director of the Bureau of Investigation (later renamed the Federal Bureau of Investigation) in 1921, he continued spying on suspected radicals, collecting information on a variety of Americans, and increasing his power over the next several decades.

Compounding the anxieties fueled by the Red scare, a medical crisis plunged Americans into panic. In late 1918, just as World War I was ending, an influenza epidemic struck the United States. Part of a worldwide contagion, the disease infected nearly 20 percent of the U.S. population and killed more than 675,000 people. Soldiers returning home from the war brought the flu virus with them. Infants and the elderly succumbed, as well as able-bodied young men and women. As the death toll mounted over the course of 1919, terror gripped the nation. Susanna Turner, a volunteer at an emergency hospital in Philadelphia, recalled: "The fear in the hearts of people just withered them. They were afraid to go out, afraid to do anything. If you asked a neighbor for help, they wouldn't do so because they weren't taking any chances. It was a horror-stricken time." A staggering 50 to 100 million people worldwide are estimated to have died from the flu before it subsided in 1920.

Racial Violence in the Postwar Era

Racial strife also heightened postwar anxieties. Drawn by the promise of wartime industrial jobs, more than 400,000 African Americans left the South beginning in 1917 and 1918 and headed north hoping to escape poverty and racial discrimination. (By 1930 another 800,000 blacks had left the South.) This exodus became known as the **great migration**. Black newspapers such as the *Chicago Defender* circulated throughout the South, offering glowing stories of the opportunities that adventurous blacks would find if they moved. Some 75,000 southern blacks heeded the call and relocated to Chicago. During World War I, many found work in steel mills, meatpacking, shipbuilding, and other heavy industries, but most were relegated to low-paying jobs. Still, as a carpenter earning $95 a month wrote from Chicago to a friend back in Hattiesburg, Mississippi: "I should have been here 20 years ago. I just begin to feel like a man." Most African American women remained employed as domestic workers, but more than 100,000 obtained manufacturing jobs.

For many blacks, however, the North was not the "promised land" they expected. Instead, they encountered bitter opposition from white migrants from the South competing for employment and scarce housing. As black and white veterans returned from the war, racial hostilities exploded. In 1919 race riots erupted in twenty-five cities throughout the country, including one in Washington, D.C., that left a deep impression on Ossian Sweet, who witnessed it firsthand.

The worst of these disturbances occurred in Chicago during what James Weldon Johnson, a poet and an NAACP official, called "Red Summer." On a hot July day, a black youth swimming at a Lake Michigan beach inadvertently crossed over into an area of water customarily reserved for whites. In response, white bathers shouted at the swimmer to return to the black section of the beach. To make their

The Influenza Epidemic, St. Louis, Missouri, 1918

When the influenza epidemic hit Missouri in October 1918, the mayor of St. Louis closed "all theaters, moving picture shows, schools, pool and billiard halls, Sunday schools, cabarets, lodges, societies [churches], public funerals, open air meetings, dance halls and conventions." Despite these precautions and efforts by the Red Cross, within a month more than 21,000 people in Missouri became ill, and 500 perished. © akg-images/The Image Works point more forcefully, they hurled stones at him. The black swimmer drowned, and word of the incident quickly spread through white and black neighborhoods in Chicago. For thirteen days, mobs of blacks and whites attacked each other, ransacked businesses, and torched homes. Over the course of the riots, at least 15 whites and 23 blacks died, 178 whites and 342 blacks were injured, and more than a thousand black families were left homeless. Against this background, D. C. Stephenson's Ku Klux Klan began to flourish in the North.

REVIEW & RELATE

What factors combined to produce the turmoil of the immediate postwar period?

What factors contributed to the rise in racial tensions that accompanied the transition from wartime to peacetime?

 LEARNINGCurve bedfordstmartins.com/hewittlawson/LC

People of Plenty

Despite the turbulence of the immediate postwar period and the persistence of underlying social and racial tensions, the 1920s were a time of vigorous economic growth. Between 1922 and 1927, the economy grew by 7 percent a year, the largest peacetime rate up to that point. Over the decade, the gross domestic product (then called the gross national product), per capita income, and the average purchasing power of wage earners all soared. At the same time, unemployment rates remained low, as producers added new workers in an effort to keep up with increasing consumer demand. Aligning themselves with big business, government officials took an active role in stimulating economic growth. Their efforts shaped and accelerated economic developments that amounted to a second industrial revolution.

Government Promotion of the Economy

The general prosperity of the 1920s owed a great deal to backing by the federal government. Republicans controlled the presidency and Congress, and though they claimed to stand for principles of laissez-faire and opposed various economic and social reforms, they were willing to use governmental power to support large corporations and the wealthy.

Senator Warren G. Harding of Ohio, who was elected president in 1920, pledged to restore "normalcy" after World War I and the tumult of the Red scare. Summing up

the Republican philosophy, Harding declared that he and his party wanted "less government in business and more business in government." Harding's cabinet appointments reflected this goal. Treasury Secretary Andrew Mellon, a banker and an aluminum company titan, believed that the government should stimulate economic growth by reducing taxes on the rich, raising tariffs to protect manufacturers from foreign competition, and trimming the budget. The Republican Congress enacted much of this agenda, reducing spending and lowering inheritance and corporate taxes. During the Harding administration, tax rates for the wealthy, which had skyrocketed during World War I, plummeted from 66 percent to 20 percent. Mellon believed that those on the lower rungs of the economic ladder would prosper once business people invested the extra money they received from tax breaks into expanding production. Supposedly, the wealth would trickle down through increased jobs and purchasing power. At the same time, Republicans turned Progressive Era regulatory agencies such as the Federal Trade Commission and the Federal Reserve Board into boosters for major corporations and financial institutions by weakening regulatory enforcement.

Secretary of Commerce Herbert Hoover had an even greater impact than Mellon in cementing the government-business partnership during the 1920s. A progressive who ably headed the Food Administration during World War I, Hoover believed that the federal government had a role to play in the economy and in lessening economic suffering. Rejecting government control of business activities, however, he insisted on voluntary cooperation between the public and private sectors. The secretary of commerce favored the creation of trade associations in which businesses would collaborate to stabilize production levels, prices, and wages. In turn, the Commerce Department would provide helpful data and information to improve productivity and trade.

Hoover's vision fit into a larger Republican effort to weaken unions by promoting voluntary business-sponsored worker welfare initiatives. For example, under the **American Plan** (the name itself implied that unions were "un-American"), some firms established health insurance and pension plans for their workers. As early as 1914, Henry Ford provided his autoworkers over twenty-two years old "a share in the profits of the house" equal to a minimum wage of $5 a day, and he cut the workday from nine hours to eight hours. Already under pressure from such tactics, unions were further damaged by a series of Supreme Court rulings that restricted strikes and overturned hard-won union victories such as child labor legislation and minimum wage laws. By 1929 union membership had dropped from approximately five million to three million, or about 10 percent of the industrial labor market.

Modern Technology and the Pioneer Spirit

From left to right sit Henry Ford, Thomas Edison, President Warren G. Harding, and Harvey Firestone on a camping trip in Maryland in 1921. Through their inventions and technological innovations, Ford, Edison, and Firestone changed the way Americans lived at the beginning of the twentieth century.   Ohio Historical Society

Scandals during the presidency of Warren G. Harding diminished its luster but did not tarnish the shine of Republican economic policy. The **Teapot Dome scandal** grabbed the most headlines. In 1921 Interior Secretary Albert Fall collaborated with Navy Secretary Edwin Denby to transfer naval oil reserves to the Interior Department. Fall then parceled out these properties to private companies. As a result, Harry F. Sinclair's Mammoth Oil Company received a lease to develop the Teapot Dome section in Wyoming. In return for this handout, Sinclair delivered more than $300,000, much of it in cash, to Fall. In the wake of congressional hearings launched by Senator Thomas J. Walsh of Montana, one of the few progressives remaining in Congress, Fall and Sinclair were convicted on a number of criminal charges and sent to jail.

Harding's sudden death from a heart attack in August 1923 brought Vice President Calvin Coolidge to the presidency. The former Massachusetts governor, who had sent state troops to quell the Boston police strike in 1919, distanced himself from the scandals of his predecessor's administration but reaffirmed Harding's economic policies. "The chief business of the American people is business," President Coolidge remarked succinctly.

Americans Become Consumers

The 1920s marked a period of economic expansion and general prosperity. National income rose from approximately $63 billion to $88 billion and per capita income jumped from $641 to $847, an increase of 32 percent. The purchasing power of wage earners climbed approximately 20 percent.

This great spurt of economic growth in the 1920s resulted from the application of technological innovation and scientific management techniques to industrial production (Figure 21.1). Perhaps the greatest innovation came with the introduction of the assembly line. First used in the automobile industry before World War I, the assembly line moved the product to a worker who performed a specific task before sending it along to the

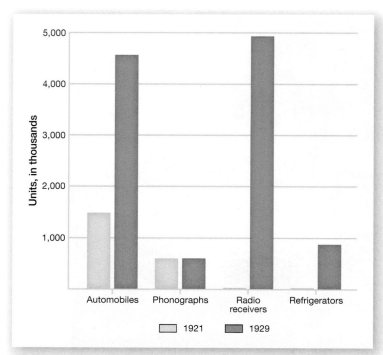

FIGURE 21.1 Production of Consumer Goods, 1921 and 1929

Rising per capita income, lower manufacturing costs, urban electrification, and advertising spurred the production of consumer goods in the 1920s. The most popular new items—automobiles and radios—brought Americans together through better transportation and communication.

next worker. This deceptively simple system, perfected by Henry Ford, saved enormous time and energy by emphasizing repetition, accuracy, and standardization. As a result, a new car rolled out of one of Ford's auto plants in less than a minute—earlier it had taken twelve and a half hours. Streamlined production lowered costs, which, in turn, allowed Ford to lower prices. The price of a new Model T dropped from $725 in 1910 to $290 in the early 1920s.

Besides the automobile, the **second industrial revolution** focused on the production of consumer-oriented goods previously considered luxuries. The electrification of urban homes created demand for a wealth of new laborsaving appliances; rural areas, most of which lacked electricity, did not benefit. Refrigerators, washing machines, toasters, and vacuum cleaners appealed to middle-class housewives whose husbands could afford to purchase them. Wristwatches replaced bulkier pocket watches. Radios became the chief source of home entertainment, and families gathered around the radio console to listen to music, news, and sports. Religious and political radio programs helped spread their particular faiths and ideologies, and those farmers equipped with electricity depended on the radio for weather reports and agricultural prices.

Although such household items changed the lives of many Americans, no single product had as profound an effect on American life in the 1920s as the automobile. Auto sales soared in the 1920s from 1.5 million to 5 million, making Henry Ford a multimillionaire and fueling the growth of related industries such as steel, rubber, petroleum, and glass. In 1929 Ford and his competitors at General Motors, Chevrolet, and Oldsmobile employed nearly 4 million workers, and around one in eight American workers toiled in factories connected to automobile production.

The automobile also changed day-to-day living patterns. Although most roads and highways consisted of dirt and contained rocks and ruts, enough were paved to extend the boundaries of suburbs farther from the city. By the end of the 1920s, around 17 percent of Americans lived in suburbia. Cars allowed families to travel to vacation destinations at greater distances from their homes. Even the roadside landscape changed to accommodate weary travelers, as gas stations, diners, and motels sprang up to serve them, and advertisers constructed billboards along the roads to remind them of what they needed. Each year, vacation resorts on the east and west coasts of Florida attracted thousands of tourists who drove south to enjoy the state's balmy climate and beautiful beaches. The use of automobile technology blended the conveniences of modern America with the primitiveness of the environment. Outdoor camping became the craze.

The automobile also provided new dating opportunities for young men and women. At the turn of the twentieth century, a young man courted a woman by going to her home and sitting with her on the sofa or out on the porch under the watchful eyes of her parents and family members. When the couple left the house, they might walk to a park and listen to a bandstand concert, again in the company of others. With the arrival of the automobile, couples could move from the couch in the parlor to the backseat of a car, away from adult supervision. Driving to a "lover's lane" in a Model T and drinking from a flask of prohibited alcohol, the young couple could explore new sexual terrain that had been denied them in the past (most likely "petting"—kissing and rubbing rather than intercourse).

Although Ford and his fellow manufacturers had succeeded in lowering prices for consumers, they still had to convince Americans to spend their hard-earned money to purchase their products. Turning for help to New York City's Madison Avenue, the location of the fledgling advertising industry, manufacturers nearly tripled their spending on advertising over the course of the 1920s. Firms pitched their products around price and quality, but they directed their efforts more than ever to the personal psychology of the consumer. Advertisers played on consumers' unexpressed fears, unfulfilled desires, hopes for success, and sexual fantasies. The producers of Listerine mouthwash transformed a product previously used to disinfect hospitals into one that fought the dreaded but made-up disease of halitosis (bad breath). Advertisers told people that they could measure success through consumption. Purchasing a General Electric (GE) all-steel refrigerator not only would preserve food longer but also would enhance the owners' reputation among their neighbors. "Happy to own it . . . proud to show it" headlined one ad explaining the virtues of GE's new product.

> **Explore**
>
> See Document 21.1 for a typical GE advertisement from 1928.

Although average wages and incomes rose during the 1920s, the majority of Americans did not have the disposable income to afford the bounty of new consumer goods. To resolve this problem, companies extended credit in dizzying amounts. By 1929 consumers purchased 60 percent of their cars and 80 percent of their radios and furniture on credit in the form of installment plans and owed a total of $3 billion. "Buy now and pay later" became the motto of corporate America. By putting a small amount down and making monthly payments with interest, people could obtain an assortment of consumer items they otherwise could not afford.

Perilous Prosperity

Prosperity in the 1920s was real enough, but behind the impressive financial indicators flashed warnings that profound danger loomed ahead. Perhaps most important, the boom was accompanied by growing income inequality. A majority of workers lived below the poverty line, and farmers plunged deeper into hard times. Corporate profits increased much faster than wages, resulting in a disproportionate share of the wealth going to the rich. The combined income of the top 1 percent of families was greater than that of the 42 percent at the bottom (Figure 21.2); 66 percent lived below the income level ($1,800 to $2,000 annually) necessary to maintain an adequate standard of living. In addition, less than 1 percent of families accumulated 34 percent of the nation's savings, while around 78 percent of families had no savings at all.

Income inequality was a critical problem because America's new mass-production economy depended on ever-increasing consumption, and higher income groups

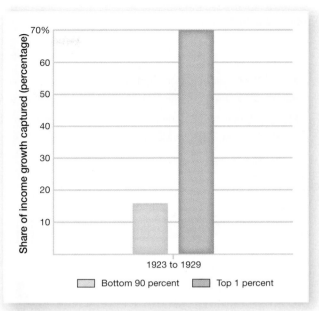

FIGURE 21.2 Income Inequality, 1923–1929

Although the U.S. economy expanded rapidly in the early 1920s, the accumulation of vast wealth among a small percentage of Americans created growing inequality. Although most Americans could purchase new consumer goods only by buying on credit, the richest 1 percent engaged in risky stock and real estate ventures to further enhance their wealth.

could consume only so much, no matter how much of the nation's wealth they controlled. While the expansion of consumer credit helped hide this fundamental weakness, the low wages earned by most Americans drove down demand over time. Cutbacks in demand forced manufacturers to reduce production, thereby reducing jobs and increasing unemployment. In the days before unemployment insurance, this placed an increased burden on families to make ends meet and dragged down the demand for consumer goods even further. By 1926, as a result of lagging purchasing power, the growth of automobile sales had begun to slow, as did new housing construction—signs of an economy heading for trouble.

At the same time, the wealthy few used their disproportionate savings to speculate in the stock market and risky real estate ventures. To encourage investments, brokers promoted buying stocks on margin (credit) and required down payments of only a fraction of the market price. Without vigilant governmental oversight, banks and lending agencies extended credit without taking into account what would happen if a financial panic occurred and they were suddenly required to call in all of their loans. To make matters worse, the banking system operated on shaky financial grounds, combining savings facilities with speculative lending operations. With minimal interference from the

DOCUMENT 21.1

General Electric Refrigerator Advertisement, 1928

The 1920s boom in the production of household goods posed a challenge for business marketers and advertisers. They had to convince consumers that items once regarded as luxuries were now necessities that would improve their lives. Many of these advertisements were directed at women who, as housewives, managed the family budget and made the purchases. The General Electric Company played a leading role in winning women over to buying their products.

Explore

Why do women need "first aid" in the kitchen?

What do the items in the refrigerator reveal about food and consumer expectations in the 1920s?

How does this ad use the authority of science to persuade consumers?

First aid in entertaining

FIRST aid in entertaining, nowadays, is a General Electric Refrigerator. If you have one, you can make those delicious, *different* salads and aspics and desserts. You can make them at your leisure—the same morning, or the day before, or whenever you wish. There's plenty of room to store them. There's the scientific cold to keep them fresh.

You will like the simplicity of the General Electric Refrigerator. It never needs oiling. It hasn't a drain-pipe or a belt or a fan. All its machinery is enclosed

in the hermetically sealed casing mounted on top of the cabinet. And there is a remarkably large shelf area because the chilling chamber is so compact. All the models are up on legs, so the floor under them can easily be cleaned.

General Electric's world-famed engineers and scientists worked for fifteen years to develop this supremely practical and

efficient refrigerator—to make it quiet, portable and economical to run.

Already it is giving flawless service in more than fifty thousand homes. Ask these users about the General Electric and make comparisons before you buy. There is a wide range of models and prices. Write us today for Booklet S-6B, which is completely descriptive.

GENERAL ⓖ ELECTRIC
Refrigerator

ELECTRIC REFRIGERATION DEPARTMENT · OF GENERAL ELECTRIC COMPANY · HANNA BUILDING · CLEVELAND, OHIO

The Advertising Archives

Put It in Context

What does this ad convey about the role of women in the 1920s?

Federal Trade Commission, business people frequently managed firms in a reckless way that created a high level of interdependence among them. For example, Samuel Insull, who owned a gas and electric utilities empire, was the chairman of the board of sixty-five companies, a director of eighty-five others, and the president of an additional seven corporations. This interlocking system of corporate ownership and control meant that the collapse of one company could bring down many others, while also imperiling the banking houses that had generously financed them.

Rampant real estate speculation in Florida foreshadowed these dangers, as private developers and the state government promoted tourism and land purchases. In many cases, investors bought properties sight unseen, as speculators and unscrupulous agents worked under the assumption that land values would continue to increase forever. However, severe storms in 1926 and 1928 abruptly halted the increase in land values. Land prices spiraled downward, speculators defaulted on bank loans, and financial institutions tottered.

Throughout the 1920s, fortunes plummeted for farmers as well. Despite the growing urbanization of the nation, farmers still made up one-third of the population. Declining world demand following the end of World War I, together with increased productivity because of the mechanization of agriculture, drove down farm prices and income. Between 1925 and 1929, falling wheat and cotton prices cut farm income in half. The collapse of farm prices had the most devastating effects on tenants and sharecroppers who were forced off their lands through mortgage foreclosures. Around three million displaced farmers migrated to cities, where they had to compete with unskilled laborers for factory jobs and often found themselves among the ranks of the unemployed.

Internationally, the United States encountered serious economic obstacles. World War I had destroyed European economies, leaving them ill equipped to repay the $11 billion they had borrowed from the United States. Much of the Allied recovery, and hence the ability to repay debts, depended on obtaining the reparations imposed on Germany at the conclusion of World War I (see chapter 20). Germany, however, was in even worse shape than France and Britain and could not meet its obligations. Without a prosperous Europe, the American economy suffered. In 1924 the U.S. government sent Charles G. Dawes, a banker and soon to become Coolidge's vice president, to negotiate with Britain, France, and Germany to find a solution to their mutual problem. Under the terms of the eventual agreement, the United States provided loans to Germany to pay its reparations. In turn, Britain and France reduced the size of Germany's payments. The result was a series of circular payments. American banks loaned money to Germany, which used the money to pay reparations to Britain and France, which, in turn, used Germany's reparations payments to repay debts owed to American banks. What appeared a satisfactory resolution at the time ultimately proved a calamity. In undertaking this revolving-door solution, American bankers added to the cycle of spiraling credit and placed themselves at the mercy of unstable European economies. Compounding the problem, Republican administrations in the 1920s supported high tariffs on imports, reducing foreign manufacturers' revenues and therefore their nations' tax receipts, making it more difficult for these countries to pay off their debts.

REVIEW & RELATE

Describe the relationship between business and government in the 1920s.

Why was a high level of consumer spending so critical to 1920s prosperity, and why was the economic expansion of the 1920s ultimately unsustainable?

LEARNINGCurve bedfordstmartins.com/hewittlawson/LC

Challenges to Social Conventions

While most of the nation ignored growing evidence of the fragility of American prosperity, the social and cultural consequences of the second industrial revolution received considerable attention, as new, distinctly modern cultural patterns emerged. Advertising and credit, two of the mainstays of modern capitalism, sought to bypass the time-honored virtues of saving and living within one's means. Conventional sexual standards came under assault from the growth of the film and automobile industries, which influenced fashion styles and dating practices. In addition to moral and social behavior, traditional racial assumptions came under attack. African American writers and artists condemned the kind of racism Ossian Sweet experienced, drew on their rich racial legacies, and produced a cultural renaissance. Other blacks, led by the Jamaican immigrant Marcus Garvey, rejected the integrationist strategy of the NAACP in favor of black nationalism.

Breaking with the Old Morality

Challenges to the virtues of thrift and sacrifice were accompanied by a transformation of the moral codes of late-nineteenth-century America, especially those relating to sex. The entertainment industry played a large role in promoting

Hollywood

Hollywood's silent movies provided audiences with graphic images of changing sexual values during the 1920s. Rudolph Valentino, pictured in this advertisement for *Blood and Sand* (1922), was the leading male heartthrob of the era. Here he embraces his costar Nita Naldi, who responds with a look of ecstasy to Valentino's touch.   Courtesy Everett Collection

relaxed attitudes toward sexual relations to a mass audience throughout the nation. The motion picture business, increasingly centered in Hollywood after 1920, attracted women and men to movie palaces where they could see swashbuckling heroes and glamorous heroines. In an era of silent movies, patrons in the nation's twenty thousand movie houses were enthralled not by the occasional dialogue printed on the screen but by the powerfully attractive images of the film stars.

Originally shown as short films for 5 cents in nickelodeons, the movies appealed to a national audience. Melodramas and comedies entertained the masses, and films such as D. W. Griffith's *Birth of a Nation* (1915) appealed to racial

prejudices by glorifying the Ku Klux Klan. By the 1920s, films had expanded into feature-length pictures, Hollywood film studios had blossomed into major corporations, and movies were shown in ornate theaters in cities and towns across the country. The star system was born, and matinee idols such as Douglas Fairbanks, Charlie Chaplin, Clara Bow, and Mary Pickford influenced fashions and hairstyles. Female stars dressed as "flappers" and wooed audiences. Representing the liberated **new woman**, flappers wore short skirts, used ample makeup (formerly associated with prostitutes), smoked cigarettes in public, drank illegal alcoholic beverages, and gyrated to jazz tunes on the dance floor.

Americans could enjoy new entertainment opportunities and still remain faithful to traditional values. By 1929 approximately 40 percent of households owned a radio and could listen to stations affiliated with the two major broadcasting networks: the Columbia Broadcasting System (CBS) and the National Broadcasting Company (NBC). Shows such as *The General Motors Family* and *The Maxwell House Hour* blended product advertising with family entertainment. *Amos 'n' Andy* garnered large audiences by satirizing black working-class life, which, intentionally or not, reinforced racist stereotypes. In cities like New York and Chicago, immigrants could tune in to foreign-language radio programs aimed at non-English-speaking ethnic groups, which offered them an outlet for preserving their identity in the face of the increasing homogeneity fostered by the national consumer culture.

The most spirited challenge to both traditional values and the modern consumer culture came from a diverse group of intellectuals known as the **Lost Generation**. Gertrude Stein coined the term to describe the disillusionment that many of her fellow writers and artists felt after the ravages of World War I. Already concerned about the impact of mass culture and corporate capitalism on individualism and free thought, they focused their talents on criticizing what they saw as the hypocrisy of old values and the conformity ushered in by the new. In the novel *This Side of Paradise* (1920), F. Scott Fitzgerald complained that his generation had "grown up to find all Gods dead, all wars fought, all faith in man shaken." In a series of novels, including *Main Street* (1920), *Babbitt* (1922), and *Elmer Gantry* (1927), Sinclair Lewis ridiculed the narrow-mindedness of small-town life, the empty materialism of businessmen, and the insincerity of evangelical preachers. Journalist Henry Louis (H. L.) Mencken picked up these subjects in the pages of his magazine, *The American Mercury*. From his vantage point in Baltimore, Maryland, he lampooned the beliefs and behavior of Middle America and groused that its residents had turned democracy into "boobocracy," or government by boobs.

While radio audiences howled with laughter over the exploits of *Amos 'n' Andy*, scholars discredited conventional wisdom about race. Challenging studies that purported to demonstrate the intellectual superiority of whites over blacks, Columbia University anthropologist Franz Boas argued that any apparent intelligence gap between the races resulted from environmental factors and not heredity. His student Ruth Benedict further argued that the culture of so-called primitive tribes such as the Pueblo Indians, which emphasized cooperation and spiritual ideals, produced a less stressful and more emotionally connected lifestyle than that of more advanced societies. The ideas of Sigmund Freud, an Austrian psychoanalyst, shifted emphasis away from culture and race to individual consciousness. His disciples stressed the role of the unconscious mind and the power of the sex drive in shaping human behavior, beliefs that gained traction not only in university education but also in advertising appeals.

The African American Renaissance

The greatest challenge to conventional notions about race came from black Americans. The influx of southern black migrants to the North spurred by World War I and continuing into the 1920s created a black cultural renaissance, with New York City's Harlem and the South Side of Chicago leading the way. Black intellectuals joined their white counterparts in criticizing conventional social and cultural norms. Gathered in Harlem—with a population of more than 120,000 African Americans in 1920 and growing every day—a group of black writers paid homage to the **New Negro**, the second generation born after emancipation. These New Negro intellectuals refused to accept white supremacy. In militant voices, they expressed pride in their race, sought to perpetuate black racial identity, and demanded full citizenship and participation in American society. Intending to enrich the culture of the United States, black writers and poets drew on themes from African American life and history for inspiration in their literary works.

Explore

See Document 21.2 for an example of Harlem Renaissance poetry.

These men and women made up the "Talented Tenth," the leaders of the black race whom W. E. B.

DOCUMENT 21.2

Claude McKay | If We Must Die, 1919

Jamaican-born writer Claude McKay moved to the United States in 1912 and influenced many writers of the Harlem Renaissance. His poems focused primarily on race relations and the lives of working-class African Americans. The following poem is one of his most powerful and well-known works, written in reaction to the Red Summer of 1919.

Explore

If we must die, let it not be like hogs
Hunted and penned in an inglorious spot,
While round us bark the mad and hungry dogs,
Making their mock at our accursèd lot.
If we must die, O let us nobly die,
So that our precious blood may not be shed
In vain; then even the monsters we defy
Shall be constrained to honor us though dead!
O kinsmen! we must meet the common foe!

Though far outnumbered let us show us brave,
And for their thousand blows deal one death-blow!
What though before us lies the open grave?
Like men we'll face the murderous, cowardly pack,
Pressed to the wall, dying, but fighting back!

Source: Claude McKay, "If We Must Die," in *Harlem Shadows: The Poems of Claude McKay* (New York: Harcourt, Brace, 1922), 53.

Interpret the Evidence

• How does McKay characterize the situation of blacks in America?
• In McKay's view, what purpose might be served by resistance in the face of overwhelming odds?

Put It in Context

How does McKay's poem reflect the ideals of the Harlem Renaissance?

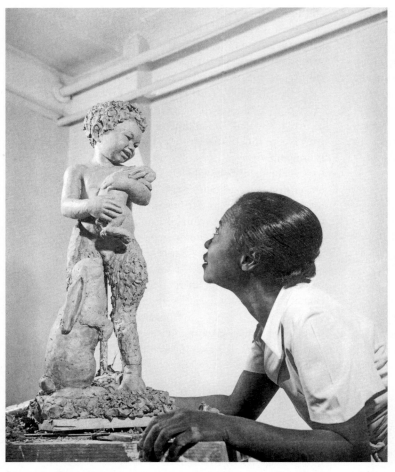

Augusta Savage
Born in Florida, Augusta Savage joined other artists in moving to New York City in the 1920s as part of the Harlem Renaissance. She took formal art classes at the Cooper Union, working mainly in clay. In addition to the sculpture of the young boy here, Savage produced busts of W. E. B. Du Bois and Marcus Garvey.   Hansel Mieth/Time & Life Pictures/Getty Images

Black music became a vibrant part of mainstream American popular culture in the 1920s. Traveling musicians such as Ferdinand "Jelly Roll" Morton, Louis Armstrong, Edward "Duke" Ellington, and singer Bessie Smith developed and popularized two of America's most original forms of music—jazz and the blues. Emerging from brothels and bars in the South, these unique compositions grew out of the everyday experiences of black life and expressed the thumping rhythms of work, pleasure, and pain. Such music did not remain confined to dance halls and clubs in black communities; it soon spread to white musicians and audiences for whom the hot beat of jazz rhythms meant emotional freedom and the expression of sexuality.

Marcus Garvey and Black Nationalism

In addition to providing a fertile ground for African American intellectuals, Harlem became the headquarters of the most significant alternative black political vision of the 1920s. In 1916 the Jamaican-born Marcus Mosiah Garvey settled in Harlem and became the leading exponent of black nationalism. In 1914 Garvey had set up the **Universal Negro Improvement Association (UNIA)** in Jamaica, an organization through which he promoted racial separation and pride. Unlike the leaders of the NAACP, who sought equal access to American institutions and cooperation with whites, Garvey favored a "Back to Africa" movement that would ultimately repatriate

Du Bois had spoken of in *The Souls of Black Folk* (1903). James Weldon Johnson, a writer and the chief executive of the NAACP, commented: "The final measure of the greatness of all peoples is the amount and standard of the literature and art they have produced." The poets, novelists, and artists of the Harlem Renaissance captured the imagination of blacks and whites alike. Many of these artists increasingly rejected white standards of taste as well as staid middle-class, black values. Writers Langston Hughes and Zora Neale Hurston in particular drew inspiration from the vernacular of African American folk life. In 1926 Hughes defiantly asserted: "We younger Negro artists who create now intend to express our dark-skinned selves without fear or shame. If white people are pleased, we are glad. If they are not, it doesn't matter."

many black Americans to their ancestral homelands on the African continent. Together with the indigenous black African majority, transplanted African Americans would help overthrow colonial rule and use their power to assist black people throughout the world.

Garvey's appeal did not rely primarily on this utopian project. Instead, the UNIA concentrated on building the economic strength of black communities in the United States through self-help. In the pages of his newspaper, *Negro World*, Garvey promoted ventures such as his Black Star Line steamship company, established in 1919. After raising more than $200,000 in less than four months, the company acquired a fleet of three less-than-seaworthy ships on which it planned to transport passengers between the United States, the West Indies, and Africa. The UNIA's companies opened up

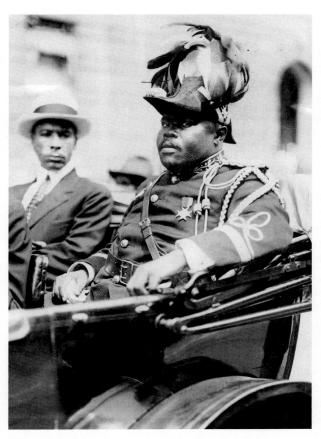

Marcus Garvey
Dressed in military regalia topped off with a plumed hat, the Jamaican immigrant Marcus Garvey embodied the spirit of black nationalism after World War I. His Universal Negro Improvement Association, headquartered in Harlem, attracted a sizable following in the United States, the Caribbean, Central America, Canada, and Africa. Garvey advocated black political and economic independence.　NY Daily News via Getty Images

blue-collar and white-collar jobs to black men and women that were generally unavailable to them in white-owned firms.

In addition to offering an outlet for dreams of economic advancement, Garvey tapped into the racial discontent of African Americans for whom living in the United States had proven so difficult. He denounced what he saw as the accommodationist efforts of the NAACP and declared, "To be a Negro is no disgrace, but an honor, and we of the UNIA do not want to become white." Indeed, he proclaimed "Black is Beautiful" and asserted that both God and Jesus were black. Ironically, the UNIA and D. C. Stephenson's Klan agreed on the necessity of racial segregation, though Garvey never accepted the premise that blacks were inferior. Garvey dressed in a military uniform with a saber dangling from his belt and a plumed hat atop his

head. His appeals to black manhood were also accompanied by a celebration of black womanhood. He set up the Black Cross Nurses, and his wife, Amy Jacques Garvey, went beyond her husband's traditional notions of femininity to extol the accomplishments of black women in politics and culture. Garveyism became the first mass African American movement in U.S. history and was especially effective in recruiting working-class blacks. UNIA branches were established in thirty-eight states throughout the North and South and attracted some 500,000 members.

Given his ideas and outspokenness, Garvey soon made powerful enemies. Du Bois and fellow members of the NAACP despised him. The black socialist labor leader A. Philip Randolph, who saw the UNIA program as just another form of exploitative capitalism, labeled Garvey an "unquestioned fool and ignoramus." Yet Garvey's downfall came from his own business practices. Convicted in 1925 of mail fraud related to his Black Star Line, Garvey served two years in federal prison until President Coolidge commuted his term and had the Jamaican citizen deported. Garvey continued to carry on his activities from England, but without his presence the UNIA lost most of its following in the United States.

REVIEW & RELATE

How did new forms of entertainment challenge traditional morality and traditional gender roles?

Describe the black cultural and intellectual renaissance that flourished in the 1920s.

✔ *LEARNINGCurve* **bedfordstmartins.com/hewittlawson/LC**

Culture Wars

Attacks on traditional cultural and racial values did not go uncontested. During this era when technological innovations overturned traditional economic values, when modes of social behavior were in a state of flux, and when white supremacy came under assault, it is not surprising that many segments of the population resisted these changes. Rallying around ethnic and racial purity, Protestant fundamentalism, and family values, defenders of an older America attempted to roll back the tide of modernity.

Nativists versus Immigrants

The 1920s experienced a surge in nativist (anti-immigrant) and racist thinking that in many ways reflected long-standing fears. The end of World War I brought a new wave of Catholic and Jewish emigration from eastern and southern Europe, triggering religious prejudice among Protestants. Just as immigrants had been linked to socialism and anarchism in the 1880s and 1890s, old-stock Americans associated these immigrants with immoral behavior and political radicalism and saw them as a threat to their traditional culture and values. Moreover, as in the late nineteenth century, native-born workers saw immigrants as a source of cheap labor that threatened their jobs and wages.

The **Sacco and Vanzetti case** provides the most dramatic evidence of this nativism. In 1920 a botched robbery at a shoe company in South Braintree, Massachusetts, resulted in the murder of the bookkeeper and guard. Police arrested Nicola Sacco, a shoemaker, and Bartolomeo Vanzetti, a fish peddler, and charged them with the crime. These two Italian immigrants shared radical political views as anarchists and World War I draft evaders. The subsequent trial revolved around their foreign birth and ideology more than the facts pertaining to their guilt or innocence. The presiding judge at the trial referred to the accused as "anarchistic bastards" and "damned dagos" (a derogatory term for "Italians"). Convicted and sentenced to death, Sacco and Vanzetti lost their appeals for a new trial. Criticism of the verdict came from all over the world. Workers in Mexico, Argentina, Uruguay, France, and Morocco organized vigils and held rallies in solidarity with the condemned men. The American minister to Venezuela reported that "practically all the lower classes regarded them as martyrs." Despite support from influential lawyers such as Harvard's Felix Frankfurter, the two men were executed in the electric chair in 1927.

The Sacco and Vanzetti case provides an extreme example of 1920s nativism, but the anti-immigrant views that contributed to the two men's conviction and execution were commonplace during the period and shared by Americans across the social spectrum. Many Americans, including Henry Ford, saw immigrants as a threat to cherished traditions. In his commitment to "One-Hundred Percent Americanism," Ford tried to preserve traditional values. He strongly supported prohibition and denounced the frenetic sounds and sexual overtones of Jazz Age music and dancing. Ford felt that immigrants were the cause of a decline in American morality. He contended that aliens did not understand "the principles which have made our [native] civilization," and he blamed the influx of foreigners for society's "marked deterioration" during the 1920s. He stirred up anti-immigrant prejudices mainly by targeting Jews. Believing that an international Jewish conspiracy was attempting to subvert non-Jewish societies, Ford serialized in his company newspaper the so-called

Protocols of the Elders of Zion, an anti-Semitic tract concocted in czarist Russia to justify pogroms against Jews. Ford continued to publish it even after the document was proven a fake in 1921.

Ford joined other nativists in supporting legislation to restrict immigration. In 1924 Congress passed the **National Origins Act**, a quota system on future immigration. The measure limited entry by any foreign group to 2 percent of the number of people of that nationality who resided in the United States in 1890. The statute's authors were interested primarily in curbing immigration from eastern and southern Europe. They chose 1890 as the benchmark for immigration because most newcomers from those two regions entered the United States after that year. Quotas established for northern Europe, about 70 percent of the total, went unfilled, while those for southern and eastern Europe could not accommodate the vast number of people who sought admission. The law continued to bar East Asian immigration altogether.

With immigration of those considered "undesirable" severely if not completely curtailed, some nativist reformers shifted their attention to Americanization, which developed into one of the largest social and political movements in American history. Speaking about immigrants, educator E. P. Cubberly said, "Our task is to break up their groups and settlements, to assimilate and amalgamate these people as a part of our American race, to implant in their children the northern-European conception of righteousness, law and order, and popular government." Business corporations conducted Americanization and naturalization classes on factory floors. Schools, patriotic societies, fraternal organizations, women's groups, and labor unions launched citizenship classes. Even the U.S. Catholic hierarchy joined the effort by prohibiting the creation of new parishes based on nationality and increasingly requiring the use of English for confessions and sermons.

In the Southwest and on the West Coast, whites aimed their Americanization efforts at the growing population of Mexican Americans. Subject to segregated education, Mexican Americans were expected to speak English in their classes. "The opening of school," an Arizona teacher's journal noted, "will provide an opportunity for all the Mexican children . . . to study under separate tutelage until they have acquired a thorough mastery of the English language." Anglo school administrators and teachers generally believed that Mexican Americans were suited for farmwork and manual trades. For Mexican Americans, therefore, Americanization meant vocational training and preparation for low-status, low-wage jobs.

Despite attempts at Americanization, ethnic groups did not dissolve into a melting pot and lose their cultural identities. First-generation Americans—the children of immigrants—learned English, enjoyed American popular culture, and dressed in fashions of the day. Yet in cities around the country where immigrants had settled, ethnic enclaves remained intact and preserved the religious practices and social customs of their residents. Americanization may have watered down the "vegetable soup" of American diversity, but it did not completely eliminate the variety and distinctiveness of its flavors.

Resurrection of the Ku Klux Klan

Nativism received its most spectacular boost from the reemergence of the Ku Klux Klan in 1915. Originally an organization dedicated to terrorizing emancipated African Americans and their white Republican allies in the South during Reconstruction, the KKK branched out during the 1920s to the North and West. In addition to blacks, the new Klan targeted Catholics and Jews, as well as anyone who was alleged to have violated community moral values. The organization consisted of a cross section of native-born Protestants primarily from the middle and working classes who sought to reverse a perceived decline in their social and economic power. Revived by W. J. Simmons, a former Methodist minister, the new Klan celebrated its founding at Stone Mountain, Georgia, near Atlanta. There, Klansmen bowed to the twin symbols of their cause, the American flag and a burning cross that represented their fiery determination to stand up for Christian morality and against all those considered "un-American." People flocked to the new KKK. By the mid-1920s, Klan membership totaled more than three million men and women. Tens of thousands of members outfitted in white sheets and pointed hoods openly paraded down Pennsylvania Avenue in Washington, D.C., the route of presidential inaugurations. Not confined to rural areas, the revived Klan counted a significant following in D. C. Stephenson's Indianapolis and Ossian Sweet's Detroit, as well as in Chicago, Denver, Portland, and Seattle. Rural dwellers who had moved into cities with large numbers of black migrants and recent immigrants found solace in Klan vows to preserve "Native, white, Protestant supremacy."

The phenomenal growth of the KKK in the 1920s probably resulted more from the desire to reestablish traditional values than from sheer hostility toward blacks. In the face of challenges to traditional values, a changing sexual morality, and the flaunting of prohibition, wives joined their husbands as devoted followers. Protestant women appreciated the Klan's message condemning abusive husbands and fathers and the group's affirmation

of the status of white Protestant women as the embodiment of virtue. In the post-suffrage era, the Klan also provided its female members with an incentive to vote by encouraging them to counteract the influence of newly enfranchised Catholic, Jewish, Latina, and African American women.

> **Explore**
>
> See Documents 21.3 and 21.4 for two perspectives on the KKK.

Like the original Klan, its successor resorted to terror tactics. Acting under cover of darkness and concealed in robes and hoods, Klansmen burned crosses to scare their victims, many of whom they beat, kidnapped, tortured, and murdered. To gain greater legitimacy and to appeal to a wider audience, the Klan also participated in electoral politics. The KKK succeeded in electing governors in Georgia and Oregon, a U.S. senator from Texas, numerous state legislators, and other officials in California, Indiana, Michigan, Ohio, and Oklahoma. Politicians routinely joined the Klan to advance their careers, whether they shared its views or not. For example, Hugo Black, a Klansman from Alabama, won election as U.S. senator and was appointed to the Supreme Court, where he accumulated a distinguished record as a progressive jurist.

Fundamentalism versus Modernism

Protestant fundamentalists also fought to uphold traditional values against modern-day incursions. Around 1910, two wealthy Los Angeles churchgoers had subsidized and distributed a series of booklets called *The Fundamentals*, incorporating many statements about the literal truth of the Bible. With three million copies in circulation nationwide, the booklets informed readers that the Bible offered a true account of the genesis and development of humankind and the world and that its words had to be taken literally. After 1920, believers of this approach to interpreting the Bible became known as "fundamentalists." Their preachers spread the message of old-time religion through carnival-like revivals, and preachers used the new medium of radio to broadcast their sermons. Fundamentalism divided many Protestant denominations, but its appeal was strongest in the Midwest and the South—the so-called Bible belt—where residents felt deeply threatened by the secular aspects of modern life that left their conventional religious teachings open to skepticism and scorn.

Nothing bothered fundamentalist Protestants as much as Charles Darwin's theory of evolution. In *On the Origin of*

Men and Women of the KKK: Two Views

While the new Ku Klux Klan grew in power and visibility, many Americans also resisted and ridiculed the organization. In the first selection, journalist Gerald Johnson describes the typical KKK member. The second selection, an excerpt from the bylaws of a Maryland chapter of the Women of the Ku Klux Klan, indicates the group's devotion to the responsibilities of traditional womanhood. Nearly half a million women joined the women's auxiliaries of the KKK.

Ku Klux Klan Wedding, 1925 Getty Images

Explore

21.3 Gerald W. Johnson | The Ku Kluxer, 1924

The Ku Klux Klan was swept beyond the racial boundaries of the Negro and flourishes now in the Middle West because it is a perfect expression of the American idea that the voice of the people is the voice of God. The belief that the average klansman is consciously affected by an appeal to his baser self is altogether erroneous. In the voice of the organizer he hears a clarion call to knightly and selfless service. It strikes him as in no wise strange that he should be so summoned; is he not, as an American citizen, of the nobility? Politics has been democratized. Social usage has been democratized. Religion has been most astoundingly democratized. Why, then, not democratize chivalry?

The klansman has already been made, in his own estimation, politically a monarch, socially a peer of the realm, spiritually a high priest. Now the Ku Klux Klan calls him to step up and for the trifling consideration of ten dollars he is made a Roland, a Lancelot, a knight-errant vowed to the succor of the oppressed, the destruction of ogres and magicians, the defense of the faith. Bursting with noble ideals and lofty aspirations, he accepts the nomination. The trouble is that this incantation doesn't work, as none of the others has worked, except in his imagination. King, aristocrat, high priest as he believes himself to be, he is neither royal, noble, nor holy. So, under his white robe and pointed hood he becomes not a Chevalier Bayard [French knight] but a thug.

Source: Gerald W. Johnson, "The Ku Kluxer," *The American Mercury*, February 1924, 209–10.

Species (1859), Darwin replaced the biblical story of creation with a scientific theory of the emergence and development of life that centered on evolution and natural selection. Fundamentalists rejected this explanation and repudiated the views of fellow Protestants who attempted to reconcile Darwinian evolution with God's Word by reading the Bible as a symbolic representation of what might have happened. Few people had actually read Darwin, and fundamentalists derided him by emphasizing the popular misconception that he had written that human beings had descended directly from apes (in fact, he maintained that simians and humans had a common ancestor). To combat any other interpretation but the biblical one, in 1925 lawmakers in Arkansas, Florida, Mississippi, Oklahoma,

Explore

21.4 Women of the Ku Klux Klan, 1927

Objects and Purposes

SECTION 1. The objects of this Order shall be to unite white female persons, native-born Gentile citizens of the United States of America, who owe no allegiance of any nature or degree to any foreign government, nation, institution, sect, ruler, person, or people; whose morals are good; whose reputations and vocations are respectable; whose habits are exemplary; who are of sound minds and 18 years or more of age, under a common oath into a Sisterhood of strict regulation, to cultivate and promote patriotism toward our Civil Government; to practice an honorable clannishness toward each other; to exemplify a practical benevolence; to shield the sanctity of the home and the chastity of womanhood; to maintain forever white supremacy; to teach and faithfully inculcate a high spiritual philosophy through an exalted ritualism, and by a practical devotion to conserve, protect, and maintain the distinctive institutions, rights, privileges, principles, traditions, and ideals of a pure Americanism.

SEC. 2. To create and maintain an institution by which the present and succeeding generations shall commemorate the great sacrifice, chivalric service, and imperishable achievements of the Ku Klux Klan and the Women of the Reconstruction period of American History, to the end that justice and honor be done the sacred memory of those who wrought through our mystic society during that period, and that their valiant accomplishments be not lost to posterity; to perpetuate their faithful courage, noble spirit, peerless principles, and faultless ideals; to hold sacred and make effective their spiritual purpose in this and future generations, that they be rightly vindicated before the world by a revelation of the whole truth.

Source: Women of the KKK (Maryland) Records, Schlesinger Library, Radcliffe Institute, Harvard University, reprinted in *Modern American Women*, ed. Susan Ware (Boston: McGraw-Hill, 2002), 136–37.

Interpret the Evidence

- How does Johnson describe the typical KKK member?
- How do each of these statements identify the central purpose of the KKK?

Put It in Context

Why did the KKK and other nativist groups appeal to so many people during the 1920s?

and Tennessee made it illegal to teach in public schools and colleges "any theory that denies the story of the Divine Creation of man as taught in the Bible."

Shortly after the anti-evolution law passed, the town of Dayton, Tennessee, decided to take advantage of it. Local business people and town boosters wanted to put their town on the map and attract new investment to the area.

They recruited John Scopes, a general science high school teacher and part-time football coach. Scopes defied the law by lecturing from a biology textbook that presented Darwin's theory. At the same time, the interests of the town boosters converged with those of the ACLU, which wanted to challenge the restrictive state statute on the grounds of free speech and academic freedom and attract new members to the organization. Together, these two very different groups succeeded in turning an ordinary judicial hearing into the "trial of the century."

The resulting trial brought Dayton more fame, much of it negative, than the planners had bargained for. When court convened in July 1925, millions of people listened over the radio to the first trial ever broadcast. Reporters from all over the country descended on Dayton to keep their readers informed of the proceedings, while cynical journalists such as H. L. Mencken ridiculed Dayton and its residents.

Inside the courtroom, a monumental confrontation took place. Clarence Darrow headed the defense team. A controversial and colorful criminal lawyer from Chicago, who in a few months would defend Ossian Sweet, Darrow doubted the existence of God. On the other side, William Jennings Bryan, three-time Democratic candidate for president and secretary of state under Woodrow Wilson, assisted the prosecution. As a Protestant fundamentalist, Bryan believed that accepting scientific evolution would undermine the moral basis of politics and that communities should have the right to determine their children's school curriculum. A Seventh-Day Adventist minister summed up what the fundamentalists considered to be at stake: "[Darwin's theory] breeds corruption, lust, immorality, greed, and such acts of criminal depravity as drug addiction, war, and atrocious acts of genocide."

The presiding judge, John T. Raulston, set the tone for the trial by beginning each session with a prayer. He ruled that scientists could not take the stand to defend evolution because he considered their testimony "hearsay," given that they had not been present at the creation. The defense nearly collapsed until Darrow called the willing Bryan to the stand as "an expert on the Bible." The clash of these two titans provided excellent theater but changed few minds. The jury took only eight minutes to declare Scopes guilty. Two weeks after the trial, Bryan died in his sleep, still convinced that his views had prevailed. Scopes's conviction was overturned by an appeals court on a technicality. Yet fundamentalists remained as certain as ever in their beliefs, and anti-evolution laws stayed in force until the 1970s. The trial had not "settled" anything. Rather, it served to highlight a cultural division over the place of religion in American society that persists to the present day.

REVIEW & RELATE

What was the connection between anti-immigrant sentiment and the defense of tradition during the 1920s?

Who challenged the new morality associated with modernization? Why?

Politics and the Fading of Prosperity

These cultural clashes tore the Democratic Party apart, leaving Republicans in command of national politics. As it attracted a growing number of urban immigrants to its ranks alongside its customary base of white southerners, the Democratic Party tried to reconcile the tensions between traditional and modern America. Its failure to do so kept Republicans in power despite growing evidence of their inability to resolve serious economic problems. Although many progressives continued to press for reform, they were all but powerless to prevent the coming economic crisis.

The Battle for the Soul of the Democratic Party

The 1924 presidential election exposed the social and cultural fault lines within the Democratic Party. Since the end of Reconstruction and the "redemption" of the South by southern Democrats, the Republican Party had ceased to compete for office in the region. Southern Democrats, along with party supporters from the rural Midwest, shared strong fundamentalist religious beliefs and an enthusiasm for prohibition that usually placed them at odds with big-city northern Democrats. The urban wing of the party increasingly represented immigrant populations that rejected prohibition as contrary to their social practices and supported political machines, which many rural Democrats found odious and an indicator of cultural degradation. These distinctions, however, were not absolute—some rural dwellers opposed prohibition, and some urbanites supported temperance.

Delegates to the 1924 Democratic convention in New York City had trouble deciding on a party platform and a presidential candidate. When urban delegates from the Northeast attempted to insert a plank condemning D. C. Stephenson's Ku Klux Klan for its intolerance, they lost by a thin margin. Proponents of this measure owed their defeat to the sizable number of convention delegates who either belonged to the Klan or had been backed by it.

The selection of the presidential ticket proved even more divisive. Urban Democrats favored the nomination of New York governor Alfred E. Smith. Smith came from an Irish Catholic immigrant family, had grown up on New York City's Lower East Side, and was sponsored by the Tammany Hall machine. The epitome of everything that rural Democrats despised, Smith further angered opponents with his outspoken denunciation of prohibition. Prohibitionists fiercely opposed Smith, and he lost the

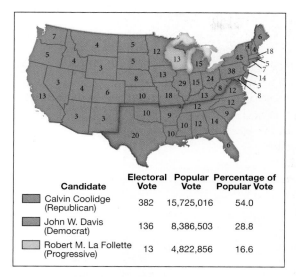

Candidate	Electoral Vote	Popular Vote	Percentage of Popular Vote
Calvin Coolidge (Republican)	382	15,725,016	54.0
John W. Davis (Democrat)	136	8,386,503	28.8
Robert M. La Follette (Progressive)	13	4,822,856	16.6

MAP 21.1　The Election of 1924

Republican Calvin Coolidge, who became president in August 1923 on the death of Warren Harding, continued Harding's policies of limited government regulation and corporate tax cuts. Coolidge easily defeated Democrat John Davis, whose strength was confined to the South. Running as the Progressive Party candidate, Senator Robert La Follette won 16 percent of the popular vote but carried only his home state of Wisconsin, with 13 electoral votes.

nomination to John W. Davis, a West Virginia Protestant and a supporter of prohibition. The intense intraparty fighting left the Democrats deeply divided going into the general election. To no one's surprise, Davis lost to Calvin Coolidge in a landslide (Map 21.1).

In 1928, however, when the Democrats met in Houston, Texas, the delicate cultural equilibrium within the Democratic Party had shifted in favor of the urban forces. With Stephenson and the Klan discredited and no longer a force in Democratic politics, the delegates nominated Al Smith as their presidential candidate. To balance the ticket, they tapped for vice president Joseph G. Robinson, a senator from Arkansas, a Protestant, and a supporter of prohibition.

The Republicans selected Herbert Hoover, one of the most popular men in the United States. His biography read like a script of the American dream. Born in Iowa to a Quaker family, he became an orphan at the age of nine and moved to Oregon to live with relatives. After graduating from Stanford University in 1895, he began a career as a prosperous mining engineer and a successful businessman. Affectionately called "the Great Humanitarian" for his European relief efforts after World War I, Hoover served as secretary of commerce during the Harding and Coolidge administrations. His name became synonymous with the Republican prosperity of the 1920s. In accepting his party's nomination for president in 1928, Hoover optimistically

declared: "We in America today are nearer to the final triumph over poverty than ever before in the history of the land." A Protestant supporter of prohibition from a small town, Hoover was everything Smith was not.

The outcome of the election proved predictable. Running on prosperity and pledging a "chicken in every pot and two cars in every garage," Hoover trounced Smith with 58 percent of the popular vote and more than 80 percent of the electoral vote. Despite the weakening economy, Smith lost usually reliable Democratic votes to religious and ethnic prejudices. The New Yorker prevailed only in Massachusetts, Rhode Island, and six southern states but failed to win his home state. A closer look at the election returns showed a significant party realignment under way. Smith succeeded in identifying the Democratic Party with urban, ethnic-minority voters and attracting them to the polls. Despite the landslide loss, he captured the twelve largest cities in the nation, all of which had gone Republican four years earlier. In another fifteen big cities, Smith did better than the Democrat ticket had done in the 1924 election, thereby encouraging the country's ethnic minorities to support the party of Thomas Jefferson and Woodrow Wilson. To break the Republicans' national dominance, the Democrats would need a candidate who appealed to both traditional and modern Americans. Smith's defeat, however, laid the foundation for future Democratic political success.

Where Have All the Progressives Gone?

The Democrats and Republicans were not the only parties that attracted voters in the 1920s. Some voters continued to cast their ballot for the Socialist Party. Others took the opportunity to voice their disapproval of Republican policies by voting for the remaining progressive candidates. Progressives did manage to hold on to seats in Congress, and in 1921 they helped pass the Shepherd-Towner Act, which appropriated federal funds to establish maternal and child centers (see chapter 19). But their efforts to restrict the power of the Supreme Court, reduce tax cuts for the wealthy, nationalize railroads, and extend agricultural relief to farmers were rebuffed by conservative legislative majorities. In 1924 reformers nominated Senator Robert M. La Follette of Wisconsin to run for president on a revived Progressive Party ticket, but he came in a distant third and won only five million popular votes and the electoral votes of his home state. The Progressive Party collapsed soon after La Follette died in 1925.

Still, progressivism managed to stay alive on the local and state levels. Gifford Pinchot, a Roosevelt ally and a champion of conservation (see chapter 19), twice

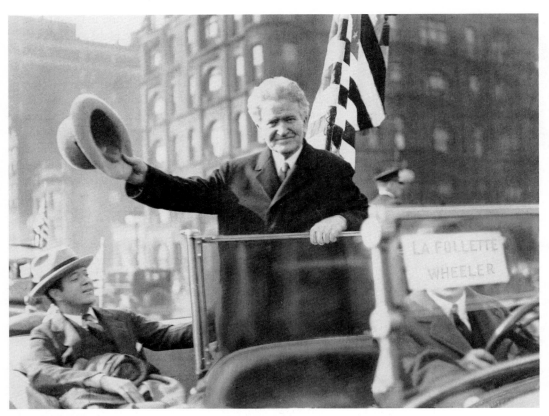

Robert M. La Follette, 1924
Wisconsin senator Robert M. La Follette, running for president on the Progressive Party ticket in 1924, campaigns in Chicago with his son, Robert Jr., seated next to him. La Follette and his running mate, Senator Burton K. Wheeler of Montana, favored higher taxes for the wealthy, collective bargaining rights for factory workers, and limits on Supreme Court power.   Library of Congress

won election as governor of Pennsylvania starting in 1922. Social workers continued their efforts to alleviate urban poverty and lobby for government assistance to the poor. Even at the national level, women in the Children's Bureau maintained the progressive legacy by supporting assistance to families and devising social welfare proposals. Progressivism did not disappear during the 1920s, but it did fight an uphill and often losing battle during an age of conservative political ascendancy. Its weakness contributed to the government's failure to check the worst corporate and financial practices, a failure that would play a role in the nation's economic collapse.

Financial Crash

On October 29, 1929, a day that became known as **Black Tuesday**, stock market prices tumbled. Over the previous five years, the rising market, bolstered by optimistic buyers, earned huge profits for investors, and the value of stocks

nearly doubled. In late October, panicked sellers sent stock prices into free fall, culminating in the selling of more than 16 million shares valued at $32 billion on October 29. Although only 2.5 percent of Americans owned stock, the stock market crash had an enormous impact on the economy and the rest of the world. Because so much of the stock boom depended on generous margin requirements (a down payment of only 5 to 10 percent), when investor-borrowers got caught short by falling prices, they could not repay the financial institutions that had extended them credit. Banks and lending agencies, with their interlocking management and overextension of credit, had difficulty withstanding the turmoil unleashed by the stock market crash.

The 1929 crash did not cause the decade-long Great Depression that followed. The seeds for the greatest economic catastrophe in American history had been planted earlier. The economy had endured a series of panics and depressions in the past, but nothing like what happened between 1929 and 1940. The causes stemmed from flaws in an economic system that produced a great disparity of wealth, inadequate consumption, overextension of credit both at home and abroad, and the government's unwillingness to relieve the plight of farmers. Republican administrations made matters worse by lowering taxes on the rich and raising tariffs to benefit manufacturers. The Federal Reserve Board exacerbated the situation by keeping interest rates high, thereby making it difficult for people to get loans and repay debts. The failure was not that of the United States alone; the depression affected capitalist nations throughout the world. The stock market collapse crushed whatever confidence the American public had that the unfettered law of supply and demand and laissez-faire economics could ensure prosperity.

REVIEW & RELATE

How did divisions within the Democratic Party contribute to Republican political dominance in the 1920s?

What underlying economic weaknesses led to the Great Depression?

 LEARNINGCurve **bedfordstmartins.com/hewittlawson/LC**

Conclusion: The Roaring Twenties

While the second industrial revolution spurred extraordinary prosperity, the 1920s ended in an unprecedented economic collapse. During the decade, industrialists produced and marketed wares in a manner that drew the mass of Americans into the economy as laborers and consumers. Automobiles, fueled by gasoline, traveled up and down streets and highways. Electricity powered household appliances and ran movie projectors in theaters throughout the nation. People living in California, Michigan, Florida, or New Jersey had similar opportunities to buy consumer products and partake in a mass culture made possible by movies and radio. Producing for a mass market, industrial giants like Henry Ford transformed the nature of work and pleasure. The assembly line revolutionized the pace of labor and turned it into a standardized routine. The automobile transformed dating patterns and opened up new opportunities for the exploration of romance and sex.

For most Americans earning very modest incomes, the fruits of the consumer revolution were beyond their reach. The image of the 1920s as an era of widespread prosperity is exaggerated. Most Americans lived at or below the poverty line and earned just enough money to acquire the bare necessities. They could live beyond their means through an ample supply of credit, but their poverty contrasted with the increasing concentration of wealth in the hands of the richest Americans. Businessmen like Henry Ford attempted to take care of their workers through higher wages and assorted benefits, but their paternalism depended on the continuation of good economic times. The stock market crash of 1929 and the ensuing Great Depression exposed the shortcomings of the corporate business world, inadequate oversight by the federal government, and an overreliance on the private sector to look after the nation's economic health.

The weaknesses of the economy, which appear clear in retrospect, were often hidden behind the clash over cultural differences. Guardians of traditional morality and values worried about the effects of more than fifty years of industrialization, immigration, and urbanization. Issues such as the enforcement of prohibition, the teaching of evolution in the schools, and whether a Catholic should be elected president dominated political discussion, while efforts to assist farmers and workers were unsuccessful. These battles marked a turning point in American history— the transition from a traditional, rural, Protestant society to an urban, ethnically and religiously diverse one. The widespread popularity of D. C. Stephenson's Ku Klux Klan throughout the South and the North demonstrated that the older America of white, northern European Protestants did not intend to relinquish political or cultural power without a struggle. At the same time, ethnic minorities represented by Al Smith had no intention of backing down. Neither did millions of African Americans, whether they joined the NAACP, as did Ossian Sweet, or supported Marcus Garvey's UNIA. During the next decade, Americans from all backgrounds would battle more than cultural threats; they would fight for their economic survival.

LEARNINGCurve
Check what you know.
bedfordstmartins.com/hewittlawson/LC

Chapter Review

Online Study Guide ▶ **bedfordstmartins.com/hewittlawson**

KEY TERMS

Red scare (p. 655)
Palmer raids (p. 656)
great migration (p. 657)
American Plan (p. 658)
Teapot Dome scandal (p. 659)
second industrial revolution (p. 660)
new woman (p. 664)
Lost Generation (p. 664)
New Negro (p. 665)
Universal Negro Improvement Association (UNIA) (p. 666)
Sacco and Vanzetti case (p. 668)
National Origins Act (p. 668)
Black Tuesday (p. 674)

REVIEW & RELATE

1. What factors combined to produce the turmoil of the immediate postwar period?

2. What factors contributed to the rise in racial tensions that accompanied the transition from wartime to peacetime?

3. Describe the relationship between business and government in the 1920s.

4. Why was a high level of consumer spending so critical to 1920s prosperity, and why was the economic expansion of the 1920s ultimately unsustainable?

5. How did new forms of entertainment challenge traditional morality and traditional gender roles?

6. Describe the black cultural and intellectual renaissance that flourished in the 1920s.

7. What was the connection between anti-immigrant sentiment and the defense of tradition during the 1920s?

8. Who challenged the new morality associated with modernization? Why?

9. How did divisions within the Democratic Party contribute to Republican political dominance in the 1920s?

10. What underlying economic weaknesses led to the Great Depression?

TIMELINE OF EVENTS

1914	Universal Negro Improvement Association (UNIA) formed
1915	Ku Klux Klan revived
1917–1918	400,000 African Americans leave South as part of great migration
1917	Russian Revolution begins
1918–1920	Worldwide influenza epidemic
1919	4 million workers go on strike nationwide
	Race riots erupt in twenty-five U.S. cities
	Radicals mail incendiary devices to prominent Americans
	Palmer raids begin
1920	American Civil Liberties Union (ACLU) formed
	David Curtis Stephenson joins the Ku Klux Klan
1920s	Harlem Renaissance
1921	J. Edgar Hoover becomes director of the Bureau of Investigation (later the FBI)
	Teapot Dome scandal
1924	National Origins Act passed
	Charles Dawes negotiates with the Allies to reduce Germany's reparations payments
1925–1929	U.S. farm income drops by 50 percent
1925	Scopes trial
1926	Ossian Sweet and family acquitted of first-degree murder charges
1927	Sacco and Vanzetti executed
1928	Democrat Al Smith loses presidential election but wins ten largest cities
1929	Stock market crash sparks Great Depression

The *Abrams* Case and the Red Scare

In August 1918, New York City police arrested five Russian immigrants and charged them with violating the Espionage and Sedition Acts passed during World War I. The defendants were part of an anarchist group called Frayhayt (Freedom). Late in the summer of 1918, the group distributed two leaflets—one in Yiddish and one in English—that criticized President Wilson and the U.S. military intervention against Russia's Bolshevik government. It also called for a general workers' strike to protest Wilson's policy. During police interrogations, Jacob Schwartz was beaten so badly that he died from his injuries. The other four defendants were tried and convicted in October 1918 and sentenced to between fifteen and twenty years in prison. When they appealed their convictions, the U.S. Supreme Court upheld the verdict. In 1921 the defendants were deported to the Soviet Union.

Abrams v. United States upheld the "clear and present danger" principle first established in *Schenck v. United States* (1919). In the *Schenck* case, Justice Oliver Wendell Holmes wrote the unanimous decision establishing that free speech could be legally restricted only if it posed a clear threat to public safety. Eight months later, Holmes changed his mind and broke with the majority of his fellow justices in their application of his "clear and present danger" test to the *Abrams* case. In his famous dissent (Document 21.7), Holmes insisted that the prosecution had failed to prove intent on the part of the anarchists to harm the United States and further argued that a threat must be "clear and *imminent* [emphasis added]" before free speech could be limited, even during wartime.

Like thousands of other anarchists, socialists, and Communists, the *Abrams* defendants were victims of the "Red scare" that suppressed radical activities during and immediately after World War I. The following documents explore different aspects of the Red scare and the *Abrams* case. As you examine these sources, consider to what extent national security concerns should allow the government to curtail free speech rights.

DOCUMENT 21.5

Mollie Steimer | Trial Testimony, 1918

Mollie Steimer, the youngest defendant in the *Abrams* case, emigrated from Russia in 1912 at the age of fifteen. Steimer worked in a shirtwaist factory in New York City's garment industry. Her discontent grew under the strain of this monotonous, low-paying work, and in 1917 she joined Frayhayt and the anarchist movement. Press reports on the trial emphasized her youthful appearance and defiant demeanor, including her refusal to stand when the judge entered the courtroom. At the proceedings, she offered the following explanation of anarchism.

ANARCHISM is a new social order where no group shall be governed by another group of people. Individual freedom shall prevail in the full sense of the word. Private ownership shall be abolished. Every person shall have an equal opportunity to develop himself well, both mentally and physically. We shall not have to struggle for our daily existence as we do now. No one shall live on the product of others. Every person shall produce as much as he can, and enjoy as much as he needs—receive according to his need. Instead of striving to get money, we shall strive towards education, towards knowledge.

While at present the people of the world are divided into various groups, calling themselves nations, while one nation defies another—in most cases considers the others as competitive—we, the workers of the world, shall stretch out our hands towards each other with brotherly love. To the fulfillment of this idea I shall devote all my energy, and, if necessary, render my life for it.

Source: *Sentenced to Twenty Years in Prison* (New York: Political Prisoners Defense and Relief Committee, 1919), 20.

DOCUMENT 21.6

"Workers—Wake Up!!" 1918

The leaflet entitled "Workers—Wake Up!!" that Frayhayt distributed in 1918 was central to the government's case against the defendants. Following is the official translation of the Yiddish document used at the trial. The prosecution allegedly translated the document in a manner that made it more explosive, whereas in more recent translations it sounds less threatening.

The preparatory work for Russia's emancipation is brought to an end by his Majesty, Mr. [Woodrow] Wilson, and the rest of the gang; dogs of all colors!

America, together with the Allies, will march to Russia, not, "God Forbid," to interfere with the Russian affairs, but to help the Czecho-Slovaks in their struggle against the Bolsheviki.

Oh, ugly hypocrites; this time they shall not succeed in fooling the Russian emigrants and the friends of Russia in America. Too visible is their audacious move.

Workers, Russian emigrants, you who had the least belief in the honesty of our government, must now throw away all confidence, must spit in the face [of] the false, hypocritic, military propaganda which has fooled you so relentlessly, calling forth your sympathy, your help, to the prosecution of the war. With the money which you have loaned, or are going to loan them, they will make bullets not only for the Germans but also for the Workers Soviets of Russia. Workers in the ammunition factories, you are producing bullets, bayonets, cannon, to murder not only the Germans, but also your dearest, best, who are in Russia and are fighting for freedom.

You who emigrated from Russia, you who are friends of Russia, will you carry on your conscience in cold blood the shame spot as a helper to choke the Workers Soviets? Will you give your consent to the inquisition-ary expedition to Russia? Will you be calm spectators to the fleecing blood from the hearts of the best sons of Russia?

America and her Allies have betrayed (the workers). Their robberish aims are clear to all men. The destruction of the Russian Revolution, that is the politics of the march to Russia.

Workers, our reply to the barbaric intervention has to be a general strike! An open challenge only will let the government know that not only the Russian worker fights for freedom, but also here in America lives the spirit of revolution.

Do not let the government scare you with their wild punishment in prisons, hanging and shooting. We must not and will not betray the splendid fighters of Russia. Workers, up to fight.

Three hundred years had the Romanoff dynasty taught us how to fight. Let all rulers remember this, from the smallest to the biggest despot, that the hand of the revolution will not shiver in a fight.

Woe unto those who will be in the way of progress. Let solidarity live!

THE REBELS

Source: Richard Polenberg, *Fighting Faiths: The Abrams Case, the Supreme Court, and Free Speech* (New York: Viking, 1987), 51–52.

DOCUMENT 21.7

Oliver Wendell Holmes | *Abrams v. United States* Dissent, 1919

The *Abrams v. United States* majority decision, written by Justice John Clarke, upheld the "clear and present danger" argument of *Schenck v. United States*. Justice Oliver Wendell Holmes wrote the *Schenck* decision; however, in the *Abrams* case he broke from the majority and argued that the government needed a much tougher standard to restrict free speech. Justice Louis Brandeis joined him in this dissent.

I N THIS CASE, sentences of twenty years' imprisonment have been imposed for the publishing of two leaflets that I believe the defendants had as much right to publish as the Government has to publish the Constitution of the United States now vainly invoked by them. Even if I am technically wrong, and enough can be squeezed from these poor and puny anonymities to turn the color of legal litmus paper, I will add, even if what I think the necessary intent were shown, the most nominal punishment seems to me all that possibly could be inflicted, unless the defendants are to be made to suffer not for what the indictment alleges, but for the creed that they avow—a creed that I believe to be the creed of ignorance and immaturity when honestly held, as I see no reason to doubt that it was held here, but which, although made the subject of examination at the trial, no one has a right even to consider in dealing with the charges before the Court.

Persecution for the expression of opinions seems to me perfectly logical. If you have no doubt of your premises or your power, and want a certain result with all your heart, you naturally express your wishes in law, and sweep away all opposition. To allow opposition by speech seems to indicate that you think the speech impotent, as when a man says that he has squared the circle, or that you do not care wholeheartedly for the result, or that you doubt either your power or your premises. But when men have realized that time has upset many fighting faiths, they may come to believe even more than they believe the very foundations of their own conduct that the ultimate good desired is better reached by free trade in ideas—that the best test of truth is the power of the thought to get itself accepted in the competition of the market, and that truth is the only ground upon which their wishes safely can be carried out. That, at any rate, is the theory of our Constitution. It is an experiment, as all life is an experiment. Every year, if not every day, we have to wager our salvation upon some prophecy based upon imperfect knowledge. While that experiment is part of our system, I think that we should be eternally vigilant against attempts to check the expression of opinions that we loathe and believe to be fraught with death, unless they so imminently threaten immediate interference with the lawful and pressing purposes of the law that an immediate check is required to save the country. . . . Only the emergency that makes it immediately dangerous to leave the correction of evil counsels to time warrants making any exception to the sweeping command, "Congress shall make no law . . . abridging the freedom of speech." Of course, I am speaking only of expressions of opinion and exhortations, which were all that were uttered here, but I regret that I cannot put into more impressive words my belief that, in their conviction upon this indictment, the defendants were deprived of their rights under the Constitution of the United States.

Source: *Abrams et al. v. United States*, 250 U.S. (1919), 629–31.

DOCUMENT 21.8

Zechariah Chafee Jr. | Freedom of Speech in Wartime, 1919

Harvard law professor Zechariah Chafee Jr. led protests against the severity of the sentences in the *Abrams* case, pointing out that the defendants were only guilty of advocating against U.S. interference in the affairs of another nation, not of inciting antiwar violence. In an article published after the *Schenck* decision, but several months before the Supreme Court's decision in the *Abrams* case, Chafee argued for the importance of protecting freedom of speech even in wartime.

THE REAL ISSUE in every free-speech controversy is this—whether the state can punish all words which have some tendency, however remote, to bring about acts in violation of law, or only words which directly incite to acts in violation of law.

If words do not become criminal until they have an immediate tendency to produce a breach of the peace, there is no need for a law of sedition, since the ordinary standards of criminal solicitation and attempt apply. Under those standards the words must bring the speaker's unlawful intention reasonably near to success. Such a limited power to punish utterances rarely satisfies the zealous in times of excitement like war. They realize that all condemnation of the war or of conscription may conceivably lead to active resistance or insubordination. Is it not better to kill the serpent in the egg? All writings that have a tendency to hinder the war must be suppressed.

Such has always been the argument of the opponents of free speech. And the most powerful weapon in their hand, since the abolition of the censorship, is this doctrine of indirect causation, under which words can be punished for a supposed bad tendency long before there is any probability that they will break out into unlawful acts. . . .

It is now clear that the First Amendment fixes limits upon the power of Congress to restrict speech either by a censorship or by a criminal statute, and if the Espionage Act exceeds those limits it is unconstitutional. It is sometimes argued that the Constitution gives Congress the power to declare war, raise armies, and support a navy, that one provision of the Constitution cannot be used to break down another

provision, and consequently freedom of speech cannot be invoked to break down the war power. I would reply that the First Amendment is just as much a part of the Constitution as the war clauses, and that it is equally accurate to say that the war clauses cannot be invoked to break down freedom of speech. The truth is that all provisions of the Constitution must be construed together so as to limit each other. In war as in peace, this process of mutual adjustment must include the Bill of Rights. There are those who believe that the Bill of Rights can be set aside in war time at the uncontrolled will of the government. The first ten amendments were drafted by men who had just been through a war. Two of these amendments [the Third and Fifth Amendments] expressly apply in war. . . .

The First Amendment protects two kinds of interests in free speech. There is an individual interest, the need of many men to express their opinions on matters vital to them if life is to be worth living, and a social interest in the attainment of truth, so that the country may not only adopt the wisest course of action but carry it out in the wisest way. This social interest is especially important in war time. Even after war has been declared there is bound to be a confused mixture of good and bad arguments in its support, and a wide difference of opinion as to its objects. Truth can be sifted out from falsehood only if the government is vigorously and constantly cross-examined, so that the fundamental issues of the struggle may be clearly defined, and the war may not be diverted to improper ends, or conducted with an undue sacrifice of life and liberty, or prolonged after its just purposes are accomplished. Legal proceedings prove that an opponent

(continued on page 682)

makes the best cross-examiner. Consequently it is a disastrous mistake to limit criticism to those who favor the war. Men bitterly hostile to it may point out evils in its management like the secret treaties, which its supporters have been too busy to unearth. The history of the last five years shows how the objects of a war may change completely during its progress, and it is well that those objects should be steadily reformulated under the influence of open discussion not only by those who demand a military victory but by pacifists who take a different view of the national welfare. Further argument for the existence of this social interest becomes unnecessary if we recall the national value of the opposition in former wars. . . .

The true boundary line of the First Amendment can be fixed only when Congress and the courts realize that the principle on which speech is classified as lawful or unlawful involves the balancing against each other of two very important social interests, in public safety and in the search for truth. Every reasonable attempt should be made to maintain both interests unimpaired, and the great interest in free speech should be sacrificed only when the interest in public safety is really imperiled, and not, as most men believe, when it is barely conceivable that it may be slightly affected. In war time, therefore, speech should be unrestricted by the censorship or by punishment, unless it is clearly liable to cause direct and dangerous interference with the conduct of the war.

Thus our problem of locating the boundary line of free speech is solved. It is fixed close to the point where words will give rise to unlawful acts.

Source: Zechariah Chafee Jr., *Freedom of Speech in War Time* (Cambridge, MA: Harvard Law Review, 1919), 948–49, 955, 958–60.

DOCUMENT 21.9

Billy Ireland | "We Can't Digest the Scum," 1919

The Red scare stoked fears that radical immigrants were a threat to the U.S. government and America's capitalist economy. In contrast to the traditional vision of America as a melting pot that would dissolve cultural differences, cartoonist Billy Ireland suggests that not all ideas or people should be assimilated into the American melting pot.

DOCUMENT 21.10

A. Mitchell Palmer | The Case against the Reds, 1920

U.S. Attorney General A. Mitchell Palmer was a leading architect of the Red scare. In response to the strikes and riots that occurred throughout 1919, in January 1920 Palmer organized a series of raids against suspected Communists, anarchists, and other foreign radicals. More than six thousand people were arrested, many of whom were later released. In an article in the *Forum* magazine, Palmer defended his actions and described his views on radicalism and its threat to American society.

Like a prairie-fire, the blaze of revolution was sweeping over every American institution of law and order a year ago. It was eating its way into the homes of the American workman, its sharp tongues of revolutionary heat were licking the altars of the churches, leaping into the belfry of the school bell, crawling into the sacred corners of American homes, seeking to replace marriage vows with libertine laws, burning up the foundations of society.

Robbery, not war, is the ideal of communism. This has been demonstrated in Russia, Germany, and in America. As a foe, the anarchist is fearless of his own life, for his creed is a fanaticism that admits no respect of any other creed. Obviously it is the creed of any criminal mind, which reasons always from motives impossible to clean thought. Crime is the degenerate factor in society.

Upon these two basic certainties, first that the "Reds" were criminal aliens, and secondly that the American Government must prevent crime, it was decided that there could be no nice distinctions drawn between the theoretical ideals of the radicals and their actual violations of our national laws. An assassin may have brilliant intellectuality, he may be able to excuse his murder or robbery with fine oratory, but any theory which excuses crime is not wanted in America. This is no place for the criminal to flourish, nor will he do so, so long as the rights of common citizenship can be exerted to prevent him.

OUR GOVERNMENT IN JEOPARDY

It has always been plain to me that when American citizens unite upon any national issue, they are generally right, but it is sometimes difficult to make the issue clear to them. If the Department of Justice could succeed in attracting the attention of our optimistic citizens to the issue of internal revolution in this country, we felt sure there would be no revolution. The Government was in jeopardy. My private information of what was being done by the organization known as the Communist Party of America, with headquarters in Chicago, of what was being done by the Communist Internationale under their manifesto planned at Moscow last March by Trotzky, Lenine, and others, addressed "To the Proletariats of All Countries," of what strides the Communist Labor Party was making, removed all doubt. In this conclusion we did not ignore the definite standards of personal liberty, of free speech, which is the very temperament and heart of the people. The evidence was examined with the utmost care, with a personal leaning toward freedom of thought and word on all questions. . . .

. . . The Department of Justice will pursue the attack of these "Reds" upon the Government of the United States with vigilance, and no alien, advocating the overthrow of existing law and order in this country, shall escape arrest and prompt deportation.

It is my belief that while they have stirred discontent in our midst, while they have caused irritating strikes, and while they have infected our social ideas with the disease of their own minds and their unclean morals, we can get rid of them! And not until we have done so shall we have removed the menace of Bolshevism for good.

Source: A. Mitchell Palmer, "The Case against the Reds," *The Forum*, February 1920, 174–75, 185.

Interpret the Evidence

1. What elements of Mollie Steimer's and Frayhayt's arguments (Documents 21.5 and 21.6) would have seemed most threatening to the court and the American public?

2. Why does Justice Oliver Wendell Holmes (Document 21.7) believe it is important to safeguard free speech rights? On what does he base his argument?

3. Where does Zechariah Chafee (Document 21.8) draw the line between free speech and unlawful activity?

4. According to A. Mitchell Palmer (Document 21.10), why is it necessary and constitutional to suppress the rights of Communists?

5. What does Billy Ireland's cartoon (Document 21.9) conclude about the success of the American melting pot?

6. Compare the statements from Mollie Steimer, Oliver Wendell Holmes, and A. Mitchell Palmer. How does each define and understand anarchism and other radical ideologies?

Put It in Context

- How did the *Abrams* case and the Red scare reflect the cultural and political anxieties of the 1920s?

Library of Congress

Carol M. Highsmith Archive, Library of Congress

Children of Mexican cotton laborers, Casa Grande, Arizona, 1937.

WPA mural, Cohen Building, Washington, D.C.

22

Depression, Dissent, and the New Deal

1929–1940

Anna Eleanor Roosevelt came from an old Dutch American family of wealthy merchants and bankers. In 1901, at the age of fifteen, she saw her uncle Theodore succeed William McKinley as president. Like other girls of her generation, Eleanor was expected to marry and become a "charming wife." Eleanor appeared well on her way toward doing so when she struck up a relationship with her distant cousin Franklin Delano Roosevelt, whom she married in 1905. Over a ten-year period, Eleanor gave birth to six children, further reinforcing her status as a traditional woman of her class.

Two events, however, set her life on a very different path than the one she had embarked on when she married Franklin. First, thirteen years into her marriage Eleanor discovered that her husband was having an affair with her social secretary, Lucy Mercer. She did not divorce him but made it clear that she would stay with him primarily as a mother to their children and a political partner. Second, in 1921 the thirty-nine-year-old Franklin contracted polio. Although he recovered, Franklin would never walk again or stand without the aid of braces. From this point on, Eleanor threw herself into public life, taking a more active role in her husband's political career and writing about personal and political issues for a range of publications.

After her husband won the presidency in 1932, Eleanor did not function as a typical First Lady. She played a very public role promoting her husband's agenda, and she also took advantage of her own extensive network of friends and acquaintances in labor

Library of Congress

Line of men inside the State Employment Service in San Francisco, California, waiting to register for benefits, 1938.

unions, civil rights organizations, and women's groups to advance a variety of causes. In many ways more liberal than her husband, Eleanor was a fierce advocate for the rights of women, minorities, workers, and the poor. Behind the scenes, she pushed her husband to move further to the political left.

Eleanor Roosevelt's proximity to power provided her with a unique position from which to confront the problems of her day. She was not, however, alone in her desire to work for social and economic justice. Luisa Moreno provides a striking example of an activist whose American story bears little resemblance to that of Eleanor Roosevelt. A native of Guatemala, Moreno moved to Mexico and then New York City, where she led a difficult life. In the midst of the Great Depression, Moreno worked as a seamstress in a sweatshop to support her young child and unemployed husband. Like tens of thousands of people disillusioned with capitalism, in 1930 she joined the Communist Party but quit several years later.

In 1935 Moreno went to Florida to organize cigar workers for the American Federation of Labor (AFL). Despite numerous successes, she grew tired of the AFL's refusal to recruit unskilled workers and jumped to the Congress of Industrial Organizations (CIO), which formed in 1935. That same year, she began working for the United Cannery, Agricultural, Packing, and Allied Workers of America (UCA-PAWA), an affiliate of the CIO. Encouraged by the federal government's establishment of the National Labor Relations Board in 1935 to safeguard union organizing, by 1943 Moreno and her colleagues in the UCAPAWA had won more than thirty elections recognizing their union among cannery workers.

Moreno also promoted the advancement of Latinos throughout the United States. In 1939 she helped create El Congreso de Pueblos de Habla Española (The Congress of Spanish-Speaking People). Besides championing equal access to jobs, education, housing, and health care, the organization pressed to end the segregation of Latinos in schools and public accommodations. Moreno was not nearly as well known as Eleanor Roosevelt, but she worked just as hard to fight poverty, exploitation, and racial bigotry on behalf of people whom President Franklin Roosevelt called "the forgotten Americans." •

photos: Library of Congress; Courtesy of Vicki L. Ruiz

WHILE THE AMERICAN HISTORIES of Eleanor Roosevelt and Luisa Moreno were very different, both of their lives were shaped in fundamental ways by the same global catastrophe, the Great Depression. The economic crisis that erupted in 1929 made a bad situation worse for the majority of Americans. Even before the Great Depression, most Americans lived at or near the poverty level, surviving month to month. By 1933, millions of Americans had lost even this tenuous hold on economic security, as unemployment reached a record 25 percent, a figure that did not include those who had stopped looking for work. Succeeding President Herbert Hoover, Franklin Roosevelt initiated policies that departed profoundly from the reliance on private charity and voluntary efforts that had characterized Republican responses to economic problems throughout the 1920s. Proclaiming the establishment of a New Deal for America, Roosevelt expanded the power of the federal government in ways that previously had taken place only during wartime, and he forged a new political order in which the Democratic Party ruled for generations to come.

The Great Depression

Herbert Hoover had the unenviable task of assuming the presidency in 1929 as the economy crumbled. Given his long history of public service, he seemed the right man for the job. Hoover, however, was unwilling to make a fundamental break with the economic approaches of the past and proved unable to effectively communicate his genuine concern for the plight of the poor. Despite his sincere efforts, the depression deepened. Among the hardest hit were minority groups already suffering from discrimination. As unemployment rose and more and more farmers lost their land, many Americans, made desperate by their economic plight and angered by the inadequate response of their government, took to the streets in protest.

Hoover Faces the Depression

National prosperity was at its peak when the Republican Hoover entered the White House in March 1929. The nation had little reason to doubt him when he boasted in his inaugural address: "We in America today are nearer to the final triumph over poverty than ever before in the history of any land. The poorhouse is vanishing from among us." These words were still ringing in the public's ears when the stock market crashed later that year.

Hoover brought to the presidency a blend of traditional and progressive ideas. He believed that government and business should form voluntary partnerships to work toward common goals. Rejecting the principle of absolute laissez-faire, he nonetheless argued that the government should extend its influence lightly over the economy—to encourage and persuade sensible behavior, but not to impose itself on the private sector.

The Great Depression sorely tested Hoover's beliefs. Having placed his faith in cooperation rather than coercion, the president relied on voluntarism to get the nation through hard economic times. Hoover hoped that management and labor, through gentle persuasion, would hold steady on prices and wages and calmly wait until the worst of the depression passed. In the meantime, for those in dire need, the president turned to local communities and private charities. Hoover expected municipal and state governments to shoulder the burden of providing relief to the needy, just as they had during previous economic downturns.

Hoover's remedies failed to rally the country back to good economic health. Initially, business people responded positively to the president's request to maintain the status quo, but when the economy did not bounce back, they lost confidence and defected. Nor did local governments and private agencies have the funds to provide relief to all those who needed it. With tax revenues in decline, some 1,300 municipalities across the country had gone bankrupt by

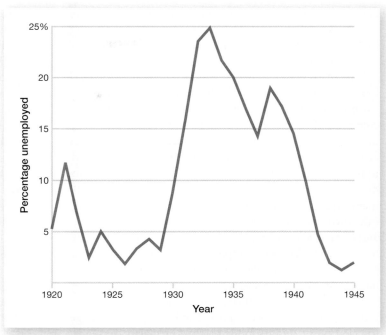

FIGURE 22.1   Unemployment, 1920–1945

Business prosperity and immigration restriction ensured low unemployment during most of the 1920s. When unemployment rose dramatically in the late 1920s, President Hoover failed to handle the crisis. During the 1930s, President Roosevelt's New Deal initiatives did lower unemployment to some extent. Still, only mobilizing the nation for war in 1941 created a significant increase in jobs.

1933. Chicago and other cities stopped paying their teachers. Benevolent societies and religious groups could handle short-term misfortunes, but they could not cope with the ongoing disaster of mass unemployment (Figure 22.1).

As confidence in recovery fell and the economy sank deeper into depression, President Hoover shifted direction. Without abandoning his belief in voluntarism, the president persuaded Congress to lower income tax rates and to allocate an unprecedented $423 million for federal public works projects. In 1929 the president signed into law the Agricultural Marketing Act, a measure aimed at raising prices for long-suffering farmers.

In general, Hoover had the right idea, but he retreated from initiating greater spending because he feared government deficits more than unemployment. With federal accounting sheets showing a rising deficit, Hoover reversed course in 1932 and joined with Congress in sharply raising income, estate, and corporate taxes on the wealthy. This effectively slowed down investment and new production, throwing millions more American workers out of jobs. The Hawley-Smoot Act passed by Congress in 1930 made matters worse. In an effort to replenish revenues and protect American farmers and companies from foreign competition, the act increased tariffs on agricultural and industrial imports. However, other countries retaliated by lifting their import duties, which hurt American companies because it diminished demand for American exports.

In an exception to his aversion to spending, Hoover lobbied Congress to create the Reconstruction Finance Corporation (RFC) to supply loans to banks in danger of collapsing, financially strapped railroads, and troubled insurance companies. By injecting federal dollars into these critical enterprises, the president and lawmakers expected to produce dividends that would trickle down from the top of the economic structure to the bottom. Renewed investment supposedly would increase production, create jobs, raise the income of workers, and generate consumption and economic recovery. In 1932 Congress gave the RFC a budget of $1.5 billion to employ people in public works projects, a significant allocation for those individuals hardest hit by the depression.

This notable departure from Republican economic philosophy fell short of its goal. The RFC spent its budget too cautiously, and its funds reached primarily those institutions that could best afford to repay the loans, ignoring the companies in the greatest difficulty. Whatever the president's intentions, wealth never trickled down. Hoover was not indifferent to the plight of others so much as he was incapable of breaking away from his ideological preconceptions. He refused to support expenditures for direct relief (what today we call welfare) and hesitated to extend assistance for work relief because he believed that it would ruin individual initiative and character.

Hoover and the United States did not face the Great Depression alone; it was a worldwide calamity. By 1933 Germany, France, and Great Britain all faced mass unemployment. In Britain, one survey showed that around 20 percent of the population lacked sufficient food, clothing, and housing. As with American agriculture, European farmers had been suffering since the 1920s from falling prices and increased debt, and the depression further exacerbated this problem. In this climate of extreme social and economic unrest, authoritarian dictators came to power in a number of European countries, including Germany, Italy, Spain, and Portugal. Each claimed that his country's social and economic problems could be solved only by placing power in the hands of a single, all-powerful leader.

Hoovervilles and Dust Storms

The depression hit all areas of the United States hard. In large cities, families crowded into apartments with no gas or electricity and little food to put on the table. In Los Angeles, people cooked their meals over wood fires in backyards. An observer in Philadelphia reported a house containing a family of eleven. "They've got no shoes, no pants," he lamented. "In the house, no chairs. My God, you go in there, you cry, that's all." In many cities, the homeless constructed makeshift housing consisting of cartons, old newspapers, and cloth—shanties that journalists derisively dubbed **Hoovervilles**. Thousands of hungry citizens wound up living under bridges in Portland, Oregon; in wrecked autos in city dumps in Brooklyn, New York, and Stockton, California; and in abandoned coal furnaces in Pittsburgh. In Chicago, a fight broke out among fifty men over scraps of food placed in the garbage outside of a restaurant.

Rural workers fared no better. Landlords in West Virginia and Kentucky evicted coal miners and their families from their homes in the dead of winter, forcing them to live in tents. Farmers in the Great Plains, who were already experiencing foreclosures, were little prepared for the even greater natural disaster that lay waste to their farms. In the early 1930s, dust storms swept through western Kansas, eastern Colorado, western Oklahoma, the Texas Panhandle, and eastern New Mexico, destroying crops and plant and animal life. The storms resulted from both climatological and human causes. A series of droughts had destroyed crops and turned the earth into sand, which gusts of wind deposited on everything that lay in their path. Though they did not realize it at the time, plains farmers, by focusing on growing wheat for income, had neglected planting trees and grasses that would have kept the earth from eroding and turning into dust. Instead, dust storms brought life to a grinding halt, blocking out the midday sun. **See Document Project 22: The Depression in Rural America, page 712**.

As the storms continued through the 1930s, most residents—approximately 75 percent—remained on the plains and rode out the blizzards of dust. Millions, however, headed for California by train, automobiles, and trucks looking for relief from the plague of swirling dirt and hoping to find jobs in the state's fruit and vegetable fields. Although they came from several states besides Oklahoma, these migrants came to be known as "Okies," a derogatory term used by those who resented and looked down on the poverty-stricken newcomers to their communities. John Steinbeck's novel *The Grapes of Wrath* (1939) portrayed the plight of the fictional Joad family, as storms and a bank foreclosure destroyed their Oklahoma farm and sent them on the road to California. "[Route] 66 is the path of a people in flight," Steinbeck wrote, "refugees from dust and shrinking land, from the thunder of tractors and shrinking ownership, from the

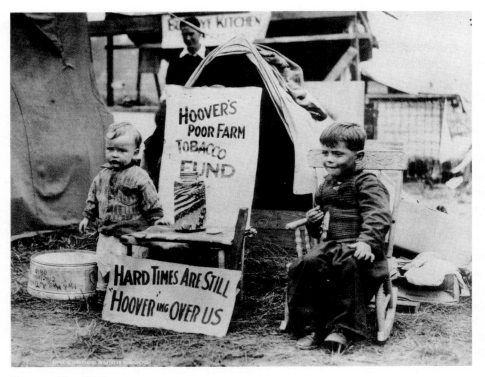

Hooverville, 1932
By the third year of the Great Depression, impoverished Americans were still living in makeshift accommodations called Hoovervilles, which popped up around the nation. These children are staying with their family in a camp in Washington, D.C. The signs target President Herbert Hoover as the source of their misery and condemn him for not taking action to relieve their economic distress.   MPI/Getty Images

few pegs to fall." Despite the great migration to the North during and after World War I, three-quarters of the black population still lived in the South. They worked mostly as farmers, but 80 percent did not own their own land. Mainly sharecroppers and tenant farmers, black southerners were mired in debt that they could not repay as crop prices plunged to record lows during the 1920s. As white landowners struggled to save their farms by introducing machinery to cut labor costs, they forced black sharecroppers off the land and into even greater poverty. Nor was the situation better for black workers employed at the lowest-paying jobs as janitors, menial laborers, maids, and laundresses. On average, African Americans earned $200 a year, less than one-quarter of the average wage of white factory workers.

The economic misfortune that African Americans experienced was compounded by the fact that they lived in a society rigidly constructed to preserve white supremacy. The 25 percent of blacks living in the North faced racial discrimination in employment, housing, and the criminal justice system, but at least they could express their opinions and desires by voting. In Chicago, the growing African American community elected a black congressman, the Republican Oscar DePriest. By contrast, black southerners remained segregated and disfranchised by law. The depression also exacerbated racial tensions, as whites and blacks competed for the shrinking number of jobs. Lynching, which had declined from fifty-nine murders of blacks in 1921 to seven in 1929, surged upward—in 1933 twenty-four blacks lost their lives to this form of terrorism.

Events in Scottsboro, Alabama, reflected the special misery African Americans faced during the Great Depression. Trouble erupted in 1931. Two young, unemployed white women, Ruby Bates and Victoria Price, snuck onto a freight train heading to Huntsville, Alabama. Before the train reached the Scottsboro depot, a fight broke out between black and white men on top of the freight car occupied by the two women. After the train pulled in to

desert's slow northward invasion, from the twisting winds that howl up out of Texas, from the floods that bring no richness to the land and steal what little richness is there." By no means did all the migrants suffer the misfortunes of the Joads, and many of them succeeded in establishing new lives in the West.

Challenges for Minorities

Given the demographics of the workforce, the overwhelming majority of Americans who lost their jobs were white men; yet racial and ethnic minorities, including African Americans, Latinos, and Asian Americans, suffered disproportionate hardship. Racial discrimination had kept these groups from achieving economic and political equality, and the Great Depression added to their woes.

Traditionally the last hired and the first fired, blacks occupied the lowest rungs on the industrial and agricultural ladders. "The depression brought everybody down a peg or two," the African American poet Langston Hughes wryly commented. "And the Negroes had but

Scottsboro, the local sheriff arrested nine black youths between the ages of twelve and twenty. Charges of assault quickly escalated into rape, when the women told authorities that the black men in custody had molested them on board the train. The accused narrowly escaped a mob lynching when the governor sent in the National Guard to ensure that they stood trial.

Going to court, however, did not guarantee a fair trial. The court-appointed attorney was less than competent and had little time to prepare his clients' cases. It probably made little difference, as the all-white male jury swiftly convicted the accused; only the youngest defendant was not sentenced to death. The Communist Party, whose membership had increased as despair over the depression mounted, rushed to defend the youths, providing legal and financial assistance for them and their families. The Supreme Court spared the lives of the **Scottsboro Nine** by overturning their guilty verdicts in 1932 on the grounds that the defendants did not have adequate legal representation and again in 1935 because blacks had been systematically excluded from the jury pool. Although Ruby Bates had recanted her testimony and there was no physical evidence of rape, retrials in 1936 and 1937 produced the same guilty verdicts, but this time the defendants did not receive the death penalty—a minor victory considering the charges. State prosecutors dismissed charges against four of the accused, all of whom had already spent six years in jail. Despite international protests against this racist injustice, the last of the remaining five did not leave jail until 1950.

Explore

See Document 22.1 for a letter from one of the Scottsboro Nine.

Racism also worsened the impact of the Great Depression on Spanish-speaking Americans. Mexicans and Mexican Americans made up the largest segment of the Latino population living in the United States at the outset of the depression. Concentrated in the Southwest and California, they worked in a variety of low-wage factory jobs and as migrant laborers in fruit and vegetable fields. The depression reduced the Mexican-born population living in the United States in two ways. The federal government began deporting unemployed workers back to Mexico, as many as 500,000, some of whom may have been American citizens. Many more returned to Mexico voluntarily when demand for labor in the United States dried up.

Those who remained endured growing hardships. Relief agencies refused to provide them with the same benefits as whites. Like African Americans, they encountered discrimination in public schools, in public accommodations, and at the ballot box. Conditions remained harshest for migrant workers toiling long hours for little pay and living in overcrowded and poorly constructed housing. Employers had little incentive to improve the situation because there were plenty of white migrant workers to fill their positions. The same held true in factories. Employers justified keeping pay low by claiming that Mexican workers would only spend pay raises on "tequila and worthless trinkets in the dime stores."

The transient nature of agricultural work and the legal vulnerability of Mexican laborers who were not citizens made it difficult for workers to organize, but Mexican American laborers engaged in dozens of strikes in California and Texas in the early 1930s. Most ended in defeat, but a few, such as a five-week strike of pecan shellers in San Antonio, Texas, led by Luisa Moreno, won better working conditions and higher wages. Despite these hard-fought victories, the condition of Latinos remained precarious.

On the West Coast, Asian Americans also remained economically and politically marginalized. Barred from entry into the United States after passage of the 1924 National Origins Act, the Japanese population remained steady. Japanese immigrants (*issei*) eked out a living as small farmers, grocers, and gardeners, despite California laws preventing them from owning land. Many college-educated *Nisei* (U.S.-born children) found few professional opportunities available to them, and they often returned to work in family businesses. The depression magnified the problem. Like other racial and ethnic minorities, the Japanese found it harder to find even the lowest-wage jobs now that unemployed whites were willing to take them. As a result, about one-fifth of Japanese immigrants returned to Japan during the 1930s.

The Chinese suffered a similar fate. They remained isolated in ethnic communities along the West Coast. Discriminated against in schools and most occupations, many operated restaurants and laundries. Chinese immigrants had been barred from entering the United States since the Chinese Exclusion Act of 1882. Yet approximately 45 percent of people of Chinese ancestry had been born in the United States and thus were citizens. During the depression, those Chinese who did not obtain assistance through governmental relief turned instead to their own community organizations and to extended families to help them through the hard times.

Filipinos, who lived mainly on the Pacific coast and worked as low-wage agricultural workers, were subject to the same kind of racial animosity as other darker-skinned minorities, despite their colonial relationship with the United States. In 1934 anti-Filipino hostility reached its height when Congress passed the

Andy Wright | Plea from One of the Scottsboro Nine, 1937

Andy Wright was nineteen when he was arrested along with eight other black youths and charged with raping two white women. Wright was twice convicted of the charges and was not paroled until 1944. In this letter to the editor of the *Nation* magazine, Wright pleads his case after his second conviction. He contends that he was framed and tries to bring the misconduct of both the police investigators and the trial judge to the attention of the public.

Explore

Dear Sirs:

I am quite sure you all have read the outcome of my trial, and seen that I was given a miscarriage of justice. I feel it is my duty to write you all the facts of my case, which you perhaps overlooked, or perhaps it was not published in the papers. I was framed, cheated, and robbed of my freedom. First, beginning March 25, 26, and 27, 1931, I wasn't charged with criminal assault on either girl, and was carried through the first, second, and third degree, and even on the basis I would gain my freedom by turning state evidence against the other eight boys. Just because I didn't know nothing, nor neither would I lie on the other boys the charge of rape was framed and placed against me on the 28th day of March, 1931.

I was tried, convicted, and given the death sentence, and in November, 1932, the Supreme Court of the United States reversed the sentence and a retrial ordered. The 19th day of July, 1937, I was retried and sentenced to 99 years' imprisonment.

Now I wish to call your attention to how the judge charged the jury. He charged them in a perjury way. Out of his one hour and twenty-five minutes summation he only mentioned acquittal three times and each time he contradicted it by saying if you juries find a doubt which goes to me reconsider it. Never did he mention a single defense witness in his hour and twenty-five minutes summation to the jury.

How can I receive justice in the state of Alabama, especially of Morgan County, when perjury is used against me and my attorneys too? And I beg you, dear friends, readers, all stick together and work and struggle together and see that justice be brought to light. Let us all pull and struggle together and see that justice be done. It is not that I hate to go to prison, but I am innocent, and the slander is being thrown on our race of people and my family, is my reason of wanting to fight harder than ever.

ANDY WRIGHT
Montgomery, Ala., July 24

Source: Andy Wright, letter to the editors, *The Nation*, August 7, 1937, 159–60.

Interpret the Evidence

- According to Wright, why did the police decide to frame him?
- Why did Wright send his letter to the *Nation*, a magazine whose readers are mostly in the North?

Put It in Context

Why was it unlikely that a black man in Alabama could receive a fair trial on the charge of raping a white woman?

Mexican Migrant Farmworkers
This photograph by Dorothea Lange shows a Mexican migrant and his child harvesting carrots in the Imperial Valley of California in 1935. Demand for Mexican labor declined during the Great Depression as displaced farmers from the Dust Bowl moved west to take jobs formerly held by Mexicans. Government deportations further decreased the number of undocumented Mexican laborers in the United States.   Copyright the Dorothea Lange Collection, the Oakland Museum of California, City of Oakland. Gift of Paul S. Taylor.

Tydings-McDuffie Act. The measure accomplished two aims at once: The act granted independence to the Philippines, and it restricted Filipino immigration into the United States.

Families under Strain

With millions of men unemployed, women faced increased family responsibilities. Stay-at-home wives had to care for their children and provide emotional support for out-of-work husbands who had lost their role as the family breadwinner. Despite the loss of income, homemakers continued their daily routines of shopping, cooking, cleaning, and child rearing.

Disproportionate male unemployment led to an increase in the importance of women's income. The depression hit male-dominated industries like steel mills and automakers the hardest. As a result, men were more likely to lose their jobs than women, who were concentrated in low-paying jobs like domestic service, nursing, and secretarial work. Although more women held on to their jobs, their often meager wages had to go further, since many now had to support unemployed fathers and husbands. During the 1930s, federal and local governments sought to increase male employment by passing laws to keep married women from holding civil service and teaching positions. Nonetheless, more and more married women entered the workplace, and by 1940 the

proportion of women in the job force had grown by about 25 percent.

As had been the case in previous decades, a higher proportion of African American women than white women worked outside the home in the 1930s. By 1940 less than 40 percent of African American women held jobs, compared to about 25 percent of white women. Racial discrimination played a key role in establishing this pattern. Black men faced higher unemployment rates than did their white counterparts, and what work was available was often limited to the lowest-paying jobs. As a result, black women faced greater pressure to supplement family incomes. Still, unemployment rates for black women reached as high as 50 percent during the 1930s. During more prosperous times, they had worked in white homes as domestic servants, but the depression forced white families to cut back on household expenses. Many African American women lost some of their domestic jobs to white working-class women who could find work nowhere else.

Despite increased burdens, most American families remained intact and discovered ways to survive the economic crisis. They pared down household budgets, made do without telephones and new clothes, and held on to their automobiles for longer periods of time. What money they managed to save they often spent on movies. Comedies, gangster movies, fantasy tales, and uplifting films helped viewers forget their troubles, if only for a few hours. Radio remained the chief source of entertainment, and radio sales doubled in the 1930s as listeners tuned in to soap operas, comedy and adventure shows, news reports, and musical programs.

The Season of Discontent

As the depression deepened, angry citizens found a variety of ways to express their discontent. Farmers had suffered economic hardship longer than any other group. Even before 1929, they had seen prices spiral downward, but in the early 1930s agricultural income plummeted 60 percent, and one-third of farmers lost their land (Figure 22.2). Some farmers decided that the time had come for drastic action. In the summer of 1932, Milo Reno, an Iowa farmer, created the Farm Holiday Association to organize farmers in order to keep their produce from going to market and thereby raise prices. Strikers blocked roads and kept reluctant farmers in line by smashing their truck windshields and headlights and slashing their tires. When law enforcement officials arrested fifty-five demonstrators in Council Bluffs, thousands of farmers marched on the jail and forced their release. The boycott spread to Nebraska and Wisconsin, and the violence increased. Despite armed attempts to prevent foreclosures and the intentional destruction of vast quantities of farm produce, the Farm Holiday Association failed to achieve its goal of raising prices.

Disgruntled urban residents also resorted to protest. Although the Communist Party remained a tiny group of just over 10,000 members in 1932, it played a large role in organizing the dispossessed. In major cities such as New York, Communists set up unemployment councils and led marches and rallies demanding jobs and food. In Harlem, the party endorsed rent strikes by African American apartment residents against their landlords. Party members did not confine their activities to the urban Northeast. They also went south to defend the Scottsboro Nine and to organize industrial workers in the steel mills of Birmingham and sharecroppers in the surrounding rural areas of Alabama. On the West Coast, Communists played an active role in the motion picture business, unionized seamen and waterfront workers, and led strikes.

One of the most visible protests of the early 1930s centered on events at the Ford factory in Dearborn, Michigan. As the depression worsened after 1930, Henry Ford, who had initially pledged to keep employee wages steady, changed his mind and reduced wages. The paternalistic Ford declared that it was "a good thing the recovery is prolonged. Otherwise people wouldn't profit by the illness." His laborers thought otherwise. On March 7, 1932, spearheaded by Communists, three thousand autoworkers marched from Detroit to Ford's River Rouge plant in nearby Dearborn. When they reached the factory town, they faced policemen

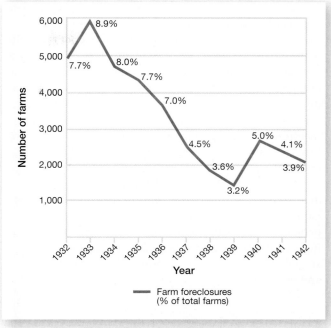

FIGURE 22.2   Farm Foreclosures, 1932–1942

A drop of 60 percent in prices led to a wave of farm foreclosures and rural protests in the early 1930s. From 1934 on, federal programs that promoted rural electrification, crop allotments, commodity loans, and mortgage credits allowed many farmers to retain their land. But tenant farmers and sharecroppers, particularly in the South, rarely benefited from these programs.

indiscriminately firing bullets and tear gas, which killed four demonstrators. The attack provoked great outrage. Around forty thousand mourners attended the funeral of the four protesters; sang the Communist anthem, the "Internationale"; and surrounded the caskets, which were draped in a red banner emblazoned with a picture of Bolshevik hero Vladimir Lenin.

Protests spread beyond Communist agitators. The federal government faced an uprising by some of the nation's most patriotic and loyal citizens—World War I veterans. Scheduled to receive a $1,000 bonus for their service, unemployed veterans could not wait until the payment date arrived in 1945. Instead, in the spring of 1932 a group of ex-soldiers from Portland, Oregon, set off on a march on Washington, D.C., to demand immediate payment of the bonus by the federal government. By the time they reached the nation's capital, the ranks of this **Bonus Army** had swelled to around twenty thousand veterans. They camped in the Anacostia Flats section of the city, constructed ramshackle shelters, and in many cases moved their families in with them. After intensive lobbying efforts, the House approved a bonus bill, but the Senate rejected it. Discouraged, many veterans abandoned the makeshift camps and returned home.

The rest of the Bonus Army remained in place until late July. The Hoover administration declined to negotiate with the demonstrators. When Hoover decided to clear the capital of the protesters, violence ensued. Rather than engaging in a measured and orderly removal, General Douglas MacArthur overstepped presidential orders and used excessive force to disperse the veterans and their families. The Third Cavalry, commanded by George S. Patton, torched tents and sent their residents fleeing from the city. The "Battle of Anacostia Flats" left more than one hundred marchers wounded and one dead.

In this one-sided battle, the biggest loser was President Hoover. Through four years of the country's worst depression, Hoover had lost touch with the American people. His cheerful words of encouragement fell increasingly on deaf ears. As workers, farmers, and veterans stirred in protest, Hoover appeared aloof, standoffish, and insensitive.

REVIEW & RELATE

How did President Hoover respond to the problems and challenges created by the Great Depression?

How did different segments of the American population experience the depression?

☑ *LEARNINGCurve* **bedfordstmartins.com/hewittlawson/LC**

The New Deal

The nation was ready for a change, and on election day 1932, with hard times showing no sign of abating, Democratic presidential candidate Franklin Delano Roosevelt defeated Hoover easily. Roosevelt's sizable victory provided him with a mandate to take the country in a bold, new direction. However, few Americans, including Roosevelt himself, knew exactly what the new president meant to do or what his pledge of a New Deal would mean for the country.

Roosevelt Restores Confidence

As a presidential candidate, Roosevelt presented no clear, coherent policy. He did not spell out how his plans for the country would differ from Hoover's, but he did refer broadly to providing a "new deal" and bringing to the White House "persistent experimentation." He pledged to put more faith "in the forgotten man at the bottom of the economic pyramid." These flights of rhetoric, however, were balanced by the Democratic candidate's harsh denunciation of Hoover for excessive governmental spending and failure to balance the budget. Roosevelt's appeal derived more from the genuine compassion he was able to convey than from the

Franklin Delano Roosevelt Campaigning in Georgia

New York governor Franklin Roosevelt greets farmers in Georgia as he campaigns for president in 1932 as the Democratic candidate. Photographers were careful not to show that Roosevelt was unable to use his legs, which were paralyzed after he contracted polio in 1921. Roosevelt forged a coalition of farmers and urban workers and easily defeated the incumbent Hoover. AP Photo specificity of his promises. In this context, Eleanor Roosevelt's evident concern for people's suffering and her history of activism made Franklin Roosevelt even more attractive.

Instead of any fixed ideology, Roosevelt followed what one historian has called "pragmatic humanism." A seasoned politician who understood the need for flexibility, Roosevelt blended principle and practicality. "It is common sense," Roosevelt explained, "to take a method and try it. If it fails, admit it frankly and try another. But above all, try something." More than any president before him, FDR, as he became affectionately known, created an expectation among Americans that the federal government would take concrete action to improve their lives. A Colorado woman expressed her appreciation to Eleanor Roosevelt: "Your husband is *great*. He seems lovable even tho' he is a 'politician.'" A textile worker echoed this sentiment: "The president isn't going to forget us." The New Deal would take its twists and turns, but Roosevelt never lost the support of the majority of Americans.

Starting with his inaugural address, in which he declared that "the only thing we have to fear is fear itself," Roosevelt took on the task of rallying the American people and restoring their confidence in the future. Using the power of radio to communicate directly with the American people, Roosevelt delivered regular **fireside chats** in which he boosted morale and informed his audience of the steps the government was taking to help solve their problems. Not limited to rhetoric, Roosevelt's **New Deal** would provide relief, put millions of people to work, raise prices for farmers, extend conservation projects, revitalize America's financial system, and rescue capitalism.

Steps toward Recovery

In March 1933, President Roosevelt issued an executive order shutting down banks for several days to calm the panic that gripped many Americans in the wake of bank failures and the loss of their life's savings. Shortly after, Congress passed the administration's Emergency Banking Act, which subjected banks to Treasury Department inspection before they reopened, reorganized the banking system, and provided federal funds to bail out banks on the brink of closing. This assertion of federal power allowed solvent banks to reopen. Boosting confidence further, Congress passed the Glass-Steagall Act in June 1933. The measure created the Federal Deposit Insurance Corporation (FDIC), insuring personal savings accounts up to $5,000, and detached commercial banks from investment banks to avoid risky speculation. The

president also sought tighter supervision of the stock market, whose collapse many blamed for sparking the Great Depression. By June 1934, Roosevelt had signed into law measures setting up the Securities and Exchange Commission (SEC) to regulate the stock market and ensure that corporations gave investors accurate information about their portfolios.

The regulation of banks and the stock exchange did not mean that Roosevelt was antibusiness. He affirmed his belief in a balanced budget and sought to avoid a $1 billion deficit by cutting government workers' salaries and lowering veterans' pensions. Roosevelt also tried to keep the budget under control by ending prohibition, which would allow the government to tax alcohol sales and eliminate the cost of enforcement. The Twenty-first Amendment, ratified in 1933, ended the more than decade-long experiment with temperance.

These initial measures restored confidence in the presidency and in the federal government's willingness and ability to redress some of the problems responsible for the economic crisis. Yet the Roosevelt administration had much more to accomplish before those hardest hit by the depression felt some relief. Roosevelt viewed the Great Depression as a crisis analogous to war and adapted many of the bureaus and commissions used during World War I to ensure productivity and mobilize popular support to fit the current economic emergency. Many former progressives lined up behind Roosevelt, including women reformers and social workers who had worked in government and private agencies during the 1920s to develop programs for mothers, children, and the poor. At his wife Eleanor's urging, Roosevelt appointed one of them, Frances Perkins, as the first woman to head a cabinet agency—the Department of Labor.

Rehabilitating agriculture and industry stood at the top of the New Deal's priority list. Farmers came first. In May 1933, Congress passed the **Agricultural Adjustment Act**, aimed at raising prices by reducing production. The Agricultural Adjustment Administration (AAA) paid farmers subsidies to produce less in the future, and for farmers who had already planted their crops (including corn, cotton, rice, tobacco, and wheat) and raised livestock, the agency paid them to plow under a portion of their harvest, slaughter hogs, and destroy dairy products. By 1935 the program succeeded in raising farm income by 50 percent. Large farmers remained the chief beneficiaries of the AAA because they could afford to cut back production. In doing so, especially in the South, they forced off the land sharecroppers who no longer had plots to farm. Even when sharecroppers managed to retain a parcel of their acreage, AAA subsidies went to

National Recovery Administration Eagles

President Roosevelt initiated the National Recovery Administration in 1933 as the center-piece of his New Deal to stimulate economic growth. The city of Miami Beach employed these bathing beauties to attract conventioneers and vacationers to its hotels. Under the NRA code, they worked a forty-hour week and showed their satisfaction by sporting the NRA blue eagle insignia on their backs.   © Bettmann/CORBIS

the landowners, who did not always distribute the designated funds owed to the sharecroppers. Though poor white farmers felt the sting of this injustice, the system of white supremacy existing in the South guaranteed that blacks suffered most.

After the Supreme Court voided the AAA in 1936 for imposing an unlawful tax on food processors in order to fund the subsidies, Congress enacted several pieces of legislation designed to limit production and provide aid to small farmers. The second AAA, passed in 1938, offered agricultural subsidies to reduce cultivation on the basis of conservation and soil erosion prevention, which overcame judicial objections. To deal with continuing rural poverty among sharecroppers and tenant farmers, Congress provided loans for displaced farmers.

The Roosevelt administration exhibited its boldest initiative in creating the **Tennessee Valley Authority (TVA)** in 1933 to bring low-cost electric power to rural areas and help redevelop the entire Tennessee River valley region through flood-control projects. In contrast to the AAA and other farm programs in which control stayed in private hands, the TVA owned and supervised the building and operation of public power plants, starting with the Muscle Shoals Dam in Alabama, which progressives had lobbied for since the 1920s. For farmers outside the Tennessee River valley, the Rural Electrification Administration helped them obtain cheap electric power starting in

1935, and for the first time tens of thousands of farmers experienced the modern conveniences that electricity brought (though most farmers would not get electric power until after World War II).

Roosevelt and Congress also acted to deal with the soil erosion problem behind the dust storms. In 1933, the Department of Interior established a Soil Erosion Service, and two years later Congress created a permanent Soil Conservation Service in the Department of Agriculture. Although these measures would prove beneficial in the long run, they did nothing to prevent even more severe storms from rolling through the Dust Bowl, as it was now known, in 1935 and 1936.

At the same time, Roosevelt concentrated on industrial recovery. He kept Hoover's RFC intact, but he went far beyond his predecessor in sanctioning government participation in the economy. In 1933 Congress passed the National Industrial Recovery Act, which established the **National Recovery Administration (NRA)**. This agency allowed business, labor, and the public (represented by government officials) to create codes to regulate production, prices, wages, hours, and collective bargaining. Designers of the NRA expected that if wages rose and prices remained stable, consumer purchasing power would climb, demand would grow, and businesses would put people back to work. For this plan to work, business people needed to keep prices steady by absorbing some of the costs of higher wages. The head of the

NRA, Hugh S. Johnson, a veteran of the War Industries Board during World War I, engaged in a highly visible public relations campaign. Johnson argued that regulatory codes were good for everyone. Like rules for a fair fight, they would "eliminate eye-gouging and knee-groining and ear-chewing in business," Johnson proclaimed. Businesses and industries that joined the NRA displayed the symbol of a blue eagle to signal their participation, and officials whipped up patriotic fervor on its behalf.

However, the NRA did not function as planned, nor did it bring the desired recovery. Businesses did not exercise the necessary restraint to keep prices steady. Large manufacturers dominated the code-making committees, and because Roosevelt had suspended enforcement of the antitrust law, they could not resist taking collective action to force smaller firms out of business. The NRA legislation guaranteed labor the right to unionize, but the agency did not vigorously enforce collective bargaining. The government failed to intervene to redress the imbalance of power between labor and management because Roosevelt depended primarily on big business to generate economic improvement. Moreover, the NRA had created codes for too many businesses, and government officials could not properly oversee them all. In 1935 the Supreme Court delivered the final blow to the NRA by declaring it an unconstitutional delegation of legislative power to the president.

Direct Assistance and Relief

Economic recovery programs were important, but they took time to take effect, and many Americans needed immediate help. Thus relief efforts and direct job creation were critical parts of the New Deal. Created in the early months of Roosevelt's term, the Federal Emergency Relief Administration (FERA) provided cash grants to states to revive their bankrupt relief efforts. Unlike Hoover's RFC, the FERA did not expect states to repay the loans, but it left administration of the programs to state and local agencies. Roosevelt chose Harry Hopkins, the chief of New York's relief agency, to head the FERA and distribute its initial $500 million appropriation. On the job for two hours, Hopkins had already spent $5 million. He did not calculate whether a particular plan "would work out in the long run," because, as he remarked, "people don't eat in the long run—they eat every day."

Harold Ickes, secretary of the interior and director of the Public Works Administration (PWA), oversaw efforts to rebuild the nation's infrastructure. Funding architects, engineers, and skilled workers, the PWA built the Grand Coulee, Boulder, and Bonneville dams in the West; the Triborough Bridge in New York City; 70 percent of all new schools constructed between 1933 and 1939; and a variety of municipal buildings, sewage plants, port facilities, and hospitals.

Yet neither the FERA nor the PWA provided enough emergency relief to the millions who faced the winter of 1933–1934 without jobs or the money to heat their homes. In response, Hopkins persuaded Roosevelt to launch a temporary program to help needy Americans get through this difficult period. Both men favored "work relief"—giving people jobs rather than direct welfare payments whenever practical. The Civil Works Administration (CWA) lasted four months, but in that brief time it employed more than 4 million people on about 400,000 projects that built 500,000 miles of roads, 40,000 schools, 3,500 playgrounds, and 1,000 airports. Montana got its state capitol building renovated, Pittsburgh erected its Cathedral of Learning, Boston's unemployed teachers went back to their classes, writers and artists remained at their desks and canvases, singers toured the nation, and ninety-four Indians restocked the Kodiak Islands off the coast of Alaska with rabbits.

Explore

See Document 22.2 for a criticism of direct relief assistance.

One of Roosevelt's most successful relief programs was the **Civilian Conservation Corps (CCC)**, created shortly after he entered the White House. The CCC recruited unmarried men between the ages of eighteen and twenty-five for a two-year stint. It removed them from relief rolls and the glut of the job market and put them to work planting forests; cleaning up beaches, rivers, and parks; and building bridges and dams. To build discipline, the U.S. army ran the CCC, furnished uniforms, and set up military-style camps. Participants received $1 per day, and the government sent $25 of the $30 in monthly wages directly to their families, helping make this the most popular of all New Deal programs. The CCC employed around 2.5 million men and lasted until 1942.

New Deal Critics

Despite the unprecedented efforts of the Roosevelt administration to spark recovery, provide relief, and encourage reform between 1933 and 1935, the country remained in depression, and unemployment still hovered around 20 percent. A liberal but not a radical, Roosevelt found himself under attack from both the left and the right. On the right, conservatives questioned New Deal spending and the growth of big government. On the left, the president's critics argued that he had not done enough to topple

DOCUMENT 22.2

Minnie Hardin | Letter to Eleanor Roosevelt, 1937

During the 1930s, Americans wrote to President Roosevelt and the First Lady in unprecedented numbers, revealing their personal desperation and their belief that the Roosevelts would respond to their individual pleas. Though most requested government assistance, not all letter writers favored the New Deal. In the following letter written to Eleanor Roosevelt in 1937, Minnie Hardin of Columbus, Indiana, expresses her frustration with direct relief programs.

Explore

How might Hardin explain the existence of poverty in America?

How does Hardin's "square deal" differ from Roosevelt's New Deal?

What impact did New Deal policies have on Hardin's life?

Mrs. Roosevelt:

I suppose from your point of view the work relief, old age pensions, slum clearance, and all the rest seems like a perfect remedy for all the ills of this country, but I would like for you to see the results, as the other half see them.

We have always had a shiftless, never-do-well class of people whose one and only aim in life is to live without work. I have been rubbing elbows with this class for nearly sixty years and have tried to help some of the most promising and have seen others try to help them, but it can't be done. We cannot help those who will not try to help themselves and if they do try, a square deal is all they need, and by the way that is all this country needs or ever has needed: a square deal for all and then, let each paddle their own canoe, or sink.

There has never been any necessity for any one who is able to work, being on relief in this locality, but there have been many eating the bread of charity and they have lived better than ever before. I have had taxpayers tell me that their children came from school and asked why they couldn't have nice lunches like the children on relief. The women and children around here have had to work at the fields to help save the crops and several women fainted while at work and at the same time we couldn't go up or down the road without stumbling over some of the reliefers, moping around carrying dirt from one side of the road to the other and back again, or else asleep. I live alone on a farm and have not raised any crops for the last two years as there was no help to be had. I am feeding the stock and have been cutting the wood to keep my home fires burning. There are several reliefers around here now who have been kicked off relief but they refuse to work unless they can get relief hours and wages, but they are so worthless no one can afford to hire them.

Source: Minnie Hardin, letter to Eleanor Roosevelt, December 14, 1937, Eleanor Roosevelt Papers, Series 190, Miscellaneous, 1937, Franklin D. Roosevelt Library.

Put It in Context

How did Hardin's beliefs about the causes of poverty shape her view of the New Deal?

wealthy corporate leaders from power and relieve the plight of the downtrodden.

The Great Depression and Hoover's inability to ameliorate its most damaging effects dealt a serious blow to the Republican Party and to the conservative opposition to federal government intervention with which it was identified. In 1934 officials of the Du Pont Corporation and General Motors formed the American Liberty League. The group, according to one of its founders, set out to educate the nation about "the value of encouraging people to work; encouraging people to get rich." From the point of view of the league's founders, the New Deal was little more than a vehicle for the spread of socialism and communism. The organization spent $1 million attacking what it considered to be Roosevelt's "dictatorial" policies and his assaults on free enterprise. The league, however, failed to attract support beyond a small group of northern industrialists, Wall Street bankers, and a few disaffected Democrats.

Roosevelt also faced criticism from the left. Communist Party membership reached its peak of around 75,000 in 1938, and though the party remained relatively small in numbers, it attracted intellectuals and artists whose voices could reach the larger public. The party's efforts to save the Scottsboro Nine boosted its appeal among African Americans. Party members also led unionizing drives in both the North and the South and displayed great talent and energy in organizing workers where resistance to unions was greatest. In the mid-1930s, the party followed the Soviet Union's antifascist foreign policy and joined with left-leaning, non-Communist groups, such as unions and civil rights organizations, to oppose the growing menace of fascism in Europe, particularly in Germany and Italy. By the end of the decade, however, the party had lost many members, as revelations about the tyrannical behavior of the Soviet dictator Joseph Stalin emerged and after the Soviet Union reversed its anti-Nazi foreign policy.

The greatest challenge to Roosevelt came from a trio of talented men who reflected diverse beliefs. Through charisma, organizational skills, or a combination of both, each of them created his own national campaign criticizing the New Deal. Francis Townsend, a retired California physician, proposed a "Cure for Depressions." In 1934 he formed the Old-Age Revolving Pensions Corporation, whose title summed up the doctor's idea. Townsend would have the government give all Americans over the age of sixty a monthly pension of $200 if they retired and spent the entire stipend each month. He promoted this scheme as a simple panacea for the ailing economy. Retirements would open up jobs for younger workers, and the income these workers received, along with the pension for the elderly, would pump ample

funds into the economy to promote recovery. The government would fund the Townsend plan with a 2 percent "transaction" or sales tax. By 1936 Townsend Clubs had attracted about 3.5 million members throughout the country, and one-fifth of all adults in the United States signed a petition endorsing the Townsend plan.

While Townsend appealed mainly to the elderly, Charles E. Coughlin attracted Catholics and a lower-middle-class following. An outspoken priest from the Detroit suburb of Royal Oak, Michigan, Father Coughlin used his popular national radio broadcasts to talk about economic and political issues. Originally a Roosevelt supporter, by 1934 Coughlin had begun criticizing the New Deal for catering to greedy bankers. He spoke to millions of radio listeners about the evils of the Roosevelt administration, the godless Communists who had allegedly infested it, and international bankers—coded language referring to Jews—who supposedly manipulated it. In 1935 Coughlin's popularity reached its peak as he organized the National Union for Social Justice, which supported monetary inflation to help debt-ridden farmers and the nationalization of banks to control lending practices. As the decade wore on, his strident anti-Semitism and his growing fondness for fascist dictatorships abroad overshadowed his economic justice message, and Catholic officials ordered him to stop broadcasting.

Father Charles E. Coughlin
Father Charles E. Coughlin spoke at Cleveland Stadium in 1936 on behalf of Ohio congressional candidates who had been endorsed by his National Union for Social Justice. Coughlin, a Catholic priest and a stern critic of President Roosevelt, advocated the nationalization of banks and other industries, protection of worker rights, and monetary reform. Despite Coughlin's outspoken opposition, Roosevelt easily won reelection in 1936.
Library of Congress

Huey Pierce Long of Louisiana, known as "the Kingfish," posed the greatest political threat to Roosevelt. Unlike Townsend and Coughlin, Long had built and operated a successful political machine, first as governor and then as U.S. senator, taking on the special interests of oil and railroad corporations in his home state. Early on he had backed Roosevelt, but Long found the New Deal wanting. "Not a single thin dime of concentrated, bloated, pompous wealth, massed in the hands of a few people," Long claimed, "has been raked down to relieve the masses." In 1934 Long established the **Share Our Wealth** society, promising to make "every man a king" by presenting families with a $5,000 homestead and a guaranteed annual income of $2,000. To accomplish this, Long proposed levying heavy income and inheritance taxes on the wealthy. Although the financial calculations behind his bold plan did not add up, Share Our Wealth clubs counted some seven million members. The swaggering senator departed from most of his segregationist southern colleagues by appealing to a coalition of disgruntled farmers, industrial workers, and African Americans (as governor of Louisiana, he supported repeal of the poll tax). Before Long could help lead a third-party campaign for president, he was shot and killed in 1935.

REVIEW & RELATE

What steps did Roosevelt take to stimulate economic recovery and provide relief to impoverished Americans during his first term in office?

What criticisms did Roosevelt's opponents level against the New Deal?

LEARNINGCurve bedfordstmartins.com/hewittlawson/LC

The New Deal Moves to the Left

Facing criticism from within his own party about the pace and effectiveness of the New Deal, and with the 1936 election looming, Roosevelt moved to the left. He adopted harsher rhetoric against recalcitrant corporate leaders; beefed up economic and social programs for the unemployed, the elderly, and the infirm; and revived measures to redress the power imbalance between management and labor. In doing so, he fashioned a political coalition that would deliver a landslide victory in 1936 and allow the Democratic Party to dominate electoral politics for the next three decades.

Expanding Relief Measures

Even though the New Deal had helped millions of people, millions of others still felt left out, as the popularity of Townsend, Coughlin, and Long indicated. "We the people voted for you," a Columbus, Ohio, worker wrote the president in disgust, "but it is a different story now. You have faded out on the masses of hungry, idle people. . . . The very rich is the only one who has benefited from your new deal."

In 1935 the president seized the opportunity to win his way back into the hearts of the "forgotten Americans"—poor farmers, industrial workers, and marginalized minority groups. Although Roosevelt favored a balanced budget, political necessity forced him to embark on deficit spending to expand the New Deal. Federal government expenditures would now exceed tax revenues, but New Dealers argued that these outlays would stimulate job creation and economic growth, which ultimately would replenish government coffers. Based on the highly successful but short-lived Civil Works Administration, the **Works Progress Administration (WPA)** provided jobs for the unemployed with a far larger budget, starting out with $5 billion. To ensure that the money would be spent, Roosevelt appointed Harry Hopkins to head the agency. Although critics condemned the WPA for employing people on unproductive "make-work" jobs and jibed that its initials stood for "We Poke Around"—a criticism not entirely unfounded—overall the WPA did a great deal of good. The agency constructed or repaired more than 100,000 public buildings, 600 airports, 500,000 miles of roads, and 100,000 bridges. The WPA employed about 8.5 million workers during its eight years of operation.

The WPA also helped artists, writers, and musicians. Under its auspices, the Federal Writers Project, the Federal Art Project, the Federal Music Project, and the Federal Theater Project encouraged the production of cultural works and helped bring them to communities and audiences throughout the country. Actors staged plays, dancers performed ballets, and musicians held recitals outside the usual centers of high culture in New York, Boston, and Chicago. Writers Richard Wright, Ralph Ellison, Clifford Odets, Saul Bellow, John Cheever, Margaret Walker, and many others nourished both their works and their stomachs while employed by the WPA. Painters created elaborate murals on the walls of post offices and other government buildings. Historians and folklorists researched and prepared city and state guides and interviewed black ex-slaves whose narratives of the system of bondage would otherwise have been lost.

New Deal Art

The Works Progress Administration, established by the Roosevelt administration in 1935, put Americans to work amid the ongoing depression. The WPA's Federal Art Project employed artists such as Ingrid E. Edwards of Minnesota, whose painting *Communications* features a newspaper boy, a telephone operator, a radio announcer, and a railroad train. Many of these works adorned public buildings.

Collection of Minnesota Historical Society. Lent by Fine Arts Collection, Public Buildings Service, U.S. General Services. Gift of Ah-Gwah Ching Archive

In addition to the WPA, the National Youth Administration (NYA) employed millions of young people. The NYA provided part-time work to 600,000 college undergraduates, 1.5 million high school students, and 2.6 million jobless youth who no longer attended school. Their work ranged from clerical assignments and repairing automobiles to building tuberculosis isolation units and renovating schools. Heading the NYA in Texas, the young Lyndon B. Johnson worked hard to expand educational and construction projects to unemployed whites and blacks. The Division of Negro Affairs, headed by the Florida educator Mary McLeod Bethune and the only minority group subsection in the NYA, ensured that African American youths would benefit from the programs sponsored by the agency.

Despite their many successes, these relief programs had a number of flaws. The WPA paid participants relatively low wages. The $660 in annual income earned by the average worker fell short of the $1,200 that a family needed to survive. In addition, the WPA limited participation to one family member. In most cases, this meant the male head of the household. As a result, women made up only about 14 percent of WPA workers, and even in the peak year of 1938, the WPA hired only 60 percent of eligible women. With the exception of the program for artists, most women hired by the WPA worked in lower-paying jobs than men.

Establishing Social Security

The elderly also required immediate relief and insurance in a country that lagged behind the rest of the industrialized world in helping its aged workforce. In August 1935, the president rectified this shortcoming and signed into law the **Social Security Act**. The measure provided that at age sixty-five, eligible workers would receive retirement payments funded by payroll taxes on employees and employers. The law also extended beyond the elderly by providing unemployment insurance for those temporarily laid off from work and welfare payments for the disabled who were permanently out of a job as well as for destitute, dependent children of single parents.

The Social Security program had significant limitations. The act excluded farm, domestic, and laundry workers, who were among the neediest Americans and were disproportionately African American. The reasons for these exclusions were largely political. The president needed southern Democrats to support this measure, and as a Mississippi newspaper observed: "The average Mississippian can't imagine himself chipping in to pay pensions for able bodied Negroes to sit around in idleness." The system of financing pensions also proved unfair. The payroll tax, which imposes the same fixed percentage on all incomes, is a regressive tax, one that falls hardest on those with lower incomes. The regressiveness of the tax proved to be an additional handicap for immediate economic recovery because the tax payments took purchasing power out of the hands of workers, whereas pension payments would not begin for several years. Social Security also disadvantaged working women, who on average earned less than men; nor did it take into account the unpaid labor of women who remained in the home to take care of their children.

Even with its flaws, Social Security revolutionized the expectations of American workers. It created a compact between the federal government and its citizens, and workers insisted that their political leaders fulfill their moral responsibilities to keep the system going. President Roosevelt recognized that the tax formula might not be economically sound, but he had a higher political objective in mind. He believed that payroll taxes would give contributors the right to collect their benefits and that "with those taxes in there, no damn politician can ever scrap my social security program." Social Security also helped create a larger middle-class constituency for Roosevelt and the Democratic Party.

Organized Labor Strikes Back

In 1935 Congress passed the **National Labor Relations Act**, also known as the Wagner Act for its leading sponsor, Senator Robert F. Wagner Sr. of New York. The law created the National Labor Relations Board (NLRB), which protected workers' right to organize labor unions without owner interference. During the 1930s, union membership rolls soared from fewer than 4 million workers to more than 10 million, including more than

800,000 women. At the outset of the depression, barely 6 percent of the labor force belonged to unions, compared with 33 percent in 1940.

Government efforts boosted this growth, but these spectacular gains were due primarily to workers' grassroots efforts set in motion by economic hard times. Workers in key industries—automobiles, steel, rubber, and textiles—took the lead. The number of striking workers during the first year of the Roosevelt administration soared from nearly 325,000 to more than 1.5 million. Organizers such as Luisa Moreno traveled the country to bring as many people as possible into the union movement. The most important development within the labor movement occurred in 1935, with the creation of the Congress of Industrial Organizations (CIO). After the American Federation of Labor (AFL), which consisted mainly of craft unions, rejected a proposal by John L. Lewis of the United Mine Workers to incorporate industrial workers under its umbrella, Lewis and representatives of seven other AFL unions defected and formed the CIO. Unlike the AFL, the new union sought to recruit a wide variety of workers without respect to race, gender, or region.

In 1937, two years after its founding, the CIO mounted a full-scale organizing campaign. More than 4.5 million workers participated in some 4,700 strikes, strangling mass-production industries. Unions found new ways to protest poor working conditions and arbitrary layoffs. Members of the United Auto Workers (UAW), a CIO affiliate, launched a **sit-down strike** against General Motors (GM) in Flint, Michigan, to win union recognition, higher wages, and better working conditions. Strikers refused to work but remained in the plants, shutting them down from the inside. Workers felt a new sense of power and confidence, a belief that they were more important than machines. "We learned we can take the plant," one striker gloated. "We already knew how to run them." When the company sent in local police forces to evict the strikers on January 11, 1937, the barricaded workers bombarded the police with spare machine parts and anything that was not bolted down. The community rallied around the strikers, and wives and daughters called "union maids" formed the Women's Emergency Brigade, which supplied sit-downers with food and water and kept up their morale. Neither the state nor the federal government interfered with the work stoppage, and after six weeks GM acknowledged defeat and recognized the UAW. Most of the other auto companies soon followed, though Henry Ford's was one of the last.

Despite some setbacks in 1937, especially in the steel industry, most strikes were settled in the union's

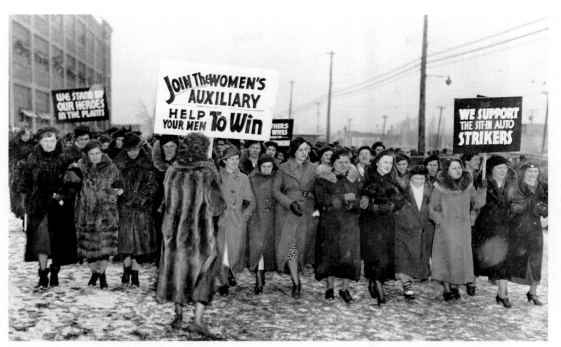

Women's Emergency Brigade

In December 1936, the United Auto Workers initiated a sit-down strike against General Motors in Flint, Michigan, for union recognition, better working conditions, and higher wages. The following month, a group of their women relatives, friends, and coworkers organized the Women's Emergency Brigade and held demonstrations and successfully rallied public support for the strikers.   © Bettmann/CORBIS

favor, and by the end of the decade "big labor," as the AFL and CIO unions were known, had become a significant force in American politics and a leading backer of the New Deal. However, this big labor/big government alliance left out non-unionized industrial and agricultural workers, many of whom were African American or other minorities and lacked adequate bargaining power. Employers often passed on the burden of higher industrial wages to consumers in the form of higher prices.

A Half Deal for Minorities

President Roosevelt made significant gestures on behalf of African Americans. He appointed Mary McLeod Bethune and Robert Weaver to staff New Deal agencies and gathered an informal "Black Cabinet" in the nation's capital to advise him on matters pertaining to race. He also reversed the racial segregation policy his Democratic predecessor Woodrow Wilson had initiated in federal offices and facilities. The Roosevelt administration established the Civil Liberties Unit (later renamed Civil Rights Section) in the Department of Justice, which investigated racial discrimination. Eleanor Roosevelt acted as a visible symbol of the White House's concern with the plight of blacks, a role that culminated in her public support for the black singer Marian Anderson. In 1939 Eleanor Roosevelt quit the Daughters of the American Revolution, a women's organization, when it refused

to allow Anderson to hold a concert in Constitution Hall in Washington, D.C. Instead, the First Lady brought Anderson to sing on the steps of the Lincoln Memorial before an integrated audience of 75,000 and to millions more on the radio.

Perhaps the greatest measure of Franklin Roosevelt's impact on African Americans came when large numbers of black voters switched from the Republican to the Democratic Party in 1936, a pattern that has lasted to the present day. "Go turn Lincoln's picture to the wall," a black observer wryly commented after the election. "That debt has been paid in full."

Yet overall the New Deal did little to break down racial inequality. President Roosevelt believed that the plight of African Americans would improve, along with all downtrodden Americans, as New Deal measures restored economic health. Black leaders disagreed. They argued that the NRA's initials stood for "Negroes Ruined Again" because the agency displaced black workers and approved lower wages for blacks than for whites. The AAA dislodged black sharecroppers, a problem later ameliorated somewhat by New Deal programs such as the Farm Security Administration. New Deal programs such as the CCC and those for building public housing maintained existing patterns of segregation. Both the Social Security Act and the Fair Labor Standards Act omitted from coverage jobs that black Americans were most likely to hold. When members of Congress did propose legislation to combat

The Indian New Deal

John Collier, commissioner of Indian affairs under President Roosevelt, favored a New Deal for Native Americans. An advocate for Indian culture, Collier implemented reform legislation that replaced the policy of Indian assimilation with that of self-determination. In this 1935 photograph, Collier watches his boss, Secretary of the Interior Harold Ickes, sign the Flathead [Montana] Indian Constitution as tribal leaders look on.
© Bettmann/CORBIS

lynching and eliminate the poll tax on voting, Roosevelt offered only lukewarm support for fear of alienating his southern Democratic allies; consequently, these bills went down to defeat.

This pattern of halfway reform persisted for other minorities. Since the end of the Indian wars in 1890 (see chapter 15), Native Americans had lived in poverty, forced onto reservations that offered few economic opportunities and where whites carried out a relentless assault on their culture. By the early 1930s, American Indians earned an average income of less than $50 a year—compared with $800 for whites—and their unemployment rate was three times higher than that of white Americans. For the most part, they lived on lands that whites had given up on as unsuitable for farming or mining. The policy of assimilation established by the Dawes Act of 1887 had exacerbated the problem by depriving Indians of their cultural identities as well as their economic livelihoods. In 1934 the federal government reversed its course. Spurred on by John Collier, the commissioner of Indian affairs, Congress passed the **Indian Reorganization Act (IRA)**, which terminated the Dawes Act, authorized self-government for those living on reservations, extended tribal landholdings, and pledged to uphold native customs and language.

Although the IRA brought economic and social improvements for Native Americans, many problems remained. Despite his considerable efforts, Collier approached Indian affairs from the top down. One historian remarked that Collier had "the zeal of a crusader who knew better than the Indians what was good for them." The Indian commissioner failed to appreciate the diversity of native tribes and administered laws that contradicted Native American political and economic practices. For example, the IRA required the tribes to operate by majority rule, whereas many of them reached decisions through consensus, which respected the views of the minority. Although 174 tribes accepted the IRA, 78 tribes, including the Seneca, Crow, and Navajo, rejected it.

Twilight of the New Deal

Roosevelt's shift to the left paid political dividends, and in 1936 the president won reelection by a landslide. His sweeping victory proved to be one of the rare critical elections that signified a fundamental political realignment. Democrats replaced Republicans as the majority party in the United States, overturning thirty-six years of Republican rule. While Roosevelt had won convincingly in 1932, not until 1936 did the president put together a stable coalition that could sustain Democratic dominance for many years to come.

In 1936 Roosevelt trounced Alfred M. Landon, the Republican governor of Kansas, and Democrats increased their congressional majorities by staggering margins. The vote broke down along class lines. Roosevelt won the votes of 80 percent of union members, 81 percent of unskilled workers, and 84 percent of people on relief, compared with only 42 percent of high-income voters. Millions of new voters came out to the polls, and most of them supported Roosevelt's New Deal coalition of the poor, farmers, urban ethnic minorities, unionists, white southerners, and African Americans.

The euphoria of his triumph, however, proved short-lived. An overconfident Roosevelt soon reached beyond his electoral mandate and within two years found himself unable to extend the New Deal. In 1937 Roosevelt asked Congress to increase the size of the Supreme Court through a **court-packing plan**. He justified this as a matter of reform, claiming that the present nine-member Court could not handle its workload, much of it generated by the avalanche of New Deal legislation. Roosevelt attributed a good deal of the problem to the advanced age of six of the nine justices, who were over seventy years old. Under his proposal, the president would make one new appointment for each judge over the age of seventy who did not retire so long as the bench did not exceed fifteen members. In reality, Roosevelt schemed to "pack" the Court with supporters to prevent it from declaring New Deal legislation such as Social Security and the Wagner Act unconstitutional.

The plan backfired. Conservatives charged Roosevelt with seeking to destroy the separation of powers enshrined in the Constitution among the executive, legislative, and judicial branches. They portrayed the president as a "dictator," which, although a distorted characterization, touched a nerve in those concerned with the rise of tyrants in Germany and Italy. In the end, the president failed to expand the Supreme Court, but he preserved his legislative accomplishments. In a series of rulings, the chastened Supreme Court approved Social Security, the Wagner Act, and other New Deal legislation. Nevertheless, the political fallout from the court-packing fight damaged the president and his plans for further legislative reform.

Explore

See Documents 22.3 and 22.4 for two views on Roosevelt's court-packing plan.

Roosevelt's court-packing plan alienated many southern Democratic members of Congress who previously had sided with the president. Traditionally

suspicious of the power of the federal government, southern lawmakers worried that Roosevelt was going too far toward centralizing power in Washington at the expense of states' rights. Southern Democrats formed a coalition with conservative northern Republicans who shared their concerns about the expansion of federal power and excessive spending on social welfare programs. Their antipathy toward labor unions, especially in the wake of the sit-down strikes, further bound them together. Although they held a minority of seats in Congress, this **conservative coalition** could block unwanted legislation by using the filibuster in the Senate (unlimited debate that could be shut down only with a two-thirds vote). The coalition could not defeat Roosevelt's **Fair Labor Standards Act** (1938), which established minimum wages at 40 cents an hour and maximum working hours at forty per week, but after 1938 these conservatives made sure that no other New Deal legislation passed.

Roosevelt also lost support because the recession of 1937 overlapped with the Supreme Court fight. When federal spending soared after passage of the WPA and other relief measures adopted in 1935, the president lost his economic nerve for deficit spending. He called for reduced spending, which increased unemployment and slowed economic recovery. At the same time, as the Social Security payroll tax took effect, it reduced the purchasing power of workers, thereby exacerbating the impact of reduced government spending. This "recession within the depression" further eroded congressional support for the New Deal.

The country was still deep in depression in 1939. Unemployment was at 17 percent, with more than 11 million people out of work. Most of those who were poor at the start of the Great Depression remained poor. Recovery came mainly to those who were temporarily impoverished as a result of the economic crisis. The distribution of wealth remained skewed toward the top. In 1933 the richest 5 percent of the population controlled 31 percent of disposable income; in 1939 the figure stood at 26 percent.

Against this backdrop of persistent difficult economic times, the president's popularity began to fade. In the midterm elections of 1938, Roosevelt campaigned against Democratic conservatives in an attempt to reinvigorate his New Deal coalition. His efforts failed to purge the conservatives he hoped to unseat and upset many ordinary citizens who associated the tactic with that used by European dictators who had recently risen to power. As the decade came to a close, Roosevelt turned his attention away from the New Deal and increasingly toward a new war in Europe that, like

DOCUMENTS 22.3 AND 22.4

Packing the Supreme Court: Two Views

In his first term, President Roosevelt secured legislation to implement his New Deal; however, by 1937 the Supreme Court had overturned several key pieces of New Deal legislation, arguing that Congress had exceeded its constitutional authority. As the Social Security Act and the National Labor Relations Act came up for review before the Court, Roosevelt tried to dilute the influence of the Court's conservative majority. Following his landslide reelection in 1936, he asked Congress to enlarge the Court so that he could appoint justices more favorable to his liberal agenda. The following cartoons take opposing positions on Roosevelt's court-packing plan.

Explore

22.3 The Great Emancipator, 1937

THE GREAT EMANCIPATOR—1937

Franklin D. Roosevelt Library

Explore

22.4 **Retire or Move Over,** 1937

To Six of the Nine

RETIRE OR MOVE OVER!

MESSAGE ON FEDERAL COURT REFORM

U.S. SUPREME COURT

A FREE AND INDEPENDENT JUDICIARY

Interpret the Evidence

- Why does the first cartoonist compare Roosevelt to Abraham Lincoln?
- How does the second cartoonist's idea of freedom differ from that of the first?

Put It in Context

How do both cartoons appeal to the hopes and fears of the American public during the late 1930s?

World War I twenty-five years earlier, threatened to engulf the entire world.

REVIEW & RELATE

Why and how did the New Deal shift to the left in 1934 and 1935?

Despite the president's landslide victory in 1936, why did the New Deal stall during Roosevelt's second term in office?

 LEARNINGCurve bedfordstmartins.com/hewittlawson/LC

Conclusion: New Deal Liberalism

Franklin Roosevelt succeeded in expanding the scope of public authority. The New Deal brought unprecedented government involvement in the lives of people, whether rich or poor. Businesses were subject to increased regulation even as they retained control over hiring and firing, production, and pricing. The federal government grew considerably during the 1930s, jumping from 605,000 employees to more than 1 million, and turned citizens' attention from local and state authorities to officials in Washington, D.C. Yet the New Deal rescued the capitalist system, doing little to alter the fundamental structure of the American economy. It left corporations, the stock market, farms, and banks in the hands of private enterprise. Indeed, by the end of the 1930s large corporations had more power over markets than ever before. Income and wealth remained unequally distributed, nearly to the same extent as it had been before Roosevelt took office in 1933.

Roosevelt forged a middle path between reactionaries and revolutionaries at a time when the fascist tyrants Adolf Hitler and Benito Mussolini gained power in Germany and Italy respectively and Joseph Stalin ruthlessly consolidated his rule in the Communist Soviet Union. By contrast, the American president expanded democratic capitalism, bringing a broader cross section of society to the decision-making table. Big business no longer held unilateral authority but instead found its power balanced by big labor, big agriculture, and big government. Roosevelt's "broker state" of multiple competing interests provided for greater democracy than a government dominated exclusively by business elites. This system did not benefit those who remained unorganized and wielded little power, but marginalized groups—African Americans, Latinos, and Native Americans—did receive greater recognition and self-determination from the federal government. Moreover, in the coming decades these groups, too, would find ways to take advantage of the power of collective action and claim a place at the bargaining table.

President Roosevelt also solidified the institution of the presidency as the focal point for public leadership. His cheerfulness, hopefulness, and pragmatism rallied millions of individuals behind him. Even after Roosevelt died in 1945, the public retained its expectation that leadership came from the White House.

Through his programs and force of personality, Franklin Roosevelt convinced Americans that he cared about their welfare and that the federal government would not ignore their suffering. With his chin cocked upward, a fedora hat on his head, and a cigarette holder protruding from his smiling mouth, Roosevelt assured the depression-weary public that it had somewhere to turn for relief. He was not universally beloved: Millions of Americans despised him because they thought he was leading the country toward socialism, and he did not solve all the problems the country faced—it would take government spending for World War II to end the depression. Still, together with his wife Eleanor, Franklin Roosevelt conveyed a sense that the American people belonged to a single community, capable of banding together to solve the country's problems, no matter how serious they were or how intractable they might seem.

Chapter Review | Online Study Guide ▶ bedfordstmartins.com/hewittlawson

KEY TERMS

Hoovervilles (p. 690)
Scottsboro Nine (p. 692)
Bonus Army (p. 695)
fireside chats (p. 697)
New Deal (p. 697)
Agricultural Adjustment Act (p. 697)
Tennessee Valley Authority (TVA) (p. 698)
National Recovery Administration (NRA) (p. 698)
Civilian Conservation Corps (CCC) (p. 699)
Share Our Wealth (p. 702)
Works Progress Administration (WPA) (p. 702)
Social Security Act (p. 703)
National Labor Relations Act (p. 704)
sit-down strike (p. 704)
Indian Reorganization Act (IRA) (p. 706)
court-packing plan (p. 707)
conservative coalition (p. 707)
Fair Labor Standards Act (p. 707)

REVIEW & RELATE

1. How did President Hoover respond to the problems and challenges created by the Great Depression?

2. How did different segments of the American population experience the depression?

3. What steps did Roosevelt take to stimulate economic recovery and provide relief to impoverished Americans during his first term in office?

4. What criticisms did Roosevelt's opponents level against the New Deal?

5. Why and how did the New Deal shift to the left in 1934 and 1935?

6. Despite the president's landslide victory in 1936, why did the New Deal stall during Roosevelt's second term in office?

TIMELINE OF EVENTS

1931	Scottsboro Nine tried for rape
1932–1939	Dust storms sweep through Great Plains
1932	Creation of Reconstruction Finance Corporation
	River Rouge autoworkers' strike
	Milo Reno creates the Farm Holiday Association
	Bonus Army marches on Washington, D.C.
1933	Roosevelt takes steps to stabilize banking and financial systems
	Agricultural Adjustment Act passed
	Federal Emergency Relief Administration (FERA) created
	Tennessee Valley Authority (TVA) created
	National Recovery Administration (NRA) created
	Civilian Conservation Corps (CCC) created
1934	Indian Reorganization Act (IRA) passed
	Francis Townsend forms Old-Age Revolving Pensions Corporation
	Huey Long establishes Share Our Wealth movement
	Securities and Exchange Commission (SEC) established
1935	Charles E. Coughlin organizes National Union for Social Justice
	Works Progress Administration (WPA) established
	Social Security Act passed
	National Labor Relations Act passed
	Congress of Industrial Organizations (CIO) founded
	Creation of the Soil Conservation Service
1937	United Auto Workers conduct sit-down strikes against General Motors in Flint, Michigan
	Roosevelt proposes to increase the size of the Supreme Court
1938	Fair Labor Standards Act passed

DOCUMENT PROJECT **22**

The Depression in Rural America

During the 1930s, rural Americans' lives were devastated by the twin disasters of the Great Depression and, in the Great Plains, the most sustained drought in American history. But both problems only deepened the already difficult lives of many farmers. Agriculture in the South had long been dominated by sharecropping, a system that hampered crop diversification and left many African American tenant farmers vulnerable to exploitation by white landowners. In the Midwest, farmers had spent decades overgrazing pastures and exhausting the soil through overproduction. Prices dropped dramatically throughout the 1920s, and farmers were the only group whose incomes fell during that decade.

When the depression hit, many farmers did not have the resources to stay on their land, and farm foreclosures tripled in the early 1930s. Sharecroppers, tenant farmers, and former farm owners left their homes to find better opportunities, and a million people left the Great Plains alone. Most ended up as migrant agricultural laborers in farms and orchards on the West Coast. Feeling overrun by refugees, California passed a law in 1937 making it a misdemeanor to bring into California any indigent person who was not a state resident. This law remained in effect until 1941.

Under the New Deal, the federal government acted in a number of ways to relieve the plight of farmers around the country. The Agricultural Adjustment Act attempted to raise crop prices and stabilize agricultural incomes by encouraging farmers to cut production. The Farm Credit Act helped some farmers refinance mortgages at a lower rate, the Rural Electrification Administration brought electricity to farm areas previously without it, and the Soil Conservation Service advised farmers on how to properly cultivate their hillsides. The report of the Great Plains Committee (Document 22.10), another Roosevelt creation, details additional recommendations for helping the agricultural economy in the Midwest.

The following documents on the lives of farmers, sharecroppers, migrants, and labor organizers during the 1930s shed light on many aspects of the Great Depression. Consider what they reveal about the challenges faced by rural Americans and how different individuals and groups responded to those problems.

DOCUMENT 22.5

Ann Marie Low | Dust Bowl Diary, 1934

When massive dust storms swept through the Midwest beginning in the early 1930s, they blew away the topsoil of a once productive farm region and created hazardous living conditions. Residents needed to clean and wash repetitively to perform even simple daily tasks. Ann Marie Low, a young woman living with her family in southeastern North Dakota, describes in her diary the monotony and difficulty of life in the Dust Bowl.

May 21, 1934, Monday . . .
Saturday Dad, Bud, and I planted an acre of potatoes. There was so much dirt in the air I couldn't see Bud only a few feet in front of me. Even the air in the house was just a haze. In the evening the wind died down, and Cap came to take me to the movie. We joked about how hard it is to get cleaned up enough to go anywhere.

The newspapers report that on May 10 there was such a strong wind the experts in Chicago estimated 12,000,000 tons of Plains soil was dumped on that city. By the next day the sun was obscured in Washington, D.C., and ships 300 miles out at sea reported dust settling on their decks.

Sunday the dust wasn't so bad. Dad and I drove cattle to the Big Pasture. Then I churned butter and baked a ham, bread, and cookies for the men, as no telling when Mama will be back.

May 30, 1934, Wednesday
Ethel got along fine, so Mama left her at the hospital and came to Jamestown by train Friday. Dad took us both home.

The mess was incredible! Dirt had blown into the house all week and lay inches deep on everything. Every towel and curtain was just black. There wasn't a clean dish or cooking utensil. There was no food. Oh, there were eggs and milk and one loaf left of the bread I baked the weekend before. I looked in the cooler box down the well (our refrigerator) and found a little ham and butter. It was late, so Mama and I cooked some ham and eggs for the men's supper because that was all we could fix in a hurry. It turned out they had been living on ham and eggs for two days.

Mama was very tired. After she had fixed starter for bread, I insisted she go to bed and I'd do all the dishes.

It took until 10 o'clock to wash all the dirty dishes. That's not wiping them—just washing them. The cupboards had to be washed out to have a clean place to put them.

Saturday was a busy day. Before starting breakfast I had to sweep and wash all the dirt off the kitchen and dining room floors, wash the stove, pancake griddle, and dining room table and chairs. There was cooking, baking, and churning to be done for those hungry men. Dad is 6 feet 4 inches tall, with a big frame. Bud is 6 feet 3 inches and almost as big-boned as Dad. We say feeding them is like filling a silo.

Mama couldn't make bread until I carried water to wash the bread mixer. I couldn't churn until the churn was washed and scalded. We just couldn't do anything until something was washed first. Every room had to have dirt almost shoveled out of it before we could wash floors and furniture.

We had no time to wash clothes, but it was necessary. I had to wash out the boiler, wash tubs, and the washing machine before we could use them. Then every towel, curtain, piece of bedding, and garment had to be taken outdoors to have as much dust as possible shaken out before washing. The cistern is dry, so I had to carry all the water we needed from the well.

Source: Ann Marie Low, *Dust Bowl Diary* (Lincoln: University of Nebraska Press, 1984), 96–97.

DOCUMENT 22.6

The Life of a White Sharecropper, 1938

In 1936 workers in the WPA's Federal Writers Project began the Folklore Project. Interviewers spoke with thousands of ordinary individuals to document their home lives, education, occupations, political and religious views, and the impact of the Great Depression on their families. Folklore Project worker Claude Dunnagan collected the following story from a white sharecropping family in Longtown, North Carolina.

I guess we been hard luck renters all our lives—me and Morrison both. They was ten young'uns in my family, and I was next to the youngest. We had it awful hard. . . . We went to Yadkin County and rented an old rundown farm for a share of what we could raise. The crops wasn't any good that year, the landlord came and got what we had raised and had the auctioneers come and sell our tools and furniture. They was a bunch of people at the sale that day from all around. I was standin' there watchin' the man sell the things when I saw a good lookin' man in overalls lookin' toward me. He watched me all durin' the sale and I knew what he was thinkin'. That was the first time I ever saw Allison. I reckon he fell in love with me right off, for we was married a few days later. Allison didn't have no true father. His mother wasn't married, and he was raised up by his kin folks. Then we moved to a little farm near Longtown, about ten miles away. The owner said we could have three-fourths of what we raised. The first two years the crops turned out pretty good so we could pay off the landlord and buy a little furniture . . . a bed and table and some chairs. Then the first baby came on. That was Hildreth. He's out in the field workin' now, suckerin' [removing sprouts] tobacco. . . . By that time, we was able to get a cow, and that came in good, for the baby was awful thin and weak. . . .

Hildreth was only six, but he could help a lot, pullin' and tyin' the tobacco, and helpin' hang it in the barn. We got out more tobacco that year than any other, but when we took it to market in Winston, they wasn't payin' but about twelve cents a pound for the best grade, so when we give the landlord his share and paid the fertilizer bill, we didn't have enough left to pay the doctor and store bill. We didn't know what we was goin' to do durin' the winter. Allison had raised a few vegetables and apples, so we canned what we could and traded the rest for some cotton cloth up at the store so the children would have something to wear that winter. Allison got a job helpin' build a barn for a neighbor, but it didn't last but two days. The neighbor gave him two second hand pairs of overalls for the work. . . .

Things are a lot better for the renter today than in the past. It used to be we couldn't get enough to eat and wear. Now we got a cow, a hog, and some chickens. Allison bought a second-hand car and every Sunday afternoon we ride somewhere. It's the only time we ever get away from home.

The landlord gives us five-sixths of what we raise, so we get along pretty good when the crops are fair. Of course we have to furnish the fertilizer and livestock. This year we had seven barns of tobacco and four acres of corn. Wheat turned out pretty good, too. We raised forty-three bushels, and I hear the price is going to be fair at the roller mill. I canned about all our extra fruits and vegetables. I reckon we still got about a hundred cans in the pantry.

Source: Library of Congress, Manuscript Division, WPA Federal Writers Project Collection.

DOCUMENT 22.7

Sharecropping Family in Washington County, Arkansas, 1935

The Resettlement Administration (later the Farm Security Administration) documented the plight of migrant farmworkers and sharecroppers in numerous photographs. The following photo, taken by the noted photojournalist Arthur Rothstein, depicts a sharecropper's wife and daughters in Washington County, Arkansas, in 1935.

Franklin D. Roosevelt Library

DOCUMENT 22.8

John Steinbeck | The Harvest Gypsies, 1936

In 1936 the *San Francisco News* hired John Steinbeck to write a series of articles on Dust Bowl migrants in California. Steinbeck toured farm sites and shantytowns, and his work on these articles formed the basis of his Pulitzer Prize–winning novel *The Grapes of Wrath*. The following selection is from the second installment of his newspaper series.

This is a family of six; a man, his wife, and four children. They live in a tent the color of the ground. Rot has set in on the canvas so that the flaps and the sides hang in tatters and are held together with bits of rusty baling wire. There is one bed in the family and that is a big tick [sack mattress] lying on the ground inside the tent.

They have one quilt and a piece of canvas for bedding. The sleeping arrangement is clever. Mother and father lie down together and two children lie between them. Then, heading the other way, the other two children lie, the littler ones. If the mother and father sleep with their legs spread wide, there is room for the legs of the children.

There is more filth here. The tent is full of flies clinging to the apple box that is the dinner table, buzzing about the foul clothes of the children, particularly the baby, who has not been bathed nor cleaned for several days. This family has been on the road longer than the builder of the paper house. There is no toilet here, but there is a clump of willows nearby where human feces lie exposed to the flies—the same flies that are in the tent.

Two weeks ago there was another child, a four year old boy. For a few weeks they had noticed that he was kind of lackadaisical, that his eyes had been feverish. They had given him the best place in the bed, between father and mother. But one night he went into convulsions and died, and the next morning the coroner's wagon took him away. It was one step down.

They know pretty well that it was a diet of fresh fruit, beans, and little else that caused his death. He had no milk for months. With this death there came a change of mind in his family. The father and mother now feel that paralyzed dullness with which the mind protects itself against too much sorrow and too much pain.

And this father will not be able to make a maximum of four hundred dollars a year any more because he is no longer alert; he isn't quick at piecework, and he is not able to fight clear of the dullness that has settled on him. His spirit is losing caste rapidly.

The dullness shows in the faces of this family, and in addition there is a sullenness that makes them taciturn. Sometimes they still start the older children off to school, but the ragged little things will not go; they hide in ditches or wander off by themselves until it is time to go back to the tent, because they are scorned in the school.

The better-dressed children shout and jeer, the teachers are quite often impatient with these additions to their duties, and the parents of the "nice" children do not want to have disease carriers in the schools.

The father of this family once had a little grocery store and his family lived in back of it so that even the children could wait on the counter. When the drought set in there was no trade for the store any more.

This is the middle class of the squatters' camp. In a few months this family will slip down to the lower class. Dignity is all gone, and spirit has turned to sullen anger before it dies.

Source: John Steinbeck, "The Harvest Gypsies," *San Francisco News*, October 7, 1936.

DOCUMENT 22.9

Frank Stokes | Let the Mexicans Organize, 1936

While union organizers made some gains in the industrial sector, they made little headway in the agricultural fields of California. Frank Stokes was a citrus grower who broke with his fellow farmers to support migrant labor organizing. In the following selection, Stokes argues in favor of unionization among migrant Mexican farmworkers.

The Mexican is to agricultural California what the Negro is to the medieval South. His treatment by the vegetable growers of the Imperial Valley is well known. What has happened to him in the San Joaquin has likewise been told. But for a time at least it appeared that the "citrus belt" was different. Then came the strike of the Mexican fruit pickers in Orange County. In its wake came the vigilantes, the night riders, the strike-breakers, the reporters whose job it was to "slant" all the stories in favor of the packers and grove owners. There followed the State Motor Patrol, which for the first time in the history of strike disorders in California set up a portable radio broadcasting station "in a secret place" in the strike area "to direct law-and-order activities." And special deputy badges blossomed as thick as Roosevelt buttons in the recent campaign.

Sheriff Jackson declared bravely: "It was the strikers themselves who drew first blood so from now on we will meet them on that basis." "This is no fight," said he, "between orchardists and pickers. It is a fight between the entire population of Orange County and a bunch of Communists." However, dozens and dozens of non-Communist Mexican fruit pickers were jailed; 116 were arrested en masse while traveling in automobiles along the highway. They were charged with riot and placed under bail of $500 each. . . . After fifteen days in jail the hearing was finally held—and the state's witnesses were able to identify only one person as having taken part in the trouble. . . . Judge Ames of the Superior Court ordered the release of all but one identified prisoner and severely criticized the authorities for holding the Mexicans in jail for so long a time when they must have known it would not be possible to identify even a small portion of the prisoners.

For weeks during the strike newspaper stories described the brave stand taken by "law-abiding citizens." These stories were adorned with such headlines as "Vigilantes Battle Citrus Strikers in War on Reds." During all this time, so far as I know, only one paper—the Los Angeles *Evening News*—defended the fruit pickers. . . .

These Mexicans were asking for a well-deserved wage increase and free transportation to and from the widely scattered groves; they also asked that tools be furnished by the employers. Finally they asked recognition of their newly formed union. Recognition of the Mexican laboring man's union, his cooperative organization formed in order that he might obtain a little more for his commodity, which is labor—here was the crucial point. The growers and packers agreed to furnish tools; they agreed to furnish transportation to and from the groves. They even agreed to a slight wage increase, which still left the workers underpaid. But recognition of the Mexican workers' union? Never! . . .

Not only in the fields are the Mexican people exploited. Not only as earners but as buyers they are looked upon as legitimate prey—for old washing machines that will not clean clothes, for old automobiles that wheeze and let down, for woolen blankets made of cotton, for last season's shop-worn wearing apparel. Gathered in villages composed of rough board shanties or drifting with the seasons from vegetable fields of the Imperial Valley to the grape vineyards of the San Joaquin, wherever they go it is the same old, pathetic story. Cheap labor!

Source: Frank Stokes, "Let the Mexicans Organize," *The Nation*, December 19, 1936, 731–32.

DOCUMENT 22.10

Report of the Great Plains Committee, 1937

Much has been written of our droughts here in Oklahoma, and how they have driven the farmers from the land. But little has been said of the other tentacles that choke off the livelihood of the small owner and the tenant. We do not wish to minimize the seriousness of these droughts and their effects on the farming population. But droughts alone would not have permanently displaced these farmers. The great majority of migrants had already become share-tenants and sharecroppers. The droughts hastened a process that had already begun. We submit the following as the cases for migratory agricultural workers:

1. *High interest rates.* Often a farmer borrows money for periods of 10 months and is charged an interest rate of 10 percent. These rates are charged when crops are good and when they fail. Through such practices the farmer loses his ownership; he becomes a tenant, then a sharecropper, then a migrant.

2. *The tenant and sharecropping system.* When share tenants are charged $33\frac{1}{3}$ percent of all corn or feed crops and 25 percent or more on cotton, plus 10 percent on all money borrowed at the bank, when sharecroppers are charged 50 to 75 percent of all he produces to the landlords, plus 10 percent for the bank's share on money invested; when these robbing practices are carried on in a community or a State, is it surprising that 33,241 farm families have left Oklahoma in the past 5 years?

3. *Land exhaustion, droughts, soil erosion, and the one-crop system of farming.* Lacking capital and equipment, small farmers have been unable to terrace their land or conduct other soil-conservation practices. The tenant and sharecropping system is chiefly responsible for the one-crop system. The landlord dictates what crops are to be planted—invariably cotton—and the tenant either plants it or gets off.

4. *Unstable markets.* Approximately a month and a half before the wheat harvest this year the price for this product was 93 cents here in Oklahoma City. But at harvest time the farmer sold his wheat for 46 cents to 60 cents per bushel, depending on the grade. . . . Kaffir [a grain sorghum] was selling

for $1.30 one month ago, and yesterday we sold some for 85 cents per hundred. . . .

It is obvious to all of us that farm prices are set by speculators. The farmer's losses at the market have contributed in no small part to the farmer losing his place on the land. Higher prices for farm products are quoted when the farmer has nothing to sell.

5. *Tractor farming.* In Creek County, Okla., we have the record of one land-owner purchasing 3 tractors and forcing 31 of his 34 tenants and croppers from the land. Most of these families left the State when neither jobs nor relief could be secured. This is over 10 families per machine, 10 families who must quit their profession and seek employment in an unfriendly, industrialized farming section of Arizona or California. Many of these families were even unable to become "Joads" [the fictional family in *The Grapes of Wrath*] in these other States, and had to seek relief from an unfriendly national administration and a more unfriendly State administration. . . .

At this hearing we will have all kinds of statistical material presented and arguments based on this material. But I am one of those who is more interested in the people, my people, than in mere figures. I do not agree with those who say "the no-good must always be weeded out." I say that all of these people, casually referred to in statistical sums, are 100-percent Americans. There are no more important problems facing us than the problem of stopping this human erosion and rehabilitating those unfortunates who have already been thrown off the land. Certainly it is un-American for Americans to be starved and dispossessed of their homes in our land of plenty. Those who seek to exploit and harass these American refugees, the migratory workers, are against our principles of democracy.

Source: U.S. Congress, House Select Committee to Investigate the Interstate Migration of Destitute Citizens (Washington: Government Printing Office, 1940–1941), 2102.

Interpret the Evidence

1. What does Ann Marie Low's description of a typical day suggest about the particular challenges women faced during the Dust Bowl era (Document 22.5)?

2. Compare the living conditions described by a white southern sharecropper (Document 22.6) to those of the migrant family described by John Steinbeck (Document 22.8). How does the poverty of the two families differ? How would you explain the differences you note?

3. Compare the sharecropper's story (Document 22.6) with the photograph of the Arkansas family (Document 22.7). Do the subjects seem to react to the Great Depression in the same way? Do they seem hopeful or hopeless?

4. According to Frank Stokes, how did the fruit packers and grove owners characterize their conflict with the Mexican farmworkers (Document 22.9)? In what ways did their characterization draw on more general conservative criticisms of the New Deal?

5. According to the Great Plains Committee testimony (Document 22.10), what role did human-caused factors play in producing the misery that accompanied the dust storms of the early 1930s?

Put It in Context

- What do these documents tell us about expectations regarding government help during the Great Depression?

background photos: pages 714 and 718, Library of Congress

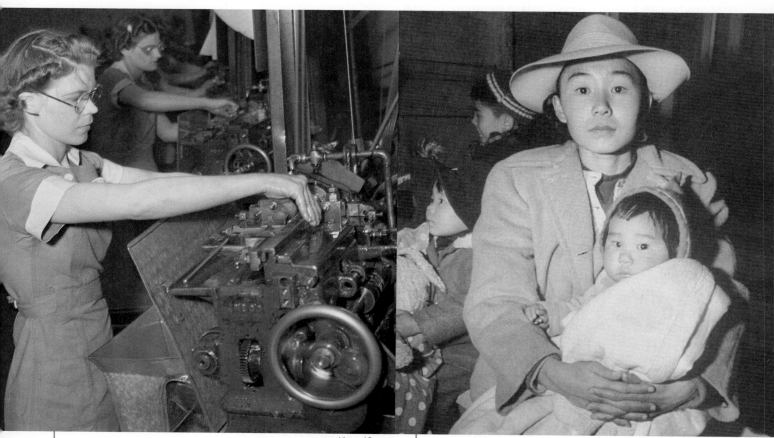

Library of Congress

Time & Life Pictures/Getty Images

Woman working at the Republic Drill and Tool Company in Chicago, Illinois, 1942.

Japanese American woman and child at internment camp, Tule Lake, California.

23
World War II
1933–1945

Tuskegee airman Edward C. Gleed, March 1945.

AMERICAN HISTORIES

One month after Japan attacked the U.S. naval base at Pearl Harbor on December 7, 1941, and the United States entered World War II, President Franklin Roosevelt approved a full-scale effort to develop an atomic bomb. As scientific director of this top-secret program, called the Manhattan Engineering District Project, physicist J. Robert Oppenheimer orchestrated the work of more than 3,000 scientists, technicians, and military personnel at the Los Alamos Laboratories near Santa Fe, New Mexico. The thirty-seven-year-old Oppenheimer, the son of German American Jews, had studied theoretical physics in England and Germany and then returned to the United States to teach physics. He was also interested and engaged in world events. When the Nazis began persecuting German Jews in the early 1930s, Oppenheimer helped Jews gain asylum in the United States.

On July 16, 1945, Oppenheimer and his team successfully tested their new weapon. The explosion, which had a force equal to more than 18,000 tons of TNT, lit up the predawn sky with a blast so powerful that it broke a window 125 miles away and so bright that a blind woman claimed she saw a flash of light. A mushroom cloud shot up 41,000 feet into the sky over ground zero, where a 1,200-foot-wide crater had formed. Oppenheimer understood that the world had been permanently transformed. Quoting from Hindu scriptures, he remembered thinking at the moment of the explosion, "I am become death, destroyer of worlds."

On August 6, 1945, Army Air Corps planes dropped an atomic bomb on the Japanese city of Hiroshima and three days later another one on Nagasaki, resulting in the deaths of more than 200,000 civilians. Profoundly shaken by the death and destruction his efforts had produced, Oppenheimer observed: "If atomic bombs are to be added to the arsenals of a warring world, or to the arsenals of nations preparing for war, then the time will come when mankind will curse the names of Los Alamos and Hiroshima."

While Oppenheimer and his team remained cloistered at Los Alamos, Fred Korematsu and some 112,000 Japanese Americans lived in internment camps, imprisoned for no other reason than their Japanese ancestry. Born in Oakland, California, in 1919 to Japanese immigrants, Fred and his three brothers grew up like many first-generation Americans. Fred's parents spoke Japanese at home and maintained the cultural traditions of their native land, while their sons learned English in public school, ate hamburgers, and played football and basketball like other children their age. After graduating from high school in 1938, Korematsu worked on the Oakland docks as a welder.

After the 1941 bombing of Pearl Harbor, residents on the West Coast turned their anger on the Japanese and Japanese Americans living among them. As assimilated as Fred Korematsu and many other Nisei (the U.S.-born children of Japanese immigrants) had become, white Americans doubted their loyalty and viewed them as a threat to national security. Korematsu could no longer get a haircut in a white-owned barbershop; the

Boilermakers Union expelled him, and he lost his job as a welder; and he was not allowed to join the U.S. coast guard because of his race.

These indignities foreshadowed events to come. On March 21, 1942, President Roosevelt issued Executive Order 9066 authorizing military commanders on the West Coast to take any measures necessary to promote national security. Consequently, officials imposed a curfew on Japanese Americans, excluded them from designated areas, and prohibited them from traveling more than twenty-five miles from their homes. On May 9, the military ordered Korematsu's family to report to Tanforan Racetrack in San Mateo, from which they would be transported to internment camps throughout the West. Although the rest of his family complied with the order, Fred refused. He adopted the name "Clyde Sarah" and claimed to be of Spanish-Hawaiian ancestry. However, Korematsu's efforts to resist internment failed. Three weeks later, he was arrested and later transferred to the Topaz internment camp in south-central Utah. Found guilty of violating the original evacuation order, Korematsu received a sentence of five years of probation. When he appealed his conviction to the U.S. Supreme Court in 1944, the high court upheld the verdict. By the time the first atomic bomb exploded over Hiroshima, the government had closed down the internment camp where Fred Korematsu lived, and he had regained his freedom. ●

photos: Hulton Archive/Getty Images; National Portrait Gallery, Smithsonian Institution/Art Resource, NY

THE AMERICAN HISTORIES of both Fred Korematsu and J. Robert Oppenheimer were shaped by the profound changes brought about by war. Korematsu was subjected to the full force of anti-Japanese sentiment that followed the attack on Pearl Harbor, while Oppenheimer played a key role in developing a weapon that he feared would lead to the destruction of mankind. Both men experienced a mixture of hope and uneasiness as they looked ahead to the postwar world.

The war that these two men experienced in such different ways marked a critical point for the United States in the twentieth century. World War II finally ended the Great Depression, cementing the trend toward government intervention in the economy that had begun with the

New Deal. With the war fought almost entirely on foreign soil, the United States converted its factories to wartime production and became the "arsenal of democracy," putting millions of Americans to work in the process, including African Americans, other minorities, and women. All Americans contributed to the war effort, whether they wanted to or not, through rationing and higher taxes. Overseas, soldiers fought fierce battles in Europe, Africa, and Asia. The combined military power of the Allies, led by the United States, Great Britain, and the Soviet Union, finally defeated the Axis nations of Germany, Italy, and Japan, but not until the fighting had killed 60 to 70 million people, more than half of whom were civilians, and ushered in the Atomic Age.

The Road toward War

The end of World War I did not bring peace and prosperity to Europe. The harsh peace terms imposed on the Central Powers in 1919 left the losers, especially Germany, deeply resentful. The war saddled both sides with a huge financial debt and produced economic instability, which contributed to the Great Depression. In the Far East, Japanese invasions of China and Southeast Asia threatened America's Open Door policy (see chapter 20). The failure of the United States to join the League of Nations dramatically reduced the organization's ability to maintain peace and stability. German expansionism in Europe in the late 1930s moved President Roosevelt and the nation toward war, but it took the Japanese attack on Pearl Harbor to bring the United States into the global conflict.

The Growing Crisis in Europe

Despite its failure to join the League of Nations, the United States did not withdraw from international affairs behind a wall of total isolationism in the 1920s. It participated in arms control negotiations; signed the Kellogg-Briand Pact, which outlawed war as an instrument of national policy but proved unenforceable; and expanded its foreign investments in Central and Latin America, Asia, the Middle East, and western Europe. In 1933 a new possibility for trade emerged when the Roosevelt administration extended diplomatic recognition to the Soviet Union (USSR).

Overall, the country did not retreat from foreign affairs so much as it refused to enter into collective security agreements that would restrain its freedom of action. To the extent that American leaders practiced isolationism, they did so mainly in the political sense of rejecting

internationalist organizations such as the League of Nations and the World Court, institutions that might require military cooperation to implement their decisions.

The experience of World War I had reinforced this brand of political isolationism, which was reflected in an outpouring of antiwar sentiments in the late 1920s and early 1930s. Best-selling novels like Ernest Hemingway's *Farewell to Arms* (1929), Erich Maria Remarque's *All Quiet on the Western Front* (1929), and Dalton Trumbo's *Johnny Got His Gun* (1939) presented graphic depictions of the horror and futility of war. Beginning in 1934, Senate investigations chaired by Gerald Nye of North Dakota concluded that bankers and munitions makers— "merchants of death" as one contemporary writer labeled them—had conspired to push the United States into war in 1917. Nye's hearings appealed to popular antibusiness sentiment in Depression-era America.

Following the Nye committee hearings, Congress passed a series of **Neutrality Acts**, each designed to make it more difficult for the United States to become entangled in European armed hostilities. In 1935 Congress prohibited the sale of munitions to either warring side and authorized the president to warn Americans against traveling on passenger liners of belligerent nations. The following year, lawmakers added private loans to the ban, and in 1937 they required belligerents to pay cash for nonmilitary purchases and ship them on their own vessels—so-called cash-and-carry provisions.

Events in Europe, however, made U.S. neutrality ever more difficult to maintain. After rising to power as chancellor of Germany in 1933, Adolf Hitler revived Germany's economic and military strength despite the Great Depression. Hitler installed National Socialism (Nazism) at home and established the empire of the Third Reich abroad. The *Führer* (Leader) whipped up patriotic fervor by scapegoating and persecuting Communists and Jews. To garner support for his actions, Hitler manipulated German feelings of humiliation for losing World War I and having been forced to sign the "war guilt" clause (see chapter 20) and pointed to the disastrous effects of the country's inflation-ridden economy. In 1936 Hitler sent troops to occupy the Rhineland between Germany and France in blatant violation of the Treaty of Versailles.

Hitler did not stop there. Citing the need for more *lebensraum* (space for living) for the Germanic people, he pushed for German expansion into eastern Europe. In March 1938, he forced Austria to unite with Germany. In September of that year, Hitler signed the Munich Accord with Great Britain and France, allowing Germany to annex the Sudetenland, the mainly German-speaking, western region of Czechoslovakia. Hitler still wanted more land and was convinced that his western European rivals would not stop him, so in March 1939 he sent German troops to invade and occupy the rest of Czechoslovakia. Hitler proved correct; Britain and France did nothing in response, in hopes that he would stop with Czechoslovakia—what critics of inaction called "appeasement."

Hitler's Italian ally, Benito Mussolini, joined him in war and conquest. In 1935 Italian troops invaded Ethiopia; deposed its leader, Emperor Haile Selassie; and occupied the small African nation. The following year, both Germany and Italy intervened in the Spanish civil war, providing military support for General Francisco Franco in his effort to overthrow the democratically elected, socialist republic of Spain. While the United States and Great Britain remained on the sidelines, only the Soviet Union officially assisted the Loyalist defenders of the Spanish republic. In violation of American law, private citizens, many of whom were Communists, volunteered to serve on the side of the Spanish Loyalists and fought on the battlefield as the Abraham Lincoln Brigade. Other sympathetic Americans, such as J. Robert Oppenheimer, feared the spread of dictatorships and provided financial assistance for the anti-Franco government. Despite these efforts, Franco's forces seized control of Spain in early 1939, another victory for Hitler and Mussolini.

The Challenge to Isolationism

As Europe drifted toward war, public opinion polls revealed that most Americans wanted to stay out of any European conflict. The president, however, thought it likely that the United States would eventually need to assist the Western democracies. Given the United States' economic dominance in the world and its dependence on international commerce, Roosevelt feared that Germany and Italy threatened a stable world order. Still, Roosevelt had to tread lightly in the face of the Neutrality Acts that Congress had passed between 1935 and 1937 and overwhelming public opposition to American involvement in Europe.

Germany's aggression in Europe eventually led to full-scale war. When Germany invaded Poland in September 1939, Britain and France declared war on Germany and Italy. Just before the invasion, the Soviet Union had signed a nonaggression agreement with Germany, which carved up Poland between the two nations and permitted the USSR to occupy the neighboring Baltic states of Latvia, Lithuania, and Estonia. Soviet leader Joseph Stalin had few illusions about Hitler's ultimate design on his own nation, but he concluded that by signing this pact he could secure his country's western borders and buy additional time. (In June 1941, the Germans broke the pact and invaded the Soviet Union.)

Roosevelt responded to the outbreak of war by reaffirming U.S. neutrality. Unlike Woodrow Wilson, however, he recognized that this position would be hard to maintain, asserting, "This nation will remain a neutral nation, but I cannot ask that every American remain neutral in thought as well," and "Even a neutral cannot be asked to close his mind or close his conscience." Despite his sympathy for the Allies, which most Americans had come to share, the president stated his hope that the United States could stay out of the war: "Let no man or woman thoughtlessly or falsely talk of Americans sending its armies to European fields."

With the United States on the sidelines, German forces marched toward victory. By the spring of 1940, German armies had launched a *blitzkrieg* (lightning war) across Europe, defeating and occupying Denmark, Norway, the Netherlands, Belgium, and Luxembourg. The greatest shock occurred in June 1940 when France fell to the German onslaught and Nazi troops marched into Paris. Britain now stood virtually alone, and its position seemed tenuous. The British had barely succeeded in evacuating their forces from France by sea when the German Luftwaffe (air force) began a relentless bombing campaign on London and other targets in the Battle of Britain.

With German victories mounting, committed opponents of American involvement in foreign wars organized the **America First Committee**. Gerald Nye helped found the organization, which attracted New Deal critics such as Father Charles Coughlin and William Lemke; business leaders who opposed Roosevelt, such as Sears, Roebuck head Robert Wood; and aviation hero Charles A. Lindbergh, who admired what Hitler had accomplished in building up the Luftwaffe. America First tapped into the feeling of isolationism and concern among a diverse group of Americans who did not want to get dragged into another foreign war.

The surrender of France and the Battle of Britain drastically changed Americans' attitude toward entering the war. Before Germany invaded France, 82 percent of Americans thought that the United States should not aid the Allies. After France's defeat, in a complete turnaround, some 80 percent of Americans favored assisting Great Britain in some way, though most expected that this aid would lead to further U.S. involvement. However, four out of five Americans polled opposed immediate entry into the war. As a result, the politically astute Roosevelt portrayed all U.S. assistance to Britain as a way to prevent American military intervention by allowing Great Britain to defeat the Germans on its own.

From September 1940 to November 1941, the Roosevelt administration helped Britain in any way it could, short of going to war against Germany. On September 2, 1940, the

America First Committee Rally, 1941

Organized in 1940, the America First Committee campaigned against U.S. entry into World War II. Led by isolationists such as North Dakota senator Gerald Nye and the popular aviator Charles Lindbergh, the group blamed eastern bankers, British sympathizers, and Jewish leaders for promoting war fever. The committee dissolved soon after this 1941 rally and the Japanese attack on Pearl Harbor. ullstein bild/The Granger Collection, New York

president sent fifty obsolete destroyers to the British in return for leases on British naval bases in Newfoundland, Bermuda, and the British West Indies. These aging warships did not have much military value, but they provided a great morale boost to the British, who were being pounded by German air attacks. Two weeks later, on September 16, Roosevelt persuaded Congress to pass the Selective Service Act, the first peacetime military draft in U.S. history, which quickly registered more than 16 million men.

This political maneuvering came as Roosevelt campaigned for an unprecedented third term in 1940. He defeated the Republican Wendell Willkie, a Wall Street lawyer who shared Roosevelt's anti-isolationist views. However, both candidates accommodated voters' desire to stay out of the European war, and Roosevelt went so far as to promise American parents: "Your boys are not going to be sent into any foreign war."

Roosevelt's campaign promises did not halt the march toward war. Roosevelt succeeded in pushing Congress to pass the **Lend-Lease Act** in March 1941. With Britain running out of money and its shipping devastated by German submarines, this measure circumvented the cash-and-carry provisions of the Neutrality Acts. The United States would lend or lease equipment, but no one expected the recipients to return the used weapons and other commodities. As one critic of the act declared, "Lending war equipment is a good deal like chewing gum, you don't really want it back!" To protect British ships

carrying American supplies, the president extended naval and air patrols in the North Atlantic. In response, German submarines began sinking U.S. ships. By May 1941, Germany and the United States were engaged in an undeclared naval war.

The United States Enters the War

Financially, militarily, and ideologically, the United States had aligned itself with Britain, and Roosevelt expected that the nation would soon be formally at war. After passage of the Lend-Lease Act, American and British military planners agreed that defeating Germany would become the top priority if the United States entered the war. In August 1941, Roosevelt and British prime minister Winston Churchill met in Newfoundland, where they signed the **Atlantic Charter**, a lofty statement of war aims that included principles of freedom of the seas, self-determination, free trade, and "freedom from fear and want"—ideals that laid the groundwork for the establishment of a postwar United Nations. At the same meeting, Roosevelt promised Churchill that the United States would protect British convoys in the North Atlantic as far as Iceland while the nation waited for a confrontation with Germany that would rally the American public in support of war. The president got what he wanted. After several attacks on American ships by German submarines in September and October, the president persuaded Congress to repeal the neutrality legislation of the 1930s and allow American ships to sail across the Atlantic to supply Great Britain. By December, the nation was close to open war with Germany.

The event that finally prompted the United States to enter the war, however, occurred not in the Atlantic but in the Pacific Ocean. For nearly a decade, U.S. relations with Japan had deteriorated over the issue of China's independence. American Christian missionaries had established their presence in China, and since the turn of the twentieth century the U.S. government had promoted the Open Door policy to protect its access to Chinese markets. The United States did little to challenge the Japanese invasion and occupation of Manchuria in 1931, but after Japanese armed forces moved farther into China in 1937, Roosevelt took action. The president skirted the Neutrality Acts by refusing to declare war, but he did supply arms to China. When a bombing raid by Japanese planes inadvertently sank the U.S. gunboat *Panay* in the Yangtze River and killed two sailors, Japan apologized, thereby temporarily reducing tensions between the two countries.

Yet relations between Japan and the United States did not substantially improve. In 1940 the Japanese government signed the Tripartite Pact with Germany and Italy, which created a mutual defense agreement among the Axis powers. That same year, Japanese troops invaded northern Indochina, and Roosevelt responded by embargoing sales

---

DOCUMENTS 23.1 AND 23.2

American Reactions to Pearl Harbor: Two Views

Few Americans would forget where they were or how they felt when they first learned of the Japanese attack on Pearl Harbor. The following documents describe the experiences of two women: Monica Conter, a U.S. army nurse on duty at Pearl Harbor during the Japanese attack, and Monica Sone, a Nisei who was a student at the University of Washington in December 1941. Sone and her family were eventually placed in an internment camp in Idaho.

Explore

23.1 Monica Conter | Letter to Her Parents, December 22, 1941

The wounded started coming in 10 minutes after the 1st attack. We called Tripler [Hospital] for more ambulances—they wanted to know if we were having "Maneuvers." Imagine! Well, the sight in our hospital I'll never forget. No arms, no legs, intestines hanging out etc. . . . In the meantime, the hangars all around us were burning—and that awful "noise." Then comes the second attack—We all fell face down on the wounded in the halls, O.R., and everywhere and heard the bombers directly over us. We (the nurses and the doctors) had no helmets nor gas masks—and it really was a "helpless" feeling. One of the soldiers who works for my ward saw me and so we shared helmets together. In the meantime, the bombs were dropping all around us and when a 500 lb. bomb dropped about CENSORED from the CENSORED, we waited for the plane to come in as it felt like it had hit us—then they were gone. CENSORED.

All our electric clocks stopped on the dot. The dead were placed in back of the hospital, the walking wounded went in trucks to Tripler, and the seriously injured in the ambulances. We used our place as an "Evacuation Hospital." . . . The mayor sent out 20 cases of whiskey so that helped some—that is, the uninjured who were going around in a daze. Of course, it was used medicinally too. We worked, and worked, and worked—and when night came on "Blackout" (I'm used to it now). . . . For a week the nurses slept in uniform on the ward in one of the officer's rooms.

Source: Lisa Grunwald and Stephen J. Adler, eds., *Women's Letters: America from the Revolutionary War to the Present* (New York: Dial Press, 2005), 548.

of aviation fuel and scrap metal, products that Japan needed for war. This embargo did not deter the Japanese; in July, they occupied the remainder of Indochina to gain access to the region's natural resources. The Roosevelt administration retaliated by freezing Japanese assets and cutting off all trade with Japan. The two countries maneuvered to the edge of war.

On the quiet Sunday morning of December 7, 1941, Japan attacked the U.S. Pacific Fleet stationed at Pearl Harbor in Honolulu, Hawaii. This surprise air and naval assault killed more than 2,400 Americans and damaged eight battleships, three cruisers, three destroyers, and nearly two hundred airplanes. The bombing raid abruptly ended

isolationism and rallied the American public behind President Roosevelt, who pronounced December 7 "a date which will live in infamy." The next day, Congress overwhelmingly voted to go to war with Japan, and on December 11 Germany and Italy declared war on the United States in response. In little more than a year after his reelection pledge to keep the country out of war, Roosevelt sent American men to fight overseas.

> **Explore**
>
> See Documents 23.1 and 23.2 for two perspectives on the bombing of Pearl Harbor.

Explore

23.2 Monica Sone | Memories of Pearl Harbor

On a peaceful Sunday morning, December 7, 1941, Henry, Sumi, and I were at choir rehearsal singing ourselves hoarse in preparation for the annual Christmas recital of Handel's "Messiah." Suddenly Chuck Mizuno, a young University of Washington student, burst into the chapel, gasping as if he had sprinted all the way up the stairs.

"Listen, everybody!" he shouted. "Japan just bombed Pearl Harbor . . . in Hawaii. It's war!"

The terrible words hit like a blockbuster, paralyzing us. Then we smiled feebly at each other, hoping this was one of Chuck's practical jokes. Miss Hara, our music director, rapped her baton impatiently on the music stand and chided him, "Now Chuck, fun's fun, but we have work to do. Please take your place. You're already half an hour late."

But Chuck strode vehemently back to the door. "I mean it, folks, honest! I just heard the news over my car radio. Reporters are talking a blue streak. Come on down and hear it for yourselves."

. . . I felt as if a fist had smashed my pleasant little existence, breaking it into jigsaw puzzle pieces. An old wound opened up again, and I found myself shrinking inwardly from my Japanese blood, the blood of an enemy. I knew instinctively that the fact that I was an American by birthright was not going to help me escape the consequences of this unhappy war.

One girl mumbled over and over again, "It can't be, God, it can't be!" Someone else was saying, "What a spot to be in! Do you think we'll be considered Japanese or Americans?"

A boy replied quietly, "We'll be Japs, same as always. But our parents are enemy aliens now, you know."

A shocked silence followed.

Source: Monica Sone, *Nisei Daughter* (Boston: Little Brown, 1953), 145–46.

Interpret the Evidence

- How did the attack on Pearl Harbor directly affect both women's lives?
- How did each woman feel about Japan and America?

Put It in Context

What does the experience of Japanese Americans during World War II indicate about constitutional guarantees of civil liberties during wartime?

REVIEW & RELATE

How did American public opinion shape Roosevelt's foreign policy in the years preceding U.S. entry into World War II?

What events in Europe and the Pacific ultimately brought the United States into World War II?

 LEARNING*Curve* bedfordstmartins.com/hewittlawson/LC

Global War

World War II pitted the "Grand Alliance" of Great Britain, the Soviet Union, the French government in exile, and the United States against the Axis powers of Germany, Japan, and Italy. The Allies consisted of the world's leading colonial power, Great Britain; the world's lone Communist nation, the Soviet Union; and the world's strongest capitalist country, the United States—ingredients for an uncomfortable alliance. From the outset, the United States deployed military forces to contain Japanese aggression, but its most immediate concern was to defeat Germany. Before battles in Europe, Asia, and four other continents concluded, more than 60 million people perished, including 405,000 Americans. Six million Jewish civilians died in the Holocaust, the Nazi regime's genocidal effort to eradicate Europe's Jewish population. The Soviet Union experienced the greatest losses—nearly 27 million soldiers and civilians, more than two-fifths of all those killed.

War in Europe

United against Hitler, the Grand Alliance divided over how quickly to mount a counterattack directly on Germany. The Soviet Union, which bore the brunt of the fighting in trying to repel the German army's invasion, demanded the speedy opening of a **second front** through France and into Germany to take the pressure off its forces. The British wanted to fight first in northern Africa and southern Europe, in part to remove Axis forces from territory that endangered their economic interests in the Mediterranean and the oil-rich Middle East and in part to buy time to rebuild their depleted fighting strength. President Roosevelt understood Soviet demands for immediately establishing a second front, but such a plan would involve fierce and bloody battles to attack the center of Axis strength. The president did not want to risk losing public support early in the war if the United States experienced heavy casualties. He approved his military advisers' plans for an invasion of France from England in 1943, but in the meantime he

agreed with Churchill to fight the Germans and Italians on the periphery of Europe.

From a military standpoint, this circuitous approach proved successful. In October 1942, British forces in North Africa overpowered the Germans at El Alamein, pushing them out of Egypt and removing their threat to the Suez Canal. The following month, British and American troops landed in Algeria and Morocco, controlled by the pro-Nazi French government, and under the British general Bernard Montgomery and the American general George S. Patton they engaged the desert forces of the German general Erwin Rommel. After some early defeats, the combined strength of British and American ground, air, and naval forces drove the Germans out of Africa in May 1943.

These military victories failed to relieve political tensions among the Allies. Although the Soviets had managed to stop the German offensive against Stalingrad, the deepest penetration of enemy troops into their country, Stalin expected the second front to begin as promised in the spring of 1943. He was bitterly disappointed when Roosevelt, hoping to replenish military resources that had been lost in North Africa, postponed the cross–English Channel invasion of France until 1944. To Stalin, it appeared as if his allies were looking to gain a double triumph by letting the Communists and Nazis beat each other into submission. Churchill's strong anti-Communist beliefs fueled Stalin's suspicions.

Instead of opening a second front in France, British, American, and Canadian troops invaded Italy from its southern tip in July 1943. Their initial victories quickly led to the removal of Mussolini and his retreat to northern Italy, where he lived under German protection (Map 23.1). Not until June 4, 1944, did the Allies occupy Rome in central Italy and force the Germans to retreat.

To overcome Stalin's dissatisfaction with the postponement of opening the second front, President Roosevelt issued orders to give the Soviets unlimited access to Lend-Lease supplies to sustain their war efforts and to care for their citizens. In November 1943, the American president and the British prime minister met with the Soviet leader in Tehran, Iran. Roosevelt and Stalin seemed to get along well. Stalin agreed to deploy troops against Japan after the war in Europe ended, and Roosevelt agreed to open the second front within six months. Churchill joined Roosevelt and Stalin in supporting the creation of an international organization to ensure postwar peace.

This time the Americans and British kept their word, and the Allies finally embarked on the second-front invasion. Under the command of General Dwight D. Eisenhower, on June 6, 1944—called **D Day**—more than 1.5 million American, British, and Canadian troops crossed the English Channel in 4,000 boats and landed on the

MAP 23.1   World War II in Europe, 1941–1945

By late 1941, the Axis powers had brought most of Europe and the Mediterranean region under their control. But between 1942 and 1945, the Allied powers drove them back. Critical victories at Leningrad and Stalingrad, in North Africa, and on the beaches of Normandy forced the retreat, and then the defeat, of the Axis powers.

beaches of Normandy, France. Paratrooper landings behind German lines and naval bombardments supported this astonishing amphibious assault. Despite deadly machine-gun fire from German troops placed on higher ground, the Allied forces managed to establish a beachhead. The bravery and discipline of the troops, along with their superior numbers, overcame the Germans and opened the way for the Allies to liberate Paris in August 1944. By the end of the year, the Allies had regained control of the rest of France and most of Belgium.

Amid these Allied victories, Roosevelt won a fourth term against Republican challenger Thomas E. Dewey, governor of New York. He dumped from the campaign

ticket his vice president, Henry A. Wallace, a liberal on economic and racial issues, and replaced him with Senator Harry S. Truman of Missouri, who was more acceptable to southern voters. Despite his declining health, Roosevelt won easily with 432 electoral votes and a margin of more than 3.5 million popular votes.

War in the Pacific

With the Soviet Union bearing the brunt of the fighting in eastern Europe, the United States shouldered the burden of fighting Japan. U.S. military commanders began a two-pronged counterattack in the Pacific in 1942. General

Douglas MacArthur, whose troops had escaped from the Philippines as Japanese forces overran the islands in May 1942, planned to regroup in Australia, head north through New Guinea, and return to the Philippines. At the same time, Admiral Chester Nimitz directed the U.S. Pacific Fleet from Hawaii toward Japanese-occupied islands in the western Pacific. If all went well, MacArthur's ground troops and Nimitz's naval forces would combine with General Curtis LeMay's air forces to overwhelm Japan.

All went according to plan in 1942. Shortly after the Philippines fell to the Japanese, the Allies won a major victory in May in the Battle of the Coral Sea, off the northwest coast of Australia. The following month, the U.S. navy achieved an even greater victory when it defeated the Japanese in the Battle of Midway Island, northwest of Hawaii. In August, the fighting moved to the Solomon Islands, east of New Guinea, where U.S. forces waged fierce battles at Guadalcanal Island. After six months of heavy casualties on both sides, the Americans finally dislodged the Japanese. By late 1944, American, Australian, and New Zealand troops had put the Japanese on the defensive with further victories in the Mariana Islands, north of Guam, and the Marshall Islands, east of the Philippines, allowing General MacArthur to return to the island that the Japanese had forced him to abandon three years earlier.

In 1945 the United States mounted its final offensive against Japan. In preparation for an invasion of the Japanese home islands, American marines won important battles on Iwo Jima and Okinawa, two strategic islands off the coast of Japan. The fighting proved costly—on Iwo Jima alone, the Japanese fought and died nearly to the last man while killing 6,000 Americans and wounding 20,000 others, demonstrating that the Japanese would ferociously defend their homeland against the American invasion planned for November. At the same time, the U.S. Army Air Corps conducted firebomb raids over Tokyo and other major cities, killing some 330,000 Japanese civilians. These attacks were conducted by newly developed B-29 bombers, which could fly more than 3,000 miles and could be dispatched from Pacific island bases captured by the U.S. military. The purpose of this strategic bombing was to destroy Japan's economic capability to sustain the war rather than to destroy their military forces. B-29s dropped bombs that set fire to Japanese buildings, which were constructed mainly of wood, and ignited firestorms that caused widespread destruction. At the same time, the navy blockaded Japan, further crippling its economy and reducing its supplies of food, medicine, and raw materials (Map 23.2). Still, the Japanese government refused to surrender and indicated its determination to resist by launching *kamikaze* attacks (suicidal airplane crashes) on American warships and airplanes.

Ending the War

With victory in sight in both Europe and the Pacific, the Allies addressed problems of postwar relations. In February 1945, Roosevelt and Churchill met with Stalin in the resort city of Yalta in the Ukraine. There they clashed over the question of the postwar government of Poland and whether to recognize the claim of the Polish government in exile in London, which the United States and Great Britain supported, or that of the pro-Soviet government, which had spent the war in the USSR. The loosely worded **Yalta Agreement** that resulted from the conference called for the establishment of permanent governments in Poland and the rest of eastern Europe through free elections. Because the USSR considered Poland vital to its national security—it had been invaded from Europe through Poland twice in the past thirty years—the Soviets interpreted the Yalta accord differently than did the Americans and the British, a difference of opinion that soon degenerated into a serious rupture in relations among the parties known as the "Big Three."

Despite this controversy, the Allies left Yalta united over other issues. They renewed their commitment to establishing the United Nations, and the Soviets reaffirmed their intention to join the war against Japan three months after Germany's surrender. The Allies also reached a tentative agreement on postwar Germany. The United States, Great Britain, the Soviet Union, and France would parcel out the defeated country into four zones, each occupied by one of the powers. They would further subdivide Berlin into four sectors because the capital city fell within the Soviet occupation area. As with the accord over Poland, the agreement concerning Germany created tension after the war.

The Yalta Conference concluded just as the final assault against Germany was under way. The Germans had launched one last offensive in mid-December 1944. Mobilizing troops from remaining outposts in Belgium, they attacked Allied forces in what became known as the Battle of the Bulge because of the way that their assault looked when sketched on Allied maps. After an initial German drive into enemy lines, American and British fighting men recovered and sent the Germans retreating across the Rhine River and back into Germany. Pushing from the west, General Eisenhower stopped at the Elbe River, where he had agreed to meet up with Red Army troops who were charging from the east to Berlin. After an intense assault by the Soviets, the German capital of Berlin fell, and on April 25 Russian and American forces linked up in Torgau on the Elbe River. They achieved this triumph two weeks after Franklin Roosevelt died at the age of sixty-three from a cerebral hemorrhage. On April 30, 1945, with Berlin shattered, Hitler committed suicide in his bunker. A few days earlier, Italian antifascist partisans had

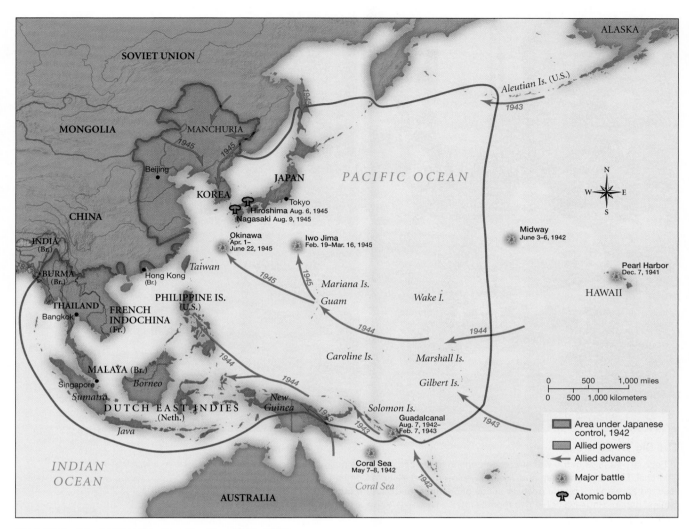

MAP 23.2 World War II in the Pacific, 1941–1945
After bombing Pearl Harbor on December 7, 1941, Japan captured the Philippines and wrenched control of Asian colonies from the British, French, and Dutch and then occupied eastern China. The Allied powers, led by U.S. forces, eventually defeated Japan by winning a series of hard-fought victories on Central Pacific islands and by bombing Hiroshima and Nagasaki.

captured and executed Mussolini in northern Italy. On May 2, German troops surrendered in Italy, and on May 7 the remnants of the German government formally surrendered. The war in Europe ended the next day.

With the war over in Europe, the United States made its final push against Japan. Since 1942, J. Robert Oppenheimer and his team of scientists and engineers had labored feverishly to construct an atomic bomb. Few people knew about this top-secret project, and Congress appropriated $2 billion without knowing its true purpose. Under Colonel Leslie Groves of the Army Corps of Engineers, the military supervised the **Manhattan Project**, which operated at five sites around the country. The need for tight security hampered the project because the military

did not want scientists in different locations to confer with one another.

Vice President Harry S. Truman did not learn about the details of the Manhattan Project until Roosevelt's death in April 1945, and in July he found out about the first atomic test while en route to a conference in Potsdam, Germany, with Stalin and Churchill. He ordered the State Department to issue a vaguely worded ultimatum to the Japanese demanding their immediate surrender or else face annihilation, though the message did not state specifically by what means. When Japan indicated that it would surrender if the United States allowed the country to retain its emperor, Hirohito, the Truman administration refused and demanded unconditional surrender. As a further blow

The Big Three at Yalta

In February 1945, with the war in Europe coming to a close, the three main Allied leaders—Winston Churchill, Franklin Roosevelt, and Joseph Stalin—met at Yalta, a Crimean city on the Black Sea. They reached agreements on the postwar status of Germany and eastern Europe and Soviet entry into the war against Japan. Roosevelt died two months later.   Franklin D. Roosevelt Library

to Japan, Stalin was preparing to send the Soviet military to attack Japanese troops in Manchuria on August 8, which would seriously weaken Japan's ability to hold out.

On August 6, before the Soviets' planned invasion, the ***Enola Gay***, an American B-29 Super Fortress bomber, dropped an atomic bomb on Hiroshima. The weapon immediately killed 80,000 civilians, and tens of thousands later died slowly from radiation poisoning. Three days later, on August 9, Japan still had not surrendered, and the Army Air Corps dropped another atomic bomb on Nagasaki, killing more than 100,000 civilians. Following these bombings and the advance of the Soviet army into Manchuria, Japan announced on August 14 that it would surrender; the formal surrender ceremony took place on September 2, 1945.

At the time, very few Americans questioned the decision to drop atomic bombs on Japan. Truman believed, probably correctly, that had Roosevelt been alive, he would have authorized use of the bombs. Newly on the job, Truman hesitated to reverse a decision already reached by

his predecessor. He reasoned that his action would save American lives because the U.S. military would not have to launch a costly invasion of Japan's home islands. He also felt justified in giving the order because he sought retaliation for the surprise attack on Pearl Harbor and for Japanese atrocities against American soldiers, especially in the Philippines. With an invasion of Japan planned for November and projections for the loss of American lives ranging from hundreds of thousands to 2 million, the servicemen slated to fight there, as well as their relatives, friends, and neighbors, welcomed Truman's decision. **See Document Project 23: The Decision to Drop the Atomic Bomb, page 747**.

Evidence of the Holocaust

The end of the war revealed the full extent and horror of Germany's calculated and methodical slaughter of certain religious, ethnic, and political groups. As Allied troops liberated Germany and Poland, they saw for themselves the

Holocaust Survivors at Mauthausen

Constructed by the Nazis in Austria, the Mauthausen-Gusen concentration camp housed Jews, Communists, homosexuals, Soviet prisoners of war, and opponents of Franco's fascist regime in Spain. Tens of thousands of prisoners died at this forced labor camp. This photograph shows surviving Spanish inmates tearing down the Nazi eagle from atop the entrance after they were liberated in May 1945.   United States Holocaust Memorial Museum

brutality of the Nazi concentration camps that Hitler had set up to execute or work to death 6 million Jews and another 5 million "undesirables"—Slavs, Poles, Gypsies, homosexuals, the physically and mentally disabled, and Communists. At Buchenwald and Dachau in Germany and at Auschwitz in Poland, the Allies encountered the skeletal remains of inmates tossed into mass graves, dead from starvation, illness, and executions. Crematoria on the premises contained the ashes of inmates first poisoned and then incinerated. Troops also freed the "living dead," those still alive but seriously ill and undernourished. One U.S. soldier reported his initial impression of the inmates: "They were . . . all skin and bones. They were sick, starving, and dying."

These horrific discoveries shocked the public, but evidence of what was happening had appeared early in the war. Journalists like Varian Fry had outlined the Nazi atrocities against the Jews several years before. "Letters, reports, tables all fit together. They add up to the most

appalling picture of mass murder in all human history," Fry wrote in the *New Republic* magazine in 1942. He called on Roosevelt and Churchill to speak out forcefully, urged the pope to excommunicate Catholics who participated in Nazi crimes, and proposed sending food to occupied countries to counter the Nazi claim that they were killing Jews and Poles because there was not enough food to go around.

The Roosevelt administration did little in response, despite receiving evidence of the Nazi death camps beginning in 1942. It chose not to send planes to bomb the concentration camps or the railroad lines leading to them, deeming it too risky militarily and too dangerous for the inmates. In a less defensible decision, the Roosevelt administration refused to relax immigration laws to allow Jews and other persecuted minorities to take refuge in the United States, and only 21,000 managed to find asylum. The State Department, which could have modified these policies, was staffed with anti-Semitic officials, and though

President Roosevelt expressed sympathy for the plight of Hitler's victims, he believed that winning the war as quickly as possible was the best way to help them.

REVIEW & RELATE

How did the Allies win the war in Europe and in the Pacific?

How did tensions among the Allies shape both their military strategy and their postwar plans?

✓ *LEARNINGCurve* **bedfordstmartins.com/hewittlawson/LC**

The Home-Front Economy

The global conflict had profound effects on the American home front. World War II ended the Great Depression, restored economic prosperity, and increased labor union membership. At the same time, it smoothed the way for a closer relationship between government and private defense contractors, later referred to as the **military-industrial complex**. The war extended U.S. influence in the world and offered new economic opportunities at home. Despite fierce and bloody military battles throughout the world, Americans kept up morale by rallying around family and community.

Managing the Wartime Economy

To mobilize for war, President Roosevelt increased federal spending to unprecedented levels. Federal government employment during the war expanded to an all-time high of 3.8 million workers, four times as many as during the New Deal, setting the foundation for a large, permanent Washington bureaucracy. War orders fueled economic growth, productivity, and employment. In 1939 the federal budget stood at $9 billion; by the end of the war, it had grown to more than $100 billion. The gross national product increased from $91 billion to $166 billion during the war (Figure 23.1), union membership rose from around 9 million to nearly 15 million, and unemployment dropped from 8 million to less than 1 million. The armed forces helped reduce unemployment significantly by enlisting 12 million men and women, 7 million of whom had been unemployed. Workers earned extra income for overtime work, but because of the rationing of consumer goods, Americans had to defer personal spending.

Prosperity was not limited to any one region. The industrial areas of the Northeast and Midwest once again boomed, as automobile factories converted to building tanks

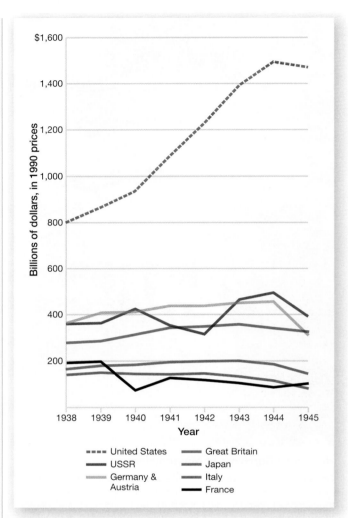

FIGURE 23.1 Real Gross Domestic Product of the Great Powers, 1938–1945

Although World War II stalled or damaged the economic productivity of most of the warring nations, the U.S. economy grew dramatically between 1938 and 1944. With all the battles taking place outside the continental United States, the demand for food, weapons, ships, airplanes, gasoline, and other items by Great Britain and other Allied powers ensured increased employment, productivity, and profits for American workers.   Data from Mark Harrison, ed., *The Economics of World War II: Six Great Powers in International Comparison* (Cambridge: Cambridge University Press, 1998), 11.

and other military vehicles, oil refineries processed gasoline to fuel them, steel and rubber companies manufactured parts to construct these vehicles and the weapons they carried, and textile and shoe plants furnished uniforms and boots for soldiers to wear. As farmers provided food for the nation and its allies, the index of farm production (which was 100 in 1939) jumped from 108 in 1940 to 126 in 1946. The economy diversified geographically. Fifteen million Americans—11 percent of the entire population—migrated between 1941 and 1945, and another 12 million left their homes and joined the armed forces. The war transformed the agricultural South into a budding industrial region. The federal government poured more than $4 billion in contracts into the South to operate military camps, contract with textile factories to clothe the military, and use its ports to build and launch warships. The availability of jobs in southern cities attracted sharecroppers and tenant farmers, black and white, away from the countryside and promoted urbanization while reducing the region's dependency on the plantation economy. In similar fashion, the West Coast prospered because it was the gateway to the Pacific war. The federal government established aircraft plants and ship-building yards in California, Oregon, and Washington, resulting in extraordinary population growth in Los Angeles, San Diego, San Francisco, Portland, and Seattle. Black and white migrants from Texas, Mississippi, and Louisiana headed west to take advantage of these opportunities.

Following the attack on Pearl Harbor, Congress passed the War Powers Act, which authorized the president to reorganize federal agencies any way he thought necessary to win the war. Roosevelt replaced the agencies he had created to combat the Great Depression with another outpouring of organizations to fight the Axis powers. In 1942 the president established the **War Production Board** to oversee the economy. The agency enticed business corporations to meet ever-increasing government orders by negotiating lucrative contracts that helped underwrite their costs, lower their taxes, and guarantee large profits. During the course of the war, corporate net profits nearly doubled. The government also suspended antitrust enforcement, giving private companies great leeway in running their enterprises. Much of the antibusiness hostility generated by the Great Depression evaporated as the Roosevelt administration recruited business executives to supervise government agencies for the token pay of $1 a year. Indeed, the close relationship between the federal government and business that emerged during the war produced the military-industrial complex— the government-business alliance that would have a vast influence on the future development of the economy.

In the first three years of the war, the United States increased military production by some 800 percent. American factories accounted for more than half of worldwide manufacturing output. On their best days, U.S. plants built a ship a day and an airplane every five minutes. By 1945 the United States had produced 86,000 tanks, nearly 300,000 airplanes, 15 million rifles and machine guns, and 6,500 ships.

Financing this enormous enterprise took considerable effort. The federal government spent more than $320 billion, ten times the cost of World War I. To pay for the war, the federal government sold $100 billion in bonds, only about half of what was needed. The rest came from increased income tax rates, which for the first time affected low- and middle-income workers who had paid little or no tax before. At the same time, the tax rate for the wealthy was boosted to 94 percent. In addition to paying higher taxes, American consumers shouldered the burden of inflation. Shortages in household and personal goods produced higher prices, which meant lower purchasing power. During the war, consumer prices jumped by 28 percent, despite the efforts of another federal agency, the Office of Price Administration, to stabilize them.

Building up the armed forces was the final ingredient in the mobilization for war. In 1940 about 250,000 soldiers were serving in the U.S. military, compared with Germany's 6 to 8 million troops. By 1945 American forces had grown to more than 12 million men and women through volun-tary enlistments and a draft of men between the ages of eighteen and forty-five. The military reflected the diversity of the U.S. population. The sons of immigrants fought alongside the sons of older-stock Americans. Although the military tried to exclude homosexuals, they managed to join the fighting forces. Some 700,000 African Americans served in the armed forces, but civilian and military officials confined them to segregated units in the army, assigned them to menial work in the navy, and excluded them from the U.S. Marine Corps. The Army Air Corps created a segregated fighting unit trained at Tuskegee Institute in Alabama, and these Tuskegee airmen, like their counter-parts among the ground forces, distinguished themselves in battle. Women could not fight in combat, but 140,000 joined the Women's Army Corps, and 100,000 joined the navy's WAVES (Women Accepted for Voluntary Emer-gency Service). In these and other service branches, women contributed mainly as nurses and performed transportation and clerical duties.

The concentration of power in the executive branch that accompanied the war effort, together with the presi-dent's expanded role in international diplomacy, fostered what historian Arthur Schlesinger Jr. termed "the imperial presidency." As commanders in chief, Roosevelt and his successors waged war and negotiated peace by controlling and manipulating the flow of information that reached Congress and the American public. Together with the burgeoning military-industrial complex, the imperial presidency redistributed power both within Washington and throughout the country at large.

The government relied on corporate executives to manage wartime economic conversion, but without the sacrifice and dedication of American workers, their efforts would have failed. The demands for wartime production combined with the departure of millions of American workers to the military created a labor shortage that gave unions increased leverage. By 1945 the membership rolls of organized

Tuskegee Airmen
Twenty black pilots, among those known as the Tuskegee airmen, line up for a photograph, which they signed. The Army Air Corps created two segregated units of African American airmen, the 442nd Bombardment Group and the 99th Pursuit Squadron. The latter flew combat missions in Europe. The success of the Tuskegee airmen contributed to the postwar desegregation of the armed forces.   Courtesy National Park Service, Museum Management Program and Tuskegee Institute National Historic Site, TUAI 31, http://www.cr.nps .gov/museum/exhibits/tuskegee/lgimage/air28.htm

labor had grown from 9 million to nearly 14 million. In 1942 the Roosevelt administration established the **National War Labor Board**, which regulated wages, hours, and working conditions and authorized the government to take over plants that refused to abide by its decisions. Unions at first refrained from striking but later in the war organized strikes to protest the disparity between workers' wages and corporate profits. In 1943 Congress responded by passing the Smith-Connally Act, which prohibited walkouts in defense industries and set a thirty-day "cooling-off" period before unions could go out on strike.

New Opportunities for Women

World War II opened up new opportunities for women in the paid workforce. Between 1940 and the peak of wartime employment in 1944, the number of employed women rose more than 50 percent to 6 million. Given severe labor

shortages caused by increased production and the exodus of male workers into the armed forces, for the first time in U.S. history married working women outnumbered single working women. At the start of the war, about half of women employees held poorly paid clerical, sales, and service jobs. Women in manufacturing labored mainly in low-wage textile and clothing factories. During the war, however, the overall number of women in manufacturing grew 141 percent; in industries producing directly for war purposes, the figure jumped by 463 percent. By contrast, the number of women in domestic service dropped by 20 percent. As women moved into defense-related jobs, their incomes also improved.

As impressive as these figures are, they do not tell the whole story. First, although married women entered the job market in record numbers, most of these workers were older and without young children. Women over the age of thirty-five accounted for 60 percent of those entering the workforce. The government did little to encourage young mothers to work, and few efforts were made to provide assistance for child care for those who did. One notable exception was the Kaiser Corporation shipyards, which operated child care facilities twenty-four hours a day. In contrast to this situation, in Great Britain child care programs were widely available. Second, openings for women in manufacturing jobs did not guarantee equality. Women received lower wages for work comparable to the work that men performed, and women did not have the same chances for advancement. Typical union benefits, such as seniority, hurt women, who were generally the most recent hires. In fact, some contracts stipulated that women's tenure in jobs previously held by men would last only for the duration of the war.

Gender stereotypes continued to dominate the workforce and society in general. Magazine covers with the image of "Rosie the Riveter," a woman with her sleeves rolled up and her biceps bulging, became a symbol for the recruitment of women, but reality proved different. The government, private employers, and mass media advertised for women workers by adapting traditional views of women to their new roles. One piece of literature suggested that an overhead crane operated "just like a gigantic clothes wringer" and that winding wire spools was very much like crocheting. Women who took war jobs were viewed not so much as war workers but as women temporarily occupying "men's jobs" during the emergency. As the war drew to a close, public relations campaigns shifted gears and encouraged the same women they had recently recruited to prepare to return home.

Explore

See Documents 23.3 and 23.4 on women's roles during World War II.

Everyday Life on the Home Front

Morale on the home front remained generally high during the war, as prosperity returned and American casualties proved relatively light compared with those of other allied nations. As in World War I, the government set up an agency, the Office of War Information, to promote patriotism and urge Americans to contribute to the war effort any way they could. Schoolchildren collected scrap metal and rubber to donate to the production of military vehicles and weapons, and families planted "victory gardens" to grow

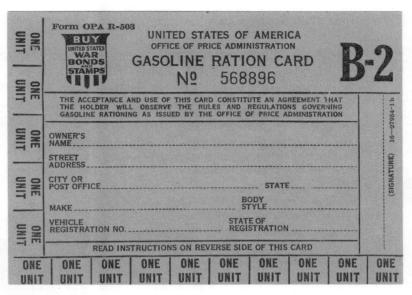

Ration Card

Gasoline rationing, administered by the Office of Price Administration, began in May 1942. Drivers holding this "B" card, such as industrial workers, were considered essential to the war effort and could purchase eight gallons a week. Nonessential drivers were allocated half that amount. By the end of July 1942, the government had issued more than 850,000 of these cards. Home Front Coupons, Rare Book, Manuscript, and Special Collections Library, Duke University

vegetables for domestic consumption. Mothers and daughters helped staff USO (United Service Organizations) dances and recreational activities for soldiers headquartered in the United States. Americans also contributed to the war effort by adhering to restrictions on the consumption of consumer goods. Rationing cards restricted purchases of gasoline for cars and for food such as meat, butter, and sugar.

Hollywood kept the American public entertained, and movie attendance reached a record high of more than 100 million viewers. Films portrayed the heroism of soldiers on battlefields in Guadalcanal and Bataan. They celebrated the courage of Russian allies in propaganda epics such as *Mission to Moscow* (1943) and explored the depth of personal and political loyalties in classics such as *Casablanca* (1943). Hollywood stars signed up for the military, and some fought overseas; others, such as Ronald Reagan, made informational films and entertained the troops. A number of Hollywood celebrities, including the comedic actor Carole Lombard, helped raise funds in war bond drives. Others such as Betty Grable kept up servicemen's spirits by posing for photos that GI's pinned up in their lockers, tents, and equipment.

For many, life went on, but not quite in the same way. Around 15 million Americans moved during the war, with more than half of them relocating out of state. With husbands at war and wives at work, many children became "latchkey kids" who stayed home alone after school until their mothers or fathers returned from their jobs. With less

DOCUMENTS 23.3 AND 23.4

Women Workers during Wartime: Two Views

During the war, women worked in industrial jobs in unprecedented numbers. Corporations and the federal government actively recruited women through posters and advertisements and promised women that factory work was something that would benefit themselves, their families, and their nation. As the Allies neared victory, however, the message changed, and women were urged to prepare to return to the home to open up jobs for returning soldiers.

Explore

23.3 Recruitment Poster, 1942

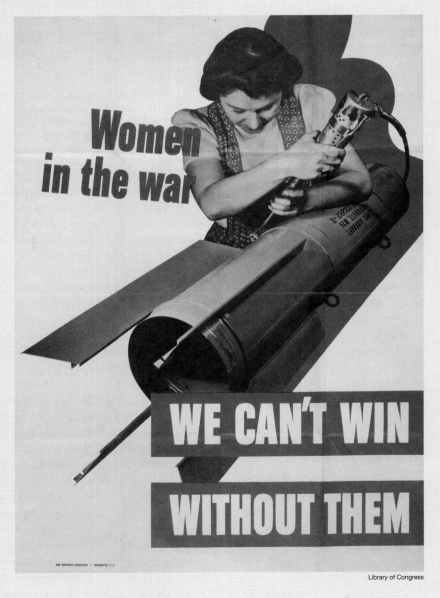

Library of Congress

Explore

23.4 ADEL Advertisement, 1944

Interpret the Evidence

- How do the messages and images of the women in the poster and the advertisement differ? Do you find any similarities?
- How does the 1942 poster portray women's transition from home to work?
- How does the 1944 advertisement emphasize the coming transition from work to home?

Put It in Context

Why were women so important in winning the war?

parental supervision, juvenile delinquency rose, resulting in increased teenage arrests for robbery, vandalism, and loitering. Prostitution flourished around military installations, and with it came more cases of sexually transmitted diseases. High school graduation rates, especially for boys, fell sharply, but many of the dropouts found jobs to add to the family income and relieve the labor shortage. With the end of the Great Depression and with more young people working, marriage rates increased, and couples wed at a younger age. By 1945 the winding down of the war and the rapidly increasing number of marriages produced the first signs of a "baby boom." At the same time, the stresses of life during wartime, including long separations of husbands and wives, also resulted in higher divorce rates.

REVIEW & RELATE

How did the war accelerate the trend that began during the New Deal toward increased government participation in the economy?

How did the war affect life on the home front for the average American?

 LEARNINGCurve bedfordstmartins.com/hewittlawson/LC

Fighting for Equality at Home

The war also had a significant impact on race relations. The fight to defeat Nazism, a doctrine based on racial prejudice and white supremacy, offered African Americans a chance to press for equal opportunity at home. By contrast, Japanese Americans experienced intensified discrimination and oppression as wartime anti-Japanese hysteria led to the internment of Japanese Americans, an erosion of their civil rights. They were freed toward the end of the war, but their incarceration left scars. Finally, Mexican Americans benefited from wartime jobs but continued to experience ethnic prejudice.

The Origins of the Civil Rights Movement

In 1941 A. Philip Randolph, the head of the Brotherhood of Sleeping Car Porters, applied his labor union experience to the struggle for civil rights. He announced that he planned to lead a 100,000-person march on Washington, D.C., in June 1941 to protest racial discrimination in government and war-related employment as well as segregation in the military. Although Randolph believed in an interracial alliance of working people, he insisted that participation in the march be open only to African Americans. He took this position because he wanted

to show that blacks could lead their own movement and to prevent the presence of white Communists from diverting attention from the message. Inching the country toward war, but not yet engaged militarily, President Roosevelt wanted to avoid any embarrassment the proposed march would bring to the forces supporting democracy and freedom. With his wife Eleanor serving as go-between, Roosevelt agreed to meet with Randolph and worked out a compromise. Randolph called off the march, and in return, on June 25, 1941, the president issued Executive Order 8802, creating the **Fair Employment Practice Committee (FEPC)**. Roosevelt refused to order the desegregation of the military, but he set up a committee to investigate inequality in the armed forces. Although the FEPC helped African Americans gain a greater share of jobs in key industries than they had before, the effect was limited because the agency did not have enforcement power.

The march on Washington movement was emblematic of rising civil rights activity. Black leaders proclaimed their own "two-front war" with the symbol of the "Double V" to represent victory against racist enemies both abroad and at home. The National Association for the Advancement of Colored People continued its policy of fighting racial discrimination in the courts. In 1944 the organization won a significant victory in a case from Texas, *Smith v. Allwright*, which outlawed all-white Democratic primary elections in the traditionally one-party South. As a result of the decision, the percentage of African Americans registered to vote in the South doubled between 1944 and 1948. In 1942 early civil rights activists also founded the interracial Congress of Racial Equality (CORE) in Chicago. CORE protested directly against racial inequality in public accommodations. Its members, including the black pacifists Bayard Rustin and James Farmer, organized "sit-ins" at restaurants and bowling alleys that refused to serve African Americans. Students at Howard University in Washington, D.C., used the same tactics, with some success, to protest racial exclusion from restaurants and cafeterias in the nation's capital. Although these demonstrations did not get the national attention that postwar protests would, they constituted the prelude to the civil rights movement.

Explore

See Document 23.5 for a letter from black soldiers on discrimination in the army.

Population shifts on the home front during World War II exacerbated racial tensions, resulting in violence. As jobs opened up throughout the country at military installations and defense plants, hundreds of thousands of African Americans moved from the rural South to the urban South, the North, and the West. Cities could not handle this rapid influx of people and failed to provide sufficient housing to

DOCUMENT 23.5

Letter from Black Soldiers, 1943

During World War II, many black soldiers and their families wrote to popular African American newspapers such as the *Pittsburgh Courier* to publicize discrimination in the armed forces. In the following letter to the editor, a group of black soldiers describes their mistreatment at an army base in Colorado, showing that racial discrimination was not confined to the South.

Explore

The Pittsburgh Courier
April 26, 1943
Dear Sirs:

We are soldiers who are stationed at Fort Logan, Colorado. We would appreciate it to the highest if our little article was printed in your paper against discrimination.

How does the treatment of these soldiers contradict the goals of the war?

We are colored soldiers who have been discriminated against terribly to the extent where we just can't possibl[y] stand any more. We're supposed to be representing part of the Army in which we're fighting for equality, justice, and humanity so as all men, no matter of race, color, or creed, can be free to worship any way that they please.

Here on the Post we're treated like dogs. We work on different positions, sometimes for 9 or 10 hours daily. In the mornings we report to one particular job and at noon we are taken from the former one into a complete[ly] new one by orders of the white N.C.O.s (meaning Non-commissioned Officers) and at these jobs we

How do the soldiers characterize their experience at the base?

work at a very tiresome task, one that is unfit even for a dog. And yet the whites which are supposed to be a labor battalion just sit down and watch us do their work.

Even in eating time we were told to remain at attention outside the messhall until the whites have finished eating, then we go and eat what's left over—food which is cold, tasteless, and even sometimes dirty from sitting on tables from left overs. . . .

Why can't we eat, live, and be respected as the whites? We're constantly being cursed at, and mocked. But yet we too have to die as well as them, and even perhaps beside them. . . .

People on the outside don't know how we boys, their boys, are being treated here and perhaps on some of the other bad camps near or far. That's the reason

What do the letter writers hope to gain?

we're writing to you to please print this article to let everyone hear our story and give us a chance. Yes, that is all we ask—a chance to prove to the whole world that we colored people are no one's fools. Just give us a chance to show our color.

Source: Philip McGuire, ed., *Taps for a Jim Crow Army: Letters from Black Soldiers in World War II* (Lexington: University Press of Kentucky, 1983), 64–65.

Put It in Context

What is the connection between the experiences described in this letter and the start of the civil rights movement?

accommodate those who migrated in search of employment. Competition between white and black workers for scarce housing spilled over into tensions in crowded transportation and recreational facilities. In 1943 the stress caused by close wartime contact between the races exploded in more than 240 riots. The most serious one occurred in Detroit, where federal troops had to restore order after whites and blacks fought with each other following a dispute at a popular amusement park that killed thirty-four people.

Struggles for Mexican Americans

Immigration from Mexico increased significantly during the war. To address labor shortages in the Southwest and on the Pacific coast, in 1942 the United States negotiated an agreement with Mexico for contract laborers (*braceros*) to enter the country for a limited time to work as farm laborers and in factories. From the Southwest, Mexican migrants found their way to industrial cities of the Midwest and California. Most U.S. residents of Mexican ancestry were, however, American citizens. Like other Americans, they settled into jobs to help fight the war, while more than 300,000 Mexican Americans served in the armed forces.

The war heightened Mexican Americans' consciousness of their civil rights. As one Mexican American World War II veteran recalled: "We were Americans, not 'spics' or 'greasers.' Because when you fight for your country in a World War, against an alien philosophy, fascism, you are an American and proud to be in America." In southern California, Ignacio Lutero Lopez, the publisher of the newspaper *El Espectador* (The Spectator), campaigned against segregation in movie theaters, swimming pools, and other public accommodations. He organized boycotts against businesses that discriminated against or excluded Mexican Americans. Wartime organizing led to the creation of the Unity Leagues, a coalition of Mexican American business owners, college students, civic leaders, and GIs that pressed for racial equality. In Texas, Mexican Americans joined the League of United Latin American Citizens (LULAC), a largely middle-class group that challenged racial discrimination and segregation in public accommodations. Members of the organization emphasized the use of negotiations to redress their grievances, but when they ran into opposition, they resorted to economic boycotts and litigation. The war encouraged LULAC to expand its operations in Arizona and throughout the Southwest.

Mexican American citizens encountered hostility from recently transplanted whites and longtime residents. Tensions were greatest in Los Angeles. A small

Zoot Suit Riots, 1943

This photograph shows two Latino youths after they were attacked by a group of sailors who slashed their clothing during the zoot suit riots in Los Angeles in June 1943. They are wearing the popular zoot suit style of wide shirt collars and baggy pants tapered at the bottom.   Hulton Archive/Getty Images

group of Mexican American teenagers joined gangs and identified themselves by wearing zoot suits—colorful, long, loose-fitting jackets with padded shoulders and baggy pants tapered at the bottom. Not all zoot-suiters were gang members, but many outside their communities failed to make this distinction. Dressed in wide-brimmed hats worn atop slicked-back hair, with pocket watches and chains dangling from their trousers, these young men offended white sensibilities of fashion and proper decorum. Sailors stationed at naval bases in southern California found their dress and swagger provocative. On the night of June 4, 1943, squads of seamen stationed in Long Beach invaded Mexican American neighborhoods in East Los Angeles, indiscriminately attacked both zoot-suiters and those not dressed in this garb on the streets, and beat them up. The police sided with the sailors and arrested Mexican American youths who tried to fight back. After four days, the **zoot suit riots** ended as civilian and military authorities restored order. In response, the Los Angeles city council banned the wearing of zoot suits in public and made it a criminal offense.

The Ordeal of Japanese Americans

World War II marked a significant crossroads for the protection of civil liberties, the freedoms people have from government interference as enshrined in the Bill of Rights. In general, the federal government did not repress civil liberties as harshly as it had during World War I, primarily because opposition to World War II was not nearly as great. The chief potential for radical dissent came from the Communist Party, but after the Germans attacked the Soviet Union in June 1941, Communists and their sympathizers rallied behind the war effort and did whatever they could to stifle any protest that threatened the goal of defeating Germany. On the other side of the political spectrum, after the attack on Pearl Harbor conservative isolationists in the America First Movement quickly threw their support behind the war.

Of the three ethnic groups associated with the Axis enemy—Japanese, Germans, and Italians—Japanese Americans received by far the worst treatment from the civilian population and state and federal officials. Germans had experienced animosity and repression on the home front during World War I (see chapter 20), but like Italian immigrants they had generally assimilated into the wider population. When baseball was the national pastime during the 1930s and 1940s, Lou Gehrig, of German ancestry, and his Italian American teammate Joe DiMaggio of the New York Yankees reigned as popular heroes. At the same time, Fiorello La Guardia, an Italian American, had a large following as mayor of New York City. In addition, German Americans and Italian Americans had spread out across the country, while Japanese Americans remained concentrated in distinct geographical pockets along the West Coast. Although German Americans and Italian Americans experienced prejudice, they had come to be considered racially white, unlike Japanese Americans. Nevertheless, the government arrested about 1,500 Italians considered "enemy aliens" and placed around 250 of them in internment camps. It also arrested more than 11,000 Germans, some of them American citizens who were considered a danger.

The **internment**, or forced relocation and detainment, of Italians and Germans in the United States paled in comparison with that of the Japanese. Nearly all people of Japanese descent lived along the West Coast. Government officials relocated all of those living there—citizens and noncitizens alike—to camps in Arizona, Arkansas, California, Colorado, Idaho, Texas, Utah, and Wyoming. In Hawaii, the site of the Japanese attack on Pearl Harbor,

the Japanese population, nearly one-third of the territory's population, was too large to transfer and instead lived under martial law. Only a thousand or so were interned. The few thousand Japanese Americans living elsewhere in the continental United States remained in their homes.

It did not matter that Fred Korematsu had been born in the United States, had a white girlfriend of Italian heritage, and counted whites among his best friends. His parents had come from Japan, and for much of the American public, his racial heritage meant that he was not a true American. As one American general put it early in the war, "A Jap's a Jap. It makes no difference whether he is an American citizen or not." Along with more than 100,000 people of Japanese descent, two-thirds of whom were American citizens, Korematsu spent most of the war in an internment camp. Unlike Nazi concentration camps, these facilities did not work inmates to death or execute them. Yet Japanese Americans lost their freedom and protection under the Bill of Rights and the Fourteenth Amendment. Distinguished American leaders—including President Roosevelt, California attorney general Earl Warren, and Supreme Court justice Hugo Black—convinced themselves that depriving Japanese Americans of their civil liberties did not result from racism. Despite scant evidence that Japanese Americans were disloyal or harbored spies or saboteurs, U.S. officials chose to believe that as a group they threatened national security. The government established a system that questioned German Americans and Italian Americans on an individual basis if their loyalty came under suspicion. By contrast, U.S. officials identified all Japanese Americans and Japanese resident aliens with the nation that had attacked Pearl Harbor, and incarcerated them. In this respect, the United States was not unique. Following the United States' lead, Canada interned its Japanese population, more than 75 percent of whom held Canadian citizenship.

For their part, Japanese Americans made the best they could out of this situation. They had been forced to dispose of their homes and sell their possessions and businesses quickly, either selling or renting them at very low prices or simply abandoning them. They left their neighborhoods with only the possessions they could carry. They lived in wooden barracks divided into one-room apartments and shared communal toilets, showers, laundry, and dining facilities. The camps provided schools, recreational activities, and opportunities for religious worship, except for Shintoism, the official religion of Japan. Some internees attempted to farm, but the arid land on which the camps were located made this nearly impossible. Inmates who worked at jobs within the camp earned monthly wages of

Japanese American Internment

This painting was made by one of the more than 10,000 Japanese American inmates at the Heart Mountain Relocation Camp in Wyoming who were interned during World War II. Most of the internees were American citizens of Japanese descent from the West Coast. The scene depicts the camp's isolation yet conveys the enduring spirit of the artist. "Heart Mt. Wyo 1943" (detail), by J. Miyauchi. Reprinted by permission of the Heart Mountain Wyoming Foundation

$12 to $19, far less than they would have received outside the camps.

Japanese Americans responded to their internment in a variety of ways. Many formed community groups, and some expressed their reactions to the emotional upheaval by writing of their experiences or displaying their feelings through artwork. Contradicting beliefs that their ancestry made them disloyal or not real Americans, some 18,000 men joined the army, and many fought gallantly in some of the war's fiercest battles on the European front with the 442nd Regiment, one of the most heavily decorated units in the military. Nisei soldiers were among the first, along with African American troops, to liberate Jews from German concentration camps. Others, like Korematsu, remained in the camps and challenged the legality of President Roosevelt's executive order, which had allowed military officials to exclude Japanese Americans from certain areas and evacuate them from their homes. Gordon Hirabayashi, a student at the University of Washington, had filed suit against the establishment of a curfew specifically targeted at Japanese Americans. In 1942 the Supreme Court rejected his appeal, as it did Korematsu's two years later. Finally, in December 1944, shortly after he won election to his fourth term as president, Roosevelt rescinded Executive Order 9066.

In contrast to the treatment of Japanese Americans, the status of Chinese Americans improved markedly during the war. With China under Japanese occupation, Congress repealed the Chinese Exclusion Act in 1943, making the Chinese the first Asians who could become naturalized citizens. Chinese American men also fought in integrated military units like their Filipino peers. For the first time, the war opened up jobs to Chinese American men and women outside their ethnic economy.

Despite the violation of the civil liberties of Japanese American citizens, the majority did not become embittered against the United States. Rather, most of the internees returned to their communities after the war and resumed their lives, still intent on pursuing the American dream from which they had been so harshly excluded; however, some 8,000 Japanese Americans renounced their U.S. citizenship and repatriated to Japan in 1945. After briefly moving to Detroit, Korematsu returned to San Leandro, California, with his wife and two children. Still, Korematsu had trouble finding regular employment because he had a criminal record for violating the exclusion order. Unlike most inmates of German concentration camps, Korematsu survived, but in the name of national security the government had established the precedent of incarcerating groups deemed "suspect." It took four decades for the U.S. government to admit its mistake and apologize, and in 1988 Congress awarded reparations of $20,000 to each of the 60,000 living internees. In 1998 President Bill Clinton awarded Korematsu the Presidential Medal of Freedom—the highest decoration a civilian can receive.

REVIEW & RELATE

- What new challenges and opportunities did the war present to minority groups?

- Why were Japanese Americans singled out as a particular threat to national security?

 LEARNINGCurve bedfordstmartins.com/hewittlawson/LC

Conclusion: The Impact of World War II

Like Woodrow Wilson before World War I, Franklin Roosevelt initially charted a course of neutrality before the United States entered World War II. Yet Roosevelt believed that the rise of European dictatorships and their expansionist pursuits throughout the world threatened American national security. He saw signs of trouble early, but responding to antiwar sentiment from lawmakers and the American public, he maneuvered carefully to keep the nation from going to war. Like President Lincoln preceding the Confederate bombardment of Fort Sumter, Roosevelt waited for a blatant enemy attack before declaring war. The Japanese attack on Pearl Harbor in 1941 provided that justification.

On the domestic front, World War II accomplished what Franklin Roosevelt's New Deal could not. Prosperity and nearly full employment returned only after the nation's factories began supplying the Allies and the United States joined in the fight against the Axis powers. Mobilization for war also completed what the New Deal had begun: the tremendous growth and centralization of power in the federal government. Washington, D.C., became the chief source of authority to which Americans looked for solutions to problems concerning economic security and financial development. Most people looked to the future with optimism following sixteen years of depression and war.

The federal government showed that it would use its authority to expand equal rights for African Americans. The war swung national power against racial discrimination, and various civil rights victories during the war served as precursors to the civil rights movement of subsequent decades. The war also heightened Mexican Americans' consciousness of oppression and led them to organize for civil rights. In neither case, however, did the war erase white prejudice.

At the same time, the federal government did not hesitate to trample on the civil liberties of Japanese Americans. The president succumbed to wartime antagonism against Japanese immigrants and their children. However, the same did not happen to the white descendants of the other Axis nations. Yet like white and black Americans, the Nisei displayed their patriotism by distinguishing themselves as soldiers on the battlefields of Europe.

The war brought women into the workforce as never before, providing a measure of independence and distancing them from their traditional roles as wives and mothers. Nevertheless, the government and private employers made it clear that they expected most female workers to give up their jobs to returning servicemen and to become homemakers once the war ended.

Finally, the war thrust the United States onto the world stage as one of the world's two major superpowers alongside the Soviet Union. This position posed new challenges. In sole possession of the atomic bomb, the most powerful weapon on the planet, and fortified by a robust economy, the United States filled the international power vacuum created by the weakening and eventual collapse of the European colonial empires. The fragile alliance that had held together the United States and the Soviet Union shattered soon after the end of World War II. The Atomic Age, which J. Robert Oppenheimer helped usher in with a powerful weapon of mass destruction, and the government oppression that Korematsu endured in the name of national security did not disappear. Rather, they expanded in new directions and shaped the lives of all Americans for decades to come.

LEARNINGCurve
Check what you know.
bedfordstmartins.com/hewittlawson/LC

Chapter Review

Online Study Guide ▶ bedfordstmartins.com/hewittlawson

KEY TERMS

Neutrality Acts (p. 723)
America First Committee (p. 724)
Lend-Lease Act (p. 725)
Atlantic Charter (p. 725)
second front (p. 728)
D Day (p. 728)
Yalta Agreement (p. 730)
Manhattan Project (p. 731)
Enola Gay (p. 732)
military-industrial complex (p. 734)
War Production Board (p. 735)
National War Labor Board (p. 736)
Fair Employment Practice Committee
  (FEPC) (p. 740)
zoot suit riots (p. 742)
internment (p. 743)

REVIEW & RELATE

1. How did American public opinion shape Roosevelt's foreign policy in the years preceding U.S. entry into World War II?

2. What events in Europe and the Pacific ultimately brought the United States into World War II?

3. How did the Allies win the war in Europe and in the Pacific?

4. How did tensions among the Allies shape both their military strategy and their postwar plans?

5. How did the war accelerate the trend that began during the New Deal toward increased government participation in the economy?

6. How did the war affect life on the home front for the average American?

7. What new challenges and opportunities did the war present to minority groups?

8. Why were Japanese Americans singled out as a particular threat to national security?

TIMELINE OF EVENTS

1933	United States extends diplomatic recognition to the Soviet Union
	Adolf Hitler becomes chancellor of Germany
1935–1937	Neutrality Acts passed
1938	Germany annexes the Sudetenland
1939	Germany occupies Czechoslovakia
	Germany and Soviet Union invade Poland; World War II begins
1940	Battle of Britain begins
	Japan, Germany, and Italy sign Tripartite Pact
1941	Lend-Lease Act passed
	Fair Employment Practice Committee (FEPC) created
	Roosevelt and Churchill sign Atlantic Charter
December 7, 1941	Japan attacks U.S. naval base at Pearl Harbor
December 11, 1941	Germany and Italy declare war on the United States
1942	Congress of Racial Equality (CORE) established
	War Production Board and National War Labor Board formed
	Roosevelt approves Manhattan Project
	Roosevelt issues order that leads to internment of Japanese Americans
1943	Zoot suit riots
	Race riots in Detroit and more than 240 cities
June 6, 1944	D Day invasion begins
1945	Final U.S. offensive against Japan, with victories at Iwo Jima and Okinawa
February 1945	Yalta Conference
May 1945	Germany surrenders
July 1945	First successful atomic bomb test
August 1945	U.S. drops atomic bombs on Hiroshima and Nagasaki
September 1945	Japan formally surrenders

The Decision to Drop the Atomic Bomb

U.S. officials became interested in nuclear weapons in the late 1930s when scientists fleeing Nazi Germany alerted President Roosevelt to German experiments in nuclear fission. The Manhattan Project—the code name given to the U.S. atomic program—was formally set up in 1942 under the direction of General Leslie Groves and physicist J. Robert Oppenheimer. The program was a massive undertaking, employing thousands of workers at sites in Chicago; Berkeley, California; Oak Ridge, Tennessee; Hanford, Washington; and, most famously, at the scientific laboratory in Los Alamos, New Mexico. It took $3 billion to create the atomic bombs. The project was so secretive that even Harry Truman didn't learn of it until he became president following Roosevelt's death.

The bombs that exploded over Hiroshima and Nagasaki in August 1945 revolutionized world history. They ended World War II, changed the nature of warfare, and altered the course of international relations. The bombs launched a nuclear arms race that continued throughout the Cold War and unleashed fears of global annihilation. The United States is the only country to use nuclear weapons against an enemy, and debates about whether the bombs were necessary began even before they were dropped. Scientists, officials in the Truman administration, military figures, and ordinary citizens all grappled with the meaning and consequences of this nuclear action. As a result of the bombing of Hiroshima and Nagasaki, more than 200,000 people, mostly civilians, were killed immediately, and even more were stricken with radiation poisoning, burns, and other injuries. More than 80 percent of the buildings in each city were flattened instantly, and permanent shadows were left on walls and pavement.

Many aspects of Truman's decision continue to be questioned and debated. Were the bombs the only way to end the war with Japan? Should the alternatives of blockading or using conventional bombs have been tried? Should the United States have given Japan an explicit warning about the bomb or demonstrated its effectiveness on an uninhabited island? Did racist attitudes about the Japanese influence the decision? Was the motive revenge or saving American lives? The following documents help explore these and other questions about America's use of atomic weapons in World War II.

DOCUMENT 23.6

Recommendations on the Immediate Use of Nuclear Weapons, June 16, 1945

Secretary of War Henry Stimson received the following memorandum from the scientific advisory panel of the Manhattan Project, a group that included J. Robert Oppenheimer. The memorandum was written one month before the successful "Trinity" test on July 16, and in it the panel recommends the use of atomic weapons against Japan.

You have asked us to comment on the initial use of the new weapon. This use, in our opinion, should be such as to promote a satisfactory adjustment of our international relations. At the same time, we recognize our obligation to our nation to use the weapons to help save American lives in the Japanese war.

(1) To accomplish these ends we recommend that before the weapons are used not only Britain, but also Russia, France, and China be advised that we have made considerable progress in our work on atomic weapons, that these may be ready to use during the present war, and that we would welcome suggestions as to how we can cooperate in making this development contribute to improved international relations.

(2) The opinions of our scientific colleagues on the initial use of these weapons are not unanimous: they range from the proposal of a purely technical demonstration to that of the military application best designed to induce surrender. Those who advocate a purely technical demonstration would wish to outlaw the use of atomic weapons, and have feared that if we use the weapons now our position in future negotiations will be prejudiced. Others emphasize the opportunity of saving American lives by immediate military use, and believe that such use will improve the international prospects, in that they are more concerned with the prevention of war than with the elimination of this specific weapon. We find ourselves closer to these latter views; we can propose no technical demonstration likely to bring an end to the war; we see no acceptable alternative to direct military use.

(3) With regard to these general aspects of the use of atomic energy, it is clear that we, as scientific men, have no proprietary rights. It is true that we are among the few citizens who have had occasion to give thoughtful consideration to these problems during the past few years. We have, however, no claim to special competence in solving the political, social, and military problems which are presented by the advent of atomic power.

Source: U.S. National Archives, Record Group 77, Records of the Chief of Engineers, Manhattan Engineer District, Harrison-Bundy file, folder #76.

DOCUMENT 23.7

Petition to the President of the United States, July 17, 1945

Some advisers urged President Truman to seek an alternative to dropping atomic bombs on Japan, such as demonstrating the weapon on an uninhabited island for Japanese and international observers or giving Japan the results of the test in New Mexico. One day after the Trinity test, seventy scientists involved in the Manhattan Project wrote to President Truman arguing against the bomb's use.

Discoveries of which the people of the United States are not aware may affect the welfare of this nation in the near future. The liberation of atomic power which has been achieved places atomic bombs in the hands of the Army. It places in your hands, as Commander-in-Chief, the fateful decision whether or not to sanction the use of such bombs in the present phase of the war against Japan.

We, the undersigned scientists, have been working in the field of atomic power. Until recently we have had to fear that the United States might be attacked by atomic bombs during this war and that her only defense might lie in a counterattack by the same means. Today, with the defeat of Germany, this danger is averted and we feel impelled to say what follows:

The war has to be brought speedily to a successful conclusion and attacks by atomic bombs may very well be an effective method of warfare. We feel, however, that such attacks on Japan could not be justified, at least not unless the terms which will be imposed after the war on Japan were made public in detail and Japan were given an opportunity to surrender.

If such public announcement gave assurance to the Japanese that they could look forward to a life devoted to peaceful pursuits in their homeland and if Japan still refused to surrender our nation might then, in certain circumstances, find itself forced to resort to the use of atomic bombs. Such a step, however, ought not to be made at any time without seriously considering the moral responsibilities which are involved.

The development of atomic power will provide the nations with new means of destruction. The atomic bombs at our disposal represent only the first step in this direction, and there is almost no limit to the destructive power which will become available in the course of their future development. Thus a nation which sets the precedent of using these newly liberated forces of nature for purposes of destruction may have to bear the responsibility of opening the door to an era of devastation on an unimaginable scale.

If after this war a situation is allowed to develop in the world which permits rival powers to be in uncontrolled possession of these new means of destruction, the cities of the United States as well as the cities of other nations will be in continuous danger of sudden annihilation. All the resources of the United States, moral and material, may have to be mobilized to prevent the advent of such a world situation. Its prevention is at present the solemn responsibility of the United States—singled out by virtue of her lead in the field of atomic power.

The added material strength which this lead gives to the United States brings with it the obligation of restraint and if we were to violate this obligation our moral position would be weakened in the eyes of the world and in our own eyes. It would then be more difficult for us to live up to our responsibility of bringing the unloosened forces of destruction under control.

In view of the foregoing, we, the undersigned, respectfully petition: first, that you exercise your power as Commander-in-Chief, to rule that the United States shall not resort to the use of atomic bombs in this war unless the terms which will be imposed upon Japan have been made public in detail and Japan knowing these terms has refused to surrender; second, that in such an event the question whether or not to use atomic bombs be decided by you in the light of the considerations presented in this petition as well as all the other moral responsibilities which are involved.

Source: U.S. National Archives, Record Group 77, Records of the Chief of Engineers, Manhattan Engineer District, Harrison-Bundy file, folder #76.

DOCUMENT 23.8

President Harry S. Truman | Press Release on the Atomic Bomb, August 6, 1945

After the first atomic bomb, nicknamed "Little Boy," was dropped on Hiroshima, President Truman released the following statement to the public. In it, Truman explains the development of the bomb, its destructive power, and why it was used against Japan. This statement was made before the second bomb was dropped on Nagasaki and before Japan's surrender.

SIXTEEN HOURS AGO an American airplane dropped one bomb on [Hiroshima] and destroyed its usefulness to the enemy. That bomb had more power than 20,000 tons of T.N.T. It had more than two thousand times the blast power of the British "Grand Slam" which is the largest bomb ever yet used in the history of warfare.

The Japanese began the war from the air at Pearl Harbor. They have been repaid many fold. And the end is not yet. With this bomb we have now added a new and revolutionary increase in destruction to supplement the growing power of our armed forces. In their present form these bombs are now in production and even more powerful forms are in development.

It is an atomic bomb. It is a harnessing of the basic power of the universe. The force from which the sun draws its power has been loosed against those who brought war to the Far East. . . .

We are now prepared to obliterate more rapidly and completely every productive enterprise the Japanese have above ground in any city. We shall destroy their docks, their factories, and their communications. Let there be no mistake; we shall completely destroy Japan's power to make war.

It was to spare the Japanese people from utter destruction that the ultimatum of July 26 was issued at Potsdam. Their leaders promptly rejected that ultimatum. If they do not now accept our terms they may expect a rain of ruin from the air, the like of which has never been seen on this earth. Behind this air attack will follow sea and land forces in such numbers and power as they have not yet seen and with the fighting skill of which they are already well aware. . . .

The fact that we can release atomic energy ushers in a new era in man's understanding of nature's forces. Atomic energy may in the future supplement the power that now comes from coal, oil, and falling water, but at present it cannot be produced on a basis to compete with them commercially. Before that comes there must be a long period of intensive research.

It has never been the habit of the scientists of this country or the policy of this Government to withhold from the world scientific knowledge. Normally, therefore, everything about the work with atomic energy would be made public.

But under present circumstances it is not intended to divulge the technical processes of production or all the military applications, pending further examination of possible methods of protecting us and the rest of the world from the danger of sudden destruction.

I shall recommend that the Congress of the United States consider promptly the establishment of an appropriate commission to control the production and use of atomic power within the United States. I shall give further consideration and make further recommendations to the Congress as to how atomic power can become a powerful and forceful influence towards the maintenance of world peace.

Source: Press Release by the White House, August 6, 1945, Ayers Papers, Truman Library.

DOCUMENT 23.9

Hiroshima, August 6, 1945

In this photograph, a survivor stands among the ruins of Hiroshima. The bomb that was dropped on the city destroyed 5 square miles and killed 70,000 to 80,000 people. Three days later, the United States dropped a second atomic bomb on Nagasaki.

AP Photo/Stanley Troutman

DOCUMENT 23.10

U.S. Strategic Bombing Survey, 1946

After the war, President Truman called for a series of surveys on the effectiveness of strategic bombing campaigns in Europe and Asia and on the effects of the atomic bombs on Hiroshima and Nagasaki. The survey on the Pacific war included interviews with Japanese military and government leaders as well as information from Japanese wartime documents. It concluded that the use of the atomic bombs was unnecessary because even without them Japan would have surrendered in the fall of 1945.

4. When Japan was defeated without invasion, a recurrent question arose as to what effect the threat of a home island invasion had had upon the surrender decision. It was contended that the threat of invasion, if not the actual operation, was a requirement to induce acceptance of the surrender terms. On this tangled issue the evidence and hindsight are clear. The fact is, of course, that Japan did surrender without invasion, and with its principal armies intact. Testimony before the Survey shows that the expected "violation of the sacred homeland" raised few fears which expedited the decision to surrender beforehand. Government and Imperial household leaders felt some concern for the "destruction of the Japanese people," but the people were already being shattered by direct air attacks. Anticipated landings were even viewed by the military with hope that they would afford a means of inflicting casualties sufficiently high to improve their chances of a negotiated peace. Preparation of defenses against landings diverted certain resources from dispersal and cushioning moves which might have partially mitigated our air blows. But in Japan's then depleted state, the diversion was not significant. The responsible leaders in power read correctly the true situation and embraced surrender well before invasion was expected.

5. So long as Germany remained in the war that fact contributed to the core of Japanese resistance. Slight evidence exists that some hope was held for a long-promised German miracle weapon. A telegram received on 6 May in the German embassy at Tokyo revealed that Hitler was dead, the promised new weapon had failed to materialize, and that Germany would surrender within a matter of hours. [Adviser Marquis Koichi] Kido believed, presumably on Japanese Army representations, that the Army would not countenance peace moves so long as Germany continued to fight. It is not clear whether this was a face-saving position, designed to avoid a prior Japanese surrender. In any case on 9 May 1945, immediately after the Nazi capitulation, General Anami, the War Minister, asked the cabinet for an Imperial conference to reconsider the war situation. The significant fact, however, is that Japan was pursuing peace before the Nazis collapsed, and the impoverishment and fragmentation of the German people had already afforded a portent of similar consequences for an intransigent Japan.

6. The Hiroshima and Nagasaki atomic bombs did not defeat Japan, nor by the testimony of the enemy leaders who ended the war did they persuade Japan to accept unconditional surrender. The Emperor [Hirohito], the lord privy seal, the prime minister, the foreign minister, and the navy minister had decided as early as May of 1945 that the war should be ended even if it meant acceptance of defeat on allied terms. The war minister and the two chiefs of staff opposed unconditional surrender. The impact of the Hiroshima attack was to bring further urgency and lubrication to the machinery of achieving peace, primarily by contributing to a situation which permitted the prime minister to bring the Emperor overtly and directly into a position where his decision for immediate acceptance of the Potsdam declaration could be used to override the remaining objectors. Thus, although the atomic bombs changed no votes of the Supreme War Direction Council concerning the Potsdam terms, they did foreshorten the war and expedite the peace. . . .

There is little point in attempting more precisely to impute Japan's unconditional surrender to any one of the numerous causes which jointly and cumulatively were responsible for Japan's disaster. Concerning the absoluteness of her defeat there can be no doubt. The time lapse between military impotence and political acceptance of the inevitable might have been shorter had the political structure of Japan permitted a more rapid and decisive determination of national policies. It seems clear, however, that air supremacy and its exploitation over Japan proper was the major factor which determined the timing of Japan's surrender and obviated any need for invasion.

Based on a detailed investigation of all the facts and supported by the testimony of the surviving Japanese leaders involved, it is the Survey's opinion that certainly prior to 31 December 1945, and in all probability prior to 1 November 1945, Japan would have surrendered even if the atomic bombs had not been dropped, even if Russia had not entered the war, and even if no invasion had been planned or contemplated.

Source: United States Strategic Bombing Survey: Japan's Struggle to End the War, July 1, 1946, Elsey Papers, Truman Library.

DOCUMENT 23.11

Father Johannes Siemes | Eyewitness Account of the Hiroshima Bombing, 1945

Father Johannes Siemes, a German priest living in Japan, wrote the following eyewitness account of the Hiroshima bombing. Siemes lived less than a mile outside the city, and after the attack he went into Hiroshima to look for other priests from his order. He gave this account to Bishop Franklin Corley, an American soldier and one of the first Americans to enter the city.

After we have had a few swallows and a little food, Fathers Stolte, Luhmer, Erlinghagen, and [I] take off once again to bring in the family. Father Kleinsorge requests that we also rescue two children who had lost their mother and who had lain near him in the park. On the way, we were greeted by strangers who had noted that we were on a mission of mercy and who praised our efforts. We now met groups of individuals who were carrying the wounded about on litters. As we arrived at the Misasa Bridge, the family that had been there were gone. They might well have been borne away in the meantime. There was a group of soldiers at work taking away those that had been sacrificed yesterday.

More than thirty hours had gone by until the first official rescue party had appeared on the scene. We find both children and take them out of the park: six-year old girl who was uninjured, and a twelve-year old girl who had been burned about the head, hands, and legs, and who had lain for thirty hours without care in the park. The left side of her face and the left eye were completely covered with blood and pus, so that we thought that she had lost the eye. When the wound was later washed, we noted that the eye was intact and that the lids had just become stuck together. On the way home, we took another group of three refugees with us. The first wanted to know, however, of what nationality we were. They, too, feared that we might be Americans who had parachuted in. When we arrived in Nagat-suka, it had just become dark.

We took under our care fifty refugees who had lost everything. The majority of them were wounded and not a few had dangerous burns. Father Rektor treated the wounds as well as he could with the few medicaments that we could, with effort, gather up. He had to confine himself in general to cleansing the wounds of puru-lent [consisting of pus] material. Even those with the smaller burns are very weak and all suffered from diarrhea. . . .

Thousands of wounded who died later could doubtless have been rescued had they received proper treatment and care, but rescue work in a catastrophe of this magnitude had not been envisioned; since the whole city had been knocked out at a blow, everything which had been prepared for emergency work was lost, and no preparation had been made for rescue work in the outlying districts. Many of the wounded also died because they had been weakened by under-nourishment and consequently lacked in strength to recover. Those who had their normal strength and who received good care slowly healed the burns which had been occasioned by the bomb. There were also cases, however, whose prognosis seemed good who died suddenly. There were also some who had only small external wounds who died within a week or later, after an inflammation of the pharynx and oral cavity had taken place. . . .

Only several cases are known to me personally where individuals who did not have external burns later died. Father Kleinsorge and Father Cieslik, who were near the center of the explosion, but who did not suffer burns, became quite weak some fourteen days after the explosion. Up to this time small incised wounds had healed normally, but thereafter the wounds which were still unhealed became worse and are to date (in September) still incompletely healed. The attending physician diagnosed it as leucopenia [a decrease in white blood cells]. There thus seems to be some truth in the statement that the radiation had some effect on the blood. I am of the opinion, however, that their generally undernourished and weakened condition was partly responsible for these findings. It was noised about that the ruins of the city emitted deadly rays and that workers who went there to aid in the clearing died, and that the central district would be uninhabitable for some time to come.

Source: Father Johannes Siemes, "Hiroshima, August 6, 1945," *Bulletin of the Atomic Scientists* 1, no. 11 (1946): 5–6.

Interpret the Evidence

1. Why do the scientists in favor of using the bomb believe it should be used against Japan (Document 23.6)?

2. What arguments do the scientists who oppose dropping the atomic bomb on Japan put forward (Document 23.7)? Under what conditions do they believe the use of the bomb would be justified?

3. How do both groups of scientists place the use of the bomb within the context of postwar international relations?

4. What reasons does Truman give for dropping the bomb (Document 23.8)?

5. According to the strategic bombing survey, what factors delayed Japan's acceptance of unconditional surrender (Document 23.10)?

6. How does what you see in the photograph of the day after the bombing of Hiroshima (Document 23.9) compare with the eyewitness account in Document 23.11? Which do you find more powerful and why?

Put It in Context

- What do you think was the primary reason the United States dropped the atomic bomb on Japan?

- After reading these documents, do you think the United States should have sought a different way to end the war? Why or why not?

background photos: pages 753 and 754, Library of Congress

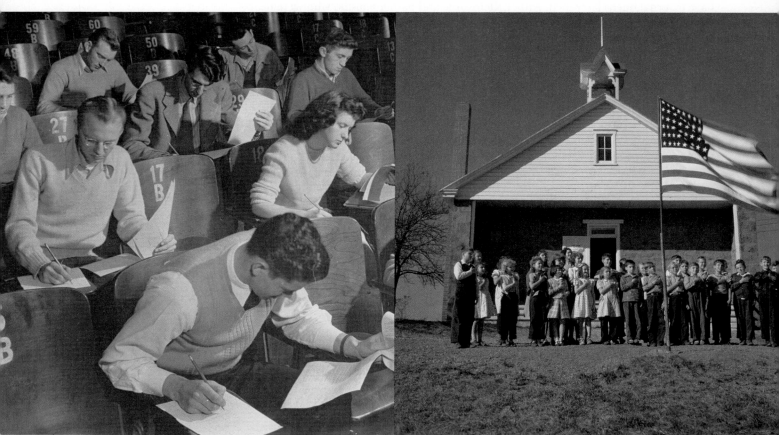

Time & Life Pictures/Getty Images

© SuperStock

War veterans and other students taking notes at the University of Iowa, 1947.

Schoolchildren reciting the pledge of allegiance, 1950s.

24

The Opening of the Cold War

1945–1954

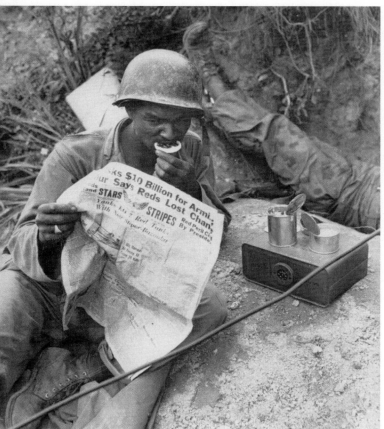

Time & Life Pictures/Getty Images

U.S. soldier in Korea, 1951.

AMERICAN HISTORIES

Did one American's fears about Soviet intentions spark a decades-long conflict that threatened the world with nuclear destruction? Certainly no one person can be held responsible for the Cold War between the United States and the Soviet Union, but George Frost Kennan played a critical role in shaping the confrontation between these two superpowers. Kennan's views were based on extensive experience with the Soviets. A graduate of Princeton University, where he majored in history, and a career diplomat, Kennan served two tours of duty at the U.S. Embassy in Moscow. During the first, from 1933 to 1937, he witnessed the brutality of the Stalin regime, as countless "enemies of the state" were arrested, exiled, or executed in Stalin's purges. His experiences convinced him that there was little basis for a positive relationship between the United States and the Soviet Union.

Kennan's second tour of duty in Moscow, from 1944 to 1946, came at a critical juncture in U.S.-Soviet relations. As the war came to a close, tensions over the nature of the postwar world escalated, and by 1946 the wartime alliance had collapsed. Against this backdrop, Kennan sent an 8,000-word telegram to Secretary of State James F. Byrnes outlining a proposal for future U.S. strategy. Convinced that Stalin was committed to expanding communism throughout the world, Kennan advised President Harry S. Truman to adopt a policy of *containment*. In Kennan's view, all Soviet efforts at expansion should be met with firm resistance. At the same time, the United States should take an active role in rebuilding the economies of war-torn Western

European countries, thereby reducing the appeal of communism to their populations. Kennan's concept of containment would become the basis for President Truman's foreign policy and would establish the initial strategic parameters of the Cold War.

Kennan, however, was not a rigid cold warrior. He soon insisted that his containment strategy had been misunderstood. As the Cold War intensified and expanded, Kennan argued that containment would work best through political and economic rather than military means. Increasingly, his views fell out of favor at the State Department, and Kennan left in 1950 in a disagreement with the Truman administration's growing militarization of the conflict with the Soviet Union.

Julius and Ethel Rosenberg were casualties of the Cold War that Kennan helped shape. Accused of passing military secrets to the Soviet Union, they were tried for espionage in an atmosphere of growing anti-Communist fervor. Ethel Greenglass and her future husband, Julius Rosenberg, both grew up in families that suffered economically during the Great Depression. During the 1930s, Ethel worked as a secretary in New York City and took part in labor union organizing. Like other young idealists of the period, she became disillusioned with capitalism and joined the Young Communist League. Julius attended the City College of New York, where he, too,

joined the Young Communist League. Three years after they met in 1936, Julius and Ethel married and started a family.

During World War II, Julius worked for the Army Signal Corps as an engineer, but his political past came back to haunt him. In 1945 he lost his job after a security investigation revealed his Communist Party membership. Five years later, the federal government charged that during World War II the Rosenbergs had provided classified information about the construction of the atomic bomb to the Soviet Union, charges that the Rosenbergs denied.

A jury found them guilty on April 5, 1951, and the presiding judge sentenced them to death under the 1917 Espionage Act, which prohibited the transmission of information "relating to the national defense" to a foreign government. Despite an international campaign for clemency and after unsuccessful appeals to the Supreme Court, on June 19, 1953, the Rosenbergs became the only two American civilians executed for espionage during the Cold War. Though recent evidence has confirmed Julius Rosenberg's role as a spy, the case against Ethel remains inconclusive. Without the heightened Cold War climate that then existed in the country, it is likely that neither would have gone to the electric chair. •

THE AMERICAN HISTORIES of both George Kennan and Julius and Ethel Rosenberg revolved around their views of communism and the Soviet Union. Kennan designed an approach to containing Soviet aggression based on his close dealings with Stalin—one that he believed would check Soviet expansion without precipitating another world war. The Rosenbergs believed in communism's promise of social and economic equality and saw the Soviet Union as a defense against Nazi aggression—views that led Julius into spying for the Soviets, a U.S. ally, during World War II. Kennan and the Rosenbergs were famous in their time and played prominent roles in the Cold War, but in at least one respect they were unexceptional. As the Cold

War deepened over the course of the 1950s, the lives of all Americans would be profoundly shaped by the epic military and ideological battle between the superpowers.

The Origins of the Cold War, 1945–1947

The wartime partnership between the United States and the Soviet Union (USSR) was an alliance of necessity. Putting aside ideological differences and a history of mutual distrust, the two nations joined forces to combat Nazi aggression. As long as the Nazi threat existed, the alliance held, but as the war ended and attention turned to the postwar world, the allies became adversaries. The two nations did not engage directly in war, but they entered into a struggle for political, economic, and military superiority known as the Cold War. In general, most Cold War maneuvers did not take place on battlefields; rather they consisted of building military and economic alliances to establish spheres of influence, stopping short of "hot wars" (actual fighting) between the United States and the Soviet Union.

Mutual Misunderstandings

Guided by competing ideological and economic values, the United States and the Soviet Union pursued their national interests on the world stage in a manner that led to dangerous confrontations. After World War II, the United States came to believe that the Soviet Union desired world revolution to spread communism, a doctrine hostile to free market individualism. At the same time, the Soviet Union viewed the United States as seeking to make the world safe for capitalism, thereby reducing Soviet chances to obtain economic resources and rebuild its war-shattered economy. Thus each nation tended to see the other's actions in the most negative light possible and to see global developments as a zero-sum game, one in which every victory for one side was necessarily a defeat for the other.

Problems had already surfaced during World War II, but President Franklin D. Roosevelt and Joseph Stalin were able to keep tensions in check (see chapter 23). The president went a long way toward defusing Stalin's concerns at the Yalta Conference in 1945. Stalin viewed the Eastern European countries that the Soviets had liberated from the Germans, especially Poland, as a buffer to protect his nation from future attacks by Germany. He refused to allow hostile, anti-Communist governments to rule these countries and wanted to maintain a regional sphere of influence favorable to Soviet foreign policy objectives. Roosevelt understood Stalin's reasoning, and he recognized political realities: The Soviet military already occupied Eastern Europe, a state of affairs that increased Stalin's bargaining position. Still, while accepting Stalin's basic position, the president insisted that the Yalta Agreement include a guarantee of free elections in Eastern Europe. Roosevelt believed in spreading democracy and freedom, but he was also a realist, and the Yalta Agreement reflected his effort to strike a delicate balance.

By contrast, his successor, Harry S. Truman, took a much less nuanced approach to U.S.-Soviet relations. He believed that the Soviets threatened "a barbarian invasion of Europe," and he intended to deter it. Stalin's ruthless purges within the Soviet Union in the 1930s and 1940s, which led to the deaths

of millions of his opponents, convinced Truman that the Soviet dictator was paranoid and extremely dangerous. President Truman did not expect the United States to achieve "100 percent of what we propose" in negotiations with the Russians, but "we should be able to get eighty-five percent." In his first meeting with Soviet foreign minister Vyacheslav Molotov in April 1945, Truman rebuked the Russians for failing to support free elections in Poland. Molotov, recoiling from the sharp tone of Truman's remarks, replied: "I have never been talked to like that in my life."

Despite this rough start, Truman did not immediately abandon the idea of cooperation with the Soviet Union. At the Potsdam Conference in Germany in July 1945, Truman and Stalin agreed on several issues (see chapter 23). The two leaders reaffirmed the concept of free elections in Eastern Europe; Soviet troop withdrawal from the oil fields of northern Iran, which bordered the USSR; and the partition of Germany into four Allied occupation zones. (Berlin was also divided into four occupation zones.) After Stalin assured Truman that he did not support the Communist revolution in China against the Western-backed government of Jiang Jieshi (Chiang Kai-shek), Truman wrote, "I can deal with Stalin. He is honest—but smart as hell."

Within six months of the war's end, the president had changed his mind, and relations between the two countries quickly soured. The United States was the only nation in the world with the atomic bomb, which it had used on Japan, and boasted the only economy reinvigorated by the war. As a result, the Truman administration believed that it held the upper hand against the Soviets and could gain most of what it wanted. With this in mind, the State Department offered the Soviets a $6 billion loan, which they needed to help rebuild their war-ravaged economy. But when the Soviets undermined free elections in Poland in 1946 and established a compliant government, the United States withdrew the offer. Soviet troops also remained in northern Iran, closing off the oil fields to potential capitalist enterprises. The failure to reach agreement over international control of atomic energy proved the last straw. Before reaching an accord, the United States wanted to make sure it would keep its atomic weapons, while the Soviets first wanted the United States to destroy its nuclear arsenal. Clearly, the former World War II allies did not trust each other, and each suspected the other of trying to gain an atomic advantage.

Truman had significantly underestimated the strength of the Soviet position. The Soviets were well on their way toward building their own atomic weapons, negating the Americans' nuclear advantage. In the meantime, until the Russians obtained the bomb, they could rely on the power of their huge army—the largest in the world—poised in Eastern Europe. The Soviets could also ignore the enticement of U.S. economic aid by taking resources from East Germany and mobilizing the Russian people to rebuild their country's industry and military. Indeed, on February 9, 1946, Stalin delivered a tough speech to rally Russians to make sacrifices to enhance national security. By asserting that communism was "a better form of organization than any non-Soviet social system," he implied, according to George Kennan, that capitalist nations could not coexist with communism and that future wars were unavoidable unless communism triumphed over capitalism.

Whether Stalin meant this speech as an unofficial declaration of a third world war was not clear, but U.S. leaders interpreted it this way. A few days after Stalin spoke, Kennan sent his 8,000-word telegram from the U.S. Embassy in Moscow to Washington, blaming the Soviets for stirring up international tensions and confirming that Stalin could not be trusted. "Driven by a neurotic view of world affairs," Kennan maintained, "[the Soviet Union] would respond only to force." The following month, on March 15, former British prime minister Winston Churchill gave a speech in Truman's home state of Missouri, which the president read in advance and presumably approved. Declaring that "an iron curtain has descended across the Continent" of Europe, Churchill observed that "there is nothing [the Russians] admire so much as strength, and there is nothing for which they have less respect than for military weakness." This comment reaffirmed Truman's sentiments expressed the previous year: "Unless Russia is faced with an iron fist and strong language another war is in the making." The message was clear: Unyielding resistance to the Soviet Union was the only way to avoid another world war.

DOCUMENTS 24.1 AND 24.2

Reactions to Soviet Policy in Europe: Two Views

By the late 1940s, tensions between the two superpowers threatened to erupt into armed conflict. Opinion within the U.S. government about how to respond to this challenge ranged widely: Some urged cooperation, while others argued for aggressive confrontation with the Soviet Union. The following selections illustrate the nature of this important postwar debate. In his famous "iron curtain" speech, Winston Churchill condemned Soviet policies in Europe. The same year, Secretary of Commerce Henry Wallace criticized aggressive responses to the Soviet Union.

Explore

24.1 Winston Churchill | The Iron Curtain, 1946

A shadow has fallen upon the scenes so lately lighted by the Allied victory. Nobody knows what Soviet Russia and its Communist international organization intends to do in the immediate future, or what are the limits, if any, to their expansive and proselytizing tendencies. I have a strong admiration and regard for the valiant Russian people and for my wartime comrade, Marshal Stalin. There is deep sympathy and goodwill in Britain—and I doubt not here also—towards the peoples of all the Russias and a resolve to persevere through many differences and rebuffs in establishing lasting friendships. We understand the Russian need to be secure on her western frontiers by the removal of all possibility of German aggression. We welcome Russia to her rightful place among the leading nations of the world. We welcome her flag upon the seas. Above all, we welcome constant, frequent, and growing contacts between the Russian people and our own people on both sides of the Atlantic. It is my duty however, for I am sure you would wish me to state the facts as I see them to you, to place before you certain facts about the present position in Europe.

From Stettin in the Baltic to Trieste in the Adriatic, an iron curtain has descended across the Continent. Behind that line lie all the capitals of the ancient states of Central and Eastern Europe. Warsaw, Berlin, Prague, Vienna, Budapest, Belgrade, Bucharest, and Sofia, all these famous cities and the populations around them lie in what I must call the Soviet sphere, and all are subject in one form or another, not only to Soviet influence but to a very high and, in many cases, increasing measure of control from Moscow.

Source: Robert Rhodes James, ed., *Winston S. Churchill: His Complete Speeches, 1897–1963*, vol. 7, *1943–1949* (New York: Chelsea House Publishers, 1974), 7290.

Not all Americans agreed with this view. Although some 60 percent of the public believed that cooperation with the Soviets was unlikely, a minority argued that a more amicable relationship was possible. Led by Roosevelt's former vice president Henry Wallace, who served as Truman's secretary of commerce, critics voiced concern about taking a "hard line" against the Soviet Union. Stalin was pursuing a policy of expansion, they agreed, but for limited reasons. Wallace claimed that the Soviets merely wanted to protect their borders by surrounding themselves with friendly countries, just as the United States had done by establishing spheres of influence in the Caribbean. Except for Poland and Romania, Stalin initially accepted an array of governments in Eastern Europe, allowing free elections in Czechoslovakia, Hungary, and, to a lesser extent, Bulgaria. Only as Cold War tensions escalated did the Soviets tighten control over all of Eastern Europe, snuffing out any semblance of democracy. Critics such as Wallace considered this outcome the result of a self-fulfilling prophecy; by misinterpreting Soviet motives, the Truman administration pushed Stalin to counter the American hard line with a hard line of his own.

Explore

See Documents 24.1 and 24.2 for comments from Winston Churchill and Henry Wallace.

The Truman Doctrine

By 1947 U.S.-Soviet relations had reached a new low. International arms control had proven futile, the United States had gone to the United Nations to pressure the Soviets

---

Explore

24.2 Henry Wallace | The Way to Peace, 1946

"Getting tough" never bought anything real and lasting—whether for schoolyard bullies or businessmen or world powers. The tougher we get, the tougher the Russians will get.

Throughout the world there are numerous reactionary elements which had hoped for Axis victory—and now profess great friendship for the United States. Yet, these enemies of yesterday and false friends of today continually try to provoke war between the United States and Russia. They have no real love of the United States. They only long for the day when the United States and Russia will destroy each other. We must not let our Russian policy be guided or influenced by those inside or outside the United States who want war with Russia. This does not mean appeasement. . . .

The real peace treaty we now need is between the United States and Russia. On our part, we should recognize that we have no more business in the political affairs of Eastern Europe than Russia has in the political affairs of Latin America, Western Europe, and the United States. We may not like what Russia does in Eastern Europe. Her type of land reform, industrial expropriation, and suppression of basic liberties offends the great majority of the people of the United States. But whether we like it or not the Russians will try to socialize their sphere of influence just as we try to democratize our sphere of influence. . . .

Russia must be convinced that we are not planning for war against her and we must be certain that Russia is not carrying on territorial expansion or world domination through native communists faithfully following every twist and turn in the Moscow party line. But in this competition, we must insist on an open door for trade throughout the world. There will always be an ideological conflict—but that is no reason why diplomats cannot work out a basis for both systems to live safely in the world side by side.

Source: Henry Wallace, "The Way to Peace," in *The Annals of America* (Chicago: Encyclopedia Britannica, 1968), 16:372–73.

Interpret the Evidence

- How does each man view the prospect of "toughness" toward the Soviet Union?
- What legitimate Soviet interests do both Wallace and Churchill acknowledge? On what policies toward the Soviets do they differ, and why?

Put It in Context

Why do you think American foreign policy conformed to Churchill's perspective in the postwar period?

to withdraw from Iran, and the rhetoric from both sides had become warlike. From the American vantage point, Soviet actions to expand communism in Eastern Europe appeared to threaten democracies in Western Europe. By contrast, the Soviets viewed the United States as seeking to extend economic control over nations close to their borders and to weaken communism in the Soviet Union.

Events in Greece allowed Truman to take the offensive and apply Kennan's policy of containment. The Mediterranean Sea linked the United Kingdom (formerly Great Britain) to the Middle East, the Suez Canal, and its Asian colonies, and the British therefore considered it vitally important to keep Greece within its sphere of influence. During the war, Churchill and Stalin had agreed that after the war the United Kingdom (UK) would resume its oversight of Greece, while the Soviets would predominate in Eastern Europe. All did not go according to plan. In 1946 a civil war broke out in Greece between the right-wing monarchy, which the UK supported, and a coalition of insurgents consisting of members of the wartime anti-Nazi resistance, Communists, and non-Communist opponents of the repressive government. Under normal conditions, the British would have provided the necessary resources to prop up the Greek government. The United Kingdom, however, was exhausted by the war and in desperate financial shape, so it had no choice but to turn to the United States for help.

The Truman administration agreed to help the UK. Although the Greeks were fighting a civil war, the president and his advisers viewed the situation differently. They believed that the presence of Communists among the Greek rebels meant that Moscow was behind the insurgency. In fact, Stalin was not aiding the revolutionaries; the assistance came from the Communist leader of Yugoslavia, Josip Broz Tito, who acted independently of the Soviets and would soon break with them. Following Kennan's lead in advocating containment, Truman incorrectly believed that all Communists around the world were ultimately controlled by the Kremlin.

While Truman was convinced that the United States had to intervene in Greece to contain the spread of communism, he still had to convince the Republican-controlled Congress and the American people to go along. In 1946 the Republicans had run on a platform of lowering taxes and cutting government spending—positions that enjoyed considerable public support and were incompatible with appropriating huge sums to support the Greek government. In order to overcome potential opposition to its plans, the Truman administration exaggerated the danger of Communist control of Greece. Truman sent Undersecretary of State Dean Acheson to testify before a congressional committee that "like apples in a barrel infected by one rotten one, the corruption of Greece would infect Iran and all to the east." The administration's presentation of the issues to the American public was even more dramatic. On March 12, 1947, Truman gave a speech to a joint session of

Congress that was broadcast over national radio to millions of listeners. He interpreted the civil war in Greece as a titanic struggle between freedom and totalitarianism that threatened the free world. "I believe," the president declared, "that it must be the policy of the United States to support free peoples who are resisting attempted subjugation by armed minorities or by outside pressures." Truman's rhetoric stretched the truth on many counts—the armed minorities to which the president referred had fought the Nazis; the Soviets did not supply the insurgents; the right-wing monarchy, propped up by the military, was hardly democratic; and the United Kingdom had long exerted "outside pressure." Truman achieved his goal of frightening both lawmakers and the public, and Congress appropriated $400 million in military aid to fortify the existing governments of Greece and neighboring Turkey.

The **Truman Doctrine**, which pledged to contain the expansion of communism, was the cornerstone of American foreign policy throughout the Cold War. The United States committed itself to shoring up governments, whether democratic or dictatorial, as long as they were avowedly anti-Communist. Americans believed that the rest of the world's nations wanted to be like the United States and therefore would not willingly accept communism, which they thought could be imposed only from the outside by the Soviet Union and never reasonably chosen from within.

Although Truman misread Soviet intentions with respect to Greece, Stalin's regime had given him cause for worry. Soviet actions that imposed communism in Poland, along with the USSR's refusal to withdraw troops from the Baltic states of Latvia, Lithuania, and Estonia, reinforced the president's concerns about Soviet expansionism and convinced many in the U.S. government that Stalin had no intention of abiding by his wartime agreements. Difficulties in negotiating with the Soviets about international control of atomic energy further worried American foreign-policy makers about Russian designs for obtaining the atomic bomb.

The Marshall Plan and Economic Containment

George Kennan's version of containment called for economic and political aid to check Communist expansion. In this context, to forestall Communist inroads and offer humanitarian assistance to Europeans facing homelessness and starvation, the Truman administration offered economic assistance to the war-torn continent. Secretary of State George Marshall recognized that if the United States did not offer help, European nations would face "economic, social, and political deterioration of a very grave character," which in turn might plunge the world and the United States, which depended heavily on European markets, into another Great Depression. In a June 1947 speech that drew heavily on Kennan's ideas, Marshall sketched out a plan to provide financial assistance to Europe. Although he invited any country, including the Soviet Union, that experienced "hunger, poverty, desperation, and chaos" to apply for aid, Marshall did not expect Stalin to ask for assistance. To do so would require the Soviets to supply information to the United States concerning the internal operations of their economy and to admit to the failure of communism.

Following up Marshall's speech, Truman asked Congress in December 1947 to authorize $17 billion for European recovery. With conservative-minded Republicans still in control of Congress, the president's spending request faced steep opposition. The Soviet Union inadvertently came to Truman's political rescue. Stalin interpreted the proposed

Marshall Plan of economic assistance as a hostile attempt by the United States to gain influence in Eastern Europe. To forestall this possibility, in late February 1948 the Soviets extinguished the remaining democracy in Eastern Europe by engineering a Communist coup in Czechoslovakia. Congressional lawmakers viewed this action as further proof of Soviet aggression. In April 1948, they approved the Marshall Plan, providing $13 billion in economic assistance to sixteen European countries over the next five years.

Explore

See Document 24.3 for the Soviet Union's reaction to the Marshall Plan.

DOCUMENT 24.3

Vyacheslav Molotov | Soviet Objections to the Marshall Plan, 1947

Shortly after Secretary of State George Marshall proposed the Marshall Plan to grant economic assistance to Europe, France and the United Kingdom invited Soviet leaders to a conference in Paris to discuss their response to General Marshall's offer. In the following selection, Soviet foreign minister Vyacheslav Molotov lays out an alternative vision of economic assistance, which implicitly rejects the Marshall Plan.

Explore

When efforts are directed toward Europe helping herself in the first place and developing her economic potentialities as well as the exchange of goods between countries, such efforts are in conformity with the interests of the countries of Europe. When, however, it is stated . . . that the decisive hold on the rehabilitation of the economic life of European countries should belong to the United States and not to the European countries themselves, such a position stands in contradiction to the interests of European countries since it might lead to a denial of their economic independence, which denial is incompatible with national sovereignty.

The Soviet delegation believes that internal measures and the national efforts of each country should have a decisive importance for the countries of Europe and not make calculations for foreign support which should be of secondary importance. The Soviet Union has always counted above all on its own powers and is known to be on a steady way of progress of its economic life.

The first form of cooperation is based on the development of political and economic relations between states possessing equal rights and in that case their national sovereignty does not suffer from foreign interference.

Such is the democratic basis for international cooperation which brings nations closer together and facilitates the task of their mutual aid.

Source: U.S. Department of State, *A Decade of American Foreign Policy: Basic Documents, 1941–1949* (Washington, D.C.: Department of State Printing Office, 1985), 969.

Interpret the Evidence

- Why does Molotov think that accepting U.S. assistance would be against the interests of European countries?
- What does Molotov claim should be the basis for international cooperation?

Put It in Context

How did the U.S. government interpret Soviet rejection of the Marshall Plan?

The Cold War Hardens, 1948–1952

After 1947, the Cold War intensified. Both sides increased military spending and took measures to enhance their military presence around the world. Fueled by growing distrust, the Soviet Union and the United States engaged in inflammatory rhetoric that added to the danger that the conflict posed to world peace. In 1950 the United States, in cooperation with the United Nations, sent troops to South Korea to turn back an invasion from the Communist North. During the late 1940s and early 1950s, the president gained expanded power to initiate wars and increase spending for military and national security agencies.

Military Containment

The New Deal and World War II had increased the power of the president and his ability to manage economic and military crises. The Cold War further strengthened the presidency and shifted the balance of governmental power to the executive branch, creating what has been called the **imperial presidency**.

As the Cold War heated up, Congress granted the president enormous authority over foreign affairs and internal security. The National Security Act, passed in 1947, created the Department of Defense as a cabinet agency (replacing the Department of War), consolidated control of the various military services under its authority, and established the Joint Chiefs of Staffs, composed of the heads of the army, navy, air force, and marines. To advise the president on military and foreign affairs, the act set up the **National Security Council (NSC)**, a group presided over by the national security adviser. The NSC also consisted of the secretaries of state, defense, the army, the navy, and the air force and any others the president might choose to designate.

In addition to this panel, the National Security Act established the Central Intelligence Agency (CIA) as part of the executive branch. Because of the nation's poor experience analyzing intelligence prior to World War II, the CIA was given the responsibility of coordinating intelligence gathering and conducting espionage abroad to counter Soviet spying operations. Another new intelligence agency, the National Security Agency, created in 1949, monitored overseas communications through the latest technological devices. Together, these agencies enhanced the president's ability to conduct foreign affairs with little congressional oversight and out of public view.

By 1948 the Truman administration had decided that an economically healthy Germany, with its great industrial potential, provided the key to a prosperous Europe

The Berlin Airlift
This group of West Berliners waits anxiously as an American C-47 cargo plane prepares to land at Tempelhof Airfield to deliver food in July 1948. The Soviets had blockaded ground transportation to the Allied sector of West Berlin, prompting President Truman to airlift supplies. Three years after the war ended, the photograph shows Germany still in ruins.   Time & Life Pictures/Getty Images

and consequently a depression-proof United States. Rebuilding postwar Germany would also fortify the eastern boundary of Europe against Soviet expansion. In mid-1948, the United States, United Kingdom, and France consolidated their occupation zones, created the Federal Republic of Germany (West Germany), and initiated economic reforms to stimulate a speedy recovery. This prompted the Soviet Union, which saw a strong Germany as a threat to its national security, to respond in a belligerent manner. Stalin closed the access roads from the border of West Germany to Berlin, located in the Soviet zone of East Germany, effectively cutting off the city from the West.

The Soviet blockade of West Berlin turned the Cold War even colder. Without provisions from the United States and its allies in West Germany, West Berliners could not survive.

In an effort to break the blockade, Truman ordered a massive airlift known as "Operation Vittles," during which American and British planes transported more than 2.5 million tons of supplies to West Berlin. After nearly a year of these flights, the **Berlin airlift** ended in the spring of 1949 when the Russians backed off and once again allowed their adversaries to supply West Berlin on the ground.

Although the two superpowers narrowly avoided war over Berlin, their subsequent actions kept the conflict alive. Both nations fashioned military alliances to keep the other at bay. In April 1949, the United States joined eleven European countries in the **North Atlantic Treaty Organization (NATO)**. A peacetime military alliance, NATO established a collective security pact in which an attack on one member was viewed as an attack on all (Map 24.1). Pledging to defend Europe,

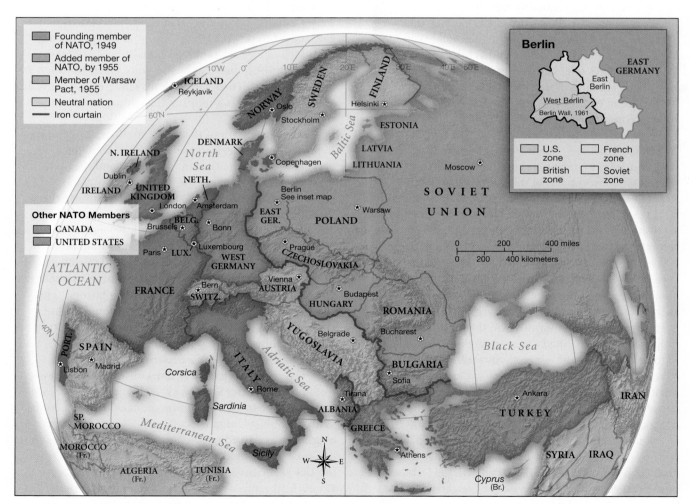

MAP 24.1   The Cold War in Europe, 1945–1955

In 1946, the four major victorious wartime allies divided Germany and Berlin into distinct sectors, leading to increasing conflict. Between 1949 and 1955, the descent of what Winston Churchill called the "iron curtain" of communism and the creation of rival security pacts headed by the United States and the Soviet Union hardened these postwar divisions into a prolonged Cold War.

Truman dispatched four army divisions to Western Europe to show his resolve against Soviet aggression. In 1949 the Russians followed suit by organizing the Council for Mutual Economic Assistance to help their satellite nations rebuild and six years later by creating the Warsaw Pact military alliance, the respective counterparts in Eastern Europe to the Marshall Plan and NATO.

Amid the growing militarization of the Cold War, 1949 brought two new shocks to the United States and its allies. First, in September the Russians successfully tested an atomic bomb. Second, Communist forces within China led by Mao Zedong and Zhou Enlai succeeded in overthrowing the U.S.-backed government of Jiang Jieshi and creating the People's Republic of China. These two events convinced many in the United States that the threat posed by communism was escalating rapidly.

In response, the National Security Council met to reevaluate U.S. strategy in fighting the Cold War. In April 1950, the NSC recommended to Truman that the United States intensify its containment policy both abroad and at home. The document it handed over to the president, entitled **NSC-68**, spelled out the need for action in ominous language. "The Soviet Union, unlike previous aspirants to hegemony," NSC-68 warned, "is animated by a new fanatic faith, antithetical to our own, and seeks to impose its absolute authority over the rest of the world. It is in this context that this Republic and its citizens . . . stand in their deepest peril." Having sketched out the dire threat posed by Russia's acquisition of the atomic bomb, the NSC made specific recommendations to combat this new challenge. NSC-68 proposed that the United States develop an even more powerful nuclear weapon, the hydrogen bomb; increase military spending; and continue to negotiate NATO-style alliances around the globe. Departing from the original guidelines for the CIA, the president's advisers proposed that the United States engage in "covert means" to foment and support "unrest and revolt in selected strategic [Soviet] satellite countries." At home, the government should prepare Americans for the Communist danger by enhancing internal security and civil defense programs.

Truman agreed with many of the principles behind NSC-68 but worried about the cost of funding it. The problem remained a political one. Though the Democrats once again controlled both houses of Congress, there was little sentiment to raise taxes and slash the economic programs established during the New Deal. However, circumstances abruptly changed when, in June 1950, shortly after the president received the NSC report, Com-munist North Korea invaded U.S.-backed South Korea. In response to this attack, Truman took the opportunity to put into practice key recommendations of NSC-68.

The Korean War

Like Germany, Korea emerged from World War II divided between U.S. and Soviet spheres of influence. Above the 38th parallel, which divided the Korean peninsula, the Communist leader Kim Il Sung ruled North Korea with support from the Soviet Union. Below that latitude, the anti-Communist leader Syngman Rhee governed South Korea. The United States supported Rhee, but with American forces occupying Japan and the Philippines, in January 1950 Secretary of State Dean Acheson did not regard South Korea as part of the vital Asian "defense perimeter" that the United States guaranteed to protect from Communist aggression. Truman had already removed remaining American troops from the country the previous year. On June 25, 1950, an emboldened Kim Il Sung sent troops to invade South Korea, seeking to unite the country under his leadership.

In the aftermath of the invasion, Korea took on new importance to American policymakers. Drawing a parallel between the situation in Korea and the appeasement of the Nazis before World War II, Truman remarked that he had seen strong nations invade the weak before and that the failure of democracies to act only encouraged aggressors. If South Korea fell, the president believed, Communist leaders would be "emboldened to override nations closer to our own shores." Thus the Truman Doctrine was now applied to Asia as it had previously been applied to Europe. This time, however, American financial aid would not be enough. It would be up to the U.S. military to contain the Communist threat.

Truman did not seek a declaration of war from Congress. According to Acheson, consulting Congress would delay matters and "weaken and confuse [our] will." Instead, Truman chose a multinational course of action. With the Soviet Union boycotting the United Nations over its refusal to admit the Communist People's Republic of China, the United States obtained authorization from the UN Security Council to send a peacekeeping force to Korea. In the absence of a declaration of war, Truman, as commander in chief, sent American troops to enforce what he called a "police action." Fifteen other countries joined UN forces, but the United States supplied the bulk of the troops, as well as their commanding officer,

General Douglas MacArthur. In reality, MacArthur reported to the president, not the United Nations.

Before MacArthur could mobilize his forces, the North Koreans had penetrated most of South Korea, except for the port of Pusan on the southwest coast of the peninsula. In a daring counterattack, on September 15, 1950, MacArthur dispatched land and sea forces to capture Inchon, northwest of Pusan on the opposite coast, to cut off North Korean supply lines. Joined by UN forces pushing out of Pusan, MacArthur's Eighth Army troops chased the enemy northward in retreat back over the 38th parallel.

Explore

See Document 24.4 for a letter from an American Red Cross worker in Korea.

Now Truman had to make a key decision. MacArthur wanted to invade North Korea, defeat the Communists, and unify the country under Syngman Rhee. Instead of sticking to his original goal of containing Communist aggression against South Korea, Truman succumbed to the lure of liberating all of Korea from the Communists. MacArthur received permission to proceed, and on October 9 his forces crossed

---

DOCUMENT 24.4

Helen Stevenson | Letter from Korea, 1951

American Red Cross worker Helen Stevenson wrote the following letter to her parents just weeks after she arrived in Korea. In her correspondence, Stevenson described her work for the Red Cross's Clubmobile unit in war-torn Pusan. Stevenson later married a New Jersey governor and served in the U.S. House of Representatives in the 1970s.

Explore

We do not let South Korean soldiers come into the club. It seems that the higher-ups feel that we would be completely taken over by them. (Of this I am not convinced.) I am glad you can't see the way that we as Americans treat the S. Koreans who work for us. It nearly kills me when I see some of the things they do to the S. K's who work for the army, and there are a great many of them. In the first place we treat these people as if we were occupying them, as if we were or had been at war with them. That is not the case at all, as you know. One day an American Major friend of mine took me out of town to see the S. Korean Officers training school. Some American officers work out there with the S. K. officers teaching them American ways, tactics, etc. The Major told me that he had talked to these S. K. officers and the general opinion among them was that they resented very much the Americans being here. And that they wanted to see their country united and as long as it was UNITED they did not care under what kind or type of government. They also told this major that they knew full well that the Americans were here for their own interests and not in any way for the interests of Korea as a whole. The S. Koreans who work for us get about four dollars a month pay. They do not get any time off and they work over 12 hours a day. The price of their own food and clothing is terribly high and all the workers are so thin and sickly looking. We scream at them in English and then get furious when they don't understand.

Source: Lisa Grunwald and Stephen Adler, eds., *Women's Letters: America from the Revolutionary War to the Present* (New York: Dial Press, 2005), 608–9.

Interpret the Evidence

- What is Stevenson's attitude about her work in Korea and about the war?
- Why would South Koreans have considered the United States to be an occupying power rather than a liberator?

Put It in Context

What impact did the Korean War have on the Cold War?

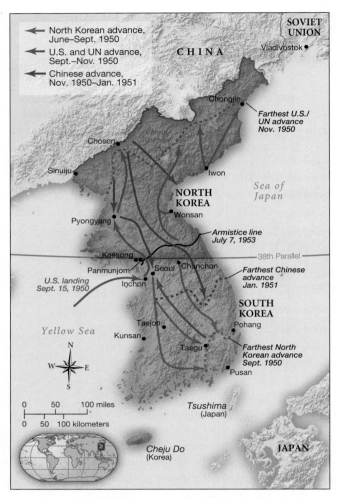

MAP 24.2 The Korean War, 1950–1953

Considered a "police action" by the United Nations, the Korean War cost the lives of nearly 37,000 U.S. troops. Approximately one million Koreans were killed, wounded, or missing. Each side pushed deep into enemy territory, but neither could achieve victory. When hostilities ceased in 1953, a demilitarized zone near the original boundary line separated North and South Korea.

the 38th parallel into North Korea. Within three weeks, UN troops marched through the country until they reached the Yalu River, which bordered China. With the U.S. military massed along their southern perimeter, the Chinese warned that they would send troops to repel the invaders if the Americans crossed the Yalu. Both General MacArthur and Secretary of State Acheson, based on faulty CIA intelligence, discounted this threat, figuring that the Chinese Communists did not want to fight another war so recently after winning their revolution. They were wrong. Truman approved MacArthur's plan to cross the Yalu, and on November 27, 1950, China sent more than 300,000 troops south into North Korea. This proved disastrous for the United States; within two months, Communist troops regained control of North Korea, allowing them once again to invade South Korea. On

January 4, 1951, the South Korean capital of Seoul fell to Chinese and North Korean troops (Map 24.2).

By the spring of 1951, the war had degenerated into a stalemate. UN forces succeeded in recapturing Seoul and repelling the Communists north of the 38th parallel. This time, with the American public anxious to end the war and with the presence of the Chinese promising an endless, bloody predicament, the president sought to replace combat with diplomacy. The American objective would be containment, not Korean unification.

Truman's change of heart infuriated General MacArthur, who was willing to risk an all-out war with China and to use nuclear weapons to win. After MacArthur spoke out publicly against Truman's policy by remarking, "There is no substitute for victory," the president removed him from command on April 11, 1951. However, even with the change in strategy and leadership, the war dragged on for two more years until July 1953, when a final armistice agreement was reached. By this time, Truman's term of office had ended.

The Korean War cost the United States 54,000 lives and $54 billion. This sacrifice of human lives and economic resources made the war unpopular among the American people. Few understood what good, if any, was accomplished. If American soldiers had to die and suffer, many Americans questioned why the Truman administration was satisfied with containment and not the expulsion of communism from Asia once and for all. When MacArthur returned to the United States, he was greeted as a hero, reflecting public dissatisfaction with a war in which fighting to a draw was represented as a victory.

The War and the Imperial Presidency

The Korean War boosted the imperial presidency by allowing the president to bypass Congress and the Constitution to initiate wars in the name of "police actions." The war allowed Truman to expand his powers as commander in chief and augmented the strength of the national security state over which he presided. As a result of the Korean conflict, the military draft became a regular feature of American life for young men over the next two decades. The expanded peacetime military was active around the globe, operating bases in Europe, Asia, and the Middle East. During the war, the military budget rose from $13.5 billion to $50 billion, strengthening the connection between economic growth and permanent mobilization to fight the Cold War. The war also permitted President Truman to reshape foreign policy along the lines sketched in NSC-68, including the extension of U.S. influence in Southeast Asia. Consequently, he authorized economic aid to support the French against Communist revolutionaries in Vietnam.

Yet the power of the imperial presidency did not go unchecked. Congress deferred to Truman on key issues of

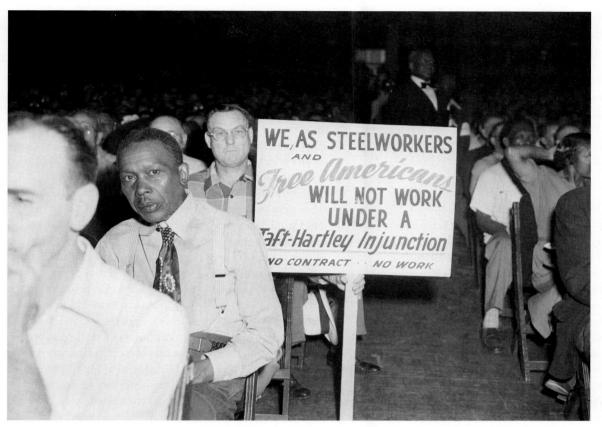

Steel Strike, 1952

In this photograph, steelworkers in Gary, Indiana, listen to a speech by CIO president Philip Murray, given on June 22, 1952. Murray promised to lead the union on strike and get a contract for its members. Five years earlier, Congress had passed the Taft-Hartley Act, which hampered union organizing. Before the steel strike could begin, President Truman seized the steel plants and placed them under federal control, an action the Supreme Court soon reversed.   © Bettmann/CORBIS

military policy, but on one important occasion the Supreme Court stepped in to restrain him. The central issue grew out of a labor dispute in the steel industry. In 1952 the United Steel Workers of America threatened to go on strike for higher wages, which would have had a serious impact on war production as well as the economy in general. On May 2, after the steel companies refused the union's demands, Truman announced the government seizure and operation of the steel mills to keep them running. He argued that as president he had the "inherent right" to take over the steel plants.

The steel companies objected and brought the matter before the Supreme Court. On June 2, 1952, the Court ruled against Truman. It held that the president did not have the intrinsic authority to seize private property, even during wartime. For the time being, the Supreme Court affirmed some limitations on the unbridled use of presidential power even during periods of war.

REVIEW & RELATE

What were the causes and consequences of the militarization of the containment strategy in the late 1940s and early 1950s?

How did the Korean War contribute to the centralization of power in the executive branch?

✔ *LEARNINGCurve* bedfordstmartins.com/hewittlawson/LC

Peacetime Challenges, 1945–1948

As the Cold War heated up overseas, at home Americans faced numerous challenges posed by the reconversion of the economy from a war footing to peacetime. Consumers experienced shortages and high prices; businesses complained about tight regulations; and labor unions sought higher wages and a greater voice in companies' decision making. African Americans attempted to build on the gains they had achieved during World War II and to secure new civil rights victories at home. The return to peace also occasioned debates about whether married women, especially those with children, should continue to work outside the home. Even as the Cold War created new anxieties, Americans tried to achieve the peace and prosperity that had eluded them for the past two decades.

Coming Home

In August 1945, 12 million troops, two-thirds of all men between the ages of eighteen and thirty-four, were in uniform. One year later, 9 million had returned to the United States. Some wanted to continue their education, most wanted jobs, and all sought to reunite with their families. They came home to a changed world. The Great Depression was over, but industries still needed to shift to peacetime production before consumers could enjoy the fruits of the new prosperity. In the meantime, consumers faced shortages and high prices. Indeed, there was no guarantee that, with the booming war industries dismantled, the depression would not return.

World War II had also exerted pressures on traditional family life. During the war, millions of women had left their homes and worked jobs that their husbands, sons, and boyfriends had vacated (see chapter 23). Most of the 150,000 women who served in the military received their discharge, and like their male counterparts they hoped to obtain employment. Many other women who had tasted the benefits of wartime employment also wanted to keep working and were reluctant to give up their positions to men.

The war disrupted other aspects of family life as well. During the war, husbands and wives had spent long periods of time apart, resulting in marital tensions and an increased divorce rate. The relaxation of parental authority during the war led to a rise in juvenile delinquency, which added to the anxieties of adults. In 1948 the noted psychiatrist William C. Menninger observed, "While we alarm ourselves with talk of . . . atom bombs, we are complacently watching the disintegration of our family life." Some observers worried that the very existence of the traditional American family was in jeopardy. These fears proved unfounded, as the baby boom of the postwar decades would dramatically demonstrate.

Economic Conversion and Labor Discontent

Before the Cold War became the focus of U.S. foreign policy in 1947, Americans worried more about economic security

than about fighting communism. In the absence of war-driven production and with the return of millions of veterans to the job market, Americans feared massive unemployment and another depression. Many families had managed to save money during the war with rationing in place, and they looked forward to spending it on consumer goods. Instead, they found shortages of manufactured items and foodstuffs as the economy moved slowly to peacetime production. Workers who had remained on the home front enjoyed rising incomes from overtime pay, but they worried about holding on to their increased earnings in peacetime.

Even before the war ended, the U.S. government took some steps to meet postwar economic challenges. In 1944, for example, Congress passed the **Servicemen's Readjustment Act**, commonly known as the GI Bill, which offered veterans educational opportunities and financial aid as they adjusted to civilian life. Overall, however, the Truman administration did not handle the economic problems of reconversion well. In the face of shortages and high prices for available commodities, the president wavered between retaining World War II price controls to benefit consumers and eliminating them to help corporate industrialists. He satisfied neither. Nor did the Employment Act of 1946 improve matters. Contrary to its name, the legislation did not guarantee jobs but merely recommended using tax policies to make adjustments to the economy and created a three-member Council of Economic Advisors to make suggestions to the president.

The president also ran into serious difficulty with labor unions. In the years immediately following the war, real incomes fell, undermined by inflation and reduced overtime hours. As corporate profits rose, workers in the steel, automobile, and fuel industries struck for higher wages and a greater voice in company policies. Truman responded harshly. Labor had been one of Franklin Roosevelt's strongest allies, but his successor put that relationship in jeopardy. In 1946 the federal government took over railroads and threatened to draft workers into the military until they stopped striking. Truman took a tough stance, but in the end union workers received a boost in pay, though it did little to relieve inflation.

Political developments forced Truman to change course. In the 1946 midterm elections, Republicans won control of the Eightieth Congress (1947–1949). Stung by this defeat, Truman sought to repair the damage his anti-union policies had done to the Democratic Party coalition. In 1947 Congress passed the **Taft-Hartley Act**. The act hampered the ability of unions to organize and limited their power to go on strike if larger, national interests were seen to be at stake. Seeking to regain labor's support, Truman vetoed the measure. Congress, however, overrode the president's veto, and the Taft-Hartley Act became law.

Veterans Return Home

After World War II, many veterans returned home, married, and started families. They went to school with funds provided by the GI Bill. This twenty-four-year-old former soldier, a student at the University of Iowa, tries to study while holding his baby daughter on his lap as his wife irons in their cramped house trailer.   Time & Life Pictures/Getty Images

The Postwar Civil Rights Struggle

With the war against Nazi racism and tyranny over, African Americans expected to win first-class citizenship in the United States. During World War II, A. Philip Randolph, a black activist and union leader, had led a successful effort to pressure the federal government to tackle discrimination. New organizations such as the **Congress of Racial Equality (CORE)** had emerged to attack racial exclusion in public accommodations, and older groups such as the National Association for the Advancement of Colored People (NAACP) had flourished by attracting new members and leading the legal battle against racial inequality. African American veterans returned home to the South determined to build on these victories, especially by extending the right to vote. "A Voteless citizen is a Voiceless citizen" became the slogan of campaigns throughout the South. Yet African Americans found that most whites resisted demands for racial equality.

Violence surfaced as the most visible evidence of many white people's determination to preserve the traditional racial order. In 1946 a race riot erupted in Columbia, Tennessee, in which blacks were killed and black businesses were burned down. In February 1946 in South Carolina, Isaac Woodard, a black veteran still in uniform and on his way home on a bus, got into an argument with the white bus driver. When the local sheriff arrived, he pounded Woodard's face with a club, permanently blinding the ex-GI. Five months later, the Ku Klux Klan in Monroe, Georgia, shot a black veteran and three members of his family to death for "acting uppity." In Mississippi, Senator Theodore Bilbo, running for reelection in the Democratic primary, told his white audiences that they could keep blacks from voting "by seeing them the night before" the election. Groups such as the NAACP and the National Association of Colored Women demanded that the president take action to combat this reign of terror.

In December 1946, after meeting with a delegation of concerned African Americans, Truman issued an executive order creating the President's Committee on Civil Rights to investigate the situation and report back to him. Truman's response reflected moral concerns and good politics: It provided the opportunity to increase Democratic Party support among African Americans, which Roosevelt had

Journey of Reconciliation, 1947

Members of the interracial Congress of Racial Equality embarked on a Journey of Reconciliation (known later as freedom rides) to desegregate interstate bus transportation in the Upper South. They met resistance and were arrested several times. In this photograph, some members of CORE appear in front of their lawyer's office in Richmond, Virginia. Bayard Rustin, an important leader of the civil rights movement, stands fourth from the right.   Used with permission of the Fellowship of Reconciliation (http://forusa.org)

first succeeded in gaining in 1936. In April 1947, while the President's Committee on Civil Rights conducted its work, Jackie Robinson achieved a milestone by becoming the first black baseball player to enter the major leagues. This accomplishment proved to be a sign of changes to come.

After extensive deliberations, the committee, which consisted of blacks and whites, northerners and southerners, issued its report, *To Secure These Rights*, on October 29, 1947. The document placed the problem of what it called "civil rights shortcomings" within the context of the Cold War, arguing that racial inequality and unrest could only aid the Soviets in their global anti-American propaganda efforts. "The United States is not so strong," the committee asserted, "the final triumph of the democratic ideal not so inevitable that we can ignore what the world thinks of us or our record." A far-reaching document, the report called for racial desegregation in the military, interstate transportation, and education, as well as extension of the right to vote. The following year, in the midst of the presidential election and once again pressured by A. Philip Randolph, the president signed an executive order to desegregate the armed forces.

Explore

See Document 24.5 for an excerpt from *To Secure These Rights.*

The Election of 1948

By supporting civil rights measures recommended by his presidential committee, Truman alienated white southern segregationists, a significant force in the Democratic Party. On the president's political right, Strom Thurmond, the governor of South Carolina, mounted a presidential challenge by heading up the States' Rights Party, known as the Dixiecrats, which threatened to take away traditional southern Democratic voters from Truman.

At the same time, Truman's conduct of foreign affairs brought criticism from the left wing of his party. Former vice president Henry Wallace ran on the Progressive Party ticket, backed by disgruntled liberals living mainly in the North who opposed Truman's hard-line Cold War policies. Besides these two independent candidates, Truman also faced the popular Republican governor of New York, Thomas E. Dewey. Under these circumstances, political pundits and public opinion polls predicted that Truman would lose the 1948 presidential election.

Truman confounded these voices of gloom by winning the election. His victory resulted from a number of factors, including his vigorous campaign style; the complacency of his Republican opponent, who placed too much faith in opinion polls; and his success in winning over many potential Thurmond and Wallace voters. Much of his victory, however, depended on the continuing power of the New Deal coalition. Truman succeeded in holding together the winning alliance that Franklin Roosevelt had first put together. He did this by stitching together a coalition of labor, minorities, farmers, and liberals and won enough votes in the South to come out ahead despite long odds. In the four-candidate race, Truman did very well in winning slightly less than 50 percent of the popular vote. Democrats also regained control of Congress.

Having won election as president in his own right and armed with a Democratic majority in Congress, Truman still faced tough opposition in his second term. A coalition of southern Democrats and conservative Republicans blocked passage of civil rights proposals and Truman's so-called Fair Deal programs, including national health insurance, federal aid to education, and agricultural reform. The president did manage to obtain budget increases for New Deal measures such as Social Security, minimum wages, and public housing.

By this time, many liberals, as a result of their experience during World War II, had made peace with cooperative corporate executives and relied on the federal government to produce prosperity by tinkering

DOCUMENT 24.5

To Secure These Rights, 1947

In 1946 President Truman appointed a committee to investigate racial discrimination and segregation in the United States. In response to the committee's lengthy report released the following year, Truman issued executive orders to desegregate federal employment and the armed services in 1948. The following excerpt from the report explains the international conditions that prompted a change in American race relations.

Explore

Why does the committee emphasize the fact that America is a nation of immigrants?

What impact does racial prejudice in the United States have worldwide?

Who does the report imply is behind the global dissemination of negative descriptions of American race relations?

The people of the United States stem from many lands. Other nations and their citizens are naturally intrigued by what has happened to their American "relatives." Discrimination against, or mistreatment of, any racial, religious, or national group in the United States is not only seen as our internal problem. The dignity of a country, a continent, or even a major portion of the world's population, may be outraged by it. A relatively few individuals here may be identified with millions of people elsewhere, and the way in which they are treated may have world-wide repercussions. We have fewer than half a million American Indians; there are 30 million more in the Western Hemisphere. Our Mexican American and Hispano groups are not large; millions in Central and South America consider them kin. We number our citizens of Oriental descent in the hundreds of thousands; their counterparts overseas are numbered in hundreds of millions. Throughout the Pacific, Latin America, Africa, the Near, Middle, and Far East, the treatment which our Negroes receive is taken as a reflection of our attitudes toward all dark-skinned peoples.

In the recent war, citizens of a dozen European nations were happy to meet Smiths, Cartiers, O'Haras, Schultzes, di Salvos, Cohens, and Sklodowskas and all the others in our armies. Each nation could share in our victories because its "sons" had helped win them. How much of this good feeling was dissipated when they found virulent prejudice among some of our troops is impossible to say.

We cannot escape the fact that our civil rights record has been an issue in world politics. The world's press and radio are full of it. This Committee has seen a multitude of samples. We and our friends have been, and are, stressing our achievements. Those with competing philosophies have stressed—and are shamelessly distorting—our shortcomings. They have not only tried to create hostility toward us among specific nations, races, and religious groups. They have tried to prove our democracy an empty fraud, and our nation a consistent oppressor of underprivileged people. This may seem ludicrous to Americans, but it is sufficiently important to worry our friends.

Source: *To Secure These Rights: The Report of the President's Committee on Civil Rights* (Washington, D.C.: Government Printing Office, 1947), 147.

Put It in Context

What impact did the Cold War have on shaping the civil rights movement?

with the economy through tax and monetary adjustments; these liberals no longer supported the more radical approaches of income redistribution or reducing corporate concentration. They practiced what historian Arthur Schlesinger Jr. labeled **vital center liberalism**, avoiding what they considered the ideological dogmatism of the extreme political left and right. Militantly anti-Stalinist, centrist liberals supported civil rights, the prosecution of Communists through due process of law, and the expansion of New Deal social welfare programs. In the end, however, preoccupation with fighting the Cold War in Europe and the hot war in Korea diverted Truman's attention from aggressively pursuing a truly liberal political agenda in Congress.

REVIEW & RELATE

What social and economic challenges did America face as it made the transition from war to peace?

Why did Truman have only limited success in implementing his domestic agenda?

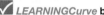 *LEARNINGCurve* bedfordstmartins.com/hewittlawson/LC

The Anti-Communist Consensus, 1945–1954

For most of Truman's second administration, fear of Communist subversion within the United States consumed domestic politics. This focus on anticommunism did not emerge abruptly; rather it carried over from policies the president had employed in fighting the Cold War during his first term in office. There was a consensus within the Truman administration that Soviet-sponsored Communists were attempting to infiltrate American society and that such efforts constituted a grave threat to capitalist and democratic values and institutions. This consensus turned into an anti-Communist obsession, as evidence of Soviet espionage came to light. In an atmosphere of fear, lawmakers and judges blurred the distinction between actual Soviet spies and political radicals who were merely attracted to Communist beliefs. In the process, these officials trampled on individual constitutional freedoms.

Loyalty and Americanism

The postwar fear of communism echoed earlier anti-Communist sentiments. The government had initiated the repressive Palmer raids during the Red scare following World War I,

which led to the deportation of immigrants sympathetic to the Communist doctrines of the Russian Revolution (see chapter 21). In 1938 conservative congressional opponents of the New Deal established the **House Committee on Un-American Activities (HUAC)** to investigate domestic communism, which they tied to the Roosevelt administration. Much of anticommunism, however, was bipartisan. In 1940 Roosevelt signed into law the **Smith Act**, which prohibited teaching or advocating the "duty, necessity, desirability, or propriety of overthrowing or destroying any government in the United States by force or violence" or belonging to any group with that aim. At the same time, President Roosevelt secretly authorized the FBI to monitor and wiretap individuals suspected of violating the act.

The Cold War produced the second Red scare. Just two weeks after his speech announcing the Truman Doctrine in March 1947, the president signed an executive order creating the **Federal Employee Loyalty Program**. Under this program, a board investigated federal employees to see if "reasonable grounds [existed] to suspect disloyalty." The attorney general compiled a list of suspect organizations to assist the board. Soviet espionage was, in fact, a cause for legitimate concern. Spies operated in both Canada and the United States during and after World II, and they had infiltrated the Manhattan Project. The Venona papers, declassified intercepts of Soviet intelligence communications first released in 1995, suggest that a cadre of government officials and federal employees worked for Soviet intelligence during the 1930s and 1940s.

The loyalty board, however, did not focus on espionage. Rather, it concentrated its attention on individuals who espoused dissenting views on a variety of political, social, and economic issues. It failed to uncover a single verifiable case of espionage or find even one actual Communist in public service. This lack of evidence did not stop the board from dismissing 378 government employees for their political beliefs and personal behavior. People lost jobs because they did not satisfactorily answer such questions as "Do you believe in racial integration?" or "Do you listen to the records of Paul Robeson?" (Robeson was an African American singer and actor who had close ties to Communists and the Soviet Union.) Some employees were dismissed because they were homosexuals and considered susceptible to blackmail by foreign agents. (Heterosexual men and women who were having extramarital affairs were not treated in the same manner.) The accused rarely faced their accusers and at times did not learn the nature of the charges against them. This disregard for due process of law spread as loyalty boards at state and municipal levels questioned and fired government employees, including public school teachers and state university professors.

Paul Robeson

Standing at a microphone and surrounded by supporters, Paul Robeson, an African American singer and a left-wing political activist, sings during a benefit concert at an abandoned golf course near Peekskill, New York, on September 4, 1949. A large group of war veterans chanting anti-Communist and racist slogans attacked members of the audience, resulting in some 140 injuries. AP Photo

Congress also investigated communism in the private sector, especially in industries that shaped public opinion. In 1947 HUAC broadened the anti-Red probe from Washington to Hollywood. Convinced that the film industry had come under Communist influence and threatened to poison the minds of millions of moviegoers, HUAC conducted hearings that attracted much publicity. HUAC cited for contempt ten witnesses, among them directors and screenwriters, for refusing to answer questions about their political beliefs and associations. These and subsequent hearings assumed the form of a ritual. The committee already had information from the FBI about the witnesses; HUAC really wanted the accused to confess their Communist heresy publicly and to show contrition by naming their associates. Those who did not comply were considered "unfriendly" witnesses and were put on an industry **blacklist** that deprived them of employment. **See Document Project 24: McCarthyism and the Hollywood Ten, page 780.**

HUAC grabbed even bigger headlines in 1948. With Republicans in charge of the committee, they launched a probe of Alger Hiss, a former State Department official in the Roosevelt administration who had accompanied the president to the Yalta Conference. The hearings resulted from charges brought by former Soviet spy Whittaker

Chambers that Hiss had passed him classified documents. Hiss denied the allegations, and President Truman dismissed them as a distraction. In fact, Democrats viewed the charges as a politically motivated attempt by Republicans to characterize the Roosevelt and Truman administrations as having been riddled with Communists.

The Democrats' concerns proved well founded. Following Truman's victory in the 1948 presidential election, first-term Republican congressman Richard M. Nixon kept the Hiss affair alive. A member of HUAC, Nixon went to Chambers's farm and discovered a cache of documents that Chambers had stored for safekeeping in a hollowed-out pumpkin. Armed with these "Pumpkin Papers," Nixon reopened the case. Hiss never wavered in maintaining his innocence, and the statute of limitations for espionage from the 1930s had expired. Nonetheless, the federal government had enough evidence to prosecute him for perjury. One trial produced a hung jury, but a second convicted Hiss; he was sentenced to five years in prison.

Hiss's downfall tarnished the Democrats, as Republicans charged them with being "soft on communism." It did not matter that Truman was a cold warrior who had advanced the doctrine of containment to stop Soviet expansionism or that he had instituted the federal loyalty program to purge Communists from government. In fact, in 1949 Truman tried to demonstrate his cold warrior credentials by authorizing the Justice Department to prosecute twelve high-ranking officials of the Communist Party for violating the Smith Act. In 1951 the Supreme Court upheld the conviction of the Communist leaders on the grounds that they posed a "clear and present danger" to the United States by advocating the violent overthrow of the government. Despite the presence of some 43,000 Communists, nearly all of them known to the FBI, out of a total population of 150 million and with no evidence of immediate danger, in *Dennis v. United States* the justices decided that "the gravity of the [Communist] evil" was enough to warrant conviction under the Smith Act.

In 1950 the Truman administration also prosecuted Julius and Ethel Rosenberg. Unlike the *Dennis* case, which involved political beliefs, the Rosenbergs were charged with espionage. When the Russians successfully tested an atomic bomb in 1949, anyone accused of helping them obtain this weapon became "Public Enemy Number One." The outbreak of the Korean War the following year, in which tens of thousands of soldiers died, made the Rosenbergs appear as conspirators to murder. After a lengthy trial in 1951, the couple received the death penalty, rather than a possible thirty-year sentence, undoubtedly because they refused to confess and because the trial took place during the war. The presiding judge, Irving Kaufman, admitted as much. In sentencing them to death, he told the Rosenbergs that their actions "caused . . . the Communist aggression in Korea, with the resultant casualties exceeding 50,000 and who knows what millions more innocent people may pay the price of your treason. Indeed, by your betrayal, you undoubtedly have altered the course of history to the disadvantage of our country."

By 1950 the anti-Communist crusade included Democrats and Republicans, liberals and conservatives. Liberals had the most to lose because conservatives could easily brand them as ideologically tainted. In his successful campaign to become a U.S. senator from California in 1950, Richard Nixon had accused his opponent, the liberal Democrat Helen Gahagan Douglas, of being "pink down to her underwear," not quite a Red but close enough. Liberal civil rights and civil liberties groups as well as labor unions were particularly vulnerable to such charges and rushed to rid their organizations of suspected Communists. Such efforts did nothing, however, to slow down conservative attacks. The conservative Republican chairman of HUAC, Harold Velde, linked the anti-Communist issue to traditional Republican fiscal policy in the slogan "Get the Reds out of Washington and Washington out of the red." In 1950 Republicans supported legislation proposed by Senator Pat McCarran, a conservative Democrat from Nevada, which

required Communist organizations to register with the federal government, established detention camps to incarcerate radicals during national emergencies, and denied passports to American citizens suspected of Communist affiliations. (As a result, singer Paul Robeson lost his right to travel abroad.) The severity of the entire measure proved too much for President Truman, and he vetoed it. Reflecting the bipartisan consensus on the issue, the Democratic-controlled Congress overrode the veto.

McCarthyism

Joseph Raymond McCarthy, a Republican senator from Wisconsin, did not create the phenomenon of postwar anticommunism, which was already in full swing from 1947 to 1950, but he served as its most public and feared voice from 1950 until 1954. Senator McCarthy used his position as the head of the Permanent Investigation Subcommittee of the Committee on Government Operations to harass current and former government officials and employees who, he claimed, collaborated with the Communist conspiracy. He had plenty of assistance from members of his own party who considered McCarthy a potent weapon in their battle to reclaim the White House. Robert A. Taft, the respected conservative Republican senator from Ohio, told McCarthy "to keep talking and if one case doesn't work [you] should proceed with another." The press also courted the young senator by giving his charges substantial coverage on the front pages of daily newspapers and then shifting the story to the back pages when McCarthy's claims turned out to be false. McCarthy bullied people, exaggerated his military service, drank too much, and did not pull his punches in making speeches—but he was not a maverick. He did seek publicity, but his anti-Communist tirades fit into mainstream Cold War politics.

Aware of the power of the Communists-in-government issue, McCarthy gave a speech in February 1950 at a Republican women's club in Wheeling, West Virginia. Waving sheets of paper in his hand, the senator announced that he had "the names of 205 men known to the Secretary of State as being members of the Communist Party and who nevertheless are still working and shaping the policy of the State Department," a claim that was based on old information. McCarthy cared more about the message than about the truth. As he continued campaigning for Republican congressional candidates across the country, he kept changing the number of alleged Communists in the government. When Senator Millard Tydings of Maryland, a Democrat who headed the Senate Foreign Relations Committee, launched an investigation of McCarthy's charges, he concluded that they were irresponsible and unfounded.

This finding did not stop McCarthy; if anything, it emboldened him to go further. He accused Tydings of being

Fighting Communism in the Movies

As part of a series of movies alerting audiences to the insidious dangers of communism, Hollywood produced *I Married a Communist* (1949). Although the story revolved around a shipping executive with a Communist past, the poster features a woman who uses her beauty to serve "a mob of terror" intent on destroying America.   Courtesy Everett Collection

"soft on communism" and campaigned against his reelection in 1952. Tydings's defeat in the election helped give McCarthy a reputation of political invincibility and scared off many critics from openly confronting him. McCarthy won reelection to the Senate, and when Republicans once again captured a majority in Congress, he became chair of the Permanent Investigations Subcommittee. Not only did he make false accusations and smear witnesses with anti-Communist allegations, but he also dispatched two aides to travel to Europe and purge what they considered disreputable books from the shelves of overseas libraries sponsored by the State Department.

McCarthy stood out among anti-Communists not for his beliefs but for his tactics. His name became synonymous with anticommunism as well as with manipulating the truth. At once jovial and sneering, McCarthy publicly hurled charges so astounding, especially coming from a U.S. senator, that people thought there must be something to them. He specialized in the "multiple untruth," a concoction of allegations so complex and convoluted that it was

impossible to refute them simply or quickly. By the time the accusations could be discredited, the damage was already done. The senator bullied and badgered witnesses, called them names, and if necessary furnished phony documents and doctored photographs linking them to known Communists.

In 1954 McCarthy finally went too far. After one of his aides got drafted and the army refused to give him a special commission, McCarthy accused the army of harboring Communists at Camp Kilmer and Fort Monmouth in New Jersey. To sort out these charges and to see whether the army had acted appropriately, McCarthy's own Senate subcommittee conducted an investigation, with the Wisconsin senator stepping down as chair. For two months, the relatively new medium of television broadcast live the army-McCarthy hearings, during which the cameras showed many viewers for the first time how reckless McCarthy had become. As his public approval declined, the Senate decided that it could no longer tolerate McCarthy's outrageous behavior and that he was making anticommunism look ridiculous at home and abroad. The famous television journalist Edward R. Murrow ran an unflattering documentary on McCarthy on his evening program on CBS, which further cast doubt on the senator's character and veracity. In December 1954, the Senate voted to censure McCarthy for conduct unbecoming a senator, having violated senatorial decorum by insulting colleagues who criticized him. McCarthy retained his seat on the subcommittee and all his Senate prerogatives, but he never again wielded substantial power. In 1957 he died from acute hepatitis, a disease related to alcoholism.

The anti-Communist consensus did not end with the execution of the Rosenbergs in 1953 or the censure of Joseph McCarthy in 1954 and his death three years later. Even J. Robert Oppenheimer, "the father of the atomic bomb" (see chapter 23), came under scrutiny. In 1954 the Atomic Energy Commission revoked Oppenheimer's security clearance for suspected, though unproven, Communist affiliations. That same year, Congress passed the Communist Control Act, which required "Communist infiltrated" groups to register with the federal government. Federal, state, and municipal governments required employees to take a loyalty oath affirming their allegiance to the United States and disavowing support for any organization that advocated the overthrow of the government. In addition, the blacklist continued in Hollywood throughout the rest of the decade. In the South, anticommunism actually flourished following the Senate's punishment of McCarthy. After the Supreme Court declared racial segregation in public schools unconstitutional in 1954, a number of southern states, including Florida and Louisiana, set up committees to investigate Communist influence in the civil rights movement. In a case concerning civil liberties, the Supreme Court still upheld HUAC's authority to investigate communism and to require witnesses who came before it to answer questions about their affiliations. Yet the Court did put a stop to the anti-Communist momentum. In 1957 the high court dealt a severe blow to enforcement of the Smith Act by ruling in *Yates v. United States* that the Justice Department could not prosecute someone for merely advocating an abstract doctrine favoring the violent overthrow of the government. In response, Congress tried, but failed, to limit the Supreme Court's jurisdiction in cases of this sort.

Even without the presence of Senator Joseph McCarthy, many Americans would have fallen victim to anti-Communist hysteria. J. Edgar Hoover and the FBI did more to fuel the second Red scare than did the Wisconsin senator. Hoover and his bureau did greater damage than McCarthy because they provided the information that Communist-hunters used throughout the government. The FBI was involved in criminal prosecutions in the *Dennis* and *Rosenberg* cases, supplied evidence to congressional committees and loyalty boards, and wiretapped suspected targets and used undercover agents to monitor and harass them. Historian Ellen Schrecker has suggested that because of the FBI's prominent role in the anti-Communist crusade we should call the attacks on suspected radicals during this period not **McCarthyism** but Hooverism.

REVIEW & RELATE

Why did fear of Communists in positions of influence escalate in the late 1940s and early 1950s?

Why was McCarthyism much more powerful than Joseph McCarthy?

✔ *LEARNINGCurve* **bedfordstmartins.com/hewittlawson/LC**

Conclusion: The Cold War and Anticommunism

Anticommunism remained a potent weapon in political affairs as long as the Cold War operated in full force. When George Kennan designed the doctrine of containment in 1946 and 1947, he had no idea that it would lead to permanent military alliances such as NATO or to a war in Korea. He viewed the Soviet Union as an unflinching ideological enemy, but he believed that it should be contained through economic rather than military means, along the lines of the Marshall Plan. When the Korean War ended in 1953, the Truman administration had already put into operation around the world the heightened military plans called for by NSC-68. Hard-line Cold War rhetoric portrayed the struggle as a battle between good and evil, summed up in the phrase "I'd rather be dead than Red." Casting the conflict in apocalyptic terms did little justice to the nature of its origins. Born out of different perceptions of national interests and mutual misunderstandings of the other side's actions, the Cold War became frozen in the language of competing moralistic assumptions and self-righteousness. Within this context, though some Americans rallied to obtain clemency for the Rosenbergs, most considered that they got just what they deserved.

The Cold War remained the backdrop for life during the 1950s. Americans accepted it and took it for granted as part of the hazard of modern everyday life. Occasionally, overseas crises riveted their attention on the perilous possibilities of atomic brinksmanship with the Soviets, but for the most part Americans focused their attention on pursuing their economic dreams and raising their families. They could not avoid the Cold War, but they would try to work around it.

Robeson's declaration of faith in socialism as a cure for racism, was a rocket that lit up the sky.

On a lucky afternoon I happened upon *The Devil in Massachusetts*, by Marion Starkey, a narrative of the Salem witch-hunt of 1692. I knew this story from my college reading, but in this darkened America it turned a completely new aspect toward me: the poetry of the hunt. Poetry may seem an odd word for a witch-hunt but I saw there was something of the marvelous in the spectacle of a whole village, if not an entire province, whose imagination was captured by a vision of something that wasn't there.

In time to come, the notion of equating the red-hunt with the witch-hunt would be condemned as a deception. There were communists and there never were witches. The deeper I moved into the 1690s, the further away drifted the America of the 50s, and, rather than the appeal of analogy, I found something different to draw my curiosity and excitement.

Anyone standing up in the Salem of 1692 and denying that witches existed would have faced immediate arrest, the hardest interrogation, and possibly the rope. Every authority not only confirmed the existence of witches but never questioned the necessity of executing them. It became obvious that to dismiss witchcraft was to forgo any understanding of how it came to pass that tens of thousands had been murdered as witches in Europe. To dismiss any relation between that episode and the hunt for subversives was to shut down an insight into not only the similar emotions but also the identical practices of both officials and victims. . . .

. . . Part of the surreality of the anti-left sweep was that it picked up people for disgrace who had already turned away from a pro-Soviet past but had no stomach for naming others who had merely shared their illusions. But the hunt had captured some significant part of the American imagination and its power demanded respect.

Source: Arthur Miller, "Are You Now or Were You Ever?," *The Guardian/The Observer* (online), June 17, 2000.

Interpret the Evidence

1. According to Ronald Reagan (Document 24.6), what threats did communism pose to American society? Why was Communist influence in entertainment seen as particularly dangerous? How should the Communist threat be handled?

2. How did the Herblock cartoon (Document 24.8) connect anti-Communist hysteria to the extinguishing of constitutional rights? Why did he see McCarthyism as a threat to American society?

3. Compare the testimonies of John Howard Lawson and Lillian Hellman (Documents 24.7 and 24.9). What were their chief objections to testifying before HUAC?

4. In what ways does Arthur Miller criticize both the right and the left (Document 24.10)?

5. In what different ways would HUAC and the witnesses appearing before it have defined "Un-American"? What gave HUAC so much power in the 1940s and 1950s?

Put It in Context

- Compare the Red scare following World War I with McCarthyism.

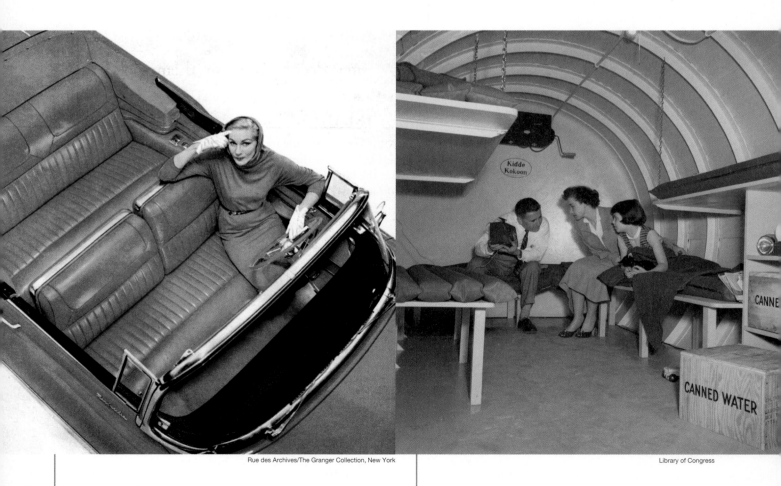

Rue des Archives/The Granger Collection, New York

Library of Congress

Buick advertisement, 1955.

Backyard bomb shelter, Garden City, New York, 1955.

25
Troubled Innocence
1950–1961

ullstein bild/The Granger Collection, New York

Teenage girl practicing with a hula hoop, 1958.

AMERICAN HISTORIES

Alan Freed shook up American youth culture in the 1950s by rebranding existing black music and making it popular with white teenagers. *Rock 'n' roll* was a slang term among African Americans for sexual intercourse, but Freed turned it into an expression of musical rebellion. In 1951, at the age of twenty-nine, Aldon (Alan) James Freed was spinning records as a disc jockey, or "deejay," at a Cleveland, Ohio, radio station. He started out playing classical music but switched to rhythm and blues, an African American music style considered "race music." Freed began calling himself Moondog, howling like a dog, and using sound effects to rattle his radio listeners. Although he initially appealed mainly to a black audience, Freed's radio show and live concerts of music he dubbed rock 'n' roll soon attracted white teenagers.

In 1954 Freed moved to New York City radio station WINS, where his evening rock 'n' roll broadcast became a number one hit. Three years later at the height of his popularity, he hosted a nationally televised rock 'n' roll program, but only briefly. The American Broadcasting Company canceled Freed's show after four telecasts because of outrage from affiliate stations in the South after the black singer Frankie Lymon was shown dancing with a white girl.

The television incident was only the start of Freed's professional problems. In 1960 Freed was brought before a congressional committee investigating "payola," a common practice among deejays of receiving gifts from record companies in exchange for playing their records. His career sank further when Freed was indicted in 1962 for commercial

**Alan Freed
and Grace Metalious**

bribery by New York State. He was found guilty, was fined $300, and received a six-month suspended jail sentence. Freed never regained his earlier stature. Impoverished and struggling with alcoholism, Freed died in 1965 at the age of forty-three.

Like Alan Freed, Grace Metalious sent shock waves through American popular culture in the 1950s. Metalious grew up in poverty in a small mill town in southern New Hampshire. In 1943, while still a teenager, she married George Metalious and became a mother and housewife. In 1956 Metalious published her first novel, *Peyton Place*. Based on her hometown, the book sold more than three million copies the first year and unsettled the literary world. Considered provocative and racy because of its discussion of sex, rape, and incest, the novel punctured myths about the straitlaced life of small-town America. It criticized small-minded conformity that enforced a double standard of sexual behavior on women.

Despite the book's popularity, which inspired a toned-down Hollywood film and a television series, Metalious was never seen as a serious writer. Detractors described her as an untalented author who disseminated filth. In response to such allegations, she countered, "If I'm a lousy writer, then an awful lot of people have lousy taste." Metalious could not reconcile her success with the criticism she received and, like Alan Freed, increasingly turned to alcohol for comfort. She wrote other novels, but they never achieved the success that *Peyton Place* had. In 1964, a year before Freed's death and just eight years after publication of *Peyton Place*, she died at age thirty-nine of cirrhosis of the liver. Both Metalious and Freed challenged notions of conventional taste, and both found their lives upended by the conservative backlash their work inspired.

photos: Michael Ochs Archives/Getty Images; Courtesy Everett Collection

RONICALLY, THE AMERICAN HISTORIES of Alan Freed and Grace Metalious, both of whom attacked conformity, were made possible by the emergence of a mass-consumption economy fueled by technological innovation. The production of inexpensive paperback books enabled *Peyton Place* to reach a broad market. The development of low-cost records made rock 'n' roll songs widely available, and the creation of handheld transistor radios allowed teenagers to listen to music—played by deejays like Alan Freed—away from their parents' supervision. Young people were not the only ones to challenge their parents' culture. Writers and musicians experimented with freer forms of artistic expression and attacked the conformity they associated with mainstream America. African Americans challenged racial segregation directly in the Supreme Court and through powerful community protests. The Cold War remained the chief feature of foreign affairs and, despite wide-ranging

prosperity, continued to generate fears for the safety and security of all Americans.

The Boom Years

The notoriety of Grace Metalious and Alan Freed came at a time of renewed economic growth and prosperity in the United States. With more disposable income than they had enjoyed in decades, American consumers responded enthusiastically to the wide range of products that advertisers promised would make their lives easier and more enjoyable. The search for the good life propelled middle-class families from cities to the suburbs. At the same time, a postwar baby boom added millions of children to the population and created a market to supply them with goods from their infancy and childhood to their teenage years.

Economic Boom

The United States emerged from World War II in strong financial shape. The gross national product (GNP) soared 250 percent between 1945 and 1960, and per capita income (total income divided by the population) grew 35 percent. During this fifteen-year period, the average real income (actual purchasing power) for American workers increased by as much as it had during the fifty years preceding World War II. Equally striking, 60 percent of Americans achieved middle-class status, and the number of salaried office workers rose 61 percent. Factory workers also experienced gains. Union membership leaped to the highest level in U.S. history, reaching nearly 17 million. In the mid-1950s, the American Federation of Labor (AFL) and the Congress of Industrial Organizations (CIO) merged to increase labor union bargaining power, and the new AFL-CIO concentrated on improving its members' income.

The affluence of the 1950s was much more equally distributed than the prosperity of the 1920s had been. As the middle class grew, the top 5 percent of wealthy families dropped in the percentage of total income they earned from 21.3 percent to 19 percent. Though poverty remained a persistent problem, the rate of poverty decreased, falling from 34 percent in 1947 to 22.1 percent in 1960 (Figure 25.1). A college education served as a critical marker of entry into the middle class. Traditionally, colleges and universities had been accessible only to the upper class. That began to change in the postwar era. Between 1940 and 1960, the number of high school students who went on to college more than doubled, with the percentage of Americans who went to college vastly exceeding that of the British and the French.

In addition to purchasing paperbacks, transistor radios, and rock 'n' roll records, consumers bought televisions. TV sets became a household staple in the 1950s, and by 1960, 87 percent of Americans owned a television. Americans also continued to purchase automobiles—75 percent owned a car, most likely one produced by General Motors, Ford, or Chrysler. With gas supplies plentiful and the price per gallon less than 30 cents, automakers concentrated on size, power, and style to compete for buyers. With more cars on the road, motels built by chains such as Holiday Inn sprang up along the highways. Fast-food establishments proliferated to feed motorists

and their families. McDonald's hamburger restaurants, which first appeared in 1940 in San Bernardino, California, became the prototypical franchise chain for roadside fast food.

Baby Boom

In 1955 Illinois governor Adlai Stevenson told the graduating class of women at Smith College that they could do their part to maintain a free society as wives and mothers. Educated women had an important role to play in maintaining a household that boosted their husband's morale. "It is home work," Stevenson declared. "You can do it in the living-room with a baby in your lap or in the kitchen with a can opener in your hand . . . while you're watching television!" The mothers of these college graduates had suffered through the Great Depression, a time when the birthrate was 40 percent lower than in the 1950s. This was soon about to change.

In the 1950s, the average age at marriage was younger than it had been in the 1930s. On average, men married for

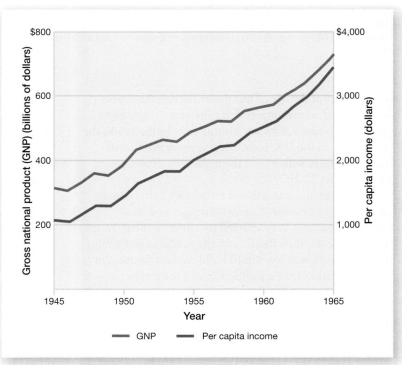

FIGURE 25.1   Economic Growth, 1945–1965

As industries shifted from war equipment to consumer goods, productivity remained high. More Americans entered the middle class in the two decades following World War II, while rising union membership ensured higher incomes for the working class. As a result, the purchasing power of most Americans increased in the immediate postwar period.

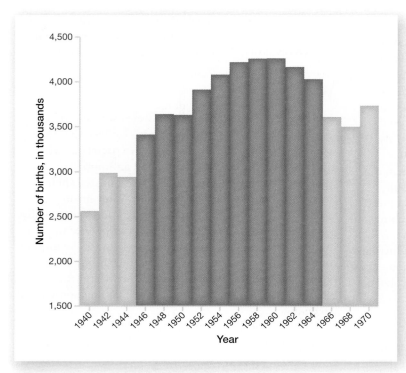

FIGURE 25.2 The Baby Boom, 1946–1964
The U.S. population increased dramatically in the postwar decades. Economic prosperity made it easier to support large families, women's early age at marriage contributed to high fertility, and improved health care led to the survival of more children.

the first time at the age of just under twenty-three, and 49 percent of women married at nineteen. Couples also produced children at an astonishing rate. In the 1950s, the growth rate in the U.S. population approached that of India, a country with one of the highest birthrates in the world (Figure 25.2).

Marriage and parenthood reflected a culture that increasingly emphasized early marriages and large families. The Cold War spurred this development. In the Atomic Age, public officials and the media urged young American men and women to build nuclear families in which the father held a paying job and the mother stayed at home and raised her growing family. Doing so would strengthen the moral fiber of the United States in its battle to contain Soviet communism. Religious leaders echoed this message. "The family that prays together stays together" became a popular refrain and served as an inducement to encourage marital fertility alongside spiritual fidelity.

Parents could also look forward to their children surviving childhood diseases that had resulted in many childhood deaths in the past. In the 1950s, children received

vaccinations against diphtheria, whooping cough, and tuberculosis before they entered school. The most serious illness affecting young children remained the crippling disease of polio, or infantile paralysis. Each year, usually around summertime, parents and children feared a renewed outbreak of the polio virus, which they believed was spread through contact at crowded swimming pools and beaches. An outbreak of polio in 1952 and 1953 infected 93,000 people nationwide. In 1955 Dr. Jonas Salk developed a successful injectable vaccine against the disease. On April 12, 1955, news bulletins interrupted scheduled television programs to announce Salk's breakthrough, and, as one writer recalled, "citizens rushed to ring church bells and fire sirens, shouted, clapped, sang, and made every kind of joyous noise they could." Dr. Albert Sabin later developed a more convenient oral vaccine, and by the mid-1960s polio was no longer a public health menace in the United States.

Suburban Boom

In 1948 real estate developer William Levitt remarked: "No man who owns his own house and lot can be a Communist. He has too much to do." Levitt did not invent the suburbs, but he promoted them as no one before him had. The economic and demographic booms encouraged migration out of the cities so that growing families could have their own homes, greater space, and a healthier environment. By 1960 nearly 60 million people, one-third of the nation's population, lived in suburbs. Residential communities outside New York City drew some 1.5 million people, and around Los Angeles the population tripled in size.

No section of the nation expanded faster than the West and the South. Attracted by the mild climate and jobs in the defense, petroleum, and chemical industries, transplanted Americans swelled the populations of California and Texas. The proliferation of air-conditioning in residences and businesses made the hot summer temperatures of these and other southern states more livable. California's population increased the most, adding nearly six million new residents between 1940 and 1960. In 1957, in a sign of the times, New York City lost two of its baseball teams, the New York Giants and the Brooklyn Dodgers, to San Francisco and Los Angeles. Retirees also flocked to California, and many others headed to Florida and Arizona. In Miami alone, the population jumped around 80 percent in the three decades after World War II. This migration to the **Sun Belt**, as the southern and western states would be called, transformed the political and social landscapes of the nation.

The extraordinary housing demand following World War II drove the suburban boom. The available housing stock could not accommodate returning veterans who married and started families. Many sought escape from crowded cities and a chance to achieve a piece of the American dream: a home with a front lawn, a backyard, and plenty of fresh air. To meet this demand, private enterprise and the federal government provided veterans and civilians opportunities to purchase their own homes.

William Levitt, a thirty-eight-year-old veteran from Long Island, New York, devised the formula for attracting home buyers to the suburbs. After World War II, Levitt, his father, and his brother saw their opportunity in the housing crunch and pioneered the idea of adapting Henry Ford's mass-production principles to the housing industry. To build his subdivision of **Levittown** in Hempstead, Long Island, twenty miles from Manhattan, he bulldozed 4,000 acres of potato fields and brought in trucks that dumped piles of building materials at exact intervals of sixty feet. Specialized crews then moved from pile to pile, each performing their assigned job. In July 1948, Levitt's workers constructed 180 houses a week, or 36 a day, in two shifts. These simple houses, placed on 60-by-100-foot lots, contained a living room, a kitchen, two bedrooms, and one bathroom. Levitt originally sold the homes for an affordable $7,990 and threw in a free television and washing machine. Mass-production methods kept prices low, and Levitt quickly sold his initial 17,000 houses and soon built other subdivisions in Pennsylvania and New Jersey. With Levitt leading the way, the production of new single-family homes nearly doubled from 937,000 in 1946 to 1.7 million in 1950.

Levitt and his fellow builders received a good deal of public help in making suburbia possible. The Federal Housing Administration, created in the 1930s, provided long-term mortgages to qualified buyers at low interest rates. After the war, the Veterans Administration offered even lower mortgage rates and did not require substantial down payments for ex-GIs to purchase a home. The federal government also cooperated by building roads that allowed drivers to commute to and from the suburbs. In 1956 the **National Interstate and Defense Highway Act** provided funds for the construction of 42,500 miles of roads throughout the country. In fashioning this policy of highway construction, Congress gave a tremendous boost not only to the development of the suburbs but also to the automobile industry. Between 1945 and 1960, the number of cars in the United States more than doubled. For many families living in suburban housing tracts, purchasing a second car became a necessity as husbands traveled by automobile to nearby cities and wives drove cars to go on errands and chauffeur their children to after-school activities.

Although millions of Americans took advantage of opportunities to move to the suburbs, millions of others could not. Levitt closed his subdivisions to African Americans. Many whites moved out of the cities because they did not want to live near the growing number of southern blacks who migrated north during World War II and the influx of Puerto Ricans who came to the United States after the war, and they did not welcome these minorities to their new communities. Levitt defended his racist exclusionary policy on business rather than on racial grounds. "I have come to know," he declared, "that if we sell one house to a Negro family, then 90 or 95 percent of our white customers will not buy into the community." Levitt was not alone in his discriminatory practices. Residents of many communities in the North purchased homes with restrictive covenants, which prohibited resale to blacks and members of other minority groups, including Hispanics, Jews, and Asian Americans. Although the Supreme Court outlawed restrictive covenants in *Shelley v. Kraemer* (1948), housing discrimination remained prevalent in urban and suburban neighborhoods. Real estate brokers steered minority buyers away from white communities, and banks refused to lend money to black purchasers who sought to move into white locales, an illegal policy called redlining.

Explore

See Documents 25.1 and 25.2 for two glimpses of 1950s suburban life.

REVIEW & RELATE

What factors contributed to the economic and population growth of the 1950s?

How did economic and demographic trends in the 1950s contribute to the growth of suburbs?

LEARNINGCurve bedfordstmartins.com/hewittlawson/LC

DOCUMENTS 25.1 AND 25.2

Living the Suburban Dream: Two Views

The postwar suburban boom eased housing shortages and gave millions the benefits of home ownership. In the 1950s, William Levitt built low-cost homes in the suburbs of New York City and Philadelphia. The following publicity photo for Levittown, Pennsylvania, just northeast of Philadelphia, is targeted at blue-collar workers. However, suburban developments largely excluded African Americans and other minorities. The restrictive covenant reprinted here is from Innis Arden, a suburban development created by the aircraft manufacturer William E. Boeing outside of Seattle, Washington. This restriction, written in 1941, remained in effect for several decades.

Explore

25.1 Levittown Advertisement, 1950s

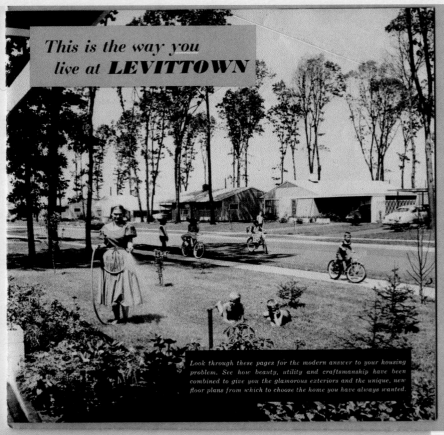

Courtesy of The State Museum of Pennsylvania, Pennsylvania Historical and Museum Commission

The Culture of the 1950s

In the 1950s, popular culture developed as the United States confronted difficult political, diplomatic, and social issues. Amid this turmoil, television played a large role in shaping people's lives, reflecting their desire for success, and depicting the era as a time of innocence. The rise of teenage culture as a powerful economic force also influenced this portrayal of the 1950s. Teenage tastes, including rock 'n' roll, and consumption patterns reinforced the impression of a simpler and more carefree time. Religion painted a similar picture, as attendance at houses of worship rose. Still, the decade held a more complex social reality. Cultural rebels—writers, actors, and musicians—emerged to challenge mainstream values. Even women did not always act the suburban parts that television and society assigned them, and religion seemed

25.2 Restrictive Covenant for Innis Arden, Seattle, 1941

RACIAL RESTRICTIONS. No property in said addition shall at any time be sold, conveyed, rented, or leased in whole or in part to any person or persons not of the White or Caucasian race. No person other than one of the White or Caucasian race shall be permitted to occupy any property in said addition or portion thereof or building thereon except a domestic servant actually employed by a person of the White or Caucasian race where the latter is an occupant of such property.

ANIMALS. No hogs, cattle, horses, sheep, goats, or similar livestock shall be permitted or maintained on said property at any time. Chicken hens, pigeons, rabbits, and other similar small livestock not exceeding a total of twenty-five in number, shall be permitted but must be kept on the premises of the owner. Not more than one dog and cat may be kept for each building site.

Source: "Segregated Seattle," Seattle Civil Rights and Labor History Project, http://depts.washington.edu/civilr/segregated.htm.

Interpret the Evidence
- According to the advertisement, what would life in Levittown be like for potential buyers?
- Under what circumstances were nonwhites allowed to live in Innis Arden?

Put It in Context
How do these contrasting impressions of suburban life reflect home-purchasing opportunities in the 1950s?

to serve more of a communal, social function than an individual, spiritual one.

The Rise of Television

Few postwar developments had a greater impact on American society and politics than the advent of television. The first commercial TV broadcast occurred in 1939, but television sets did not become widely available until after World War II. The three major television networks—the Columbia Broadcasting System (CBS), the National Broadcasting Company (NBC), and the American Broadcasting Company (ABC)—offered programs nationwide that appealed to mainstream tastes while occasionally challenging the public with serious drama, music, and documentaries. During the 1950s, congressional investigations became a staple of television, and none provided a better morality tale than

Family Television Time

In the 1950s, television became an important part of family leisure. Families watched television in black and white, without a remote control, and could tune in to only a handful of channels. Some programs appealed only to children, others to adults, and some, like the western shown on the screen here, to the entire family.   © ClassicStock.com/SuperStock

coverage of the army-McCarthy hearings in 1954 (see chapter 24). In the same manner, television networks began to feature intense presidential campaign coverage, from the national nominating conventions to election day vote tallies, and political advertisements began to fill the airwaves.

If many Americans recall the 1950s as a time of innocence, they have in mind television shows aimed at children, such as *Howdy Doody*, *Superman*, *Hopalong Cassidy*, *The Cisco Kid*, and *The Lone Ranger*. In the course of a half hour, the casts performed in shows that pitted good versus evil and in which honesty and decency triumphed. These youth-oriented television programs showcased a simple world of moral absolutes.

In similar fashion, adults enjoyed evening television shows that depicted old-fashioned families entertaining themselves, mediating quarrels sensibly and peacefully, and relying on the wisdom of parents. In *The Adventures of Ozzie and Harriet*, the Nelsons raised two clean-cut sons. In *Father Knows Best*, the Andersons—

a father and mother and their three children—lived a tranquil life in the suburbs, and the father solved whatever dilemmas arose. The same held true for the Cleaver family on *Leave It to Beaver*. In *I Love Lucy*, the show's namesake, played by Lucille Ball, and her female sidekick tried to outwit their husbands on a weekly basis. Despite the focus on the women and the sympathy they engendered, men usually won this battle of the sexes. Television portrayed working-class families in grittier fashion on shows such as *The Life of Riley*, whose lead character worked at a factory, and *The Honeymooners*, whose male protagonists were a bus driver and a sewer worker. Nevertheless, like their middle-class counterparts, these families stayed together and worked out their problems despite their more challenging financial circumstances.

By contrast, African American families received little attention on television. Black female actors usually appeared as maids, and the one show that featured an all-black cast, *The Amos 'n' Andy Show*, generally portrayed African

Americans according to the racial stereotypes of the period. American Indians faced similar difficulties. Few appeared on television, and those who did served mainly as targets for "heroic" cowboys defending the West from "savage" Indians. When Indians did appear, white actors often played them. There were exceptions. Tonto, the Lone Ranger's sidekick, was played by Jay Silverheels, a Canadian Mohawk; he offered a sympathetic character, mainly because he grunted his approval and showed his loyalty to his *kimosabe* (trusty scout). With the notable exception of Cuban American musician Desi Arnaz (Lucille Ball's husband and her costar in *I Love Lucy*), minorities such as Latinos, Native Americans, and Asians rarely appeared in television series.

Wild Ones on the Big Screen

If young people in the 1950s were expected to behave like Ozzie and Harriet Nelson's sons, Ricky and David, or the Cleaver boys, the popular culture industry also provided teenagers with alternative role models. Hollywood films offered several. In *Rebel without a Cause* (1955), actor James Dean portrayed Jim Stark, a seventeen-year-old filled with anguish about his role in life. A sensitive but misunderstood young man, Stark muses that he wants "just one day when I wasn't all confused . . . [when] I wasn't ashamed of everything . . . [when] I felt I belonged some place." After making only three films, Dean died in a car crash, further enhancing his mystique among young people. *The Wild One* (1954), which starred Marlon Brando as Johnny Strabler, also popularized youthful angst. Strabler, the leather-outfitted leader of a motorcycle gang, rides into a small town, hoping to shake it up. When asked by a local resident, "What are you rebelling against?" Strabler coolly replies, "Whaddya got?" Real gangs did exist on the streets of New York and other major cities. Composed of working-class members from various ethnic and racial backgrounds, these gangs were highly organized, controlled their neighborhood turfs, and engaged in "rumbles" (fights) with intruders. These battles came to Broadway with the production of *West Side Story* (1957), which pitted a white gang against a Puerto Rican gang in a musical version of *Romeo and Juliet*; its popularity later spawned a Hollywood film.

Hollywood generally did not portray women as rebels; rather they appeared as mothers, understanding girlfriends, and dutiful wives. If they sought a career, like many of the women played by actor Doris Day, they pursued it only as long as necessary to meet the right man. Yet the film industry did offer a more tantalizing woman, a sexual being who displayed her attributes, albeit in decorous fashion, to seduce and outwit men. Marilyn Monroe played such a woman in *The Seven Year Itch* (1955), as did Elizabeth Taylor in *Cat on a Hot Tin Roof* (1958), revealing that women also had a powerful libido, though in the end they became domesticated or paid a terrible price.

The Influence of Teenage Culture

In 1941 *Popular Science* magazine coined the term *teenager*, and by the middle of the next decade members of this age group viewed themselves not as prospective adults but as a distinct group with its own identity, patterns of behavior, and tastes in music and fashion. Postwar prosperity provided teenagers with money to support their own choices and styles. In 1956 teenage boys were estimated to have a weekly income from family allowances or part-time jobs of $8.96 a week, up from $2.41 in 1944. Four years later, *Seventeen* magazine surveyed teenage girls and reported that they earned $9.53 a week. In 1959 *Life* magazine found that teenagers had $10 billion at their disposal, "a billion more than the total sales of GM [General Motors]." **See Document Project 25: Teenagers in Postwar America, page 815.**

Teenagers owned 10 million record players, more than 1 million TV sets, 13 million cameras, and what *Life* called "a fantastic array of garish and often expensive baubles and amusements." They spent 16 percent of their disposable income on entertainment, particularly the purchase of rock 'n' roll records. The comic book industry also attracted a huge audience among teenagers by selling inexpensive, illustrated, brief, and easy-to-read pulp fiction geared toward romance and action adventure.

Public high schools reinforced teenage identity. Following World War II, high school attendance grew. In 1930, 50 percent of working-class children attended high school; thirty years later, the figure had jumped to 90 percent. Also, from 1940 to 1960, the percentage of black youths attending high school doubled. For the first time, white middle-class teenagers saw the fashions and heard the language of working-class youths close-up and both emulated and feared what they encountered. Their parents told them to avoid young people who smoked cigarettes, dressed in blue jeans, wore leather jackets, and used expressions like "man" and "cat" to address each other, and to keep away from young women who wore tight skirts and sweaters. Nobody wanted to run afoul of such students in school bathrooms or on the playgrounds, but their clothes, hairdos, and swagger appealed to high school teenagers, many of whom incorporated them into their own behavior.

More than anything else, rock 'n' roll music set teenagers apart from their elders. The pop singers of the 1940s and early 1950s—such as Frank Sinatra, Perry Como, Rosemary Clooney, and Patti Page, who had appealed to both adolescents and parents—lost much of their teenage audience after 1954 to rock 'n' roll, with its heavy downbeat and lyrics evoking teenage passion and sexuality. Black artists such as Chuck Berry, Little Richard, and Antoine "Fats" Domino and groups such as the Platters, the Channels, the Chords, the Chantels, and the Teenagers popularized the sound of classic, up-tempo rock and its soaring, harmonic variation known as doo-wop.

Although blacks pioneered the sound, the music entered the mainstream largely through white artists who added rural flavor to rhythm and blues. Elvis Presley was not the first white man to sing rock 'n' roll, but he became the most famous. Born in Tupelo, Mississippi, and living in Memphis, Tennessee, Elvis adapted the fashion and sensuality of the black performers he encountered to his own style. Elvis's snarling singing and wild pelvic gyrations excited young people, both black and white, while upsetting their parents. In an era when matters of sex remained private or were not discussed at all and when African Americans were still treated as second-class citizens, a

white man singing "black" music and shaking his body to the frenetic tempo of the music caused alarm. When Elvis sang on the popular *Ed Sullivan Show* in 1956, cameras were allowed to show him only from the waist up to uphold standards of decency. Four years later while Elvis was in the army, Congress targeted rock 'n' roll through its investigation of payola and the notorious deejay Alan Freed.

The Lives of Women

Throughout the 1950s, movies, women's magazines, mainstream newspapers, and medical and psychological experts informed women that only by embracing domesticity could they achieve personal fulfillment. Dr. Benjamin Spock's best-selling *Common Sense Book of Baby and Child Care* (1946) advised mothers that their children would reach their full potential only if wives stayed at home and watched over their offspring. In another best seller, *Modern Women: The Lost Sex* (1947), Ferdinand

Women in the Home and in the Workplace

In the 1950s, married women were encouraged to stay at home. Modern appliances like this refrigerator (right) supposedly made housework less difficult, but wives had to spend a great deal of time keeping it fully stocked and attending to other household chores. With all the new devices at their disposal, wives were expected to keep the home neat and spotless, while caring for their children. But not all married women stayed at home and tended the family. Senator Margaret Chase Smith (above) was an influential Republican senator from Maine who took on Senator Joseph McCarthy in Congress and challenged his harsh anti-Communist methods. Here she is engaged in serious deliberations with Democratic Majority Leader Lyndon B. Johnson at a Senate hearing in 1957. above: Time & Life Pictures/Getty Images; right: Hulton/Archive/Getty Images

Lundberg and Marynia Farnham called the independent woman "a contradiction in terms." A 1951 study of corporate executives found that most businessmen viewed the ideal wife as one who devoted herself to her husband's career. College newspapers described female undergraduates as distraught if they did not become engaged by their senior year. Certainly many women professed to find such lives fulfilling, but not all women were so content. Many experienced anxiety and depression, and, in their despair, some turned to alcohol and tranquilizers. Far from satisfied, these women suffered from what the social critic Betty Friedan would later call "a problem that has no name," a malady that derived not from any personal failing but from the unrewarding roles women were expected to play.

Not all women fit the stereotype, however. Although most married women with families did not work during the 1950s, the proportion of working wives doubled from 15 percent in 1940 to 30 percent in 1960, with the greatest increase coming in women over the age of thirty-five. Married women were more likely to work if they were African American or came from working-class immigrant families. Moreover, women's magazines did not offer readers a unified message of domesticity. Alongside articles about and advertisements directed at stay-at-home mothers, these periodicals profiled career women who served in politics, such as Maine senator Margaret Chase Smith, the African American educator Mary McLeod Bethune, and sports figures such as the golf and tennis great Babe (Mildred) Didrikson Zaharias. At the same time, working women played significant roles in labor unions, where they formulated plans to reduce disparities between men's and women's income and to provide a wage for housewives, recognizing the unpaid work they did at home in maintaining the family. Many other women joined women's clubs and organizations like the Young Women's Christian Association (YWCA), where they engaged in charitable and public service activities. Some participated in political organizations, such as Henry Wallace's Progressive Party, and peace groups, such as the Women's International League for Peace and Freedom, to campaign against the violence caused by racial discrimination at home and Cold War rivalries abroad.

Religious Revival

Along with marriage and the family, religion experienced a revival in the postwar United States. The arms race between the United States and the Soviet Union heightened the dangers of international conflict for ordinary citizens, and the social and economic changes that accompanied the Cold War intensified personal anxiety. Churchgoing underscored the contrast between the United States, a nation of religious worship, and the "godless" communism of the Soviet Union. The link between religion and Americanism prompted Congress in 1954 to add "under God" to the pledge of allegiance and to make "In God We Trust" the national motto. Even President Dwight D. Eisenhower joined a church for the first time in his life.

Americans turned in great numbers to religious worship. Between 1940 and 1950, church and synagogue membership rose by 78 percent, and more than 95 percent of the population professed a belief in God. Yet religious affiliation appeared to reflect a greater emphasis on togetherness than on specific doctrinal beliefs. Theologian Will Herberg wrote that this religious revival constituted "religiousness without religion." It offered a way to overcome isolation and embrace community in an increasingly alienating world. "The people in the suburbs want to feel psychologically secure, adjusted, at home in their environment," Herberg explained. "Being religious and joining a church is . . . a fundamental way of 'adjusting' and 'belonging.'"

Television also helped spread religiosity into millions of homes. The Catholic bishop Fulton J. Sheen spoke to a weekly television audience of ten million and alternated his message of "a life worth living" with attacks on atheistic Communists. The Methodist minister Norman Vincent Peale, also a popular TV figure, combined traditional religious faith with self-help remedies prescribed in his best-selling book *The Power of Positive Thinking* (1952). The Reverend Billy Graham, a preacher from Charlotte, North Carolina, who became the greatest evangelist of his era, was a traveling minister who blended his call for Americans to accept Jesus Christ into their hearts with fervent anticommunism. Graham used his considerable oratorical powers to preach at huge outdoor crusades in baseball parks and large arenas, which were broadcast on television. Religious Americans derived a variety of meanings from their religious experiences, but they embraced Americanism as their national religion. A good American, one magazine proclaimed, could not be "un-religious."

Explore

See Document 25.3 for Billy Graham's interpretation of America's problems in the 1950s.

DOCUMENT 25.3

Billy Graham | What's Wrong with Our World? 1958

Billy Graham, the most famous preacher of his generation, began speaking to packed auditoriums in the late 1940s. Known for his huge revival-style meetings, or crusades, Graham used mass media to reach national and international audiences through radio programs, television specials, movies, and newspaper columns. This excerpt from a 1958 speech shows Graham as a social critic. He laments Americans' unhappiness despite their high standard of living, and he locates the problem in personal sin rather than in economic and political institutions.

Explore

As a nation, as a human race, what's wrong with our world? . . . Our crime rate is increasing in city after city across the nation.

What causes those problems? What is back of it? Why cannot we solve our problems?

We in America have the highest standard of living in the world.

We are a prosperous nation. We have educational advantages. We have everything, and yet something is wrong.

We are not a happy people.

We have more boredom per square inch in this country than any country in the world.

Our divorce rate is the highest, indicating our homes are basically unhappy. . . .

We're facing problems within ourselves. Many people today are searching for happiness. They're searching for peace of mind. They're searching for joy, and they're not finding it. They've tried money, they've tried other things in life, but they haven't been able to find the peace, the relaxation, the joy, that they want.

What's wrong? What's happened? What's wrong with Man? What's wrong with the world in which we live?

I believe that the "United Nations" is doing the best it can, but I believe the "United Nations" is only dealing with symptoms of something deeper that is wrong with the world.

. . . I think all over the world men want peace, but somehow peace doesn't come.

We put out a fire in the Middle East and it breaks out again in the Far East. We put it out in the Far East and it breaks out again somewhere else. And it seems we're jumping from fire to fire. We're trying to solve the problems of the world but we make the mistake of treating symptoms!

The race problem is a symptom. War is a symptom. Crime is a symptom. The sociological problem is a symptom. Something deeper is wrong. . . .

What is the cause? The Bible has an answer. Jesus had an answer. Jesus said, "All these evil things come from within" and they devour the individual and they devour the society.

The Bible teaches that something is wrong with human nature. Something is wrong with Man himself. What is that something?

The Bible says that man has a disease and that disease is called S-I-N—"sin."

Now, ladies and gentlemen, that is what is wrong with the world tonight.

Source: Billy Graham, "What's Wrong with Our World?," *The Charlotte Observer*, September 28, 1958, 10.

Interpret the Evidence

• Why does Graham believe that Americans are unhappy?

• How does Graham's belief that "human nature" is the cause of the problem limit the solutions he might recommend?

Put It in Context

Why might Graham's message about personal sin as the source of war and social tensions have appealed to his audience during the 1950s?

Beats and Other Nonconformists

As many Americans migrated to the suburbs, spent money on leisure and entertainment, and cultivated religion, a small group of young poets, writers, intellectuals, musicians, and artists attacked mainstream politics and culture. Known as **beats** (derived from "beaten down"), they attacked white middle-class society with stinging critiques of what they considered the sterility and conformity of American life. In 1956 Allen Ginsberg began his epic poem *Howl* with the line "I saw the best minds of my generation destroyed by madness, starving hysterical naked." In his novel *On the Road* (1957), Jack Kerouac, a friend of Ginsberg's, praised the individual who pursued authentic experiences and mind-expanding consciousness through drugs, sexual experimentation, and living in the moment. At a time when whiteness was not just a skin color but a standard of beauty and virtue, the beats and authors such as Norman Mailer looked to African Americans as cultural icons, embracing jazz music and the spontaneity and coolness they attributed to inner-city blacks. The beats formed their own artistic enclaves in New York City's Greenwich Village and San Francisco's North Beach and Haight-Ashbury districts. Wherever they lived, they provided a lifestyle that a younger generation of political and cultural rebels would adopt in the 1960s.

The beat writers frequently read their poems and prose to the rhythms of jazz, reflecting both their affinity with African American culture and the innovative explorations taking place in music. From the big bands of the 1930s and 1940s, postwar jazz musicians formed smaller trios, quartets, and quintets and experimented with sounds more suitable for serious listening than for dancing. The bebop rhythms of trumpeter Dizzy Gillespie and alto saxophonist Charlie Parker revolutionized jazz and reflected the accompanying black rebellion against white supremacy. Trumpeter Miles Davis and tenor saxophonist John Coltrane experimented with more complex and textured forms of this music and took it to new heights. Like rock 'n' roll musicians, these black artists broke down racial barriers as their music crossed over to white audiences.

Homosexuals also attempted to live nonconformist sexual lifestyles, albeit clandestinely. According to studies by researcher Dr. Alfred Kinsey of Indiana University, homosexuals made up approximately 10 percent of the adult population. During World War II, gay men and

Recording *1958 Miles*

Jazz underwent great changes in the 1950s and became a soundtrack to the literary rebels of the beat generation. This 1958 recording session features four of the greatest jazz musicians of their era. From left to right, John Coltrane plays the tenor saxophone, Nat "Cannonball" Adderley the alto saxophone, Miles Davis (the leader) the trumpet, and Bill Evans the piano. Rue des Archives/The Granger Collection, New York lesbians had the opportunity to meet other homosexuals in the military and in venues that attracted gay soldiers. Though homosexuality remained taboo and public displays of it were a crime, politically radical gay men organized against homophobia after the war. In 1951 they formed the Mattachine Society in Los Angeles, which then spread to the East Coast. In 1954 a group of lesbians founded the Daughters of Bilitis in San Francisco. Because of police harassment, most homosexuals refused to reveal their sexual orientation, which made sense practically but reduced their ability to counter antihomosexual discrimination.

Alfred Kinsey also shattered myths about conformity in the private conduct of heterosexuals. In *Sexual Behavior in the Human Female* (1953), Kinsey revealed that many women rejected the double standard that allowed men, but not women, to lose their virginity before marriage. Fifty percent of the women he interviewed had had sexual intercourse before marriage, and 25 percent had had extramarital affairs. Kinsey's findings were supported by other data. Between 1940 and 1960, the frequency of out-of-wedlock births among all women rose from 7.1 newborns to 21.6 newborns per thousand women of childbearing age. The tawdry relations that Grace Metalious depicted in *Peyton Place* merely reflected what many Americans practiced but did not talk about. The brewing sexual revolution further went public in 1953 with the publication of *Playboy* magazine, founded by Hugh Hefner. Through a combination of serious articles and photographs of nude women, the magazine provided its chiefly male readers with a guide to pursuing sexual pleasure and a sophisticated lifestyle.

Like Metalious, many writers denounced the conformity and shallowness they found in suburban America. Novelist Sloan Wilson wrote about the alienating experience of suburban life in *The Man in the Gray Flannel Suit* (1955). "Without talking about it much," Wilson wrote of his fictional suburban couple, "they both began to think of the house as a trap, and they no more enjoyed refurbishing it than a prisoner would delight in shining up the bars of his cell." In J. D. Salinger's novel *Catcher in the Rye* (1951), the young protagonist, Holden Caulfield, mocks the phoniness of the adult world while ending up in a mental institution. Journalists and scholars joined in the criticism. Such critics often overstated the conformity that characterized the suburbs by minimizing the ethnic, religious, and political diversity of their residents. Yet they tapped into a growing feeling, especially among a new generation of young people, of the dangers of a mass culture based on standardization, compliance, and bureaucratization.

REVIEW & RELATE

What trends in American popular culture did the television shows and popular music of the 1950s reflect?	How did artists, writers, and social critics challenge the mainstream politics and culture of the 1950s?

The Civil Rights Movement

African Americans wanted what most other Americans desired after World War II—the opportunity to make a decent living, buy a nice home, raise a healthy family, and get the best education for their children. Yet blacks faced much greater obstacles than did whites in obtaining these dreams, particularly in the South, where African Americans attended separate and unequal schools, faced discrimination if not outright exclusion from public accommodations, were not permitted to vote, and encountered vigilante violence. Determined to eliminate these injustices, black Americans mounted a campaign against white supremacy in the decades after World War II. African Americans increasingly viewed their struggle as part of an international freedom movement of black people in Africa and other nonwhites in the Middle East and Asia to obtain their freedom from Western colonial rulers.

School Segregation and the Supreme Court

Led by the National Association for the Advancement of Colored People (NAACP), African Americans launched a prolonged assault on school segregation. Pursuing a strategy designed in the 1930s by its chief lawyer, Charles Hamilton Houston, the association filed lawsuits against states that excluded blacks from publicly funded law schools and universities. After victories in Missouri and Maryland, Houston's successor, Thurgood Marshall, convinced the Supreme Court in 1950 to disband the separate law school that Texas had set up for blacks and to allow them to attend the University of Texas Law School. At the same time, the Court also eliminated separate facilities for black students at the University of Oklahoma graduate school and ruled against segregation in interstate rail transportation.

Before African Americans could attend college, they had to obtain a first-class education in public schools. All-black schools typically lacked the resources provided to white schools. The NAACP understood that without federal intervention southern officials would never live up to the "separate but equal doctrine" asserted in *Plessy v. Ferguson* (1896). African Americans sought to integrate schools not because they wanted their children to sit next to white students in classrooms and adopt their ways, but because they believed that integration offered the best and quickest way to secure quality education.

In fighting segregated education, the NAACP drew on grassroots organizing techniques in southern communities. In the late 1940s, black families in towns throughout the South joined together to pressure white officials to provide buses to transport children to school, to raise the salaries of black teachers, and to furnish classrooms with critical supplies. Led by black activists in South Carolina and Virginia, the NAACP filed lawsuits seeking to overturn *Plessy*. The association added cases from Delaware and Kansas, where a measure of segregation persisted, as well as from Washington, D.C., where the federal government was responsible for maintaining segregated schools in the nation's capital.

On May 17, 1954, in **Brown v. Board of Education of Topeka, Kansas**, the Supreme Court overturned *Plessy*. In a unanimous decision read by Chief Justice Earl Warren, the Court concluded that "in the field of public education the doctrine of 'separate but equal' has no place. Separate educational facilities are inherently unequal." This ruling undercut the legal foundation for segregation and officially placed the law on the side of those who sought racial equality. Nevertheless, the ruling did not end the controversy; in fact, it led to more battles over segregation. In 1955 the Court issued a follow-up opinion calling for implementation with "all deliberate speed." But, it left enforcement of *Brown* to federal district courts in the South, which consisted mainly of white southerners who espoused segregationist views. As a result, southern officials emphasized "deliberate" rather than "speed" and slowed the implementation of the *Brown* decision.

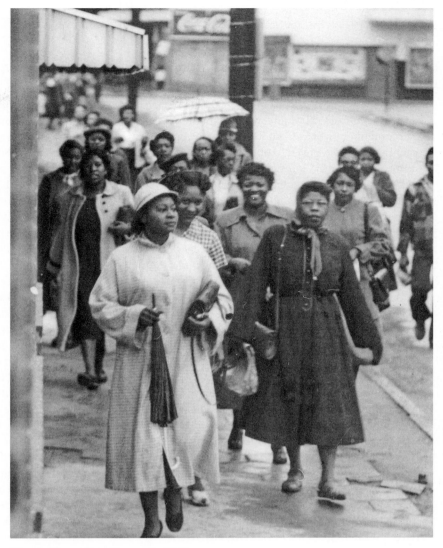

Montgomery Bus Boycott, 1956

Two months after African American residents of Montgomery, Alabama, began their boycott of the city buses to protest segregation and mistreatment, the black community kept up its boycott despite violence and intimidation. Black women had made up the majority of bus riders, and this photograph, taken on February 1, 1956, shows many of them walking to work or going shopping. Time & Life Pictures/Getty Images

The Montgomery Bus Boycott

The *Brown* decision encouraged African Americans to protest against other forms of racial discrimination. In 1955 in Montgomery, Alabama, the Women's Political Council, a group of middle-class and professional black women, petitioned the city commission to improve bus service for black passengers. Among other things, they wanted blacks not to have to give up their seats to white passengers who boarded the bus after black passengers did. Their requests went unheeded until December 1, 1955, when Rosa Parks, a black seamstress and an NAACP activist, refused to give up her seat to a white man. Parks's arrest rallied civic, labor, and religious groups around her and sparked a bus boycott that involved nearly the entire black community. Instead of riding buses, black commuters walked to work or joined car pools. One elderly woman reportedly declined a ride and insisted on walking, explaining, "My feet are tired, but my soul is rested." White officials refused to capitulate and fought back by arresting leaders of the **Montgomery Improvement Association,** the organization that coordinated the protest. Other whites hurled insults at blacks and engaged in violence. After more than a year of conflict, the Supreme Court ruled in favor of the complete desegregation of Montgomery's buses.

Out of this landmark struggle, Martin Luther King Jr. emerged as the civil rights movement's most charismatic leader. The son of a prominent Atlanta minister, King had graduated from the historically black Morehouse College and received a doctorate in theology from Boston University.

Twenty-six years old at the time of Parks's arrest, King was a recent arrival in Montgomery and the pastor of the prestigious Dexter Avenue Baptist Church. He did not seek to lead the boycott, but instead he had it thrust upon him. In Dr. King, Montgomery's blacks had found a man whose personal courage and power of oratory could inspire nearly all segments of the African American community. Though King was familiar with the nonviolent methods of the Indian revolutionary Mohandas Gandhi and the civil disobedience of the nineteenth-century writer Henry David Thoreau, he drew his inspiration and commitment to these principles mainly from the black church and secular leaders such as A. Philip Randolph and Bayard Rustin. King understood how to convey the goals of the civil rights movement to sympathetic white Americans, but his vision and passion grew out of black communities. At the outset of the Montgomery bus boycott, King noted proudly the achievement of African Americans: "When the history books are written in future generations, the historians will have to pause and say 'There lived a great people—a Black people—who injected new meaning and dignity into the veins of civilization.'"

The Montgomery bus boycott made King a national civil rights leader, but it did not guarantee him further success. In 1957 King and a like-minded group of southern black ministers formed the **Southern Christian Leadership Conference (SCLC)** to spread nonviolent protest throughout the region, but except in a few cities, such as Tallahassee, Florida, bus boycott spinoffs did not take hold.

White Resistance to Desegregation

Segregationists responded forcefully to halt black efforts to eliminate Jim Crow. In 1956, 101 southern congressmen issued a manifesto declaring the 1954 *Brown* opinion "a clear abuse of judicial power" and pledging to resist its implementation through "lawful means." Other southerners went beyond the law, as events in Little Rock, Arkansas, showed. In 1957 a federal court approved a plan submitted by the Little Rock School Board to integrate Central High School. However, the governor of Arkansas, Orval Faubus, obstructed the court ruling by sending the state National Guard to keep out nine black students chosen to attend Central High. Faced with blatant state resistance to federal authority, President Eisenhower, a lukewarm supporter of school desegregation, placed the National Guard under federal control and sent in the 101st Airborne Division to restore order after a mob blocked the students from entering the school. The black students, who became known as the **Little Rock Nine**, attended classes for the year under the protection of the National Guard but still encountered considerable harassment from white pupils inside the school. In June 1958, one of the black students, Ernest Green, graduated, but Governor Faubus and the state legislature shut down the school for a year until the Supreme Court in 1959 ordered its reopening. In defiance of the high court, other school districts, such as Prince Edward County, Virginia, chose to close their public schools rather than desegregate. By the end of the decade, public schools in the South remained mostly segregated, and only a token number of black students in a handful of states attended school with whites.

The white South used other forms of violence and intimidation to preserve segregation. The third incarnation of the Ku Klux Klan (KKK) appeared after World War II to strike back at growing African American challenges to white supremacy. This terrorist group threatened, injured, and killed those blacks they considered "uppity." Following the *Brown* decision, segregationists also formed the White Citizens' Council (WCC). The WCC drew members largely from businessmen and professionals. Rather than condoning murder and violent confrontation, the WCC generally relied on intimidating blacks by threatening to fire them from jobs or denying them credit from banks. In Alabama, WCC members launched a campaign against radio stations playing the kind of rock 'n' roll music that Alan Freed popularized in New York City because they believed that it fostered close interracial contact. Reflecting much of the sentiment in the region, an Alabama segregationist called rock 'n' roll "the basic, heavy beat music of Negroes," which, if left unchecked, would result in the downfall of "the entire moral structure . . . the white man has built."

The WCC and the KKK created a racial climate in the deep South that encouraged whites to believe they could get away with murder to defend white supremacy. In the summer of 1955, Emmett Till, a fourteen-year-old from Chicago who was visiting his great-uncle in Mississippi, was killed because he allegedly flirted with a white woman in a country store. Although the two accused killers were brought to trial, an all-white jury quickly acquitted them. Elsewhere in Mississippi that same year, an NAACP official, George Lee, was killed for organizing voter registration drives; the crime was never prosecuted.

The Sit-Ins

With boycotts petering out and white violence rising, African Americans, especially high school and college students, developed new techniques to confront discrimination, including sit-ins, in which protesters seat themselves in a strategic spot and refuse to move until their demands are met or they are forcibly evicted. In 1958 the NAACP organized a sit-in against segregated lunch counters in Oklahoma City, and in 1959 the Congress of Racial Equality (CORE) did the same in Miami. However, mass demonstrations did not really get off the ground until February 1960, when four students at North Carolina A&T University in Greensboro waged sit-ins at the whites-only lunch counters in Woolworth and Kress department stores. Their protests sparked similar efforts throughout the Southeast, expanding to more than two hundred cities within a year (Map 25.1).

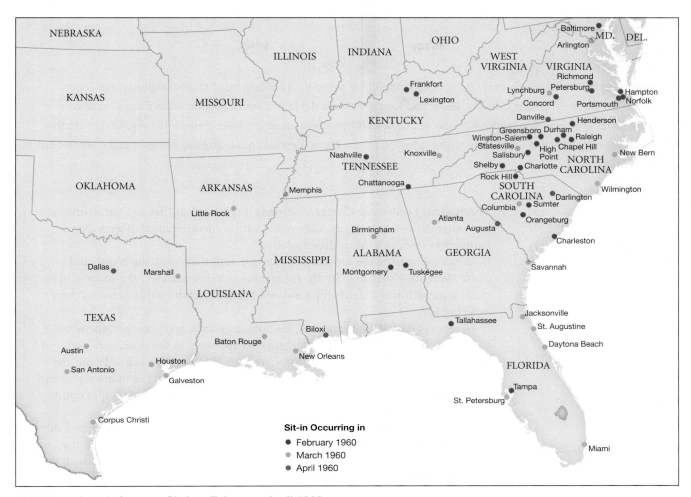

MAP 25.1   Lunch Counter Sit-Ins, February–April 1960

After starting slowly in the late 1950s, lunch counter sit-ins exploded in 1960 following a sit-in by college students in Greensboro, North Carolina. Within three months, sit-ins erupted in fifty-eight cities across the South. The participation of high school and college students revitalized the civil rights movement and led to the formation of the Student Nonviolent Coordinating Committee in April 1960.

A few months after the sit-ins began, a number of their participants formed the **Student Nonviolent Coordinating Committee (SNCC).** The organization's young members sought not only to challenge racial segregation in the South but also to create interracial communities based on economic equality and political democracy. This generation of black and white sit-in veterans came of age in the 1950s at a time when the democratic rhetoric of America's role in the Cold War and the Supreme Court's decision in the *Brown* case raised their expectations for racial equality. Yet these young activists often saw their hopes dashed by numerous examples of southern segregationist resistance, including the 1955 murder of Emmett Till, an incident that both horrified and helped mobilize them to fight for black equality. "Emmett Till was only three years older than me and I identified with him," recalled Cleveland Sellers, a SNCC staff member from

South Carolina. "I tried to put myself in his place and imagine what he was thinking when those white men took him from his home that night. . . . I couldn't get over the fact that the men who were accused of killing him had not been punished at all."

Explore

See Document 25.4 for more on SNCC's core goals.

REVIEW & RELATE

What strategies did African Americans adopt in the 1950s to fight segregation and discrimination?

How and why did white southerners resist efforts to end segregation?

 LEARNINGCurve bedfordstmartins.com/hewittlawson/LC

DOCUMENT 25.4

Ella Baker | Bigger Than a Hamburger, 1960

Soon after the first lunch counter sit-ins, activist Ella Baker called for a conference of student organizers at Shaw University in Raleigh, North Carolina. Baker had fought for black rights and equality for decades through local and national groups, including the NAACP and SCLC. At the Shaw conference, she helped students establish the Student Nonviolent Coordinating Committee. In the following article, Baker summarizes an address she gave at the conference on SNCC's goals.

Explore

What is the significance of the article's title?

The Student Leadership Conference made it crystal clear that current sit-ins and other demonstrations are concerned with something much bigger than a hamburger or even a giant-sized Coke.

Whatever may be the difference in approach to their goal, the Negro and white students, North and South, are seeking to rid America of the scourge of racial segregation and discrimination—not only at lunch counters, but in every aspect of life.

In reports, casual conversations, discussion groups, and speeches, the sense and the spirit of the following statement that appeared in the initial newsletter of the students at Barber-Scotia College, Concord, N.C., were re-echoed time and again: "We want the world to know that we no longer accept the inferior position of second-class citizenship. We are willing to go to jail, be ridiculed, spat upon, and even suffer physical violence to obtain First Class Citizenship."

By and large, this feeling that they have a destined date with freedom, was not limited to a drive for personal freedom, or even freedom for the Negro in the South. Repeatedly it was emphasized that the movement was concerned with the moral implications of racial discrimination for the "whole world" and the "Human Race."

This universality of approach was linked with a perceptive recognition that "it is important to keep the movement democratic and to avoid struggles for personal leadership."

What concerns did students cite about cooperating with adults?

It was further evident that desire for supportive cooperation from adult leaders and the adult community was also tempered by apprehension that adults might try to "capture" the student movement. The students showed willingness to be met on the basis of equality, but were intolerant of anything that smacked of manipulation or domination.

According to Baker, what problems do "leader-centered groups" seem to create?

This inclination toward group-centered leadership, rather than toward a leader-centered group pattern of organization, was refreshing indeed to those of the older group who bear the scars of the battle, the frustrations and the disillusionment that come when the prophetic leader turns out to have heavy feet of clay.

Source: Ella Baker, "Bigger Than a Hamburger," *Southern Patriot*, June 1960, 4.

Put It in Context

How did SNCC's goals as expressed here represent a change from earlier efforts to achieve racial equality?

The Eisenhower Era

Despite the existence of civil rights protesters, rock 'n' roll upstarts, intellectual dissenters, and sexual revolutionaries, the 1950s seemed to many a tranquil, even dull period—one commentator referred to it as "the bland leading the bland." This impression owes a great deal to the leadership of President Dwight D. Eisenhower. Serving two terms from 1953 to 1961, Eisenhower, or "Ike" as he was affectionately called, convinced the majority of Americans that their country was in good hands regardless of political turbulence at home and heated international conflicts abroad.

Modern Republicanism

President Eisenhower, a World War II hero, radiated strength and trust, qualities the American people found very attractive as they rebuilt their lives and established families in the 1950s. Nominated by the Republican Party in 1952, the sixty-two-year-old Eisenhower shrewdly balanced his ticket by choosing as his running mate California senator Richard M. Nixon, a man twenty-three years his junior who had risen in politics by attacking Democrats as soft on communism. On election day, Eisenhower coasted to victory, winning 55 percent of the popular vote and 83 percent of the electoral vote. Despite Eisenhower's personal popularity, the Republicans managed to win only slim majorities in the Senate and the House. Within two years, they had lost even this slight edge in both houses, and the Democrats regained control of Congress.

With a limited electoral mandate, the president adopted what one of his speechwriters called **Modern Republicanism**, which tried to fit the traditional Republican Party ideals of individualism and fiscal restraint within the broad framework of Franklin Roosevelt's New Deal. With Democrats in control of Congress after 1954, Republicans agreed to raise Social Security benefits and to include coverage for some ten million additional workers. Congress and the president retained another New Deal mainstay, the minimum wage, and increased it from 75 cents to $1 an hour. Departing from traditional Republican criticism of big government, the Eisenhower administration added the Department of Health, Education, and Welfare to the cabinet in 1953. The president justified expanding the federal government in domestic matters as part of fighting the Cold War. In 1958 Eisenhower signed into law the National Defense Education Act, which provided aid for instruction in science, math, and foreign languages and graduate fellowships and loans for college students. He portrayed the new law as a way to catch up with the Soviets, who the previous year had successfully launched the first artificial satellite, called *Sputnik*, into outer space.

Eisenhower and the Cold War

In foreign affairs, Eisenhower perpetuated Truman's containment doctrine while at the same time espousing the contradictory principle of "rolling back" communism in Eastern Europe. However, when Hungarians rose up against their Soviet-backed regime in 1956, the U.S. government did little more than offering encouragement and allowing approximately eighty thousand Hungarian refugees to enter the country. Rather than pushing back communism, the Eisenhower administration expanded the doctrine of containment around the world by entering into treaties to establish regional defense pacts. In 1954 the Southeast Asia Treaty Organization was formed to protect Australia, France, Great Britain, New Zealand, Pakistan, the Philippines, and Thailand from Communist assault. In 1959 the Central Treaty Organization brought Iraq, Iran, Turkey, and once again Pakistan within the U.S. defense perimeter.

Eisenhower's commitment to fiscal discipline had a profound effect on his foreign policy. The president worried that the alliance among government, defense contractors, and research universities—which he dubbed "the military-industrial complex"—would bankrupt the economy and undermine individual freedom. With this in mind, he implemented the **New Look** strategy, which placed a higher priority on building a nuclear arsenal and delivery system than on the more expensive task of maintaining and deploying armed forces on the ground throughout the world. Nuclear missiles launched from the air by U.S. air force bombers or fired from submarines would give the United States, as Secretary of Defense Charles Wilson asserted, "a bigger bang for the buck." With the nation now armed with nuclear weapons, the Eisenhower administration threatened "massive retaliation" in the event of Communist aggression.

The New Look may have saved money and slowed the rate of defense spending, but it had serious flaws. First, it placed a premium on "brinksmanship," taking Communist enemies to the precipice of nuclear destruction, risking the death of millions, and hoping the other side would back down. Second, massive retaliation did not work for small-scale conflicts. For instance, in the event of a confrontation in Berlin, would the United States launch nuclear missiles toward Germany and expose its European allies in West Germany and France to nuclear contamination? Third, the buildup of nuclear warheads provoked an arms race by encouraging the Soviet Union to do the same. Peace depended on the superpowers terrifying each other with the threat of nuclear annihilation—that is, if one country attacked the other, retaliation was guaranteed to result in shared obliteration. This strategy was known as **mutually assured destruction**, and its acronym—**MAD**—summed up its nightmarish qualities. As each nuclear power increased its capacity to destroy the other many times over, the

Civil Defense Drills

During the Cold War, school-children took part in civil defense drills. When the teacher yelled "duck and cover," children scrambled under their desks. In the nuclear age, few questioned whether these drills would protect people from atomic radiation. This 1952 photograph shows students and their teacher in a Newark, New Jersey, classroom participating in a statewide air raid test. © Bettmann/CORBIS

potential for mistakes and errors in judgment increased, threatening a nuclear holocaust that would leave little to rebuild. Fortunately, Eisenhower used the threat of massive retaliation judiciously, mainly against the Chinese rather than the Soviets. In 1953, after the United States threatened to deploy nuclear weapons against China, China agreed to an armistice that ended the fighting in Korea; two years later, similar American threats kept the Chinese from attacking Taiwan, where Jiang Jieshi's Nationalist government ruled in exile.

National security concerns occupied a good deal of the president's time. Fearing that a Soviet nuclear attack could wipe out nearly a third of the population before the United States could retaliate, the Eisenhower administration stepped up civil defense efforts. Schoolchildren took part in "duck and cover" drills, in which teachers shouted "Take cover" and students hid under their desks. In the meantime, both the United States and the Soviet Union began producing intercontinental ballistic missiles armed with nuclear warheads. They also stepped up aboveground tests of nuclear weapons, which contaminated the atmosphere with dangerous radioactive particles.

Despite doomsday rhetoric of massive retaliation, Eisenhower generally relied more on diplomacy than on military action. Stalin's death in 1953 and his eventual replacement by Nikita Khrushchev in 1955 permitted détente, or a relaxation of tensions, between the two superpowers. In July 1955, Eisenhower and Khrushchev, together with British and French leaders, gathered in Geneva to discuss arms control. It was the first meeting of an American president and a Soviet head of state since the end of World War II. Nothing concrete came out of this summit, but Eisenhower and Khrushchev did ease tensions between the two nations. In a speech to Communist officials two years later, Khrushchev denounced the excesses of Stalin's totalitarian rule and reinforced hopes for a new era of peaceful coexistence between the Cold War antagonists. Khrushchev also visited the United States in 1959, yet peaceful coexistence remained precarious. Just as President Eisenhower was about to begin his own tour of the Soviet Union in 1960, the Soviets shot down an American U-2 spy plane flying over their country. Eisenhower canceled his trip, and tensions resumed.

Cold War Interventions

While relations between the Soviet Union and the United States thawed and then cooled during the Eisenhower era, the Cold War advanced into new regions. In a manner first suggested in NSC-68 (see chapter 24), the Eisenhower administration deployed the CIA to help topple governments considered pro-Communist as well as to promote U.S. economic interests. For example, after Iranian prime minister Mohammed Mossadegh nationalized foreign oil corporations in 1953, the CIA engineered a successful coup that ousted his government and installed the pro-American

The Kitchen Debate

Soviet premier Nikita Khrushchev, second on the left, talks with Vice President Richard Nixon, second on the right, at a U.S. exhibit in Moscow on July 24, 1959. The two leaders argued about the relative merits of capitalism and communism, while looking at an American kitchen that displayed the latest washing machine. Khrushchev, pointing his finger at Nixon, appears unimpressed. Time & Life Pictures/Getty Images

Shah Mohammad Reza Pahlavi in his place. Mossadegh was not a Communist, but by overthrowing him American oil companies obtained 40 percent of Iran's oil revenue.

In 1954 fruit and sugar replaced oil as the catalyst for U.S. intervention. The elected socialist regime of Jacobo Arbenz Guzmán in Guatemala had seized 225,000 acres of land held by the United Fruit Company, a powerful American company in which Secretary of State John Foster Dulles and his brother, CIA Director Allen Dulles, held stock. According to the Dulles brothers, the land's seizure by the Guatemalan government posed a threat to the nearby Panama Canal. Eisenhower was unwilling to send in troops, but he allowed the CIA to hatch a plot that resulted in a coup d'état, or government overthrow, that installed a right-wing military regime in Guatemala, which safeguarded both the Panama Canal and the United Fruit Company.

The success of the CIA's covert efforts in Guatemala prompted the Eisenhower administration to plan a similar action in Cuba, ninety miles off the coast of Florida. In 1959 the Cold War inched closer to the United States as Fidel Castro led an uprising and came to power in Cuba after overthrowing the American-backed dictator Fulgencio

Batista. A Cuban nationalist in the tradition of José Martí, Castro sought to regain full control over his country's economic resources, including those owned by U.S. corporations. He appropriated $1 billion worth of American property and signed a trade agreement with the Soviet Union. To consolidate his political rule, Castro jailed opponents and installed a Communist regime, forcing a large number of his adversaries to immigrate to Miami. In 1960 President Eisenhower authorized the CIA to design a clandestine operation to overthrow the Castro government, but he left office before the invasion could occur.

The efforts of Iranian, Guatemalan, and Cuban leaders to seize control of their countries' resources were but a few examples of the surge of nationalism that swept through former European colonies in the 1950s. Following World War II, revolutionary nationalists in the Middle East, Africa, and Southeast Asia toppled colonial governments and wielded the power of their newly liberated regimes to take charge of their own development. The United States and the Soviet Union each tried to gain influence over these emerging nations. Many newly independent countries tried to practice neutrality in foreign affairs, accepting aid from both of the Cold War protagonists. Nonetheless, they were often drawn into East-West conflicts.

Such was the case in Egypt, which achieved independence from Great Britain in 1952. Two years later under General Gamal Abdel Nasser, the country sought to modernize its economy by building the hydroelectric Aswan Dam on the Nile River. Nasser welcomed financial backing from the United States and the Soviet Union, but the Eisenhower administration refused to contribute so long as the Egyptians accepted Soviet assistance. In 1956 Nasser, falling short of funds, sent troops to take over the Suez Canal, the waterway run by Great Britain and through which the bulk of Western Europe's oil was shipped. He intended to pay for the dam by collecting tolls from canal users. In retaliation, Britain and France, the two European powers most affected by the seizure, invaded Egypt on October 29, 1956. Locked in a struggle with Egypt and other Arab nations since its creation in 1948, Israel joined in the attack. The invading forces—all U.S. allies—had not warned the Eisenhower administration of their plans. Coming at the same time as the Soviet crack-down against the Hungarian revolution, the British-French-Israeli assault placed the United States in the difficult position of condemning the Soviets for intervening in Hungary while its anti-Communist partners waged war in Suez. Instead, Eisenhower cooperated with the United Nations to negotiate a cease-fire and engineer a pullout of the invading forces in Egypt. Ultimately, the Soviets proved the winners in this Cold War skirmish. The Suez invasion revived memories of European imperialism and fueled anti-Western sentiments and pan-Arab nationalism (a sense of unity among Arabs across national boundaries), which worked to the Soviets' advantage. Nasser obtained financial assistance from the Soviets and built the Aswan Dam.

The Eisenhower administration soon moved to counter growing Soviet power in the region. In 1957, fearing increasing Communist influence in the oil-rich Middle East, Congress approved the **Eisenhower Doctrine**, which gave the president a free hand to use U.S. military forces in the Middle East "against overt armed aggression from any nation controlled by International Communism," as he remarked to Congress. In effect, the Eisenhower administration was more concerned with protecting access to oil fields from hostile Arab nationalist leaders than with any Communist incursion. In 1958, when an anti-American, non-Communist regime came to power in Iraq, the president sent fourteen thousand marines to neighboring Lebanon to prevent a similar outcome there. A military realist, Eisenhower made his choice for intervention carefully—the invasion required limited force and allowed a speedy exit without any fatalities.

Just before Eisenhower left office in January 1961, his administration intervened in a civil war in the newly independent Congo. This former colony of Belgium held valuable mineral resources, which Belgium and the United States still coveted. After the Congo's first prime minister, Patrice Lumumba, stated his intentions to remain neutral in the Cold War, President Eisenhower and CIA Director Allen Dulles declared him unreliable in the conflict with the Soviet Union. With the support of Belgian military troops and encouragement from the United States, the resource-rich province of Katanga seceded from the Congo in 1960. After the Congolese military, under the leadership of Joseph Mobuto, overthrew Lumumba's government, the CIA launched an operation that culminated in the execution of Lumumba on January 17, 1961. Several years later, Mobuto became president of the country, changed its name to Zaire, and allied with the West. The Eisenhower administration had extended the Cold War to central Africa in a covert, but nonetheless bloody, manner.

Early U.S. Intervention in Vietnam

Eisenhower's intervention in Vietnam would have profound, long-term consequences for the United States. By the 1950s, Vietnamese revolutionaries (the Vietminh) had been fighting for independence from the French for decades. They were led by Ho Chi Minh, a revolutionary who had studied Communist doctrine in the Soviet Union but was not controlled by the Soviets. In fact, he modeled his 1945 Vietnamese Declaration of Independence on that of the United States. Ho's overriding objective was the liberation of Vietnam along socialist principles. In 1954 the Vietminh defeated the French at the Battle of Dien Bien Phu. With the backing of the United States, the Soviet Union, and China, both sides agreed to divide Vietnam at the seventeenth parallel and hold free elections to unite the country in 1956.

President Eisenhower believed that if Vietnam fell to the Communists, the rest of Southeast Asia and Japan would "go over very quickly" like "a row of dominoes," threatening American strategic power in the Far East as well as free access to Asian markets. Convinced that Ho Chi Minh and his followers would win free elections, the Eisenhower administration installed the anti-French, anti-Communist Ngo Dinh Diem to lead South Vietnam and then supported his regime's refusal to hold national elections in 1956. The anti-Communist interests of the United States had trumped its democratic promises. With the country now permanently divided, Eisenhower funneled economic aid to Diem to undertake needed land reforms that would strengthen his government and weaken

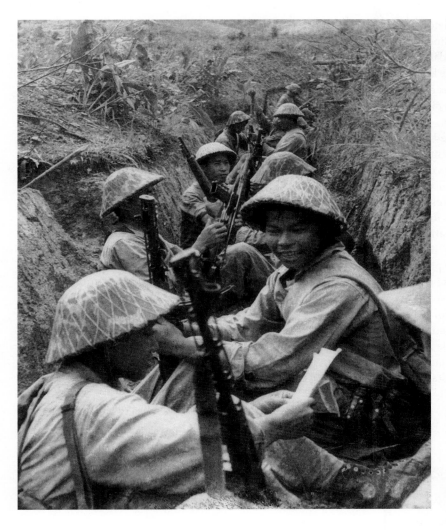

The Battle of Dien Bien Phu

This photograph shows Vietnamese soldiers resting in a trench at Dien Bien Phu, site of the pivotal battle at which French colonial forces were defeated. Fighting began on March 13, 1954, and ended on May 7, when French troops surrendered. This photo, like most of those taken of the battle, was restaged shortly after the action, mainly for propaganda purposes. AFP/Getty Images

the appeal of Ho Chi Minh. The president also dispatched CIA agents and military advisers to help the South Vietnamese government set up security forces, train military units, and extend educational opportunities. However, Diem used most of the money to consolidate his power rather than implement reforms, which only widened opposition to his regime from Communists and non-Communists alike. This prompted Ho Chi Minh in 1959 to support the creation in the South of the National Liberation Front, or **Vietcong**, to wage a military insurgency against Diem. By the end of the decade, the Eisenhower administration had created a major diplomatic problem with no clear plan for its resolution.

The Election of 1960

Even after experiencing eight years of dramatic challenges in both foreign and domestic affairs, Eisenhower remained popular. In 1956 voters had returned Eisenhower to the

White House with greater support than in 1952. Once again, Eisenhower's personal popularity did not carry over to the Republican Party, as Democrats increased their control over Congress. Eisenhower, however, could not run for a third term, barred by the Twenty-second Amendment (1951), and Vice President Richard M. Nixon ran as the Republican candidate for president in 1960. Unlike Eisenhower, Nixon was not universally liked or respected. His manipulation of the anti-Communist issue and his reputation for unsavory political combat drew the scorn of Democrats, especially liberals. Moreover, Nixon had to fend off charges that Republicans, as embodied in the seventy-year-old Eisenhower, were out-of-date and out of new ideas.

Running as the Democratic candidate for president in 1960, Senator John F. Kennedy of Massachusetts promised to instill renewed "vigor" in the White House and get the country moving again. Yet Kennedy did not differ much from his Republican rival on domestic and foreign policy issues. Kennedy's willingness to employ a rhetoric of high-minded change did not seem to be dampened by the fact that he had not compiled a distinguished or courageous record in the Senate, that his family's fortune had paved the way for his political career, and that he had earned a well-justified reputation in Washington as a playboy and womanizer.

The outcome of the 1960 election turned on several factors. The country was experiencing a slight economic recession, reviving memories in older voters of the Great Depression, which had begun with the Republican Hoover in power. In addition, presidential candidates faced off on television for the first time, participating in four televised debates. As the leading medium for information, TV emphasized visual style and presentation. With Nixon having just recovered from a stay in the hospital and looking haggard, Kennedy in the first debate convinced a majority of television viewers that he possessed the presidential bearing for the job. Nixon performed better in the next three debates, but the damage had been done. Still, Kennedy had to overcome considerable religious prejudice to win the election. No Catholic had ever won the presidency, and the prejudices of Protestants,

especially in the South, threatened to divert critical votes from Kennedy's Democratic base. While many southern Democrats did support Nixon, Kennedy balanced out these defections by gaining votes from the nation's Catholics, especially in northern states rich in electoral votes (Map 25.2).

Race also exerted a critical influence. Nixon and Kennedy had similar records on civil rights, and if anything, Nixon's was slightly stronger. However, on October 19, 1960, when Atlanta police arrested Martin Luther King Jr. for participating in a restaurant sit-in, Kennedy sprang to his defense, whereas Nixon kept his distance. Kennedy telephoned the civil rights leader's wife to offer his sympathy and used his influence to get King released from jail. As a result, King's father, a Protestant minister who had intended to vote against the Catholic Kennedy, switched his position and endorsed the Democrat. In addition to the elder King, Kennedy won back for Democrats 7 percent of black voters who had supported Eisenhower in 1956. Kennedy won by a margin of less than 1 percent of the popular vote, underscoring the importance of the African American electorate.

REVIEW & RELATE

Why did Eisenhower adopt a moderate domestic agenda? What were his most notable accomplishments?

How did Eisenhower use the CIA and covert actions to protect and expand American influence around the world?

LEARNINGCurve bedfordstmartins.com/hewittlawson/LC

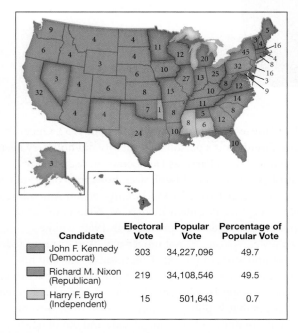

Candidate	Electoral Vote	Popular Vote	Percentage of Popular Vote
John F. Kennedy (Democrat)	303	34,227,096	49.7
Richard M. Nixon (Republican)	219	34,108,546	49.5
Harry F. Byrd (Independent)	15	501,643	0.7

MAP 25.2 The Election of 1960

The 1960 presidential candidates differed little on major policy issues. John F. Kennedy gained the White House by winning back black voters who had supported Eisenhower, gaining crucial support from Catholic voters across the country, and appearing more presidential on the first televised debate in history. Still his margin of victory was razor thin.

Conclusion: Cold War Politics and Culture

Following the end of World War II, the return of peace and prosperity fostered a baby boom that sent families scrambling for new housing and increasingly away from the cities. Suburbs grew as housing developers such as William Levitt built affordable, mass-produced homes in the suburbs and as the federal government provided new highways that allowed suburban residents to commute to their jobs in the cities. With increased income, consumers purchased the latest models in automobiles as well as newly introduced televisions, reshaping how they spent their leisure time. As the baby boom generation entered their teenage years, their sheer numbers and general affluence helped make them a significant economic and cultural force. They poured their dollars into clothes, music, and other forms of entertainment, which reinforced their identity as teenagers and set them apart from adults.

The increasingly distinct teenage culture owed a great deal to African Americans, who contributed to the development of rock 'n' roll and revolutionized jazz, thereby providing a standard for teenage rebellion and attacks on mainstream values by the beats. Yet African Americans remained most focused on tearing down the legal and institutional foundations of white supremacy. First in the courts and then in the streets, they confronted segregation and disfranchisement in the South. By the end of the 1950s, African Americans had persuaded the Supreme Court to reverse the doctrine of "separate but equal" that buttressed Jim Crow; they also won significant victories in desegregating buses in Montgomery, schools in Little Rock, and lunch counters in Greensboro. Black teenagers reinvigorated the civil rights movement through their boldness and energy, opening the path for even greater racial changes in the coming decade.

In addition to struggles over racial equality, the 1950s witnessed serious tensions at home and overseas. Teenage cultural rebellion; sexual revolution; McCarthyite witch-hunts; a bloody war in Korea; foreign crises in the Middle East, Eastern Europe, and Southeast Asia; clandestine operations in Iran, Guatemala, and the Congo—all of these confronted the citizens of Alan Freed's and Grace Metalious's America. Nevertheless, the popular image of the 1950s as a tranquil and innocent period persists, mainly because of the presence of President Dwight Eisenhower as a symbol for the age. A cheerful, grandfatherly patriarch, Eisenhower in this version of historical memory reflects a kinder and gentler time. The Republican Eisenhower provided moderate leadership that helped the country adjust to the changes it was undergoing. His critics complained that the nation had lost its spirit of adventure, had misplaced its ability to distinguish between community and conformity, had failed to live up to ideals of racial and economic justice, and had relinquished its primary place in the world. Nevertheless, most Americans emerging from decades of depression and war felt satisfied with the new lives they were building. Despite upheavals at home and abroad, they still liked Ike.

When Eisenhower left office in 1961, a new decade began with a Democratic president in charge. Yet the challenges that Eisenhower had faced and the diplomatic, social, and cultural forces that propelled them continued to confront his successors. During the following years, many of the teenagers and young people who had benefited from the peace and prosperity of the 1950s would lead the way in questioning the role of the United States in world affairs and its commitment to democracy, freedom, and equality at home.

LEARNINGCurve
Check what you know.
bedfordstmartins.com/hewittlawson/LC

Chapter Review

Online Study Guide ▶ bedfordstmartins.com/hewittlawson

KEY TERMS

Sun Belt (p. 793)

Levittown (p. 793)

National Interstate and Defense Highway Act (p. 793)

beats (p. 801)

Brown v. Board of Education of Topeka, Kansas (p. 803)

Montgomery Improvement Association (p. 803)

Southern Christian Leadership Conference (SCLC) (p. 804)

Little Rock Nine (p. 804)

Student Nonviolent Coordinating Committee (SNCC) (p. 805)

Modern Republicanism (p. 807)

New Look (p. 807)

mutually assured destruction (MAD) (p. 807)

Eisenhower Doctrine (p. 810)

Vietcong (p. 811)

REVIEW & RELATE

1. What factors contributed to the economic and population growth of the 1950s?

2. How did economic and demographic trends in the 1950s contribute to the growth of suburbs?

3. What trends in American popular culture did the television shows and popular music of the 1950s reflect?

4. How did artists, writers, and social critics challenge the mainstream politics and culture of the 1950s?

5. What strategies did African Americans adopt in the 1950s to fight segregation and discrimination?

6. How and why did white southerners resist efforts to end segregation?

7. Why did Eisenhower adopt a moderate domestic agenda? What were his most notable accomplishments?

8. How did Eisenhower use the CIA and covert actions to protect and expand American influence around the world?

TIMELINE OF EVENTS

1940–1960	Migration to Sun Belt swells region's population
1945–1960	U.S. gross national product soars 250 percent; 60 percent of Americans achieve middle-class status; union membership reaches new high
1951–1954	Alan Freed promotes rock 'n' roll with radio show and concerts
1953	CIA coup puts Shah Mohammad Reza Pahlavi in power in Iran
1954–1958	Eisenhower adopts Modern Republicanism and expands domestic programs
1954	CIA plot results in a military takeover of Guatemala
	Brown v. Board of Education of Topeka, Kansas Supreme Court ruling
1955–1956	Montgomery bus boycott
1955	Jonas Salk develops polio vaccine
	Emmett Till murdered
1956	Grace Metalious publishes *Peyton Place*
	National Interstate and Defense Highway Act passed
	U.S. begins supporting anti-Communist government of South Vietnam
1957	Martin Luther King Jr. and other black ministers form Southern Christian Leadership Council (SCLC)
	Eisenhower uses federal troops to enforce school desegregation in Little Rock, Arkansas
	Soviet Union launches *Sputnik*
	Congress approves Eisenhower Doctrine
1958	Eisenhower sends U.S. marines into Lebanon
1959	Fidel Castro takes power in Cuba
1960	U-2 spy plane shot down over Soviet Union
	Student Nonviolent Coordinating Committee (SNCC) formed
1960–1961	U.S. intervenes in civil war in Congo

DOCUMENT PROJECT **25**

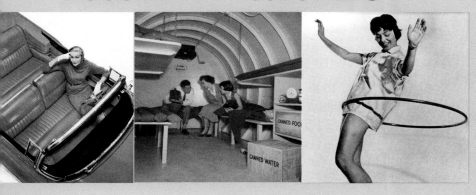

Teenagers in Postwar America

"There are many different opinions about just what is the most exclusive club in America these days," observed Dick Clark in his book *Your Happiest Years* (1959). But for Clark, the most exclusive and important club was the one he called "Teenagers of America, Inc." Clark's appraisal of American society in 1959 may have been self-serving—after all, his career hinged largely on appealing to teen audiences— but he was not alone in his belief in the significance of teenagers in postwar American society.

Even now, pop culture often portrays the 1950s as a simpler time when girls wore poodle skirts and swooned over Elvis Presley while boys raced hot-rod cars and took their dates to the malt shop. In this vision, teens were concerned with little more than increasing their popularity, "going steady," and watching *American Bandstand*. As the following documents illustrate, there is much to support this interpretation of postwar teen culture. Young people made rock 'n' roll into an enduring and lucrative entertainment industry, shaped the advertising and manufacture of products, and were the focus of numerous television shows and movies.

But there are other, more complicated images of teen life in this era. For one, juvenile delinquency was seen by many as a serious problem. Actor James Dean's *Rebel without a Cause* competed with singer Pat Boone's squeaky-clean haircut and white shoes. In 1959 actor Sandra Dee portrayed both a perky Malibu surfer in *Gidget* and an unwed pregnant teen in *A Summer Place*. Teens also grew up under the looming threat of the Cold War, the Korean War, and McCarthyism. African Americans helped popularize rock 'n' roll, but in Little Rock, Arkansas, and elsewhere in the South black teenagers risked their lives to desegregate public schools.

The following sources consider different aspects of teen life and postwar culture in the 1950s. They provide examples of the importance of teenagers as consumers and reveal some of the concerns adults expressed about their interests and desires. They also offer illustrations of teenagers in the 1950s who had more on their mind than just dating and having a good time.

DOCUMENT 25.5

Dick Clark | *Your Happiest Years*, 1959

By 1959 Dick Clark was a nationally popular disc jockey and host of television's *American Bandstand*. Always seen in a suit and tie, Clark, with his clean-cut good looks, projected a more wholesome vision of rock 'n' roll than did many of his contemporaries, such as Alan Freed. Clark's advice book for teenagers includes instruction on manners, makeup, and getting along with parents and other teens, as well as advice on romantic relationships.

We've mentioned before that it is very important to build a wide circle of friends, both fellows and girls. There are two reasons for this, but one is basic to dating. That is, the more fellows or girls you meet, the better the possibility that one or two might consider you what we called "date bait." The other reason, and it's a long shot, is that having a wide circle of friends, you meet more different types of people and learn how to adjust to them. This pays off after the teen years are past and you are either at work or away at school. But in order to get yourself into this teenage world of dating, let's just say you'll grow very lonely if you lock yourself away from eligible fellows or girls.

You've joined the staff of the school paper, or you are a member of a crowd of fellows that seem to attract a liberal following of the fair sex to your athletic contests. Or, on the distaff [female] side, you've a fine collection of girl friends—they're especially fine if they have at least one or two brothers of dating age. If you haven't quite reached that stage of teenage paradise yet, there are such events as community dances, or mixed school or church activities, that bring manly blips on your radarscope. In other words, you've gotten out of your shell and into the teenage swim. Don't be shy. You know that all the other fellows and girls your own age feel the same way you do. Remember, no self-pity. Braces on your teeth can't dim the glow of a sparkling personality, and neither can a shortage of new dresses or suits be an alibi for what is really a lack of effort on your part. Your fellow teenagers are eager to find sincere friends, and if you can prove that you are one then you definitely classify as "date bait." There is a phrase that I heard from General Carlos P. Romulo, the Philippines' famed patriot and Ambassador to the United States, and I think it applies here. "A stranger," the General said, "is a friend that I haven't met." It's a wonderful application of the Golden Rule, and it's one sentence that can carry a teenager through a lot of embarrassing uncertainty.

Accepting your fellow teenagers as friends, known or unknown, is another step toward that all-important phone call or whispered conference in the hall at school. You know the one I mean. It may begin, "Uh, Margie . . . uh, this Saturday night . . . uh, well, some of us were . . ." And a date is born.

Source: Dick Clark, *Your Happiest Years* (New York: Random House, 1959), 100–101.

DOCUMENT 25.6

Richard Gehman | The Nine Billion Dollars in Hot Little Hands, 1957

In the 1950s, teenagers were identified for the first time as a distinct and important consumer market. Advertising agencies and manufacturers studied teen spending habits on products such as movies, clothes, and records, and as the following article suggests, teenagers influenced purchases and popular culture well beyond their own experiences.

WHOLE INDUSTRIES are devoted exclusively to pleasing teenagers. Relatively untalented performers have become the highest-paid stars in the country simply because teenagers idolize them. Our eating habits have changed drastically; many families now eat the way teenagers do—from trays, in front of the TV set.

Currently there are three organizations in New York devoted exclusively to polling teenagers, discovering their opinions and tastes, and selling this information to manufacturers and advertising agencies. . . .

One watch company, whose products had not been striking the fancy of the nation's youth, designed a whole new line of wrist watches. Before long, word got around that this company's watches were *the* ones to have, and sales began to rise—even, to the manufacturer's surprise, in its adult line.

"The adults heard the kids talking about the watches and decided they must be pretty good," one dealer explains.

This illustrates another huge factor in the teens' influence. Kids are better-educated, better-informed, and, in the majority of cases, more alert today than at any previous time in history.

Also, they are more articulate. Schools encourage them to express their opinions and preferences. Consequently, adults respect them more, and listen when they talk about new inventions and products. A manufacturer of farm equipment tells of a salesman who visited a farmer to try to interest him in buying a tractor. The farmer said that if his teenaged son approved of the tractor, he would buy it. "This is going to be a cinch," the salesman thought—but to his surprise, the boy's reaction was negative. "That tractor of yours just won't do the work we need to do," he said. No sale.

Many of the innovations in Detroit-produced cars in recent years have come about as a result of the teenagers' interest in hot rods, says a publisher of motor magazines. "Four-barrel carburetors, twin exhausts, and the so-called 'power packages' found in many new models stem directly from hot rod activity," the publisher says.

Home design, too, is directly influenced by what teenagers want and don't want. A New Jersey contractor last year decided to build himself the house he had always wanted. It was to cost $200,000 and include all the ultra-modern features a house can possibly have. He hired an architect and set men to work on the foundation. Then one day his daughter came home from high school in tears. "Daddy," she said, "is it true we're going to have the biggest house in town? Everybody'll think we're snobs and climbers!" Then and there the contractor abandoned his plans for the house.

Nowadays, that contractor and hundreds of his contemporaries build houses with teenagers uppermost in their minds. They provide separate entrances to bedroom wings, so that the children won't track mud through the main part of the house; they build in special playrooms. The furniture manufacturers follow suit with special pieces that are sturdy enough to withstand teenage sprawling and covered with dirt-resistant fabrics. "There is no question about it," says one builder; "teenagers have taken over the house." He might well have carried it a few steps further. They've taken over everything.

Source: Richard Gehman, "The Nine Billion Dollars in Hot Little Hands," *Cosmopolitan*, November 1957, 72, 77–78.

DOCUMENT 25.7

Chevrolet Advertisement, 1954

Automobile manufacturers did not design cars specifically with teenagers in mind, but they did target the teen market for sales. Colorful, powerful, and sleek models were especially appealing to teenagers who considered cars a central part of their dating experience. The phrase "You're only young twice" appealed not only to youths but also to adults who wanted to stay young. As the previous document indicates, teenagers often influenced the purchases their parents made, and this advertisement appears to be aware of this influence.

Ever see a prettier car than the Chevrolet Bel Air Sport Coupe? And this is just one of a great line of Chevrolet beauties. Best choice in the field.

You're only young <u>twice</u>!

Once when you take your first battered old jalopy to your heart . . . and once again when you put your first brand-new Chevrolet on parade! After that—your motoring life is young for good! You've discovered the Fountain of Youth on wheels.

WHAT'S CHEVROLET GOT THAT YOUNG PEOPLE GO FOR?

First of all: It's smooth! Real cool! It looks as a car ought to look that's loaded with youngsters who love the feel of a spirited pick-up and the power of broad-shouldered brakes. Chevrolet is the <u>only</u> low-priced car in the world with a Fisher Body.

And what a pleasant surprise to discover that you can run the new Chevrolet with the kind of money that fits a young man's budget. And, of course, everybody knows that Chevrolet's original cost is less than any other line in the low-price field.

It's the only low-priced car with a full length box-girder frame for *extra safety*.

And if you're interested in those new automatic power features a family car ought to have, you'll find that Chevrolet offers them all—optional at extra cost if you want them.

YOUR MONEY'S WORTH IN FUN, TOO!

When you put your money in a Chevrolet you're putting it into the closest thing there is to a savings bank on wheels! You'll get your money's worth in fun all its long life, and a trade-in value that will make you realize all over again that nothing—no, nothing—has ever topped Chevrolet for VALUE.

Why don't you drop around to your dealer's and take a ride in a new Chevrolet? . . . Chevrolet Division of General Motors, Detroit 2, Michigan.

SAFER STOPPING, TOO! The going's great and so is the stopping! Those broad-shouldered Chevrolet brakes are actually the largest in the low-price field. That's to give you easier stops and safer control-anywhere, any time!

YEAR AFTER YEAR MORE PEOPLE BUY CHEVROLETS THAN ANY OTHER CAR!

DOCUMENT 25.8

Charlotte Jones | Letter on Elvis, 1957

Nothing highlighted the growing generation gap more than rock 'n' roll. When Elvis Presley burst onto the music scene in the mid-1950s, adults criticized his music and gyrating hips, while teenage boys dressed to imitate his style, and teenage girls screamed and fainted at his concerts. In 1957 Charlotte Jones, an admiring fan, wrote the following letter to the conservative newspaper columnist George Sokolsky in response to Sokolsky's criticism of Presley's popularity.

There are too many people saying that Elvis is going to die out. When Elvis dies out is when the sun quits burning.

You say everybody is forgotten that is once great; George Washington has never been forgotten and nobody can be as great a president or as long remembered as he. Nobody can ever take his place or do what he did. Well, it's the same with Elvis. He'll always be remembered and nobody has ever [done] or ever will do the same thing as Elvis has.

Elvis is the king of popularity and we (teens of America) love him and we'll see he lives forever. Not his body but his name. Adults won't admit he's so great, because they're jealous! They know that their top singers weren't as great as Elvis. They're mad because their taste isn't quite as good as ours.

Look at James Dean, been dead for a year and he's bigger now than he ever was.

God gifted Elvis to us and you oughta thank him, not tear down the greatest thing the world has ever known: Elvis Presley!!!!!!

Scornfully yours,
Charlotte Jones

P.S.: And if you're over 30, you're old. You're certainly not young.

Source: George E. Sokolsky, "Teenager Puts Rap on Suggestion Elvis on Way Out," *Milwaukee Sentinel*, March 11, 1957, 5.

DOCUMENT 25.9

Todd Gitlin | Reflections on the 1950s, 1987

Todd Gitlin was born in 1943 and grew up in the Bronx, where he attended the prestigious Bronx High School of Science in the late 1950s. By the end of the decade, Gitlin had started questioning American domestic and foreign policies and began moving in the direction of the radicalism that he would embrace in the 1960s. In this excerpt from his book on the 1960s, Gitlin recalls the political disillusionment he was beginning to feel as a teenager.

On New Year's Eve, as 1958 slipped into 1959, I wasn't especially aware I was living in the dead, dreary Fifties. I was a high school senior about to turn sixteen. I had little sense of living in any kind of "Fifties" at all; I wasn't old enough to think in decades. I was simply living my life: striving for grades, wondering about sex, matching my exploits against those—real and imagined—of my rivals, watching the tides of adolescence rip through me. The only threshold I thought about was the one I would cross later that year, on the way to college. I was not living in history, but in biography.

Which is not to say I was devoid of political interests. I read *The New York Times* and my parents were liberal. I stayed up late on election nights and rooted for Democrats almost as passionately as I followed the New York Giants baseball team (until they broke my heart by running off to San Francisco in 1958). I thought President Dwight David Eisenhower was a genial deadhead, a semiliterate fuddy-duddy who deserved to be chastised almost as much for excessive golfing and tangled sentences as for embracing *Generalísimo* Franco [Spanish dictator Francisco Franco]. I thought Richard Nixon was sinister. I delighted in Jules Feiffer's [a cartoonist and writer] worldly spoofs of Eisenhower's syntax, the phone company's arrogance, and the middle class's clichés. I liked Herblock's liberal cartoons, including

one in which [presidential adviser] Bernard Baruch said that Eisenhower's stinginess with the military budget would make the United States "the richest man in the graveyard." A friend introduced me to H. L. Mencken's tilts at the philistine American "booboisie," and when I wrote the valedictory speech at the Bronx High School of Science later that year, the only quotation was from Mencken: "We live in a land of abounding quackeries."

My closest friends, the children of Jewish civil servants and skilled workers, held similar opinions. As we celebrated the coming of 1959, around midnight, in a fragment of news squeezed into Guy Lombardo's orchestral schmaltz, we saw the black-and-white footage of bearded Cubans wearing fatigues, smoking big cigars, grinning big grins to the cheers of throngs deliriously happy at the news that Batista had fled; and we cheered too. The overthrow of a brutal dictator, yes. But more, on the faces of the striding, strutting *barbudos* [bearded men] surrounded by adoring crowds we read redemption—a revolt of young people, underdogs, who might just cleanse one scrap of earth of the bloodletting and misery we had heard about all our lives. From a living room in the Bronx we saluted our unruly champions.

Source: Todd Gitlin, *The Sixties: Years of Hope, Days of Rage* (New York: Bantam, 1987), 1–2.

DOCUMENT 25.10

The Desegregation of Central High School, 1957

In 1957 nine black teenagers attempted to desegregate Central High School in Little Rock, Arkansas, pursuant to a federal court order. This photograph captures fifteen-year-old Elizabeth Eckford, one of the Little Rock Nine, surrounded by an angry white crowd on the first day of school. The photo also shows an enraged white student, Hazel Bryan, shouting at her to go home. Neither Eckford nor the other black students managed to attend school that day, but they entered Central High after President Eisenhower sent in federal troops to protect them.

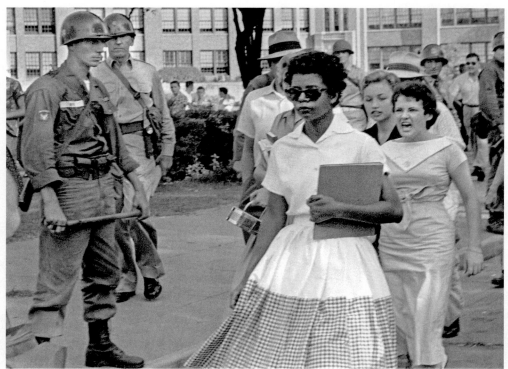

Lloyd Dinkins/The Commercial Appeal/Landov

Interpret the Evidence

1. What information in these documents confirms commonly held beliefs about teenagers in the 1950s?

2. What information in these documents challenges the conventional wisdom about teenagers in the 1950s?

3. Documents 25.5 and 25.7 speak specifically to teenagers. How do they differ, either in tone or in content, from those written *about* teens (Document 25.6) or *by* teens (Document 25.8)?

4. What do Documents 25.6 and 25.8 tell us about generational differences?

5. How much do these documents tell us about racial differences among teenagers in the postwar era?

6. What do Documents 25.5 and 25.10 reveal about gender roles and expectations within teenage culture in the 1950s?

Put It in Context

How do these documents show the way teenagers shaped the larger post–World War II society?

background photo: page 819, Library of Congress

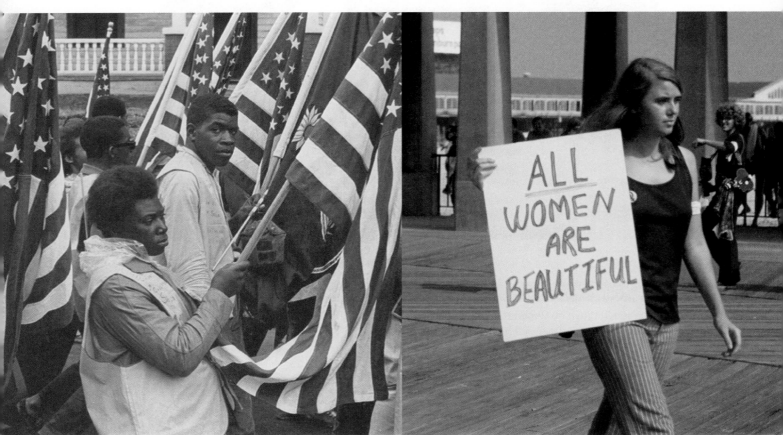

Robert Abbott Sengstacke/Getty Images

Santi Visalli Inc./Getty Images

Demonstrators carry American flags on the march from Selma to Montgomery to support voters' rights, 1965.

Protester at the Miss America Pageant at Atlantic City, New Jersey, 1969.

26

The Liberal Consensus and Its Challengers

1960–1973

Time & Life Pictures/Getty Images

U.S. military adviser with a South Vietnamese soldier of the 5th Airborne Brigade, 1972.

AMERICAN HISTORIES

How did a Republican politician who advocated the internment of Japanese Americans during World War II end up presiding over the most liberal Supreme Court in U.S. history? As attorney general of California at the outset of World War II, Earl Warren helped convince President Franklin D. Roosevelt to order the relocation of 110,000 Japanese Americans. After the war, as governor, he continued to fight against perceived threats to national security by joining the anti-Communist crusade. In 1953 President Dwight D. Eisenhower appointed Warren to be chief justice of the Supreme Court, a choice that many observers saw as a safe conservative pick by a safe conservative president.

As chief justice, however, Warren defied expectations and instead led the Court in a liberal direction. In 1954 Warren wrote the landmark opinion ordering school desegregation in *Brown v. Board of Education of Topeka, Kansas.* Departing from his own strong anti-Communist record, Warren upheld the rights of political dissenters and extended the boundaries of free speech. The Warren Court did not shrink from controversy, and its rulings expanding the rights of accused criminals, banning prayer in public school classrooms, and upholding birth control as a right of privacy evoked harsh criticism from the police, religious fundamentalists, and conservative politicians.

Unlike Earl Warren, Bayard Rustin worked outside of regular political and social channels to achieve change. Raised by his Quaker grandparents in Pennsylvania, Rustin began his career as an activist for social justice in

1937 when he moved to New York City to work as a youth organizer. He joined the Young Communist League because of its commitment to economic justice, racial equality, and international peace, but the pacifist Rustin quit the organization in 1941 when the party supported U.S. intervention in World War II and retreated on its fight against racial discrimination during the war.

In 1942 Rustin helped found the Congress of Racial Equality (CORE), an interracial organization that pioneered nonviolent, direct-action protests against racial bias. A committed pacifist, Rustin was imprisoned from 1943 to 1946 for declining to perform alternative service after he refused to register for the military draft. Prison strengthened his determination to challenge racial injustice through unconventional means. After his release, he continued to push for racial equality, and in 1947 Rustin helped plan and lead the Journey of Reconciliation, which challenged segregation on interstate buses in the South (see chapter 24). In the 1950s and 1960s, he became an adviser to Martin Luther King Jr. and a major strategist in the civil rights movement in his own right.

Rustin remained active in various causes throughout his life. One of his last efforts was perhaps his most personal: the struggle against antigay prejudice. As a homosexual, Rustin had to conceal his sexual identity at a time when the public and his political allies rejected homosexuals. Rustin often had to work behind the scenes to avoid unfavorable publicity, and even Dr. King on occasion kept his distance from him. In the 1980s, as the gay liberation movement grew more vocal, Rustin spoke out for tolerance and equality until his death in 1987. ●

photos: Robert S. Oakes for the National Geographic Society, Collection of the Supreme Court of the United States; Library of Congress

THE AMERICAN HISTORIES of Earl Warren and Bayard Rustin demonstrate the complexity of social change. The federal government had the power to encourage social movements by interpreting the Constitution, enacting legislation, and enforcing the law in a manner that eliminated barriers to racial, sexual, and political equality. Yet federal action likely would not have happened without the pressure applied by activists like Rustin. At the same time, efforts to promote equality and social justice produced a strong reaction from conservatives who feared that their political and social values were under assault. By the end of the 1960s, liberal reformers had achieved many of their objectives, but they had also triggered a stiff challenge from conservative opponents who sought to roll back those gains and pursue their own policies of small government, low taxes, and self-help.

The Politics of Liberalism

In 1960 the liberal agendas of Presidents Franklin Roosevelt and Harry Truman remained unfinished. Hoping to build on the legacy of the New Deal, liberals sought to increase the role of the federal government in the economy, education, and health care. Most liberals supported a staunchly anti-Communist foreign policy, differing with Republicans more over means than over ends. Indeed, when Democrats recaptured the White House in 1960, they seized opportunities in Cuba and Southeast Asia to vigorously challenge the expansion of Soviet influence.

Kennedy's New Frontier

With victory in World War II and the revival of economic prosperity, liberal thinkers regained confidence in capitalism. Many saw the postwar American free-enterprise system as different from the old-style capitalism that had existed before Franklin Roosevelt's New Deal. In their view, this new "reform capitalism," or democratic capitalism, created abundance for all and not just for a few elites. Rather than pushing for the redistribution of wealth, liberals now called on the government to help create conditions conducive to economic growth and increased productivity. In this context, the liberal economist John Kenneth Galbraith argued in *The Affluent Society* (1958) that increased public investments in education, research, and development were the key to American prosperity and progress.

These ideas guided the thinking of Democratic politicians such as Senator John F. Kennedy of Massachusetts. Elected president in 1960, the forty-three-year-old Kennedy brought good looks, charm, a beautiful wife, and young children to the White House—presenting a public image that matched the kind of nuclear family that Americans tuned in to watch on their television sets during the 1950s. Yet this was no ordinary family. The Kennedy family had numerous estates, and the president's father had used his fortune to bankroll his son John's political ambitions, first as a Massachusetts congressman, then as a U.S. senator, and finally as president. As president, John Kennedy pledged a **New Frontier** to battle "tyranny, poverty, disease, and war," but lacking strong majorities in Congress, he contented himself with making small gains on the New Deal foundation established by Franklin Roosevelt. Congress expanded unemployment benefits, increased the minimum wage, extended Social Security benefits, and raised appropriations for public housing, but Kennedy's caution disappointed many liberals.

The Kennedy administration showed greater zeal in fighting the Cold War abroad. The president believed that the same reform capitalism that had worked well in the United States should become a global model, especially in newly developing nations in Asia, Africa, and the Middle East. Communism, like fascism before it, posed a fundamental threat to American interests and to other countries' ability to emulate the economic miracle of the United States. The faith of liberals in American ingenuity, willpower, technological superiority, and moral righteousness encouraged them to reshape the "free world" in America's image.

President Kennedy's first Cold War battle took place in Cuba. During the 1960 campaign, Kennedy criticized the Eisenhower administration for allowing Fidel Castro to establish a Communist dictatorship in Cuba—despite Kennedy's knowledge of a secret CIA plan, devised by the Eisenhower administration, to topple Castro from power. After becoming president, Kennedy approved the scheme that Eisenhower had already set in motion.

The operation ended disastrously. On April 17, 1961, the invasion force of between 1,400 and 1,500 Cuban exiles, trained by the CIA, landed by boat at the Bay of Pigs on Cuba's southwest coast. Kennedy refused to provide backup military forces for fear of revealing America's role in the attack. After three days of fighting, Castro's troops defeated the insurgents. CIA planners had underestimated Cuban popular support for Castro, falsely believing that the invasion would inspire a national uprising against the Communist regime. The Kennedy administration had blundered its way into a bitter foreign policy defeat.

Two months later, Kennedy met Soviet leader Nikita Khrushchev at a summit meeting in Vienna. At the conference, Khrushchev took advantage of the president's embarrassing defeat in Cuba to press his own demands. The confrontational summit meeting increased tensions between the superpowers. Returning from Vienna, Kennedy persuaded Congress to increase the defense budget, dispatch additional troops to Europe, and bolster civil defense. In August, the Soviets responded by constructing a wall through Berlin, making it more difficult for refugees to flee from East Berlin to West Berlin, but they did not close off U.S. access to West Berlin. After the building of the Berlin Wall, tensions seemed to subside for a time, only to spike again the following year in a confrontation over Cuba that brought the world to the brink of nuclear disaster.

Following the Bay of Pigs disaster, the United States continued its efforts to topple the Castro regime. Such attempts were uniformly unsuccessful, but a wary Castro decided to invite the Soviet Union to install short- and intermediate-range missiles in his country to protect against further U.S. incursion. On October 22, 1962, Kennedy went on national television to inform the American people that Soviet missile sites were under construction in Cuba. The Kennedy administration decided to blockade Cuba to prevent Soviet ships from supplying the deadly missile warheads that would make the missiles fully operational. If this effort failed and Soviet ships defied the blockade, the president would order air strikes on Cuba. Ordinary Americans, particularly those within striking distance of Cuban-based Soviet missiles, nervously contemplated the very real possibility of nuclear destruction.

On the brink of nuclear war, both sides decided to compromise. Khrushchev agreed to remove the missiles, and Kennedy pledged not to invade Cuba and secretly promised to dismantle U.S. missile sites in Turkey that were aimed at the Soviet Union. The outcome did not please everyone. Castro, who still feared U.S. intervention, remained disappointed, as did Soviet hard-line leaders who believed that Khrushchev had displayed weakness. (Two years later, they deposed him.) The rest of the world breathed a sigh of relief, and Kennedy and Khrushchev, having stepped back from the edge of nuclear holocaust, worked to ease tensions further. In 1963 they signed a Partial Nuclear Test Ban Treaty—which prohibited atmospheric but not underground testing—and installed an electronic "hot line" to ensure swift communications between Washington and Moscow.

Explore

See Document 26.1 for one cartoonist's commentary on the Soviet removal of missiles from Cuba.

DOCUMENT 26.1

Edmund Valtman | The Cuban Missile Crisis, 1962

For thirteen days in October 1962, the world held its breath while President Kennedy and Soviet premier Khrushchev traded threats over the presence of nuclear weapons in Cuba. Khrushchev eventually backed down and removed the missiles. Two days after the crisis ended, the following cartoon by Edmund Valtman appeared in the *Hartford Times*.

Explore

Why might Khrushchev tell Castro, "This hurts me more than it hurts you!"?

What does the placement of the missiles suggest about their importance to Cuba?

What does the position of both characters suggest about the power relationship between Castro and Khrushchev?

Library of Congress

Put It in Context

How did the Cuban missile crisis affect Kennedy's and Khrushchev's thinking about the Cold War?

Containment in Southeast Asia

In addition to Cuba, Kennedy inherited the policy of containing communism in Southeast Asia. He shared his predecessors' belief that the Soviet Union was behind wars of national liberation throughout the third world. Like Eisenhower, Kennedy believed that if Communists toppled one regime in Asia it would produce a "domino effect," with one country after another falling to the Communists. Kennedy, a World War II veteran, also believed that aggressive nations that attacked weaker ones threatened world peace unless they were challenged.

Kennedy's containment efforts ran into difficulty in Vietnam because the United States did not control the situation on the ground. After supporting Ngo Dinh Diem as president of South Vietnam in 1955, the United States poured more than $1 billion into the country to implement land reform and create a stable government capable of withstanding Communist opposition from the Vietcong and North Vietnamese leader Ho Chi Minh's Communist forces in North Vietnam. However, Diem spent the money on building up military and personal security forces to suppress all political opposition. In 1961 Kennedy sent military advisers to help the South Vietnamese fight the Communists, but the situation deteriorated in 1963 when the Catholic Diem prohibited the country's Buddhist majority from holding religious celebrations. In protest, Buddhist monks committed suicide by setting themselves on fire, a grisly display captured on television news programs in the United States. With political opposition mounting against Diem's oppressive regime and the war going poorly, the Kennedy administration endorsed a military coup to replace the Diem government with one more capable of fighting Communists. On November 1, 1963, the coup leaders removed Diem from office, assassinated the deposed president and key members of his regime, and installed a military government.

Diem's death, however, did little to improve the worsening war against the Communists. The Vietcong had more support in the rural countryside than did the South Vietnamese government because the rebels promised land reform and recruited local peasants disturbed by the corruption and ruthlessness of the Diem regime. The Kennedy administration committed itself to supporting Diem's successor, but by late November 1963 Kennedy seemed ambivalent about what to do next. He was torn between sending more American troops and finding a way to negotiate a peace.

This ambivalence was reflected in Kennedy's more general effort to balance his hard-line anti-Communist policies with new outreach efforts to inspire developing nations to follow a democratic path. The Peace Corps program sent thousands of volunteers to teach and advise developing nations, and Kennedy's Alliance for Progress supplied economic aid to emerging democracies in Latin America. In June 1963, Kennedy announced his departure from his earlier militant Cold War stance in a commencement address at American University. Instead of describing a bipolar world of good and evil, Kennedy envisioned a "world safe for diversity. For in the final analysis, our most basic common link is that we all inhabit this small planet. We all breathe the same air. We all cherish our children's future and we are all mortal."

On November 22, 1963, three weeks after the assassination of Diem, Lee Harvey Oswald murdered Kennedy as he rode in an open motorcade in Dallas, Texas. The fatal shots from the assassin's rifle brought the nation to a standstill and prompted an outpouring of public grief not seen since President Roosevelt died in office in 1945. In death, Kennedy achieved immense popularity, and many Americans viewed him as a martyr. Yet Kennedy had left many problems unresolved. His legislative agenda, including civil rights, remained unfulfilled, and at the time of his death there were 16,000 American military advisers in Vietnam.

Johnson Escalates the War in Vietnam

Kennedy's successor, Lyndon B. Johnson, faced a difficult decision about Vietnam. Privately, the new president harbored reservations about fighting in Vietnam, but he was fearful of being considered soft on communism and was concerned that a demonstration of weakness would jeopardize congressional support for his domestic plans. Although President Johnson eventually concluded that more U.S. forces had to be sent to Vietnam, he hesitated to act immediately. Instead, he waited for the right moment to rally Congress and the American public behind an escalation of the war.

That moment came in August 1964. On August 2, North Vietnamese gunboats sixty miles off the North Vietnamese coast in the Gulf of Tonkin attacked an American spy ship. Two days later, another U.S. destroyer reported coming under torpedo attack, but because of stormy weather this second ship was not certain that it had actually been fired on. Neither ship suffered any damage. In fact, when informed of the assaults, the president responded: "For all I know, our navy might have been shooting at whales out there." Despite the considerable uncertainty about what actually happened, Johnson seized the opportunity to prompt Congress to authorize military action. On August 7, with only two dissenting votes, Congress passed the **Gulf of Tonkin Resolution**, which empowered the president to "repel any armed attacks against the forces of the United States and to prevent further aggression." In effect, Congress provided Johnson with unlimited power to make military decisions regarding Vietnam.

After winning election in 1964, President Johnson stepped up U.S. military action. In March 1965, with North Vietnamese forces flooding into the South, the president initiated Operation Rolling Thunder, a massive bombing campaign over North Vietnam and infiltration routes into the South along the Vietnamese borders with Cambodia and Laos, known as the Ho Chi Minh Trail. For more than three years, American planes dropped a million tons of bombs on North Vietnam, more than the total amount the United States used in World War II. Despite this massive firepower, the operation proved ineffective. A largely agricultural country, North Vietnam did not have the type of industrial targets best suited for air attacks. It stored its vital military resources under-ground, and the North Vietnamese were able to recon-struct rudimentary bridges and roads to maintain the flow of troops into the South within hours after U.S. bombers had pounded them.

Responding to the need to protect American air bases and the persistent ineffectiveness of the South Vietnamese government and military, Johnson deployed ever-increasing numbers of ground troops to Vietnam. In 1963, when

Johnson became president, 16,000 American troops were serving in Vietnam; this number grew to 380,000 in 1966, to 485,000 in 1967, and to 536,000 in 1968, with Johnson hoping that each new infusion would be the last. An estimated 200,000 North Vietnamese reached draft age annually, and Hanoi replenished its troops to counter the U.S. escalation. The U.S. military also deployed napalm bombs, which spewed burning jellied gasoline, and Agent Orange, a chemical defoliant that denuded the Vietnamese countryside and produced long-term adverse health effects for those who came in contact with it, including American soldiers. These attacks added to the resentment of the South Vietnamese peasants living in the countryside and helped the Vietcong gain new recruits.

The United States confronted a challenging guerrilla war in Vietnam. The Vietcong fought at night and blended in during the day as ordinary residents of cities and villages. They did not provide a visible target, and they recruited women and men of all ages, making it difficult for U.S. ground forces to distinguish friend from foe. To meet this challenge, the military, under the direction of General William C. Westmoreland, estab-lished "strategic hamlets" to separate the Vietcong from noncombatants. Troops moved residents out of their villages to a new location, set up a defense perimeter

My Lai Massacre, 1968
On March 16, 1968, U.S. army soldiers killed hundreds of unarmed civilians—most of them women, children, and the elderly—in the village of My Lai. The soldiers left bodies piled in ditches that ran around the village. The massacre became public in 1969, but only one soldier was convicted by a military tribunal.   Time & Life/Getty Images

around it, and assumed that anyone found outside this zone must be the enemy. Westmoreland then instituted "search and destroy" missions throughout the countryside to defeat the Vietcong. In the end, these policies did little to advance the U.S. military effort and alienated the population they were designed to safeguard.

Explore

> See Document 26.2 for one American soldier's experience in Vietnam.

On the ground, frustration also bred racism, as many American soldiers could not relate to the Vietnamese way of life and dismissed the enemy as "gooks." Lieutenant Philip Caputo later admitted that he could order his men to burn the thatch and bamboo shacks the Vietnamese lived in because to him a "home had brick or frame walls, a window, a lawn, a TV antenna on the roof." This attitude pushed some of the troops over the line between legitimate wartime practices and murder. Frustrated by rising casualties from an enemy they could not see, some American soldiers indiscriminately burned down villages and killed noncombatant civilians. Such disreputable behavior peaked in March 1968 with the My Lai massacre, when an American platoon murdered between 347 and 504 unarmed Vietnamese civilians in the village of My Lai.

DOCUMENT 26.2

George Olsen | Letter Home from Vietnam, 1969

George Olsen sent the following letter to his girlfriend shortly after he was sent to Vietnam in August 1969. The previous year, more than 16,000 American soldiers were killed, the largest one-year total of the war. By the time Olsen arrived in Vietnam, many Americans believed that the United States should withdraw its troops, and antiwar protests in America had escalated dramatically. Olsen was killed in action in March 1970.

Explore

31 Aug '69

Dear Red,

Last Monday I went on my first hunter-killer operation. . . . The frightening thing about it all is that it is so very easy to kill in war. There's no remorse, no theatrical "washing of the hands" to get rid of nonexistent blood, not even any regrets. When it happens, you are more afraid than you've ever been in your life—my hands shook so much I had trouble reloading. . . . You're scared, really scared, and there's no thinking about it. You kill because that little SOB is doing his best to kill you and you desperately want to live, to go home, to get drunk or walk down the street on a date again. And suddenly the grenades aren't going off any more, the weapons stop and, unbelievably fast it seems, it's all over. . . .

I have truly come to envy the honest pacifist who honestly believes that no killing is permissible and can, with a clear conscience, stay home and not take part in these conflicts. I wish I could do the same, but I can't see letting another take my place and my risks over here. . . . The only reason pacifists such as the Amish can even live in an orderly society is because someone—be they police or soldiers—is taking risks to keep the wolves away. . . . I guess that's why I'm over here, why I fought so hard to come here, and why, even though I'm scared most of the time, I'm content to be here.

Source: Bernard Edelman, ed., *Dear America: Letters Home from Vietnam* (New York: Pocket Books, 1985), 204–5.

Interpret the Evidence

- According to Olsen, why is it both easy and difficult to kill in wartime?
- Why does Olsen think it is important for him to fight?

Put It in Context

Why did Americans become disillusioned with the war in Vietnam?

On January 31, 1968, the Buddhist New Year of Tet, some 67,000 Communist forces mounted a surprise offensive throughout South Vietnam that targeted major population centers (Map 26.1). For six hours, a suicide squadron of Vietcong surrounded the U.S. Embassy in Saigon. U.S. forces finally repelled the **Tet Offensive**, but the battle proved psychologically costly to the United States. Following the Tet Offensive, the most revered television news anchor of the era, Walter Cronkite of CBS, turned against the war and expressed the doubts of a growing number of viewers when he announced: "To say that we are mired in stalemate seems the only reasonable, yet unsatisfactory conclusion."

Tet marked the beginning of the end of the war's escalation. On March 31, 1968, President Johnson ordered a halt to the bombing campaign and called for peace negotiations. He also stunned the nation by announcing that he would not seek reelection. By the time he left the White House in 1969, peace negotiations had stalled and some 36,000 Americans had died in combat, along with 52,000 South Vietnamese troops.

REVIEW & RELATE

How did President Kennedy's domestic agenda reflect the liberal political ideology of the early 1960s?

How and why did the United States escalate its role in the Vietnam War?

LEARNINGCurve bedfordstmartins.com/hewittlawson/LC

MAP 26.1   The Vietnam War, 1968
The United States wielded vastly more military personnel and weaponry than the Vietcong and North Vietnamese but faced a formidable challenge in fighting a guerrilla war in a foreign country. Massive American bombing failed to defeat the North Vietnamese or stop their troop movements and supply lines along the Ho Chi Minh Trail. The 1968 Tet Offensive demonstrated the shortcomings in the U.S. strategy.

Civil Rights

Back home, the most critical issue facing the nation in the early 1960s was the intensification of the civil rights movement. As a candidate, Kennedy had promised vigorous action on civil rights, but as president he did little to follow through on his promises. With southern Democrats occupying key positions in Congress and threatening to block any civil rights proposals, Kennedy hesitated to upset this critical component of his political base. Following Kennedy's death in 1963, President Johnson succeeded in breaking the legislative logjam and signed into law three major pieces of civil rights legislation. He did so under considerable pressure from the civil rights movement.

Freedom Rides

The Congress of Racial Equality took the offensive on May 4, 1961. Similar to Bayard Rustin's efforts in the 1940s, CORE mounted racially integrated **Freedom Rides** to test whether facilities in the South, from Virginia to Louisiana, were complying with the 1960 Supreme Court ruling that outlawed segregated bus and train stations serving passengers who were traveling interstate. CORE had alerted the Justice Department and the FBI of its plans, but the riders received no protection when Klan-dominated mobs in Anniston and Birmingham, Alabama, attacked two buses containing activists, seriously wounding several passengers.

Freedom Rides, 1961

On May 4, 1961, two buses of black and white riders left Washington, D.C., and headed for New Orleans to desegregate bus terminal facilities along the route. When one of the buses arrived in Anniston, Alabama, it was attacked and burned by white mobs, forcing the passengers to flee for safety. Despite the violence, the Freedom Rides continued and grew in scope.   Library of Congress

After safety concerns forced CORE to forgo the rest of the trip, members of the Student Nonviolent Coordinating Committee (SNCC) rushed to Birmingham to continue the bus rides. The Kennedy administration urged them to reconsider, but Diane Nash, a SNCC founder, explained that although the group realized the peril of resuming the journey, "we can't let them stop us with violence. If we do, the movement is dead." When the replenished busload of riders reached Montgomery on May 20, they were brutally assaulted by a mob. Dr. Martin Luther King Jr., who supported the rides but had not participated in them, subsequently held a rally in a Montgomery church, which became the target of renewed white attacks that threatened the lives of King and the Freedom Riders inside the building. Faced with the prospect of serious bloodshed, the Kennedy administration dispatched federal marshals to the scene and persuaded the governor to call out the Alabama National Guard to ensure the safety of everyone in the church.

The president and his brother, Attorney General Robert Kennedy, worked out a compromise to let the rides continue with minimal violence and publicity; at the same time, Robert Kennedy petitioned the Interstate Commerce Commission (ICC) to issue an order prohibiting segregated transportation facilities, which went into effect in November 1961. Despite the ICC declaration, many southern communities refused to comply. When Freedom Riders encountered opposition in Albany, Georgia, in the fall of 1961, SNCC workers remained in Albany and helped local leaders organize residents of the town against segregation and other forms of racial discrimination. Even with the assistance of Dr. King and the Southern Christian Leadership Conference (SCLC), the Albany movement stalled, as the Kennedy administration refused to provide support.

The Government Responds on Civil Rights

Despite the setback in Albany, the civil rights movement kept up pressure on other fronts. In September 1962, Mississippi governor Ross Barnett tried to thwart the registration of James Meredith as an undergraduate at the

University of Mississippi. Barnett's obstruction precipitated a riot on campus, and as Eisenhower had done at Little Rock, President Kennedy dispatched army troops and federalized the Mississippi National Guard to restore order, but not before two bystanders were killed.

The following year, King and the SCLC joined the Reverend Fred Shuttlesworth's freedom movement in Birmingham, Alabama, in its battle against employment discrimination, segregation in public accommodations, and police brutality. With the white supremacist Eugene "Bull" Connor in charge of law enforcement, civil rights protesters, including children ranging in age from six to sixteen, encountered violent resistance, the use of vicious police dogs, and high-powered water hoses. Connor ordered mass arrests, including Dr. King's, prompting the minister to write his famous "Letter from Birmingham Jail," in which he justified the use of nonviolent direct action. Seeking to defuse the crisis and concerned about America's image abroad, President Kennedy sent an emissary in early May 1963 to negotiate a peaceful solution that granted concessions to Birmingham blacks and ended the demonstrations. On Sunday, September 15, 1963, however, a few months after the successful end of the conflict, the Ku Klux Klan dynamited Birmingham's Sixteenth Street Baptist Church, a freedom movement staging ground. The blast killed four young girls attending services.

Meanwhile, after several years of caution, the president finally decided to speak out about the nation's duty to guarantee equal rights regardless of race. On June 11, 1963, shortly after negotiating the Birmingham agreement, Kennedy delivered a nationally televised address. He acknowledged that the country faced a "moral crisis" heightened by the events in Birmingham, and he noted the difficulty of preaching "freedom around the world" while "this is a land of the free except for Negroes." He proposed congressional legislation to end segregation in public accommodations, increase federal power to promote school desegregation, and broaden the right to vote.

Events on the day Kennedy delivered his powerful speech reinforced the need for swift action. Earlier that morning, Alabama governor George C. Wallace, a segregationist, had stood in front of the administration building at the University of Alabama to block the entrance of two black undergraduates. To uphold the federal court decree ordering their admission, Kennedy deployed federal marshals and the Alabama National Guard, and Wallace, having dramatized his point, stepped aside. Victory soon turned into tragedy. Later that evening, the president learned of the killing of Medgar Evers, the head of the NAACP in Mississippi, who was shot in the driveway of his Jackson home by the white supremacist Byron de la Beckwith. (Following two trials, de la Beckwith remained free until 1994, when he was retried and convicted for Evers's murder.)

Nonetheless, Congress was still unwilling to act. To increase pressure on lawmakers, civil rights organizations held a **March on Washington for Jobs and Freedom** on August 28, 1963, carrying out an idea first proposed by A. Philip Randolph in 1941 (see chapter 23). With Randolph as honorary chair, his associate Bayard Rustin directed the proceedings, delivering 250,000 black and white peaceful protesters to a rally in front of the Lincoln Memorial. Two speakers in particular caught the attention of the crowd. John Lewis, the chairman of SNCC, expressed the frustration of militant blacks with both the Kennedy administration and Congress. "The revolution is at hand. . . . We will not wait for the President, nor the Justice Department, nor Congress," Lewis asserted. "But we will take matters into our own hands." In a more conciliatory tone, King delivered a speech expressing his dream for racial and religious brotherhood. Still, King issued a stern warning to "those who hope that the Negro needed to blow off steam and will now be content. . . . There will be neither rest nor tranquility in America until the Negro is granted his citizenship rights. The whirlwinds of revolt will continue to shake the foundations of our nation until the bright day of justice emerges."

Freedom Summer and Voting Rights

Following Kennedy's death and three months after the March on Washington, President Johnson took charge of the pending civil rights legislation. Under Johnson's leadership, a bipartisan coalition turned back a southern filibuster (a tactic that delays or prevents action in Congress) in the Senate and passed the **Civil Rights Act of 1964**. The law prohibited discrimination in public accommodations, increased federal enforcement of school desegregation and the right to vote, and created the Community Relations Service, a federal agency authorized to help resolve racial conflicts. The act also contained a final measure to combat employment discrimination on the basis of race and sex.

Yet even as President Johnson signed the 1964 Civil Rights Act into law on July 2, black freedom forces launched a new offensive to secure the right to vote in the South. The 1964 act contained a voting rights provision but did little to address the main problems of the discriminatory use of literacy tests and poll taxes and the biased administration of voter registration procedures that kept the majority of southern blacks from voting. Three years earlier, the Kennedy administration had brokered a deal to secure private funding for voter registration drives in the South directed by the Atlanta-based Voter Education Project. Civil rights workers believed that the Justice

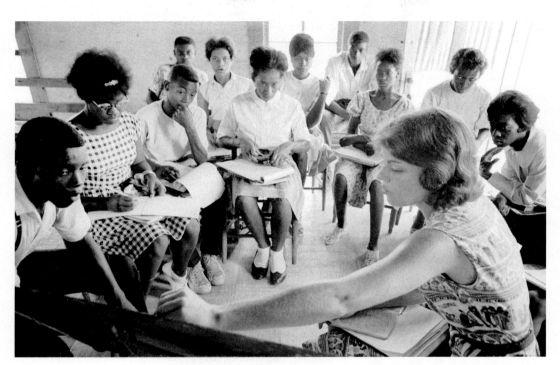

Freedom Schools, 1964

In Mileston, Mississippi, summer volunteer Martha Honey teaches a freedom school class that included Eddie Carthan (far left), who later became mayor of nearby Tchula. Because the state provided black students a limited education, these schools, staffed by volunteers, offered an opportunity to learn basic reading, writing, and arithmetic skills as well as African American history and culture. © Matt Heron/Take Stock/The Image Works

Department would provide federal protection for voter drives, but the Kennedy and Johnson administrations let them down. Beatings, killings, arson, and arrests became a routine response to voting rights efforts. Although the Justice Department filed lawsuits against recalcitrant voter registrars and police officers, the government refused to send in federal personnel or instruct the FBI to safeguard vulnerable civil rights workers.

To focus national attention on this problem, SNCC, CORE, the NAACP, and the SCLC launched the **Freedom Summer** project in Mississippi. They assigned eight hundred volunteers from around the nation, mainly white college students, to work on voter registration drives and in "freedom schools" to improve education for rural black youngsters stuck in inferior, segregated schools. White supremacists fought back against what they perceived as an enemy invasion. In late June 1964, the Ku Klux Klan, in collusion with local law enforcement officials, killed three civil rights workers. This tragedy brought national attention, and President Johnson pressed the usually uncooperative FBI to find the culprits, which it did. However, civil rights workers continued to encounter white violence and harassment throughout Freedom Summer. **See Document Project 26: Freedom Summer, page 849.**

One outcome of the Freedom Summer project was the creation of the **Mississippi Freedom Democratic Party (MFDP)**. Because the regular all-white state Democratic Party excluded blacks, the civil rights coalition formed an alternative Democratic Party open to everyone. In August 1964, the mostly black MFDP sent a delegation to the Democratic National Convention meeting in Atlantic City, New Jersey, to challenge the seating of the all-white delegation from Mississippi. One of the MFDP delegates, Fannie Lou Hamer, who had lost her job on a Mississippi plantation for her voter registration activities, offered passionate testimony broadcast on television. To avoid a bruising political fight, Johnson hammered out a compromise that gave the MFDP two general at-large seats, imposed a loyalty oath on members of the regular delegation to support the Democratic presidential ticket, and prohibited racial discrimination in the future by any state Democratic Party. Although both sides rejected the compromise, four years later an integrated delegation, which included Hamer, represented Mississippi at the Democratic National Convention in Chicago.

Freedom Summer highlighted the problem of disfranchisement, but it took further demonstrations in Selma, Alabama, to resolve it. After state troopers shot and killed a black voting rights demonstrator in February 1965, Dr. King called for a march from Selma to the capital of Montgomery to petition Governor George Wallace to end the violence and allow blacks to vote. Local law enforcement officials answered their peaceful protests with arrests and beatings. On Sunday, March 7, as black and white marchers left Selma, the sheriff's forces sprayed them with tear gas, beat them, and sent them running for their lives

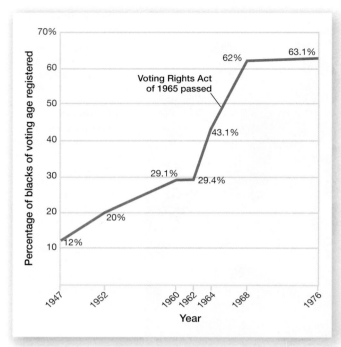

FIGURE 26.1 Black Voter Registration in the South, 1947–1976

After World War II, the percentage of black adults registered to vote in the South slowly but steadily increased, largely as a result of grassroots voting drives. Despite the Kennedy administration's support for voter registration drives, a majority of southern blacks remained prohibited from voting in 1964. The passage of the 1965 Voting Rights Act removed barriers such as literacy tests and poll taxes, strengthened the federal government's enforcement powers, and enabled more than 60 percent of southern blacks to vote by the late 1960s. Source: Data from David Garrow, *Protest at Selma* (New Haven: Yale University Press, 1978), and U.S. Department of Commerce, Bureau of the Census, *Statistical Abstract of the United States*, 1976.

back to town. A few days later, a white clergyman who had joined the protesters was killed on the streets of Selma by a group of white thugs. On March 21, following another failed attempt to march to Montgomery, King led protesters on the fifty-mile hike to the state capital, where they arrived safely four days later. Tragically, after the march, the Ku Klux Klan murdered a white female marcher from Michigan.

Events in Selma prompted President Johnson to take action. On March 15, he addressed a joint session of Congress and told lawmakers and a nationally televised audience that the black "cause must be our cause too. Because it is not just Negroes, but really it is all of us, who must overcome the crippling legacy of bigotry and injustice." In the words of the civil rights movement anthem, Johnson added, "And we shall overcome." On August 6, 1965, the president signed the **Voting Rights Act**, which banned the use of literacy tests for voter registration,

authorized a federal lawsuit against the poll tax (which succeeded in 1966), empowered federal officials to register disfranchised voters, and required seven southern states to submit any voting changes to Washington before they went into effect. With strong federal enforcement of the law, by 1968 a majority of African Americans and nearly two-thirds of black Mississippians could vote in the South (Figure 26.1).

REVIEW & RELATE

- What role did the federal government play in advancing the cause of racial equality in the early 1960s?

- How did civil rights activists pressure state and federal government officials to enact their agenda?

✓ *LEARNINGCurve* bedfordstmartins.com/hewittlawson/LC

Reforming the Social Order

President Johnson carried liberal reform to its greatest heights, drawing on Kennedy's legacy and his own considerable political skills to win passage of the most important items on the liberal agenda. While Johnson pressed ahead in the legislative arena, Chief Justice Earl Warren's Supreme Court issued rulings that extended social justice to minorities and the economically oppressed and favored those who believed in a firm separation of church and state, in free speech, and in a right to privacy.

The Great Society

In an address at the University of Michigan on May 22, 1964, President Johnson sketched out his dream for the **Great Society**, one that "rests on abundance and liberty for all. It demands an end to poverty and racial justice, to which we are totally committed in our time. But that is just the beginning." According to Johnson, increasing the power and wealth of America was not enough. He saw the Great Society as "a place where the city of man serves not only the needs of the body and the demands of commerce but the desire for beauty and the hunger for community." Besides poverty and race, he outlined three broad areas in need of reform: education, the environment, and cities.

Johnson did not hesitate to approve plans to develop Kennedy's unfinished fight against poverty. Kennedy had persuaded lawmakers to provide federal aid to poor regions such as Appalachia. In designing the Economic Opportunity Act of 1964, Johnson wanted to offer the poor "a hand up, not a handout." His program provided job training, remedial education (later to include the preschool program Head Start), a domestic Peace Corps called Volunteers in Service to America (VISTA), and a Community Action Program that empowered the poor to shape policies affecting their own communities. The antipoverty program helped reduce the proportion of poor people from 20 percent in 1963 to 13 percent five years later, and it helped reduce the rate of black poverty from 40 percent to 20 percent during this same period.

Johnson intended to fight the War on Poverty through the engine of economic growth. In 1962 Congress had passed the Revenue Act, which gave more than $1 billion in tax breaks to businesses. Kennedy had agreed to the targeted tax reduction because he believed it would encourage businesses to plow added savings into new investments and to expand production, thereby creating new jobs. Johnson's tax cut, which applied across the board, stimulated the economy and sent the gross national product soaring from $591 billion in 1963 to $977 billion by the end of the decade. Thus the logic of economic expansion rather than redistribution guided Johnson's War on Poverty.

Despite considerable success, Johnson's program failed to meet liberal expectations. It would have taken an annual appropriation of about $11 billion to lift every needy person above the poverty line. To reduce opposition from cost-minded legislators who wanted to starve his programs if they could not stop them, Johnson asked Congress for just under $1 billion a year. Because the president refused to

press lawmakers harder for money, his ability to fight the War on Poverty was severely limited.

Whatever the limitations, Johnson campaigned on his antipoverty and civil rights record in his bid to recapture the White House in 1964. His Republican opponent, Senator Barry M. Goldwater of Arizona, personified the conservative right wing of the Republican Party and rejected the Modern Republicanism identified with President Eisenhower (see chapter 25). The Arizona senator condemned big government, supported states' rights, and accused liberals of not waging the Cold War forcefully enough. His aggressive conservatism appealed to his grassroots base in small-town America, especially in southern California, the Southwest, and the South. His tough rhetoric, however, scared off moderate Republicans, resulting in a landslide for Johnson on election day, as well as considerable Democratic majorities in Congress.

Flush with victory, Johnson moved quickly and achieved impressive results. To cite only a few examples, the Eighty-ninth Congress (1965–1967) provided federal aid to public schools; subsidized health care for the elderly and the poor by creating Medicare and Medicaid; expanded voting rights for African Americans in the South; authorized funds to cities for housing, jobs, education, mass transportation, crime prevention, and recreation; raised the minimum wage; created national endowments for the fine arts and humanities; and adopted regulations to preserve clean air and water supplies. The 1965 Immigration Act

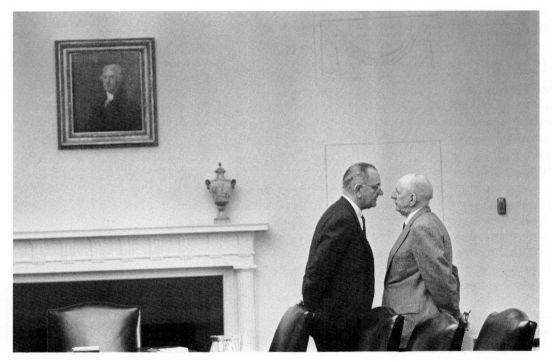

The Johnson Treatment

At six feet four inches tall, Lyndon Johnson towered over most of his colleagues. As Senate majority leader, he became famous for putting pressure on lawmakers and cajoling them into submission. This 1963 photograph shows President Johnson leaning over his former Senate mentor, Richard B. Russell of Georgia, and firmly making his point in pursuit of his legislative agenda. LBJ Library photo by Yoichi Okamoto

TABLE 26.1   Major Great Society Measures, 1964–1968

Year	Legislation or Order	Purpose
1964	Civil Rights Act	Prohibited discrimination in public accommodations, education, and employment
	Economic Opportunity Act	Established War on Poverty agencies: Head Start, VISTA, Job Corps, and Community Action Program
1965	Elementary and Secondary Education Act	Federal funding for elementary and secondary schools
	Medical Care Act	Provided Medicare health insurance for citizens 65 years and older and Medicaid health benefits for the poor
	Voting Rights Act	Banned literacy tests for voting, authorized federal registrars to be sent into seven southern states, and monitored voting changes in these states
	Executive Order 11246	Required employers to take affirmative action to promote equal opportunity and remedy the effects of past discrimination
	Immigration and Nationality Act	Abolished quotas on immigration that reduced immigration from non-Western and southern and eastern European nations
	Water Quality Act	Established and enforced federal water quality standards
	Air Quality Act	Established air pollution standards for motor vehicles
	National Arts and Humanities Act	Established National Endowment of the Humanities and National Endowment of the Arts to support the work of scholars, writers, artists, and musicians
1966	Model Cities Act	Approved funding for the rehabilitation of inner cities
1967	Executive Order 11375	Expanded affirmative action regulations to include women
1968	Civil Rights Act	Outlawed discrimination in housing

repealed discriminatory national origins quotas established in 1924, resulting in a shift of immigration from Europe to Asia and Central and South America (Table 26.1).

The Warren Court

The Warren Court reflected this high tide of liberalism. The Court affirmed the constitutionality of the Voting Rights Act and struck down the poll tax as a voting requirement in 1966. A year later, the justices overturned state laws prohibiting interracial marriages. And in 1968, fourteen years after the *Brown* school desegregation decision, they ruled that school districts in the South could no longer maintain racially exclusive schools and must desegregate immediately. In a series of cases, the Warren Court ensured fairer legislative representation for blacks and whites by removing the disproportionate power that rural districts had held over urban districts.

The Supreme Court's most controversial rulings dealt with the criminal justice system, religion, and private sexual practices, all of which involved liberal interpretations of the individual freedoms guaranteed by the Bill of Rights. Strengthening the rights of criminal defendants, the justices ruled in *Gideon v. Wainwright* (1963) that states had to provide indigents accused of felonies with an attorney, and in *Miranda v. Arizona* (1966) they ordered the police to advise suspects of their constitutional rights.

The Court also moved into new, controversial territory concerning school prayer, contraception, and pornography. In 1962 the Court outlawed a nondenominational Christian prayer recited in New York State schools as a violation of the separation of church and state guaranteed by the First Amendment. Three years later, in *Griswold v. Connecticut*, the justices struck down a state law that banned the sale of contraceptives because such laws, they contended, infringed on an individual's right to privacy. In a 1966 case reversing Massachusetts's ban of an erotic novel, the Supreme Court ruled that states could not prohibit what they deemed pornographic material unless it was "utterly without redeeming social value," a standard that opened the door for the dissemination of sexually explicit books, magazines, and films. These verdicts unleashed a firestorm of criticism, especially from religious groups that accused the Warren Court of undermining traditional values of faith and decency.

REVIEW & RELATE

What problems and challenges did Johnson's Great Society legislation target?

In what ways did the Warren Court's rulings advance the liberal agenda?

 LEARNINGCurve bedfordstmartins.com/hewittlawson/LC

Challenges to the Liberal Center

Even at its peak in the 1960s, liberalism faced major challenges from both the left and the right. A generation of young activists, mainly in colleges and universities, became impatient with what they saw as the slow pace of social progress and were increasingly disturbed by the escalation of the Vietnam War. At the same time, the right contended that liberals had instituted reforms that diminished individual initiative and benefited racial minorities at the expense of the white middle class. They disparaged liberals for not winning the Vietnam War and depicted the left as unpatriotic and out of step with mainstream American values. By 1969 liberalism and the left were in retreat, and Richard M. Nixon, a political conservative, had captured the White House.

Movements on the Left

The civil rights movement had inspired many young people to activism. Combining ideals of freedom, equality, and community with direct-action protest, civil rights activists offered a model for those seeking to address a variety of problems, including the Cold War threat of nuclear devastation, the loss of individual autonomy in a corporate society, racism, poverty, sexism, and the poisoning of the environment. The formation of SNCC in 1960 illuminated the possibilities for personal and social transformation and offered a movement culture founded on democracy.

Tom Hayden helped apply the ideals of SNCC to predominantly white college campuses. After spending the summer of 1961 registering voters in Mississippi and Georgia, the University of Michigan graduate student returned to campus eager to recruit like-minded students who questioned America's commitment to democracy. "Beyond lunch counter demonstrations," Hayden wrote, "there are more serious evils which must be ripped out by any means: exploitation, socially destructive capital, evil political and legal structure, and myopic liberalism which is anti-revolutionary."

Hayden became an influential leader of the **Students for a Democratic Society (SDS)**, which advocated the

formation of a "New Left." They considered the "Old Left," which revolved around the Communist Party, as autocratic and no longer relevant. In its **Port Huron Statement** (1962), SDS condemned mainstream liberal politics, Cold War foreign policy, racism, and research-oriented universities that cared little for their undergraduates. It called for the adoption of "participatory democracy," which would return power to the people. SDS argued that the age of the military-industrial complex, with its mega-universities and giant corporations, had created a new educated class of alienated white-collar workers and college students perfectly suited to lead the revolution.

The New Left never consisted of one central organization such as SDS; after all, many protesters challenged the very idea of centralized authority. In fact, SDS did not initiate the New Left's most dramatic, early protest. In 1964 the University of California at Berkeley banned political activities just outside the main campus entrance in response to CORE protests against racial bias in local hiring. When CORE defied the prohibition, campus police arrested its leader, prompting a massive student uprising. The university's prohibition also spurred students to form the **Free Speech Movement (FSM)**, which held rallies in front of the administration building, culminating in a nonviolent, civil rights–style sit-in to assert their right to participate in such activities. When California governor Edmund "Pat" Brown dispatched a large force of state and county police to evict the demonstrators, students and faculty joined together in protest and forced the university administration to yield to FSM's demands for amnesty and reform. By the end of the decade, hundreds of demonstrations had erupted on campuses throughout the nation, culminating in 1968 in a bloody confrontation at Columbia University between students and New York City police. Unlike protests in the South aimed at reactionary white supremacists, campus revolts targeted liberals, dismissing them as obstacles to genuine social change.

The Vietnam War accelerated student radicalism, and college campuses provided a strategic setting for antiwar activities. Like most Americans in the mid-1960s, undergraduates had only a dim awareness of U.S. activity in Vietnam. Yet all college men were eligible for the draft once they graduated and lost their student deferment. As more troops were sent to Vietnam, student concern intensified.

Protests escalated in 1966 as President Johnson authorized an additional 250,000-troop buildup in Vietnam. This mobilization required higher draft calls, which began to affect more college men. With induction into the military a looming possibility, student protesters engaged in a variety of activities. Some burned draft cards; disrupted attempts by outside firms, such as the CIA and Dow Chemical Company (which made napalm), to recruit on campus; or

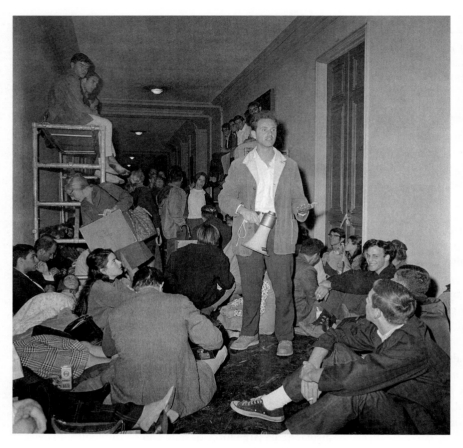

The Berkeley Free Speech Movement

Mario Savio, a student leader at the University of California at Berkeley and a Freedom Summer volunteer, stands among demonstrators sitting in at Sproul Hall on December 3, 1964, to protest university curbs on free speech. A day earlier, Savio had declared: "There's a time when the operation of the machine becomes so odious . . . you've got to put your bodies upon the gears . . . and you've got to make it stop." AP Photo/Robert Houston

campaigned against the presence on campus of Reserve Officers' Training Corps (ROTC), which prepared future military leaders. Others resisted the draft by fleeing to Canada, and still others engaged in various forms of civil disobedience. Most college students, however, were not activists—between 1965 and 1968, only 20 percent of college students attended demonstrations. Nevertheless, the activist minority received wide media attention and helped raise awareness about the difficulty of waging the Vietnam War abroad and maintaining domestic tranquillity at home.

By the end of 1967, as the number of troops in Vietnam approached half a million, protests increased. Antiwar sentiment had spread to faculty, artists, writers, business people, and elected officials. Earlier that year in April, Martin Luther King Jr. delivered a powerful antiwar address at Riverside Church in New York City. "The world now demands," King declared, ". . . that we admit that we have been wrong from the beginning of our adventure in Vietnam, that we have been detrimental to the life of the Vietnamese people." In 1968 SDS split into factions, with the most prominent of them, the **Weathermen**, going underground and adopting violent tactics.

The New Left's challenge to liberal politics attracted many students, and the **counterculture**'s rejection of conventional middle-class values of work, sexual restraint, and faith in reason captivated even more. Cultural rebels emphasized living in the present, immediate gratification, authenticity of feelings, and reaching a higher consciousness through mind-altering drugs like marijuana and LSD. These youth rebels, popularly called "hippies," mocked their elders in the slogan "Don't trust anyone over thirty." Despite differences in approach, both the New Left and the counterculture expressed concerns about modern technology, bureaucratization, and the possibility of nuclear annihilation and sought new means of creating political, social, and personal liberation.

Rock 'n' roll became the soundtrack of the counterculture. In 1964 Bob Dylan's song "The Times They Are A-Changin'" became an anthem for youth rebellion, just as his "Blowin' in the Wind" did for the civil rights movement. In 1964 the Beatles, a British quartet influenced by 1950s black and white rock 'n' rollers, came to the United States and revolutionized popular music. Originally singing tuneful compositions of teenage love and angst, the Beatles embraced the counterculture and began writing songs

```
SELECTIVE SERVICE SYSTEM
NOTICE OF CLASSIFICATION
This is to certify that
STEVEN      F.     LAWSON
(First name)  (Middle initial)  (Last name)

Selective Service No.

50 | 22 | 45 | 246

is classified in Class        1A

until
by Local Board unless otherwise
checked below:
☐ by Appeal Board
   vote of _____ to _____
☐ by President
       AUG 1 9 1970
(Date of mailing)

(Member, Executive Secretary, or clerk of
              local board)

(Registrant's signature)

SSS Form 110 (Rev. 5-25-67)
(Previous printings are obsolete)
(Approval not required)
```

(Fold along this line)

Draft Card

In 1963 Steven F. Lawson reached the age of eighteen and registered with his draft board, but as a college undergraduate he received a student deferment (II-S). With draft calls climbing due to the escalation of the Vietnam War, Lawson like many others was reclassified to I-A status—"available for military service." When a draft lottery was introduced in 1969, he drew a high number and was not drafted.　Courtesy of Steven F. Lawson

about alienation and politics, flavoring them with the drug-inspired sounds of psychedelic music. The Beatles launched a "British invasion," which also brought the Rolling Stones, who offered a harder-edged and raunchier sound than did the Beatles. Although most of the songs that reached the top ten on the record charts did not undermine traditional values, the music of groups like the Beatles, the Rolling Stones, the Who, the Grateful Dead, Jefferson Airplane, and the Doors spread counterculture messages of youth rebellion. At the same time, young black and white rebels embraced "soul music," black dance music popularized through the African American–owned Motown Records in Detroit and the white-owned Stax Records in Memphis.

The counterculture viewed the elimination of sexual restrictions as essential for transforming personal and social behavior. The 1960s generation did not invent sexual freedom, but it did a great deal to shatter time-honored moral codes of monogamy, fidelity, and moderation. Promiscuity—casual sex, group sex, extramarital affairs, public nudity—and open-throated vulgarity tested public tolerance. Yet within limits, the popular culture reflected these changes. The Broadway production of the musical *Hair* showed frontal nudity, the movie industry adopted ratings of "X" and "R" that made films with nudity and profane language available to a wider audience, and new television comedy shows featured sketches including risqué content and double entendres. With a nod from the Warren Court's easing definitions of pornography, counterculture writers assaulted the boundaries of "good taste."

With sexual conduct in flux, society had difficulty maintaining the double standard of behavior that privileged men over women. The counterculture gave many women a chance to pursue and enjoy sexual pleasure that had long been denied to them. The availability of birth control pills for women, introduced in 1960, made much of this sexual freedom possible. Although sexual liberation still carried more risks for women than for men, increased openness in discussing sexuality allowed many women to gain greater control over their bodies and their relationships.

Women's Liberation

Struggles in the 1960s for racial equality, peace, economic justice, and cultural and sexual freedom helped revive the fight for women's emancipation. Despite passage of the Nineteenth Amendment in 1920, which gave women the right to vote (see chapter 19), women did not have equal access to employment and education or control over reproduction. Nor did they have sufficient political power to remove the remaining obstacles to full equality. By 1960 nearly 40 percent of all women held jobs—representing one-third of the labor force—and women made up 35 percent of college enrollments. Subsequently, the social movements of the 1960s—civil rights, the New Left, and the counterculture—included large numbers of women and provided them with experience, connections, principles, and grievances that would lead women to create their own movement for liberation.

The federal government played a significant role in addressing gender discrimination. In 1961 President Kennedy appointed the **Commission on the Status of Women**. The commission's report, *American Women*, issued in 1963, reaffirmed the primary role of women in raising the family but cataloged the inequities women faced in the workplace. In 1963 Congress passed the Equal Pay Act, which required employers to give men and women equal pay for equal work. The following year, the 1964 Civil Rights Act opened up further opportunities when it prohibited sexual bias in employment and created the Equal Employment Opportunity Commission (EEOC). However, women remained divided over the need for the Equal Rights Amendment (ERA), first proposed in 1923 by suffragist Alice Paul. The Commission on the Status of Women refused to endorse it largely because labor union women believed that adopting the ERA would eliminate laws that specifically protected women workers with respect to hours, wages, and safety conditions.

In 1963 Betty Friedan published a landmark work in the history of the women's rights movement, *The Feminine Mystique*, a book that questioned society's prescribed gender roles. In *The Feminine Mystique*, she described the isolation and alienation experienced by her female friends and associates, raising the consciousness of many women, particularly college graduates and professionals. However, not all women saw themselves reflected in Friedan's book. Many working-class women from African American and other minority families had not had the opportunity to attend college and had to work to help support their families, and younger women had not yet experienced the burdens of domestic isolation.

Nevertheless, in October 1966, Betty Friedan and like-minded women formed the **National Organization for Women (NOW)**. With Friedan as president, NOW dedicated itself to moving society toward "true equality for all women in America, and toward a fully equal partnership of the sexes." NOW also called on the EEOC to enforce women's employment rights more vigorously and favored passage of the ERA, maternity leave rights in employment, the establishment of child care centers, and reproductive rights. Although NOW advocated job training programs and assistance for impoverished women, it attracted a mainly middle-class white membership. Some blacks were among its charter members, but most African American women chose to concentrate on first eliminating racial barriers that affected black women and men alike. Some union women also continued to

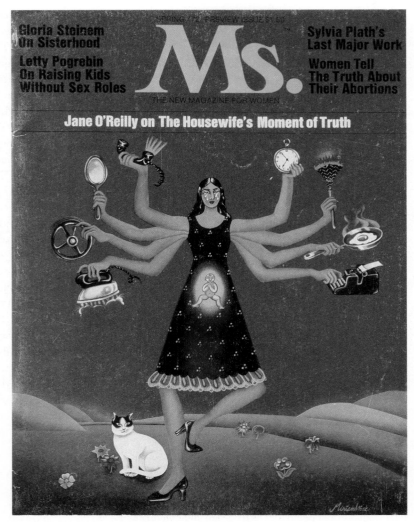

The Feminist Movement

In 1972 Gloria Steinem, a founder of NOW, established *Ms.* magazine in hope of attracting readers from across the feminist political spectrum. In this premiere issue, women's art and poetry appear alongside articles on sisterhood, child rearing, and abortion. The cover illustrates the demands on housewives who juggle domestic chores with paid employment and the pressure to remain attractive. The Granger Collection, New York

oppose the ERA, and antiabortion advocates wanted to steer clear of NOW's support for reproductive rights. Despite these concerns, between 1966 and 1971 NOW's membership increased dramatically from 1,000 to 15,000.

Supporters of women's equality drew lessons from the black freedom struggle. SNCC empowered women staff through community-organizing projects, but even within the civil rights movement women had not always been treated equally, often being assigned clerical duties. Women came up against even greater discrimination in the antiwar movement. Men held a higher status in such groups because women were not eligible for the draft. Ironically, men's claims of moral advantage justified many of them in seeking sexual favors. "Girls say yes to guys who say no," quipped draft-resisting men who sought to put women in their traditional sexual place.

As a result of these experiences, radical women formed their own, mainly local organizations. They created "consciousness-raising" groups that allowed them to share their experiences of oppression in the household, the workplace, the university, and movement organizations. These women's liberationists went beyond NOW's emphasis on legal equality and attacked male domination, or patriarchy, as the primary source of women's subordination. They criticized the nuclear family and cultural values that glorified women as the object of male sexual desires, and they protested creatively against discrimination. In 1968 radical feminists picketed the popular Miss America contest in Atlantic City, New Jersey, the epitome of male conceptions of female beauty, and set up a "Freedom Trash Can" into which they threw undergarments and cosmetics. Radical groups such as the Redstockings condemned all men as oppressors and formed separate female collectives to affirm their identities as women.

In 1973 feminists won a major battle in the Supreme Court over a woman's right to control reproduction. In *Roe v. Wade*, the high court ruled that states could not prevent a woman from obtaining an abortion in the first three months of pregnancy but could impose some limits in the next two trimesters. In furthering the constitutional right of privacy for women, the justices classified abortion as a private medical issue between a patient and her doctor. This decision marked a victory for a woman's right to choose to terminate her pregnancy, but it also stirred up a fierce reaction from women and men who considered abortion to be the murder of an unborn child. Although the basic principle of the right to an abortion has remained intact, legal and cultural battles have raged to the present day.

Power to the People

In addition to stimulating feminist consciousness, the civil rights movement emboldened other oppressed groups to emancipate themselves. African Americans led the way in influencing the liberationist struggles of Latinos, Indians, and gay men and women.

Malcolm X shaped the direction that many African Americans would take in seeking independence and power. Born Malcolm Little, he had engaged in a life of crime, which landed him in prison. Inside jail, he converted to the Nation of Islam, a religious sect based partly on Muslim teachings and partly on the belief that white people were

devils (not a doctrine associated with orthodox Islam). After his release from jail, Malcolm rejected his "slave name" and substituted the letter *X* to symbolize his unknown African forebears. A charismatic leader, Minister Malcolm helped convert thousands of disciples in black ghettos by denouncing whites and encouraging blacks to embrace their African cultural heritage and beauty as a people. Favoring self-defense over nonviolence, he criticized civil rights leaders for failing to protect their women, their children, and themselves. After 1963, Malcolm X broke away from the Nation of Islam, visited the Middle East and Africa and accepted the teachings of traditional Islam, moderated his rhetoric against all whites as devils, but remained committed to black self-determination. He had already influenced the growing number of disillusioned young black activists when, in 1965, members of the Nation of Islam murdered him, apparently in revenge for challenging the organization.

Black militants, echoing Malcolm X's ideas, further challenged the liberal consensus on race. They renounced King's and Rustin's ideas, rejecting their principles of integration and nonviolence in favor of black power and self-defense. Instead of welcoming whites within their organizations, black radicals believed that African Americans had to assert their independence from white America. In 1966 SNCC decided to expel whites and create an all-black organization. That same year, Stokely Carmichael, SNCC's chairman, proclaimed the rallying cry of "black power" as the central goal of the freedom struggle, linking the cause of African American freedom to revolutionary conflicts in Cuba, Africa, and Vietnam.

Black power seemed menacing to most whites. Its emergence in the midst of riots in black ghettos, which erupted across the nation starting in the mid-1960s, underscored the concern. Few white Americans understood the horrific conditions that led to riots in Harlem and Rochester, New York, in 1964; in Los Angeles in 1965; and in Cleveland, Chicago, Detroit, Newark, and Tampa in the following two years. Black northerners still faced problems of high unemployment, dilapidated housing, and police mistreatment, which civil rights legislation had done nothing to correct. While whites perceived the ghetto uprisings solely as an exercise in criminal behavior, many blacks viewed the violence as an expression of political discontent—as rebellions, not riots. The Kerner Commission, appointed by President Johnson to assess urban disorders and chaired by Governor Otto Kerner of Illinois, concluded in 1968 that white racism remained at the heart of the problem: "Our nation is moving toward two societies, one black, one white—separate and unequal."

New groups emerged to take up the cause of black power. In 1966 Huey P. Newton and Bobby Seale, two black college students in Oakland, California, formed the **Black Panther Party**. Like Malcolm X and Stokely Carmichael, the Panthers linked their cause to revolutionary movements around the world. Dressed in black leather, sporting black berets, and carrying guns, the Panthers appealed mainly to black men. They did not, however, rely on armed confrontation and bravado alone. The Panthers established day care centers and health facilities, which gained the admiration of many in their communities. Much of this good work was overshadowed by violent confrontations with the police, which led to the deaths of Panthers in shootouts and the imprisonment of key party officials. By the early 1970s, local and federal government crackdowns on the Black Panthers had destabilized the organization and reduced its influence.

Black militants were not the only African Americans to clash with the government. After 1965, King increasingly criticized the Johnson administration for waging war in Vietnam and failing to fight the War on Poverty more vigorously at home. In 1968 he prepared to mount a massive Poor People's March on Washington when he was shot and killed by James Earl Ray in Memphis, where he was supporting demonstrations for striking sanitation workers. The death of King furthered black disillusionment. In the wake of his murder, riots again erupted in hundreds of cities throughout the country. Little noticed amid the fiery turbulence, President Johnson signed into law the 1968 Fair Housing Act, the final piece of civil rights legislation of his term.

The African American freedom movement inspired Latinos struggling for equality and advancement. During the 1960s, the size of the Spanish-speaking population in the United States tripled from three million to nine million. Hispanic Americans were a diverse group who hailed from many countries and backgrounds. In the 1950s, Cesar Chavez had emerged as the leader of oppressed Mexican farmworkers in California. In seeking the right to organize a union and gain higher wages and better working conditions, Chavez shared King's nonviolent principles. In 1962 Chavez formed the National Farm Workers Association, and in 1965 the union called a strike against California grape growers, one that attracted national support and lasted five years before reaching a successful settlement.

Younger Mexican Americans, especially those in cities such as Los Angeles and other western *barrios* (ghettos), supported Chavez's economic goals but challenged older political leaders who sought cultural assimilation. Borrowing from the Black Panthers,

Mexican Americans formed the Brown Berets, a self-defense organization. As a sign of their increasing militancy and independence, in 1969 some 1,500 activists gathered in Denver and declared themselves *Chicanos*, a term that expressed their cultural pride and identity, instead of Mexican Americans. Chicanos created a new political party, **La Raza Unida (The United Race)**, to promote their interests, and the party and its allies sponsored demonstrations to fight for jobs, bilingual education, and the creation of Chicano studies programs in colleges. Chicano and other Spanish-language communities also took advantage of the protections of the Voting Rights Act, which, in 1975, was amended to include sections of the country—from New York to California to Florida and Texas—where Hispanic literacy in English and voter registration were low.

American Indians also joined the upsurge of

Explore

See Document 26.3 for a statement on Chicano self-identity.

activism and ethnic nationalism. By 1970 some 800,000 people identified themselves as American Indians, many of whom lived in poverty on reservations. They suffered from inadequate housing, high alcoholism rates, low life expectancy, staggering unemployment, and lack of education. Conscious of their heritage before the arrival of white people, determined to halt their continued deterioration, and seeking to assert "red" pride, they established the **American Indian Movement (AIM)** in 1968. The following year, AIM protesters occupied the abandoned prison island of Alcatraz in San Francisco Bay, where they remained until 1971. In 1972 AIM occupied the headquarters of the Federal Bureau of Indian Affairs in Washington, D.C., where protesters presented twenty demands, ranging from reparations for treaty violations to abolition of the bureau. AIM demonstrators also seized the village of Wounded Knee, South Dakota, the scene of the 1890 massacre of the Sioux residents by the U.S. army (see chapter 15), to dramatize the impoverished living conditions on the reservation. They held on for more than seventy days with eleven hostages until a shootout with the FBI ended the confrontation, killing one protester and wounding another.

The results of the red power movement proved mixed. Demonstrations focused media attention on the plight of American Indians but did little to halt their downward spiral. Nevertheless, courts became more sensitive to Indian claims and protected mineral and fishing rights on reservations. Still, in the early 1970s the

DOCUMENT 26.3

Chicano Student Movement of Aztlán, 1969

In April 1969, a group of students met at the University of California at Santa Barbara and formed the *Movimiento Estudiantil Chicano de Aztlán* (MEChA; Chicano Student Movement of Aztlán). MEChA organizers drafted "El Plan de Santa Barbara," excerpted below, which set out their basic philosophy and objectives. Their goals included using the term *Chicano* instead of *Mexican American* as a sign of cultural nationalism and political consciousness, creating Chicano studies departments at colleges and universities, and organizing other MEChA groups in the United States.

Explore

For decades Mexican people in the United States struggled to realize the "American Dream." And some—a few—have. But the cost, the ultimate cost of assimilation, required turning away from *el barrio* [one's neighborhood] and *la colonia* [one's community]. In the meantime, due to the racist structure of this society, to our essentially different life style, and to the socioeconomic functions assigned to our community by Anglo-American society—as suppliers of cheap labor and a dumping ground for the small-time capitalist entrepreneur—the *barrio* and *colonia* remained exploited, impoverished, and marginal.

As a result, the self-determination of our community is now the only acceptable mandate for social and political action; it is the essence of Chicano commitment. Culturally, the word *Chicano*, in the past a pejorative and class-bound adjective, has now become the root idea of a new cultural identity for our people. It also reveals a growing

solidarity and the development of a common social praxis [customary conduct]. The widespread use of the term *Chicano* today signals a rebirth of pride and confidence. *Chicanismo* simply embodies an ancient truth: that man is never closer to his true self as when he is close to his community.

Chicanismo draws its faith and strength from two main sources: from the just struggle of our people and from an objective analysis of our community's strategic needs. We recognize that without a strategic use of education, an education that places value on what we value, we will not realize our destiny. Chicanos recognize the central importance of institutions of higher learning to modern progress, in this case, to the development of our community. But we go further: we believe that higher education must contribute to the information of a complete man who truly values life and freedom.

Source: Carlos Muñoz Jr., *Youth, Identity, Power: The Chicano Movement* (London: Verso, 1989), 191–92.

Interpret the Evidence

- Why does MEChA focus on the use of the term *Chicano*, and what does it hope to gain by its usage?
- Why did MEChA reject, at least in part, the goal of assimilation into mainstream American society?

Put It in Context

What connections does MEChA make between cultural awareness and political activism?

---

average annual income of American Indian families hovered around $1,500.

Unlike African Americans, Chicanos, and American Indians, homosexuals were not distinguished by the color of their skin. Estimated at 10 percent of the population, gays and lesbians remained invisible to the rest of society. Homosexuals were a target of repression

during the Cold War, and the government treated them harshly and considered their sexual identity a threat to the American way of life. In the 1950s, gay men and women created their own political and cultural organizations and frequented bars and taverns outside mainstream commercial culture, but most lesbians and gay men like Bayard Rustin hid their identities. It was not

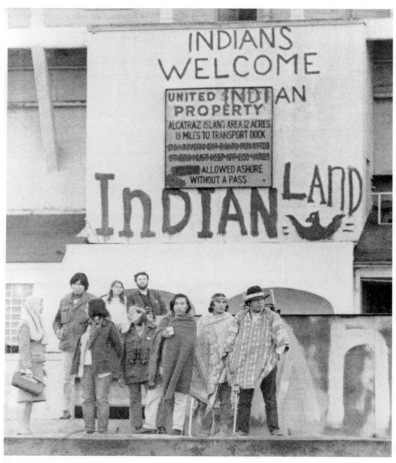

Native American Power

Drawing on the civil rights movement, this group of Native Americans occupied the former prison at Alcatraz Island on November 25, 1969. Among their demands, they offered to buy the island for $24 in beads and cloth—a reference to the purchase of Manhattan Island in 1626—and turn it into an Indian educational and cultural center.   AP Photo

The Revival of Conservatism

These diverse social movements did a great deal to change the political and cultural landscapes of the United States, but they did not go unchallenged. Many mainstream Americans worried about black militancy, opposed liberalism, and were even more dismayed by the radical offshoots they spawned. Generally overshadowed by more colorful protests for progressive causes, conservatives soon attracted support from many Americans who did not see change as progress. Many believed that the political leadership of the nation did not speak for them about what constituted a great society.

Conservatism had suffered a severe political blow with the ascendancy of Franklin Roosevelt's New Deal liberalism. Yet as conservatives lost political influence, they joined together to keep alive and publicize their beliefs. The brand of conservatism that emerged in the 1960s united libertarian support for a laissez-faire political economy and opposition to social welfare policies with moralistic concerns for defeating communism and defending religious devotion, moral decency, and family values. Unlike earlier conservatives, the new generation believed that the United States had to escalate the struggle against the evil of godless communism anywhere it posed a threat in the world, but they opposed internationalism as represented in the United Nations.

Conservative religious activists who built grassroots organizations to combat liberalism joined forces with political and intellectual conservatives such as William F. Buckley, the founder of the *National Review*, an influential journal of conservative ideas. The Reverend Billy Joe Hargis's Christian Crusade and Dr. Frederick Charles Schwartz's Christian Anti-Communist Crusade, both formed in the early 1950s, spun conspiracy theories about how the eastern liberal establishment intended to sell the country out to the Communists by supporting the United Nations, foreign aid, Social Security, and civil rights. The John Birch Society, named after a Baptist missionary and U.S. military intelligence officer killed during World War II by Communists in China, packaged these ideas in periodicals and radio broadcasts throughout the country and urged readers and listeners to remain vigilant to attacks against their freedom.

In the late 1950s and early 1960s, the conservative revival grew, mostly unnoticed, at the grassroots level in the

until 1969 that they took a giant step toward asserting their collective grievances in a very visible fashion. Police regularly cracked down on the **Stonewall Tavern** in New York City's Greenwich Village, but gay patrons battled back on June 27 in a riot that the *Village Voice* called "a kind of liberation, as the gay brigade emerged from the bars, back rooms, and bedrooms of the Village and became street people." In the manner of black power and the New Left, homosexuals organized the Gay Liberation Front, voiced pride in being gay, and demanded equality of opportunity regardless of sexual orientation.

As with other oppressed groups, gays achieved victories slowly and unevenly. In the decades following the 1960s, homosexuals faced discrimination in employment, could not marry or receive domestic benefits, and were subject to violence for public displays of affection.

suburbs of southern California and the Southwest. Bolstered by the postwar economic boom that centered around the military research and development of the Cold War, these towns in the Sun Belt attracted college-educated engineers, technicians, managers, and other professionals from the Midwest (or Rust Belt) seeking new economic opportunities. These migrants brought with them Republican loyalties as well as traditional conservative political and moral values. Women played a large part in conservative causes, especially in protesting against public school curricula that they believed encouraged secularism over religion, sex education over abstinence, and anti-Americanism over patriotism. Young housewives built an extensive network of conservative study groups.

In addition, the conservative revival, like the New Left, found fertile recruiting ground on college campuses. In October 1960, some ninety young conservatives met at William Buckley's estate in Sharon, Connecticut, to draw up a manifesto of their beliefs. The Sharon Statement affirmed the conservative doctrines of states' rights, the free market, and anticommunism. Participants at the conference formed the **Young Americans for Freedom (YAF)**, which six months later boasted 27,000 members on one hundred college campuses, far more than were in SDS in 1960. The *National Review* became its bible as subscriptions to Buckley's journal tripled to more than 90,000 by 1964. In 1962 the YAF filled Madison Square Garden to listen to a speech by the one politician who excited them: Republican senator Barry M. Goldwater of Arizona.

Explore

See Documents 26.4 and 26.5 to compare Johnson's ideas on the Great Society with a statement from the Young Americans for Freedom.

Goldwater's book *The Conscience of a Conservative* (1960) attacked New Deal liberalism and advocated abolishing Social Security; dismantling the Tennessee Valley Authority, the government-owned public power utility; and eliminating the progressive income tax. His firm belief in states' rights put him on record against the ruling in *Brown v. Board of Education of Topeka, Kansas* and prompted him to vote against the Civil Rights Act of 1964, positions that won him increasing support from conservative white southerners. However, Goldwater's advocacy of small government did not prevent him from supporting increased military spending to halt the spread of communism abroad. The senator may have anticipated growing concerns of government excess, but he was ahead of his time. His defeat to Lyndon Johnson by a landslide in the 1964 presidential election indicated that most voters perceived Goldwater's brand of conservatism as too extreme and were not yet ready to support it.

The election of 1964 also brought George C. Wallace onto the national stage as a leading architect of the conservative revival. As Democratic governor of Alabama, the segregationist Wallace had supported states' rights and opposed federal intervention to reshape social and political affairs. Wallace began to attract white northerners fed up with rising black militancy, forced busing to promote school integration, and open housing laws to desegregate their neighborhoods. Running in the Democratic presidential primaries in 1964, the Alabama governor had no chance to win, but he garnered 34 percent of the votes in Wisconsin, 30 percent in Indiana, and 43 percent in Maryland.

More so than Goldwater, Wallace united a populist message against the political establishment with concern for working-class Americans. Wallace voters identified with the governor as an "outsider," despised by liberal elites as uncouth, uncultured, and unrespectable. Many of them also backed Wallace for attacking privileged college students who, he claimed, mocked patriotism, violated sexual taboos, and looked down on hardworking, churchgoing, law-abiding Americans. How could "all those rich kids—from the fancy suburbs," one father wondered, "[avoid the draft] when my son has to go over there and maybe get his head shot off?" Each in his own way, George Wallace and Barry Goldwater waged political campaigns against liberals for undermining the economic freedom of middle- and working-class whites and coddling what they considered "racial extremists" and "countercultural barbarians."

REVIEW & RELATE

- How did organizations on the left challenge social, cultural, and economic norms in the 1960s?

- What groups were attracted to the 1960s conservative movement? Why?

☑ *LEARNINGCurve* bedfordstmartins.com/hewittlawson/LC

Conclusion: Liberalism and Its Discontents

The presidencies of John Kennedy and Lyndon Johnson marked the high point of liberal reform. Kennedy's New Frontier and Johnson's Great Society expanded the power of the national state to provide both compassionate government and bureaucratic regulation. Liberalism permitted greater freedom for racial, ethnic, and sexual minorities; expanded educational opportunities for the disadvantaged; reduced poverty; extended health care; and began to clean up the environment. However, liberalism imposed a degree of federal oversight that seemed too restrictive and expensive to many Americans. Johnson's escalation of the Vietnam War weakened many of these accomplishments and fractured the liberal consensus of the 1960s.

Kennedy and Johnson did not achieve liberal triumphs by themselves. The civil rights movement, with unsung heroes like Bayard Rustin, forced the federal government into action by creating crises and raising the stakes for preserving domestic tranquillity. In addition, Earl Warren's Supreme Court affirmed the constitutionality of major pieces of reform legislation and charted a new course for expanding the guarantees of the Bill of Rights.

Although the Vietnam War tarnished liberalism, the struggles of African Americans, women, Chicanos, Indians, and gays continued. Indeed, the civil rights movement spurred other exploited groups to seek greater freedom, and they flourished in the late 1960s and early 1970s despite the waning of the liberal consensus. Even the counterculture, which lost its most extreme elements to drugs and

DOCUMENTS 26.4 AND 26.5

Liberalism and Conservatism: Two Views

President Johnson's major domestic initiative, the Great Society, was designed to address the problems of poverty and discrimination in postwar America and rally the nation's youth behind it, as he expressed in a 1964 commencement address at the University of Michigan. His social vision reflected the major principles of liberalism in the 1960s. In 1960, at a gathering in Sharon, Connecticut, young conservatives presented their own ideas on how to tackle the social and moral problems affecting the country and its future.

Explore

26.4 Lyndon B. Johnson | The Great Society, 1964

The Great Society rests on abundance and liberty for all. It demands an end to poverty and racial injustice, to which we are totally committed in our time. But that is just the beginning.

The Great Society is a place where every child can find knowledge to enrich his mind and to enlarge his talents. It is a place where leisure is a welcome chance to build and reflect, not a feared cause of boredom and restlessness. It is a place where the city of man serves not only the needs of the body and the demands of commerce but the desire for beauty and the hunger for community.

It is a place where man can renew contact with nature. It is a place which honors creation for its own sake and for what it adds to the understanding of the race. It is a place where men are more concerned with the quality of their goals than the quantity of their goods. . . .

So I want to talk to you today about three places where we begin to build the Great Society—in our cities, in our countryside, and in our classrooms. . . .

The solution to these problems does not rest on a massive program in Washington, nor can it rely solely on the strained resources of local authority. They require us to create new concepts of cooperation, a creative federalism, between the National Capital and the leaders of local communities. . . .

So, will you join in the battle to give every citizen the full equality which God enjoins and the law requires, whatever his belief, or race, or the color of his skin?

Will you join in the battle to give every citizen an escape from the crushing weight of poverty?

Will you join in the battle to make it possible for all nations to live in enduring peace—as neighbors and not as mortal enemies?

Will you join in the battle to build the Great Society, to prove that our material progress is only the foundation on which we will build a richer life of mind and spirit?

There are those timid souls who say this battle cannot be won; that we are condemned to a soulless wealth. I do not agree. We have the power to shape the civilization that we want.

Source: *Public Papers of the Presidents of the United States: Lyndon B. Johnson, 1963–1964* (Washington, D.C.: Government Printing Office, 1965), 1:704, 706.

overindulgence, saw its styles, music, and attitudes toward pleasure blended into mainstream consumer culture.

Liberalism produced unparalleled accomplishments but planted the seeds for its own unraveling. During the 1960s, liberal policies and programs generated powerful counterattacks from radicals and conservatives alike. Indeed, over the next twenty-five years conservatives mobilized the American electorate and gained power by attacking liberal political, economic, and cultural values.

The liberal ascendancy proved short-lived, but its impact on the United States has had a lasting effect.

Rather than encompassing any one political and social philosophy, the decade of the 1960s was a time when reform, revolution, and reaction intermingled. Although the era remains known for radicalism and excess, it also saw the revival of conservatism as a force that would dominate politics for the rest of the twentieth century and into the beginning of the next millennium.

Explore

26.5 The Sharon Statement, 1960

In this time of moral and political crises, it is the responsibility of the youth of America to affirm certain eternal truths.

We, as young conservatives, believe:

That foremost among the transcendent values is the individual's use of his God-given free will, whence derives his right to be free from the restrictions of arbitrary force;

That liberty is indivisible, and that political freedom cannot long exist without economic freedom;

That the purpose of government is to protect those freedoms through the preservation of internal order, the provision of national defense, and the administration of justice;

That when government ventures beyond these rightful functions, it accumulates power, which tends to diminish order and liberty;

That the Constitution of the United States is the best arrangement yet devised for empowering government to fulfill its proper role, while restraining it from the concentration and abuse of power;

That the genius of the Constitution—the division of powers—is summed up in the clause that reserves primacy to the several states, or to the people, in those spheres not specifically delegated to the Federal government;

That the market economy, allocating resources by the free play of supply and demand, is the single economic system compatible with the requirements of personal freedom and constitutional government, and that it is at the same time the most productive supplier of human needs;

That when government interferes with the work of the market economy, it tends to reduce the moral and physical strength of the nation; that when it takes from one man to bestow on another, it diminishes the incentive of the first, the integrity of the second, and the moral autonomy of both.

Source: Young Americans for Freedom, "The Sharon Statement," *National Review*, September 1960, 173.

Interpret the Evidence

- What does Johnson see as the major responsibility of government?
- What do the authors of the Sharon Statement see as the major responsibility of government?

Put It in Context

What do these documents reveal about the major differences between liberal and conservative political philosophies in the 1960s?

Chapter Review

Online Study Guide ▶ bedfordstmartins.com/hewittlawson

KEY TERMS

New Frontier (p. 825)
Gulf of Tonkin Resolution (p. 827)
Tet Offensive (p. 830)
Freedom Rides (p. 830)
March on Washington for Jobs and Freedom (p. 832)
Civil Rights Act of 1964 (p. 832)
Freedom Summer (p. 833)
Mississippi Freedom Democratic Party (MFDP) (p. 833)
Voting Rights Act (p. 834)
Great Society (p. 834)
Students for a Democratic Society (SDS) (p. 837)
Port Huron Statement (p. 837)
Free Speech Movement (FSM) (p. 837)
Weathermen (p. 838)
counterculture (p. 838)
Commission on the Status of Women (p. 839)
National Organization for Women (NOW) (p. 840)
Roe v. Wade (p. 841)
Black Panther Party (p. 842)
La Raza Unida (The United Race) (p. 842)
American Indian Movement (AIM) (p. 842)
Stonewall Tavern (p. 844)
Young Americans for Freedom (YAF) (p. 845)

REVIEW & RELATE

1. How did President Kennedy's domestic agenda reflect the liberal political ideology of the early 1960s?

2. How and why did the United States escalate its role in the Vietnam War?

3. What role did the federal government play in advancing the cause of racial equality in the early 1960s?

4. How did civil rights activists pressure state and federal government officials to enact their agenda?

5. What problems and challenges did Johnson's Great Society legislation target?

6. In what ways did the Warren Court's rulings advance the liberal agenda?

7. How did organizations on the left challenge social, cultural, and economic norms in the 1960s?

8. What groups were attracted to the 1960s conservative movement? Why?

TIMELINE OF EVENTS

1960	Young Americans for Freedom founded; Sharon Statement issued
1961	Kennedy sends military advisers to South Vietnam
	Cuban exile invasion force lands at Bay of Pigs
	CORE mounts Freedom Rides
	Soviets build Berlin Wall
1962	Students for a Democratic Society (SDS) issues Port Huron Statement
	Cuban missile crisis
1963–1968	U.S. troop levels in Vietnam rise from 16,000 to 536,000
1963	Betty Friedan publishes *The Feminine Mystique*
	U.S. and Soviet Union agree to Partial Nuclear Test Ban Treaty
	March on Washington for Jobs and Freedom
	John F. Kennedy assassinated by Lee Harvey Oswald; Lyndon B. Johnson becomes president
1964–1966	Great Society domestic programs enacted
1964	Civil Rights Act of 1964 passed
	Freedom Summer project in Mississippi
	Congress passes Gulf of Tonkin Resolution
1965	Operation Rolling Thunder begins
	Voting Rights Act passed
	Griswold v. Connecticut Supreme Court decision
1966	Black Panther Party formed
	National Organization for Women (NOW) formed
1968	American Indian Movement (AIM) founded
	Martin Luther King Jr. assassinated
	Tet Offensive begins in Vietnam
1969	Gays fight police at Stonewall Tavern
1973	*Roe v. Wade* Supreme Court decision

DOCUMENT PROJECT 26

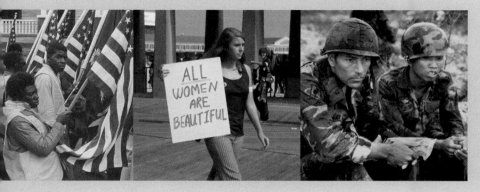

Freedom Summer

In June 1964, white college students gathered at the Western College for Women in Oxford, Ohio, to train for a massive voter registration project in Mississippi. Freedom Summer, as it was called, was organized by the Student Nonviolent Coordinating Committee, the Congress of Racial Equality, the National Association for the Advancement of Colored People, and the Southern Christian Leadership Conference. Working under an umbrella organization, the Congress of Federated Organizations (COFO), the project focused on political rights, particularly the right to vote. COFO set up freedom schools, which taught voter literacy, organizing techniques, and basic reading and writing skills. The decision to use white volunteers was a deliberate one to put more activists on the ground and, more important, draw national attention to the cause. The activities of Freedom Summer volunteers provoked violence and resistance. Perhaps the most well-known acts of violence were the murders of three civil rights workers: James Chaney, a local black activist; and Michael Schwerner and Andrew Goodman, two northern whites.

Also, black activists formed the interracial Mississippi Freedom Democratic Party (MFDP), which sent its own delegates to the Democratic National Convention in Atlantic City, New Jersey, and sought official recognition by the convention to replace the all-white delegation. Offered a compromise, the MFDP refused it and returned home but supported Lyndon Johnson's election.

Although few black Mississippians successfully registered to vote and the MFDP was denied official recognition at the Democratic National Convention, Freedom Summer did publicize the plight of black communities in Mississippi and throughout the South, and this publicity contributed to the passage of the Voting Rights Act of 1965. As you examine the following documents, consider whether you think the campaign was a success.

DOCUMENT 26.6

Prospectus for Mississippi Freedom Summer, 1964

Civil rights organizers carefully prepared for Freedom Summer, knowing that such a large campaign against intransigent disfranchisement in Mississippi would require extensive planning and coordination. The following selection is from an internal document of the Student Nonviolent Coordinating Committee that summarizes the purpose and strategies of Freedom Summer. It highlights the goals of voter registration and freedom schools.

It has become evident to the civil rights groups involved in the struggle for freedom in Mississippi that political and social justice cannot be won without the massive aid of the country as a whole, backed by the power and authority of the federal government. Little hope exists that the political leaders of Mississippi will steer even a moderate course in the near future (Governor Johnson's [Mississippi governor Paul Johnson] inaugural speech notwithstanding); in fact, the contrary seems true: as the winds of change grow stronger, the threatened political elite of Mississippi becomes more intransigent and fanatical in its support of the status quo. The closed society of Mississippi is, as Professor [James] Silver asserts, without the moral resources to reform itself. And Negro efforts to win the right to vote cannot succeed against the extensive legal weapons and police powers of local and state officials without a nationwide mobilization of support.

A program is planned for this summer which will involve the massive participation of Americans dedicated to the elimination of racial oppression. Scores of college students, law students, medical students, teachers, professors, ministers, technicians, folk artists, and lawyers from all over the country have already volunteered to work in Mississippi this summer—and hundreds more are being recruited. . . .

Why this summer?

Mississippi at this juncture in the movement has received too little attention—that is, attention to what the state's attitude really is—and has presented COFO with a major policy decision. Either the civil rights struggle has to continue, as it has for the past few years, with small projects in selected communities with no real progress on any fronts, or [there must be a] task force of such a size as to force either the state and the municipal governments to change their social and legal structures, or the Federal Government to intervene on behalf of the constitutional rights of its citizens.

Since 1964 is an election year, the clear-cut issue of voting rights should be brought out in the open. Many SNCC and CORE workers in Mississippi hold the view that Negroes will never vote in large numbers until Federal marshals intervene. At any rate, many Americans must be made to realize that the voting rights they so often take for granted involve considerable risk for Negroes in the South. In the larger context of the national civil rights movement, enough progress has been made during the last year that there can be no turning back. Major victories in Mississippi, recognized as the stronghold of racial intolerance in the South, would speed immeasurably the breaking down of legal and social discrimination in both North and South. . . .

Direction of the Project . . .

Voter Registration: This will be the most concentrated level of activity. Voter registration workers will be involved in an intensive summer drive to encourage as many Negroes as possible to register. They will participate in COFO's Freedom Registration, launched in early February, to register over 400,000 Negroes on Freedom Registration books. These books will be set up in local Negro establishments and will have simplified standards of registration (the literacy test and the requirement demanding an interpretation of a section of the Mississippi Constitution will be eliminated).

Freedom Registration books will serve as the basis of a challenge of the official books of the state and the validity of "official" elections this fall. Finally, registration workers will assist in the campaigns of Freedom candidates who are expected to run for seats in all five of the State's congressional districts and for the seat of Senator John Stennis, who is up for re-election.

Freedom Schools:

1. *General Description.* About 25 Freedom Schools are planned, of two varieties: day schools in about 20–25 towns (commitments still pending in some communities) and one or two boarding, or residential, schools on college campuses. Although the local communities can provide school buildings, some furnishings, and staff housing (and, for residential schools, student housing), all equipment, supplies, and staff will have to come from outside. A nationwide recruitment program is underway to find and train the people and solicit the equipment needed. In the schools, the typical day will be hard study in the morning, an afternoon break (because it's too hot for an academic program), and less formal evening activities.

Source: Prospectus for the Mississippi Freedom Summer, Miller (Michael J.) Civil Rights Collection, McCain Library and Archives, University of Southern Mississippi.

DOCUMENT 26.7

Nancy Ellin | Letter Describing Freedom Summer, 1964

Setting up freedom schools throughout Mississippi was a key project of Freedom Summer. The schools in Hattiesburg were staffed by many northern white volunteers, including Nancy and Joseph Ellin. Both originally from New York City, Nancy and Joseph met at Yale University, where Joseph received his doctorate in philosophy in 1962. At the time of Freedom Summer, Joseph was a philosophy professor at Western Michigan University. The following selection is from a letter written by Nancy to Joseph's parents shortly after they arrived in Mississippi.

June 30

Dear Dr. and Mrs. Ellin,

It was nice to get your letter today; we hope you will write often. I'm sure Joe will write to you any minute now, but I thought I might as well, too.

We got here OK, though we were frightened most of the way, quite unnecessarily. It was the people who came down in integrated cars who had the unpleasant time—refused service, cars following them, etc. We came down with a very nice girl who just graduated from Smith [College] and who did quite a bit of driving.

We are currently hard at work getting the Freedom Schools organized. Joe and another boy have everyone typing up stencils of the Constitution, the Declaration of Independence, etc. The school enrollment is over 150; we are having official registration Thursday. The philosophy is to take everyone who comes; we will be teaching adults in the evening. There are 10 teachers, 8 more expected from New York City on Thursday. We also intend to recruit a few local people.

I, too, am sorry things came to such a pass. We felt terrible about causing you all such anguish, but we felt the decision was ours to make, and though we were very afraid and doubtful at Oxford [in Ohio], we made the decision to come. You must know that you were not the only parents who were worried, and some kids did drop out, one from our group, in fact, who was underage and couldn't get his parents' consent. Now that we are here we feel more than ever that coming here was the right thing to do. Even if we don't teach a single child (and I think the odds are heavily against that) we still will have accomplished something in showing the people of Hattiesburg that they should not hate whites. Even our own group leaders, Carolyn and Arthur Reese, who are Detroit Negroes (schoolteachers), were very anti-white until Oxford, Ohio. (Carolyn has been extremely frightened much of the time we have been here.) The people of Hattiesburg are militant and eager; our landlady told us last night about a woman who had attempted to register to vote 17 times before she made it.

Things here are pretty horrible. The Negro section, where we are, smells and looks more than a little like India. The house we are staying in (free) is pretty good-sized but very dilapidated—creaky floors, etc. It has a bathroom—some don't. Our landlady is registered; her husband has tried but hasn't made it yet. Everyone agrees that things here would be much worse right this minute if it weren't for our presence and the pressure exerted on the govt. on our behalf by our rich Northern parents. Negroes in the movement tend to lose their jobs. We feel—rightly or wrongly—that our place is here, in the heart of the struggle. No man is an island . . .

Otherwise, there isn't much news. We have been to one mass meeting and are cutting another one tonight to make stencils. Another job we have before us is organizing the library—there are tremendous quantities of books. We haven't had much contact yet, aside from smiles and handshakes, with the regular Negro community, so I haven't much else to report. The leaders we have met are terrific.

Thank Mary and everyone for praying for us.

Love,
Nancy

Source: Letter from Joseph and Nancy Ellin to Dr. and Mrs. Ellin, Joseph and Nancy Ellin Freedom Summer Collection, McCain Library and Archives, University of Southern Mississippi.

DOCUMENT 26.8

Letter from a Freedom Summer Volunteer, 1964

The following letter is from an unknown Freedom Summer volunteer in Meridian, Mississippi. Written the day after the FBI discovered the bodies of slain civil rights activists James Chaney, Michael Schwerner, and Andrew Goodman, the letter describes how the local community remembered "Mickey" Schwerner and "Jimmy" Chaney.

Meridian, August 5

At the Freedom school and at the community center, many of the kids had known Mickey and almost all knew Jimmy Chaney. That day we asked the kids to describe Mickey and Jimmy because we had never known them.

"Mickey was a big guy. He wore blue jeans all the time." . . . I asked the kids, "What did his eyes look like?" and they told me they were "friendly eyes" "nice eyes" ("nice" is a lovely word in a Mississippi accent). "Mickey was a man who was at home everywhere and with anybody," said the 17-year-old girl I stay with. The littlest kids, the 6, 7, 8 year olds, tell about how he played "Frankenstein" with them or took them for drives or talked with them about Freedom. Many of the teenage boys were delinquents until Mickey went down to the bars and jails and showed them that one person at least would respect them if they began to fight for something important. . . . And the grown-ups too, trusted him. The lady I stay with tells with pride of how Mickey and Rita [his wife] came to supper at their house, and police cars circled around the house all during the meal. But Mickey could make them feel glad to take the risk.

People talk less about James Chaney here, but feel more. The kids describe a boy who played with them—whom everyone respected but who never had to join in fights to maintain this respect—a quiet boy but very sharp and very understanding when he did speak. Mostly we know James through his sisters and especially his 12-year-old brother, Ben. Today Ben was in the Freedom School. At lunchtime the kids have a jazz band (piano, washtub bass, cardboard boxes and bongos as drums) and tiny Ben was there leading it all even with his broken arm, with so much energy and rhythm that even Senator Eastland [Senator James Eastland of Mississippi] would have had to stop and listen if he'd been walking by.

Source: Elizabeth Sutherland, ed., *Letters from Mississippi* (New York: McGraw-Hill, 1965), 190.

DOCUMENT 26.9

White Southerners Respond to Freedom Summer, 1964

As Freedom Summer activists began arriving in Mississippi, newspapers throughout the South ran editorials and articles condemning the volunteers. The following article appeared in a South Carolina newspaper and is representative of the ways in which white southerners characterized Freedom Summer. It mentions the National Council of Churches, a federation of white and black Christian churches that supported many civil rights and peace causes in the postwar era, including Freedom Summer.

This week the vanguard of a youthful army left the rolling hill country of southwestern Ohio, where volunteers had spent several weeks being indoctrinated and incensed, for the flat Delta land of Mississippi. The Summer Project, a joint effort of the Student Non-Violent Coordinating Committee (SNICK) and the National Council of Churches, was on the march. . . .

"The real aim of SNICK and the other more extreme Negro organizations is to secure the military occupation of Mississippi by federal troops." This is not the expressed judgment of Mississippi Governor Paul Johnson or even of Senator James Eastland. The words are those of Joseph Alsop, the liberal columnist [from the *Washington Post*]. Mr. Alsop, however much he may desire civil rights for Negroes, knows that no good can come from this Summer Project, controlled as it is by the most militant of the many civil rights groups and the one whose ranks include, according to Mr. Alsop, more than a few dedicated Communists.

It would be comforting to believe that the young persons involved in this project understand something of what is going on behind the scenes. It would be much easier then to dismiss their possible fate from the mind. But the facts will not allow such optimism.

"Last summer I went back to London for three months and did nothing," one recruit told a *Washington Post* reporter. "It was unhealthy. This summer I want to do something."

Another young recruit said he didn't think he could live with himself if he didn't do something about Mississippi. A third, a young lady studying theology, said she was going because of her belief that "the SNICK people are living a life that is relevant to the New Testament." Just how accurate is this rosy view?

The crusade leaders say publicly that the main thrust of the summer invasion will be directed at voter discrimination in Mississippi, where only 6.6 percent of Negroes of voting age are registered to vote. Such an effort, conducted with forbearance and directed at helping the Negro improve himself, might produce some good. Judging by the record, however, SNICK is short on forbearance and uncommonly long on making trouble. Nor is the National Council of Churches likely to provide much in the way of restraint.

The Council has invested $260,000 in this project, and it wants more out of that investment than a handful of votes. At a Baltimore meeting last February, during which the Summer Project was under discussion, Council members talked of "social redevelopment" in Mississippi, of applying "corrective treatment" to the Delta region.

"The main problem at this point," the Council's own report of the Baltimore meeting said, "is the concentration of wealth among the few, e.g., on an average, 5 percent of the farms control 50 percent of all the farmland."

Voting? This has nothing to do with voting. The Council is speaking of agrarian reform of the sort that socialists promote.

From this, the goals of the Summer Project appear to be two-fold: first, indoctrination in socialist economics; second, military occupation of Mississippi if that can be arranged. This is no longer a struggle of black and white. If the reports of even the most liberal observers are to be believed, the Reds predominate and the nation can anticipate a long, hot summer indeed.

Source: "'Freedom' to the Delta," *Charleston Post*, June 24, 1964.

DOCUMENT 26.10

Fannie Lou Hamer | Address to the Democratic National Convention Credentials Committee, 1964

At the 1964 Democratic National Convention, Mississippi Freedom Democratic Party (MFDP) members attempted to unseat the official all-white Mississippi delegation. Several MFDP members testified before the convention's credentials committee, including Fannie Lou Hamer. Hamer's testimony began in front of a national television audience, but that coverage ended when President Johnson quickly held a press conference to divert attention from the controversy. On the evening news, however, the major networks carried stories about Hamer and the MFDP. Though the MFDP was not recognized in 1964, four years later Hamer led the party's official delegation at the Democratic National Convention. In the following selection, Hamer tells of her arrest in Winona, Mississippi, as she traveled home from a voter registration workshop.

I was carried to the county jail and put in the booking room. They left some of the people in the booking room and began to place us in cells. I was placed in a cell with a young woman called Miss Euvester Simpson. After I was placed in the cell, I began to hear sounds of licks and screams. I could hear the sounds of licks and horrible screams. And I could hear somebody say, "Can you say, 'yes, sir,' nigger? Can you say 'yes, sir'?" And they would say other horrible names.

She would say, "Yes, I can say 'yes, sir.'"

"So, well, say it."

She said, "I don't know you well enough." They beat her, I don't know how long. And after a while she began to pray, and asked God to have mercy on those people.

And it wasn't too long before three white men came to my cell. One of these men was a state highway patrolman and he asked me where I was from. And I told him Ruleville. He said, "We are going to check this." And they left my cell and it wasn't too long before they came back. He said, "You's from Ruleville all right," and he used a curse word. And he said, "We are going to make you wish you was dead."

I was carried out of that cell into another cell where they had two Negro prisoners. The state highway patrolmen ordered the first Negro to take the blackjack [police baton]. The first Negro prisoner ordered me, by orders from the state highway patrolman, for me to lay down on a bunk bed on my face.

And I laid on my face and the first Negro began to beat. And I was beat by the first Negro until he was exhausted. I was holding my hands behind me at that time on my left side, because I suffered from polio when I was six years old. After the first Negro had beat until he was exhausted, the state highway patrolman ordered the second Negro to take the blackjack. The second Negro began to beat and I began to work my feet, and the state highway patrolman ordered the first Negro [who] had beat me to sit on my feet—to keep me from working my feet. I began to scream and one white man got up and began to beat me in my head and tell me to hush.

One white man—my dress had worked up high— he walked over and pulled my dress, I pulled my dress down, and he pulled my dress back up.

I was in jail when Medgar Evers was murdered.

All of this is on account of we want to register, to become first-class citizens. And if the Freedom Democratic Party is not seated now, I question America. Is this America, the land of the free and the home of the brave, where we have to sleep with our telephones off of the hooks because our lives be threatened daily, because we want to live as decent human beings, in America? Thank you.

Source: Megan Parker Brooks and David W. Houck, eds., *The Speeches of Fannie Lou Hamer: To Tell It like It Is* (Jackson: University Press of Mississippi, 2011), 44–45.

DOCUMENT 26.11

Lyndon B. Johnson | Monitoring the MFDP Challenge, 1964

President Johnson feared that the MFDP challenge at the 1964 Democratic National Convention would prove divisive and lessen his chances of winning the South in the upcoming election. To maintain unity, he instructed Senator Hubert Humphrey of Minnesota, a respected liberal and civil rights supporter, to work out a compromise. In this telephone conversation on August 9, 1964, with Walter Reuther, the head of the United Auto Workers and a power broker at the convention, an irritated Johnson explains his reasoning for working out a deal.

JOHNSON   If you and Hubert Humphrey have got any leadership, you'd get Joe Rauh [MFDP lawyer] off that damn television. The only thing that can really screw us good is to seat that group of challengers from Mississippi. . . . He said he's going to take it to the convention floor. Now there's not a damn vote that we get by seating these folks. What we want to do is elect some Congressmen to keep 'em from repealing this [1964 Civil Rights] act. And who's seated at this convention don't amount to a damn. Only reason I would let Mississippi [all-white delegation] come in is because I don't want to run off fourteen border states, like Oklahoma and Kentucky. . . . Incidentally this Governor [Mississippi governor Paul Johnson] has done everything I've asked him to do in Mississippi. We've broken that case [the Chaney, Schwerner, and Goodman murders]. I talk to him two or three times a week. Now he's not for [me]. But I can't say that he hasn't listened to us and he hasn't cooperated.

REUTHER   Exactly. . . . We'll lose Mississippi, but the impact on the other Southern states—

JOHNSON   That's all I'm worried about. . . . I've got to carry Georgia. . . . I've got to carry Texas. . . . We don't want to cut off our nose to spite our face. If they give us four years, I'll guarantee the Freedom delegation somebody representing views like that will be seated four years from now. But we can't do it all before breakfast.

Source: Michael R. Beschloss, ed., *Taking Charge: The Johnson White House Tapes, 1963–1964* (New York: Simon and Schuster, 1997), 510–11.

Interpret the Evidence

1. What did local blacks think of white volunteers in the Freedom Summer project (Documents 26.7 and 26.8)? What were the advantages and disadvantages of bringing white volunteers to Mississippi?

2. Why were voter registration and political organizing the focus of Freedom Summer (Document 26.6)? Why did the project also include freedom schools?

3. What arguments did the *Charleston Post* (Document 26.9) make to discredit Freedom Summer?

4. How did Fannie Lou Hamer use the testimony of her experience in a Mississippi jail (Document 26.10) to gain support for the Mississippi Freedom Democratic Party?

5. Do you think President Johnson's views toward seating the MFDP delegation (Document 26.11) were consistent with his vision of the Great Society? Explain.

Put It in Context

- In what ways did Freedom Summer succeed? In what ways did it fail?

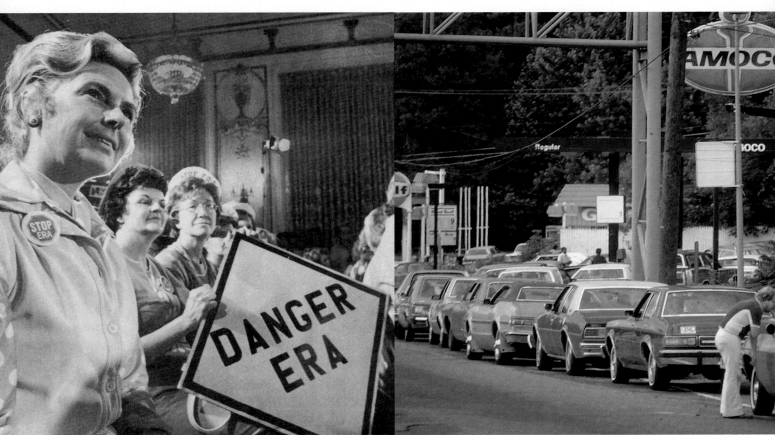

Time & Life Pictures/Getty Images

Time & Life Pictures/Getty Images

Political activist Phyllis Schlafly and other women at a government hearing on the Equal Rights Amendment in Kansas City, Missouri, 1976.

Line of cars waiting for gas during a fuel shortage, 1979.

27

The Conservative Ascendancy

1968–1992

Spencer Grant/Getty Images

Attendants observe a moment of prayer during the New England Rally for God, Family, and Country in Boston, Massachusetts, 1970.

AMERICAN HISTORIES

Allan Bakke was not a political ideologue or an activist. He had always played by the rules. Born in Minnesota in 1940, Bakke grew up in a white middle-class family, earned a degree in mechanical engineering, and served in Vietnam. When his tour of duty was over, Bakke returned home, found an engineering job in Sunnyvale, California, and received a master's degree from Stanford University. However, he had not satisfied his great ambition—to become a physician.

In 1972 Bakke applied to two California medical schools and was turned down, probably because at age thirty-two he was considered too old. The next year, he applied to twelve schools but was rejected by all of them, including the University of California at Davis. Bakke learned that of the one hundred available spaces in the incoming class, the university awarded sixteen spots to minority group members, consisting mainly of African Americans, Chicanos, and Asian Americans. Contending that the policy amounted to reverse discrimination, he sued the University of California at Davis for violating his constitutional rights. In his challenge to the university's admission policy, Bakke complained: "I realize that the rationale for these quotas is that they attempt to atone for past racial discrimination, but insisting on a new racial bias in favor of minorities is not a just situation." In 1978 the U.S. Supreme Court ruled in his favor, and Bakke successfully completed his studies and graduated with a medical degree.

Like Allan Bakke, Anita Faye Hill did not seek celebrity, yet like Bakke she, too, would gain notoriety in a

859

Allan Bakke
and Anita Hill

cause not of her own making. Born in Okla-homa in 1956, Hill grew up in a large family whose ancestors included Creek Indians and former slaves. Like other African Americans in the state, she encountered racial segregation when she attended school, but her parents encouraged her to work hard and abide by strong religious and moral values.

A bookish and determined young woman, Hill graduated from Yale Law School in 1980. The following year, she went to work in the Office of Civil Rights at the Department of Education. Her boss, Clarence Thomas, was an African Ameri-can supporter of President Ronald Reagan. When Thomas moved to the Equal Employ-ment Opportunity Commission in May 1982, Hill transferred as well. Although a pragmatic moderate who privately favored affirmative action, she tried not to make waves and defended the positions that the conservative Thomas implemented to further reduce the scope of affirmative action in the aftermath of the *Bakke* case.

Anita Hill would have remained an obscure public servant had President George H. W. Bush not nominated Thomas to the Supreme Court in 1991. During the course of Thomas's Senate confirmation hearing, Hill testified before the Senate Judiciary Committee and a nationally televised audi-ence that Thomas had made unwanted sex-ual advances to her on and off the job. Disturbed by Thomas's harassment and sexual impro-priety, Hill had quit her job in 1983 and returned to Oklahoma to teach at a law school. It was difficult for this usually shy black woman to publicly describe these embarrassing moments concerning a high-ranking black man, but her courage was not rewarded. Black and white conservatives defended Thomas and attacked Hill's credibility, and Thomas won confirmation by a 52–48 vote. Nevertheless, she became a hero for many working women who faced similar incidents of sexual bias and harassment. •

photos: © Bettmann/CORBIS; UPI/Landov

ALLAN BAKKE and Anita Hill were not engaged in politics in the usual sense of the word. Nonetheless, their American histories took on profound political importance in the larger context of the rise and ascendancy of conservatism in the late twentieth century. Scoring their first national victory with the election of Richard Nixon in 1968, conservatives became the domi-nant force on the political landscape with the election of Ronald Reagan in 1980. Reagan led a New Right coalition that meshed the traditional economic conservatism of lower taxes, deregulation, and anti-unionism with the concerns of religious conservatives over abortion and family values. By 1992 conservatives had built upon the judicial victory of Allan Bakke and brushed back the complaint of Anita Hill in reshaping the nation's political priorities. Still, they had neither silenced their progressive critics nor eliminated the impact of liberal achievements from the 1960s.

Richard M. Nixon, War, and Politics, 1969–1974

Richard Nixon won the presidency in 1968 by forging a conservative coalition behind him, blaming liberals for the radical excesses of the 1960s. While continuing to fight Communists in Vietnam, Nixon improved relations with the Soviet Union and China, creating a thaw in the Cold War. At home, Nixon mixed conservatism with pragmatic politics, supporting some liberal measures while defending the virtues of limited government and traditional values. Nixon won reelection in 1972 by a landslide, but his victory was short-lived. In an effort to ensure electoral success, the Nixon administration engaged in illegal activities that subsequently came to light in the Watergate scandal. Nixon was forced to resign, and the conservative movement suffered a temporary setback.

The Election of President Nixon

The year 1968 was a turbulent one. In February, police shot indiscriminately into a crowd gathered for civil rights protests at South Carolina State University in Orangeburg, killing three students in the so-called Orangeburg massacre. The following month, student protests at Columbia University led to a violent confrontation with the New York City police. On April 4, the murder of Martin Luther King Jr. sparked an outburst of rioting by blacks in more than one hundred cities throughout the country (see chapter 26). The assassination of Democratic presidential aspirant Robert Kennedy in June further heightened the mood of despair. Adding to the unrest, demonstrators gathered in Chicago in August at the Democratic National Convention to press for an antiwar plank in the party platform. Thousands of protesters were beaten and arrested by Chicago police officers, who violently released their frustrations on the crowds. Many Americans watched in horror as television networks broadcast the bloody clashes, but a majority of viewers sided with the police rather than the protesters.

Similar protests occurred around the world. In early 1968, university students outside of Paris protested educational policies and what they perceived as their second-class status. When students at the Sorbonne in Paris joined them in the streets, police attacked them viciously. In June, French president Charles de Gaulle sent in tanks to break up the strikes but also instituted political and economic reforms. Protests erupted during the spring in Prague, Czechoslovakia, as well. President Alexander Dubček, vowing to reform the Communist regime by initiating "socialism with a human face," lifted press censorship, guaranteed free elections, and encouraged artists and writers to express themselves freely. Unaccustomed to such dissent and fearful it would spread to other nations within its imperial orbit, the Soviet Union sent its military into Prague in August 1968 to crush the reforms. Czechoslovakian protesters were no match for Soviet forces, and the brief experiment in freedom remembered as the "Prague Spring" came to a violent end. During the same year, student-led demonstrations erupted in Yugoslavia, Poland, West Germany, Italy, Spain, Japan, and Mexico.

It was against this backdrop of protest, violence, and civil unrest that Richard Nixon ran for president against the Democratic nominee Hubert H. Humphrey, who was Johnson's vice president, and the independent candidate, George C. Wallace, the segregationist governor of Alabama and a popular archconservative. To outflank Wallace on the right, Nixon appealed to disaffected Democrats as well as traditional Republicans. He declared himself the "law and order" candidate, a phrase that became a code for reining in black militancy. To win southern supporters, he pledged to ease up on enforcing federal civil rights legislation and opposed forced busing to achieve racial integration in schools. He criticized antiwar protesters and promised to end the Vietnam War with honor (without disclosing exactly how he would achieve this goal). Seeking to portray the Democrats as the party of social and cultural radicalism, Nixon geared his campaign message to the "silent majority" of voters—what one political analyst characterized as "the unyoung, the unpoor, and unblack."

Although Nixon won 301 electoral votes, 110 more than Humphrey, none of the three candidates received a majority of the popular vote (Map 27.1). Yet Nixon and Wallace together received about 57 percent of the popular vote, a dramatic shift to the right compared with Johnson's landslide victory just four years earlier. Nixon's election ushered in more than two decades of Republican presidential rule, interrupted only by scandal. The New Left, which had captured the imagination of many of America's young people, would give way to the **New Right**, an assortment of old and new conservatives, overwhelmingly white, who were determined to contain, if not roll back, the Great Society.

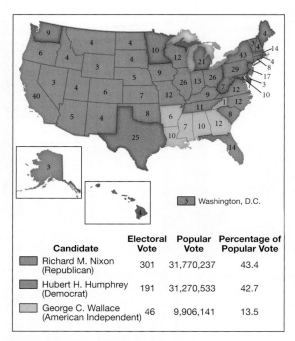

Candidate	Electoral Vote	Popular Vote	Percentage of Popular Vote
Richard M. Nixon (Republican)	301	31,770,237	43.4
Hubert H. Humphrey (Democrat)	191	31,270,533	42.7
George C. Wallace (American Independent)	46	9,906,141	13.5

MAP 27.1   The Election of 1968

Democratic presidential candidate Hubert Humphrey lost across the South as white voters turned to Republican Richard Nixon or segregationist George Wallace. Many working-class whites in the North and West also shifted their allegiance to these "law and order" candidates, rejecting the civil rights and antipoverty agendas promoted by President Johnson and blaming Democrats for the turmoil over the Vietnam War.

The Failure of Vietnamization

Vietnam plagued Nixon as it had his Democratic predecessor. Despite intimations during the campaign that he had a secret plan to end the war, Nixon's approach to Vietnam turned out to look much the same as Johnson's. Henry Kissinger, who served first as national security adviser and then as secretary of state, continued peace talks with the North Vietnamese, which had been initiated by Johnson. Over the next four years, Nixon and Kissinger devised a strategy that removed U.S. ground forces and turned over greater responsibility for the fighting to the South Vietnamese army, a process called **Vietnamization**.

Vietnamization did not, however, mean an end to U.S. belligerence in the region. In 1969, at the same time that American troop levels were being drawn down, the president ordered secret bombing raids in Cambodia, a neutral country adjacent to South Vietnam that contained enemy forces and parts of the Ho Chi Minh Trail. Meant to pressure the North Vietnamese into accepting U.S. peace

terms, the bombing accomplished little in the mountainous jungle. In April 1970, Nixon ordered the invasion of Cambodia, which destabilized the country and eventually brought to power the Communist Khmer Rouge, who later slaughtered two million Cambodians. In 1971 the United States sponsored the South Vietnamese invasion of Laos, another neutral neighbor that harbored North Vietnamese troops and supply lines, which again yielded no battlefield gains. Finally, in December 1972, shortly before Christmas, the United States carried out a massive eleven-day bombing campaign of targets in North Vietnam meant to force the North Vietnamese government to come to a peace accord.

The intense bombing of North Vietnam did end formal U.S. involvement in the war. An agreement signed on January 27, 1973, stipulated that the United States would remove all American troops, the North Vietnamese would return captured U.S. soldiers, and North and South Vietnam would strive for peaceful national unification. Nixon and Kissinger could now claim that they had

The Fall of Saigon, 1975

On April 29, 1975, the day before Communist troops took control of Saigon, crowds of South Vietnamese, many of whom had supported the United States, scramble to climb the wall of the U.S. Embassy. They were making a desperate attempt to get to evacuation helicopters, but with space limited on available aircraft, many of these people were left behind. AP Photo/Neal Ulevich achieved "peace with honor," ending U.S. involvement in Vietnam without compromising America's credibility with its anti-Communist allies around the world. In fact, peace had not been achieved, and the United States had failed in its stated goal of preventing a Communist takeover of South Vietnam. The war in Vietnam continued, and in 1975 North Vietnamese and Vietcong forces captured Saigon, resulting in a Communist victory. This outcome came at a terrible cost. Some 58,000 American soldiers, 215,000 South Vietnamese soldiers, 1 million North Vietnamese and Vietcong soldiers, and an estimated 4 million South and North Vietnamese civilians were killed in the conflict.

The Nixon administration's war efforts generated great controversy at home. In 1969 the president eliminated most draft deferments and introduced an impartial lottery system. This procedure was more equitable, but it exposed a wider range of young men to the draft. More important, the invasion of Cambodia touched off widespread campus demonstrations in May 1970. At Kent State University in Ohio, four student protesters were shot and killed by the National Guard. Large crowds of antiwar demonstrators descended on Washington in 1969 and 1971, though the president refused to heed their message. Nevertheless, the American public, and not just radicals, had turned against the war. By 1972 more than 70 percent of those polled believed that the Vietnam War was a mistake, and 31 percent disapproved of Nixon's handling of it. Growing numbers of Vietnam veterans also spoke out against the war. Contributing to this disillusionment, in 1971 the *New York Times* and the *Washington Post* published a classified report known as the **Pentagon Papers**. This document, leaked by former Defense Department analyst Daniel Ellsberg, confirmed that the Kennedy and Johnson administrations had misled the public about the origins and nature of the Vietnam War. The Nixon administration tried, unsuccessfully, to block its publication. Congress reflected growing disapproval for the war by repealing the Gulf of Tonkin Resolution in 1970 after the Cambodian invasion. In 1973 Congress passed the **War Powers Act**, which required the president to consult with Congress within forty-eight hours of deploying military forces and to obtain a declaration of war from Congress if troops remained on foreign soil beyond sixty days. That same year, as the U.S. combat mission in Vietnam drew to a close, President Nixon disbanded the draft and created an all-volunteer military.

Cold War Realism and Détente

As Nixon maneuvered to end the Vietnam War, he embarked on a parallel effort to improve relations with his Cold War Communist enemies. Nixon had begun his political career as a fierce anti-Communist, but he also considered himself a realist in foreign affairs. He was concerned less about promoting abstract ideals of democracy than about fashioning a stable world order based on a balance of power. With this in mind, Nixon and Secretary of State Kissinger worked to establish closer relations with both the People's Republic of China and the Soviet Union, hoping each power could be persuaded to pressure the North Vietnamese to accept an American peace settlement and end the war quickly. In addition, with the Soviet Union and China competing for influence in Asia, Nixon sought to exploit this conflict to keep these nuclear powers divided.

Nixon and Kissinger's plans succeeded in many ways. Their efforts to use great-power diplomacy to pressure the North Vietnamese into concessions failed, but their greatest triumph came in easing tensions with the country's Cold War adversaries. Through secret maneuvering, Kissinger prepared the way for Nixon to make the bold move of visiting mainland China in 1972, the first president to do so since the Cold War began. The meeting set in motion a new relationship between the capitalist and Communist nations. After blocking the People's Republic of China's admission to the United Nations for twenty-two years, the United States announced that it would no longer oppose China's entry to the world organization. This cautious renewal of relations between the two countries benefited both. It opened up possibilities of American access to the huge China market, and for the Chinese it promised trade with the United States.

Shaken by the movement toward closer relations between China and the United States, Soviet premier Leonid Brezhnev invited President Nixon to Moscow in May 1972, the first time an American president had visited the Soviet Union since 1945. The main topic of discussion concerned arms control, and with the Soviet Union eager to make a deal in the aftermath of Nixon's trip to China, the two sides worked out the historic **Strategic Arms Limitation Treaty (SALT I)**, the first to curtail nuclear arms production during the Cold War. The pact restricted the number of antiballistic missiles that each nation could deploy and froze the number of intercontinental ballistic missiles and submarine-based missiles for five years, with each side agreeing to pursue nuclear "sufficiency" rather than "superiority."

Nixon's diplomatic initiatives, however, failed to resolve festering problems in the Middle East, an area of strategic concern to both the United States and the Soviet Union. Since its victory in the Six-Day War of 1967, Israel had occupied territory once controlled by Egypt and Syria as well as the former Palestinian capital of Jerusalem. On October 6, 1973, during the start of the Jewish High Holidays of Yom Kippur, Egyptian and Syrian troops, fortified with Soviet arms, caught the Israelis off guard and quickly managed to recapture territory lost in 1967. An Israeli counterattack, reinforced by a shipment of $2 billion of American weapons, repelled Arab forces, and the Israeli military stood ready to destroy the Egyptian army. To avoid a complete breakdown in the balance of power, the United States and the Soviet Union agreed to broker a cease-fire that left the situation the same as before the war.

U.S. involvement in the struggle between Israel and its Arab enemies exacerbated economic troubles at home. On October 17, 1973, in the midst of the Yom Kippur War, the Arab-dominated **Organization of Petroleum Exporting Countries (OPEC)** imposed an oil embargo on the United States as punishment for its support of Israel. As a result of the embargo, the price of oil skyrocketed, and reduced oil supplies produced long lines at the gas pumps. The effect of high oil prices rippled through the economy, leading to increased inflation and unemployment, which rose from 5 to 7 percent. The embargo also affected America's allies in Western Europe, which imported 80 percent of its oil supply from Arab states, compared with 12 percent for the United States. The crisis lasted until May 1974, when OPEC lifted its embargo following six months of diplomacy by Kissinger.

The United States preferred to support stability over democracy when its strategic or economic interests were at stake. Under Nixon's leadership, the United States supported repressive regimes in Nicaragua, South Africa, the Philippines, and Iran. In Chile, the United States overthrew the democratically elected socialist president Salvador Allende, who was murdered in a CIA-backed operation in 1973. The coup brought nearly two decades of dictatorial rule to that country.

Pragmatic Conservatism at Home

On the domestic front, Nixon had pledged during his 1968 campaign to "reverse the flow of power and resources from the states and communities to Washington" and redirect "power and resources" back to the American people, a key objective of conservatism. He kept his promise by dismantling Great Society social programs, cutting funds for the War on Poverty, and eliminating the Office of Economic Opportunity. In 1972 the president adopted a program of revenue sharing, which transferred federal tax revenues to the states to use as they wished. Hoping to rein in the liberal Warren Court, Nixon nominated conservative justices, such as William Rehnquist and Lewis Powell, to the Supreme Court.

However, in several areas Nixon departed from conservatives who favored limited government. In 1970 he persuaded Congress to pass the Environmental Protection Act, which strengthened federal oversight of environmental programs throughout the country. In 1972 the federal government increased its responsibility for protecting the health and safety of American workers through the creation of the Occupational Safety and Health Administration (OSHA). The Consumer Products Safety Commission was established to provide added safety for the buying public. The president also signed a law banning cigarette advertising on radio and television because of the link between smoking and cancer.

Nixon applied this pragmatic conservatism to racial issues. The president proposed legislation that prevented the use of busing to promote school desegregation, which the Democratic Congress rejected. In general, he supported "benign neglect" concerning the issue of race

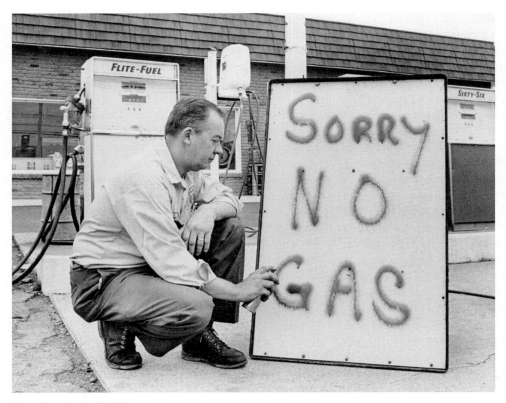

Gas Shortages, 1973

A gas station owner in Perkasie, Pennsylvania, lets his customers know he is out of gas. OPEC's 1973 oil embargo during the Yom Kippur War caused gas shortages and soaring prices in the United States. Motorists scrambling to find available supplies at gas stations created long lines. AP Photo and therefore rejected new legislative attempts to remove the vestiges of racial discrimination. In this way, Nixon courted southern conservatives in an attempt to deter George Wallace from mounting another third-party challenge in 1972. Still, Nixon moved back to the political center with efforts that furthered civil rights. Expanding **affirmative action** programs begun under the Johnson administration, he adopted plans that required construction companies and unions to recruit minority workers according to their percentage in the local labor force. His support of affirmative action was part of a broader approach to encourage "black capitalism," a concept designed to convince African Americans to seek opportunity within the free-enterprise system. Moreover, in 1970 Nixon signed the extension of the 1965 Voting Rights Act, thereby renewing the law that had provided suffrage to the majority of African Americans in the South. The law also lowered the voting age from twenty-one to eighteen for national elections. In 1971 the Twenty-sixth Amendment was ratified to lower the voting age for state and local elections as well.

The Nixon administration also veered away from the traditional Republican free market philosophy by resorting to wage and price controls to curb rising inflation brought on, for the most part, by increased military spending during the Vietnam War. In 1971 the president declared a ninety-day freeze on wages and prices, placed a temporary 10 percent surtax on imports, and let the value of the dollar drop on the international market, leading to increased U.S. exports. Taken together, these measures stabilized consumer prices, reduced unemployment, and boosted the gross national product. Although these proved to be only short-term gains, they improved Nixon's prospects for reelection.

The Nixon Landslide and Disgrace, 1972–1974

By appealing to voters across the political spectrum, Nixon won a monumental victory in 1972. The president invigorated the "silent majority" by demonizing his opponents and encouraging Vice President Spiro Agnew to aggressively pursue Nixon's strategy of polarization. Agnew called protesters "kooks" and "social misfits" and attacked the media and Nixon critics with heated rhetoric. As Nixon had hoped, George Wallace rejected a third-party bid and ran in the Democratic primaries. Wallace won impressive victories in North Carolina, Florida, Tennessee, Maryland, and Michigan, but his campaign ended after an assassination attempt left him paralyzed. With Wallace out of the race, the Democrats helped Nixon look more centrist by nominating George McGovern, a liberal antiwar senator from South Dakota, who ran a generally inept campaign.

The election marked the personal triumph of Richard Nixon. Winning in a landslide, he captured more than 60 percent of the popular vote and nearly all of the electoral votes. Democrats retained control of Congress but were trounced in their bid for the White House. However, Nixon would have little time to savor his victory, for within the next two years his conduct in the campaign would come back to destroy his presidency.

In the early hours of June 17, 1972, five men broke into Democratic Party headquarters in the Watergate apartment complex in Washington, D.C. What appeared initially as a routine robbery turned into the most infamous political scandal of the twentieth century. It was eventually revealed that the break-in had been authorized by the Committee for the Re-Election of the President in an attempt to steal documents from the Democrats.

Whether President Nixon knew about the break-in in advance and approved it remains in dispute, but he did authorize a cover-up of his administration's involvement. Nixon ordered his chief of staff, H. R. Haldeman, to get the CIA and FBI to back off from a thorough investigation of the incident by claiming that it would breach national security. To silence the burglars at their trials, the president promised them $400,000 and hinted at a presidential pardon after their conviction.

Nixon embarked on the cover-up to protect himself from revelations of his administration's other illegal activities. Several of the Watergate burglars belonged to a secret band of operatives known as "the plumbers," which had been formed in 1971 and authorized by the president. Their mission was to find and plug up unwelcome information leaks from government officials. On their first secret operation, the plumbers broke into the office of Daniel Ellsberg's psychiatrist to look for embarrassing personal information with which to discredit Ellsberg, who had leaked the *Pentagon Papers*. The president had other unsavory matters to hide. In an effort to contain leaks about the administration's secret bombing of Cambodia in 1969, the White House had illegally wiretapped its own officials and members of the press.

Watergate did not become a major scandal until after the election. The trial judge forced one of the burglars to reveal their backers. This revelation led two *Washington Post* reporters, Bob Woodward and Carl Bernstein, to doggedly investigate the link between the administration and the plumbers. With the help of Mark Felt, a top FBI official whose identity long remained secret and whom the reporters called "Deep Throat," Woodward and Bernstein succeeded in exposing the true nature of the crime. With the president still denying any knowledge of the offense, the Senate created a special committee in February 1973 to investigate the scandal. Televised hearings absorbed the public. White House counsel John Dean, whom Nixon had fired, testified about discussing the cover-up with the president and his

Nixon Resigns, 1974

On August 8, 1974, President Richard M. Nixon announced his resignation on national television. His decision came after the House Judiciary Committee voted to impeach Nixon and as he was rapidly losing support in both houses of Congress. Before leaving the White House the next day, Nixon bid farewell to his cabinet members and White House staff. Nixon chokes up as his wife Pat (partially visible) and his daughter Tricia look on.   AP Photo

closest advisers. His testimony proved accurate after the committee learned that Nixon had secretly taped all Oval Office conversations. When the president refused to release the tapes to a special prosecutor, the Supreme Court ruled against him. In the meantime, the hearings and investigations produced a number of political casualties. Nixon's attorney general, John Mitchell, and his closest advisers, H. R. Haldeman and John Ehrlichman, resigned, and twenty-five administration members went to jail.

The eventual release of the tapes finally revealed the truth about Nixon's cover-up, and the House Judiciary Committee voted to bring articles of impeachment to the House of Representatives. After concluding that the House would vote to impeach him and the Senate would very likely convict him, Nixon resigned on August 9, 1974. After receiving overwhelming support from the American electorate less than two years earlier, Richard Nixon left the White House in disgrace.

Vice President Gerald Ford served out Nixon's remaining term. The Republican representative from Michigan had replaced Vice President Spiro Agnew after Agnew resigned in 1973 following charges that he had taken illegal kickbacks while governor of Maryland. Ford chose Nelson A. Rockefeller, the moderate Republican governor of New York, as his vice president. In the wake of the Watergate scandal, the nation now had both a president and a vice president who had never been elected to those offices.

President Ford's most controversial and defining act took place shortly after he entered the White House. Explaining to the country that he wanted to quickly end the "national nightmare" stemming from Watergate, Ford pardoned Nixon for any criminal offenses he might have committed as president. Rather than healing the nation's wounds, this preemptive pardon polarized Americans and cost Ford considerable political capital. Ford also wrestled with a troubled economy as Americans once again experienced rising prices and high unemployment.

REVIEW & RELATE

Who made up the New Right coalition that brought Nixon to power? How did Nixon appeal to the New Right?

How did Nixon's pragmatism shape both his foreign and domestic policies?

LEARNINGCurve bedfordstmartins.com/hewittlawson/LC

The Challenges of the 1970s

Though deeply disillusioned by Vietnam and the Watergate scandal, most Americans hoped that, with these disasters behind them, better times lay ahead. Nixon's resignation did not, however, mark the beginning of a new era of peace and prosperity. Under the leadership of the Democratic president Jimmy Carter, the economy worsened as oil-producing nations in the Persian Gulf and Latin America raised the price of petroleum. Carter's efforts to revive the economy and rally the country behind energy conservation were ineffective, sharpening Republicans' attack on his policies and presidency. Activists on both the left and the right continued to fight over the role of the federal government in economic affairs as well as over the racial and cultural issues that divided the nation.

Jimmy Carter and the Limits of Affluence

Despite his political shortcomings, Gerald Ford received the Republican presidential nomination in 1976 and ran against James Earl (Jimmy) Carter, a little-known former governor of Georgia, who used his "outsider" status to his advantage. Shaping his campaign with Watergate in mind, Carter stressed character over economic issues and promised voters that he would run the government honestly, truthfully, and morally. As a postsegregationist governor of Georgia, Carter won the support of the family of Martin Luther King Jr. and other black leaders. Carter needed all the help he could get and eked out a narrow victory.

The greatest challenge Carter faced once in office was a faltering economy. America's consumer-oriented economy depended on cheap energy, a substantial portion of which came from sources outside the United States. By the 1970s, four-fifths of the world's oil supply came from Saudi Arabia,

Iran, Iraq, and Kuwait, all members of OPEC. The organization had been formed in 1960 by these Persian Gulf countries together with Venezuela, and it used its control of petroleum supplies to set world prices. By the time Carter became president, the cost of a barrel of oil had jumped to around $30. American drivers who had paid 30 cents a gallon for gas in 1970 paid more than four times that amount ten years later.

Energy concerns helped reshape American industry. With energy prices rising, American manufacturers sought ways to reduce costs by moving their factories to Mexico, Central and South America, and several Asian nations that offered cheaper labor and lower energy costs. This outmigration of American manufacturing had two significant consequences. First, it weakened the American labor movement, particularly in heavy industry. In the 1970s, union membership dropped from 28 to 23 percent of the workforce and continued to decline over the next decade. Second, this process of deindustrialization accelerated a significant population shift that had begun during World War II from the old industrial areas of the Northeast and the Midwest (the Rust Belt) to the South and the Southwest (the Sun Belt), where cheaper costs and lower wages were enormously attractive to businesses (Map 27.2). Only 14 percent of southern workers were unionized in a region with a long history of opposition to labor organizing. The

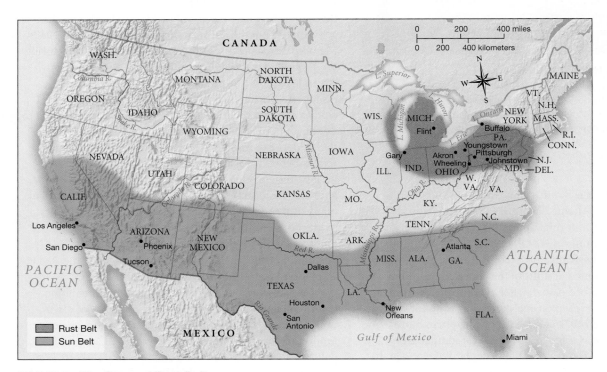

MAP 27.2   The Sun and Rust Belts

Dramatic economic and demographic shifts during the 1970s led to industrial development and population growth in the "Sun Belt" in the South and Southwest at the expense of the "Rust Belt" in the Northeast and Midwest. As manufacturers sought cheap, non-unionized labor, they moved factories to the South or overseas while defense industries and agribusiness fueled growth from Texas to California.

President Carter's Fireside Chat, 1977

In February 1977, reminiscent of Franklin D. Roosevelt's fireside chats of the 1930s, President Jimmy Carter addressed the nation during a fuel shortage. He sought to identify himself with the average American by donning a simple cardigan sweater. Carter asked viewers to save energy by turning down their thermostats and wearing sweaters.   Jimmy Carter Library

North's loss was the South's gain, and cities such as Houston, Texas; Atlanta, Georgia; Phoenix, Arizona; and San Diego, California, flourished, while the steel and auto towns of Youngstown, Ohio; Flint, Michigan; and Johnstown, Pennsylvania, decayed.

These monumental shifts in the American economy produced widespread pain. Higher gasoline prices affected all businesses that relied on energy, leading to serious inflation. Between 1974 and 1980, housing prices more than doubled, and the average cost of a new car jumped from $3,900 to $5,770. To maintain their standard of living in the face of rising inflation and stagnant wages, many Americans went into debt, using a new innovation, the credit card, to borrow more than $300 billion. The American economy had gone through inflationary spirals before, but they were

usually accompanied by high employment, with wages helping to drive up prices. In the 1970s, however, rising prices were accompanied by growing unemployment, a situation that economists called "stagflation." Joblessness had risen to 9 percent on the eve of Carter's election and stood at 7 percent when he ran for reelection in 1980. Traditionally, remedies to control inflation increased unemployment, yet most unemployment cures also spurred inflation. With both occurring at the same time, economists were confounded, and many Americans felt they had lost control over their economy. In 1978, 55 percent of survey respondents declared, "Next year will be worse than this year."

President Carter had no better solutions than did his predecessor. To reduce dependency on foreign oil, in 1977 Carter devised a plan for energy self-sufficiency, which he called the "moral equivalent of war." Critics poked fun at the proposal by reducing the president's words to the acronym MEOW, suggesting that it had all the bite of a pussycat. A more substantial accomplishment came on August 4, 1977, when Carter signed into law the creation of the Department of Energy, with responsibilities covering research, development, and conservation of energy.

The Persistence of Liberalism

Despite the elections of Richard Nixon and the economic hard times that many encountered in the 1970s, political activism did not die out with the end of the militant 1960s. Many of the changes sought by liberals and radicals during the 1960s had entered the political and cultural mainstreams. Nor did the influence of the counterculture disappear. During the 1970s, long hairstyles and colorful clothes also entered the mainstream, and rock continued to dominate popular music. American youth and many of their elders experimented with recreational drugs, and the remaining sexual taboos of the 1960s fell. Many parents became resigned to seeing their daughters and sons living with boyfriends or girlfriends before getting married. And many of those same parents sought to expand their own sexual horizons by engaging in extramarital affairs or divorcing their spouses. The divorce rate increased 116 percent in the decade after 1965; in 1979 the rate peaked at 23 divorces per 1,000 married couples.

Rock music, long linked to sexual experimentation, continued to dominate the era. The popularity of disco music, glamorized by John Travolta in the blockbuster motion picture *Saturday Night Fever* (1977), emphasized dance beats over social messages, much like early rock 'n' roll. However, listeners could still get deeper meaning and engaging melodies from the works of singer-songwriters, who crafted and recorded their own songs. The decade inspired artists such as Bruce Springsteen, Jackson Browne, and Billy Joel, whose performing energy and songs of loss, loneliness, urban decay, and adventure carried folk-rock music in new directions.

The antiwar movement and counterculture influenced popular culture in other ways. The film *M*A*S*H* (1970), though dealing with the Korean War, was a thinly veiled satire of the horrors of the Vietnam War, and in the late 1970s filmmakers began producing movies specifically about Vietnam and the toll the war took on ordinary Americans who served there. The television sitcom *All in the Family* gave American viewers the character of Archie Bunker, an opinionated blue-collar worker, in a comedy that dramatized the contemporary political and cultural war pitting conservatives against liberals. The show recounted the battle of the generations as Archie taunted his hippie-looking son-in-law with politically incorrect remarks about religious, racial, and ethnic minorities, feminists, and liberals.

The battles fought in the fictional Bunker household played out in real life. In the 1970s, the women's movement gained strength, but it also attracted powerful opponents. The 1973 Supreme Court victory for abortion rights in *Roe v. Wade* (see chapter 26) mobilized women on all sides of the issue. Pro-choice advocates pointed out that previous laws criminalizing abortion exposed pregnant women who sought the procedure to unsanitary and dangerous methods of ending pregnancies. However, *Roe v. Wade* produced an equally strong reaction from abortion opponents. Pro-life advocates believed that a fetus was a human being and must be granted full protection from what they considered to be murder. In 1976 Congress responded to abortion opponents by passing legislation prohibiting the use of federal funds for impoverished women seeking to terminate their pregnancies.

Feminists engaged in other debates in this decade, often clashing with more conservative women. The National Organization for Women (NOW) and its allies succeeded in getting thirty-five states out of a necessary thirty-eight to ratify the **Equal Rights Amendment (ERA)**, which prevented the abridgment of "equality of rights under law . . . by the United States or any State on the basis of sex." In response, other women activists formed their own movement to block ratification. Phyllis Schlafly, a conservative activist, founded the Stop ERA organization. She argued that the ERA would create a "unisex society" and deprive "women of the rights they already have, such as the right of a wife to be supported by her husband," attend a single-sex college, use women's-only bathrooms, and avoid military combat. Despite the inroads made by feminists, traditional notions of femininity appealed to many women and to male-dominated legislatures. The remaining states refused to ratify the ERA, thus killing the amendment in 1982, when the ratification period expired.

Despite the failure to obtain ratification of the ERA, feminists achieved significant victories. In 1972 Congress passed the Educational Amendments Act. Title IX of this law prohibited colleges and universities that received federal funds from discriminating on the basis of sex, leading to substantial advances in women's athletics. Many more women sought relief against job discrimination through the Equal Employment Opportunity Commission, resulting in major victories against such firms as the American Telephone and Telegraph Company. NOW membership continued to grow, and the number of battered women's shelters and rape crisis centers multiplied in towns and cities across the country. Women saw their ranks increase on college campuses, in both undergraduate and professional schools. Women also began entering politics in large enough numbers, especially at the local and state levels, to justify the formation of the National Women's Political Caucus in 1971. At the national level, women such as Shirley Chisholm and Geraldine Ferraro of New York, Barbara Jordan of Texas, and Patricia Schroeder of Colorado won seats in Congress. Women's political associations—such as Emily's List, founded in 1984, and the Fund for a Feminist Majority, founded in 1987—saw their memberships and donations soar, especially after Anita Hill testified against the nomination of Clarence Thomas to the Supreme Court.

At the same time, women of color sought to broaden the definition of feminism to include struggles against race and class oppression as well as sex discrimination. In 1974 a group of black feminists, led by author Barbara Smith, organized the Combahee River Collective and proclaimed: "We . . . often find it difficult to separate race from class from sex oppression because in our lives they are most often experienced simultaneously." Chicana and other Latina feminists drew strength from African American women in extending women's liberation beyond the confines of the white middle class. In 1987 feminist poet and writer Gloria Anzaldúa wrote: "Though I'll defend my race and culture when they are attacked by non-mexicanos . . . I abhor some of my culture's ways, how it cripples its women . . . our strengths used against us, lowly [women] bearing humility with dignity."

Explore

See Document 27.1 for an excerpt from the Combahee River Collective.

Another outgrowth of 1960s liberal activism that flourished in the 1970s was the effort to clean up and preserve the environment. The publication of Rachel Carson's *Silent Spring* in 1962 had renewed awareness of what Progressive Era reformers called conservation (see chapter 19). Carson expanded the concept of conservation

DOCUMENT 27.1

Combahee River Collective | *A Black Feminist Statement*, 1977

The Combahee River Collective was founded in 1974 as an expression of black feminism rooted in socialism. The group, operated mainly in the Boston area, contended that sexism had many sources: capitalism, racism, patriarchy, and enforced heterosexuality. Although many of the group's members were lesbians, they rejected lesbian separatism called for by some white lesbians. They proclaimed racial solidarity with African American men, but, as this statement shows, they recognized the difficulties of allying with black men against sexism.

Explore

Why do these black feminists think they are at a disadvantage?

The major source of difficulty in our political work is that we are not just trying to fight oppression on one front or even two, but instead to address a whole range of oppressions. We do not have racial, sexual, heterosexual, or class privilege to rely upon, nor do we have even the minimal access to resources and power that groups who possess any one of these types of privilege have.

The psychological toll of being a black woman and the difficulties this presents in reaching political consciousness and doing political work can never be underestimated. There is a very low value placed upon black women's psyches in this society, which is both racist and sexist. As an early group member once said, "We are all damaged people merely by virtue of being black women." . . .

Why do black feminists say that black men feel threatened by them?

The reaction of black men to feminism has been notoriously negative. They are, of course, even more threatened than black women by the possibility that black feminists might organize around our own needs. They realize that they might not only lose valuable and hard-working allies in their struggles but that they might also be forced to change their habitually sexist ways of interacting with and oppressing black women. Accusations that black feminism divides the black struggle are powerful deterrents to the growth of an autonomous black women's movement.

Still, hundreds of women have been active at different times during the three-year existence of our group. And every black woman who came, came out of a strongly felt need for some level of possibility that did not previously exist in her life. . . .

According to this statement, what do white feminists have to do?

One issue that is of major concern to us and that we have begun to publicly address is racism in the white women's movement. As black feminists we are made constantly and painfully aware of how little effort white women have made to understand and combat their racism, which requires among other things that they have a more than superficial comprehension of race, color, and black history and culture. Eliminating racism in the white women's movement is by definition work for white women to do, but we will continue to speak to and demand accountability on this issue.

Source: Zillah R. Eisenstein, ed., *Capitalist Patriarchy and the Case for Socialist Feminism* (New York: Monthly Press, 1978), 367–69, 371–72.

Put It in Context

How did tensions within the feminist movement reflect broader social tensions on women's issues in the 1970s?

Three Mile Island Nuclear Plant, 1979

On March 28, 1979, the Three Mile Island nuclear power plant, outside Harrisburg, Pennsylvania, started leaking radioactive steam that contaminated the surrounding area. The governor called for a voluntary evacuation within a twenty-mile distance. The cooling tower of the nuclear plant stands behind an abandoned playground, where children had been playing only days earlier.   AP Photo

to include ecology, which addressed the relationships of human beings and other organisms to their environments. By exploring these connections, she offered a revealing look at the devastating effects of powerful pesticides, especially DDT, on birds and fish, as well as on the human food chain and water supply.

This new environmental movement not only focused on open spaces and national parks but also sought to publicize urban environmental problems. By 1970, 53 percent of Americans considered air and water pollution to be one of the top issues facing the country, up from only 17 percent five years earlier. Responding to this shift in public opinion, in 1971 President Nixon established the **Environmental Protection Agency (EPA)** and signed the Clean Air Act, which regulated auto emissions. Two years later, Congress banned the sale of DDT.

Not everyone embraced environmentalism. As the EPA toughened emission standards, automobile manufacturers complained that the regulations forced them to raise prices and hurt an industry that was already feeling the threat of foreign competition, especially from Japan. Workers were also affected, as declining sales forced companies to lay off employees. Similarly, passage of the Endangered Species Act of 1973 pitted timber companies in the Northwest against environmentalists. The new law prevented the federal government from funding any projects that threatened the habitat of animals at risk of extinction.

Several disasters heightened public demands for stronger government oversight of the environment. In

1978 women living near Love Canal outside of Niagara Falls, New York, complained about unusually high rates of illnesses and birth defects in their community. Investigations revealed that their housing development had been constructed on top of a toxic waste dump. This discovery spawned grassroots efforts to clean up this area as well as other contaminated communities. In 1980 Congress responded by passing the Comprehensive Environmental Response, Compensation, and Liability Act (known as Superfund) to clean up sites contaminated with hazardous substances. Further inquiries showed that the presence of such poisonous waste dumps disproportionately affected minorities and the poor. Critics called the placement of these waste locations near African American and other minority communities "environmental racism" and launched a movement for environmental justice.

The most dangerous threat came in March 1979 at the Three Mile Island nuclear plant near Harrisburg, Pennsylvania. A broken valve at the plant leaked coolant and threatened the meltdown of the reactor's nuclear core. As officials quickly evacuated residents from the surrounding area, employees at the plant narrowly averted catastrophe by fixing the problem before an explosion occurred. Grassroots activists, such as the Clamshell Alliance in New Hampshire, protested and raised public awareness against the construction of additional power facilities. They also convinced existing utility companies to slow down their plans for expanding the output of nuclear power.

Shirley Chisholm, 1968

On November 6, 1968, Shirley Chisholm won election to the House of Representatives from a predominantly black district in Brooklyn, New York, becoming the first African American woman in Congress. This photo shows Chisholm (center) surrounded by campaign workers flashing the victory sign.   AP Photo

Black mayors were elected in Atlanta and New Orleans as well as in smaller municipal and county governments in the South where African Americans could scarcely vote a decade earlier. These mayors appointed black officials, improved public health, and filled government jobs and contracts through affirmative action programs. At the same time, the number of Latino American and Asian American elected officials increased, and as with African Americans, most held office at the state and local levels.

The issue of school busing highlighted the persistence of racial discrimination. In the fifteen years following the landmark decision in *Brown v. Board of Education of Topeka, Kansas* in 1954 (see chapter 25), few schools had been integrated. Starting in 1969, the U.S. Supreme Court ruled that genuine racial integration of the public schools must no longer be delayed. In 1971 the Court went even further in *Swann v. Charlotte-Mecklenburg Board of Education* by requiring school districts to bus pupils to achieve integration. Cities such as Charlotte, North Carolina; Lexington, Kentucky; and Tampa, Florida, embraced the ruling and carefully planned for it to succeed.

However, the decision was more controversial in other municipalities around the nation. The civil rights movement had primarily addressed injustices in the South, but it also exposed racism as a national problem. There were no Jim Crow laws in the North, but in many northern communities racially discriminatory housing policies created segregated neighborhoods and, thus, segregated schools. When white parents in the Detroit suburbs objected to busing their children to inner-city, predominantly black schools, the Supreme Court in 1974 departed from the *Swann* case and prohibited busing across distinct school district boundaries. This ruling created a serious problem for integration efforts because many whites were fleeing the cities and moving to the suburbs where few blacks lived.

As the conflict over school integration intensified, violence broke out in communities throughout the country. In Boston, Massachusetts, busing opponents tapped into the racial and class resentments of the largely white working-class population of South Boston, which was paired with the black

Racial Struggles Continue

The civil rights struggle did not end with the last great interracial march in Selma, Alabama, in 1965 or the death of Martin Luther King Jr. in 1968. The civil rights coalition of organizations that banded together in the 1960s had disintegrated, but the National Association for the Advancement of Colored People remained active, as did local organizations in communities nationwide. The 1965 Voting Rights Act, through the election of black officials, provided a significant path for the continuation of the civil rights movement. A black candidate in South Carolina summed up electoral politics as the new form of activism. "There's an inherent value in office holding," he declared. "A race of people excluded from public office will always be second class." By 1992 there were more than 7,500 black elected officials in the United States. Many of them had participated in the civil rights movement and subsequently worked to gain for their constituents the economic benefits that integration and affirmative action had not yet achieved.

community of Roxbury for busing, leaving mainly middle- and upper-class white communities unaffected. In the fall of 1974, battles broke out inside and outside the schools. Antibusing protesters gathered in front of the Federal Building in downtown Boston, threw eggs and tomatoes, and cursed Senator Edward Kennedy, a busing supporter who sent his children to private school. "You're a disgrace to the Irish," one protester shouted. "Let your daughter get bussed [to Roxbury] so she can get raped." Despite the violence, schools stayed open, and for the next three decades Boston remained under court order to continue busing.

Along with busing, affirmative action generated fierce controversy, as the case of Allan Bakke showed. From 1970 to 1977, with the acceleration of affirmative action programs, the number of African Americans attending college doubled, constituting nearly 10 percent of the student body, a few percentage points lower than the proportion of blacks in the national population. Though blacks still earned lower incomes than the average white family, black family income as a percent of white family income had grown from 55.1 percent in 1965 to 61.5 percent ten years later. African Americans, however, still had a long way to go to catch up with whites. The situation was even worse for those who did not reach middle-class status: About 30 percent of African Americans slid deeper into poverty during the decade.

Despite the persistence of economic inequality, many whites believed that affirmative action placed them at a disadvantage with blacks in the educational and economic marketplaces. In particular, many white men condemned policies that they thought recruited blacks at their expense. "Talk about rights; we've got no rights," a white Detroit policeman stated in voicing his disapproval over an affirmative action decision in favor of blacks. Polls showed that although most whites favored equal treatment of blacks, they disapproved of affirmative action as a form of "reverse discrimination." **See Document Project 27: The Affirmative Action Debate, page 884**.

The furor over affirmative action did not end with the *Bakke* case, and over the next three decades affirmative action opponents succeeded in narrowing the use of racial considerations in employment and education. However, they did so without Bakke, who chose to live a very private life with his family and refused to take up the larger cause against affirmative action with which his name became identified.

REVIEW & RELATE

- What issues and trends shaped the presidency of Jimmy Carter?

- How and why did the social and cultural developments of the 1960s continue to create conflict and controversy in the 1970s?

The Conservative Political Ascendancy

The backlash against affirmative action and the ERA confirmed that liberal reformers were losing ground to conservatives. By the early 1990s, liberalism had become identified with special interests and elitism, and conservatives could boast of numerous successes. The election of former California governor Ronald Reagan as president in 1980 reflected the spectacular growth in political power of the New Right, finishing what Barry Goldwater had started in his unsuccessful bid for the presidency in 1964 (see chapter 26). Reagan pushed the conservative economic agenda of lower taxes and business deregulation alongside the New Right's concern for traditional religious and family values. His presidency installed conservatism as the dominant political ideology for the remainder of the twentieth century.

The New Right Revival

The New Right emerged from a mixture of forces: the revolt against high taxes, the backlash against the growth of the federal government, the disillusionment of former liberal intellectuals known as neoconservatives, and the growth of the Christian Right. In the 1970s, working- and middle-class white resentment against antiwar protesters, hippies, black power militants, and feminist agitators found a new target in big government spending and high taxes. During the 1970s, taxation claimed 30 percent of the gross national product, up 6 percent from 1960. Although Americans still paid far less in taxes than their counterparts in Western Europe, and even though tax rates had fallen since World War II, Americans objected to rising state and federal taxes. Leading the tax revolt was the Sun Belt state of California. In a 1978 referendum, California voters passed Proposition 13, a measure that reduced property taxes and placed strict limits on the ability of local governments to raise them in the future. In the wake of Proposition 13, a dozen states enacted similar measures.

Economic conservatives also set their sights on reducing the federal income tax. They supported cutting personal and corporate taxes by a third in the belief that reducing taxes would encourage new investment and job creation. "Supply-side" economists, such as Arthur Laffer, argued that lowering tax rates would actually boost tax receipts: With lower taxes, companies and investors would have more capital to invest, leading to expanded job growth; with increased employment, more people would be paying taxes. At the same time, supply-side conservatives called for reduced government spending, especially in the social service sector, to ensure balanced budgets and to eliminate what they saw as unnecessary spending on domestic programs.

The New Right also benefited by the defection of disillusioned liberals. Labeled **neoconservatives**, intellectuals such as Irving Kristol, Norman Podhoretz, and Nathan Glazer reversed course and condemned the Great Society programs that they had originally supported. They believed that federal policies had aggravated rather than improved the problems government planners intended to solve. Of particular concern to many neoconservatives were affirmative action programs, the domination of campus debate and discourse by New Left radicals, and left-wing criticism of the use of American military and economic might to advance U.S. interests overseas.

Perhaps the greatest spark igniting the New Right came from socially conservative religious believers, mainly evangelical Christians and Catholics. Phyllis Schlafly—a Catholic, a former Goldwater supporter, and an ERA opponent—played a major role in connecting the political conservatism of the 1960s with the social conservatism of the following decade. Yet evangelical Christians most often provided the leadership and core support for this political movement. Evangelicals considered themselves to have been "born again"—literally experiencing Jesus Christ's saving presence inside of them. By the end of the 1970s, evangelical Christians numbered around 50 million, about a quarter of the population. The Christian Right opposed abortion, gay rights, and sex education; attacked Supreme Court rulings banning prayer in the public schools; denounced Darwin's theory of evolution in favor of divine creationism; and supported the traditional role of women as mothers and homemakers. Certainly not all evangelical Christians held all of these beliefs; for example, President Jimmy Carter, a born-again Christian, did not. Still, conservative Christians believed that the liberals and radicals of the 1960s had spread the secular creed of individual rights and personal fulfillment at the expense of traditional Christian values.

Social conservatives worried that the traditional nuclear family was in danger, as households consisting of married couples with children declined from 30 percent in the 1970s to 23 percent thirty years later, and the divorce rate soared. The number of unmarried couples living together doubled over the last quarter of the twentieth century, and the percentage of children born to single mothers jumped from 18 in 1980 to 40 in 2007. This increase was part of a trend in developed countries worldwide, and among these nations the United States ranked in the middle between Iceland at the top and Japan at the bottom.

Since the 1950s, Billy Graham, a charismatic Southern Baptist evangelist from North Carolina, had used television to conduct nationwide crusades that attracted millions of followers. Television became an even greater instrument in the hands of New Right Christian preachers in the 1970s and 1980s. The Reverend Pat Robertson of Virginia founded the Christian Broadcasting Network, and ministers such as

Jerry Falwell used the airwaves to great effect. What distinguished Falwell and Robertson from earlier evangelists like Graham was their fusion of religion and electoral politics. In 1979 Falwell founded the Moral Majority, an organization that backed political candidates who supported a "family values" social agenda. Within two years of its creation, the Moral Majority counted four million members who were eager to organize in support of New Right politicians. The alliance of economic, intellectual, and religious conservatives offered a formidable challenge to liberalism.

Explore

See Document 27.2 for a statement from Jerry Falwell.

The Triumph of Ronald Reagan

Ronald Reagan's presidential victory in 1980 consolidated the growing New Right coalition and reshaped American politics for a generation to come. The former movie actor had transformed himself from a New Deal Democrat into a conservative Republican politician when he ran for governor of California in 1966. As governor, he implemented conservative ideas of free enterprise and small government and denounced Johnson's Great Society for threatening private property and individual liberty. "Government," Reagan

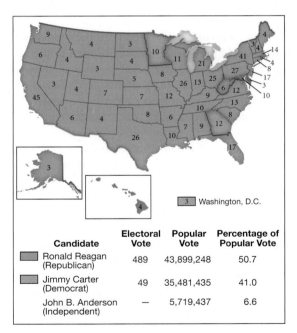

Candidate	Electoral Vote	Popular Vote	Percentage of Popular Vote
Ronald Reagan (Republican)	489	43,899,248	50.7
Jimmy Carter (Democrat)	49	35,481,435	41.0
John B. Anderson (Independent)	—	5,719,437	6.6

MAP 27.3   The Election of 1980

Ronald Reagan won 50.7 percent of the popular vote in the 1980 election, but his margin of victory over Jimmy Carter was much greater in the electoral vote. Reagan won the votes of the South and many disaffected Democrats in the urban North. A third-party candidate, John Anderson of Illinois, won 6.6 percent of the popular vote, demonstrating significant disapproval with both major parties.

DOCUMENT 27.2

Jerry Falwell | We Must Return to Traditional Religious Values, 1980

Socially conservative evangelical Christians opposed the feminist movement, abortion rights, gay rights, and other forces they believed contributed to the secularization of American society. Southern Baptist preacher Jerry Falwell was one of the Christian Right's most powerful leaders. He founded the Thomas Road Baptist Church and Liberty University, in Lynchburg, Virginia, as well as the Moral Majority political organization. The following selection illustrates Falwell's merging of religious beliefs with a conservative political agenda.

Explore

We must reverse the trend America finds herself in today. Young people between the ages of twenty-five and forty have been born and reared in a different world than Americans of years past. The television set has been their primary baby-sitter. From the television set they have learned situation ethics and immorality—they have learned a loss of respect for human life. They have learned to disrespect the family as God has established it. They have been educated in a public-school system that is permeated with secular humanism. They have been taught that the Bible is just another book of literature. They have been taught that there are no absolutes in our world today. They have been introduced to the drug culture. They have been reared by the family and by the public school in a society that is greatly void of discipline and character-building. These same young people have been reared under the influence of a government that has taught them socialism and welfarism. They

have been taught to believe that the world owes them a living whether they work or not. . . .

It is now time to take a stand on certain moral issues, and we can only stand if we have leaders. We must stand against the Equal Rights Amendment, the feminist revolution, and the homosexual revolution. We must have a revival in this country. . . .

As a preacher of the Gospel, I not only believe in prayer and preaching, I also believe in good citizenship. If a labor union in America has the right to organize and improve its working conditions, then I believe that the churches and the pastors, the priests, and the rabbis of America have a responsibility, not just the right, to see to it that the moral climate and conscience of Americans is such that this nation can be healed inwardly. If it is healed inwardly, then it will heal itself outwardly.

Source: Jerry Falwell, *Listen America!* (New York: Doubleday, 1980), 17–18.

Interpret the Evidence

- According to Falwell, what are the biggest problems facing American society?
- What solutions does Falwell propose?

Put It in Context

What contribution did Falwell make in expanding the base of the New Right?

observed, "is like a baby, an alimentary canal with a big appetite at one end and no sense of responsibility at the other." His winning combination of support for conservative economic and social issues carried him to the presidency.

Reagan triumphed over Jimmy Carter and John Anderson, a moderate Republican who ran as an independent candidate (Map 27.3). The high unemployment and inflation of the late 1970s worked in Reagan's favor. Reagan appealed to a coalition of conservative Republicans

and disaffected Democrats, promising to cut taxes and reduce spending, to relax federal supervision over civil rights programs, and to end what was left of expensive Great Society measures and affirmative action. Finally, he energized members of the religious right, who flocked to the polls to support Reagan's demands for voluntary prayer in the public schools, defeat of the Equal Rights Amendment, and a constitutional amendment to outlaw abortion.

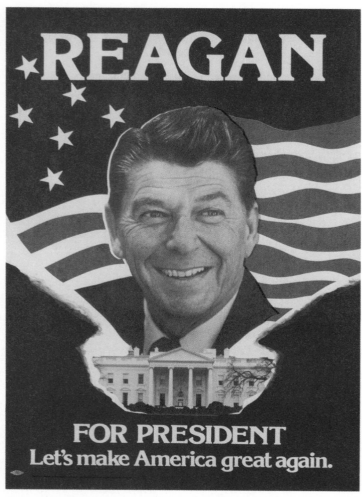

Ronald Reagan Campaign Poster, 1980

This 1980 campaign poster captures one of Ronald Reagan's central themes: to make America great again, referring to the discontent many Americans felt over stagflation and energy shortages as well as the hostage crisis in Iran.   Courtesy of the Ronald Reagan Presidential Foundation

Reagan's first priority, however, was stimulating the stagnant economy. The president's strategy, known as **Reaganomics**, reflected the ideas of supply-side economists and conservative Republicans. Stating that "government is not the solution to our problem; government is the problem," Reagan asked Congress for a huge income tax cut of 30 percent over three years, a reduction in spending for domestic programs of more than $40 billion, and new monetary policies to lower rising rates for loans.

The president did not operate in isolation from the rest of the world. He learned a great deal from Margaret Thatcher, the British prime minister who took office two years before Reagan. Thatcher combated inflation by slashing welfare programs, selling off publicly owned companies, and cutting back health and education programs. An advocate of

supply-side economics, Thatcher reduced income taxes on the wealthy by more than 50 percent to encourage new investment. West Germany also moved toward the right under Chancellor Helmut Kohl, who reined in welfare spending. In the 1980s, Reaganomics and Thatcherism dominated the United States and the two most powerful nations of Western Europe.

In March 1981, Reagan survived a nearly fatal assassin's bullet. More popular than ever after his recovery, the president persuaded the Democratic House and the Republican Senate to pass his economic measures in slightly modified form. The initial results were disastrous—unemployment rose to 9.5 percent in the wake of government cutbacks in spending. However, the government's tight money policies, as engineered by the Federal Reserve Board, reduced inflation from 14 percent in 1980 to 4 percent in 1984. By 1983 the unemployment rate had also fallen, while the gross national product grew by a healthy 4.3 percent, an indication that the recession of the previous two years had ended.

The success of Reaganomics came at the expense of the poor and the lower middle class. The Reagan administration slashed federal spending by cutting benefits that affected mainly the poor and marginal workers dependent on government supplements. The president reduced spending for food stamps, school lunches, Aid to Families with Dependent Children (welfare), and Medicaid, while maintaining programs that middle-class voters relied on, such as Medicare and Social Security. However, rather than diminishing the government, the savings that came from reduced social spending went into increased military appropriations. Together with lower taxes, these expenditures benefited large corporations that received government military contracts and favorable tax write-offs.

As a result of Reagan's economic policies, financial institutions and the stock market earned huge profits. The Reagan administration relaxed antitrust regulations, encouraging corporate mergers to a degree unseen since the Great Depression. Fueled by falling interest rates, the stock market created wealth for many investors. The number of millionaires doubled during the 1980s, as the top 1 percent of families gained control of 42 percent of the nation's wealth and 60 percent of corporate stock. Reflecting this phenomenal accumulation of riches, television produced melodramas depicting the lives of oil barons (such as *Dallas* and *Dynasty*), whose characters lived glamorous lives filled with intrigue and extravagance. In *Wall Street* (1987), a film that captured the money ethic of the period, Gordon Gekko, the main character, utters the memorable line summing up the moment: "Greed, for lack of a better word, is good. Greed is right. Greed works."

In reality, however, greed did not work for most people. The gap between the rich and the poor widened. During the 1980s, the nation's share of poor people rose from 11.7 percent to 13.5 percent, representing 33 million Americans. Severe cutbacks in government social programs that had alleviated suffering in the past worsened the plight of the poor. Poverty disproportionately affected women and minorities. The number of homeless people grew to as many as 400,000 during the 1980s, as chronically unemployed workers, the mentally ill, and single mothers sought shelter in subways, under bridges, and in parks. While the rich got richer and the poor got poorer, the middle class diminished in size. From a high of 53 percent of families in the early 1970s, the middle class shrank to 49 percent in 1985.

The Reagan administration's relaxed regulation of the corporate sector also contributed to the unbalanced economy. Federal agencies concerned with environmental protection, consumer product reliability, and occupational safety saw their key functions shifted to the states, which made them less effective. The president also aided big business by challenging labor unions. In 1981 air traffic controllers went on strike to gain higher wages and improved safety conditions. In response, the president fired the strikers who refused to return to work, and in their place he hired new controllers. Reagan's anti-union actions both reflected and encouraged a decline in union membership throughout the 1980s, with union membership falling to its lowest level since the New Deal (16 percent). Without union protection, wages failed to keep up with inflation, further increasing the gap between rich and poor.

Explore

> See Documents 27.3 and 27.4 on the state of the nation in the 1980s.

Reagan's landslide victory over Democratic candidate Walter Mondale in 1984 sealed the national political transition from liberalism to conservatism. Voters responded overwhelmingly to the improving economy, Reagan's defense of traditional social values, and his boundless optimism about America's future. Despite the landslide, the election was notable for the nomination of Representative Geraldine Ferraro of New York as Mondale's Democratic running mate, the first woman to run on a major party ticket for national office.

Reagan's second term did not produce changes as significant as did his first term. Democrats still controlled the House and in 1986 recaptured the Senate. The Reagan administration focused on foreign affairs and the continued Cold War with the Soviet Union, thus escalating defense spending. Most of the Reagan economic revolution continued as before, but with serious consequences: The federal deficit mushroomed, and by 1989 the nation was saddled with a $2.8 trillion debt, a situation that jeopardized the country's financial independence and the economic well-being of succeeding generations.

The president also reshaped the future through his nominations to the U.S. Supreme Court. Starting with the choice of Sandra Day O'Connor, the Court's first female justice, in 1981, Reagan's appointments moved the Court in a more conservative direction. The elevation of Associate Justice William Rehnquist to chief justice in 1986 reinforced this trend, which would have significant consequences for decades to come.

The Implementation of Social Conservatism

Throughout his two terms, President Reagan pushed the New Right's social agenda with mixed success. Conservatives blamed political liberalism and an increasingly secular society for what they saw as a decline in family values. Their solution was a renewed focus on conservative Christian principles. In addition to trying to remove evolution and sex education from the classroom and bring in prayer and patriotism, the New Right stepped up its opposition to abortion. The Reagan administration required family planning agencies seeking federal funding to notify parents of children under age eighteen before dispensing birth control, cut off financial aid to international organizations supporting abortion, and provided funds for "chastity clinics" that preached sexual abstinence. Despite these efforts, conservatives could not convince the Supreme Court to overturn *Roe v. Wade*.

Social conservatives also felt threatened by more tolerant views of homosexuality. The gay rights movement, which began in the 1960s, strengthened during the 1970s as thousands of gay men and lesbians made known their sexual orientation, fought discrimination, and expressed pride in their sexual identity. However, the gay rights movement also inspired personal and political attacks. Then, in the early 1980s, physicians traced an outbreak of a deadly illness among gay men to a virus that attacked the immune system (human immunodeficiency virus, or HIV), making it vulnerable to infections that were usually fatal. This disease, called **acquired immune deficiency syndrome (AIDS)**, was transmitted through bodily fluids during sexual intercourse, through blood transfusions, and by intravenous drug use. Scientists could not explain why the disease initially showed up among gay men in the United States; however, New Right critics insisted that

DOCUMENTS 27.3 AND 27.4

Morning in America: Two Views

In the 1980s, as the nation reeled in the aftermath of Watergate and the Vietnam War as well as the more immediate crises of oil shortages and stagflation, Ronald Reagan promised voters that better times were coming. In his first inaugural address, Reagan reasserted his pledges to lower taxes, reduce the size of the federal government, and restore American pride. By 1984 Reagan and his supporters were ready to claim victory, seeing in the return of economic growth vindication of their ideas and optimism. New York governor Mario Cuomo's keynote address at the Democratic National Convention, however, portrays a very different picture.

Explore

27.3 Ronald Reagan | First Inaugural Address, January 20, 1981

The business of our nation goes forward. These United States are confronted with an economic affliction of great proportions. We suffer from the longest and one of the worst sustained inflations in our national history. It distorts our economic decisions, penalizes thrift, and crushes the struggling young and the fixed-income elderly alike. It threatens to shatter the lives of millions of our people.

Idle industries have cast workers into unemployment, human misery, and personal indignity. Those who do work are denied a fair return for their labor by a tax system which penalizes successful achievement and keeps us from maintaining full productivity. . . .

In this present crisis, government is not the solution to our problem; government is the problem. From time to time, we've been tempted to believe that society has become too complex to be managed by self-rule, that government by an elite group is superior to government for, by, and of the people.

Well, if no one among us is capable of governing himself, then who among us has the capacity to govern someone else? All of us together, in and out of government, must bear the burden. The solutions we seek must be equitable, with no one group singled out to pay a higher price. . . .

It is my intention to curb the size and influence of the Federal establishment and to demand recognition of the distinction between the powers granted to the Federal Government and those reserved to the States or to the people. All of us need to be reminded that the Federal Government did not create the States; the States created the Federal Government.

Now, so there will be no misunderstanding, it's not my intention to do away with government. It is rather to make it work—work with us, not over us; to stand by our side, not ride on our back. Government can and must provide opportunity, not smother it; foster productivity, not stifle it.

Source: Michael Waldman, ed., *My Fellow Americans: The Most Important Speeches of America's Presidents, from George Washington to George W. Bush* (Naperville, IL: Sourcebooks, 2003), 247–49.

AIDS was a plague visited on sexual deviants by an angry God. "The poor homosexuals," mocked Pat Buchanan, a Reagan adviser. "They have declared war on nature and now nature is exacting an awful retribution." As the epidemic spread beyond the gay community, mainly through blood transfusions and illegal intravenous drug use, gay rights organizers and their heterosexual allies raised research money and public awareness. By the early 1990s, medical advances had begun to extend the lives of AIDS patients and manage the disease.

Increased immigration also troubled social conservatives as another reflection of the general societal breakdown. The number of immigrants to the United States rose dramatically in the 1970s and 1980s following the relaxation of foreign quota restrictions after 1965 (Figure 27.1). During these decades, immigrants came mainly from

27.4 Mario Cuomo | Speech to the Democratic National Convention, July 16, 1984

Ten days ago, President Reagan admitted that although some people in this country seemed to be doing well nowadays, others were unhappy, and even worried, about themselves, their families, and their futures.

The president said he didn't understand that fear. He said, "Why, this country is a shining city on a hill."

The president is right. In many ways we *are* "a shining city on a hill."

But the hard truth is that not everyone is sharing in this city's splendor and glory.

A shining city is perhaps all the president sees from the portico of the White House and the veranda of his ranch, where everyone seems to be doing well.

But there's another part of the city, the part where some people can't pay their mortgages and most young people can't afford one, where students can't afford the education they need and middle-class parents watch the dreams they hold for their children evaporate.

In this part of the city there are more poor than ever, more families in trouble, more and more people who need help but can't find it.

Even worse: there are elderly people who tremble in the basements of the houses there.

There are people who sleep in the city's streets, in the gutter, where the glitter doesn't show. . . .

In fact, Mr. President, this nation is more a "Tale of Two Cities" than it is a "shining city on a hill."

Maybe if you visited more places, Mr. President, you'd understand.

Maybe if you went to Appalachia, where some people still live in sheds, and to Lackawanna, where thousands of unemployed steel workers wonder why we subsidized foreign steel while we surrender their dignity to unemployment and welfare checks. . . .

Maybe, Mr. President.

But I'm afraid not.

Because, the truth is, this is how we were warned it would be.

President Reagan told us from the very beginning that he believed in a kind of social Darwinism. Survival of the fittest. "Government can't do everything," we were told. "So it should settle for taking care of the strong and hope that economic ambition and charity will do the rest. Make the rich richer and what falls from their table will be enough for the middle class and those trying to make it into the middle class."

Source: Mario Cuomo, *More Than Words: The Speeches of Mario Cuomo* (New York: St. Martin's Press, 1993), 21–23.

Interpret the Evidence

- How do Reagan's and Cuomo's views of American society and the role of government differ?
- What are Cuomo's chief criticisms of Reagan?

Put It in Context

Why do you think Reagan's views triumphed politically over Cuomo's?

Mexico, Central America, the Caribbean, and eastern and southern Asia and tended to settle in California, Florida, Texas, New York, and New Jersey. Like those who came nearly a century before, most sought economic opportunity, political freedom, and escape from wars; and like their predecessors, they brought with them foreign languages, their native cultural practices, and poverty. By 1990 one-third of Los Angeles's and New York City's populations were foreign-born, figures similar to the high numbers of European immigrants at the turn of the twentieth century.

As happened during previous immigration waves, many Americans whose ancestors had immigrated to the United States generations earlier expressed hostility toward the new immigrants. The New Right provoked traditional fears that immigrants took away jobs and depressed wages, and

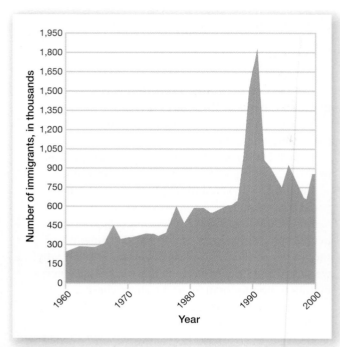

FIGURE 27.1 Immigrant Arrivals to the United States, 1960–2000

Following the relaxation of foreign quota restrictions after 1965, immigration to the United States rose dramatically in the 1970s and 1980s, peaking in the early 1990s. Between 1970 and 2000, nearly 21 million immigrants arrived in the United States, mainly from Mexico, Central America, the Caribbean, and eastern and southern Asia. Source: Data from *2000 Statistical Yearbook of the Immigration and Naturalization Service.*

questioned whether these culturally diverse people could assimilate into American society. Cities and states, led by California, enacted laws making English their official language. The migration of illegal immigrants intensified the controversy. In 1985 the Reagan administration, with bipartisan congressional support, fashioned a compromise that extended amnesty to undocumented aliens residing in the United States for a specified period and allowed them to acquire legal status. At the same time, the act penalized employers who hired new illegal workers. The measure allowed Reagan and the Republicans to appeal to Latino voters in the Sun Belt states while convincing the New Right that the administration intended to halt further undocumented immigration.

The Presidency of George H. W. Bush

After Reagan left office, his two-term vice president, George H. W. Bush, carried on his legacy. The son of a former senator from Connecticut, Bush made a fortune in the Texas oil business and began his political career as a member of Congress in the mid-1960s. After losing the Republican nomination to Reagan in 1980, Bush joined the ticket as vice president. In doing so, he abandoned his moderate Republican political views and became a loyal follower of Reaganomics. In his 1988 presidential campaign against Michael Dukakis, the Democratic governor of Massachusetts, Bush defended conservative principles when he promised: "Read my lips: No new taxes." The Republican candidate attacked Dukakis for his liberal positions and accused him of being soft on crime. Bush also affirmed his own opposition to abortion and support for gun rights and the death penalty. At the same time, however, he also called for a "kinder, gentler nation" in dealing with social justice and the environment.

Once in office, George Bush had to deal with problems that he inherited from his predecessor. Reagan's economic programs and military spending had left the nation with a mounting federal budget deficit, which reached nearly $300 billion in 1992 and slowed economic growth, resulting in another recession in 1990. Unemployment reached 7 percent, and state and local governments had difficulty paying for the educational, health, and social services that the Reagan and Bush administrations had transferred to them. To reverse the downward spiral, Bush abandoned his "no new taxes" pledge. In 1990 he supported a deficit reduction package that included more than $130 billion in new taxes, which failed to solve the economic problems and angered Reagan conservatives who had never fully trusted Bush. He also departed from anti-Washington conservatives when he signed the Americans with Disabilities Act (1990), extending an assortment of protections to some 40 million Americans with physical and mental handicaps.

Bush had a mixed record on the environment. In 1989 he continued supporting oil drilling after the oil tanker *Exxon Valdez* struck a reef off the coast of Alaska, dumping nearly 11 million gallons of oil into Prince William Sound. By contrast, in 1990 the president signed the Clean Air Act, which reduced emissions from automobiles and power plants. Two years later, however, the president opposed international efforts to limit carbon dioxide emissions, greenhouse gases that contribute to climate change.

Bush also courted conservatives in his nomination of Clarence Thomas to fill the Supreme Court vacancy left by Justice Thurgood Marshall, the first African American justice. Thomas belonged to a rising group of conservative blacks who shared Republican views supporting private enterprise and the free market system and opposing affirmative action. As chief of the Equal Employment Opportunity Commission under Reagan, Thomas had generally weakened the agency's enforcement of racial and gender equality in the workplace. He also opposed abortion and denounced welfare. Anita Hill's charges of sexual harassment did not stop his advancement. Following his confirmation battle in 1991, Thomas became one of the most conservative members of the Court.

ACT UP Protest, 1989
Amid the AIDS epidemic in the gay community, the militant group ACT UP (AIDS Coalition to Unleash Power) campaigned for better funding of programs to fight the disease. In this 1989 photo, a protester falls to the ground as police break up a demonstration in New York City.　Chester Higgins Jr./The New York Times/Redux

Despite Bush's overtures to conservatives, his popularity plummeted to 34 percent in 1992 based largely on his inability to revive the sagging economy. He ran for reelection against Governor William Jefferson (Bill) Clinton of Arkansas, a candidate skilled in the art of political maneuvering. Learning from the mistakes of Michael Dukakis, Clinton ran as a centrist Democrat who promised to reduce the federal deficit by raising taxes on the wealthy and who supported conservative social policies such as the death penalty, tough measures against crime, and welfare reform. Though he did pledge to extend health care and opposed discrimination against homosexuals, Clinton relied on his mainstream southern Democratic credentials to deflect any claims that he was a liberal. Bush also faced a challenge from the independent candidate Ross Perot, a wealthy self-made businessman from Texas, whose campaign against rising government deficits won 19 percent of the popular vote, mostly at Bush's expense. In turn, Clinton defeated the incumbent by a two-to-one electoral margin.

REVIEW & RELATE

What was Reaganomics, and what were its most important long-term consequences?

How did conservative ideas shape the social, cultural, and political landscape of the 1980s and 1990s?

✓ *LEARNINGCurve* **bedfordstmartins.com/hewittlawson/LC**

Conclusion: The Conservative Legacy

The defeat of George Bush in 1992 did not signal the end of the conservative political consensus of the previous twenty years. The Nixon-Reagan-Bush era had succeeded in dismantling most of Lyndon Johnson's Great Society, and what it did not disassemble these Republican administrations starved by underfunding. President Reagan managed to reorient the political discourse in the country by turning liberalism into an outmoded idea and a pejorative label. The conservatism that Reagan had rallied behind in the unsuccessful Goldwater campaign of 1964 now provided the political instrument with which Republicans defeated Democrats. The Democratic presidential administration of Jimmy Carter acknowledged the conservative notions of limited government and a deregulated market economy while embracing key conservative social values, such as faith in God and prayer. Both Carter and Bill Clinton, who won in 1992, departed from conservatives on some key issues concerning the economy, race, and gender, but neither of them portrayed himself as the heir of the liberal ideals promoted by Franklin Roosevelt, Harry Truman, and Lyndon Johnson.

The movement toward conservatism had been slow and sporadic. Nixon's pragmatic course and his downfall following the Watergate scandal stalled the march toward greater conservatism, and indeed his expediency angered many conservatives to his political right. Reagan represented the triumph of the New Right and transformed the politics of resentment toward the excesses of the 1960s into the politics of revivalism, convincing many that traditional values once again might guide the nation. In constructing this winning coalition, Reagan tapped into the political awakening of the Christian Right, led by evangelicals and Catholics.

The conservative political ascendancy, however, did not stifle dissent. For much of the 1970s and 1980s, Democrats controlled Congress and tried to restrain conservative presidents. The Supreme Court shifted in a more conservative direction, but the Court did not reject the precedents established by the Warren Court. Conservative justices limited controversial decisions on affirmative action and abortion but did not overturn their constitutional foundations. Civil rights reformers, feminists, environmentalists, and antinuclear activists continued to press their concerns and achieve victories.

The New Right bestowed a mixed legacy. Although the Reagan administration reduced inflation and revived economic growth, it burdened the country with unsupportable budget deficits that damaged economic growth and international trade. Tax and spending cuts further enriched the wealthy but hurt the poor and the middle class. Fiscal and monetary policies encouraged widespread speculation on Wall Street and increased the power of giant corporations over political and economic life. Americans learned about the dangers to the environment, took some measures to correct them, but generally refused to alter their lifestyles. African Americans and women broke through barriers that denied them equal access to education and politics, but they confronted white male opposition to further progress.

Yet ordinary people of all backgrounds still made a difference. Allan Bakke was not a conservative ideologue, but his desire to go to medical school helped reshape affirmative action and stimulate a controversy that lasted far beyond his graduation from medical school. Anita Hill rode the conservative wave that brought Reagan to power. However, when she was subjected to sexual harassment, she broke ranks with conservatives and testified against the nomination of Clarence Thomas. Her assertions failed to derail his appointment to the Supreme Court, but her testimony encouraged more women to challenge sexual harassment.

Conservative successes on the home front did not take place in a vacuum. The rise of conservatism coincided with political shifts taking place in the United Kingdom and West Germany. Moreover, conservatives came to power amid major changes occurring in foreign affairs, most notably the proliferation and then the cessation of the Cold War.

LEARNINGCurve
Check what you know.
bedfordstmartins.com/hewittlawson/LC

Chapter Review

Online Study Guide ▶ bedfordstmartins.com/hewittlawson

KEY TERMS

New Right (p. 861)
Vietnamization (p. 862)
Pentagon Papers (p. 863)
War Powers Act (p. 863)
Strategic Arms Limitation Treaty (SALT I) (p. 863)
Organization of Petroleum Exporting Countries
   (OPEC) (p. 864)
affirmative action (p. 865)
Watergate (p. 865)
Equal Rights Amendment (ERA) (p. 869)
Environmental Protection Agency (EPA) (p. 871)
neoconservatives (p. 874)
Reaganomics (p. 876)
acquired immune deficiency syndrome (AIDS) (p. 877)

REVIEW & RELATE

1. Who made up the New Right coalition that brought Nixon to power? How did Nixon appeal to the New Right?

2. How did Nixon's pragmatism shape both his foreign and domestic policies?

3. What issues and trends shaped the presidency of Jimmy Carter?

4. How and why did the social and cultural developments of the 1960s continue to create conflict and controversy in the 1970s?

5. What was Reaganomics, and what were its most important long-term consequences?

6. How did conservative ideas shape the social, cultural, and political landscape of the 1980s and 1990s?

TIMELINE OF EVENTS

1970	Nixon orders invasion of Cambodia
	Four students shot by National Guardsmen at Kent State University
	Congress repeals Gulf of Tonkin Resolution
1971	Environmental Protection Agency (EPA) created
	New York Times and *Washington Post* publish the *Pentagon Papers*
1972	Nixon visits China
	U.S. and Soviet Union sign the Strategic Arms Limitation Treaty (SALT I)
	Watergate break-in
1973	Endangered Species Act passed
	Congress passes the War Powers Act
	U.S. supports Israel in Yom Kippur War
	U.S. agrees to withdraw from Vietnam
1973–1974	OPEC oil embargo against the United States creates gas shortages
1974	Nixon resigns
1975	North Vietnam defeats South Vietnam
1977	Department of Energy created
1978	Proposition 13 passed in California
	Allan Bakke wins his affirmative action case
1979	Divorce rate peaks at 23 divorces per 1,000 married couples
	Moral Majority founded
	Three Mile Island nuclear accident
1981	Reagan fires striking air traffic controllers
	Reagan survives assassination attempt
1982	Ratification period expires for Equal Rights Amendment
1991	Senate confirmation hearing for Clarence Thomas

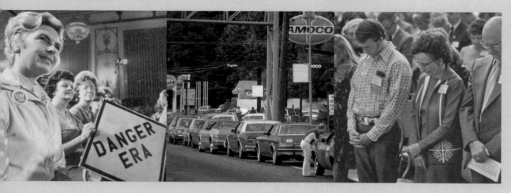

The Affirmative Action Debate

President Kennedy first used the term *affirmative action* to assert the need for positive or "affirmative" action to end racial discrimination in American society. While affirmative action takes various forms, it contains racial or gender guidelines as a way to measure compliance in recruitment programs in employment, government contracts, and school admissions.

Affirmative action became federal policy in 1965 after President Johnson issued Executive Order 11246. During his presidency, Johnson also added gender as a category for affirmative action. President Nixon expanded these programs further and upheld provisions that set affirmative action standards for contractors bidding on federally funded projects. During his administration, affirmative action policies were extended to include people with disabilities. Although affirmative action has always been a contentious topic, as Documents 27.7, 27.8, and 27.9 demonstrate, it came under increasing attack beginning in the late 1970s, and many programs across the country have been dismantled since then.

Opponents consider affirmative action to be "reverse discrimination" and argue that preferential treatment based on race, ethnicity, or gender is exactly what rights-based movements of the 1960s and 1970s fought against. They assert that all hiring and admissions decisions should be based only on individual qualifications, though the exact criteria for those qualifications vary. Those who favor affirmative action argue that it is important and necessary to redress past and present discrimination, and they point out that white men continue to control most positions of economic and political power in the United States. They also argue that creating more diverse schools and workplaces benefits the entire society. As you read the following documents, consider whether affirmative action is needed to ensure equality in American society and whether it has worked as a policy. If not affirmative action, then what should be substituted in its place?

DOCUMENT 27.5

Lyndon B. Johnson | Freedom Is Not Enough, 1965

President Johnson helped pass the Civil Rights Act of 1964 and the Voting Rights Act of 1965, both of which eliminated many forms of racial discrimination. In June 1965, he gave a commencement speech at Howard University, a historically black college in Washington, D.C., that set out a more aggressive policy to achieve racial equality and outlined his reasons for instituting affirmative action.

The voting rights bill will be the latest, and among the most important, in a long series of victories. But this victory—as Winston Churchill said of another triumph for freedom—"is not the end. It is not even the beginning of the end. But it is, perhaps, the end of the beginning."

That beginning is freedom; and the barriers to that freedom are tumbling down. Freedom is the right to share, share fully and equally, in American society—to vote, to hold a job, to enter a public place, to go to school. It is the right to be treated in every part of our national life as a person equal in dignity and promise to all others.

But freedom is not enough. You do not wipe away the scars of centuries by saying: Now you are free to go where you want, and do as you desire, and choose the leaders you please.

You do not take a person who, for years, has been hobbled by chains and liberate him, bring him up to the starting line of a race and then say, "you are free to compete with all the others," and still justly believe that you have been completely fair.

Thus it is not enough just to open the gates of opportunity. All our citizens must have the ability to walk through those gates.

This is the next and the more profound stage of the battle for civil rights. We seek not just freedom but opportunity. We seek not just legal equity but human ability, not just equality as a right and a theory but equality as a fact and equality as a result.

For the task is to give 20 million Negroes the same chance as every other American to learn and grow, to work and share in society, to develop their abilities—physical, mental, and spiritual, and to pursue their individual happiness.

To this end equal opportunity is essential, but not enough, not enough. Men and women of all races are born with the same range of abilities. But ability is not just the product of birth. Ability is stretched or stunted by the family that you live with, and the neighborhood you live in—by the school you go to and the poverty or the richness of your surroundings. It is the product of a hundred unseen forces playing upon the little infant, the child, and finally the man.

Source: *Public Papers of the Presidents of the United States: Lyndon B. Johnson, 1965* (Washington, D.C.: Government Printing Office, 1966), 2:635–36.

DOCUMENT 27.6

Title IX of the Education Amendments Regulations, 1975

In 1972 Title IX of the Education Amendments Act prohibited gender discrimination in public and private educational institutions that receive federal financial aid. Although it originally covered education in general, many individuals and groups used the law to successfully challenge male dominance in high school and college athletics. The regulations have been expanded over the years, and Title IX is credited with substantially increasing the number and visibility of female athletes in American society. In the following selection from the 1975 regulations, Congress clarifies the meaning of the provisions in Title IX.

Section 86.37 Athletic scholarships or grants-in-aid must provide reasonable opportunities for each sex in proportion to the students of each sex participating in interscholastic or intercollegiate athletics. However, separate awards for members of each sex may be provided as part of separate athletic teams. . . .

Section 86.41 . . . A recipient may operate or sponsor separate teams for each sex where selection is based on *competitive skill* or the *activity involved is a contact sport.* However, where a recipient operates or sponsors a team in a particular sport for only one sex and athletic opportunities for the other sex have previously been limited, members of the excluded sex must be allowed to try out for the team offered *unless the sport involved is a contact sport.* Contact sports include boxing, wrestling, rugby, ice hockey, football, basketball, and other sports mainly involving bodily contact. . . .

Unequal aggregate expenditures for each sex, or unequal expenditures for male and female teams does not constitute noncompliance with this section, but the failure to provide necessary funds for teams for one sex may be considered in assessing equality of athletic opportunity.

Source: Education Committee of the States, *A Digest of Federal Laws and Regulations Affecting Equal Rights for Women in Education* (Denver, CO: Education Commission of the States, 1976), 16–21.

DOCUMENT 27.7

Nathan Glazer | *Affirmative Discrimination*, 1975

Affirmative action opponents viewed it as a form of reverse discrimination and believed that college admissions and hiring should be based on the merit of individual applicants, not on a previous history of racial discrimination against any single group. Nathan Glazer, a sociologist, was part of a group of neoconservatives who insisted that affirmative action led to the imposition of racial quotas and a departure from the color-blind goals that Martin Luther King Jr. was said to favor. In the following excerpt, Glazer explains his objections to affirmative action.

We have created two racial and ethnic classes in this country to replace the disgraceful pattern of the past in which some groups were subjected to an official and open discrimination. The two new classes are those groups that are entitled to statistical parity in certain key areas on the basis of race, color, and national origin, and those groups that are not. The consequences of such a development can be foreseen: They are already, in some measure, upon us. Those groups that are not considered eligible for special benefits become resentful. If one could draw a neat line between those who have suffered from discrimination and those who have not, the matter would be simpler. Most immigrant groups have had periods in which they were discriminated against. For the Irish and the Jews, for example, these periods lasted a long time. Nor is it the case that all the groups that are now recorded as deserving official protection have suffered discrimination, or in the same way. . . .

The protected groups include variously the descendants of free immigrants, conquered peoples, and slaves, and a single group may include the descendants of all three categories (e.g., the Puerto Ricans). Do free immigrants who come to this country voluntarily deserve the same protected treatment as the descendants of conquered people and slaves? The point is that racial and ethnic groups make poor categories for the design of public policy. They include a range of individuals who have different legal bases for claims for redress and remedy of grievances. If the categories are designed to correct the injustices of the past, they do not work.

They do not work to correct the injustices of the present either, for some groups defined by race and ethnicity do not seem to need redress on the basis of their economic, occupational, and educational position. The Asian Americans have indeed been subjected to discrimination, legal and unofficial alike. But Chinese and Japanese Americans rank high in economic status, occupational status, educational status. (This does not prevent members of these groups from claiming the benefits that now accrue to them because they form a specially protected category under affirmative action programs.) If they were included in the protected category because they have faced discrimination, then groups in the unprotected categories also deserve inclusion. If they were included because they suffer from a poor economic, occupational, and educational position, they were included in error. So if these ethnic and racial categories have been designed to group individuals with some especially deprived current condition, they do not work well. Just as the Chinese and Japanese and Indians (from India) do not need the protection of the "Asian American" category, the Cubans do not need the protection of the Spanish-surnamed category, the middle-class blacks the protection of the Negro category, in order to get equal treatment today in education and employment. The inequalities created by the use of these categories became sharply evident in 1975 when many private colleges and universities tried to cut back on special aid for racially defined groups, who did indeed include many in need, but also included many in no greater need than "white" or "other" students. But the creation of a special benefit, whether needed or not, is not to be given up easily: Black students occupied school buildings and demanded that the privileges given on

(continued on page 888)

the basis of race be retained. This is part of the evil of the creation of especially benefited ethnic and racial categories. . . .

Compensation for the past is a dangerous principle. It can be extended indefinitely and make for endless trouble. Who is to determine what is proper compensation for the American Indian, the black, the Mexican American, the Chinese or Japanese American? When it is established that the full status of equality is extended to every individual, regardless of race, color, or national origin, and that special opportunity is also available to any individual on the basis of individual need, again regardless of race, color, or national origin, one has done all that justice and equity call for and that is consistent with a harmonious multigroup society.

Source: Nathan Glazer, *Affirmative Discrimination: Ethnic Inequality and Public Policy* (Cambridge, MA: Harvard University Press, 1975), 98–100.

DOCUMENT 27.8

Lewis Powell | Opinion in the *Bakke* Case, 1978

In *Regents of the University of California v. Allan Bakke*, the first major U.S. Supreme Court decision on affirmative action in education, Justice Lewis Powell crafted a compromise to satisfy a majority of the deeply divided Court. The 5–4 decision ruled in Bakke's favor and required the University of California at Davis to admit him. Satisfying neither affirmative action opponents nor its supporters, Powell struck down the university's quota system while still allowing universities to consider race and diversity as important elements in their admissions policies. In the following selection, Powell discusses quotas and an affirmative action program that the Court considers constitutionally valid.

The experience of other university admissions programs, which take race into account in achieving the educational diversity valued by the First Amendment, demonstrates that the assignment of a fixed number of places to a minority group is not a necessary means toward that end. An illuminating example is found in the Harvard College program:

In recent years, Harvard College has expanded the concept of diversity to include students from disadvantaged economic, racial, and ethnic groups. Harvard College now recruits not only Californians or Louisianans but also blacks and Chicanos and other minority students.

In practice, this new definition of diversity has meant that race has been a factor in some admission decisions. When the Committee on Admissions reviews the large middle group of applicants who are "admissible" and deemed capable of doing good work in their courses, the race of an applicant may tip the balance in his favor just as geographic origin or a life spent on a farm may tip the balance in other candidates' cases. A farm boy from Idaho can bring something to Harvard College that a Bostonian cannot offer. Similarly, a black student can usually bring something that a white person cannot offer. . . .

In Harvard College admissions, the Committee has not set target quotas for the number of blacks, or of musicians, football players, physicists, or Californians to be admitted in a given year. . . . But that awareness [of the necessity of including more than a token number of black students] does not mean that the Committee sets a minimum number of blacks or of people from west of the Mississippi who are to be admitted. It means only that, in choosing among thousands of applicants who are not only "admissible" academically but have other strong qualities, the Committee, with a number of criteria in mind, pays some attention to distribution among many types and categories of students.

In such an admissions program, race or ethnic background may be deemed a "plus" in a particular applicant's file, yet it does not insulate the individual from comparison with all other candidates for the available seats. The file of a particular black applicant may be examined for his potential contribution to diversity without the factor of race being decisive when compared, for example, with that of an applicant identified as an Italian-American if the latter is thought to exhibit qualities more likely to promote beneficial educational pluralism. Such qualities could include exceptional personal talents, unique work or service experience, leadership potential, maturity, demonstrated compassion, a history of overcoming disadvantage, ability to communicate with the poor, or other qualifications deemed important. In short, an admissions program operated in this way is flexible enough to consider all pertinent elements of diversity in light of the particular qualifications of each applicant, and to place them on the same footing for consideration,

although not necessarily according them the same weight. Indeed, the weight attributed to a particular quality may vary from year to year depending upon the "mix" both of the student body and the applicants for the incoming class.

This kind of program treats each applicant as an individual in the admissions process. The applicant who loses out on the last available seat to another candidate receiving a "plus" on the basis of ethnic background will not have been foreclosed from all consideration for that seat simply because he was not the right color or had the wrong surname. It would mean only that his combined qualifications, which may have included similar nonobjective factors, did not outweigh those of the other applicant. His qualifications would have been weighed fairly and competitively, and he would have no basis to complain of unequal treatment under the Fourteenth Amendment.

It has been suggested that an admissions program which considers race only as one factor is simply a subtle and more sophisticated—but no less effective—means of according racial preference than the Davis program. A facial [readily observable] intent to discriminate, however, is evident in petitioner's preference program, and not denied in this case. No such facial infirmity exists in an admissions program where race or ethnic background is simply one element—to be weighed fairly against other elements—in the selection process. . . . And a court would not assume that a university, professing to employ a facially nondiscriminatory admissions policy, would operate it as a cover for the functional equivalent of a quota system. In short, good faith would be presumed in the absence of a showing to the contrary in the manner permitted by our cases.

Source: *Regents of the University of California v. Allan Bakke*, 438 U.S. 265 (1978).

DOCUMENT 27.9

Nell Irvin Painter | Whites Say I Must Be on Easy Street, 1981

Since 1967, affirmative action programs have addressed discrimination based on sex as well as race. Nell Irvin Painter received her doctorate in history from Harvard University and subsequently taught at the University of Pennsylvania, the University of North Carolina, and Princeton University. Despite these accomplishments, she heard complaints from white men that her success depended on the preferences she received because of her race and sex. In the following selection, she describes the dilemma facing many African American women and defends affirmative action.

I've always thought affirmative action made a lot of sense, because discrimination against black people and women was prolonged and thorough. But I've been hearing talk in the last several years that lets me know that not everyone shares my views. The first time I noticed it was shortly after I had moved to Philadelphia, where I used to live. One evening I attended a lecture—I no longer remember the topic—but I recall that I arrived early and was doing what I did often that fall. I worked at polishing my dissertation. In those days I regularly carried chapters and a nicely sharpened pencil around with me. I sat with pencil and typescript, scratching out awkward phrases and trying out new ones.

Next to me sat a white man of about 35, whose absorption in my work increased steadily. He watched me intently—kindly—for several moments. "Is that your dissertation?" I said yes, it was. "Good luck in getting it accepted," he said. I said that it had already been accepted, thank you.

Still friendly, he wished me luck in finding a job. I appreciated his concern, but I already had a job. Where? At Penn, for I was then a beginning assistant professor at the University of Pennsylvania. "Aren't you lucky," said the man, a little less generously, "you got a job at a good university." I agreed. Jobs in history were, still are, hard to find.

While cognizant of the job squeeze, I never questioned the justice of my position. I should have a job, and a good one. I had worked hard as a graduate student and had written a decent dissertation. I knew foreign languages, had traveled widely, and had taught and published. I thought I had been hired because I was a promising young historian. Unlike the man beside me, I didn't think my teaching at a first-rate university required an extraordinary explanation.

"I have a doctorate in history," he resumed, "but I couldn't get an academic job." With regret he added that he worked in school administration. I said I was sorry he hadn't been able to find the job he wanted. He said: "It must be great to be black and female, because of affirmative action. You count twice." I couldn't think of an appropriate response to that line of reasoning, for this was the first time I'd met it face to face. I wished the lecture would start. I was embarrassed. Did this man really mean to imply that I had my job at his expense? The edge of competition in his voice made me squirm.

He said that he had received his doctorate from Temple, and yet he had no teaching job, and where was my degree from? "Harvard," I said. It was his time not to reply. I waited a moment for his answer, then returned to my chapter.

Now I live in North Carolina, but I still hear contradictory talk about affirmative action. Last spring I was having lunch with some black Carolina undergraduates. One young woman surprised me by deploring affirmative action. I wondered why. "White students and professors think we only got into the University of North Carolina because we're black," she complained, "and they don't believe we're truly qualified." She said that she knew that she was qualified and fully deserved to be at Carolina. She fulfilled all the regular admissions requirements. It was the stigma of affirmative action that bothered her; without it other students wouldn't assume she was unqualified.

Another student said that the stigma of affirmative action extended to black faculty as well. She had heard white students doubting the abilities of black professors. Indeed, she herself tended to wait for black professors to disprove her assumption that they did not know their fields. She was convinced that without affirmative action, students would assume black faculty to be as good as white.

That's what I've been hearing from whites and blacks. White people tell me I must be on easy street because I'm black and female. (I do not believe I've ever heard that from a black person, although some blacks believe that black women have an easier time in the white world than black men. I don't think so.) White people tell me, "You're a twofer." On the other side of the color line, every black student knows that he or she is fully qualified—I once thought that way myself. It is just the other black people who need affirmative action to get in. No one, not blacks, not whites, benefits from affirmative action, or so it would seem. . . .

I am one of the few people I know who will admit to having been helped by affirmative action. To do so is usually tantamount to admitting deficiency. To hear people talk, affirmative action exists only to employ and promote the otherwise unqualified, but I don't see it that way at all. I'm black and female, yet I was hired by two history departments that had no black members before the late 60's, never mind females. Affirmative action cleared the way. . . .

. . . The civil rights movement and the feminist movement have created a new climate that permitted affirmative action, which, in turn, opened areas previously reserved for white men. Skirts and dark skins appeared in new settings in the 1970's, but in significant numbers only after affirmative action mandated the changes and made them thinkable. Without affirmative action, it never would have occurred to any large, white research university to consider me for professional employment, despite my degree, languages, publications, charm, grace, despite my qualifications.

My Philadelphia white man and my Carolina black women would be surprised to discover the convergence of their views. I doubt that they know that their convictions are older than affirmative action. I wish I could take them back to the early 60's and let them see that they're reciting the same old white-male-superiority line, fixed up to fit conditions that include a policy called affirmative action. Actually, I will not have to take those people back in time at all, for the Reagan Administration's proposed dismantling of affirmative action fuses the future and the past. If they achieve their stated goals, we will have the same old discrimination, unneedful of new clothes.

Source: Nell Irvin Painter, "Whites Say I Must Be on Easy Street," *New York Times*, December 10, 1981.

DOCUMENT 27.10

Bob Dole | Call to End Affirmative Action, 1995

Kansas Republican senator Robert Dole supported affirmative action for much of his career, but by 1995 his views had changed. In March 1995 he gave a speech on the Senate floor calling for an end to affirmative action policies. At the end of the speech he asked two Senate colleagues to request hearings on Johnson's Executive Order 11246, which had established requirements for nondiscriminatory practices in hiring among U.S. government contractors and required large contractors to implement affirmative action plans. In 1996 Dole ran unsuccessfully against Bill Clinton for the presidency.

Mr. President, to his credit, President Clinton has initiated a long-overdue review of all Federal affirmative action laws.

After nearly 30 years of government-sanctioned quotas, timetables, set-asides, and other racial preferences, the American people sense all too clearly that the race-counting game has gone too far. The President is responding to these pressures, and his review could not have come at a more propitious time. . . .

[L]et's remember that to raise questions about affirmative action is not to challenge our antidiscrimination laws. Discrimination is illegal. Those who discriminate ought to be punished. And those who are individual victims of illegal discrimination have every right to receive the remedial relief they deserve.

Unfortunately, America is not the color-blind society we would all like it to be. Discrimination continues to be an undeniable part of American life.

But fighting discrimination should never become an excuse for abandoning the color-blind ideal. Expanding opportunity should never be used to justify dividing Americans by race, by gender, by ethnic background. Race-preferential policies, no matter how well-intentioned, demean individual accomplishment. They ignore individual character. And they are absolutely poisonous to race relations in our great country. You cannot cure the evil of discrimination with more discrimination.

Mr. President, last December, I asked the Congressional Research Service [CRS] to provide me with a list of every Federal law and regulation that grants a preference to individuals on the basis of race, sex, national origin, or ethnic background. Frankly, I was surprised to learn that such a list had never been compiled before, which, I suppose, speaks volumes about how delicate this issue can be.

Earlier this year, the CRS responded to my request with a list of more than 160 preference laws, ranging from Federal procurement regulations, to the RTC's bank-ownership policies, to the Department of Transportation's contracting rules. Even NASA has gotten into the act, earmarking 8 percent of the total value of its contracts each year to minority-owned and female-owned firms on the theory that these firms are presumptively disadvantaged. They may not be disadvantaged at all.

As a follow-up to the CRS report, I have written to my colleagues, Senators Bond and Kassebaum, requesting hearings on the most prominent programs identified in the report—the Small Business Administration's section 8(A) program and Executive order 11246, which has been interpreted to require Federal contractors to adopt timetables and goals in minority- and female-hiring.

These hearings, I expect, will demonstrate that there are other, more equitable ways to expand opportunity, without resorting to policies that grant preferences to individuals simply because they happen to be members of certain groups. And unless the hearings produce some powerful evidence to the contrary, it is my judgment that the section 8(a) program should be repealed outright. . . .

I intend to introduce legislation later this year that will force the Federal Government to live up to the color-blind ideal by prohibiting it from granting preferential treatment to any person, simply because of his or her membership in a certain favored group. . . .

So, Mr. President, the coming debate over affirmative action will be much more than just a debate over reverse discrimination. It will be a debate that focuses us to answer a fundamental question: What kind of country do we want America to be?

Do we work toward a color-blind society? I hope so. A society that judges people by their talents, their sense of honor, their hopes and dreams, as individuals? Or do we continue down the path of group rights, group entitlements—special rights for some—judging people not by their character or intellect, but by something irrelevant: the color of their skin?

Source: 104th Congress., 1st Sess., *Congressional Record* (March 15, 1995): S 3929.

Interpret the Evidence

1. Why did Lyndon Johnson institute affirmative action policies in the 1960s (Document 27.5)?

2. Why does Nell Irvin Painter support affirmative action (Document 27.9)?

3. Why do supporters of affirmative action (Documents 27.5 and 27.9) reject the belief that affirmative action creates a stigma of inferiority in those who receive its benefits?

4. Documents 27.7, 27.9, and 27.10 give powerful arguments for and against affirmative action. Compare their characterizations of affirmative action and the language they use to describe it.

5. How do the different documents view quotas? Why are quotas such a touchstone for the affirmative action controversy? What are the differences between quotas and guidelines?

6. Why does Supreme Court justice Lewis Powell think that diversity is a permissible goal for affirmative action (Document 27.8)? Do you think that taking diversity into account is more justifiable than considering remedies based strictly on race and sex? Why or why not?

Put It in Context

- Based on what you have read in the chapter and in these documents, how might affirmative action have influenced the lives of your parents and grandparents?

AP Photo/Ira Schwartz

© Owen Franken/CORBIS

President Ronald Reagan greets a baby held by Soviet leader Mikhail Gorbachev during a visit to Moscow, 1988.

A worker tests a camera at a joint Chinese-German plant in Qingdao, China, 1985.

28
Ending the Cold War
1977–1991

Boston Globe via Getty Images

A boy waves to soldiers on the Berlin Wall, 1989.

AMERICAN HISTORIES

As secretary of state, George Pratt Shultz presided over the end of the Cold War. A skilled mediator, Shultz believed in the brand of hard-nosed diplomacy practiced by Henry Kissinger during the Nixon administration, asserting that "negotiations are a euphemism for capitulation if the shadow of power is not cast across the bargaining table." After graduating from Princeton with an economics degree in 1942, the twenty-two-year-old Shultz joined the Marine Corps and served in the Pacific during World War II. Three years later, Captain Shultz returned home, got married, and earned a Ph.D. in industrial economics. Shultz taught at the Massachusetts Institute of Technology and the University of Chicago and published several books on labor and wage issues. In 1955 he joined President Eisenhower's Council of Economic Advisors, the first of many government posts he would fill.

Known for his judicious temperament and bipartisanship, Shultz, a Republican, served under Democratic presidents John F. Kennedy and Lyndon B. Johnson, as well as Republican president Richard Nixon, who appointed him secretary of labor. With Nixon's resignation in 1974, Shultz left government for the corporate world.

In 1982 Shultz returned to Washington to serve as President Ronald Reagan's secretary of state. Like Reagan, Shultz believed that the United States needed to reassert itself as a global power and rebound from the insecurity and self-doubt that followed the Vietnam War. The president believed that a tough approach would bring peace, and he revived the fiery rhetoric and military preparedness of the darkest days of the Cold War. As a seasoned economist, Shultz doubted that the Soviet Union was financially able to sustain its military strength, and his predictions proved correct. Faced with an escalating arms race, a fresh group of Soviet leaders decided to pursue peaceful relations, a decision that had great repercussions for the internal structure of the Soviet Union and the nations subject to its control.

While President Reagan and Secretary of State Shultz advocated confrontation with the Soviet Union, Barbara Deming challenged their efforts and devoted her life to promoting peace in a far different manner. She was born in 1917, three years earlier than Shultz, to a middle-class family living in New York City. Deming attended Quaker schools before graduating from Bennington College with a degree in theater and literature. She became an outspoken proponent of nuclear disarmament, feminism, civil rights, and pacifism. Her radical political beliefs and her recognition that she was a lesbian at the age of sixteen placed her outside the social and cultural mainstream. She lived in a women's commune and mobilized heterosexual and gay women to demonstrate for peaceful coexistence with the Soviet Union.

In the 1980s, Deming applied her nonviolent, pacifist beliefs against Reagan and Shultz's muscular approach to fighting the Cold War. "We can put *more* pressure on the antagonist for whom we show human concern," Deming argued. As part of a worldwide campaign against the deployment of nuclear weapons, she joined the Women's Encampment for a Future of Peace and Justice, which opened in western New York in 1983 next to an army depot that stored nuclear missiles. On July 30, 1983, Deming led a march of seventy-five women from the camp into the small town of Waterloo. "Four miles into our walk," she recalled, "our way was blocked by several hundred townspeople brandishing American flags and chanting, 'Commies, go home!'" The marchers then sat down in the style of nonviolent protest and engaged their opponents in dialogue to no avail, as the police arrested Deming and fifty-three other protesters. Demonstrations continued throughout the rest of the summer, inspiring protests in other American communities and throughout Europe. •

THE AMERICAN HISTORIES of George Shultz and Barbara Deming were shaped in profound ways by decades of conflict between the United States and the Soviet Union. Both Shultz and Deming believed that the conflict was one of the defining issues of their times, and both were convinced that their approach was the best way to achieve lasting global peace.

The Cold War that Shultz and Deming were dedicated to ending underwent significant changes in the decades following the Nixon administration's reduction of tensions with the Soviet Union. In the late 1970s, President Jimmy Carter emphasized the moralistic diplomacy of human rights, but by the end of his term he had increased the size of the U.S. military in response to Soviet aggression in Afghanistan. His successor, Ronald Reagan, employed harsher rhetoric and accelerated the military buildup begun under Carter. However, Reagan would have been far less successful had it not been for the willingness of Soviet leader Mikhail Gorbachev to join him in ending the Cold War. With the ultimate collapse of the Soviet Union and its empire, the United States became the world's sole superpower. At the same time, the United States had to operate in an increasingly globalized world. Embracing new challenges, the United States tested its strength in Central America, the Middle East, and the Persian Gulf.

Carter's Diplomacy, 1977–1980

Drawing on the foreign policies of Gerald Ford and Richard Nixon, President Jimmy Carter sought to negotiate with the Soviets over arms reduction while at the same time challenging them to do more to protect human rights. In practice, Carter found this balancing act difficult to sustain, and despite his desire to find ways to cooperate with the Soviets, relations between the superpowers deteriorated over the course of his term in office. Trouble in the Persian Gulf also added to the Carter administration's woes.

The Perils of Détente

Carter made human rights a cornerstone of his foreign policy, and he was vocal in his criticism of the Soviet Union for violating the human rights requirements of the Helsinki accords that President Ford and Soviet leader Leonid Brezhnev had signed in 1975. His emphasis on human rights extended to other regimes as well. Unlike previous presidents who had supported dictatorial governments as long as they were anti-Communist, Carter intended to hold such regimes to a higher moral standard. Thus the Carter administration cut off military and economic aid to repressive regimes in Argentina, Uruguay, and Ethiopia. Still, Carter was not entirely consistent in his application of moral standards to diplomacy. Important U.S. allies around the world such as the Philippines, South Korea, and South Africa were hardly models of democracy, but national security concerns kept the president from severing ties with them.

One way that Carter tried to set an example of responsible moral leadership was by signing an agreement to return control of the Panama Canal Zone to Panama at the end of 1999. The treaty that President Theodore Roosevelt negotiated in 1903 gave the United States control over this ten-mile piece of Panamanian land forever (see chapter 20). Panamanians resented this affront to their sovereignty, and Carter considered the occupation as a vestige of colonialism. Conservative critics viewed the transfer of land as a sign of weakness, but after extended debate the Senate ratified the treaty to relinquish the canal.

The president's pursuit of **détente**, or the easing of tensions, with the Soviet Union was less successful. In 1978 the Carter administration extended full diplomatic recognition to the People's Republic of China. Abandoning the United States' traditional ally of Taiwan, Carter sought to drive a greater wedge between China and the Soviet Union. Nevertheless, Carter did not give up on cooperation with the Soviets. In June 1979, Carter and Brezhnev signed **SALT II**, a new strategic arms limitation treaty. Six months later, however, the Soviet Union invaded Afghanistan to bolster its pro-Communist Afghan regime. President Carter viewed this action as a violation of international law and a threat to Middle East oil supplies and persuaded the Senate to drop consideration of SALT II. To counter Soviet aggression in Afghanistan, Carter obtained from Congress

Afghan Mujahideen, January 1980

On December 25, 1979, Soviet troops invaded Afghanistan in order to suppress mujahideen guerrillas who were trying to overthrow the nation's secular, pro-Soviet regime. These rebel forces were among the guerrillas who defeated the Soviets after a decade of warfare and eventually established an Islamic theocracy. © Pascal Manoukian/Sygma/Corbis a 5 percent increase in military spending. The Carter administration also reduced grain sales to the USSR and led a boycott of the 1980 Olympic Games in Moscow to punish the Soviet Union for its invasion of Afghanistan.

Of perhaps the greatest long-term importance was President Carter's decision to authorize the CIA to provide covert military and economic assistance to Afghan rebels resisting the Soviet invasion. Chief among these groups were the *mujahideen*, or warriors who wage jihad. Although portrayed as freedom fighters, these Islamic fundamentalists (including a group known as the Taliban) did not support democracy in the Western sense, and many of them were dedicated to creating a theocratic Islamic nation in Afghanistan. Among the mujahideen who received assistance from the United States was Osama bin Laden, a Saudi Arabian Islamic fundamentalist.

In ordering these CIA operations, Carter ignored recent revelations about questionable intelligence practices. Responding to presidential excesses stemming from the Vietnam War and the Watergate scandal, the Senate had held hearings in 1975 into clandestine CIA and FBI activities at home and abroad. Led by Frank Church of Idaho, the Senate Select Committee to Study Governmental Operations with Respect to Intelligence Activities (known as the Church Committee) issued reports revealing that both intelligence agencies had illegally spied on Americans and that the CIA had fomented revolution abroad, contrary to the provisions of its charter. Despite the Church Committee's findings, Carter revived some of these murky practices to combat the Soviets in Afghanistan.

Challenges in the Middle East

Before President Carter attempted to restrain the Soviet Union in Afghanistan, he did have some notable diplomatic successes. Five years after the 1973 Yom Kippur War (see chapter 27), with relations between Israel and its Arab neighbors in a deadlock, Carter invited the leaders of Israel and Egypt to the United States. Following two weeks of discussions in September 1978 at the presidential retreat at Camp David, Maryland, Israeli prime minister Menachem Begin and Egyptian president Anwar Sadat reached an agreement on a "framework for peace." For the first time in its history, Egypt would extend diplomatic recognition to Israel in exchange for Israel's agreement to return the Sinai peninsula to Egypt, which Israel had captured and occupied since 1967. Carter facilitated Sadat's acceptance of the **Camp David accords** by promising to extend foreign aid to Egypt. The treaty, however, left unresolved controversial issues between Israelis and Arabs concerning the establishment of a Palestinian state and control of Jerusalem.

Whatever success Carter had in promoting peace in the Middle East suffered a serious setback in the Persian Gulf

nation of Iran. In 1953 the CIA helped overthrow Iran's democratically elected president, replacing him with a monarch and staunch ally, Mohammad Reza Pahlavi, the shah of Iran. For more than two decades, the shah ruled Iran with U.S. support, seeking to construct a modern, secular state allied with the United States. In doing so, he used repressive measures against Islamic fundamentalists, deploying his secret police to imprison, torture, and exile dissenters. The shah's lavish lifestyle stood in contrast to the poverty of most Iranians, and in 1979 revolutionary forces headed by Ayatollah Ruholla Khomeini, an Islamic fundamentalist exiled by the shah, overthrew his government. Khomeini intended to end the growing secularism in Iran and reshape the nation according to strict Islamic law.

When the deposed shah needed treatment for terminal cancer, President Carter invited him to the United States for medical assistance as a humanitarian gesture, despite warnings from the Khomeini government that it would consider this invitation a hostile action. On November 4, 1979, the ayatollah ordered fundamentalist Muslim students to seize the U.S. Embassy in Tehran and hold its fifty-two occupants hostage until the United States returned the shah to Iran to stand trial. Rather than submit to this violation of international law, President Carter retaliated by freezing all Iranian assets in American banks, breaking off diplomatic relations, and imposing a trade embargo. Carter's response did nothing to free the hostages, and the cutoff of Iranian oil shipments contributed to a 130 percent increase in the price of gasoline in the United States. For most Americans, the oil embargo meant shortages and high gas prices. In response, Khomeini incited Iranian nationalism by denouncing the United States as "the Great Satan." As the impasse dragged on and with the presidential election of 1980 fast approaching, Carter became desperate. After a failed U.S. rescue attempt, Khomeini's guards separated the hostages, making any more rescue efforts impossible. Further humiliating the president, Khomeini released the hostages on January 20, 1981, the inauguration day of Carter's successor, Ronald Reagan.

Explore

See Document 28.1 to read about one hostage's experience.

Despite good intentions and some notable achievements, Jimmy Carter left office with many of his foreign policy objectives unfulfilled. His administration was inconsistent in its approach to the Soviet Union, with attempts at improving relations, as evidenced in the SALT II talks, undermined by moral outrage at the Soviets for invading Afghanistan. The Camp David accords marked a high point of Carter's diplomatic efforts; however, his policies satisfied neither liberals nor conservatives in the

DOCUMENT 28.1

Robert Ode | Iran Hostage Diary, 1979–1980

In November 1979, Iranian students stormed the U.S. Embassy in Tehran and held fifty-two Americans hostage for 444 days. Their demands included the surrender of the recently deposed shah, who was in the United States for medical care. At the time of his capture, American hostage Robert Ode was a retired diplomat who was on special assignment in Tehran. He was released in January 1981 along with the other hostages. While he was in captivity, Ode kept a diary, which included the following entries.

Explore

November 4, 1979
We were taken back to the Compound, being pushed and hurried along the way and forced to put our hands above our heads and then marched to the Embassy residence. After arriving at the residence I had my hands tied behind my back so tightly with nylon cord that circulation was cut off. I was taken upstairs and put alone in a rear bedroom and after a short time was blindfolded. After protesting strongly that the cord was too tight the cord was removed and the blindfold taken off when they tried to feed me some dates and I refused to eat anything I couldn't see. I strongly protested the violation of my diplomatic immunity, but these protests were ignored. I then was required to sit in a chair facing the bedroom wall. Then another older student came in and when I again protested the violation of my diplomatic immunity he confiscated my U.S. Mission Tehran I.D. card. My hands were again tied and I was taken to the Embassy living room on the ground floor where a number of other hostages were gathered. Some students attempted to talk with us, stating how they didn't hate Americans—only our U.S. Government, President Carter, etc. We were given sandwiches and that night I slept on the living room floor. We were not permitted to talk to our fellow hostages and from then on our hands were tied day and night and

only removed while we were eating or had to go to the bathroom. . . .

April 28, 1980
Nothing special has happened since my being moved to the new (less desirable room) except that I forgot to mention that about a week or 10 days ago we had hasps [metal fasteners] applied to the doors of our room and are now padlocked in the room as an extra security precaution! So with the bars on our windows and our doors being padlocked, it is more like a prison than ever!

[*A year later, the hostages were still in captivity.*]
October 21, 1980 (353rd Day!!!!)
Still no more mail today. Thirty-three days with only one letter from my wife and only 10 others from other family members, friends, and strangers. Every day is exactly the same as the one before and the one after. Mohsen came in Monday, October 20 and said we could take showers. However, I have decided not to go through the hassle anymore of being blindfolded, put into a car, stumbling around, and then have to shower in a filthy bathroom used by countless student-terrorists. I am just going to make my daily sponge baths do even though it is cold water.

Source: Robert Ode, "Iran Hostage's Diary," 1979–1980, Jimmy Carter Library, http://www.jimmycarterlibrary.gov/documents/r_ode/index.phtml.

Interpret the Evidence

- How does Ode react when he is initially taken hostage? How does he describe the Iranian students?
- Based on this entry, do you think that Ode grew resigned to his captivity over time? Why or why not?

Put It in Context

How did the hostage crisis expose the weakness in the United States' ability to defend its interests throughout the world?

United States, and the Iran fiasco helped ensure Carter's defeat in 1980 (see chapter 27).

REVIEW & RELATE

How did Carter's foreign policy differ from that of Ford and Nixon?

How did events in Afghanistan and Iran undermine the Carter administration?

 LEARNINGCurve bedfordstmartins.com/hewittlawson/LC

Reagan's Cold War Policy, 1981–1988

Ronald Reagan entered the White House determined to offer a direct challenge to the Soviets. Reagan and Secretary of State George Shultz believed that détente would become feasible only after the United States achieved military supremacy over the Soviet Union. Reagan also took strong measures to fight communism around the globe, from Central America to the Middle East. Yet military superiority alone would not defeat the Soviet Union. A shift of leadership within the USSR, as well as a worldwide protest movement for nuclear disarmament, involving people like Barbara Deming, helped bring an end to the Cold War and prepare the way for the dissolution of the Soviet empire.

"The Evil Empire"

In running for president in 1980, Reagan wrapped his hard-line anti-Communist message in the rhetoric of peace. "I've called for whatever it takes to be so strong that no other nation will dare violate the peace," he told the Veterans of Foreign Wars Convention on August 18, 1980. Still, he made it clear that he did not intend to pursue peace at any price; it "must not be a peace of humiliation and gradual surrender." Once in the White House, Reagan left no doubt about his anti-Communist stance. He called the Soviet Union "the evil empire," regarding it as "the focus of evil in the modern world." The president planned to confront that evil with both words and deeds, backing up his rhetoric with a massive military buildup.

In a show of moral and economic might, Reagan proposed the largest military budget in American history. Under the Reagan administration, the defense budget grew about 7 percent per year, increasing from $157 billion in 1981 to around $282 billion in 1988. Reagan clearly intended to win the Cold War by outspending the Soviets, even if it meant running up huge deficits that greatly burdened the U.S. economy (see chapter 27).

The president sought to expand the Cold War by developing new weapons to be deployed in outer space. He proposed a Strategic Defense Initiative (SDI), or "Star Wars," as it was dubbed, to create an orbiting shield of antiballistic missiles, which even Secretary of State Shultz privately called "lunacy." Seeming more like a page out of science fiction, the SDI was never carried out, though the government spent $17 billion on research.

Reagan was unyielding in his initial dealings with the Soviet Union, and negotiations between the superpowers moved slowly and unevenly. The Reagan administration's initial "zero option" proposal called for the Soviets to dismantle all of their intermediate-range missiles in exchange for the United States agreeing to refrain from deploying any new medium-range missiles. The administration presented this option merely for show, expecting the Soviets to reject it. However, in 1982, after the Soviets accepted the principle of "zero option," Reagan sent negotiators to begin Strategic Arms Reduction Talks (START). Influenced by antinuclear protests in Europe, which had a great impact on European governments, the Americans proposed shelving the deployment of 572 Pershing II and cruise missiles in Europe in return for the Soviets' dismantling of Eastern European–based intermediate-range ballistic missiles that were targeted at Western Europe. The Soviets viewed this offer as perpetuating American nuclear superiority and rejected it.

Relations between the two superpowers deteriorated in September 1983 when a Soviet fighter jet shot down a South Korean passenger airliner, killing 269 people. The Soviets charged that the plane had veered off course and violated their airspace on a trip from Anchorage, Alaska, to Seoul, South Korea. Although the disaster resulted mainly from Soviet mistakes, Reagan chose to condemn this attack as further proof of the malign intentions of the USSR, and country singer Lee Greenwood wrote the patriotic song "God Bless the USA" in support of the country and of Reagan. The United States sent additional missiles to bases in West Germany, Great Britain, and Italy; in response, the Soviets abandoned the disarmament talks and replenished their nuclear arsenal in Czechoslovakia and East Germany. More symbolically, the Soviets boycotted the 1984 Olympic Games in Los Angeles, in retaliation for the U.S. boycott of the Olympics in Moscow four years earlier. As the two adversaries swung from peace talks to threats of nuclear confrontation, one European journalist observed: "The second Cold War has begun."

Human Rights and the Fight against Communism

The Reagan administration extended its firm Cold War position throughout the world, emphasizing anticommunism often at the expense of human rights. The president saw threats of Soviet intervention in Central America and the Middle East, and he aimed to contain them. As had former presidents John Kennedy, Lyndon Johnson, and Richard Nixon, Reagan exploited the fear of communism in Central America and the Caribbean, where for nearly a century the United States had guarded its sphere of influence. During the 1980s, the United States continued its economic isolation of Cuba via the trade embargo, and it sought to prevent other Communist or leftist governments from emerging in Central America and the Caribbean. In doing so, the Reagan administration interfered in the internal affairs of small nations struggling to lift themselves from the poverty caused by decades of oppressive rule that had benefited private companies and commercial interests in the United States.

In the late 1970s, Nicaraguan revolutionaries, known as the National Liberation Front or Sandinistas, had overthrown the tyrannical government of General Anastasio Somoza, a brutal dictator who had suppressed dissent and tortured opponents. President Jimmy Carter, who had originally supported Somoza's overthrow, halted all aid to Nicaragua in 1980 after the Sandinistas began nationalizing foreign companies and drawing closer to Cuba. In the early years of the Reagan administration, Secretary of State Shultz suggested a U.S. invasion of Nicaragua, reflecting the administration's belief that the Sandinistas were "Soviet proxies" and that the revolution in Nicaragua had been sponsored by Moscow. Rather than invade, Reagan adopted a more indirect but no less violent approach. In 1982 he authorized the CIA to train approximately two thousand guerrilla forces outside the country, known as Contras (Counterrevolutionaries), to overthrow the Sandinista government. Although Reagan praised the Contras as "the moral equivalent of our Founding Fathers," the group consisted of pro-Somoza reactionaries as well as anti-Marxist democrats who blew up bridges and oil dumps, burned crops, and killed civilians. In 1982 Congress, unwilling to support such actions, passed the **Boland Amendment**, which prohibited direct aid to the Contras, thereby limiting the president's ability to aid the anti-Sandinista forces.

Proponents of the Boland Amendment drew on the lessons of the Vietnam War. Recalling that President Johnson had manipulated Congress and the public to support intervention in a civil war conducted by guerrillas, supporters of the amendment sought to prevent Reagan from producing another disaster of this kind. Members of the Reagan administration viewed Vietnam differently. They believed that the United States had to restore its honor and credibility following the defeat in Vietnam, especially in fighting Communists in its own backyard. In the face of congressional opposition, Reagan and his advisers came up with a plan that would secretly fund the efforts of their military surrogates in Nicaragua.

Elsewhere in Central America, the Reagan administration supported a corrupt right-wing government in El Salvador that, in an effort to put down an insurgency, sanctioned military death squads and killed forty thousand people during the 1980s. Despite the failings and abuses of the El Salvadoran government, Reagan insisted that Communist regimes in Nicaragua and Cuba were behind the Salvadoran insurgents. The United States sent more than $5 billion in aid to El Salvador and trained its military leaders to combat guerrilla forces.

While many Americans supported Reagan's strong anti-Communist stance, others opposed to the president's policy mobilized protests. Marches, rallies, and teach-ins were organized in cities and college campuses nationwide. U.S.-sponsored wars also drove many people to flee their dangerous, poverty-stricken countries and seek asylum in the United States. Between 1984 and 1990, 45,000 Salvadorans and 9,500 Guatemalans applied for asylum in the United States, but because the United States supported the established governments in those two nations, nearly all requests for refugee status were denied. Approximately five hundred American churches and synagogues established a sanctuary movement to provide safe haven for those fleeing Central American civil wars. Other Americans, especially in California and Texas, began to view the influx of refugees from Central America with alarm. This immigration, both legal and illegal, meant an increase in medical and educational costs for state and local communities, which taxpayers considered a burden.

In addition to financing secret wars in Central America, on October 25, 1983, Reagan sent 7,000 marines to invade the tiny 133-square-mile Caribbean island of Grenada. After a coup toppled the leftist government of Maurice Bishop, who had received Cuban and Soviet aid, the United States stepped in, ostensibly to protect American medical school students in Grenada from political instability following the coup. A swift victory in Grenada boosted Reagan's popularity and installed a pro-American government.

In Reagan's worldview, securing human rights was less important than fighting communism. Thus Reagan supported repressive governments in the Middle East, Asia, Latin America, and Africa without reservations. Reagan embraced the distinction made by his ambassador to the United Nations, Jeane Kirkpatrick, between non-Communist "authoritarian" nations, which were acceptable, and Communist "totalitarian" regimes, which were not. The difference remained fuzzy in practice, particularly in South Africa, where a white totalitarian government ruled over the black majority. Reagan considered the South African government an example of an acceptable authoritarianism, even though it practiced apartheid (white supremacy and racial separation) and torture. The fact that the South African Communist Party had joined the fight against apartheid reinforced Reagan's desire to support the white-minority, anti-Communist government. Interested in the country's vast mineral wealth, Reagan opted for what he called "constructive engagement"

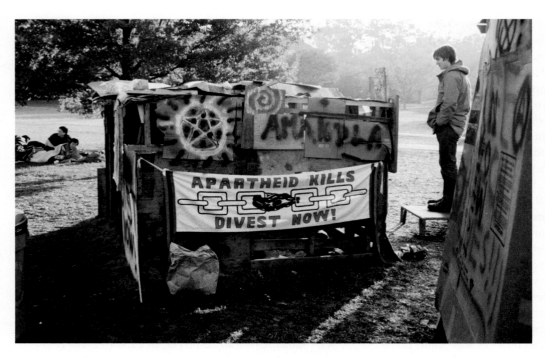

Antiapartheid Protest, Cornell University

In 1986 students on college campuses such as Cornell protested apartheid in South Africa. They constructed shantytowns to highlight the poverty of nonwhite South Africans. Their immediate goal was to persuade their universities to remove their investments in companies that did business in South Africa.   David Lyons

with South Africa, meaning that the United States would maintain and expand trade with a nation whose government had been condemned by the United Nations for its racist practices. The Reagan administration did so even as protesters across the United States and the world spoke out against South Africa's repressive white-majority government and campaigned for divestment of public and corporate funds from South African companies.

As early as 1977, the Reverend Louis Sullivan, an African American clergyman from Philadelphia and a board member of General Motors, convinced the company, the largest employer of blacks in South Africa, to treat its employees equally and in a nonsegregated manner. Supporters of this approach campaigned to persuade other companies doing business in South Africa to adopt what became known as the Sullivan Principles and to get investment funds to withdraw their portfolios from the apartheid nation. In the mid-1980s, students on U.S. college campuses nationwide joined the **divestment movement** by building "shantytowns" to protest the squalid, segregated living conditions of black South Africans. They also conducted demonstrations to demand that universities remove investments in South Africa from their endowment funds. Antiapartheid forces staged similar protests against municipal and state governments. At the same time, numerous African American officials and their allies conducted sit-ins at the South African Embassy in Washington, D.C. These efforts were largely successful. Between 1984 and 1988, the number of colleges and universities divesting either partially or fully from South Africa tripled from 53 to 155. In 1986 Congress passed the Comprehensive

Anti-Apartheid Act, which prohibited new trade and investment in South Africa. President Reagan vetoed it, but in testimony to the strength of this popular grassroots movement, Congress overrode the president's veto.

Fighting International Terrorism

Two days before the Grenada invasion in 1983, the U.S. military suffered a grievous blow halfway around the world. In the tiny country of Lebanon, wedged between Syrian occupation on its northern border and the Palestine Liberation Organization's (PLO) fight against Israel to the south, a civil war raged between Christians and Muslims. Reagan believed that stability in the region was in America's national interest. With this in mind, in 1982 the Reagan administration sent 800 marines, as part of a multilateral force that included French and Italian troops, to keep the peace, but fighting continued in Beirut between Christian and Muslim militias. On October 23, 1983, a suicide bomber drove a truck into a marine barracks, killing 241 soldiers. Reagan withdrew the remaining troops.

The removal of troops did not end threats to Americans in the Middle East. Terrorism had become an ever-present danger, especially since the Iranian hostage crisis in 1979–1980. In 1985, 17 American citizens were killed in terrorist assaults, and 154 were injured. In June 1985, Shi'ite Muslim extremists hijacked a TWA airliner in Athens with 39 Americans on board and flew it to Beirut. The Israeli government acceded to the hijackers' demands to release Shi'ite prisoners in its jails, and the crisis ended safely for the hostages. That same year, PLO members hijacked an

Bombing of Marine Barracks, Lebanon, 1983
On October 23, 1983, an Islamic terrorist group ignited two truck bombs that blasted U.S. marine barracks in Beirut, killing 241. Here rescuers search for survivors in the wreckage of the U.S. marine command. The troops were part of a multilateral peacekeeping force during the Lebanese civil war. President Reagan removed American forces after the bombings.   AP Photo/Souki

Italian cruise ship in the Mediterranean. Before the dangerous situation was resolved, an elderly American man in a wheelchair was killed and his body dumped in the sea.

In response, the Reagan administration targeted the North African country of Libya for retaliation. Its military leader, Muammar al-Qaddafi, supported the Palestinian cause and provided sanctuary for terrorists. In 1981 a squadron of Libyan planes attacked a U.S. naval flotilla conducting maneuvers off Libyan shores, and American pilots shot down two enemy planes. The Reagan administration placed a trade embargo on Libya, and Secretary of State Shultz remarked: "We have to put Qaddafi in a box and close the lid." In 1986, after the bombing of a nightclub in West Berlin killed 2 American servicemen and injured 230, Reagan charged that Qaddafi was responsible. In late April, the United States retaliated by sending planes to bomb the Libyan capital of Tripoli. The military strongman survived, but one of his daughters perished in the attack. Following the bombing, Qaddafi took a much lower profile against the

United States. Reagan had demonstrated his nation's military might despite the retreat in Lebanon (Map 28.1).

The Reagan administration's efforts to fight communism in Central America and terrorism in the Middle East continued unabated. Despite passage of the Boland Amendment in 1982 and its extension in 1984, the president continued to support the Nicaraguan Contras. By 1985 the Contras numbered somewhere between 10,000 and 20,000 troops and relied almost entirely on U.S. assistance. Barred from providing direct military or economic aid to the Contras, Reagan ordered the CIA and the National Security Council (NSC) to raise money from anti-Communist leaders abroad and wealthy conservatives at home. This effort, called "Project Democracy," raised millions of dollars. In violation of federal law, CIA director William Casey also authorized his agency to continue training the Contras in assassination techniques and other methods of subversion.

In the meantime, the situation in Lebanon remained critical as the strife caused by civil war led to the seizing of

MAP 28.1   The United States in the Middle East, 1978–1991

The United States has historically needed access to the rich oil reserves of the Middle East. From the 1970s to the 1990s, both Democratic and Republican administrations were committed to the security of Israel, supportive of Afghan rebels fighting Soviet invaders, and opposed to the rising power of Islamic regimes. These principles often led to contradictory policies that further embroiled the United States in Middle East affairs.

American hostages. By mid-1984, seven Americans, including the CIA bureau chief in Beirut, had been kidnapped by Shi'ite Muslims financed by Iran. Since 1980, Iran, a Shi'ite nation, had been engaged in a protracted war with Iraq, which was ruled by military leader Saddam Hussein and his Sunni Muslim party, the chief rival to the Shi'ites. With relations between the United States and Iran having deteriorated in the aftermath of the 1979 coup, the Reagan administration backed Iraq in this war. The fate of the hostages, however, motivated Reagan to make a deal with Iran. In late 1985, Reagan's national security adviser Robert McFarlane negotiated secretly with an Iranian intermediary for the United States to sell antitank missiles to Iran in exchange for the Shi'ite government using its influence to induce the Muslim kidnappers to release the hostages. This covert bargain produced mixed success. Two Americans were freed by the end of 1986, but by then another three had been captured.

Had the matter ended there, the secret deal might never have come to light. However, NSC aide Lieutenant Colonel Oliver North developed a plan to transfer the proceeds from the arms-for-hostages deal to fund the Contras and circumvent the Boland Amendment. Despite opposition from Secretary of State Shultz, Reagan liked North's plan, although the president seemed vague about the details, and some $10 million to $20 million of Iranian money flowed into the hands of the Contras.

In 1986 information about the **Iran-Contra** connection came to light. **See Document Project 28: The Iran-Contra Scandal, page 918.** Not since the Watergate scandal had a presidential administration received such intense media scrutiny. In the summer of 1987, televised Senate hearings exposed much of the tangled, covert dealings with Iran. In 1988 a special federal prosecutor indicted NSC adviser Vice Admiral John Poindexter (who had replaced McFarlane), North, and several others on charges ranging from perjury to conspiracy to obstruct justice. However, Reagan did not suffer the same fate or disgrace as had Nixon. Certainly the president knew what had been going on and had even approved it, but what he said publicly about his responsibility was circumscribed: "A few months ago, I told the American people I did not trade arms for hostages. My heart and best intentions still tell me that is true, but the facts and the evidence tell me it is not."

The Nuclear Freeze Movement

Despite his tough talk and military buildup, Reagan was not immune to public pressure. Rising protests against nuclear weapons in the United States and Europe in the early 1980s revealed a public increasingly anxious about the possibility of nuclear confrontation with the Soviet Union. At the end of the Carter administration, the United States had promised NATO that it would station new missiles in England, Italy, West Germany, and Belgium. Coupled with his confrontational stance against the Soviet Union, Reagan's decision to implement this policy sparked enormous protest. The campaign for nuclear disarmament included men and women, but women played a particularly strong leadership role in opposing nuclear proliferation. In 1981 peace activists set up camp at Greenham Common in England outside of one of the military bases prepared to house the arriving missiles. With twenty such camps in England, the disarmament forces organized nonviolent protests, including marches and sit-ins. The peace camp at Greenham Common became the model for the Women's Encampment for a Future of Peace and Justice at Seneca Falls, where Barbara Deming and other activists staged demonstrations. Protesters engaged in various forms of nonviolent expression, including singing, dancing, and performing skits to affirm women's solidarity for peace. As the participation of Deming as well as those at Greenham Common showed, women came together not only to promote disarmament but also to empower themselves and create communities based on mutual respect, trust, equality, and nonviolence.

These activities were part of a larger **nuclear freeze movement** that began in 1980. Its proponents called for a "mutual freeze on the testing, production, and deployment of nuclear weapons and of missiles and aircraft designed primarily to deliver nuclear weapons." Grassroots activists also held town meetings throughout the United States to mobilize ordinary citizens to speak out against nuclear proliferation. In 1982 some 750,000 people rallied in New York City's Central Park, the largest demonstration of its kind, to support a nuclear freeze resolution presented at the United Nations. Despite opposition from the United States and its NATO allies, measures favoring the freeze easily passed in the UN General Assembly. In the 1982 elections, peace groups placed nonbinding, nuclear freeze referenda on local ballots, which passed with wide majorities. The nuclear freeze movement's momentum carried over to Congress, where the House of Representatives narrowly rejected an "immediate freeze" by only two votes. Catholic bishops in the United States sent a pastoral letter to their parishioners condemning the spread of nuclear armaments. Even hard-line anti-Communists like Republican senator and former presidential candidate Barry Goldwater of Arizona joined the critics. "I'm not one of those freeze-the-nukes nuts," he explained in opposing new missile production, "but I think we have enough."

Explore

See Documents 28.2 and 28.3 to read about two nuclear freeze efforts.

Women's Peace Encampment Vigil

On October 24, 1983, protesters from the Women's Encampment for a Future of Peace and Justice held a candlelight vigil outside the Seneca Army Depot in Romulus, New York. Originally organized by feminist women, the protests also drew men. Together they campaigned to shut down the base, which was used as a munitions storage and disposal facility. In 1995 the military closed the depot.   AP Photo

Demonstrations in the United States and in Europe influenced Reagan. According to a 1982 public opinion poll, 57 percent of Americans favored an immediate nuclear freeze. Reflecting this sentiment, a 1983 television drama, *The Day After*, graphically portrayed the devastating horror of a nuclear attack on America. Reagan acknowledged that he was more inclined to reconsider deploying missiles abroad because European leaders felt pressure from protesters in their home countries. Ironically, the president credited Europeans' sentiments on the matter while claiming to ignore widespread efforts of domestic opponents such as Barbara Deming. However, the freeze movement inside and outside the United States created a favorable climate in which

the president and Soviet leaders could negotiate a genuine plan for nuclear disarmament by the end of the decade.

The Road to Nuclear De-escalation

As frightening as this massive arms buildup was and despite the continuation of peace protests, Ronald Reagan won reelection in 1984 by a landslide (see chapter 27). Following his enormous victory, the popular Reagan softened his militant stance and became more amenable to negotiating with the USSR. Like Nixon, Reagan came to office with a well-deserved reputation as a fervent anti-Communist and left the White House having eased tensions between the

DOCUMENTS 28.2 AND 28.3

The Nuclear Freeze Movement: Two Views

In 1982, 30 percent of American voters considered nuclear freeze referenda in ten states and thirty-seven cities and counties. The nuclear freeze movement called on the United States and the Soviet Union to mutually halt the production, testing, and deployment of nuclear weapons. A nonbinding referendum in New Jersey passed overwhelmingly in every county. In addition to initiating ballot measures, the nuclear freeze campaign won the support of the Catholic Church, which issued a pastoral letter in 1983.

Explore

28.2 New Jersey Referendum on Nuclear Freeze, 1982

Public Question No. 1: Freeze on Nuclear Arms Escalation

Do you support a mutual United States–Soviet Union nuclear weapons "freeze" and urge the government of the United States:

(1) to propose to the government of the Soviet Union that both countries immediately agree to a mutual, verifiable halt of all further testing, production, and deployment of nuclear warheads, missiles, and delivery systems as a first step toward mutual, balanced reduction, and

(2) to apply the money saved to human needs and tax reduction?

Interpretive Statement

"This non-binding referendum, if approved by the public, would demonstrate the voters' support of a nuclear weapons freeze and would direct the Secretary of State to transmit the results of these voters' opinions on this question to the President of the United States, the Speaker of the House of Representatives, and President of the United States Senate no later than twenty (20) days after the conclusion of the election."

Source: "New Jersey Nuclear Freeze Ballot," 1982, http://www.initiativeforchange.org/ProtestOnBallot.htm.

United States and the Soviet Union. It took a president with impeccable credentials in fighting communism to reduce Cold War conflicts. Had a liberal or even a moderate Democratic president copied Reagan's actions, he would have been seen as a traitor for succumbing to what many considered the godless Soviet villains. Reagan, even more than Nixon, espoused conservative principles during his presidency, but he refused to let rigid dogma interfere with more pragmatic considerations to foster peace. Notwithstanding his aggressive, moralistic rhetoric, he perceived the limits of America's power in the post-Vietnam era, as evidenced by his decision to invade a very weak Grenada rather than Cuba, Nicaragua, or El Salvador, and he quickly

withdrew U.S. marines from Lebanon rather than risk a wider war. By the time President Reagan left office, little remained of the Cold War.

In the mid-1980s, powerful changes were sweeping through the Soviet Union, which helped bring the Cold War to a close. In September 1985, Mikhail Gorbachev became general secretary of the Communist Party and head of the Soviet Union. The first Soviet chief of state born after the 1917 Bolshevik Revolution, Gorbachev introduced a program of economic and political reform. Through *glasnost* (openness) and *perestroika* (restructuring), the Soviet leader hoped to reduce massive state control over the declining economy and to extend democratic elections and

Explore

28.3 United States Conference of Catholic Bishops | Pastoral Letter on War and Peace, 1983

What are we saying? Fundamentally, we are saying that the decisions about nuclear weapons are among the most pressing moral questions of our age. While these decisions have obvious military and political aspects, they involve fundamental moral choices. In simple terms, we are saying that good ends (defending one's country, protecting freedom, etc.) cannot justify immoral means (the use of weapons which kill indiscriminately and threaten whole societies). We fear that our world and nation are headed in the wrong direction. More weapons with greater destructive potential are produced every day. More and more nations are seeking to become nuclear powers. In our quest for more and more security we fear we are actually becoming less and less secure. . . .

On Promoting Peace

1. We support immediate, bilateral verifiable agreements to halt the testing, production, and

deployment of new nuclear weapons systems. This recommendation is not to be identified with any specific political initiative.

2. We support efforts to achieve deep cuts in the arsenals of both superpowers; efforts should concentrate first on systems which threaten the retaliatory forces of either major power.

3. We support early and successful conclusion of negotiations of a comprehensive test ban treaty.

4. We urge new efforts to prevent the spread of nuclear weapons in the world, and to control the conventional arms race, particularly the conventional arms trade.

5. We support, in an increasingly interdependent world, political and economic policies designed to protect human dignity and to promote the human rights of every person, especially the least among us.

Source: "The Challenge of Peace: God's Promise and Our Response," United States Conference of Catholic Bishops, 1983.

Interpret the Evidence

- What did voters in New Jersey hope to accomplish with a nonbinding referendum? Do you think the nonbinding nature of the measure made much difference to the outcome of the vote?
- Why did the Catholic Church take such a strong position in support of the nuclear freeze? How do their goals compare with those of the New Jersey referendum?

Put It in Context

What impact did the nuclear freeze movement have on the Cold War?

freedom of speech and freedom of the press. Gorbachev understood that the success of his reforms depended on reducing Cold War tensions with the United States and slowing the arms escalation that was bankrupting the Soviet economy. Gorbachev's *glasnost* brought the popular American musical performer Billy Joel to the Soviet Union in August 1987, staging the first rock concert in the country.

The changes that Gorbachev brought to the internal affairs of the Soviet Union carried over to the international arena. From 1986 to 1988, the Soviet leader negotiated in person with the American president, something that had not happened during Reagan's first term. In 1986 at a summit in Reykjavik, Iceland, the two leaders agreed to cut the number of strategic nuclear missiles in half. Gorbachev even proposed to eliminate his nation's entire nuclear stockpile of weapons if Reagan terminated the SDI program, an offer Reagan declined. Despite widespread skepticism in the scientific community about the practicality of the SDI, Reagan sincerely believed that it offered the best hope of preventing nuclear warfare. In 1987 the two sides negotiated an Interme-diate Nuclear Forces Treaty, which provided for the destruc-tion of existing intermediate-range missiles and on-site inspections to ensure compliance. The height of détente came in December 1987, when Gorbachev traveled to the United States to take part in the treaty-signing ceremony. Reagan no longer referred to the USSR as "the evil empire," and Gorbachev impressed Americans with his personal charm and by demonstrating the media savvy associated with American politicians. The following year, Reagan flew to the Soviet Union and hugged his new friend Mikhail at Lenin's Tomb and told reporters, "They've changed," referring to the once and not-so-distant "evil empire." Citizens of the two adversarial nations breathed a collective sigh of relief; at long last, the Cold War appeared to be winding down.

REVIEW & RELATE

- How did anticommunism shape Ronald Reagan's foreign policy?
- What role did ordinary citizens play in prompting the superpowers to move toward nuclear de-escalation?

LEARNINGCurve bedfordstmartins.com/hewittlawson/LC

The Fall of the Iron Curtain

When George H. W. Bush, Reagan's vice president and successor, took office in January 1989, he encountered a very different Soviet Union from the one Ronald Reagan had faced a decade earlier. The USSR was undergoing an internal revolution, one that allowed Bush and the United States to take on a new role in a world that was no longer divided between capitalist and Communist nations and their allies. The United States led the formation of new global partner-ships that included the former Soviet Union. Globalization became the hallmark of the post–Cold War era, replacing previously dualistic economic and political systems, with mixed consequences. Following the collapse of the old world order, local and regional conflicts long held in check by the Cold War broke out along religious, racial, and ethnic lines.

The Breakup of the Soviet Union

Bush's first year in office coincided with upheavals in the Soviet-controlled Communist bloc, with Poland leading the way. In 1980 Polish dockworker Lech Walesa organized **Solidarity**, a trade union movement that conducted a series of popular strikes that forced the Communist government to recognize the group. Solidarity had ten million members and attracted various opponents of the Communist regime, including working-class democrats, Catholics, and nation-alists who favored breaking ties with the Soviet Union. In 1981 Soviet leaders, disturbed by Solidarity's growing strength, forced the Polish government to crack down on the organization, arrest Walesa, and ban Solidarity. However, in 1989 Walesa and Solidarity were still alive and seized on the changes ushered in by Mikhail Gorbachev's *glasnost* in the USSR to press their demands for democracy in Poland. This time, with Gorbachev in command, the Soviets refused to intervene, and Poland conducted its first free elections since the beginning of the Cold War, electing Lech Walesa as president of the country. In July 1989, Gorbachev further broke from the past and announced that the Soviet Union would respect the national sovereignty of all the nations in the Warsaw Pact, which the Soviet Union had controlled since the late 1940s. "There is no universal road toward socialism," the Soviet chief declared.

Explore

See Document 28.4 for Gorbachev's statement to the United Nations on *glasnost* and *perestroika*.

Gorbachev's proclamation spurred the end of commu-nism throughout Eastern Europe. Within the next year, Soviet-sponsored regimes fell peacefully in Hungary and Czechoslovakia, and elected governments replaced them. In Bulgaria, government officials dropped the word *Commu-nist* from their party's name and held free elections, which brought reformers to power. Only in Romania did Com-munist rulers put up a fight. There, it took a violent popular uprising to topple the brutal dictator Nicolae Ceausescu. The pent-up animosity was so great that Romanian revolutionaries executed Ceausescu and his wife in 1989. The Baltic states of Latvia, Lithuania, and Estonia, which

Mikhail Gorbachev | Speech to the United Nations, 1988

Soviet leader Mikhail Gorbachev instituted two major reform movements, called *glasnost* and *perestroika*. *Glasnost* was meant to transform the Soviet political system by creating more governmental openness and transparency, while *perestroika* referred to the restructuring of the Soviet economy. In December 1988, Gorbachev stunned the world when he discussed these changes at the United Nations and outlined plans to reduce Soviet military units in Eastern Europe.

Explore

What does Gorbachev's statement about constructing a state based on the rule of law imply about conditions in the Soviet Union prior to *glasnost*?

We have gone substantially and deeply into the business of constructing a socialist state based on the rule of law. A whole series of new laws has been prepared or is at a completion stage. Many of them come into force as early as 1989, and we trust that they will correspond to the highest standards from the point of view of ensuring the rights of the individual. Soviet democracy is to acquire a firm, normative base. This means such acts as the Law on Freedom of Conscience, on glasnost, on public associations and organizations, and on much else. There are now no people in places of imprisonment in the country who have been sentenced for their political or religious convictions. It is proposed to include in the drafts of the new laws additional guarantees ruling out any form or persecution on these bases. . . . We intend to expand the Soviet Union's participation in the monitoring mechanism on human rights in the United Nations and within the framework of the pan-European process. We consider that the jurisdiction of the International Court in The Hague with respect to interpreting and applying agreements in the field of human rights should be obligatory for all states.

What new possibilities did a free exchange of information represent for Soviet citizens?

Within the Helsinki process, we are also examining an end to jamming of all the foreign radio broadcasts to the Soviet Union. On the whole, our credo is as follows: Political problems should be solved only by political means, and human problems only in a humane way. . . . Now about the most important topic, without which no problem of the coming century can be resolved: disarmament. . . .

What impact would the withdrawal of Soviet troops from the USSR's satellite nations have on those countries?

Today I can inform you of the following: The Soviet Union has made a decision on reducing its armed forces. In the next two years, their numerical strength will be reduced by 500,000 persons, and the volume of conventional arms will also be cut considerably. These reductions will be made on a unilateral basis. . . . By agreement with our allies in the Warsaw Pact, we have made the decision to withdraw six tank divisions from the GDR [East Germany], Czechoslovakia, and Hungary, and to disband them by 1991. Assault landing formations and units, and a number of others, including assault river-crossing forces, with their armaments and combat equipment, will also be withdrawn from the groups of Soviet forces situated in those countries.

Source: "Address by Mikhail Gorbachev at the 43rd U.N. General Assembly Session," December 7, 1988, http://legacy.wilsoncenter.org/coldwarfiles/index-34441.html.

Put It in Context

What is Gorbachev's vision of the future of the Soviet Union? What role did he hope a reformed Soviet Union would play in the world?

the Soviets had incorporated into the USSR at the outset of World War II, also regained their independence, signaling the geographical breakup of the Soviet Union itself.

Perhaps the most striking symbolism in the dismantling of the Soviet empire came in Germany, a country that had been divided between East and West states since 1945 and had been the scene of confrontations between the two superpowers throughout the Cold War (see chapters 24 and 26). With Communist governments collapsing around them, East Germans demonstrated against the regime of Erich Honecker. With no Soviet help forthcoming, Honecker decided to open the border between East and West Germany. On November 9, 1989, East and West Germans flocked to the Berlin Wall and jubilantly joined workers in knocking down the concrete barricade that divided the city. A year later, East and West Germany merged under the democratic, capitalist Federal Republic of Germany, the nation that the United States and its anti-Communist allies had set up after World War II.

Gorbachev also brought an end to the costly nine-year Soviet-Afghan War. More than 14,000 Soviet troops had died in the war, and more than 450,000 suffered from wounds and diseases. The war cost the Soviets more than $20 billion, which severely strained their already ailing economy. When the Soviets withdrew their last troops on February 15, 1989, they left Afghanistan in shambles. One million Afghans had perished, and another 5 million fled the country for Pakistan and Iran, resulting in the political destabilization of Afghanistan. Following a civil war, the Taliban, a group of Sunni Muslim fundamentalists, came to power in the mid-1990s and established a theocratic regime that, among other things, strictly regulated what women could wear in public and denied them educational and professional opportunities. The Taliban also provided sanctuary for many of the mujahideen rebels who had fought against the Soviets, including Osama bin Laden, who would use the country as a base for his al-Qaeda organization to promote terrorism against the United States.

Meanwhile, the Soviet Union disintegrated. Free elections were held in 1990, which ironically threatened Gorbachev's own power by bringing non-Communists to local and national political offices. Although an advocate of economic reform and political openness, Gorbachev remained a Communist and was committed to preserving the USSR. Challenges to Gorbachev came from both ends of the political spectrum. Boris Yeltsin, his former protégé, led the non-Communist forces that wanted Gorbachev to move more quickly in adopting capitalism; on the other side, hard-line generals in the Soviet army disapproved of Gorbachev's reforms and his cooperation with the United States. On August 18, 1991, a group of conspirators from the army, the Communist Party, and the KGB (the Soviet intelligence agency) staged a coup against Gorbachev,

placed him under house arrest, and surrounded the parliament building with troops. Yeltsin, the president of the Russian Republic, rallied fellow legislators and Muscovites against the plotters and brought the uprising to a peaceful end. After Gorbachev was set free, he resigned in December 1991. Following the official dissolution of the Soviet Union, Yeltsin engineered the formation of the Commonwealth of Independent States (CIS), consisting of the Russian Federation and eleven of fifteen former Soviet republics (the Baltic states of Latvia, Lithuania, and Estonia did not join). Later that month, the CIS removed the hammer and sickle, the symbol of communism, from its flag. With the Soviet Union dismantled, Yeltsin, as head of the Russian Federation and the CIS, expanded the democratic and free market reforms initiated by Gorbachev (Map 28.2).

Despite his fall from power, Gorbachev deserves a great deal of credit for ending the Cold War. In bringing economic and political reforms to the Soviet Union, he opened the way for greater dialogue with the United States on arms control. His refusal to intervene when communism collapsed in Eastern Europe ensured that the nations in the region would follow their own course toward independence and democracy. He paid a high price for his efforts to restructure his country, as the reforms he set in motion ultimately led to his overthrow and the breakup of the Soviet Union. Yet he must be recognized as one of the prime movers in bringing the Cold War to an end.

Before Gorbachev left office, he completed one last agreement with the United States to curb nuclear arms. In mid-1991, just before conspirators staged their abortive coup, Gorbachev met with President Bush, who had traveled to Moscow to sign a strategic arms reduction treaty. Under this pact, each side agreed to reduce its bombers and missiles by one-third and to trim its conventional military forces. This accord led to a second strategic arms reduction treaty, signed in 1993. Gorbachev's successor, Boris Yeltsin, met with Bush in January 1993, and the two agreed to destroy their countries' stockpile of multiple-warhead intercontinental missiles within a decade.

Globalization and the New World Order

With the end of the Cold War, cooperation replaced economic and political rivalry between capitalist and Communist nations in a new era of **globalization**—the extension of economic, political, and cultural relationships among nations, through commerce, migration, and communication. In 1976 the major industrialized democracies had formed the Group of Seven (G7). Consisting of the United States, the United Kingdom, France, West Germany, Italy, Japan, and Canada, the G7 nations met annually to discuss common problems related to issues of global concern, such

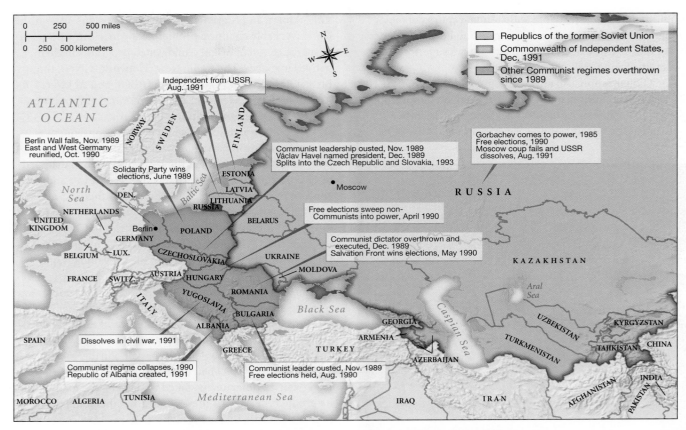

0   250   500 miles

0   250   500 kilometers

Republics of the former Soviet Union

Commonwealth of Independent States, Dec. 1991

Other Communist regimes overthrown since 1989

ATLANTIC OCEAN

Independent from USSR, Aug. 1991

NORWAY   SWEDEN   FINLAND

Berlin Wall falls, Nov. 1989 East and West Germany reunified, Oct. 1990

Communist leadership ousted, Nov. 1989 Václav Havel named president, Dec. 1989 Splits into the Czech Republic and Slovakia, 1993

Gorbachev comes to power, 1985 Free elections, 1990 Moscow coup fails and USSR dissolves, Aug. 1991

Solidarity Party wins elections, June 1989

ESTONIA

North Sea   DEN.   LATVIA   RUSSIA

LITHUANIA

NETHERLANDS   RUSSIA   BELARUS

Moscow   RUSSIA

UNITED KINGDOM   Berlin   POLAND

Free elections sweep non-Communists into power, April 1990

GERMANY

BELGIUM   LUX.   CZECHOSLOVAKIA   UKRAINE

Communist dictator overthrown and executed, Dec. 1989 Salvation Front wins elections, May 1990

KAZAKHSTAN

FRANCE   SWITZ.   AUSTRIA   HUNGARY   MOLDOVA

Aral Sea

ITALY   YUGOSLAVIA   ROMANIA

Black Sea   UZBEKISTAN   KYRGYZSTAN

BULGARIA

SPAIN   ALBANIA   GEORGIA   TURKMENISTAN   TAJIKISTAN   CHINA

Dissolves in civil war, 1991

GREECE   ARMENIA   Caspian Sea

TURKEY   AZERBAIJAN   AFGHANISTAN   INDIA

Communist regime collapses, 1990 Republic of Albania created, 1991

Communist leader ousted, Nov. 1989 Free elections held, Aug. 1990

MOROCCO   ALGERIA   TUNISIA   Mediterranean Sea   IRAQ   IRAN   PAKISTAN

MAP 28.2   The Fall of Communism in Eastern Europe and the Soviet Union, 1989–1991

The collapse of Communist regimes in eastern Europe was due in part to political and economic reforms initiated by Soviet Premier Mikhail Gorbachev, including agreements with the United States to reduce nuclear arms. These changes inspired demands for free elections that were supported by popular uprisings, first in Poland and then in other former Soviet satellites.

as trade, health, energy, the environment, and economic and social development. After the fall of communism, Russia joined the organization, which became known as G8. This group of countries represented only 14 percent of the globe's population but produced 60 percent of the world's economic output. Four of the G8 members—the United States, the United Kingdom, Russia, and France—controlled more than 95 percent of the nuclear weapons in the world.

The United States took an active lead in promoting the World Trade Organization (WTO). The WTO emerged from the General Agreement on Tariffs and Trade, a multilateral agreement fashioned after World War II to encourage tariff reductions and free trade. Created in 1995, the WTO consists of more than 150 nations and seeks "to ensure that trade flows as smoothly, predictably and freely as possible." The policies of the WTO generally benefit wealthier nations, such as the United States. From 1978 to 2000, the value of U.S. exports and imports jumped from 17 percent to 25 percent of the gross national product.

Globalization was accompanied by the extraordinary growth of **multinational (or transnational) corporations**—companies that operate production facilities or deliver services in more than one country. Between 1970 and 2000, the number of such firms soared from 7,000 to well over 60,000. By 2000 the 500 largest corporations in the world generated more than $11 trillion in revenues, owned more than $33 trillion in assets, and employed 35.5 million people. American companies left their cultural and social imprint on the rest of the world. Walmart greeted shoppers in more than 1,200 stores outside the United States, and McDonald's changed global eating habits with its more than 1,000 fast-food restaurants worldwide. Traveling abroad, American tourists marveled at local inhabitants in Europe, Asia, and Africa wearing T-shirts and baseball caps with the logos of American companies. As American firms penetrated other countries with their products, foreign companies changed the economic landscape of the United States. For instance, by the twenty-first century Japanese automobiles, led by Toyota and Honda, captured a major share of the American market, surpassing Ford and General Motors, once the hallmark of the country's superior manufacturing and salesmanship.

Globalization also affected popular culture. In the 1990s, reality shows, many of which originated in Europe, became a staple of American television. British imports included the hugely popular *American Idol*. At the same time, American programs were shown as reruns all over the world. As cable channels proliferated, American viewers of Hispanic or Asian origin could watch programs in their native languages. The Cable News Network (CNN), the British Broadcasting Corporation (BBC), and Al Jazeera, an Arabic-language television channel, competed for viewers with specially designed international broadcasts.

Globalization also had some negative consequences. Organized labor in particular suffered a severe blow. By 2004 union membership in the United States had dropped to 12.5 percent of the industrial workforce. Fewer and fewer consumer goods bore the label "Made in America," as multinational companies shifted manufacturing jobs to low-wage workers in third world countries in Central America, East Asia, and Southeast Asia. Many of these foreign workers earned more than the prevailing wages in their countries, but by Western standards their pay was extremely low. There were few or no regulations governing working conditions or the use of child labor, and many foreign factories resembled the sweatshops of early-twentieth-century America. Not surprisingly, workers in the United States could not compete in this market. Furthermore, China, which by 2007 had become a prime source for American manufacturing, failed to regulate the quality of its products closely. Chinese-made toys, including the popular Thomas the Train, showed up in U.S. stores with excessive lead paint and had to be returned before endangering millions of children.

Globalization also posed a danger to the world's environment. As poorer nations sought to take advantage of the West's appetite for low-cost consumer goods, they industrialized rapidly and chaotically, with little concern for the excessive pollution that accompanied their efforts. The landscapes of some countries were transformed beyond recognition. The desire for wood products and the expansion of large-scale farming eliminated one-third of Brazil's rain forests. The health of indigenous people suffered wherever globalization-related manufacturing appeared. In Taiwan and China, chemical by-products of factories and farms turned rivers into polluted sources of drinking water and killed the rivers' fish and plants.

The older, industrialized nations added their share to the environmental damage. Besides using nuclear power, Americans consumed electricity and gas produced overwhelmingly from coal and petroleum. Gas-guzzling automobiles, and particularly sport-utility vehicles (SUVs) beginning in the 1990s, further harmed the environment. The burning of fossil fuels by cars and factories released greenhouse gases, which has raised the temperature of the atmosphere and the oceans and contributed to the phenomenon known as global warming. Most scientists believe that global warming has led to the melting of the polar ice

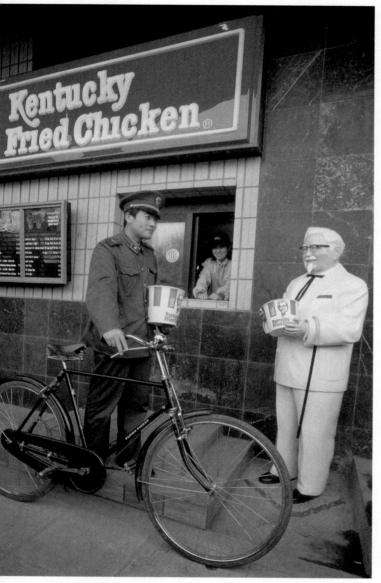

Globalization, 1980s

Following the efforts of Presidents Nixon, Ford, and Carter to normalize relations with Communist China, companies established commercial enterprises there, including American fast-food chain restaurants. Here a soldier, standing beside a replica of Colonel Sanders, picks up his order at the bike ride-up window of a Kentucky Fried Chicken restaurant. © Dave Bartruff/CORBIS caps and threatens the existence of human and animal survival on the planet. However, after the industrialized nations of the world signed the Kyoto Protocol in 1998 to curtail greenhouse-gas emissions, the U.S. Senate refused to ratify it. Critics of the agreement maintained that it did not address the newly emerging industrial countries that polluted heavily and thus was unfair to the United States.

Globalization also highlighted health problems such as the AIDS epidemic. By the outset of the twenty-first century, approximately 33.2 million people worldwide suffered from the disease, though the number of new cases diagnosed annually had dropped to 2.5 million from more than 5 million a few years earlier. Africa remained the continent with the largest number of AIDS patients and the center of the epidemic. Initially concentrated in gay men, intravenous drug users, and sex workers, AIDS constituted a continual though diminished threat. Increased education and the development of more effective pharmaceuticals to treat the illness reduced cases and prolonged the lives of those affected by the disease. Though treatments were more widely available in prosperous countries like the United States, agencies such as the United Nations and the World Health Organization, together with nongovernmental groups such as Partners in Health, were instrumental in offering relief in developing countries.

Globalization did not mean the end of regional cooperation. To boost their economic might, western European nations formed the **European Union (EU)** in 1993, and by 2007 twenty-seven countries had joined the EU. The EU allowed people to move freely by abolishing passport control and customs checks for residents traveling from one member state to another. The organization encouraged free trade and investment. In 1999 the EU introduced a common currency, the euro, which has been adopted by thirteen nations. In 2007 the EU had representation in the G8, contained a population of 500 million, and accounted for approximately 31 percent of the world's output of goods and services.

To strengthen its trading position, the United States formed its own regional economic partnership in North America. In 1993, together with the governments of Mexico and Canada, the U.S. Congress ratified the **North American Free Trade Agreement (NAFTA)**, and it went into effect the following year. The agreement removed tariffs and other obstacles to commerce and investment among the three countries to encourage trade. NAFTA produced noteworthy gains: Between 1994 and 2004, trade among NAFTA nations increased nearly 130 percent. Although income disparity remains large between Mexico and the United States, Mexico has seen a significant drop in poverty rates and a rise in real income. At the same time, NAFTA has harmed workers in the United States. From 1994 to

2007, net manufacturing jobs dropped by 3,654,000, as U.S. companies outsourced their production to plants in Mexico, taking advantage of the low wage and benefits structure.

Managing Conflict after the Cold War

The end of the Cold War left the United States as the only remaining superpower. Though Reagan's Cold War defense spending had created huge deficits (see chapter 27), the United States emerged from the Cold War with its economic and military strength intact. With the power vacuum created by the breakup of the Soviet Union, the question remained how the United States would use its strength to preserve world order and maintain peace.

In several areas of the globe, the move toward democracy that had begun in the late 1980s proceeded peacefully into the 1990s. The oppressive, racist system of apartheid fell in South Africa, and antiapartheid activist Nelson Mandela was released after twenty-seven years in prison to become president of the country in 1994. In 1990 Chilean dictator Augusto Pinochet stepped down as president of Chile and ceded control to a democratically elected candidate. That same year, the pro-Communist Sandinista government lost at the polls in Nicaragua, and in 1992 the ruling regime in El Salvador signed a peace accord with the rebels.

The end of the Cold War allowed President Bush to turn his attention to explosive issues in the Middle East. The president brought the Israelis and Palestinians together to sign an agreement providing for eventual Palestinian self-government in the Gaza Strip and the West Bank. In doing so, the United States for the first time officially recognized Yasser Arafat, the head of the PLO, whom both the Israelis and the Americans had considered a terrorist.

Before Bush left the White House in 1993, he had deployed military forces in both the Caribbean and the Persian Gulf, confident that the United States could exert its influence without a challenge from the former Soviet Union. During the 1980s, the United States had developed a precarious relationship with Panamanian general Manuel Noriega. Noriega played the United States against the Soviet Union in this region that was vital to American security. Although he channeled aid to the Contras with the approval and support of the CIA, he angered the Reagan administration by maintaining close ties with Cuba. Noriega cooperated with the U.S. Drug Enforcement Agency in halting shipments of cocaine from Latin America headed for the United States at the same time that he collaborated with Latin American drug kingpins to elude U.S. agents and launder the drug lords' profits. In 1988 two Florida grand juries indicted the Panamanian leader on charges of drug smuggling and bribery, pressuring President Reagan to cut off aid to Panama and to ask Noriega to resign. Not only did Noriega refuse to step down, but he also nullified the results of the 1989 presidential election in Panama and declared himself the nation's "maximum leader."

After the United States tried unsuccessfully to foment an internal coup against Noriega, in 1989 the Panamanian leader proclaimed a "state of war" between the United States and his country. The situation worsened in mid-December when a U.S. marine was killed on his way home from a restaurant, allegedly by Panamanian defense forces. On December 28, 1989, President Bush launched Operation Just Cause, sending some 27,000 marines to invade Panama. Bush justified the invasion as necessary to protect the Panama Canal and the lives of American citizens, as well as to halt the drug traffic promoted by Noriega. In reality, the main purpose of the mission was to overthrow and capture the Panamanian dictator. In Operation Just Cause, the United States easily defeated a much weaker enemy. The U.S. government installed a new regime, and the marines captured Noriega and sent him back to Florida to stand trial on the drug charges. In 1992 he was found guilty and sent to prison.

Flexing military muscle in Panama was more feasible than doing so in China. President Bush believed that the acceleration of trade relations that followed full U.S. diplomatic recognition of Communist China in 1978 would prompt the kind of democratic reforms that swept through the Soviet Union in the 1980s. His expectation proved far too optimistic. In May 1989, university students in Beijing and other major cities in China held large-scale protests to demand political and economic reforms in the country. Some 200,000 demonstrators consisting of students, intellectuals, and workers gathered in the capital city's huge Tiananmen Square, where they constructed a papier-mâché figure resembling the Statue of Liberty and sang songs borrowed from the African American civil rights movement. Deng Xiaoping, Mao Zedong's successor, cracked down on the demonstrations by declaring martial law and dispatching the army to disperse the protesters. Peaceful activists were mowed down by machine guns and stampeded by tanks. Rather than displaying the toughness he showed in Panama, Bush merely issued a temporary ban on sales of weapons and nonmilitary items to China. When outrage over the Tiananmen Square massacre subsided, the president restored normal trade relations.

By contrast, the Bush administration's most forceful military intervention came in Iraq. Maintaining a steady flow of oil from the Persian Gulf was vital to U.S. strategic interests. During the prolonged Iraq-Iran War in the 1980s, the Reagan administration had switched allegiance from one belligerent to the other to ensure that neither side emerged too powerful. Though the administration had orchestrated the arms-for-hostages deal with Iran, it had also courted the Iraqi dictator Saddam Hussein. U.S. support for Hussein ended in 1990, after Iraq sent 100,000 troops to invade the small oil-producing nation of Kuwait, on the southern border of Iraq.

President Bush responded aggressively. He compared Saddam Hussein to Adolf Hitler and warned the Iraqis that their invasion "will not stand." Oil was at the heart of the matter. Hussein needed to revitalize the Iraqi economy, which was devastated after a decade of war with Iran. In conquering Kuwait, which held huge oil reserves, Hussein would control one-quarter of the world output of the "black gold." Bush feared that the Iraqi dictator would also attempt to overrun Kuwait's neighbor Saudi Arabia, an American ally, thereby giving Iraq control of half of the world's oil supply. Bush was also concerned that an emboldened Saddam Hussein would then upset the delicate balance of power in the Middle East and pose a threat to Israel by supporting the Palestinians. The Iraqis were rumored to be quickly developing nuclear weapons, which Hussein could use against Israel.

Rather than act unilaterally, President Bush organized a multilateral coalition against Iraqi aggression. Secretary of State James Baker persuaded the United Nations—including the Soviet Union and China, the United States' former Cold War adversaries—to adopt a resolution calling for Iraqi withdrawal from Kuwait and imposing economic sanctions. Thirty-eight nations, including the Arab countries of Egypt, Saudi Arabia, Syria, and Kuwait, contributed 160,000 troops, roughly 24 percent of the 700,000 allied forces that were deployed in Saudi Arabia in preparation for an invasion if Iraq did not comply. Hussein's bellicosity against an Islamic nation won him few allies in the Middle East.

With military forces stationed in Saudi Arabia, Bush gave Hussein a deadline of January 15, 1991, to withdraw from Kuwait or else risk attack. However, the president faced serious opposition at home against waging a war for oil. Demonstrations occurred throughout the nation, and most Americans supported the continued implementation of economic sanctions, which were already causing serious hardships for the Iraqi people. In the face of widespread opposition, the president requested congressional authorization for military operations against Iraq. Lawmakers were also divided, but after long debate they narrowly approved Bush's request.

Saddam Hussein let the deadline pass. On January 16, **Operation Desert Storm** began when the United States launched air attacks on Baghdad and other key targets in Iraq. After a month of bombing, Hussein still refused to capitulate, so a ground offensive was launched on February

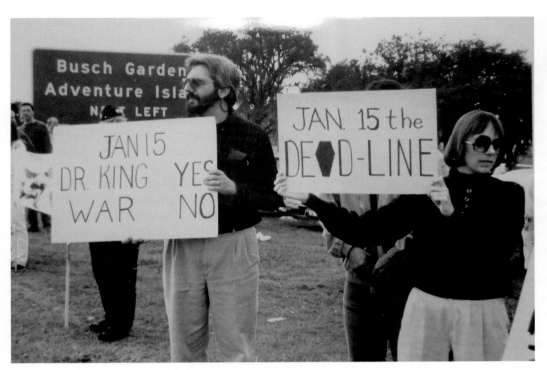

Gulf War Protests, 1991

The United States gave Iraq a January 15, 1991, deadline to withdraw from Kuwait or face military force. Protesters at the University of South Florida in Tampa favored continued diplomatic efforts. They carry signs that refer to the January 15 deadline, which also is the birthday of Martin Luther King Jr., a critic of U.S. militarism. Courtesy of Steven Lawson and Nancy Hewitt

24, 1991. Under the command of General Norman H. Schwarzkopf, more than 500,000 allied troops moved into Kuwait and easily drove Iraqi forces out of that nation; they then moved into southern Iraq. Although Hussein had confidently promised that the U.S.-led military assault would encounter the "mother of all battles," the vastly outmatched Iraqi army, worn out from its ten-year war with Iran, was quickly defeated. Desperate for help, Hussein ordered the firing of Scud missiles on Israel to provoke it into war, which he hoped would drive a wedge between the United States and its Arab allies. Despite sustaining some casualties, Israel refrained from retaliation. The ground war ended within one hundred hours, and Iraq surrendered. An estimated 100,000 Iraqis died; by contrast, 136 Americans perished (see Map 28.1 on page 904).

With the war over quickly, President Bush resisted pressure to march to Baghdad and overthrow Saddam Hussein. Bush's stated goal had been to liberate Kuwait; he did not wish to fight a war in the heart of Iraq. The administration believed that such an expedition would involve house-to-house, urban guerrilla warfare. Marching on Baghdad would also entail battling against Hussein's elite Republican Guard, not the weaker conscripts who had put up little resistance in Kuwait. Bush's Arab allies opposed expanding the war, and the president did not want to risk losing their support. Finally, getting rid of Hussein might make matters worse by leaving Iran and its Muslim fundamentalist rulers the dominant power in the region.

For these reasons, President Bush held Schwarzkopf's troops in place.

The Gulf War preserved the U.S. lifeline to oil in the Persian Gulf. President Bush and his supporters concluded that the United States had the determination to make its military presence felt throughout the world. Bush and the chairman of the Joint Chiefs of Staff, General Colin Powell, understood that the United States had succeeded because it had pieced together a genuine coalition of nations, including Arab ones, to coordinate diplomatic and military action. Military leaders had a clear and defined mission— the liberation of Kuwait—as well as adequate troops and supplies. When they carried out their purpose, the war was over. However, American withdrawal later allowed Saddam Hussein to slaughter thousands of Iraqi rebels, including Kurds and Shi'ites, to whom Bush had promised support. In effect, the Bush administration had applied the Cold War policy of limited containment in dealing with Hussein. The end of the Cold War and peaceful relations with former adversaries in Moscow and Beijing made possible the largest and most successful U.S. military intervention since the war in Vietnam.

REVIEW & RELATE

- What led to the end of Communist rule in Eastern Europe and the breakup of the Soviet Union?

- How did the end of the Cold War contribute to the growth of globalization?

Conclusion: Farewell to the Cold War

The Cold War between the United States and the Soviet and Chinese Communists occupied the attention of two generations of Americans from 1945 to 1991. Citizens in these nations faced the nightmare of nuclear holocaust caused by even small missteps between the adversaries. But some unlikely people were responsible for ending the Cold War. Ronald Reagan, a militant anti-Communist crusader, together with his pragmatic and steady secretary of state, George Shultz, guided the United States through a policy of heightened military preparedness in order to push the Soviet Union toward peace. It was a dangerous gambit, but it worked; diplomacy rather than armed conflict prevailed. Reagan's Cold War strategy succeeded largely because during the 1980s an enlightened leader, Mikhail Gorbachev, governed the Soviet Union. He envisioned the end of the Cold War as a means of bringing political and economic reform to his beleaguered and bankrupt nation. What Gorbachev began, his successor, Boris Yeltsin, finished: the dismantling of the Soviet Union and its empire, and the infusion of democracy and capitalism into Russia.

The activism of ordinary people around the world also helped transform the relationship between the superpowers. Antinuclear protesters in Western Europe and the United States, including Barbara Deming and her feminist cadre at the Seneca Falls Women's Encampment, kept up pressure on Western leaders to make continued nuclear expansion unacceptable. In Eastern Europe, Polish dockworker Lech Walesa and other fighters for democracy broke from the Soviet orbit and tore down the bricks and barbed-wire fences of the iron curtain. Who won the Cold War? Clearly, the United States did, thereby gaining dominance as the world's sole superpower. Yet this did not necessarily guarantee peace. In assuming this preeminent role, the United States faced new threats to international security from governments and insurgents seeking to rebuild nations along ethnic and religious lines in the Balkans, the Middle East, the Persian Gulf, and Africa. Ironically, the bipolar Cold War in some ways had meant a more stable and manageable world presided over by the two superpowers. The collapse of the Soviet empire created a power vacuum that would be filled by a variety of unchecked and combustible local and regional forces intent on challenging the political and economic dominance of the United States and, even more sweeping, the values of Western civilization. At the same time, as globalization and digital technology shrank the world economically and culturally, the United States became the chief target of those who wanted to contain the spread of Western values. Terrorism, which transcended national borders, replaced communism as the leading enemy of the United States and its allies.

Chapter Review

Online Study Guide ▶ bedfordstmartins.com/hewittlawson

KEY TERMS

détente (p. 897)
SALT II (p. 897)
mujahideen (p. 898)
Camp David accords (p. 898)
Boland Amendment (p. 901)
divestment movement (p. 902)
Iran-Contra (p. 904)
nuclear freeze movement (p. 905)
glasnost (p. 907)
perestroika (p. 907)
Solidarity (p. 908)
globalization (p. 910)
multinational (or transnational) corporations (p. 911)
European Union (EU) (p. 913)
North American Free Trade Agreement (NAFTA) (p. 913)
Operation Desert Storm (p. 914)

REVIEW & RELATE

1. How did Carter's foreign policy differ from that of Ford and Nixon?

2. How did events in Afghanistan and Iran undermine the Carter administration?

3. How did anticommunism shape Ronald Reagan's foreign policy?

4. What role did ordinary citizens play in prompting the superpowers to move toward nuclear de-escalation?

5. What led to the end of Communist rule in Eastern Europe and the breakup of the Soviet Union?

6. How did the end of the Cold War contribute to the growth of globalization?

TIMELINE OF EVENTS

1975	U.S. and USSR sign Helsinki accords
1978	Camp David accords between Israel and Egypt
1979	U.S. Embassy staff in Tehran taken hostage
	U.S. and USSR sign SALT II; Congress does not ratify
	Soviet Union invades Afghanistan
1980	Solidarity founded in Poland
1982	Boland Amendment passed
	750,000 attend nuclear freeze rally in New York City's Central Park
1983	Suicide bomb attack in Lebanon kills 241 U.S. soldiers
	U.S. invasion of Grenada
1985	Reagan administration sells arms to Iran for release of hostages and to fund Nicaraguan Contras
	Mikhail Gorbachev assumes leadership of the Soviet Union
1987	Senate hearings on Iran-Contra affair
	U.S. and Soviet Union sign Intermediate Nuclear Forces Treaty
1989	Tiananmen Square protests and crackdown in China
	Fall of the Berlin Wall
1990–1991	Soviet Union dismantled
1991	U.S. pushes Iraq out of Kuwait
1993	European Union (EU) formed
1994	North Atlantic Free Trade Agreement (NAFTA) goes into effect

The Iran-Contra Scandal

On November 3, 1986, the Lebanese magazine *Ash-Shiraa* revealed a secret arms-for-hostages deal between the United States and Iran. As the scandal unfolded, it was revealed that the profits from these arms sales had been illegally diverted to aid anti-Sandinista rebels (called Contras) in Nicaragua. For the next year, the Iran-Contra scandal, as it was known, played out in the press as questions of governmental conspiracy, abuse of power, and a White House cover-up swirled around the Reagan administration.

Since the early 1980s, the Central Intelligence Agency had been funding, arming, and training groups of dissident forces opposing the leftist Nicaraguan government. After Congress passed the Boland Amendment, which prohibited further aid to the Contras, the Reagan administration then looked for other ways to continue its support for the rebels, eventually funneling sales from the Iranian arms sales.

Less than a month after the story broke, President Reagan appointed a three-person committee to investigate the allegations. The Tower Commission—named after commission member John Tower, a Republican senator from Texas—spent several months calling witnesses and poring over classified documents. Unsatisfied with the Tower Commission's work, the U.S. Senate and House of Representatives established their own joint investigative committee and held hearings in the summer of 1987. Both the Tower Commission and the congressional committee concluded that neither Reagan nor Vice President George H. W. Bush was aware of the illegal funding of the Contras, though Reagan was sharply criticized as a poor administrator who needed to exert more control over his staff.

Several of Reagan's top officials were eventually indicted on a variety of felony accounts, including lying to Congress, destroying evidence, and obstructing justice. In all, eleven men were convicted or pleaded guilty. In late 1992, then President George H. W. Bush pardoned six men indicted or convicted as part of the Iran-Contra scandal.

DOCUMENT 28.5

The Boland Amendment, 1982

Alarmed at the CIA's involvement in the Nicaraguan civil war, Congress passed a measure in 1982 to limit funding and support for these activities. Offered by Edward Boland, a Democratic representative from Massachusetts, the Boland Amendment prohibited the CIA or any government agency from providing military aid or advice to the Contra rebels.

Amendment to H.R. 7355, Offered December 8, 1982

A substitute amendment to the Harkin amendment [which also prohibited support of military activity in Nicaragua] to prohibit the CIA or Defense Department to use funds of the bill to furnish military equipment, military training or advice, or other support for military activities, to any group or individual, not part of a country's armed forces, for the purpose of overthrowing the government of Nicaragua or provoking a military exchange between Nicaragua and Honduras. The Harkin amendment has prohibited support of any military activity in Nicaragua.

Source: House Amendment 974, 97th Congress (1981–1982).

DOCUMENT 28.6

CIA Freedom Fighter's Manual, 1983

The CIA's support for the Contras included training in sabotage to disrupt Nicaraguan government and society. In 1983 the CIA prepared a Freedom Fighter's Manual and air-dropped thousands of pamphlets over Nicaragua. Promising "minimal risk for the combatant," the manual's advice ranged from passive and mundane techniques— such as showing up late for work, spreading false rumors, and plugging up toilets with sponges—to more aggressive methods of sabotage, shown here.

PUT NAILS ON ROADS AND HIGHWAYS

REGAR CLAVOS EN LOS CAMINOS Y CARRETERAS

PUT DIRT INTO GASOLINE TANKS

ECHARLE TIERRA AL TANQUE DE GASOLINA

COLOCAR CLAVOS JUNTO A LOS NEUMÁTICOS DE VEHÍCULOS ESTACIONADOS

PUT NAILS NEXT TO THE TIRES OF PARKED VEHICLES

ECHAR AGUA EN EL TANQUE DE GASOLINA

PUT WATER IN GASOLINE TANKS

DOCUMENT 28.7

Tower Commission Report, 1987

As the scandal unfolded, President Reagan appointed a three-member commission to investigate the allegations. In addition to Senator Tower, the Tower Commission included Edmund Muskie, a former secretary of state, and Brent Scowcroft, a former national security adviser to President Ford. More than seventy witnesses testified, and Reagan appeared before the commission in December 1986. At the center of the scandal was Lieutenant Colonel Oliver North, a marine assigned to the National Security Council and the professed coordinator of the arms sales and the diversion of funds to the Contras. When the commission released its report in February 1987, it concluded that while Reagan should have been more directly aware of the actions of his advisers, he was not aware of the illegal diversion of funds to the Contras.

The President's management style is to put the principal responsibility for policy review and implementation on the shoulders of his advisors. Nevertheless, with such a complex, high-risk operation and so much at stake, the President should have insured that the N.S.C. [National Security Council] system did not fail him. He did not force his policy to undergo the most critical review of which the N.S.C. participants and the process were capable. At no time did he insist upon accountability and performance review. Had the President chosen to drive the N.S.C. system, the outcome could well have been different. As it was, the most powerful features of the N.S.C. system—providing comprehensive analysis, alternatives, and follow-up—were not utilized. . . .

The board found considerable reason to question the actions of Lt. Col. North in the aftermath of the disclosure. The board has no evidence to either confirm or refute that Lt. Col. North destroyed documents on the initiative in an effort to conceal facts from threatened investigations. The board found indications that Lt. Col. North was involved in an effort, over time, to conceal or withhold important information. The files of Lt. Col. North contained much of the historical documentation that the board used to construct its narrative. Moreover, Lt. Col. North was the primary U.S. Government official involved in the details of the operation. The chronology he produced has many inaccuracies. These "histories" were to be the basis of the "full" story of the Iran initiative. These inaccuracies lend some evidence to the proposition that Lt. Col. North, either on his own or at the behest of others, actively sought to conceal important information.

Out of concern for the protection of classified material, [CIA] Director [William] Casey and [National Security Adviser Vice Admiral (VADM) John] Poindexter were to brief only the Congressional intelligence committees on the "full" story; [Casey] before the committees and VADM Poindexter in private sessions with the chairmen and vice chairmen. [Casey] and VADM Poindexter undertook to do this on November 21, 1986. It appears from the copy of [Casey's] testimony and notes of VADM Poindexter's meetings that they did not fully relate the nature of events as they had occurred. The result is an understandable perception that they were not forthcoming.

The board is also concerned about various notes that appear to be missing. VADM Poindexter was the official note taker in some key meetings, yet no notes for the meetings can be found. The reason for the lack of such notes remains unknown to the board. If they were written, they may contain very important information. We have no way of knowing if they exist.

Source: President's Special Review Board, *The Tower Commission Report* (New York: New York Times Books, 1987), 84–86.

DOCUMENT 28.8

Ronald Reagan | Speech on Iran-Contra, 1987

A few weeks after the Tower Commission released its report, President Reagan went on television and spoke about the Iran-Contra scandal. Although he had appeared on television during the commission's hearings, this was the first time he spoke directly to the American people about the scandal. He discussed the Tower Commission report as well as the steps he was taking to address the problems it identified about his administration and management style.

I've studied the Board's report. Its findings are honest, convincing, and highly critical; and I accept them. And tonight I want to share with you my thoughts on these findings and report to you on the actions I'm taking to implement the Board's recommendations.

First, let me say I take full responsibility for my own actions and for those of my administration. As angry as I may be about activities undertaken without my knowledge, I am still accountable for those activities. As disappointed as I may be in some who served me, I'm still the one who must answer to the American people for this behavior. And as personally distasteful as I find secret bank accounts and diverted funds—well, as the Navy would say, this happened on my watch.

Let's start with the part that is the most controversial. A few months ago I told the American people I did not trade arms for hostages. My heart and my best intentions still tell me that's true, but the facts and the evidence tell me it is not. As the Tower board reported, what began as a strategic opening to Iran deteriorated, in its implementation, into trading arms for hostages. This runs counter to my own beliefs, to administration policy, and to the original strategy we had in mind. There are reasons why it happened, but no excuses. It was a mistake. . . .

Now, another major aspect of the Board's findings regards the transfer of funds to the Nicaraguan contras. The Tower board wasn't able to find out what happened to this money, so the facts here will be left to the continuing investigations of the court-appointed Independent Counsel and the two congressional investigating committees. I'm confident the truth will come out about this matter, as well. As I told the Tower board, I didn't know about any diversion of funds to the contras. But as President, I cannot escape responsibility.

Much has been said about my management style, a style that's worked successfully for me during 8 years as Governor of California and for most of my Presidency. The way I work is to identify the problem, find the right individuals to do the job, and then let them go to it. I've found this invariably brings out the best in people. They seem to rise to their full capability, and in the long run you get more done. . . .

I'm taking action in three basic areas: personnel, national security policy, and the process for making sure that the system works. First, personnel—I've brought in an accomplished and highly respected new team here at the White House. They bring new blood, new energy, and new credibility and experience. . . .

Now, what should happen when you make a mistake is this: You take your knocks, you learn your lessons, and then you move on. That's the healthiest way to deal with a problem. This in no way diminishes the importance of the other continuing investigations, but the business of our country and our people must proceed. I've gotten this message from Republicans and Democrats in Congress, from allies around the world, and—if we're reading the signals right—even from the Soviets. And of course, I've heard the message from you, the American people. You know, by the time you reach my age, you've made plenty of mistakes. And if you've lived your life properly—so, you learn. You put things in perspective. You pull your energies together. You change. You go forward.

Source: "Address to the Nation on the Iran Arms and Contra Aid Controversy," March 4, 1987, http://www.pbs.org/wgbh/americanexperience/features/primary-resources/reagan-iran-contra.

DOCUMENT 28.9

Oliver North | Testimony to Congress, July 1987

As the Iran-Contra scandal intensified, Lieutenant Colonel Oliver North appeared before the joint congressional committee in the summer of 1987 and admitted his role as a chief operator in the Iran-Contra affair. He also admitted that he had lied to Congress and had shredded incriminating documents, but he defended himself as a soldier in service to his country. North was eventually indicted and convicted on three felony counts, though his conviction was overturned on appeal.

QUESTION: Is it correct to say that following the enactment of the Boland Amendment, our support for the war in Nicaragua did not end and that you were the person in the United States Government who managed it?

Answer: Starting in the spring of 1984, well before the Boland proscription of no appropriated funds made available to the D.O.D. [Department of Defense] and the C.I.A. etc., I was already engaged in supporting the Nicaraguan resistance and the democratic outcome in Nicaragua. I did so as part of a covert operation. It was carried out starting as early as the spring of '84, when we ran out of money and people started to look in Nicaragua, in Honduras and Guatemala, El Salvador, and Costa Rica for some sign of what the Americans were really going to do, and that that help began much earlier than the most rigorous of the Boland proscriptions. And yes, it was carried out covertly, and it was carried out in such a way as to insure that the heads of state and the political leadership in Nicaragua—in Central America—recognized the United States was going to meet the commitments of the President's foreign policy.

And the President's foreign policy was that we are going to achieve a democratic outcome in Nicaragua and that our support for the Nicaraguan freedom fighters was going to continue, and that I was given the job of holding them together in body and soul. And it slowly transitioned into a more difficult task as time went on and as the C.I.A. had to withdraw further and further from that support, until finally we got to the point in October when I was the only person left talking to them. . . .

Question: Do you know whether or not the President was aware of your activities seeking funds and operational support for the contras, from third countries?

Answer: I do not know.

Question: Were you ever—

Answer: I assumed that he did.

Question: . . . What was the basis of your assumption?

Answer: Just that there was a lot going on and it was very obvious that the Nicaraguan resistance survived—I sent forward innumerable documents, some of which you've just shown us as exhibits, that demonstrated that I was keeping my superiors fully informed, as to what was going on.

Source: "Iran-Contra Hearings: 'I Came Here to Tell You the Truth'; The Colonel States His Case: Country and Orders above All," *New York Times*, July 8, 1987, A8.

George Mitchell | Response to Oliver North, 1987

Maine senator George Mitchell joined the joint House and Senate committee investigating the Iran-Contra affair in 1987. During Oliver North's testimony, Mitchell listened to North's characterization of his activities and support for the Contras as the true patriotic course of action. In Mitchell's response to North, he discusses the meaning of patriotism in a democratic society.

My time is nearly up and I want to make some closing observations, because you have, as I indicated, expressed several points of view with respect to which there are other points of view, and I think they ought to be expressed, and I would like to do that now.

You have talked here often and eloquently about the need for a democratic outcome in Nicaragua. There is no disagreement on that. There is disagreement as how best to achieve that objective. Many Americans agree with the President's policy; many do not. Many patriotic Americans, strongly anti-Communist, believe there's a better way to contain the Sandinistas, to bring about a democratic outcome in Nicaragua and to bring peace to Central America.

And many patriotic Americans are concerned that in the pursuit of democracy abroad we not compromise it in any way here at home. You and others have urged consistency in our policies, you have said repeatedly that if we are not consistent our allies and other nations will question our reliability. That is a real concern. But if it's bad to change policies, it's worse to have two different policies at the same time: one public policy and an opposite policy in private. It's difficult to conceive of a greater inconsistency than that. It's hard to imagine anything that would give our allies more cause to consider us unreliable than that we say one thing in public and secretly do the opposite. And that's exactly what was done when arms were sold to Iran and arms were swapped for hostages.

Now, you have talked a lot about patriotism and the love of our country. Most nations derive from a single tribe, a single race; they practice a single religion. Common racial, ethnic, religious heritages are the glue of nationhood for many. The United States is different; we have all races, all religions, we have a limited common heritage. The glue of nationhood for us is the American ideal of individual liberty and equal justice. The rule of law is critical in our society. It's the great equalizer, because in America everybody is equal before the law. We must never allow the end to justify the means where the law is concerned. However important and noble an objective, and surely democracy abroad is important and is noble, it cannot be achieved at the expense of the rule of law in our country. And our diversity is very broad.

You talked about your background and it was really very compelling, and is obviously one of the reasons why the American people are attracted to you.

Let me tell you a story from my background. Before I entered the Senate, I had the great honor of serving as a federal judge. In that position I had great power. The one I most enjoyed exercising was the power to make people American citizens. From time to time I presided at what we call naturalization ceremonies; they're citizenship ceremonies. These are people who came from all over the world, risked their lives, sometimes left their families and their fortunes behind to come here. They had gone through the required procedures, and I, in the final act, administered to them the oath of allegiance to the United States, and I made them American citizens. To this moment, to this moment it was the most exciting thing I've ever done in my life.

Ceremonies were always moving for me because my mother was an immigrant, my father the orphan son of immigrants. Neither of them had any education, and they worked at very menial tasks in our society. But because of the openness of America, because of equal justice under law in America, I sit here today a United States Senator. And after every one of these ceremonies I made it a point to speak to these new Americans, I asked them why they came, how they came, and their stories, each of them, were inspiring. I think you would be interested and moved by them given the views you have expressed on this country.

And when I asked them why they came they said several things, mostly two. The first is they said we came because here in America everybody has a chance, opportunity. And they also said over and over again, particularly people from totalitarian societies, we came here because here in America you can criticize the government without looking over your shoulder. Freedom to disagree with the government.

Now, you have addressed several pleas to this committee, very eloquently. None more eloquent than last Friday when in response to a question by Representative [Richard] Cheney you asked that Congress not cut off aid to the Contras for the love of God and for the love of country. I now address a plea to you. Of all the qualities which the American people find compelling about you, none is more impressive than your obvious deep devotion to this country. Please remember that others share that devotion and recognize that it is possible for an American to disagree with you on aid to the Contras and still love God and still love this country just as much as you do.

Although he's regularly asked to do so, God does not take sides in American politics. And in America, disagreement with the policies of the government is not evidence of lack of patriotism.

I want to repeat that: in America, disagreement with the policies of the Government is not evidence of lack of patriotism.

Indeed, it is the very fact that Americans can criticize their government openly and without fear of reprisal that is the essence of our freedom, and that will keep us free.

Now, I have one final plea. Debate this issue forcefully and vigorously as you have and as you surely will, but, please, do it in a way that respects the patriotism and the motives of those who disagree with you, as you would have them respect yours.

Source: Iran-Contra Investigation, Joint Hearings Part II, July 10, 13, and 14, 1987: Continued Testimony of Oliver L. North and Robert C. McFarlane, 31–46.

Interpret the Evidence

1. What was the goal of the Boland Amendment (Document 28.5), and was its wording sufficient to meet that goal? Why or why not?

2. What, if anything, surprises you about the Freedom Fighter's Manual (Document 28.6)? Why would it focus on these specific activities, and do you think they were effective?

3. What does the Tower Commission conclude about Ronald Reagan's management style (Document 28.7)? How does Reagan respond (Document 28.8)?

4. Why did Oliver North assume that President Reagan knew about his activities (Document 28.9)? How does his testimony compare with what Reagan says he knew (Document 28.8)? Can they both be right?

5. Why does George Mitchell focus on the rule of law in his speech (Document 28.10)? How does he relate that idea to patriotism?

Put It in Context

• Compare the Iran-Contra scandal with Watergate (chapter 27). How did Reagan's presidency survive such a scandal when Nixon's did not?

background photo: page 919, Library of Congress

LEARNINGCurve
Check what you know.
bedfordstmartins.com/hewittlawson/LC

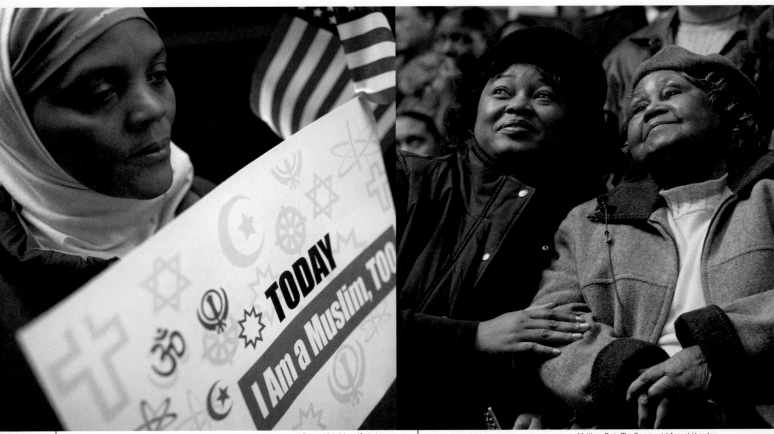

Robert Nickelsberg/Getty Images

Matthew Craig/The Commercial Appeal / Landov

One of many demonstrators of all faiths marching against the House Committee on Homeland Security's hearings on the radicalization of American Muslims, 2011.

A mother and daughter watch the inauguration of President Barack Obama at the National Civil Rights Museum in Memphis, Tennessee, 2009.

29

The Challenges of a New Century

1993 to the present

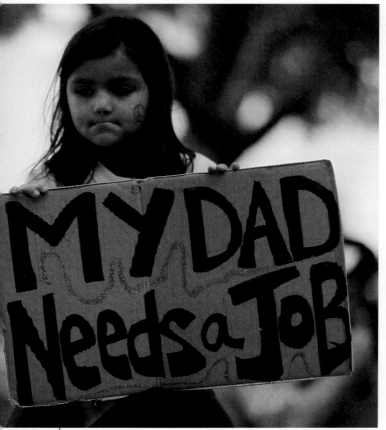

A girl sits on her father's shoulders at an Occupy Miami protest in Miami, Florida, 2011.

AMERICAN HISTORIES

William Henry Gates III started tinkering with computers at age thirteen. At that time in the late 1960s, computers were big, bulky machines that filled entire rooms. As a teenager in 1969, the enterprising Gates and some of his friends set up a business to make computerized traffic counters to gauge the speed of automobiles and other vehicles, for which they earned $20,000.

His brilliant mathematical mind and entrepreneurial inclinations led Gates to enroll at Harvard, where those same qualities soon led him to drop out. He spent more time at the university's computer center than he did in class, and in 1974 he became interested in microcomputers as an alternative to large conventional computers. A year later, Gates went to Albuquerque, New Mexico, and formed a computer software company called Microsoft (an amalgam of *microcomputer* and *software*). He envisioned the microcomputer on every office desktop and in homes throughout America. Gates actively pursued the lucrative financial rewards that microcomputers would bring, in contrast to other microcomputer pioneers who did not seek commercial gain and shared information and software with one another freely and unconditionally.

Bill Gates succeeded beyond all expectations. In 1980 Microsoft, now headquartered in Redmond, Washington, collaborated with International Business Machines (IBM) to create a software package for IBM's new line of personal computers. Additional technological breakthroughs came rapidly. Microsoft joined the financial boom of the 1980s and in 1986 became a publicly traded company on the New York Stock Exchange. Within a

Bill Gates and
Kristen Breitweiser

decade, Gates became the richest man in America, and like other industrial titans a century earlier, he has donated generously to fund philanthropic activities worldwide.

Despite the enormous benefits of computer technology, the digital revolution has had unforeseen consequences. The terrorists who attacked the World Trade Center and the Pentagon on September 11, 2001, communicated through e-mail and cell phones and trained on computerized flight simulators. They belonged to al-Qaeda, an international terror network that spread its ideology and raised and transferred money over the Internet.

Kristen Breitweiser was a young housewife and mother living in suburban New Jersey on September 11, 2001 (9/11). Her husband, Ron, a senior vice president at an investment management service, worked in Tower Two of the World Trade Center. When one of the planes commandeered by terrorists crashed into the building, her husband died in the fiery collapse of the building, leaving her a widow with a two-year-old daughter. Breitweiser's loss transformed her from a grieving victim and a stay-at-home mother into a political activist.

She started attending meetings of the Victim Compensation Fund established by the federal government following 9/11. She met Mindy Kleinberg, Lorie Van Auken, and Patty Casazza, widows like herself living in New Jersey. The "Jersey Girls," as they became known, addressed concerns over victims' compensation but soon confronted larger political issues. Seeking more than financial compensation for their losses, they demanded to know how the 9/11 attacks could have happened and what the federal government might have done to prevent them. Breitweiser and her colleagues favored an investigation by an independent commission to gather information about what had occurred and to make recommendations to prevent other attacks. However, they found themselves in opposition to President George W. Bush, who initially resisted the creation of such a commission.

Undeterred, the four women mounted a vigorous campaign to pressure the White House and Congress to form a national commission. Breitweiser testified before the Joint Congressional Intelligence Committee to garner support. The women's perseverance paid off: In November 2002, Congress established a bipartisan commission that President Bush signed into law.

However, the commission's final report in 2004 disappointed Breitweiser. She called the report "hollow" and criticized President Bush for not fully and openly cooperating with the investigation. Although Breitweiser had voted for Bush in the 2000 election and considered herself a conservative, her rapid political education since 9/11 turned her against his candidacy in 2004. She also spoke out against the Iraq War, which the administration had initiated in 2003 in response to the 9/11 attacks. Breitweiser continued her political activism as a blog writer for *The Huffington Post*. In this way, this housewife from New Jersey shared her views with millions of people through technology that Bill Gates's generation had developed. •

photos: Dennis Brack/Landov; Reuters/Hyungwon Kang/Landov

THE AMERICAN HISTORIES of Bill Gates and Kristen Breitweiser were deeply affected by the twin forces of digital technology and terror that dominated life in the United States and throughout the world at the start of the twenty-first century. Computers, the Internet, and cell phone technology reformulated commerce and social relations, fostering the globalization that emerged after the Cold War (see chapter 28). Google, the Web, Facebook, and Twitter became household words and broke down domestic and global barriers that twentieth-century technology had not yet demolished. Computer technology revolutionized political communication and organization, mobilized ordinary citizens into action, and expanded opportunities for disgruntled and oppressed citizens of foreign countries to overthrow despotic rulers. Driven by new computer models for trading in financial securities, the stock market grew highly volatile, and downturns in the economy became greater in intensity and scope. At the same time, the threat of terrorism continued to preoccupy the United States and its allies around the world, and their governments used the latest technologies to monitor suspected terrorists. Ordinary people paid for this increased surveillance each time they boarded an airplane and were subjected to intimate security searches.

Transforming American Society

The decade of the 1990s was a period of great economic growth and technological advancement in the United States. Computers stood at the center of the technological revolution of the late twentieth and early twenty-first centuries, allowing both small and large businesses to reach new markets and transform the workplace. Digital technology also altered the personal habits of individuals in the way they worked, purchased goods and services, communicated, and spent their leisure time. As the Internet and World Wide Web connected Americans to the rest of the world, corporate leaders embraced globalization as the key to economic prosperity. They put together business mergers so that their companies could operate more powerfully in the international market. Government officials generally supported their efforts by reducing regulations on business and financial practices, thus encouraging greater risk taking and easing the way for freer trade overseas. Globalization not only thrust American business enterprises outward but also brought a new population of immigrants to the United States.

The Computer Revolution

The first working computers were developed for military purposes during World War II and the Cold War and were enormous in size and cost. Engineers began to resolve the size issue with the creation of transistors. Invented by Bell Laboratories in the late 1940s, these silicon pieces of equipment came into widespread use in running computers during the 1960s. As companies manufactured smaller and smaller silicon chips, computers became faster, cheaper, and more reliable. The design of integrated circuits in the 1970s led to the production of microcomputers in which a silicon chip the size of a nail head did the work once performed by huge computers. Bill Gates was not the only one to recognize the potential market of microcomputers for home and business use. Steve Jobs, like Gates a college dropout, founded Apple Computer Company in 1976. By 1980 the company had become a publicly traded corporation, turning its founder into a multimillionaire.

Microchips and digital technology found a market beyond home and office computers. Beginning in the 1980s, computers replaced the mechanical devices that ran household appliances such as washing machines, dishwashers, and refrigerators. Over the next twenty years, computers operated everything from standard appliances such as televisions and telephones, to new electronic gadgets such as VCR and CD players, fax machines, cell phones, and iPods. Computers controlled traffic lights on the streets and air traffic in the skies. They changed the leisure patterns of youth: Many young people preferred to play video games at home, rather than engage in outside activities. Consumers purchased goods online, and companies such as Amazon sold merchandise through cyberspace without any actual retail stores. Computers became the stars of movies such as *The Matrix* (1999), *A.I. Artificial Intelligence* (2001), and *Iron Man* (2008). In 2010 *The Social Network* became a hit in portraying the life of Mark Zuckerberg, the primary developer of the social media Web site Facebook, which in 2012 had 900 million users worldwide.

The Internet—an open, global series of interconnected computer networks that transmit data, information, electronic mail, and other services—made social networking possible. The Internet grew out of military research in the 1970s, when the Department of Defense constructed a system of computer servers connected to one another throughout the United States. The main objective of this network was to preserve military communications in the event of a Soviet nuclear attack. At the end of the Cold War, the Internet was repurposed for nonmilitary use, and it now links government, academic, business, and organizational systems. In 1991 the World Wide Web came into existence as a way to access the Internet and share documents and images. Search engines like Google and Yahoo were developed to allow computer users to "surf the Net" and gain access to Web pages. Consumers could shop online as they once had in stores, and researchers could find information previously available only in libraries. Politicians learned how to use the Internet to raise campaign funds and spread their messages to voters more widely and more quickly than they had been able to do in person or on television. Terrorist groups, such as al-Qaeda, also went online. In 2010 around 75 percent of people in the United States used the Internet, as did nearly 2 billion people worldwide, about a quarter of the globe's population.

The Digital Revolution

Digital technology revolutionized business and personal communications. Introduced in the 1990s, smartphones combine the functions of cell phones with those of a computer, and they appeal to users of all ages. Using their smartphones, this family can make phone calls, send text messages, take photos and videos, listen to music, surf the Web, and download applications. Compassionate Eye Foundation/Jetta Productions/Getty Images

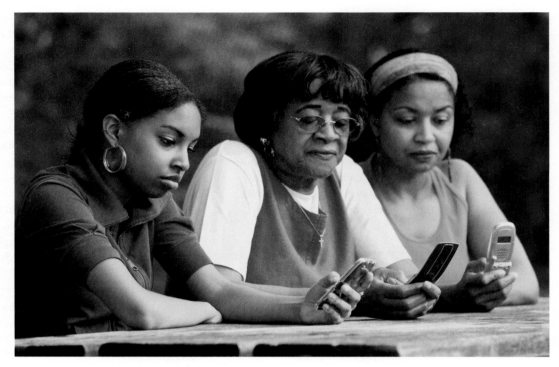

Digital communication revolutionized globalization. Bill Gates's computer software programs, along with the Internet and World Wide Web, dramatically reduced the time it took for trading partners around the world to converse and make business decisions. Consumers in the United States called customer service operators stationed in India and other remote sites. E-mail largely replaced postal mail, allowing Americans to instantly contact relatives, friends, or professional and business associates around the country or the world.

Business Consolidation

The incredible growth of the computer industry led to increased business consolidation, making it possible for large firms to communicate instantly within the United States and throughout the world and to keep control over their far-flung operations. In addition, the federal government aided the merger process by relaxing financial regulation. Media companies took the greatest advantage of this situation. In 1990 the giant Warner Communications merged with Time Life to create an entertainment empire that included a film studio (Warner Brothers), a television cable network (Home Box Office), a music company (Atlantic Records), a baseball team (the Atlanta Braves), and several magazines (*Time, Sports Illustrated*, and *People*). Before Warner Communications combined with the Internet service provider America Online (AOL) in

2006, it had topped $21 billion annually in sales. Several other media conglomerates formed during this period as well. The Australian-born Rupert Murdoch, who already owned considerable holdings in his home country and in Great Britain, moved his operations to the United States. Murdoch soon purchased the Fox Broadcasting Company to go along with a satellite dish company; a movie studio; a variety of newspapers, including the *New York Post* and the *Wall Street Journal*; and thirty television stations. Media mergers mirrored the trend in the rest of the economy. The estimated number of business mergers rose dramatically from 1,529 in 1991 to 4,500 in 1998. The market value of these transactions in 1998 was approximately $2 trillion, compared with $600 billion for 1989, the previous peak year for consolidation.

Corporate consolidation brought corporate malfeasance, as some chief executives of major companies abused their power by expanding their companies too quickly and making risky financial deals, which put workers and stockholders in jeopardy. Such practices led to a number of scandals, including one involving Enron. Enron was the product of a merger in 1985 between Houston Natural Gas and InterNorth, a gas company headquartered in Omaha, Nebraska. Operating out of Houston, Texas, Enron benefited from the deregulation of the gas and electric industry in the 1990s, which brought exorbitant profits and encouraged corporate greed. As Enron thrived, its prices shot up and its stock soared, earning the company more than

$50 billion in 2001. In October of that year, information began to trickle out about insider trading, faulty business deals, and questionable accounting practices. As these revelations mounted, Enron's stock and its credit rating plunged, jeopardizing the solvency of the company. In December 2001, the once mighty Enron filed for bankruptcy and fired four thousand employees; its top two executives were subsequently convicted on charges of criminal fraud. This scandal affected companies beyond Enron, leading to the conviction of executives from Enron's accounting firm, Arthur Andersen, and another Andersen client, WorldCom.

The Changing American Population

At the same time as the technological revolution helped transform the U.S. economy and society, an influx of immigrants began to greatly alter the composition of the American population. Since passage of the Immigration Act of 1965 (see chapter 26), the country had experienced a wave of immigration comparable to that at the turn of the twentieth century. As the population of the United States grew from 202 million to 300 million between 1970 and 2006, immigrants accounted for some 28 million of the increase. They came to live in the United States for much the same reasons as those who had journeyed before: to seek economic opportunity and to find political and religious freedom.

Most newcomers who came in the 1980s and 1990s arrived from Latin America and South and East Asia; relatively few Europeans (approximately 2 million) moved to the United States, though their numbers increased after the collapse of the Soviet empire in the early 1990s. Poverty and political unrest pushed migrants out of Mexico, Central America, and the Caribbean. The prizewinning film *El Norte* (1983) dramatized the plight of undocumented Guatemalan Indians who traveled through Mexico to settle in California. Yet most others took advantage of a provision in the 1965 act that permitted them to join family members already settled in the United States. At the beginning of the twenty-first century, Latinos (35 million) had surpassed African Americans (34 million) as the nation's largest minority group. However, with the arrival of Caribbean

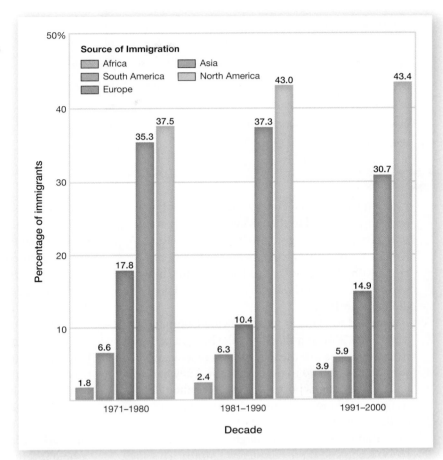

FIGURE 29.1   Immigrant Growth by Home Region, 1971–2000

In the late twentieth century, immigration to the United States increased significantly, especially from North America (which in this figure includes Mexico, Central America, and the Caribbean). Residents of East and South Asia formed the second largest group of immigrants while Africans arrived in small but growing numbers.   Source: Data from *2000 Statistical Yearbook of the Immigration and Naturalization Service.*

and African immigrants, black America was also becoming more diverse in this period.

Explore

See Document 29.1 for one immigrant's experience in low-wage factory work.

In addition to the 16 million immigrants who came from south of the U.S. border, another 9 million headed eastward from Asian nations, including China, South Korea, and the Philippines, together with refugees from the Vietnam War and Cambodia. By 2007 an estimated 1.6 million Indians from South Asia had immigrated to the United States, most arriving after the 1960s. Indian Americans became the third-largest Asian American group behind Chinese and Filipinos. Another 1 to 2 million people came from predominantly Islamic nations such as Pakistan, Lebanon, Iraq, and Iran (Figure 29.1).

DOCUMENT 29.1

Bo Yee | The New American Sweatshop, 1994

Bo Yee came to the United States from Hong Kong and worked as a seamstress. When her employer laid off workers without paying back wages Yee joined with a local immigrant women's organization to fight for outstanding payments. In a 1994 interview she described conditions in the California garment factory where she was paid five dollars to create dresses that retailed for $175.

Explore

I started working at a factory a month after I got here. I immigrated to the US because of my two sons. They were not going to be happy in Hong Kong after the 1997 changeover [the transfer of Hong Kong from the United Kingdom to China]. My husband did not want to come to the US but he did come in 1985.

I started working at Lucky Sewing Company in June 1986. Working there was like being a prisoner in a sealed cage. All the windows were locked. They wouldn't let you go to the bathroom. They had "No loud talking" signs posted. There were about 20 of us there working ten hours a day, seven days a week, endlessly, without rest. Most of the workers were from mainland China, although some came from Hong Kong and there were a few Latinos. The boss' wife created a tense, competitive atmosphere between the workers. She would praise some people and downgrade others. Because of my experience, I can work faster than newer workers from China

who are not as skillful. They would sacrifice their lunch and break time to catch up. I hated the way the boss made us compete. There were three of us in one department who had to produce 200 pieces. They would push us to see who could finish first. They were getting people to exploit themselves. How disgusting! I hate this!

I couldn't communicate with the Latino workers, but you can have fun without speaking each other's language. You motion. You use body language and whatever method you can. The relations with Latinos were better. We were not forced to compete with each other.

I thought America was a very advanced country, but working in sweatshops here, I see that the garment industry is very backward compared to Hong Kong.

Source: Miriam Ching Yoon Louie, *Sweatshop Warriors: Immigrant Women Workers Take On the Global Factory* (Cambridge, MA: South End Press, 2001), 49–50.

Interpret the Evidence

- Why did Yee come to the United States?
- How did Yee's boss get workers to exploit themselves?

Put It in Context

Compare Yee's experience to sweatshops that existed a century earlier in the United States as described in chapter 18.

Like their predecessors, new immigrants formed ethnic and religious enclaves. California displayed this fresh face of immigration most vividly. Latinos and Asians had long settled there, and by 2001, 27 percent of the state's population was foreign-born. The majority of Californians consisted of Latinos, Asian Americans, and African Americans, with whites in the minority. In addition to California and the Southwest, immigrants flocked to northeastern and midwestern cities—New York City, Jersey City, Chicago, and Detroit—as they had in the past. However, they now fanned out through the Southeast, adding to the growing populations of Atlanta, Raleigh-Durham, Charlotte, Columbia, and Memphis and providing these cities with an unprecedented ethnic mixture. Like immigrants before them, they created their own businesses, spoke their own languages, and retained their own religious and cultural practices.

They also encountered hostility from many native-born Americans. Some workers felt threatened by immigrants who took jobs, both commercial and agricultural, at lower wages. Middle-class taxpayers complained that the flood of impoverished immigrants placed the burden on them to fund the social services—schools, welfare, public health—that the newcomers required. Some of the children and grandchildren of immigrants who had assimilated into American culture resented foreigners who pushed for bilingual education and public signs and instructions in their native languages. Immigration critics also complained about the influx of illegal foreign residents among the immigrant population. Besides breaking the law, these critics argued, undocumented immigrants further depressed wages and taxed public resources.

California led the way in rolling back the effects of immigration. In 1986 Californians approved Proposition 63, which declared English to be the state's official language. Thirty states passed similar laws. In 1994 California voters approved Proposition 186, which prohibited illegal residents from attending public schools and using any social services except emergency health facilities. This proposal never went into effect because federal courts ruled it unconstitutional. Also, some conservative Republicans like President Ronald Reagan, former governor of California, along with agribusiness and other corporate interests that relied on cheap immigrant labor to keep their operating costs low, opposed such severe measures.

REVIEW & RELATE

How have computers changed life in the United States?

How has globalization affected business consolidation and immigration?

✔ *LEARNINGCurve* bedfordstmartins.com/hewittlawson/LC

Politics at the End of the Twentieth Century

The baby boom generation that produced Bill Gates and Kristen Breitweiser also brought President Bill Clinton (and his successors George W. Bush and Barack Obama). The first president born after 1945, Clinton had to deal with the challenges facing the post–Cold War world. He embraced globalization as the key to economic prosperity and showed his readiness to promote and defend U.S. national security. Despite achieving general prosperity and peace, Clinton could not escape the political polarization that divided the American electorate, and his tenure in office only made this schism worse.

The Clinton Presidency

Born in Arkansas in 1946, William Jefferson (Bill) Clinton served six terms as Democratic governor of his home state. As governor, Clinton spoke out for equal opportunity and improved education and economic development. After defeating President George H. W. Bush in 1992 (see chapter 27), Clinton entered the White House brimming with energy and enthusiasm. An admirer of President John F. Kennedy, Clinton echoed Kennedy's sentiments in his inaugural address: "Today a new generation raised in the shadow of the Cold War assumes new responsibilities in a world warmed by the sunshine of freedom but threatened still by ancient hatreds and new plagues."

President Clinton failed in his first attempt to achieve his goals. Against powerful congressional opposition, he backed away from ordering the admission of gays and lesbians into the military, though many already served secretly. Under pressure, the president instead devised the policy of **"don't ask, don't tell,"** which permitted homosexuals to serve in the armed forces so long as they kept their sexual orientation a secret. Gay service members did not benefit from this compromise and continued to encounter discrimination in the military.

Clinton had even less success in reforming health care. Since President Harry Truman had first proposed a system of universal health care coverage in the late 1940s (see chapter 24), the American Medical Association and private insurance companies had succeeded in blocking passage of this and all subsequent plans, despite the general approval of the American public. The Clinton administration recommended a system of universal medical coverage based on "managed competition"—the establishment of regional health care cooperatives to purchase low-cost, private insurance paid for largely by employers. Although Clinton's plan did not advocate "socialized medicine" (government-run medical care) as many critics charged, the plan nonetheless went down to defeat.

President Clinton was more successful in achieving his goals in other areas, some of which were no less controversial. In 1993, reversing Reagan-Bush policies, President Clinton signed executive orders allowing physicians in federally funded clinics to advise patients about abortion; authorizing military hospitals to perform abortions; and funding UN programs that included abortions. Clinton also demonstrated that women's rights were not incompatible with family values. He approved the 1993 Family and Medical Leave Act, which allowed parents to take up to twelve weeks of unpaid leave to care for newborn children without risk of losing their jobs.

Clinton tried to appeal to voters across the political spectrum on other issues. He signed a tough anticrime law that funded the recruitment of an additional 100,000 police officers to patrol city streets, while supporting gun control legislation. Managing to overcome the powerful lobby of the National Rifle Association, in 1993 Clinton signed the Brady Bill (named after Ronald Reagan's aide who was shot in the attempted assassination of the president in 1981), which banned the sale of semiautomatic weapons and imposed a five-day waiting period to check the background of gun buyers.

The president achieved even greater success in promoting racial diversity. He appointed African Americans to high-level positions in his cabinet—his selection of four African Americans at one time was unprecedented. His "rainbow administration" welcomed women and minorities to other important posts. Born in the segregated South, Clinton had become a strong advocate of affirmative action and did what he could to protect it from conservative challenges in the states and the courts.

Clinton's fiscal policies ushered in a period of economic growth and prosperity, which ended the recession of the early 1990s. With congressional support, the president reduced domestic and defense spending by $500 billion, while raising taxes on wealthy individuals and corporations. By the end of the 1990s, the Clinton administration had eliminated the deficit, the gross domestic product was rising 3 percent annually, unemployment dropped from 6 percent to 4 percent, and the stock market reached record highs.

President Clinton's accomplishments aroused fierce opposition from conservatives. Right-wing talk radio hosts criticized the president and his wife, Hillary Rodham Clinton, a lawyer and leader in the effort to reform health care. Conservatives blamed Clinton for all they considered wrong in society—feminism, abortion, affirmative action, and secularism. Rush Limbaugh, a popular conservative talk-show host, donned the self-proclaimed mantle of the "angry white male." His rhetoric respected few boundaries, even on publicly owned airwaves, where he uttered comments such as "Feminism was established to allow unattractive women access to mainstream society." Clinton's personal life also provided ammunition for his opponents. Rumors of marital infidelity hounded him, and questions about his and his wife's pre-presidential dealings in a controversial real estate development project known as Whitewater prompted the appointment in 1994 of a special prosecutor to investigate allegations of impropriety.

Facing conservative opposition, the president and the Democratic Party fared poorly in the 1994 congressional elections. Republicans, led by House Minority Leader Newt Gingrich of Georgia, championed the **Contract with America**. This document embraced conservative principles of a constitutional amendment for a balanced budget, reduced welfare spending, lower taxes, and term limits for lawmakers. Democrats lost fifty-four seats in the House, and for the first time since 1952 Republicans captured a majority of both houses of Congress. This election also underscored the increasing electoral influence of white evangelical Christians, who turned out to vote in large numbers for Republican candidates.

Stung by this defeat, Clinton tried to outmaneuver congressional Republicans by shifting rightward politically and championing welfare reform. In 1996 he signed the **Personal Responsibility and Work Opportunity Reconciliation Act**, which abolished the Aid to Families with Dependent Children provision of the Social Security law, the basis for welfare in the United States since the New Deal. The measure required adults on the welfare rolls to find work within two years or lose the benefits provided to families earning less than $7,700. Welfare had provided Republicans with a wedge issue to divide the Democratic electorate, and Clinton diminished its effect by supporting reform. Also in 1996, the president approved the Defense of Marriage Act, which denied married same-sex couples the federal benefits granted to heterosexual married couples, including Social Security survivor's benefits.

In adopting such positions as deficit reduction, welfare reform, and antigay legislation, Clinton ensured his reelection in 1996. Running against Republican senator Robert Dole of Kansas, a military veteran of World War II, and the independent candidate Ross Perot, Clinton captured 49 percent of the popular vote and 379 electoral votes. Dole received 41 percent of the vote, and Perot came in a distant third with 8 percent, a sharp decline from the 19 percent he had received four years earlier (see chapter 27).

Global Challenges and Economic Renewal

Clinton faced numerous foreign policy challenges during his two terms in office. As the first president elected to office in the post–Cold War era, Clinton could approach trouble spots without the rigid anti-Communist views of his predecessors. Increasingly, the problems facing the United States did not result from customary military aggression by one nation against another; rather, the greatest threats came from the implosion of national governments into factionalism and genocide, as well as the dangers posed by Islamic extremists.

At first, the Clinton administration acted cautiously. During a civil war in the African nation of Rwanda, Hutu extremists dispatched armed militias to exterminate the ethnic Tutsi population. The United States watched from the sidelines, along with most of the rest of the world. The slaughter of more than 800,000 Tutsis and moderate Hutus brought condemnation but little action other than the United Nations' attempt to evacuate refugees from the massacre. Following this tragedy, Hollywood told the story of this genocide in the movie *Hotel Rwanda* (2004), which occasioned sympathy for the plight of the Rwandan victims, if not shame for the inaction of the United States.

By contrast, Clinton responded boldly to violence in the Balkans, an area considered more vital to U.S. national security than Rwanda. Along with the collapse of Eastern European regimes in 1989, Yugoslavia splintered into religious and ethnic pieces after the crumbling of the ruling Communist regime. The predominantly Roman Catholic states of Slovenia and Croatia declared their independence from the largely Russian Orthodox Serbian population in Yugoslavia. In 1992 the mainly Muslim territory of Bosnia-Herzegovina also broke away, much to the chagrin of its substantial Serbian population (Map 29.1). This unleashed a civil war between Serb and Croatian minorities and the Muslim-dominated Bosnian government. Supported by Slobodan Milošević, the leader of the neighboring province of Serbia, Bosnian Serbs wrested control of large parts of the region and slaughtered tens of thousands of Muslims through what they euphemistically called **ethnic cleansing**.

MAP 29.1   The Breakup of Yugoslavia, 1991–2008
With the collapse of Communist control of Yugoslavia in 1989, the country splintered along ethnic and religious lines, eventually forming seven separate nations. A civil war between Serbia and Croatia ended in 1995, but Serbs then attacked Muslims in Bosnia and Kosovo.

In 1995, following three years of violence, Clinton sponsored NATO bombing raids against the Serbs and dispatched 20,000 American troops as part of a multilateral peacekeeping force. At the same time, the president brokered a peace agreement, known as the **Dayton Peace Accords**, among Serbia, Croatia, and Bosnia at a conference in Dayton, Ohio. In 1999 renewed conflict erupted when Milošević's Serbian government attacked the province of Kosovo to eliminate its Albanian Muslim residents. Clinton and NATO responded by initiating air strikes against the Serbs and placing troops on the ground, actions that preserved Kosovo's independence. (Milošević was later brought before the World Court to face trial for war crimes but died before the court reached a verdict.)

The United States faced an even graver danger from Islamic extremists intent on waging a religious struggle (jihad) of terror against their perceived enemies and establishing a transnational Muslim government, or caliphate. Former presidents Jimmy Carter in Iran and Ronald Reagan in Lebanon had experienced the wrath of radical Muslims (see chapter 28). The United States' close relationship with Israel placed it high on the list of terrorist targets, along with pro-American Muslim governments in Egypt, Pakistan, and Indonesia. In 1993 Islamic militants orchestrated the bombing of the World Trade Center's underground garage, which killed six people and injured more than one thousand. Five years later, terrorists blew up American embassies in the African nations of Kenya and Tanzania, killing hundreds and injuring thousands of local workers and residents. In retaliation, Clinton ordered air strikes against terrorist bases in Sudan and Afghanistan. However, the danger persisted. In 2000 al-Qaeda terrorists blew a gaping hole in the side of the USS *Cole*, a U.S. destroyer anchored in Yemen, killing seventeen American sailors.

International terrorism did not lead to the undoing of President Clinton, but more mundane, sexual indiscretions nearly brought him down. Starting in 1995, Clinton had engaged in consensual sexual relations with Monica Lewinsky, a twenty-two-year-old White House intern. Clinton denied these charges under oath and before a national television audience, but when Lewinsky testified about the details of their sexual encounters, the president recanted his earlier statements that he had never had "sexual relations with *that* woman." After an independent prosecutor concluded that Clinton had committed perjury and obstructed justice, the Republican-controlled House voted to impeach the president on December 19, 1998, the first time it had done so in 130 years (see chapter 14). However, on February 12, 1999, Republicans in the Senate failed to muster the necessary two-thirds vote to convict Clinton on the impeachment charges.

Despite his impeachment, Clinton left the country in more prosperous shape than he had found it. At the height of the sex scandal in 1998, the unemployment rate fell to 4.3 percent, the lowest level since the early 1970s. The rate of home ownership reached a record-setting nearly 67 percent. As the "misery index"—a compilation of unemployment and inflation—fell, the gross domestic product grew by more than $250 billion. By 1999 the stock market's Dow Jones average reached a historic 10,000 points, up 2,000 points from just two years before. The Clinton administration boasted that its economic policies had succeeded in canceling the Reagan-Bush budget deficit, yielding a surplus of $230 billion for the fiscal year 2000. This boom, however, did not affect everyone equally. African Americans and Latinos lagged behind whites economically. The gap between rich and poor widened, as the wealthiest 13,000 American families earned as much income as the poorest 20 million. Despite these shortcomings, most Americans seemed pleased with the economic renaissance of the Clinton years.

REVIEW & RELATE

How did conflicts between Democrats and Republicans affect President Clinton's accomplishments?
How did the end of the Cold War shape President Clinton's foreign policies?

 LEARNINGCurve bedfordstmartins.com/hewittlawson/LC

The New Millennium

Following the prosperous but turbulent Clinton years, Americans looked forward to celebrating the new millennium with hope for the future. Yet this did not happen. Within two years, the country endured a bruising presidential election, experienced unprecedented terrorism at home, and engaged in two wars abroad. The second baby boomer president, George W. Bush, left the country as politically divided as had his predecessor.

George W. Bush and Compassionate Conservatism

In the first presidential election of the new century, the Democratic candidate, Vice President Al Gore, ran against George W. Bush, the Republican governor of Texas and son of the forty-first president. This election marked the first contest between members of the baby boom generation, but in many ways politics remained the same. Candidates began

to use the latest technology—the Internet and sophisticated phone banks to mobilize voters—but they rehashed issues stemming from the Clinton years. Gore ran on the coattails of the Clinton prosperity, endorsed affirmative action, was pro-choice on women's reproductive rights, and warned of the need to protect the environment. Presenting himself as a "compassionate conservative," Bush opposed abortion, gay rights, and affirmative action while at the same time supporting faith-based reform initiatives in education and social welfare. Also in the race was Ralph Nader, an anticorporate activist who ran under the banner of the Green Party, a party formed in 1991 in support of grassroots democracy, environmentalism, social justice, and gender equality. According to Nader, Gore and Bush were "Tweedledee and Tweedledum—they look and act the same, so it doesn't matter who you get." Despite this claim, Nader appealed to much the same constituency as did Gore.

Nader's candidacy drew votes away from Gore, but fraud and partisanship hurt the Democrats even more. Gore won a narrow plurality of the popular vote (48.4 percent) compared with 47.8 percent for Bush and 2.7 percent for Nader. However, Bush won a slim majority of the electoral votes: 271 to 267. The key state in this Republican victory was Florida, where Bush outpolled Gore by fewer than 500 popular votes. Counties with high proportions of African Americans and the poor encountered the greatest difficulty and outright discrimination in voting, and in these areas voters were more likely to support Gore. A subsequent recount of the vote might have benefited Bush because Republicans controlled the state government. (Jeb Bush, the Republican candidate's younger brother, was Florida's governor, and Republicans held a majority in the legislature.) Eventually, litigation over the recount reached the U.S. Supreme Court, and on December 12, 2000, more than a month after the election, the Court proclaimed Bush the winner in a decision that clearly reflected the preferences of the conservative justices appointed by Ronald Reagan and George H. W. Bush.

George W. Bush did not view his slim, contested victory cautiously. Rather, he intended to appeal mainly to his conservative political base and govern as boldly as if he had received a resounding electoral mandate. Republicans still controlled the House, whereas a Republican defection in the Senate gave the Democrats a one-vote majority. According to the veteran political reporter Ronald Brownstein, Bush and his congressional leaders "would rather pass legislation as close as possible to his preferences on a virtual party-line basis than make concessions to reduce political tensions or broaden his support among Democrats."

The president promoted the agenda of the evangelical Christian wing of the Republican Party. He spoke out against gay marriage, abortion, and federal support for stem cell

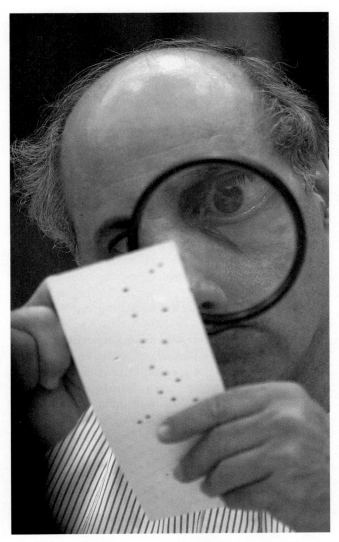

Hanging Chads and the 2000 Presidential Election

The outcome of the 2000 presidential election between George W. Bush and Al Gore hinged on who won Florida. The closeness of the vote required a recount, and election officials, including this one in Broward County, had to scrutinize ballots closely to figure out the intentions of voters who left a hanging chad (paper fragment) on the punch-card ballot.   AP Photo/Alan Diaz

research, a scientific procedure that used discarded embryos to find cures for diseases. The president created a special office in the White House to coordinate faith-based initiatives, programs that provided religious institutions with federal funds for social service activities without violating the First Amendment's separation of church and state.

At the turn of the twenty-first century, a growing number of churchgoers were attending **megachurches**. These congregations, mainly Protestant, each contained 2,000 or more worshippers and reflected the American impulse for building large-scale organizations, the same passion for size as could be seen in corporate consolidations. Between 1970 and 2005, the number of megachurches jumped from 50 to more than 1,300, with California, Texas, and Florida taking the lead. The establishment of massive churches was part of a worldwide movement, with South Korea home to the largest congregation. Joel Osteen—the evangelical pastor of Lakewood Church in Houston, Texas, the largest megachurch in the United States—drew average weekly audiences of 43,000 people, with sermons available in English and Spanish. Preaching in a former professional basketball arena and using the latest technology, Osteen stood under giant video screens that projected his image. He and other pastors of megachurches have earned enormous wealth from preaching and writing, which their followers consider justified. "Many preachers tell us that God loves us, but Osteen makes us believe that God loves us. And this is why he is so successful," one observer reflected.

While courting such people of faith, Bush did not neglect economic conservatives. The Republican Congress gave the president tax-cut proposals to sign in 2001 and 2003, measures that favored the wealthiest Americans. Yet to maintain a balanced budget, the cardinal principle of fiscal conservatism, these tax cuts would have required a substantial reduction in spending, which Bush and Congress chose not to do. Furthermore, continued deregulation of business encouraged unsavory and harmful activities that resulted in corporate scandals and risky financial practices.

At the same time, Bush showed the compassionate side of his conservatism. Like Clinton's cabinet appointments, Bush's appointments reflected racial, ethnic, and sexual diversity. They included African Americans as secretary of state (Colin Powell), national security adviser (Condoleezza Rice, who later succeeded Powell as secretary of state), and secretary of education (Rod Paige). In addition, the president chose women to head the Departments of Agriculture, Interior, and Labor and also appointed one Latino and two Asian Americans to his cabinet.

In 2002 the president signed the No Child Left Behind Act, which raised federal appropriations for the education of students in primary and secondary schools, especially in underprivileged areas. The law imposed federal criteria for evaluating teachers and school programs, relying on standardized testing to do so. Another display of compassionate conservatism came in the 2003 passage of the Medicare Prescription Drug, Improvement, and Modernization Act. The law was projected to cost more than $400 billion over a ten-year period to lower the cost of prescription drugs to some 40 million senior citizens under the 1965 Medicare Act and received support from the American Association of Retired Persons (AARP).

The United States at War

President Bush ultimately spent little of his presidency focusing on domestic issues because events originating from abroad vaulted him into the role of wartime president. To make up for his lack of experience in foreign affairs, Bush relied heavily on Vice President Richard (Dick) Cheney, Secretary of Defense Donald Rumsfeld, and Condoleezza Rice. In running for election in 2000, Bush had pledged: "I would be very careful about using our troops as nation builders. I believe the role of the military is to fight and win war and therefore prevent war from happening in the first place." However, Bush's closest advisers had other ideas and sought to reshape critical parts of the post–Cold War world through preemptive force, most notably in the Persian Gulf.

After the attacks on the World Trade Center and the Pentagon on September 11, 2001, the president abandoned his campaign promise to use U.S. troops cautiously and followed the counsel of his advisers. The violence that killed Kristen Breitweiser's husband and thousands of others on that day changed the direction of U.S. foreign and domestic policies. The country undertook a war on terror, one that led to protracted and costly conflicts in Afghanistan and Iraq and the erosion of civil liberties at home. As part of that effort, in 2002 Congress created a cabinet-level superagency, the Department of Homeland Security,

responsible for developing a national strategy against further terrorist threats. Congress also enacted into law a key recommendation of the national commission that Breitweiser and the Jersey Girls pressured the government to establish. In 2004 Congress created the Office of the Director of National Intelligence to coordinate the work of security agencies more effectively.

In the immediate aftermath of the September 11 terrorist attacks, Bush acted decisively. The president dispatched U.S. troops to Afghanistan, whose Taliban leaders refused to turn over Osama bin Laden and other terrorists operating training centers in the country. A combination of anti-Taliban warlords and U.S. military special forces, backed up by American aircraft, toppled the Taliban regime and installed a pro-American government; however, the United States did not immediately capture the elusive bin Laden, who escaped somewhere in the remote territory of Pakistan.

On the home front, the war on terror prompted passage of the **Patriot Act** in October 2001. The measure eased restrictions on domestic and foreign intelligence gathering and expanded the authority of law enforcement and immigration officials in detaining and deporting immigrants suspected of terrorism-related acts. The act gave law enforcement agencies nearly unlimited authority to wiretap telephones, retrieve e-mail messages, and search the medical, financial, and library borrowing records of

President Bush at Ground Zero

On September 14, 2001, President George W. Bush toured the wreckage of the destroyed World Trade Center. Standing on a pile of rubble, he heard firefighters, police officers, and other rescuers shout, "USA, USA." He responded: "I can hear you. The rest of the world hears you. And the people who knocked these buildings down will hear all of us soon." Reuters/ Win McNamee/Landov individuals, including U.S. citizens, suspected of involvement in terrorism overseas or at home. The computer age had provided terrorist networks like al-Qaeda with the means to communicate quickly through electronic mail and cell phones across national boundaries and to raise money and launder it into safe bank accounts online. Computer technology also gave U.S. intelligence agencies ways to monitor these communications and transactions.

Amid rising anti-Muslim sentiments, the overwhelming majority of Americans supported the Patriot Act. In the weeks and months following September 11, some people committed acts of violence against mosques, Arab American community centers and businesses, and individual Muslims and people thought to be Muslims (such as Sikhs). Near Chicago, a crowd of about three hundred anti-Arab youths waved flags, shouted "USA, USA," and attempted to march on a mosque. In this atmosphere, some critics complained about the harsh provisions of the Patriot Act, comparing them to the measures restricting civil liberties during the Red scare following World War I (see chapter 21). Nevertheless, in 2006 Congress renewed the act with only minor changes.

President Bush and his advisers, particularly Vice President Cheney and Secretary of Defense Rumsfeld, did not believe that the defeat of the Taliban in Afghanistan had ended the war on terror. Rather, they saw it as part of a larger plan to reshape the politics of the Middle East and Persian Gulf regions along pro-American lines. In doing so, the United States and its European allies would ensure the flow of cheap oil in order to satisfy the energy demands of consumers in these countries. Furthermore, by replacing authoritarian regimes with democratic governments in places like Iraq and Afghanistan, the Bush administration envisioned a domino effect that would lead to the toppling of reactionary leaders throughout the region. The establishment of pro-American, democratic nations, according to this strategy, would defeat extremist Islamic powers, thereby paving the way for resolving deep-seated, ongoing conflicts between Arabs and Israelis. In crafting this strategy, the Bush administration departed from the well-established, post–World War II policy of containing enemies short of going to war. Instead, the **Bush Doctrine** proposed undertaking preemptive war against despotic governments deemed a threat to U.S. national security, even if that danger was not imminent.

Following this doctrine, President Bush declared in January 2002 that Iraq was part of an "axis of evil," along with Iran and North Korea. Although the United States had supported Saddam Hussein in Iraq's war against Iran in the 1980s, Bush considered the Iraqi dictator to be in the same terrorist camp with Osama bin Laden. Little had changed in Iraq since the 1980s, but President Bush sought to complete the job that his father had started and then retreated from in the 1991 Gulf War—removing Hussein from power. The Iraqi leader was considered too undependable to protect U.S. oil interests in the region. Removing him would also open a path to overthrowing the radical Islamic government of neighboring Iran, which had embarrassed the United States in 1979 and remained its sworn enemy (see chapter 28).

Over the next two years, Bush convinced Congress and a majority of the American people that Iraq presented an immediate danger to the security of the United States in its effort to fight global terrorism. He did so by falsely connecting Saddam Hussein to the 9/11 al-Qaeda terrorists. The president also accused Iraq of being well along the way to building and stockpiling "weapons of mass destruction." Even after UN inspectors examined alleged nuclear and chemical weapons facilities in Iraq and found nothing harmful, the Bush administration remained adamant. Further, the government manipulated questionable intelligence information to defend its claims. In a speech to the United Nations based on dubious and inaccurate information, Secretary of State Powell charged that intelligence services had gathered direct evidence that Iraq was working on a nuclear device. **See Document Project 29: The Uses of September 11, page 952.**

Challenging the Bush administration's assumptions and allegations about Iraq, antiwar critics staged mass demonstrations in major cities throughout the country, but with little success. Most Americans gave the president the benefit of the doubt. At the very least, they agreed with Bush that Saddam Hussein was "evil" and that his removal was justified. Thus in March 2003, after a congressional vote of approval, U.S. military aircraft unleashed massive bombing attacks on Baghdad as part of the Bush-Rumsfeld strategy of "shock and awe." Unlike the 1991 Gulf War, in which the first President Bush had responded to the Iraqi invasion of Kuwait and led a broad coalition of nations, including Arab countries (see chapter 28), the United States did not wait for any overt act of aggression and created merely a nominal alliance of nations, with only Great Britain supplying significant combat troops. Nevertheless, within weeks Hussein went into hiding, prompting Bush to declare that "major combat operations" had ended in Iraq.

This triumphant declaration proved premature, although Hussein was captured several months later. Despite the presence of 130,000 U.S. and 30,000 British troops, the war dragged on. More American soldiers (more than 4,000) died after the president proclaimed victory than had died during the invasion. The perception of the United States as an occupying power destabilized Iraq, leading to a civil war between the country's Shi'ite Muslim majority, which had been persecuted under Saddam Hussein, and its Sunni minority, which Hussein represented. In the northern part of the nation, the Kurdish majority, another group brutalized by Hussein, also battled Sunnis. Moreover, al-Qaeda forces, which previously had been absent from the country, joined the fray.

Explore

See Document 29.2 for one reporter's description of life in war-torn Iraq.

The U.S. occupation and attempts at nation building, something that Bush during the 2000 campaign vowed he would not support, caused serious problems. American soldiers staffing jails containing Iraqi war prisoners, such as Abu Ghraib, were caught in photographs abusing their captives. The reconstituted Iraqi army and police lacked experience and harbored rebels within their ranks. Absent a military draft, Bush could not put sufficient active-duty troops into Iraq without exhausting them through extended tours of duty. In 2004 the military began relying on National Guard units to meet troop requirements, and they eventually constituted about 40 percent of the U.S. armed forces in Iraq. To make up for staffing shortages, the Pentagon outsourced to private companies jobs that would normally be performed by military personnel. American companies profited immensely from construction projects; from supplying troops with housing, meals, and uniforms; and from providing security for high-ranking military and diplomatic personnel. The Defense Department awarded contracts without competitive bidding to companies such as Halliburton, which had close ties to Vice President Cheney.

Amid a protracted war in Iraq, President Bush won reelection in 2004 by promising to finish the course of action he had started in Iraq. Bush argued that to do less would encourage terrorists, subvert burgeoning democracy in Iraq and Afghanistan, and dishonor the troops who had been killed and wounded. Although the Democratic presidential candidate, Senator John Kerry of Massachusetts, criticized Bush's handling of Iraq, Bush eked out a victory; however, this time, unlike four years before, the president won a majority of the popular vote (50.7 percent).

Bush's Second Term

Bush won reelection, but over the next four years his credibility suffered. Several issues—the continued presence of sectarian violence in Iraq, the lack of progress in training Iraqi troops and police to safeguard civilians, the mounting death tolls, and the failure of the U.S.-supported Iraqi government to work out a political solution to the country's problems—turned the majority of Americans against the

war. Even when in 2007 the president ordered an increase of 30,000 troops, known as "the surge," which succeeded in reducing mayhem in Baghdad and its vicinity, many Americans had had enough. In 2008 polls showed that 54 percent of Americans considered the invasion of Iraq a mistake, and 49 percent wanted U.S. troops to return home (compared with 47 percent who opposed withdrawal).

However, the president seemed impervious to criticism. The Bush administration continued to enforce the Patriot Act with little concern for the protection of privacy and civil liberties, and it justified its actions on the belief that in a time of war the president had few limits on his power. Bush also refused to back down from the policy of incarcerating suspected al-Qaeda rebels in the U.S. military base in Guantánamo, Cuba. The facility housed more than six hundred men classified as "enemy combatants," who were subject to extreme interrogation and were deprived of legal counsel. This policy changed somewhat when the Supreme Court, in *Hamdan v. Rumsfeld* (2006), ruled that the military tribunals established by the president to prosecute Guantánamo prisoners were unconstitutional. Shortly after, Congress passed legislation providing a small measure of protection for the four hundred prisoners who remained in Guantánamo.

As Bush's handling of the Iraq War generated rising disapproval, his management of a major natural disaster further diminished his popularity. On August 29, 2005, **Hurricane Katrina** slammed into the Gulf coast states of Louisiana and Mississippi. This powerful storm devastated New Orleans, a city with a population of nearly 500,000, a majority of whom were African American. A thirty-foot flood surge caused poorly maintained levees to break, placing large areas of the city underwater. Despite the evacuation of hundreds of thousands of people from New Orleans before the hurricane struck, approximately 50,000 residents remained trapped by the flood. Not only did local and state officials respond slowly and ineptly, but so, too, did the federal government in providing assistance to those trapped in the city.

In the days after the storm hit, chaos reigned in New Orleans. Evacuees were housed in the Superdome football stadium and a municipal auditorium without adequate food, water, and sanitary conditions, and the scenes of despair were broadcast on national television. The flooding killed at least 1,800 residents of the Gulf coast, New Orleans's population dropped by around 130,000 residents, and critics blamed the president for his lack of leadership and slow response to the disaster. Some argued that just as Bush had failed to manage the war in Iraq, he also lacked the ability to handle the Katrina catastrophe. Overall, Hurricane Katrina was just as much a human-made disaster as a natural one.

Farnaz Fassihi | Report from Baghdad, 2004

After U.S. forces ousted Saddam Hussein in 2003, civil war broke out between rival religious sects of Sunni and Shi'ite Muslims. Many Iraqis viewed the United States as an occupying power despite efforts to reconstruct the war-torn nation and promote free elections. In an e-mail to friends in the United States, *Wall Street Journal* correspondent Farnaz Fassihi presents a frank assessment of the deteriorating conditions in Baghdad in September 2004.

Explore

Being a foreign correspondent in Baghdad these days is like being under virtual house arrest. Forget about the reasons that lured me to this job: a chance to see the world, explore the exotic, meet new people in far away lands, discover their ways, and tell stories that could make a difference.

Little by little, day-by-day, being based in Iraq has defied all those reasons. I am house bound. I leave when I have a very good reason to and a scheduled interview. I avoid going to people's homes and never walk in the streets. I can't go grocery shopping any more, can't eat in restaurants, can't strike a conversation with strangers, can't look for stories, can't drive in anything but a full armored car, can't go to scenes of breaking news stories, can't be stuck in traffic, can't speak English outside, can't take a road trip, can't say I'm an American, can't linger at checkpoints, can't be curious about what people are saying, doing, feeling. And can't and can't.

How do conditions in Baghdad affect Fassihi's ability to report on the war?

There has been one too many close calls, including a car bomb so near our house that it blew out all the windows. So now my most pressing concern every day is not to write a kick-ass story but to stay alive and make sure our Iraqi employees stay alive. In Baghdad I am a security personnel first, a reporter second. . . .

Iraqis like to call this mess "the situation." When asked "how are things?" they reply: "the situation is very bad."

Why do the Iraqis think the war is going badly?

What they mean by situation is this: the Iraqi government doesn't control most Iraqi cities, there are several car bombs going off each day around the country killing and injuring scores of innocent people, the country's roads are becoming impassable and littered by hundreds of landmines and explosive devices aimed to kill American soldiers, there are assassinations, kidnappings, and beheadings. The situation, basically, means a raging barbaric guerilla war. In four days, 110 people died and over 300 got injured in Baghdad alone. The numbers are so shocking that the ministry of health—which was attempting an exercise of public transparency by releasing the numbers—has now stopped disclosing them.

What are some of the challenges of rebuilding Iraq?

Insurgents now attack Americans 87 times a day. . . . As for reconstruction: firstly it's so unsafe for foreigners to operate that almost all projects have come to a halt. After two years, of the $18 billion Congress appropriated for Iraq reconstruction only about $1 billion or so has been spent and a chunk has now been reallocated for improving security, a sign of just how bad things are going here. . . .

Source: Lisa Grunwald and Stephen J. Adler, eds., *Women's Letters: America from the Revolutionary War to the Present* (New York: Dial Press, 2005), 758–60.

Put It in Context

How does this document challenge the Bush administration's views on the Iraq War?

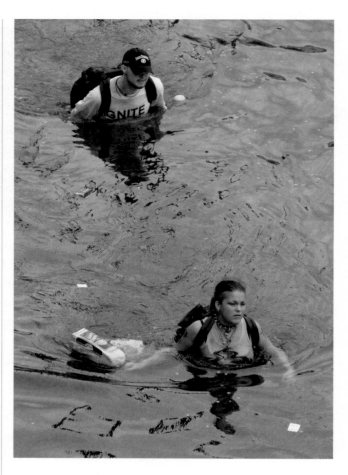

Two Perceptions of New Orleans Looting

Some members of the media were guilty of racial profiling in their reporting of the aftermath of Hurricane Katrina. Compare the original caption for the photo on the left ("A young man walks through chest-deep floodwater after looting a grocery store in New Orleans") with the one on the right ("Two residents wade through chest-deep water after finding bread and soda from a local grocery store after Hurricane Katrina came through the area in New Orleans"). Racial identity appears to be the only distinction between who was "looting" and who was "finding."   left: AP Photo/ Dave Martin; right: Chris Graythen/Getty Images

Displeased with the Bush administration, voters elected a Democratic majority to the House and Senate in 2006, yet little changed. American troops remained in Iraq and Afghanistan. Mobilization for the war on terror had become a permanent part of life in the United States, much like the growth of the national security state during the Cold War (see chapter 24). However, not all Americans experienced the war equally. With military enlistments at low levels, the men and women who served in Iraq and Afghanistan were disproportionately poor and from minority communities. At the same time, Osama bin Laden remained alive and in hiding, and al-Qaeda had regrouped in Pakistan and Yemen. The Bush administration did little to address the perennial problem of Israeli-Palestinian relations, one of the chief elements that fueled terrorism and Islamic radicalism. Making the situation even more combustible, in 2006 Hamas (the Islamic Resistance Movement), which the United States considered an anti-Semitic, terrorist organization, won Palestinian parliamentary elections and posed a new threat to peace in the Middle East.

With turmoil continuing in the Middle East and the Persian Gulf, the threat of nuclear proliferation grew. Iraq did not have nuclear weapons, but Iran sought to develop nuclear capabilities. Iranian leaders claimed that they wanted nuclear technology for peaceful purposes, but the Bush administration believed that Iran's real purpose was to build nuclear devices to attack Israel and

establish its supremacy in the region. The election in April 2006 of Mahmoud Ahmadinejad, an avowed enemy of Israel, as president of Iran reinforced Bush's fears. Pakistan, a country that already had nuclear weapons, also proved troublesome. Although an ally of the United States, Pakistan was largely ineffective in removing al-Qaeda and Taliban forces from their bases along the country's border with Afghanistan. Equally disturbing, a high-ranking nuclear scientist in Pakistan had previously sold information to North Korea, one of the states in Bush's "axis of evil." North Korea, a totalitarian nation and one of the few remaining Communist dictatorships left from the Cold War era, conducted underground nuclear tests in 2006.

REVIEW & RELATE

How did President Bush put compassionate conservatism into action?

How did the war on terror prompt U.S. leaders to rethink America's position in the world?

 LEARNINGCurve bedfordstmartins.com/hewittlawson/LC

Challenges Ahead

The changes brought by the digital technology of Bill Gates and the war on terror following September 11 had become firmly embedded in the United States and throughout an interconnected, globalized world. In 2008 a new concern emerged with the arrival of the worldwide Great Recession. At the same time, many Americans rallied behind the presidential candidacy of Barack Obama with renewed hope. Obama's election reflected sweeping demographic changes in the United States and brought reform, but Obama's victory did not eliminate the deep political and cultural divisions in the nation or eradicate pervasive economic and social inequality.

The Great Recession

In 2008 the boom times of the early years of the twenty-first century came to a sudden halt. The stock market's Dow Jones average, which had hit a high of 14,000, fell 6,000 points, the steepest percentage drop since 1931. Americans who had invested their money in the stock market lost trillions of dollars. The stock market crash plunged investment firms into crisis. Lehman Brothers, a financial services firm founded in 1850, lost more than $2 billion and went bankrupt. The gross domestic product fell by about 6 percent, a loss too great for the economy to absorb quickly. Americans lost their jobs as consumer spending decreased,

and many forfeited their homes when they could no longer afford to pay their mortgages. Unemployment jumped from 4.9 percent in January 2008 to 7.6 percent a year later. Confronted by this spiraling disaster, President Bush approved a $700 billion bailout plan to rescue the nation's largest banks and brokerage houses.

The causes of the **Great Recession** were many and had developed over a long period. Since the Reagan presidency, the federal government had relaxed regulation of the financial industry. The Clinton administration supported repeal of the Glass-Steagall Act (see chapter 22). This measure, enacted during the New Deal, had separated commercial and investment banking to protect small business people and American families and to avoid the intense financial speculation that preceded the stock market crash of 1929 and the Great Depression. The Federal Reserve Bank encouraged excessive borrowing through keeping interest rates very low and relaxed its oversight of Wall Street practices that placed ordinary investors' money at risk. Investment houses developed elaborate computer models that produced new and risky kinds of financial instruments, which went unregulated and whose complex nature few people understood. Insurance companies such as American International Group marketed so-called credit default swaps as protection for risky securities, exacerbating the financial crisis. In addition, some financial managers engaged in corrupt practices. One of the most notorious, securities broker Bernard Madoff, swindled investors out of billions of dollars through phony securities dealings.

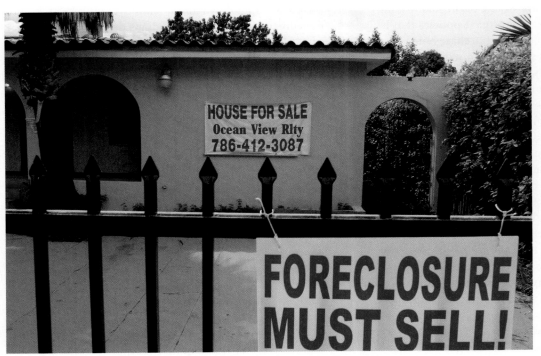

The Housing Bubble Bursts

The housing bubble of the early twenty-first century burst in 2006. By 2007 the owners of this Miami home could no longer afford to pay their mortgage, and like millions around the country they lost their home. Risky lending practices, including subprime mortgages and real estate speculation, triggered the housing collapse. California, Florida, Michigan, and Nevada posted the highest rates of foreclosures.   Joe Raedle/Getty Images

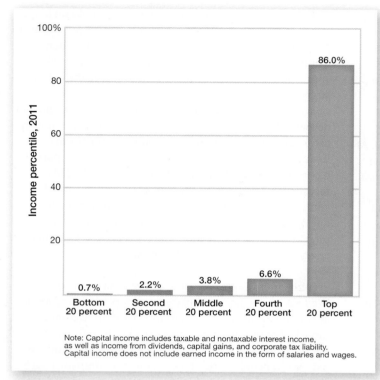

FIGURE 29.2　Wealth Inequality (Capital Income), 2011

The decline of American manufacturing and the expansion of the low-wage service sector, combined with the rise of high-tech industries and unregulated investment banking, led to growing disparities of wealth in the early twenty-first century. Disparities exist even within the top 20 percentile, as the top 1 percent controlled more than half of all capital income in 2011.

securities industry and greater economic equality to bolster consumer spending. But this was not the case. Wealth remained concentrated in relatively few hands. In 2007 the top 1 percent of households owned 34.6 percent of all privately held wealth, and the next 19 percent held 50.5 percent. Thus 80 percent of Americans owned only 15 percent of the wealth, and the gap between rich and poor widened further. The poverty rate stood at around 13 percent (and as high as 20 percent for those under eighteen years of age). This maldistribution of wealth made it extremely difficult to support an economy that required ever-expanding purchasing power and produced steadily rising personal debt (Figure 29.2).

In the age of globalization, the Great Recession spread rapidly throughout the world. Great Britain's banking system teetered on the edge of collapse. Some of the other nations in the European Union (EU)—most notably Greece and Spain, which were the most heavily in debt—verged on bankruptcy and had to be rescued by stronger EU nations. Ireland, whose economy had leaped in the early years of the twenty-first century, abruptly fell on hard times. In providing financial assistance to its member states, the EU required countries such as Greece to slash spending for government services and to lower minimum wages. Even in China, where the economy had boomed as a result of globalization, businesses shut down and unemployment rose as consumer demand for its products declined in the wake of worldwide recession.

The Rise of Barack Obama

In the midst of the Great Recession, the United States held the 2008 presidential election. The Republican candidate, John McCain, was a Vietnam War hero and a longtime senator from Arizona. His Democratic opponent was Barack Obama, who was a young boy during the Vietnam War and had served a mere four years in the Senate from Illinois. For their vice presidential running mates, McCain chose Sarah Palin, the first-term governor of Alaska, and Obama selected Joseph Biden, the senior senator from Delaware. Whoever won would represent a break with tradition. If McCain triumphed, for the first time a woman would serve as vice president. An Obama victory would place an African American in the White House for the first time in history.

In the end, Obama overcame lingering racial prejudices in the country by speaking eloquently about his background

Consumers also shared some of the blame. Many took advantage of the easy mortgage policies that had been devised to allow buyers to purchase homes beyond their means. Known as **subprime mortgages**, these loans appealed to borrowers with low incomes or poor credit ratings, especially minorities, who historically had had difficulty obtaining mortgages and personal loans. On the surface, subprime mortgages appeared to make possible the American dream of home ownership. However, when the housing market collapsed, they turned into the nightmare of home foreclosure as many homeowners ended up owing banks and mortgage companies much more than their homes were worth. Investment banks, which had bundled risky mortgages together for speculative purposes, made the situation even worse. Enticed by the easy availability of credit, consumers also went heavily into personal debt to finance purchases of new technology-driven goods, such as personal computers, smartphones, and larger and larger digital televisions.

The economy might have experienced a less severe downturn if there had been stricter regulation of the as an interracial child, the son of an immigrant from Kenya and the grandson of a World War II veteran from Kansas. He also refuted charges that he was a Muslim (he is a Christian), that he was not born in the United States (he was born in Hawaii), and that he associated with terrorists (in the 1990s, he had participated in a few Chicago civic engagements with a past 1960s radical). The former community organizer succeeded in building a nationwide, grassroots political movement through digital technology. He raised an enormous amount of campaign money from ordinary donors through the Internet and used Web sites and text messaging to mobilize his supporters. Obama won the presidential election most of all because the public blamed the Bush administration for the recession, and Obama offered hope—"Yes we can" was his campaign slogan—for economic recovery. Obama captured 53 percent of the popular vote, obtaining a majority of votes from African Americans, Latinos, women, and the young, who turned out in record numbers, and a comfortable 365 electoral votes. The Democrats also scored big victories in the House and Senate.

Yet the election of President Obama did not erase the impact of generations of racism from the United States or usher in what some have called a "postracial" America. From 1975 to 2002, the number of black elected officials in the United States increased from around 3,500 to more than 9,000. African Americans had also made significant economic progress as a result of antidiscrimination laws and affirmative action, expanding the size of the black middle class. However, the racial gap in wealth, education, and rates of incarceration remained wide. In 2006 the median income for blacks was $32,132, compared with $50,673 for whites. About 75 percent of whites owned their home, compared with slightly less than 50 percent for blacks, a reflection of the continued disparity in wealth between the races. By 2008 approximately 24 percent of African Americans (compared with 8 percent of whites) lived in poverty, nearly double the national poverty rate of 12.7 percent. The percentage of whites who received a bachelor's degree was almost double that for blacks. More than 28 percent of black men were expected to be imprisoned during their lifetime, compared with 4 percent for whites. More than half the prison population in the United States is black and another quarter

Latino, far out of proportion with their percentages among the total U.S. population.

Despite the persistence of racism, President Obama achieved notable victories during his first term in office. He continued the Bush administration's bailout of collapsing banks and investment firms and expanded it to include American automobile companies, which within three years bounced back, became profitable again, and began paying back the government for the bailout. The president supported passage of an economic stimulus plan that provided federal funds to state and local governments to create jobs and keep their employees, including teachers, on the public payroll. Congress also extended the period of unemployment insurance benefits. More controversially, President Obama pushed Congress to pass a health care

The Election of Barack Obama

On the evening of November 4, 2008, after Barack Obama won the 2008 presidential election, he gave his victory speech at Grant Park in his home city of Chicago, Illinois, before a crowd of approximately 240,000 people. The first African American to be elected president, Obama echoed the words in speeches by Martin Luther King Jr. and Abraham Lincoln.   AP Photo/David Guttenfelder reform measure, which mandated that all Americans had to obtain health insurance and that no one could be denied coverage for a preexisting condition. He also signed into law repeal of the "don't ask, don't tell" policy, which discriminated against gays in the military. Although the Supreme Court in 2003 had declared unconstitutional a Texas law making homosexual acts a crime, the issue of same-sex marriage remained unresolved. Initially Obama supported civil unions rather than gay marriage, but in 2012 he declared his support for same-sex marriage.

In foreign affairs, the president appointed Hillary Clinton, the former First Lady and a senator from New York, as secretary of state. The U.S. military increased combat troop withdrawals from Iraq and turned over security for the country to the newly elected Iraqi government. At the same time, the Obama administration stepped up the war in Afghanistan by increasing U.S. troop levels, which led to a rise in casualties. Still, the president pledged withdrawal of combat soldiers by 2014. His most dramatic success came in 2011, when U.S. special forces killed Osama bin Laden in his hideout in Pakistan. The Obama administration also persuaded the Senate to approve the renewal of a nuclear disarmament treaty with Russia.

President Obama continued to encounter vigorous political opposition. Most Republican lawmakers refused to support his economic stimulus and health care reform bills. A group of Republican conservatives formed the **Tea Party movement**, which they named after colonial Americans who sought to topple British rule. Its followers attacked the president as a "socialist" for what they perceived as an effort to expand federal control over the economy and diminish individual liberty with passage of the health care act. The Fox News media empire, owned by Rupert Murdoch, backed this movement and its leaders, such as Sarah Palin and talk-show host Glenn Beck.

Obama encountered growing political difficulties because the economy remained stagnant. The president did save the financial system from collapse, and the stock market had rebounded by 2012, but unemployment remained over 8 percent (a drop from its high of 10.2 percent). As millions of people remained out of work, a resurgent Wall Street rewarded its managers and employees with big financial bonuses. Large corporations earned millions of dollars in profits but did not create new jobs. The 2010 midterm elections illustrated the growing dissatisfaction of American voters, as Republicans regained control of the House and the Democratic majority in the Senate narrowed. The Tea Party flexed its electoral muscle in successfully campaigning for Republican congressional and gubernatorial candidates who supported its positions. Exit polls showed that 41 percent of the voters endorsed the Tea Party movement. Governor Scott Walker of Wisconsin, backed by the Tea Party, took aim at public employee unions in his state and signed into law a measure limiting

Same-Sex Marriage

A lesbian couple from St. Louis, Missouri, gets married on May 1, 2009, in Iowa City, Iowa. Joining them on what they called the "Show Me Marriage Equality Bus," another sixteen same-sex couples from Missouri also rode to Iowa City to get married. By June 2012, Connecticut, Iowa, Massachusetts, New Hampshire, New York, Vermont, Washington, and Washington, D.C., had authorized same-sex marriage.   AP Photo/The Gazette, Brian Ray collective bargaining. (In 2012 his opponents failed to win a recall election to remove him from office.)

Dissent also came from the left. In 2011 protesters in cities around the nation launched the **Occupy Wall Street** movement, which attacked corporate greed, economic inequality, and the inability of the federal government to relieve the widespread suffering. Many in the movement were inspired to act by massive cuts in education spending, crippling state budget deficits and declining tax revenues that slashed social services, decaying infrastructure, and crushing student loan debts. These and other Americans continued to be concerned about environmental issues, including dependence on foreign oil, global warming, and air and water pollution.

With unemployment remaining high, economic growth moving at a slow pace, and a number of European economies still in recession and unable to pay mounting debts, the economy loomed as the top issue in the 2012 presidential election. The Republican nominee, Mitt Romney, the former governor of Massachusetts, appealed to conservative voters by opposing Obama's economic programs, including health care reform, and by embracing the social agenda of the Christian Right. Although admitting that much remained to be done, Obama defended his record on creating new jobs, reducing unemployment, and rescuing the automobile industry. He also criticized economic inequality in the country and promised to raise taxes on the rich. Despite the slower-than-expected economic recovery, Barack Obama won reelection by holding together his coalition of African American, Latino, female, young, and lower-income voters.

Explore

See Documents 29.3 and 29.4 for testimonies from the Great Recession.

An Unfinished Agenda

The United States will continue to face serious tests to its international leadership in the twenty-first century. Terrorism remains a potent threat. Iraq has yet to prove that it can survive as a stable nation in the absence of a strong American military presence, and the outcome of the war against al-Qaeda and the Taliban in Afghanistan

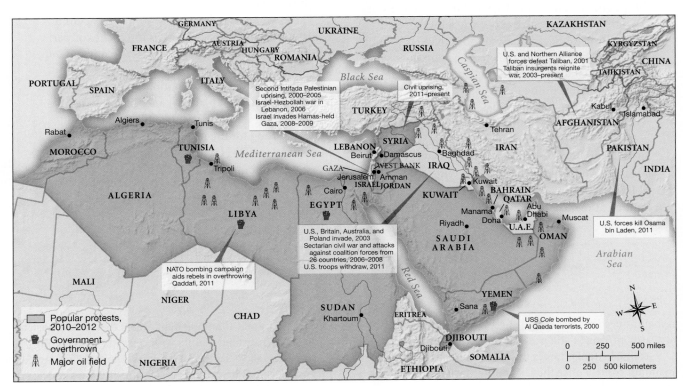

MAP 29.2 The Middle East, 2000–2012

Since 2000, the Middle East has been marked by both terrorism and democratic uprisings. After 9/11 the United States tried to transform Iraq and Afghanistan by military might, which led to prolonged wars. Yet popular rebellions in 2011, led by young people and fueled by new technology, created hope that change was possible. However, as of 2012 the most brutal government repression of the uprisings continued in Syria.

DOCUMENTS 29.3 AND 29.4

The Great Recession: Two Views

For generations of Americans, education has provided an opportunity for upward mobility. During the Great Recession, many people with college degrees found themselves deep in debt with few job opportunities. Prospects for people without degrees were even worse, as these two selections show. The first tells the story of Alice, who was born in Korea and has a bachelor's degree in architecture. She was interviewed by Melissa K. McDonough, who transcribed and edited the conversation for the blog RecessionGrads. The second entry, from a different blog, is by an anonymous navy veteran and substitute schoolteacher.

Explore

29.3 Alice | RecessionGrads Interview, April 21, 2011

I thought I would get a job, right after college. I graduated college, I have a degree, I should get a job. But that wasn't the case. And my parents thought I would get a job, be independent and those kind of things. But I moved in with my parents and my parents were *very* . . . upset, in a way, and very disappointed. They didn't say it, but, because I was the oldest kid, they were expecting a lot more. . . .

And [my job search] lasted more than six months. And, then your parents start to say, you know, you shouldn't just look for planning and architecture, why are you just doing that? You should just work somewhere else. And they just kind of keep telling you. And it's kind of annoying. *She laughs.* Because I do have a goal to get some experience in planning and eventually get a full time job. It was very, very stressful. And, you know, you have your younger siblings with you too. It's kind of like . . . they're looking at me like I'm a bad example, you know? . . .

I thought, you go to elementary, middle school, high school, college and get a job. I thought that was the whole thing and you don't really have to *try* to do it. I thought if you get good grades in college then you automatically get a job, but that wasn't the case. I'm a pretty positive, optimistic person, so I was like, 2 to 3 months, I'll get a job. You know? I'll get a job. I was pretty optimistic. And then that kind of diminishes every month. *She laughs.*

There weren't many full time positions opening. Most of the positions were either internship or part time or temporary positions. So it was really difficult, but even if it was just internship, part time, temporary positions, competition was amazing. Like, I apply for [assistant planner] and they call me for an interview and I went there, there were like, 20, 30 people waiting for the interview. If you think about how many people already applied and they selected those people to interview, I was awed. I was awed.

Source: http://recessiongrads.blogspot.com/2011_04_01_archive.html.

remains questionable. Despite Osama bin Laden's death, al-Qaeda in Yemen still poses a serious danger, and U.S.-trained Afghan forces must demonstrate that they can maintain control once the U.S. military withdraws. If Iran succeeds in developing nuclear weapons, it will present an even greater threat, as will the continuing stalemate between the Israeli government and the Palestinians in reaching agreement over issues of peace and land that have been unresolved since 1967.

In 2011 great changes swept across the Middle East, as young people, armed mainly with cell phones and connected through social media networks, peacefully toppled pro-Western but despotic governments in Egypt and Tunisia. In Libya, armed rebels succeeded in overthrowing the government of the dictator Muammar al-Qaddafi. Elsewhere, a hostile North Korea has developed nuclear weapons. Prolonged instability in the Middle East, the Persian Gulf, and Asia is harmful to U.S. security

29.4 Anonymous | We Are the 99 Percent Blog, November 5, 2011

I am 36 years old. I have a husband and two children, ages 13 and 11, and live in an apartment on a university campus.

I have an extruded disc in my back that presses on my sciatic nerve and leaves me in constant pain, making me unable to stand for more than 20 minutes at a time. My husband and I are both veterans of the US Navy, having served our country honorably and proudly. We are unable to afford medical insurance so we use the VA [Veterans Administration]. We don't qualify for dental insurance through them and both have several missing and broken teeth, as well as numerous abscesses.

Our children have healthcare through the state's medical insurance for needy families. We rely on housing assistance to be able to afford our apartment. We only qualify for food stamps because of our children as adults cannot qualify without steady 32+ hours per week jobs.

We were raised to believe that a college education would make you more successful and able to achieve the American Dream. I have a bachelor's degree and am certified to teach elementary education and middle school science and social studies. I will graduate in a month with a master's degree in educational technology and over $70,000 in debt. My husband has two bachelor's degrees and is working toward a master's and his debt is equivalent to mine.

He works as an adjunct professor at a university because he cannot find regular, steady employment. I am a substitute teacher in the local school district because I am "overqualified" for other work and cannot find a full time teaching position.

We both work at the whim of our employers on an as needed basis. We are literally living paycheck to paycheck, unable to have savings of any sort. My family and I are the 99%.

Source: "We Are the 99 Percent," http://wearethe99percent.tumblr.com/page/30.

Interpret the Evidence

- How has each woman pursued economic advancement?
- What challenges does each woman face in overcoming her economic problems?

Put It in Context

What effect has the Great Recession had on the middle class?

interests and to achieving lasting peace in these regions (Map 29.2).

Whatever happens in the war on terror, the United States still faces challenges of globalization. China, a nation of 1.3 billion people, is contesting American economic supremacy. As China flourishes economically, American workers have lost jobs, and the Chinese have amassed a nearly $200 billion trade surplus with the United States. China also owns a substantial portion of America's national

debt, a situation that further alters the balance of economic power between the two nations. In addition, the growth of manufacturing and the market economy in China has resulted in the rising consumption of oil and gasoline, thereby adding to soaring fuel prices in the United States.

Along with the United States and China, the rest of the world faces the problem of climate change and ultimately the survival of the planet. Global warming during the twentieth century resulted mainly from emissions of greenhouse gases into the atmosphere and the erosion of the ozone layer. As temperatures climb, they cause a rise in the sea level, the melting of glaciers, extreme fluctuations of weather, and famines. Powerful hurricanes such as Katrina have been attributed to rising temperatures in the Atlantic Ocean and Caribbean. Disruptions in industrial production caused by storms and the subsequent expense of rebuilding have a negative impact on the U.S. and world economies.

As the twenty-first century unfolds, immigration will continue to arouse considerable political controversy. Immigration restrictionists, particularly in Arizona and California, support such policies as building a fence along the U.S.-Mexican border and strengthening the administration of immigration laws. Supporters of immigration reform favor amnesty for illegal residents who have lived in this country for a designated period and have jobs, opening up a path to citizenship. At the heart of this issue is the question that has always existed during periods of intense foreign immigration, especially from non-English-speaking nations: Do the nation's vitality and character still depend on welcoming a new generation of foreigners to make their living and their home in the United States? Whatever the answer, by the end of the twenty-first century the population of the United States will look much different. The percentage of Latinos and Asian Americans will increase, while that of whites and blacks will decline. In 2012 the U.S. Census Bureau reported that nonwhite babies made up the majority of births for the first time. If present trends continue, the country's racial and ethnic composition will become much more mixed through intermarriage. In 2010 the Census Bureau reported that one of seven new marriages, or 14.6 percent, was interracial or interethnic. In 1961, when Barack Obama was born, the figure for interracial marriages was less than one in a thousand. And, as for the institution of marriage, we can expect its legal recognition to expand to gays, although in 2012 voters approved state referenda that rejected same-sex marriage.

REVIEW & RELATE

What were the causes and consequences of the Great Recession?

What effects did the election and presidency of Barack Obama have on American politics and society?

 LEARNINGCurve bedfordstmartins.com/hewittlawson/LC

Conclusion: Technology and Terror in a Global Society

Since 1993, Americans have faced new forms of globalization, new technologies, and new modes of warfare. The computer revolution that Bill Gates helped initiate

changed the way Americans gather information, communicate ideas, purchase goods, and conduct business. It has also shaped national and international conflicts. The September 11, 2001, attacks on the World Trade Center and the Pentagon demonstrated that terrorists could use computers and digital equipment to wreak havoc on the most powerful nation in the world. At the same time, Kristen Breitweiser used the Internet to mobilize public support for the families of 9/11 victims. And Barack Obama's 2008 presidential campaign, protesters demonstrating against various Middle East dictatorships, and the leaders of the Tea Party and Occupy Wall Street movements also used technology to inspire men and women to join their causes.

Along with the computer revolution, globalization has encouraged vast economic transformation throughout the world. Presidents as politically different as Bill Clinton and George W. Bush supported deregulation, free trade, and other policies that fostered corporate mergers that allowed businesses to reach beyond U.S. borders for cheap labor, raw materials, and markets in new and more profitable ways. While the 1990s witnessed the fruits of the new global economy, by 2008 the dangers of financial speculation and intertwined national economies became striking in the onset of the Great Recession. This economic collapse has underscored the inequalities of wealth that continue to exist and grow larger, aggravated by racial, ethnic, and gender disparities. Gripped by ongoing partisan deadlock, U.S. lawmakers have been unable to address the troublesome problems of unemployment, budget deficits, health care, global warming, immigration reform, energy consumption, and the protection of civil liberties.

Throughout its history, the United States has shown great strength in developing and adapting to new technology, with the computers of Bill Gates and other digital pioneers only the latest. At the same time, the nation has incorporated diverse populations into its midst, redefined old cultural identities and created new ones, expanded civil rights and civil liberties, extended economic opportunities, and joined other nations to fight military aggression and address common international concerns. The election of Barack Obama in 2008 shows that the nation has progressed significantly from the Reconstruction era to the present. Still, many problems remain before the United States achieves the "more perfect union" that the Founders and their successors envisioned. Ordinary Americans such as Kristen Breitweiser and many others who came before her have tried to make this country live up to its principles. The United States will have to draw on the many histories of its diverse peoples if it expects to continue to exert leadership in the world and maintain its greatness into the twenty-first century.

LEARNING*Curve*
Check what you know.
bedfordstmartins.com/hewittlawson/LC

Chapter Review

Online Study Guide ▶ bedfordstmartins.com/hewittlawson

KEY TERMS

"don't ask, don't tell" (p. 933)
Contract with America (p. 934)
Personal Responsibility and Work Opportunity
   Reconciliation Act (p. 934)
ethnic cleansing (p. 935)
Dayton Peace Accords (p. 935)
megachurches (p. 937)
Patriot Act (p. 938)
Bush Doctrine (p. 939)
Hurricane Katrina (p. 940)
Great Recession (p. 943)
subprime mortgages (p. 944)
Tea Party movement (p. 946)
Occupy Wall Street (p. 947)

REVIEW & RELATE

1. How have computers changed life in the United States?

2. How has globalization affected business consolidation and immigration?

3. How did conflicts between Democrats and Republicans affect President Clinton's accomplishments?

4. How did the end of the Cold War shape President Clinton's foreign policies?

5. How did President Bush put compassionate conservatism into action?

6. How did the war on terror prompt U.S. leaders to rethink America's position in the world?

7. What were the causes and consequences of the Great Recession?

8. What effects did the election and presidency of Barack Obama have on American politics and society?

TIMELINE OF EVENTS

1975	Microsoft formed
1976	Apple Computer Company formed
1980–1990s	Immigration surges from Mexico, Central America, the Caribbean, and South and East Asia
1991	World Wide Web comes into existence
1993–2011	"Don't ask, don't tell" policy enacted
1994	Contract with America announced; Republicans win control of Congress
1995	Dayton Peace Accords
1996	Personal Responsibility and Work Reconciliation Act reforms welfare
	Defense of Marriage Act
1998	President Clinton impeached
2000	al-Qaeda bombs USS *Cole* in Yemen
	Supreme Court rules in favor of George W. Bush in contested presidential election
2001	September 11 al-Qaeda attacks on World Trade Center and Pentagon
	U.S. troops invade Afghanistan; Patriot Act passed
2002	No Child Left Behind Act passed
2003–2011	War in Iraq
2005	Hurricane Katrina hits Gulf coast
2008	Great Recession begins
	Barack Obama elected president
	Tea Party movement formed
2009	Congress passes health care reform act
2011	Osama bin Laden killed by U.S. special forces
	Occupy Wall Street movement formed
2012	U.S. Census Bureau reports majority of nonwhite births for first time in U.S. history

The Uses of September 11

The terrorist attacks on the morning of September 11, 2001, killed three thousand people and left the American nation reeling. Millions spent that morning and the days that followed glued to their television sets, watching repeated images of the World Trade Center, the Pentagon, and scattered wreckage in Pennsylvania. Police and firefighters flocked to the Pentagon and Ground Zero to aid in rescue and recovery efforts. Rumors began circulating immediately about various terrorist groups or nations that might be responsible, and it was quickly discovered that the terrorist organization al-Qaeda, under the direction of Osama bin Laden, had carried out the attacks.

Americans reacted to the events in various ways, and official responses were immediate. The Bush administration launched the war on terror, which included the creation of the Department of Homeland Security, passage of the Patriot Act, and the invasion of Afghanistan. In the aftermath of the attacks, more than eighty thousand Arabs and Muslims living in the United States were fingerprinted and registered with the federal government. President Bush, believing that Saddam Hussein was linked to both the terrorism and al-Qaeda, launched an American invasion of Iraq in the spring of 2003.

Individuals and communities nationwide responded with an outpouring of grief. Throughout the nation, communities held ceremonies, candlelight vigils, and marches. Impromptu memorials appeared in New York City and Washington, D.C., and photos of the missing filled subway stations and parks. Many businesses and individuals prominently displayed American flags as people searched for ways to find meaning in the attacks.

The following documents present different responses to September 11, from official responses to cultural commentary on the events. As you read these documents, consider how the authors understand the attacks in the larger international context. How do the authors' different backgrounds influence their responses? In what ways do these documents speak to one another?

DOCUMENT 29.5

George W. Bush | The Axis of Evil, 2002

Four months after the September 11 attacks, President Bush delivered his annual State of the Union message, in which he expressed the lingering shock and outrage that many Americans felt and discussed his administration's actions, particularly the war in Afghanistan. He also issued a warning to those nations he deemed "an axis of evil"—North Korea, Iran, and Iraq. He accused Iraq of developing weapons of mass destruction, a charge that he used to support the American invasion of Iraq in 2003.

While the most visible military action is in Afghanistan, America is acting elsewhere. We now have troops in the Philippines, helping to train that country's armed forces to go after terrorist cells that have executed an American and still hold hostages. Our soldiers, working with the Bosnian Government, seized terrorists who were plotting to bomb our Embassy. Our Navy is patrolling the coast of Africa to block the shipment of weapons and the establishment of terrorist camps in Somalia.

My hope is that all nations will heed our call and eliminate the terrorist parasites who threaten their countries and our own. Many nations are acting forcefully. Pakistan is now cracking down on terror, and I admire the strong leadership of President [Pervez] Musharraf. But some governments will be timid in the face of terror. And make no mistake about it: If they do not act, America will.

Our second goal is to prevent regimes that sponsor terror from threatening America or our friends and allies with weapons of mass destruction. Some of these regimes have been pretty quiet since September the 11th, but we know their true nature.

North Korea is a regime arming with missiles and weapons of mass destruction, while starving its citizens.

Iran aggressively pursues these weapons and exports terror, while an unelected few repress the Iranian people's hope for freedom.

Iraq continues to flaunt its hostility toward America and to support terror. The Iraqi regime has plotted to develop anthrax and nerve gas and nuclear weapons for over a decade. This is a regime that has already used poison gas to murder thousands of its own citizens, leaving the bodies of mothers huddled over their dead children. This is a regime that agreed to international inspections, then kicked out the inspectors. This is a regime that has something to hide from the civilized world.

States like these and their terrorist allies constitute an axis of evil, arming to threaten the peace of the world. By seeking weapons of mass destruction, these regimes pose a grave and growing danger. They could provide these arms to terrorists, giving them the means to match their hatred. They could attack our allies or attempt to blackmail the United States. In any of these cases, the price of indifference would be catastrophic.

We will work closely with our coalition to deny terrorists and their state sponsors the materials, technology, and expertise to make and deliver weapons of mass destruction. We will develop and deploy effective missile defenses to protect America and our allies from sudden attack. And all nations should know: America will do what is necessary to ensure our Nation's security.

We'll be deliberate, yet time is not on our side. I will not wait on events while dangers gather. I will not stand by as peril draws closer and closer. The United States of America will not permit the world's most dangerous regimes to threaten us with the world's most destructive weapons.

Source: "Address before a Joint Session of the Congress on the State of the Union, January 29, 2002," *Weekly Compilation of Presidential Documents*, vol. 38, no. 5 (Washington, D.C.: Government Printing Office, Monday, February 4, 2002), 135.

DOCUMENT 29.6

Diana Hoffman | "The Power of Freedom," 2002

The September 11 attacks inspired thousands of poems, essays, and songs that expressed sorrow for the victims and resolve that the tragedy would make America a stronger nation. The following poem by Diana Hoffman, which reflects these sentiments, appeared on a memorial Web site in 2002.

I know you're celebrating
what your evil deeds have wrought
But with the devastation
something else you've also brought

For nothing is more powerful
than Americans who unite
Who put aside their differences
and for freedom fight

Each defenseless victim whose
untimely death you caused
And every fallen hero
whose brave life was lost

Has only served to strengthen
our national resolve
Each freedom-loving citizen
will surely get involved

You've galvanized our nation
into a force so strong
We'll end your reign of terror
although the fight is long

For every heart that's broken
ten million will stand tall
and every tear that's falling
is the mortar for it all

And when this war is over
one thing I know is sure
Our country will be greater
and our freedom will endure

Source: Diana Hoffman, "The Power of Freedom," http://911neverforget.tripod.com/neverforgotten/id3.html.

DOCUMENT 29.7

Daniel Harris | The Kitschification of September 11, 2001

Amid the outpouring of September 11 cultural and artistic expression, writer Daniel Harris criticized much of it as empty kitsch, or art that is considered overly sentimental and tasteless. His article on the "kitschification" of September 11 appeared on *Salon.com*, an online news and entertainment magazine.

Within minutes after the collapse of the World Trade Center, inspirational songs, propagandistic images designed to feed the fires of patriotic fury, and poetry commemorating the victims began to proliferate on radio, television, and the Internet. The Dixie Chicks performed an a cappella rendition of "The Star Spangled Banner"; car-window decals appeared featuring a lugubrious poodle with a glistening tear as large as a gum drop rolling mournfully down its cheek; refrigerator magnets of Old Glory flooded the market ("buy two and get a third one FREE!"); and the unofficial laureates of the World Wide Web brought the Internet to a crawl by posting thousands of elegies with such lyrics as "May America's flag forever fly unfurled, / May Heaven be our perished souls' 'Windows on the World'!" Gigabytes of odes to the lost firemen and celebrations of American resolve turned the information superhighway into a parking lot:

My Daddy's Flag

Arriving home from work and a trip to the store,

My 5 year old daughter greeted me at the door.

"Hi daddy!" she smiled, "what's in the bag?"

"Well, daddy has brought home the American flag."

With a puzzled look she asked "What does it do?"

I answered, "it's our country's colors, red, white, and blue.

This flag on our house will protect you my dear,

It has magical powers to keep away fear."

Does an event as catastrophic as this one require the rhetoric of kitsch to make it less horrendous? Do we need the overkill of ribbons and commemorative quilts, haloed seraphim perched on top of the burning towers, and teddy bears in firefighter helmets waving flags, in order to forget the final minutes of bond traders, restaurant workers, and secretaries screaming in elevators filling with smoke, standing in the frames of broken windows on the 90th floor waiting for help, and staggering down the stairwells covered in third-degree burns? Perhaps saccharine images of sobbing Statues of Liberty

(continued on page 956)

and posters that announce "we will never forget when the Eagle cried" make the incident more palatable, more "aesthetic" in a sense, decorated with the mortician's reassuringly familiar stock in trade. Through kitsch, we avert our eyes from tragedy, transforming the unspeakable ugliness of diseases, accidents, and wars into something poetic and noble, into pat stories whose happy endings offer enduring lessons in courage and resilience.

And yet while kitsch may serve to anesthetize us to the macabre spectacle of perfectly manicured severed hands embedded in the mud and charred bodies dropping out of windows, it may conceal another agenda. The strident sentimentality of kitsch makes the unsaid impermissible and silences dissenting opinions, which cannot withstand the emotional vehemence of its rhetoric. It not only beautifies ghoulish images, it whitewashes the political context of the attack which, when portrayed as a pure instance of gratuitous sadism, of inexpiable wickedness, appears to have had no cause, no ultimate goal. Four months to Bush's "crusade," despite clear successes, we remain far from certain about what, in the long run, we hope to achieve.

Source: Daniel Harris, "The Kitschification of September 11," in *Afterwords: Stories and Reports from 9/11 and Beyond*, compiled by the Editors of *Salon.com* and David Talbot (New York: Washington Square Press, 2002), 203–5.

DOCUMENT 29.8

Khaled Abou El Fadl | Response to September 11, 2001

Arab Americans and Muslims became targets of violence, racial profiling, surveillance, and even deportation in the wake of the September 11 attacks. Khaled Abou El Fadl is a law professor at the University of California at Los Angeles and a leading expert on Islamic law. In the following reflection, he recalls how he felt on September 11 and how being a Muslim shaped his response to the attacks.

My reaction very soon after it happened was anguished hope that Muslims were not involved in this. And actually I remember very distinctly sort of a degree of feeling ashamed about having that hope, because you would like to respond to something like this at a human and universal level. You would like to feel like, Muslim or not Muslim, this is just terrible, period. It's really irrelevant who has done this. But because of what I knew, what it's going to mean for Muslims, I knew that the sort of hyphenation of whether a Muslim did this or not was going to make a big difference for me, for my friends, for my family, for my son. That's a reality. And the agony of it has not subsided because the worst fears, that this is going to open a door of much suffering for many human beings, has fully materialized. . . .

The word *fear* describes everything. There is fear of fellow citizens being killed. There is fear that you yourself will be the subject of a terrorist attack. Terrorism doesn't have an exemption clause for Arabs or Muslims. If I was on that plane that day, the fact that I was Arab or Muslim wouldn't have made an iota of difference. So you run the risk of being the victim of a terrorist attack as much as any other member of society. But you now also run the risk of being blamed for it, just simply by the fact that you're Arab or Muslim. . . .

We belong on this plane and on our seat, you don't. You're here because we allow you to be here. It's as if it's a privilege. You're different, it's a privilege that you are allowed on this plane. And when I started wearing suits and ties consistently, regardless of how long or short the flight is, I've noticed that the treatment has gotten better. But it's always anxiety producing, not just for the normal security concerns, but because it's an unknown sum. You just don't know whether you're going to run into someone who's going to say something rude, something hurtful, whether you're going to sit next to someone who asks to change seats, which has happened to me, because they don't feel comfortable sitting next to you. Every time you pick up something from your travel bag, or you take out a magazine, or take out a book, they look like they're going to have a heart attack. Or constantly staring at you. It's just, it's an extremely anxiety producing experience and the irony of it is that if, God forbid, there is a terrorist attack, and I am on a plane, I'm just like everyone else, I die just like everyone else.

Source: "Face to Face: Stories from the Aftermath of Infamy," ITVS Interactive, http://archive.itvs.org/facetoface/stories/khaled.html.

DOCUMENT 29.9

Anti-Muslim Discrimination, 2011

The terrorist attacks on September 11 incited anti-Muslim sentiment among many Americans. Although President Bush made it clear that the enemy was al-Qaeda and not Muslims in general, the passage of the Patriot Act and the roundup and deportation of Arab and Muslim immigrants reflected an underlying hostility to Muslim Americans. This cartoon, which appeared in a Florida newspaper, compares discrimination against Muslims to the prejudice that Japanese Americans experienced during World War II.

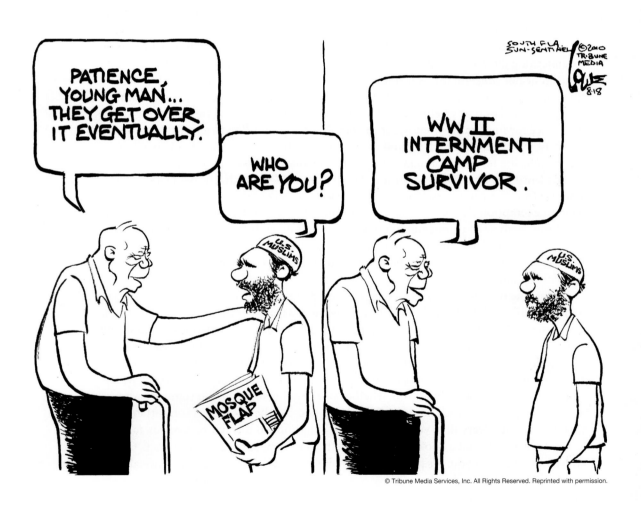

DOCUMENT 29.10

Brian Gallagher | Hundred-Mile Marine, 2012

In 2006 construction began on the National September 11 Memorial and Museum, located on the former site of the World Trade Center. The memorial was dedicated on the tenth anniversary of the attacks and has been visited by millions of people. Brian Gallagher, who grew up in New York City and served in the Marine Corps, explains his plan to honor the memory and sacrifices of those who died in the attacks and the servicemembers who fought in Iraq and Afghanistan. On May 26, 2012, he achieved his goal of running one hundred miles around the World Trade Center site.

At the time of its completion, One World Trade Center, or what is commonly known as the Freedom Tower, will soon scrape the New York City skyline at 1,776 feet. The height of the tower symbolically represents the year that [the] Continental Congress formally adopted the Declaration of Independence, charting a path of freedom for this great nation.

For centuries, we've enjoyed the fruits of liberty, which was due in large part to brave men and women who proudly serve in our military forces. Freedom is not, nor shall ever be, free. Protecting it bears a price. The price paid is not in currency, but in sacrifice. Sacrifice from the few, selfless warriors whose actions speak volumes—their dedication without reserve. They are the sons and daughters of our nation who risk their lives to protect ours and the freedoms we enjoy.

They come home wounded, forever changed. As these wounded warriors return home, many face difficult times. Their fight continues long after their time in service.

What do you do for those service members who provided the blanket of freedom that protects us and has been physically or mentally injured? How do you ensure their sacrifices do not fade from our memory?

(continued on page 960)

I asked myself the same questions and created an event to help spread awareness to the actions of our heroes.

On May 26, [2012] this Memorial Day weekend, I will execute a one-man, 100-mile run under 30 hours, circling around the World Trade Center to support wounded warriors and their families and to honor the sacrifices of our heroes who have shown the courage, commitment, and dedication that has been the hallmark and strength of our nation.

The height of the One World Trade Center symbolically represents the birth of America. It is my hope that my 100-mile journey is the first step to raise funds for the National September 11 Memorial & Museum and two other organizations that help assist our wounded warriors and their families.

As former Pres. Ronald Reagan once said, "Freedom is never more than one generation away from extinction. We didn't pass it to our children in the bloodstream. It must be fought for, protected, and handed on for them to do the same."

Please help me support those who have fought for and protected our freedom. Together, we can show these great warriors the enduring respect they deserve.

Source: "Marine Runs 100 Miles in Support of Memorial, Wounded Service Members," *The Memo Blog*, http://www.911memorial.org/blog/marine-runs-100-miles-support-911-memorial-and-wounded-military.

Interpret the Evidence

1. Of the three nations that George W. Bush characterizes as "an axis of evil" (Document 29.5), why do you think his administration chose to invade Iraq?

2. What do you think of Daniel Harris's assessment of September 11 responses as kitsch (Document 29.7)? What purposes does kitsch serve? What might Harris say about Diana Hoffman's poem (Document 29.6)?

3. How does being a Muslim shape Khaled Abou El Fadl's reaction to September 11 (Document 29.8)?

4. Why does the cartoonist in Document 29.9 compare the Muslim experience following September 11 to that of Japanese Americans interned in World War II camps?

5. How does Brian Gallagher draw on history to memorialize September 11 (Document 29.10)? How might his memories of September 11 differ from those of El Fadl?

Put It in Context

- Compare the treatment of Muslim Americans after September 11 with the experience of German Americans during World War I and Japanese Americans during World War II.

- How did the attacks on September 11 change America?

background photos: pages 954 and 956, Library of Congress

The Declaration of Independence

In Congress, July 4, 1776.

The unanimous Declaration of the thirteen united States of America,

When in the course of human events, it becomes necessary for one people to dissolve the political bands which have connected them with another, and to assume, among the powers of the earth, the separate and equal station to which the laws of nature and of nature's God entitle them, a decent respect to the opinions of mankind requires that they should declare the causes which impel them to the separation.

We hold these truths to be self-evident, that all men are created equal; that they are endowed by their Creator with certain unalienable rights; that among these, are life, liberty, and the pursuit of happiness. That, to secure these rights, governments are instituted among men, deriving their just powers from the consent of the governed; that, whenever any form of government becomes destructive of these ends, it is the right of the people to alter or to abolish it, and to institute a new government, laying its foundation on such principles, and organizing its powers in such form, as to them shall seem most likely to effect their safety and happiness. Prudence, indeed, will dictate that governments long established, should not be changed for light and transient causes; and, accordingly, all experience hath shown, that mankind are more disposed to suffer, while evils are sufferable, than to right themselves by abolishing the forms to which they are accustomed. But, when a long train of abuses and usurpations, pursuing invariably the same object, evinces a design to reduce them under absolute despotism, it is their right, it is their duty, to throw off such government and to provide new guards for their future security. Such has been the patient sufferance of these colonies, and such is now the necessity which constrains them to alter their former systems of government. The history of the present King of Great Britain is a history of repeated injuries and usurpations, all having, in direct object, the establishment of an absolute tyranny over these States. To prove this, let facts be submitted to a candid world: He has refused his assent to laws the most wholesome and necessary for the public good.

He has forbidden his governors to pass laws of immediate and pressing importance, unless suspended in their operation till his assent should be obtained; and, when so suspended, he has utterly neglected to attend to them.

He has refused to pass other laws for the accommodation of large districts of people, unless those people would relinquish the right of representation in the legislature; a right inestimable to them, and formidable to tyrants only.

He has called together legislative bodies at places unusual, uncomfortable, and distant from the depository of their public records, for the sole purpose of fatiguing them into compliance with his measures.

He has dissolved representative houses repeatedly for opposing, with manly firmness, his invasions on the rights of the people.

He has refused, for a long time after such dissolutions, to cause others to be elected; whereby the legislative powers, incapable of annihilation, have returned to the people at large for their exercise; the state remaining in the meantime exposed to all the danger of invasion from without, and convulsions within.

He has endeavoured to prevent the population of these States; for that purpose, obstructing the laws for naturalization of foreigners, refusing to pass others to encourage their migration hither, and raising the conditions of new appropriations of lands.

He has obstructed the administration of justice, by refusing his assent to laws for establishing judiciary powers.

He has made judges dependent on his will alone, for the tenure of their offices, and the amount and payment of their salaries.

He has erected a multitude of new offices, and sent hither swarms of officers to harass our people, and eat out their substance.

He has kept among us, in times of peace, standing armies, without the consent of our legislature.

He has affected to render the military independent of, and superior to, the civil power.

He has combined, with others, to subject us to a jurisdiction foreign to our Constitution, and unacknowledged by our laws; giving his assent to their acts of pretended legislation:

For quartering large bodies of armed troops among us:

For protecting them by a mock trial, from punishment, for any murders which they should commit on the inhabitants of these States:

For cutting off our trade with all parts of the world:

For imposing taxes on us without our consent:

For depriving us, in many cases, of the benefit of trial by jury:

For transporting us beyond seas to be tried for pretended offences:

For abolishing the free system of English laws in a neighboring province, establishing therein an arbitrary government, and enlarging its boundaries, so as to render it at once an example and fit instrument for introducing the same absolute rule into these colonies:

For taking away our charters, abolishing our most valuable laws, and altering, fundamentally, the powers of our governments:

For suspending our own legislatures, and declaring themselves invested with power to legislate for us in all cases whatsoever.

He has abdicated government here, by declaring us out of his protection, and waging war against us.

He has plundered our seas, ravaged our coasts, burnt our towns, and destroyed the lives of our people.

He is, at this time, transporting large armies of foreign mercenaries to complete the works of death, desolation, and tyranny, already begun, with circumstances of cruelty and perfidy scarcely paralleled in the most barbarous ages, and totally unworthy the head of a civilized nation.

He has constrained our fellow citizens, taken captive on the high seas, to bear arms against their country, to become the executioners of their friends, and brethren, or to fall themselves by their hands.

He has excited domestic insurrections amongst us, and has endeavored to bring on the inhabitants of our frontiers, the merciless Indian savages, whose known rule of warfare is an undistinguished destruction of all ages, sexes, and conditions.

In every stage of these oppressions, we have petitioned for redress; in the most humble terms; our repeated petitions have been answered only by repeated injury. A prince, whose character is thus marked by every act which may define a tyrant, is unfit to be the ruler of a free people.

Nor have we been wanting in attention to our British brethren. We have warned them, from time to time, of attempts made by their legislature to extend an unwarrantable jurisdiction over us. We have reminded them of the circumstances of our emigration and settlement here. We have appealed to their native justice and magnanimity, and we have conjured them, by the ties of our common kindred, to disavow these usurpations, which would inevitably interrupt our connections and correspondence. They, too, have been deaf to the voice of justice and consanguinity. We must, therefore, acquiesce in the necessity which denounces our separation, and hold them as we hold the rest of mankind, enemies in war, in peace, friends.

We, therefore, the representatives of the United States of America, in general Congress assembled, appealing to the Supreme Judge of the world for the rectitude of our intentions, do, in the name, and by authority of the good people of these colonies, solemnly publish and declare, that these united colonies are, and of right ought to be, free and independent states: that they are absolved from all allegiance to the British Crown, and that all political connection between them and the state of Great Britain is, and ought to be, totally dissolved; and that, as free and independent states, they have full power to levy war, conclude peace, contract alliances, establish commerce, and to do all other acts and things which independent states may of right do. And, for the support of this declaration, with a firm reliance on the protection of Divine Providence, we mutually pledge to each other our lives, our fortunes, and our sacred honor.

The foregoing Declaration was, by order of Congress, engrossed, and signed by the following members:

JOHN HANCOCK

New Hampshire
Josiah Bartlett
William Whipple
Matthew Thornton

Massachusetts Bay
Samuel Adams
John Adams
Robert Treat Paine
Elbridge Gerry

Rhode Island
Stephen Hopkins
William Ellery

Connecticut
Roger Sherman
Samuel Huntington
William Williams
Oliver Wolcott

New York
William Floyd
Phillip Livingston
Francis Lewis
Lewis Morris

New Jersey
Richard Stockton
John Witherspoon
Francis Hopkinson

John Hart
Abraham Clark

Pennsylvania
Robert Morris
Benjamin Rush
Benjamin Franklin
John Morton
George Clymer
James Smith
George Taylor
James Wilson
George Ross
Caesar Rodney
George Read
Thomas M'Kean

Maryland
Samuel Chase
William Paca
Thomas Stone
Charles Carroll, of Carrollton

North Carolina
William Hooper
Joseph Hewes
John Penn

South Carolina
Edward Rutledge
Thomas Heyward, Jr.
Thomas Lynch, Jr.
Arthur Middleton

Virginia
George Wythe
Richard Henry Lee
Thomas Jefferson
Benjamin Harrison
Thomas Nelson, Jr.
Francis Lightfoot Lee
Carter Braxton

Georgia
Button Gwinnett
Lyman Hall
George Walton

Resolved, That copies of the Declaration be sent to the several assemblies, conventions, and committees, or councils of safety, and to the several commanding officers of the continental troops; that it be proclaimed in each of the United States, at the head of the army.

The Articles of Confederation and Perpetual Union

Agreed to in Congress, November 15, 1777.
Ratified March 1781.

Between the states of New Hampshire, Massachusetts Bay, Rhode Island and Providence Plantations, Connecticut, New York, New Jersey, Pennsylvania, Delaware, Maryland, Virginia, North Carolina, South Carolina, Georgia.*

Article 1
The stile of this confederacy shall be "The United States of America."

Article 2
Each State retains its sovereignty, freedom and independence, and every power, jurisdiction, and right, which is not by this confederation expressly delegated to the United States, in Congress assembled.

Article 3
The said states hereby severally enter into a firm league of friendship with each other for their common defence, the security of their liberties and their mutual and general welfare; binding themselves to assist each other against all force offered to, or attacks made upon them, or any of them, on account of religion, sovereignty, trade, or any other pretence whatever.

Article 4
The better to secure and perpetuate mutual friendship and intercourse among the people of the different states in this

*This copy of the final draft of the Articles of Confederation is taken from the Journals, 9:907–925, November 15, 1777.

union, the free inhabitants of each of these states, paupers, vagabonds, and fugitives from justice excepted, shall be entitled to all privileges and immunities of free citizens in the several states; and the people of each State shall have free ingress and regress to and from any other State, and shall enjoy therein all the privileges of trade and commerce, subject to the same duties, impositions, and restrictions, as the inhabitants thereof respectively; provided, that such restrictions shall not extend so far as to prevent the removal of property, imported into any State, to any other State of which the owner is an inhabitant; provided also, that no imposition, duties, or restriction, shall be laid by any State on the property of the United States, or either of them. If any person guilty of, or charged with treason, felony, or other high misdemeanor in any State, shall flee from justice and be found in any of the United States, he shall, upon demand of the governor or executive power of the State from which he fled, be delivered up and removed to the State having jurisdiction of his offence. Full faith and credit shall be given in each of these states to the records, acts, and judicial proceedings of the courts and magistrates of every other State.

Article 5
For the more convenient management of the general interests of the United States, delegates shall be annually appointed, in such manner as the legislature of each State shall direct, to meet in Congress, on the 1st Monday in November in every year, with a power reserved to each State to recall its delegates, or any of them, at any time within the year, and to send others in their stead for the remainder of the year.

No State shall be represented in Congress by less than two, nor by more than seven members; and no person shall be capable of being a delegate for more than three years in any term of six years; nor shall any person, being a delegate, be capable of holding any office under the United States, for which he, or any other for his benefit, receives any salary, fees, or emolument of any kind.

Each State shall maintain its own delegates in a meeting of the states, and while they act as members of the committee of the states.

In determining questions in the United States, in Congress assembled, each State shall have one vote.

Freedom of speech and debate in Congress shall not be impeached or questioned in any court or place out of Congress: and the members of Congress shall be protected in their persons from arrests and imprisonments, during the time of their going to and from, and attendance on Congress, except for treason, felony, or breach of the peace.

Article 6

No State, without the consent of the United States, in Congress assembled, shall send any embassy to, or receive any embassy from, or enter into any conference, agreement, alliance, or treaty with any king, prince, or state; nor shall any person, holding any office of profit or trust under the United States, or any of them, accept of any present, emolument, office or title, of any kind whatever, from any king, prince, or foreign state; nor shall the United States, in Congress assembled, or any of them, grant any title of nobility.

No two or more states shall enter into any treaty, confederation, or alliance, whatever, between them, without the consent of the United States, in Congress assembled, specifying accurately the purposes for which the same is to be entered into, and how long it shall continue.

No state shall lay any imposts or duties which may interfere with any stipulations in treaties entered into by the United States, in Congress assembled, with any king, prince, or state, in pursuance of any treaties already proposed by Congress to the courts of France and Spain.

No vessels of war shall be kept up in time of peace by any State, except such number only as shall be deemed necessary by the United States, in Congress assembled, for the defence of such State or its trade; nor shall any body of forces be kept up by any State, in time of peace, except such number only as, in the judgment of the United States, in Congress assembled, shall be deemed requisite to garrison the forts necessary for the defence of such State; but every State shall always keep up a well regulated and disciplined militia, sufficiently armed and accoutred, and shall provide, and constantly have ready for use, in public stores, a due number of field pieces and tents, and a proper quantity of arms, ammunition and camp equipage.

No State shall engage in any war without the consent of the United States, in Congress assembled, unless such State be actually invaded by enemies, or shall have received certain advice of a resolution being formed by some nation of Indians to invade such State, and the danger is so imminent as not to admit of a delay till the United States, in Congress assembled, can be consulted; nor shall any State grant commissions to any ships or vessels of war, nor letters of marque or reprisal, except it be after a declaration of war by the United States, in Congress assembled, and then only against the kingdom or state, and the subjects thereof, against which war has been so declared, and under such regulations as shall be established by the United States, in Congress assembled, unless such State be infested by pirates, in which case vessels of war may be fitted out for that occasion, and kept so long as the danger shall continue, or until the United States, in Congress assembled, shall determine otherwise.

Article 7

When land forces are raised by any State for the common defence, all officers of or under the rank of colonel, shall be appointed by the legislature of each State respectively, by whom such forces shall be raised, or in such manner as such State shall direct; and all vacancies shall be filled up by the State which first made the appointment.

Article 8

All charges of war and all other expences, that shall be incurred for the common defence or general welfare, and allowed by the United States, in Congress assembled, shall be defrayed out of a common treasury, which shall be supplied by the several states, in proportion to the value of all land within each State, granted to or surveyed for any person, as such land and the buildings and improvements thereon shall be estimated according to such mode as the United States, in Congress assembled, shall, from time to time, direct and appoint.

The taxes for paying that proportion shall be laid and levied by the authority and direction of the legislatures of the several states, within the time agreed upon by the United States, in Congress assembled.

Article 9

The United States, in Congress assembled, shall have the sole and exclusive right and power of determining on peace and war, except in the cases mentioned in the 6th article; of sending and receiving ambassadors; entering into treaties and alliances, provided that no treaty of commerce shall be made, whereby the legislative power of the respective states shall be restrained from imposing such imposts and duties on foreigners as their own people are subjected to, or from prohibiting the exportation or importation of any species of goods or commodities whatsoever; of establishing rules for deciding, in all cases, what captures on land or water shall be legal, and in what manner prizes, taken by land or naval forces in the service of the United States, shall be divided or appropriated; of granting letters of marque and reprisal in times of peace; appointing courts for the trial of piracies and felonies committed on the high seas, and establishing courts for receiving and determining, finally, appeals in all cases of captures; provided, that no member of Congress shall be appointed a judge of any of the said courts.

The United States, in Congress assembled, shall also be the last resort on appeal in all disputes and differences now subsisting, or that hereafter may arise between two or more states concerning boundary, jurisdiction or any other cause whatever; which authority shall always be exercised in the manner following: whenever the legislative or executive authority, or lawful agent of any State, in controversy with another, shall present a petition to Congress, stating the matter in question, and praying for a hearing, notice thereof shall be given, by order of Congress, to the legislative or executive authority of the other State in controversy, and a day assigned for the appearance of the parties by their lawful agents, who shall then be directed to appoint, by joint consent, commissioners or judges to constitute a court for hearing and determining the matter in question; but, if they cannot agree, Congress shall name three persons out of each of the United States, and from the list of such persons each party shall alternately strike out one, the petitioners beginning, until the number shall be reduced to thirteen; and from that number not less than seven, nor more than nine names, as Congress shall direct, shall, in the presence of Congress, be drawn out by lot; and the persons whose names shall be so drawn, or any five of them, shall be commissioners or judges to hear and finally determine the controversy, so always as a major part of the judges who shall hear the cause shall agree in the determination; and if either party shall neglect to attend at the day appointed, without shewing reasons which Congress shall judge sufficient, or, being present, shall refuse to strike, the Congress shall proceed to nominate three persons out of each State, and the secretary of Congress shall strike in behalf of such party absent or refusing; and the judgment and sentence of the court to be appointed, in the manner before prescribed, shall be final and conclusive; and if any of the parties shall refuse to submit to the authority of such court, or to appear or defend their claim or cause, the court shall nevertheless proceed to pronounce sentence or judgment, which shall, in like manner, be final and decisive, the judgment or sentence and other proceedings begin, in either case, transmitted to Congress, and lodged among the acts of Congress for the security of the parties concerned: provided, that every commissioner, before he sits in

judgment, shall take an oath, to be administered by one of the judges of the supreme or superior court of the State where the cause shall be tried, "well and truly to hear and determine the matter in question, according to the best of his judgment, without favour, affection, or hope of reward:" provided, also, that no State shall be deprived of territory for the benefit of the United States.

All controversies concerning the private right of soil, claimed under different grants of two or more states, whose jurisdictions, as they may respect such lands and the states which passed such grants, are adjusted, the said grants, or either of them, being at the same time claimed to have originated antecedent to such settlement of jurisdiction, shall, on the petition of either party to the Congress of the United States, be finally determined, as near as may be, in the same manner as is before prescribed for deciding disputes respecting territorial jurisdiction between different states.

The United States, in Congress assembled, shall also have the sole and exclusive right and power of regulating the alloy and value of coin struck by their own authority, or by that of the respective states; fixing the standard of weights and measures throughout the United States; regulating the trade and managing all affairs with the Indians not members of any of the states; provided that the legislative right of any State within its own limits be not infringed or violated; establishing and regulating post offices from one State to another throughout all the United States, and exacting such postage on the papers passing through the same as may be requisite to defray the expences of the said office; appointing all officers of the land forces in the service of the United States, excepting regimental officers; appointing all the officers of the naval forces, and commissioning all officers whatever in the service of the United States; making rules for the government and regulation of the said land and naval forces, and directing their operations.

The United States, in Congress assembled, shall have authority to appoint a committee to sit in the recess of Congress, to be denominated "a Committee of the States," and to consist of one delegate from each State, and to appoint such other committees and civil officers as may be necessary for managing the general affairs of the United States, under their direction; to appoint one of their number to preside; provided that no person be allowed to serve in the office of president more than one year in any term of three years; to ascertain the necessary sums of money to be raised for the service of the United States, and to appropriate and apply the same for defraying the public expences; to borrow money or emit bills on the credit of the United States, transmitting, every half year, to the respective states, an account of the sums of money so borrowed or emitted; to build and equip a navy; to agree upon the number of land forces, and to make requisitions from each State for its quota, in proportion to the number of white inhabitants in such State; which requisitions shall be binding; and thereupon, the legislature of each State shall appoint the regimental officers, raise the men, and cloathe, arm, and equip them in a soldier-like manner, at the expence of the United States; and the officers and men so cloathed, armed, and equipped, shall march to the place appointed and within the time agreed on by the United States, in Congress assembled; but if the United States, in Congress assembled, shall, on consideration of circum-stances, judge proper that any State should not raise men, or should raise a smaller number than its quota, and that any other State should raise a greater number of men than the quota thereof, such extra number shall be raised, officered, cloathed, armed, and equipped in the same manner as the quota of such State, unless the legislature of such State shall judge that such extra number cannot be safely spared out of the same, in which case they shall raise, officer, cloathe, arm, and equip as many of such extra number as they judge can be safely spared. And the officers and men so cloathed, armed, and equipped, shall march to the place appointed and within the time agreed on by the United States, in Congress assembled.

The United States, in Congress assembled, shall never engage in a war, nor grant letters of marque and reprisal in time of peace, nor enter into any treaties or alliances, nor coin money, nor regulate the value thereof, nor ascertain the sums and expences necessary for the defence and welfare of the United States, or any of them: nor emit bills, nor borrow money on the credit of the United States, nor appropriate money, nor agree upon the number of vessels of war to be built or purchased, or the number of land or sea forces to be raised, nor appoint a commander in chief of the army or navy, unless nine states assent to the same; nor shall a question on any other point, except for adjourning from day to day, be determined, unless by the votes of a majority of the United States, in Congress assembled.

The Congress of the United States shall have power to adjourn to any time within the year, and to any place within the United States, so that no period of adjournment be for a longer duration than the space of six months, and shall publish the journal of their proceedings monthly, except such parts thereof, relating to treaties, alliances or military operations, as, in their judgment, require secrecy; and the yeas and nays of the delegates of each State on any question shall be entered on the journal, when it is desired by any delegate; and the delegates of a State, or any of them, at his, or their request, shall be furnished with a transcript of the said journal, except such parts as are above excepted, to lay before the legislatures of the several states.

Article 10

The committee of the states, or any nine of them, shall be authorized to execute, in the recess of Congress, such of the powers of Congress as the United States, in Congress assembled, by the consent of nine states, shall, from time to time, think expedient to vest them with; provided, that no power be delegated to the said committee, for the exercise of which, by the articles of confederation, the voice of nine states, in the Congress of the United States assembled, is requisite.

Article 11

Canada acceding to this confederation, and joining in the measures of the United States, shall be admitted into and entitled to all the advantages of this union; but no other colony shall be admitted into the same, unless such admis-sion be agreed to by nine states.

Article 12

All bills of credit emitted, monies borrowed and debts contracted by, or under the authority of Congress before the assembling of the United States, in pursuance of the present confederation, shall be deemed and considered as a charge against the United States, for payment and satisfaction whereof the said United States and the public faith are hereby solemnly pledged.

Article 13

Every State shall abide by the determinations of the United States, in Congress assembled, on all questions which, by this confederation, are submitted to them. And the articles of this confederation shall be inviolably observed by every State, and the union shall be perpetual; nor shall any alteration at any time hereafter be made in any of them, unless such alteration be agreed to in a Congress of the United States, and be afterwards confirmed by the legisla-tures of every State.

These articles shall be proposed to the legislatures of all the United States, to be considered, and if approved of by them, they are advised to authorize their delegates to ratify the same in the Congress of the United States; which being done, the same shall become conclusive.

The Constitution of the United States*

Agreed to by Philadelphia Convention, September 17, 1787. Implemented March 4, 1789.

Preamble

We the people of the United States, in order to form a more perfect union, establish justice, insure domestic tranquility, provide for the common defense, promote the general welfare, and secure the blessings of liberty to ourselves and our posterity, do ordain and establish this Constitution for the United States of America.

Article I

Section 1. All legislative powers herein granted shall be vested in a Congress of the United States, which shall consist of a Senate and a House of Representatives.

Section 2. The House of Representatives shall be composed of members chosen every second year by the people of the several States, and the electors in each State shall have the qualifications requisite for electors of the most numerous branch of the State Legislature.

No person shall be a Representative who shall not have attained to the age of twenty-five years, and been seven years a citizen of the United States, and who shall not, when elected, be an inhabitant of that State in which he shall be chosen.

Representatives and direct taxes shall be apportioned among the several States which may be included within this Union, according to their respective numbers, *which shall be determined by adding to the whole number of free persons, including those bound to service for a term of years and excluding Indians not taxed, three-fifths of all other persons.* The actual enumeration shall be made within three years after the first meeting of the Congress of the United States, and within every subsequent term of ten years, in such manner as they shall by law direct. The number of Representatives shall not exceed one for every thirty thousand, but each State shall have at least one Representative; and until such enumeration shall be made, *the State of New Hampshire shall be entitled to choose three, Massachusetts eight, Rhode Island and Providence Plantations one, Connecticut five, New York six, New Jersey four, Pennsylvania eight, Delaware one, Maryland six, Virginia ten, North Carolina five, South Carolina five, and Georgia three.*

When vacancies happen in the representation from any State, the Executive authority thereof shall issue writs of election to fill such vacancies.

The House of Representatives shall choose their Speaker and other officers; and shall have the sole power of impeachment.

Section 3. The Senate of the United States shall be composed of two Senators from each State, *chosen by the legislature thereof,* for six years; and each Senator shall have one vote.

Immediately after they shall be assembled in consequence of the first election, they shall be divided as equally as may be into three classes. The seats of the Senators of the first class shall be vacated at the expiration of the second year, of the second class at the expiration of the fourth year, and of the third class at the expiration of the sixth year, so that one-third may be chosen every second year; and if vacancies happen by resignation or otherwise, during the recess of the legislature of any State, the Executive thereof may make temporary appointments until the next meeting of the legislature, which shall then fill such vacancies.

No person shall be a Senator who shall not have attained to the age of thirty years, and been nine years a citizen of the United States, and who shall not, when elected, be an inhabitant of that State for which he shall be chosen.

The Vice-President of the United States shall be President of the Senate, but shall have no vote, unless they be equally divided.

The Senate shall choose their other officers, and also a President pro tempore, in the absence of the Vice-President, or when he shall exercise the office of President of the United States.

The Senate shall have the sole power to try all impeachments. When sitting for that purpose, they shall be on oath or affirmation. When the President of the United States is tried, the Chief Justice shall preside: and no person shall be convicted without the concurrence of two-thirds of the members present.

Judgment in cases of impeachment shall not extend further than to removal from the office, and disqualification to hold and enjoy any office of honor, trust or profit under the United States: but the party convicted shall nevertheless be liable and subject to indictment, trial, judgment and punishment, according to law.

Section 4. The times, places and manner of holding elections for Senators and Representatives shall be prescribed in each State by the legislature thereof; but the Congress may at any time by law make or alter such regulations, except as to the places of choosing Senators.

*Passages no longer in effect are in italic type.

The Congress shall assemble at least once in every year, and such meeting *shall be on the first Monday in December, unless they shall by law appoint a different day.*

Section 5. Each house shall be the judge of the elections, returns and qualifications of its own members, and a majority of each shall constitute a quorum to do business; but a smaller number may adjourn from day to day, and may be authorized to compel the attendance of absent members, in such manner, and under such penalties, as each house may provide.

Each house may determine the rules of its proceedings, punish its members for disorderly behavior, and with the concurrence of two-thirds, expel a member.

Each house shall keep a journal of its proceedings, and from time to time publish the same, excepting such parts as may in their judgment require secrecy; and the yeas and nays of the members of either house on any question shall, at the desire of one fifth of those present, be entered on the journal.

Neither house, during the session of Congress, shall, without the consent of the other, adjourn for more than three days, nor to any other place than that in which the two houses shall be sitting.

Section 6. The Senators and Representatives shall receive a compensation for their services, to be ascertained by law and paid out of the treasury of the United States. They shall in all cases except treason, felony and breach of the peace, be privileged from arrest during their attendance at the session of their respective houses, and in going to and returning from the same; and for any speech or debate in either house, they shall not be questioned in any other place.

No Senator or Representative shall, during the time for which he was elected, be appointed to any civil office under the authority of the United States, which shall have been created, or the emoluments whereof shall have been increased, during such time; and no person holding any office under the United States shall be a member of either house during his continuance in office.

Section 7. All bills for raising revenue shall originate in the House of Representatives; but the Senate may propose or concur with amendments as on other bills.

Every bill which shall have passed the House of Representatives and the Senate, shall, before it become a law, be presented to the President of the United States; if he approve he shall sign it, but if not he shall return it with objections to that house in which it shall have originated, who shall enter the objections at large on their journal, and proceed to reconsider it. If after such reconsideration two-thirds of that house shall agree to pass the bill, it shall be sent, together with

the objections, to the other house, by which it shall likewise be reconsidered, and, if approved by two-thirds of that house, it shall become a law. But in all such cases the votes of both houses shall be determined by yeas and nays, and the names of the persons voting for and against the bill shall be entered on the journal of each house respectively. If any bill shall not be returned by the President within ten days (Sundays excepted) after it shall have been presented to him, the same shall be a law, in like manner as if he had signed it, unless the Congress by their adjournment prevent its return, in which case it shall not be a law.

Every order, resolution, or vote to which the concurrence of the Senate and House of Representatives may be necessary (except on a question of adjournment) shall be presented to the President of the United States; and before the same shall take effect, shall be approved by him, or being disapproved by him, shall be repassed by two-thirds of the Senate and House of Representatives, according to the rules and limitations prescribed in the case of a bill.

Section 8. The Congress shall have power

To lay and collect taxes, duties, imposts, and excises, to pay the debts and provide for the common defense and general welfare of the United States; but all duties, imposts and excises shall be uniform throughout the United States;

To borrow money on the credit of the United States;

To regulate commerce with foreign nations, and among the several States, and with the Indian tribes;

To establish an uniform rule of naturalization, and uniform laws on the subject of bankruptcies throughout the United States;

To coin money, regulate the value thereof, and of foreign coin, and fix the standard of weights and measures;

To provide for the punishment of counterfeiting the securities and current coin of the United States;

To establish post offices and post roads;

To promote the progress of science and useful arts by securing for limited times to authors and inventors the exclusive right to their respective writings and discoveries;

To constitute tribunals inferior to the Supreme Court;

To define and punish piracies and felonies committed on the high seas and offences against the law of nations;

To declare war, grant letters of marque and reprisal, and make rules concerning captures on land and water;

To raise and support armies, but no appropriation of money to that use shall be for a longer term than two years;

To provide and maintain a navy;

To make rules for the government and regulation of the land and naval forces;

To provide for calling forth the militia to execute the laws of the Union, suppress insurrections and repel invasions;

To provide for organizing, arming, and disciplining the militia, and for governing such part of them as may be employed in the service of the United States, reserving to the States respectively the appointment of the officers, and the authority of training the militia according to the discipline prescribed by Congress;

To exercise exclusive legislation in all cases whatsoever, over such district (not exceeding ten miles square) as may, by cession of particular States, and the acceptance of Congress, become the seat of the government of the United States, and to exercise like authority over all places purchased by the consent of the legislature of the State, in which the same shall be, for erection of forts, magazines, arsenals, dock-yards, and other needful buildings;—and

To make all laws which shall be necessary and proper for carrying into execution the foregoing powers, and all other powers vested by this Constitution in the government of the United States, or in any department or officer thereof.

Section 9. *The migration or importation of such persons as any of the States now existing shall think proper to admit shall not be prohibited by the Congress prior to the year one thousand eight hundred and eight; but a tax or duty may be imposed on such importation, not exceeding ten dollars for each person.*

The privilege of the writ of habeas corpus shall not be suspended, unless when in cases of rebellion or invasion the public safety may require it.

No bill of attainder or ex post facto law shall be passed.

No capitation, or other direct, tax shall be laid, unless in proportion to the census or enumeration herein before directed to be taken.

No tax or duty shall be laid on articles exported from any State.

No preference shall be given by any regulation of commerce or revenue to the ports of one State over those of another; nor shall vessels bound to, or from, one State be obliged to enter, clear, or pay duties in another.

No money shall be drawn from the treasury, but in consequence of appropriations made by law; and a regular statement and account of the receipts and expenditures of all public money shall be published from time to time.

No title of nobility shall be granted by the United States: and no person holding any office of profit or trust under them, shall, without the consent of the Congress, accept of any present, emolument, office, or title, of any kind whatever, from any king, prince, or foreign state.

Section 10. No State shall enter into any treaty, alliance, or confederation; grant letters of marque and reprisal; coin money; emit bills of credit; make anything but gold and silver coin a tender in payment of debts; pass any bill of attainder, ex post facto law, or law impairing the obligation of contracts, or grant any title of nobility.

No State shall, without the consent of Congress, lay any imposts or duties on imports or exports, except what may be absolutely necessary for executing its inspection laws: and the net produce of all duties and imposts, laid by any State on imports or exports, shall be for the use of the treasury of the United States; and all such laws shall be subject to the revision and control of the Congress.

No State shall, without the consent of Congress, lay any duty of tonnage, keep troops, or ships of war in time of peace, enter into any agreement or compact with another State, or with a foreign power, or engage in war, unless actually invaded, or in such imminent danger as will not admit of delay.

Article II

Section 1. The executive power shall be vested in a President of the United States of America. He shall hold his office during the term of four years, and, together with the Vice-President, chosen for the same term, be elected as follows:

Each State shall appoint, in such manner as the legislature thereof may direct, a number of electors, equal to the whole number of Senators and Representatives to which the State may be entitled in the Congress; but no Senator or Representative, or person holding an office of trust or profit under the United States, shall be appointed an elector.

The electors shall meet in their respective States, and vote by ballot for two persons, of whom one at least shall not be an inhabitant of the same State with themselves. And they shall make a list of all the persons voted for, and of the number of votes for each; which list they shall sign and certify, and transmit sealed to the seat of government of the United States, directed to the President of the Senate. The President of the Senate shall, in the presence of the Senate and House of Representatives, open all the certificates, and the votes shall then be counted. The person having the greatest number of votes shall be the President, if such number be a majority of the whole number of electors appointed; and if there be more than one who have such majority, and have an equal number of votes, then the House of Representatives shall immediately choose by ballot one of them for President; and if no person have a majority, then from the five highest on the list said house shall in like manner choose the President. But in choosing the President the votes shall be taken by States, the representation from each State having one vote; a quorum for this purpose shall consist of a member or members from two-thirds of the States, and a majority of all the States shall be necessary to a choice. In every case, after the choice of the President, the person having the greatest number of votes of the electors shall be the Vice-President. But if there should remain two or more who have equal votes, the Senate shall choose from them by ballot the Vice-President.

The Congress may determine the time of choosing the electors, and the day on which they shall give their votes; which day shall be the same throughout the United States.

No person except a natural-born citizen, *or a citizen of the United States at the time of the adoption of this Constitution,* shall be eligible to the office of President; neither shall any person be eligible to that office who shall not have attained to the age of thirty-five years, and been fourteen years a resident within the United States.

In cases of the removal of the President from office or of his death, resignation, or inability to discharge the powers and duties of the said office, the same shall devolve on the Vice-President, and the Congress may by law provide for the case of removal, death, resignation, or inability, both of the President and Vice-President, declaring what officer shall then act as President, and such officer shall act accordingly, until the disability be removed, or a President shall be elected.

The President shall, at stated times, receive for his services a compensation, which shall neither be increased nor diminished during the period for which he shall have been elected, and he shall not receive within that period any other emolument from the United States, or any of them.

Before he enter on the execution of his office, he shall take the following oath or affirmation:—"I do solemnly swear (or affirm) that I will faithfully execute the office of the President of the United States, and will to the best of my ability preserve, protect and defend the Constitution of the United States."

Section 2. The President shall be commander in chief of the army and navy of the United States, and of the militia of the several States, when called into the actual service of the United States; he may require the opinion, in writing, of the principal officer in each of the executive departments, upon any subject relating to the duties of their respective offices, and he shall have power to grant reprieves and pardons for offenses against the United States, except in cases of impeachment.

He shall have power, by and with the advice and consent of the Senate, to make treaties, provided two-thirds of the Senators present concur; and he shall nominate, and by and with the advice and consent of the Senate, shall appoint ambassadors, other public ministers and consuls, judges of the Supreme Court, and all other officers of the United States, whose appointments are not herein otherwise provided for, and which shall be established by law: but Congress may by law vest the appointment of such inferior officers, as they think proper, in the President alone, in the courts of law, or in the heads of departments.

The President shall have power to fill up all vacancies that may happen during the recess of the Senate, by granting commissions which shall expire at the end of their next session.

Section 3. He shall from time to time give to the Congress information of the state of the Union, and recommend to their consideration such measures as he shall judge necessary and expedient; he may, on extraordinary occasions, convene both houses, or either of them, and in case of disagreement between them, with respect to the time of adjournment, he may adjourn them to such time as he shall think proper; he shall receive ambassadors and other public ministers; he shall take care that the laws be faithfully executed, and shall commission all the officers of the United States.

Section 4. The President, Vice-President and all civil officers of the United States shall be removed from office on impeachment for, and on conviction of, treason, bribery, or other high crimes and misdemeanors.

Article III

Section 1. The judicial power of the United States shall be vested in one Supreme Court, and in such inferior courts as the Congress may from time to time ordain and establish. The judges, both of the Supreme and inferior courts, shall hold their offices during good behavior, and shall, at stated times, receive for their services a compensation which shall not be diminished during their continuance in office.

Section 2. The judicial power shall extend to all cases, in law and equity, arising under this Constitution, the laws of the United States, and treaties made, or which shall be made, under their authority;—to all cases affecting ambassadors, other public ministers and consuls;—to all cases of admiralty and maritime jurisdiction;—to controversies to which the United States shall be a party;—to controversies between two or more States;—between a State and citizens of another State;—between citizens of different States;—between citizens of the same State claiming lands under grants of different States, and between a State, or the citizens thereof, and foreign states, citizens or subjects.

In all cases affecting ambassadors, other public ministers and consuls, and those in which a State shall be party, the Supreme Court shall have original jurisdiction. In all the other cases before mentioned, the Supreme Court shall have appellate jurisdiction, both as to law and fact, with such exceptions, and under such regulations, as the Congress shall make.

The trial of all crimes, except in cases of impeachment, shall be by jury; and such trial shall be held in the State where said crimes shall have been committed; but when not committed within any State, the trial shall be at such place or places as the Congress may by Law have directed.

Section 3. Treason against the United States shall consist only in levying war against them, or in adhering to their enemies, giving them aid and comfort. No person shall be convicted of treason unless on the testimony of two witnesses to the same overt act, or on confession in open court.

The Congress shall have power to declare the punishment of treason, but no attainder of treason shall work corruption of blood, or forfeiture except during the life of the person attainted.

Article IV

Section 1. Full faith and credit shall be given in each State to the public acts, records, and judicial proceedings of every other State. And the Congress may by general laws prescribe the manner in which such acts, records, and proceedings shall be proved, and the effect thereof.

Section 2. The citizens of each State shall be entitled to all privileges and immunities of citizens in the several States.

A person charged in any State with treason, felony, or other crime, who shall flee from justice, and be found in another State, shall on demand of the executive authority of the State from which he fled, be delivered up, to be removed to the State having jurisdiction of the crime.

No Person held to service or labor in one State, under the laws thereof, escaping into another, shall, in consequence of any law or regulation therein, be discharged from such service or labor, but shall be delivered up on claim of the party to whom such service or labor may be due.

Section 3. New States may be admitted by the Congress into this Union; but no new State shall be formed or erected within the jurisdiction of any other State; nor any State be formed by the junction of two or more States, or parts of States, without the consent of the legislatures of the States concerned as well as of the Congress.

The Congress shall have power to dispose of and make all needful rules and regulations respecting the territory or other property belonging to the United States; and nothing in this Constitution shall be so construed as to prejudice any claims of the United States, or of any particular State.

Section 4. The United States shall guarantee to every State in this Union a republican form of government, and shall protect each of them against invasion; and on application of the legislature, or of the executive (when the legislature cannot be convened), against domestic violence.

Article V

The Congress, whenever two-thirds of both houses shall deem it necessary, shall propose amendments to this Constitution, or, on the application of the legislatures of two-thirds of the several States, shall call a convention for proposing amendments, which, in either case, shall be valid to all intents and purposes, as part of this Constitution, when ratified by the legislatures of three-fourths of the several States, or by conventions in three-fourths thereof, as the one or the other mode of ratification may be proposed by the Congress; *provided that no amendments which may be made prior to the year one thousand eight hundred and eight shall in any manner affect the first and fourth clauses in the ninth section of the first article;* and that no State, without its consent, shall be deprived of its equal suffrage in the Senate.

Article VI

All debts contracted and engagements entered into, before the adoption of this Constitution, shall be as valid against the United States under this Constitution, as under the Confederation.

This Constitution, and the laws of the United States which shall be made in pursuance thereof; and all treaties made, or which shall be made, under the authority of the United States, shall be the supreme law of the land; and the judges in every State shall be bound thereby, anything in the Constitution or laws of any State to the contrary notwithstanding.

The Senators and Representatives before mentioned, and the members of the several State legislatures, and all executive and judicial officers, both of the United States and of the several States, shall be bound by oath or affirmation to support this Constitution; but no religious test shall ever be required as a qualification to any office or public trust under the United States.

Article VII

The ratification of the conventions of nine States shall be sufficient for the establishment of this Constitution between the States so ratifying the same.

Done in convention by the unanimous consent of the States present, the seventeenth day of September in the year of our Lord one thousand seven hundred and eighty-seven and of the Independence of the United States of America the twelfth. In witness whereof we have hereunto subscribed our names.

GEORGE WASHINGTON, President and Deputy from Virginia

New Hampshire
John Langdon
Nicholas Gilman

Massachusetts
Nathaniel Gorham
Rufus King

Connecticut
William Samuel
 Johnson
Roger Sherman

New York
Alexander Hamilton

New Jersey
William Livingston
David Brearley
William Paterson
Jonathan Dayton

Pennsylvania
Benjamin Franklin
Thomas Mifflin
Robert Morris
George Clymer
Thomas FitzSimons
Jared Ingersoll
James Wilson
Gouverneur Morris

Delaware
George Read
Gunning Bedford, Jr.
John Dickinson
Richard Bassett
Jacob Broom

Maryland
James McHenry
Daniel of St. Thomas Jenifer
Daniel Carroll

Virginia
John Blair
James Madison, Jr.

North Carolina
William Blount
Richard Dobbs Spaight
Hugh Williamson

South Carolina
John Rutledge
Charles Cotesworth Pinckney
Charles Pinckney
Pierce Butler

Georgia
William Few
Abraham Baldwin

Amendments to the Constitution
(including six unratified amendments)

Amendment I
[Ratified 1791]

Congress shall make no law respecting an establishment of religion, or prohibiting the free exercise thereof; or abridging the freedom of speech, or of the press; or the right of the people peaceably to assemble, and to petition the government for a redress of grievances.

Amendment II
[Ratified 1791]

A well-regulated militia being necessary to the security of a free State, the right of the people to keep and bear arms shall not be infringed.

Amendment III
[Ratified 1791]

No soldier shall, in time of peace, be quartered in any house without the consent of the owner, nor in time of war, but in a manner to be prescribed by law.

Amendment IV
[Ratified 1791]

The right of the people to be secure in their persons, houses, papers, and effects, against unreasonable searches and seizures, shall not be violated, and no warrants shall issue but upon probable cause, supported by oath or affirmation, and particularly describing the place to be searched, and the persons or things to be seized.

Amendment V
[Ratified 1791]

No person shall be held to answer for a capital, or otherwise infamous crime, unless on a presentment or indictment of a grand jury, except in cases arising in the land or naval forces, or in the militia, when in actual service in time of war or public danger; nor shall any person be subject for the same offence to be twice put in jeopardy of life or limb; nor shall be compelled in any criminal case to be a witness against himself, nor be deprived of life, liberty, or property, without due process of law; nor shall private property be taken for public use without just compensation.

Amendment VI
[Ratified 1791]

In all criminal prosecutions, the accused shall enjoy the right to a speedy and public trial, by an impartial jury of the State and district wherein the crime shall have been committed, which district shall have been previously ascertained by law, and to be informed of the nature and cause of the accusation; to be confronted with the witnesses against him; to have compulsory process for obtaining witnesses in his favor, and to have the assistance of counsel for his defence.

Amendment VII
[Ratified 1791]

In suits at common law, where the value in controversy shall exceed twenty dollars, the right of trial by jury shall be preserved, and no fact tried by a jury shall be otherwise reexamined in any court of the United States, than according to the rules of the common law.

Amendment VIII
[Ratified 1791]

Excessive bail shall not be required, nor excessive fines imposed, nor cruel and unusual punishments inflicted.

Amendment IX
[Ratified 1791]

The enumeration in the Constitution, of certain rights, shall not be construed to deny or disparage others retained by the people.

Amendment X
[Ratified 1791]

The powers not delegated to the United States by the Constitution, nor prohibited by it to the States, are reserved to the States respectively, or to the people.

Unratified Amendment
[Reapportionment Amendment (proposed by Congress September 25, 1789, along with the Bill of Rights)]

After the first enumeration required by the first article of the Constitution, there shall be one Representative for every thirty thousand, until the number shall amount to one hundred, after which the proportion shall be so regulated by Congress, that there shall be not less than one hundred Representatives, nor less than one Representative for every forty thousand persons, until the number of Representatives shall amount to two hundred; after which the proportion shall be so regulated by Congress, that there shall not be less than two hundred Representatives, nor more than one Representative for every fifty thousand persons.

Amendment XI
[Ratified 1798]

The judicial power of the United States shall not be construed to extend to any suit in law or equity, commenced or prosecuted against one of the United States by citizens of another State, or by citizens or subjects of any foreign state.

Amendment XII
[Ratified 1804]

The electors shall meet in their respective States, and vote by ballot for President and Vice-President, one of whom, at least, shall not be an inhabitant of the same State with themselves; they shall name in their ballots the person voted for as President, and in distinct ballots the person voted for as Vice-President, and they shall make distinct lists of all persons voted for as President, and of all persons voted for as Vice-President, and of the number of votes for each, which lists they shall sign and certify, and transmit sealed to the seat of government of the United States, directed to the President of the Senate;—the President of the Senate shall, in the presence of the Senate and House of Representatives, open all the certificates and the votes shall then be counted;—the person having the greatest number of votes for President shall be the President, if such number be a majority of the whole number of electors appointed; and if no person have such majority, then from the persons having the highest numbers not exceeding three on the list of those voted for as President, the House of Representatives shall choose immediately, by ballot, the President. But in choosing the President, the votes shall be taken by States, the representation from each State having one vote; a quorum for this purpose shall consist of a member or members from two-thirds of the States, and a majority of all the States shall be necessary to a choice. And if the House of Representatives shall not choose a President whenever the right of choice shall devolve upon them, before *the fourth day of March* next following, then the Vice-President shall act as President, as in the case of the death or other constitutional disability of the President.

The person having the greatest number of votes as Vice-President shall be the Vice-President, if such number be a majority of the whole number of electors appointed; and if no person have a majority, then from the two highest numbers on the list the Senate shall choose the Vice-President; a quorum for the purpose shall consist of two-thirds of the whole number of Senators, and a majority of the whole number shall be necessary to a choice. But no person constitutionally ineligible to the office of President shall be eligible to that of Vice-President of the United States.

Unratified Amendment
[Titles of Nobility Amendment (proposed by Congress May 1, 1810)]

If any citizen of the United States shall accept, claim, receive or retain any title of nobility or honor or shall, without the consent of Congress, accept and retain any present, pension, office or emolument of any kind whatever, from any emperor, king, prince or foreign power, such person shall cease to be a citizen of the United States, and shall be incapable of holding any office of trust or profit under them or either of them.

Unratified Amendment
[Corwin Amendment (proposed by Congress March 2, 1861)]

No amendment shall be made to the Constitution which will authorize or give to Congress the power to abolish or interfere, within any State, with the domestic institutions thereof, including that of persons held to labor or service by the laws of said State.

Amendment XIII
[Ratified 1865]

Section 1. Neither slavery nor involuntary servitude, except as a punishment for crime whereof the party shall have been duly convicted, shall exist within the United States, or any place subject to their jurisdiction.

Section 2. Congress shall have power to enforce this article by appropriate legislation.

Amendment XIV
[Ratified 1868]

Section 1. All persons born or naturalized in the United States, and subject to the jurisdiction thereof, are citizens of the United States and of the State wherein they reside. No State shall make or enforce any law which shall abridge the privileges or immunities of citizens of the United States; nor shall any State deprive any person of life, liberty, or property, without due process of law; nor deny to any person within its jurisdiction the equal protection of the laws.

Section 2. Representatives shall be appointed among the several States according to their respective numbers, counting the whole number of persons in each State, excluding Indians not taxed. But when the right to vote at any election for the choice of Electors for President and Vice-President of the United States, Representatives in Congress, the executive and judicial officers of a State, or the members of the legislature thereof, is denied to any of the *male* inhabitants of such State, being *twenty-one* years of age and citizens of the United States, or in any way abridged, except for participation in rebellion, or other crime, the basis of representation therein shall be reduced in the proportion which the number of such male citizens shall bear to the whole number of *male* citizens *twenty-one* years of age in such State.

Section 3. No person shall be a Senator or Representative in Congress, or Elector of President and Vice-President, or hold any office, civil or military, under the United States, or under any State, who, having previously taken an oath, as a member of Congress, or as an officer of the United States, or as a member of any State legislature, or as an executive or judicial officer of any State, to support the Constitution of the United States, shall have engaged in insurrection or rebellion against the same, or given aid or comfort to the enemies thereof. Congress may, by a vote of two-thirds of each house, remove such disability.

Section 4. The validity of the public debt of the United States, authorized by law, including debts incurred for payment of pensions and bounties for services in suppressing insurrection or rebellion, shall not be questioned. But neither the United States nor any State shall assume or pay any debt or obligation incurred in aid of insurrection or rebellion against the United States, or any claim for the loss or emancipation of any slave; but all such debts, obligations, and claims shall be held illegal and void.

Section 5. The Congress shall have power to enforce, by appropriate legislation, the provisions of this article.

Amendment XV
[Ratified 1870]

Section 1. The right of citizens of the United States to vote shall not be denied or abridged by the United States or by any State on account of race, color, or previous condition of servitude.

Section 2. The Congress shall have power to enforce this article by appropriate legislation.

Amendment XVI
[Ratified 1913]

The Congress shall have power to lay and collect taxes on incomes, from whatever source derived, without apportionment among the several States, and without regard to any census or enumeration.

Amendment XVII
[Ratified 1913]

Section 1. The Senate of the United States shall be composed of two Senators from each State, elected by the people thereof, for six years; and each Senator shall have one vote. The electors in each State shall have the qualifications requisite for electors of [voters for] the most numerous branch of the State legislatures.

Section 2. When vacancies happen in the representation of any State in the Senate, the executive authority of such State shall issue writs of election to fill such vacancies: Provided, that the Legislature of any State may empower the executive thereof to make temporary appointments until the people fill the vacancies by election as the Legislature may direct.

Section 3. *This amendment shall not be so construed as to affect the election or term of any Senator chosen before it becomes valid as part of the Constitution.*

Amendment XVIII
[Ratified 1919; repealed 1933 by Amendment XXI]

Section 1. *After one year from the ratification of this article the manufacture, sale, or transportation of intoxicating liquors within, the importation thereof into, or the exportation thereof from the United States and all territory subject to the jurisdiction thereof, for beverage purposes, is hereby prohibited.*

Section 2. *The Congress and the several States shall have concurrent power to enforce this article by appropriate legislation.*

Section 3. *This article shall be inoperative unless it shall have been ratified as an amendment to the Constitution by the legislatures of the several States, as provided by the Constitution, within seven years from the date of the submission thereof to the States by the Congress.*

Amendment XIX
[Ratified 1920]

Section 1. The right of citizens of the United States to vote shall not be denied or abridged by the United States or by any State on account of sex.

Section 2. Congress shall have the power to enforce this article by appropriate legislation.

Unratified Amendment
[Child Labor Amendment (proposed by Congress June 2, 1924)]

Section 1. *The Congress shall have power to limit, regulate, and prohibit the labor of persons under eighteen years of age.*

Section 2. *The power of the several States is unimpaired by this article except that the operation of State laws shall be suspended to the extent necessary to give effect to legislation enacted by Congress.*

Amendment XX
[Ratified 1933]

Section 1. The terms of the President and Vice-President shall end at noon on the 20th day of January, and the terms of Senators and Representatives at noon on the 3rd day of January, of the years in which such terms would have ended if this article had not been ratified; and the terms of their successors shall then begin.

Section 2. The Congress shall assemble at least once in every year, and such meeting shall begin at noon on the 3rd day of January, unless they shall by law appoint a different day.

Section 3. If, at the time fixed for the beginning of the term of the President, the President-elect shall have died, the Vice-President-elect shall become President. If a President shall not have been chosen before the time fixed for the beginning of his term, or if the President-elect shall have failed to qualify, then the Vice-President-elect shall act as President until a President shall have qualified; and the Congress may by law provide for the case wherein neither a President-elect nor a Vice-President-elect shall have qualified, declaring who shall then act as President, or the manner in which one who is to act shall be selected, and such person shall act accordingly until a President or Vice-President shall have qualified.

Section 4. The Congress may by law provide for the case of the death of any of the persons from whom the House of Representatives may choose a President whenever the right of choice shall have devolved upon them, and for the case of the death of any of the persons from whom the Senate may choose a Vice-President whenever the right of choice shall have devolved upon them.

Section 5. Sections 1 and 2 shall take effect on the 15th day of October following the ratification of this article.

Section 6. This article shall be inoperative unless it shall have been ratified as an amendment to the Constitution by the Legislatures of three-fourths of the several States within seven years from the date of its submission.

Amendment XXI
[Ratified 1933]

Section 1. The eighteenth article of amendment to the Constitution of the United States is hereby repealed.

Section 2. The transportation or importation into any State, Territory, or Possession of the United States for delivery or use therein of intoxicating liquors, in violation of the laws thereof, is hereby prohibited.

Section 3. This article shall be inoperative unless it shall have been ratified as an amendment to the Constitution by conventions in the several States, as provided in the Constitution, within seven years from the date of the submission thereof to the States by the Congress.

Amendment XXII
[Ratified 1951]

Section 1. No person shall be elected to the office of the President more than twice, and no person who has held the office of President, or acted as President, for more than two years of a term to which some other person was elected President shall be elected to the office of President more than once. But this article shall not apply to any person holding the office of President when this Article was proposed by the Congress, and shall not prevent any person who may be holding the office of President, or acting as President, during the term within which this Article becomes operative from holding the office of President or acting as President during the remainder of such term.

Section 2. This article shall be inoperative unless it shall have been ratified as an amendment to the Constitution by the legislatures of three-fourths of the several States within seven years from the date of its submission to the States by the Congress.

Amendment XXIII
[Ratified 1961]

Section 1. The District constituting the seat of Government of the United States shall appoint in such manner as the Congress may direct: A number of electors of President and Vice-President equal to the whole number of Senators and Representatives in Congress to which the District would be entitled if it were a State, but in no event more than the least populous State; they shall be in addition to those appointed by the States, but they shall be considered for the purposes of the election of President and Vice-President, to be electors appointed by a State; and they shall meet in the District and perform such duties as provided by the twelfth article of amendment.

Section 2. The Congress shall have the power to enforce this article by appropriate legislation.

Amendment XXIV
[Ratified 1964]

Section 1. The right of citizens of the United States to vote in any primary or other election for President or Vice-President, for electors for President or Vice-President, or for Senator or Representative in Congress, shall not be denied or abridged by the United States or any State by reason of failure to pay any poll tax or other tax.

Section 2. The Congress shall have the power to enforce this article by appropriate legislation.

Amendment XXV
[Ratified 1967]

Section 1. In case of the removal of the President from office or of his death or resignation, the Vice-President shall become President.

Section 2. Whenever there is a vacancy in the office of the Vice-President, the President shall nominate a Vice-President who shall take office upon confirmation by a majority vote of both Houses of Congress.

Section 3. Whenever the President transmits to the President pro tempore of the Senate and the Speaker of the House of Representatives his written declaration that he is unable to discharge the powers and duties of his office, and until he transmits to them a written declaration to the contrary, such powers and duties shall be discharged by the Vice-President as Acting President.

Section 4. Whenever the Vice-President and a majority of either the principal officers of the executive departments or of such other body as Congress may by law provide, transmit to the President pro tempore of the Senate and the Speaker of the House of Representatives their written declaration that the President is unable to discharge the powers and duties of his office, the Vice-President shall immediately assume the powers and duties of the office as Acting President.

Thereafter, when the President transmits to the President pro tempore of the Senate and the Speaker of the House of Representatives his written declaration that no inability exists, he shall resume the powers and duties of his office unless the Vice-President and a majority of either the principal officers of the executive department[s] or of such other body as Congress may by law provide, transmit within four days to the President pro tempore of the Senate and the Speaker of the House of Representatives their written declaration that the President is unable to discharge the powers and duties of his office. Thereupon Congress shall decide the issue, assembling within forty-eight hours for that purpose if not in session. If the Congress, within twenty-one days after receipt of the latter written declaration, or, if Congress is not in session, within twenty-one days after Congress is required to assemble, determines by two-thirds vote of both Houses that the President is unable to discharge the powers and duties of his office, the Vice-President shall continue to discharge the same as Acting President; otherwise, the President shall resume the powers and duties of his office.

Amendment XXVI
[Ratified 1971]

Section 1. The right of citizens of the United States, who are eighteen years of age or older, to vote shall not be denied or abridged by the United States or by any State on account of age.

Section 2. The Congress shall have power to enforce this article by appropriate legislation.

Unratified Amendment
[Equal Rights Amendment (proposed by Congress March 22, 1972; seven-year deadline for ratification extended to June 30, 1982)]

Section 1. *Equality of rights under the law shall not be denied or abridged by the United States or by any State on account of sex.*

Section 2. *The Congress shall have the power to enforce, by appropriate legislation, the provisions of this article.*

Section 3. *This amendment shall take effect two years after the date of ratification.*

Unratified Amendment
[D.C. Statehood Amendment (proposed by Congress August 22, 1978)]

Section 1. *For purposes of representation in the Congress, election of the President and Vice-President, and article V of this Constitution, the District constituting the seat of government of the United States shall be treated as though it were a State.*

Section 2. *The exercise of the rights and powers conferred under this article shall be by the people of the District constituting the seat of government, and as shall be provided by Congress.*

Section 3. *The twenty-third article of amendment to the Constitution of the United States is hereby repealed.*

Section 4. *This article shall be inoperative, unless it shall have been ratified as an amendment to the Constitution by the legislatures of three-fourths of the several states within seven years from the date of its submission.*

Amendment XXVII
[Ratified 1992]

No law, varying the compensation for the services of the Senators and Representatives, shall take effect, until an election of Representatives shall have intervened.

Admission of States to the Union

State	Year of Admission	State	Year of Admission
Delaware	1787	Michigan	1837
Pennsylvania	1787	Florida	1845
New Jersey	1787	Texas	1845
Georgia	1788	Iowa	1846
Connecticut	1788	Wisconsin	1848
Massachusetts	1788	California	1850
Maryland	1788	Minnesota	1858
South Carolina	1788	Oregon	1859
New Hampshire	1788	Kansas	1861
Virginia	1788	West Virginia	1863
New York	1788	Nevada	1864
North Carolina	1789	Nebraska	1867
Rhode Island	1790	Colorado	1876
Vermont	1791	North Dakota	1889
Kentucky	1792	South Dakota	1889
Tennessee	1796	Montana	1889
Ohio	1803	Washington	1889
Louisiana	1812	Idaho	1890
Indiana	1816	Wyoming	1890
Mississippi	1817	Utah	1896
Illinois	1818	Oklahoma	1907
Alabama	1819	New Mexico	1912
Maine	1820	Arizona	1912
Missouri	1821	Alaska	1959
Arkansas	1836	Hawaii	1959

Presidents of the United States

President	Term	President	Term
George Washington	1789–1797	Benjamin Harrison	1889–1893
John Adams	1797–1801	Grover Cleveland	1893–1897
Thomas Jefferson	1801–1809	William McKinley	1897–1901
James Madison	1809–1817	Theodore Roosevelt	1901–1909
James Monroe	1817–1825	William H. Taft	1909–1913
John Quincy Adams	1825–1829	Woodrow Wilson	1913–1921
Andrew Jackson	1829–1837	Warren G. Harding	1921–1923
Martin Van Buren	1837–1841	Calvin Coolidge	1923–1929
William H. Harrison	1841	Herbert Hoover	1929–1933
John Tyler	1841–1845	Franklin D. Roosevelt	1933–1945
James K. Polk	1845–1849	Harry S. Truman	1945–1953
Zachary Taylor	1849–1850	Dwight D. Eisenhower	1953–1961
Millard Fillmore	1850–1853	John F. Kennedy	1961–1963
Franklin Pierce	1853–1857	Lyndon B. Johnson	1963–1969
James Buchanan	1857–1861	Richard M. Nixon	1969–1974
Abraham Lincoln	1861–1865	Gerald R. Ford	1974–1977
Andrew Johnson	1865–1869	Jimmy Carter	1977–1981
Ulysses S. Grant	1869–1877	Ronald Reagan	1981–1989
Rutherford B. Hayes	1877–1881	George H. W. Bush	1989–1993
James A. Garfield	1881	Bill Clinton	1993–2001
Chester A. Arthur	1881–1885	George W. Bush	2001–2009
Grover Cleveland	1885–1889	Barack Obama	2009–

acquired immune deficiency syndrome (AIDS) Immune disorder that reached epidemic proportions in the United States in the 1980s. (p. 877)

affirmative action Programs meant to overcome historical patterns of discrimination against minorities and women in education and employment. By establishing guidelines for hiring and college admissions, the government sought to advance equal opportunities for minorities and women. (p. 865)

Agricultural Adjustment Act New Deal legislation that raised prices for farm produce by paying farmers subsidies to reduce production. Large farmers reaped most of the benefits from the act. The Supreme Court declared it unconstitutional in 1936. (p. 697)

Alamo Texas fort captured by General Santa Anna on March 6, 1836, from rebel defenders. Sensationalist accounts of the siege of the Alamo increased popular support in the United States for Texas independence. (p. 310)

Albany Congress June 1754 meeting in Albany, New York, of Iroquois and colonial representatives meant to facilitate better relations between Britain and the Iroquois Confederacy. Benjamin Franklin also put forward a plan for colonial union that was never implemented. (p. 131)

Alien and Sedition Acts 1798 security acts passed by the Federalist-controlled Congress. The Alien Act allowed the president to imprison or deport noncitizens; the Sedition Act placed significant restrictions on political speech. (p. 213)

America First Committee Isolationist organization founded by Senator Gerald Nye in 1940 to keep the United States out of World War II. (p. 724)

American Anti-Slavery Society (AASS) Abolitionist society founded by William Lloyd Garrison in 1833 that became the most important northern abolitionist organization of the period. (p. 346)

American Colonization Society (ACS) Organization formed in 1817 to establish colonies of freed slaves and freeborn blacks in Africa. The ACS was led by a group of white elites whose primary goal was to rid the nation of African Americans. (p. 233)

American Equal Rights Association Group of black and white women and men formed in 1866 to promote gender and racial equality. The organization split in 1869 over support for the Fifteenth Amendment. (p. 438)

American Federation of Labor (AFL) Trade union federation founded in 1886. Led by its first president, Samuel Gompers, the AFL sought to organize skilled workers into trade-specific unions. (p. 534)

American Indian Movement (AIM) An American Indian group, formed in 1968, that promoted "red power" and condemned the United States for its continued mistreatment of Native Americans. (p. 842)

American Plan Voluntary program initiated by businesses in the early twentieth century to protect worker welfare. The American Plan was meant to undermine the appeal of labor unions. (p. 658)

American Protective League (APL) An organization of private citizens that cooperated with the Justice Department and the Bureau of Investigation during World War I to spy on German residents suspected of disloyal behavior. (p. 639)

American System Plan proposed by Henry Clay to promote the U.S. economy by combining federally funded internal improvements to aid farmers with federal tariffs to protect U.S. manufacturing and a national bank to oversee economic development. (p. 265)

American system of manufacturing Production system focused on water-powered machinery, division of labor, and the use of interchangeable parts. The introduction of the American system in the early nineteenth century greatly increased the productivity of American manufacturing. (p. 244)

American Woman Suffrage Association Organization founded in 1869 to support ratification of the Fifteenth Amendment and campaign for women's suffrage. (p. 438)

Anti-Imperialist League An organization founded in 1898 to oppose annexation of the Philippines. Some feared that annexation would bring competition from cheap labor; others considered Filipinos racially inferior and the Philippines unsuitable as an American territory. (p. 628)

Antifederalists Opponents of ratification of the Constitution. Antifederalists were generally more rural and less wealthy than the Federalists. (p. 206)

Appeal . . . to the Colored Citizens Radical abolitionist pamphlet published by David Walker in 1829. Walker's work inspired some white abolitionists to take a more radical stance on slavery. (p. 346)

Articles of Confederation Plan for national government proposed by the Continental Congress in 1777 and ratified in March 1781. The Articles of Confederation gave the national government limited powers, reflecting widespread fear of centralized authority. (p. 174)

Atlantic Charter August 1941 agreement between Franklin Roosevelt and Winston Churchill that outlined potential war aims and cemented the relationship between the United States and Britain. (p. 725)

Aztecs Spanish term for the Mexica, an indigenous people who built an empire in present-day Mexico in the centuries before the arrival of the Spaniards. The Aztecs built their empire through conquest. (p. 5)

Bacon's Rebellion 1676 uprising in Virginia led by Nathaniel Bacon. Bacon and his followers, many of whom were former servants, were upset by the Virginia governor's unwillingness to send troops to intervene in conflicts between settlers and Indians and by the lack of representation of western settlers in the House of Burgesses. (p. 47)

Battle of Saratoga Site of key Revolutionary War battle. The patriot victory at Saratoga in October 1777 provided hope that the colonists could prevail and increased the chances that the French would formally join the patriot side. (p. 173)

Battle of Shiloh April 1862 battle in Tennessee that provided the Union entrance to the Mississippi valley. Shiloh was the bloodiest battle in American history to that point. (p. 402)

Battle of the Little Big Horn 1876 battle in the Montana Territory in which Lieutenant Colonel George Armstrong Custer and his troops were massacred by Lakota Sioux. (p. 466)

beats A small group of young poets, writers, intellectuals, musicians, and artists who attacked mainstream American politics and culture in the 1950s. (p. 801)

benign neglect British colonial policy from about 1700 to 1760 that relaxed supervision of internal colonial affairs as long as the North American colonies produced sufficient raw materials and revenue; also known as *salutary neglect.* (p. 140)

Beringia Land bridge that linked Siberia and Alaska during the Wisconsin period. Migrants from northeast Asia used this bridge to travel to North America. (p. 5)

Berlin airlift During the Berlin blockade by the Soviets from 1948 to 1949, the U.S. and British governments dispatched their air forces to transport food and supplies to West Berlin. (p. 765)

Bill of Rights The first ten amendments to the Constitution. These ten amendments helped reassure Americans who feared that the federal government established under the Constitution would infringe on the rights of individuals and states. (p. 207)

black codes Racial laws passed in the immediate aftermath of the Civil War by southern legislatures. The black codes were intended to reduce free African Americans to a condition as close to slavery as possible. (p. 432)

Black Death The epidemic of bubonic plague that swept through Europe beginning in the mid-fourteenth century and wiped out roughly half of Europe's population. (p. 10)

Black Panther Party Organization founded in 1966 by Huey P. Newton and Bobby Seale to advance the black power movement in black communities. (p. 842)

Black Tuesday October 29, 1929, crash of the American stock market. The 1929 stock market crash marked the beginning of the Great Depression. (p. 674)

blacklist Informal list of individuals barred from employment in the entertainment industry in the late 1940s and early 1950s as a result of their suspected Communist connections. (p. 775)

Bleeding Kansas The Kansas Territory during a period of violent conflicts over the fate of slavery in the mid-1850s. The violence in Kansas intensified the sectional division over slavery. (p. 376)

Boland Amendment 1982 act of Congress prohibiting direct aid to the Nicaraguan Contra forces. (p. 901)

Bonus Army World War I veterans who marched on Washington, D.C., in 1932 to demand immediate payment of their service bonuses. President Hoover refused to negotiate and instructed the U.S. army to clear the capital of protesters, leading to a violent clash. (p. 695)

boss Leader of a political machine. Men like "Boss" George Washington Plunkitt of New York's Tammany Hall wielded enormous power over city life. (p. 577)

Boston Massacre 1770 clash between colonial protesters and British soldiers in Boston that led to the death of five colonists. The bloody conflict was used to promote the patriot cause. (p. 146)

Brown v. Board of Education of Topeka, Kansas Landmark 1954 Supreme Court case that overturned the "separate but equal" principle established by *Plessy v. Ferguson* and applied to public schools. Few schools in the South were racially desegregated for more than a decade. (p. 803)

buffalo soldiers African American cavalrymen who fought in the West against the Indians in the 1870s and 1880s and served with distinction. (p. 466)

bully pulpit Term used by Theodore Roosevelt to describe the office of the presidency. Roosevelt believed that the president should use his office as a platform to promote his programs and rally public opinion. (p. 607)

Bush Doctrine President George W. Bush's proposal to engage in preemptive war against despotic governments, such as Iraq, deemed to threaten U.S. national security, even if the danger was not imminent. (p. 939)

Californios Spanish and Mexican residents of California. Before the nineteenth century, Californios made up California's economic and political elite. Their position, however, deteriorated after the conclusion of the Mexican-American War in 1848. (p. 479)

Camp David accords 1978 peace accord between Israel and Egypt facilitated by the mediation of President Jimmy Carter. (p. 898)

carpetbaggers Derogatory term for white Northerners who moved to the South in the years following the Civil War. Many white Southerners believed that such migrants were intent on exploiting their suffering. (p. 440)

Chinese Exclusion Act 1882 act that banned Chinese immigration into the United States and prohibited those Chinese already in the country from becoming naturalized American citizens. (p. 481)

Church of England National church established by Henry VIII after he split with the Catholic Church. (p. 37)

civic housekeeping Idea promoted by Jane Addams for urban reform by using women's traditional skills as domestic managers; caregivers for children, the elderly, and the needy; and community builders. (p. 594)

Civil Rights Act of 1964 Wide-ranging civil rights act that, among other things, prohibited discrimination in public accommodations and employment and increased federal enforcement of school desegregation. (p. 832)

Civilian Conservation Corps (CCC) New Deal work program that hired young, unmarried men to work on conservation projects. The CCC employed about 2.5 million men and lasted until 1942. (p. 699)

Coercive Acts (Intolerable Acts) 1774 act of Parliament passed in response to the Boston Tea Party. The Coercive Acts were meant to force the colonists into submission, but they only resulted in increased resistance. Colonial patriots called them the Intolerable Acts. (p. 149)

collective bargaining The process of negotiation between labor unions and employers. (p. 532)

Columbian exchange The biological exchange between the Americas and the rest of the world. Although the initial impact of the Columbian exchange was strongest in the Americas and Europe, it was soon felt all over the world. (p. 18)

Commission on the Status of Women Commission appointed by President Kennedy in 1961. The commission's 1963 report, *American Women*, highlighted employment discrimination against women and recommended legislation requiring equal pay for equal work regardless of sex. (p. 839)

committee of correspondence Type of committee first established in Massachusetts to circulate concerns and reports of protests and other events to leaders in other colonies in the aftermath of the Sugar Act. (p. 141)

Committee on Public Information (CPI) Committee established in 1917 to create propaganda and promote censorship in order to generate enthusiasm for World War I and stifle antiwar dissent. (p. 639)

Common Sense Pamphlet arguing in favor of independence written by Thomas Paine and published in 1776. *Common Sense* was widely read and had an important impact on the debate over declaring independence from Britain. (p. 165)

Compromise of 1850 Series of acts following California's application for admission as a free state. Meant to quell sectional tensions over slavery, the act was intended to provide something for all sides but ended up fueling more conflicts. (p. 368)

Compromise of 1877 Compromise between Republicans and southern Democrats that resulted in the election of Rutherford B. Hayes. Southern Democrats agreed to support Hayes in the disputed presidential election in exchange for his promise to end Reconstruction. (p. 446)

Comstock Lode Massive silver deposit discovered in the Sierra Nevada in the late 1850s. (p. 469)

Confederate States of America Nation established in 1861 by the eleven slave states that seceded between December 1860 and April 1861. (p. 381)

Congress of Racial Equality (CORE) Civil rights organization, founded in 1942, that fought against racial exclusion in public accommodations. The emergence of organizations like CORE signaled a new phase in the civil rights struggle. (p. 771)

conquistadors Spanish soldiers who were central to the conquest of the civilizations of the Americas. Once conquest was complete, conquistadors often extracted wealth from the people and lands they now ruled. (p. 20)

conservative coalition Alliance of southern Democrats and conservative northern Republicans in Congress that thwarted passage of New Deal legislation after 1938. (p. 707)

Continental Congress Congress convened in Philadelphia in 1774 in response to the Coercive Acts. The delegates hoped to reestablish the freedoms colonists had enjoyed in earlier times. (p. 149)

contraband Designation assigned to escaped slaves by Union general Benjamin Butler in May 1861. By designating slaves as property forfeited by the act of rebellion, the Union was able to strike at slavery without proclaiming a general emancipation. (p. 399)

Contract with America A document that called for reduced welfare spending, lower taxes, term limits for lawmakers, and a constitutional amendment for a balanced budget. In preparation for the 1994 midterm congressional elections, Republicans, led by Representative Newt Gingrich, drew up this proposal. (p. 934)

convict lease The system used by southern governments to furnish mainly African American prison labor to plantation owners and industrialists and to raise revenue for the states. In practice, convict labor replaced slavery as the means of providing a forced labor supply. (p. 497)

Copperheads Northern Democrats who did not support the Union war effort. Such Democrats enjoyed considerable support in eastern cities and parts of the Midwest. (p. 409)

corporation A form of business ownership in which the liability of shareholders in a company is limited to their individual investments. The formation of corporations in the late nineteenth century greatly stimulated investment in industry. (p. 499)

Corps of Discovery Expedition organized by the U.S. government to explore the Louisiana Territory. Led by Meriwether Lewis and William Clark, the expedition set out in May 1804 and journeyed to the Pacific coast and back by 1806 with the aid of interpreters like Sacagawea. (p. 237)

cotton gin Machine invented by Eli Whitney in 1793 to deseed short-staple cotton. The cotton gin dramatically reduced the time and labor involved in deseeding, facilitating the expansion of cotton production in the South and West. (p. 243)

counterculture Young cultural rebels of the 1960s who rejected conventional moral and sexual values and used drugs to reach a higher consciousness. These so-called hippies bonded together in their style of clothes and taste in rock 'n' roll music. (p. 838)

court-packing plan Proposal by President Franklin Roosevelt in 1937 to increase the size of the Supreme Court and reduce its opposition to New Deal legislation. Congress failed to pass the measure, and the scheme increased resentment toward Roosevelt. (p. 707)

Coxey's army 1894 protest movement led by Jacob Coxey. Coxey and five hundred supporters marched from Ohio to Washington, D.C., to protest the lack of government response to the depression of 1893. (p. 544)

Crusades Eleventh- and twelfth-century campaigns to reclaim the Holy Land for the Roman Catholic Church. The Crusades were, on the whole, a military failure, but they did stimulate trade and inspire Europeans to seek better connections with the larger world. (p. 9)

Cuba Libre Vision of Cuban independence developed by José Martí, who hoped that Cuban independence would bring with it greater social and racial equality. (p. 626)

D Day June 6, 1944, invasion of German-occupied France by Allied forces. The D Day landings opened up a second front in Europe and marked a major turning point in World War II. (p. 728)

Dawes Act 1887 act that ended federal recognition of tribal sovereignty and divided Indian land into 160-acre parcels to be distributed to Indian heads of household. The act dramatically reduced the amount of Indian-controlled land and undermined Indian social and cultural institutions. (p. 467)

Dayton Peace Accords 1995 peace agreement ending the war in Bosnia that emerged from a conference hosted by President Bill Clinton in Dayton, Ohio. (p. 935)

Declaration of Independence Document declaring the independence of the colonies from Great Britain. Drafted by Thomas Jefferson and then debated and revised by the Continental Congress, the Declaration was made public on July 4, 1776. (p. 166)

Declaration of Sentiments Call for women's rights in marriage, family, religion, politics, and law issued at the 1848 Seneca Falls convention. It was signed by 100 of the 300 participants. (p. 348)

Democratic-Republican Party Political party that emerged out of opposition to Federalist policies in the 1790s. The Democratic-Republicans chose Thomas Jefferson as their presidential candidate in 1796, 1800, and 1804. (p. 211)

Democrats and National Republicans Two parties that resulted from the split of the Democratic-Republicans in the early 1820s. Andrew Jackson emerged as the leader of the Democrats. (p. 275)

depression of 1893 Severe economic downturn triggered by railroad and bank failures. The severity of the depression, combined with the failure of the federal government to offer an adequate response, led to the realignment of American politics. (p. 544)

deskilling The replacement of skilled labor with unskilled labor and machines. (p. 333)

détente An easing of tense relations with the Soviet Union during the Cold War. This process moved unevenly through the 1970s and early 1980s but accelerated when Soviet leader Mikhail Gorbachev came to power in the mid-1980s. (p. 897)

divestment movement 1980s campaign against apartheid by ending investments by U.S. corporations, universities, and municipalities in South Africa. (p. 902)

dollar diplomacy Term used by President Taft to describe the economic focus of his foreign policy. Taft hoped to use economic policies and the control of foreign assets by American companies to influence Latin American nations. (p. 633)

"don't ask, don't tell" The official policy toward gays in the U.S. military established by President Bill Clinton in 1993. The policy prohibited discrimination against homosexuals as long as they did not reveal their sexual identity, but it banned openly gay men and women from serving in the armed forces. It was repealed by President Barack Obama in 2011. (p. 933)

***Dred Scott* decision** 1857 Supreme Court case centered on the status of Dred Scott and his family. In its ruling, the Court denied the claim that black men had any rights and blocked Congress from excluding slavery from any territory. (p. 378)

Dunmore's Proclamation 1775 proclamation issued by the British commander Lord Dunmore that offered freedom to all enslaved African Americans who joined the British army. The proclamation heightened concerns among some patriots about the consequences of independence. (p. 165)

Eisenhower Doctrine A doctrine guiding intervention in the Middle East. In 1957 Congress granted President Dwight Eisenhower the power to send military forces into the Middle East to combat Communist aggression. Eisenhower sent U.S. marines into Lebanon in 1958 under this doctrine. (p. 810)

Emancipation Proclamation January 1, 1863, proclamation that declared all slaves in areas still in rebellion "forever free." While stopping short of abolishing slavery, the Emancipation Proclamation was, nonetheless, seen by blacks and abolitionists as a great victory. (p. 403)

Embargo Act 1807 act that prohibited American ships from leaving their home ports until Britain and France repealed restrictions on U.S. trade. The act had a devastating impact on American commerce. (p. 239)

encomiendas System first established by Columbus by which Spanish leaders in the Americas received land and the labor of all Indians residing on it. From the Indian point of view, the encomienda system amounted to little more than enslavement. (p. 14)

Enlightenment European cultural movement that emphasized rational and scientific thinking over traditional religion and superstition. Enlightenment thought appealed to many colonial elites. (p. 112)

Enola Gay American B-29 bomber that dropped an atomic bomb on Hiroshima on August 6, 1945. The dropping of a second bomb on Nagasaki three days later led to Japan's surrender. (p. 732)

Enrollment Act March 1863 Union draft law that provided for draftees to be selected by an impartial lottery. A loophole in the law that allowed wealthy Americans to escape service by paying $300 or hiring a substitute created widespread resentment. (p. 408)

Enterprise of the Indies Columbus's proposal to sail west across the Atlantic to Japan and China. In 1492 Columbus gained support for the venture from Ferdinand and Isabella of Spain. (p. 14)

Environmental Protection Agency (EPA) Federal agency established by Richard Nixon in 1971 to regulate activities that resulted in pollution or other environmental degradation. (p. 871)

Equal Rights Amendment (ERA) A proposed amendment that prevented the abridgment of "equality of rights under law . . . by the United States or any State on the basis of sex." Not enough states had ratified the amendment by 1982, when the ratification period expired, so it was not adopted. (p. 869)

Erie Canal Canal built in the early 1820s that made water transport from the Great Lakes to New York City possible. The success of the Erie Canal inspired many similar projects and ensured New York City's place as the premier international port in the United States. (p. 265)

Espionage Act 1917 act that prohibited antiwar activities, including opposing the military draft. It punished speech critical of the war as well as deliberate actions of sabotage and spying. (p. 639)

ethnic cleansing Ridding an area of a particular ethnic minority in order to achieve ethnic homogeneity. In the civil war between Serbs and Croatians in Bosnia from 1992 to 1995, the Serbian military attempted to eliminate the Croatian population through murder, rape, and expulsion. (p. 935)

eugenics The pseudo-science of producing genetic improvement in the human population through selective breeding. Proponents of eugenics often saw ethnic and racial minorities as genetically "undesirable" and inferior. (p. 570)

European Union (EU) Organization formed by European nations in 1993 to boost their economic and political power. Member nations took steps to facilitate free trade, investment, and migration among EU states. (p. 913)

Exodusters Blacks who migrated from the South to Kansas in 1879 seeking land and a better way of life. (p. 441)

Fair Employment Practice Committee (FEPC) Committee established in 1941 to help African Americans gain a greater share of wartime industrial jobs. (p. 740)

Fair Labor Standards Act 1938 law that provided a minimum wage of 40 cents an hour and a forty-hour workweek for employees in businesses engaged in interstate commerce. (p. 707)

Farmers' Alliances Regional organizations formed in the late nineteenth century to advance the interests of farmers. The most prominent of these organizations were the Northwestern Farmers' Alliance, the Southern Farmers' Alliance, and the Colored Farmers' Alliance. (p. 540)

Federal Employee Loyalty Program Program established by President Truman in 1947 to investigate federal employees suspected of disloyalty. (p. 774)

Federalists Supporters of ratification of the Constitution, many of whom came from urban and commercial backgrounds. (p. 206)

Field Order Number 15 Order issued by General Sherman in January 1865 setting aside more than 400,000 acres of Confederate land to be divided into plots for former slaves. Sherman's order came in response to pressure from African American leaders. (p. 414)

Fifteenth Amendment Amendment to the Constitution prohibiting the abridgment of a citizen's right to vote on the basis of "race, color, or previous condition of servitude." From the 1870s on, southern states devised numerous strategies for circumventing the Fifteenth Amendment. (p. 438)

fireside chats Radio addresses by Franklin Roosevelt during the depression. Roosevelt's addresses boosted morale and informed the public about government efforts to help ease their difficulties. (p. 697)

Fort Sumter Union fort that guarded the harbor in Charleston, South Carolina. The Confederacy's decision to fire on the fort and block resupply in April 1861 marked the beginning of the Civil War. (p. 395)

Fourteen Points The core principles President Wilson saw as the basis for lasting peace, including freedom of the seas, open diplomacy, and self-determination for colonial peoples. (p. 639)

Fourteenth Amendment Amendment to the Constitution defining citizenship and protecting individual civil and political rights from abridgment by the states. Adopted during Reconstruction, the Fourteenth Amendment overturned the *Dred Scott* decision. (p. 436)

Free Speech Movement (FSM) Movement protesting policies instituted by the University of California at Berkeley that restricted free speech. In 1964 students at Berkeley conducted sit-ins and held rallies against these policies. (p. 837)

Freedmen's Bureau Federal agency created in 1865 to provide ex-slaves with economic and legal resources. The Freedmen's Bureau played an active role in shaping black life in the postwar South. (p. 427)

Freedom Rides Integrated bus rides through the South organized by CORE in 1961 to test compliance with Supreme Court rulings on segregation. (p. 830)

Freedom Summer 1964 civil rights project in Mississippi launched by SNCC, CORE, the SCLC, and the NAACP. Some eight hundred volunteers, mainly white college students, worked on voter registration drives and in freedom schools to improve education for rural black youngsters. (p. 833)

Fugitive Slave Act of 1850 Act strengthening earlier fugitive slave laws, passed as part of the Compromise of 1850. The Fugitive Slave Act provoked widespread anger in the North and intensified sectional tensions. (p. 368)

gag rule Rule passed by the House of Representatives in 1836 to table, or postpone action on, all antislavery petitions without hearing them read in order to stifle debate over slavery. It was renewed annually until it was rescinded in 1844. (p. 311)

Gettysburg Key July 1863 battle that helped turn the tide for the Union. Union victory at Gettysburg, combined with a victory at Vicksburg that same month, positioned the Union to push farther into the South. (p. 410)

ghettos Neighborhoods dominated by a single ethnic, racial, or class group. (p. 565)

Ghost Dance Religious ritual performed by the Paiute Indians in the late nineteenth century. Following a vision he received in 1888, the prophet Wovoka believed that performing the Ghost Dance would cause whites to disappear and allow Indians to regain control of their lands. (p. 468)

Gilded Age Term coined by Mark Twain and Charles Dudley Warner to describe the late nineteenth century. The term referred to the opulent and often ostentatious lifestyles of the era's superrich. (p. 505)

glasnost Policy of political "openness" initiated by Soviet leader Mikhail Gorbachev in the 1980s. Under *glasnost*, the Soviet Union extended democratic elections, freedom of speech, and freedom of the press. (p. 907)

globalization The extension of economic, political, and cultural relationships among nations, through commerce, migration, and communication. Globalization expanded in the late twentieth century because of free trade agreements and the relaxation of immigration restrictions. (p. 910)

Glorious Revolution 1688 rebellion that forced James II from the English throne and replaced him with William and Mary. The Glorious Revolution led to greater political and commercial autonomy for the British colonies. (p. 67)

gold rush The rapid influx of migrants into California after the discovery of gold in 1848. Migrants came from all over the world seeking riches. (p. 365)

"The Gospel of Wealth" 1889 essay by Andrew Carnegie in which he argued that the rich should act as stewards of the wealth they earned, using their surplus income for the benefit of the community. (p. 504)

Grangers Members of an organization founded in 1867 to meet the social and cultural needs of farmers. Grangers took an active role in the promotion of the economic and political interests of farmers. (p. 539)

Great Awakening Series of religious revivals in colonial America that began in 1720 and lasted to about 1750. (p. 114)

great migration Population shift of more than 400,000 African Americans who left the South beginning in 1917–1918 and headed north and west hoping to escape poverty and racial discrimination. During the 1920s another 800,000 blacks left the South. (p. 657)

Great Plains Semiarid territory in central North America. (p. 461)

Great Recession The severe economic decline in the United States and throughout the world that began in 2008, leading to bank failures, high unemployment, home foreclosures, and large federal deficits. (p. 943)

Great Society President Lyndon Johnson's vision of social, economic, and cultural progress in the United States. (p. 834)

greenbacks U.S. treasury notes issued by the federal government during the Civil War. Using its new control over the currency and banking systems, the federal government issued large quantities of greenbacks during the war, contributing to inflation. (p. 405)

Gulf of Tonkin Resolution 1964 congressional resolution giving President Lyndon Johnson wide discretion in the use of U.S. forces in Vietnam. The resolution followed reported attacks by North Vietnamese gunboats on two American destroyers. (p. 826)

Haitian Revolution Revolt against French rule by free and enslaved blacks in the 1790s on the island of Saint Domingue. The revolution led in 1803 to the establishment of Haiti, the first independent black-led nation in the Americas. (p. 236)

Harpers Ferry, Virginia Site of the federal arsenal that was the target of John Brown's 1859 raid. Brown hoped to rouse the region's slave population to a violent uprising. (p. 379)

Hartford Convention 1814 convention of Federalists opposed to the War of 1812. Delegates to the convention considered a number of constitutional amendments, as well as the possibility of secession. (p. 262)

Haymarket Square Site of 1886 rally and violence. In the aftermath of the events in Haymarket Square, the union movement in the United States went into temporary decline. (p. 533)

Hetch Hetchy valley Site of a controversial dam built to supply San Francisco with water and power in the aftermath of the 1906 earthquake. The dam was built over the objections of preservationists such as John Muir. (p. 606)

Homestead Act 1862 act that established procedures for distributing 160-acre lots to western settlers, on condition that they develop and farm their land, as an incentive for western migration. (p. 474)

Homestead strike 1892 strike by steelworkers at Andrew Carnegie's Homestead steel factory. The strike collapsed after a failed assassination attempt on Carnegie's plant manager, Henry Clay Frick. (p. 534)

Hoovervilles Shantytowns that sprang up in the years following the 1929 stock market crash. Many Americans believed that President Hoover did not do enough to relieve the suffering that accompanied the Great Depression. (p. 690)

Hopewell people Indian people who established a thriving culture near the Mississippi River in the early centuries C.E. (p. 7)

horizontal integration The ownership of as many firms as possible in a given industry by a single owner. John D. Rockefeller pursued a strategy of horizontal integration when he bought up rival oil refineries. (p. 499)

horticulture A form of agriculture in which people work small plots of land with simple tools. (p. 5)

House Committee on Un-American Activities (HUAC) House committee established in 1938 to investigate domestic communism. After World War II, HUAC conducted highly publicized investigations of Communist influence in government and the entertainment industry. (p. 774)

House of Burgesses Local governing body in Virginia established by the English crown in 1619. (p. 44)

Hull House Settlement house established in 1889 by Jane Addams and Ellen Starr. Hull House inspired a generation of young women to work directly in immigrant communities. (p. 594)

Hurricane Katrina 2005 storm that hit the Gulf coast states of Louisiana, Mississippi, and Alabama. The hurricane caused massive flooding in New Orleans after levees broke. Federal, state, and local government responses to the storm were inadequate and highlighted racial and class inequities. (p. 940)

imperial presidency Term used to describe the growth of presidential powers during the Cold War, particularly with respect to war-making powers and the conduct of national security. (p. 764)

import duty Tax imposed on goods imported into the colonies, paid by the importer rather than directly by the consumer; also known as a *tariff*. (p. 140)

impressment The forced enlistment of civilians into the army or navy. The impressment of residents of colonial seaports into the British navy was a major source of complaint in the eighteenth century. (p. 118)

Incas Andean people who built an empire in the centuries before the arrival of the Spaniards. At the height of their power in the fifteenth century, the Incas controlled some sixteen million people. (p. 7)

indentured servants Servants contracted to work for a set period of time without pay. Many early migrants to the English colonies indentured themselves in exchange for the price of passage to North America. (p. 44)

Indian Removal Act 1830 act by which Indian peoples in the East were forced to exchange their lands for territory west of the Mississippi River. Andrew Jackson was an ardent supporter of Indian removal. (p. 281)

Indian Reorganization Act (IRA) 1934 act that ended the Dawes Act, authorized self-government for those living on reservations, extended tribal landholdings, and pledged to uphold native customs and language. (p. 706)

Industrial Workers of the World (IWW) Organization that grew out of the activities of the Western Federation of Miners in the 1890s and formed by Eugene V. Debs. The IWW attempted to unite all skilled and unskilled workers in an effort to overthrow capitalism. (p. 536)

internment The relocation of persons seen as a threat to national security to isolated camps during World War II. Nearly all people of Japanese descent living on the West Coast were forced to sell or abandon their possessions and relocate to internment camps during the war. (p. 743)

Interstate Commerce Commission (ICC) Regulatory commission established by Congress in 1887. The commission investigated interstate shipping, required railroads to make their rates public, and could bring lawsuits to force shippers to reduce "unreasonable" fares. (p. 539)

Intolerable Acts See Coercive Acts.

Iran-Contra Reagan administration scandal involving the funneling of funds from an illegal arms-for-hostages deal with Iran to the Nicaraguan Contras in the mid-1980s. (p. 904)

Jamestown The first successful English colony in North America. Settled in 1607, Jamestown was founded by soldiers and adventurers under the leadership of Captain John Smith. (p. 42)

Jay Treaty 1796 treaty that required British forces to withdraw from U.S. soil, required American repayment of debts to British firms, and limited U.S. trade with the British West Indies. (p. 212)

Jim Crow Late-nineteenth-century statutes that established legally defined racial segregation in the South. Jim Crow legislation helped ensure the social and economic inferiority of southern blacks. (p. 509)

jingoists Superpatriotic supporters of the expansion and use of military power. Jingoists such as Theodore Roosevelt longed for a war in which they could demonstrate America's strength and prove their own masculinity. (p. 624)

Joint Electoral Commission Commission created by Congress to resolve the disputed presidential election of 1876. The commission consisted of five senators, five House members, and five Supreme Court justices—seven Republicans, seven Democrats, and one independent. The commission sided with the Republican presidential candidate, Rutherford B. Hayes. (p. 446)

Judiciary Act of 1801 Act passed by the Federalist-controlled Congress to expand the federal court system by creating sixteen circuit (regional) courts, with new judges appointed for each, just before Democratic-Republicans took control of the presidency and Congress. (p. 239)

Kansas-Nebraska Act 1854 act creating the territories of Kansas and Nebraska out of what was then Indian land. The act stipulated that the issue of slavery would be settled by a popular referendum in each territory. (p. 373)

King Philip's War 1675–1676 conflict between New England settlers and the region's Indians. The settlers were the eventual victors, but fighting was fierce and casualties on both sides were high. (p. 55)

King William's War 1689–1697 war that began as a conflict over competing French and English interests on the European continent but soon spread to the American frontier. Both sides pulled Indian allies into the war. (p. 71)

Knights of the Ku Klux Klan (KKK) Organization formed in 1865 by General Nathan Bedford Forrest to enforce prewar racial norms. Members of the KKK used threats and violence to intimidate blacks and white Republicans. (p. 443)

La Raza Unida (The United Race) A Chicano political party, formed in 1969, that advocated job opportunities for Chicanos, bilingual education, and Chicano cultural studies programs in universities. (p. 842)

laissez-faire French for "let things alone." Advocates of laissez-faire believed that the marketplace should be left to regulate itself, allowing individuals to pursue their own self-interest without any government restraint or interference. (p. 503)

League of Nations The international organization proposed by Woodrow Wilson after the end of World War I to ensure world peace and security in the future through mutual agreement. The United States failed to join the league because Wilson and his opponents in Congress could not work out a compromise. (p. 640)

Lend-Lease Act March 1941 law permitting the United States to lend or lease military equipment and other commodities to Great Britain and its allies. Its passage marked the end of American neutrality before the U.S. entered World War II. (p. 725)

Levittown Suburban subdivision built in Long Island, New York, in the 1950s in response to the postwar housing shortage. Subsequent Levittowns were built in Pennsylvania and New Jersey. (p. 793)

Liberal Republicans Political group organized to challenge the reelection of President Grant in 1872. The Liberal Republicans called for an end to federal efforts at Reconstruction in the South. (p. 445)

Liberator Radical abolitionist newspaper launched by William Lloyd Garrison in 1831. Through the *Liberator*, Garrison called for immediate, uncompensated emancipation of slaves. (p. 346)

Liberty Party Antislavery political party formed in 1840. The Liberty Party, along with the Free-Soil Party, helped place slavery at the center of national political debates. (p. 349)

Little Rock Nine Nine African American students who, in 1957, became the first black students to attend Central High School in Little Rock, Arkansas. Federal troops were required to overcome the resistance of white officials and to protect the students. (p. 804)

Long Drive Cattle drive from the grazing lands of Texas to rail depots in Kansas. Once in Kansas, the cattle were shipped eastward to slaughterhouses in Chicago. (p. 471)

Lost Generation A term used by the writer Gertrude Stein to describe the writers and artists disillusioned with the consumer culture of the 1920s. (p. 664)

Louisiana Territory Vast territory stretching from the Mississippi River to the Rocky Mountains and from New Orleans to present-day Montana that the United States purchased from France in 1803, doubling the size of the nation. (p. 236)

loyalist A colonial supporter of the British during the Revolutionary War. Loyalists came from all economic backgrounds and had a variety of motives for siding with the British. (p. 169)

Manhattan Project Code name for the secret program to develop an atomic bomb. The project was launched in 1942 and directed by the United States with the assistance of Great Britain and Canada. (p. 731)

manifest destiny Term coined by John L. O'Sullivan in 1845 to describe what he saw as the nation's God-given right to expand its borders. Throughout the nineteenth century, the concept of manifest destiny was used to justify U.S. expansion. (p. 313)

Marbury v. Madison 1803 Supreme Court decision that established the authority of the Supreme Court to rule on the constitutionality of federal laws. (p. 239)

March on Washington for Jobs and Freedom August 28, 1963, rally by civil rights organizations in Washington, D.C., that brought increased national attention to the movement. (p. 832)

Marshall Plan Post–World War II European economic aid package developed by Secretary of State George Marshall. The plan helped rebuild Western Europe and served American political and economic interests in the process. (p. 763)

Maya People who established large cities in the Yucatán peninsula. Mayan civilization was strongest between 300 and 800 C.E. (p. 7)

Mayflower Compact Written constitution created by the Pilgrims upon their arrival in Plymouth. The Mayflower Compact was the first written constitution adopted in North America. (p. 49)

McCarthyism Term used to describe the harassment and persecution of suspected political radicals. Senator Joseph McCarthy was one of many prominent government figures who helped incite anti-Communist hysteria in the early 1950s. (p. 778)

McCulloch v. Maryland 1819 Supreme Court decision that reinforced the federal government's ability to employ an expansive understanding of the implied powers clause of the Constitution. (p. 239)

megachurches Mainly Protestant congregations containing at least two thousand members. The number of megachurches in the United States increased dramatically during the 1980s and 1990s. (p. 937)

melting pot Popular metaphor for immigrant assimilation into American society. According to this ideal, all immigrants underwent a process of Americanization that produced a homogeneous society. (p. 570)

mercantilism Economic system centered on the maintenance of a favorable balance of trade for the home country, with more gold and silver flowing into that country than flowed out. Seventeenth- and eighteenth-century British colonial policy was heavily shaped by mercantilism. (p. 76)

Mexican revolution 1911 revolution in Mexico, which led to nearly a decade of bloodshed and civil war. (p. 634)

Middle Passage The brutal voyage of slave ships laden with human cargo from Africa to the Americas. The voyage was the middle segment in a triangular journey that began in Europe, went first to Africa, then to the Americas, and finally back to Europe. (p. 77)

military-industrial complex The government-business alliance related to the military and national defense that developed out of World War II and that greatly influenced future development of the U.S. economy. (p. 734)

Mississippi Freedom Democratic Party (MFDP) Political party formed in 1964 to challenge the all-white state Democratic Party for seats at the 1964 Democratic presidential convention and run candidates for public office. Although unsuccessful in 1964, MFDP efforts led to subsequent reform of the Democratic Party and the seating of an interracial, convention delegation from Mississippi in 1968. (p. 833)

Missouri Compromise 1820 act that allowed Missouri to enter the Union as a slave state and Maine to enter as a free state and established the southern border of Missouri as the boundary between slave and free states throughout the Louisiana Territory. (p. 272)

Modern Republicanism The political approach of President Dwight Eisenhower that tried to fit traditional Republican Party ideals of individualism and fiscal restraint within the broad framework of the New Deal. (p. 807)

Monroe Doctrine Assertion by President James Monroe in 1823 that the Western Hemisphere was part of the U.S. sphere of influence. Although the United States lacked the power to back up this claim, it signaled an intention to challenge Europeans for authority in the Atlantic world. (p. 267)

Montgomery Improvement Association Organization founded in Montgomery, Alabama, in 1955 to coordinate the boycott of city buses by African Americans. (p. 803)

Mormons Religious sect that migrated to Utah to escape religious persecution; also known as the Church of Jesus Christ of Latter-Day Saints. (p. 478)

muckrakers Investigative journalists who specialized in exposing corruption, scandal, and vice. Muckrakers helped build public support for progressive causes. (p. 593)

mujahideen Religiously inspired Afghan rebels who resisted the Soviet invasion of Afghanistan in 1979. (p. 898)

multinational (or transnational) corporations Companies that operate production facilities or deliver services in more than one country. Between 1970 and 2000, the number of such firms increased ninefold. (p. 911)

multiplier effect The diverse changes spurred by a single invention, including other inventions it spawns and the broader economic, social, and political transformations it fuels. (p. 242)

mutual aid societies Voluntary associations that provide a variety of economic and social benefits to their members. (p. 565)

mutually assured destruction (MAD) Defense strategy built around the threat of a massive nuclear retaliatory strike. Adoption of the doctrine of mutually assured destruction contributed to the escalation of the nuclear arms race during the Cold War. (p. 807)

Nat Turner's rebellion 1831 slave uprising in Virginia led by Nat Turner. Turner's rebellion instilled panic among white Southerners, leading to tighter control of African Americans and reconsideration of the institution of slavery. (p. 302)

National Association for the Advancement of Colored People (NAACP) Organization founded by W. E. B. Du Bois, Ida B. Wells, Jane Addams, and others in 1909 to fight for racial equality. The NAACP strategy focused on fighting discrimination through the courts. (p. 602)

National Interstate and Defense Highway Act 1956 act that provided funds for construction of 42,500 miles of roads throughout the United States. (p. 793)

National Labor Relations Act 1935 act (also known as the Wagner Act) that created the National Labor Relations Board (NLRB). The NLRB protected workers' right to organize labor unions without owner interference. (p. 704)

National Organization for Women (NOW) Feminist organization formed in 1966 by Betty Friedan and like-minded activists. (p. 840)

National Origins Act 1924 act establishing immigration quotas by national origin. The act was intended to severely limit immigration from southern and eastern Europe as well as prohibit all immigration from East Asia. (p. 668)

National Recovery Administration (NRA) New Deal agency established in 1933 to create codes to regulate production, prices, wages, hours, and collective bargaining. The NRA failed to produce the intended results and was eventually ruled unconstitutional. (p. 698)

National Republicans *See* Democrats and National Republicans.

National Road Road constructed using federal funds that ran from western Maryland through southwestern Pennsylvania to Wheeling, West Virginia; also called the Cumberland Road. Completed in 1818, the road was part of a larger push to improve the nation's infrastructure. (p. 242)

National Security Council (NSC) Council created by the 1947 National Security Act to advise the president on military and foreign affairs. The NSC consists of the national security adviser and the secretaries of state, defense, the army, the navy, and the air force. (p. 764)

National War Labor Board (NWLB) Government agency created in 1918 to settle labor disputes. The NWLB consisted of representatives from unions, corporations, and the public. (p. 638)

National War Labor Board Board established in 1942 to oversee labor-management relations during World War II. The board regulated wages, hours, and working conditions and authorized the government to take over plants that refused to abide by its decisions. (p. 736)

National Woman Suffrage Association Organization founded in 1869 to support women's voting rights. Founders Susan B. Anthony and Elizabeth Cady Stanton objected to the Fifteenth Amendment because it did not provide suffrage for women. (p. 438)

nativism The belief that foreigners pose a serious danger to a nation's society and culture. Nativist sentiment rose in the United States as the size and diversity of the immigrant population grew. (p. 568)

nativists Anti-immigrant Americans who launched public campaigns against foreigners in the 1840s. Nativism emerged as a response to increased immigration to the United States in the 1830s and 1840s, particularly the large influx of Catholic immigrants. (p. 337)

Navigation Acts Acts passed by Parliament in the 1650s and 1660s that prohibited smuggling, established guidelines for legal commerce, and set duties on trade items. In the 1760s, British authorities sought to fully enforce these laws, leading to resistance by colonists. (p. 140)

neoconservatives Disillusioned liberals who condemned the Great Society programs they had originally supported. Neoconservatives were particularly concerned about affirmative action programs, the domination of campus discourse by New Left radicals, and left-wing criticism of the use of American military and economic might to advance U.S. interests overseas. (p. 874)

Neutrality Act 1793 act prohibiting ships of belligerent nations—including France and Great Britain—from using American ports. The act was meant to help keep America out of the conflict between France and Great Britain and to enhance U.S. commerce. (p. 210)

Neutrality Acts Legislation passed between 1935 and 1937 to make it more difficult for the United States to become entangled in overseas conflicts. The Neutrality Acts reflected the strength of isolationist sentiment in 1930s America. (p. 723)

New Deal The policies and programs that Franklin Roosevelt initiated to combat the Great Depression. The New Deal represented a dramatic expansion of the role of government in American society. (p. 697)

New Freedom Term used by Woodrow Wilson to describe his limited-government, progressive agenda. Wilson's New Freedom was offered as an alternative to Theodore Roosevelt's New Nationalism. (p. 610)

New Frontier President Kennedy's domestic agenda. Kennedy promised to battle "tyranny, poverty, disease, and war," but, lacking strong majorities in Congress, he achieved relatively modest results. (p. 825)

New Light clergy Colonial clergy who called for religious revivals and emphasized the emotional aspects of spiritual commitment. The New Lights were leaders in the Great Awakening. (p. 112)

New Look The foreign policy strategy implemented by President Dwight Eisenhower that emphasized the development and deployment of nuclear weapons in an effort to cut military spending. (p. 807)

New Nationalism Agenda articulated by Theodore Roosevelt in his 1912 presidential campaign. Roosevelt called for increased regulation of large corporations, a more active role for the president, and the extension of social justice using the power of the federal government. (p. 610)

New Negro 1920s term for the second generation of African Americans born after emancipation and who stood up for their rights. (p. 665)

New Right The conservative coalition of old and new conservatives, as well as disaffected Democrats. The New Right came to power with the election of Ronald Reagan in 1980. (p. 861)

New South Term popularized by newspaper editor Henry Grady in the 1880s, a proponent of the modernization of the southern economy. Grady believed that industrial development would lead to the emergence of a "New South." (p. 497)

new woman 1920s term for the modern, sexually liberated woman. The new woman, popularized in movies and magazines, flouted traditional morality. (p. 664)

Noble Order of the Knights of Labor Labor organization founded in 1869 by Uriah Stephens. The Knights sought to include all workers in one giant union. (p. 532)

Non-Intercourse Act Act passed by Congress in 1809 allowing Americans to trade with every nation except France and Britain. The act failed to stop the seizure of American ships or improve the economy. (p. 261)

North American Free Trade Agreement (NAFTA) Free trade agreement approved in 1993 by the United States, Canada, and Mexico. (p. 913)

North Atlantic Treaty Organization (NATO) Cold War military alliance intended to enhance the collective security of the United States and Western Europe. (p. 765)

Northwest Land Ordinance (1785 and 1787) Act of the confederation congress that provided for the survey, sale, and eventual division into states of the Northwest Territory. The 1787 act clarified the process by which territories could become states. (p. 198)

NSC-68 April 1950 National Security Council document that advocated the intensification of the policy of containment both at home and abroad. (p. 766)

nuclear freeze movement 1980s protests calling for a mutual freeze on the testing, production, and deployment of nuclear weapons and of missiles and aircraft designed primarily to deliver nuclear weapons. (p. 905)

nullification The doctrine that individual states have the right to declare federal laws unconstitutional and, therefore, void within their borders. South Carolina attempted to invoke the doctrine of nullification in response to the tariff of 1832. (p. 278)

Occupy Wall Street A loose coalition of progressive and radical forces that emerged in 2011 in New York City and around the country to protest corporate greed and federal policies that benefit the very wealthy. (p. 947)

Old Light clergy Colonial clergy from established churches who supported the religious status quo in the early eighteenth century. (p. 112)

Open Door 1899 policy in which Secretary of State John Hay informed the nations occupying China that the United States had the right of equal trade in China. (p. 631)

Operation Desert Storm Code name of the 1991 allied air and ground military offensive that pushed Iraqi forces out of Kuwait. (p. 914)

Oregon Trail The route west from the Missouri River to the Oregon Territory. By 1860, some 350,000 Americans had made the three- to six-month journey along the trail. (p. 363)

Organization of Petroleum Exporting Countries (OPEC) Organization formed by oil-producing countries to control the price and supply of oil on the global market. (p. 864)

Palmer raids Government roundup of some 6,000 suspected alien radicals in 1919–1920, ordered by Attorney General A. Mitchell Palmer and his assistant J. Edgar Hoover. The raids resulted in the deportation of 556 immigrants. (p. 656)

panic of 1819 The nation's first severe recession. The panic of 1819 lasted four years and resulted from irresponsible banking practices and the declining demand for American goods, including cotton, abroad. (p. 268)

panic of 1837 Severe economic recession that began shortly after Martin Van Buren's presidential inauguration. The panic of 1837 started in the South and was rooted in the changing fortunes of American cotton in Great Britain. (p. 311)

patriarchal family Model of the family in which fathers have absolute authority over wives, children, and servants. Most colonial Americans accepted the patriarchal model of the family, at least as an ideal. (p. 102)

Patriot Act 2001 law passed in response to the September 11 terror attacks. It eased restrictions on domestic and foreign intelligence gathering and expanded governmental power to deport immigrants. (p. 938)

Peace of Paris 1763 peace treaty that brought the Seven Years' War to a close. Under the terms of the treaty, Britain gained control of North America east of the Mississippi River and of present-day Canada. (p. 133)

Pendleton Civil Service Reform Act 1883 act that required federal jobs to be awarded on the basis of merit through competitive exams rather than through political connections. (p. 579)

Pentagon Papers Classified report on U.S. involvement in Vietnam leaked to the press in 1971. The report confirmed that the Kennedy and Johnson administrations had misled the public about the origins and nature of the Vietnam War. (p. 863)

Pequot War 1636–1637 conflict between New England settlers, their Narragansett allies, and the Pequots. The English saw the Pequots as both a threat and an obstacle to further English expansion. (p. 53)

perestroika Policy of economic "restructuring" initiated by Soviet leader Mikhail Gorbachev. Gorbachev hoped that by reducing state control he could revive the Soviet economy. (p. 907)

Personal Responsibility and Work Opportunity Reconciliation Act 1996 act reforming the welfare system in the United States. The law required adults on the welfare rolls to find work within two years or lose their welfare benefits. (p. 934)

Petticoat Affair 1829 political conflict over Jackson's appointment of John Eaton as secretary of war. Eaton was married to a woman of allegedly questionable character, and the wives of many prominent Washington politicians organized a campaign to snub her. (p. 278)

Pietists German Protestants who decried the power of established churches and urged individuals to follow their heart rather than their head in spiritual matters. Pietism had a profound influence on the leaders of the Great Awakening. (p. 112)

Pilgrims Group of English religious dissenters who established a settlement at Plymouth, Massachusetts, in 1620. Unlike more mainstream Protestants, the Pilgrims were Separatists who aimed to sever all connections with the Church of England. (p. 49)

Pinckney Treaty 1796 treaty that defined the boundary between U.S. and Spanish territory in the South and opened the Mississippi River and New Orleans to U.S. shipping. (p. 212)

Platt Amendment 1901 act of Congress limiting Cuban sovereignty. American officials pressured Cuban leaders to incorporate the amendment into the Cuban constitution. (p. 628)

Plessy v. Ferguson 1896 Supreme Court ruling that upheld the legality of Jim Crow legislation. The Court ruled that as long as states provided "equal but separate" facilities for whites and blacks, Jim Crow laws did not violate the equal protection clause of the Fourteenth Amendment. (p. 509)

political machine Urban political organizations that dominated many late-nineteenth-century cities. Machines provided needed services to the urban poor, but they also fostered corruption, crime, and inefficiency. (p. 577)

Populists The People's Party of America, formed in 1892. The Populists sought to appeal to both farmers and industrial workers. (p. 541)

Port Huron Statement Students for a Democratic Society manifesto written in 1962 that condemned liberal politics, Cold War foreign policy, racism, and research-oriented universities. It called for the adoption of "participatory democracy." (p. 837)

Powhatan Confederacy Large and powerful Indian confederation in Virginia. The Jamestown settlers had a complicated and contentious relationship with the leaders of the Powhatan Confederacy. (p. 43)

pragmatism Philosophy that holds that truth can be discovered only through experience and that the value of ideas should be measured by their practical consequences. Pragmatism had a significant influence on the progressives. (p. 593)

Proclamation Line of 1763 Act of Parliament that restricted colonial settlement west of the Appalachian Mountains. The Proclamation Line sparked protests from rich and poor colonists alike. (p. 135)

Proclamation of Amnesty and Reconstruction 1863 proclamation that established the basic parameters of President Lincoln's approach to Reconstruction. Lincoln's plan would have readmitted the South to the Union on relatively lenient terms. (p. 431)

Progressive Party Third party formed by Theodore Roosevelt in 1912 to facilitate his candidacy for president. Nicknamed the "Bull Moose Party," the Progressive Party split the Republican vote, allowing Democrat Woodrow Wilson to win the election. (p. 610)

proprietary colonies Colonies granted to individuals, rather than held directly by the crown or given to chartered companies. Proprietors of such colonies, such as William Penn of Pennsylvania, had considerable leeway to distribute land and govern as they pleased. (p. 67)

Protestantism Religious movement initiated in the early sixteenth century that resulted in a permanent division within European Christianity. Protestants differed with Catholics over the nature of salvation, the role of priests, and the organization of the church. (p. 37)

Pueblo revolt 1680 uprising of Pueblo Indians against Spanish forces in New Mexico that led to the Spaniards' temporary retreat from the area. The uprising was sparked by mistreatment and the suppression of Indian culture and religion. (p. 70)

Pullman strike 1894 strike by workers against the Pullman railcar company. When the strike disrupted rail service nation-wide, threatening the delivery of the mail, President Cleveland ordered federal troops to get the railroads moving again. (p. 535)

Puritans Radical English Protestants who hoped to reform the Church of England. The first Puritan settlers in the Americas arrived in Massachusetts in 1630. (p. 50)

Reaganomics Ronald Reagan's economic policies based on the theories of supply-side economists and centered on tax cuts and cuts to domestic programs. (p. 876)

Red scare The fear of Communist-inspired radicalism in the wake of the Russian Revolution. The Red scare following World War I culminated in the Palmer raids on suspected radicals. (p. 655)

Redeemers White, conservative Democrats who challenged and overthrew Republican rule in the South during Reconstruction. (p. 443)

redemptioners Immigrants who borrowed money from shipping agents to cover the costs of transport to America, loans that were repaid, or "redeemed," by colonial employers. Redemptioners worked for their "redeemers" for a set number of years. (p. 81)

Regulators Local organizations formed in North and South Carolina to protest and resist unpopular policies. After first seeking redress through official institutions, Regulators went on to establish militias and other institutions of self-governance. (p. 137)

Renaissance The cultural and intellectual flowering that began in Italy in the fifteenth century and then spread north. The Renaissance occurred at the same time that European rulers were pushing for greater political unification of their states. (p. 10)

Republican Party Party formed in 1854 that was committed to stopping the expansion of slavery and advocated economic development and internal improvements. Although their appeal was limited to the North, the Republicans quickly became a major political force. (p. 373)

Roe v. Wade The 1973 Supreme Court opinion that affirmed a woman's constitutional right to abortion. (p. 841)

Roosevelt Corollary 1904 addition to the Monroe Doctrine that affirmed the right of the United States to intervene in the internal affairs of Caribbean and Latin American countries to preserve order and protect American interests. (p. 631)

Sacco and Vanzetti case 1920 case in which Nicola Sacco and Bartolomeo Vanzetti were convicted of robbery and murder. The trial centered on the defendants' foreign birth and political views, rather than the facts pertaining to their guilt or innocence. (p. 668)

SALT II 1979 strategic arms limitation treaty agreed on by President Jimmy Carter and Soviet leader Leonid Brezhnev. After the Soviet Union invaded Afghanistan, Carter persuaded the Senate not to ratify the treaty. (p. 897)

scalawags Derisive term for white Southerners who supported Reconstruction. (p. 440)

Scottsboro Nine Nine African American youths convicted of raping two white women in Scottsboro, Alabama, in 1931. The Communist Party played a key role in defending the Scottsboro Nine and in bringing national and international attention to their case. (p. 692)

seasoning The period of time in which newly arrived slaves regained their strength, adapted to their new environments, and were absorbed into American slave culture. (p. 78)

Second Continental Congress Assembly of colonial representatives that served as a national government during the Revolutionary War. Despite limited formal powers, the Continental Congress coordinated the war effort and conducted negotiations with outside powers. (p. 164)

second front Beginning in 1942, Stalin wanted an immediate invasion by U.S., British, and Canadian forces into German-occupied France to take pressure off the Soviet forces fighting the Germans on the eastern front. The attack in western Europe did not begin until 1944, fostering resentment in Stalin. (p. 728)

Second Great Awakening Evangelical revival movement that began in the South in the early nineteenth century and then spread to the North. The social and economic changes of the first half of the nineteenth century were a major spur to religious revivals, which in turn spurred social reform movements. (p. 339)

second industrial revolution Revolution in technology and productivity that reshaped the American economy in the early twentieth century. (p. 660)

Second Seminole War 1835–1842 war between the Seminoles, including fugitive slaves who had joined the tribe, and the U.S. government over whether the Seminoles would be forced to leave Florida and settle west of the Mississippi River. Despite substantial investments of men, money, and resources, it took seven years for the United States to achieve victory. (p. 307)

Sedition Act 1918 act appended to the Espionage Act. It punished individuals for expressing opinions deemed hostile to the U.S. government, flag, or military. (p. 639)

separate spheres The notion that men and women should occupy separate social, economic, and political spheres. According to this middle-class ideal, men were best suited for the public world of business and politics, while women were meant to manage the home. (p. 331)

Servicemen's Readjustment Act 1944 act that offered educational opportunities and financial aid to veterans as they readjusted to civilian life. Known as the GI Bill, the law helped millions of veterans build new lives after the war. (p. 770)

settlement houses Community centers established by urban reformers in the late nineteenth century. Settlement house organizers resided in the institutions they created and were often female, middle-class, and college educated. (p. 579)

Share Our Wealth Plan devised by Senator Huey Long of Louisiana to provide families with a $5,000 homestead and a guaranteed annual income of $2,000. These results would be achieved by taxing the wealthy. (p. 702)

sharecropping A system that emerged as the dominant mode of agricultural production in the South in the years after the Civil War. Under the sharecropping system, sharecroppers received tools and supplies from landowners in exchange for a share of the eventual harvest. (p. 441)

Shays's Rebellion 1786 rebellion by western Massachusetts farmers caused primarily by economic turmoil in the aftermath of the Revolutionary War. (p. 203)

Sherman Antitrust Act 1890 act that outlawed monopolies that prevented free competition in interstate commerce. (p. 500)

sit-down strike A strike in which workers occupy their place of employment. In 1937 the United Auto Workers conducted sit-down strikes in Flint, Michigan, against General Motors to gain union recognition, higher wages, and better working conditions. The union won its demands. (p. 704)

skilled workers Workers with particular training and skills. Skilled workers were paid more and were more difficult for owners to replace than unskilled workers. (p. 529)

skyscrapers Buildings more than ten stories high that first appeared in U.S. cities in the late nineteenth century. Urban crowding and high prices for land stimulated the drive to construct taller buildings. (p. 573)

Smith Act 1940 act that prohibited teaching or advocating the violent overthrow of the U.S. government or belonging to any group with that aim. (p. 774)

social gospel Religious movement that advocated the application of Christian teachings to social and economic problems. The ideals of the social gospel inspired many progressive reformers. (p. 593)

Social Security Act Landmark 1935 act that created retirement pensions for most Americans, as well as unemployment insurance. (p. 703)

Solidarity Polish trade union movement led by Lech Walesa. During the 1980s, Solidarity played a central role in ending Communist rule in Poland. (p. 908)

Sons of Liberty Boston organization first formed to protest the Stamp Act. The Sons of Liberty spread to other colonies and played an important role in the unrest leading to the American Revolution. (p. 142)

Southern Christian Leadership Conference (SCLC) Organization founded in 1957 by Martin Luther King Jr. and other black ministers to encourage nonviolent protests against racial segregation and disfranchisement in the South. (p. 804)

spectral evidence Evidence given by spirits acting through possessed individuals. A number of the accused in the 1692 Salem witch trials were convicted on the basis of spectral evidence. (p. 99)

spoils system Patronage system introduced by Andrew Jackson in which federal offices were awarded on the basis of political loyalty. The system remained in place until the late nineteenth century. (p. 278)

Stamp Act 1765 act of Parliament that imposed a duty on all transactions involving paper items. The Stamp Act prompted widespread, coordinated protests and was eventually repealed. (p. 141)

Stonewall Tavern The gay bar in Greenwich Village in New York City where, in 1969, its patrons fought the police in response to harassment. This encounter helped launch the gay liberation movement. (p. 844)

Stono rebellion 1739 uprising by African American slaves in South Carolina. In the aftermath of the uprising, white fear of slave revolts intensified. (p. 87)

Strategic Arms Limitation Treaty (SALT I) 1972 agreement between the United States and Soviet Union to curtail nuclear arms production during the Cold War. The pact froze for five years the number of antiballistic missiles (ABMs), intercontinental ballistic missiles (ICBMs), and submarine-based missiles that each nation could deploy. (p. 863)

Student Nonviolent Coordinating Committee (SNCC) Civil rights organization that grew out of the sit-ins of 1960. The organization focused on taking direct action and political organizing to achieve its goals. (p. 805)

Students for a Democratic Society (SDS) Student activist organization formed in the early 1960s that advocated the formation of a "New Left" that would overturn the social and political status quo. (p. 837)

subprime mortgages Mortgages that are normally made out to borrowers with lower credit ratings. During the early twenty-first century, banks and mortgage companies devised lenient lending policies to allow buyers to purchase homes beyond their means. (p. 944)

subtreasury system A proposal by the Farmers' Alliances in the 1880s for the federal government to extend loans to farmers and store their crops in warehouses until prices rose and they could buy back and sell their crops to repay their debts. (p. 541)

suffragists Supporters of voting rights for women. Campaigns for women's suffrage gained strength in the late nineteenth and early twentieth centuries and culminated in ratification of the Nineteenth Amendment in 1920. (p. 596)

Sugar Act 1764 act of Parliament that imposed an import tax on sugar, coffee, wines, and other luxury items. The Sugar Act sparked colonial protests that would escalate over time as new revenue measures were enacted. (p. 140)

Sun Belt The southern and western part of the United States. After World War II, millions of Americans moved to the Sun Belt, drawn by the region's climate and jobs in the defense, petroleum, and chemical industries. (p. 793)

sweatshops Small factories or shops in which workers toiled under adverse conditions. Business owners, particularly in the garment industry, turned tenement apartments into sweatshops. (p. 575)

syncretic culture A hybrid culture that combines elements of previously distinct cultures. Enslaved African Americans created a syncretic culture by combining elements of African, West Indian, and European cultures. (p. 301)

Taft-Hartley Act 1947 law that curtailed unions' ability to organize. It prevented unions from barring employment to non-union members and authorized the federal government to halt a strike for eighty days if it interfered with the national interest. (p. 770)

Tea Party movement A loose coalition of conservative and libertarian forces that arose around 2008. Generally working within the Republican Party, the Tea Party advocates small government, low taxes, and reduced federal deficits. (p. 946)

Teapot Dome scandal Oil and land scandal during the Harding administration that highlighted the close ties between big business and the federal government in the early 1920s. (p. 659)

Tejanos Mexican residents of Texas. Although some Tejano elites allied themselves with American settlers, most American settlers resisted the adoption of Tejano culture. (p. 310)

Teller Amendment Amendment to the 1898 declaration of war against Spain stipulating that Cuba should be free and independent. The amendment was largely ignored in the aftermath of America's victory. (p. 628)

temperance The movement to moderate and then ban the sale and consumption of alcohol. The American temperance movement emerged in the early nineteenth century as part of the larger push for improving society from the 1820s to the 1850s. (p. 340)

tenements Multifamily apartment buildings that housed many poor urban dwellers at the turn of the twentieth century. Tenements were crowded, uncomfortable, and dangerous. (p. 574)

Tennessee Valley Authority (TVA) New Deal agency that brought low-cost electricity to rural Americans and redeveloped the Tennessee River valley through flood-control projects. The agency built, owned, and supervised a number of power plants and dams. (p. 698)

Tenure of Office Act Law passed by Congress in 1867 to prevent President Andrew Johnson from removing cabinet members sympathetic to the Republican Party's approach to congressional Reconstruction without Senate approval. Johnson was impeached, but not convicted, for violating the act. (p. 437)

Tet Offensive January 31, 1968, offensive mounted by Vietcong and North Vietnamese forces against population centers in South Vietnam. The offensive was turned back, but it shocked many Americans and increased public opposition to the war. (p. 830)

Thirteenth Amendment Amendment to the Constitution abolishing slavery. The Thirteenth Amendment was passed in January 1865 and sent to the states for ratification. (pp. 415, 431)

three-fifths compromise Compromise between northern and southern delegates to the 1787 Constitutional Convention to count enslaved persons as three-fifths of a free person in apportioning representation in the House of Representatives and taxation by the federal government. (p. 205)

To Secure These Rights Report issued by President Truman's Committee on Civil Rights in 1947 that advocated extending racial equality. Among its recommendations was the desegregation of the military, which Truman instituted by executive order in 1948. (p. 772)

total war The strategy of attacking civilian as well as military targets. Engaging in a war of attrition to wear down the Confederacy, General Grant and his commanders used this strategy in 1864 and 1865. (p. 413)

Townshend Act 1767 act of Parliament that instituted an import tax on a range of items including glass, lead, paint, paper, and tea. The Townshend Act prompted a boycott of British goods and contributed to violence between British soldiers and colonists. (p. 143)

Trail of Tears The forced march of some 15,000 Cherokees from Georgia to Indian Territory. Inadequate planning, food, water, sanitation, and medicine led to the deaths of thousands of Cherokees. (p. 309)

transcendentalism A movement founded by Ralph Waldo Emerson in the 1830s that proposed that individuals look inside themselves and to nature for spiritual and moral guidance rather than to the dogmas of formal religion. Transcendentalism attracted a number of important American writers and artists to its vision. (p. 341)

transcontinental railroad A railroad linking the East and West Coasts of North America. Completed in 1869, the transcontinental railroad facilitated the flow of migrants and the development of economic connections between the West and the East. (p. 462)

Treaty of Fort Laramie 1851 treaty that sought to confine tribes on the northern plains to designated areas in an attempt to keep white settlers from encroaching on their land. In 1868, the second Treaty of Fort Laramie gave northern tribes control over the "Great Reservation" in parts of present-day Montana, Wyoming, North Dakota, and South Dakota. (p. 465)

Treaty of Guadalupe Hidalgo 1848 treaty ending the Mexican-American War. By the terms of the treaty, the United States acquired control over Texas north and east of the Rio Grande plus the New Mexico territory, which included present-day Arizona and New Mexico and parts of Utah, Nevada, and Colorado. The treaty also ceded Alta California, which had declared itself an independent republic during the war, to the United States. (p. 316)

Treaty of New Echota 1836 treaty in which a group of Cherokee men agreed to exchange their land in the Southeast for money and land in Indian Territory. Despite the fact that the treaty was obtained without tribal sanction, it was approved by the U.S. Congress. (p. 308)

Treaty of Paris 1783 treaty that formally ended the conflict between Britain and its North American colonies. The newly established United States gained benefits from the treaty. (p. 182)

Triangle Shirtwaist Company Site of an infamous industrial fire in New York City in 1911. Inadequate fire safety provisions in the factory led to the deaths of 146 workers. (p. 575)

Truman Doctrine U.S. pledge to contain the expansion of communism around the world. Based on the idea of containment, the Truman Doctrine was the cornerstone of American foreign policy throughout the Cold War. (p. 762)

Tuskegee Institute African American educational institute founded in 1881 by Booker T. Washington. Following Washington's philosophy, the Tuskegee Institute focused on teaching industrious habits and practical job skills. (p. 599)

U.S. Sanitary Commission Federal organization established in June 1861 to improve and coordinate the medical care of Union soldiers. Northern women played a key role in the commission. (p. 405)

Uncle Tom's Cabin Novel published in 1852 by Harriet Beecher Stowe. Meant to publicize the evils of slavery, the novel struck an emotional chord in the North and was an international best seller. (p. 372)

underground railroad A series of routes from southern plantation areas to northern free states and Canada along which abolitionist supporters, known as conductors, provided hiding places and transportation for runaway slaves seeking freedom. (p. 346)

unions Groups of workers seeking rights and benefits from their employers through their collective efforts. (p. 532)

Universal Negro Improvement Association (UNIA) Organization founded by Marcus Garvey in 1914 to promote black self-help, pan-Africanism, and racial separatism. (p. 666)

unskilled workers Workers with little or no specific expertise. Unskilled workers, many of whom were immigrants, made up the vast majority of the late-nineteenth-century industrial workforce. (p. 529)

utopian societies Communities formed in the first half of the nineteenth century to embody alternative social and economic visions and to create models for society at large to follow. (p. 344)

Valley Forge Site of Continental Army winter encampment in 1777–1778. Despite the harsh conditions, the Continental Army emerged from its encampment at Valley Forge as a more effective fighting force. (p. 173)

vertical integration The control of all elements in a supply chain by a single firm. For example, Andrew Carnegie, a vertically integrated steel producer, sought to own suppliers of all the raw materials used in steel production. (p. 499)

Vietcong The popular name for the National Liberation Front (NLF) in South Vietnam, which was formed in 1959. The Vietcong waged a military insurgency against the U.S.-backed president, Ngo Dinh Diem, and received support from Ho Chi Minh, the leader of North Vietnam. (p. 811)

Vietnamization President Richard Nixon's strategy of turning over greater responsibility for the fighting of the Vietnam War to the South Vietnamese army. (p. 862)

Virginia Plan Plan put forth at the beginning of the 1787 Constitutional Convention that introduced the ideas of a strong central government, a bicameral legislature, and a system of representation based on population. (p. 204)

vital center liberalism Political ideology of Harry Truman supporters who took a middle political ground between the extreme right and left. Vital center liberals supported the Cold War, favored civil rights measures and federal government support for public housing and medical care, and opposed McCarthyism while supporting domestic anticommunism efforts. (p. 774)

Voting Rights Act 1965 act that eliminated many of the obstacles to African American voting in the South and resulted in dramatic increases in black participation in the electoral process. (p. 834)

Walking Purchase 1737 treaty that allowed Pennsylvania to expand its boundaries at the expense of the Delaware Indians. The treaty, quite possibly a forgery, allowed the British to add territory that could be walked off in a day and a half. (p. 111)

War Industries Board (WIB) Government commission created in 1917 to supervise the purchase of military supplies and oversee the conversion of the economy to meet wartime demands. The WIB embodied a government-business partnership that lasted beyond World War I. (p. 637)

War of the Spanish Succession 1702–1713 war over control of Spain and its colonies; also called Queen Anne's War. Although the Treaty of Utrecht that ended the war in 1713 was intended to bring peace through the establishment of a balance of power, imperial conflict continued to escalate. (p. 71)

War Powers Act 1973 act that required the president to consult with Congress within forty-eight hours of deploying military forces and to obtain a declaration of war from Congress if troops remained on foreign soil beyond sixty days. (p. 863)

War Production Board Board established in 1942 to oversee the economy during World War II. The War Production Board was part of a larger effort to convert American industry to the production of war materials. (p. 735)

Watergate Scandal and cover-up that forced the resignation of Richard Nixon in 1974. The scandal revolved around a break-in at Democratic Party headquarters in 1972 and subsequent efforts to conceal the administration's involvement in the break-in. (p. 865)

Weathermen A group advocating the use of revolutionary violence, formed in 1968 by dissident members of Students for a Democratic Society (SDS). The Weathermen went underground to avoid criminal prosecution. (p. 838)

Whig Party Political party formed in the 1830s to challenge the power of the Democratic Party. The Whigs attempted to forge a diverse coalition from around the country by promoting commercial interests and moral reforms. (p. 307)

Whiskey Rebellion Uprising by western Pennsylvania farmers who led protests against the excise tax on whiskey in the early 1790s. (p. 211)

white-collar workers Managerial, clerical, and technical workers. The creation of large numbers of white-collar jobs in the late nineteenth century was the key factor in the expansion of the American middle class. (p. 506)

Wilmot Proviso 1846 proposal by Democratic congressman David Wilmot of Pennsylvania to outlaw slavery in all territory acquired from Mexico. The proposal was defeated, but the fight over its adoption foreshadowed the sectional conflicts of the 1850s. (p. 316)

Woman's Christian Temperance Union (WCTU) Organization founded in 1874 to campaign for a ban on the sale and consumption of alcohol. In the late nineteenth century, under Frances Willard's leadership, the WCTU supported a broad social reform agenda. (p. 602)

Women's National Loyal League Organization founded by abolitionist women during the Civil War to press Lincoln and Congress to enact universal emancipation. (p. 408)

Works Progress Administration (WPA) New Deal agency established in 1935 to put unemployed Americans to work on public projects ranging from construction to the arts. (p. 702)

XYZ affair 1798 incident in which French agents demanded bribes before meeting with American diplomatic representatives. (p. 213)

Yalta Agreement Agreement negotiated at the 1945 Yalta Conference by Roosevelt, Churchill, and Stalin about the fate of postwar eastern Europe. The Yalta Agreement did little to ease growing tensions between the Soviet Union and its Western allies. (p. 730)

yellow journalism Sensationalist news accounts meant to provoke an emotional response in readers. Yellow journalism contributed to the growth of public support for American intervention in Cuba in 1898. (p. 627)

yeomen farmers Southern independent landowners who did not own slaves. Although yeomen farmers had connections to the South's plantation economy, many realized that their interests were not always identical to those of the planter elite. (p. 303)

Yorktown Site of decisive patriot victory. The surrender of British forces on October 19, 1781, at Yorktown, Virginia, effectively sealed the patriot victory in the Revolutionary War. (p. 181)

Young Americans for Freedom (YAF) A group of young conservatives from college campuses formed in 1960 in Sharon, Connecticut. It favored free market principles, states' rights, and anticommunism. (p. 845)

Zimmermann telegram 1917 telegram in which Germany offered Mexico an alliance in the event that the United States entered World War I. The telegram's publication in American newspapers helped build public support for war. (p. 635)

zoot suit riots Series of riots in 1943 in Los Angeles, California, sparked by white hostility toward Mexican Americans. White sailors attacked Mexican American teenagers who dressed in zoot suits—suits with long jackets with padded shoulders and baggy pants tapered at the bottom. (p. 742)

Chapter 25

Document 25.2: Courtesy of Seattle Civil Rights and Labor History Project, University of Washington. http://depts.washington.edu/civilr/InnisArden.htm.

Document 25.3: From "What's Wrong with Our World?" by Billy Graham, September 28, 1958. Reprinted with permission from the *Charlotte Observer*. Copyright owned by the Charlotte Observer.

Document 25.6: "The Nine Billion Dollars in Hot Little Hands" by Richard Gehman, from *Cosmopolitan*, November 1957. Courtesy of Christian Gehman.

Document 25.8: From George E. Sokolsky, "Teenager Puts Rap on Suggestion Elvis on Way Out," *Milwaukee Sentinel,* March 11, 1967.

Document 25.9: From *The Sixties: Years of Hope, Days of Rage* by Todd Gitlin, copyright © 1987 by Todd Gitlin. Used by permission of Bantam Books, a division of Random House, Inc.

Chapter 26

Document 26.2: From *Dear America: Letters Home from Vietnam*, edited by Bernard Edelman for the New York Vietnam Veterans Memorial Commission; W. W. Norton & Company, 1985. Used by permission of Bernard Edelman.

Document 26.5: From "The Sharon Statement," 1960. Courtesy of Young America's Foundation.

Document 26.6: From "Prospectus for Mississippi Freedom Summer," the Michael J. Miller Civil Rights Collection. Courtesy of Archives and Special Collections, The University of Mississippi.

Document 26.7: "Letter from Joseph and Nancy Ellin to Dr. and Mrs. Ellin," June 30, 1964. Used by permission of David Ellin.

Document 26.8: Excerpt from *Letters from Mississippi*, edited by Elizabeth Sutherland Martínez. Original edition copyright © 1965 and renewed 1993 by Elizabeth Sutherland Martínez. New edition copyright © 2002 by Elizabeth Sutherland Martínez. Reprinted with the permission of The Permissions Company, Inc., on behalf of Zephyr Press, www.zephyrpress.org.

Document 26.9: From "'Freedom' to the Delta," *Charleston Post*, June 26, 1964.

Chapter 27

Document 27.1: From *Capitalist Patriarchy and the Case for Socialist Feminism*, edited by Zillah R. Eisenstein. Reprinted with permission of the Monthly Review Foundation.

Document 27.4: "A Tale of Two Cities" from *More Than Words: The Speeches of Mario Cuomo* by Mario Cuomo. ©1993 by Mario Cuomo. Reprinted by permission of St. Martin's Press. All rights reserved.

Document 27.7: From *Affirmative Discrimination: Ethnic Inequality and Public Policy* by Nathan Glazer (Cambridge, MA: Harvard University Press, 1975). Reprinted with permission of Perseus Books in the format textbook by Copyright Clearance Center.

Document 27.9: "Whites Say I Must Be on Easy Street" by Nell Irvin Painter, as it appeared in *The New York Times*, December 10, 1981. Used by permission of Nell Irvin Painter.

Chapter 28

Document 28.3: Adapted from *Pastoral Letter on War and Peace*, "The Challenge of Peace: God's Promise and Our Response" by The National Conference of Catholic Bishops. Copyright © 1983 by the United States Conference of Catholic Bishops, Inc. Used by permission.

Chapter 29

Document 29.1: From *Sweatshop Warriors: Immigrant Women Workers Take On the Global Factory* by Miriam Ching Yoon Louie.

Document 29.2: "Report from Baghdad" by Farnaz Fassihi, 2004. Courtesy of Farnaz Fassihi.

Document 29.3: RecessionGrads interview by Melissa K. McDonough, April 21, 2011. Used by permission of Melissa K. McDonough.

Document 29.4: "We Are the 99 Percent," November 5, 2011, anonymous. Courtesy of Priscilla Grim.

Document 29.6: "The Power of Freedom" by Diana Hoffman, 2002. By permission of Diana Hoffman.

Document 29.7: From "The Kitschification of September 11" by Daniel Harris, Jan. 25, 2002. This article first appeared in Salon.com, at http://www.Salon.com. An online version remains in the Salon archives. Reprinted with permission.

Document 29.8: From "Face to Face: Stories from the Aftermath of Infamy" by Khaled Abou El Fadl. Courtesy of Dr. Khaled Abou El Fadl.

Document 29.10: From "Marine Runs 100 Miles in Support of Memorial, Wounded Service Members" by Brian Gallagher. Courtesy of Brian Gallagher.

A Note about the Index: Names of individuals appear in boldface. Letters in parentheses following page numbers refer to documents *(d)*, figures *(f)*, illustrations *(i)*, maps *(m)*, and tables *(t)*.

Peale, Norman Vincent, 799
Pearce, Charles H., 431
Pearl Harbor
 American reactions to attack on, 726, 727
 Japanese bombing of, 721, 723, 726, 727
 naval base at, 623
Pendleton Civil Service Reform Act (1883), 579
Penn, William, Jr., 67, 110–111
Penn, William, Sr., 67
Pennsylvania, 67, 69(t)
 abolition in, 175
 Civil War in, 410, 411(m)
 German colonists in, 82(d)
 Indian and immigrant settlements in, 110
 legislature in, 175
 Tuscarora appeal to, 73(d)
Pennsylvania Dutch, arts of, 110(i)
Pennsylvania Gazette, 80, 131(i)
Pennsylvania Railroad, 493
Penobscot Indians, 228
Pensions
 in Great Depression, 701
 for mothers and widows, 596
Pentagon, September 11, 2001, attack on, 938
Pentagon Papers, 863, 865
Peonage, 599
People of color, anti-imperialists and, 629
Peoples. *See also* Immigrants and immigration; Migration; specific groups
 diversity of, 109–110
 movement to west, 241–242
People's Party of America. *See* Populists
People's Republic of China, 766. *See also* China
Pequot Indians, 55, 57
Pequot War, 53, 54(i)
Per capita income, growth of, 791
Perestroika, 907–908
Perkins, Frances, 697
Permanent Investigation Subcommittee of the Committee on Government Operations, 776
Perot, Ross
 1992 election and, 881
 1996 election and, 934
Perry, Jim, 471–474
Perry, Matthew C., 371
Pershing, John
 in Mexico, 634
 in World War I, 637
Persian Gulf region, 867, 948
Persian Gulf War. *See* Gulf War
Personal liberty, Wilson and, 638, 642
Personal Responsibility and Work Opportunity Reconciliation Act (1996), 934

Peru, 5, 267
 figure whistle from, 5(i)
 Inca in, 5
 Pizarro in, 20
Peter, Hugh, 53
Peters, Thomas, "Petition to British Cabinet," 183(d)
Petersburg, siege of (1864), 413, 414
Petition(s)
 antislavery, 293, 328, 346, 347, 415
 antitariff, 288(d)
 gag rule for antislavery, 311, 347
 for Hawaiian self-rule, 644, 645–646(d)
 supporting Cherokee rights, 307, 308(d)
"Petition from Free Blacks of Charleston," 202(d)
"Petition of Abigail Faulkner" (Faulkner), 100(d)
"Petition of the Women's Councils to the Cherokee National Council," 308(d)
"Petition to British Cabinet" (Peters), 183(d)
"Petition to Free an Indian Slave, 1675" (Nahaton), 61(d)
"Petition to the President of the United States," 749(d)
Petroleum. *See* Oil and oil industry
Petticoat Affair, 278
Peyton Place (Metalious), 790, 802
Pfundheler, Nora, 476
Philadelphia, 329, 577(i)
 African Americans in, 331, 572
 Centennial Exposition (1876) in, 566
 Constitutional Convention at, 204–205
 First Continental Congress in, 149–151
 nativist–Irish Catholic violence in, 337
 politics in, 118
 population of, 241, 570
 race riot in, 274, 331
 in Revolution, 171, 177, 178
Philadelphia convention, 204–205
Philadelphia Female Anti-Slavery Society, 346
Philadelphia Negro, The, 600
Philanthropy, Carnegie and, 494, 504, 522
Philip II (Spain), 23, 39, 40
Philip, King. *See* Metacom
Philippine-American War (1899–1902), 628–630, 650
Philippines, 864
 colonization by U.S., 644
 immigration from, 931
 independence for, 694
 Magellan and, 17
 Seven Years' War and, 131–137
 U.S. annexation of, 628–629
 in World War II, 730
Phillips, Wendell, 438

Phips, William, 99–100
Phoenix (Cherokee), 281(i)
Phonograph, 497
Photography
 in Civil War, 404(i), 406(i)
 of wagon train, 363(i)
Photojournalism, Riis and, 588
Physicians. *See* Doctors
Pickett, George, 410
Pickett's Charge, 410, 411(m)
Piecework, 531
Pierce, Franklin, 373, 377
 1852 election and, 371
 expansionism of, 368, 371–372
Pietists, 112
Pike, Zebulon, 238, 238(m)
Pilgrims, 49–50, 51
Pilgrim's Progress (Bunyan), 594
Pinchot, Gifford, 591–592, 592(i), 593, 605, 610, 612, 673–674
 Hetch Hetchy valley damming and, 606
 Taft and, 609
Pinckney, Charles (father), 88
Pinckney, Charles Cotesworth (son), 91
 1800 election and, 214
Pinckney, Eliza Lucas, 66, 78–80, 88, 90
 "Letter to Charles Cotesworth Pinckney, 1785," 91(d)
Pinckney, Thomas, 212, 213
Pinckney Treaty (1796), 212
Pine Ridge Reservation, 468
Pingree, Hazen, 605
Pinkerton detectives, 526(i), 535
Pinochet, Augusto, 913
Pioneers, 461
 legacy of, 482
 to West, 363–365
 women as, 471, 475(i), 476, 527(i)
Piracy, Barbary pirates and, 195
Piri Reis (map), 27, 30(i)
Pitt, Fort, 134
Pitt, William, 132–133
Pittsburgh
 as Fort Duquesne, 130, 133
 Whiskey Rebellion and, 218
Pittsburgh Courier, 572
 "Letter from Black Soldiers" to, 741(d)
"Pittsburgh Resolution, The," 220(d)
Pizarro, Francisco, 20
Plains, 7. *See also* Great Plains
Plains Indians. *See also* Great Plains
 Catlin paintings of, 342
 culture and society of, 463–465
 Kansas-Nebraska Act and, 373
Plan of Union (Franklin), 131
Plantation slavery. *See also* Slaves and slavery
 in Barbados, 46

THE CONTEMPORARY WORLD

CANADA

Greenland
(Den.)

ICELAND

UNITED
KINGDOM

IRELAND

FRANCE

SPAIN

PORTUGAL

Alaska
(U.S.)

UNITED STATES

ATLANTIC
OCEAN

Azores
(Port.)

MOROCCO

Bermuda (U.K.)

Canary Is.
(Sp.)

Western Sahara
(Mor.)

MEXICO

Hawaii (U.S.)

BAHAMAS
DOMINICAN
REPUBLIC
HAITI
CUBA
JAMAICA
BELIZE
HONDURAS
GUATEMALA
EL SALVADOR   NICARAGUA
COSTA RICA
PANAMA

Puerto Rico (U.S.)
ST. KITTS AND NEVIS
ANTIGUA AND BARBUDA
Guadeloupe (Fr.)   DOMINICA
Martinique (Fr.)
ST. LUCIA   ST. VINCENT AND THE GRENADINES
BARBADOS
GRENADA
TRINIDAD AND TOBAGO
GUYANA
SURINAME
French Guiana (Fr.)

MAURITANIA

CAPE
VERDE   SENEGAL

GAMBIA   MAL

GUINEA-BISSAU

GUINEA
SIERRA LEONE

LIBERIA
CÔTE D'IVOIRE

BURKINA FASO
GHANA

VENEZUELA

COLOMBIA

PACIFIC OCEAN

Galápagos Is.
(Ec.)   ECUADOR

Equator

PERU

BRAZIL

SAMOA

BOLIVIA

TONGA

PARAGUAY

CHILE

Easter I.
(Chile)

N
W   E
S

URUGUAY

ATLANTIC
OCEAN

0   1,500   3,000 miles
0   1,500   3,000 kilometers

ARGENTINA

Falkland Is.
(U.K.)

80°N

60°N

40°N

20°N

0°

20°S

40°S

60°S

80°S

160°W   140°W   120°W   100°W   80°W   60°W   40°W   20°W

ARCTIC OCEAN

RUSSIAN FEDERATION

NORWAY
SWEDEN
FINLAND
ESTONIA
LATVIA
LITHUANIA
DEN.
GERMANY
LUX.
POLAND
BELARUS
CZ.
SLK.
UKRAINE
AUS.
HUNG.
MOLDOVA
SLN.
ITZ.
ITALY
CR.
SE.
ROMANIA
B.H.
MO. KO.
BULGARIA
ALB.
MAC.
GREECE
GEORGIA
ARMENIA
AZERBAIJAN
TURKEY

KAZAKHSTAN

UZBEKISTAN
KYRGYZSTAN
TURKMENISTAN
TAJIKISTAN

MONGOLIA

N. KOREA
S. KOREA

JAPAN

PACIFIC OCEAN

TUNISIA
MALTA
CYPRUS
ISRAEL
SYRIA
LEBANON
IRAQ
West Bank
Gaza Strip
JORDAN
KUWAIT
BAHRAIN
IRAN
AFGHANISTAN
PAKISTAN

CHINA

Taiwan

LIBYA
EGYPT
SAUDI ARABIA
QATAR
UNITED ARAB
EMIRATES
OMAN

INDIA

NEPAL
BHUTAN
BANGLADESH
MYANMAR
(BURMA)
LAOS
VIETNAM

Mariana Is.
(U.S.)

Guam
(U.S.)

MARSHALL
IS.

ERIA
NIGER
CHAD
SUDAN
YEMEN
DJIBOUTI
ERITREA

THAILAND
CAMBODIA

PHILIPPINES

GERIA
ENIN
OGO
CENTRAL
AFRICAN REP.
SOUTH
SUDAN
ETHIOPIA
SOMALIA

SRI
LANKA
MALDIVES

BRUNEI

PALAU

FEDERATED STATES
OF MICRONESIA

CAMEROON
NEA
GABON
CONGO
RWANDA
UGANDA
KENYA
DEM. REP. OF
THE CONGO

MALAYSIA

SINGAPORE

NAURU
KIRIBATI

SÃO
OMÉ
RINCIPE
BURUNDI
TANZANIA
COMOROS
SEYCHELLES

INDONESIA

PAPUA
NEW
GUINEA

TUVALU

SOLOMON
IS.

ANGOLA
ZAMBIA
MALAWI

INDIAN OCEAN

TIMOR
LESTE

VANUATU

FIJI

NAMIBIA
ZIMBABWE
BOTSWANA
MADAGASCAR
MAURITIUS

New Caledonia
(Fr.)

MOZAMBIQUE
SWAZILAND
SOUTH
AFRICA
LESOTHO

AUSTRALIA

NEW
ZEALAND

Tasmania
(Aust.)

ABBREVIATIONS

ALB.	ALBANIA
AUS.	AUSTRIA
BEL.	BELGIUM
B.H.	BOSNIA AND HERZEGOVINA
CR.	CROATIA
CZ.	CZECH REPUBLIC
DEN.	DENMARK
HUNG.	HUNGARY
KO.	KOSOVO
LUX.	LUXEMBOURG
MAC.	MACEDONIA
MO.	MONTENEGRO
NETH.	NETHERLANDS
SE.	SERBIA
SLK.	SLOVAKIA
SLN.	SLOVENIA
SWITZ.	SWITZERLAND

ANTARCTICA

20°E   40°E   60°E   80°E   100°E   120°E   140°E   160°E

About the authors

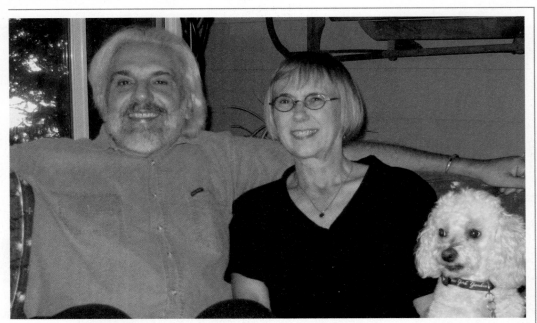

Authors Steven F. Lawson and Nancy A. Hewitt outside the couple's home with their trusty consultant, Scooter.

Nancy A. Hewitt (Ph.D., University of Pennsylvania) is professor of history and of Women's and Gender Studies at Rutgers University. Her publications include *Southern Discomfort: Women's Activism in Tampa, Florida, 1880s–1920s,* for which she received the Julia Cherry Spruill Prize from the Southern Association of Women Historians; *Women's Activism and Social Change: Rochester, New York, 1822–1872*; and the edited volume *No Permanent Waves: Recasting Histories of U.S. Feminism.* She is currently working on a biography of the nineteenth-century radical activist Amy Post and a book that recasts the U.S. woman suffrage movement.

Steven F. Lawson (Ph.D., Columbia University) is professor emeritus of history at Rutgers University. His research interests include U.S. politics since 1945 and the history of the civil rights movement, with a particular focus on black politics and the interplay between civil rights and political culture in the mid-twentieth century. He is the author of many works, including *Running for Freedom: Civil Rights and Black Politics in America since 1941*; *Black Ballots: Voting Rights in the South, 1944–1969*; and *In Pursuit of Power: Southern Blacks and Electoral Politics, 1965–1982.*